Interesting

Accurate

Up-to-Date

COMPTON'S

PICTURED ENCYCLOPEDIA
AND FACT-INDEX

*To Inspire Ambition,
to Stimulate the Imagination, to Provide the
Inquiring Mind with Accurate Information
Told in an Interesting Style, and Thus
Lead into Broader Fields of Knowledge—
Such Is the Purpose of This Work.*

Volume 1

Text: A—Animal Tracks

Fact-Index: A—Annamese

F. E. COMPTON CO.,
DIVISION OF ENCYCLOPÆDIA BRITANNICA, INC.

WILLIAM BENTON, Publisher

Chicago / Toronto / Rome / Sydney / Tokyo

Editor's Preface

COMPTON'S ENCYCLOPEDIA is a home and school encyclopedia. It has been designed and written to help you in many ways. Every article, every picture, and every feature of this work has been included because of its usefulness to some part of family or school life.

All Compton material has been prepared in the interests of children and young people. Much of it will be used at some time or another by the young people themselves. Some parts will be used mainly by adults—parents or teachers—to help children help themselves. Still other parts will be used by adults and young people together in enriching family and school life. Many times parents and teachers need satisfying and stimulating answers to children's questions to keep the child interested in further learning. Compton's has a wealth of material to do this. Every feature of the encyclopedia can be used in many different ways to fit the needs of the family and the school. Compton's is a reference work in which answers to thousands of questions can be found quickly and accurately.

1. Material to Be Used by Children and Young People

The great bulk of the encyclopedia has been prepared for easy *use by the child or young person* himself. Articles of this type are designed to provide the information needed at the particular age and grade levels where the subject or interest usually arises. These materials result from thorough study of school courses at all educational levels and continuing study of child interests at all ages. The text and illustrations are developed together to make sure that the material is truly explanatory, readable, and easily understood by its intended users.

Because the purpose of this encyclopedia is to carry the young person beyond his present level of information into the realm of exciting new ideas, the reader is never left with the bare bones of mere definition. Any words necessary to do this are explained in terms the young person can understand. All articles are written at the lowest reading level that can effectively give the needed information. For those topics which are studied at more than one grade level, the more advanced material is put later in the article. Thus a child or young person can learn what he needs to know at any particular time with the reading skill he then has.

2. Material to Be Used with Children

Almost all the material in the encyclopedia can be *used with children*. It is a well-known fact that the ability of a child to understand goes far beyond his ability to read. The young child and the child whose interests extend beyond his reading ability can be helped easily if the parent or teacher will read the article to him and talk it over as they go along. Retarded readers and nonreaders can also gain significantly when the encyclopedia is used *with* them. One need not allow reading handicaps to limit the learning of a child when learning can be encouraged so easily. At times the interest generated by adult attention and by suitable materials will motivate the child to further effort and ultimate success in reading itself.

The preschool readiness program is another important and productive use of Compton material with children. By looking at pictures together and by reading and explaining simple concepts that interest the preschool child, parents go a long way in preparing their child for a successful school experience. Valuable skills of listening and talking are learned. Vocabulary is developed. Interests are aroused. When the child goes to school he already has the interest, the foundation skills, and the information on which to build his school learning.

i

3. *Material to Be Used in the Interests of Children*

Helping children to grow and develop into wholesome, healthy, competent maturity is the pleasant privilege of the family, the church, and the school. It is a cooperative effort in which each must do its share in order to achieve the best results. To cooperate fully each must understand the aims and methods of the others. All who are concerned with children must know how children grow, how they develop, what can be expected of them at different ages, how to foster interests, and how to guide them to success.

A generous amount of material to help adults understand these problems is included in this encyclopedia. The material reflects the best of modern thinking on child development and family living. It is a safe guide to understanding the problems of parents, schools, and children. School aims and practices are explained, and parents are encouraged to cooperate effectively in the interests of their children.

There are articles written for adults on all important phases of family life from Baby Care to Adolescence; Vacations to Vocations. There is a wealth of general and specific information to add zest to family life. Using Compton's together can weld a family into a unit. The creation and sharing of family interests truly change a house into a home.

HOW COMPTON'S IS ARRANGED

Compton's has been designed for ease of use by young people. There are 24 conveniently sized volumes. Each volume has two main parts, and they are equally important. The first part has the main text. The second part is the famous Compton Easy Reference Fact-Index. Both contain information important to you, and both should be consulted when you seek specific facts or all the facts available.

The Main Text

The main text is an alphabetical arrangement of principal articles. The purpose of each article is to bring many related facts together into a coordinated explanation of a main topic. Related facts are put into a setting which gives them meaning. Because the facts are brought together they are more easily understood and easier to remember. They are related to other facts to provide memory pegs.

The main text has thousands of illustrations. Although the pictures are beautiful, that is not the reason for their inclusion. Each has been carefully selected and prepared for the meaning it adds to the topic. Each has been included because it aids in understanding, simplifies a principle, or gives information that could not be given as well in words at the reading level at which the article has been written. Each illustration carries with it a few lines of explanatory text. This text should always be carefully read to get the most from the illustration.

Included in the individual articles of the main text are many cross-references to other articles. These supplementary references should be read faithfully because they too have information which adds to some aspect of the topic.

Reference-Outlines and Bibliographies

Following many of the main text articles are Reference-Outlines and Bibliographies. These are study guides and reading guides which lead the reader to a systematic survey of fields of interest too large or too detailed to have been included in one article. The Reference-Outlines refer to other articles in Compton's Encyclopedia. The Bibliographies refer to significant books in print and usually available at local libraries.

The Easy Reference Fact-Index

The Fact-Index is the key that unlocks the door to the wealth of information in this encyclopedia. Knowing how to use an index is an important skill. No matter how much information may be included in a publication, the information has little value unless it can be found quickly and easily when it is needed. An index is the only possible way to make *single* facts and *all* the facts findable in a single book or in a set of books.

The Fact-Index is an alphabetical list. It gives the exact volume and page number for almost two hundred thousand individual text references. Every main idea is shown in boldface (heavy) type. This is called a main entry. In lighter type, following the main entries, are alphabetically arranged subentries, which divide the main entry into its parts.

Almost every topic for which you seek information is related to many other topics. Some of the information which you may want will be in related articles. Let us suppose that you are interested in Copper and want to find all the information in Compton's Encyclopedia. First you locate Copper in the Fact-Index. Under Copper you will find the subentries which give you the volumes and pages on which you will find the facts you want to know. The references are to articles in all volumes which have information on the subject. Without the index it is unlikely that you would have thought of so many articles in which information was to be found. You might have missed the very fact you wanted. By using the index you can locate a single fact or all the facts.

The Fact-Index has been built to save you time, trouble, and difficulty in hunting through long articles and different articles to find information. Many times you will need to look only in the Fact-Index. Many thousands of short articles, called Fact Entries, are in the Fact-Index itself. These Fact Entries often give the information you want without looking further. Some identify and give short biographies of people, both living and dead, or locate places and give their populations and industries. Many others pronounce, identify, locate, define, and give important facts about things, events, processes, and principles.

The numerous tables in the Fact-Index bring together information about important people and events and facts about classes of things to make comparisons easy.

Many topics are listed in more than one way for easy finding. For instance, Robinson Crusoe can be found as 'Robinson Crusoe' in the R section of the Fact-Index. It can also be found under Crusoe, Robinson; or under Defoe, Daniel, its author; or under Friday, another character in the story.

Pictures are indicated by the word *picture* or *color picture*. The volume and page number which follow show where they can be found. A picture reference is intended to call attention to details in the legend under the picture as well as to the picture itself. The legend should always be carefully read.

The pronunciations given are those preferred by the Merriam-Webster dictionaries. The diacritics (pronunciation marks) used are those given in the Key to Pronunciation at the front of each volume and in the Fact-Index. Alternative pronunciations are also given. In recent years hundreds of geographical names have been changed, either officially or by custom. Both old and new names are listed at the appropriate places in the alphabet. Populations are those of the latest available census or official estimate. Distances between points are map or air distances, not distances by highway or railroad.

THE PUBLISHER AND HIS AIMS

The first edition of Compton's Encyclopedia was published in 1922. For many years prior to that date the Compton organization published other well-known children's reference books. Each established new standards in books for young people.

Our sole aim has always been to publish the finest home and school encyclopedia that can be built. All the resources, skills, and efforts of the Compton organization are devoted to making Compton's Encyclopedia and its annual supplements serve the interests of young people in families, in schools, in libraries, and in youth-serving organizations.

With large permanent editorial and art staffs, outstanding specialists as contributors and consultants, professional advisory groups for areas of interest, panels of experts in special fields of knowledge, and extensive consultation with individual scholars, we have consistently maintained the encyclopedia at the highest quality. Each edition of Compton's Encyclopedia uses the most recent advances in the graphic arts, from papermaking to color printing. Each retains the unique features of earlier editions and by revision and expansion keeps them up-to-date in fact and spirit. This edition has also added many new articles and features to explain the events and developments of our times.

Young people and adults with the interests of children high in their hearts use Compton's Encyclopedia effectively throughout the free world. This fact is both a satisfaction and a challenge to the entire editorial staff.

Donald E. Lawson

Editor in Chief

Photograph by Fabian Bachrach

Donald E. Lawson

EDITOR IN CHIEF

COMPTON'S ENCYCLOPEDIA

Editorial Staff

Editor in Chief
DONALD E. LAWSON, B.A.

Staff Editor 1952–57; Editorial Supervisor 1957–59; Managing Editor 1959–64; Editor 1964–65; newspaper editor 1939–41; member Air Force counterintelligence 1941–45; house organ editor 1946–52; short-story writer, novelist, and author of books for young people; author, 'A Brand for the Burning', 'Young People in the White House', 'The United States in World War I', 'The United States in World War II', 'The United States in the Korean War', 'Famous American Political Families', 'The War of 1812', 'Frances Perkins: First Lady of the Cabinet', 'Great Air Battles'.

Administrative Director
VERNE L. PORE, B.S.

Fact-Index 1956–57; Staff Editor 1959–60; Chief, Department of Statistical Research 1960–65; Assistant to the Editor in Chief 1966–67.

Managing Editor
EUGENE ZUCKER, B.A., M.A.

Chief Proofreader 1960–65; Chief Copy Editor 1965–66; Assistant Editor 1966–67; United States Army 1943–45; Social Studies Teacher 1949–52; technical writer, encyclopedia and magazine editor, research director 1952–60.

Assistant Managing Editor
AUDREY MITCHELL

Copy Editor 1964–66; Assistant Editor 1966–67; newspaper editor, reporter, columnist, production coordinator, art director, copywriter.

Art Director
BERNARD S. HOLLIDAY

Staff Picture-Layout Editor 1960–65; graduate, American Academy of Art, Bauhaus School of Design; Art Director, 'Chicago Daily News' 1941–46.

Staff Editors
MARCELLA ALBERT
SAMUEL ALLEN
MICHAEL FLEISHER
KENNETH R. HUFF
FRANK LITTLER
MURIEL LOIS McKUNE
LUKE V. MATRANGA
WILLIAM O. WOOD
MARGARET ZIEMER
JOSEPH A. ZULLO

Fact-Index Staff
MAYBELLE TAYLOR, *Editor*
RITA KOWALSKI
RALPH NOEL
SUSAN DE WOLFE
FRANCIS E. YOUNG

Librarian
WAYNE M. HARTWELL

Production Supervisor
KENNETH B. ALWOOD

Production Editors
BARBARA J. GARDETTO, *Chief*
BARBARA ANNE ALPERT
LINDA CANTER
CONSTANCE HALL
MARY RADAKOVIC
DARLENE STILLE

Graphic Arts Supervisor
THEODORE MASSON

Picture Procurement
ALBERTO MENOCAL

Manuscript Preparation
EUNICE MITCHELL
KATHERYN L. ADERONMU

HOWARD L. GOODKIND
Executive Vice-President, Editorial

LEONARD R. HARRIS
Vice-President, Editorial

Consultants and Contributors

Art Contributors

WILLARD ARNOLD
STANLEY M. ARTHURS
ERNEST W. BECK
WILLIAM J. BEECHER
FRED BOND
REX I. BRASHER
MATILDA BREUER
L. LESLIE BROOKE
GERALD CARVETH
JAMES H. DAUGHERTY
CLIFFE EITEL
AL FINCHER
CLARENCE M. FLATEN
FRANCES FOY
CHESTER GILLIAM
VELINO HERRERA

BOB HINES
ALLAN HOUSER
A. F. HURFORD
MIRIAM HURFORD
ELIZABETH ORTON
   JONES
FRED KABOTIE
W. LANGDON KIHN
GLADYS McHUGH
C. P. MALTMAN
BARBARA MAYNARD
GERALD NAILOR
R. H. PALENSKE
FRED A. PETRICK
HENRY C. PITZ
ELIOT F. PORTER

ARTHUR RAHNFELD
ERWIN C. RENDALL
EDWARD RINKER
STEELE SAVAGE
LEE SAYLOR
ANDREW STANDING
   SOLDIER
DONALD STEBBING
PAUL STRAYER
LOWELL STUMPF
SU ZAN N. SWAIN
JAMES G. TEASON
ELAN TUITE
THOMAS W. VOTER
ROLAND WHITEHORSE
MILO WINTER

Editorial Consultants and Contributors

ACADEMY OF MOTION PICTURE ARTS AND SCIENCES
(by Special Committee)

Motion Pictures

CLIFFORD ROSE ADAMS, A.B., A.M., PH.D.

Family; Marriage

Professor of Psychology, and in charge of marriage coun-
seling, School of Education, Pennsylvania State University; author, 'How to Pick a Mate', 'Making Marriage
Work', 'Looking Ahead to Marriage', etc.

CHARLES ANDERSON ALDRICH, M.D.

Baby Care

Late Professor of Pediatrics, Mayo Foundation Graduate
School, University of Minnesota; coauthor, 'Cultivating
the Child's Appetite', 'Babies Are Human Beings'.

ARTHUR A. ALLEN, M.A., PH.D.

Birds

Professor of Ornithology, Cornell University; author,
'The Book of Bird Life', 'American Bird Biographies'.

CLIFFORD J. ALLUM

Airplane Models

Technical Director, Academy of Model Aeronautics;
editor, 'Model Aviation'.

BOWER ALY, B.S., A.M., PH.D.

Public Speaking

Professor of Speech, University of Oregon; executive
secretary, National University Extension Association.

A. W. ANDERSON, B.S.

Fish Technology

Chief, Branch of Commercial Fisheries, U. S. Fish and
Wildlife Service, Department of the Interior; author of
many technical articles on fish.

CONSULTANTS AND CONTRIBUTORS

JEAN M. ARBO
Art
Graduate, The Chicago Academy of Fine Arts, The Art Institute of Chicago; art editor and illustrator of children's books.

MAX BACHRACH
Fur Industry
Late fur consultant and lecturer; member, Committee D-13, American Society for Testing Materials; president, New York Microscopical Society; author, 'Fur', 'Selling Furs Successfully', 'The Fur Digest'.

HERBERT B. BAIN, B.A.
Meat; Meat Industry
Director of Public Relations, American Meat Institute; formerly director of public relations, American Dental Association.

AUGUSTA BAKER, B.S. IN ED., B.S. IN L.S.
Negroes Bibliography
Coordinator, Children's Services, New York Public Library; author, 'Books About Negro Life for Children' and magazine articles.

ROBERT H. BAKER, A.M., PH.D.
Astronomy
Professor of Astronomy, University of Illinois; author, 'An Introduction to Astronomy', 'When the Stars Come Out', etc.

ELMAAR H. BAKKEN
Boy Scouts of America
Late Director, Division of Relationships, Boy Scouts of America.

ANN BARZEL, PH.B.
Ballet; Dance
Writer and critic; lecturer on the dance, University of Chicago; editorial staff, 'Dance Magazine'; contributor to 'Dance Index' and 'Dance Encyclopedia'.

W. W. BAUER, M.D.
Anatomy; Health
Late Consultant to the Director of the Division of Environmental Medicine, American Medical Association.

ROBERT F. BEATTIE, B.A.
Skiing
Coach, U. S. ski team, 1964 Olympics (Alpine events); Director of Skiing Activities, University of Colorado; formerly coach, U. S. ski team for world championships (1962).

ROBERT O. BEATTY, B.S., M.S.
Fishing
Formerly Conservation Director, Izaak Walton League of America, Inc.; editor, 'Outdoor America'.

WILLARD W. BEATTY, B.S., A.M., HON. ED.D.
American Indians
Late Deputy Director in Charge of Fundamental Education Training Centers, Department of Education, UNESCO, Paris; formerly chief, Branch of Education, Bureau of Indian Affairs, U. S. Department of the Interior; editor, 'Indian Education'; author of texts, pamphlets.

ERNEST W. BECK, B.S., M.A.
Anatomy
Free-lance medical illustrator; Art Director, G. D. Searle & Company.

FRANCES OBERHOLTZER BELSEY, A.B.
Social Studies; Geography
Social Studies Supervisor and staff writer; formerly manuscript editor, 'Journal of the American Medical Association'; contributor to magazines.

STEPHEN VINCENT BENÉT, M.A.
Poetry
Late author, 'Young Adventure', 'Five Men and Pompey', 'The Beginning of Wisdom', 'Spanish Bayonet', 'John Brown's Body' (Pulitzer prize, 1929), 'Ballads and Poems 1915–1930', 'Johnny Pye and the Fool Killer', 'Western Star' (Pulitzer prize, 1944).

WILLIAM ROSE BENÉT, M.A., LITT.D.
Biographies
Late contributing editor, 'Saturday Review of Literature'; editor, 'Poems for Youth', 'The Dust Which Is God' (Pulitzer prize, 1942).

ROBERT J. BENFORD, M.D.
Antibiotics; Drugs
Director of Medical Relations, Pharmaceutical Manufacturers Association, Washington, D. C.

ADAM S. BENNION, M.A., PH.D.
Mormons
Late Superintendent, Latter-day Saints' School; member, Latter-day Saints' General Board of Education; author, 'What It Means to Be a Mormon'.

F. LEE BENNS, A.M., PH.D., LITT.D., F.R.H.S.
Modern History
Professor of History, Indiana University.

EMMETT A. BETTS, A.B., A.M., PH.D.
Reading; Phonics
Research Professor, School of Education, University of Miami; editor in chief, 'Education'; formerly director, Betts Reading Clinic, Haverford, Pa.; senior author, 'Betts Basic Readers', 'American Adventure Series'.

KENNETH BOLDT, B.S.
Aerospace Fuels
Consultant, Fuels and Lubricants, Pure Oil Company Research Center.

CONSULTANTS AND CONTRIBUTORS

ROGER W. BOLZ, M.E.

Automation

Editor, 'Automation'; author, 'Production Processes'; member, American Society of Mechanical Engineers, Institute of Radio Engineers, Instrument Society of America, National Society of Professional Engineers.

FRED E. BOND

Photography

Color photographer and author; member, California Color Society; fellow, Photographic Society of America; received 1956 La Belle award for contributions to color photography.

JACK BOOKBINDER, B.S., M.F.A.

The Arts; Sculpture

Director, Division of Art Education, Philadelphia Public Schools; lecturer, Pennsylvania Academy of Fine Arts; paintings and lithographs in many collections; author, 'Invitation to the Arts'.

CHRISTY BORTH

Automobile; Automobile Industry

Formerly Assistant Managing Director, Automobile Manufacturers Association; author, 'Masters of Mass Production', 'True Steel', 'Pioneers of Plenty'.

ELEANOR BOYKIN, A.B.

Conversation; Etiquette; Letter Writing

Journalist and lecturer; formerly Secretary of Public Relations Committee, National Council of Teachers of English; instructor, Columbia University.

FRANK B. BRADY

Airplane Instruments

Director, Airport Equipment Program, General Precision Equipment Corporation.

JAMES ALBERT BRAMMELL, B.S., M.A.

Maps

Geographer, U. S. Government; Chief of Geography Branch, U. S. Department of State.

STANLEY H. BRAMS

Automobile Careers

Editor and Publisher, 'Detroit Labor Trends'.

JAMES H. BREASTED, A.M., PH.D., LL.D.

Archaeology

Late Professor of Egyptology, Oriental History; director, Oriental Institute, University of Chicago.

CHARLES K. BRIGHTBILL, B.A., M.A.

Games; Parks and Playgrounds

Late head, Department of Recreation, University of Illinois; chairman, National Recreation Policies Committee; formerly president, American Recreation Society, National Director of Recreation, Veterans Administration; author, 'Community Recreation', etc.

CALVIN CHARLES BROWN, B.S., CH.E.

Metals and Alloys

Chief Control Metallurgist, Open Hearth and Blooming Mills, Inland Steel Company; formerly instructor in Metallurgy and Statistics, Purdue University.

ROBERT G. BROWN

Telemetry

Associate Director of Development Engineering, AC Spark Plug Division, General Motors Corporation; member, Executive Committee, National Telemetering Conference; coauthor, 'Analysis and Design of Feedback Control Systems', 'Servomechanism Analysis'.

W. NORMAN BROWN, A.B., PH.D.

Pakistan

Chairman of the South Asia Regional Studies Department, University of Pennsylvania; editor, 'India, Pakistan, Ceylon'.

REV. PATRICK WILLIAM BROWNE, S.T.D., PH.D.

Papacy; Monasticism

Late editor, 'Catholic Historical Review'; author, 'Story of Labrador', 'History of Newfoundland'.

LEO J. BRUECKNER, B.A., M.A., PH.D.

Arithmetic

Late Professor of Education, University of Minnesota; coauthor of arithmetic textbooks widely used in Canadian and American schools; author, 'Making Arithmetic Meaningful', etc.

LESLIE A. BRYAN, PH.D., LL.B.

Airplane; Aviation Meteorology

Director, Institute of Aviation, University of Illinois; author and aviation consultant; Colonel, U. S. Air Force Reserve.

HELEN BUCKLER, A.B.

Camp Fire Girls

Associate Director, National Public Relations Division, Camp Fire Girls, Inc.

JOHN W. BUNN, B.S.

Basketball

Editor, 'NCAA Basketball Guide'.

EDWARD M. L. BURCHARD, B.A., M.A., PH.D.

Psychoanalysis

Associate Professor of Psychology, Queens College; member, Low Cost Psychoanalytic Service, William Alanson White Institute of Psychiatry, New York; president, Society of Projective Techniques, 1951–52.

JOHN ANGUS BURRELL, A.B.

Biographies

Late Associate Professor of English, Columbia University; coauthor, 'Dead Reckoning in Fiction', 'Adventure or Experience', 'Modern Fiction'.

J. S. Butz, Jr., B.S., Ae.E.
Airplane Flight Controls; Airplane Flight Theory
Engineering Editor, 'Aviation Week and Space Technology'.

Noble Cain, M.A.
Musical Theory
Writer, lecturer, conductor, composer, and arranger; formerly director, A Cappella Choir, Chicago; author, 'Science of Music', 'Goethe and Music'.

Robert L. Calvert
Boy Scouts of America
National Director, Editorial Service, Boy Scouts of America.

R. Milton Carleton, Ph.D.
Gardens
Director of Research, Vaughan Garden Research Center, Chicago, Ill.; fellow, Royal Horticultural Society; director, Men's Garden Clubs of America; president, Chicago Horticultural Society; author and coauthor of many books and articles on gardening.

Carl Carmer, M.A., Litt.D., L.H.D.
American Folklore
Editor, 'Rivers of America Series'; author, 'Listen for a Lonesome Drum', 'The Hudson', 'America Sings', 'Too Many Cherries', 'Hurricane Luck', etc.

Leon Carnovsky, A.B., Ph.D.
Biographies
Professor of Library Science, Graduate Library School, University of Chicago.

Sid Cato
Bus
News Editor, The Greyhound Corporation.

W. Linwood Chase, A.B., A.M., Ph.D.
History
Formerly Professor of Education, Boston University; educational consultant, 'History on the March' series; formerly president, National Council for the Social Studies; contributor to educational journals.

Carl M. Christenson
Airplane Safety
Assistant Vice-President, Flight Operations, United Air Lines, Inc.

Evert B. Clark
Aerospace Industry
Space Technology Editor, 'Aviation Week and Space Technology'.

Charles N. Cofer, A.B., A.M., Ph.D.
Personality
Professor of Psychology, University of Maryland.

Warren H. Cole, M.D.
Surgery
Surgeon in Chief, Research and Educational Hospitals, University of Illinois College of Medicine.

Frank B. Cookson, Ph.D.
Music
Professor of Theory and Composition and Chairman of Department of Theory and Composition, School of Music, Northwestern University; managing editor, 'Educational Music Magazine'.

John Niessink Cooper, A.B., Ph.D.
Physics
Professor of Physics, U. S. Naval Postgraduate School, Monterey, Calif.; formerly research physicist, Manhattan Project, Radiation Laboratory, University of California.

Robert I. Crane, B.A., M.A., Ph.D.
India
Professor of History, Duke University; formerly assistant professor, Department of History, and member of Policy Committee, Research Center on Economic Development and Cultural Change, University of Chicago.

Robert M. Cunningham, Jr., Ph.B.
Hospitals
Managing Editor, 'Modern Hospital Magazine'; lecturer, hospital administration, Northwestern University, University of Chicago; formerly associate editor, 'Hygeia'; contributor to national magazines.

Alice Dalgliesh, B.S., A.M.
Biographies
Formerly Editor of Books for Younger Readers, Charles Scribner's Sons; instructor in Literature for Children, Teachers College, Columbia University; author, 'A Book for Jennifer' and other books for children.

Marietta Daniels, A.B., B.S. in L.S., M.A.
Libraries in the Americas (Latin America)
Associate Librarian, Columbus Memorial Library, Pan American Union, Washington, D. C.

James Henry Daugherty
Biographies
Author and illustrator, 'Daniel Boone' (Newbery medal, 1940), 'Abraham Lincoln', 'Poor Richard', 'Andy and the Lion'; illustrator of many books for children.

Mary Gould Davis
Storytelling; Biographies
Late lecturer on Storytelling; formerly Supervisor of Storytelling, New York Public Library; compiler, 'The Girls' Book of Verse'; author, 'The Truce of the Wolf', 'The Handsome Donkey', 'Sandy's Kingdom'.

Marguerite de Angeli
Nursery Rhymes; Mother Goose
Illustrator and author of children's books.

CONSULTANTS AND CONTRIBUTORS

HILARY J. DEASON, A.B., A.M., PH.D.

Science Bibliography

Director of Libraries, American Association for the Advancement of Science, Washington, D. C.

JOHN J. DEBOER, A.B., A.M., PH.D.

Report Writing

Professor of Education, University of Illinois.

JOHN L. DE JONG

Bank

Late Associate Director, News Bureau, American Bankers Association.

NICHOLAS DEWITT, B.A., M.A., PH.D.

Russia; Russian History

Department of Economics, Indiana University; formerly member, Russian Research Center, Harvard University.

LEON T. DICKINSON, PH.D.

American Literature

Chairman, Department of English, University of Missouri.

WAYNE DINSMORE, B.S.A., M.S.A., J.D.

Horses

Consultant on Horses, Pastures, Equine Nutrition, and Riding; executive secretary, Horse Association of America; coauthor, 'A History of the Percheron Horse', etc.

W. E. DOHERTY, JR.

Glider

Sales Manager, Commercial Aircraft, Schweizer Aircraft Corporation; director, Soaring School, Elmira, N. Y.

EDGAR A. DOLL, PD.M., PH.D.

Educational Psychology

Consulting Psychologist, Bellingham Public Schools, Bellingham, Wash.; formerly president, American Association on Mental Deficiency; author, 'Clinical Studies in Feeble-Mindedness', 'The Growth of Intelligence'.

LUCY E. DRISCOLL, M.A.

Factors

Assistant Superintendent, Cook County (Illinois) Schools.

DOROTHY DRUMMOND, B.A., M.A.

South America

Coauthor, 'The World Today: Its Patterns and Cultures'; formerly teacher of geography; assistant editor, 'Focus'.

RUTH SAWYER DURAND, B.S.

Storytelling

Author and professional storyteller; specialist in Irish folk tales; 'Roller Skates' (Newbery medal, 1937), 'The Way of the Storyteller', 'The Long Christmas', etc.

JEANETTE EATON, A.B., A.M.

Biographies

Author, 'That Lively Man, Ben Franklin', 'Young Lafayette', 'Narcissa Whitman, Pioneer of Oregon', 'Gandhi: Fighter Without a Sword', etc.

RICHARD EDGREN, PH.D.

Biology

Endocrinologist, Division of Biological Research, G. D. Searle & Company.

MARGARET A. EDWARDS, A.B., A.M., B.S. IN L.S.

Reading for Young Adults

Formerly Coordinator of Work with Young People, Enoch Pratt Free Library, Baltimore, Md.

DAVID I. EGGENBERGER, B.S.

Flags; Military Subjects

Executive Editor, Encyclopedia and Library Division of McGraw-Hill; author, 'Flags of the U.S.A.', 'A Dictionary of Battles'.

GLADYS ENGLISH

Literary Biographies

Late instructor, Graduate Department of Library Science, Immaculate Heart College, Los Angeles; formerly Department Librarian, Work with Children, Los Angeles Public Library.

EVAN EVANS, A.B., A.M., LL.D.

Aviation

Executive Director, National Aerospace Education Council; contributor to professional magazines.

PAUL L. EVANS, B.S.

Tennessee Valley Authority

Director of Information, Tennessee Valley Authority; formerly professor of journalism, Ohio Wesleyan University.

JOHN C. EWERS, A.B., M.A.

American Indians

Associate Curator of Ethnology, Smithsonian Institution; formerly with Office of Indian Affairs; curator, Museum of the Plains Indian, Montana; field curator, Museum Division, National Park Service.

DELMER STATER FAHRNEY, B.S., M.S.

Guided Missiles

Rear Admiral, U. S. Navy (retired); pioneer work in guided missiles and pilotless aircraft.

LEONARD V. FARLEY

Circus

Museum Librarian, Hertzberg Circus Collection, San Antonio (Texas) Public Library; Historian, Circus Fans Association of America.

CARROLL LANE FENTON, B.S., PH.D.

Life; Prehistoric Life

Formerly Assistant Professor of Physical Sciences, University of Buffalo; geologist, Rutgers University and

CONSULTANTS AND CONTRIBUTORS

New Jersey State Museum; associate editor, 'American Midland Naturalist'; author, 'The World of Fossils', 'Prehistoric World', etc.; coauthor, 'Giants of Geology', etc.

C. B. FERGUSSON, M.A. (OXON.)

Canada

Assistant Archivist for Nova Scotia; lecturer in Contemporary History, Nova Scotia Technical College; lecturer in Canadian and Nova Scotian History, Nova Scotia Summer School for Teachers; author, 'The Establishment of Negroes in Nova Scotia'.

LESTER E. FISHER, D.V.M.

Zoology; Veterinary Medicine

Director, Lincoln Park Zoological Gardens, Chicago, Ill.

CLARENCE M. FLATEN, PH.D.

Nature Study

Supervisor of Photography and Science Film Writer-Photographer-Editor, Audio-Visual Center; Assistant Professor in AV Communications and Educational Media, School of Education, Indiana University.

JOHN M. FOGG, JR., B.S., PH.D.

Plant Life

Director, Morris Arboretum; formerly vice-provost and dean of the College of Arts and Sciences, University of Pennsylvania; author, 'Weeds of Lawn and Garden'.

CHARLES ALFRED FORD, B.Sc., M.A., PH.D.

Chairman, Compton Advisory Boards

Formerly Editor in Chief, Compton's Pictured Encyclopedia.

GENEVIEVE FOSTER, B.A.

Biographies

Author and illustrator, 'George Washington's World', 'Abraham Lincoln's World', 'Augustus Caesar's World', 'George Washington: an Initial Biography', 'Abraham Lincoln: an Initial Biography'.

FRANK NUGENT FREEMAN, M.A., PH.D.

Handwriting

Late Dean of the College of Education, University of California; author, 'Psychology of the Teaching of Handwriting', 'How to Teach Handwriting', etc.

HYMAN GABAI, B.A., M.A., PH.D.

Algebra; Mathematics; Numeration Systems and Numbers

Professor of Mathematics, University of Illinois; member, University of Illinois Committee on School Mathematics, Urbana, Ill.

ROMA GANS, B.S., PH.D.

Reading

Professor of Education, Teachers College, Columbia University; author, 'Critical Reading in the Intermediate Grades', 'Guiding Children's Reading Through Experience', 'Reading Is Fun'; coauthor, 'Teaching Children in Nursery School, Kindergarten, and Primary Grades'.

ALFRED B. GARRETT, B.S., M.S., PH.D.

Chemistry

Professor and Head of Division of General Chemistry, Ohio State University; coauthor, 'Essentials of Chemistry', etc.

ROBERT MALCOLM GAY, A.B., A.M., LITT.D.

Shakespeare

Emeritus Professor of English, Simmons College; author, 'Reading and Writing'; editor, Anthony Trollope's 'The Warden', etc.

IGNACE JAY GELB, PH.D.

Alphabet; Babylonia and Assyria; Writing

Professor of Assyriology, University of Chicago; member, Société Asiatique, Finnish Oriental Society; author, 'Hittite Hieroglyphs' 3v., 'Study of Writing'; editor, 'Chicago Assyrian Dictionary'.

JACK A. GERTZ

Airports; Air Traffic Control

Chief, Office of Public Affairs, Federal Aviation Agency.

MRS. STANLEY GIBSON

Cats

Secretary-Treasurer, The American Cat Association, Inc.; president, Beresford Cat Club of America.

WRIGHT D. GIFFORD, JR., B.S., M.S.

Parachute

Engineering Office Manager, Pioneer Parachute Company.

JAMES E. GILLEY, B.S.

Coal; Mines and Mining

Mining engineer, U. S. Bureau of Mines, Department of the Interior.

NORTON S. GINSBURG, PH.D.

Southeast Asia

Associate Professor, Department of Geography, University of Chicago.

MARGUERITA GOFORTH

Cats

Formerly all-breed judge, Cat Fanciers' Association, Inc.; cat breeder; originator of Himalayan breed; president, San Diego Cat Fanciers, Inc.; animal painter and sculptor.

HERB GRAFFIS

Golf

Formerly editor, 'Golfdom'; formerly president, Golf Writers' Association of America; coauthor, 'Better Golf Through Practice'.

STEPHEN V. GRANCSAY

Armor

Curator of Arms and Armor, Metropolitan Museum of Art, New York; consultant to Chief of U. S. Army Ordnance; author, 'The Armor of Galiot de Genouilhac', etc.

CONSULTANTS AND CONTRIBUTORS

JACOB C. HOLPER, A.B., M.A., PH.D.
Vaccines
Research virologist, Abbott Laboratories, Research Division.

F. LOUIS HOOVER, B.S., A.M., D.ED.
Design
Professor of Art and Director of Division of Art Education, Illinois State University; formerly editor, 'Arts and Activities'.

PHILIP S. HOPKINS
Airplane History
Director, National Air Museum, Smithsonian Institution.

MARION HORTON, A.B., B.L.S.
Literary Biographies; Bibliographies
Visiting Professor, School of Library Science, University of Southern California.

JOHN H. HOWARD, B.S., M.S.
Calculating Machines
Associate Director of Research, Burroughs Corporation; computers chairman, Institute of Radio Engineers.

PAUL HOWARD, A.B., B.S. IN L.S., M.A.
Libraries in the Americas (United States)
Librarian, U. S. Department of the Interior Library, Washington, D. C.

FRANK W. HUBBARD, A.B., A.M., PH.D.
Safety
Director, Research Division, National Education Association.

H. GORDON HULLFISH, A.B., A.M., PH.D.
Education
Late Professor of Education, Ohio State University; editor, 'Educational Freedom in an Age of Anxiety'.

ERLING M. HUNT, A.M., PH.D.
History
Professor of History and Head of the Department of Teaching of Social Science, Teachers College, Columbia University; formerly editor, 'Social Education' and 'Social Studies'; coauthor, 'The World History'.

ELIZABETH B. HURLOCK, A.B., M.A., PH.D.
Child Development
Associate in Psychology, The Graduate School, University of Pennsylvania; Child Training Editor, 'Today's Health'; author, 'Child Development', 'Modern Ways with Children', etc.

MARSH JEANNERET, B.A.
Canadian History
Director, University of Toronto Press, Toronto; author, 'Story of Canada', 'From Cartier to Champlain'.

ROBERT I. JOHNSON, A.B.
Moon; Planets; Nebulae
Formerly Director, Adler Planetarium and Astronomical Museum, Chicago, Ill.; author, lecturer, inventor in field of astronomy.

WILLIAM CUMMING JOHNSON, JR., B.S., E.E.
Balloon
Engineering Specialist, Goodyear Aircraft Corporation.

SEYMOUR JONES
Art
Late art editor for various reference works, including Compton's Encyclopedia.

SARA C. JOYNER, A.B., M.A.
The Arts
Professor of Art, Department of Art, University of Georgia; formerly Supervisor of Art Education, State Department of Education, Richmond, Va.; author, 'Art and the Child', 'Report in Primary Colors', etc.

WILL JUDY, A.B., LL.B.
Dogs
Formerly Editor and Publisher, 'Dog World Magazine'; author, 'Dog Encyclopedia' and other works on dogs.

EDMUND JOSEPH JURICA, PH.D.
Plant and Animal Diseases
Professor of Zoology and Chemistry, St. Procopius College, Lisle, Ill.

HILARY STANISLAUS JURICA, PH.D.
Plant and Animal Diseases
Professor of Botany and Head of the Department of Biology, St. Procopius College, Lisle, Ill.

N. B. JUSTER, B.S. IN CH.E.
Iron and Steel, Properties of
Superintendent, Technical Service Department, Inland Steel Company, Chicago, Ill.

HANS H. KANNEGIESSER
Berlin; Germany
Production Manager, Velhagen & Klasing, West Berlin, Germany.

JAMES A. KEELER
Automobile Models
Member, Research and Development Department, Revell, Incorporated; builder of prizewinning models; contributor, 'Rod and Custom Magazine'.

MAHMOUD R. KHATER, B.A., M.A., PH.D.
Modern Egypt
Professor of Education, University of Cairo, Cairo, Egypt.

ROBERT E. KINGERY, B.S.
Hobbies
Formerly Special Assistant to the Director, New York Public Library; author, 'How-to-do-it Books: a Selected Guide'.

CONSULTANTS AND CONTRIBUTORS

CARL F. KLINCK, M.A., PH.D.

Canadian Literature

Head of English Department, University of Western Ontario, London, Ontario.

ROYCE H. KNAPP, B.Sc., M.A., ED.D.

Citizenship

Professor of Education, Teachers College, University of Nebraska; formerly member, executive board, National Council for the Social Studies; director, the Nebraska Citizenship project; American Legion's Boys' State programs on citizenship.

JOHN A. KNAUSS, B.S., M.A., PH.D.

Oceanography

Dean, Graduate School of Oceanography, Narragansett Marine Laboratory, University of Rhode Island.

LORENTZ BENNETT KNOUFF, A.B., J.D., LL.M.

Pottery and Porcelain

Formerly Associate Editor, 'Corpus Juris'; member, English Ceramic Circle.

CLYDE F. KOHN, B.A., M.A., PH.D.

Asia; Argentina; Australia; Geography; Latitude and Longitude

Department of Geography, State University of Iowa; lecturer; coauthor, 'The World Today: Its Patterns and Cultures', etc.

DALE C. KRAUSS, B.S., M.S., PH.D.

Oceanography

Assistant Professor, Graduate School of Oceanography, Narragansett Marine Laboratory, University of Rhode Island.

IRVING B. KRAVIS, PH.D.

Economics

Associate Dean, Wharton School of Finance and Commerce, University of Pennsylvania.

ANN M. LALLY, B.A., M.A., PH.D.

The Arts

Principal, Marshall High School, Chicago; lecturer, De Paul University; member, Editorial Advisory Board, Junior Arts and Activities; formerly Director of Art, Chicago Public Schools; author, 'The Development of Personal Security Through Art', 1953 Yearbook, National Art Education Association, etc.

GRACE LANGDON, B.Sc., M.A., PH.D.

Toys

Child Development Consultant for American Toy Institute; instructor, Arizona State University; member, board of Advisory Editors of 'Parents Magazine'; coauthor, 'These Well-Adjusted Children', 'The Discipline of Well-Adjusted Children'; syndicated newspaper columnist.

GLENN C. LANGE, B.S.J., M.S.J., M.B.A.

Air Force Academy; Laundry

Lieutenant Colonel, USAF Reserve; Air Force Academy Liaison Officer; formerly public relations and editorial manager, American Institute of Laundering; instructor, University of Detroit, Chicago Evening Junior Colleges.

MARION F. LANSING, A.B., A.M.

American Colonial Life

Author, 'America in the World', 'Makers of America', 'Great Moments in Freedom', and many other historical books for girls and boys.

STEPHEN BUTLER LEACOCK, PH.D., LITT.D., LL.D., D.C.L.

Biographies

Late professor, McGill University; author, 'Elements of Political Science', 'Literary Lapses', 'Nonsense Novels', 'Essays and Literary Studies', 'Charles Dickens', etc.

ROBERT WARD LEEPER, A.B., M.A., PH.D.

Emotion

Professor of Psychology, University of Oregon; author, 'Lewin's Topological and Vector Psychology', 'Psychology of Personality'.

LEORA LEWIS

Literature

Formerly Staff Director of Library Service; director, South Dakota Library Commission; editor, 'South Dakota Library Bulletin'; president, League of Library Commissions.

WILLY LEY

Guided Missiles; Rockets; Space Travel

Writer, lecturer, and consultant in field of rockets and space travel; author, 'Rockets, Missiles and Space Travel', 'Conquest of Space'; coauthor, 'Lands Beyond'.

MIRIAM LICHTHEIM, A.B., M.A., PH.D.

Ancient Egypt

Research Associate, Department of Oriental Languages and Literature, University of Chicago.

C. C. LINGARD, M.A., PH.D.

Canadian Statistics

Director, Information Services Division, Dominion Bureau of Statistics, Ottawa; editor, 'Canada Year Book'; author, 'Territorial Government of Canada', 'Canada and World Affairs'.

W. W. LIVENGOOD, A.B.

Education

Director, American Book Company and Audio-Education, Inc., formerly editor in chief; member, Society for Study of Education, Society of Teachers of English.

JOSEPH A. LIVINGSTON, A.B.

Stocks and Bonds

Financial Editor, 'Philadelphia Bulletin'; syndicated financial columnist; economist, 'Business Week'.

CONSULTANTS AND CONTRIBUTORS

ROBERT M. LOEBELSON, B.A.

Airplane Pilot and Crew; Airplane Power Plants; Airplane Propeller; Helicopter; Jet Propulsion

Military-Industry Editor, 'Space/Aeronautics Magazine'; Washington editor, 'Business/Commercial Aviation Magazine'; President, Aviation Writers Association.

ROBERT GRANT LONG, B.A., A.M., PH.D.

Latin America

Associate Professor of Geography, Department of Geology and Geography, University of Tennessee; coauthor, 'An Introduction to World Geography'.

T. MORRIS LONGSTRETH, B.A.

Weather

Member, the American Meteorological Society; author, 'Reading the Weather', 'Knowing the Weather'.

JOHN F. LOOSBROCK, PH.B.

United States Air Force

Editor, 'Air Force Magazine and Space Digest'; lecturer and author of articles on the U. S. Air Force.

NOLA LUXFORD, O.B.E.

New Zealand

Roving correspondent, New Zealand Free Lance; writer for 'Baltimore News' and other newspapers; honorary vice-president, British-American Co-operation movement; president, New Zealand Society of North America.

JOHN LYMAN, B.S., M.S., PH.D.

Ship and Shipping

Oceanographic Coordinator, U. S. Bureau of Commercial Fisheries; member Steamship Historical Society of America.

IRINA B-M LYNCH, PH.D.

Russian Literature

Associate Professor of Russian and Chairman of the Department of Russian, Wellesley College; research fellow in Mathematical Linguistics, Harvard University.

JUSTIN MCCARTHY

Coal; Mines and Mining

Editor, 'United Mine Workers Journal'; formerly director, United Mine Workers News Bureau; reporter; radio news writer.

ROBERT A. MCCLEARY, B.A., M.D., PH.D.

Brain; Nerves

Professor, Departments of Psychology and Physiology, University of Chicago.

HARRY M. MCDONALD, B.S., M.A.

Agriculture

Supervisor of Vocational Agricultural Education, Maryland State Department of Education.

DONALD B. MACMILLAN, A.M., SC.D., F.R.G.S.

Arctic Regions; Polar Exploration

Explorer, lecturer; formerly Professor of Anthropology, Bowdoin College; leader of many Arctic expeditions; author, 'Four Years in the White North', etc.

RUSSELL B. MCNEILL, A.B., M.B.A.

Industrial Systems

Vice-President of Administration, Houdaille Industries, Inc.; formerly manager, Production and Devices group, Rand Corporation; faculty of Harvard Graduate School of Business Administration; Industrial Systems consultant.

WALTER MACPEEK

Boy Scouts of America

Assistant to the Director, Editorial Service, Boy Scouts of America.

TONY MARCH

United States Army

Editor, 'Army Times'.

JANE N. MARSHALL, A.B., M.A.

Aerospace Careers

Author, magazine articles for 'NEA Journal' and others; editor, 'Skylights' and other publications of the National Aerospace Education Council.

THOMAS H. W. MARTIN, B.A., D.PAED.

Canada

President, Associated Programmers of Canada Ltd.; lecturer on Instructional Techniques and Practices, College of Education, University of Toronto; chairman, Social Studies Curriculum Committee for Toronto.

ARTHUR B. MAYS, M.A.

Woodworking

Professor of Industrial Education, University of Illinois; author, 'The Problem of Industrial Education', 'Introduction to Vocational Education', etc.

FREDERIC G. MELCHER

Literary Awards

Late Chairman of the Board of R. R. Bowker Company, publishers of 'Publishers' Weekly' and 'Library Journal'; founder of Newbery and Caldecott medals; honorary life member of the American Library Association.

W. C. MENTZER

Airplane Airframe

Vice-President, Engineering, United Air Lines, Inc.

DONALD H. MENZEL, A.B., A.M., PH.D.

Astronomy

Director, Harvard Observatory, Cambridge, Mass.; author and editor of many astronomical and astrophysical publications; director and member of many solar eclipse expeditions.

RAY O. MERTES, B.S., M.A.

Airlines

Director, School and College Service, Public Relations Division, United Air Lines, Inc.; member, executive board, National Aviation Education Council; consultant to U. S. Armed Forces Institute.

HARRY MILGROM, PH.D.

Atom

Supervisor, Elementary Science, Board of Education of New York City.

MARION E. MILLER, B.A., M.A.

The Arts

Director of Art Education, Denver Public Schools; formerly president, Department of Art Education, National Education Association; member, Art Committee, Motion Picture Commission, American Council on Education; member, Educational Staff, Metropolitan Museum of Art.

JIM MITCHELL

Hunting

Editor, 'Hunting and Fishing'; Outdoor Editor, 'Chicago Daily News'.

GEORGE J. MOHR, B.S., M.D.

Baby Care

Associate Professor, University of Illinois School of Medicine; formerly director, Pittsburgh Child Guidance Center; clinical director, Institute for Juvenile Research, Chicago; member, American Academy of Pediatrics, American Psychoanalytic Association.

R. KATHLEEN MOLZ, B.S., M.A., M.A.L.S.

Libraries

Editor, 'Wilson Library Bulletin', H. W. Wilson Company, New York.

RICHARD MOODY, M.A.

Theater

Professor of Speech and Director of University Theatre, Indiana University.

ANNE CARROLL MOORE, L.H.D., LITT.D.

Literature for Children

Late Superintendent of Work with Children, New York Public Library; lecturer, literary critic; author, 'The Three Owls', 'My Roads to Childhood', etc.

PERCY A. MORRIS

Shells

Chief Preparator in Invertebrate Paleontology and Assistant in Conchology, Peabody Museum of Natural History, Yale University; author, 'What Shell Is That?', 'Field Guide to the Shells', etc.

W. MORRIS

United States Marine Corps

Colonel, U. S. Marine Corps.

ROBERT L. MORTON, B.S., A.M., PH.D.

Arithmetic

Professor of Education, Ohio University; formerly professor of Mathematics; coauthor of arithmetic textbooks; author, 'Teaching Children Arithmetic', etc.

W. L. MORTON, LITT.B., M.A.

Canada

Professor of Canadian History and Chairman of the Department of History, University of Manitoba, Winnipeg; editor, 'The Voice of Dafoe'; author, 'The Progressive Party in Canada'.

JOHN MULHOLLAND

Magic

Editor, 'The Sphinx'; lecturer on magic; author, 'Quicker than the Eye', 'Story of Magic', etc.

JOSÉ MUNDA

Philippine Islands

Chief, Reference Division, National Library, Commonwealth of the Philippines.

NORMAN LESLIE MUNN, A.M., PH.D.

Psychology

Professor of Psychology, Head, Department of Psychology, Bowdoin College; author, 'An Introduction to Animal Psychology', 'Psychological Development', etc.

ROBERT CUSHMAN MURPHY, PH.B., A.M., D.SC.

Birds

Chairman, Department of Birds, American Museum of Natural History; formerly president, National Audubon Society; author, 'Oceanic Birds of South America', etc.

ARTHUR WILFORD NAGLER, A.M., TH.D., D.D.

Church History

Professor of Church History, Garrett Biblical Institute.

FRANK NELICK, PH.D.

English Literature

Professor of English, University of Kansas.

JOHN J. NELLIGAN

Police

Captain, Head of Special Investigation Section, Traffic Division, Chicago Police Department.

ELIZABETH NESBITT, B.A., M.A., B.S. IN L.S.

Folk Tales

Formerly Associate Dean, Library School, Carnegie Institute of Technology.

CURTIS PUTNAM NETTELS, PH.D.

American History

Professor of American History, Cornell University; member, editorial board, 'A History of American Economic Life', 'Journal of Economic History'.

CONSULTANTS AND CONTRIBUTORS

OTTO NEURATH, PH.D.

Visual Education

Late Director, International Foundation for Visual Education; editor in chief, International Encyclopedia of Unified Science; author, 'International Picture Language'.

M. B. NEUWORTH

Coal-Tar Products

Manager, Organic Research, Consolidation Coal Company, Inc.

ALLAN NEVINS, A.M., LITT.D., LL.D.

American History; Franklin D. Roosevelt

Formerly Professor of American History, Columbia University; Chief Public Affairs Officer, American Embassy, London; Harmsworth Professor of American History, 1940–41, Oxford University; professor of American History, Cornell University; author, 'Grover Cleveland' (Pulitzer prize, 1933), 'Hamilton Fish' (Pulitzer prize, 1937), 'A Brief History of the United States', 'Ordeal of the Union' (Scribner prize, 1946).

T. ERNEST NEWLAND, A.B., A.M., PH.D.

Intelligence Tests; Mental Deficiency; Exceptional Children

Professor of Educational Psychology, University of Illinois.

ROBERT J. NORRISH, B.S.

Livestock

Official, International Live Stock Exposition, International Dairy Show, International Kennel Club Dog Show, Chicago.

DELBERT OBERTEUFFER, A.B., A.M., PH.D.

Health Education and Physical Education

Professor of Physical Education, Ohio State University.

ALI OTHMAN, M.A.

Mohammedanism

Liaison Officer, Arab Information Center, New York City; formerly headmaster, Amiriah High School, Palestine; fellow, Ford Foundation, for study of "Authority and Public Consensus in Islam."

JACQUELINE OVERTON

Biographies

Late Librarian, Children's Library, Robert Bacon Memorial, Westbury, N. Y.; author, 'Life of Robert Louis Stevenson for Boys and Girls', etc.

THOMAS PARK, S.B., PH.D.

Insects

Professor, Department of Zoology, University of Chicago.

WALTER G. PATTON, A.B.

Automobile Bodies and Accessories; Automobile Chassis; Automobile Power Plant; Automobile Power Train

Technical writer, Society of Automotive Engineers, Inc.; engineering editor, 'SAE Journal'.

J. J. PEYTON

United States Army

Captain, U. S. Army.

VELMA PHILLIPS, PH.B., A.M., PH.D.

Food

Professor of Home Management and Family Finance, San Fernando Valley State College; formerly dean, College of Home Economics, Washington State University.

ESTHER J. PIERCY, B.A., B.S. IN L.S.

Libraries, History of

Chief of Processing Division, Enoch Pratt Free Library, Baltimore, Md.

WILLARD J. PIERSON, JR., B.S., PH.D.

Ocean Waves and Tides

Professor of Oceanography, Department of Meteorology and Oceanography, New York University.

ALBERT PILTZ, A.B., M.ED., D.ED.

Science

Professor of Science Education, Johns Hopkins University.

ALTON W. POTTER, B.S., M.B.A., LL.B.

Legal Terms

Member (inactive), State Bar of Michigan; Chicago, Illinois State, and American Bar associations.

PITMAN B. POTTER, A.M., PH.D.

Political Science

Dean, Graduate Division, American University, Beirut; formerly professor of International Organization, Graduate Institute of International Studies, Geneva; author, 'An Introduction to the Study of International Organization', 'International Civics', etc.

DAVID M. PRATT, B.A., A.M., PH.D.

Oceanography

Professor, Graduate School of Oceanography, Narragansett Marine Laboratory, University of Rhode Island.

SIDNEY L. PRESSEY, PH.D.

Teaching Machines

Professor of Psychology, College of Education, Ohio State University.

CONSULTANTS AND CONTRIBUTORS

DONALDA PUTNAM, B.S. IN L.S., M.A.

Canada

Extension Librarian, Provincial Library, Regina, Saskatchewan.

GEORGE I. QUIMBY, A.B.. M.A.

American Indians

Curator of Ethnology, Thomas Burke Memorial Washington State Museum, and Professor of Anthropology, University of Washington; formerly Curator of North American Archaeology and Ethnology, Field Museum of Natural History, Chicago.

ROBERT J. QUINN

Fire Department

Fire Commissioner, Chicago Fire Department.

STANLEY RACHESKY, B.S., M.S.

Insecticides

Area adviser on pesticides, Extension Entomologist, University of Illinois; Executive Secretary, Illinois Pest Control Association.

BURTON RASCOE

Biographies

Late literary and drama critic; author, 'Theodore Dreiser', 'Titans of Literature', 'Prometheans', etc.

WILLIAM M. RASSCHAERT, ED.D.

Science

Supervisor of Research, Department of Instructional Research, Detroit Public Schools.

HAIM REINGOLD, A.B., M.A., PH.D.

Calculus

Chairman of Department of Mathematics, Illinois Institute of Technology; coauthor, 'Basic Mathematics for Engineering'.

ROBERT RIENOW, A.B., M.A., PH.D.

International Relations; United States Government

Professor of Political Science, State University College for Teachers, Albany, N. Y.; author, 'Calling All Citizens', 'American Government in Today's World', etc.

ALICE SANDERSON RIVOIRE, B.S., M.S.

Cooking

Homemaking Specialist, Program Department, Girl Scouts of the United States of America, National Headquarters.

DAVID M. ROBB, PH.D.

Architecture

Chairman, Department of Art History, University of Pennsylvania.

HOWARD ROBINSON, A.B., A.M., PH.D., LL.D.

English History

Lecturer on History, University of Queensland, Brisbane, Australia; emeritus head of department and dean of College of Liberal Arts, Oberlin College.

FORD A. ROCKWELL, B.A., B.S. IN L.S.

Pirates

Librarian, Wichita City Library; instructor in Public Library Administration, Emporia State Teachers College.

E. J. ROLAND, ADMIRAL

United States Coast Guard

Commandant, U. S. Coast Guard

JEAN CAROLYN ROOS

Bibliographies

Formerly Supervisor of Service to Youth, Cleveland Public Library; author, 'Thirty Books for Young People'; editor, 'By Way of Introduction'; compiler, 'Background Readings for American History', 'What Shall We Read Next?'.

EULALIE STEINMETZ ROSS, A.B., B.L.S.

Bibliographies

Director of Work with Children, Public Library of Cincinnati and Hamilton County; compiler, fourth edition of 'Stories: a List of Stories to Tell and to Read Aloud'.

NEIL P. RUZIC, B.S.J.

International Geophysical Year

Editor and Publisher, 'Industrial Research Magazine'.

JOSÉ J. SARMIENTO, M.D.

Anesthetics

Staff Anesthesiologist, St. James Hospital, Chicago Heights, Ill.

FRANCES CLARKE SAYERS

Biographies; Mythology; Reading

Formerly Lecturer on Children's Literature, English Department, and Lecturer, Library Work with Children, School of Library Service, University of California at Los Angeles; author, 'Bluebonnets for Lucinda', 'Tag-Along Tooloo', 'Sally Tait'.

DAVID R. SCHINK, B.A., M.S., PH.D.

Oceanography

Assistant Research Professor, Graduate School of Oceanography, Narragansett Marine Laboratory, University of Rhode Island.

F. WAGNER SCHLESINGER, PH.B.

Relativity

Formerly Director, Adler Planetarium, Chicago; Director, Fels Planetarium, Philadelphia.

WILBUR SCHRAMM, A.B., A.M., PH.D.

Writing, Communication by

Director, Department of Communication and Journalism, Institute for Communication Research, Stanford University; author.

ALBERT H. SCHWICHTENBERG, M.D.

Aerospace Medicine

Head, Department of Aerospace Medicine, Lovelace Foundation for Medical Education; member, American Board of Preventive Medicine; fellow, Aerospace Medicine; formerly Command Surgeon, Air Defense Command; Brigadier General (retired), U. S. Air Force (Medical Corps).

ROBERT E. SCUDDER, B.A., B.S. IN L.S., M.A.

Libraries of the World

Head, Social Science and History Department, Free Library of Philadelphia.

PAUL BIGELOW SEARS, A.M., PH.D.

Land Use; Ecology

Conservation Program, Yale University Program; author, 'Deserts on the March', 'This Is Our World', etc.

J. CONRAD SEEGERS, A.B., PH.D., LITT.D., LL.D.

Language Arts

Consultant on University Administration, Valparaiso University; formerly President of Muhlenberg College; Dean of Teachers College, Temple University; author, 'Vocabulary Problems in the Elementary Schools'.

ALBERT E. SHAW, E.E., PH.D.

Electron Physics

Industrial consultant; formerly senior physicist, Argonne National Laboratory; assistant professor, Physics Department, University of Chicago; contributor to journals in electron physics.

PHILIP A. SHELLEY, PH.D.

German Literature

Professor of German and Comparative Literature and Head of the Department of German, Pennsylvania State University.

MARTHA SHEPARD, B.A., B.L.S.

Libraries in the Americas (Canada)

Director of Reference Service, National Library Public Archives of Canada, Ottawa.

FREDERICK C. SHERMAN

Navy and related subjects

Late Admiral, U. S. Navy; military writer and analyst; author, 'Combat Command: the American Aircraft Carriers in the Pacific War'.

LOUIS SHORES, A.B., B.S. IN L.S., PH.D.

Reference Books

Dean, Library School, Florida State University; author, 'Basic Reference Sources'.

MARY E. SILVERTHORN, B.A., B.S. IN L.S., A.M.

Bibliographies

Associate Professor of Library Science, The Library School, Ontario College of Education, University of Toronto.

PARKE H. SIMER, M.D., PH.D.

Anatomy

Professor of Anatomy, University of Illinois College of Medicine.

GEORGE EATON SIMPSON, B.S., M.A., PH.D.

Sociology

Professor of Sociology and Anthropology and head of the department, Oberlin College; author, 'The Negro in the Philadelphia Press'; coauthor, 'Racial and Cultural Minorities'.

GRACE SANDS SMITH, B.A., M.A.

The Arts

Director of Art Education, Houston Public Schools; instructor in Art Education, University of Houston; past president, Texas Art Educators Association; regional chairman, Scholastic Art Awards.

HERBERT A. SMITH, PH.D.

Science

Director of Professional Studies, Colorado State University, Fort Collins, Colorado.

WHITNEY SMITH, JR., A.B., A.M.

Flags

Director, Flag Research Center; Editor, 'The Flag Bulletin'; formerly managing editor, 'Contemporary Photographer'; North American representative, Conseil Héraldique du Luxembourg; contributor to foreign heraldic journals; consultant to the U. S. Committee for UNICEF.

SMITHSONIAN INSTITUTION

Airplane History

National Air Museum staff.

ROBERT SNEDIGAR

Snakes

Late Curator of Reptiles, Amphibians, and Invertebrates, Chicago Zoological Park, Brookfield, Ill.; author, 'Our Small Native Animals', 'Life in the Forest'.

FRED D. SNYDER, B.A.

United States Navy

Lieutenant Commander, U. S. Navy.

CONSULTANTS AND CONTRIBUTORS

FRANK ENGLAND SORENSON, M.A., PH.D.
Brazil; International Cooperation
Director of Summer Session, chairman of Department of Educational Services, and lecturer in Geography, University of Nebraska; formerly Director of Education, Foreign Service Technicians staff of the Technical Cooperation Administration of the U. S. Department of State; coauthor, 'Our Neighbors' series of elementary geographies; U. S. staff member, UNESCO Seminar for Teaching Geography.

LAWRENCE D. STEEFEL, A.B., PH.D.
World War I
Professor of History, University of Minnesota; author, 'The Schleswig-Holstein Question'.

EVELYN STEFANSSON (MRS. VILHJALMUR STEFANSSON)
Northmen
Librarian, The Stefansson Library; author, 'Here Is Alaska', 'Within the Circle'.

VILHJALMUR STEFANSSON, A.B., A.M., PH.D., LL.D., L.H.D.
Biographies
Late anthropologist, geographer, Arctic explorer; author, 'My Life with the Eskimo', 'The Friendly Arctic', 'Greenland', etc.

WALLACE E. STEGNER, A.B., A.M., PH.D.
Creative Writing
Professor of English, Stanford University; editor, compiler, and contributor; author of numerous books; awarded Guggenheim Fellowship 1950, 1952, 1959.

RALPH STEIN
Automobile Racing and Rallies
Automobile Editor, 'This Week Magazine'; author, 'The Treasury of the Automobile'.

DAVID BARNARD STEINMAN, B.S., A.M., PH.D., C.E., Sc.D., D.ENG., D.Sc. ENG., LL.D., F.R.S.A.
Bridges
Late consulting engineer and bridgebuilder; author, 'Bridges and Their Builders', 'Famous Bridges of the World', 'Suspension Bridges', etc.

ELWYN FRANKLIN STERLING, A.B., A.M., PH.D.
French Literature
Assistant Professor, Romance Languages and Literature, Colgate University.

KURT STERN, M.D.
Diseases; Allergy
Professor of Pathology, University of Illinois College of Medicine.

MARTIN DELAWAY STEVERS, PH.B.
Science
Formerly Managing Editor, Compton's Pictured Encyclopedia; author, 'Steel Trails', 'Sea Lanes', etc.

LINDLEY J. STILES, A.B., A.M., ED.D.
Teaching
Dean, School of Education, University of Wisconsin; author, compiler, and contributor.

MERVIN K. STRICKLER, B.Sc., PH.D.
Civil Aviation
Chief, Aviation Education Division, Office of General Aviation Affairs, Federal Aviation Administration.

FELIX STUNGEVICIUS, B.A., M.A., M.B.A.
Uruguay
Consul of Uruguay, Chicago; President, International Language Communications Center; formerly lecturer in Political Science, Northwestern University; vice-president, Pan American Board of Education.

JAMES O. SWAIN, B.A., M.A., PH.D.
Latin American Literature; Spanish Literature
Professor of Romance Languages, University of Tennessee; executive secretary, Spanish Honor Society, Sigma Delta Pi.

RALPH BROWNLEE SWAIN, B.S., M.S., PH.D.
Insects
Late entomologist, New Jersey; formerly entomologist, Mississippi; agent, Bureau of Entomology and Plant Quarantine, U. S. Department of Agriculture, Utah; author, 'The Insect Guide'.

GEORGE W. TAYLOR, PH.D.
Labor
Professor of Industry, University of Pennsylvania; formerly chairman, National War Labor Board and National Wage Stabilization Board; president, Industrial Relations Research Association.

HERBERT J. TAYLOR
Yukon
Territorial Secretary, Government of the Yukon Territory, Canada.

JOHN J. TEAL, JR., B.S., M.A.
Musk-Ox
Research Professor of Animal Husbandry and Human Ecology, University of Alaska; President, Institute of Northern Agricultural Research, Huntington Center, Vt.

NEGLEY K. TEETERS, B.Sc., M.A., PH.D.
Prisons
Professor of Sociology, Temple University.

LEWIS H. THOMAS, M.A.
Canada
Professor of History, Regina College, Saskatchewan.

MARY P. THOMAS
Coal
Educational Assistant, Education Division of the National Coal Association; author of articles on coal.

CAPTAIN ROBERT THOMSON
Salvation Army
Assistant Editor, 'The War Cry'.

GLADYS TIPTON, B.F.A., M.S. IN MUS., D.ED.
Music
Professor of Music Education, Teachers College, Columbia University; author, 'RCA Basic Record Library for Elementary Schools', 'Adventures in Music'.

ARTHUR J. TODD, B.L., PH.D.
Sociology
Late Professor of Sociology, Northwestern University; author, 'Theories of Social Progress', 'The Scientific Spirit and Social Work', 'Industry and Society', etc.

THEODORE W. TORREY, A.B., M.A., PH.D.
Embryology
Professor and Chairman, Department of Zoology, Indiana University; author, 'Morphogenesis of the Vertebrates'; research papers on embryology and histology.

JOHN W. TURRENTINE, M.S., PH.D.
Agricultural Chemistry
Emeritus President, Chairman, American Potash Institute, Inc.; formerly in charge of potash investigations, U. S. Department of Agriculture.

ROGER A. VAN BEVER, M.S.
Science
Instructor of Science, Wayne School, Detroit, Mich.

RUPERT BAYLESS VANCE, A.M., PH.D., LL.D.
Population
Professor of Sociology, University of North Carolina; past president, American Sociological Society, Population Association of America; author, 'Human Geography of the South', 'All These People', etc.

EUGENE VAN CLEEF, S.B., PH.D.
Geographical Names
Professor of Geography, Ohio State University; author, 'The Story of the Weather', 'Finland, the Republic Farthest North', 'Trade Centers and Trade Routes'.

CARL VAN DOREN, A.B., PH.D.
Biographies
Late Associate in English, Columbia University; formerly managing editor, 'Cambridge History of American Literature'; author, 'Contemporary American Novelists', 'James Branch Cabell', 'Sinclair Lewis', 'American Literature', 'Benjamin Franklin' (Pulitzer prize, 1939).

HENRY VAN ENGEN, A.B., M.A., PH.D.
High School Mathematics
Head of Department of Mathematics, Iowa State Teachers College; coauthor, 'Numbers in Action', 'Numbers We See'.

JAMES VEEDER, B.S., M.A.
4-H Clubs
Director of Information, National 4-H Service Committee.

RUTH HILL VIGUERS, A.B., B.S. IN L.S.
Children's Literature
Former editor, 'Horn Book Magazine'; lecturer on Library Service to Children, Department of Library Science, Simmons College.

HOWARD P. VINCENT, PH.D.
Literature
Chairman, Department of Language, Literature, and Philosophy, Illinois Institute of Technology; author, 'The Trying-Out of Moby-Dick'; general editor, 'Collected Works of Herman Melville'.

P. V. H. WEEMS
Navigation; Log, Ship's
Captain, U. S. Navy (retired); conducted first class in Space Navigation at U. S. Naval Academy; designer of navigation devices; founder of Weems System of Navigation, Inc.; codeveloper, 'Air Almanac'; author, 'Air Navigation', 'Star Altitude Curves', 'Line of Position Book'; coauthor, 'Marine Navigation'.

VERNON I. WEIHE, B.Sc. IN E.E.
Aviation Navigation
Director, Air Traffic Control and Navigation Programs, General Precision, Inc.; staff consultant, Air Transport Association of America; fellow, Institute of Radio Engineers.

DANIEL S. WENTZ II, B.A.
Aerospace Research and Development; Wind Tunnel
Information Officer, Ames Research Center, National Aeronautics and Space Administration; associate member, Aviation Writers Association; writer and reporter in fields of aeronautical and space activities.

HELEN WESSELLS
Library Organizations
Library consultant, New York; formerly editor, 'Library Journal'.

JOHN H. WHITE, JR.
Automobile History
Curator of Land Transportation, United States National Museum, Smithsonian Institution.

EUGENE WHITMORE
Clowns
Writer, editor, and reporter; formerly editor, 'American Business Magazine'; first managing editor, 'Sales Man-

agement Magazine'; author, books on sales, advertising, and personnel management and magazine articles on clowns, circuses, and railroads.

FARIDA A. WILEY
Natural Science

Instructor, Department of Education, Director of Field and Laboratory Courses in Natural Science and Conservation, American Museum of Natural History; field instructor in Ecology, National Audubon Society Camp of Maine; author, 'Ferns of Northeastern United States'.

BLANCHE COLTON WILLIAMS, A.M., PH.D.
Biographies

Late Head of Department of English, Hunter College of the City of New York; author, 'George Eliot: a Biography', etc.; formerly editor, 'O. Henry Memorial Award Prize Stories'.

MENTOR L. WILLIAMS, A.B., M.A., PH.D.
Literature

Late Associate Professor of English, Illinois Institute of Technology; Fulbright lecturer in American Literature, University of Sydney, Australia; coauthor, 'A History of American Literature'.

T. HARRY WILLIAMS, B.E., PH.M., PH.D.
History

Professor of History, Louisiana State University; member, Southern Historical Association, Mississippi Valley Historical Association, Abraham Lincoln Association, American Military Institute; author, 'Lincoln and the Radicals', 'Lincoln and His Generals'.

ROBERT W. WIRTZ, B.S.
Mathematics; Numeration Systems and Numbers

Professor of Mathematics, University of Illinois; member, University of Illinois Committee on School Mathematics, Urbana, Ill.; coauthor of a widely used series of textbooks based on the new mathematics.

VAL W. WOODWARD, B.S., M.S., PH.D.
Genetics

Professor, Department of Genetics, University of Minnesota; contributor to professional journals.

K. C. WU, B.A., M.A., PH.D.
China

Lecturer and author of articles on China; formerly Nationalist Chinese government official and governor of Formosa; mayor of Chungking, Hankow, and Shanghai; author, 'The Lane of Eternal Stability'.

JOHN COOK WYLLIE, B.A.
Thomas Jefferson

Librarian, University of Virginia; member of Advisory Council for Princeton 'Papers of Thomas Jefferson'; book editor, 'Richmond News Leader'; author of numerous bibliographic articles.

READ W. WYNN, B.A.
Civil Air Patrol

Director, Public Information, National Headquarters, Civil Air Patrol, Auxiliary of U. S. Air Force, Ellington Air Force Base, Texas; public information specialist, U. S. Naval Reserve.

CLARENCE MARSHALL YOUNG, LL.B.
Aviation

Aeronautics official; formerly manager, Pacific Division, Pan American Airways Company; Assistant Secretary of Commerce for Aeronautics.

EDWIN ZIEGFELD, B.S.L.A., B.S. IN ED., M.L.A., PH.D.
The Arts; Painting

Professor of Fine Arts and head of Department of Fine and Industrial Arts, Teachers College, Columbia University; formerly president, National Art Education Association; coauthor, 'Art Today', 'Art for Daily Living'; editor, 'Art Education Today', 'UNESCO Handbook on Art Education'.

JANET HULL ZIMMERMANN, A.B.
Birds; Nature Study; Canada

Formerly staff Natural History Supervisor and writer; secretary and director, Illinois Audubon Society; member, Chicago Ornithological Society; contributor to periodicals.

GEORGE FREDERICK ZOOK, A.M., PH.D., LL.D.
World War I

Late President, American Council on Education; member, U. S. National Commission for UNESCO; formerly U. S. Commissioner of Education.

HAROLD ZYSKIND, B.A., M.A.
Nation

Assistant Professor of Humanities in the College, Director of Curriculum Development at University College, University of Chicago.

CONSULTANTS AND CONTRIBUTORS

Canadian Advisory Board

CLARE R. MACLEOD, B.A., B.PAED.

Chairman, Canadian Advisory Board; Superintendent of Public Schools and Director of Education, Windsor, Ontario.

HAROLD S. BAKER, B.A., M.A., PH.D.

Dean, Faculty of Education, University of Alberta, Calgary, Alberta.

W. B. BAKER, B.S.A.

Director, Center for Community Studies, University of Saskatchewan, Saskatoon, Saskatchewan.

CHARLES BILODEAU, LL.D.

Département de l'Instruction publique, Province of Quebec.

GUY HENSON, B.A.

Director, The Institute of Public Affairs, Dalhousie University, Halifax, Nova Scotia.

MARSH JEANNERET, B.A.

Director, University of Toronto Press, Toronto, Ontario; author, 'Story of Canada', 'From Cartier to Champlain'; coauthor, 'Canada in North America', 2v.

RANTON MCINTOSH, B.A., M.ED., PH.D.

Department of Education, University of British Columbia, Vancouver, British Columbia; general editor, 'Canadian Reading Development Series'.

Advisers for Curriculum Correlation

EMMETT A. BETTS, A.B., A.M., PH.D.

Research Professor, School of Education, University of Miami; Editor in Chief, 'Education', Coral Gables, Fla.

WILLIAM H. BRISTOW, B.S., A.M., ED.D.

Assistant Superintendent, Bureau of Curriculum Development, New York City Public Schools, New York, N. Y.

W. LINWOOD CHASE, A.B., A.M., PH.D.

Formerly Professor of Education, Boston University, Boston, Mass.

JOHN J. DEBOER, A.B., A.M., PH.D.

Professor of Education, University of Illinois, Urbana, Ill.

LLOYD DENNIS

Principal, Bowmore Road Public School, Toronto, Ontario, Canada.

EDWIN H. FRIEDRICH, B.A., M.A.

Director of Curriculum Services, New Orleans Public Schools, New Orleans, La.; a John Hay fellow.

WILLIAM T. GRUHN, B.S., A.M., PH.D.

Professor of Education, University of Connecticut, Storrs, Conn.

RICHARD G. HANSEN, B.S., A.M., PH.D.

Superintendent of Schools, School District 107, Highland Park, Ill.

PAULINE HILLIARD, B.S., A.M., ED.D.

Professor of Elementary Education, University of Florida, Gainesville, Fla.

HOWARDINE G. HOFFMAN, A.B., B.S., M.S., ED.D.

Director, Division of Elementary Education, County of Los Angeles Public Schools, Los Angeles, Calif.

ROYCE H. KNAPP, B.S., A.M., ED.D.

Professor of Education, Department of Secondary Education, Teachers College, University of Nebraska, Lincoln, Neb.

PAUL J. MISNER, A.B., A.M., PH.D.

Professor of Education, Western Michigan University; formerly Superintendent of Schools, Glencoe, Ill.

HENRY J. OTTO, A.B., A.M., PH.D.

Graduate Advisor, College of Education, University of Texas, Austin, Tex.

Publishers' Acknowledgments

THE PICTURES in these volumes form a pictorial legion of honor, an elite corps chosen from the world's army of illustrations. For photographs alone, the Art Staff examines thousands of pictures each year to make the selection. They come from all parts of the world—from explorers and famous travelers, men of science, official archives, specialists—in short, from every source known to experts. To this great number of photographs there have been added large numbers of explanatory drawings, graphs, maps, and pictures. From this rare array the editors have gradually selected and kept only the best—the pictures you see in this edition. For every illustration you find here, you may know that more than a hundred were discarded.

In order to carry out with accuracy and completeness many educational features which had never before been attempted, whole series of photographs and drawings were specially prepared under the direct supervision of the Art and Editorial staffs. In the selection and preparation of these pictures the guiding principle was that each should serve either to explain and emphasize the text or to provide additional information. The captions and legends that accompany the pictures are designed to point out significant details of the subject illustrated. In this way text and picture form a closely knit and powerful educational alliance.

The publishers of this work feel a profound sense of gratitude to those whose cooperation has made possible these excellent illustrations. They regret that limitations of space make it necessary to confine acknowledgments to the special cases listed below.

CREDITS GIVEN

A. C. Gilbert Co.
A. Devaney, Inc.
A. I. Root Co.
Abbott, Chuck
Abbott, Randall W.
Abbott Laboratories
Abernathy, J. F.
Abrams Aerial Survey Corp.
Adams, Marcus
Adler Planetarium and Astronomical Museum
Aerial Photographers, Inc.
Aero Commander
Aerofilms, Ltd.
Aero o/y Press Information (Helsinki)
Aero Service Corp.
Agencia Geral Do Ultramar (Lisbon)
Agriculture, U. S. Dept. of
Aircraft Radio Corp.
Air Development Center, U. S.
Air Force, U. S.
Air France
Akeley, Delia J.
Alabama C. of C.
Alaska Pictorial Service
Alaska Visitors Assoc.
Alberta Dept. of Industry and Development
Alberta Government
Albuquerque C. of C.
Alexander Graham Bell Assoc. for the Deaf, Inc.
Allan Hancock Foundation
Allen, Arthur A.
Allen, O. N.
Allen B. DuMont Laboratories, Inc.
Allis-Chalmers Mfg. Co.
Allison Div., General Motors Corp.
All-Pets Magazine

Aluminium Ltd.
Aluminum Co. of America
Alvina Lenke Studio
Amarillo C. of C.
Amber Guild, Ltd.
American Ace, Maryland Farm
American Airlines
American Antiquarian Soc.
American Artist Magazine
American Assoc. for the Advancement of Science
American Barge Line Co.
American Battle Monument Commission
American Bee Journal
American Book Co.
American Brahman Breeders' Assoc.
American Bridge Div., U. S. Steel Corp.
American Cancer Soc.
American Canoe Assoc.
American Car and Foundry Co.
American Carpet Inst.
American Character Doll Co.
American Cocoa Research Inst.
American Cyanamid Co.
American Dairy Assoc.
American Dental Assoc.
American Drycleaner
American Express Co.
American Forest Products Industries
American Forestry Assoc.
American Genetic Assoc.
American Geographical Soc.
American Guernsey Cattle Club
American Heart Assoc.
American Hereford Assoc.
American House
American Humane Assoc.
American Inst. of Architecture

American Inst. of Baking
American Inst. of Laundering
American Inst. of Steel Construction
American Iron and Steel Inst.
American Jersey Cattle Club
American Legion
American Library Assoc.
American Medical Assoc.
American Meter Co.
American Motors Corp.
American Museum of Natural History
American National Theatre and Academy
American Petroleum Inst.
American Pigeon Journal
American Polled Hereford Assoc.
American Publications, Inc.
American Red Cross
American Scenic and Historic Preservation Soc.
American Spice Trade Assoc.
American-Swedish News
American Telephone & Telegraph Co.
American Tobacco Co.
American Toy Inst.
American Veterinarians Medical Assoc.
American Vocational Assoc.
American Walnut Mfrs. Assoc.
Ames Aeronautical Laboratory
AMF Pinspotters, Inc.
Amon Carter Museum of Western Art
Anaconda Co., The
Anderson, Gustav
Aquarium Stock Co., Inc.
Arabian American Oil Co.
Argonne National Laboratory
Arizona, University of
Arizona Photographic Associates, Inc.
Arkansas, University of

Arkansas Publicity and Parks
  Commission
Arkansas Rice Growers Cooperative
  Assoc.
Armco Steel Corp.
Armed Forces Inst. of Pathology
Armour & Co.
Armour Research Foundation
Armstrong Cork Co.
Army, U. S.
Army Times
Arnold, Rus
Arnold Arboretum
Arnold Ryan Chalpant & Associates
Arnold Schwinn & Co.
Arthurs, Stanley M.
Art Reference Bureau, Inc.
Arts Council of Great Britain
Asheville C. of C.
Asia Inst.
Asia Magazine
Ask, Gilbert
Asphalt Inst.
Assoc. of American Railroads
Asuc Photography
Atkeson, Ray
Atlanta C. of C.
Atomic Energy Commission, U. S.
Atwell, Harry
Audubon Naturalist Soc. of the
  Central Atlantic States, Inc.
Augusta (Ga.) C. of C.
Austin C. of C.
Australian Consolidated Press, Ltd.
Australian News & Information
  Bureau
Austrian State Tourist Bureau
Authenticated News International
Automobile Mfrs. Assoc.
Aviation Electric Ltd.
Ayrshire Breeders' Assoc.

B. De Rothschild Foundation for
  the Arts and Sciences, Inc.
B. F. Goodrich Co.
Babcock & Wilcox
Babson Bros. Co.
Bach, Lorena
Bagley Studios
Baha'i Temple
Baigdens
Bailey, Bernadine
Bakelite Co., Div. of Union Carbide
  Corp.
Baker, Robert H.
Baldwin Piano and Organ Co.
Ball Brothers Co.
Baltimore Assoc. of Commerce
Baltimore Public Schools
Banking Magazine
Bank of Montreal
Bantam Books, Inc.
Barry, David F.
Barzel, Ann
Battelle Memorial Inst.
Batton, Barton, Durstine & Osborn,
  Inc.
Bausch & Lomb Optical Co.
Beake-Huntington, Inc.
Becker, Gerald W.
Beech Aircraft Corp.
Behlen Mfg. Co.
Belgian Government Information
  Center

Belgian National Tourist Bureau
Bell Aircraft Corp.
Bell Helicopter Corp.
Bell Telephone Laboratories, Inc.
Bellingrath Gardens
Bendix Corp.
Berko Studio
Bernard L. Lewis, Inc.
Bernheim, Marc & Evelyne
Berry Schools
Bethlehem Steel Corp.
Better Homes and Gardens
Better Living Magazine
Bettmann Archive
Beverly Studio
Bibliothèque Nationale (Paris)
Bigelow-Sanford Carpet Co.
Biological Survey, U. S. Bureau of
Birmingham C. of C.
Bituminous Coal Inst.
Black & Decker Mfg. Co.
Black Star
Blue Bird Doll Hospital
Boatmen's National Bank of St.
  Louis
Bodine, A. Aubrey
Bodleian Library
Boeing Co.
Boise C. of C.
Bolens Products Div., Food
  Machinery & Chemical Corp.
Bolz, Roger W.
Bond, Fred E.
Bookbinder, Jack
Book of Knowledge (London)
Boston Globe
Boston Museum of Fine Arts
Boston Photo News Co.
Boston Public Library
Boughton, Beryl
Bourke-White, Margaret
Bowaters Southern Paper Corp.
Bowman Dairy Co.
Boy Scouts of America
Bradford-LaRiviere, Inc.
Bradshaw, Henry E.
Brandt, C.
Bremerton Public School District
Bridal Cave
British & Irish Railways, Inc.
British Central Office of Information
British Columbia Electric Co., Ltd.
British Columbia Government
British Columbia Government Travel
  Bureau
British Combine
British Council Press Div., British
  Information Services
British Museum
Brooke, L. Leslie
Brookhaven National Laboratory
Brooklyn Museum
Brooklyn Public Library
Brooks, H. M.
Brown, F. N. M.
Brown, Lewis R.
Brown & Bigelow
Brown Brothers
Brownell, L. W.
Brown Swiss Breeders' Assoc.
Brown University
Buchsbaum, Ralph
Buckbee-Mears Co.
Bucyrus-Erie Co.

Budd Photographer
Buehler Corp.
Buffalo Museum of Science
Buffalo Soc. of Natural Science
Bumiller, Ted
Bureau of Industrial Service
Burg, Amos
Burgess Battery Co.
Burleigh Brooks, Inc.
Burnell & Co., Inc.
Butcher, Devereux
Butler University

C. D. Gammon Co.
C. S. Hammond & Co., Inc.
Cadillac Motor Car Div., General
  Motors Corp.
Calgary (Alta.) Public Library
California, University of
California Div. of Highways
California Dried Fruit Research Inst.
California Fruit Growers Exchange
California Highways & Public Works
California Inst. of Technology
California Institution for Men
Californians, Inc.
California Prune and Apricot Growers
  Assoc.
Calvoss, Ulrich
Camera Clix, Inc.
Camera Hawaii
Camera Press (London)
Camp Fire Girls, Inc.
Canadian Bureau of Geology &
  Topography
Canadian Bureau of Information
Canadian Consulate General
Canadian Dept. of Agriculture
Canadian Dept. of Mines and
  Resources
Canadian Dept. of National Defence
Canadian Dept. of Resources &
  Development, Forestry Branch
Canadian Dominion Bureau of
  Statistics
Canadian Government Travel Bureau
Canadian National Railways
Canadian Pacific Airlines
Canadian Pacific Railway
Canadian Royal Air Force
Canadian Royal Army
Canadian Royal Navy
Cape Cod (Mass.) C. of C.
Capital Press Service
Capitol Records, Inc.
Carborundum Co.
Carnation Co.
Carnegie Institution of Washington
  (D. C.)
Carter Oil Co.
Cartwright & Co.
Casa de Portugal
Case Inst. of Technology
Caterpillar Tractor Co.
Census, U. S. Bureau of the
Central City (Colo.) Opera House
  Assoc.
Central Office of Information
  (London)
Central Press Photos Ltd.
Central Scientific Co.
Century Photos
Cessna Aircraft Co.
Chace, Lynwood M.

Chadde, Fred
Champion Aircraft Corp.
Champion Paper & Fiber Co.
Charles Pfizer & Co., Inc.
Charles Scribner's Sons
Charleston (S. C.) C. of C.
Chase Manhattan Bank Museum of Moneys of the World
Chesapeake & Ohio Railway Co.
Chevrolet Motor Div., General Motors Corp.
Chicago, Art Inst. of
Chicago, University of
Chicago Aerial Industries, Inc.
Chicago Aerial Survey
Chicago Architectural Photographing Co.
Chicago Assoc. of Commerce & Industry
Chicago Board of Education
Chicago Board of Trade
Chicago Burlington & Quincy Railroad Co.
Chicago Civic Opera Co.
Chicago Div. of Bridges & Viaducts
Chicago Fire Dept.
Chicago Historical Soc.
Chicago Housing Authority
Chicago Lighting Inst.
Chicago Mercantile Exchange
Chicago Musical Instrument Co.
Chicago Park District
Chicago Police Dept.
Chicago Public Library
Chicago Roller Skate Co.
Chicago Transit Authority
Chicago Tribune
Chicago Wesley Memorial Hospital
Chris-Craft Corp.
Christian Endeavor
Christian Science Publishing Soc.
Chrysler Building Corp.
Chrysler Corp.
Church, A.
Cincinnati, University of
Cincinnati Milling Machine Co.
Cities Service Oil Co.
City Museum and Art Gallery (Birmingham, England)
Civic Center Redevelopment Corp. (St. Louis, Mo.)
Civil Aeronautics Administration
Civil Air Patrol
Clark Art Inst.
Clarke, Cornelia
Cleff, Bernie
Cleveland C. of C.
Cleveland Cliffs Iron Co.
Coast Guard, U. S.
Coleman Co., Inc.
Colonial Trailer Corp.
Colonial Williamsburg
Colorado Springs C. of C.
Colorado State Advertising and Publicity Dept.
Columbia Pix
Columbia Records
Columbus (Ohio) C. of C.
Combine Photos
Combustion Engineering, Inc.
Commander Gatti Expeditions
Commerce, U. S. Dept. of
Commissariat Général au Tourisme
Commonwealth Edison Co.

Communicable Disease Center
Community Fund-Red Cross Joint Appeal
Conant, Roger and Isabelle Hunt
Confederation Life Assoc. Collection (Canada)
Connecticut Development Commission
Connecticut State Dept. of Education
Consolidated Mining and Smelting Co. of Canada, Ltd.
Consolidated Vultee Aircraft Corp.
Consulate General of Japan (New York)
Consumer Cooperative Assoc.
Container Corp. of America
Convair Div. of General Dynamics Corp.
Cooperative League of U. S. A.
Corcoran Gallery of Art
Cornell College
Cornell University
Corning Glass Works
Corps of Engineers, U. S. Army
Courier Journal & Louisville Times
Coward-McCann, Inc.
Craft Horizons
Crane, Donn P.
Crocker-Hamilton Papers Inc.
Cruickshank, Allan D.
Culver Service
Cunningham & Walsh, Inc.
Curry, John Steuart
Curta Co., The
Curtis & Cameron, Inc.
Curtis Publishing Co.
Cushing, Charles Phelps

D. V. Burrell Seed Growers Co.
Dalgliesh, Alice
Dallas C. of C.
Dallas Independent School Dist.
Dallas Public Library
Dalrymple, Byron
Dartmouth College
Davis, Albert
Decatur Public Library
Deere & Co.
Defense, U. S. Dept. of
DeLaMater, Mabel
Delaware River Port Authority
Delaware State Development Dept.
Delta Air Lines
Denver C. of C.
Denver Public Library
Desert Sea News Bureau
Des Moines C. of C.
Detroit Convention and Tourist Bureau
Detroit Inst. of Arts
Detroit News-Times
Detroit Publishing
Detroit Zoological Park
Dexter Press, Inc.
Diamond Match Div. of Diamond National Corp.
Diamond T Motor Truck Co.
Dickason, Deane
Dinkin, Luba
Dinsmore, Wayne
Dixon Pencil Co.
DoALL Co.
Dodd, Mead & Co.
Dole Pineapple Co.

Donner Crédit
Doremus & Co.
Doubleday & Co., Inc.
Dow Chemical Co.
Down Beat Magazine
Downtown Gallery
Draper Corp.
Dravo Corp.
Dry Zero Corp.
Duluth C. of C.
Dumont Laboratories
Durant's Photo Shop & Studio

E. B. Crocker Art Gallery
E. I. du Pont de Nemours & Co., Inc.
E. P. Dutton & Co., Inc.
Eastern Air Lines
Eastern Brahman Assoc.
Eastman Chemical Products, Inc.
Eastman Kodak Co.
Eberhard Faber Co.
Ebony Magazine
Ecke, Dr. Herbert
Eclectic Magazine
Edgerton, Germeshausen & Grier
Edison Electric Inst.
Edward Hines Lumber Co.
Eisenbeiss, Hermann (Germany)
El Dorado (Ark.) C. of C.
Electro-Motive Div., General Motors Corp.
Electro-Optical Systems, Inc.
Elgin National Watch Co.
Eli Lilly & Co.
Ellicott Machine Corp.
Elliott & Fry (London)
Emhart Mfg. Co.
Encyclopaedia Britannica Films, Inc.
Engineering & Mining Journal
Enterprise (Ala.) C. of C.
Escanaba (Mich.) C. of C.
Esquire, Inc.
Estey Organ Corp.
European Picture Service
Evanston Board of Education
Evening Bulletin
Evinrude Motors, Div. of Outboard Marine Corp.
Ewing Galloway
Exakta Camera Co.
Ezra Stoller Associates

Fair, Paul J.
Fairbanks Family in America, Inc.
Fairbanks Morse, Div. of Colt Industries, Inc.
Fairchild Aerial Surveys, Inc.
Fairchild Camera & Instrument Corp.
Farm Equipment Inst.
Federal Aviation Agency
Federal Bureau of Investigation
Federal Reserve Bank of New York
Feher, Joseph
Fenton, Carroll Lane
Fenton, Mildred Adams
Field Museum of Natural History (Chicago)
Finnish National Travel Office
Fire Engineering Co.
Firestone Tire & Rubber Co.
First Church of Christ, Scientist
First Federal Savings and Loan Assoc.
First National Bank of Chicago
Fish and Wildlife Service, U. S.

Fisher, Arthur H.
Fisher, W. A.
Fisher Body Craftsman's Guild
Fisher Scientific Co.
Florida, University of
Florida Citrus Commission
Florida State News Bureau
Fogg, Tyler
Fogg Museum of Art
Folger Shakespeare Library
Folk Arts Center, Inc.
Food Machinery & Chemical Corp.
Foote, Cone & Belding
Ford Foundation
Ford Motor Co.
Forest Preserve Dist. of Cook County
    (Ill.)
Forest Service, U. S.
Fort Ticonderoga Museum
Fortune Magazine
Fort Wayne C. of C.
Fort Worth C. of C.
Four-H Service Committee, Inc.
Foxboro Co.
France Actuelle
Frank, Carl
Frank, Kenneth
Frank C. Nahser, Inc.
Franklin Inst.
Frantzen, Earl A.
Frederick Warne & Co., Inc.
Freelance Photographers Guild, Inc.
Free Library of Philadelphia
Freeport Sulphur Co.
Free Public Library (East Orange,
    N. J.)
French Embassy Press & Information
    Div.
French Government Tourist Office
French National Railroads
Friden, Inc.
Friedman-Abeles
Frigidaire Div., General Motors Corp.
Fritzsche Brothers, Inc.
Fruitlands and Wayside Museum,
    Inc.
Fuller & Smith & Ross, Inc.
Furniture Mfrs. Assoc.
Future Farmers of America

G. Bell & Sons, Ltd.
G. Schirmer, Inc.
Galérie Louise Leiris
Gallery of Portraits
Garrett Corp.
Garrison, Richard
Gendreau, Philip D.
General Biological Supply House
General Dynamics Corp.
General Electric Co.
General Electric Research Laboratory
General Electric X-Ray Corp.
General Foods Corp.
General Motors Corp.
Genereux, Paul E.
Geological Survey, U. S.
Georgia, University of
Georgia Forestry Commission
Georgia Marble Co.
Georgian Bay Line
Georgia Power Co.
Gerard, John H.
German Consulate General
German Tourist Information Office

Germantown Academy
Gerster, Dr. George
Gildersleeve, L. G.
Gillette, Guy
Gillham Advertising Agency
Gilpin, Laura
Ginn & Co.
Girl Scouts of the U. S. A.
Glencoe (Ill.) Public Schools
Globe Photos, Inc.
Gloucester C. of C.
Goell, Theresa
Goforth, Marguerita
Golby, Bob
Goldstein, H.
Golf Digest Magazine
Golfing Magazine
Goodall Fabrics
Goodman Mfg. Co.
Goodman Theatre, Art Inst. of
    Chicago
Goodrich, Alice
Goodyear Aircraft Corp.
Goodyear News Service
Goodyear Tire & Rubber Co.
Gorham Co.
Goro, Fritz
Goss Co.
Gottscho-Schleisner, Inc.
Grace Line
Graflex, Inc.
Gramstorff Brothers
Grand Rapids C. of C.
Graphic House, Inc.
Gray, Johnnie M.
Gray Dove, The
Greater Boston C. of C.
Greater North Dakota Assoc.
Greater Pittsburgh C. of C.
Greater Vancouver (B. C.) Tourist
    Assoc.
Greater Vermont Assoc.
Great Northern Railway
Great Western Sugar Co.
Greensboro C. of C.
Greenwald, Inc.
Gregynog Press
Grenfell Assoc. of America
Gresham Committee, Royal Exchange
    (London)
Greyhound Corp.
Griffin's Photos
Grumman Aircraft Engineering Corp.
Gulfgate Shopping City (Houston)
Guthman Studios

H. Armstrong Roberts
H. A. Robins Co.
H. H. Bennett Studio
H. P. Hood & Sons
H. R. Harmer, Inc.
H. W. Wilson Co.
Haeger Potteries, Inc.
Hahn, Charless
Hall, Eugene J.
Hall, Robert B., Jr.
Halliday Historic Photo Co.
Halliwell, James O.
Hallmark Antique Valentine
    Collection
Hal Porter Photos
Hamilton Standard Propellers
Hamilton Wright Organization, Inc.
Hammond Organ Co.

Hampton Beach C. of C.
Haney, George
Hansen, H. Lee
Harcourt, Brace & World, Inc.
Harley-Davidson Motor Co.
Harold M. Lambert Studios
Harper & Row Publishers, Inc.
Harper's Magazine
Harrack, J. J.
Harrington, Richard
Harris & Ewing
Harrisburg C. of C.
Harris Pictures
Harry N. Abrams, Inc.
Hartford Special Machinery Co.
Hartwell Collection
Harvard College Library
Harvard University
Harvey, Fred
Hastings, Sue
Hawaiian Pineapple Co.
Hawaii Visitors Bureau
Hawkins, J. Allen
Hayes Memorial Library
Hazen, Delmer
Health, Education, and Welfare,
    U. S. Dept. of
Hedrich-Blessing
Heilman, Grant
Helena C. of C.
Helio Aircraft Corp.
Hendricks, Hodge
Henle, Fritz
Henry Ford Museum
Herbert Photo, Inc.
Herbert Photos
Herrick, Margaret
Hershey Chocolate Corp.
Herter, Albert
Hertzberg Circus Collection
Hess, Chester Newton
Hess, John
Hess, Lilo
Hildebrand
Hiller Aircraft Corp.
Hillman, George T.
Hispanic Soc. of America
Historical Pictures Service
Historical Soc. of Pennsylvania
Hobbies Magazine
Hoffman, Malvina
Hohenberger, Frank M.
Holiday Magazine
Holzman, Frank
Homer Laughlin China Co.
Homestake Mining Co.
Honegars
Hoppe, E. O.
Horse and Mule Assoc. of America
Horydczak
Hosmer, Paul
Hotpoint Co., Div. of General
    Electric Co.
Hougen's Ltd.
Hough, R. B.
Hough & Sanborn
Houghton Mifflin Co.
House of Photography
Housing and Urban Development,
    U. S. Dept. of
Houston, Roger
Houston C. of C.
Houston Museum of Fine Arts
Howard, John H.

PUBLISHERS' ACKNOWLEDGMENTS

Howard University
Howe & Lescaze, Architects
Hudson's Bay Co.
Humane Soc. of Illinois
Hunn, Max
Hunter, George
Hunt Foods, Inc.
Huntington Library and
    Art Gallery
Hurok Attractions, Inc.

I. de Wys, Inc.
Iceland, Legation of (Washington,
    D. C.)
Iceland Tourist Bureau (Reykjavik)
Idaho, University of
Idaho State C. of C.
Ideal Toy Corp.
Ilford, Ltd.
Illinois, University of
Illinois Bell Telephone Co.
Illinois Central R.R. Co.
Illinois Education Assoc.
Illinois State Dept. of Public Health
Illinois State Dept. of Public Works
    and Buildings
Illinois State Div. of Dept. Reports
Illinois State Div. of Parks &
    Memorials
Illinois State Employment Service
Illinois State Penitentiary
Illinois Tollway
Illustrated London News
Imperial Oil, Ltd.
India, Government of
Indiana Dept. of Conservation
Indian Affairs, U. S. Bureau of
Indiana Historical Soc.
Indianapolis C. of C.
Indianapolis Motor Speedway Corp.
Indiana State Police Dept.
Indiana University
Indonesia, Republic of
Ingersoll-Rand Co. (Canada)
Inland Steel Co.
Inst. of Human Development
Instituto Nacional del Libro
    Español
Instructor Magazine
Insurance Co. of North America
Interior, U. S. Dept. of the
International Assoc. of Chiefs of
    Police
International Bank for Reconstruction
    and Development
International Business Machines
    Corp.
International Civil Aviation
    Organization
International Cooperation
    Administration
International Engineering, Inc.
International Film Service
International Harvester Co.
International Ladies' Garment
    Workers' Union
International News Photos
International Newsreel
International Nickel Co., Inc.
Intertype Co.
Iowa Development Commission
Irish Tourist Assoc.
Israel Consulate
Italian State Tourist Office

J. B. Lippincott Co.
J. C. Allen & Sons
J. C. Deagan, Inc.
J. H. Day Co., Inc.
J. Horace McFarland Co.
Jackson & Perkins
Jacksonville (Fla.) C. of C.
James Lees and Sons
James Monroe Memorial Foundation,
    Inc.
James Press
James S. Robbins & Associates, Inc.
Jamestown Foundation
Janion, Aubrey P.
Japan Tourist Assoc.
Jedd, Joseph
Jefferys, C. W. (from Imperial Oil
    Collection)
Jeffries, T. A.
Jensen Mfg. Co.
Jerichau, Elizabeth
Jewel Companies, Inc.
John and Mable Ringling Museum of
    Art
John B. Stetson Co.
John Deere, Moline, Ill.
John Donat Photography
John Hancock Mutual Life
    Insurance Co.
John L. Van Zant and Associates
John Mather Lipton Co.
John Morell & Co.
John Reid & Associates
Johns Hopkins Hospital
John Swenson Granite Co., Inc.
Jones & Lamson Machine Co.
Jones & Laughlin Steel Corp.
Journal of Pediatrics
Joy Mfg. Co.
Judy Publishing Co.
Juneau C. of C.
Justice, U. S. Dept of (Bureau of
    Prisons)

Kabel, John
Kaiser Aluminum & Chemical Sales,
    Inc.
Kaiser Services
Kaiser Steel Corp.
Kalamazoo Sled Co.
Kane, Henry B.
Kannegiesser, Hans
Kansas, University of
Kansas City (Mo.) Public Library
Kansas Industrial Development
    Commission
Kaufmann & Fabry Co.
Kay Laboratories
Kay Musical Instrument Co.
Kehr, E. H.
Keinigsberg, Leon
Kenmore Assoc.
Kennebec Journal
Kennecott Copper Corp.
Kentucky, University of
Kenyon, Katharine M.
Kepes, Juliet
Keystone Pictures, Inc.
Keystone View Co.
Kimberly-Clark Corp.
Kitchen Kreeper Co.
Klep, Rolf
KLM Aerocarto N. V.
Klots, Alexander B.

Knoll Associates, Inc.
Knopf, Alfred A., Inc.
Knouff, Lorentz Bennett
Kollsman Instrument Corp.
Korling, Torkel
Korth, Fred G.

Labor, U. S. Dept. of
Lafayette Ltd.
Lancaster (Pa.) C. of C.
Langley Aeronautical Laboratory
Lansing State Journal
Lanston Monotype Co.
Lanza, Anthony
Laredo C. of C.
La Tour, Cy
La Varre, William
Lawrence, Ralph E.
LeBlang, Sedge
Lederle Laboratories, Div. of
    American Cyanamid Co.
Lee-Norse Co.
Les Éditions Mondiales
Lewis, Frank
Lewis, Frederic
Libbey-Owens-Ford Glass Co.
Library of Congress
Lick Observatory
Liebes, Dorothy
Life Magazine
Lighthall, Allison
Lincoln National Life Insurance Co.
Lincoln Park (Chicago) Zoo
Linde Air Products Co.
Link Aviation, Inc., Div. of
    General Precision Equipment Corp.
Link-Belt Co.
Literary Magazine
Little League Baseball, Inc.
Little Rock C. of C.
Lockheed Aircraft Corp.
Lockwood Greene Engineers, Inc.
Lomen Brothers
London Electrotype Agency
London Royal Academy
London Sphere
London Times
Longacre and Herring
Long Island State Park Commission
Longmans, Green & Co.
Lorant, Stefan
Los Angeles C. of C.
Los Angeles County Air Pollution
    Control Dist.
Los Angeles County C. of C.
Los Angeles Times News Bureau
Louisiana State Dept. of Commerce
    and Industry
Louisville (Ga.) C. of C.
Louisville (Ga.) Free Public Library
Louisville (Ky.) C. of C.
Lowell Observatory
Lubbock C. of C.
Luedeke Studio
Lukens Steel Co.
Lyon-Healy

McCormick International
McCulloch Brothers
McDonnell Douglas Corp.
McGraw-Hill Book Co.
Mackinac Bridge Authority
McManigal, J. W.
Macmillan Co.

McNally, Terence J.
Macrae Smith Co.
Madison (Wis.) Public Schools
Madsen, Edna
Magazine Publishers Assoc., Inc.
Magnum Photos, Inc.
Maine Development Commission
Malak
Mammoth Cave Operating Committee
Maney, Richard
Manitoba Dept. of Industry and
    Commerce
Manley, Ray
Marine Biological Laboratory
    (England)
Marine Corps, U. S.
Mariners' Museum
Marine Studios
Maritime Commission, U. S.
Markow Photography
Martin, Keith
Marx, M. Richard
Maryland Dept. of Information
Maryland Historical Soc.
Massachusetts, University of
Massachusetts Dept. of Commerce
Massachusetts Inst. of Technology
Massie-Missouri Resources Div.
Masters in Art
May, Charles
Mead Corp.
Mee, Arthur
Meister Bräuser Sports Car Racing
    Team
Mélançon, Louis
Melchers, Mrs. Gari
Menninger Foundation
Mercersburg Academy Press Club
Merck & Co., Inc.
Mergenthaler Linotype Co.
Meridian (Miss.) C. of C.
Merkel, H. W.
Merrill Lynch, Pierce, Fenner &
    Smith Inc.
Metro-Goldwyn-Mayer, Inc.
Metropolitan Fair & Exposition
    Authority
Metropolitan Life Insurance Co.
Metropolitan Museum of Art
Metropolitan Opera Assoc., Inc.
Metropolitan Water District of
    Southern California
Miami Beach News Bureau
Miami Conservancy District
Miami-Metro News Bureau
Miami Seaquarium
Michaud, Joe
Michigan, University of
Michigan Dept. of Conservation
Michigan State University
Michigan Tourist Council
Middlebury College
Mignard
Mili, Gjon
Millar, Ronald
Milwaukee Public Museum
Mines, U. S. Bureau of
Mine Safety Appliances Co.
Minneapolis C. of C.
Minneapolis Sunday Tribune
Minnesota, University of
Minnesota Dept. of Business
    Research and Development
Minnesota Div. of Publicity

Mishkin
Mississippi Agricultural and
    Industrial Board
Mississippi Library Commission
Missouri, University of
Mobile C. of C.
Mobile Homes Mfg. Assoc.
Mobil Oil Corp.
Modernage, Vanadium Corp. of
    America
Modern Pharmacy
Mohr, Charles
Monkmeyer Press Photo Service
Monotype, Ltd.
Monsanto Chemical Co.
Montana State University
Montgomery C. of C.
Montpelier (Vt.) Board of Historic
    Sites
Montpelier National Life Insurance
    Co.
Montreal, Municipal Tourist Office of
Moore-McCormack Lines, Inc.
Moran Towing & Transportation Co.
Morey, Humm & Warwick, Inc.
Morgan, C. Ray
Morrison, A. Q.
Morse, Norman K.
Morton Salt Co.
Motorola, Inc.
Mount Wilson Observatory
Muench, David
Muench, Josef
Mukoyama, Terno
Mulholland, John
Museum of Modern Art
Museum of Negro History and Art
Museum of Science and Industry
    (Chicago)
Museum of the American Indian,
    Heye Foundation
Music Corp. of America

N. W. Ayer & Son, Inc.
Nash, Ernest
Nashville C. of C.
Nashville Public Library
National Academy of Sciences
National Advisory Committee for
    Aeronautics
National Aeronautics and Space
    Administration
National Archives
National Art Gallery (Canada)
National Assoc. of Audubon Societies
National Audubon Soc.
National Aviation Education Council
National Biscuit Co.
National Broadcasting Corp.
National Bureau of Standards
National Capital Commission
    (Canada)
National Cash Register Co.
National Citizens Committee for
    Educational Television
National Coal Assoc.
National Committee for Careers in
    Medical Technology
National Congress of Parents and
    Teachers
National Cotton Council of America
National Cottonseed Products Assoc.,
    Inc.
National Education Assoc.

National Film Board of Canada
National Gallery (London)
National Gallery of Art
National Garden Bureau
National Geographic Magazine
National Geographic Soc.
National Girl Scout News Bureau
National Homes Corp.
National Housing Center Library
National Inst. of Drycleaning, Inc.
National Inst. of Health
National Library of Medicine
National Life Insurance Co.
National Machine Tool Builders
    Assoc.
National Maritime Museum
National Museum of Archaeology
    (Mexico)
National Observer
National Park Service
National Radio Astronomy
    Observatory
National Recreation Assoc.
National Red Cross
National Rifle Assoc.
National Safety Council
National Science Foundation
National Science Teacher Assoc.
National Screen Service Corp.
National Shoe Mfrs. Assoc.
National Soybean Crop Improvement
    Council
Natural Rubber Bureau
Nature in Pictures
Navy, U. S.
Nebraska, University of
Nebraska State Dept. of Roads and
    Irrigation
Nebraska State Div. of Resources
Nebraska State Historical Soc.
Nemec, George P.
Neon Products, Inc.
Nestor Johnson Mfg. Co.
Netherlands Information Service
Neurath
Nevada State Highway Dept.
Newark News
Newark Public Library
New Bedford Times
Newberry Library (Chicago)
New Brunswick Travel Bureau
New England Mutual Life Insurance
    Co.
New Hampshire, University of
New Hampshire Planning &
    Development Commission
New Jersey State Dept. of Conserva-
    tion & Economic Development
New Jersey Turnpike Authority
Newman, Arnold
Newman Kraft Studio
New Mexico State Tourist Bureau
New Orleans C. of C.
New Orleans Times-Picayune
Newport News Shipbuilding and
    Dry Dock Co.
New York City Ballet Co.
New York City Board of Education
New York City Board of Water
    Supply
New York City Dept. of Public
    Works
New York Convention & Visitors
    Bureau

PUBLISHERS' ACKNOWLEDGMENTS

New York Cotton Exchange
New York Daily News
New York Herald Tribune
New York Historical Soc.
New York Housing Authority
New York Philharmonic Orchestra
New York Public Library
New York Shipbuilding Corp.
New York State Dept. of Commerce
New York State Thruway Authority
New York Stock Exchange
New York Times
New York Zoological Soc.
New Zealand Embassy
Niagara Falls Convention &
    Visitors Service
Niagara Frontier State Park Com-
    mission
Nickel, Richard
Norair Div. of Northrop Aircraft, Inc.
North American Aviation, Inc.
North American Lace Co.
North Carolina Dept. of Conservation
    & Development
North Dakota, University of
Northern Paper Mills
Northwestern University
Northwestern University Medical
    School
Northwest Orient Airlines
Norwegian Information Service
Notre Dame, University of
Nova Scotia Information Service

O. E. M. Photo
Oak Brook Polo Club
Oakland C. of C.
Oakland Park Dept.
Oak Ridge Inst. of Nuclear Studies
Oberlin College
O'Connor, Jack
Office of Economic Opportunity
Office of the City Representative
    (Philadelphia)
Ogden, H. A.
Ogden, William S.
Ohio Agricultural Experiment
    Station
Ohio Brass Co.
Ohio Development & Publicity
    Commission
Ohio Leather Co.
Ohio State University
Oil Well Supply Co.
Oklahoma, University of
Oklahoma Planning & Resources
    Board
Oliver Corp.
Oliver Plow Works
Omaha C. of C.
Ontario Dept. of Planning &
    Development, Conservation Branch
Ontario Dept. of Travel & Publicity
Ontario Hydro-Electric Power
    Commission
Ontario Public Archives
Opp Cotton Mills
Ordeman, Les T.
Oregon, University of
Oregon State Highway Commission
Oriental Inst.
Orient & Occident
Orne, Harold
Oscar, Marcus

Ottawa Journal
Outdoor Advertising Assoc. of
    America
Overton, Jacqueline
Owens-Corning Fiberglas Corp.
Owens-Illinois Glass Co.
P. & A. Photos
Pach Brothers
Pacific Gas & Electric Co.
Pakistan, Embassy of
Palmer Chemical & Equipment Co.
Palomar Pictures
Panagra
Panama Canal Co.
Pan-American Coffee Bureau
Pan American Petroleum Corp.
Pan American Union
Pan American World Airways System
Pan-Pacific Press Bureau
Paquette, Edward
Parachutes, Inc.
Parke, Davis & Co.
Parker, Elinor
Parker, Maynard L.
Parker, Paul
Partridge, Basil
Passmore, Lee
Patterson Publishing Co.
Paul, George F.
Paul Popper, Ltd.
Peace Corps
Pennsylvania Historical and
    Museum Commission
Pennsylvania New York Central R. R.
Pennsylvania State Dept. of
    Commerce
Peoples and Places Magazine
Peoples Gas Light & Coke Co.
Peoria Assoc. of Commerce
Perkins & Will
Peter Pauper Press
Peter Persch & Sons Co.
Phaidon Press Ltd. (London)
Pharmaceutical Mfrs. Assoc.
Philadelphia C. of C.
Philadelphia Museum of Art
Philadelphia Zoo
Philippine Tourist and Travel
    Assoc., Inc.
Philips Electronics, Instruments Div.
Phoenix C. of C.
Photographic History Service
Photo-Representatives
Photo Researchers, Inc.
Photo Service Co.
Pickett & Eckel, Inc.
Pictorial Parade, Inc.
Pictured Knowledge
Pierpont Morgan Library
Pillsbury Co.
Pioneer Parachute Co., Inc.
Piper Aircraft Corp.
Pittsburgh, University of
Pittsburgh C. of C.
Pittsburgh Plate Glass Co.
Pitz, Henry C.
Pix, Inc.
Plymouth Cordage Co.
Polaroid Corp.
Polk's Studio
Popular Photography
Popular Science Monthly
Porter, Eliot F.
Portland Cement Assoc.

Portland (Ore.) Public Schools
Port of Detroit Commission
Port of New York Authority
Port of Seattle
Post Office Dept., U. S.
Pote, Louise
Power Authority of the State of
    New York
Pratt & Whitney Aircraft
Preservation Soc. of Newport
    County (R. I.)
Press Assoc., Inc.
Preston, William G.
Primary Educational Service
Public Archives of Canada
Public Health Service, U. S.
Public Photo Service
Public Roads, U. S. Bureau of
Public Service Co. of Northern
    Illinois
Publisher's Photo Service
Publix Pictorial Service
Pueblo (Colo.) C. of C.
Puerto Rico, Commonwealth of
Puerto Rico News Service
Pullman Standard
Putman Publishing Co.

Q. M. Food & Container Inst.
Quebec Provincial Publicity Bureau
Queens Borough Public Library

R. G. LeTourneau, Inc.
R. R. Donnelley & Sons Co.
Radio City Music Hall
Radio Corp. of America
Radio Times Hulton Picture Library
    (London)
Ragsdale, Fred H.
Rand McNally & Co.
Random House
Ran Studio
Rapho Guillumette
Raven Industries, Inc.
Raytheon Co.
R E A Express
Réalités Magazine
Reclamation, U. S. Bureau of
Record Press
Red Poll Cattle Club of America
Redwood Empire Assoc.
Reeves, James E.
Regina (Sask.) C. of C.
Reno C. of C.
Rensselaer Polytechnic Inst.
Republic Flow Meters Co.
Republic Steel Corp.
Revell, Inc.
Revillon Frères
Rheem Mfg. Co.
Rhode Island, University of
Rhode Island Development Council
Rice, Pearl
Richie, Robert Yarnall
Richmond C. of C.
Ring Guild of America
Ringling Bros. and Barnum & Bailey
Rinker, Edward
Rittase, William M.
Roach, O.
Roads and Streets Magazine
Robinson, Gus
Roche
Rochester Public Library
Rockefeller Center, Inc.

Rockefeller Foundation
Rock Island Lines
Rock of Ages Corp.
Rockwell, F. F.
Rockwell Mfg. Co.
Rodd, Emma Zvorist
Rogers, Mrs. Walter
Rogers, Lunt & Bowlen
Rohm & Haas Co.
Rolls-Royce, Inc.
Rondot, Edward E.
Rose, Ben
Ross, John G.
Ross Hall Studio
Rowland, Frank
Royal Dutch Airlines
Royal Greek Embassy
Royal McBee Corp.
Roy Bernard Co., Inc.
Rubenstein, Harry
Rumel, Hal
Rutgers University

S. C. Johnson & Son, Inc.
Sacramento C. of C.
Sailors, Robert D.
St. Charles Mfg. Co.
St. Dunstan's University (Canada)
St. Elizabeth's Hospital (Washington, D. C.)
St. Lawrence Seaway Development Corp.
St. Louis City Art Museum
St. Paul C. of C.
St. Simons Island C. of C.
Salvation Army
San Antonio C. of C.
Sanborn, Elwin R.
San Diego Zoo
Sanford, Eric M.
San Francisco C. of C.
San Francisco Housing Authority
San Francisco International Airport
Santa Barbara C. of C.
Santa Fe Railway
Sarony-Burroughs
Saskatchewan Dept. of Industry & Information
Saudi Arabian Public Relations Bureau
Savage, Steele
Savannah C. of C.
Sawders, James
Scacheri, Mario
Schalek, Alice
Scherl & Roth, Inc.
School Dist. of Philadelphia
Schroder, Hugo H.
Schutt, Paul
Schweizer Aircraft Corp.
Science Illustrated
Science Service, Inc.
Scientific American
Scott, Henry D.
Scottsbluff (Neb.) C. of C.
Scott Wilson & Associates
Scranton C. of C.
Scrivener Press (England)
Seagrave Corp.
Seattle C. of C.
Seely Service
Sentinel Publishing Co.
Service Général de l'Information (Morocco)

Sesera Studios
Sets in Order Magazine
Seymour, John
Sheldon, H. H.
Shell Oil Co.
Sherrit Flag Co., Inc.
Shostal
Shriber, Anne
Shufeldt
Shure Brothers, Inc.
Signal Corps, U. S. Army
Sikorsky Aircraft Div.
Simon & Schuster, Inc.
Sinclair Refining Co.
Singer Sewing Machine Co.
Sioux City C. of C.
Sioux Falls C. of C.
Ski Industries of America
Skokie Public Library
Small Homes Council, University of Illinois
Smith, Ida
Smith, Kline & French Laboratories
Smithsonian Institution
Smith Studios
Soc. for the Preservation of New England Antiquities
Soc. of American Bacteriologists
Soil Conservation Service
South Africa Government Information Office
South African Tourist Corp.
South Bend Lathe Works
South Carolina State Dept. of Education
South Carolina State Development Board
South Dakota Dept. of Highways
Southern Bell Telephone & Telegraph Co.
Southern California, University of
Southern Methodist University
Southern Pacific Railroad
Southwest Museum
Sovfoto
Spanish National Tourist Office
Sparger, Celia
Spence Air Photos
Spencer, Hugh
Sperry Gyroscope Co.
Springfield (Ill.) Historical Soc.
Squire Haskins
Stack's Coins
Standard Brands, Inc.
Standard Oil Co. (Ind.)
Standard Oil Co. (N. J.)
Standard Studios
Stanford Research Inst.
Stanford University
Stanley Tools
Stapleton, William
State, U. S. Dept. of
Staten Island Historical Soc.
State Street (Chicago) Council
Steelways
Steinman, D. B.
Steinway & Sons
Stephens College
Sternig, John
Stevens Enterprises, Inc.
Stewarts Commercial Photographers, Inc.
Stewart-Warner Corp.
Stock, R. P.

Stone Mountain Memorial Park
Stoy, Werner
Stratford (Ont.) C. of C.
Stuart Motors, Inc.
Studebaker Corp.
Sugar Research Foundation, Inc.
Sunday Pictorial (London)
Sunkist Growers
Sun Valley News Bureau
Sutton, Sam R.
Swain, Ralph B.
Swain, Su Zan N.
Swedish Information Service
Swedish National Travel Office
Swift & Co.
Swiss Federal Railways
Swiss National Tourist Office
Sylvania Electric Products, Inc.
Syracuse C. of C.

Tabor & Prang
Tampa C. of C.
Taylor Instrument Companies
Tea Council of the U. S. A.
Teale, Edwin Way
Tennessee Conservation Dept.
Tennessee Eastman Co.
Tennessee Valley Authority
Testa, Angelo
Texaco, Inc.
Texas, University of
Texas Highway Dept.
Texas Longhorn Cavern
Thomas, Arthur H.
Thomas A. Edison Industries
Thomas Jefferson Memorial Foundation
Thompson, William
Thomson, Paul
Three Lions, Inc.
Timber Structures, Inc.
Time, Inc.
Tisdale, E.
Title Guarantee Co.
Today's Health
Tokheim Corp.
Toledo, University of
Tootons Studios (Canada)
Topical Press Agency, Ltd.
Toronto (Ont.) Board of Education
Toronto Dominion Bank
Toronto Public Library
Toronto Star Syndicate
Torrey, Helen
Torrington Co.
Trans World Airlines
Travel & Industrial Development Assoc. of Great Britain & Ireland
Travel Magazine
Trefts, Charles
Triangle Photo Service
Triborough Bridge and Tunnel Authority
Troy, John P.
Tulsa C. of C.
Turkish Information Office
Twentieth Century Fox Film Corp.
Twin Falls C. of C.

Ulysses Book Shop
Underwood & Underwood
Underwriters' Laboratories, Inc.
UNESCO
Union Pacific R. R.
Union Special Machine Co.

PUBLISHERS' ACKNOWLEDGMENTS

Union Title Insurance Co.
United Air Lines
United Fruit Co.
United Nations
United Press International
United Shoe Machinery Corp.
U. S. Divers Corp.
U. S. Lines, Inc.
U. S. Machine Corp.
U. S. Military Academy
U. S. Naval Academy
U. S. Naval Academy Museum
U. S. Naval Observatory
U. S. Navy Submarine Library &
   Museum
U. S. Secret Service
U. S. Steel Corp.
U. S. Testing Co., Inc.
Universal International Films, Inc.
Universal Match Corp.
University Museum (Pa.)
Urban, Julian
Urquhart, Kenneth Trist
Utah, University of
Utah Dept. of Publicity & Industrial
   Development

Valdiosera
Valley Forge State Park
Vancouver (B. C.) Public Library
Vandamm Studio
Vanilla Bean Assoc. of America, Inc.
Van Riper, Walker
Van Zele, Helen
VariTyper Corp.
Vaughan's Seed Co.
Venezuela Embassy Information
   Service
Verbelke
Vermont Development Commission
Veterans Administration
Vickers, Inc.
Viking Press, Inc.
Virginia Dept. of Conservation and
   Development
Virginia Dept. of Highways
Virginia State C. of C.
Volkswagen of America, Inc.
Voureo Glass Co.

W. A. Mansell & Co.

W. A. Sheaffer Pen Co.
W. Atlee Burpee Co.
W. R. Scott, Inc.
W. W. Kimball Co.
Walker, Evangeline
Walt Disney Productions
Walter Baker Co.
Wanberg, Dr. C. W.
Ward, Fred
Ward's Natural Science
   Establishment, Inc.
Warner, Al
Warner Brothers
Washburn, Bradford
Washington, University of
Washington (D. C.) Board of Trade
Washington Convention & Visitors
   Bureau
Washington State Advertising
   Commission
Washington State Progress Commission
Waterman Co.
Wayne State University
Weather Bureau, U. S.
Webcor, Inc.
Weeks, Ethelyn
Weimer, Charles Perry
Weller, Paul
WENR Television
Werckmeister
Wesley Bowman Studio, Inc.
Western Cartridge Co.
Western Design and Electronics
Western Electric Co.
Western Pine Assoc.
Western Printing and Lithographing
   Co.
Western Union Telegraph Co.
Western Ways
Westinghouse Broadcasting Co.
Westinghouse Electric Corp.
West Virginia Conservation
   Commission
West Virginia Industrial and
   Publicity Commission
Weyerhaeuser Timber Co.
WGN, Inc.
Wheat Flour Inst.
Whirlpool Corp.
White, Harper
White & Renner

White Motor Co.
Whizzer Motor Co.
Wichita C. of C.
Wichita City Library
Wide World Photos
Wilder & Wentworth
Will & Baumer Candle Co., Inc.
Williams, Maynard Owen
William Strange Co.
Wilson, Douglas P.
Wilson Co.
Winchester Repeating Arms Co.
Windsor Star
Wine Inst.
Wisconsin, University of
Wisconsin Assoc. of Commerce
Wisconsin Conservation Dept.
Wisconsin State Historical Soc.
Wolfe Commercial Photo Service
Woltz Aerial Photo Service, Inc.
Womack, Dr. C. Ray
Woodhead Photos
Woods, Samuel
Woods Hole Oceanographic Inst.
Wool Bureau
World Health Organization
World Publishing Co.
Worthington Pump Co.
Wright, Joe
Wright Air Development Div. of Air
   Research & Development Command
Wurlitzer Co.
Wyman-Gordon Co.
Wyoming, University of
Wyoming State Dept. of Commerce
   and Industry
Wyoming Travel Commission

Yale University Press
Yerkes Observatory
YMCA
York Corp.
York University (Canada)
Yorkville High School of Women
   Service Trades
Yosemite Park & Curry Co.
Youngstown C. of C.
YWCA

Zaharis
Zehrt, Jack
Zeiss, Carl

THE PUBLISHERS also desire to acknowledge the courtesy of those who have given special permission for the use of copyrighted text and picture matter, as follows:

FOR ADDITIONAL Publishers' Acknowledgments of picture credits, see end of Volume 24.

A. S. Barnes and Co., Inc., for adaptation of drawings from 'The Outdoor Encyclopedia' T-105.

American Heritage Publishing Co., Inc., for adaptation of map from 'Picture History of the Civil War' A-449.

Atlantic, Little, Brown & Co., for illustration from 'Ounce, Dice, Trice', by Alastair Reid (© 1958 by Alastair Reid and Ben Shahn) R-107; for drawing by Juliet Kepes from 'Laughing Time', by William Jay Smith (© 1953 by the Curtis Publishing Co.) © 1953, 1955 by William Jay Smith) R-105.

Curtis Publishing Co., for reproduction of photograph from Holiday Magazine (© 1955) C-193.

Doubleday and Co., Inc., for poem 'As toilsome I wandered Virginia's woods' from 'Leaves of Grass', by Walt Whitman P-407; for reproduction of color drawings from 'The Insect Guide', by Ralph B. Swain I-199-202; for permission (with Mrs. George Bambridge) to quote from 'Just So Stories', by Rudyard Kipling (© 1900 by Rudyard Kipling) R-105.

Harcourt, Brace & Co., for adaptation of chart from 'Women and Men' (© 1933, 1934 by Amram Scheinfeld) C-267; for adaptation of charts from 'Life: an Introduction to Biology', by Simpson Pittendrigh and Tiffany (© 1957) A-417-19; for adaptation of

drawings from 'The Dancing Bees', by Karl von Frisch B-106-7.

Harcourt, Brace & World, Inc., for reproduction of book jackets for 'The Education of Hyman Kaplan', artist Leo Manso R-112e; and 'A Fall of Moondust', artist Arthur Hawkins R-112i.

Harper & Brothers, for quote from the introduction to 'A Little Book of Necessary Nonsense', by Burges Johnson R-107; for basic material from chart page 89 of 'Oil for the World', by Schackne and Drake (© 1960) P-241.

PUBLISHERS' ACKNOWLEDGMENTS

Henry Holt and Co., for poem 'The Cherry Tree' from 'A Shropshire Lad', by A. E. Housman P-405.

Houghton Mifflin Co., for poem 'The Sonnet', by R. W. Gilder P-406.

Ilford, Ltd., and A. C. Black & Co. (London), for reproduction of X-ray photographs from 'Anatomy and Ballet', by Celia Sparger B-33.

Jeppesen & Co., for adaptations and reproductions of illustrations from 'Marine Navigation', by P. V. H. Weems and C. V. Lee (© 1958) N-85-7.

Little, Brown & Co., for 'The Clam', by Ogden Nash (© 1962 by Ogden Nash) N-15a; for poem 'I'll Tell You How the Sun Rose', from 'Poems by Emily Dickinson', edited by Martha Dickinson Bianchi and Alfred Leete Hampson R-107; for illustration from 'Favorite Fairy Tales Told in France', by Virginia Haviland (text © 1959 by Virginia Haviland, illustrations © 1959 by Roger Duvoisin) R-109c; for illustration from 'Le Hibou et la poussiquette', by Francis Steegmuller (text © 1959, 1961 by Francis Steegmuller, illustrations © 1961 by Barbara Cooney) R-111e.

McGraw-Hill Book Co., Inc., for stills from the film series 'Child Development', produced by the Text-Film Dept. A-34-6, C-265-79, M-174-6, P-385; for reproduction of diagram of salt process from 'Chemical Process Industries', by R. N. Shreve (© 1945) H-287.

Macmillan Co., for reproduction of line drawing of a trip lever from 'Technical Drawing', by Henry C. Spencer (© 1952) M-202.

Parke, Davis & Co., for reproduction of painting by Robert A. Thom from 'A History of Pharmacy in Pictures', by George A. Bender P-248b.

Pei, Mario, for adaptation of map from article "Swahili," in Holiday Magazine, April 1959 A-89.

Rand McNally & Co., for reproduction of book jacket for 'Aku-Aku', by Thor Heyerdahl (© 1958 by Thor Heyerdahl) R-112f.

Teachers College, Columbia University, for quote from 'Reading Is Fun', by Roma Gans R-103.

Viking Press, for adaptations and reproductions of illustrations from 'Across the Space Frontier' and 'Conquest of the Moon', edited by Cornelius Ryan (© Crowell-Collier 1952, 1953) S-348c-d.

HERE AND THERE IN VOLUME 1

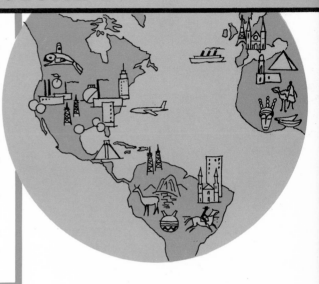

AT ODD TIMES when you are just looking for "something interesting to read," without any special plan in mind, this list will help you. With this as a guide, you may visit faraway countries, watch people at their work and play, meet famous persons of ancient and modern times, review history's most brilliant incidents, explore the marvels of nature and science, play games—in short, find whatever suits your fancy of the moment. This list is not intended to serve as a table of contents, an index, or a study guide. For these purposes consult the Fact-Index and the Reference-Outlines.

HERE AND THERE IN VOLUME 1

The Plant and Animal Kingdoms

The Wide World of Facts

Marvels of Science and Invention

The Arts

At Home and Abroad

How do animals become extinct?   423.

How many hours of solo flying are required for a civilian pilot's license?   186.

What is the lowest form of animal life?   370.

Why was Alaska called "Seward's folly"?   232.

Are bathrooms really modern conveniences?   44.

How much of the Territory of Alaska was owned by the United States government?   230.

Where can you dip fresh water from the Atlantic Ocean?   293.

Which is the largest state in the Union?   224.

What president of the United States was the son of another president?   20.

What two emperors agreed in 1807 to divide the world between them?   255.

What easy experiment will prove that fire uses oxygen?   120 drawing.

What are some requirements for airline stewardesses?   187.

What was the "Gordian knot"?   256 picture.

What American city had the first fire-fighting organization?   322.

What mythical nation did women rule?   294.

How did a flyswatter change the history of Algeria?   274.

What is the "philosopher's stone"?   252.

How does a pilot get his airplane under control when it stalls?   163, 164 picture.

How long is a newly hatched alligator?   279 picture.

Which is the most plentiful metal in the earth's crust?   290.

What goddess dressed her son as a girl to keep him from fighting in the Trojan War?   10.

How is alcohol denatured?   254.

What is the difference between a plant and an animal?   400.

What is a sampler?   328 picture.

Which bird has the greatest wingspread?   244.

Why are coins not made of pure gold and silver?   282.

What are the most primitive forms of the plant kingdom?   261.

What is a trundle bed?   328 picture.

Which character in 'Little Women' represents the author?   254.

Which animals live the longest?   414 pictograph.

What is the name of the highest peak in the Andes?   394 picture.

What nut-bearing tree belongs to the rose family?   283.

What were the "salt boxes" of the American colonial period?   325 picture.

How many bones are there in the human skeleton?   373.

What does "parity" mean to a farmer?   113.

In approximately what century was writing invented?   387.

What are the differences between a configuration, a mock-up, and a prototype?   54.

On what continent is the Great Rift Valley?   73.

Does the century plant bloom only after it is 100 years of age?   100.

What legendary animal has a single horn projecting from the center of its forehead?   430.

What national historic site in Quincy, Mass., was the home of two presidents of the United States?   23 picture.

What poem, written by Oliver Wendell Holmes, saved the American frigate *Constitution* from demolition?   349.

What are the three kinds of muscles found in the human body?   373.

What famous battle was won because of the effectiveness of the longbow against heavily armored knights?   100.

How did the aeolian harp get its name?   45.

What woman, according to the Bible, bore her only child when she was 90 years of age?   6.

How many kinds of animals inhabit the earth?   424.

What is a part-time farm?   102.

What kinds of fuels are used in jet engines?   53.

What is the "vegetable lamb"? Is it based on fact or fable?   430.

What ocean bird is usually protected by sailors because of an old superstition?   244.

Who were the Sophists?   7.

What makes alfalfa a desirable crop?   259.

What large animal escapes from its enemies by digging underground?   2.

Where is the abacus still used in business?   3.

What was the last important animal to be domesticated by man?   422.

How does the government attempt to dispose of the farm surplus?   114.

Where is the world's most important telephone?   128 picture.

What woman helped establish the world's first Juvenile Court?   26.

What crop compensated the early Jamestown settlers for their failure to find gold and silver in Virginia?   306.

How do mammals differ from other vertebrates?   428.

What city is called the "rubber capital of the world"?   205.

KEY TO PRONUNCIATION

Pronunciations have been indicated in the body of this work
only for words which present special difficulties.
For the pronunciation of other words, consult the FACT-INDEX.
Marked letters are sounded as in the following words:
cāpe, ăt, fär, fȧst, whạt, fạll; mē, yĕt, fẽrn, thêre;
īce, bĭt; rōw, wȯn, fôr, nŏt, dọ; cūre, bŭt, rụde, fụll, bûrn; out;
ü = French *u*, German *ü*; ġem, ḡo; *th*in, *th*en;
ṅ = French nasal (Jeaṅ); *zh* = French *j* (*z* in azure); K = German guttural *ch*.

AACHEN (ä′κĕn), **West Germany.** The most important gateway in and out of West Germany is the ancient city of Aachen, or Aix-la-Chapelle. It is located in low hills, close to the point where the borders of the Netherlands, Belgium, and West Germany meet. It dates back to the days of the Romans, who built luxurious bathhouses around the hot sulfur springs that rise there.

Charlemagne, the first Holy Roman emperor, is generally believed to have been born in Aachen. He started building the famous cathedral in 796. He made the city the center of European culture and the capital of his dominions north of the Alps. Because of his fondness for the city, he exempted its citizens from military service and taxation and even from imprisonment. The great empire builder died here in 814 and was buried in a chapel attached to the cathedral.

After his death Norman invaders partially destroyed the rising cathedral, but it was restored by Emperor Otto III in 983. According to tradition, Otto opened Charlemagne's tomb and, to his amazement and terror, saw the body sitting upright in a huge marble chair, clothed in white robes, holding a scepter and wearing a crown. Frightened by the sight, Otto had the tomb closed. It remained untouched until it was reopened by Barbarossa 160 years later. He removed the chair, crown, and scepter. They were used in the coronation ceremonies of 32 succeeding Holy Roman emperors, held in the old Rathaus, or Town Hall.

In the 14th century, Aachen, then an important member of the Hanseatic League, controlled the territory between the Meuse and the Rhine rivers. Three treaties of Aix-la-Chapelle were signed at congresses of European powers held here. The first, in 1668, ended the War of Devolution between France and Spain. The second, in 1748, decided peace terms for the war of the Austrian Succession. The objective of the third, in 1818, was to bring order out of the disorganized conditions that followed the Napoleonic wars.

After this period, Aachen lost all political and military significance. Then, toward the close of the 19th century, the development of rich coal deposits in the nearby hills transformed the city into an important industrial and railroad center. Soon almost all kinds of iron and steel products and textiles, glass, and leather were manufactured.

The Effect of Two World Wars

Its peaceful commercial role underwent another change in 1914, when the Germans launched from Aachen their surprise attack on Belgium at the beginning of World War I. Again, in 1940, it was one of the vantage points from which Nazi armies overran Belgium and Holland. Its strategic position as Germany's most westerly city, as well as its network of highways and railway lines, made it in turn a target for attack by the Allies when they started their victorious march into Germany. Hitler himself

FAMED RESTING PLACE OF EMPEROR CHARLEMAGNE
The cathedral at Aachen was begun by Charlemagne and later rebuilt. His bones rest in the chapel at center. Damaged in World War II, the cathedral was afterward repaired.

signed a death sentence for the city by sending a "no surrender" order to the troops that were defending it. Aachen was finally taken by United States Army divisions on Oct. 21, 1944, after a savage battering by American artillery units. Charlemagne's cathedral, from which his shrine and relics had been removed to safety, was one of the few buildings still standing. It was badly damaged. After the war Aachen began rebuilding its industries. Population (prewar), about 163,000; (1963 estimate), 174,300.

AARDVARK (*ärd′värk*). The aardvark, or "earth pig," is one of Africa's strangest animals. Its thick body is thinly covered with stiff hair. Its back is arched. The animal's strong legs are short and stumpy. Its head has huge donkeylike ears, a long snout, and drooping eyelids with long lashes. Its naked tail tapers to a point from a thick base. From tip of tail to snout the animal measures about six feet. It weighs about 100 pounds.

The Boer settlers in South Africa, who found this odd mammal rooting about at dusk among termite mounds, gave it the name aardvark. In Dutch the word means "earth pig." The animal is also called

AN AARDVARK AND TERMITE CASTLES
An aardvark uses its powerful claws to tear down the stout walls of a termite castle. As the termites emerge, it laps them up with its long, sticky, and extensible tongue.

"ant bear." Aardvarks live throughout Africa south of the Sahara in any country where they can find their favorite food of termites. They feed by night and sleep in underground burrows by day. They have powerful front legs, armed with four strong claws on each forefoot. With these claws they tear open termite mounds which man can break into only with a pickax. They escape from enemies by digging underground. Their tough skin protects them from the bites of soldier termites. Since the females bear only one offspring a year, aardvarks are not common.

There are two species. The Cape aardvark lives in southeastern and western Africa. The northern, or Ethiopian, aardvark is found in central and eastern Africa. Aardvarks are classified in an order by themselves, the *Tubulidentata*, meaning "tube-toothed." The tubular teeth are without enamel or roots. The scientific name of the Cape aardvark is *Orycteropus capensis;* of the northern aardvark, *O. aethiopicus.*

AARDWOLF (*ärd′wulf*). The aardwolf, or "earth wolf," is related to the hyena. It lives in open sandy plains and brush country across southern Africa from Somalia on the east to Angola on the west. It derives its Dutch name from its habit of digging a burrow in the earth. Unlike the hyena, it is mild and timid. Its weak jaws and small teeth are adapted to feeding on termites and other insects and on well-rotted carrion. It hunts by night.

The aardwolf measures about two feet in length and 20 inches at shoulder height. It has large, erect ears, a pointed muzzle, and a short, bushy tail. Its long, coarse fur is light gray or buff in color with dark brown stripes. Along its sloping back is an erect mane of long hairs. From scent glands under its tail it can emit an evil-smelling fluid as a means of warding off an attack. The female aardwolf bears a litter of two to four pups in the late fall.

Aardwolves belong to the family *Hyaenidae*. Their scientific name is *Proteles cristatus.*

ABACUS (*ăb′a-kŭs*). Before the Hindu-Arabic numeration system was used, men counted, added, and subtracted with an abacus. (The name comes from the Greek word *abax*, meaning "board" or "calculating table.") The Greeks and Romans used pebbles or metal disks as counters. They moved these on marked boards to work out problems. Later the counters were strung on wires mounted in a frame.

Men used this device instead of working out their problems in writing because they could not "carry ten" conveniently with their cumbersome system of writing numbers. For example, how would you add 13 to 69 if you had to use the corresponding Roman numerals XIII and LXIX? (The article Numeration Systems and Numbers describes some of the early systems and symbols that men devised for counting.)

The ancient Egyptians, Hindus, and Chinese also used the abacus. The introduction of the Hindu-Arabic system of numeration, with the use of zero as a number, made written calculations easier, and the

A MODERN CHINESE ABACUS

In this type of abacus, beads above the dividing bar count 5; those below count 1. To be counted, a bead must be next to the bar, as shown at the right, where the number 182 is set out. The beads available on each wire add up to 15, not 10. This provides for "carrying ten," as shown in the example below.

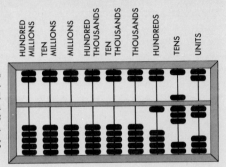

EXAMPLE:
Add 67 to 182

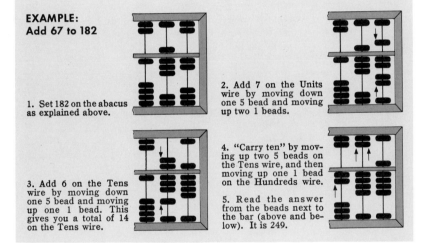

1. Set 182 on the abacus as explained above.

2. Add 7 on the Units wire by moving down one 5 bead and moving up two 1 beads.

3. Add 6 on the Tens wire by moving down one 5 bead and moving up one 1 bead. This gives you a total of 14 on the Tens wire.

4. "Carry ten" by moving up two 5 beads on the Tens wire, and then moving up one 1 bead on the Hundreds wire.

5. Read the answer from the beads next to the bar (above and below). It is 249.

abacus passed out of use in Europe. However, people in the Orient, Russia, and the Middle East still use it —particularly in business.

The early abacus had ten counters to a wire. The modern form has a dividing bar. Counters above the bar count five; those below, one. It is unnecessary to handle counters larger than five in value.

ABADAN (*ä-bä-dän'*), **Iran.** One of the great centers in the Middle East for the refining of petroleum and the shipment of petroleum products is Abadan. It is located on an island of the same name in the Shatt-al-'Arab, a stream formed by the junction of the Tigris and Euphrates rivers.

Abadan's development dates from 1909. In that year it became the site of the huge refinery erected by the Anglo-Persian Oil Company for processing petroleum brought by pipeline from oil fields in southwestern Iran.

Before the development of the oil-refining center of Abadan, the 40-mile-long island was a mass of mudflats surrounded by groves of date palms. Despite a hot and humid summertime climate, the city has grown rapidly. (*See also* Iran.) Population (1963 estimate), 302,189.

ABALONE (*ăb-ạ-lō'nē*). Of all the Pacific coast mollusks, the abalone is one of the most useful. The pearly, iridescent inner surface of the shell is prized in the manufacture of jewelry, buttons, and mother-of-pearl inlays. The abalone is also an important seafood.

The abalone is a gastropod (stomach-footed) mollusk with a single shell (*see* Mollusks). The opening of the flattened spiral shell is broad and ear-shaped. Hence abalones are also known as "ear shells" and "sea ears." The big muscle attached to the shell becomes the abalone steak, which is considered a delicacy in California.

The single large disklike foot on the underside of the shell is surrounded by a fringe of tentacles which are sense organs of the shellfish. The eyes are on stalks near the outer base of the tentacles. Water flowing over the gills on the underside passes out the top of the shell through a row of holes along the left margin. Some of the tentacles also extend through these holes.

The abalone spends most of its life in an undersea cave or clinging to a rock or reef. Its food consists of seaweed and microscopic marine life. These shellfish were once in danger of extermination. Protective laws now prohibit taking them before they have reached a minimum size.

California has three important species of abalone. The red abalone (scientific name, *Haliotis rufescens*) measures ten inches or more in length. Its shell is red on the outside and green mottled with pink on the inside. The blue abalone (*H. fulgens*) and the black abalone (*H. cracherodii*) attain a maximum size of five or six inches. (For picture in color of the black abalone shell, *see* Shell.)

ABBOTT, Sir John Joseph Caldwell (1821–1893).

"I hate politics," Sir John Abbott once wrote. "I hate notoriety, public meetings . . . everything that is apparently the necessary incident of politics—except doing public work to the best of my ability." Abbott's long life of public service to Canada was climaxed in 1891 when, as leader of the Conservative party, he succeeded Sir John A. Macdonald as prime minister (*see* Macdonald).

John Joseph Caldwell Abbott was born on March 12, 1821, in St. Andrews, in the county of Argenteuil, Lower Canada (now Quebec). He was the eldest son of the Rev. Joseph Abbott and Harriet Bradford Abbott. He received his early education in St. Andrews and in Montreal, then entered McGill University. He took his law degree in 1847 and was received as advocate to the bar of Montreal the same year. In 1849 he married Mary Bethune. They had six children.

Abbott was named queen's counsel in 1862. He served as counsel for the Canadian Pacific Railway from 1880 to 1887, when he became a director. For several years he was dean of the Faculty of Law at McGill University. He held the office of mayor of Montreal from 1887 to 1889.

From Law to Public Life

One of Abbott's first political acts was to sign, in 1849, an annexation manifesto which favored the union of Canada with the United States. The union movement, brought on by a business depression, lasted only a short time. In 1859 Abbott was elected to the Legislative Assembly of Canada.

As legal adviser to Hugh Allan, one of the builders of the Canadian Pacific Railway, Abbott was implicated in the Pacific Scandal of 1873 (*see* Canadian History). One of his confidential clerks furnished the evidence that brought about the fall of the Macdonald government in that year and the defeat of Abbott in the elections of 1874. In 1881 Abbott was returned to the House of Commons, and in 1887 he was appointed to the Dominion Senate.

A Brief but Productive Term as Premier

Abbott was 70 years of age and in declining health when he became prime minister. During his short term of office he accomplished a major revision of the jury law. He drafted an act which is the basis of Canadian law on insolvency today. His other reforms concerned the administration of justice.

On Dec. 5, 1892, Abbott resigned as prime minister because of ill health. That same year he was created a knight commander of the Order of St. Michael and St. George. He died in Montreal on Oct. 30, 1893.

ABBREVIATIONS.

Ancient monuments and manuscripts show that men began to abbreviate words very soon after alphabetic writing became general. In writing and printing today, thousands of words and phrases are abbreviated.

Often the last parts of words are dropped, as in shortening *Oklahoma* to *Okla.* Sometimes all except the initials are omitted, as in shortening *South Dakota* to *S. D.*, *page* to *p.*, and *west* to *w.* Words also are telescoped, as in contracting *year* to *yr.*, *quart* to *qt.*, and *hogshead* to *hhd.* Abbreviations of foreign words may be substituted, such as *lb.* for *pound*, from the Latin word *libra.* (For list of common abbreviations, *see* Abbreviations table in Fact-Index.)

ABELARD, Peter (1079–1142).

It was early in the 12th century. The morning bell had rung in the small cathedral of Paris. From the taverns and boardinghouses came a throng of students. They poured into nearby enclosures and seated themselves on the straw-strewn floors of the classrooms to hear lectures by the masters of the cathedral school (the forerunner of the famous University of Paris). Books were few in those days, and most teaching was by lectures. Thus for six or seven hours each day the students took notes on waxed tablets, which they held on the knee.

Of all the teachers, Peter Abelard was the favorite. The eldest son of a minor lord in Brittany, he had forsaken the life of a noble to be a scholar. He had studied in Paris and had soon surpassed his teacher. At the age of 22 he became a master and teacher.

He was skilled in theology, but he was especially brilliant in logic. Students flocked to hear him, and learned men everywhere read handwritten copies of his book 'Sic et Non' (Yes and No). The book was so named for its "Yes" and "No" answers from the teachings of the Church Fathers to such questions as:

Is God one, or no?

Is God a substance, or no?

Are the flesh and blood of Christ in very truth and essence present in the sacrament of the altar, or no?

His Wife, Héloïse

Then came an unhappy love affair with one of his pupils, the brilliant Héloïse (1101–64). Because marriage would interfere with Abelard's career, the lovers were married secretly. Their secret was soon discovered, however, and they were forced to part.

Abelard's habit of challenging his colleagues irritated them, and they attacked his doctrines, particularly his thesis that nothing should be accepted unless it could be proved. They claimed that religious faith should come first. Bernard of Clairvaux (later St. Bernard), his most bitter opponent, finally convinced the church to condemn a number of his teachings. Abelard then retired to the Benedictine monastery at Cluny. The noble character of Héloïse, who for some 40 years was a nun, is shown in her letters to Abelard. Abelard died in 1142. When Héloïse died, in 1164, she was buried at his side.

BALMORAL CASTLE, IN ABERDEENSHIRE
This granite castle on the River Dee is the summer residence of Britain's royal family. It was built in 1855 for Queen Victoria.

The term "Balmoral" comes from the Gaelic word meaning "the majestic dwelling." Its architectural style is Scots baronial.

ABERDEEN (ăb-ẽr-dēn′), **Scotland.** The chief seaport of northern Scotland is Aberdeen. It is the capital of the county of Aberdeenshire and the largest city in northeastern Scotland.

It is situated on the North Sea coast, between the River Don, to the north, and the Dee, to the south. The mouths of the two rivers are about 1½ miles apart. The valley of the Dee gives easy access, by rail and by road, to the varied beauty of the Highlands. The Don is spanned by the 14th-century Bridge of Balgownie (Auld Brig o' Don), and the Dee by the 16th-century Bridge of Dee.

Places of Interest and Industries

Aberdeen is called the Granite City because nearly all its buildings are made of the pale granite that is quarried nearby. The square solid buildings that line Union Street, in the New City, date chiefly from the 19th century. Marischal College, founded in 1593, is a gray granite building with many kinds of spires and pinnacles, each topped with a little gilt flag.

To the north are the narrow, twisting streets of the Old Town. Here many buildings date from the 16th century or earlier. The plain stone cathedral, St. Machar's, was begun in the 14th century. King's College, founded in 1494, joined with Marischal College in 1858 to form Aberdeen University.

In the morning trawlers, bringing in haddock, cod, plaice, and hake, crowd Aberdeen's harbor. Also important, in addition to fishing, are weaving woolens, papermaking, tanning, machinery manufacturing, shipbuilding, granite quarrying, and curing and canning of the abundant fish catch. Population (1961 census), 185,390.

ABERRATION. The word "aberration" comes from the Latin *aberrare*, meaning "to stray." Scientists use this word to describe many events in which certain phenomena "stray from a normal course." Psychologists and psychiatrists often identify particular behavior in mental disorders as aberrations (*see* Mental Health). Astronomers and physicists refer to "straying phenomena" associated with the study of light as aberrations (*see* Light).

Aberrations in Astronomy

When a person looks at a star, he does not see its actual position in space—he sees its *apparent* position. Nor does he see the star itself—he sees the light coming from it (*see* Star).

Rays of light coming from a star are bent as they pass through the earth's atmosphere. Any object seen by means of such curved rays will appear displaced from its true position. This apparent displacement is called an aberration.

If the earth were not moving, a star could easily

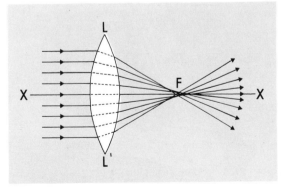

SPHERICAL ABERRATION
In spherical aberration the rays nearer the edge of a spherical convex lens come to a focus slightly nearer the lens.

5

be observed by merely looking through a telescope pointed directly at it. The earth moves, however. So does the eyepiece of the telescope. Thus to see a star, the observer must slant the telescope slightly. This puts it in proper position to receive the light rays coming from the star. The angle between the actual and the apparent position of a star is the *angle of aberration*.

Optical Aberration

An *optical aberration* is one in which an optical system—such as a mirror or a lens—fails to form an image of a point as a point, a straight line as a straight line, or an angle as an equal angle. There are five types of optical aberrations, also known as *third-order aberrations*. They are:

Spherical Aberration. A perfect spherical surface can never form a faithful image of an object. This defect is caused by the curved geometric form of the surface. The light rays most influenced by this defect are those which make the largest angle with the optical axis. (*See also* Lens, subhead "Focus and Optical Center.")

Astigmatism. Rays proceeding from a point source form an area instead of a point in an astigmatism. This aberration may involve: (1) a lens defect in which there is a difference in the radius of curvature as seen in one plane observed from another plane; (2) aberration of a spherical lens in which the image of a point not lying on the optical axis is a pair of short lines at right angles to each other and at slightly different distances from the lens; and (3) in an electron-beam tube, a focus defect in which the electrons in different axial planes come to focus at different points. (For discussion of astigmatism in the human eye, *see* Eye, subhead "Optical Defects of the Eye.")

Coma. Skew, or slanting, rays originating from a point on an object do not meet at the same point on the image plane but rather in a pear-shaped dot—the "coma."

Curvature of Field. If a system is corrected so that there is no spherical aberration, coma, or astigmatism, the images of off-axis points will lie on a curved surface called the Petzval surface (*see* Lens, subhead "Remedying Aberrations of Lenses").

Distortion. Variation in magnification with the distance from the axis causes this aberration.

Chromatic Aberration

The distance from the center of a lens to the principal focus is called the *focal length* of the lens. In the diagram on the preceding page the focal length of the lens would be a distance from the center of the lens to point F.

A simple lens has a different focal length for each different wavelength of light. Therefore, if a lens is adjusted so that the image is properly focused for red light, the image will be slightly out of focus for violet and other colors. This defect is called *chromatic aberration*.

Chromatic aberration also pertains to other media. The refractive index of any medium depends upon the wavelength (color) of the light (*see* Lens, subhead "How Lens Action Is Figured"). Thus all the properties of a refracting optical system will vary with wavelength. Dispersion of the material of the lens may cause all light from one point on an object to fail to form an image at a point. (*See also* Color.)

ABRAHAM. The story of Abraham is told in Genesis, the first book of the Bible (chaps. xi–xxv). Abraham was the first of the Hebrew tribal leaders (patriarchs) and is regarded as the father of the Jewish people.

Abraham was born at Ur, in Mesopotamia. He was already married to Sarah when his family moved to Syria. There his father, Terah, died. The Lord told Abraham: "Get thee . . . unto a land that I will shew thee, and I will make of thee a great nation." So Abraham set off with his tents and flocks. Lot, his brother's son, went with him. When they reached Canaan (Palestine), the Lord told Abraham, "Unto thy seed will I give this land."

Finally a famine drove Abraham and Lot to Egypt. They returned so rich in sheep, oxen, asses, camels, and servants that Canaan could not support them; so Lot went east to Sodom, in the Jordan Valley. (Lot's wife was turned into a pillar of salt when Sodom and Gomorrah were destroyed.)

The Bible says that Sarah was 90 years old when she bore her only child, Isaac. (Her maidservant, Hagar, was the mother of Abraham's older son, Ishmael.) Isaac was still a child when God "did tempt Abraham," telling him to offer his son as a burned sacrifice. Abraham took Isaac up a mountain, laid the wood, and lifted a knife to slay him; but an angel stopped him, saying, "Now I know thou fearest God." (*See also* Jews.)

ABRAHAM AND ISAAC
This relief sculpture by Ghiberti is from one of the Baptistery doors in Florence. It shows the angel stopping the sacrifice.

ABYSSIN'IA. Ethiopia, now an independent kingdom in East Africa, was long known as Abyssinia. Abyssinia is an Arab word meaning "mongrel." The Arabs scornfully gave this name to the Christians of Ethiopia when they conquered Egypt in A.D. 675. Europeans also used the name Abyssinia for several centuries, although the name was never recognized in Ethiopia. (*See also* Ethiopia.)

ACACIA (*ạ-kā'sha*). About 450 species of acacia are scattered through the warm regions of the world. Most of them are shrubs or small trees. Some are matted plants a few inches high. All are thorny and pod-bearing. The tiny sweet-smelling blossoms cluster together in fluffy balls or cylinder shapes. They range in color from deep yellow to almost white. The leaves are usually grayish and fernlike. The acacia is quick-growing and short-lived.

Australia has about 300 species of acacia. The early settlers called them *wattles* because they used the pliant branches to make wattle-and-daub huts. The golden wattle is Australia's national flower.

In the southwestern United States acacias are grown in many parks and gardens. The ornamental species were imported from Australia. The native catclaw (*Texas mimosa*) grows wild and is heartily disliked because of its strong hooked spines. The Arizona Indians, however, made meal of the pods. Smaller acacias are eaten by cattle and horses.

Gum arabic is obtained from an African species (*see* Gums and Resins). The Australians get tannin, used for tanning leather, from the bark of some species and make furniture of the hard, dark "blackwood" acacia. The wood of an Indian species is the chief source of catechu, a dye for true khaki. France grows several kinds for perfume.

The genus acacia belongs to the mimosa tribe of the pea family (*Leguminosae*). The black locust is sometimes called "false acacia" (*see* Locust Tree). The plant that florists call mimosa is actually an acacia.

ACACIAS THRIVE ON AFRICA'S SAVANNAS
Here and there in the semiarid grasslands of Africa grows a lonely acacia tree. One species yields gum arabic.

ACADEMY. Before the time of Plato ambitious young Athenians depended for their higher education upon the Sophists. The Sophists were traveling lecturers who went from city to city giving instruction in oratory and philosophy. They were always sure to find an audience in one of the three great public gymnasiums in the suburbs of Athens, where young men trained for athletic contests. The large buildings were set in beautiful enclosed grounds; and the covered walks and olive groves came to be the usual meeting places for teachers and students.

When Plato returned to Athens from his travels, about 387 B.C., he settled in a house near a gymnasium called the Academy, about a mile northwest of the city walls. He organized a college with a definite membership which met sometimes in the walks of the Academy and sometimes in his own house or garden. (*See* Plato.) Other philosophers followed his example in choosing a fixed place for their lectures and discussions. Aristotle, a pupil of Plato, set up his school in the Lyceum, a gymnasium east of the city.

How Greek Tradition Survives

The names associated with these Greek schools and discussion groups have been carried down to our own times with a wide variety of meanings. The Germans, for example, use the word gymnasium not for a place for athletic exercises but for a secondary school (*gÿm-nä'zĭ-ụm*). In France lycée (*lē-sā'*) is a secondary school. In the United States lyceum once meant a group that met for lectures and discussion. Today it refers to a program of planned lectures and concerts.

The word academy is used in England and America for many private secondary schools and for institutions where special training is provided, such as riding academies and military or naval academies. It is also used in a more general way in several languages for learned societies formed to promote knowledge and culture or to advance some particular art or science.

Modern Academies of Arts and Letters

Of these learned societies the most famous is the French Academy, an association of literary men established by Cardinal Richelieu in 1635. Four years later its members began work on a dictionary. Since new words had to be approved by them before being accepted as good usage, they exercised careful control over the French language. On the death of an academician the remaining members voted on a writer to take his place. Election to this group of "forty immortals" came to be regarded the highest honor a French writer could receive. In the 19th century the French Academy became associated with four other academies—of Inscriptions, of Science, of Fine Arts, and of Moral and Political Sciences—to form the Institute of France. The Academy of Fine Arts is best known for its famous school, the École des Beaux-Arts.

Another great modern academy is England's Royal Academy of Arts, devoted to painting, sculpture, and architecture. Its membership also is limited to 40. When an artist is elected he presents to the Academy a specimen of his work, called his diploma work, and receives a diploma signed by the sovereign. The Royal Academy provides instruction for students in its schools in Burlington House.

The oldest academy of this sort in the United States is the National Academy of Design, which conducts a school of design in New York City. It was founded in 1825 and incorporated under its present name in 1828. Its membership is limited to 250, including painters, sculptors, architects, and graphic artists.

The American Academy of Arts and Letters was founded in 1904 and incorporated under an act of Congress in 1916. Its membership is limited to 50.

ACADIA. The French were the first Europeans to explore the St. Lawrence River and settle in Canada. To protect the entrance to the great river they needed to hold also the region around the Gulf of St. Lawrence. They gave the name *Acadie* (in English, Acadia) to the land south of the Gulf. It included what is now Nova Scotia and New Brunswick.

In 1605 the French built a fort, Port Royal, at the mouth of the Annapolis River (*see* Nova Scotia). By 1668 a few dozen French families had settled in the beautiful Annapolis Valley. Instead of clearing the forest, they built dikes on the low-lying land and transformed the marshes into rich meadows. The soil was fertile, and game and fish were plentiful.

Because of its geographical position, Acadia at once became involved in the long struggle between the British and French for possession of the North American continent. In 1621 James I of England granted all Acadia to Sir William Alexander, who renamed it Nova Scotia. Time after time Port Royal was conquered by the English and retaken by the French. The Acadians took no part in the wars. They also lived in peace with the friendly Micmac Indians.

The final struggle for North America began in 1754 (*see* French and Indian War). The English were in control of Acadia when the war started. The Acadians were French in language and customs. The English feared that French priests and missionaries would persuade the Acadians and Indians to enter the war.

In 1755 the English authorities in Acadia demanded that each Acadian take an oath of allegiance to England. All who refused were deported. About 6,000 were shipped to English colonies along the Atlantic coast, from Massachusetts to South Carolina. Some made their way to Louisiana to live with the French settlers there. Their descendants are called Cajuns, many of whom still speak a French dialect. Others went back to Acadia.

Longfellow's 'Evangeline: A Tale of Acadie'

Henry Wadsworth Longfellow published 'Evangeline' in 1847. It became widely popular. It tells of the wanderings of two lovers who were separated when the Acadians were deported by the English.

Evangeline, the heroine, and her lover, Gabriel, lived in the village of Grand Pré. Evangeline kept house for her father, Benedict Bellefontaine, a farmer. Gabriel was the son of Basil, the village blacksmith.

On the day that Evangeline and Gabriel were celebrating their betrothal, the English summoned all the men of Grand Pré to the church. There they were held prisoners for five days. Then they were herded on to ships. That night the English burned the houses and barns in Grand Pré, and Evangeline's father died. The next day Evangeline was put on a ship with other exiles.

Evangeline spent the rest of her life wandering in search of her lover. She found his father, Basil, in Louisiana; but he did not know where Gabriel was.

> Sometimes she spake with those who had seen
> her beloved and known him,
> But it was long ago, in some far-off place
> or forgotten.
> . . . .
> Fair was she and young, when in hope began
> the long journey;
> Faded was she and old, when in disappointment
> it ended.

Finally Evangeline became a sister of mercy in Philadelphia, Pa. There, in an almshouse, she found her lover, Gabriel, dying:

> Vainly he strove to rise; and Evangeline,
> kneeling beside him,
> Kissed his dying lips, and laid his head on
> her bosom.

A MEMORIAL TO 'EVANGELINE'
A statue of Evangeline, the heroine of Longfellow's poem, stands in front of this old chapel of the Acadians at Grand Pré, in Nova Scotia. The site is now a memorial park.

THE ACANTHUS IN ART AND ARCHITECTURE
The graceful leaf of the acanthus (left) inspired formal designs (center) often used in art and architecture. Capitals of Corinthian columns (right) were decorated with the acanthus.

ACANTHUS. The leaf of the acanthus plant was carved in marble on the capitals of the Greek Corinthian columns. It is often used as decoration in art, architecture, furniture, and household objects. The acanthus plant grows three to four feet tall. The leaves cluster around the stem and curl outward and upward. They are about two feet long and a foot across. They have deep-cut, sharply notched edges and look somewhat like an enlarged holly leaf. Acanthus flowers are densely clustered on a spike sometimes 18 inches tall. They are tubular shaped, varying in color from white to lilac, purple, and rose.

The acanthus is native to Mediterranean lands, Africa, and the warm regions of Asia. In the United States it is grown in greenhouses and in the gardens of the South. The word comes from a Greek word meaning "sharp point" or "thorn."

About 2,000 species of the family *Acanthaceae* are found throughout the temperate and tropical regions of the world. The scientific name of the silver thistle, known to the Greeks, is *Acanthus spinosus*. The plant used by the Romans in their decorations is *Acanthus mollis*. A group of common wildflowers in the United States, the ruellias, belong to the acanthus family.

ACCOUNTING. Money records for a home or simple business may be kept by methods shown in the article on Bookkeeping. Larger businesses usually need more complex systems to account for all their many financial activities. The man who sets up, controls, and interprets these systems is the *accountant*.

He prepares tax reports and financial statements showing whether the company is making or losing money. He determines the actual cost of producing or selling goods. He tests the reliability of the records. He may be a *private accountant*, working for one company, or a *public accountant*, serving many companies as a professional consultant or advisor. About 13 per cent of the persons giving their occupation as "accountant" in the United States census are C.P.A.'s. This means they have passed a state examination and hold a license as a certified public accountant. Some states also register public accountants who are not certified.

An accountant performs many different tasks. In *auditing*, he examines and verifies records. A public accountant also expresses a professional opinion on whether the company's financial statements are fairly presented. In *cost accounting* he finds the cost of a product, service, department, or process. He also computes the separate costs of labor, materials, and overhead.

Budgetary control is often administered by a *controller*, sometimes called *comptroller*. He sets up the plan to estimate how much money a company may need for operations in the future and to control spending. Later he compares the actual spending with the budget estimate. Accountants who do *system installation* set up the ways of keeping records to provide information needed for payroll, cost, and taxes. *Tax accounting* requires the study of laws affecting taxes.

For further reading: 'Accounting for Non-Accountants', by J. N. Myer (N.Y. Univ. Press, 1957); 'Handbook of Accounting Methods', by J. K. Lasser (Van Nostrand, 1964); and 'Principles of Accounting', by H. A. Finney and H. E. Miller (Prentice-Hall, 1963).

ACETYLENE. One of the most active and useful of gases is acetylene. As a fuel, it is capable of giving either a very brilliant light or an intensely hot flame, depending upon the way it is burned. It serves also as a raw material from which important plastics and other valuable substances are made.

Acetylene is produced by adding water to calcium carbide. When burned in a simple jet, it gives an intensely white flame. Before portable electric lamps were perfected, the so-called "carbide lamps" were widely used by miners, with water from a small reservoir dripping down on lumps of calcium carbide placed in the base of the lamp. Lights for buoys and the headlamps of early automobiles operated on the same principle. Later the carbide generators were often replaced by cylinders containing the acetylene gas dissolved under pressure in acetone.

Acetylene is a compound of carbon and hydrogen (C_2H_2). The flame owes its brilliance to the exceptionally large number of carbon particles that are set free inside the flame. Unable to burn up immediately because air does not reach them, they glow intensely in the flame's heat. If, however, enough oxygen is used with the acetylene to consume this free carbon, the flame loses in brilliance but gains in heat. The *oxyacetylene* blowpipe, or torch, gives one of the hottest known flames (6,300° F.). It can cut through the hardest steel by burning away the metal in its path. The flame may also be used for welding. In a cutting torch, the oxygen is fed around the outside of the flame so that it not only helps to burn the acetylene more rapidly but helps also to oxidize or burn the metal to be cut. In a welding torch the oxygen is fed to the interior of the flame and only in such quantity as will be consumed there; so the metal melts instead of burning (*see* Welding).

Acetylene is the raw material out of which acetaldehyde is manufactured, which in turn may be made into acetic acid. It is a basic material in the preparation of many *vinyl* compounds of great importance

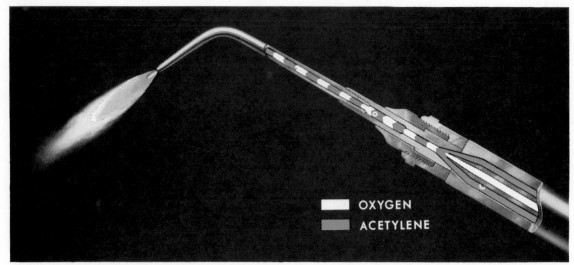

OXYGEN

ACETYLENE

THE OXYACETYLENE TORCH USED FOR WELDING

This drawing, somewhat simplified for the sake of clarity, shows how oxygen and acetylene are mixed in the torch. The two gases come through hoses from pressure tanks, and the quantity of each can be regulated with a valve. For most welding a "neutral flame" is used, with enough oxygen to consume all the acetylene. In the so-called "cutting torch," an extra stream of pure oxygen is supplied at the nozzle so that metal touched by the flame burns up instead of merely melting.

in the field of plastics (*see* Plastics). One of these, vinyl acetylene, led to the manufacture of the first synthetic rubbers (*see* Rubber).

Calcium carbide and water react to form acetylene and calcium hydroxide (slaked lime) as follows:

$$CaC_2 + 2H_2O \longrightarrow C_2H_2 + Ca(OH)_2$$

As acetylene is formed, it absorbs heat from the surroundings and converts the heat into chemical energy. This reaction is described as *endothermic* (from Greek *endo-*, "within" plus *thermos*, "heat") and is opposite to an *exothermic* reaction, which gives off heat to the surroundings. When the acetylene is burned, the absorbed energy is released as heat.

Pure acetylene is a colorless gas with a sweet odor somewhat similar to that of ether. It is poisonous and weighs about nine tenths as much as air. Under high pressures, acetylene is easily dissolved in the liquid acetone. It is shipped and sold in cylinders. It escapes freely from the solvent on reduction of pressure.

ACHILLES (*ȧ-kĭl′ēz*). Of all the Greeks who fought against Troy, the bravest and most handsome was Achilles. Part of his story has come down to us from Homer's 'Iliad'; the rest, from other Greek and Roman authors (*see* Homer).

Achilles' mother was the goddess Thetis, a sea nymph or Nereid, one of the 50 daughters of Nereus and Doris. His father was Peleus, king of Thessaly. Though not a god himself, Peleus was a grandson of Zeus, the lord of heaven. It was at the wedding feast of Thetis and Peleus that the goddess Eris (Discord) hurled among the guests a golden apple which was to cause the Trojan War (*see* Trojan War).

Soon after the birth of Achilles, Thetis tried to outwit the Fates, who had foretold that war would cut down her son in his prime. So that no weapon might ever wound him, she dipped her babe in the black waters of the Styx, a river which flowed around the underworld. Only the heel by which she held him was untouched by the magic waters, and this was the only part of his body that could be wounded. Hence we still use the expression "Achilles' heel" to mean a vulnerable point.

During boyhood and youth, Achilles was trained in speech and in the arts of war by his father's friend, Phoenix, fugitive son of Amyntor, king of Argos. He was also taught by Chiron the centaur, who was half man and half horse (*see* Centaurs). Under his kindly counsel, the boy grew expert in riding, hunting, music, and the art of healing.

A Trick That Failed

When the Trojan War began, Achilles was tall, handsome, and strong. The warriors marveled at his strength and wished to see him test it on the field of battle. But his mother, fearing the decree of the Fates, dressed him as a girl and hid him among the maidens at the court of the king of Scyros (*sī′rŏs*).

The trick did not succeed. Odysseus, shrewdest of the Greeks, came to the court disguised as a peddler. When he had spread his wares before the girls, a sudden trumpet blast was sounded. The girls screamed and fled, but Achilles betrayed himself by seizing a sword and spear from the peddler's stock. So, yielding to his destiny, the young hero joined his countrymen before Troy and took command of his father's men, the Myrmidons. (Homer does not mention the hiding of Achilles, but has him go directly to war from the court of his father.)

Achilles and his men set an example of bravery for all the other Greeks. He raided the coast of Troy with his many ships and sacked a number of cities. Then he quarreled with Agamemnon, the leader of the Greeks, over a captive maid, Briseis (*brī-sē′ĭs*), whom he loved. When she was taken from him, he withdrew his followers from the fight and sulked in his tent. As a result the Greek armies were driven back to their ships by the Trojans.

The Death of Patroclus

At last, moved by the plight of the Greeks, Achilles entrusted his men and his armor to Patroclus, his best friend. Thus, when Patroclus led the Myrmidons into battle, the Trojans mistook him for Achilles and fled in panic. Patroclus pressed his victory too far, however, and was killed by Hector, the leader of the Trojans. The body was stripped, and Achilles' armor became the prize of Hector.

Angered and stricken by grief, Achilles roused himself and vowed to kill Hector. Meanwhile his goddess-mother, Thetis, hastened to Olympus to beg a new suit of armor from Hephaestus, the god of the forge. The lame god, grateful to Thetis, who had once saved his life, went to his forge and made a suit of armor and a marvelous shield of bronze.

Clad in his new armor, Achilles went into battle. He slew many Trojans, and the rest—all save Hector —fled within their city. The story of how Achilles killed Hector is told elsewhere (*see* Hector).

Though the Trojans had now lost their leader, they were able to continue fighting with the help of other nations. Achilles broke the strength of these allies by killing Memnon, prince of the Ethiopians, and Penthesilea, queen of the Amazons (*see* Amazons).

The Hero Meets His Doom

Achilles was now weary of war and, moreover, had fallen in love with Polyxena, sister of Hector. To win her in marriage he consented to ask the Greeks

ACHILLES ARMS FOR BATTLE WITH HECTOR
The armor of Achilles was lost in combat by Patroclus. Achilles' mother, Thetis, had Hephaestus, the god of metalworking, forge a new armor in bronze. Here Thetis presents it to her son.

to make peace. He was in the temple arranging for the marriage when Hector's brother, Paris, shot him with a poisoned arrow in the only vulnerable part of his body—the heel. Thus, the hero met the doom foretold by the Fates. The Achilles tendon, named for the hero, connects the calf to the heel (*see* Tendon).

ACIDS AND BASES—Their Actions and Uses

ACIDS AND ALKALIES (or BASES). Acids and bases are two groups of chemical compounds. Each group has many different members. Acids and bases react together to produce entirely new products. Acids, bases, and the products of their reactions are vital to many life processes and valuable to industry.

The Properties of Acids

An acid is defined as a substance containing hydrogen that dissociates (breaks up) in water to produce hydrogen ions. It may also be defined as a compound in which the hydrogen can be replaced by a metal. The other part of the compound is called the *acid radical*. For example, in sulfuric acid (H_2SO_4) one atom of sulfur and four of oxygen form the acid radical which is joined to two atoms of hydrogen.

A typical metal-acid reaction occurs when zinc is placed in a solution of sulfuric acid. Hydrogen is released as a gas and zinc unites with the acid radical to form zinc sulfate:

$$H_2SO_4 + Zn \longrightarrow ZnSO_4 + H_2$$

The strongest acids are the *mineral*, or *inorganic*,

acids. These include sulfuric acid, nitric acid, and hydrochloric acid. More important to life are hundreds of weaker *organic* acids. These include acetic acid (in vinegar), citric acid (in lemons), lactic acid (in sour milk), and the amino acids (in proteins).

The Properties of Bases

A base is a substance containing the hydroxide ion, OH^-, or the hydroxyl group, OH, which dissociates in water as the hydroxide ion, OH^-. Basic solutions have a characteristic brackish taste. The hydroxides of metals are metal compounds that have the hydroxyl group, and they are bases. Hydroxides of the metals lithium, sodium, potassium, rubidium, and cesium have the special name of alkalies. The hydroxides of beryllium, magnesium, calcium, strontium, and barium are called alkaline earths. A basic solution is also called an alkaline solution.

Acid-Base Reactions

From these brief descriptions it can be seen why acids and bases react so readily with each other. An acid has hydrogen to exchange for a metal. A base has a metal to exchange for hydrogen. When the two react the exchange takes place. These reactions or exchanges are sometimes violent. Acids and bases react to form compounds which are called *salts*. The reaction of sodium hydroxide and sulfuric acid produces a salt, sodium sulfate (Na_2SO_4), and water:

$$2NaOH + H_2SO_4 \longrightarrow Na_2SO_4 + 2H_2O$$

Another typical acid-base reaction is that between calcium hydroxide and phosphoric acid to produce calcium phosphate and water:

$$3Ca(OH)_2 + 2H_3PO_4 \longrightarrow Ca_3(PO_4)_2 + 6H_2O$$

Acids and bases react freely in aqueous (water) solutions. It is said that when an acid dissociates, it forms an acid radical and a hydrogen ion. Actually, the hydrogen ion (H^+) does not exist in large concentrations in the aqueous solution. Instead, the hydrogen ion attaches itself to a water molecule to form the hydronium ion, H_3O^+. It is customary, however, to simplify reaction equations by using the symbol for the hydrogen ion, H^+. When a base dissociates it produces an hydroxide ion (OH) with a negative charge and a metal ion with a positive charge. The hydrogen ion and the hydroxide ion combine to form a molecule of water. The negative acid radical and the positive metal ion can then form a salt.

Indicators and Neutrality

Acids and bases can cause many organic substances to change color. For example, if lemon juice is added to tea, the tea becomes lighter in color. This occurs because the acid in the lemon juice changes the color of a substance in the tea from dark brown to light brown. The reaction can be reversed by adding an alkaline substance, such as baking soda ($NaHCO_3$), to the tea. This addition restores the original color. A substance that changes color when an acid or base is added to it is called an *indicator*.

Litmus paper is a common indicator. It turns red in an acid solution and blue in a basic solution. A solution which gives litmus paper a color midway between red and blue is called a neutral solution. It is a solution that contains hydrogen ions and hydroxide ions in equal amounts. Thus, a solution with an excess of hydrogen ions is an acid solution. A solution with an excess of hydroxide ions is a basic solution.

Pure water is a neutral solution. It ionizes slightly and releases an equal number of hydrogen and hydroxide ions. The concentration of these ions has been measured and found to be 1×10^{-7}. Instead of saying that the hydrogen ion concentration in pure water is 1×10^{-7}, it is customary to say that the pH of water is 7. The pH is the logarithm of the reciprocal of the hydrogen ion concentration. It is written:

$$pH = \log \frac{1}{[H^+]}$$

Since water has a pH of 7 and is neutral, solutions with pH less than 7 are acid, and solutions with pH greater than 7 are basic. (*See also* Hydrochloric Acid; Nitric Acid; Sulfuric Acid.)

ACONCAGUA, HIGHEST POINT IN THE AMERICAS
The floor of this valley in Chile is itself higher than most mountains in North America. Beyond it, just over the border in Argentina, soars Aconcagua's mighty peak. Aconcagua is the highest summit in the Western Hemisphere.

ACONCAGUA (ăk-ŭn-kä′ḡwạ). The highest mountain in South America and in the entire Western Hemisphere is the extinct volcanic peak Aconcagua. It towers in the southern Andes in Argentina near the Chilean border. Its height is 22,834 feet. This is more than 2,500 feet higher than Mount McKinley, which is the highest peak in North America. The upper slopes of the mountain are continuously covered with snow. The peak of Aconcagua was first scaled in 1897.

A river in Chile as well as Aconcagua Province of Chile are named for the mountain. The province is a large producer of fruit and tobacco and is famed for its wines and cattle. (*See also* Andes.)

ACROPOLIS. More than 2,300 years ago, in the Age of Pericles, the Greeks created the most beautiful temples and statues in the ancient world from white marble. The best of these stood upon the Acropolis, a small plateau in the heart of Athens. The Acropolis displayed more treasures of art than any other public place of comparable size.

An oblong mass of rock, the Acropolis looks very much like a pedestal. It rises abruptly about 500 feet above the city. The top is almost flat. It measures 1,000 feet long and 460 feet wide, covering less than eight acres. Ten miles to the northeast

THE ACROPOLIS TODAY AND LONG AGO

This is how the ancient Acropolis of Athens looks today. From its highest level (right) rise the ruins of the Parthenon to recall the Golden Age of Pericles. Seen at the left are other historic structures, notably the remainder of the gateway, or Propylaea. This can be seen as it was in ancient times in the middle of the picture below. The Parthenon is at the upper right.

This is the way the Acropolis looked about 400 B.C. The Propylaea, with its six rows of pillars, is in the center. At its left stands Phidias' bronze statue of Athena Promachos. Far behind the statue rises the Erechtheum, a stately temple of Athena. At the right front is the tiny temple of Athena Nike, which shows its graceful Ionic pillars.

towers Mount Pentelicus, which supplied the white Pentelic marble for the temples and the statues.

The earliest people of Athens, perhaps 4,000 years ago, walled in the Acropolis as a kind of fort. Here their first kings ruled, and here in later years were the chief shrines of Athena (see Athena).

More than 2,500 years ago, the goddess' shrines began to rise. The *Hecatompedon* ("temple measuring 100 feet") was completed about 600 B.C. Only 90 years later, the Lacedaemonians found the Acropolis covered with marble temples and dwellings. They destroyed the dwellings, but they paused in awe and silence before the temples. Then they went on their way, leaving them unharmed.

In 480 B.C., the Persians burned or smashed everything on the Acropolis and killed its defenders. But in two days, legend says, the ashes of Athena's sacred olive tree near the ruined Hecatompedon put forth a bright new shoot more than a yard in length.

Like the olive tree, the Acropolis was quickly renewed. Within 13 years Themistocles and Cimon had rebuilt the walls and cleared away the ruins. Now it was ready for the Age of Pericles (see Pericles).

At first, Pericles was too busy with politics and war to do much about the Acropolis. Finally, in 447 B.C., he gave orders to start work. He placed the sculptor Phidias in charge, assisted by the architects Ictinus, Mnesicles, and Callicrates (see Phidias).

Several years before, Phidias had erected on the Acropolis a 30-foot bronze statue of *Athena Promachos* (see Athena). Her helmet and her spear were plainly visible from Cape Sunium, some 15 miles away.

13

In 447 B.C. Phidias began to build a shrine to Athena. This Doric temple, called the *Parthenon* ("dwelling of the maiden"), was opened in 438 B.C. It was 228 feet long, 101 feet wide, and 65 feet high (for picture, *see* Architecture). Many classic American memorials, churches, and bank buildings have used features of its design.

The Parthenon's Sculptures

On the western pediment of the new temple stood statues of Athena and Poseidon. The eastern pediment represented Athena's birth. Relief carvings, 92 in all, studded the outside of the temple. Along the portico, between the temple's outside columns and its walls, was a frieze. It extended around the top of the walls, 39 feet above the portico floor, and was 524 feet long and 3 feet 3½ inches wide. Its 350 people and 125 horses represented the Panathenaic procession that carried a new gown to Athena each year.

In the temple itself (the *cella*) was a statue of *Athena Parthenos*, 40 feet tall. Its body was of ivory, its dress of gold. Its right hand held a statue of *Nike*, goddess of victory, and its left hand rested upon a 20-foot shield. In 437–432 B.C. a majestic gate, the *Propylaea*, was erected at the west end of the Acropolis. The *Temple of Athena Nike* was finished about 410 B.C. It was only 27 feet long, 18½ feet wide, and 23 feet high, a little gem of Ionic design. The *Erechtheum*, built in 421–407 B.C., was named for Erechtheus, foster son of Athena and king of Athens. Six marble statues, 7½ feet tall, served as pillars on its Porch of the Maidens (for picture, *see* Athens).

Later History

By the 5th century A.D. the Byzantines had carried to Constantinople the statues of Athena Promachos and Athena Parthenos and had made the Parthenon a Christian church. Ten centuries later the Turks made it a mosque. In 1687, under attack by the Venetians, the Turks stored gunpowder in the mosque. Struck by a cannon ball, it exploded, killing 300 men. The roof, walls, and 16 columns lay in ruin.

In 1801 Lord Elgin, British ambassador to Turkey, got permission to remove "a few blocks of stone with inscriptions and figures." Actually he almost stripped the Parthenon of its frieze, pediment, sculptures, and relief carvings. He took a frieze from the Athena Nike temple, which the Turks had torn down in 1687. From the Erechtheum he took a marble maiden and a pillar of the eastern portico. In 1816 these Elgin marbles went to the British Museum.

Freed from Turkey in 1829, Greece began to redeem the ruins. The Athena Nike temple was rebuilt in 1835–36. The Acropolis Museum (opened 1878) was built north of the Parthenon. In the 20th century the American School of Classical Studies rebuilt part of the Erechtheum, wrecked by war and storms. The Propylaea, in ruins since 1645, has been partly repaired. Some fallen pillars have been restored in the Parthenon, but it is still empty and roofless. It suffered further damage in World War II.

ADAM AND EVE. The story of Adam and Eve is told in Genesis, the first book of the Bible. According to Genesis ii, God formed Adam "of the dust of the ground, and breathed into his nostrils the breath of life." Then God planted the Garden of Eden and took Adam to it. "It is not good," said God, "that man should be alone." While Adam slept, God took one of Adam's ribs and made a woman, Eve.

God told Adam he might eat the fruits of all the trees except one. This was the tree of the knowledge of good and evil. Chapter iii tells how a serpent tempted Eve to eat the forbidden fruit and how she

THE 'FALL OF MAN' AND 'EXPULSION', BY MICHELANGELO

At the left, Adam and Eve, tempted by the serpent, reach for the forbidden fruit. At the right, overcome with shame, they are driven from the Garden of Eden by an angel. The picture is on the ceiling of the Sistine Chapel in the Vatican, Rome.

gave some to Adam, who also ate. God said, "Behold, the man has become as one of us, to know good and evil." In order that Adam might not eat also of the tree of life, and live forever, God expelled the couple from paradise. Later they had three sons: Cain, Abel (who was killed by Cain), and Seth.

Adam and Eve are not mentioned in the story of creation in Genesis i, which says: "God created man in his own image . . . male and female created he them." It is not clear from this passage whether "man" means mankind in general or a single couple. The Adam and Eve story seems to be found also in old Hebrew tradition. The ancient Sumerians had a myth somewhat similar (*see* Babylonia and Assyria). Theologians later used the story of "Adam's fall" to justify the doctrine of original sin.

ADAMS, Charles Francis (1807–1886). Grandson of the second president of the United States and son of the sixth president, Charles Francis Adams was himself a noted statesman. His greatest years of public service were those spent as minister to Great Britain during the trying period of the American Civil War.

Adams was born Aug. 18, 1807, in Boston, Mass. At the age of two, he was taken to Russia, where his father, John Quincy Adams, served as American minister. He stayed six years and learned to speak French well. (French was then the first language for educated Russians.) In 1815 his father was appointed minister to England. Young Charles went to an English school for two years. In 1817 they returned to the United States, and his father began service as secretary of state under President Monroe. The boy attended Boston Latin School and later Harvard College, from which he was graduated in 1825.

He studied law and in 1829 was admitted to the bar. The same year he married Abigail Brown, a daughter of Peter Chardon Brooks, one of the wealthiest men in Boston. Their sons carried on the traditions of the distinguished Adams family. (*See also* Adams Family.)

For five years Adams served in the Massachusetts legislature. In 1848 he was the Free Soil party candidate for vice-president. When the Republican party was formed he joined it and was elected to Congress. President Lincoln appointed him minister to Great Britain in 1861. He served until 1868.

Adams in England

Adams found most Englishmen hostile or indifferent to the American Federal government in its war with the South. Early in the Civil War the British government had granted equal rights as a belligerent to the Confederacy. The prime minister and the foreign secretary only awaited a favorable time to recognize the independence of the South.

The Federal blockade of Southern ports forced the Lancashire, England, cotton mills to shut down for lack of raw cotton. The mill owners loudly demanded that Great Britain lift the blockade.

The hardest problem Adams had to solve, however, concerned the Confederate cruiser *Alabama*. This vessel, built in Britain, was allowed to go to sea and to begin a career of destruction against Federal shipping. With patience, understanding, and good sense, Adams worked out the dispute in terms largely favorable to the United States. His last public service was as a member of the Geneva arbitration tribunal, 1871–72. This group fixed the amount of damages which Britain was to pay for permitting the *Alabama* to escape. (*See also* 'Alabama' Claims.)

ADAMS, Henry (1838–1918). During his lifetime Henry Adams was known chiefly as a historian and as a member of a great American family (*see* Adams Family). After his death he was recognized as a major figure in American literature. His fame rests mainly on two books: 'The Education of Henry Adams' and 'Mont-Saint-Michel and Chartres'.

Henry Adams was born Feb. 16, 1838, in Boston, Mass. As a child, he said, he felt he really belonged to Quincy, Mass., where his grandfather, John Quincy Adams, lived. His grandfather and his great-grandfather, John Adams, had been presidents of the United States. His father was Charles Francis Adams, a noted statesman (*see* Adams, Charles Francis).

After graduating from Harvard (1858), Henry Adams studied in Germany and toured Europe. From 1861 to 1868 he was in London serving as secretary to his father, who was minister to Great Britain. From 1870 to 1877 he taught medieval history at Harvard and edited the *North American Review*. He married Marian Hooper in 1872. In 1877 they moved to Washington, D.C. In 1891 Adams completed his nine-volume 'History of the United States During the Administrations of Thomas Jefferson and James Madison'.

Grieved by his wife's death, in 1885, Adams spent many of his later years traveling throughout the world. The cathedrals in France awakened his interest in the spirit of the 12th century. In 1904 he had printed privately a limited edition of 'Mont-Saint-Michel and Chartres' to give to his friends. Two years later he gave them privately printed copies of 'The Education of Henry Adams'. This book was not published until after his death. Adams died March 27, 1918, in Washington, D.C.

JOHN ADAMS—

2nd President of

the United States

John Adams

ADAMS, John (1735–1826; president 1797–1801). The second president of the United States was John Adams, lawyer and diplomat. Adams' public career lasted more than 35 years. He was second only to George Washington in making a place for the young United States among the nations of the world. In his devotion to our country he was second to none.

Adams was a Federalist. He, like other Federalists, believed in a strong central government. However, he was independent and decided issues for himself in the interests of his country and often against the interests of his party. Adams was defeated for a second term as president because he defied party power to act for the nation's good.

Massachusetts Boy and Man

John Adams was born Oct. 19, 1735, in Braintree (now Quincy), Mass. He was the eldest of three sons, children of John and Susanna Boylston Adams. Young John attended a "dame" school and later went to the Free Latin School. He was handy around cattle and horses, helping with the milking and feeding. He was handy in the kitchen too, building fires and cleaning up. In summer he went down to the bay to watch the sailing ships come in. In winter he skated on the frozen creeks. He flew homemade kites, collected birds' eggs, and always had a whittling knife in hand.

When he entered Harvard College, he intended to become a minister. By the time he was graduated, he had given up the idea. He taught school until he could make up his mind about his future. Adams taught in Worcester, Mass., about 60 miles west of Boston. After a year he began to study law under James Putnam, the town's leading lawyer. He kept on teaching and spent his after-school hours in Putnam's office.

Two years later he was admitted to the bar and settled in Braintree to practice. When he was 29 he married Abigail Smith, a minister's daughter. She was

JOHN ADAMS' ADMINISTRATION
1797–1801

X Y Z Affair and naval war
with France (1798–1800)
Alien and Sedition laws passed (1798)
Kentucky and Virginia
nullification resolutions
Death of Washington (1799)
Capital moved from Philadelphia
to Washington, D.C. (1800)
Federalist party split
Adams defeated for re-election
John Marshall made Chief Justice
of Supreme Court (1801)

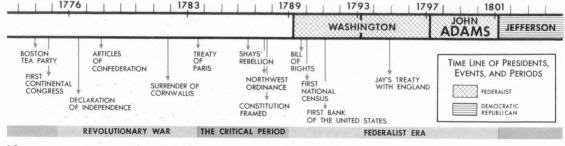

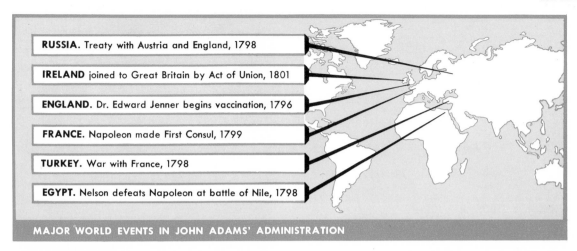

RUSSIA. Treaty with Austria and England, 1798

IRELAND joined to Great Britain by Act of Union, 1801

ENGLAND. Dr. Edward Jenner begins vaccination, 1796

FRANCE. Napoleon made First Consul, 1799

TURKEY. War with France, 1798

EGYPT. Nelson defeats Napoleon at battle of Nile, 1798

MAJOR WORLD EVENTS IN JOHN ADAMS' ADMINISTRATION

only 20, but she had schooled herself well in politics and literature (*see* White House, sections "Hostesses of the White House" and "Children in the White House"). They had four children: Abigail, John Quincy, Charles, and Thomas (*see* Adams, John Quincy).

Revolutionary War Service

Adams' first political post came when he was appointed one of the town attorneys to argue the legality of the Stamp Act (*see* Stamp Act). He also defended a British officer and seven enlisted men who fired on a rioting Boston mob. Five Bostonians were killed in the fracas, soon known as the Boston Massacre. Adams secured the outright acquittal of six men. The other two, convicted of manslaughter, were branded on the thumbs and released. Despite the unpopularity of the British, Adams was admired for his courage in defending them.

In 1774 Adams was elected a delegate to the Continental Congress. There he met other delegates and learned how they felt about the government of the American Colonies. The next year, at the second meeting, these feelings and beliefs grew into a declaration of war. It was Adams, a Massachusetts man, who nominated George Washington of Virginia as commanding general of the Continental army.

PUBLIC SERVANT
Drafting the Declaration of Independence, in Philadelphia in 1776, are, left to right, Benjamin Franklin, Thomas Jefferson, Robert R. Livingston, John Adams, and Roger Sherman.

John Singleton Copley, famous American artist, painted this portrait of John Adams (right) as American envoy to England. It shows Adams in middle age, serving his new nation with zeal.

Important Events

in the Administration of

John Adams

The John Adams family moved into the White House in November 1800. They were the first to live there.

TROUBLE ABROAD

Adams congratulates Charles C. Pinckney, U. S. envoy to France, on successful end of the XYZ Affair.

War with France actually broke out on the high seas. An uneasy peace was declared before either country was invaded.

TROUBLE AT HOME

John Fries led a revolt against taxes. Adams pardoned him after conviction.

Alien and Sedition laws, designed to stop criticism of Congress, were unpopular.

Kentucky and Virginia passed resolutions against Alien and Sedition laws.

HIGH LIGHTS OF THE PERIOD

Benjamin Stoddert became first secretary of the Navy. Ship is *Constitution*.

Charles Newbold patented cast-iron plow, replacing iron-plated wooden plow.

John Marshall, eminent lawyer, chosen chief justice of Supreme Court.

In 1777 Adams was made commissioner to France, serving with Benjamin Franklin and Arthur Lee. Soon he was authorized to work out treaties of peace and commerce with Britain. Britain was not ready to make peace, so Adams went to Holland to raise money for America. He was successful. Holland and France were the only countries to recognize the United States as an independent nation before the war's end.

Peace with England finally came. Adams was appointed minister to the Court of St. James's in London. His wife and daughter joined him. Adams found it hard to deal with the British, and when his term was up he did not seek a second one.

Vice-President and President

Adams returned to be elected vice-president under George Washington. In 1792 Washington and Adams were re-elected. Adams worked hard as vice-president. He presided over all Senate meetings and cast his vote some 20 times to break ties.

Political parties arose under Washington. Adams and Alexander Hamilton became leaders of the Federalist party (*see* Hamilton, Alexander). They were opposed to Thomas Jefferson and his Democratic-Republican party (*see* Jefferson). In 1797 Adams became president, with Jefferson as vice-president.

Despite Adams' great ability and patriotism, he was never popular. He was often vain and blunt. The Jefferson men charged him with wanting to confine power to "the rich, the well-born, and the able." He did not get along well with Hamilton, and as a result the party was hopelessly split. There was increasing friction with France, once the nation's closest friend. The four years of Adams' presidency made up one of the stormiest periods in American history.

For a brief time the nation was truly united. In 1798 the country rallied behind Adams as he defied

ADAMS IN OLD AGE
This portrait of John Adams in retirement was painted by Samuel F. B. Morse, later to win fame for his telegraph invention but then well known as a portrait painter.

the increasingly insolent French. Their demands for bribes led the American envoy Charles C. Pinckney to utter his famous "Millions for defense, but not one cent for tribute" (*see* 'XYZ' Affair).

Peace with France was made in 1800, but taxation to support the war had brought complications. In Pennsylvania a man named Fries had led a rebellion against taxes. He and others were convicted of treason. The Federalists cried for their execution, but Adams pardoned them. The Federalists also pressed the tyrannical Alien and Sedition laws over Adams' objections (*see* Alien and Sedition Laws).

The Virginia and Kentucky legislatures passed resolutions asking other states to join them in declaring the Alien and Sedition laws illegal. These later proved important in the nullification and secession doctrines used by the South in the slavery question.

Adams Loses Election

In the election of 1800 Jefferson received 73 electoral votes to Adams' 65. Adams spent the rest of his life in retirement. He renewed his friendship with Jefferson, and they wrote to each other often. Adams died July 4, 1826, on the 50th anniversary of the birth of the United States. Jefferson died the same day, a few hours earlier. Adams, not knowing this, murmured as he died, "Thomas Jefferson still lives."

Two good books about John Adams are C. D. Bowen's 'John Adams and the American Revolution' (Little, 1950) and Page Smith's 'John Adams', 2v. (Doubleday, 1962).

BIRTHPLACE OF THE ADAMSES
John Adams was born in 1735 in Braintree (now Quincy), Mass., in the house at the left. His son John Quincy Adams was born in 1767 in the house at the right.

JOHN QUINCY ADAMS—

6th President of

the United States

ADAMS, John Quincy (1767–1848; president 1825–1829). Son of the second president of the United States, John Quincy Adams was the sixth president. His whole adult life was devoted to his country's service. Diplomat, senator, president—these posts were only steps on the road to greatness. His best years in public office came after his presidency, when he was elected to the House of Representatives. He served for 17 years, above party politics and concerned only for his country's good.

Until after his presidency, Adams was always respected, sometimes admired, but rarely liked. Then public attitude toward him slowly changed. People around him and finally the whole nation began to see the honesty and devotion beneath his crusty surface. As elder statesman he received the affection that was never his before.

Boyhood in Politics

John Quincy Adams was born July 11, 1767, in Braintree (now Quincy), Mass. He was the second of four children—a girl and three boys. From infancy, young John saw history being made. Often he was taken to Boston Common to see the hated British soldiers parade. He heard his father tell about the Boston Massacre and the Boston Tea Party just after they happened. During the Revolution he saw the fires of Charlestown and heard the noise of Bunker Hill.

In 1778 John Quincy went with his diplomat father to France and later to Holland. When he was 14 he accompanied Francis Dana, commissioner to Russia, to the St. Petersburg court. He served as secretary and French interpreter. After a 14-month stay he traveled alone in Europe.

In 1785 John Adams was appointed minister to Great Britain. John Quincy went home alone to attend Harvard College. His college days were busy and happy. He debated often, saw much of his friends,

and practiced on his flute. He was graduated at 20.

Clearly, the lifework for Adams was law. He entered the office of Theophilus Parsons (later chief justice of Massachusetts), studied for three years, and was admitted to the bar. Clients were few at first, so he occupied his time by writing political articles, signing them with such names as Publicola, Marcellus, Columbus, and Barneveld. President Washington read the articles and appointed Adams minister to Holland in 1794. He was then only 27 years old.

Service Abroad and at Home

With his brother Thomas, Adams sailed for Europe. From Holland he reported on conditions during the French occupation. Back in London, he met Louisa Catherine Johnson, daughter of the American consul. She was a high-spirited girl, brilliant and sensitive. They were married July 26, 1797. (See also White

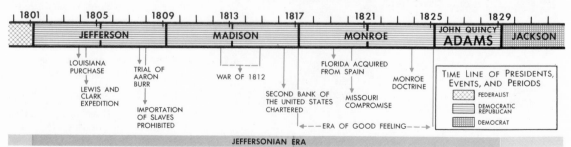

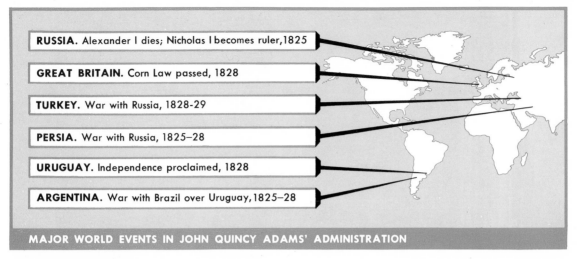

RUSSIA. Alexander I dies; Nicholas I becomes ruler, 1825

GREAT BRITAIN. Corn Law passed, 1828

TURKEY. War with Russia, 1828-29

PERSIA. War with Russia, 1825–28

URUGUAY. Independence proclaimed, 1828

ARGENTINA. War with Brazil over Uruguay, 1825–28

MAJOR WORLD EVENTS IN JOHN QUINCY ADAMS' ADMINISTRATION

House, section "Hostesses of the White House.")

Adams took his bride to Berlin, where he served as minister to the Prussian court. He worked out a treaty, read much, and traveled with his wife through Germany. Their first child, George Washington Adams, was born in Berlin in 1801. The same year they returned to Boston and Adams' law practice.

Senator and Diplomat

He was soon back in politics, first in the Massachusetts State Senate, then in 1803 in the United States Senate. At once he was drawn into the fight over the government of the newly acquired Louisiana Territory. Adams fought unsuccessfully to give the new land a democratic form of government.

The Federalist party was against him. Its members hated him for supporting the Democratic-Republican action against the British attack on the American frigate *Chesapeake*. Adams also supported Jefferson's embargo policy. Yet he remained independent, neither Federalist nor wholly Democratic-Republican. In 1808 he resigned from the Senate and went home to practice law.

In Washington and Boston society Adams was stiff and ill at ease. He had no skill at small talk. With his family and close friends, however, he was easy and sociable. He liked to read aloud before small groups. Children loved him and he them. During these

---

JOHN QUINCY ADAMS' ADMINISTRATION
1825–1829
Clay appointed secretary of state
Erie Canal completed (1825)
Early efforts toward
Pan American co-operation
Bunker Hill monument erected
Steam railway construction begun
Tariff becomes a burning issue
(1828)
Beginning of Democratic and
Whig parties
Adams defeated for re-election
by rising power of West

---

years his sons John and Charles Francis were born. (*See also* White House, section "Children in the White House"; Adams, Charles Francis.)

In 1809 President Madison appointed him minister to Russia. Adams saw Napoleon invade Russia and followed the news of his disastrous retreat from Moscow. At the close of the War of 1812 he was named to the commission which was to work out a peace with Britain. The commission met with the British at Ghent, Belgium, and in four months hammered out the Treaty of Ghent. The terms were generally favorable to America (see War of 1812).

From 1815 to 1817 Adams served as minister to Great Britain. The Adamses lived quietly in a country house in Ealing, in London, and sent their sons to English schools. Adams worked hard to strengthen the peace between Britain and the United States.

President Monroe appointed Adams secretary of state in 1817. His first important task was to defend Andrew Jackson in his supposedly unlawful raid of Spanish-held Florida. He won the administration to his view and quieted Spain and Britain. Next he induced Spain to cede Florida to the United States. He fought for the Missouri Compromise and helped write the Monroe Doctrine (see Missouri Compromise; Monroe Doctrine).

Sixth President

In 1824 Adams was one of four candidates for the presidency. The others were Andrew Jackson, W. H. Crawford, and Henry Clay. Jackson received the most electoral votes, but not a plurality. Adams was second. The election was turned over to the House of Representatives, and Adams won. He was accused of bargaining with Clay, and Jackson used the accusation with telling effect in the 1828 campaign.

Quarrels between Jackson's supporters (who later formed the Democratic party) and those of Adams (who became Whigs) were intense. The Democrats blocked every bill started by Adams. The South was beginning to unite against him. He hated slavery, wanted a high tariff, and worked for internal improve-

Important Events

in the Administration of

John Quincy Adams

In Boston patriotic citizens erected Bunker Hill Memorial. It is a stone shaft commemorating Revolutionary War battle.

NEW METHODS OF TRAVEL

Ceremonies celebrated completion of Erie Canal linking New York City with Great Lakes. Boat trip took eight days.

Construction began on the Baltimore and Ohio Railroad, first common carrier (for public use) railroad in U. S.

ADMINISTRATION FACES HOSTILE NATION

A farmer chases a federal revenue officer off his land. The states were beginning to resent power of federal government.

The Tariff of Abominations, set up for defeat by Jackson forces, actually passed and was signed into law by Adams.

ADAMS INVOLVED IN MANY TROUBLES

Adams and Jackson men debate. Jackson men were out to discredit Adams.

U. S. delegates failed to reach Panama Congress, first Pan-American meeting.

Henry Clay helped Adams take office. For this he was accused of corruption.

THE HOUSE AND THE MAN
In Quincy, Mass., stands the home (left) of both John Adams and John Quincy Adams. It is now a national historic site. Here (right) is John Quincy Adams as he appeared shortly before his death in 1848. The photograph is an early daguerreotype.

ments—all against Southern interests. Few positive measures were enacted in Adams' administration.

In 1828 Jackson's followers set up a tariff bill, called the Tariff of Abominations, intending to defeat it. This would be a way to discredit Adams and help defeat him in the 1828 election. To their astonishment the bill passed and was signed by Adams.

While he was in office Adams lived quietly. He rose about 5:00 A M. and in summer went for a swim in the Potomac. Then he read his Bible and wrote in his diary. After breakfast he met with his Cabinet. He ate dinner in company, received visitors, and read a good deal. In the late afternoon he walked or rode his horse and played billiards with his sons. In the election of 1828 he lost to Andrew Jackson, who had 178 electoral votes to Adams' 83.

Seventeen Years in the House

Adams retired—permanently, he thought. His retirement was brief. In 1831 he was elected to the House of Representatives and held his seat until his death in 1848. Asked if he felt lowered by becoming a representative after having been president, he replied, "No person could be degraded by serving the people as a representative. . . . Nor, in my opinion, would an ex-president . . . be degraded by serving as a selectman . . . if elected thereto by the people."

At once Adams was appointed chairman of the Committee on Manufactures. He fought for the tariff against the Southern forces, already drifting toward secession. The Southerners placed a "gag rule" on petitions relating to slavery. Adams fought the gag rule until its repeal in 1844. He stood almost alone against Andrew Jackson's abolition of the Bank of the United States. In the 27th Congress Adams was made chairman of the House Committee on Foreign Affairs.

Adams won the title of Old Man Eloquent—not for his skill as a speaker but for the vast amount of information in his talks. In old age he made a poor appearance. He was short, fat, and bald; his voice was shrill and disagreeable. Yet his rugged honesty and patriotism were plain for all to see.

In 1847 Adams suffered a stroke in Boston and a second one a year later in the House of Representatives in Washington. He died Feb. 23, 1848.

Good chapters on the life of Adams are included in: 'Presidents of the United States', by J. T. and B. M. McConnell (Crowell, 1961); James Morgan's 'Our Presidents' (Macmillan, 1958); and C. A. Beard's 'Presidents in American History' (Messner, 1961).

ADAMS, Samuel (1722–1803). One of the firebrands of the American Revolution was Sam Adams. He helped to start it and he helped to keep it going—by speeches, newspaper articles, and behind-the-scene maneuvers. He combined great ideals with shrewd politics, and he worked hard to help America change from a British colony into an independent nation.

Adams was born Sept. 27, 1722, in Boston, Mass. His father was a well-to-do brewer and active in politics himself. Samuel was one of 12 children. The boy attended Boston Grammar School, and in 1736 he entered Harvard College. He was graduated in 1740. Three years later he went back and studied for a Master of Arts degree. He was already thinking of revolution, for he chose as his thesis subject:

"Whether it be lawful to resist the Supreme Magistrate, if the Commonwealth cannot otherwise be preserved."

Samuel Adams had little inclination for the brewery business he inherited from his father and ran into debt. His first wife died, leaving two children. His second wife practiced strict economy and gratefully accepted food and clothing from her neighbors. Adams devoted himself to public affairs. As a member of the Caucus, a political group that met in an attic, he learned the arts of the politician.

Samuel Adams as Patriot and Statesman

Adams' influence was due largely to his skill as a writer and to his passionate faith in the cause he served. In 1764 he was chosen to write Boston's protest against England's proposed Stamp Act. In 1765 he was elected to the Massachusetts colonial assembly and became the leader of opposition to the British government. In local politics he was called "the man of the town meeting." He brought about the creation in Boston in 1772 of a "committee of correspondence" to rouse public opinion. Other New England towns followed Boston's lead. Adams' famous "circular letter" appealed to all the colonies to join in action against the crown. In 1773 Adams presided over the mass meeting that gave the signal for the Boston Tea Party. (*See also* Revolution, American.)

As a delegate to the First and the Second Continental Congress, Adams fought for colonial independence. For his first trip to Philadelphia, one friend gave him money and another outfitted him with clothes. About this time his friends also built him a new barn and repaired his house.

Adams signed the Declaration of Independence, and in 1788 secured the ratification of the Constitution by Massachusetts. In 1794 he was elected governor of his state. He died Oct. 2, 1803, as poor as he had lived.

Samuel Adams was related to the prominent Adams family. His grandfather was a brother of the grandfather of John Adams, second president of the United States.

ADAMS FAMILY. The Adams family is unique in the United States. Through four generations its members made important contributions to the nation's history and culture. Some won distinction in public service. Almost all were writers.

The family's story begins with Henry Adams, an English farmer. About 1636 he arrived in Boston with his wife and nine children and was granted land at Wollaston (now in Quincy). When he died, he left a small house and barn, a cow and a calf, a few pigs, a silver spoon, and some old books. His descendants

were hard-working, pious farmers, unknown outside their village. Suddenly in the fifth generation the family leaped into prominence.

Two Presidents and a Distinguished Diplomat

In 1751 John Adams, at considerable sacrifice, sent his oldest son, John, to Harvard College. He expected the boy to enter the ministry. Instead, John studied law, took a leading part in the Continental Congress, and succeeded George Washington as president of the United States (*see* Adams, John). It is not unusual for a farmer's son to become president. John Adams, however, lived to see his son John Quincy elected president (*see* Adams, John Quincy).

John Quincy's son Charles Francis served his country as minister to Great Britain throughout the Civil War (*see* Adams, Charles Francis). After retiring from public life he edited and published, in ten volumes, the works of his grandfather John Adams and the letters of his grandmother Abigail Smith Adams (*see* White House, section "Hostesses of the White House"). He also published his father's famous diary, 'Memoirs of John Quincy Adams'.

The Fourth Generation

John Quincy Adams II was the only one of Charles Francis Adams' four distinguished sons who did not become a writer. He served three terms in the Massachusetts state legislature.

Charles Francis Adams, Jr., became president of the Union Pacific Railroad but devoted most of his time to writing. In addition to works on railroads, he wrote two books on Massachusetts history and a biography of his father, 'Life of Charles Francis Adams'.

Henry Adams also became a writer and historian (*see* Adams, Henry). His most famous book, 'The Education of Henry Adams', is an American classic.

THE LONG ROOM IN THE ADAMS FAMILY'S "OLD HOUSE"
Furnishings reflect the tastes of all four generations that occupied the house. The portrait to the right of the fireplace is of Abigail Smith Adams.

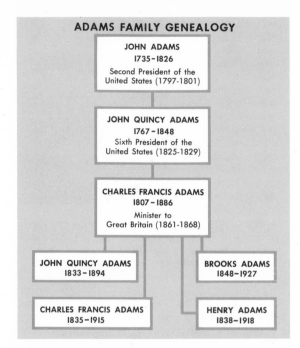

ADAMS FAMILY GENEALOGY

JOHN ADAMS
1735-1826
Second President of the
United States (1797-1801)

JOHN QUINCY ADAMS
1767-1848
Sixth President of the
United States (1825-1829)

CHARLES FRANCIS ADAMS
1807-1886
Minister to
Great Britain (1861-1868)

JOHN QUINCY ADAMS
1833-1894

BROOKS ADAMS
1848-1927

CHARLES FRANCIS ADAMS
1835-1915

HENRY ADAMS
1838-1918

Brooks Adams served as his father's secretary in England. In 'Law of Civilization and Decay' he tried to work out a theory of scientific laws governing history.

The Adams National Historic Site

The Adams National Historic Site is in Quincy, Mass., about eight miles south of Boston. It covers five acres. On it are the Adams house, a library, stables, an orchard, and a garden. Thousands of Americans visit the site each year to see how this great American family lived.

The oldest part of the house was built in 1731 by Maj. Leonard Vassall, a West Indian sugar planter. John Adams bought it in 1787 and named it Peacefield. Later generations called it affectionately the Old House. (For picture, *see* Adams, John Quincy.)

The original house had two stories in front and an attic. In back the roof swept down almost to the ground. John Adams built the gabled ell containing the Long Room, East Entry, and upstairs study. Charles F. Adams added the stone library, overlooking his grandmother's garden, and the stone stable.

The furnishings are from various periods. Much of the furniture and many of the art objects were acquired by the Adamses in Europe. The Adams family maintained the Old House as a memorial from 1927 to 1946, when title was vested in the United States.

ADDAMS, Jane (1860–1935). "When I'm grown up, I'm going to have a big house, but I don't want it to be near other pretty houses. I'm going to live right next door to poor folks," cried a frail, thoughtful girl of six to her father. The child was Jane Addams, and she was seeing poverty for the first time, in the street back of the factories at Freeport, Ill.

Jane Addams was born Sept. 6, 1860, in Cedarville, Ill. Her father, John Huy Addams, was a wealthy miller, a state senator, and a friend of Abraham Lincoln. Jane was the youngest of five children. From infancy she suffered from a slight spinal curvature. After graduation from Rockford Seminary (now Rockford College) in Illinois, her health broke, and for two years she was an invalid.

In 1883 she went to Europe to travel and study. The hunger and misery she found in the great cities impressed her more than did their famous museums or historic relics. Her childhood resolve to live among the poor was confirmed by a stay at Toynbee Hall in London, the first social settlement in the world (*see* Social Settlements).

The Beginning of Hull-House

In the fall of 1889 she settled with a school friend, Ellen Gates Starr, in a shabby old mansion on the

JANE ADDAMS WITH HER YOUNG FRIENDS AT HULL-HOUSE
In her later years, despite ill-health, Jane Addams continued to spend much of her time with the young people at Hull-House, the social settlement she founded. Children enjoyed her company and responded warmly to her charm and sincerity.

near West Side of Chicago among tenements and sweatshops. Their neighbors were folk of a dozen races, who called the place "the old Hull house" after its builder Charles Hull. So Hull-House was adopted as the name for what was to be the most famous social settlement in the United States.

At first the neighbors were suspicious and unfriendly. Before long, however, they saw that Jane Addams' friendliness was sincere and practical. A kindergarten and a day nursery were started. Wealthy people, university professors, students, and businessmen contributed time and money to Hull-House.

The Work of Hull-House

Hull-House fed the hungry and nursed the sick, guided the bewildered foreigner and the wayward boy or girl. Jane Addams became a garbage inspector so she could get the filthy streets cleaned up. She campaigned against the sweatshops and corrupt politicians. She and her associates at Hull-House helped to put through the first factory legislation in Illinois and to establish in Chicago the world's first Juvenile Court.

Jane Addams became one of the most deeply loved and famous Americans of her time. Universities honored her with degrees. Visitors from all over the world came to see her at Hull-House, crowds in many countries heard her talk simply and directly, and thousands read 'Twenty Years at Hull-House', her most famous book.

During World War I Jane Addams courageously faced bitter criticism when she urged that the issues which led to war be settled by negotiation rather than by bloodshed. After the war she continued to spread her ideals as president of the Women's International League for Peace and Freedom. In 1931 she was awarded the Nobel Peace prize jointly with Dr. Nicholas Murray Butler.

For 46 years Jane Addams managed the settlement. At the time of her death it had expanded to cover a city block, with buildings centered around a courtyard. Ellen Starr had been forced by ill-health to retire, six years before Jane Addams' death. Others remained to carry on the work at Hull-House and thus to keep alive the memory of a great woman.

A Memorial to Jane Addams

In 1961 plans were laid to tear down Hull-House to make room for a Chicago campus of the University of Illinois. Despite worldwide protests the properties were sold in 1963. The original Hull-House building, however, was preserved as a memorial to Jane Addams. Hull-House settlement work continues in new locations.

Jane Addams' best-known writings are 'Democracy and Social Ethics' (1902); 'Newer Ideals of Peace' (1907); 'The Spirit of Youth and the City Streets' (1909); 'Twenty Years at Hull-House' (1910); 'A New Conscience and an Ancient Evil' (1911); 'The Second Twenty Years at Hull-House' (1930); 'The Excellent Becomes the Permanent' (1932).

ADDISON, Joseph

(1672–1719). Among the famous London coffeehouses which sprang up in the early 18th century, "Button's" holds a high place in the history of English literature. It was a favorite meeting place for the poet and essayist Joseph Addison and for four or five of his companions. Here they would often sit, enjoying leisurely discussions.

Addison, the leading spirit of this group, was a gentleman of culture. Except for his last few years, which were marked by literary and political quarrels, his life was tranquil and pleasant. He was born at Milston, Wiltshire, where his father was rector. He spent a studious youth and entered Oxford University. There he became known for the charm of his verse. After touring Europe, he entered politics as a Whig. The publication of his poem 'The Campaign', celebrating the victory at Blenheim, won him much popular and political favor. From then on Addison held many offices, the most important being that of secretary of state for Ireland in 1717.

It is not, however, for his statesmanship or for his poetry or for his tragedy 'Cato', so famous in their day, that Addison is still loved. It was rather in his essays that he reached his highest powers.

'The Tatler' and 'The Spectator'

A school friend of Addison's, Sir Richard Steele, sensed that the growing sociability of the times, as shown by the popularity of the coffeehouses, had prepared the way for a paper which would discuss news, politics, and society. So in 1709 he inaugurated such a journal, The Tatler. Addison soon became a contributor. After The Tatler was discontinued in 1711, he and Steele started another paper, The Spectator. This combination of editors was ideal. Steele, an Irishman, was brilliant, impulsive, and had many ideas. Addison was of a calmer temperament and could develop gracefully the ideas and characters suggested by Steele. The Spectator contained no news, but only light, often gently satirical essays. Imaginary members of the Spectator Club discussed all kinds of subjects, from training young ladies in the use of fans to the appreciation of Milton. The leading member of the club was the courteous, well-loved Sir Roger de Coverley, a cultured country gentleman.

Addison's style has always been greatly praised. Samuel Johnson wrote: "Whoever wishes to attain an English style, familiar but not coarse, and elegant but not ostentatious, must give his days and nights to the study of Addison."

Addison also wrote a number of popular hymns. Of these 'The Spacious Firmament on High' and the 'Traveler's Hymn' are still well known.

ADDITION— A Basic Arithmetic Skill

The simplest way to find the sum of 28 pennies and 15 pennies is to count them.

The quickest way is to write the two numbers as an addition example and add them.

ADDITION. The girl in the picture had 28 pennies. Then she received 15 pennies as a gift. How can she find the total number of pennies she now has?

Let us suppose the girl does not know how to add. She spreads all the pennies on the table in a single large group and counts them one by one or perhaps by twos. This takes time, but when she is finished she will know the total number in the two groups. In the picture at the right, we see that she has written the two numbers as an addition example and added them. This is a much faster way to find the total.

Addition is actually only a fast method of counting. We use it when we know the amounts in two or more groups and want to combine them into one group.

To work the example above, there are several things that a child must know. He must know the meaning of the numbers. Thus 28 means 2 tens and 8 ones. He must know how to arrange the numbers in the example correctly, so that the figures in ones' place are one under the other in a straight line; likewise, the figures in tens' place must be one under the other. This is necessary because only figures having the same place value can be added. (For more information about place value, see Numeration Systems and Numbers.)

The child must also know several basic addition facts, namely that $8+5=13$; 1 (carried) $+2=3$; and $3+1=4$. In adding the 8 and 5 in ones' place, the sum is 13. He must think of the 13 as 1 ten and 3 ones, write the 3 in the sum in the ones' place, and carry the 1 ten to tens' place in the example. Then he must complete the example by adding this 1 to the 2 and 1 that are already given in tens' place. The

sum he gets is 43. This is the same number as the total found by counting the two groups of pennies one by one.

Learning the Meaning of Addition Facts

The young child learns the meaning of addition most easily by using the process in his activities in daily life, in the home and elsewhere (see Arithmetic). Addition is used in many games to find the score. It is used in buying and selling. Studies of the uses of arithmetic by children have shown that addition is the process they use most frequently in activities both in and out of school.

The meaning of addition facts can be taught very easily. Imagine a young child playing with a group of 5 blocks. He can be led to see that the 5 blocks can be made into a number of different groups. Thus, he can see that the 5 blocks can be grouped as 4 and 1; as 3 and 2; as 2 and 3; as 2, 2, and 1; and as 1 and 4. When a child gets the idea that a large group consists of smaller groups of different sizes, he is learning the first step in addition. Next, he should be taught to make drawings showing various ways of grouping 5 objects. Later, he should be asked to tell how many dots there are in each part of a drawing, such as the domino at the right, and also how many there are in all. Finally, he must learn how to read and write the basic number fact itself, using numbers and signs as shown by the example beside the domino.

$$\begin{array}{r} 2 \\ +3 \\ \hline 5 \end{array}$$

Steps in Learning an Addition Fact

1. Introduce the new fact in a social situation. Give the child a need for learning it. Have him use it in a game or in buying at the store.
2. Have the child show the two numbers to be added by grouping small objects, such as pennies, blocks, toothpicks, toys, sticks, or cardboard disks. Then have him count to find the total number.
3. Have the child make a drawing which reproduces the number fact. For example, he may draw a picture of objects, such as balls, sticks, stars, circles, or large dots, or he may draw groups of tally marks (| | | |).

TERMS USED IN ADDITION

$$\left.\begin{array}{r} 2 \\ +3 \end{array}\right\} Addends$$
$$\frac{}{5}\ Sum$$

$$\begin{array}{r} 2 \\ +3 \\ \hline \end{array}\ An\ addition\ grouping$$

The plus sign (+) says "add."

$$\begin{array}{r} 2 \\ +3 \\ \hline 5 \end{array}\ An\ addition\ fact$$

4. After a number fact has been made meaningful by the activities in steps 1, 2, and 3, have the child write the complete fact using numbers, the plus symbol (+), and the line separating the addends from the sum.

5. Have the child show that the sum is correct by using other facts that he has previously learned. For example, 5+4=9 because 4+4=8 and 5 is 1 more than 4.

6. For practice, have the child use the number fact whenever the opportunity arises—in problems, in social situations, and in group activities.

7. Finally, include the new fact in systematic practice with examples and problems.

The larger the sum, the more difficult is the fact. The facts should therefore be presented as families. Teach first as a group all addition facts whose sum is 5. Then teach the facts whose sum is 6, then 7, and so on for all facts.

Practicing Difficult Addition Facts

Special practice work should be done on any facts that the child does not learn quickly. In order to be able to work larger addition examples, the child must be able to give the sums for all addition groupings promptly and correctly. There should be no guessing at answers and no counting to find sums. The rate at which children give answers will increase as they grow older. Very young children cannot possibly give answers as rapidly as adults are able to give them after years of practice.

The hundred addition facts which must be learned are given in the chart on the opposite page. Children of all ages can use this chart to do special work with these facts. Because the answers are given, the learners can score their own work very easily.

Carrying and Column Addition

Gradually, step by step, the child should learn to work more difficult and longer examples. In all work with whole numbers, he will use the basic addition facts.

For each step described below, the thinking to be done in working the example is given in detail. Notice the emphasis placed on the arrangement of the numbers. (For diagrams which illustrate the meaning of place value and the use of zero as a placeholder, *see* Numeration Systems and Numbers.)

SPECIAL HELPS IN LEARNING ADDITION FACTS

The row of addition facts below illustrates some general ideas that will help children to learn and remember many of the addition facts. We call these ideas *generalizations*.

$$\begin{array}{ccccccccc} 1 & 4 & 0 & 5 & 4 & 7 & 8 & 8 & 9 \\ \underline{5} & \underline{1} & \underline{6} & \underline{0} & \underline{7} & \underline{4} & \underline{8} & \underline{9} & \underline{5} \\ 6 & 5 & 6 & 5 & 11 & 11 & 16 & 17 & 14 \end{array}$$

Begin with the first statement below. Give other addition facts that prove that the statement is true. Do the same for the other statements.

When we add a number to 1, or 1 to a number, the sum is 1 more than the number. The facts 1+5=6 and 4+1=5 show this.

When we add a number to 0, or 0 to a number, the sum is the same as the number.

The sum of any two numbers, such as 7+4, is the same as the sum of the reverse, 4+7.

We call 8+8 a double and 8+9 a near double. Use the doubles to learn the sums of the near doubles. Thus, the sum of 8+9 is 1 more than the sum of 8+8 because 9 is 1 more than 8.

Adding 9 to a number or a number to 9 is the same as adding 10 to a number and then taking 1 away from the sum.

The sum of two odd numbers or of two even numbers is always even. (Even numbers are those that divide evenly by 2, leaving no remainder.)

The sum of an odd number and an even number is always an odd number.

Step I. Adding two easy numbers:

12
+14
——
26

Begin at the right with the ones' column. Think: 2 and 4 are 6. Write 6 in ones' place in the answer space.
Then add the tens. 1+1=2. Write 2 in tens' place in the answer space. The sum is 26.

Step II. Carrying to tens' place:

1
28
+45
——
73

Begin at the right. Think: 8 and 5 are 13. Because 13 is 1 ten and 3 ones, write 3 in ones' place in the sum and remember (carry) the 1 ten. (This is shown above the 2 in the example.) Now add the 1 to the 2 in 28. This is 3. Then think: 3 and 4 are 7. Write 7 in tens' place in the sum. The answer is 73.

CARRYING TO TENS' PLACE (STEP II)—SHOWN WITH PLACE-VALUE POCKETS

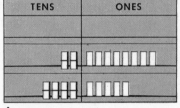
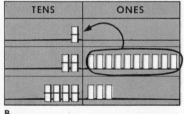
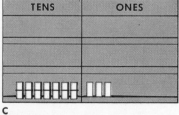

A
In the ones' pockets are single cards. In the tens' pockets are bundles of ten cards. In A the top row shows 28 as 2 tens and 8 ones; the bottom row shows 45 as 4 tens and 5 ones.

B

In B we see the 13 cards in ones' place regrouped as 1 ten and 3 ones. Ten of the 13 ones are then bundled and carried to tens' place. C shows the sum, 73, as 7 tens and 3 ones.

C

HOW TO PRACTICE THE 100 ADDITION FACTS

After the meaning of a new fact has been learned, the fact should be included in systematic practice and drill exercises. Special work with this chart will increase both speed and accuracy in working longer addition examples.

1. Begin with row 1. Read the first fact. Then close your eyes and say the fact to yourself several times. Write any fact you find difficult several times on a sheet of paper.

2. Write all the addition facts for which the sums are 6. Then write the facts whose sums are 7; then 8, 9, 10, 11, 12, 13, 14, 15, 16, 17, 18.

3. Cover the answers of a row of facts with a strip of paper and write the sums on the paper. Then slide the paper down and compare your answers with those in the printed table. Do special work on all facts that you answer incorrectly or for which you can not give the answers quickly or without counting.

4. Cover the answers to a row of facts with a card. Give the answer to the first fact. Then slide the card one space to the right to see whether your answer is correct. Do the same for the remaining facts in the row. This oral drill will speed up your work because you will not have to take the time to write the answers.

5. Have someone read the groupings to you one at a time without the answers. You say the sum and the person reading to you checks it. Write down the groupings for which you give incorrect answers and make test-study cards for them (see below).

0+2=2	0+7=7	0+3=3	0+9=9	0+0=0	0+6=6	0+4=4	0+8=8	0+1=1	0+5=5
1+9=10	1+6=7	1+3=4	1+7=8	1+0=1	1+4=5	1+8=9	1+1=2	1+2=3	1+5=6
2+0=2	2+5=7	2+3=5	2+7=9	2+8=10	2+1=3	2+4=6	2+6=8	2+9=11	2+2=4
3+7=10	3+9=12	3+3=6	3+5=8	3+6=9	3+0=3	3+1=4	3+8=11	3+4=7	3+2=5
4+0=4	4+9=13	4+5=9	4+8=12	4+3=7	4+6=10	4+2=6	4+7=11	4+4=8	4+1=5
5+4=9	5+0=5	5+9=14	5+2=7	5+7=12	5+6=11	5+3=8	5+8=13	5+1=6	5+5=10
6+2=8	6+0=6	6+6=12	6+9=15	6+3=9	6+1=7	6+4=10	6+8=14	6+5=11	6+7=13
7+1=8	7+8=15	7+4=11	7+9=16	7+3=10	7+6=13	7+2=9	7+5=12	7+0=7	7+7=14
8+1=9	8+0=8	8+8=16	8+4=12	8+9=17	8+6=14	8+2=10	8+5=13	8+3=11	8+7=15
9+0=9	9+9=18	9+5=14	9+8=17	9+1=10	9+4=13	9+7=16	9+3=12	9+6=15	9+2=11

HOW TO MAKE AND USE TEST-STUDY CARDS

On one side of a 3 × 5 inch card write the example without the answer. This is the test side. On the other side of the card write the example with the answer. This is the study side. Use objects or markers to test the answer for any fact that you are not sure of.

Stack the cards with the test sides face up. State the answer to the example on the top card, then turn it over to see whether your answer is correct. Put aside those you answer correctly and quickly. Replace at the bottom of the stack, or put in a separate pile, those that need further study.

TEST SIDE

STUDY SIDE

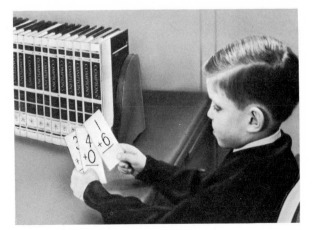

29

ADDITION

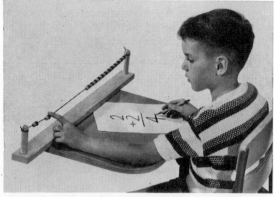

ADDING WITH A BEAD COUNTER
For this boy 2 and 4 are not just numbers—they are quantities. The counting device helps to make arithmetic meaningful.

The meaning of the carrying step can be shown in various ways, including the use of coins.

```
  1
 28     Use dimes and pennies to show each of the two
+45     numbers. First find the total number of pen-
 73     nies. This is 13. Change the 13 pennies to 1
        dime and 3 pennies. Then there are in all 7
        dimes and 3 pennies.
```

When the child understands the meaning of carrying from ones' place, he learns very quickly the meaning and the process of carrying to hundreds' place.

Step III. Carrying to hundreds' place only:

```
   1
  364   The sum of 6 tens and 9 tens is 15 tens.
+ 293   Fifteen tens are 1 hundred (10 tens) and 5
  657   tens. Write 5. Carry 1 to hundreds' place.
```

Step IV. Carrying to both tens' and hundreds' places:

```
  1 1
  365   The sum of 5 ones and 9 ones is 14 ones, or
+ 289   1 ten and 4 ones. Write 4 and carry 1 to
  654   tens' place. The sum of the 1, 6, and 8 in
        tens' place is 15 tens. Write 5 and carry 1 to
        hundreds' place.
```

In the examples above, the numbers carried are shown. Writing these numbers is a learning aid that gives meaning to the step. It should not be used after the step is understood because it slows the process.

When a child understands all the steps in the process of adding to two numbers, he is ready to learn to add longer columns of figures.

Step V. Simple column addition:

```
  3     Begin at the top and add down.
  2     See 3 and 2. Think: 5. Then add the 5 you
+ 4     think to the 4 you see.
  9     Write 9 as the sum.
```

Children must be given special help in learning to remember a sum and then to add a seen number to it.

*Step VI. Adding a two-place number you think to a
          one-place number:*

```
  5     Begin at the top and add down.
  7     See 5 and 7. Think: 12. Then add the 12 you
+ 4     think to the 4 you see.
 16     Write 16.
```

This new step involves "adding by endings," since the addition of 12 and 4 requires the addition of the 2 in 12 to the 4.

Step VII. Bridging the tens:

```
  9     See 9 and 7. Think: 16.
  7     Then add the 16 you think to the 8 you see.
+ 8     The sum of 16 and 8 is more than 20. It
 24     is 24.
```

By "bridging the tens" we mean the finding of sums that are in the next higher decade (ten). For example, the sum of 16+8 is in the next higher ten than 16; that is, it is in the 20's.

Children need special help in adding by endings both with and without bridging the tens. The pinwheel game shown at the right provides excellent practice. The circles with the various numbers may be written on the blackboard or on paper. Then several children should state the sums found by adding the number in the inner circle, 16, to each of the outer numbers. Any other number can be substituted for the 16 for further practice. A short daily drill of this kind will result in a rapid mastery of the process.

Step VIII. More difficult column addition:

The examples in column addition given below require the child to use not only the steps in adding by endings presented above, but also the methods of carrying that are used in the addition of only two numbers. The reader should work the examples and try to see the new steps involved in each of them before reading the paragraph below the examples.

A	B	C	D	E
31	33	328	291	378
14	25	113	270	154
23	24	237	148	388
68	82	678	709	920

In A, which is a very easy example, there is no carrying or adding by endings. In B, there is no adding by endings, but there is carrying to tens' place. In C, there is adding by endings and also carrying to tens' place. In D, there is bridging of tens in tens' place and carrying to hundreds' place. In E, there is bridging of tens in both ones' and tens' places and also carrying to both tens' and hundreds' places. Thus, A is seen to be a very simple example, while E is a very complex and difficult example, requiring the use of many underlying skills.

The simplest way to check an answer to any addition example is to go over the work a second time by adding from the bottom up.

All steps in the process of addition of decimals, including the carrying step, are the same as for whole numbers. The main point to watch is the placement of the decimal point in the sum. (*See also* Decimals; Arithmetic; Numeration Systems and Numbers; Subtraction; Multiplication; Division; Fractions.)

```
3.8
2.7
6.5
```

ADE, George (1866–1944). The writer George Ade had much in common with his fellow Indianan James Whitcomb Riley. Both men were famous for their use of dialect and for the down-to-earth quality of their writing. Both got their start working on newspapers. Neither of them ever married.

George Ade was born in Kentland, Ind., on Feb. 9, 1866. In 1887 he was graduated from Purdue University and went to work on a newspaper in Lafayette, Ind. In 1890 he moved to Chicago and took a job with the *Morning News*, which later became the *Record*. It was in a column begun in 1893 that Ade developed his colloquial, humorous style of writing. His characters were city dwellers who talked in the slang of the time. His themes were satirical, attacking pretentiousness. Three books compiled from this column were: 'Artie' (1896), 'Pink Marsh' (1897), and 'Doc Horne' (1899).

The author's 'Fables in Slang' also first appeared in his newspaper column. These "fables" were patterned after Aesop's and carried flippant "morals." They appeared in book form in 1900. Two sequels were published later.

Ade retired from newspaper work in 1900. Travels in the Orient furnished inspiration for his comic opera 'The Sultan of Sulu' (1902). He was elected to the National Institute of Arts and Letters in 1908. In 1915 he settled on a farm near his birthplace.

Ade received an honorary degree from Purdue University in 1926 and one from Indiana University in 1928. He died in Kentland on May 16, 1944.

1866	George Ade born
1883	James W. Riley's first book of poems published
1890	Ade begins Chicago newspaper work
1898	First of 'Fables in Slang' appears
1908	Ade elected to National Institute of Arts and Letters
1914	World War I begins
1926	Ade receives honorary degree from Purdue University
1944	Ade dies

VICTORIA SQUARE, ADELAIDE
This statue of Capt. Charles Sturt, famed British explorer of Australia, stands in Victoria Square in Adelaide.

ADELAIDE, Australia. The capital of South Australia and the fourth largest city in Australia is Adelaide. It was the first city on the continent to be incorporated, in 1840.

Adelaide is in the southeastern part of Australia, near the middle of the eastern side of the Gulf of St. Vincent. The city lies on a coastal lowland with the Mount Lofty Ranges to the east. Adelaide is bounded on all sides by parklands, which separate it from its surrounding suburbs.

The Plan of the City

Adelaide was designed by the first South Australian surveyor general, Col. William Light, shortly after the colony was founded in 1836. It was named for Queen Adelaide, the wife of King William IV.

The city is laid out in two square sections, north and south, separated by the Torrens River. The southern half of Adelaide has become its principal business center. Each section is divided into blocks, with gardens appearing where the main streets intersect.

The Torrens River, dammed and made into a lake, adds to the charm of the city. The main thoroughfare, King William Street, runs north and south, intersecting Victoria Square.

There are many fine buildings in Adelaide, including the Anglican Cathedral of St. Peter, the Roman Catholic Cathedral of St. Francis Xavier, government buildings, and the State War Memorial, dedicated to South Australians who died in World War I.

South Australia's Houses of Parliament are built of locally hewn granite and marble. The University of Adelaide and the South Australian Museum are other points of interest.

There are many flourishing industries in the city. Dairy products from the surrounding countryside are processed here. Machine shops, textile mills, furniture factories, and railroad yards also provide employment.

The climate is pleasant. Winters are short, wet, and cool; summers are long, dry, and hot. Freezing temperatures seldom occur in Adelaide. (*See also* Australia.) Population, including suburbs (1961 census), 587,957.

ADEN (*ä'd'n*). The southern entrance to the Red Sea and the Suez Canal is the Gulf of Aden, an arm of the Arabian Sea. (For map, *see* Arabia.) On the gulf, at the southern tip of the Arabian peninsula, stands the seaport of Aden, a major city in the People's Republic of South Yemen. It was the capital of the 75-square-mile state of Aden until South Yemen was created in 1967, absorbing the state.

Aden is one of the hottest places on earth. It lies in the center of an extinct volcano on one of the two small peninsulas that enclose Aden Bay, its harbor. It is an important shipping point for the Arabian peninsula, but its chief business is fueling ships and planes. Aden was long a British naval base. After the Suez crisis of 1956 it became Britain's chief Middle Eastern military base (*see* Suez Canal).

From British Rule to Independence

Aden was occupied by the British in 1839 to safeguard their trade with India from pirates. In 1937 the city and the surrounding British-held territory became a British crown colony. After World War II the British prepared the colony for self-government. In 1963 Aden became a state in the Federation of South Arabia, a group of some 20 tribal districts under British sovereignty. The federation was to become independent from Great Britain in 1968. (*See also* Arab Federations.)

As independence approached, two rival extremist groups—the Front for the Liberation of Occupied South Yemen and the National Liberation Front—mounted terrorist campaigns for the control of Aden and the federation. Under increasing terrorist pressure, the British forces were withdrawn from Aden in November 1967. Independence came on November 28. The National Liberation Front, which gained control, named Qahtan al-Shaabi as president and changed the federation's name to People's Republic of South Yemen. Population of the city of Aden (1962 estimate), 150,000. (*See also* Arabia and the Arabs.)

ADENAUER, Konrad

(1876–1967). After World War II Germany lay in ruins. To Konrad Adenauer belongs much of the credit for raising West Germany to a position of economic prosperity and making it a respected free-world ally.

Konrad Adenauer was born on Jan. 5, 1876, in Cologne, Germany. He was one of four children. His father, Konrad, was a law clerk. The Adenauers were a pious Roman Catholic family. Young Konrad attended St. Aposteln Gymnasium in Cologne and the universities of Freiburg, Munich, and Bonn. He was graduated with a law degree. Married twice, he had four sons and three daughters.

Political Career

Adenauer was elected deputy mayor of Cologne in 1906, senior deputy mayor in 1911, and lord high mayor in 1917, a post he held for 16 years. From 1917 to 1933 he was also a member of the provincial diet and a representative in the Prussian State Council, of which he became president in 1928.

When the Nazis came to power in 1933, Adenauer was stripped of all his political positions. He was imprisoned in 1934 and again in 1944. After the war he helped organize a new party, the Christian Democratic Union. In 1948 he became president of the parliamentary council to draft a constitution for West Germany. In 1949 he became West Germany's first chancellor. In 1961 he was narrowly reelected to his fourth consecutive term. He retired as chancellor in October 1963. He died on April 19, 1967.

1876	Adenauer born
1914	World War I begins
1917	Adenauer elected mayor of Cologne
1918	World War I ends
1934	Adenauer imprisoned by Nazis
1939	World War II begins
1944	Adenauer again imprisoned by Nazis
1945	World War II ends
1949 -63	Adenauer serves as chancellor of West Germany
1967	Adenauer dies

SUMMER IN THE ADIRONDACKS
Summer visitors to the Adirondack Mountains ride ski lifts to the top of Whiteface Mountain for the scenic view.

ADIRONDACK (ăd-ĭ-rŏn′ dăk) **MOUNTAINS.** The Adirondack wilderness of northeastern New York State is one of the nation's great playgrounds. It is a region of wild beauty, larger than Connecticut. Rugged mountain scenery, good hunting and fishing, and skiing and other winter sports bring hundreds of thousands of visitors each year to the Adirondack Forest Preserve, more than two million acres in area. There are few permanent residents in the Adirondacks.

Although they are sometimes considered part of the Appalachian chain, the Adirondack Mountains belong geologically to the Laurentian Plateau (Canadian Shield) of Canada, from which they are separated by the St. Lawrence River (*see* Laurentian Plateau). They form the watershed between the St. Lawrence River and the Hudson River.

The peaks of the Adirondacks are scattered singly or in small groups or short ridges. The highest is Mount Marcy, 5,344 feet; 41 others rise 4,000 feet or more. Major rivers in the area are the Grass, Oswegatchie, Raquette, Salmon, Ausable, Hudson, and Sacandaga.

Rounded hillocks, high mountain lakes, and deep valleys tell of the work of ancient glaciers. Swift streams have made narrow, rugged cuts in the bedrock, which is largely crystalline limestone and granite. The area has deposits of iron and graphite.

Fine highways make all parts of the region accessible. One road leads to the top of Whiteface Mountain (4,872 feet). This peak stands at the head of Lake Placid, the site of a famous winter resort. Lake Placid is also one of the sources of the Ausable River, which is noted for its picturesque Ausable Chasm.

The Adirondack area is heavily forested and abounds in wildlife. This fact, combined with the pleasant summer climate and the heavy winter snows, has contributed to the Adirondacks' popularity with tourists. (*See also* New York.)

ADJECTIVE. The group of words called adjectives makes up one of the eight "parts of speech" (*see* Grammar). Adjectives are used to *modify* (describe or limit) the meaning of a noun or pronoun. They answer such questions as: what kind? (*pretty new* dress); which one? (*this* one, *that* one, *yonder* tree); how many? (*thirty*, or *30* people); who owns it? (*my* house, *its* shape). The three little words called "articles" are also classed as adjectives. The definite article is *the*. The indefinite articles are *a* and *an*.

Usually the adjective is placed just before the noun it modifies. When it follows a verb (it can only follow a "linking verb") it is called a *predicate adjective:* The soup is *hot*. It smells *good*. (*See also* Verb.)

Degrees of Comparison

Many adjectives change their form to show *comparison*, or *degree:*

Positive degree: *fine*
Comparative degree: *finer*
Superlative degree: *finest*

When the addition of *er* or *est* would make the word too long or awkward, *more* and *most* are used instead: *more rugged, more beautiful* (comparative); *most rugged, most beautiful* (superlative).

Some adjectives are compared irregularly: *bad, worse, worst; good, better, best; little, less, least; much, more, most*. A few should not be compared at all. An object may be *square* or *perfect*. It cannot be *more* square or *more* perfect. When only two things are compared, the comparative should be used: John is the *taller* of two boys, the *tallest* of three.

Nouns and Verbs Used as Adjectives

In the English language, nouns may be used as adjectives without changing their form; for example, *door* chain, *birthday* cake, *college* course. When a suffix is added to a noun to form an adjective, the meaning is somewhat changed; for example, harm*ful*, harm*less*, critic*al*, boy*ish*, bird*like*, bulb*ous*, dream*y*. When a proper noun, such as *India*, is used as an adjective, the word is called a proper adjective and is capitalized: *India* ink, *Indian* clubs. (*See also* Noun.)

Verbs used as adjectives take the form of the present participle (deserv*ing* person) or the past participle (deserv*ed* praise).

33

ADOLESCENCE—
The Teen Age

Adolescent girls and boys enjoy dating at social affairs and at sports events such as high-school basketball and football games.

ADOLESCENCE. The period of transition when the individual puts away childish things and prepares for the duties and responsibilities of adult life is known as adolescence. At this time he is neither child nor adult. The word comes from the Latin word *adolescere*, meaning "to grow to maturity." It is customary to subdivide adolescence into three periods.

Preadolescence, or **puberty,** is the time of sexual maturing. It usually extends over a period of approximately two years, from 11 to 13 in girls and from 12 to 14 in boys. It coincides roughly with the junior-high-school age. At this time there are bodily changes and frequently unsocial behavior.

Early adolescence extends from the time of sexual maturity to the age of $16\frac{1}{2}$. It is characterized by new interests and gradual maturing of behavior. It coincides with the high-school age.

Late adolescence extends from $16\frac{1}{2}$ years to 21 years. In general, it coincides with the college age.

Physical Development

A year or two before the child becomes sexually mature, four types of changes take place in his body. These changes are caused by increased activity of the pituitary gland (*see* Hormones).

Increase in height and weight. The "adolescent growth spurt" takes place mainly before the child is sexually mature, with the greatest increase in the year preceding maturity. The two years after maturity are characterized by a slowing down in growth. From then until age 17 for girls and age 20 or 21 for boys, increases in height and weight are slight.

Changes in bodily proportions. Gradually, and at different rates, the various parts of the body assume their mature proportions. The hands, feet, upper part of the head, and nose reach mature size first, with the lower part of the face, the shoulders, and arms and legs attaining mature size last. When height and weight increases have been completed, bodily proportions are also complete.

Development of primary sex characteristics. At puberty the sex organs grow to adult size and become mature in function.

Development of secondary sex characteristics. The secondary sex characteristics play no direct role in reproduction. In boys hair appears on the face and body, voice and skin texture change, and the muscles in the shoulders, arms, and legs develop. Girls develop breasts and broader hips.

Emotions and Family Relationships

The adolescent years have been characterized as a period of great "storm and stress," believed to be due to the physical changes taking place in the body at this time. Now it is' widely agreed that emotional tensions come more from environmental than from physical causes.

The adolescent above all wants to become independent. He resents being treated as a child and demands the rights and privileges of a "grown-up." He wants to go to parties, have dates, visit places of entertainment his parents may not approve of, spend his time with the "crowd," and use the family car. He wants to stay out late, select his own friends, and dress as he and his friends consider correct. He resents questioning as "snooping into his affairs"; any advice is interpreted as "bossing." All this results in constant friction and strained family relationships.

The adolescent is often jealous of older brothers and sisters, for he feels that they are shown favoritism by his parents. Younger brothers and sisters embarrass him. He objects to their looks, their manner of speech, their behavior, and he does not hesitate to show how he feels. Bickering, criticizing, and name calling result.

Gradually, as he is given more freedom, the adolescent's tensions grow less. Much depends upon the understanding shown by parents in handling family frictions. If stress lasts into late adolescence, it shows the youth is not making good adjustments.

Social Behavior

At no time in life is it so important to have friends and be popular as it is in adolescence. The unpopular adolescent is desperately unhappy. He may try to compensate for lack of friends by developing some absorbing hobby; he may study hard; or he may fall back on the companionship of his parents or of younger children. None is a truly satisfying form of compensation.

This is the age of "cliques," or small groups composed of two or more individuals of the same sex. They consider themselves "best friends" and are inseparable. When an interest in doing things with members of the opposite sex develops, toward the middle of adolescence, cliques of girls combine with cliques of boys to form the adolescent "crowd." It is they who plan the social activities and who decide which boys and girls will be included. The adolescent who belongs to no clique or crowd misses out on the good times of his contemporaries.

Schools and churches establish clubs to bring young people together. To a limited extent, the unaccepted adolescent finds such clubs a compensation. But here too he runs into the clique and he often loses interest when he is made to feel like an outsider.

The social group to which the adolescent belongs has a powerful influence. He follows in a slavish manner the dress, the manner of speech, and the behavior of his group. Because each group feels that it is superior to every other group, snobbishness and prejudice are common. Only as the cliques break up with the beginning of pairing off and "going steady" does the adolescent feel that he can be himself.

Some Adolescent Interests

Social interests consist of talking to friends, going to parties, loafing around with the crowd, eating with them, doing what they do, and trying to reform the family, the school, and the community. The adolescent frequently becomes keenly interested in politics, religion, and world affairs.

Active, organized sports become of interest. If he cannot make the football or basketball team, the next best thing is to watch others play. Dancing, bowling, skating, and any recreation that can be carried out with members of the opposite sex are popular. As the years pass and study or work consumes more time, there is more interest in such recreations as the motion pictures, radio, television, and reading.

Selecting his lifework, planning his education, finding a job and getting started in it are absorbing interests. His first vocational aims may be unrealistic and based on glamor. Gradually he takes into account his own abilities. (*See also* Vocations.)

Moral Standards and Religious Doubts

The child conforms to the moral codes of society because he learns that it is to his advantage to do so. Only as childhood draws to a close does he have a guilty conscience about doing things he knows are wrong, even if he is not caught and punished. By contrast the adolescent is an idealist. He has high moral standards for himself and for everyone else. When his family or friends fall below these standards, he is intolerant. When he falls below his standards, he is oppressed by feelings of guilt.

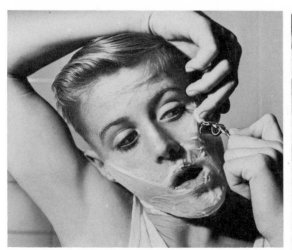

BECOMING CONSCIOUS OF ONE'S "LOOKS"
Social life—being part of the "in crowd"—is important to the adolescent. Because being accepted by the group and by the opposite sex depends so much on appearance, the adolescent becomes self-conscious about his looks and may spend much time grooming before a mirror. The adolescent is also concerned with clothes, often following the styles of the crowd.

ADOLESCENCE

TEEN-AGERS' BAND
By participating in such group activities as dancing or playing in a band, teen-age boys and girls develop confidence.

BABY-SITTING TEEN-AGER
In caring for her young charge, this baby-sitter gains valuable experience that will be extremely useful in her adult life.

In spite of these lofty ideals, the adolescent frequently misbehaves—to get revenge on someone he believes has treated him unfairly; to test those in authority; to see if he is able to break rules without being caught; or to keep the favor of friends who do the same things. Whatever the motive, the adolescent knows he is doing wrong.

In spite of the popular belief that juvenile delinquency is very widespread today, a relatively small percentage of adolescents find themselves in the hands of the law. Those who do are usually poorly adjusted children who come from homes where parents are separated or badly adjusted or from homes where little or no discipline is given. Frequently they are poor students who try to compensate for their poor school

grades by truancy or by doing things to attract the attention of their more successful classmates. Often they come from the lower socioeconomic groups who lack personal acceptance. They band together in gangs to seek pleasure through excitement and lawlessness because the healthy pleasures of their contemporaries are denied them.

The simplified religion taught to a child does not meet the needs of a mature person. It is inevitable that some revision in religious beliefs will occur. Because adolescence is the age when traditionally the individual joins the church, this is the time when social pressures are brought to bear on him to think about religion. The adolescent re-evaluates his childhood faith, often rejecting part of it, and even changing to a different faith than that of his parents.

Sex Interests

As a result of sexual maturity, there is a strong interest in members of the opposite sex, which follows a slow and predictable pattern. At first there is concentration of affection on a member of the same sex but of slightly older age. This is the "crush" stage which comes at puberty. It is followed by affection for a member of the opposite sex, of an older age, and generally known to the adolescent only by reputation. This is the stage of "hero-worshiping" a movie star, an athletic hero, or a national figure.

By mid-adolescence affection is concentrated on members of the opposite sex of the same age as the adolescent. This is the "boy-crazy" or "girl-crazy" stage, when there is a strong desire to be admired by all members of the opposite sex. The adolescent wants to date, regardless of with whom. After a year or two of this exciting new experience, affection is usually concentrated on one individual of the opposite sex of the same age, and the adolescent "goes steady."

Developing a Wholesome Personality

Adolescence is the critical age in the personality development of the individual. The foundations are laid during the childhood days, but they are not yet so well established that they cannot be changed if there is a strong desire to do so (*see* Personality).

To achieve a desirable and healthy concept of self the adolescent needs the encouragement and feeling of security that come with a wholesome family life. Every adolescent has a tendency to feel insecure. He needs someone to whom he can turn for advice and understanding. (*See also* Child Development; Family.)

Books About Adolescence

Bauer, W. W. Moving into Manhood (Doubleday, 1963).
Duvall, E. R. Love and the Facts of Life (Assoc. Press, 1963).
Fedder, Ruth. You, the Person You Want To Be (Whittlesey, 1957).
Gesell, A. L. and others. Youth: the Years from Ten to Sixteen (Harper, 1956).
Landis, J. T. and M. G. Teen-Agers' Guide to Living (Prentice-Hall, 1957).
Landis, P. H. Understanding Teen-Agers (Appleton, 1955).
Smaridge, N. A. Looking at You (Abingdon, 1962).

ADONIS GOING TO THE CHASE
In this picture by Benjamin West, Adonis is shown going into the forest in search of wild game. The handsome god was killed by a wild boar he had wounded with his spear.

ADONIS (*a-dō'nĭs*). According to Greek and Phoenician mythology, the handsomest of the gods was a youth named Adonis. His name came from the Semitic word *adonay*, meaning "my lord, my master."

Adonis was born of a tree, into which his mother had transformed herself. His relationship to a tree established the belief that his spirit lived in vegetative matter—particularly in the seed of corn. The annual Phoenician festival of Adonia commemorated Adonis as a god of fertility and plenty.

The goddess Aphrodite first saw Adonis at his birth. She was so taken by his beauty that she hid him in a coffer, or treasure chest. She told this secret to Persephone, another goddess. Unknown to Aphrodite, Persephone opened the coffer. When she beheld Adonis she was also struck by his beauty. She kidnaped him and refused to give him up. Aphrodite appealed to the god Zeus, who decreed that Adonis must spend half of each year on earth with Aphrodite and the other half in the underworld with Persephone. It was said that flowers bloomed and birds sang when Adonis walked the earth and all nature drooped when he returned to the underworld.

Aphrodite tried vainly to dissuade Adonis from his passion for hunting dangerous game. One day he was killed by a wild boar he had wounded with his spear. As Aphrodite knelt over him, anemones sprang from the ground where her tears had fallen.

ADRIATIC (*ā-drĭ-ăt'ĭk*) **SEA.** Italy is separated from Yugoslavia and Albania by a baylike arm of the Mediterranean—the Adriatic Sea. About 500 miles long, its width varies from 40 to 110 miles. Its maximum depth is 5,200 feet.

The Adriatic extends from its northerly head, the Gulf of Venice, southeastward to the Strait of Otranto, which leads to the Ionian Sea. The Po and the Adige rivers empty into the Adriatic at its head.

The western, or Italian, coast is low and straight. The principal Italian ports on the Adriatic are Bari, Brindisi, and Venice. The eastern, or Yugoslav-Albanian, coast is rocky and mountainous. It has numerous inlets and offshore islands. Rijeka, Split, Dubrovnik, and Kotor are the main Yugoslav ports. The chief Albanian ports are Durazzo and Valona. The free port of Trieste is also on the Adriatic.

The coasts of the Adriatic are important resort areas. The sunny, island-fringed Dalmatian coastal region of Yugoslavia is an especially popular tourist attraction. (For maps, *see* Europe; Italy.)

ADVERB. An adverb is a word that modifies a verb, an adjective, or another adverb. In "act fairly" the adverb *fairly* modifies the verb *act*. In "fairly good" it modifies the adjective *good*. In "fairly well" it modifies the adverb *well*. Adverbs usually answer the questions "How?" "When?" "Where?" "Why?" or "How much?"

Most adverbs are formed by adding the suffix *ly* to an adjective, for example, *great* (adjective), *greatly* (adverb); *real* (adjective), *really* (adverb). Some, however, have the same form as adjectives. *Fast*, for example, is an adjective in "fast train" and an adverb in "runs fast."

The chief difficulty in the use of adverbs comes from confusing them with adjectives. "Real kind" and "doing fine" are common mistakes for "really kind" or "very kind" and "doing well." Another error is using an adverb when an adjective is needed. The so-called *linking verbs* (such as *be*) should be followed by adjectives. These are verbs that have little meaning in themselves and serve only to connect subject and predicate. People say, for example, "The candy is *sweet*," or "tastes *sweet*" (not *sweetly*); "He turned *pale*"; "He appeared *weary*"; "She felt *sick*." When the verb, rather than the subject, is modified, an adverb is used: "He turned *quickly*," "He appeared *suddenly*." (*See also* Verb.)

Adverbs, like adjectives, can be compared in three degrees (*see* Adjective). For adverbs *more* or *less* is generally used for the comparative degree ("more quickly," "less quickly"), and *most* or *least* for the superlative degree ("most quickly," "least quickly"). A few adverbs are compared like adjectives; for example, "He worked faster," "He worked fastest." (*See also* Grammar.)

Here an advertising copy writer discusses the layout of an advertisement with the art director of the account.

ADVERTISING—An Aid to Selling

ADVERTISING.   Merchants have advertised their wares for hundreds of years. Yet advertising did not become a great social and economic force until less than a century ago. In this sense of the word, advertising is a product of the modern industrial age. Because it influences greatly the ways in which the people spend their money, it has become an essential partner of modern commerce and industry.

A good way to get an appreciation of the power of advertising and the work it does is to list some of its results—both good and bad—as they have been analyzed by economists and sociologists.

Some Good and Bad Points of Advertising

1. Skillful advertising of a desirable article ensures that a great many people at once will want to buy it. This enables the manufacturer to plan ahead and to lay in materials and machines on a large scale. He can also turn out vast quantities of the article at a much lower price than would be possible if he had to wait for people to discover slowly the value of his wares. This benefits the consumer by giving him the advantage of the lower manufacturing cost made possible by mass production. On the other hand, much the same procedure may be used to unload inferior

merchandise upon the public before any large proportion of individual consumers can find out for themselves the low quality of what they are buying.

2. Advertising establishes in the public mind standards of quality for staple articles. Thus it prevents the purchase of products of inferior grade. On the other hand, once a brand of merchandise has been established by large-scale advertising, it enjoys what may be called a psychological monopoly. The maker of a competing new product of still better quality may be unable to spend for advertising the huge sum necessary to overcome that advantage.

3. The standard of living is raised by advertising. It creates a desire for more healthful and more varied foods, better clothing, a more attractive personal appearance, and more comfortable homes. To get these, people work harder and spend money more wisely. The other side of this picture is that advertising is equally effective in persuading people to indulge in extravagance. Its frequent appeals to vanity and social rivalry tend also to lower social standards.

4. Advertising helps retail merchants. When they lay in stocks of well-advertised products they can be more certain of a continued demand for them. When, however, several competing brands of the same article are all well advertised, a merchant has to keep them all in stock. This increases his investment in stock, or *inventory*, and forces up his merchandise price.

5. New lines of merchandise can be rapidly brought to public attention through advertising. But adver-

tising also causes much property to be discarded while it is still useful. Many automobile and clothing manufacturers, for example, seek to persuade people that last year's cars or suits are out of date.

6. Many advertisements spread knowledge of useful facts. They bring inventions and scientific discoveries to public attention, foster health, and teach hygiene. Many others, however, are founded on scientific fakery. They stir up senseless fears of disease and induce people to use worthless and often injurious drugs.

7. Newspapers, magazines, and radio and television broadcasting are largely supported by advertising. Without it, these agencies of information and entertainment would be crippled or destroyed. This dependence upon advertisers, however, gives these same agencies undue control over public opinion.

Many other pros and cons of this kind could be listed. But these suffice to suggest the part that advertising plays in people's lives, the vast power it wields, and the social responsibilities it bears.

Techniques of Advertising—Price Appeal

Most people think that advertising is intended to *sell* goods. Good advertising, however, conceals this purpose and works rather to inspire a *desire to buy*. What advertising men call the *appeal of the ad* is designed to arouse one of the desires which prompt human conduct on commercial levels—the desire for comfort, wealth, social position, and health. Advertisements can be classified into types which use *price appeal, reason why*, and *suggestion*.

Price, or bargain, appeal is used by many retail stores. Grocers know they need not persuade people to buy food. Instead, the retailers use advertising to draw customers to their particular stores by promising lower prices, better quality, or superior service. On favorite shopping days, merchants may offer special bargains at a loss (loss-leaders), hoping that the bargain hunters will also buy other articles.

Clothing is often advertised similarly; but quality and style are emphasized. Style is especially stressed in advertising women's clothing, since the desire to be in style is strong in most women. "Exclusive" shops often urge that only a limited number of garments are available. This assures buyers that the garments offered will not become common.

Reason-Why and Suggestion Advertising

To sell a new article that competes with similar things already in use, advertisers must present to buyers a definite reason for changing to the new brand. They must persuade shavers, for example, that the new razor will give a better shave or is easier to keep clean. A great part of all automobile advertising is of the reason-why kind. Each manufacturer must explain to his old customers why his car is still "the best." He must give owners of other cars a strong argument for switching over. Scientific tests may be presented to support claims. Dramatic proofs are often used.

OLD STYLE ADVERTISING
This advertisement, dating from the 1800's, reflects the elaborate taste of the period. Its appeal is through suggestion.

"Nonbreakable" fountain pens were first advertised by having men write with pens which had been dropped from airplanes and run over by heavy buses.

Suggestion advertising is widely used, particularly for luxury articles. The suggestion may come from a series of pictures showing the product used in smart homes, clubs, hotels, or restaurants. The public is expected to feel that the product must be exceptional if it enjoys favor in such places.

Another type of suggestion appeal offers a "new, easy way" to avoid embarrassment, win popularity, or get ahead in life. Patent-medicine advertising often uses the fear motive by suggesting that the reader may have some disease which the medicine will relieve.

Testimonials are used freely with both reason-why and suggestion advertising. They may obviously have been bought. Advertisers believe, however, that the public either does not detect or does not resent the deception. Slogans, or catch phrases, are common. They help the reader remember the product.

Many Mediums Used by Advertisers

The particular means used to get an advertisement before the public is called the *medium*. Newspapers, popular magazines, billboards, streetcar and bus cards, broadcasting, and slides in motion-picture theaters are considered *general mediums* because they reach the general public. They are used when the product is sold through retail stores and when presumably nearly everybody is a possible customer. If an expensive article such as a refrigerator is sold through a limited number of dealers, newspapers are particularly suitable. A list of dealers in the community can be printed in each newspaper.

General mediums are too expensive to use for advertising many products which can be sold to only a few people. Such products are advertised in *trade papers*. These publications are devoted to a certain trade or line of business. Thus a manufacturer of printing equipment will rarely advertise it outside of the printing trade journals. *Class mediums* are used similarly. They include mediums which appeal to children, to sportsmen, to professional people, and to other groups which have similar tastes and habits.

OLD-FASHIONED POSTER
This outdoor advertisement of 1831 is cluttered with details. Only people who had the time to stand and look could read it all.

A common form of advertising is sampling. A food manufacturer may introduce a new brand by offering free samples in stores or through door-to-door agents. He may also use newspaper, magazine, or broadcast advertisements inviting people to send for samples.

Direct-Mail Advertising

Much advertising is of the kind called *direct-mail*. Here the first step is to obtain lists of names and addresses of persons most likely to be interested in the advertiser's product. The advertising material is sent to these people in the form of letters or circulars. To inspire confidence and dispel hesitation, the advertiser usually offers to send the article with a money-back guarantee or offers to accept payment after a short free trial.

Either method is safer for both the advertiser and the buyer than one might think. Experience has shown that most people will pay for an article if satisfied. If an advertiser persistently fails to make good on a money-back offer, the post-office authorities will issue a fraud order barring him from using the mails. Some of the greatest retail businesses in America have been built up by direct-mail selling.

Mail-order advertisers get names and addresses of possible customers through advertisements in magazines and newspapers. A reader is told, for example, that if he sends in his name and address on a coupon attached to the advertisement he will receive an interesting booklet free. Every coupon received is then followed up by direct-mail appeals or by the visit of a salesman. Such advertising usually carries a tiny symbol on the coupon or a phrase such as Dept. J in the address. These keys differ with each advertisement. When coupons or letters come in, the advertiser knows which advertisements brought results.

The Fight Against Fraud

Misrepresentation in advertising has been fought for years by the United States government, by honest advertisers, and by various organizations. One result of this fight was the United States Pure Food and Drug Act of 1906 (*see* Pure Food Laws). The Federal Trade Commission also forbids many fraudulent or unfair practices (*see* Federal Trade Commission). Better Business bureaus of states and cities are alert to detect and expose fraud in advertising.

Certain magazines require advertisers to prove the claims made for their products, often by laboratory tests, before the advertising is accepted for publication. A "seal of approval" may be granted to every product deemed acceptable. Reputable newspapers refuse objectionable forms of advertising. Sometimes they prosecute advertisers for fraudulent statements. Radio and television stations censor all advertising.

Some organizations inform consumers about the quality of advertised products. They give monthly reports on selected classes of products and special information when it is requested. Consumers can thus inform themselves about products. Many rely only upon advertising in reputable mediums. In this way

WILL THEY BE WHAT THEY WANT TO BE?

WE MUST HAVE FIRST-RATE SCHOOLS!

A PUBLIC SERVICE OF OUTDOOR ADVERTISING

Outdoor Advertising

A MODERN BILLBOARD
This modern outdoor advertisement, which will be read by people speeding past in cars, is simple and contains few words.

they can guard themselves against most advertising frauds and gross exaggerations.

It is hard for the law, the press, or broadcasters to draw the line in the fields of cosmetic and patent-medicine advertising. The medical profession often has to issue warnings against widely advertised preparations for self-treatment without prescription.

The Advertising Business

Retail stores and direct-mail advertisers usually maintain their own advertising departments. Radio and television stations and the larger newspapers will prepare programs or advertisements for advertisers. Much of the nation's advertising, however, is prepared by *advertising agencies.*

Before the Civil War newspapers and magazines sold blocks of space to agents at a discount from the regular rates. The agents resold the space to advertisers and when necessary prepared the advertisements. Later, copy writing became their chief function. The publishers continued to allow them the discount and refused it to advertisers seeking to place business directly. Publishers prefer to deal with a few agents rather than with many single advertisers. Under this system the advertiser gets agency service as well as space. The agency's income comes from the discount given it by publishers—usually 15 per cent.

Advertising placed under this arrangement is called *national* advertising. Most newspapers will not give agency discounts on local advertising placed by retailers. Hence retailers must maintain their own advertising departments. The newspapers usually give them a rate less than the national rate.

Organization of the Advertising Agency

Writing advertisements is not the only work done by an advertising agency. The advertising business includes much more than this, and so the larger agencies must maintain several departments.

First among these departments is the staff of *contact men*, or account executives. They handle the agency's relations with its clients, or "accounts." The word "account" in the advertising business means a client and his affairs, taken together. These men draw upon the other departments for everything the client needs and must keep the client satisfied. They are also expected to get new clients.

The staff of the *merchandising department* must have a thorough knowledge of merchandising in all its branches, such as retail, direct-mail, and house-to-house selling. This department watches for possible new markets for a client's wares and recommends style or other changes. It may also suggest new merchandising plans.

The *space-buyer* is in charge of placing a client's advertising before the public. An important duty is selecting the best mediums to use. No profit can be expected, for example, from offering expensive perfumes or custom-built cars in a magazine read principally by people of low income. Magazines or conservative newspapers read largely by wealthier people are poor mediums for advertisements of overalls. A great help to the space-buyer is the Audit Bureau of Circulations. This agency furnishes newspapers and magazines with certified audits of their circulations. The audits assure space-buyers that the medium has in each locality the amount of circulation it claims.

Departments for Copy and for Art

The actual writing of advertisements is done by *copy writers*. All the work of the other departments depends finally for its success upon the ability of the

GOETHE on ignorance

Great Ideas of Western Man...ONE OF A SERIES

THERE IS NOTHING MORE FRIGHTFUL THAN IGNORANCE IN ACTION

ARTIST: ANTONIO FRASCONI   (CRITICISMS, REFLECTIONS, AND MAXIMS, 1826.)

Container Corporation of America

INSTITUTIONAL AD
This advertisement is one of a series of fine paintings used to build good will and respect for the advertiser.

copy writer to prepare effective copy. Some of the largest salaries are paid to good copy writers.

The *art director* procures the pictures and arranges the typography of advertising. He must know which artists and photographers can do the most effective work for each class of product. He must decide whether a startling or a dignified typography or "dress" will be more effective in a given case. He must also devise new and striking illustrations.

Departments for Broadcasting and Publicity

Larger agencies maintain special departments for preparing radio and television broadcasts. This work involves helping to prepare the programs, procuring the entertainers, and checking the results (*see* Radio; Television).

Some agencies maintain publicity departments to get free mention of advertisers and their products in newspapers and magazines. Such work is so highly specialized, however, that advertising agencies usually confine their efforts to getting publicity in trade papers and special departments of newspapers, such as the automobile section. The more difficult work of getting publicity in the general news is entrusted to specialists called *publicity agents* or *public relations counselors*.

These men may undertake tasks as complicated as popularizing a candidate for the presidency. Propaganda on topics ranging from eating apples to waging war is originated and spread by these specialists in mass psychology.

Except in copy writing, a talent for writing counts less in advertising than an ability to create sound merchandising ideas and to anticipate trends in public taste. Also important is ability to handle business contacts successfully.

Training in merchandising and in copy writing is offered by many colleges and universities. Special schools teach advertising art, style designing, and other specialties. Such training is good but it only prepares the student to make a beginning in advertising work. Actual selling experience is extremely helpful. Service in the advertising department of a retail store is also good training.

Advertising in American Life

Advertising is a vast industry, especially in the United States. In no other country is it so highly developed or so widely used. Some form of advertising is employed by nearly every American business and by many noncommercial organizations, such as colleges and charitable societies. Government agencies use advertising to announce bond issues and public services. States and cities conduct "campaigns" to attract tourists and new industries.

Advertising employs many thousands of people, both directly and indirectly. About 80,000 work in agencies, outdoor-advertising companies, and miscellaneous firms. People with specialized talents, such as actors and painters, are often employed for particular jobs. Involved in advertising too are many of the more than 850,000 people in the printing and publishing industry. The same is true of thousands of workers in the vast radio and television field.

The Advertising Council

The Advertising Council is a nonprofit organization. Its purpose is to win public support for worthy causes. It was formed in 1941 by various advertising associations to aid the government in war drives. Later it supported Community Chest drives, campaigns for better schools, and many other causes.

Its slogans reach almost everyone. They remind him to "Drive carefully . . . the life you save may be your own"; "Give your blood—call the Red Cross"; "Remember—Only you can prevent forest fires!" Advertising agencies supply free creative talent to the Council's campaigns. Television, radio, newspapers, and magazines give the Council free time or space. (*See also* Magazines; Newspapers.)

AEGEAN CIVILIZATION— Bronze Age Culture

AEGEAN CIVILIZATION. Europe's earliest civilization appeared on the coasts and islands of the Aegean Sea. Here, while Western Europe was still in the Stone Age, the Minoan-Mycenaean peoples achieved a highly organized Bronze Age culture.

Two different civilizations flourished in this region some 2,000 years before the Christian Era. One is known as *Minoan*, because its center at Cnossus on the island of Crete was the legendary home of King Minos, son of Zeus and Europa. The other is called *Mycenaean*, after Mycenae in Greece (the city of King Agamemnon, the Achaeans' leader in the Trojan War).

The Mycenaeans, or Achaeans, had invaded the Greek mainland from the north about 2000 B.C. The center of their culture was Mycenae. The city flourished from about 1500 to 1100 B.C. Before 1400 B.C the Mycenaeans conquered the Minoans, and about 1200 B.C. they sacked Troy (*see* Trojan War).

Mycenae and Other Achaean Cities

In 1876 Heinrich Schliemann began excavating Mycenae (*see* Schliemann). Alan J. B. Wace continued the work in the 20th century. Still visible today is the acropolis, with its broken stone walls and Lion Gate. Within the walls Schliemann uncovered the graves of bodies covered with gold masks, breastplates, armbands, and girdles. In the graves of the women were golden diadems, golden laurel leaves, and exquisite ornaments shaped like animals, flowers, butterflies, and cuttlefish.

Schliemann thought he had found the burial place of Agamemnon and his followers. Later study proved the bodies belonged to a period 400 years earlier than the Trojan War. Rulers of another dynasty were buried outside the walls in strange beehive tombs.

MINOAN-MYCENAEAN CIVILIZATION
+ IMPORTANT CENTERS ABOUT 1400 B.C.

MINOAN ACHIEVEMENTS
Here are a porch of the palace of Cnossus and a snake goddess.

Other great cities of the same period were Pylos, the legendary home of King Nestor, and Tiryns. It is not known to what extent Mycenae controlled other centers of the Achaean civilization. Trade extended to Sicily, Egypt, Palestine, Troy, Cyprus, and Macedonia. Mycenaeans settled on Cyprus and at Miletus on the coast of Asia Minor.

Scholars once believed that the Mycenaeans were illiterate. The evidences of culture in their massive walled cities, their fine goldwork, pottery, and vases were attributed to the influence of the Minoans, who conquered the mainland about 1600 B.C.

Deciphering the Mycenaean Writings

In 1952 great light was thrown on the Mycenaean civilization by the deciphering of an ancient writing on clay tablets, known as Linear Script B. Michael Ventris, a young English architect, accomplished the task on which scholars had labored for 50 years. These tablets were among some 2,000 uncovered at Cnossus on Crete by Sir Arthur Evans, beginning in 1900. With them were tablets in an older writing, which Evans called Linear Script A, and some still older hieroglyphics. Linear Scripts A and B are in a kind of writing which uses symbols for syllables. In 1939 about 600 more tablets in Linear Script B were found at Pylos, on the Greek mainland, and in 1952 and 1953 some were discovered at Mycenae.

Ventris found that Linear Script B is an *archaic Greek dialect*. It is the oldest Indo-European system of writing yet discovered. The language is at a stage 700 years older than the earliest classical Greek.

THE LION GATE AT MYCENAE
A huge gate pierces the stone wall around the acropolis of Mycenae, where Agamemnon ruled. Above the lintel are two lions, their forepaws on an altar.

The tablets appeared at Cnossus because the Mycenaeans had conquered the Minoans.

The tablets are only inventories of palace storerooms and arsenals. They reveal a great deal about the life of the Mycenaeans, however. They engaged in agriculture, industry, commerce, and war. At the head of the society was a king. Under him was a "leader of the people," perhaps an army commander. There were landowning barons, tenants, servants and slaves, priests and priestesses. There were many trades and professions. The Mycenaeans worshiped Zeus, Hera, Poseidon, Ares, Artemis, and Athena.

The Minoan Civilization

The language of Linear Script A has not yet been identified, and it is uncertain where the Minoans originated. They lived on Crete from about 2500 B.C. to 1400 B.C., when they were conquered by Mycenaeans from the Greek mainland. By 1600 B.C. they were a world power. Prosperity depended upon seafaring and trade, especially with the East and with Egypt. Minoan influence spread also to the Greek mainland.

Evans' excavations at Cnossus revealed a great palace which covered six acres. White columns and walls frescoed in rich colors rose several stories high above the harbor. There were no walls, as in the Mycenaean cities. The palace and surrounding city were protected by a powerful navy.

Evans found storerooms with huge oil jars still in place, elaborate bathrooms, ventilation and drainage systems, and waste disposal chutes. The pottery was as fine as porcelain. Paintings on walls and pottery showed the "modern" dress of the women, with puffed sleeves and flounced skirts.

The Myth of the Labyrinth

The Minoans worshiped a mother goddess, whose symbol was the double-bladed ax, called a *labrys*. The name of the symbol and the maze of rooms in the palace recall the story of the labyrinth. According to Greek mythology, Daedalus built a labyrinth for Minos to house the man-eating Minotaur, half man and half bull (*see* Theseus). Painted on the palace walls are pictures of male and female acrobats vaulting over the backs of bulls. This sport may have given rise to the myth. (For picture of one of the frescoes, *see* Design.) After the Greeks conquered the Minoans such stories became a part of their mythology.

End of Minoan-Mycenaean Civilizations

About 1100 B.C. Greece was overrun by an invasion of barbaric tribes from the north. The Dorians and later the Ionians occupied the areas where the Minoan-Mycenaean cultures had flourished. Greece was not to be as rich and powerful again until the golden age of Pericles, in the 5th century B.C. (*See also* Archaeology.)

THE AEGIS OF ATHENA
Cloaking her shoulders, Athena's aegis was said to repel her enemies.

AEGIS (*ē'ǰĭs*). A shield-like piece of equipment that was worn by certain gods and goddesses is described in Homer's 'Iliad' as an *aegis*. In Greek mythology the aegis is particularly identified with the god Zeus and the goddess Athena. It was said to be made of a shaggy goatskin, to which tassels or certain other ornaments might be attached.

The aegis worn by Zeus was indestructible. It was made by Hephaestus, the god of fire and of the forge, who was also believed to be the blacksmith and the artisan of Olympus. The aegis that he devised for Zeus was a fearful, cloudlike mantle. When Zeus shook it, violent thunderstorms were produced.

Athena's aegis is often represented as a goatskin breastplate. It was surrounded by serpents and had a horrible gorgon's head in its center.

AENEAS (*ē-nē'ás*). In mythology Aeneas was regarded as a Roman god. Homer's 'Iliad' compares him with the legendary Hector. He is the hero of Vergil's 'Aeneid' but was revered by the Romans long before the 'Aeneid' was written. They called him *Jupiter indiges*—"the founder of the race."

Aeneas was not of Roman origin. Anchises, his father, was a member of the Trojan royal house. His mother was the goddess Aphrodite. Anchises was sworn never to reveal his marriage to Aphrodite. When Aeneas was born, however, Anchises boasted to his companions. In punishment, he was blinded.

When Troy was conquered in the Trojan War, Aeneas led his warriors out of the burning city, carrying his blind father on his shoulders. Aeneas and his companions then roamed the Mediterranean area for seven years in search of a new homeland. His ships were wrecked off the African coast, near Carthage. Dido, the Carthaginian queen, fell deeply in love with Aeneas and begged him to stay. When he left, Dido killed herself in grief.

Aeneas and his companions settled briefly in Thrace, Crete, and Sicily. They finally came to the land of Latium, on the banks of the Tiber. King Latinus made them welcome. Aeneas aided the ruler in his struggles against the Rutuli. Later, Aeneas married Lavinia, daughter of Latinus. He inherited the kingdom after Latinus died, reigning happily and successfully over his united Trojans and Latins. He was killed in a battle with the Etruscans.

AEOLUS (*ē'ō-lŭs*). According to a story told in the 'Odyssey', Aeolus was given command of the four winds by Zeus. With them he lived on a brass-walled island (the modern Stromboli, north of Sicily). His four charges were Boreas, the fierce north wind; Notus, the rainy south wind; Eurus, the bleak east wind; and Zephyrus, the gentle wind from the west.

Once Odysseus (Ulysses) touched at the island in the course of his wandering return from Troy. Aeolus wanted to hasten Odysseus' return home, so he gave him the unfavorable winds—the north, south, and east—safely confined in an oxhide bag.

Release of the Unfavorable Winds

With the west wind blowing steadily and the other winds safely imprisoned, Odysseus' ship flew swiftly homeward. Then on the tenth day the sailors, believing a treasure was in the bag, opened it while Odysseus slept. The released winds then blew the ship back to the island. There Aeolus, angry at the abuse of his kindness, refused further aid. (*See also* Odysseus.)

From Aeolus is named the aeolian harp, a musical instrument made by stretching catgut strings or wires over a thin sounding box. The strings are tuned as in a violin. When placed in a partially closed window, where there is a draft of air, the passing of the wind over its strings produces strange and melancholy musical sounds, varying with the rise and fall of the breeze.

THE KEEPER OF THE WINDS
The myth of Aeolus, who was the legendary custodian of the four winds, was the inspiration for this work by the noted French sculptor Claude Michel.

45

AEROSOLS. Clouds in the sky and sprays squirted from a can are both *aerosols*. The word means a liquid or a solid finely dispersed in air, in a stable state called a colloid (*see* Colloids).

A cloud is a natural aerosol of water droplets dispersed in air. Smoke contains solid particles of carbon and ash. Fog with smoke and certain other chemicals in it is the disagreeable and harmful aerosol called *smog*.

Man-made aerosols include insecticides and sprays for absorbing odors and for applying protective coatings. Related products (air bubbles in liquids) are whipped cream, shaving lather, sirups, and tooth paste.

How Cans Supply Aerosols

For supplying man-made aerosols, the product to be dispensed is held in a container under pressure from some gas (called a *propellant*). When a valve is released, the gas drives out the product as a spray or foam.

Some commercial aerosols store the propelling gas under pressure in the can. It fills the space above the product when the can is sealed. The gas expands as the product is used. Pressure is continually lost, however, and this may have an undesirable effect on some sprays or foams.

For uniform pressure, the product is mixed with the propellant. It may be a liquid that evaporates rapidly into the space left as the product is used. The same effect is obtained if a suitable gas under enough pressure is dissolved in the product. The gas must evaporate to keep up the pressure.

Types of Propellants

If the product is for human use, the propellant must be one that has been approved by the Federal Food and Drug Administration. Before he introduces any new propellant, the manufacturer must prove it to be harmless. He must show by exhaustive scientific tests that the propellant is not toxic (poisonous) or irritating. If it has a noticeable taste or odor or if it alters the product in any way, the Food and Drug Administration withholds approval. The propellants most commonly used are carbon dioxide, nitrogen, and nitrous oxide (for aerosols such as whipped cream).

If the product is not for human use as a food, medicine, or cosmetic, any gas that does not harm the product may serve as a propellant. The gas often is a freon that dissolves in the product. A freon is a hydrocarbon such as methane (CH_4), with atoms of chlorine (Cl) and fluorine (F) substituted for atoms of hydrogen (H). The one most commonly used is

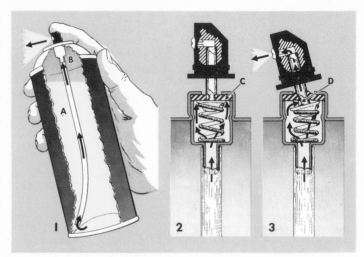

HOW AN AEROSOL DISPENSER WORKS
1. The can holds the product (A). The propellant gas above it (B) supplies pressure. 2. A rubber gasket (C) cuts off the flow of the product. 3. Pushing over the valve stem moves the gasket and opens an outlet (D) to the nozzle. The gas pressure drives the product up the dip-stick tube and out the nozzle.

DETECTING OZONE WITH BENT RUBBER
Ozone produced in smog from automobile exhausts makes bent rubber crack. The time it takes to start cracking in a standard test piece of bent rubber (left to right) measures the amount of ozone that is present in a cloud of smog.

freon-12 (CCl_2F_2). It is also a good refrigerant (*see* Refrigeration).

Character and Causes of Smogs

Smog can damage many substances and be dangerous to plant and animal life. A cloud of chemically laden smog stings the eyes and makes breathing disagreeable. If smogs occur over regions where much coal is burned and industries discharge gaseous wastes, the harmful gases are usually sulfur dioxide and oxides of nitrogen. Automobile exhausts contribute incompletely burned portions of fuel.

The worst smogs occur in regions where sunshine is abundant and strong but winds are light. Here atmospheric inversions often hold a mass of air stationary over the region. (During an inversion, heavy air lies over lighter air and pins it down.) The sunshine turns some of the fumes from automobile exhausts into ozone. The increase of ozone in the stagnant air causes most of the damage. The only efficient way to check ozone formation is by insuring complete burning of automobile fuel. (*See also* Fog; Smoke.)

AEROSPACE—The Total Expanse Beyond the Earth's Surface

AEROSPACE. The earth's atmosphere is usually referred to as "the air" (*see* Air; Atmosphere). "Airman," "airplane," and "air force" are some of the names of persons, machines, and organizations concerned with manned air travel.

Man-made vehicles have gone beyond the "air." They have entered interplanetary regions outside the earth's atmosphere. Man himself has actually traveled in a vehicle through outer space. Therefore, a whole new terminology, or system of names, is being devised to describe the technology and science of all space beyond the earth's surface.

Aerospace is such a word. It describes all the regions beyond the earth's surface. It includes the atmosphere and the vast expanse of outer space.

FACT FINDER FOR AEROSPACE ARTICLES

The subject of aerospace is a broad one. Readers will find exactly what they want to know about it in the many articles listed here.

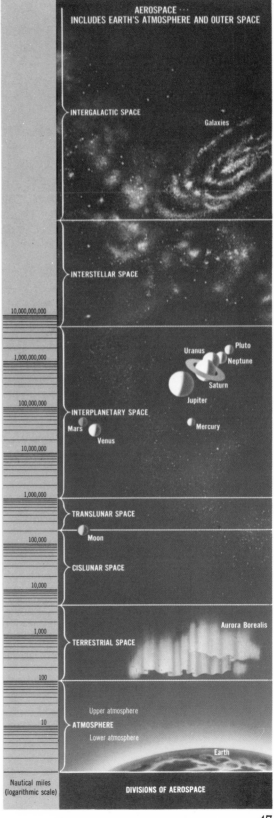

AEROSPACE · · · INCLUDES EARTH'S ATMOSPHERE AND OUTER SPACE

INTERGALACTIC SPACE — Galaxies

INTERSTELLAR SPACE

INTERPLANETARY SPACE — Uranus, Pluto, Neptune, Saturn, Jupiter, Mercury, Mars, Venus

TRANSLUNAR SPACE — Moon

CISLUNAR SPACE

TERRESTRIAL SPACE — Aurora Borealis

ATMOSPHERE — Upper atmosphere, Lower atmosphere, Earth

Nautical miles (logarithmic scale)

10,000,000,000
1,000,000,000
100,000,000
10,000,000
1,000,000
100,000
10,000
1,000
100
10

DIVISIONS OF AEROSPACE

This pilot is testing the MC-2 full-pressure space suit in the heat chamber at Wright-Patterson Air Force Base, Ohio. Such suits will protect men flying in outer space from the effects of heat, cold, altitude, and gravity.

AEROSPACE CAREERS— Jobs with Aircraft and Spacecraft

AEROSPACE CAREERS. All occupations dealing with the manufacture and operation of aircraft and spacecraft are called *aerospace careers*. About one million men and women work on civilian aerospace jobs. Thousands of servicemen and women are in military aerospace work.

About three fourths of the civilians are in the aircraft and parts manufacturing industry. The remainder are airmen. These include pilots and nonpilots, such as mechanics and air traffic control operators.

Occupations in aviation are found both in the air and on the ground. The major fields are aircraft and missile manufacturing, air transportation, federal government aviation, and general aviation. Examples of aerospace careers are described on the pages that follow.

Today's airplane mechanics little resemble those of the early days of flying when they repaired engines with pliers, screw driver, and baling wire. Here mechanics are receiving instruction on complex jet-engine simulators.

Aircraft and Missile Manufacturing Occupations

These occupations are concerned with the manufacture of airframes, engines, electronic systems, and accessories for aircraft and missiles. Scientists, engineers, mathematicians, and technicians work on research, design, and testing. Mechanics make the parts and assemble them.

Aerodynamics Engineer. Studies aircraft and missile flight performances with models in wind tunnel.

Assembler. Puts together parts of aircraft and missiles.

Chemist. Develops or tests aircraft and rocket fuels and materials such as plastics and ceramics.

Design Engineer. Plans shape, size, and structure of aircraft and missile airframes.

Design Layout Draftsman. Makes designs to engineers' specifications.

Electronics Engineer. Designs sensing and control devices.

Equipment Engineer. Designs heating, pressurizing, hydraulic, and oxygen-equipment systems.

Flight Line Mechanic. Prepares airplane for test flight after final assembly.

Inspector. Checks materials from suppliers and finished parts.

Jig and Fixture Builder. Makes jigs to hold work or to guide tools in production or assembly.

Mathematician. Develops formulas for engineering design problems; records wind tunnel data; analyzes flight test results.

Metallurgist. Develops or tests metals and alloys used for parts.

Mock-Up Builder. Makes full-size aircraft and spacecraft models for solving engineering problems.

Model Builder. Makes scale models for wind tunnel testing.

Physicist. Works on scientific problems for aircraft and missiles, such as overcoming heat barrier.

Power Plant Engineer. Designs piston, jet, turboprop, ram-jet, or rocket engines and their parts.

Sheet-Metal Fabricator. Cuts and shapes aircraft and missile parts from sheet metal.

Structures Engineer. Checks strength of materials with vibration and stress and strain tests.

Technical Illustrator. Makes drawings for operation handbooks.

Test Pilot. Flies aircraft to test flight performance.

Tool- and Diemaker. Makes tools and dies for machine parts.

Tool Designer. Designs tools for making aircraft or missile parts.

Weight Engineer. Studies weight and center of gravity of aircraft and missiles under different loads.

AERODYNAMICS ENGINEER

ASSEMBLER

MATHEMATICIAN

Air Transportation Occupations

These occupations involve the transportation of passengers, mail, and freight by scheduled and nonscheduled airlines, charter aircraft, and air-cargo carriers. About 80 per cent of these are ground jobs.

Air Cargo Agent. Supervises cargo terminal; records airfreight and arranges for delivery.

Aircraft Instrument Technician. Installs, repairs, and tests aircraft instruments.

Aircraft Maintenance Inspector. Checks aircraft parts and the work of mechanics and technicians.

Aircraft Mechanic. Services aircraft airframes and engines.

Aircraft Radio Technician. Installs and repairs radio equipment.

Airline Station Manager. Is in charge of ground and flight operations for his airline at his station.

Check Pilot. Observes pilot's efficiency on check flights, trains new pilots in company regulations.

Copilot. Assists pilot in operation of flight controls; watches instruments and weather; keeps log.

Flight Dispatcher. Plans flight with pilot; authorizes take-offs or cancels flights; advises pilots in air on weather or route changes.

Flight Engineer. Is responsible for in-flight operation of engines and aircraft systems.

Flight Simulator Instructor. Trains pilots and checks their skills, using a flight simulator.

Ground Radio Operator. Operates airline station radio equipment.

Meteorologist. Makes weather reports to pilot and dispatcher.

Navigator. Plots course; reports position; estimates arrival time.

MODEL BUILDER

FLIGHT DISPATCHER

AIR-BORNE WEATHER OPERATOR

FLIGHT NURSE

ROCKET SPECIALIST

AIR TRAFFIC CONTROLLER

MAINTENANCE INSPECTOR

Operations Agent. Oversees loading and unloading; checks distribution of aircraft load and fuel.

Pilot. Is in command of plane; is responsible for safety of passengers and cargo; makes flight plan and preflight check of aircraft; operates controls; supervises crew.

Propeller Specialist. Repairs and checks propellers and governors.

Ramp Serviceman. Handles cargo and baggage; refuels aircraft.

Reservations Clerk. Makes flight reservations for airline passengers.

Stewardess or Steward. Checks passengers' names and destinations; enforces safety rules; serves food; oversees riders' comfort.

Teletype Operator. Runs airline's teletype equipment.

Ticket Agent. Sells tickets; weighs and tags baggage; answers questions on schedules and fares.

Traffic Representative. Promotes airline travel; calls on customers; arranges charter flights.

Aviation Occupations in the Federal Government

The federal government offers hundreds of occupations in aviation. Most of them are in the armed forces. The others are civilian occupations with government agencies. Most of the civilian jobs are concerned with air safety or with aerospace research and development.

Military Aviation

Many aviation occupations in the armed forces are similar to those in air transportation. All the armed services require pilots, mechanics, meteorologists, radio operators, etc. Many careers are open to women. Some aviation occupations not found in civilian life are:

Air-Borne Weather Operator. Operates weather instruments aboard weather reconnaissance plane.

Aviation Boatswain's Mate. Handles aircraft aboard carriers and at naval air stations.

Aviation Machinist's Mate. Participates in rescue work aboard Coast Guard helicopters.

Bomber Navigator. Keeps plane on course; locates target; drops bombs; directs return course.

Fighter Pilot. Operates jet plane to intercept enemy craft or missiles.

Flight Nurse. Attends sick or injured military personnel in flight.

Guided Missile Mechanic. Installs, maintains, tests, and repairs guided missile control systems.

Parachute Rigger. Packs personnel, cargo, and aircraft parachutes.

Paramedic. Parachutes to give medical aid; rescues injured or lost persons in rough country.

Rocket Specialist. Installs, inspects, and repairs liquid propellant rockets.

Federal Aviation Administration

This agency employs thousands of workers who direct air traffic, maintain navigational aids, check pilot compliance with safety rules, or certify worthiness of aircraft.

Air Traffic Controller. Mans airport control tower, air route traffic control center, and communications station.

Airways Engineer. Plans electronic navigational aids, such as radar, instrument landing systems, and airport approach lighting.

Airways Flight Inspector. Pilots aircraft to check navigational aids, such as radio beacons and ground-controlled approach systems.

Electromechanic. Maintains teletype equipment, landing lights, beacons, and stand-by generators.

Electronics Inspector. Examines airline's compliance with safety rules for electronic equipment; checks competency of electronics repairmen; inspects electronic equipment of general aviation craft.

Electronics Installation Technician. Installs air navigational aids, such as radar, approach lighting, and communications equipment.

Electronics Maintenance Technician. Maintains navigational aids and communications equipment, such as radar and radio beacons.

Engineering Flight Test Inspector. Checks worthiness of new aircraft for certification purposes.

Maintenance Inspector. Checks airline maintenance practices, training methods, spare-parts stock; inspects aircraft engines, systems, instruments; checks compliance with safety rules in general aviation.

Manufacturing Inspector. Examines aircraft parts, engines, systems, and instruments as produced.

Operations Inspector. Oversees airline flight operations; tests general aviation pilots and instructors.

Planning Engineer. Plans airport construction and improvements.

Program Officer. Estimates costs of construction or improvements at airports.

Civil Aeronautics Board

Occupations with the Civil Aeronautics Board deal with awarding of airline routes, approval of flight schedules, and establishment of fares. They also involve the determination of rates to be paid by the Post Office Department to the airlines for hauling airmail.

Economist. Studies airline operating costs, revenues, and profits when airlines request changes in fares, routes, and services.

Statistician. Gathers statistics for decisions on airline fares, routes, and services.

National Aeronautics and Space Administration

Occupations with NASA are concerned with the research and development of advanced aircraft or with the design and testing of space vehicles for nonmilitary use. NASA employs thousands of scientists, engineers, and technicians.

Aeronautical Research Scientist. Carries on aircraft design research in chemistry, electronics, physics, metallurgy, and other areas.

Space Research Scientist. Conducts research on space travel problems, such as satellite guidance, propulsion, launching, and tracking.

OPERATIONS INSPECTOR

PLANNING ENGINEER

General Aviation Occupations

These occupations have to do with the flight of aircraft other than military or airline. All sizes of aircraft are included, from the light plane used for sport or for farming to the four-engine executive transport. In each case the airplane is a tool that helps do the job better.

Aerial Fire Fighter. Observes forest fires from air; directs fire fighters on ground by radio; dumps water or chemicals on fires.

Aerial Prospector. Uses air-borne electronic instruments to locate and map mineral deposit areas.

Aerial Sight-Seeing Guide. Conducts sight-seeing tours in aircraft.

Agricultural Pilot. Sprays, dusts, fertilizes, or seeds crops and orchards.

Air Taxi Operator. Provides air taxi service for the public.

Executive Pilot. Flies aircraft owned by business firms.

Flying Instructor. Teaches student pilots how to fly.

Helicopter Pilot. Carries loads to otherwise inaccessible areas.

Pipeline Patrol Pilot. Inspects oil pipelines from low-flying plane.

Skywriter. Pilots skywriting aircraft; releases chemicals.

AGRICULTURAL PILOT

Related Occupations

These occupations are closely connected with aviation. They contribute necessary or desirable services to all areas of aviation.

Air Cargo Forwarder. Delivers airfreight to and from airlines

Aircraft Conversion Specialist. Makes major changes on used aircraft; installs new interiors and other improvements; converts transports to executive or cargo planes.

Aircraft Designer. Designs interiors of aircraft.

Aircraft Salesman. Demonstrates light planes to customers; sells aircraft parts and accessories.

Airport Operator. Manages airport services; administers airport regulations.

Aviation Educationist. Assists schools, teachers, and youth groups to increase knowledge of aviation.

Aviation Writer. Reports on new developments in aviation and space exploration for newspapers, magazines, and books.

Flight Safety Research Specialist. Studies air accidents; promotes safety by recommending improved procedures and design.

State Aeronautics Director. Promotes aviation within his state; administers state regulations; aids communities in building airports.

AIR TAXI OPERATOR

AVIATION WRITER

AEROSPACE FUELS

AEROSPACE FUELS. Aircraft that fly within the earth's atmosphere and spaceships that travel in outer space require fuels to power them. The reciprocating, or piston-type, aircraft engine uses gasoline (*see* Airplane Power Plants; Gasoline). This petroleum substance produces heat by burning. The heat energy is converted into pressure energy which produces mechanical power to turn a propeller.

Jet engines use kerosene or a gasoline and kerosene mixture (*see* Jet Propulsion). They also change heat to pressure energy but use expanding gases directly.

Rocket engines also propel aircraft or spacecraft by using the jet thrust (*see* Rockets). They burn a wide range of fuels. Under development are nuclear and ion power plants (*see* Space Travel; Aerospace Research and Development).

The Douglas DC-8 jet airliner has ten fuel tanks located in the wings. They are quickly filled through two pressure feeding points on the underside of each wing.

Aviation Gasoline

Until World War II aviation gasoline underwent little change (*see* Petroleum). The octane rating, however, was increased from about 50 to 91. The *octane number* is the antiknock value of a fuel. Knocking indicates that combustion in the cylinder is too rapid. The higher the octane number the greater is the fuel's ability to reduce engine knock. Octane numbers range from 0 to 100. Tetraethyl lead is added to give the proper octane number. The larger aircraft require fuels of higher than 100 octane. There-

"SERVICE STATIONS" IN THE SKY
Refueling in mid-air increases the range of fighters and bombers. At left, an Air Force Boeing KC-97 tanker feeds a McDonnell F-101A Voodoo through a flying boom. At right is a close-up of a Boeing B-52 Stratofortress hooked up to a boom.

fore, a new scale called the *performance number scale* was devised to rate fuels above 100.

Aircraft engines, like those of automobiles, require different grades of fuel. The aviation gasoline now used is graded 81/87, 91/98, 100/130, and, for the newer planes, such as the Boeing Stratocruiser, 115/145.

Aircraft engine developments created the dual number fuel rating. The first number is the "lean mixture rating." It indicates how the fuel resists knocking with the engine adjusted for economy while cruising. The second number is the "rich mixture rating." It designates antiknock quality with the engine at maximum power during take-off and climb.

Jets Burn Kerosene

The first jet engines used a special kerosene. Since the early jets were military aircraft and the petroleum industry was set up to produce gasoline, a compromise fuel was developed. It was a combination of gasoline and kerosene called JP-4. Most jet airliners burn highly refined kerosene.

Exotic Fuels of Rockets and Spaceships

Rocket engines carry their own supply of oxygen in the form of chemical oxidizers, which enable them to burn materials not usually considered aircraft fuels. These range from solids, such as synthetic rubber, to liquids, such as alcohol, kerosene mixtures, hydrazine, and analine. The common oxidizers used to burn liquid fuels include liquid oxygen, hydrogen peroxide, and nitric acid.

Liquid fuels generally produce more energy and power than the solid fuels used in present-day rocket engines. High-energy solid fuels being considered for future space vehicles include uranium for nuclear engines and cesium for ion engines. The nuclear reactor may be used to furnish heat for a jet engine; or the products of the nuclear reaction may serve as the propellant.

Fuels with Greater Heat Content

Chemists are attempting to develop fuels with greater heat content. Planes using such fuels could carry lighter fuel loads and more passengers and would be able to fly longer without refueling. A large automobile may get 10 to 15 miles per gallon of gasoline, whereas a Douglas DC-7 flying at 300 miles per hour will get only about a half mile per gallon and a

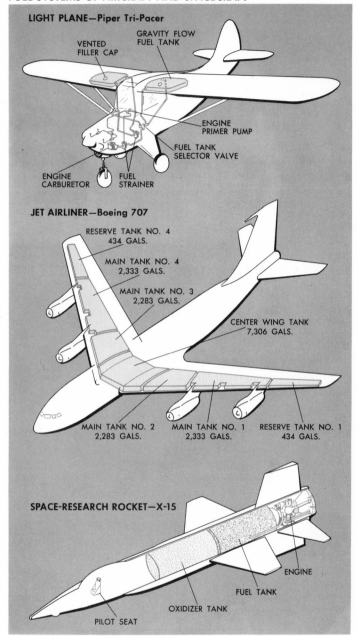

FUEL SYSTEMS OF AIRCRAFT AND SPACECRAFT

LIGHT PLANE—Piper Tri-Pacer

GRAVITY FLOW FUEL TANK
VENTED FILLER CAP
ENGINE PRIMER PUMP
FUEL TANK SELECTOR VALVE
ENGINE CARBURETOR
FUEL STRAINER

JET AIRLINER—Boeing 707

RESERVE TANK NO. 4 434 GALS.
MAIN TANK NO. 4 2,333 GALS.
MAIN TANK NO. 3 2,283 GALS.
CENTER WING TANK 7,306 GALS.
MAIN TANK NO. 2 2,283 GALS.
MAIN TANK NO. 1 2,333 GALS.
RESERVE TANK NO. 1 434 GALS.

SPACE-RESEARCH ROCKET—X-15

ENGINE
FUEL TANK
OXIDIZER TANK
PILOT SEAT

jet transport will get only about a quarter mile per gallon. Jet airliners carry up to 23,000 gallons, or 138,000 pounds, of fuel. Jet engine fuel consumption is measured in pounds per hour, which is indicated on the plane's instrument panel.

Fueling Systems

Aircraft are refueled from tank trucks or *hydrant systems*. The faster hydrant systems pump fuel from airport storage tanks directly to the aircraft through underground pipes. They can fuel a plane at the rate of 600 gallons per minute.

Mechanics are shown at work on the final assembly line of Douglas DC-8 jet airliners at a West coast aircraft plant.

AEROSPACE INDUSTRY —Building Aircraft and Spacecraft

AEROSPACE INDUSTRY. The research, design, and production of airplanes, missiles, and spacecraft constitute the *aerospace industry* (*see* Aerospace). Until shortly after World War II it was called the *aircraft* or *aviation industry*. Increasing production of missiles and spacecraft by the same manufacturers that formerly made only aircraft has resulted in the new name (*see* Guided Missiles; Space Travel). In 1959 the Aircraft Industries Association was re-named the Aerospace Industries Association to reflect the changing nature of its members' products.

It is a young industry, little more than half a century old. Its birthplace is the tiny bicycle shop of Orville and Wilbur Wright in Dayton, Ohio, where they built the first successful airplane. Today an aerospace manufacturing plant is like a small city. Its offices, warehouses, factories, and other buildings stretch for blocks.

How Air and Space Vehicles Are Built

Vehicles that travel through the air or through space have the same basic structure—an airframe, engine, propeller (if any), and equipment (*see* Airplane). A jet airplane has many thousands of parts. It therefore takes a long time—sometimes four or five years or more—to initiate, develop, and produce an aerospace vehicle. This is called *lead time*.

The important preliminary steps before manufacturing itself begins are research and development, including engineering and testing (*see* Aerospace Research and Development). Military or business leaders first specify the characteristics of the vehicle they want built. In a military plane fast take-off, supersonic speed, armament, and bomb load are important. In an airliner the number of passengers and cargo weight are considered. Manufacturers of aerospace vehicles often develop their own design ideas.

The engineering department may have a thousand specialists. They prepare drawings that show the *configuration*, or general outlines, of the vehicle. Scale models are made for testing in a wind tunnel (*see* Wind Tunnel). Next a *mock-up*, or full-sized replica, is built. Accuracy of calculations is checked with electronic computers, slide rules, and graphs.

Draftsmen then draw blueprints. A medium-sized jet plane may require up to 18,000 blueprints. An experimental model, or *prototype*, is constructed. Test pilots prove its airworthiness in actual flight.

A GUIDED-MISSILE ASSEMBLY PLANT
A three-stage intercontinental ballistic missile, its solid-fuel engines already loaded, is being assembled at a Boeing plant.

The production of the vehicle takes careful planning. Plant layout experts make a miniature scale model of the plant to solve production problems. Contracts are let to subcontractors who will supply the parts. Workers are trained (*see* Aerospace Careers).

Machines, tools, fixtures, and jigs are ordered. *Fixtures* are devices for holding parts during machining or assembly. A *jig* is a device for guiding a tool, such as a drill. Huge hydraulic presses, two stories high and exerting 3,000 tons of pressure, are used to form as many as 24 parts from a sheet of metal at one time. The metal parts are anodized to give them a tough, thin film which prevents corrosion and bonds paint. They are heat-treated to make them stronger and sprayed with paint to protect them.

When production begins the factory is a noisy and busy place. People work with riveting guns, mechanical hammers, saws, and many other tools. Overhead cranes carry materials. Tractors, trailers, and lift trucks move supplies.

In different shops and departments in the plant, parts are built into sections called subassemblies. Routers constantly check on supplies. Hundreds of inspectors examine parts and assemblies.

The aerospace manufacturing industry has borrowed the assembly-line method from the automobile makers. As the vehicle moves down the line, assemblers, riveters, and welders fit sections to it—the nose, fuselage, wings, tail, engines, and so on—until the craft is completed. It is then test-flown.

AN ENGINEERING DEPARTMENT
In the Aerospace Age hundreds of specialized engineers are required to design, produce, and test a single complex airplane or missile.

History of the Aerospace Industry

About a year after their first successful flight the Wright brothers began negotiations with the United States government to build an airplane (*see* Airplane History). The United States Army signed a contract for a Wright plane in 1908. Glenn H. Curtiss became a competitor of the Wrights and later one of the leading aircraft manufacturers in the United States.

By 1914 there were 16 aircraft manufacturers in the United States. In the next two years they had produced fewer than 1,000 airplanes. During World War I American pilots flew Allied planes. Few

A GIANT PLANT OF THE AEROSPACE INDUSTRY
This sprawling plant of the Douglas Aircraft Company in Santa Monica, Calif., covers acres of ground. Thousands of people work in the offices, warehouses, hangars, and factory shops. Among them are riveters, welders, mechanics, and inspectors.

American-built planes were used in combat, although the United States produced about 14,000 planes and flying boats. The greatest American contribution was the 12-cylinder 400-horsepower Liberty engine. After the war the aircraft industry decreased substantially. Surplus war planes glutted the market.

After Charles A. Lindbergh's transatlantic flight in 1927 interest in aviation boomed (see Lindbergh). By 1929 the industry had greatly expanded, but production dropped during the depression of the 1930's.

The development of economical multiengine planes, such as the Boeing 247 and Douglas DC-2 and DC-3, stimulated the growth of airlines and aircraft production. Military aircraft orders also increased in the period before World War II as nations rearmed.

Production Soars in World War II

When Germany attacked France, President F. D. Roosevelt called on the industry to produce a staggering 50,000 planes a year (see World War II). In its whole history it had made less than 45,000. By 1944, however, its production was almost double this goal. During the entire war it made some 300,000 military aircraft. In 1943 the industry had 1,345,600 employees. The manufacture of aircraft had become one of the nation's leading industries.

After the war the aviation industry curtailed production drastically. By 1949 output had dropped to 6,100. When the Korean conflict broke out in 1950 the industry again increased production. More than 19,000 military aircraft were built during the war.

In the 1950's significant developments included the conversion of commercial airlines from propeller and piston-engine aircraft to jet planes (see Jet Pro-

pulsion; Airplane Power Plants; Rockets). The greatest growth in aviation was in smaller planes used for private and business flying (see Aviation). Helicopter production also increased. The aviation industry became the aerospace industry as the United States and Russia raced to produce intercontinental supersonic missiles and earth-girdling satellites.

The Aerospace Industry Today

About 15 missile, space-vehicle, and aircraft companies make military and civilian aerospace products, with only six of these concerns manufacturing for civilian customers. There are six major weapon contractors and the same number of concerns producing propulsion systems and aircraft engines. Many of these companies work in partnership as vehicles become more complex. They also depend upon specialized suppliers for many items. About 100,000 smaller firms make parts for the primary producers. The aerospace industry employs over 700,000 persons.

The leading manufacturers of airframes for missiles, space vehicles, and aircraft include Boeing, Douglas, General Dynamics, Grumman, Hughes, Ling-Temco Vought, Martin-Marietta, McDonnell, North American, Northrop, and Republic. Lockheed is the leading maker of missiles and rockets. Among the producers of private airplanes are Beech, Cessna, and Piper. Bell, Hiller, Kaman, and Sikorsky manufacture helicopters. Engine makers include Aerojet-General, Continental Motors, United Aircraft, and Curtiss-Wright.

The federal government is the major customer for missiles, space vehicles, aircraft, and their compo-

BIRTHPLACE OF THE AEROSPACE INDUSTRY

These interior and exterior views show the small bicycle shop in Dayton, Ohio, where the Wright brothers made parts for the first successful airplane. Henry Ford had the original shop moved to his historic Greenfield Village at Dearborn, Mich.

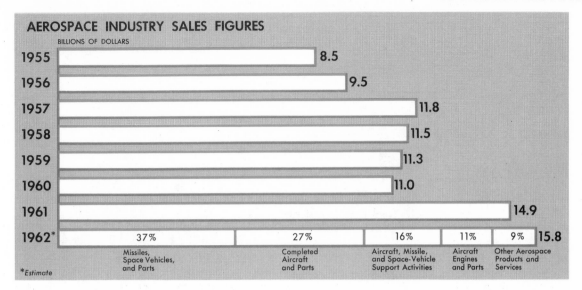

AEROSPACE INDUSTRY SALES FIGURES

BILLIONS OF DOLLARS

Year	Sales
1955	8.5
1956	9.5
1957	11.8
1958	11.5
1959	11.3
1960	11.0
1961	14.9
1962*	15.8

1962*: 37% Missiles, Space Vehicles, and Parts | 27% Completed Aircraft and Parts | 16% Aircraft, Missile, and Space-Vehicle Support Activities | 11% Aircraft Engines and Parts | 9% Other Aerospace Products and Services

*Estimate

nents. More than 80 percent of the aerospace industry's annual sales of these vehicles and parts, totaling about 12 billion dollars, are made to the government. In 1962 the aerospace industry produced about 8,500 airplanes—6,500 civil and 2,000 military.

Private Industry in the Satellite Program

In 1962, after the launching of the privately developed Telstar communications satellite, Congress passed the Communications Satellite Act. This authorized the formation of a private corporation, the first time such a step had been taken by the government. On Feb. 1, 1963, the Communications Satellite Corporation (COMSAT) was chartered.

On April 6, 1965, COMSAT launched Early Bird, the world's first commercial communications satellite. The satellite relayed telephone messages and television and other transmissions between North America and Europe. The Early Bird program is an international venture. It is supported by many nations, each of which has its own ground station. A global system of communications satellites is under way.

New Production Techniques

Aerospace industry companies have done research in manufacturing methods as well as in design. Several are exploring the use of *explosive forming* to shape hard missile metals. These require even more power to mold them than the tremendous force of hydraulic presses. The release of a great amount of electrical energy in a few millionths of a second under water produces an explosion similar to lightning. This "spark" creates a shock wave that travels rapidly through the water, pushing the metal into a mold.

Another development is the *honeycomb panel* for wings and fuselages. The skins of both aircraft and missiles need to be more durable to withstand stress at higher speeds, but strong metals are heavy. Designers join cells of thin aluminum or stainless steel to resemble a honeycomb. Thin layers of metal are

stretched across the open ends of the cells and bonded to them by heat to form a honeycomb "sandwich." It is lighter than a solid piece of metal of the same thickness but is very strong. The *brazing* technique devised for honeycomb panels is widely used. It eliminates drilling, punching, rolling, and welding.

Automation, or the use of electronic and mechanical devices to control machine operations, also has had a major effect on the industry (*see* Automation). Parts can be cut, drilled, or punched more precisely and quickly in this way than by a human operator.

UNITED STATES AIRCRAFT PRODUCTION

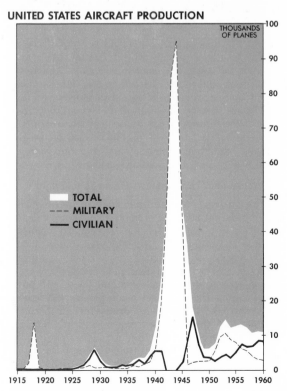

THOUSANDS OF PLANES

TOTAL
MILITARY
CIVILIAN

AEROSPACE
MEDICINE—
The Human
Reaction
to Flight

This 50-foot human centrifuge is in the Navy's Aviation Medical Acceleration Laboratory at Johnsville, Pa. Here acceleration effects on human tolerances are studied.

AEROSPACE MEDICINE. Man is not a flying animal but he has learned to fly in aircraft. He has even gone beyond the atmosphere in a spacecraft. Such flying subjects his body to unusual physical, mental, and emotional strains. The branch of medical science concerned with the effects of flight upon human beings both within and beyond the atmosphere is called *aerospace medicine*. A medical officer who specializes in this field is a *flight surgeon*.

The health of persons who fly within the atmosphere is the concern of *aviation medicine*. Among the hazards it studies are altitude, speed, fatigue, noise and vibration, airsickness, and toxic substances.

The health of people who will fly beyond the atmosphere of the earth is the concern of *space medicine*. It involves the study of problems such as weightlessness, radiation, isolation, and the provision for food, water, and air in a sealed space capsule.

Pressure and Temperature Hazards of Flight

The dangers of high-altitude flight include hypoxia, decompression sickness, and extreme temperatures. *Hypoxia* is a lack of enough oxygen to maintain normal body processes. Mild hypoxia causes a mistaken feeling of well-being coupled with confusion and poor co-ordination and judgment. Severe hypoxia leads to unconsciousness and death. Hypoxia results from the decrease in air pressure at higher altitudes. As the pressure drops the air becomes thinner and there is less oxygen present. Oxygen masks can protect fliers from hypoxia up to about 43,000 feet. Above that altitude a pressure suit must be worn or the cabin must be pressurized to permit satisfactory breathing and adequate oxygen intake.

An airman making a rapid climb into the thinner air above 25,000 feet may also be subject to *decompression sickness*, or *aeroembolism*. This is similar to the "bends" experienced by deep-sea divers who surface too quickly (*see* Diving, Deep-Sea). The fast reduction of atmospheric pressure causes formation of gas bubbles, largely nitrogen, in the body tissues and fluids. This produces aching joints, itching, coughing and choking, blurred vision, paralysis, and in severe cases unconsciousness and death. A pressurized cabin prevents decompression sickness.

A sudden loss of pressure at high altitudes produces *explosive decompression*. If a broken window or skin puncture allows the cabin pressure to fall, the occupants may experience hypoxia and decompression sickness. Pilots of pressurized aircraft wear oxygen masks as a precaution and passengers have emergency masks.

Another hazard is *temperature extremes*. High-altitude flights may encounter temperatures of −80° F. or lower. Electrically heated suits for the crew and heated cabins protect against the cold. High-speed flights or re-entry of a space capsule into the atmosphere produces intense heat. This requires special clothing, refrigeration, insulation, and heat-dispersing devices.

Acceleration and Other Hazards

If an aircraft flies at a constant speed its occupants feel no bodily effects. If, however, the rate of speed or the direction of flight is changed suddenly there may be human stresses.

An increase in velocity, or rate of speed, is called *acceleration*. Negative acceleration, or decreasing speed, is called *deceleration*. Acceleration forces react on the body in three directions—head to foot, chest to back, and side to side. Acceleration produces a pull like gravity. It is measured in *g* (gravity) units. One *g* is equal to the pull of gravity in a body at rest on the earth's surface.

Human tolerance to acceleration varies with the direction and duration of the force. In a tight turn or pull-out from a steep dive, a *blackout* may occur. This temporary loss of vision and eventual unconsciousness are caused by blood rushing from the head. To combat this a pilot may wear a G-suit, which exerts pressure on the abdomen and legs to prevent the pooling of blood in the lower body. In a steep dive a *redout* may occur. This reddening of vision and possible loss of consciousness result from the blood rushing to the head. An airman can withstand a force of several hundred g's for a fraction of a second if it builds up gradually. Lap belts, harnesses, helmets, and a supported body position help fliers tolerate acceleration stresses.

Emergency escape from high-speed aircraft requires an *ejection seat.* Beyond the speed of sound the airman must be enclosed in a capsule if he is to survive wind blast and deceleration. An explosive charge propels the seat or capsule and pilot clear of the tail.

Fatigue is a problem on long flights. Noise and vibration add to fatigue. Vibration may cause physical disturbances. Noise may impair hearing sensitivity. Cabin insulation, ear plugs, helmets, and radio headsets protect aircrews from excessive noise.

Turbulent air may cause airsickness, nausea, and discomfort. Toxic compounds such as carbon monoxide from engines or fumes from fire extinguishers must be kept from the cabin. Powerful fuels must be handled with care. Oxygen for breathing must be pure.

Hazards of Flight in Space

Space travelers encounter weightlessness. They float in the capsule, free of the earth's gravity at zero-g. In the closed cabin they must process carbon dioxide and other human wastes chemically or by photosynthesis into oxygen, water, and food. Astronauts must be trained to guard against the mental confusion that comes with isolation and confinement. They must also be protected against radiation.

Research Devices and Organizations

Research tools for aerospace medical problems are highly specialized. Low-pressure chambers duplicate the rarefied atmosphere at high altitudes. Human centrifuges produce acceleration forces. Rocket-powered sleds test high acceleration and deceleration effects. Vertical accelerators simulate vibration stress. Closed cabins duplicate isolation conditions. Radios send data to ground stations from measuring devices attached to animals and human beings in flight. Alan B. Shepard and other astronauts of Project Mercury had long training before the first American space flight was made in 1961 (*see* Aerospace Research and Development; Space Travel).

In the United States aerospace medicine is practiced by military and civilian branches of the federal government, educational institutions, research institutes, airlines, and aircraft manufacturers.

The Air Force maintains the School of Aviation Medicine, Aero Medical Laboratory, Holloman Field Laboratory, and Arctic Aerospace Medical Laboratory. The Navy has the School of Naval Aviation Medicine, Aviation Medical Acceleration Laboratories, and Equipment and Material Laboratories.

VERTICAL ACCELERATOR AND ROCKET SLED
The vertical accelerator (left) at Wright Air Development Center's Aero Medical Laboratory, Ohio, simulates re-entry buffeting of spacecraft. With the rocket sled (right), at Holloman Air Force Base, N. M., deceleration effects are tested.

AEROSPACE RESEARCH AND DEVELOPMENT

AEROSPACE RESEARCH AND DEVELOPMENT. Flight by man resulted from the study and experiments of patient and curious dreamers. When, in 1961, man finally was able to fly in outer space, it came about because of *research* and *development*. This is the systematic search for scientific principles as well as their application in a practical way.

The new word *aerospace* describes those regions, both within and beyond the earth's atmosphere, in which man has attempted to fly (*see* Aerospace). Various vehicles fly in aerospace. *Aircraft* are machines designed to go through the atmosphere of the earth (*see* Airplane). *Spacecraft* are devices, unmanned or manned, for flight in outer space (*see* Guided Missiles; Space Travel). *Space-air vehicles* operate both within and above the atmosphere.

Night skies blaze with flames from a test firing of the Titan Intercontinental Ballistic Missile. This test stand is at a rocket plant in Sacramento, Calif.

Steps in Research and Development

Research is of two types, basic and applied (*see* Science). *Basic research* attempts to discover fundamental principles. *Applied research* tries to find uses for these principles. When research has shown that it is feasible to construct an aerospace vehicle, *development* begins (*see* Aerospace Industry).

Development goes through three main stages— engineering, production, and testing. In the *engineering stage* the vehicle is designed and blueprints are made. Frequently a *mock-up* is built. This is a non-flying model, sometimes in full size. Then the engineers develop a *prototype*. This is the master model which serves as the pattern for production.

Manufacturing begins with the *production stage*. Before the assembly lines turn out the vehicle in quantity, it goes through the *testing stage*. Tests show whether the craft will perform as planned. The steps from research through development are not clearly separated but go on at the same time.

Fields of Research

Aerospace research concerns itself with many fields of investigation. They involve the aeronautical or space vehicle, its performance, and its pilot. Research on vehicles includes aerodynamics, propulsion systems, structures, and materials. When the craft is in flight the communication and navigation systems and operating and meteorological problems are investigated. Research on the pilot involves his reactions to flight.

Aerodynamics is concerned with the forces acting on a vehicle in motion in the air (*see* Airplane Flight Theory). It attempts to discover the most efficient shape for flight. Designers increase speed by *streamlining* the craft (*see* Streamlining). Thus it offers the least resistance, or drag, to air. Streamlining is particularly important in supersonic flight. When an airplane flies near, at, or beyond the speed of sound, it creates shock waves. The air piles up because it cannot move aside quickly enough to make space for the airplane. Shock waves resist motion through them and therefore cause drag.

Propulsion, Structure, and Materials

Propulsion research has played a key role in man's growing ability to move through and beyond the atmosphere (*see* Airplane Power Plants). Reciprocating engines have progressed from the 12-horsepower engine of the Wright brothers to the 3,500-h.p. propeller-driven airliners of today. Jet engines are now capable of 30,000 pounds of thrust, or 30,000 h.p. at 375 miles an hour (*see* Jet Propulsion).

Structural research has resulted in new techniques for forming the frame and skin of aircraft. Thinner wings for higher speed meant that rib and skin construction had to be replaced by panels machined from heavy slabs of solid metal alloys. Swept-back wings like those of the B-52 are flexible yet strong.

On each square foot of wing surface a fighter plane may support 110 pounds of pressure on take-off and 70 pounds in landing. Designers allow a margin of strength well beyond what may be needed in flight.

The search for new materials goes hand in hand with structural research. Aluminum alloys used in World War II airplanes are excellent for subsonic flying. Supersonic flight, however, subjects a plane to much higher temperatures, and stronger metals are needed. Today stainless steel, molybdenum, and titanium are being used. The X-15 research rocket plane is built with a nickel alloy, Inconel-X, which will withstand temperatures of 1,000° F.

Operation Problems and Pilot Research

The advent of jet aircraft has created a demand for communication and navigation facilities geared to flights at higher speeds. Communication with satellites has developed to a high stage. For example, in 1960 Pioneer V sent information 5 million miles to earth, and its transmitters were designed to send a signal 50 million miles. Even better equipment, however, is needed for the vast reaches of outer space.

Advances in the speed of aircraft bring new operating problems for research to solve. Higher cruising speeds mean higher landing speeds; therefore pilot control of high-performance aircraft during landings must be improved. Many airliners carry instruments to measure air speeds and altitudes during flight from take-off to landing. These records promote safety in day-to-day operations.

In meteorology much research remains to be done (see Aviation Meteorology). High-speed aircraft fly quickly through a wide range of weather conditions of which the pilot must be kept constantly informed.

A great step forward in meteorological research was the launching in 1960 of the world's first weather observation satellite, Tiros I, by the National Aeronautics and Space Administration (NASA). As Tiros I orbited it photographed the clouds covering the earth. Meteorologists study such photographs for a more complete picture of global weather.

Advanced aeronautical and space vehicles require an understanding of human reactions to high gravity conditions, weightlessness, disorientation, confinement, and other unfamiliar experiences (see Aerospace Medicine).

History of Research and Development

Throughout the history of man's attempt to fly, he not only experimented with flying machines but also developed the scientific foundations of flight (see Airplane History). As early as the 4th century B.C., Aristotle studied hydrodynamics, from which the science of aerodynamics springs. *Hydrodynamics* deals with fluids in motion. Later contributors to this science included Leonardo da Vinci, Galileo, Sir Isaac Newton, Johann and Daniel Bernoulli, Leonhard Euler, and Jean le Rond d'Alembert.

In the 19th century interest in science and aeronautics grew. Investigators of fluid flow included Augustin Louis Cauchy, Sir G. G. Stokes, Hermann von Helmholtz, and Gustav Robert Kirchhoff.

Sir George Cayley was one of the first experimenters to see the problem of flight clearly. In 1809 he stated that the solution to flight would be "to make a surface support a given weight by the application of power to the resistence of air." He suggested the use of a propeller and an "explosion" engine. Cayley experimented with gliders and models. Francis H. Wenham built the first wind tunnel in 1871.

In 1883 Sir Osborne Reynolds determined that fluid flow is either laminar (smooth) or turbulent. He expressed the type of flow as a ratio between the velocity, density, and length of a fluid stream and the viscosity of the fluid. Today this fraction is called the *Reynolds number*. It is important in relating wind-tunnel research with scale models to the actual flights of full-sized vehicles.

Ernst Mach was the first to do laboratory research in the motion of fluids at supersonic speeds. In 1887 he photographed shock waves at the nose of a projectile in flight. Later he experimented with a model in a

STRESS TEST ON THE WING OF A JET AIRLINER
Simulated flight stress tests are made on airplanes by loading them with weights to determine structural fatigue. Aircraft designers allow a high margin of safety.

PRINCIPAL UNITED STATES GOVERNMENT RESEARCH AND DEVELOPMENT CENTERS

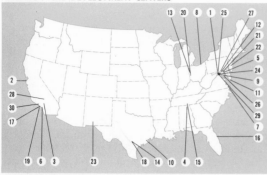

Federal Aviation Administration
1. FAA headquarters, Washington, D. C.

National Aeronautics and Space Administration
2. Ames Research Center, Moffett Field, Calif.
3. Flight Research Center, Edwards, Calif.
4. George C. Marshall Space Flight Center, Huntsville, Ala.
5. Goddard Space Flight Center, Greenbelt, Md.
6. Jet Propulsion Laboratory, California Institute of Technology, Pasadena, Calif.
7. Langley Research Center, Langley Field, Va.
8. Lewis Research Center, Cleveland, Ohio
9. NASA headquarters, Washington, D. C.
10. Manned Spacecraft Center, Houston, Tex.
11. Wallops Station, Wallops Island, Va.

National Bureau of Standards
12. NBS headquarters, Washington, D. C.

United States Air Force
13. Aeronautical Systems Center, Wright-Patterson AFB, Dayton, Ohio
14. Aerospace Medical Center, Brooks AFB, Tex.
15. Arnold Engineering Development Center, Tullahoma, Tenn.
16. John F. Kennedy Space Center, Cape Kennedy, Fla.
17. Ballistic Missile Division, Inglewood, Calif.
18. School of Aviation Medicine, Brooks AFB, Tex.
19. Space Technology Laboratory, Inglewood, Calif.
20. Wright Air Development Division, Wright-Patterson AFB, Dayton, Ohio

United States Army
21. Army Ballistic Laboratory, Aberdeen, Md.
22. Signal Research and Development Laboratory, Fort Monmouth, N. J.
23. White Sands Missile Range, Las Cruces, N. M.

United States Department of Defense
24. Advanced Research Projects Agency, Washington, D. C.

United States Navy
25. David W. Taylor Model Basin, Carderock, Md.
26. Naval Air Test Center, Naval Air Station, Patuxent River, Md.
27. Naval Ordnance Laboratory, Silver Spring, Md.
28. Naval Ordnance Test Station, China Lake, Calif.
29. Naval Research Laboratory, Washington, D. C.
30. Pacific Missile Range, Point Mugu, Calif.

supersonic jet of air. His work is recognized in the term *Mach number*. It designates flight speeds in relation to the speed of sound. The principle of lift and drag was developed in 1894 by F. W. Lanchester.

Samuel P. Langley spent many years studying air resistance before he built powered models (*see* Langley). His experiments ended in his ill-fated attempts at full-scale flight in 1903.

The Wright brothers familiarized themselves with the earlier experiments and theories on flight (*see* Wright Brothers). Dissatisfied with the scientific data, they built a wind tunnel. Their tests of airfoil shapes contributed to their successful flights.

Since the age of flight began in 1903, a vast organization of scientific and technological specialists has emerged to study the flight of aircraft and spacecraft. Research has become so complex that it is usually undertaken by teams rather than by individuals. The high cost of research and military requirements make it primarily a matter of government sponsorship.

Research Institutions

Aerospace research in the United States is carried on by many civilian and military governmental agencies and private institutions. The major research organization is the National Aeronautics and Space Administration. Congress created NASA as an independent civilian agency in 1958. NASA operations are divided into four major programs—Space Sciences, Applications, Manned Space Flight, and Advanced Research and Technology. There is also an Office of Tracking and Data Acquisition. The programs are conducted at nine research centers.

Ames Research Center: gas dynamics; automatic stabilization, guidance, and control of space vehicles; biomedical and biophysical research.

Flight Research Center: flight-evaluation tests of research aircraft such as the X-15.

George C. Marshall Space Flight Center: launch-vehicle systems; spacecraft structures and materials.

Goddard Space Flight Center: emphasis on earth, sun, and astronomy aspects of space-science program; tracking and data-gathering functions.

Jet Propulsion Laboratory: emphasis on deep-space exploration, including moon and interplanetary flights.

Langley Research Center: aerodynamics of re-entry vehicles; spacecraft structures and materials.

Lewis Research Center: propulsion and power-plant research for space vehicles, including nuclear rockets.

Manned Spacecraft Center: responsibility for spacecraft for Projects Mercury, Gemini, and Apollo.

Wallops Station: launching smaller earth satellites; firing sounding rockets.

The Department of Defense and the three military services that are a part of it—the Air Force, Navy, and Army—also engage in aerospace research. The Advanced Research Projects Agency, an organization within the Defense Department, is responsible for all projects that relate to advanced space research.

Other governmental agencies engaged in aerospace research and development are the Federal Aviation Agency, Civil Aeronautics Board, United States Weather Bureau, and National Bureau of Standards.

Private research organizations include educational institutions, industrial groups, and laboratories

SOME UNUSUAL TYPES OF EXPERIMENTAL FLYING MACHINES

HILLER X-18 "TILT WING." The rotors tilt up for vertical take-off (left) and forward for horizontal flight (right).

PIASECKI VZ-8P "AIRGEEP." This wingless vehicle rises vertically on two columns of air supplied by two rotors.

GOODYEAR INFLATOPLANE. This rubberized fabric plane (above) is blown up like a balloon. It flies at 72 mph (bottom).

and foundations. Among these are the Battelle Memorial Institute, IIT (Illinois Institute of Technology) Research Institute, Stanford Research Institute, Rand Corporation, and Brookings Institution.

Research Abroad

Most of the major European countries, including Russia, have some aerospace research activity under government, industrial, or university sponsorship. In the Far East, Japan has a growing interest in research. The United Nations is making an effort to co-ordinate aerospace work throughout the world.

Tools for Research

Many specialized facilities and instruments have been developed for aerospace research. The chief tool in the first half of the 20th century was the wind tunnel (see Wind Tunnel). New facilities that reach beyond the speed limitations of the wind tunnel have been invented. The wind tunnel, however, is far from being outmoded. No matter how far space vehicles travel they must slow down for landing. Their flying qualities over their entire range of speed must be investigated.

The evolution of power plants from piston engines through jets and to rockets and other space propulsion systems has called for new research techniques. Test cells, strong enough to withstand high temperatures and thrust, have been devised for jet and rocket engines. Fuel and lubricant research requires chemical and mechanical laboratory equipment. Lubricants are being tested for atomic radiation reaction to learn whether spacecraft will require special types.

Structural research laboratories use large machines for twisting or crushing a part under study. Quartz-lamp heaters generate the high temperatures typical of those expected in high-speed flights. Research on material is seeking new metals, plastics, and cermets (ceramic-metal combinations) that will retain their strength under extreme temperatures.

Flight testing is a useful research technique because measurements can be made under actual flight conditions. It is the earliest aeronautical research method. Today experimental aircraft are so thoroughly instrumented that they are flying laboratories.

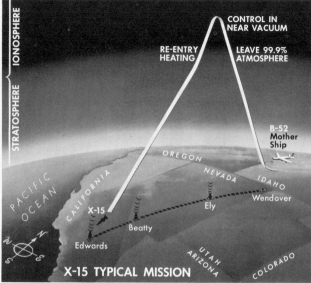

X-15 TYPICAL MISSION

CONTROL IN NEAR VACUUM

RE-ENTRY HEATING

LEAVE 99.9% ATMOSPHERE

IONOSPHERE

STRATOSPHERE

B-52 Mother Ship

PACIFIC OCEAN

OREGON

NEVADA

IDAHO

CALIFORNIA

UTAH

ARIZONA

COLORADO

X-15

Ely

Wendover

Beatty

Edwards

SOARING INTO OUTER SPACE

In 1962, for the first time, the North American X-15 flew into outer space, nearly 60 miles above the earth. The rocket plane is carried into the air by a B-52 and then launched.

Frequently the test pilots are aeronautical engineers.

Other important facilities are aeromedical laboratories, including those of the military and NASA. They explore the effects of aerospace flight on pilots.

Many instruments have been devised to measure the results of experiments. In wind tunnel work an optical device called a *schlieren system* makes visible the shock-wave pattern at supersonic speeds. High-intensity electric sparks produce shock-wave pictures in one ten-millionth of a second for studying models launched from guns at 16,000 mph. A wide range of mechanical instruments measure forces on models in wind tunnels. New electronic devices are used for small quantities and short periods of time.

Pinched-in Fuselages and Blunt Noses

In recent years new principles of design have appeared. Richard T. Whitcomb, then with the National Advisory Committee for Aeronautics, discovered the *area rule* in 1951. It reduced by 25 per cent the drag on a plane approaching the speed of sound. The combined cross-sectional area of the wing and fuselage should be no greater than that of an ideal body of minimum drag. Aircraft designers apply the rule by pinching in the fuselage where the wings are attached.

H. Julian Allen, also of NACA, proposed the *blunt*

nose-cone shape in 1952 as a way to protect a missile from friction as it re-enters the atmosphere. A slim, sharp-nosed shape would burn like a needle point held in a flame. He found that a blunt shape creates high drag and a heavy shock wave which dissipates heat. A nose cone developed later is made of material which can be *ablated*, or vaporized, during re-entry. This cuts down on drag. The ablating nose cone is longer and more pointed than the blunt type.

New applications of the *boundary-layer-control* principle were made in the 1950's. The idea that a film of slow-moving air clings to a wing dates back to Sir Osborne Reynolds. In experimental planes the boundary layer has been mechanically removed, leaving air of higher velocity to flow and provide more lift.

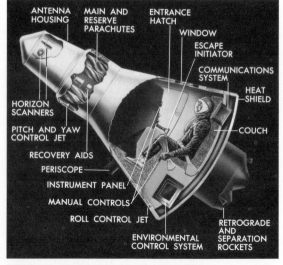

ANTENNA HOUSING

MAIN AND RESERVE PARACHUTES

ENTRANCE HATCH

WINDOW

ESCAPE INITIATOR

COMMUNICATIONS SYSTEM

HEAT SHIELD

HORIZON SCANNERS

PITCH AND YAW CONTROL JET

RECOVERY AIDS

PERISCOPE

INSTRUMENT PANEL

MANUAL CONTROLS

ROLL CONTROL JET

COUCH

ENVIRONMENTAL CONTROL SYSTEM

RETROGRADE AND SEPARATION ROCKETS

PROJECT MERCURY SPACE CAPSULE

A similar capsule, named the Friendship 7, carried American astronaut John H. Glenn, Jr., into orbit on Feb. 20, 1962.

In the early 1960's a new design to reduce air-friction drag, called Laminar Flow Control (LFC), was successfully tested. The air flow is drawn into slots in the wing surfaces and is expelled through nacelles at the rear. The Northrop X-21A used this design.

Aircraft of Advanced Design

Experiments are continually being conducted with unusual aerospace vehicles. *Ground-effect machines* hover above the earth or water on an air cushion created by the downdraft of fans. Such vehicles include the Bell SK-1 Hydroskimmer and the English-built SR-N3 Hovercraft.

Many experimental *VTOL* (vertical take-off and landing) and *STOL* (short take-off and landing) aircraft have been designed and built. The Ryan XV-5A uses fans in its wings to gain vertical lift. The Bell X-22A and Curtiss-Wright X-19 use tiltable propellers. The Ling-Temco-Vought XC-142A employs a movable "tilt wing" that points the propellers upward or forward. The Piasecki VZ-8P AirGeep, a "flying jeep," uses ducted fans for vertical flight.

Advanced power plants are also under continuous development. The ram-jet engine is capable of much greater speeds than the turbojet engine. It is used in the Air Force's supersonic interceptor Bomarc missile. Rocket engines which develop high thrust have been used in the Bell X-1, the first airplane to fly faster than sound, and in the North American X-15 research airplane. A more advanced version, the X-15A-2, is also rocket-powered.

In 1964 the Lockheed YF-12A and SR-71 were unveiled. These planes reached speeds of more than 2,000 miles an hour (over Mach 3) and altitudes above 70,000 feet. Many parts were made of titanium and special steels to resist the heat generated at high speed. Such materials will be used in the supersonic transport (SST) now under development in the United States.

SPACESHIP POWERED BY ION ROCKETS
Scientists are working on ion propulsion for spacecraft. The discharge of ionized atomic particles will furnish the thrust.

The experimental North American XB-70 Valkyrie, one of the largest and heaviest planes ever made, also used titanium and special steels. In 1965 development began on the Lockheed C-5A military transport. A civilian version will carry 900 passengers.

Satellites and Man in Space

The Air Force, Navy, and NASA have launched many artificial satellites in research programs. The Tiros satellites, for example, relay pictures of clouds to the earth as an aid in weather forecasting.

The first man to orbit the earth was Russia's Maj. Yuri Gagarin, on April 12, 1961. The first United States manned orbital flight, under Project Mercury, took place on Feb. 20, 1962, when astronaut John H. Glenn, Jr., orbited the earth. Three more manned orbital flights followed, completing the Project Mercury program in 1963. The more advanced Project Gemini began in 1964. It was to be followed by Project Apollo moon shots. (*See also* Space Travel.)

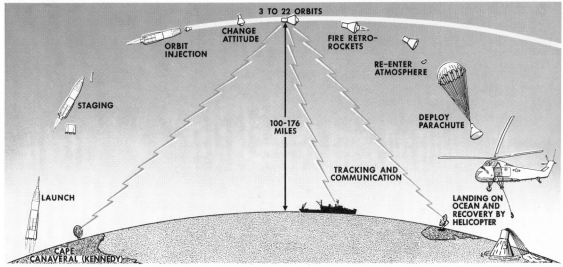

GENERAL PLAN FOR PROJECT MERCURY SPACE FLIGHTS
The first United States manned orbital flight, in 1962, was preceded by two manned suborbital flights in 1961. The final flight under Project Mercury was made by Leroy Gordon Cooper, Jr., who completed 22 orbits during May 15-16, 1963.

THE GOD OF MEDICINE AND HIS SYMBOL
The serpent was sacred to Aesculapius, god of medicine, because it was supposed to have healing powers. The god's clublike staff, with a serpent coiled round it, is a symbol of medicine.

AESCULAPIUS (ĕs-kū-lā′pĭ-ŭs). The Greek god of medicine, Asclepius, is more generally known by his Latin name, Aesculapius. In art he appears holding a staff with a serpent coiled around it. The serpent, or snake, was sacred to him. It symbolized renewal of youth because it casts off its skin.

Aesculapius was the son of Apollo and Coronis. The centaur Chiron brought him up and taught him the art of healing. His daughter Hygeia personified health, and his daughter Panacea, healing. Two of his sons appear in Homer's 'Iliad' as physicians in the Greek army. Their supposed descendants, called Asclepiadae, formed a large order of priest-physicians. The sacred secrets of medicine belonged only to them and were passed on from father to son.

The Asclepiadae practiced their art in magnificent temples of health, called Asclepieia. The temples were actually sanatoriums equipped with gymnasiums, baths, and even theaters. The patient was first put to sleep. His dream, interpreted by the priests, was supposed to furnish directions for treatment. All cures were recorded as miracles. In the course of time the priests probably accumulated considerable medical knowledge and skill.

AESOP (ē′sŏp). The great master of fables was Aesop. When he looked into the bright eyes of animals, Aesop, like a dreamy child, could imagine them behaving much like human creatures. One of the tales that has entertained the world for ages is the one about the frogs who asked the great god Zeus for a ruler. Zeus tossed them a log to be their king. They first feared it, then despised its stillness, and squatted on it.

After some time they again sent messengers who requested the god to appoint another king. This time Zeus sent an eel to the pond. He was an easy-going, good-natured fellow, and the frogs thought that he

too made a very poor king. So they sent a third time to the god to ask for a different ruler. Zeus was now out of patience and sent them a stork, who each day ate up a frog or two until soon there were none left to croak and complain.

This story, which is said to refer to the seizure of power over Athens by the tyrant Pisistratus, is a very good example of Aesop's fables. Tradition says that Aesop, who lived from about 620 to 560 B.C., was originally a Greek slave, ugly and deformed in body but of brilliant mind. In his fables, moral lessons and bits of wisdom are conveyed in such a forceful and delightful way that they have been translated into almost all languages.

Aesop was freed by his master after a time. He gained such a reputation that he was invited to live at the court of Croesus, king of Lydia. His end came, it is said, when Croesus sent him to the temple of Apollo, at Delphi. There he so aroused the anger of the Delphians that he was thrown from a cliff.

Aesop did not write out his fables but recited them, and they were handed down from memory. More than two centuries later an Athenian wrote down the fables as they were told. Later Babrius, a Greek, made another collection. For a thousand years they were lost; then a copy of Babrius' collection was found in a monastery on Mount Athos in 1844. From this copy later translations have been made. (*See also* Fables.)

AESOP AND HIS FABLED ANIMALS
In his fables Aesop made his animals talk and act like human beings with human weaknesses and virtues.

On this modern road, hacked from the barren mountains, a caravan plods toward Kabul.

the south is the longest. The Kabul waters the fertile valleys and basins around Kabul and Jalalabad.

Temperatures range widely. In summer the hot sun beats down on rock and sand, raising temperatures to 115° F. or higher. In winter temperatures drop below zero in the windswept uplands. The lowlands have milder winters. It is then that their meager rains fall. Though the highlands get snow in January and February and rain in March and April, their moisture is less than 20 inches a year.

How the People Live

About 95 percent of the people depend upon agricultural or pastoral activities for a living, but only 14 percent of the land in Afghanistan is cultivated. The remainder is either too rugged or too dry for farming. Mountain meadows and steppeland, however, afford pasture for stock raising. Afghanistan has vast herds of sheep, goats, cattle, horses, and camels—perhaps 30 million head. Of these, sheep number more than 18 million.

The two chief types of sheep are the Karakul and the fat-tailed sheep. The skins of newborn Karakul lambs are one of the chief exports. Called Persian lamb in the United States, they are widely used in coats. The herders use the wool and skins of the fat-tailed sheep for clothing and the flesh for meat. The rendered fat from the tails is used like butter.

Millions of the sheep raisers are nomads (see Nomads). They take their flocks to the mountain meadows for fresh grass in the dry summer. When cold nips the air they load their families, goods, and tents on camels and donkeys and start the long trip to the warm lowlands. Many thousands cross national boundaries on this journey, to find pasture on the Pakistan plains.

The farmers live in the fertile valleys or on the plain wherever a stream or wells can be tapped for irrigation water. With water, the farmers can raise two crops a year. In the early summer, they harvest autumn-planted wheat, barley, and lentils. Summer-grown crops include millet, corn, sorghum, rice, tobacco, cotton, sugar beets, fruits, and melons.

Aided by United States loans, the government is striving to improve farming and increase the food supply. The huge Helmand Valley project aims to supply water for 800 square miles of desert. (Irrigation canals existed here centuries ago, before they were destroyed by invaders and neglect.) Despite difficulties with the soil and drainage along the Helmand, about one thousand landless families have been settled there. The United Nations Food and

AFGHANISTAN—Rugged Asian Buffer State

AFGHANISTAN. Few travelers visit rugged Afghanistan. The country lies high amid the mountains and deserts of Central Asia far from a seacoast. For centuries its people have kept their old ways of life. Only recently have they begun to accept modern ideas, methods, and machines.

Afghanistan is bounded on the north by Russia (U.S.S.R.), on the west by Iran, and on the south and east by Pakistan. A slender panhandle on the northeast stretches to Red China's Sinkiang province.

The country has not been measured, but its area is estimated at about 250,000 square miles. It is thus larger than France. Its population of 15,227,000 (1964 estimate) is less than a third that of France. Kabul, the capital, has 400,000 inhabitants.

The Land and the Climate

About four fifths of the country is mountainous. From the lofty Pamir mountain knot in the northeast, the giant Hindu Kush range spreads westward across the country. It is highest in and near Pakistan, where many peaks are more than three miles in altitude. Plains and valleys spread out from the central highlands. The southwest lowland is desert.

The rivers rise in the snow-capped mountains. Those in the north flow toward the Amu-Dar'ya (river), which forms part of the Russian frontier. The Helmand in

Agriculture Organization has helped introduce better farming methods and equipment.

Resources and Transportation

Valuable minerals lie buried in Afghanistan's mountains, but only minor amounts have been taken out. Some salt, coal, gold, talc, and asbestos have been mined. The finest lapis lazuli is found here. A survey by American geologists revealed six oil basins.

Most products are made in workshops by handworkers. They weave cloth, shawls, and carpets; work leather goods; fashion copper vessels and gold and silver ornaments; and tailor sheepskin coats, called *postins*. The government has fostered the building of factories to produce textiles, sugar, soap, matches, cement, and brick. New hydroelectric projects promise ample power.

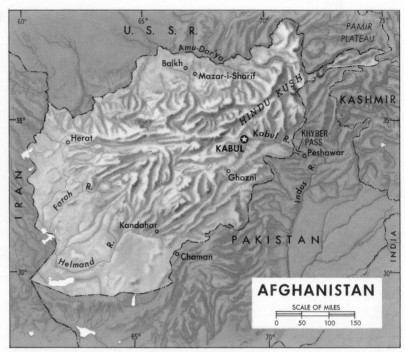

Transportation is a problem in mountainous Afghanistan. There are no railways and only a few good roads. Transport by camel and donkey is still important.

The chief exports are Karakul skins, wool, cotton, and fruits. The leading imports include textiles, machinery, vehicles, and petroleum.

There are no railways, and highways are hard to build in this mountainous land. Kabul is linked with Peshawar, Pakistan, by way of the famous Khyber Pass. A road built with Soviet aid leads north from Kabul to the Russian border; a section of it runs through the Salang Tunnel, completed in 1964. The road from Kabul to Kandahar was built with American aid; the section from Kandahar to Kushka, in the U.S.S.R., with Russian aid. These new surfaces have been laid over the old "ring" route, which encircled the central mountains and linked Kabul with Ghazni, Kandahar, Herat, Balkh, and Mazar-i-Sharif.

Peoples, Languages, and Religion

The Pathans have been termed the only true Afghans. They are of the white race and claim to be related to the Hebrews. From the Durani, a Pathan tribe, come the nation's rulers. Turkish peoples, the Uzbeks and the Turkomans, farm the plains north of the Hindu Kush. The Ghilzai, along the Pakistan frontier, may also be of Turkish origin. The Tadzhiks, near Iran, are of Persian descent. The Hazaras, a Mongol people left behind after the invasion of Genghis Khan, live in the central highlands. The Kaffirs, a fair-haired folk possibly of Greek origin, dwell in the high mountains northeast of Kabul.

The official languages of Afghanistan are Pashto and Dari, spoken by 80 percent of the people. Pashto, or Pushtu, is the native tongue of the Pathans; Dari is a Persian dialect. Uzbek is spoken in the north. Most Afghans are Sunnite Moslems (*see* Mohammed and Mohammedanism).

Government and Education

Afghanistan is a constitutional monarchy. Under the 1964 constitution, the lower house of parliament and most of the upper house are elected. The king appoints some upper-house members and the prime

A 173-FOOT BUDDHA IN THE BAMIAN VALLEY
Buddhist monks who lived in caves in this cliff 2,000 years ago carved this huge statue. It was later defaced by invaders.

minister. Royalty is barred from high public office.

Illiteracy is widespread in Afghanistan, but the number of free elementary schools is increasing. For advanced study, Afghans go to Kabul University.

History of Afghanistan

Remains of buried villages tell archaeologists that settled folk lived in the area well over 5,000 years ago. The land was invaded by nomadic tribes and world conquerors. Into it came Alexander the Great, Genghis Khan, Timur Leng, and Baber (see Alexander the Great; Mongols; Huns). Through its mountain passes China's trade flowed west and south.

The modern kingdom dates from 1747 when Ahmad Shah freed the country from Persian domination. To preserve their independence, the Afghans shut the country off from the outside world.

In the 19th century Afghanistan was caught in the rivalry of great empires. Russia, on the north, threatened Britain's control over India, to the east. Britain waged two bloody wars (1838–42 and 1878–80) to gain control over the country. Finally the British bought Afghanistan's friendship by paying a large annual subsidy to the king. The country remained independent, but Britain controlled its foreign relations and guaranteed its frontiers.

Afghanistan in the 20th Century

When Amanullah ascended the throne in 1919, he declared war on Great Britain. The British defeated him but soon recognized Afghanistan as an independent state. Amanullah turned to internal reform and attempted to modernize his country. The mullahs, the religious teachers and leaders, incited a revolt against him, and he abdicated in 1929. Mohammed Zahir Shah became king when his father, Nadir Shah, was assassinated in 1933. After World War II he intensified efforts to modernize the economy.

Afghanistan has maintained a policy of noninvolvement in the cold war. Except for an interruption in its diplomatic relations with Pakistan (1961–63), it has remained on friendly terms with its neighbors and with both democratic and communist countries in the west. Afghanistan has received economic and technical aid from the United States, Soviet Russia, Communist China, West Germany, Poland, and Czechoslovakia. Soviet friends aided not only road-building, but also the construction of grain mills and airports, oil prospecting, and the modernization of the Afghan army and air force. The less extensive American aid program included assistance for highway construction, agricultural research, education, and the Helmand Valley project.

The Westernization policy begun by Amanullah made important advances. In 1965, under a new constitution, women were able to vote and to run for political office; four were elected to the National Assembly. Kubra Noorzai became the nation's first woman cabinet minister when she was appointed minister of public health in 1966.

AFGHANISTAN FACT SUMMARY

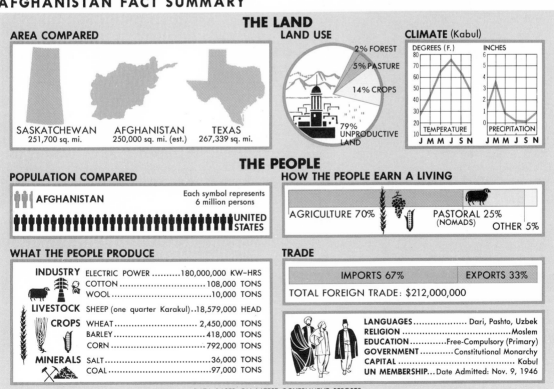

THE LAND

AREA COMPARED

SASKATCHEWAN 251,700 sq. mi.
AFGHANISTAN 250,000 sq. mi. (est.)
TEXAS 267,339 sq. mi.

LAND USE

2% FOREST
5% PASTURE
14% CROPS
79% UNPRODUCTIVE LAND

CLIMATE (Kabul)

DEGREES (F.) — TEMPERATURE — J M M J S N
INCHES — PRECIPITATION — J M M J S N

THE PEOPLE

POPULATION COMPARED

AFGHANISTAN
UNITED STATES
Each symbol represents 6 million persons

HOW THE PEOPLE EARN A LIVING

AGRICULTURE 70%
PASTORAL 25% (NOMADS)
OTHER 5%

WHAT THE PEOPLE PRODUCE

INDUSTRY
ELECTRIC POWER ....180,000,000 KW-HRS
COTTON ....108,000 TONS
WOOL ....10,000 TONS
LIVESTOCK SHEEP (one quarter Karakul)..18,579,000 HEAD
CROPS WHEAT............................ 2,450,000 TONS
BARLEY...............................418,000 TONS
CORN ....792,000 TONS
MINERALS SALT....................................36,000 TONS
COAL ....97,000 TONS

TRADE

IMPORTS 67%
EXPORTS 33%
TOTAL FOREIGN TRADE: $212,000,000

LANGUAGES .... Dari, Pashto, Uzbek
RELIGION ....Moslem
EDUCATION............Free-Compulsory (Primary)
GOVERNMENT ....Constitutional Monarchy
CAPITAL .... Kabul
UN MEMBERSHIP...Date Admitted: Nov. 9, 1946

DATA BASED ON LATEST GOVERNMENT REPORTS

Cape Town, on Table Bay, is the southern gateway to Africa. Mountains curve around the center of the city. From left to right are Devil's Peak, flat-topped Table Mountain, and pointed Lion's Head. In the distance is the Cape of Good Hope.

AFRICA—
The Awakening Giant

AFRICA. One of the outstanding historical trends since World War II has been the political awakening of Africa. As a British prime minister, Harold Macmillan, aptly described it: "The wind of change is blowing through the continent."

As the winds of freedom swept across Africa, old empires crumbled and new nations sprang into being. For some of these lands the transition to independence was orderly. For others it was accompanied by unrest and bloodshed.

The second largest continent of the world, Africa is a great storehouse of natural resources. For centuries the riches of other continents have been exploited, but the wealth of Africa is relatively undeveloped. Thus it is a land of the future.

The people who lived in North Africa in ancient times knew little about the people in the south. This was because they were separated by a great desert, the Sahara. Some people crossed it, but only a very few. The south remained a land of mystery until Europeans began to explore it in the 15th century.

Gradually, over the next 300 years, the countries of

Europe divided the African lands among themselves. The colonial empires were at their peak toward the end of the 19th century. Then the native Africans began to weary of European rule. They wanted to govern themselves. The cries for self-government grew louder and louder, and colonial controls were gradually lessened. But by this time it was too late. Aflame with the spirit of nationalism, many African peoples now wanted complete independence of European govern-

Extent.—From Ras Guern Djediane (37°20′53″ N.) to Cape Agulhas (34°50′ S.); and from Cape Verde (17°33′ W.) to Ras Hafun (51°25′ E.). Length, 5,000 miles; breadth, 4,700 miles; area estimated at about 11,600,000 square miles.

Population.—Estimated (1962) at 269,000,000.

Sahara.—Area, 3,500,000 square miles, largest desert in world.

Chief Rivers.—Nile (3,473 miles); Congo (about 3,000 miles—greatest volume of water of any river except the Amazon); Niger (2,600 miles); Zambezi (about 1,600 miles).

Highest Mountains.—Kilimanjaro, Kibo peak (19,340 feet); Kenya (17,058 feet); Mt. Margherita (16,795 feet).

Largest Lakes.—Victoria (26,830 sq. mi.), second largest freshwater lake in world; Tanganyika (12,700 sq. mi.).

Greatest Cataract.—Victoria Falls on Zambezi River, 355 feet high and more than one mile wide.

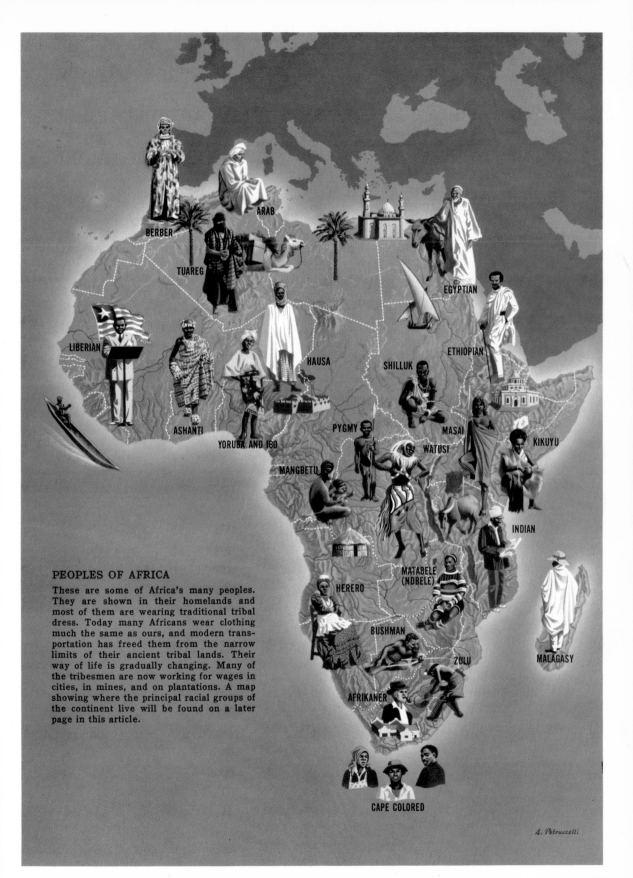

PEOPLES OF AFRICA

These are some of Africa's many peoples. They are shown in their homelands and most of them are wearing traditional tribal dress. Today many Africans wear clothing much the same as ours, and modern transportation has freed them from the narrow limits of their ancient tribal lands. Their way of life is gradually changing. Many of the tribesmen are now working for wages in cities, in mines, and on plantations. A map showing where the principal racial groups of the continent live will be found on a later page in this article.

BERBER

ARAB

TUAREG

EGYPTIAN

LIBERIAN

HAUSA

SHILLUK

ETHIOPIAN

ASHANTI

YORUBA AND IBO

PYGMY

MASAI

WATUSI

KIKUYU

MANGBETU

INDIAN

HERERO

MATABELE (NDBELE)

BUSHMAN

ZULU

MALAGASY

AFRIKANER

CAPE COLORED

A. Petruccelli

ANKOLI CATTLE IN UGANDA
Long-horned, humpless cattle are bred by the Watusi, Buganda, and other pastoral tribes of East Africa.

A BLACK RHINOCEROS IN ZULULAND
The ill-tempered rhinoceros will charge at almost anything. They are found in eastern Africa from Ethiopia to the Transvaal.

GIRAFFES ROAM EAST AFRICAN GRASSLANDS
Herds of spotted giraffes lope about the plains of eastern Africa from the Sahara to the Zambezi River in Mozambique.

ments. Before World War II only four countries—Ethiopia, Liberia, South Africa, and Egypt—were independent. The war set in motion forces that resulted in the breakup of the great European empires in Africa. In the decades following the close of World War II nearly 40 colonies of France, Britain, Belgium, Italy, and Spain became free nations. Seventeen of them won their independence in the single year 1960.

A Water-Encircled Continent

Africa is surrounded by water except for the Isthmus of Suez, in the northeast, which connects it with Asia. The Suez Canal is usually said to be the dividing line between the continents. North of Africa, separating it from Europe, is the Mediterranean Sea. The Red Sea is on the northeast, the Indian Ocean on the east, and the Atlantic Ocean on the west.

Africa is the only continent almost cut in two by the equator. More of it lies north of the equator than south of it because of the bulge in the west, but the points farthest north and south are about the same distance from the equator. Thus most of Africa lies in the tropics.

ELEPHANTS IN A KENYA GAME RESERVE
African elephants are usually dark gray. This herd looks reddish because they have been rolling in the mud of a river in the huge Tsavo National Park.

A MIGHTY EAST AFRICAN HUNTER
Huge, shaggy-maned lions roam the vast Serengeti Plains of Tanzania. They usually hunt antelope and other prey at night.

The African region includes one large island—Madagascar. The islands in the Indian Ocean are Zanzibar, Pemba, the Comoros, Réunion, Mauritius, the Seychelles, and Socotra. In the Gulf of Guinea are Annobón, Fernando Po, Príncipe, and São Tomé. In the Atlantic off the northwest coast are the Canary Islands, Cape Verde Islands, and Madeira.

Africa—A Great Plateau

Africa has few great indentations or peninsulas. It is occupied almost entirely by a great plateau. This tableland is higher in the south and east than in the north and west. For the most part it is surrounded by a narrow coastal plain. There are no lofty mountain chains like those of the Americas, Europe, and Asia.

In the northwest are the Atlas Mountains. This series of fold mountains is an extension of the Alpine system of Europe. In the northeastern part of the plateau are the Ethiopian highlands. South of these are Mounts Elgon, Kenya, and Kilimanjaro, which are of volcanic origin. The 19,340-foot Mount Kilimanjaro, near the equator, is the highest elevation in Africa. The Ruwenzori chain (the legendary Mountains of the Moon) is nonvolcanic. The only large range in the southeast is the Drakensberg.

The Great Rift Valley

In eastern Africa, running south from the Red Sea into Mozambique, is a long, narrow split in the earth's surface called the Great Rift Valley. Its origin has intrigued geologists. One theory is that the deep trench occurred when a great crustal arch, which had been upfolded over eastern Africa, collapsed. Another explanation is that the tensional pull of moving continental land masses caused the massive fissure. (*See also* Geology.)

The Rift Valley enters Africa between the Ethiopian highlands and the Somaliland ranges. In Ethiopia and Kenya the depression holds Lake Rudolf, and, farther south, Lake Nyasa. In a western branch is a chain of lakes including Albert, Edward, Kivu, and Tanganyika.

Between branches of the Rift Valley on a plateau is Lake Victoria. It is the largest lake in Africa and the second largest body of fresh water in the world. This system of lakes in the Valley is second in size only to that of the Great Lakes of North America. (*See also* Tanganyika, Lake; Victoria, Lake.)

Another major lake of Africa is Lake Chad, south

73

MOROCCANS IN OLD MARRAKESH
The historic Koutoubia Mosque tower looms over a date market.
Marrakesh is in the foothills of the Great Atlas Mountains.

A NOMAD ARAB OF THE SUDAN
A Hadendowa tribesman (sometimes called a Fuzzy-Wuzzy) rides
a camel in the Nubian Desert between the Nile and the Red Sea.

ZULUS OF SOUTH AFRICA IN THEIR VILLAGE, OR KRAAL
One large Zulu family lives in the oval grass huts of this kraal.
The brightly dressed people have gathered to do a ceremonial
dance for the head of the clan (the Paramount Chief). Zululand is in Natal in South Africa.

74

of the Sahara. It is a shallow fresh-water lake in the center of an inland drainage basin.

A Land of Great Deserts and Rivers

In Africa are the most extensive desert regions in the world. The Sahara, largest desert on earth, extends across northern Africa between the Atlantic Ocean and the Red Sea (*see* Sahara; Deserts). Its eastern extensions are known as the Libyan, Arabian, and Nubian deserts. In Botswana, near the southern tip of Africa, is the Kalahari Desert. Along the Atlantic coast of South-West Africa is the Namib Desert. The cold Benguela Current in the Atlantic Ocean is responsible for its dryness.

The rivers of Africa are unique. Most of them rise on the plateau and are navigable over it. At the plateau's edge, they drop to the coastal plain in rapids or falls. Thus few rivers are navigable near the coast. This hindered exploration of Africa.

Africa's most important rivers are the Nile, draining into the Mediterranean Sea; the Senegal, Niger, Congo, and Orange, discharging into the Atlantic Ocean; and the Zambezi and Limpopo, emptying into the Indian Ocean. The 3,473-mile Nile is the longest river in Africa (*see* Nile River). Next in length is the Congo. It drains an enormous basin, second in the world in size only to that of the Amazon (*see* Congo River). The third longest river in Africa is the Niger (*see* Niger River).

A Tropical Climate

The latitude of Africa affects its climate more than does its altitude, except in the eastern African upland. Since Africa straddles the equator, three fourths of the continent lies in the tropics. The climatic regions that spread out from the equator to the north and south are much the same. The seasons, however, are reversed. Thus it is summer in the north when it is winter in the south.

Variations in rainfall are so important that vegetation zones and natural regions correspond closely to climatic belts. The principal natural regions are rain forest, grassland, desert, and Mediterranean.

In the middle of Africa and on the central west coast, great heat and heavy rains produce the equatorial rain forest (*see* Climate; Rainfall). Eastern equatorial Africa, however, has a temperate climate because of its high land. There are even snow-capped mountains almost at the equator. These highlands capture the moisture of the southeast trade winds, causing heavy rainfall on the southeast coast.

On the north and south edges of the equatorial forests the heavy rains diminish. The trees here are mixed with grasses. Gradually the trees disappear and vast subtropical grasslands stretch for many miles to the north and south. The rainfall is much lighter and there are both wet and dry seasons. The northern grasslands are called the *savanna*. The grasslands of South Africa are called the *veld*. (*See also* Grasslands.)

North of the savanna is the hot, dry Sahara, while in southern Africa are the desert regions of Kalahari and Namib. The northwestern and southeastern coasts have a Mediterranean climate. Summers are warm and dry; winters are mild and rainy.

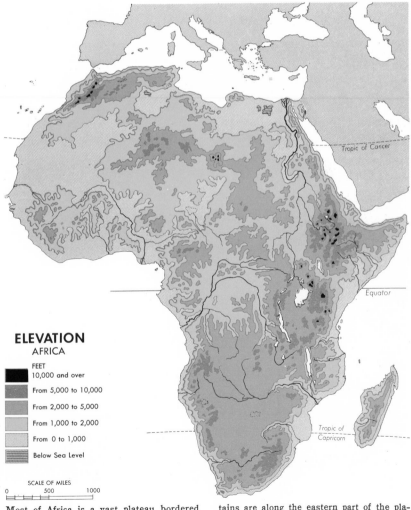

ELEVATION
AFRICA

FEET
- 10,000 and over
- From 5,000 to 10,000
- From 2,000 to 5,000
- From 1,000 to 2,000
- From 0 to 1,000
- Below Sea Level

SCALE OF MILES
0   500   1000

Tropic of Cancer

Equator

Tropic of Capricorn

Most of Africa is a vast plateau bordered by narrow coastal lowlands. The chief mountains are along the eastern part of the plateau and in the northwest.

African Peoples and Where They Live

ALTHOUGH Africa is the second largest continent in area, in population it ranks fourth. The 1962 estimate for Africa was 269,000,000 inhabitants. The figure can only be roughly estimated. In many parts of the continent an accurate count has never been made.

More than two thirds of the Africans are *Negroid*, or black, peoples. The Sahara long kept Africa's white and Negro races apart. North of the desert lived the *Caucasoid*, or white, peoples. The black peoples lived south of the desert. Through many centuries of moving about, however, whites and Negroes mixed with one another. Today many Africans are a mixture of both races (*see* Races of Mankind).

The many peoples of Africa can be understood best by studying the continent, section by section from north to south. Africa may be divided by geography and climate into three general regions. These are northern Africa along the Mediterranean and Red seas; the desert lands of the Sahara; and Negro Africa,

including the semitropical Sudan, equatorial central Africa, the grasslands (veld) of South Africa, and the coastal plains of Africa's southern tip. The European settlements are scattered throughout the continent, but most of them are in the extreme north and south.

Peoples of North Africa

Native white Africans live in what is sometimes called Arab, or Moslem, Africa. This region lies between the Mediterranean and the northern fringes of the Sahara. It extends through the northeastern Sudan into the Ethiopian plateau.

North Africans are divided into Hamites and Semites. It is said they were named for Noah's sons Ham and Shem.

Hamites are divided into two groups, according to the language they speak. One is Berber, the other Cushitic. The Berbers include the Kabyle, Siwans, Tibu, and Tuareg. The principal Cushitic peoples are the Galla and the Somali.

Semites include most Ethiopians, some Egyptians, and the Arab tribes that wander throughout the land. For centuries Hamites and Semites mingled with one another and with Negroes from the south. Now there is a great confusion of racial heritage.

Berbers and Arabs. Most northern Africans are Berbers or Arabs or a mixture of the two. Northern Africa was once called Barbary (land of the Berbers). When Arabs from Asia invaded Barbary in the Middle Ages they brought the religion of Mohammed with them. Today Mohammedanism is one of the most powerful influences in northern Africa (*see* Mohammed; Islam). Semitic Arabs intermarried with Hamitic Berbers, and in many places the ancient Berber language was replaced by Arabic. Most Hamito-Semitic peoples are farmers or herders.

The walled cities of Barbary are usually crowded trading centers near the coast. In the mountain villages the houses are attached to one another and rise in a series of steps up the steep hillsides.

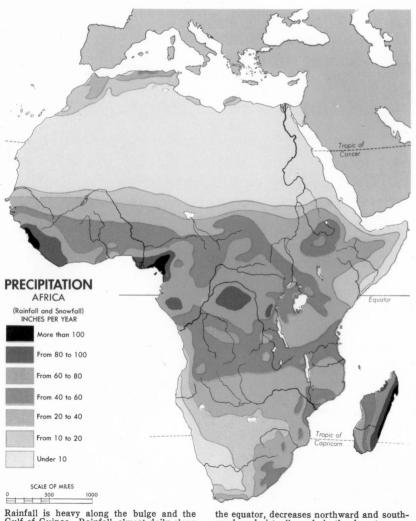

PRECIPITATION
AFRICA
(Rainfall and Snowfall)
INCHES PER YEAR

- More than 100
- From 80 to 100
- From 60 to 80
- From 40 to 60
- From 20 to 40
- From 10 to 20
- Under 10

SCALE OF MILES
0   500   1000

Rainfall is heavy along the bulge and the Gulf of Guinea. Rainfall, almost daily along the equator, decreases northward and southward, and virtually ends in the deserts.

MATABELE FAMILY AT HOME
The Matabele live in the Transvaal, Zambia, and Rhodesia. Notice the wall decoration and the coins on the baby's head.

WATUSI—AFRICA'S TALLEST PEOPLE
The Watusi men sometimes grow taller than seven feet. The fancy hair style adds to their height.

Farming in the coastal region is made possible by winter rains and by irrigation. Farther inland, rainfall is scanty and grasslands prevail. Arabs here live in tents made of camel's hair and leather and graze their sheep, camels, goats, cattle, and donkeys. Gradually the grasslands give way to the desert, where only an occasional oasis raises dusty palms to the cloudless sky. (*See also* Morocco; Algeria; Tunisia; Libya; Egypt; Ethiopia.)

Life in the Desert

People are as scarce in the Sahara as water. They are usually nomads or live in an oasis.

An oasis is a desert garden made possible by an occasional spring. Much of the precious water is used to cultivate these gardens. An oasis may look like a small fortress shaded by palms. It may have buildings several stories high. Oasis dwellers are farmers. They grow fruits and vegetables. They also grow crops such as alfalfa to feed the hungry camels of passing caravans. They get goods from the outside world by trading with the caravans. The Nile Valley is the largest oasis in the world. (*See also* Egypt; Sahara; Deserts.)

Nomads are always moving about the desert to find food for their sheep and camels. In a few places there is enough grass for grazing. When the animals have eaten all there is in one place, they must be moved to new grazing grounds. Nomads live in tents. They get vegetables, fruits, and other supplies when they stop to trade at an oasis. (*See also* Nomads.)

Negro Africa

Negro Africa begins where the sands of the southern Sahara merge with the semitropical grasslands (savanna) of the Sudan. The equatorial west coast is low, hot, and wet. The central equatorial region is a steaming rain forest. The equatorial eastern high-

lands are mostly cool and temperate. South of the equatorial regions are more grasslands—the South African veld—and the coastal plains of the South Atlantic and Indian oceans.

Between the Sahara and the equator live the Sudanese and so-called "true" Negroes. From the equator southward live the many tribes of the Bantu. Pygmies are found in the equatorial rain forest. Small groups of Bushmen and Hottentots live in southern Africa.

"True" Negroes and Sudanese. The Negro of western Africa is said to be the "purest" Negro type. In this

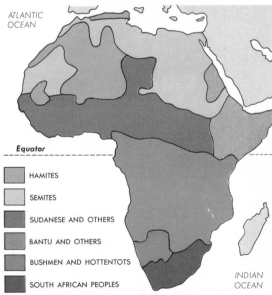

ATLANTIC OCEAN

Equator

INDIAN OCEAN

HAMITES

SEMITES

SUDANESE AND OTHERS

BANTU AND OTHERS

BUSHMEN AND HOTTENTOTS

SOUTH AFRICAN PEOPLES

RACES OF AFRICA
Hamites and Semites are Caucasoid (white) peoples. Sudanese and Bantu are Negroid. Bushmen and Hottentots are considered Negroid. European whites live mainly in the coastal regions of northern and southern Africa and the eastern highlands. (For South African peoples, *see* South Africa.)

coastal belt north and south of the equator there has been the least racial mixture. Northward and eastward in the savanna regions of the western Sudan, the mixture with Hamitic people increases. Farther east are Hausa-speaking Mohammedan kingdoms with a Hamito-Negroid ruling class and a more noticeably Negroid people. In the easternmost regions of the Sudan and in the lands at the headwaters of the Nile live still other Hamito-Negroid tribes.

Primitive tribes of these regions live in villages of crude huts, their ways of life unchanged for centuries. There are also cities with elaborately decorated houses of dried bricks—a legacy from the great Negro and Hamite empires of the past. (*See also* Ghana; Nigeria; Liberia; Ivory Coast; Sierra Leone; Guinea; Niger; Senegal; Somali Republic; Upper Volta; Sudan; Kenya; Mali; Central African Republic; Chad; Gambia; Togo; Uganda.)

The Bantu. Most of Negro Africa is occupied by the Bantu. There are several hundred tribes that extend southward from the equatorial forests to the Cape of Good Hope Province, in South Africa. They speak variants of a common language and include warlike hunters-cattle breeders and settled farmers.

European civilization has greatly disrupted tribal life in many areas of the continent. However, in some regions where white rule prevails, semiautonomous tribal "reserves" have been set aside. In these the economy is basically agricultural. In South Africa the reserves, occupied by Bantu, are known as *bantustans*. (*See also* Botswana; Congo River; Congo, Republic of; Congo, Democratic Republic of the; Rhodesia; Gabon; Lesotho; Malawi; Zambia; Angola; Mozambique; South Africa; Swaziland; Tanzania; Burundi; Rwanda.)

Primitive Peoples of Negroid Stock. There are three primitive groups—Hottentots, Bushmen, and Pygmies. The first two, almost extinct, live in the western Cape of Good Hope region and in the Kalahari Desert.

Hottentots are a nomadic pastoral people. They are believed by some to be a cross between Bushmen and Hamites. Bushmen are nomadic hunters, somewhat shorter than Hottentots. The shy little Pygmies live in the depths of the equatorial rain forest, mostly in the upper Congo region. (*See also* Pygmy.)

Europeans in Africa

For some 300 years Europeans have settled the fringes and some interior parts of Africa. In most cases they considered their residence temporary and looked forward to returning to their homeland.

This is still true almost everywhere in Africa where there are white settlements and administrations except in the republic of South Africa and in Rhodesia. The strong sense of nationalism common to South African whites (whether Afrikaner or British) is unique —South Africa *is* their homeland. The problems created by these unusual situations are discussed in the articles on South Africa and Kenya.

The Fact Summary at the end of this article gives the racial groups, languages, and religions of the people in each of Africa's political subdivisions.

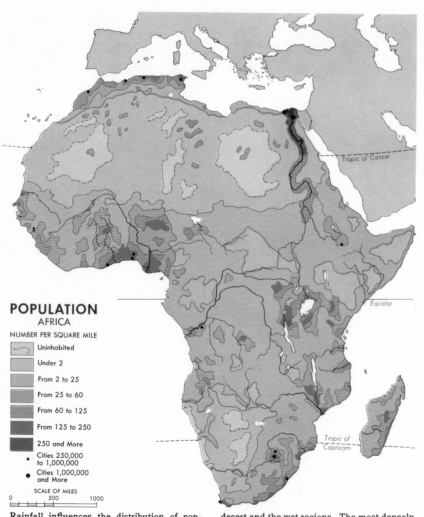

POPULATION
AFRICA

NUMBER PER SQUARE MILE

Uninhabited

Under 2

From 2 to 25

From 25 to 60

From 60 to 125

From 125 to 250

250 and More

• Cities 250,000 to 1,000,000

● Cities 1,000,000 and More

SCALE OF MILES

0   500   1000

Rainfall influences the distribution of population. Scanty population occurs in the desert and the wet regions. The most densely settled area is the fertile Nile Valley.

MODERN FARMING IN EAST AFRICA
A field of beans on a farm in the Kenya highlands has been contour-plowed to keep the soil from being washed or blown away. New food plants, such as corn, were introduced from America.

GOLD AND URANIUM MINING IN SOUTH AFRICA
The cyanide tanks in the foreground dissolve gold from its ore. The reduction plant in the background uses sulfuric acid to extract uranium from the slag that is left.

Plants, Animals, and Minerals

AFRICA is rich in plant and mineral resources. These products were long overlooked because of the spectacular mineral finds—particularly gold and diamonds. With World War II the colonial powers examined the resources of their territories more closely. Agricultural and industrial developments were started in many areas. The other continents have been steadily draining their resources, but Africa is still a great storehouse of undeveloped natural wealth.

Plants and Animals

The great natural divisions of Africa have different plant and animal life. The hot and wet jungle is rich in plant products such as rubber, mahogany, palm oil, teakwood, and gum arabic. The jungle is the home of gorillas, chimpanzees, and other members of the monkey family. There are also many insects, snakes, and bright birds. (*See also* Congo River.)

On the edges of the forests, where the grasslands begin, herds of elephants roam and crocodiles sun themselves on the banks of the warm rivers. Hippopotamuses are found in groups in many of the rivers.

The semiarid grasslands, or savannas, are mostly cattle-grazing country except where dams and irrigation have made crop farming possible. Among the many animals are lions, giraffes, and rhinoceroses. There are also zebras and many varieties of antelopes.

Acacia, thorn trees, and the scrub plants of the deserts have no value. Desert growth for man's use is confined largely to the oases. Animals are the camel, jackal, and small beasts of prey (*see* Sahara). Mediterranean lands produce grains, fruits, and vegetables. The cork oak is important in northern Africa.

The eastern highlands drop to the tropical southeast coast. Here there is a wide range of crops, including tea, coffee, cloves, rice, and tobacco. Most ivory comes from East Africa. (*See also* Kenya; Ivory; for a list of Africa's chief plants and animals, *see* Reference-Outline which follows this article.)

A Wealth of Minerals and Water Power

Africa has immense mineral resources that have never been fully exploited. It is rich in rare and strategic minerals but poor in mineral fuels. Africa is the leading continent in the production of diamonds, gold, and cobalt. The Democratic Republic of the Congo is the world's principal producer of industrial diamonds. Also important are the Republic of Congo and South Africa. South Africa is the chief gold-mining country in the world. Other leaders are Ghana, Rhodesia, and the Democratic Republic of the Congo. From the Democratic Republic of the Congo also comes about half the world's cobalt. Zambia and Morocco are other major producers.

79

A HIPPOPOTAMUS FAMILY IN EAST-CENTRAL AFRICA

Hippopotamus means "river horse." This family is wading in the warm, muddy waters of the Semliki River. The river flows out of Lake Edward and most of its course is through Albert National Park. Sir Henry M. Stanley explored the Semliki in 1888.

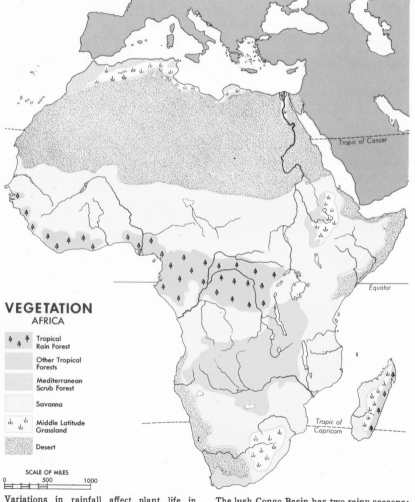

VEGETATION
AFRICA

- Tropical Rain Forest
- Other Tropical Forests
- Mediterranean Scrub Forest
- Savanna
- Middle Latitude Grassland
- Desert

SCALE OF MILES
0   500   1000

Variations in rainfall affect plant life in Africa. Most of the arid regions are barren.

The lush Congo Basin has two rainy seasons; and the grassy savannas, wet and dry periods.

Zambia and the Democratic Republic of the Congo are among the principal copper-producing nations of the world. South Africa and Rhodesia are world leaders in the mining of chromite. South Africa, Ghana, Gabon, and the Democratic Republic of the Congo are among the world's leading producers of manganese. South Africa is a prime source of antimony. South Africa and Rhodesia are major asbestos producers. The Democratic Republic of the Congo and Nigeria are leading tin producers.

South Africa and South-West Africa account for much of the world's vanadium production. South Africa also is Africa's main source of uranium. Morocco and Tunisia lead in producing phosphate rock. Bauxite is mined chiefly in Ghana and Guinea.

The continent's iron ore comes from South Africa, Liberia, Algeria, Sierra Leone, and Morocco. Lead is mined chiefly in Morocco and South-West Africa, and zinc in the Democratic Republic of the Congo, Morocco, Algeria, and Zambia. Africa's principal coal mines

80

are in South Africa and Rhodesia. Libya is the leading African petroleum producer, and output is also quite sizable in Algeria, Nigeria, and Egypt. There is much oil prospecting.

Africa has the least amount of developed water-power, but its potential is second only to that of Asia (*see* Waterpower). Central Africa, with heavy rainfall, has tremendous resources. The Congo Basin has about one fourth of the world's potential power. The Nile and the Zambezi are other great sources.

Discovery, Exploration, and Colonization

THE civilization of ancient Egypt rose in the Nile Valley about 5,000 years ago (*see* Egypt, Ancient). In 814 B.C. Phoenician traders founded the city of Carthage. Still later, Greeks, Romans, Vandals, and Arabs occupied the northern fringe of the Dark Continent (*see* Ancient History). This region was a great granary, which fed much of the ancient Mediterranean world. Great cities were built. Art and science flourished. Christianity was established and later succeeded by Mohammedanism. The people of this ancient Mediterranean world stayed on the northern coastal plain. The greater part of Africa remained a land of mystery to them.

In the Middle Ages Arab traders landed on the east coast. It was during this period that Zimbabwe and other stone cities were built in the region now called Rhodesia. The ruins of these centers indicate that the people were engaged chiefly in the mining and smelting of gold. The so-called Age of Discovery began in the 15th century when Portuguese mariners explored the western and southern coasts of Africa.

The Age of Discovery

Early in the 15th century, Prince Henry of Portugal organized a series of expeditions to explore Africa's west coast (*see* Henry the Navigator). Bartholomew Diaz rounded the Cape of Good Hope in 1488, and Vasco da Gama reached India in 1498 (*see* Diaz, Bartholomew; Gama). A century and a half later, in 1652, the Dutch settled Cape Town, the first permanent colony in South Africa (*see* South Africa).

The slave trade and the barter for gold and ivory which followed the Portuguese discoveries did not lead to colonization. Arabs overthrew Christianity in northern Africa in the 7th century, leaving only traces in the Coptic church of Egypt and Ethiopia. The Turks, in turn, overthrew the Arabs in the 16th century. Only in South Africa and in a few Portuguese settlements on the east coast had Europeans gained a foothold. Europe in the 18th century was so busy with its own wars that it virtually forgot Africa.

Then, in the course of the Napoleonic wars, Great Britain occupied and later took possession of the Dutch colony at the Cape of Good Hope. The powers of Europe were slowly becoming aware of the advantages to be gained in getting control of African territories. Slavery was abolished throughout the British Empire in 1833 (*see* Slavery). The period of great explorations had begun.

Exploration in the 18th and 19th Centuries

The first real forays into the interior of Africa were made by two Scotsmen, James Bruce and Mungo Park. Late in the 18th century Bruce explored the sources of the Nile and Park explored the Niger. David Livingstone was the most famous explorer of all. In 1849 he crossed the Kalahari from south to north and began his travels through the great waterways of the upper Zambezi and the southern lakes. Livingstone disappeared about 1869, and a New York newspaper reporter, Henry M. Stanley, was sent to find

AFRICAN CHILDREN AT SCHOOL IN UGANDA
An African teacher is using a blackboard to teach these children their native tongue, Luganda. This mission school is in the province of Buganda.

GRASS HUTS ON THE RUZIZI
The huts of this village are shaped to resist the hard rains of the region. The river flows into Lake Tanganyika.

A SKYSCRAPER IN WEST AFRICA
This gleaming white skyscraper with lacy iron balconies is an administration building in Dakar, capital of Senegal.

him (*see* Livingstone; Stanley). Stanley later explored the Congo region.

In 1869 two events again drew Europe's attention to Africa. The Suez Canal was opened and diamonds were discovered in South Africa (*see* Suez Canal; South Africa).

The European Scramble for Africa's Lands

Leopold II of Belgium started the race for African lands when he seized the vast Congo region in the 1880's and began to exploit its wealth (*see* Congo River; Congo, Democratic Republic of the). A newly unified and aggressive Germany saw in Africa one of the last areas open for colonization. Britain, already in control of South Africa, and France, in possession of Algeria, sought more territory.

Belgium and France clashed in the Congo. Germany blocked Britain in eastern Africa. Britain checked France in the Sudan and supported Portugal's claims at the mouth of the Congo. Italy seized the Red Sea coast of Ethiopia.

To put an end to the confusion, a conference of the powers was called at Berlin in 1884. It laid down rules under which annexations should be valid. It was agreed that each nation would notify the other signatory nations of its projects for colonization, outlining the territories for which it intended to be responsible and defining where its "sphere of influence" was to extend.

During the next 15 years most of Africa was divided among six European nations, after war had been narrowly averted several times. France obtained control of northwest Africa and the north bank of the Congo, as well as the island of Madagascar. Britain held Egypt, where it had intervened in 1882 (*see* Egypt). It consolidated its possessions in southern Africa, opened a large new colony in eastern Africa, and established itself at the mouth of the Niger. Leopold II considered the Congo as his personal property until he transferred it to Belgium as a colony in 1908. Portugal retained Angola in the west and Mozambique in the east. Italy held a large slice of Somaliland and a small strip (Eritrea) on the Red Sea. Later it acquired Tripoli (Libya) through a war with Turkey in 1911–12.

Germany's large holdings defeated for a time Britain's desire for an all-British strip from Cape Town to Cairo. During World War I Germany's lands were taken over by Britain, France, Belgium, and Portugal. They became League of Nations mandates.

After World War II, all except South-West Africa were made United Nations trusteeships. Defeated Italy lost its colonies, including Ethiopia, which regained its freedom as an independent nation. Through the United Nations Libya became an independent state in 1951. Eritrea joined a federation with Ethiopia in 1952.

Transportation Transforms Africa

The pattern of African life, particularly of the Negroid peoples, has been radically altered by rapid advances in transportation and communication. Perhaps no other continent has undergone so much change in so short a time.

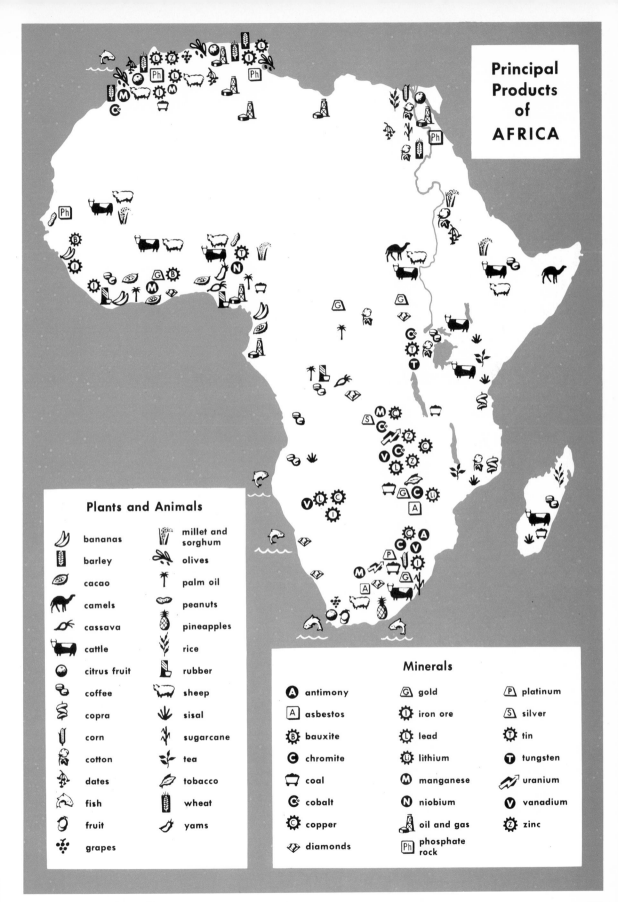

Principal Products of AFRICA

Plants and Animals

- bananas
- barley
- cacao
- camels
- cassava
- cattle
- citrus fruit
- coffee
- copra
- corn
- cotton
- dates
- fish
- fruit
- grapes
- millet and sorghum
- olives
- palm oil
- peanuts
- pineapples
- rice
- rubber
- sheep
- sisal
- sugarcane
- tea
- tobacco
- wheat
- yams

Minerals

- **A** antimony
- **A** asbestos
- **B** bauxite
- **C** chromite
- coal
- **C** cobalt
- copper
- diamonds
- **G** gold
- **I** iron ore
- **L** lead
- **Li** lithium
- **M** manganese
- **N** niobium
- oil and gas
- **Ph** phosphate rock
- **P** platinum
- **S** silver
- **Sn** tin
- **T** tungsten
- uranium
- **V** vanadium
- **Z** zinc

83

Before World War II many people in the heartland of Africa traveled mostly on the great river and lake systems. There were few roads and practically no railroads except in extreme northern and southern Africa. Even today Africa has fewer miles of railroad than any other continent except Australia. There are connecting lines in Morocco, Algeria, and Tunisia and in the system of South Africa, which extends north into Zambia, Angola, and the Democratic Republic of the Congo. Elsewhere usually narrow-gauge lines link ports with interior mining and trading centers. They rarely join with other railroads.

The construction of highways and the expansion of air transport facilities were important developments after World War II. Today international airlines serve almost every nation in Africa.

A THRIVING AFRICAN PORT
Lagos, the capital of Nigeria, is also the chief port. Petroleum and cacao are Nigeria's leading exports.

The effects of these new means of transportation have been many. Tribal organization has been disrupted. Even in the heart of the continent a journey that once took several days or weeks can now be made in hours. Africans who once led a primitive agricultural existence within a small area can now travel to places where industrial labor is in demand.

The African Giant Awakens

This era in Africa's history might be compared to the ending of the Middle Ages and feudalism in Europe. People no longer live in isolated tribes. They now move about freely in large numbers. They seek new patterns of life as the old ones are destroyed.

In the political turmoil that followed World War II, many colonies became independent. In the first 14 years after the war, six new nations were born: Libya (1951); Sudan, Morocco, and Tunisia (1956); Ghana (1957); and Guinea (1958). Eritrea became a province of Ethiopia (*see* Ethiopia).

Seventeen new states were created in 1960. Of these, 14 were former French territories. They were Cameroon, Central African Republic, Chad, Republic of Congo, Dahomey, Gabon, Ivory Coast, Malagasy Republic, Mali, Mauritania, Niger, Senegal, Togo, and Upper Volta. In the same year Nigeria became independent; the Somali Republic was formed from the British and Italian Somalilands; and the Belgian Congo became the Democratic Republic of the Congo.

Other Changes in Africa

In 1956 the Suez Canal was nationalized by Egypt (*see* Suez Canal). In 1958 Egypt and the Asian nation of Syria formed the United Arab Republic (UAR). Yemen, on the Arabian peninsula, federated with the UAR but remained independent. In 1961

Syria revolted and withdrew from the federation. Later that year Egypt dissolved its tie with Yemen but retained the name United Arab Republic.

Among the states in the Commonwealth of Nations in 1961, Northern Cameroons voted to join Nigeria, and Southern Cameroons merged with Cameroon. The former British dominion, the Union of South Africa, declared itself a republic. Sierra Leone and Tanganyika were granted independence.

Algeria won its freedom when the struggle between the Algerian nationalists and the French ended in 1962. The Belgian trusteeship of Ruanda-Urundi became the independent nations of Rwanda and Burundi. Uganda also became free in 1962.

In 1963 Kenya and Zanzibar were freed from British rule. The Federation of Rhodesia and Nyasaland was dissolved at the end of the year. In 1964 Nyasaland became the independent nation of Malawi, Northern Rhodesia the independent nation of Zambia. Tanganyika and Zanzibar merged in 1964 to form the United Republic of Tanzania. In 1965 Gambia was granted its independence, and Rhodesia unilaterally declared itself independent from Britain. Bechuanaland and Basutoland achieved freedom in 1966, becoming Botswana and Lesotho, respectively. (*See also* Nations Formed Since World War II table in Fact-Index.)

Africa's fledgling nations were, on the whole, ill-prepared for independence. Political upheavals were frequent. By the mid-1960's several of the republics had fallen under the control of military dictators. (*See also* individual articles on these countries. For the current status of each of the political subdivisions of Africa, *see* Africa Fact Summary.)

AFRICA FACT SUMMARY

Nations and Colonies of Africa

LOCATION OF NATIONS AND COLONIES LISTED BELOW

NAME, AREA, AND POPULATION	PEOPLE AND LANGUAGE	EDUCATION AND RELIGION	GOVERNMENT	PRODUCTS
AFARS AND ISSAS, TERRITORY OF THE Area: 8,494 sq. mi. Population: 67,300	**People:** Danakils (nomads); Somalis; Arabs; Europeans **Languages:** Somali; Arabic; French	**Schools:** 29 **Students:** 4,799 **Illiteracy:** 95–99% **Religion:** Moslem	**Political Status:** Former French Somaliland, 1946–67; became Territory of the Afars and Issas within French Republic, 1967 **Capital:** Djibouti **UN:** Nonmember	Salt; sheep; goats; hides; coffee, dates; fish
ALGERIA Area: 919,353 sq. mi. Population: 10,453,000	**People:** Mostly Arabs and Berbers **Languages:** Arabic; Berber; French	**Schools:** 11,483 **Students:** 1,336,472 **Illiteracy:** 80% **Religions:** Moslem; Roman Catholic	**Political Status:** Former French possession; began revolt, 1954; independent, 1962 **Capital:** Algiers **UN:** Admitted 1962	Wheat, tobacco; sheep; crude oil, iron ore, phosphates; wine; cement; olive oil; zinc
ANGOLA (Portuguese West Africa) Area: 481,352 sq. mi. Population: 5,119,000	**People:** Mostly Bantu; some Bushmen; Europeans **Languages:** Bantu; Portuguese	**Schools:** 2,131 **Students:** 119,309 **Illiteracy:** 95–99% **Religions:** Pagan; Roman Catholic	**Political Status:** Portuguese overseas province; includes Cabinda exclave; discovered by Portuguese, 1482; colony became province, 1951 **Capital:** Luanda **UN:** Nonmember	Coffee, sisal, corn, palm oil and kernels, cotton, sugar, beans; diamonds, salt; fish
ASCENSION Area: 34 sq. mi. Population: 382	**People:** Europeans; St. Helenans; no native peoples **Language:** English	**Schools:** Statistics not available **Religion:** Anglican	**Political Status:** Dependency of St. Helena (British colony) since 1922; discovered by Portuguese, 1501; inhabited by British, 1815 **UN:** Nonmember	Sea turtles; vegetables
BOTSWANA Area: 222,000 sq. mi. Population: 576,000	**People:** Almost all Negroes (Bantu); Europeans **Languages:** Bantu; Bushman; English	**Schools:** 253 **Students:** 64,320 **Illiteracy:** 75–80% **Religions:** Christian; tribal	**Political Status:** Former British protectorate (Bechuanaland); became independent, 1966 **Capital:** Gaberones **UN:** Admitted 1966	Sorghum, corn, beans, melons; cattle; butter, hides, skins; gold, silver, asbestos
BURUNDI Area: 10,747 sq. mi. Population: 2,780,000	**People:** Bahutu; Watusi **Languages:** Bantu; Hamitic; French	**Schools:** 1,304 **Students:** 114,015 **Illiteracy:** 90–95% **Religions:** Tribal; Roman Catholic; Anglican	**Political Status:** Former southern part of Ruanda-Urundi, UN trust territory administered by Belgium; became independent kingdom, 1962 **Capital:** Bujumbura **UN:** Admitted 1962	Coffee; cattle, sheep, goats; cassava; tin; bananas; pyrethrum
CAMEROON Area: 183,377 sq. mi. Population: 5,300,000	**People:** Mainly Negroes; Arabs; Europeans **Languages:** Sudanic; Bantu; Arabic; French; English	**Schools:** 3,092 **Students:** 708,676 **Illiteracy:** 90–95% **Religions:** Tribal; Moslem; Christian	**Political Status:** Former French UN trusteeship, became independent, 1960; absorbed British Southern Cameroons, 1961 **Capital:** Yaoundé **UN:** Admitted 1960	Cacao, palm oil and kernels, coffee, bananas, rubber, cassava; cattle; timber; aluminum
CANARY ISLANDS Area: 2,808 sq. mi.; archipelago of 7 major islands Population: 944,448	**People:** Original Hamitic population absorbed by Spaniards **Language:** Spanish	**Education:** Statistics not available **Religion:** Roman Catholic	**Political Status:** Made two provinces of Spain, 1927; acquired by Spain in 15th century **Capitals:** Las Palmas and Santa Cruz de Tenerife **UN:** Nonmember	Bananas, tomatoes, sugar, fruits; wine; fish
CAPE VERDE ISLANDS Area: 1,557 sq. mi.; 10 islands, 5 islets Population: 218,000	**People:** About 70% mulattoes; 28% Negroes; 2% Europeans **Language:** Portuguese	**Schools:** 286 **Students:** 12,507 **Illiteracy:** 79% **Religion:** Roman Catholic	**Political Status:** Portuguese overseas province; discovered by Portuguese, 1456; colony became province, 1951 **Capital:** Praia **UN:** Nonmember	Coffee, oranges, sugar; castor oil; hides
CENTRAL AFRICAN REPUBLIC Area: 238,224 sq. mi. Population: 1,320,000	**People:** Mostly Negroes; Europeans **Languages:** Negro dialects; hybrid Sango; French	**Schools:** 590 **Students:** 110,664 **Illiteracy:** 95–99% **Religions:** Chiefly animist; Roman Catholic	**Political Status:** Former territory (Ubangi-Shari) in French Equatorial Africa, became republic, 1958; independent, 1960; in French Community **Capital:** Bangui **UN:** Admitted 1960	Coffee, cotton, peanuts, sisal, palm kernels; cattle, sheep; lumber; diamonds, gold

Nations and Colonies of Africa—continued

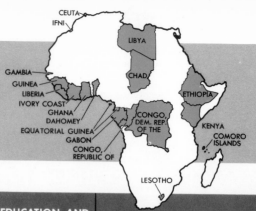

CEUTA
IFNI
LIBYA
GAMBIA
GUINEA
CHAD
LIBERIA
IVORY COAST
GHANA
ETHIOPIA
DAHOMEY
EQUATORIAL GUINEA
CONGO, DEM. REP. OF THE
GABON
KENYA
CONGO, REPUBLIC OF
COMORO ISLANDS
LESOTHO

LOCATION OF NATIONS AND COLONIES LISTED ON THESE TWO PAGES

NAME, AREA, AND POPULATION	PEOPLE AND LANGUAGE	EDUCATION AND RELIGION	GOVERNMENT	PRODUCTS
CEUTA Area: 7.3 sq. mi. Population: 73,182	**People:** Predominantly Spanish **Language:** Spanish	Schools: 88 Students: 7,887 Illiteracy: 39% Religion: Roman Catholic	**Political Status:** City is Spanish possession opposite Gibraltar; part of province of Cadiz; enclave in Morocco; ceded by Portugal to Spain, 1580 UN: Nonmember	Fish
CHAD Area: 495,754 sq. mi. Population: 2,797,521	**People:** North—Arabs; south—Negroes **Languages:** Negro dialects; Arabic; French	Schools: 458 Students: 133,830 Illiteracy: 90% Religions: Moslem; animist	**Political Status:** Former territory (Tchad) in French Equatorial Africa, became republic, 1958; independent, 1960; in French Community **Capital:** Fort-Lamy UN: Admitted 1960	Cotton, millet, sorghum, peanuts, sweet potatoes, dates; sheep, cattle; fish; gum arabic
COMORO ISLANDS Area: 838 sq. mi.; 4 islands, several islets Population: 183,133	**People:** Mainly mixed Arab, Negro, and Malagasy stock **Languages:** Arabic-Swahili; French	Schools: 59 Students: 7,129 Illiteracy: 75–80% Religions: Largely Moslem; Christian	**Political Status:** French overseas territory since 1947; protectorate, 1886; colony, 1912; attached to Madagascar, 1914 **Capital:** Moroni UN: Nonmember	Vanilla, copra, sisal, sugar, perfume plants, coffee, cacao, rice; timber; fish; rum
CONGO, DEMOCRATIC REPUBLIC OF THE Area: 905,381 sq. mi. Population: 15,007,000	**People:** Bantu; Sudanese; Pygmies; Europeans **Languages:** Bantu; French; Flemish	Schools: 12,154 Students: 2,100,409 Illiteracy: 83% Religions: Mostly animist; Christian	**Political Status:** Former colony (Belgian Congo), since 1908, became republic, 1960; seized by King Leopold, 1884–85 **Capital:** Kinshasa (Léopoldville) UN: Admitted 1960	Cassava, cotton, coffee, palm oil and kernels, rubber; copper, industrial diamonds, tin, cobalt; fish; timber
CONGO, REPUBLIC OF Area: 132,047 sq. mi. Population: 1,009,700	**People:** Mainly Bantu; Pygmies; Europeans **Languages:** Bantu; French	Schools: 637 Students: 120,237 Illiteracy: 95–99% Religions: Largely animist; Christian	**Political Status:** Former territory (Middle Congo) in French Equatorial Africa, became republic, 1958; independent, 1960; in French Community **Capital:** Brazzaville UN: Admitted 1960	Lumber; palm oil and kernels, peanuts, tobacco; lead, phosphates; hydroelectric power
DAHOMEY Area: 43,483 sq. mi. Population: 2,300,000	**People:** Chiefly Negroes; Europeans **Languages:** Many spoken (Ewe, Yoruba, etc.); French	Schools: 594 Students: 107,127 Illiteracy: 95–99% Religions: Animist; Christian; Moslem	**Political Status:** Former territory in French West Africa, since 1904, became republic, 1958; independent, 1960 **Capital:** Porto-Novo UN: Admitted 1960	Palm oil and kernels, coffee, corn, cassava, yams, peanuts; cattle, sheep, goats; gold
EQUATORIAL GUINEA Area: 10,830 sq. mi. Population: 245,989	**People:** Mainly Negroes (Bubi and Fang); many immigrants; Europeans **Languages:** Bantu; Spanish; English	Schools: 170 Students: 27,271 Illiteracy: 75–80% Religions: Tribal; Roman Catholic	**Political Status:** Spanish colony, comprising Fernando Po and Río Muni; acquired by Spain 1778 and 1885 respectively **Capital:** Santa Isabel UN: Nonmember	Cacao, coffee, tobacco, vegetables, fruits, palm oil and kernels; cabinet woods
ETHIOPIA Area: 457,267 sq. mi. Population: 22,200,000	**People:** Many ethnic groups (Amhara, Galla, etc.) **Languages:** Amharic; English	Schools: 1,579 Students: 361,024 Illiteracy: 95–99% Religions: Coptic Christian; Moslem	**Political Status:** Empire; independent since ancient times (except in 1936–41 after conquest by Italy) **Capital:** Addis Ababa UN: Admitted 1945	Coffee, cereals, cotton, oilseeds, corn; cattle, sheep, goats; hides, skins; gold
GABON Area: 103,089 sq. mi. Population: 468,000	**People:** Mainly Bantu; Pygmies; Fang; Europeans **Languages:** Bantu; Fang; French	Schools: 648 Students: 78,065 Illiteracy: 85% Religions: Mainly animist; Christian	**Political Status:** Former territory in French Equatorial Africa, became republic, 1958; independent, 1960; in French Community **Capital:** Libreville UN: Admitted 1960	Okoumé and other woods; plywood; cacao, coffee, cassava; petroleum, gold; whales; ivory
GAMBIA Area: 4,003 sq. mi. Population: 330,000	**People:** Chief tribe, Mandingo; Wolof; Serahuli; Fula; Jola **Languages:** Sudanic; English	Schools: 93 Students: 14,729 Illiteracy: 90–95% Religions: Moslem; tribal; Christian	**Political Status:** Former British protectorate (since 1902); became independent, 1965; British dominant since 17th century **Capital:** Bathurst UN: Admitted 1965	Peanuts, palm kernels, millet; cattle, sheep, goats; hides; beeswax; ilmenite; fish

AFRICA FACT SUMMARY

NAME, AREA, AND POPULATION	PEOPLE AND LANGUAGE	EDUCATION AND RELIGION	GOVERNMENT	PRODUCTS
GHANA **Area:** 91,843 sq. mi. **Population:** 7,945,000	**People:** Mainly Negroes; Europeans **Languages:** Many Negro dialects; English	**Schools:** 8,986 **Students:** 1,061,376 **Illiteracy:** 77% **Religions:** Animist; Moslem; Christian	**Political Status:** British colony, Gold Coast, and UN trust territory, British Togoland, became dominion, 1957; republic, 1960 **Capital:** Accra **UN:** Admitted 1957	Cacao, palm oil, millet, corn; cattle; gold, manganese, industrial diamonds, bauxite; timber; fish
GUINEA **Area:** 94,926 sq. mi. **Population:** 3,357,000	**People:** Negroes (Fula, Malinke, Susu); Europeans **Languages:** Sudanic; French; English	**Schools:** 1,712 **Students:** 199,781 **Illiteracy:** 90% **Religions:** Animist; Moslem; Christian	**Political Status:** Former territory in French West Africa, became independent, 1958 **Capital:** Conakry **UN:** Admitted 1958	Rice, bananas, coffee, palm oil; cattle; bauxite, iron, diamonds, gold, aluminum; fish
IFNI **Area:** 579 sq. mi.; small enclave on coast of Morocco **Population:** 49,889	**People:** Berbers; Spaniards **Languages:** Berber; Arabic; Spanish	**Schools** (primary): 27 **Students** (primary): 1,072 **Religion:** Moslem	**Political Status:** Territory in Spanish West Africa, became province, 1958; under Spanish since 1860 **Capital:** Sidi Ifni **UN:** Nonmember	Alfalfa, corn, wheat, barley, tomatoes; fish
IVORY COAST **Area:** 124,503 sq. mi. **Population:** 3,665,000	**People:** Mainly Negroes; Europeans **Languages:** Many Negro dialects; French	**Schools:** 1,940 **Students:** 371,385 **Illiteracy:** 95–99% **Religions:** Animist; Moslem; Christian	**Political Status:** Former territory in French West Africa, became republic, 1958; independent, 1960 **Capital:** Abidjan **UN:** Admitted 1960	Coffee, cacao, bananas; cattle, sheep, goats; diamonds, gold, manganese; mahogany; fish
KENYA **Area:** 224,960 sq. mi. **Population:** 9,643,000	**People:** Mainly Negroes and Hamites; Asians; Europeans **Languages:** English; Swahili; Hindustani	**Schools:** 5,514 **Students:** 1,068,981 **Illiteracy:** 75–80% **Religions:** Pagan; Christian; Moslem; Hindu	**Political Status:** Former British colony, became independent, 1963 **Capital:** Nairobi **UN:** Admitted 1963	Coffee, tea, sisal, wattle, pyrethrum; cattle, sheep; hides, skins; soda ash
LESOTHO **Area:** 11,716 sq. mi. **Population:** 745,000	**People:** Almost all Negroes (Bantu); Europeans **Languages:** Bantu (Sesuto); English	**Schools:** 1,106 **Students:** 156,991 **Illiteracy:** 15% **Religions:** Christian; tribal	**Political Status:** Former self-governing British colony (Basutoland); became independent, 1966 **Capital:** Maseru **UN:** Admitted 1966	Wheat, corn, sorghum, oats, barley, beans, peas; livestock; wool, mohair, hides, skins
LIBERIA **Area:** 43,000 sq. mi. **Population:** 1,310,000	**People:** Mainly Negroes **Languages:** English; 28 tribal dialects	**Schools:** 813 **Students:** 80,515 **Illiteracy:** 95% **Religions:** Mostly pagan; Christian; Moslem	**Political Status:** Founded by American Colonization Society as settlement for ex-slaves, 1822; first Negro republic in Africa, 1847 **Capital:** Monrovia **UN:** Admitted 1945	Rubber, palm oil and kernels, coffee, cacao, rice, cassava; iron ore, gold, diamonds; timber; fish
LIBYA **Area:** 679,360 sq. mi. **Population:** 1,682,000	**People:** Mainly Arabs and Berbers; Negroes; Italians; Jews **Languages:** Arabic; Berber; Italian; English	**Schools:** 691 **Students:** 139,463 **Illiteracy:** 86% **Religions:** Mostly Moslem; Christian	**Political Status:** Constitutional monarchy; under Italians, 1911–42, British-French, 1942–51; independent, 1951 **Cocapitals:** Tripoli, Benghazi **UN:** Admitted 1955	Cereals, peanuts, olives, esparto, dates; sheep, goats, camels; petroleum, salt; fish, sponges

LAND USE

FOREST 25%   PASTURE 20%   CROPS 8%   OTHER 47%

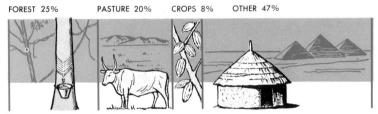

CROSS SECTION OF AFRICA (NEAR THE EQUATOR)

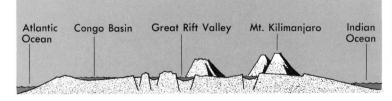

Atlantic Ocean   Congo Basin   Great Rift Valley   Mt. Kilimanjaro   Indian Ocean

AFRICA IS ABOUT THREE TIMES AS LARGE AS THE UNITED STATES

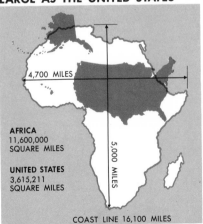

4,700 MILES

5,000 MILES

AFRICA 11,600,000 SQUARE MILES

UNITED STATES 3,615,211 SQUARE MILES

COAST LINE 16,100 MILES

87

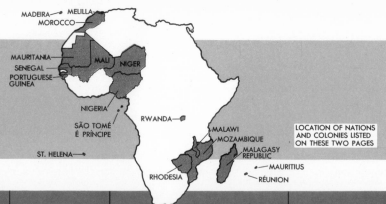

Nations and Colonies of Africa—continued

LOCATION OF NATIONS AND COLONIES LISTED ON THESE TWO PAGES

NAME, AREA, AND POPULATION	PEOPLE AND LANGUAGE	EDUCATION AND RELIGION	GOVERNMENT	PRODUCTS
MADEIRA Area: 308 sq. mi.; 2 inhabited islands, 2 barren islets **Population:** 268,937	**People:** Mulattoes (Portuguese and Negro); Moors; Italians **Languages:** Portuguese; English	**Education:** Statistics not available **Religion:** Roman Catholic	**Political Status:** Constitutes Funchal, one of 22 districts of Portugal; discovered by Portuguese, 1418 **Capital:** Funchal **UN:** Nonmember	Wine; sugar, bananas; dairy cattle; embroidery, wickerwork; fish
MALAGASY REPUBLIC Area: 227,700 sq. mi. **Population:** 6,615,000	**People:** Mainly Malagasy tribes (Hova); French; Asians **Languages:** Malagasy; French	**Schools:** 2,803 **Students:** 476,407 **Illiteracy:** 67% **Religions:** Mainly Christian; pagan	**Political Status:** Former French overseas territory, became republic, 1958; independent, 1960; in French Community **Capital:** Tananarive **UN:** Admitted 1960	Rice, coffee, vanilla, peanuts, cloves, cassava, sugar, tobacco; cattle; graphite, mica, uranium
MALAWI Area: 45,747 sq. mi. **Population:** 3,900,000	**People:** Mainly Negroes (Bantu); Europeans; Asians **Languages:** Bantu (Nyanja); English	**Schools:** 2,316 **Students:** 370,318 **Illiteracy:** 50% **Religions:** Tribal; Moslem; Christian	**Political Status:** Former British protectorate and self-governing colony; in Federation of Rhodesia and Nyasaland, 1953–63; became independent, 1964 **Capital:** Zomba **UN:** Admitted 1964	Tobacco, tea, tung oil, corn, peanuts, cotton, rice; goats, cattle, pigs; coal; fish
MALI Area: 464,873 sq. mi. **Population:** 4,305,000	**People:** Negroes; Hamites; Europeans (mostly French) **Languages:** French; Sudanic; Hamitic; Arabic	**Schools:** 859 **Students:** 127,296 **Illiteracy** 95–99% **Religions:** Moslem; animist; Christian	**Political Status:** French Sudan became republic, 1958; Mali Federation (Sudan, Senegal) formed, 1959; split, 1960; Sudan became Mali **Capital:** Bamako **UN:** Admitted 1960	Millet, rice, peanuts, cotton; cattle, sheep, goats; hides; gold, salt, iron ore; fish
MAURITANIA Area: 419,230 sq. mi. **Population:** 770,000	**People:** Mainly Moors; Negroes; non-Africans (French) **Languages:** Arabic; French	**Schools:** 276 **Students:** 20,037 **Illiteracy:** 95–99% **Religion:** Moslem	**Political Status:** Former territory in French West Africa, became republic, 1958; independent, 1960 **Capital:** Nouakchott **UN:** Admitted 1961	Millet, corn, dates, gum arabic; sheep, goats, cattle, camels; iron ore, copper; fish
MAURITIUS Area: 791 sq. mi.; island and dependencies **Population:** 780,000	**People:** Mainly Indo-Mauritians; French; English; Chinese **Languages:** French; English; Indo-Aryan	**Schools:** 736 **Students:** 176,806 **Illiteracy:** 48% **Religions:** Hindu; Roman Catholic	**Political Status:** Former British colony, became independent, 1968; includes Rodrigues and lesser dependencies **Capital:** Port Louis **UN:** Nonmember	Sugar, tea, tobacco, aloe fiber; rum; timber; fish
MELILLA Area: 4.6 sq. mi. **Population:** 79,056	**People:** Predominantly Spanish **Language:** Spanish	**Schools:** 106 **Students:** 9,221 **Illiteracy:** 36% **Religion:** Roman Catholic	**Political Status:** City is Spanish possession; administered from province of Málaga; enclave in Morocco; conquered by Spain, 1497 **UN:** Nonmember	Fish
MOROCCO Area: 171,305 sq. mi. **Population:** 13,451,000	**People:** Mainly Berbers; Arabs; Jews; Europeans **Languages:** Arabic; Berber; French; Spanish	**Schools:** 1,428 **Students:** 1,180,262 **Illiteracy:** 85% **Religions:** Moslem; Roman Catholic	**Political Status:** French and Spanish Moroccos, established 1912, Tangier international zone, 1923, united in independent monarchy, 1956 **Capital:** Rabat **UN:** Admitted 1956	Cereals, citrus fruits, cork, olives; wine; sheep, goats; phosphates, manganese, antimony; fish
MOZAMBIQUE (**Portuguese East Africa**) Area: 302,328 sq. mi. **Population:** 6,914,000	**People:** Mainly Bantu; Europeans; Asians **Languages:** Bantu; Portuguese	**Schools:** 3,023 **Students:** 431,625 **Illiteracy:** 97% **Religions:** Tribal; Roman Catholic; Moslem	**Political Status:** Portuguese colony, became overseas province, 1951; claimed by Vasco da Gama, 1498 **Capital:** Lourenço Marques **UN:** Nonmember	Sugar, cotton, copra, sisal, corn, cassava, fruits; cattle, goats; coal, berylniobium; lumber; fish
NIGER Area: 458,993 sq. mi. **Population:** 3,250,000	**People:** 75% Negroes (Hausa); Fulani; Tuareg; Europeans **Languages:** French; Sudanic; Tuareg	**Schools:** 493 **Students:** 52,895 **Illiteracy:** 95–99% **Religions:** Moslem; animist	**Political Status:** Former territory in French West Africa, became republic, 1958; independent, 1960 **Capital:** Niamey **UN:** Admitted 1960	Peanuts, millet, cotton, cassava, rice; goats, sheep, cattle; hides; tin, tungsten, salt

AFRICA FACT SUMMARY

NAME, AREA, AND POPULATION	PEOPLE AND LANGUAGE	EDUCATION AND RELIGION	GOVERNMENT	PRODUCTS
NIGERIA Area: 356,669 sq. mi. Population: 55,620,268	People: Mainly Negroes (Hausa); Fulani; Arabs Languages: Hausa; Ibo; Yoruba; Arabic; English	Schools: 17,086 Students: 3,140,875 Illiteracy: 85–90% Religions: Moslem; Christian; animist	Political Status: Former British colony; won independence, 1960; joined by Northern Cameroons, 1961; became republic, 1963 Capital: Lagos UN: Admitted 1960	Peanuts, cacao, palm oil and kernels, yams; goats; cattle, sheep; tin, niobium, petroleum; timber
PORTUGUESE GUINEA Area: 13,948 sq. mi.; includes Bissagos Islands Population: 524,000	People: Mainly Negroes; mulattoes; Europeans Languages: Sudanic; Portuguese	Schools: 230 Students: 22,002 Illiteracy: 99% Religions: Moslem; animist	Political Status: Portuguese colony, became overseas province, 1951 Capital: Bissau UN: Nonmember	Rice, palm oil and kernels, peanuts, rubber; cattle, pigs, goats, sheep; hides; beeswax
RÉUNION Area: 969 sq. mi. Population: 370,000	People: 97% Creole (mostly French); Negroes; Indians; Chinese; Malagasy; Kaffirs Language: French	Schools: 394 Students: 85,904 Illiteracy: 61% Religion: Roman Catholic	Political Status: French overseas department since 1946; under French since 1642; name changed from Bourbon, 1848 Capital: St. Denis UN: Nonmember	Rum; sugar, essential oils, vanilla, cassava
RHODESIA Area: 150,333 sq. mi. Population: 4,460,000	People: Mainly Negroes (Bantu); Europeans; Asians; coloreds Languages: Bantu; English	Schools: 3,531 Students: 3,140,875 Illiteracy: 75–80% Religions: Tribal; Christian	Political Status: British colony since 1923; in Federation of Rhodesia and Nyasaland,1953–63; unilaterally declared itself independent, 1965. Capital: Salisbury UN: Nonmember	Tobacco, corn, cotton; cattle, goats, sheep; asbestos, gold, chromite, coal, copper; teak
RWANDA Area: 10,169 sq. mi. Population: 3,200,000	People: Bahutu; Watusi Languages: Bantu; Hamitic; French	Schools: Statistics not available Students: 363,030 Illiteracy: 90–95% Religions: Tribal; Christian	Political Status: Former northern part of Ruanda-Urundi, UN trust territory administered by Belgium; became independent republic, 1962 Capital: Kigali UN: Admitted 1962	Coffee; cattle, sheep, goats; cassava; tungsten; bananas; pyrethrum
ST. HELENA (excluding dependencies) Area: 47 sq. mi. Population: 5,000	People: Europeans; Asians; Negroes Language: English	Schools: 15 Students: 1,100 Illiteracy: 1% Religion: Anglican	Political Status: British colony; administers dependencies—Ascension, Tristan da Cunha; settled by British, 1659 Capital: Jamestown UN: Nonmember	Flax; livestock; rope, twine; lace, embroidery
SÃO TOMÉ É PRÍNCIPE Area: 372 sq. mi. Population: 56,000	People: Mainly Negroes; mulattoes; Europeans Languages: Bantu; Portuguese	Schools: 32 Students: 5,626 Illiteracy: 80–85% Religions: Tribal; Roman Catholic	Political Status: Colony became overseas province of Portugal, 1951; discovered by Portuguese, 1470–71 Capital: São Tomé UN: Nonmember	Cacao, coffee, palm oil and kernels, coconuts, copra, cinchona; pigs, oxen, sheep, goats
SENEGAL Area: 76,124 sq. mi. Population: 3,280,000	People: Mainly Negroes (Wolof, Peul, Serer); Europeans Languages: Sudanic; French; Arabic	Schools: 479 Students: 235,958 Illiteracy: 95–99% Religions: Animist; Moslem; Christian	Political Status: Former territory in French West Africa, became republic, 1958; independent, 1960; in French Community (see Mali) Capital: Dakar UN: Admitted 1960	Peanuts, rice, cassava, palm oil; cattle, sheep, goats; phosphates, limestone, titanium

RELIGIONS OF AFRICA

(MILLIONS OF MEMBERS)
0 10 20 30 40 50 60 70 80 90

MOSLEM 38%

PRIMITIVE 32%

CHRISTIAN* 14%

HINDU less than 1%

JEWISH less than 1%

CONFUCIAN less than 1%

TAOIST less than 1%

OTHERS OR NONE 15%

*Roman Catholic 21,461,000
Protestant 6,795,262
Eastern Orthodox 5,868,089

LANGUAGES OF AFRICA

Language families and leading tongues

HAMITO-SEMITIC

HAUSA

AFRICAN NEGRO

SWAHILI

MALAYO-POLYNESIAN

INDO-EUROPEAN

HOTTENTOT-BUSHMAN

ZULU

KEY

Arabic
Berber
Cushitic
Ethiopic
Sudanic
Bantu
Malagasy
English and Afrikaans

Nations and Colonies of Africa—continued

TUNISIA
UNITED ARAB REPUBLIC (EGYPT)
SPANISH SAHARA
UPPER VOLTA
SIERRA LEONE
TOGO
SUDAN
UGANDA
SOMALI REPUBLIC
SEYCHELLES
ZAMBIA
TANZANIA

TRISTAN DA CUNHA

SOUTH-WEST AFRICA
SOUTH AFRICA
SWAZILAND

LOCATION OF NATIONS AND COLONIES LISTED ON THESE TWO PAGES

NAME, AREA, AND POPULATION	PEOPLE AND LANGUAGE	EDUCATION AND RELIGION	GOVERNMENT	PRODUCTS
SEYCHELLES Area: 156 sq. mi. Population: 46,000	**People:** Mainly Europeans; Negroes; Indians; Chinese **Languages:** English; French; Creole	**Schools:** 52 **Students:** 8,036 **Illiteracy:** 60–65% **Religion:** Roman Catholic	**Political Status:** British colony with dependencies; settled by British, 1794; several islands transferred to British Indian Ocean Territory, 1966 **Capital:** Victoria **UN:** Nonmember	Copra, cinnamon, vanilla, patchouli; cattle, pigs, goats, poultry; guano; turtles, fish
SIERRA LEONE Area: 27,925 sq. mi. Population: 2,180,355	**People:** Mainly Negroes; Asians; Europeans **Languages:** Sudanic; English; Krio	**Schools:** 964 **Students:** 137,481 **Illiteracy:** 90–95% **Religions:** Tribal; Moslem; Christian	**Political Status:** British colony, 1808, and protectorate, 1896, became republic in Commonwealth, 1961 **Capital:** Freetown **UN:** Admitted 1961	Palm oil and kernels, piassava, kola nuts, ginger; livestock; iron ore, diamonds, chromite
SOMALI REPUBLIC Area: 246,202 sq. mi. Population: 2,350,000	**People:** Mainly Somalis; Arabs; Indians; Italians **Languages:** Somali; Arabic; Italian	**Schools:** 278 **Students:** 33,040 **Illiteracy:** 90–95% **Religion:** Moslem	**Political Status:** Italian Somaliland (UN trust territory) and British Somaliland (protectorate) formed Somali Republic, 1960 **Capital:** Mogadishu **UN:** Admitted 1960	Livestock; hides, skins; bananas, corn, sugar, cotton; aromatic woods; tuna, shark
SOUTH AFRICA Area: 472,359 sq. mi. Population: 17,474,000	**People:** Negroes; Europeans; coloreds; Asians **Languages:** Afrikaans; English; Bantu	**Schools:** 13,498 **Students:** 3,059,664 **Illiteracy:** 55–60% **Religions:** Dutch Reformed; Anglican; animist	**Political Status:** Dominion became republic outside British Commonwealth, 1961 **Capitals:** Cape Town (legislative), Pretoria (administrative) **UN:** Admitted 1945	Corn, wheat, sugar, grapes and other fruits; sheep, cattle; wool; gold, diamonds, coal, copper, tin
SOUTH-WEST AFRICA Area: 318,099 sq. mi. Population: 554,000	**People:** Mainly Negroes (Bantu); coloreds; Europeans **Languages:** Bantu; Afrikaans; English; German	**Schools:** 189 **Students:** 58,612 **Illiteracy:** 75–80% **Religions:** Tribal; Christian	**Political Status:** Administered by South Africa under 1919 League of Nations mandate; German Southwest Africa, 1892–1915 **Capital:** Windhoek **UN:** Nonmember	Wheat; sheep, cattle, goats; diamonds, lead, manganese, tin, zinc; lobster; seal
SPANISH SAHARA Area: 102,703 sq. mi. Population: 23,793	**People:** Berbers; Arabs; Spaniards **Languages:** Berber; Arabic; Spanish; French	**Schools** (primary): 39 **Students** (primary): 1,719 **Illiteracy:** 95–99% **Religion:** Moslem	**Political Status:** Territory (comprising 2 regions—Río de Oro and Saguia el Hamra) in Spanish West Africa, became overseas province, 1958 **Capital:** El Aaiúm **UN:** Nonmember	Barley, corn, cacao; sheep, goats, camels; fish
SUDAN Area: 967,500 sq. mi. Population: 12,470,000	**People:** Mainly Arabs; Nilotic Negroes **Languages:** Arabic; Sudanic; English	**Schools:** 3,142 **Students:** 562,481 **Illiteracy:** 86.7% **Religions:** Moslem; tribal; Christian	**Political Status:** Former Anglo-Egyptian Sudan, became Republic of the Sudan, 1956; condominium of Britain and Egypt, 1899 **Capital:** Khartoum **UN:** Admitted 1956	Cotton, gum arabic, peanuts, sesame, sorghum; cattle, sheep, goats, camels; gold
SWAZILAND Area: 6,704 sq. mi. Population: 292,000	**People:** Mostly Bantu; Europeans **Languages:** Bantu (Swazi); English; Afrikaans	**Schools:** 381 **Students:** 50,999 **Illiteracy:** 80–85% **Religions:** Tribal; Protestant	**Political Status:** Protectorate; under British since 1907. **Capital:** Mbabane **UN:** Nonmember	Cotton, rice, fruits, tobacco, corn, peanuts; cattle, goats, sheep; asbestos, tin; timber
TANZANIA Area: 362,820 sq. mi. Population: 10,514,000	**People:** Mainly Bantu; Europeans **Languages:** Swahili; Bantu; Arabic; English	**Schools:** 3,256 **Students:** 724,576 **Illiteracy:** 90–95% **Religions:** Animist; Moslem; Christian; Hindu	**Political Status:** Tanganyika (independent, 1961) and Zanzibar (independent, 1963), both formerly British-controlled; merged in 1964 **Capital:** Dar es Salaam **UN:** Admitted 1964*	Sisal, coffee, cotton, cloves, copra, sugar; fish, cattle, sheep; hides, diamonds, gold, lead; timber; jewelry
TOGO Area: 22,008 sq. mi. Population: 1,620,000	**People:** North—Sudanese; south—Negroes (Ewe); Europeans **Languages:** Sudanic; Ewe; French	**Schools:** 933 **Students:** 162,056 **Illiteracy:** 90–95% **Religions:** Tribal; Moslem; Roman Catholic	**Political Status:** Former French Togoland, UN trust territory since 1946, became republic, 1958; independent, 1960 **Capital:** Lomé **UN:** Admitted 1960	Coffee, cacao, cotton, palm oil, cassava, peanuts; cattle, sheep, goats; phosphates; fish

*Tanganyika admitted 1961, Zanzibar admitted 1963; one seat after countries merged.

AFRICA FACT SUMMARY

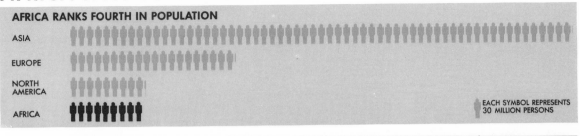

ASIA

EUROPE

NORTH AMERICA

AFRICA

EACH SYMBOL REPRESENTS 30 MILLION PERSONS

NAME, AREA, AND POPULATION	PEOPLE AND LANGUAGE	EDUCATION AND RELIGION	GOVERNMENT	PRODUCTS
TRISTAN DA CUNHA **Area:** 81 sq. mi. **Population:** 257	**People:** Europeans **Language:** English	**School:** 1 **Students:** 60 **Religion:** Anglican	**Political Status:** British possession (Tristan de Cunha, Inaccessible, Nightingale, and Gough islands); dependency of St. Helena colony since 1938 **UN:** Nonmember	Potatoes, fruits; cattle, sheep, poultry; crayfish
TUNISIA **Area:** 48,332 sq. mi. **Population:** 4,565,000	**People:** Mainly Arabs and Berbers; 7% Europeans (French, Italian) **Languages:** Arabic; Berber; French	**Schools:** 1,980 **Students:** 729,172 **Illiteracy:** 40% **Religions:** Moslem; Roman Catholic	**Political Status:** Became French protectorate in 1881; independent monarchy, 1956; republic, 1957 **Capital:** Tunis **UN:** Admitted 1956	Wheat, barley, olives, dates, esparto, cork; wine; sheep, goats; phosphates, iron ore; fish
UGANDA **Area:** 93,981 sq. mi. **Population:** 7,551,000	**People:** 99% Negroes (Bantu); Indians; whites **Languages:** English; Luganda	**Schools:** 3,101 **Students:** 524,629 **Illiteracy:** 70-75% **Religions:** Tribal; Christian	**Political Status:** Former British protectorate in British East Africa, became independent, 1962 **Capital:** Kampala **UN:** Admitted 1962	Coffee, cotton, tea, sugar; cattle; copper, tin, tungsten; hydroelectric power; timber; fish
UNITED ARAB REPUBLIC (Egypt) **Area:** 386,101 sq. mi. **Population:** 30,083,419	**People:** Mainly Hamitic Arabs **Languages:** Arabic; English; French	**Schools:** 9,743 **Students:** 4,086,840 **Illiteracy:** 75-80% **Religions:** Moslem; Coptic Christian	**Political Status:** Egypt became kingdom, 1922; republic, 1953 **Capital:** Cairo **UN:** Admitted 1945 (as Egypt)	Cotton, wheat, corn, sugar, rice, fruits; cattle, buffalo, sheep; phosphates, petroleum; fish
UPPER VOLTA **Area:** 105,839 sq. mi. **Population:** 4,500,000	**People:** Mainly Negroes (Mossi); non-Africans **Languages:** Sudanic; French	**Schools:** 564 **Students:** 86,414 **Illiteracy:** 95-99% **Religions:** Animist; Moslem; Christian	**Political Status:** Former territory in French West Africa, became republic, 1958; independent, 1960 **Capital:** Ouagadougou **UN:** Admitted 1960	Sorghum, millet, corn, shea nuts and butter, cotton, peanuts; livestock; gold, manganese, bauxite; fish
ZAMBIA **Area:** 288,130 sq. mi. **Population:** 3,494,380	**People:** Mainly Negroes (Bantu); Europeans; Asians; coloreds **Languages:** Bantu; English	**Schools:** 1,984 **Students:** 420,882 **Illiteracy:** 60% **Religions:** Tribal; Christian	**Political Status:** Former British protectorate; in Federation of Rhodesia and Nyasaland, 1953-63; became independent, 1964 **Capital:** Lusaka **UN:** Admitted 1964	Corn, tobacco; cattle; hides; copper, cobalt, zinc, lead; hydroelectric power; timber; fish

AFRICA IS RICH IN RESOURCES African production as percent of world total

PRODUCT	AFRICA	REST OF WORLD	LEADING AFRICAN PRODUCERS
TIN	13%	87%	Nigeria, Dem. Rep. of the Congo, South Africa
ASBESTOS	19%	81%	South Africa, Rhodesia, Swaziland
URANIUM*	20%	80%	South Africa, Dem. Rep. of the Congo, Malagasy Rep.
COPPER	25%	75%	Zambia, Dem. Rep. of the Congo, South Africa
MANGANESE	27%	73%	South Africa, Gabon, Ghana
ANTIMONY	35%	65%	South Africa, Morocco, Rhodesia
GOLD	48%	52%	South Africa, Ghana, Rhodesia
CHROMITE	54%	46%	South Africa, Rhodesia, Sudan
PALM OIL	55%	45%	Nigeria, Dem. Rep. of the Congo
SISAL	65%	35%	Tanzania, Angola, Kenya
NIOBIUM AND TANTALUM	75%	25%	Nigeria, Dem. Rep. of the Congo, Mozambique
COBALT	76%	24%	Dem. Rep. of the Congo, Zambia, Morocco
CACAO	78%	22%	Ghana, Nigeria, Ivory Coast
INDUSTRIAL DIAMONDS	98%	2%	Dem. Rep. of the Congo, Rep. of Congo, South Africa

*Free-world estimate

AFRICA FACT SUMMARY

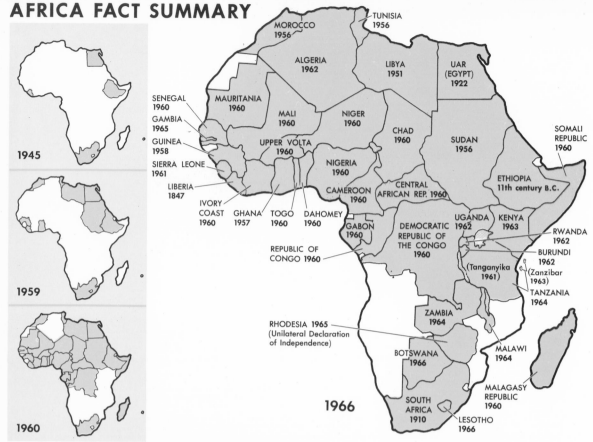

AFRICA'S MARCH TO INDEPENDENCE — Independent Nations Are Shaded

SIGNIFICANT DATES IN AFRICA'S HISTORY

About 3100 B.C.—Upper and lower kingdoms of Egypt unite under Menes, first Egyptian pharaoh.

814 B.C.—Phoenicians found Carthage.

730 B.C.(?)—Ethiopians conquer Egypt; ousted by Assyrians, 671 B.C.

630 B.C.—Greeks found Cyrenaica (Libya).

525 B.C.—Persia conquers Egypt.

332 B.C.—Alexander the Great conquers Egypt.

146 B.C.—Carthage destroyed by Romans.

51 B.C.—Cleopatra becomes queen of Egypt.

A.D. 639—Arabs invade Egypt; begin colonization of Africa's east coast, 700's.

1000's—Founding of Timbuktu in West Africa.

1109—Crusaders take Tripoli after 5-year siege.

1307–32—Height of Mali (Mandingo) Empire in West Africa; Songhoy (Gao) Empire, 1493–1528.

1400's—Emergence of Monomotapa-Zimbabwe Empire in Zambezi Basin.

1418—Prince Henry the Navigator begins explorations of African coast.

1488—Bartholomew Diaz rounds Cape of Good Hope.

1491—Portuguese settle in Angola.

1500's—Turks win much of North Africa.

1626—French settle in Senegal.

1652—Dutch settle Cape Town.

1798–99—Napoleon campaigns in Egypt.

1807—Britain abolishes slave trade; slavery, 1833.

1822—Liberia founded by the American Colonization Society as home for free Negroes.

1847—Liberia becomes first free modern African nation.

1869—Suez Canal formally opened. Diamond fields discovered at Kimberley, South Africa.

1880's–90's—European powers partition much of Africa.

1899–1902—Dutch defeat in Boer War makes Transvaal and Orange Free State British colonies.

1910—Union of South Africa founded.

1911–12—Italy takes Libya.

1919—German colonies become League of Nations mandates.

1936—Italy conquers Ethiopia; driven out, 1941.

1940—North Africa becomes battleground in World War II; Axis surrenders, 1943.

1952—Eritrea joins federation with Ethiopia.

1953—Federation of Rhodesia and Nyasaland formed.

1956—Egypt seizes Suez Canal.

1958—Egypt and Syria form United Arab Republic (UAR).

1960—Civil war and United Nations intervention in Republic of the Congo.

1961—South Africa withdraws from British Commonwealth of Nations. Syria revolts against Egypt, withdraws from UAR.

1962—Algeria wins independence after 8-year revolt. Ruanda-Urundi becomes two nations—Rwanda and Burundi.

1963—Organization of African Unity (OAU) founded. Federation of Rhodesia and Nyasaland dissolved.

1964—Tanganyika and Zanzibar merge to form the United Republic of Tanzania.

1965—Rhodesia breaks away from British rule.

AFRICA*

Abécher, Chad	13,000	E 3
Abeokuta, Nigeria	84,451	C 4
Abercorn, Zambia	1,120	F 5
Abidjan (cap.), Ivory Cst.	†212,000	B 4
Abu Hamed, Sudan		F 3
Accra (cap.), Ghana	337,828	B 4
Addis Ababa (cap.), Eth.	504,900	F 4
Aden (gulf)		G 3
Adrar, Algeria	2,107	B 2
Adwa, Eth.	6,000	F 3
Afars and Issas, Terr. of the	67,300	G 3
Agadem, Niger		D 3
Agadès, Niger	6,600	C 3
Agadir, Mor.	16,722	A 1
Agulhas (cape), S. Africa		D 8
Ahaggar (mts.), Algeria		C 2
Aïn-Salah, Algeria	5,374	C 2
Air (plateau), Niger		C 3
Albert (lake)		E 4
Aldabra (isls.), Br. Ind. Ocean Terr.	100	G 6
Alexandria, Egypt	1,516,234	E 1
Algeria	10,453,000	C 1
Algiers (cap.), Algeria	†883,879	C 1
Alula, Somali Rep.	2,000	G 3
Amber (cape), Malag. Rep.		G 6
Ambriz, Angola	2,196	D 5
Ambrizete, Angola	1,147	D 5
Angola	5,119,000	D 6
Anjouan (isl.), Com. Is.	52,646	G 6
Ankober, Eth.	3,000	F 4
Annaba, Algeria	†164,844	C 1
Annobón (isl.), Eq. Guin.	1,415	C 5
António Enes, Moz.	21,219	F 6
Antsirabe, Malag. Rep.	18,683	G 6
Araouane, Mali		B 3
Arusha, Tanzania	10,038	F 5
Ascension (isl.), St. Helena	382	A 5
Ashanti (reg.), Ghana	1,109,133	B 4
Asmara, Eth.	143,000	F 3
Aswan, Egypt	25,397	F 2
Aswan (dam), Egypt		F 2
Asyut, Egypt	121,000	F 2
Atbara, Sudan	36,298	F 3
Atlantic (ocean)		B 5
Atlas (mts.)		B 1
Aujila, Libya	1,502	E 2
Azbine (Air) (plateau), Niger		C 3
Bab el Mandeb (str.)		G 3
Babanusa, Sudan		E 3
Bagamoyo, Tanzania	5,000	F 5
Baidoa, Somali Rep.	10,000	G 4
Bakel, Sen.	2,400	A 3
Bamako, (cap.), Mali	88,500	B 3
Bandiagara, Mali	4,500	B 3
Bandundu, Dem. Rep. of the Congo		D 5
Bangui (cap.), C. Af. Rep.	111,266	D 4
Bangweulu (lake), Zambia		F 6
Bardera, Somali Rep.	3,500	G 4
Baro, Nigeria		C 4
Basoko, Dem. Rep. of the Congo		E 4
Bata, Equat. Guinea	27,024	D 4
Bathurst (cap.), Gambia	28,896	A 3
Bauchi, Nigeria	10,000	D 3
Béchar, Algeria	19,227	B 1
Beira, Moz.	†59,329	F 6
Belet Uen, Somali Rep.	9,400	G 4
Bender Beila, Somali Rep.	250	G 4
Benghazi (cap.), Libya	137,295	D 1
Benguela, Angola	14,690	D 6
Beni Suef, Egypt	78,800	F 2
Benin City, Nigeria	53,753	C 4
Benue (river)		C 4
Berber, Sudan	10,977	F 3
Berbera, Somali Rep.	20,000	G 3
Bethlehem, S. Africa	24,125	E 7
Bilma, Niger	1,300	D 3
Bingerville, Ivory Cst.	2,500	B 4
Biskra, Algeria	55,073	C 1
Bissagos (isls.), Port. Guin.	9,763	A 3
Bissau (cap.), Port. Guin.	†57,917	A 3
Bizerte, Tunisia	45,800	C 1
Black Volta (river), Upp. Volta		B 4
Blanc (cape)		A 2
Blantyre Malawi	†62,300	F 6
Bloemfontein (cap.), O.F.S., S. Africa	†145,273	E 7
Blue Nile (river)		F 3
Boa Vista (isl.), C. Verde Is.	2,779	G 8
Bobo-Dioulasso, Upper Volta	56,100	B 3
Bojador (cape), Sp. Sah.		A 2
Boma, Dem. Rep. of the Congo	33,143	D 5
Bon (cape), Tunisia		D 1
Bondo, Dem. Rep. of the Congo		E 4
Booué, Gabon	900	D 4
Bosaso, Somali Rep.		G 3
Botswana	576,000	E 7
Bouaké, Ivory Cst.	45,340	B 4
Brak, Libya		D 2
Brava (isl.), C. Verde Is.	8,528	G 9
Brava, Somali Rep.	6,100	G 4
Brazzaville (cap.), Congo, Rep. of	135,638	D 5
British Indian Oc. Terr.	1,131	G 5
Broken Hill, Zambia	43,160	E 6
Buchanan, Liberia	2,000	A 4
Buea, Cam.	3,000	C 4
Bujumbura (cap.), Burundi	†47,036	F 5
Bukama, Dem. Rep. of the Congo		E 5
Bukavu, Dem. Rep. of the Congo	60,575	E 5
Bulawayo, Rhodesia	153,470	E 7
Buram, Sudan		E 3
Burao, Somali Rep.	12,000	G 4
Burundi	2,780,000	F 5
Buta, Dem. Rep. of the Congo	10,845	E 4
Cabinda, Angola	46,238	D 5
Cairo (cap.), U.A.R.	3,348,779	E 2
Calvinia, S. Africa	5,202	D 8
Cameroon	5,300,000	D 4
Cameroon (mt.), Cam.		D 4
Canary (isls.), Spain	944,448	A 2
Cape Coast, Ghana	41,230	B 4
Cape of Good Hope (prov.), S. Af.	‡3,936,226	E 8
Cape Town (cap.), S. Af.	†807,211	D 8
Cape Verde (isls.)	218,000	G 8
Carmona, Angola		D 5
Carnot, C. Af. Rep.	4,000	D 4
Casablanca, Mor.	1,037,303	B 1
Cazombo, Angola	2,212	E 6
Central African Rep.	1,320,000	D 4
Ceuta, Spain	73,182	B 1
Chad	2,797,521	D 3
Chad (lake)		D 3
Chinde, Moz.	1,450	F 6
Chinguetti, Maur.	600	A 3
Comoro Islands	183,133	G 6
Conakry (cap.), Guinea	78,000	A 4
Congo (river)		D 4
Congo, Dem. Rep. of the	15,007,000	E 5
Congo, Rep. of	1,009,700	D 5
Constantine, Algeria	†223,259	C 1
Cotonou, Dahomey	109,328	C 4
Cradock, S. Africa	19,561	E 8
Cubango (river), Angola		D 6
Cyrenaica (reg.), Libya		D 1
Cyrene (Shahat), Libya		E 1
Dabou, Ivory Cst.	4,500	B 4
Dahomey	2,300,000	C 4
Dakar (cap.), Sen.	298,280	A 3
Damietta, Egypt	77,200	F 1
Dar es Salaam (cap.), Tanzania	128,742	F 5
De Aar, S. Africa	14,510	E 8
Debra Markos, Eth.	10,000	F 3
Debra Tabor, Eth.	9,000	F 3
Deim Zubeir, Sudan		E 4
Delgado (cape), Moz.		G 6
Derna, Libya	15,218	E 1
Desertas (isls.), Madeira		A 1
Diégo-Suarez, Malag. Rep.	28,772	G 6
Dikwa, Nigeria		D 3
Diourbel, Sen.	28,560	A 3
Dire Dawa, Eth.	40,000	G 4
Djado, Niger		D 2
Djado (plateau), Niger		D 2
Djanet, Algeria	509	C 2
Djenné, Mali	8,042	B 3
Djibouti (cap.), Terr. of the Afars and Issas	31,300	G 3
Dodoma, Tanzania	13,445	F 5
Dongola, Sudan	3,350	F 3
Dori, Upper Volta	3,500	B 3
Douala, Cam.	119,076	D 4
Durban, S. Africa	†681,492	F 7
East London, S. Af.	†116,056	E 8
Ebolowa, Cam.		D 4
Ed Da'ein, Sudan		E 3
Ed Damer, Sudan	5,458	F 3
Ed Dueim, Sudan	12,319	F 3
Edward (lake)		E 5
Egypt (U.A.R.)	30,083,419	E 2
Eil, Somali Rep.	350	G 4
El Aaiúm (cap.), Sp. Sah.	†5,251	A 2
El Djouf (desert), Mali		B 2
El Faiyûm, Egypt	100,100	E 2
El Fasher, Sudan	26,161	E 3
El Gatrun, Libya		D 2
El Goléa, Algeria	11,527	C 1
El Jadida, Mor.	41,812	B 1
El Jauf, Libya	2,500	E 2
El Kharga, Egypt	6,686	E 2
El Minya, Egypt	93,300	E 2
El Obeid, Sudan	52,372	E 3
El Quseir, Egypt	5,388	F 2
Elgon (mt.)		F 4
Emi Koussi (mt.), Chad		D 3
Entebbe, Uganda	7,942	F 5
Enugu, Nigeria	62,764	C 4
Equatorial Guinea	245,989	C 4
Er Roseires, Sudan		F 3
Eritrea (prov.), Eth.	1,422,300	F 3
Espargos, C. Verde Is.		G 8
Essaouira, Mor.	29,309	A 1
Ethiopia	22,200,000	F 4
Etosha Pan (salt dep.), S.-W. Af.		D 6
Europa (isl.), France		G 7
Famaka, Sudan		F 3
Farafangana, Malag. Rep.	8,871	G 7
Fernando Po (terr.), Equat. Guinea	62,612	C 4
Fez, Mor.	224,865	B 1
Fezzan (reg.), Libya		D 2
Fianarantsoa, Malag. Rep.	36,189	G 7
Fifth Cataract (falls), Sudan		F 3
Figuig, Mor.	12,108	B 1
Fogo (isl.), C. Verde Is.	23,022	G 9
Fort-Archambault, Chad	20,412	D 4
Fort-Crampel, C. Afr. Rep.	5,000	D 4
Fort-Dauphin, Malag. Rep.	11,190	G 7
Fort-Flatters, Algeria	362	C 2
Fort Hall, Kenya	5,389	F 5
Kort Jameson, Zambia	3,710	F 6
Fort Johnston, Malawi	670	F 6
Fort-Lamy (cap.), Chad	88,142	D 3
Fort Rosebery, Zambia	1,270	E 6
Fort Victoria, Rhod.	5,410	F 7
Fourth Cataract (falls), Sudan		F 3
Franceville, Gabon	2,790	D 5
Freetown (cap.), S. Leone	127,917	A 4
Fria (cape), S.-W. Af.		D 6
Fuerteventura (isl.), Canary Is.	18,138	A 2
Funchal (cap.), Madeira	43,301	A 1
Gaberones (cap.), Botswana	3,849	E 7
Gabès, Tunisia	24,420	D 1
Gabon	468,000	D 5
Gambela, Eth.	600	F 4
Gambia	330,000	A 3
Gamboma, Congo, Rep. of	1,700	D 5
Gao, Mali	12,839	C 3
Gardula, Eth.	4,000	F 4
Garoua, Cam.	7,000	D 4
Germiston, S. Africa	†214,393	E 7
Ghadames, Libya	2,272	D 1
Ghana	7,945,000	B 4
Ghardaia, Algeria	15,076	C 1
Gharian, Libya	†43,747	D 1
Ghat, Libya	1,503	D 2
Gibeon, S.-W. Af.	541	D 7
Gibraltar (str.)		B 1
Gobabis, S.-W. Af.	2,054	D 7
Gondar, Eth.	13,000	F 3
Good Hope (cape), S. Af.		D 8
Goundam, Mali	6,842	B 3
Graaff-Reinet, S. Africa	16,936	E 8
Grahamstown, S. Africa	32,611	E 8
Grand Canary (isl.), Canary Is.	400,837	A 2
Grand Comoro (isl.), Comoro Is.	66,265	G 6
Great Eastern Erg (desert)		C 2
Great Western Erg (desert)		B 2
Greenville, Liberia		A 4
Grootfontein, S.-W. Af.	1,550	D 6
Guardafui (cape), Somali Rep.		H 3
Guinea	3,357,000	A 3
Guinea (gulf)		C 4
Gwelo, Rhodesia	24,100	E 6
Hafun, Ras (cape), Somali Rep.		H 3
Haiya Junction, Sudan		F 3
Harar, Eth.	40,000	G 4
Harghessa, Somali Rep.	30,000	G 4
Hell-Ville, Malag. Rep.	8,572	G 6
Henrique de Carvalho, Angola		E 5
Homs, Libya	†12,918	D 1
Hon, Libya	†3,681	D 2
Hopetown, S. Africa	2,631	E 7
Ibadan, Nigeria	459,196	C 4
Iférouane, Niger	2,000	C 3
Ifni (prov.), Spain	49,889	A 2
Iguidi Erg (desert)		B 2
Ilorin, Nigeria	40,994	C 4
Impfondo, Congo, Rep. of	2,000	D 4
Indian (ocean)		F 7
Inhambane, Moz.	†21,992	F 7
Inongo, Dem. Rep. of the Congo		D 5
Irumu, Dem. Rep. of the Congo		E 4
Itala, Somali Rep.	500	G 4
Ivory Coast	3,665,000	B 4
Jarabub, Libya	196	E 1
Jebel 'Uweinat (mt.)		E 2
Jimma, Eth.	8,000	F 4
Jinja, Uganda	8,410	F 4
Johannesburg, S. Africa	†1,152,525	E 7
Jos, Nigeria	38,527	C 4
Juba, Sudan	10,660	F 4
Kabalo, Dem. Rep. of the Congo		E 5
Kabinda, Dem. Rep. of the Congo		E 5
Kaduna, Nigeria	38,794	C 3
Kalahari (desert)		E 7
Kalemie, Dem. Rep. of the Congo	29,934	E 5
Kambove, Dem. Rep. of the Congo	9,195	E 6
Kampala (cap.), Uganda	22,094	F 4
Kankan, Guinea	25,000	B 4
Kano, Nigeria	130,173	C 3
Kaolack, Sen.	69,560	A 3
Kapanga, Dem. Rep. of the Congo		E 5
Kariba (lake)		E 6
Karonga, Malawi		F 5
Kasai (river)		E 5
Kasama, Zambia	1,800	F 5
Kasanga, Tanzania		F 5
Kasempa, Zambia	1,200	E 6
Kasongo, Dem. Rep. of the Congo		E 5
Kassala ,Sudan	40,612	F 3
Katanga (reg.), Dem. Rep. of the Congo	1,743,733	E 5
Katsina, Nigeria	52,672	C 3
Kaura Namoda, Nigeria		C 3
Kayes, Mali	24,218	A 3
Keetmanshoop, S.-W. Af.	5,191	D 7
Kénitra (Port-Lyautey), Mor.	88,533	B 1
Kenya	9,643,000	F 4
Kenya (mt.), Kenya		F 5
Khartoum (cap.), Sudan	132,000	F 3
Khartoum North, Sudan	39,082	F 3
Kidal, Mali	800	C 3
Kigali (cap.), Rwanda	14,000	F 5
Kilimanjaro (mt.), Tanz.		F 5
Kilindini, Kenya		G 5
Kilwa Kivinje, Tanz.	3,500	F 5
Kimberley, S. Africa	75,376	E 7
Kindu-Port Empain, Dem. Rep. of the Congo	19,385	E 5
King William's Town, S. Africa	14,678	E 8
Kinshasa (cap.), Dem. Rep. of the Congo	402,492	D 5
Kioga (lake), Uganda		F 4
Kisangani, Dem. Rep. of the Congo	126,533	E 4
Kismayu, Somali Rep.	10,386	G 5
Kisumu, Kenya	23,200	F 5
Kita, Mali	5,230	B 3
Kivu (lake)		E 5
Kodok, Sudan		F 4
Koforidua, Ghana	34,856	C 4
Kong, Ivory Cst.	4,073	B 4
Kongolo, Dem. Rep. of the Congo	10,434	E 5
Kosti, Sudan	22,688	F 3
Koulikoro, Mali	6,144	B 3
Kouroussa, Guinea	5,500	A 3
Kufra (oasis), Libya		E 2
Kumasi, Ghana	180,642	B 4
La Palma (isl.), Can. Is.	67,141	A 2
Ladysmith, S. Africa	22,955	F 7
Laghouat, Algeria	20,594	C 1
Lagos (cap.), Nigeria	410,000	C 4
Lai, Chad	5,021	D 4
Lamu, Kenya	5,828	G 5
Las Palmas (cap.), Can. Is.	166,236	A 2
Lastoursville, Gabon	2,000	D 5
Lealui, Zambia		E 6
Léopoldville (Kinshasa) (cap.), Dem. Rep. of the Congo	402,492	D 5
Lesotho	745,000	E 7
Libenge, Dem. Rep. of the Congo		D 4
Liberia	1,310,000	B 4
Libreville (cap.), Gabon	†31,027	C 4
Libya	1,682,000	D 2
Libyan (desert)		E 2
Likasi, Dem. Rep. of the Congo	80,075	E 6

*All population figures are taken from the latest official census or estimate available. For date and source of a population figure, *see* article on the appropriate country. †Including suburbs. ‡Excluding Walvis Bay.

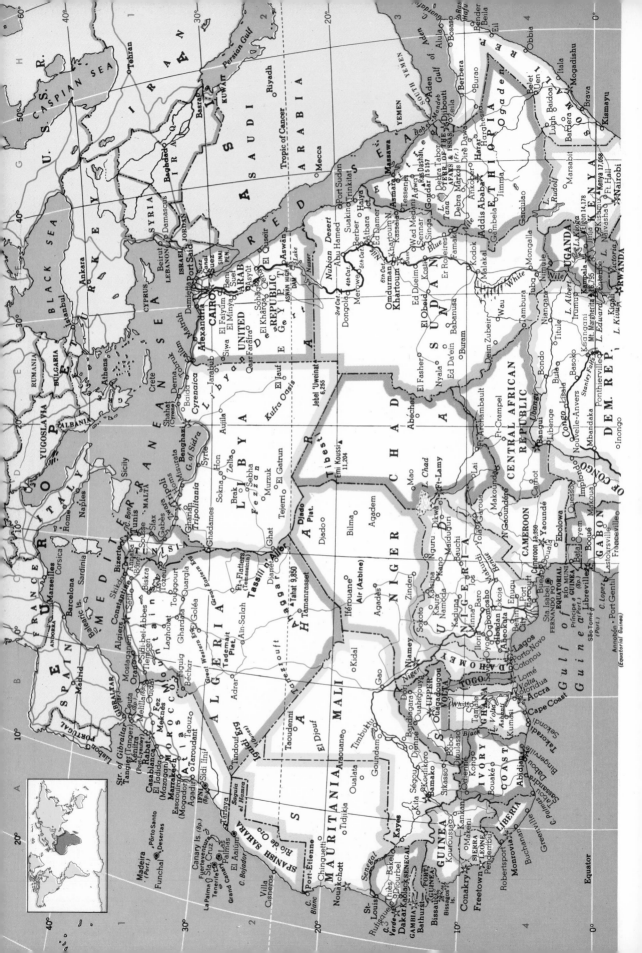

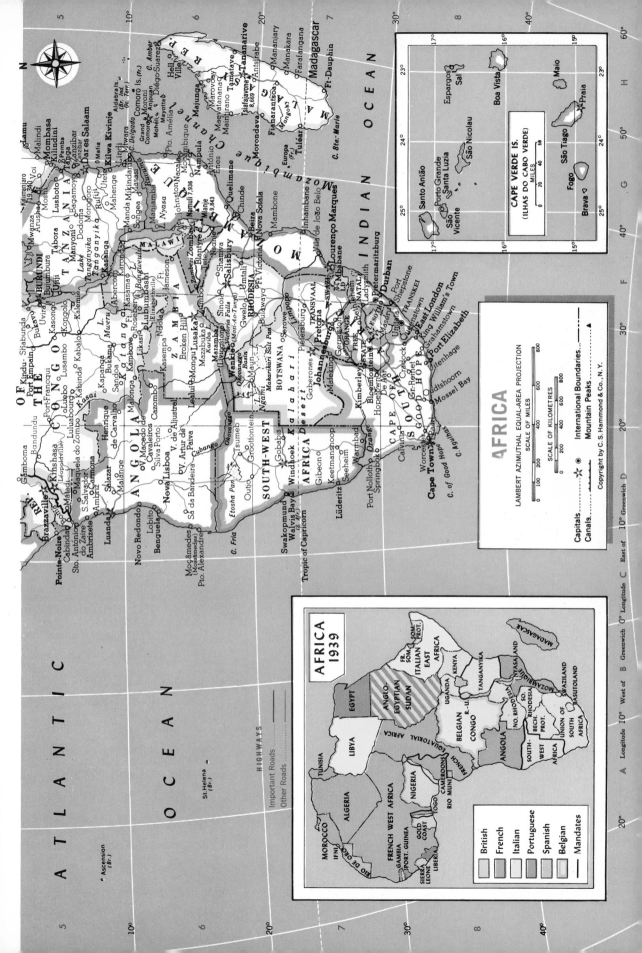

AFRICA*—*Continued*

Limpopo (river)		E 6
Lindi, Tanzania	10,315	G 5
Lisala, Dem. Rep. of the Congo		E 4
Livingstone (Maramba), Zambia	33,400	E 6
Lobito, Angola	23,897	D 6
Lokoja, Nigeria		C 4
Lomé (cap.), Togo	80,000	C 4
Lopez (cape), Gabon		C 5
Lourenço Marques (cap.), Moz.	†183,798	F 7
Luanda (cap.), Angola	224,540	D 5
Lubumbashi, Dem. Rep. of the Congo	183,711	E 6
Lüderitz, S.-W. Af.	3,604	D 7
Luebo, Dem. Rep. of the Congo		E 5
Lugh, Somali Rep.	5,000	G 4
Luluabourg, Dem. Rep. of the Congo	115,049	E 5
Lusaka (cap.), Zambia	110,600	E 6
Lusambo, Dem. Rep. of the Congo	9,395	E 5
Lushoto, Tanzania		F 5
Madagascar (isl.), Malag. Rep.	5,070,806	G 7
Madeira (isl.), Port.	265,432	A 1
Maevatanana, Malag. Rep.	2,775	G 6
Mafeking, S. Africa	8,362	E 7
Mafia (isl.), Tanzania		G 5
Mahenge, Tanzania		F 5
Maiduguri, Nigeria	54,646	D 3
Maintirano, Malag. Rep.	2,742	G 6
Maio (isl.), C. Verde Is.	2,237	H 9
Majunga, Malag. Rep.	34,119	G 6
Makarikari (salt dep.), Botswana		E 7
Makeni, S. Leone	12,304	A 4
Makoua, Congo, Rep. of	2,000	D 4
Makounda, C. Af. Rep.		D 4
Makurdi, Nigeria		C 4
Malagasy Rep.	6,615,000	G 7
Malakal, Sudan	9,680	F 4
Malange, Angola	9,473	D 5
Malawi	3,900,000	F 6
Mali	4,305,000	B 3
Malindi, Kenya	5,818	G 5
Malonga, Dem. Rep. of the Congo		E 6
Mambone, Moz.		F 7
Manakara, Malag. Rep.	11,507	G 7
Mananjary, Malag. Rep.	15,579	G 7
Manda, Tanzania		F 6
Mangoky (river), Malag. Rep.		G 7
Maniamba, Moz.	9,579	F 6
Manyoni, Tanzania		F 5
Mao, Chad	4,015	D 3
Maquela do Zombo, Angola	1,103	D 5
Maramba (Livingstone), Zambia	33,400	E 6
Margherita (mt.)		E 4
Marovoay, Malag. Rep.	13,960	G 6
Marrakech, Mor.	253,141	B 1
Marsabit, Kenya		F 4
Masasi, Tanzania		F 6
Maseru (cap.), Lesotho	10,000	E 8
Massawa, Eth.	15,216	F 3
Matadi, Dem. Rep. of the Congo	60,295	D 5
Matruh, Egypt	3,047	E 1
Maun, Botswana		E 7
Mauritania	770,000	A 3
Mayotte (isl.), Comoro Is.	17,477	G 6
Mazabuka, Zambia	1,830	E 6
Mazagan (El Jadida), Mor.	41,812	B 1
Mbabane (cap.), Swaz.	8,390	F 7
Mbandaka, Dem. Rep. of the Congo	51,359	D 4
Mediterranean (sea)		D 1
Meknès, Mor.	186,837	B 1
Melilla, Spain	79,056	B 1
Merowe, Sudan	1,620	F 3
Mikindani, Tanzania	4,807	F 6
Minna, Nigeria		C 4
Misurata, Libya	†53,874	D 1
Mlanje (mt.), Moz.		F 6
Moçambique, Moz.	†12,493	G 6
Moçamedes, Angola	8,576	D 6
Mogadishu (cap.), Somali Rep.	120,649	G 4
Mogador (Essaouira), Mor.	29,309	A 1
Mohéli (isl.), Comoro Is.	5,256	G 6
Molepolole, Botswana	29,625	E 7
Mombasa, Kenya	178,400	G 5
Mongalla, Sudan		F 4
Mongu, Zambia	1,440	E 6
Monrovia (cap.), Liberia	41,391	A 4
Morocco	13,451,000	B 1
Morogoro, Tanzania	14,507	F 5
Morondava, Malag. Rep.	10,683	G 6
Moroni (cap.), Comoro Is.	6,545	G 6
Moshi, Tanzania	13,726	F 5
Mosi-Ao-Tunya (Victoria) (falls)		E 6
Mossâmedes (Moçamedes), Angola	8,576	D 6
Mossel Bay, S. Africa	12,225	E 8
Mostaganem, Algeria	64,786	B 1
Mozambique	6,914,000	F 6
Mozambique (channel)		G 6
Mtwara, Tanzania	10,459	G 5
Murzuk, Libya	2,832	D 2
Mwanza, Tanzania	19,877	F 5
Mweru (lake)		E 5
N'Gaoundéré, Cam.	9,000	D 4
Nacala, Moz.	61,420	F 6
Nairobi (cap.), Kenya	266,700	F 5
Naivasha, Kenya		F 5
Nampula, Moz.	†104,777	G 6
Namuli (mt.), Moz.		E 6
Nasser (lake)		F 2
Natal (prov.), S. Af.	2,979,920	F 7
Ndola, Zambia	87,420	E 6
Ngami (lake), Botswana		E 7
Nguru, Nigeria	23,084	D 3
Niamey (cap.), Niger	41,975	C 3
Niangara, Dem. Rep. of the Congo		E 4
Niger	3,250,000	C 3
Niger (river)		C 3
Nigeria	55,620,268	C 3
Nile (river)		F 2
Nimule, Sudan		F 4
Nouakchott (cap.), Maur.	6,095	A 3
Nouvelle-Anvers, Dem. Rep. of the Congo		D 4
Nova Lisboa, Angola	28,296	D 6
Nova Sofala, Moz.	13,711	F 7
Novo Redondo, Angola	1,016	D 6
Nsanje, Malawi	3,790	F 6
Nubian (desert), Sudan		F 2
Nyala, Sudan	12,278	E 3
Nyasa (lake)		F 6
Obbia, Somali Rep.	3,000	G 4
Odienné, Ivory Cst.	6,000	B 4
Ogaden (reg.), Eth.		G 4
Ogbomosho, Nigeria	139,535	C 4
Okovanggo (basin), Botswana		E 6
Okovanggo (river)		D 6
Omdurman, Sudan	162,000	F 3
Oran, Algeria	†392,637	B 1
Orange (river)		D 7
Orange Free State (prov.), S. Af.	1,386,547	E 7
Ouagadougou (cap.), Upper Volta	63,000	B 3
Ouahigouya, Upper Volta	11,837	B 3
Oualata, Maur.	1,285	B 3
Ouargla, Algeria	7,931	C 1
Oudtshoorn, S. Africa	22,229	E 8
Ouesso, Congo, Rep. of	2,800	D 4
Oujda, Mor.	130,544	B 1
Outjo, S.-W. Af.	1,412	D 6
Oyem, Gabon	3,050	D 4
Oyo, Nigeria	72,133	C 4
Paarl, S. Africa	41,540	D 8
Palmas (cape)		B 4
Pemba (isl.), Tanzania	133,858	G 5
Pendembu, S. Leone	2,696	A 4
Pietermaritzburg (cap.), Natal, S. Africa	†128,598	F 7
Pietersburg, S. Africa	28,071	E 7
Pointe-Noire, Congo, Rep. of	54,643	D 5
Ponthierville, Dem. Rep. of the Congo		E 5
Port Elizabeth, S. Africa	†290,693	E 8
Port-Étienne, Maur.	7,680	A 2
Port-Francqui Dem. Rep. of the Congo		E 5
Port-Gentil, Gabon	20,732	C 5
Port Harcourt, Nigeria	71,634	C 4
Port-Lyautey (Kénitra), Mor.	88,533	B 1
Port Nolloth, S. Africa	2,624	D 7
Port Said, Egypt	245,318	F 1
Port Shepstone, S. Africa	4,266	F 8
Port Sudan, Sudan	53,800	F 3
Pôrto Alexandre, Angola	2,894	D 6
Porto Amélia, Moz.	†21,027	G 6
Porto Grande, C. Verde Is.		G 8
Porto-Novo (cap.), Dahomey	69,500	C 4
Pôrto Santo (isl.), Madeira	3,505	A 1
Portuguese Guinea	524,000	A 3
Praia (cap.), C. Verde Is.	37,102	G 9
Pretoria (cap.), S. Af.	†422,590	E 7
Príncipe é São Tomé	56,000	C 4
Qasr Farâfra, Egypt		E 2
Qena, Egypt	56,100	F 2
Queenstown, S. Africa	33,182	E 8
Quelimane, Moz.	†64,183	F 6
Rabat (cap.), Mor.	238,453	B 1
Ras Dashan (mt.), Eth.		F 3
Ras Hafun (cape), Somali Rep.		G 3
Red (sea)		F 2
Rhodesia	4,460,000	E 6
Río de Oro (reg.), Sp. Sah.		A 2
Río Muni (terr.), Equat. Guinea	183,377	C 4
Robertsport, Liberia		A 4
Rudolf (lake)		F 4
Rufiji (river), Tanzania		F 5
Rufisque, Sen.	49,660	A 3
Ruvuma (river)		F 6
Rwanda	3,200,000	F 5
Sá da Bandeira, Angola	11,654	D 6
Saguia el Hamra (reg.), Sp. Sah.		A 2
Sahara (desert)		D 2
Saint Helena	5,000	B 6
Saint-Louis, Sen.	58,000	A 3
Sainte-Marie (cape), Malag. Rep.		G 7
Sal (isl.), C. Verde Is.	1,121	G 8
Salazar, Angola		D 5
Salisbury (cap.), Rhodesia	174,860	F 6
Salum, Egypt		E 1
Sandoa, Dem. Rep. of the Congo		E 5
Santa Cruz (cap.), Can. Is.	82,620	A 2
Santa Isabel (cap.), Equat. Guinea	37,237	C 4
Santa Luzia (isl.), C. Verde Is.		G 8
Santo Antão (isl.), C. Verde Is.		G 8
Santo Antônio do Zaire, Angola	528	D 5
São Nicolau (isl.), C. Verde Is.	14,846	G 8
São Salvador, Angola	2,965	D 5
São Tiago (isl.), C. Verde Is.		G 9
São Tomé é Príncipe	56,000	C 4
São Vicente (isl.), C. Verde Is.	15,848	F 8
Sassandra, Ivory Cst.	5,300	B 4
Savé, Dahomey	30,117	C 4
Sebha, Libya	7,193	D 2
Seeheim, S.-W. Af.		D 7
Ségou, Mali	20,200	B 3
Sekondi, Ghana	34,513	B 4
Senegal	3,280,000	A 3
Senegal (river)		A 3
Sennar, Sudan	8,093	F 3
Serowe, Botswana	34,182	E 7
Sétif, Algeria	82,340	C 1
Sfax, Tunisia	75,500	D 1
Shabunda, Dem. Rep. of the Congo		E 5
Shahat (Cyrene), Libya		E 1
Shamva, Rhodesia	750	F 6
Sidi-bel-Abbes, Algeria	†105,357	C 1
Sidi Ifni (cap.), Ifni	12,751	B 2
Sidra (gulf)		D 1
Sierra Leone	2,180,355	A 4
Sikasso, Mali	13,085	B 3
Silva Porto, Angola	8,840	D 6
Sinai (pen.), Egypt		F 2
Singa, Sudan	9,436	F 3
Sinoia, Rhodesia	7,830	E 6
Siwa, Egypt	878	E 2
Sixth Cataract (falls), Sudan		F 3
Skikda, Algeria	80,281	C 1
Sohâg, Egypt	59,300	F 2
Sokna, Libya	1,250	D 2
Sokoto, Nigeria	47,643	C 3
Somali Republic	2,350,000	G 4
Songea, Tanzania		F 6
Sousse, Tunisia	48,172	D 1
South Africa	‡17,474,000	E 8
South-West Africa	§554,000	D 7
Spanish Sahara (prov.), Spain	23,793	A 2
Springbok, S. Africa	3,116	D 7
Stanley (falls), Dem. Rep. of the Congo		E 4
Suakin, Sudan	4,228	F 3
Sudan	12,470,000	E 3
Sudan (reg.)		E 3
Suez, Egypt	203,610	F 1
Suez (canal), Egypt		F 1
Swakopmund, S.-W. Af.	2,965	D 7
Swaziland	292,000	F 7
Syrte, Libya	†27,062	D 1
Tabora, Tanzania	15,361	F 5
Tabou, Ivory Cst.	3,000	B 4
Tademait (plat.)		C 2
Tahat (mt,). Algeria		C 2
Takoradi, Ghana	40,937	B 4
Tamale, Ghana	40,443	B 4
Tamanrasset, Algeria	2,760	C 2
Tamatave, Malag. Rep.	39,627	G 6
Tambura, Sudan		E 4
Tana (lake), Eth.		F 3
Tananarive (cap.), Malag. Rep.	298,813	G 6
Tanezrouft (desert)		C 2
Tanga, Tanzania	38,053	G 5
Tanganyika (reg.), Tanzania	10,179,000	F 5
Tanganyika (lake)		F 5
Tangier (Tanger), Mor.	147,946	B 1
Tanzania	10,514,000	F 5
Taoudenni, Mali		B 2
Taouz, Mor.		B 1
Tarfaya, Mor.	1,521	A 2
Taroudannt, Mor.	17,141	B 1
Tassili n'Ajjer (mts.), Alg.		C 2
Tejerri, Libya	140	D 2
Temassinin (Fort-Flatters), Algeria	362	C 2
Tenerife (isl.), Can. Is.	387,767	A 2
Tessenei, Eth.	1,850	F 3
Tete, Moz.	2,761	F 6
Thiès, Sen.	69,140	A 3
Third Cataract (falls), Sudan		F 2
Tibesti (mts.), Chad		D 2
Tidjikja, Maur.	5,900	A 3
Timbuktu, Mali	8,735	B 3
Tindouf, Algeria	1,872	B 2
Titule, Dem. Rep. of the Congo		E 4
Tlemcen, Algeria	70,930	C 1
Tobruk, Libya	4,990	E 1
Togo	1,620,000	C 4
Touggourt, Algeria	18,353	C 1
Tozeur, Tunisia	12,464	C 1
Transkei (prov.), S. Af.	1,439,195	E 8
Transvaal (prov.), S. Af.	6,273,477	E 7
Trinkitat, Sudan		F 3
Tripoli (cap.), Libya	213,506	D 1
Tripolitania (reg.), Libya		D 1
Tsiafajavona (mt.), Malag. Rep.		G 6
Tsumeb, S.-W. Af.	931	D 6
Tuléar, Malag. Rep.	33,850	G 7
Tunis (cap.), Tunisia	480,500	D 1
Tunis, Tunisia	†632,100	D 1
Tunisia	4,565,000	C 1
Ubangi (river)		E 4
Uganda	7,551,000	F 4
Uitenhage, S. Africa	48,755	E 8
Ujiji, Tanzania	25,000	F 5
Umtali, Rhodesia	34,150	F 6
Umtata (cap.), Transkei, S. Africa	12.221	E 8
United Arab Rep.	30,083,419	E 2
Upper Volta	4,500,000	B 3
Utete, Tanzania		F 5
Uvira, Dem. Rep. of the Congo		E 5
'Uweinat, Jebel (mt.)		E 2
Vaal (river), S. Af.		E 7
Verde (cape), Sen.		A 3
Victoria (falls)		E 6
Victoria (lake)		F 5
Vila Artur de Paiva, Angola		D 6
Vila de Aljustrel, Angola		D 6
Vila de João Belo, Moz.	†48,891	F 7
Vila Macedo de Cavaleiros, Angola		D 6
Villa Cisneros, Sp. Sah.	1,961	A 2
Voi, Kenya		F 5
Volta (lake), Ghana		B 4
Volta (river), Ghana		C 4
Wad Medani, Sudan		F 3
Walvis Bay, S. Africa	12,648	D 7
Walvis Bay, Wal. Bay, S. Africa	12,234	D 7
Wankie, Rhodesia	16,590	E 6
Warmbad, S.-W. Af.	546	D 7
Wau, Sudan	8,009	E 4
White Nile (river)		F 4
White Volta (river)		B 4
Windhoek (cap.), S.-W. Af.	35,916	D 7
Worcester, S. Africa	32,274	D 8
Yaoundé (cap.), Cam.	53,833	D 4
Yola, Nigeria		D 4
Zambezi (river)		F 6
Zambia	3,494,380	E 6
Zanzibar, Tanz.	57,923	G 5
Zanzibar (isl.), Tanz.	165,253	G 5
Zeila, Somali Rep.	5,000	G 3
Zella, Libya	2,450	D 2
Zinder, Niger	16,271	C 3
Zomba (cap.), Malawi	†22,000	F 6
Zumbo,. Moz.		E 6
Zwara, Libya	10,816	D 1

*All population figures are taken from the latest official census or estimate available. For date and source of a population figure, *see* article on the appropriate country. †Including suburbs. ‡Excluding Walvis Bay. §Including Walvis Bay.

REFERENCE-OUTLINE FOR STUDY OF AFRICA

POLITICAL DIVISIONS OF AFRICA

I. **Independent nations** A-84, maps A-94-5, 92, lists A-85-91: Algeria A-273; Botswana B-280; Burundi B-385; Cameroon C-59; Central African Republic C-192b; Chad C-203; Democratic Republic of the Congo C-510; Republic of Congo C-512; Dahomey D-1a; Egypt (UAR) E-108; Ethiopia E-293; Gabon G-1; Gambia G-8; Ghana G-258; Guinea G-258; Ivory Coast I-345; Kenya K-44; Lesotho L-196b; Liberia L-204; Libya L-248; Malagasy Republic M-67, M-23; Malawi M-67a; Mali M-69; Mauritania M-177a; Mauritius M-177a; Morocco M-489; Niger N-285; Nigeria N-286; Rwanda R-366a; Senegal S-108a; Sierra Leone S-192a; Somali Republic S-256; South Africa S-263 (Cape of Good Hope C-130a, Natal N-16, Orange Free State O-474, Transvaal T-249); Sudan S-501; Swaziland S-522; Tanzania T-16, T-15, Z-353; Togo T-191; Tunisia T-289; Uganda U-1; Upper Volta U-211; Zambia Z-353

Note: For members of the Commonwealth of Nations, see Commonwealth of Nations table B-338

II. **British:** Rhodesia (declared itself independent) R-195; St. Helena A-89; Seychelles A-90; Swaziland S-522

III. **French:** Comoro Islands A-86; Territory of the Afars and Issas A-85; A-90; Réunion A-89

IV. **Portuguese:** Angola A-399; Cape Verde Islands C-130b; Madeira M-23; Mozambique M-538; Portuguese Guinea A-89; São Tomé é Príncipe A-89

V. **South Africa trusteeship:** South-West Africa A-90

VI. **Spanish:** Canary Islands C-122; Equatorial Guinea A-86; Ifni A-87; Spanish Sahara A-90

THE LAND AND THE PEOPLE

I. **Location and size** A-72, map A-87: location in world, map W-242-3; political divisions, map A-94-5; air distances, polar-projection map A-794

II. **Structure of the land** A-72-3, 75, list A-70, map A-75
   A. **Mountains and plateaus** A-73, map A-75: Atlas Mountains A-73, M-489, A-273, map A-274; Ethiopian plateau E-293; Sudan and Congo highlands S-501, C-510, C-512, picture A-80; Great Rift Valley A-73, U-1; East African highlands A-73, U-1, K-44 (Mount Kilimanjaro A-73, picture T-16); Ruwenzori R-366a; South African plateau S-263, O-474, map S-264 (Drakensberg A-73, N-16, Table Mountain C-130b, picture A-70)
   B. **Sahara** (including Libyan, Nubian, and Arabian deserts) S-14-16a, A-75, L-248, E-108, map E-109
   C. **Rivers** A-75, map A-75: Congo C-513; Niger N-287; Nile N-289; Zambezi Z-353 (Victoria Falls V-315, W-73a-b, color picture W-73c); Orange, Limpopo, and Senegal (Fact-Index)
   D. **Lakes** A-73, 75, U-1, map A-94-5: Chad A-73, 75; Tanganyika T-15; Victoria V-314; Nyasa (Fact-Index)

E. **Coastline and islands** A-72-3, map A-94-5: Atlantic Ocean A-669; Mediterranean Sea M-216; Red Sea R-120; Gulf of Aden A-32; Indian Ocean I-105; Canary Islands C-122; Cape of Good Hope C-130a, picture A-70; Cape Verde Islands C-130b; Madagascar M-23, M-67, map M-67; Madeira M-23; Mauritius M-177a; Zanzibar and Pemba Z-353. See names of smaller islands in Fact-Index

F. **How the land changed through the ages** G-62, E-117: former land bridge to Europe S-349; Great Rift Valley A-73; Sahara's Ice Age S-16, M-76

III. **The tropical and subtropical climates of Africa** A-72, 75: rainfall R-88, 89, map A-76
   A. **Mediterranean and subtropical regions in North Africa** A-75, A-273, E-110, L-248, M-489, T-289: hot *sirocco* and *khamsin* winds from the deserts W-183, S-15
   B. **The desert regions** A-75, 77, D-92a: Sahara S-14-16a; *harmattan* (northeast trade wind) W-183, S-15
   C. **The Sudan savanna** S-501, G-192
   D. **The Congo River basin and Niger River rain forest** A-75, C-394, C-510, C-512, C-513-14, N-288
   E. **Subtropical and temperate regions in east-central and southern Africa** A-75, 77: East African highlands U-1, K-44; Ethiopia E-293; South African veld and coastal plains S-263-4, C-130b, N-16

IV. **Plants** A-79, C-510, C-513-14, G-192, M-23, S-264, map A-80: acacia A-7; bamboo B-48; banana B-51; banyan tree B-63; cacao C-9; clove C-410; coffee plant C-426; cork oak C-573; corn (mealies) C-574; date palm D-37; ebony E-43; esparto grass A-273, L-248; lotus L-357; mahogany M-50; millet M-325; olive O-450; orange O-472; palm P-84; papyrus P-108; peanut (groundnut) P-146; pyrethrum I-195; rubber R-301; sisal S-206; tamarind T-13. See also names of other plants in Fact-Index

V. **Animals** A-79, C-514, G-121, G-192, M-23, S-264, map A-418, color pictures A-72-3, A-404, picture G-51: wildlife sanctuaries N-23, C-510, G-161, T-15, picture A-80, N-22
   A. **Mammals:** aardvark A-2; aardwolf A-2; antelope family (dikdik, eland, gazelle, gemsbok, gnu, kudu, sable antelope, springbok) A-442, pictures A-443; wild ass A-641; baboon B-1; wild boar B-227; buffalo B-361; camel C-56c; chimpanzee C-288; elephant E-174, color pictures A-72; giraffe G-127, color picture A-72; gorilla G-160; hippopotamus H-158, picture A-80; hyena H-288; jackal J-347; jerboa K-2; lemur L-188; leopard L-196a; lion L-296, pictures A-73, L-297; monkey M-437; okapi G-128; rhinoceros R-178, color picture A-72; zebra Z-354
   B. **Birds:** guinea fowl G-259; ibis I-3; ostrich O-505d; parrot P-133; plover P-391, picture C-610; secretary bird S-105; shrike S-186; weaverbird W-90
   C. **Reptiles:** chameleon C-204b; cobra C-422; crocodile C-610; lizard L-318; python P-544; viper V-328, color picture S-226
   D. **Fish:** mudfish M-539
   E. **Insects:** driver ant A-437; termite T-106; tsetse fly T-283

VICTORIA FALLS

THE SAHARA

VASCO DA GAMA

XIV. **World War II:** struggle in the Mediterranean W-270, 274, L-249, map W-274; battle of El Alamein W-273, 287; invasion of North Africa (1942) W-273, 287, picture W-288

XV. **Italy loses African colonies** I-343e, A-82: independence restored to Ethiopia E-295

XVI. **Political awakening of Africa** A-70, 72, 84, maps A-92

A. **French Union replaces colonial empire** F-415

AFRICAN LEADERS

B. **Racial strife** S-263, 267: Mau Mau terror K-45

C. **Libya gains independence (1951)** L-249

D. **Eritrea federated with Ethiopia (1952)** E-293

E. **Egypt becomes a republic** E-325, 326: Arab federations A-468, A-84

F. **Sudan, Morocco, and Tunisia win independence (1956)** S-503, M-489, T-289

G. **Suez Canal crisis** A-84, S-504, E-250-1, U-24

H. **Ghana wins independence (1957)** G-121

I. **Guinea gains independence (1958)** G-258

J. **Seventeen new independent nations rise on African continent in 1960** A-84, C-59, C-192b, C-203, C-510, C-512, D-1a, G-1, I-345, M-67, M-70, M-177a, N-285, N-286, S-108a, S-256, T-191, U-211: United Nations troops sent to the Congo U-25, C-511

K. **Ten African nations gain independence between 1961 and 1964** A-84, S-192b, T-15, A-273, R-366a, B-385, U-1, K-44, M-67a, Z-353

L. **Tanganyika and Zanzibar merge (1964)** T-16

M. **Gambia (1965) and Botswana and Lesotho (1966) gain independence** G-8, B-280, L-196b

BIBLIOGRAPHY FOR AFRICA

Books for Younger Readers

Arundel, Jocelyn. The Wildlife of Africa (Hastings House, 1965).

Glubok, Shirley. The Art of Africa (Harper, 1965).

Kimble, G. H. T. and Steel, Ronald. Tropical Africa Today (McGraw, 1966).

Kittler, G. D. Equatorial Africa (Nelson, 1964).

Lens, Sidney. Africa: Awakening Giant (Putnam, 1962).

Paton, Alan. The Land and People of South Africa (Lippincott, 1964).

Sutton, Felix. The Illustrated Book About Africa (Grosset, 1962).

Thompson, E. B. Africa: Past and Present (Houghton, 1966).

Vlahos, Olivia. African Beginnings (Viking, 1967).

Books for Advanced Students and Teachers

Bohannan, Paul. Africa and Africans (Doubleday, 1964).

Brown, Leslie. Africa: a Natural History (Random, 1965).

Davidson, Basil. African Kingdoms (Time, 1966).

Davidson, Basil, ed. The African Past (Little, 1964).

Davidson, Basil. A Guide to African History (Doubleday, 1965).

Hatch, J. C. Africa Today and Tomorrow (Praeger, 1965).

Kaula, E. M. Leaders of the New Africa (World, 1966).

Legum, Colin, ed. Africa (Praeger, 1966).

McEwan, P. J. M. and Sutcliffe, R. B., eds. Modern Africa (Crowell, 1966).

Mountjoy, A. B. Africa: a New Geographical Survey (Praeger, 1967).

Nielsen, W. A. Africa (Atheneum, 1966).

Nolen, Barbara, ed. Africa Is People (Dutton, 1967).

Roedelberger, F. A. and Groschoff, V. I. African Wildlife (Viking, 1965).

Sterling, Thomas. Exploration of Africa (Harper, 1963).

Turnbull, C. M. The Lonely African (Simon & Schuster, 1962).

Turnbull, C. M. The Peoples of Africa (World Pub., 1962).

Welch, Galbraith. Africa Before They Came (Morrow, 1965).

AGASSIZ (ăg′a-sē), **Jean Louis Rodolphe** (1807–1873). The interests of the celebrated Swiss-American naturalist Louis Agassiz ranged from fish to glaciers. He was the greatest authority of his day on zoology and geology. In addition, he was an outstanding teacher.

Louis Agassiz was born May 28, 1807, in the little Swiss village of Môtiers, not far from Lake Neuchâtel. His father was a pastor. As a boy Louis loved birds and animals, fishes and insects. He delighted in collecting specimens and searching for new creatures.

Agassiz studied medicine at the universities of Zurich, Heidelberg, and Munich. His greatest enthusiasm, however, was for zoology. He welcomed the opportunity in 1829 to edit a work on Brazilian fishes at the invitation of a well-known naturalist. This was followed by an extended investigation of European fishes. He studied not only living specimens but also fossil fishes preserved in rocks. This led to an interest in geology.

Agassiz spent a summer in a hut on the edge of a glacier. There, in the midst of dangers and privations, he studied the glacier's action. His research helped establish the theory that at different times the greater part of Europe and other northern continents was covered by vast sheets of ice (*see* Ice Age).

Agassiz became professor of natural history at Neuchâtel in 1832. He remained there until 1846, when he came to America to deliver a series of lectures in Boston. In 1848 he accepted the chair of natural history at Harvard University.

The many ties which he formed in America and the abundant opportunities for scientific research led him to refuse tempting offers to return to Europe. He lived in America until the end of his life. Besides teaching, Agassiz wrote extensively, delivered

1807 Agassiz born

1809 Charles Darwin born

1846 Agassiz comes to America

1861-65 American Civil War

1873 Agassiz dies

popular lectures on scientific subjects, and engaged in scientific expeditions in various parts of the United States and Brazil. He was the first director of the Museum of Comparative Zoology at Harvard; it is often called the Agassiz Museum. When urged to turn his great scientific knowledge to financial profit, he impatiently replied that he "had no time to make money."

Studying Science Directly from Nature

A few months before his death Agassiz established a summer school of science on the island of Penikese in Buzzards Bay, off the southeast coast of Massachusetts. This was the first school for studying science directly from specimens and in close contact with nature. It made vital and attractive the study of natural science.

Agassiz died at Cambridge in 1873. On his grave were placed a boulder that came from the glacier near the spot where his hut once stood and pine trees sent from his old home in Switzerland.

His son Alexander (1835–1910) was also a distinguished naturalist and writer. From 1874 to 1897 he was chief curator of the Museum of Comparative Zoology which his father had founded.

Louis Agassiz's most important American publications are 'Methods of Study in Natural History'; 'Geological Sketches'; 'The Structure of Animal Life'; 'A Journey in Brazil' (with his wife, Elizabeth Agassiz); 'Contributions to the Natural History of the United States' (only four volumes of the ten planned were completed).

AGAVE (*a-gā′vē*). The most familiar species of this group of plants is the American aloe. It is known as the century plant through a mistaken idea that it blooms only after reaching 100 years of age. Actually the time of blooming depends upon the plant's vigor and the conditions under which it grows. In warm countries flowers appear in a few years. In colder climates it requires from 40 to 60 years. After blooming the plant dies. Some agaves bloom occasionally. Still others flower year after year.

Agaves grow in the arid regions of the Southwestern United States, Mexico, and Central America. The more than 300 species are widely cultivated for ornamental purposes. In their native Mexico they are among the most useful of plants. Two species are grown for the fibers sisal and henequen (*see* Sisal). Pulque, a common drink, is the fermented sap of the maguey, a species of agave. Mescal and tequila are distilled beverages made from the sap. The juice of the leaves lathers in water and is used in washing.

The century plant has thick, fleshy leaves, edged and tipped with sharp spines. They grow in a tight rosette, each leaf 5 to 7 feet long. The stem is short and thick. At the time of flowering the stem springs up 20 to 30 feet. It is many-branched and bears clusters of greenish-yellow flowers. The flower has a 6-parted, funnel-shaped perianth, 3 stamens, and a 3-lobed stigma. When the plant has flowered the

THE AGAVE PLANT IN BLOOM
The American aloe, an agave, grows in the arid Southwest. Its stalk rises from a rosette of leaves to bear flower clusters.

leaves die, but suckers are frequently produced from the base of the stem which become new plants.

The agave is a genus of the amaryllis family, *Amaryllidaceae*. The scientific name of the century plant is *Agave americana*.

AGINCOURT (*ăg′in-kōrt*), **Battle of.** The third great English victory over the French in the Hundred Years' War was won Oct. 25, 1415, near the village of Agincourt in northern France. The young king Henry V had recently succeeded to the insecure Lancastrian throne of England. On the advice of his father, Henry IV, he resolved, in the words of Shakespeare, "to busy giddy minds with foreign quarrels" by reviving England's claim to the French throne.

Henry's forces landed in Normandy and captured the port of Harfleur. Enroute to the port of Calais (then held by England), their way was blocked by a great French army. The French knights, four times as numerous as the English foot soldiers, foolishly dismounted. They advanced in their heavy armor through the deep mud of newly plowed fields. Three times they came on, in a narrow defile between two woods. Three times they were forced back by clouds of arrows let fly by skilled English archers. More than 5,000 Frenchmen were killed, including many princes and nobles. The English lost only 113 men.

This decisive battle, along with Crécy and Poitiers, proved the superiority of the longbow over the crossbow. It hastened the end of the heavily armored knight, the military basis of feudalism. (*See also* Hundred Years' War; Henry, Kings of England.)

Beauty and Efficiency on an American Farm

AGRICULTURE—How Farmers Feed the World

AGRICULTURE. The world's oldest and most important industry is agriculture. People depend upon the farmer for food. He also supplies raw materials for clothing and other things they need. The word "agriculture" comes from the Latin words *ager* ("field") and *cultura* ("cultivation"). It therefore means "cultivation of the fields."

It is hard to believe that once there were no farmers. In the earliest days people lived by hunting for fruit, nuts, fish, game, and other wild foods. If wild foods were scarce, many starved. Gradually people learned to tend flocks and herds and to grow plants from seeds. When food became more plentiful, some people could live in cities and make goods. They traded goods with the farmers for food. From this *division of labor* came the present way of life.

Some men used their new leisure to observe, to think, to experiment. As the centuries passed, man began to develop the beginnings of science, religion, government, and art. These became the foundations of modern civilization. (*See also* Civilization; Family.)

A Changing Industry

Today agriculture is an industry that changes almost constantly. This is especially true in the United States and in other advanced countries. Modern farmers use machines for the hard work that once strained the muscles of men and animals. Improved seeds, commercial fertilizers, and wiser management of land and water help them increase crop yields. Better breeding and feeding practices make their animals more productive. Insecticides, pesticides, and chemical weed killers help farmers destroy plant and animal enemies. (*See also* Farm Machinery; Fertilizers.)

American farmers continually seek more productive, speedier, and easier methods. They use all the resources of modern science and technology. Government and private research institutions attack the problems of agriculture and find many solutions. Manufacturers produce new equipment. Schools, colleges, and extension services teach farmers to use modern principles and methods.

Mounting Output and the Surplus Problem

The results of this agricultural revolution have been astounding. From 1900 to 1960 the country's net farm production (crops and livestock) more than doubled. The rise in crop production was accomplished by almost doubling the average yield per acre. The actual number of acres used for crops changed little. Meanwhile mechanization on farms caused the labor force to be cut in half.

101

CONTRASTS IN HAYING—MUSCLES VERSUS MACHINES

The Swiss family (left) cannot use machines on their steep farm. Everyone works hard to gather a bundle of hay for the cow. One

American farmer with machines has cut and raked his big hay crop. Now he is baling it into cylindrical bundles (right).

The ever-increasing output brought the problem of a mounting agricultural surplus. The American farmer produces more each year than can be economically sold and consumed. Under federal government farm-aid plans, much of the surplus is stored in granaries and warehouses. More than a two-year supply of wheat was in storage by the 1960's.

KINDS OF FARMS

Around the world two thirds of the people are farmers. Most of them engage in *subsistence farming*. This means that they raise plants and animals to furnish their families with food and other supplies. They consume their varied output and have little to sell or to trade for other goods. Subsistence farms were common in the United States at one time, but there are few such farms today.

An increasing number of American farm families operate *part-time farms*. They raise crops and animals for food and perhaps grow a cash crop, though they get most of their income from other employment. (*See also* Farm Life.)

Commercial Farms

Two thirds of American farmers practice *commercial farming*. Commercial farms produce about 97 per cent of the country's agricultural output. These farms are operated much like other industries. The members of the farm family produce the commodities that will be the most profitable. They sell their products and buy the things they need.

Some commercial farms are big factories in the field. They may be owned by a company or by an individual as an investment. Men are hired to run the giant machines and automatic equipment that do the work. The number of hired laborers has decreased with the use of machinery. Most American farms, however, are still operated by families. A farm operator may own or rent his land. Those who rent are called renters, tenant farmers, or sharecroppers.

Specialized and General Farms

In a country as large as the United States, farms vary widely in climate, land surface, soil, water

STORAGE FOR THE HUGE GRAIN SURPLUS

Scientific methods and power machinery enable United States farmers to raise bigger crops than the country can use. The

Middle West is dotted with "bin farms" like this. Here the government stores surplus corn purchased to support prices.

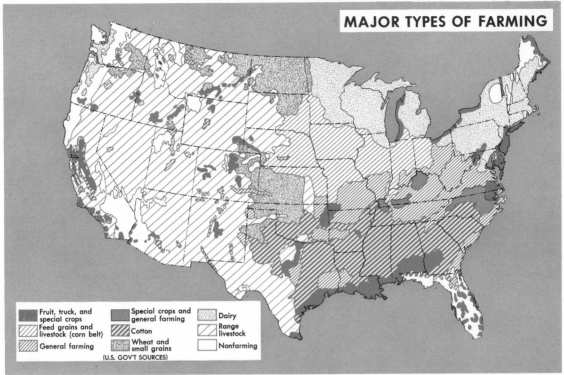

MAJOR TYPES OF FARMING

Legend:
- Fruit, truck, and special crops
- Feed grains and livestock (corn belt)
- General farming
- Special crops and general farming
- Cotton
- Wheat and small grains
- Dairy
- Range livestock
- Nonfarming

(U.S. GOV'T SOURCES)

This map shows types of farming usual in most regions of the United States. Specialization in Hawaii is based on water supply. Alaska has general and dairy farms in a few favorable areas.

supply, convenience to market, and other characteristics. The article United States discusses the various geographic regions of the country and the kinds of farms found in each. The article Farm Life describes activities on various specialized farms.

The map on this page shows regions where different kinds of *specialized farms* are most numerous: Commercial farmers concentrate on the kind of farming best suited to the land and climate, to their technical skills, and to their financial investment.

The United States Department of Agriculture classifies a specialized farm according to the commodity that accounts for 50 per cent or more of its gross sales. No region is limited to a single type of farm. Indeed few farms are limited to one crop or commodity. Where output is varied and no one source of revenue produces more than half a farm's income, it is classed as a *general farm*. The general farmer grows varied crops to use the different kinds of soils or surfaces on his land and to employ his time and machinery most efficiently.

Some General Farm Areas and Their Crops

The map shows a broad area of general farms stretching across the eastern part of the United States, about midway between the northern and southern borders. This area contains much hilly or rough land not suited to big fields of grain or other *clean-cultivated*, or row, crops. Farmers here tend to raise field crops on their level acres and use the steeper land for pasture. Rough, rocky hills may be left wooded or planted as tree farms.

Good farmers here have reclaimed much badly eroded sloping land by fertilizing it and planting hay and forage crops. Stock raising has increased. Near the cities dairy herds are kept. The steep, hilly regions of the Appalachian Highlands and the Ozark-Ouachita Plateau contain many subsistence farms.

Cash Crops and Specialized Machines

Different cash crops are mixed in the general farm systems. They include tobacco, potatoes, sugar beets, dry beans, peanuts, rice, and sugar cane. The choice of one or more depends upon climate, soil, market opportunities, and financing.

In areas devoted to tobacco and general farming, usually only a small proportion of the land is in tobacco. The plant requires a great deal of labor, and it saps the soil's fertility. (*See also* Tobacco.)

Sugar cane is raised on general farms of the warm, moist Gulf coast. In tropical Hawaii the cane is cultivated on large special farms or plantations. Sugar beets are grown chiefly on irrigated land in the Western states. (*See also* Sugar.)

In the United States specialized machines help produce cash crops with a minimum of man-hours of labor. In foreign lands these crops are often raised by the methods of past centuries. Rice, for instance, is harvested and threshed swiftly by combine in the United States. In the ricelands of Asia the work requires a host of laborers, using the sickle, flail, and other crude tools. (*See also* Rice.)

103

AUTOMATIC MACHINES ON A STOCK FARM

Heated air is forced through shelled corn in this drier. Power from a tractor operates the loading and unloading machinery.

Here chopped forage is piled on a stack silo. Heavy black plastic film protects and preserves the silage until it is fed.

This farmer operates an auger that fills the feeder bins. His hogs fatten rapidly because feed is always in the trough.

Cotton Farming

Across the South, where the annual growing season is 200 or more days, cotton plantations have long been the chief type of specialized farm. Important changes in cotton-growing methods in the last few decades have brought great changes to the South. Machinery for planting, cultivating, and picking the crop is now in common use. Acreage for cotton has been increased in areas where farms are large and level enough to use the big machines. These areas include the Mississippi Delta, the Blackland Prairies and High Plains of Texas, and the irrigated cotton sections of New Mexico, Arizona, and California.

In the eastern part of the cotton belt, less land is in cotton fields and more in pasture, feed grains, and diversified crops. Stock raising has increased, and tree farming makes the wood lots profitable. Many of the sharecroppers and hired hands who worked the cotton crop before mechanization have left the South for jobs in the North. (*See also* Cotton.)

Farming in the Corn Belt

A fertile, level-to-rolling area extends east and west from the Mississippi Valley in the heart of the country. It is popularly known as the corn belt, for corn is the principal crop. Soybeans, wheat, oats, grasses, legumes, and other commodities are also raised. The farmer changes, or rotates, the crop on a field each year to maintain soil productivity.

Some farms are *cash-grain farms*. Their operators sell the corn, oats, wheat, and soybeans. Other farms are *feed-grain and livestock farms*. On this type, farmers feed hogs or cattle on the grain and then market the stock. The big, level farms of the corn belt are well suited to machinery. The prosperous owners have modern equipment and practice the latest farming methods. The use of hybrid corn seed alone has increased the average yield per acre more than 150 percent since the 1930's. (*See also* Corn.)

Wheat Farming

West of the corn belt stretches the rich, level area of the Great Plains, where there is too little rainfall for corn or general farming. Wheat is the principal crop. Winter wheat is sown in the south; spring wheat, in the north. The Columbia River basin of the Pacific Northwest is another rich spring wheat section.

The wheat farms have benefited greatly from improved seeds and specialized machinery. Tractor-powered machines are used to prepare and fertilize the soil, to drill the seed, and to combine, or harvest, the grain. With machinery, wheat farming now takes less than two man-hours of labor to the acre. Since the grain does not have to be cultivated as do many other crops, wheat farmers may live away from their land and work at other jobs.

Drought is a threat to the wheat belt. In dry periods the crop may wither and the tilled land blow away. Modern farmers have learned scientific methods for conserving moisture and preventing erosion. These

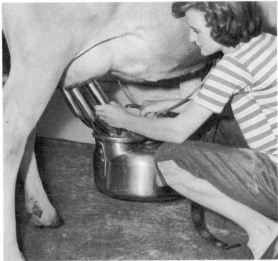

METHODS USED ON UP-TO-DATE SPECIALIZED FARMS
The poultry house (left) resembles a factory assembly line. The farmer gathers the eggs each hen lays and marks her record on a card. She eats a scientifically prepared ration from the trough. A dairy farm girl (right) adjusts a power milker.

include terracing, strip cropping, and summer fallowing. In addition to wheat, the leading crops in the belt are oats, rye, barley, flax, and grain sorghums. (*See also* Wheat; Oats; Rye; Barley; Flax; Sorghum.)

Dairy Farming

North, northeast, and east of the corn belt lies a region containing three fifths of the country's dairy farms. Its climate is more cool and moist than that of the corn belt. Its rough lands are better suited to pasture or hay than to clean-cultivated crops.

Much of the dairy belt is convenient to the manufacturing cities of the Northeast. Fluid milk is marketed in the cities. In the western part of the belt much of the milk is sent to creameries, condenseries, and cheese factories for processing. Dairy farmers have large investments in modern buildings, machinery, and electrical equipment. They have adopted new methods of herd management and feeding that have increased their output. (*See also* Milk Production.)

Fluid milk is also produced near cities in most parts of the country. In Alaska, where the climate makes farming difficult, dairying is one of the chief agricultural activities.

Cattle and Sheep Ranching

The ranch country of the Western United States lies in a belt 500 to 1,000 miles wide, stretching from Canada to Mexico. Most of this region is too high and cold, too rocky and rugged, or too dry for cultivation. On grasslands here ranchers raise about one fifth of the country's cattle and

nearly half its sheep. Ranches often contain thousands of acres. The stock graze on ranches and on open ranges, such as the national forests. Cowboys and sheepherders guard the herds and flocks.

The ranches seldom have barns or other shelter for the stock. The animals suffer when winter blizzards are severe. When drought strikes and the water supply fails, the stock may have to be shipped away. Some ranches have irrigated land, where hay or forage crops are raised. The cattle and sheep may be marketed directly from the ranches, or calves and lambs may be sent to corn belt feed lots for fattening. (*See also* Cattle; Sheep.)

A FLYING RANCHER CHECKS THE WATER SUPPLY
Here a rancher is using an airplane to watch his pasture, water supply, and stock. Many farmers who use airplanes belong to the Flying Farmers of America.

105

Truck Farming and Fruitgrowing

Farms where vegetables, fruits, and other specialties are grown are widely distributed throughout the United States. Many truck farms are found near cities. The Coastal Plain farms of New Jersey, Delaware, Maryland, and Virginia are examples. Vegetables and fruits are also raised in the South and Southwest, where the climate permits winter crops. Warm, irrigated regions in the West are especially productive (*see* Imperial Valley). Fruitgrowing farms range from the citrus groves of Florida to the cherry and apple orchards of Washington and the pineapple plantations of Hawaii.

Harvesting these crops requires much more labor than a family farm can supply. Migrant farm workers follow the ripening crops, moving from place to place to do this work. The output may be sold fresh, or it may be quick-frozen or canned. (*See also* Food Preservation; Fruit; Fruitgrowing; articles on various fruits and vegetables.)

Modern Poultry Raising

Poultry raising is also widespread. Like dairy and truck farms, poultry farms are often located near cities. Specialized broiler-chicken, egg, and breeding farms have increased tremendously in recent years.

Advances in the breeding, feeding, and care of poultry have led to increases in meat and eggs to the unit of feed. Annual egg output per hen rose about five dozen during the 1950's. The amount of feed needed to produce 100 pounds of meat decreased about 30 per cent. Although more chickens are raised than any other poultry, a large number of farms specialize in turkeys, ducks, Cornish hens, and other fowl. (*See also* Poultry.)

Contract Farming

A modern development in poultry raising is contract farming for a packing house, chain-store system, or other processing and marketing organization. The organization supplies the farmer with chicks, feed, and expert advice. It gets the total output and pays the farmer a contract price for each dozen of eggs or each pound of poultry.

Other farmers may raise crops or animals under contract. Some grow specific vegetables or fruits for a canning or freezing firm. Still others raise hops for a brewery, sugar beets for a refinery, or grapes for a winery. The contract farmer is relieved of much responsibility and risk, but he loses his former independence of action. Dairymen or cattle raisers may sell their livestock to investors and then care for the stock under contract.

TRENDS IN AMERICAN AGRICULTURE

In many parts of the world farmers have difficulty raising enough food to feed the people. This has been true throughout history. In the United States, however, farmers produce more food and fiber than the people need. The ambitious American farmer steadily raises the yield per acre by improving his methods. Each year the output increases an average of 2 per cent. The country's population increase averages about 1.8 per cent a year. Thus the surplus gets larger every year despite federal laws controlling the number of acres that can be used for certain crops.

Increasing production is far from new to American agriculture. Between 1870 and 1920 the volume of farm output tripled. In these years the total cropland and the number of horses and mules working on farms also increased three times. The reasons for

CHEMICAL WEED CONTROL AND PASTURE IMPROVEMENT
In the test cornfield (left) chemicals sprayed between the right-hand rows killed the weeds. The sod seeder (right) cuts a narrow furrow in a pasture, drops in seed, and covers it. It fertilizes the sod with anhydrous ammonia from the tank.

these increases were the spread of farming into Western lands and the opening of fertile acres in the corn belt by drainage projects.

Land Released as Draft Animals Vanish

Cropland acreage reached a level in 1920 from which there has been little change. After that date, however, the number of work horses and mules declined steadily as tractors, trucks, and automobiles became the chief sources of farm power. Feed for these animals had absorbed one fifth of the total crop acreage in 1920. By 1940 draft animal numbers had dropped until only one tenth of the cropland was needed to produce their feed. Millions of acres of cropland, together with much pasture land, and large amounts of labor were released for other crops.

Mechanization of farm work and other scientific progress led to a 10 per cent growth in average crop production per acre between 1920 and 1940. Output per animal (as milk per cow and eggs per hen) rose more than a third. This was due to improved livestock breeding and management.

Speedy Output Growth in 1940's and 1950's

The revolution in farm methods gained even greater speed during and after World War II. In the prosperous 1940's and 1950's farmers bought machines, installed electrical equipment, and adopted better farming techniques. The number of tractors increased 230 per cent. The shift from animal power to mechanical power was virtually completed. Ingenious new machines were purchased to handle farm chores. Farm investment per worker soared from about $3,400 to $21,300 (current dollars).

Machines enabled the farmer to do much more work in a given amount of time. A man with a two-horse plow could turn the soil of 1½ acres in a day; one with a tractor-drawn plow, 21 acres. The increase in output per man-hour in agriculture in the 1950's was 2½ times as great as in all other industries. By 1960 each farm worker raised enough food and fiber for about 26 persons.

Farm owners, seeing the need for greater acreage to use their machines efficiently, bought or rented extra land. Farms increased in size but decreased in number. In 1940 they averaged about 175 acres; in 1959, 303 acres. The number of commercial farms decreased from 4,700,000 in 1930 to 3,710,000 in 1959. By 1959 an estimated one third of all farms had become residential or part-time farms, farms whose owners had other employment. (*See also* Farm Machinery.)

Improved Seeds and Livestock

Better crop varieties and improved seeds played an important part in the increase of about 30 per cent in crop production per acre between 1950 and 1960. Varieties of cotton, vegetable-oil crops, and sugar crops changed almost completely in this period. Seventy per cent of the acreage is now planted in seed varieties unknown 20 years ago. Best known

Hours of Labor to Each Acre in Harvesting Wheat

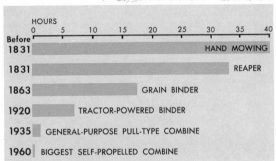

This chart shows how machinery has reduced the farmer's work. Mowing an acre of wheat took 40 hours before 1831. A big combine now cuts and threshes an acre in six to eight minutes.

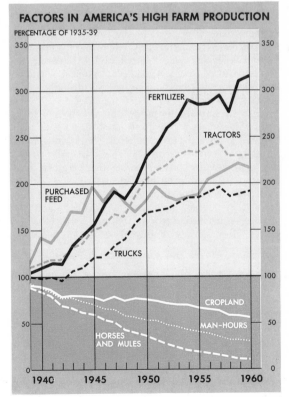

In the past 20 years man-hours, animal power, and cropland needed per unit of production have decreased. Necessary purchases—power machines, feed, and fertilizer—have increased.

RECLAIMED DESERT LAND IN UTAH
Some of the finest fruit orchards in the country are in the irrigated valleys of the arid West. The rough unwatered land bears only dry grass and brush.

new chemical is tested to be sure that no harmful residue will poison treated food plants. Natural enemies have been introduced from abroad to fight the pests. (*See also* Fungicides; Insecticides; Insects, section on harmful insects; Scale Insects.)

Improvement in storage methods, especially for cereals and hay, has cut losses from molds, insects, and rodents. Crop driers are widely used.

Insects, mites, and ticks that attack domestic animals cost stock raisers millions of dollars annually. Control methods have been worked out to free the animals from several types of pests. Gains in weight and increases in milk production have resulted. Antibiotics are given animals in feed and as medicine. By checking and preventing disease, the antibiotics promote growth, weight, and efficient use of feed.

Weed Killers and Growth Regulators

Research has shown ways to regulate or control the growth of plants by means of chemicals. Such regulators may be used to increase the size of fruits. Hormones retard the falling of fruit. This extends the harvest period.

The use of chemicals to kill weeds has saved farm labor and has led to crop increases. The application of chemicals began on a large scale after the discovery in 1944 that 2,4-D (2,4 dichlorophenoxyacetic acid) kills some weeds but not grasses. Since that time more than 100 weed killers have been developed. They may be applied by special machines before or after the crop plant emerges. Care must be taken with chemicals that harm the crop. (*See also* Weeds.)

Fertilizers and Lime Swell Farm Output

Agricultural experts credit greater and more scientific use of fertilizers and lime with about one fifth of the increase in farm production since 1940. Liming of acid soils in humid areas became general around 1900. In 1957 some 23 million tons were applied. In that year the fertilizer industry produced 22 million tons of commercial fertilizers.

Modern farmers take soil samples from their fields and send them to soil laboratories. These laboratories are usually operated by the states. After testing the samples the technicians recommend a fertilizer mixture in terms of pounds per acre of nitrogen, phosphorus, and potassium. These are the chief elements used by plants. Modern fertilizers may also contain small amounts of minor elements, called micronutrients or trace elements. Many machines have been developed for applying fertilizers to various crops.

Because draft animals have been replaced by mechanical power, there has been a decrease in animal manure, the most valuable organic fertilizer. This has

of the improved seeds is hybrid corn, which is planted on more than 90 per cent of the total corn acreage.

Government experimental laboratories and commercial seed companies shared in the research and development of the high-yield plant stocks. Varieties were developed that would resist cold, drought, plant diseases, and pests.

Improvements in livestock and in the efficiency with which stock utilize feed added greatly to farm output. Special-purpose stock were developed through selective breeding. These included cattle that were able to thrive in subtropical regions, hogs that yielded lean bacon instead of lard, and turkeys that were small and broad-breasted. Average milk production per cow increased one fourth, and egg production per hen rose about 40 per cent. (*See also* Cattle; Hog; Turkey; Poultry.)

Protecting Plants and Animals from Pests

Better control of plant and animal diseases and pests aided the increase in output. New chemical "killers" were introduced. Inorganic chemicals were generally used before 1945. Organic chemicals developed later included chlorinated hydrocarbons, such as toxaphene and benzene hexachloride. They also included organic phosphates, such as parathion.

The use of airplanes in spraying made the work more efficient. A thousand acres can be sprayed for grasshopper control in a matter of minutes. Research in insecticides must go on continuously, since the insects tend to develop immunity to the sprays. Each

increased the demand for chemical fertilizers. To return organic matter to the soil, farmers plow under cornstalks, alfalfa, clover, and other "green manure" plants. Residue from the processing of plants and animals is used as organic fertilizer. Waste from fish canneries and meat-packing houses is widely used. (*See also* Fertilizers.)

Soil and Water Management

American farmers have become more expert in soil and water management in the past half century. The science of agronomy deals with land management. The huge yields today are partly due to using the latest methods on the best land.

Farmers plan the allotment of their acreage so areas with infertile soil, poor drainage, steep slopes, or other disadvantages are put into pasture and woods rather than into plow crops. They do strip cropping and terracing to hold the rainfall and to prevent or check erosion. The farmers of a district may join in conservation projects with federal aid. (*See also* Conservation, subhead "How Soil Conservation Works.")

Irrigation in the West and the East

Irrigation has long played an important part in the agriculture of the low-rainfall Western states. Individual farmers and groups of farmers may get water for their fields from streams and wells. Others may get water from one of the large federal or state irrigation projects. These systems dam and impound the snow-fed mountain rivers of the area and send their waters through canals to the fields. About two thirds of the increase in irrigated acreage after 1949 was in the West. (*See also* Irrigation and Reclamation; for map, *see* United States, section "Western Basins and Plateaus.")

RECORDS AND ACCOUNTING ON THE FARM
Good farmers keep careful records. This man uses his records in preparing his income tax return. Records are needed to tell whether a cow is paying her way or a machine is profitable.

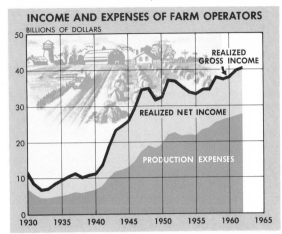

INCOME AND EXPENSES OF FARM OPERATORS

The gross income of American farmers has risen greatly in the past 30 years. Modern methods, however, require high production costs. This trims the amount of net income.

Until recent years farms in the more humid East relied entirely upon rainfall for moisture. Since World War II many Eastern farmers have turned to irrigation. It insures more dependable crops and high yields in times of drought. An estimated 33,000,000 acres of cropland in the United States are irrigated.

Capital Outlay and Expense

The successful farmer must be a careful businessman as well as a trained agriculturist. The young man who selects farming as a career makes a large investment in order to enter his chosen field.

Machines and equipment for scientific farming are expensive. The up-to-date farmer also must spend a great deal of money on fertilizer, improved seeds and livestock, special feeds, insect sprays, tractor fuel, irrigation piping, and special buildings. These buildings may include a milking parlor and poultry house. Careful accounting is required in order to show the farmer whether the "input" into a crop—or into the farm as a whole—is warranted by the value of the "output."

The price per acre of farm real estate (including land, buildings, and other improvements) rose to record highs in the 1950's and 1960's. Net income, however, changed little. A part of the rise in real estate was due to the rise in the general price level. The demand for land for nonfarm uses also boosted the average price. About a million acres of farm land are taken each year for residential and industrial development, highways, and similar projects.

Farm Credit

Few farmers pay cash for their land. Borrowed money amounted to more than 60 per cent of the farm purchase price in the 1950's. Interest on loans adds to the cost of operating the farm.

The farm owner continues to need money or credit after he settles on the new farm. He has seeds, fertilizer, stock feed, and other supplies to buy. The farm renter also needs money for the portion of ma-

AGRICULTURE

chinery or livestock he must supply. It may be months before money comes in from crops or animals. Government and private agencies assist the farmers in securing this needed credit. (*See also* Farm Credit.)

Records and Accounts

The modern farm family finds it necessary to keep numerous records. This task often falls to the wife or older sons or daughters. The farmer needs data for income tax returns and as a basis for making decisions. The dairy farmer may weigh and record the yield of every cow at each milking in order to keep only the most productive animals. The poultry farmer may tally the number of eggs each hen lays and then cull the poor layers. The grain farmer must know the cost of seed, fertilizer, weed spray, labor, machinery depreciation, and other production items to calculate his profit on a bumper crop.

After a careful study of investment, costs, and output, a farmer may make major changes in his operations. The grain farmer, for example, may decide to rent more land to get greater use from his machines. If his yield is high and the price is low, he may buy feeder cattle to use the grain. He may decide to plant soybeans or another crop instead of grain the next year. A series of poor yearly results may reveal that the output of a small farm is not paying a fair wage for his labor. He may then decide to get other employment and use his land as a part-time farm.

Modern Marketing

Marketing has changed as much over the years as other aspects of farming. A century ago much of the farmer's output was sold and consumed at the nearest marketing town. He might deliver barrels of potatoes and apples directly to the housewife. He might sell grain to a nearby mill, a steer or hog to the local slaughterhouse, eggs and butter to the crossroad store. In some parts of the world the farmer still carries his small surplus to a town market. There he trades or sells it to his neighbors.

In the United States the roadside vegetable stand is the chief remnant of direct sale from farmer to consumer. In general the farmer's output reaches the market through the hands of many businesses. These collect, store, transport, process, finance, and deliver it before it is sold to the consumer.

This system is necessary because people use few commodities in the form in which they come from the farm. People want meat—not a steer; bread—not wheat; a dress or a coat—not cotton or wool. A farm's product may be used thousands of miles away, completely changed in form. More than a million commercial firms are engaged in agricultural marketing and processing. (*See also* Trade; Food Processing; Meat Industry; Cold Storage; Food Buying.)

Sharing the Food Dollar

The people who handle farm produce en route to the American consumer or to the foreign importer must be paid for the many services they perform. About 60 per cent of every dollar people spend for farm commodities goes to the people who buy, handle, sell, package, and advertise it. This leaves 40 per cent for those who raise the produce.

To avoid dealing with commercial buyers and processors, farm groups often organize co-operatives to handle the processing and selling of their produce.

A STEER AUCTION IN INDIANA
The cattle auction is one link in the complete food marketing system in the United States. Here packing-house representatives are bidding on the steers in the ring. The farmer must market his crops and stock favorably to make a profit.

Profits are prorated among the co-operative members. Farm co-operatives may also sell the farmer such quantity items as fertilizer, seed, and gasoline. (*See* also Co-operative Societies.)

Good Management in Marketing

To sell his produce most advantageously, the farmer needs to understand the market for his particular commodities. He must keep in touch with changing prices in order to sell at the most favorable time. The federal Agricultural Marketing Service issues reports on the production and prices of crops and livestock. It also forecasts future output and furnishes market news to newspapers and radio broadcasters. Boards of trade, or commodity exchanges, in the cities issue reports of prices for current sales and "futures" on grains, cotton, soybeans, and many other commodities (*see* Boards of Trade).

The Agricultural Marketing Service has played an important role in setting standards and grades. The Service also inspects many foods for wholesomeness. The farmer increases his profits by producing commodities that meet high standards.

TRENDS IN WORLD AGRICULTURE

The revolution in agricultural technology that swelled United States output so greatly has been spreading to other countries. Today the cultivated lands of the world are producing much more abundantly than they did at the outbreak of World War II. New production records are being made in wheat, rice, corn, soybeans, sugar, coffee, cacao beans, tea, and cottonseed. Meat and livestock products are increasing.

In spite of this encouraging progress, from one third to one half of the world's people still receive insufficient food. This is partly because the world's population is growing so fast. (It has increased more than 40 per cent since the end of World War II.) Another reason why so many people go hungry is that the technological advancement and increasing production are largely limited to certain parts of the world. Most of the hunger, however, exists in the other parts. (*See also* Food Resources.)

The big steps forward are being made in the advanced countries and areas of the world—the United States, Canada, much of Western Europe, Australia and New Zealand, and parts of South America. Several nations have set up price supports to encourage production. Machines, improved seeds, and poultry breeding stock have been purchased from the United States by less advanced countries. Mechanization is spreading in Europe. The number of tractors in Europe today, excluding Russia, is about $3\frac{1}{2}$ million. Before World War II there were only 200,000.

Using modern methods, Canada has increased its agricultural output greatly since the prewar years. It has a considerable annual surplus and is one of the leading food exporters of the world. It is noted for the big wheat and other grain crops of its Prairie Provinces. Canada's western mountains are an important ranching area, and its east has dairy, fruit, and general farms. Both the national and provincial governments carry on extensive farm-aid programs.

Poor Farming and Hungry People

Most of the hunger occurs in lands where people till the soil much as their forefathers did hundreds of years ago. These people live in crowded Asian countries, in parts of Africa and Eastern Europe, and in some countries of Central and South America.

The soil has been eroded and sapped of its fertility. Often water is scarce. Land belongs to the few under outworn landownership systems. Money is too scarce for the purchase of machinery, improved seeds, or fertilizer. If it were available, laborsaving machinery would further impoverish farming folk with no other opportunities for employment.

International Movements

Since World War II modern farming methods have been spread by national and international organizations. Numerous countries have set up development programs and five-year plans to improve agriculture, marketing, and processing. Nations that attained independence after the war have been especially eager to improve their economies. Irrigation systems have

LAND RECLAMATION IN INDIA'S FIVE-YEAR PLAN
India borrowed funds from the World Bank for tractor plows to break the sod of millions of acres of kans grass. The farmer in the oxcart has gathered the tough roots.

NEW WAYS AND OLD IN FOREIGN AGRICULTURE

Since World War II Japan has improved its farm methods and increased its food output. With the new tractor (left) a rice field is prepared for a second crop in one tenth the time required by animal power. The Moroccan farmer (right) has hitched a camel and horse to his wooden plow. Morocco's climate is too dry and the soil too worn for good crops.

been built by many countries, notably India, Pakistan, Israel, and Egypt. Some have received loans from the World Bank and loans or grants from wealthy countries such as the United States.

The Food and Agriculture Organization and the World Health Organization of the United Nations are working to extend new farming methods and to fight diseases and pests. Active in improving agriculture in specific regions of the world are the British Commonwealth, the Colombo Plan nations, and the Organization of American States. Agencies of the Organization of American States maintain numerous technical institutions. These include the Inter-American Institute of Agricultural Sciences in Costa Rica and the Pan American Foot and Mouth Disease Center in Brazil.

The economic and technical-aid programs carried on by the United States are supervised by the State Department's Agency for International Development (AID). Agricultural experts are sent to work with farmers of other lands and show how modern methods may be applied to help solve their problems. They introduce improved seeds and better implements and devices to take the place of primitive farming and household equipment. Philanthropic organizations such as the Ford Foundation and the Rockefeller Foundation are also active in giving technical assistance abroad. (For information on the crops and agricultural methods of foreign countries, *see* articles on the various countries; *see* in Fact-Index international agencies mentioned.)

Farming in Communist Countries

Communist governments have worked to improve agriculture and increase the supply of food and fiber in the countries they rule. They have set up large co-operative and state farms, which use the labor and land of former private owners. In many cases they have met with resistance. Crop results have not come up to the expectation of leaders. Russia's output of grain per acre is one third less than in Western Europe where intensive farming is carried on. Seeking to improve production, the Soviet government ended the system whereby collective farms had to give grain to the state at low prices. The government also abolished its tractor stations.

Communist China set up the "commune" system. Peasant families are deprived of their property and housed in dormitories. Men and women alike work in the fields or on state projects under Communist supervisors. (*See also* Russia; China, People's Republic of.)

HOW GOVERNMENT AIDS AGRICULTURE

The welfare of a country is dependent upon the success of its agriculture. Most nations therefore have federal departments designed to help the farmers solve their problems. The United States Department of Agriculture is one of the most outstanding in the world.

Within the United States Department of Agriculture are numerous divisions, generally called bureaus, services, or administrations. Their activities and responsibilities are discussed in the article United States Government, section "Department of Agriculture." Most divisions assist in problems dealing with farm methods, but several carry on programs to aid the farmers financially. Each of the 50 states also has agricultural departments. Federal and state departments co-operate with each other and with local committees, farmers' organizations, and individual farm families.

Research in Agriculture

The United States Department of Agriculture is most famous for its research and educational activities. Areas of research include crops, farm and land management, livestock, human nutrition and home economics, and utilization of agricultural products. Large staffs of scientists carry on this work at the great Beltsville, Md., research center, in laboratories and field stations throughout the United States, and in several foreign countries. State agricultural experiment stations work on local problems and join with other state stations in doing regional research.

Discoveries of government scientists have played an important role in the growth of farm output. Stockbreeding experiments have produced efficient types of animals that provide more meat, milk, and other livestock products than previous varieties. The scientists have "tailored" crops to fit the needs and demands of consumers, processors, and machine cultivation. They have combed the world for disease-resistant seeds that will thrive in the United States soils and climates. They have discovered pesticides, medicines, and other cures for diseases of plants and animals. Utilization Research and Development laboratories work to discover new industrial uses for farm produce.

Publications and Extension Work

Federal and state agricultural departments bring the results of their research to the farm family through broad programs of publishing and extension work. All offer free or inexpensive bulletins on thousands of practical farm topics.

The extension service is a co-operative undertaking of federal and state departments. Each agricultural county in the nation is served by extension workers. They are usually the county agent, a man, and the home demonstration agent, a woman. They work directly with farm families in meetings and in farm or home consultations and demonstrations. The latest scientific knowledge is thus quickly made available to the farmer.

State extension staffs usually contain experts in agronomy, soils, livestock, landscaping, youth organizations, community improvement, wildlife conservation, and other topics of rural interest. A specialist often works with the county agent in setting up a demonstration of a new method on a local farm. Thus the neighborhood can study its use.

Aid in Conservation and Marketing

Assistance in land and water management and in watershed protection is supplied by the Soil Conservation Service and the Agricultural Stabilization and Conservation Service (*see* Conservation). The United States Forest Service helps in the management of private and public woodlands (*see* Forests and Forestry).

Aid in the marketing of farm crops is supplied by the Agricultural Marketing Service and the Foreign Agricultural Service. The Farmer Cooperative Service assists the marketing co-operatives. The Commodity Exchange Authority supervises transactions of the commodity markets, or boards of trade.

Aid in Economic Problems

Programs to aid the farmer's financial problems were introduced in 1929 and the 1930's, during the country's severe economic depression. They have been continued and revised over the years, as mounting crop surpluses threatened a slump in prices that would impoverish the farmer and the businesses that were dependent upon him.

Laws to provide various types of aid are passed by Congress. Programs are altered as political control of the legislature changes. The administration of the programs is in the hands of the secretary of agriculture. In the 1950's and 1960's about seven cents of the annual budget dollar was allocated to agricultural expenditures.

The federal government places price supports under certain farm commodities. Commodities given support have included grains, soybeans, cottonseed and other oilseeds, peanuts, cotton, tobacco, butter, cheese, dried milk, wool, mohair, and honey. Support prices are based upon a parity formula. "Parity" is the ratio between the prices farmers receive for their crops and the prices they must pay for things they need. The government selected the period from August 1909 to July 1914 as a time when farm prices were in a fair ratio with farming costs. This is the base period for the parity prices.

TESTING A FIELD'S FERTILITY
Here a county agricultural agent is showing a farmer how to take a sample of soil and how to prepare a conservation survey map. A laboratory will test the soil's plant food content and recommend a proper fertilizer.

From 1938 to 1941 prices were supported at a sliding scale of from 52.5 to 75 per cent of parity. During World War II the supports were set at 90 per cent to encourage production to help feed the armed forces and the Allies. Later a flexible system ranging from 75 to 90 per cent was voted.

Price Support and Soil Bank Plan

The Commodity Credit Corporation (CCC) is the government agency that handles commodity price agreements with the farmer. To get the support price, the farmer must usually agree to plant only a fixed acreage base in the crop. This does not necessarily reduce his output, as modern techniques permit him to raise more per acre.

The CCC offers to buy supported crops or to lend the farmer money on them at the support prices. If the farmer pledges a crop for a loan, he will pay the loan when it comes due if the market price is high enough to give him a profit on the crop. If the market price is lower than the support price, he allows the CCC to take full rights to the commodity.

Under the soil bank plan, passed by Congress in 1956, a farmer could withdraw land from production for 3-, 5-, or 10-year periods and receive rental payments. He planted it with grass, trees, or other vegetation that would help prevent erosion and aid fertility. New soil bank leasing ended in 1960. Under 1962 legislation, farmers could obtain loans to turn surplus cropland into recreation areas.

Efforts to Dispose of the Farm Surplus

The Agricultural Stabilization and Conservation Service assists in price support activities. It stores and ships commodities and tries to dispose of them. It is difficult to sell them on the world market at the supported price. Food is given to school lunch programs, to families on public assistance rolls, and to welfare institutions. Under Public Law 480

TESTING INSECTICIDE RESIDUE ON FOOD
This technician of the Agricultural Research Service is finding out whether a commercial insect spray leaves a harmful chemical on the food crops treated. Such tests help protect the health of consumers.

food and fiber are sold abroad for foreign currencies. The currencies may then be loaned to the recipient countries. Food is also given to countries that suffer from such disasters as floods and droughts.

There are difficulties even in giving away surplus food. Costs for transporting food run high. Friendly nations may complain that the American government is ruining their market for a commodity by giving it away or selling it at cut-rate prices.

In 1961 the government owned about 6.8 billion dollars' worth of commodities. Their storage and handling cost 460 million dollars that year.

Federal Aid in Farm Credit

The federal government helps the farmer obtain low-cost credit. The Farmers Home Administration lends money to farmers to buy, improve, and operate farms in cases where credit is not available from other lenders. The Farm Credit Administration supervises a nationwide system of co-operative lending associations. The Rural Electrification Administration makes loans to companies and co-operatives to take electric power and telephone service to rural districts. The Federal Crop Insurance Corporation offers to insure crops against loss from natural hazards. (*See also* Farm Credit.)

AGRICULTURAL EDUCATION

In the United States young people may study agriculture in high school and in college. Under the Smith-Hughes Act of 1917, the federal government grants funds to high schools for teaching vocational agriculture. The program is supervised by the Office of Education of the United States Department of Health, Education, and Welfare and by the respective state departments of education.

Students learn by doing. Their courses are coordinated with farming programs supervised by the teacher. Students carry on long-term productive projects, such as raising livestock as a business venture. They also undertake improvement projects to increase the value and efficiency of the farm. Examples include the building of a poultry house or the repair of farm machinery, using skills learned in shop class. In addition they conduct a variety of supplementary farm practices. They learn to keep records and figure profits and losses. They grade, process, and market their produce.

High-school vocational agriculture departments also offer evening classes to young farmers and adult farmers in the community. These classes help bring practicing operators up to date on information, methods, skills, and practices.

Professional Agriculture Colleges

In each state at least one college or university offers professional agricultural training. These institutions developed as

ACTIVITIES IN HIGH-SCHOOL VOCATIONAL AGRICULTURE
In addition to his classes each student in vocational agriculture carries on farm projects supervised by the teacher. The teacher (left) checks the weight gained by the hogs the boy is raising for market. This student (right) displays his fine corn.

a result of the Morrill Act of 1862, in which Congress provided public land grants to state colleges which would teach agriculture and mechanical arts (*see* Land Grant; Education). Later legislation provided additional federal aid.

The state experiment stations are connected with the agricultural colleges. They carry on research in laboratories and on experimental farms.

Vocations in Agriculture

Most men and women graduates in agriculture take up farming as a lifework. There are, however, a wide variety of related occupations to which they may turn their training and knowledge. The United States Department of Agriculture is the largest employer of professional agriculturists. It hires specialists for research, inspection, and other jobs in its far-flung program. State departments, agricultural education, and extension work offer a wide range of jobs.

Businesses catering to the farmer or utilizing farm products need graduates for research, production, marketing, and servicing work. Agricultural publishing requires people with a knowledge of modern farming to write and edit farm publications. Graduates may also work in radio, television, motion pictures, and advertising.

Farm Organizations

Farm boys and girls learn farming methods and develop as rural leaders through the work of their young people's clubs. Boys in vocational agriculture courses are eligible to join the Future Farmers of America.

The 4-H Clubs, sponsored by the United States Department of Agriculture and state agricultural colleges, carry on extensive programs in farming and homemaking. The Juvenile Grange, sponsored by the National Grange, is another farm youth group. (*See also* Future Farmers of America; 4-H Clubs.)

Adult farmers have independent dues-supported organizations for advancing their welfare. The three principal groups are the National Grange, organized in 1867; the American Farm Bureau Federation, begun in 1919; and the Farmers Union, set up as a national organization in 1906. (*See also* Farm Bureau Federation; Farmers Union.)

WORKING IN THE HIGH-SCHOOL SHOP
Shopwork is important in the vocational agriculture course. These students are learning to adjust and repair farm machinery.

REFERENCE-OUTLINE FOR STUDY OF AGRICULTURE

THE BUSINESS OF FARMING

AGRICULTURE

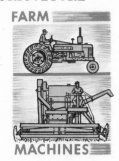

FARM MACHINES

THRESHING GRAIN

BIBLIOGRAPHY FOR AGRICULTURE
Books for Younger Readers

Boyd-Orr, John. The Wonderful World of Food (Garden City, 1958).
Colby, C. B. Soil Savers (Coward-McCann, 1957).
Eberle, Irmengarde. Basketful: the Story of Our Foods (Crowell, 1946).
Floethe, L. L. The Farmer and His Cows (Scribner, 1957).
Gorsline, D. W. Farm Boy (Viking, 1950).
Gringhuis, R. H. Of Cabbages and Cattle (Dial, 1962).
Ipcar, Dahlov. One Horse Farm (Doubleday, 1950).
Ipcar, Dahlov. Ten Big Farms (Knopf, 1958).

Books for Advanced Students and Teachers

Arnold, Pauline and White, Percival. Food: America's Biggest Business (Holiday, 1959).
Cannon, G. C. Great Men of Modern Agriculture (Macmillan, 1959).
Curwen, E. C. and Hatt, Gudmund. Plough and Pasture (Abelard, 1953).
Ethyl Corporation. Food for America's Future (McGraw, 1960).
Fite, G. C. The Farmers' Frontier, 1865–1900 (Holt, 1966).
Haberman, J. J. Farmer's Veterinary Handbook (Prentice-Hall, 1953).
Helfman, E. S. Land, People and History (McKay, 1962).
Longhouse, A. D. and Roehl, L. M. Farmer's Shop Book (Bruce, 1953).
Lord, Russell. The Care of the Earth (Nelson, 1962).
Sloane, Eric. Seasons of America Past (Wilfred Funk, 1958).
Smith, H. P. Farm Machinery and Equipment (McGraw, 1964).
Terrell, J. U. The United States Department of Agriculture (Duell, 1966).
Walden, H. T. Native Inheritance (Harper, 1966).

AIR—
What It Is and
What It Does

The Gases That Make Up Air	
NITROGEN	78%
OXYGEN	21%
ARGON	.93%
CARBON DIOXIDE AND OTHERS	.07%

In addition to nitrogen, oxygen, argon, and carbon dioxide, the composition of air includes traces of hydrogen, neon, krypton, helium, ozone, and xenon.

AIR. In countless tasks, from running blast furnaces to blowing up tires, people use air. Airplanes and kites need it to fly. The sound of thunder or a clap of hands requires air to be heard. Birds, fish, dogs, and man would die without it. Trees, flowers, and grass also need air to live.

Human beings are in contact with air every second that they live. It is all around, and it extends upward for many miles as the earth's atmosphere (*see* Atmosphere). Sometimes, on a windy day, people feel it brushing against their skin. They can hear it move when the wind howls or a tire blows out. Most of the time, however, people are completely unaware of the air, because it has no color, taste, or odor. They even think of a container of air as being empty.

What Is Air?

This invisible substance called air is really a mixture of several gases. Each gas is present in the form of separate, tiny particles called *molecules*. The molecules are much too small to be seen even with

HEATED AIR EXPANDS

Heat causes air in the bottle to expand. As the air requires more room, it flows into the balloon and inflates it.

the most powerful microscope. They make up for their small size, however, by being present in tremendous numbers. Scientists estimate that one cubic inch of ordinary air contains about 300 billion billion of them. They are so tiny, however, that there is plenty of space between them.

Under ordinary conditions, each molecule has energy enough to shoot through space at a speed of about 1,000 miles an hour. Very few molecules, however, travel far in a straight line at this speed. One reason is that the earth's force of gravity holds most of them within a few miles of the ground in spite of their speed. In this space they fly about, colliding with each other at a tremendous rate. In usual situations near the ground, each molecule collides with other molecules about 5 billion times a second.

Different Elements That Make Up Air

The molecules of two different elements, nitrogen and oxygen, make up about 99 per cent of the air. The rest includes small amounts of argon and carbon dioxide. (Other gases such as hydrogen, neon, krypton, helium, ozone, and xenon are present in traces.)

Oxygen is the life-giving element in the air. It helps plants make food and helps animals use these substances as though they were fuel. The heat given off by this process supplies energy, just as the burning of gasoline keeps an engine running. Oxygen supports fire and other chemical changes in matter. It also causes metals to rust. (*See also* Oxygen.)

Certain compounds of nitrogen help build tissue in living things. Nitrogen also serves to dilute the oxygen in the air. Plants, men, and animals are used to the diluted mixture and would soon "burn out" if they lived in pure oxygen. Indeed, the living world would soon burn up, for in pure oxygen every spark or flash of lightning would start raging fires which could never be controlled. (*See also* Nitrogen.)

Carbon dioxide is formed by the union of oxygen and carbon. Every fire produces it, as do the bodies of men and animals. They give it off in every breath they expel. Plants use the carbon in it for making food and give back the oxygen to the air. Thus they continually renew the supply of oxygen. (*See also* Carbon; Plants.)

Most air contains water vapor. The amount varies greatly from time to time and place to place. Air also contains dust, pollen, spores, bacteria, and other bits of solid and liquid matter.

The Properties of Air

Air can be compressed almost without limit. All the air in a space as big as a house can be squeezed into a small tank. On the other hand, air can expand almost indefinitely. If all the air were taken from inside a house and then one cubic foot of air were supplied, it would expand throughout the building.

This *elastic* quality comes from the nature of air as a mass of flying molecules. It can be compressed because there is plenty of space between the molecules. Pressure simply squeezes them closer together. A mass of air also will expand to fill any space which has fewer molecules. The colliding molecules merely spread out.

Although the molecules in air are unbelievably tiny, they still have weight; and there are many of them. Therefore any given mass of air has weight. At sea level and at standard pressure and temperature (29.921 inches of mercury and 59° F.) a cubic foot of air weighs about .0765 pounds. This is a little more than one ounce.

A vacuum is a space from which all matter, including air, has been removed. The concept of a complete, or "perfect," vacuum (zero internal pressure) is useful for many theoretical purposes. In practice, however, there is no equipment that can remove all the air from an airtight container. A confined space with almost all air removed from it is described as a "high vacuum" and is equal to a very *low* pressure. High vacuum techniques and compressed-air equipment have many uses in industrial plants and laboratories. (*See also* Vacuum; Pneumatic Appliances.)

Compressed Air

Air compressors serve numerous purposes in the home and in industry. A simple type is the hand pump used to inflate bicycle tires. To show that air

COMPRESSED AIR PRODUCES A FOUNTAIN

A glass tube is drawn into a nozzle. Air is blown through the nozzle into a stoppered bottle containing water. The compressed air produces a fountain.

has weight, let the air out of a basketball until it is quite soft. Weigh it on sensitive scales. Now pump it hard and weigh it again. It will be heavier by the weight of the extra air pumped into it. Similarly, every bit of extra air inside an automobile tire (the air that shows a pressure above zero on a tire gauge) adds to the weight of the tire.

In the toy air gun, bullets are fired with compressed air instead of gunpowder. A lever attached to the piston forces the air into a chamber, usually in the stock, and compresses it. When the trigger is pulled, a valve opens and the compressed air enters the barrel, forcing the bullet out.

Compressed air is used in manufacturing plants for a wide variety of purposes. It is used for paint spraying, for laundry and dry-cleaning equipment, and for heating-control units. Compressed air provides the power to drive many small tools, including grinders, drills, wrenches, and hoists. Stone blocks are engraved by blasts of compressed air. Bottling plants use it to operate their filling machines. Foundries depend upon it as power for hoisting operations and for cleaning molds, core boxes, and tools. Railroads

FLAME TAKES OXYGEN FROM THE AIR

A tube covered with a piece of rubber is placed over a flame and into putty. The hot air makes the rubber bulge. When the air cools, the loss of oxygen used by the flame causes a partial vacuum. Outside pressure pushes the rubber downward.

CARBON DIOXIDE PUTS OUT FIRE

A candle, baking soda, and water are placed in a glass. Vinegar is added, forming carbon dioxide, which smothers the flame.

use compressed air for many tasks. It operates pneumatic switches and serves to retard and charge air brakes. When air is compressed and also reduced to a temperature of about −312° F. it becomes a liquid with odd properties (*see* Liquid Air).

Air Pollution

Although air supports animal and plant life, it can also help produce effects that harm all living things. In a single year in the United States millions of tons of rubbish and wastes are poured into the air. When air is carrying such foreign particles it is said to be *polluted*.

Pollution arises from many sources. The burning of gasoline in automobiles causes harmful gases and combustion products. From cement and metal factories come millions of particles that are carried off in the air. Chemical plants produce gaseous by-products that are toxic when the concentration is high enough. Smoke from locomotives and from trash fires and garbage incinerators increases pollution.

As the United States becomes more and more industrialized, air pollution will increase and new health hazards will develop. City officials have the responsibility of enforcing laws to limit air pollution for the protection of the people.

A Demonstration of Atmospheric Pressure

Many interesting experiments with air can be performed with materials that are available in almost any home. For example, place a sheet of paper over the top of a glass filled with water. Hold the paper firmly in place and turn the glass upside down. Now the water will remain in the glass even if the paper is not held. This is because the paper prevents air from entering the glass. If the water ran out, it would create a vacuum. This demonstrates that pressure of air against the paper is greater than the weight of the water.

More Demonstrations of Air Pressure

To show the increase of air pressure under certain conditions, tie a rubber balloon onto the neck of an empty pop bottle. Place the bottle in a pan of warm water and set the pan on a hot burner. This heats the water, the bottle, and the air inside the bottle. As the air is heated, it expands and fills the balloon.

An experiment can be performed to show the power of air pressure. Boil a cup of water in an open can. The heated vapor expands and some flows out. Carefully put on the cover, making the can airtight. Next place the can into a sink and drench it with cold water. This causes the vapor to contract and create a vacuum inside the container. The air pressure on the outside will then crumple the can.

Compressed Air Produces a Fountain

Still another experiment demonstrates the effects of compressed air. Hold a glass tube over a gas flame until the glass softens. Then draw it thin

AIR PRESSURE CRUMPLES CAN

A cup of water is boiled in an open can. Heated vapor expands and some escapes. Then the container is sealed. Cold water is poured onto it. The heated vapor contracts, creating a vacuum inside the can. Air pressure on the outside crumples it.

FIRE NEEDS AIR SUPPLY

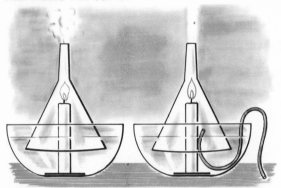

A candle flame under a glass funnel in a bowl of water smothers. A rubber tube is needed to supply air for combustion.

PRESSURE MAKES TEST TUBE SINK

A test tube is filled with water until it barely floats upside down in a container of water. For fine adjustment, air is blown in with a medicine dropper. Rubber is tied over the container's mouth. Pressure on the rubber causes the tube to sink.

and break it off to leave a small nozzle. Next fit the tube into a stopper, which is used to plug a bottle that is partially filled with water. The nozzle end points up, and the other end extends into the water.

Blowing through the nozzle into the bottle compresses the air. When blowing stops, the compressed air forces water out, making a fountain. The action is prolonged because of the tube's fine tip.

A Strange Diver

A diving experiment was devised by the French scientist René Descartes in the 17th century. To perform this experiment, pour water into a test tube until it will barely float. Place it upside down in a tall container of water and tie a piece of rubber over the mouth of the container.

Pressure on the rubber will compress the air in the container and in the test tube. This forces some water into the tube and makes it sink until the pressure is released. The air in the test tube displaces just enough water to balance the tube's weight. Archimedes discovered the principle some 2,000 years ago. (*See also* Archimedes; Liquid.)

Air Contains Oxygen

Oxygen in the air supports combustion. To demonstrate this, tie a piece of rubber over one end of a glass tube open on both ends. Next, insert a small candle into a piece of putty. Then light the candle, place the open end of the tube over the candle, and push the tube into the putty.

As the flame consumes oxygen, it heats up the other gases in the air and the rubber bulges outward. When the gases cool, there is a partial vacuum in the tube because of the loss of oxygen. Pressure from the outside air then forces the rubber into the tube.

Carbon Dioxide Suffocates Flame

Carbon dioxide extinguishes fire. To prove this, stand a candle upright inside a glass. Pour a little water mixed with baking soda into the glass. Light the candle. Next pour vinegar into the baking soda and water mixture. This forms carbon dioxide. When carbon dioxide fills the glass, the flame suffocates from lack of oxygen. This principle is used in some fire extinguishers.

To show how fire needs a steady supply of air, stand a candle in a bowl of water. Light the candle and lower a glass funnel over it down into the water. Soon the flame smokes and goes out from lack of oxygen. Now relight the candle and lead an empty tube from outside the bowl into the funnel near the flame. This will keep the flame burning by supplying air (and oxygen) for combustion.

The Egg Trick

A final experiment can be performed with an egg and a milk bottle. Light a long strip of wax paper or newspaper and drop it into the empty bottle. When the paper has burned, place a hard-boiled egg (with the shell removed) small end down on the mouth of the bottle. In a few seconds the egg will start moving down into the neck. Soon it will pop into the bottle.

The egg moves into the bottle because the burning paper heated the air inside the bottle, driving some of it out. When the flame died, the air cooled and contracted. Since the egg was now sealing the bottle, air pressure forced it down the neck.

AIR CONDITIONING —Man-Made Indoor Weather

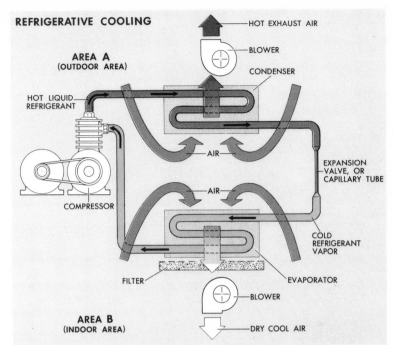

REFRIGERATIVE COOLING

HOT EXHAUST AIR

AREA A (OUTDOOR AREA)

BLOWER

CONDENSER

HOT LIQUID REFRIGERANT

AIR

EXPANSION VALVE, OR CAPILLARY TUBE

COMPRESSOR

AIR

COLD REFRIGERANT VAPOR

FILTER

EVAPORATOR

AREA B (INDOOR AREA)

BLOWER

DRY COOL AIR

Refrigerant vapor becomes hot when it is compressed. It is cooled by air forced over the condenser and then escapes through a small tube or valve opening to a cooling coil, or evaporator. Indoor air passing over the cooling coil transfers heat to the refrigerant. The hot refrigerant repeats the compression-expansion cycle.

AIR CONDITIONING. Man is the only animal that lives in all kinds of climates. He is able to do this because he protects himself from extreme heat and cold. Sometimes he changes the qualities of the air in indoor places. The control that man exercises over the air in houses, offices, stores, theaters, trains, automobiles, and airplanes is called air conditioning.

Air conditioning has a wide range of uses. These include conditioning operations both for human comfort and for many industrial processes.

Human Comfort Conditions

If a man is to remain alive and comfortable, he must lose heat to his surroundings about as fast as he generates it. If he loses body heat too rapidly his temperature will decrease and he may freeze. If he loses heat too slowly, his temperature will increase and his heart may be overworked.

Tests have determined that most people, when relaxed, find the following air temperature, humidity, and velocity rates agreeable: temperatures and humidities ranging from 71° F. with slightly over one per cent of moisture per pound of dry air (70 per cent relative humidity) to $83\frac{1}{2}°$ with about $\frac{7}{10}$ of one per cent of moisture (30 per cent relative humidity). Agreeable air velocities range from 15 to 35 feet per minute. Many home units can meet these requirements even in extreme weather conditions.

Uses in Industry

Low temperatures and humidities are often needed for storing perishables such as fruits and furs. Printing operations may require extremely constant humidity for control of paper shrinkage and for uniform operation in processes such as collotype and offset lithography. These processes rely on moisture for proper ink transfer. Bakeries and the tobacco and cotton industries require high humidities. Constant temperature control is necessary in many factories where metals are worked to very close tolerances. High filtration is often required in the chemical and other industries. This removes dust particles and crystals which might otherwise be harmful to chemical processes or human life.

Circulation of Air

Control of *circulation* and *pollution* as well as of *temperature* and *humidity* is the function of air-conditioning systems. Circulation of air is a basic requirement of all systems. Enclosed air may be recirculated. It can be diluted with fresh air through natural or forced ventilation. Water vapor, carbon dioxide, dust, and other matter may be added to it or taken from it. It may be heated or cooled.

In most air-conditioning systems some recirculated air is used; the remainder is fresh outdoor air. The circulation, or movement, may be *natural*, caused by the tendency of warm air to travel upward, or it may be *forced*. Natural circulation is sometimes used in heating systems, but cooling systems ordinarily employ fans or blowers.

Air motion alone can have a slight cooling effect on the human body. But the velocity must be high to the point of discomfort if the effect is to be helpful.

The blower power needed to move air is determined by the amount of *resistance* to the flow of air. Cooling coils, ducts, and many other parts of an air-conditioning system resist air motion.

Filtration of Air

Filters are used in all but the simplest systems to remove dust, pollen, spores, and other particles

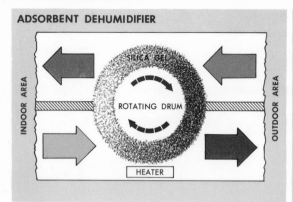

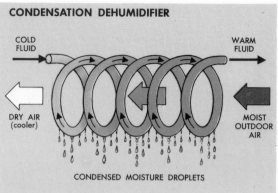

A typical adsorbent dehumidifier uses a drying chemical such as silica gel to capture moisture by capillary action (left).

Moisture condenses on a cooling coil and drips to a drain (right). Cool air can hold less moisture than warm air.

from air. *Fibrous* filters contain closely spaced fibers of glass or other materials to trap bits of dirt. Most of the filters in small, modern air-conditioning units are fibrous. *Viscous* filters use a thin film of oil, which is generally coated on a metal honeycomb, to trap dirt.

Electrostatic filters consist of a grid of wires carrying a high-voltage current to ionize particles. The charged particles are then attracted to oppositely charged collector plates, from which they may be continuously washed. Electrostatic filters are often used in industrial air conditioning.

Air washers employ sprays of water to trap particles and wash them away. The air passing through the spray is cleaned, cooled, and increased in humidity. Air washers are used industrially when high humidity is desirable.

Cooling and Dehumidifying Air

When people speak of air conditioning, they usually refer to *cooling*. Properly, however, it also includes *heating, filtering, circulating, humidifying,* and *dehumidifying*. (*See also* Heat; Heating and Ventilating.)

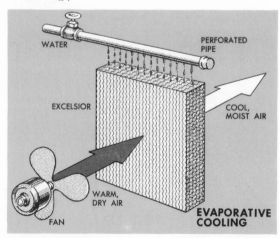

When warm, dry air is forced to pass through a moist area, it is cooled by evaporation. In the process the air is also cleaned and its moisture content increased.

Cooling and dehumidifying are most important in hot weather. They can make summer temperatures bearable even in the hottest of climatic zones.

Most present-day air conditioners employ a cold fluid circulating through a coil of tubing. Warm air passing around the tubing transfers heat to the fluid. The warmed fluid is ordinarily cooled and recirculated through the coil in a continuous process called *refrigeration*. (*See also* Refrigeration.)

Warm air is able to hold more moisture than cold air is. Consequently it is likely to be damper in warm weather than in cold weather. Moist air makes cooling by evaporation of perspiration very difficult, so the effect of high humidity on the human body is to increase discomfort.

When warm air passes over a cooling coil, its temperature falls to a point where it can no longer hold all the moisture it contains. Moisture then condenses on the coil in the form of droplets, which may be drained away.

Cooling by Refrigeration

Refrigeration air conditioners make use of the relationship between the *volume* of a substance and its capacity for holding heat. This is most easily demonstrated in the case of *gases*.

If a weight of gas at a given temperature is suddenly compressed, it attains a higher temperature momentarily. Then it loses heat to its surroundings. If the same weight of gas is suddenly expanded, its temperature will momentarily decrease.

Many refrigeration units employ fluids which take the form of gases part of the time and liquids part of the time. This change from gas to liquid can involve large degrees of compression and expansion and equally large amounts of heat.

Compressor Air Conditioners

Most modern refrigeration air conditioners in homes and factories make use of *compressor* cooling systems. In these, a gas called a *refrigerant* is alternately compressed and expanded. In the process the *temperature* of the refrigerant successively increases and decreases. At high pressures and temperatures, the refrigerant is in a partly *liquid* state. At low pressures and temperatures the refrigerant is in a *gaseous* state. The refrigerant enters a cooling coil as a gas and absorbs heat from the air flowing around the coil.

Upon leaving the cooling coil, the refrigerant is compressed by a device which resembles a bicycle pump in operation. After compression the hot refrigerant enters a *condenser*, usually located outside the cooled area. Now partly a liquid, it transfers heat to outdoor air.

Steam-Jet Air Conditioners

Steam-jet refrigeration coolers employ *water* as a refrigerant. The water is vaporized at low temperature in a partial vacuum, induced by a strong jet of superheated steam. The process is similar to compressor refrigeration, except that *low* pressures are used to expand a refrigerant which is *liquid* at ordinary room temperatures and pressures.

Steam-jet coolers lend themselves well to systems that employ a boiler for heating purposes. The same boiler may be used to produce steam both for heating and for cooling. In addition, the same piping may serve for the transmission of hot *and* cold fluids. Large factory-size models are the only steam-jet coolers currently available.

Air-Cycle Air Conditioners

Air-cycle refrigeration is commonly employed to cool high-speed aircraft, such as military jets. The speed of the craft compresses air in a forward-facing tube. This compressed air is then used as a refrigerant. Operation resembles that of an ordinary compressor cooler, except that the refrigerant, air, does not liquefy. In this case air is cooled by air.

Absorption-System Air Conditioners

Heat, supplied by gas or oil burners, may be used to make the necessary changes of pressure of a refrigerant. In absorption-system coolers a liquid absorbs the refrigerant vapor. The liquid is heated to drive out the vapor, sending it through a closed system under pressure. Other steps are similar to compressor refrigeration.

Absorption systems are coming into wider use in homes. They offer the mechanical advantage of few moving parts, and gas or oil fuels may be low in cost.

Cooling Condensers

Refrigerant systems are essentially *pumps* which transfer heat

from one area to another. In fact, heat may be pumped *into* a building by a device called a *heat pump*. (*See also* Heating and Ventilating.)

When an enclosed area is cooled, heat from it is transferred to the outdoors. The more efficient the transfer, the cooler the indoor air. Heat removal from refrigerant to outdoor air is accomplished in a *condenser*.

Air-cooled condensers are usually employed in small air conditioners. Heat is transferred to the outdoors from refrigerant in a coil of finned tubing.

Water-cooled condensers use water, flowing through tubing within a refrigerant chamber, to convey heat to outdoor air. The water may, in turn, be cooled in a device which resembles an automobile radiator, but evaporative cooling is more common for large systems.

In evaporative cooling, water is pumped to a high, narrow outdoor structure called a *cooling tower*. The water is released from the top of the tower in a fine spray. Air blown through the water causes some of it to evaporate. The water is cooled in the process. Fresh water is added to the tower to replace the small amount lost by evaporation. Cooling towers are frequently seen atop large factories and office buildings.

Heat Pumps

As has been noted, all refrigeration systems are essentially pumps which transfer heat from one place to another. The process of cooling is reversible;

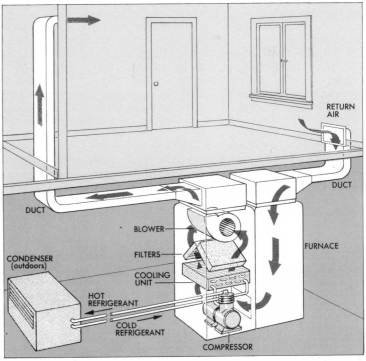

CENTRAL AIR CONDITIONER WITH DUCTS
Air conditioners vary greatly in size and capacity. A central home system contains heating, cooling, filtering, and distributing units.

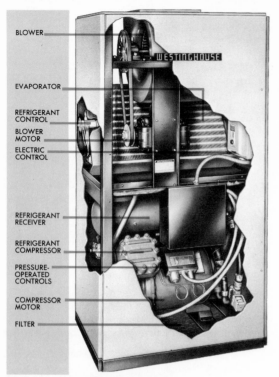

BLOWER

EVAPORATOR

REFRIGERANT
CONTROL

BLOWER
MOTOR

ELECTRIC
CONTROL

REFRIGERANT
RECEIVER

REFRIGERANT
COMPRESSOR

PRESSURE-
OPERATED
CONTROLS

COMPRESSOR
MOTOR

FILTER

UNITARY AIR CONDITIONER
Unitary air conditioners contain all the equipment needed for cooling an area. Examples are window and console systems.

that is, a refrigeration system may be used to transfer heat *into* an enclosure. In fact, the same system may be used for cooling in summer and for heating in winter. Air-cooled condensers and cooling coils are basically very similar. In heat-pump systems an indoor cooling coil functions as a heating condenser in winter, while the outdoor condenser functions as a cooling coil.

The outdoor cooling coil-condenser combination in a heat-pump system may be buried in the ground or located in a well or a stream. Temperatures are usually more regular in such locations because earth and water can store large amounts of heat. Heat pumps are usually located in areas with heavy cooling requirements and moderate heating needs. Florida, for example, has many such installations. (*See also* Heating and Ventilating.)

Central, Local, and Zone Systems

Large central air-conditioning systems simultaneously condition the air in many rooms of a large structure. These units are usually controlled automatically. Sensitive *thermostats* and *hygrostats* (switches which respond to changes in temperature and moisture) are used to switch equipment on or off, depending upon need. In addition, central or local control of air circulation may be available. Large systems are usually assembled from individual parts made by different manufacturers. Some, however, are available in complete packaged units.

Indoor air conditions may be regulated by small window, console, or cabinet air conditioners, operated in individual rooms. These local systems are often controlled by hand, being turned on only when room air becomes uncomfortably warm.

Certain industrial operations may call for completely different air conditions in different rooms of a building. Zone systems, frequently made up of two or more large air conditioners, are able to meet these special cases.

Air-Conditioning Requirements

The different mechanical units which comprise an air-conditioning system may vary enormously in *capacity*. One cooling unit, for example, may be able to rid an enclosure of ten times as much heat as another. Equipment should be selected to meet, but should not exceed, individual needs.

Air-conditioning requirements for human comfort depend upon many variable factors. Among them are:

1. The temperature, humidity, and wind conditions of the area in which the enclosure is located.

2. The construction of the enclosure, its position with respect to the sun's path, and the amount of air which can enter naturally through cracks in windows and doors.

3. The operations carried on within the enclosure (cooking, manufacturing processes, and so forth).

4. The number of persons inside the enclosure, their personal habits (such as smoking), and their individual requirements.

A good air-conditioning estimator understands the effects of climate and weather, structural engineering, and even physiology. Additional factors, such as the presence of an existing duct system, may also have to be taken into account. For these reasons professional contractors are usually called on to design and install large central systems both in homes and in commercial buildings.

Capacity Ratings; Automobile Air Conditioners

Modern air-conditioning equipment is rated in British thermal units (B.T.U.) (*see* Heat). Formerly, cooling systems were also rated in tons, one ton of cooling capacity equaling 12,000 B.T.U. per hour.

Many factors affect the cooling requirements of a structure. For this reason, the determination of capacity requirements can be made only on an individual basis. As a rough gauge, however, a single-story, three-bedroom house of conventional wood construction, located in the Northern United States, requires air-conditioning equipment with a cooling capacity of approximately 30,000 B.T.U. per hour.

Air-conditioning units in automobiles are scaled-down versions of the compressor cooling systems found in homes. In addition to a compressor and a condenser, however, air conditioners used in automobiles have an *evaporator*. The many-finned evaporator, filled with refrigerant cooled by the condenser, absorbs heat from outside air passing through it. The air thus cooled is blown into the automobile's interior.

The AIR FORCE
of the United States

An Atlas Space Launch Vehicle (SLV), used to boost spacecraft into orbit, is shown in position above racks of piping which will be assembled as part of the rocket's hydraulic, pneumatic, and electrical systems.

AIR FORCE, UNITED STATES. In this age of air power, the military strength of a nation depends largely upon the size and quality of its air force. Yet the airplane was invented only a little more than 60 years ago (see Airplane History).

The fighters, bombers, and missiles of the United States armed services are the defensive shield guarding against air attacks. They are also the offensive sword ready to retaliate against an aggressor.

The military air power of the United States is provided by the Air Force, Navy, Marine Corps, and Army (see Navy, United States; Marine Corps, United States; Army, United States). Of these, the United States Air Force (USAF) is the most powerful.

The USAF operates a mixed force of airplanes and missiles (see Guided Missiles). The airplane has undergone rapid development as a modern weapon of

war. As advances have been made in missilery, however, emphasis has gradually turned away from the traditional types of manned aircraft.

Research and development programs continually result in the production of advanced aircraft and new weapons. Airplanes of the USAF carry such weapons as missiles and nuclear and thermonuclear bombs. In addition, new types of machine guns and nonnuclear bombs have been developed. The USAF also has rockets for attacking enemy targets in the air or on the ground.

AIRCRAFT INSIGNIA IDENTIFY A NATION'S AIR FORCE

AUSTRALIA

FIN FLASH

WINGS AND FUSELAGE

CANADA
Air Force and Navy

FIN FLASH

WINGS AND FUSELAGE

CHINA, COMMUNIST

WINGS AND FUSELAGE

CHINA, NATIONALIST

RUDDER

WINGS AND FUSELAGE

FRANCE
Air Force and Navy

RUDDER

WINGS AND FUSELAGE

GERMANY, WEST

FIN FLASH

WINGS AND FUSELAGE

GREAT BRITAIN
Air Force and Navy

FIN FLASH
WINGS AND FUSELAGE

ITALY

RUDDER

WINGS AND FUSELAGE

JAPAN
Defense Forces

RUDDER

WINGS AND FUSELAGE

MEXICO

RUDDER

WINGS

RUSSIA

WINGS, FUSELAGE, AND RUDDER

UNITED STATES
Air Force, Navy, and Army

WINGS AND FUSELAGE

MIGHTY MUSCLES OF THE AIR FORCE
Aircraft and missiles make up the might of the Air Force. The
Convair F-102 Delta Dagger, shown here, carries Falcon missiles.

How the Air Force Is Organized

The three components of the United States Department of Defense are the departments of the Army, the Navy, and the Air Force. The Department of the Air Force is headed by a civilian secretary. He is appointed by the president and approved by the Senate.

The Air Force's top military man is the chief of staff, a four-star general. He and a group of officers supervise a wide range of Air Force duties in the United States and overseas.

WORLD'S MOST IMPORTANT TELEPHONE
Over this "red phone" of the Strategic Air Command at Offutt
AFB, Neb., would go orders if an enemy attacked.

Major Commands of the Air Force

Sixteen major commands, or functional organizations, are responsible for specific areas of the Air Force's mission to defend the United States. They may be grouped into combat, overseas, training, and support commands, according to their primary functions. The basic combat organizations are the Strategic Air, Tactical Air, and Air Defense commands.

Strategic Air Command

The Strategic Air Command (SAC) is designed to strike at the enemy so that his ability or will to make war is destroyed. SAC is the mainstay of the free-world policy called nuclear deterrence. This means that if the United States or its Allies were attacked, SAC airplanes carrying nuclear bombs would immediately inflict paralyzing blows against the enemy. Military bases, factories, communication and transportation facilities, and population centers, deep within the aggressor's territory, would be the primary objectives.

SAC headquarters are at Offutt Air Force Base (AFB), Omaha, Neb.

SAC is made up of four air forces in the United States and abroad, one overseas-based air division, and a missile division. SAC's Second Air Force has its headquarters at Barksdale AFB La. The headquarters of the Eighth Air Force are at Westover AFB, Mass. The headquarters of the Fifteenth Air Force are at March AFB, Calif. Overseas are the Sixteenth Air Force, Torrejón Air Base, Spain; and the 3d Air Division at Andersen AFB, Guam. The 1st Strategic Aerospace Division is located at Vandenberg AFB, Calif.

The Aircraft of SAC

The Strategic Air Command has fleets of heavy bombers and long-range missiles in a state of combat readiness day and night. The Boeing B-52 Stratofortress became SAC's chief bomber in the mid-1950's. The B-52 has a range of 12,500 miles, a bomb-carrying capacity of more than ten tons, and a ceiling above 60,000 feet. Eight jet engines give the B-52 a speed in excess of 650 miles an hour. The plane carries a crew of six. It can strike against a target anywhere on the globe within hours after takeoff. The range of the B-52 is greatly increased when the plane is refueled in flight by the jet-powered Boeing KC-135 Stratotanker.

In 1960 the Convair B-58 Hustler was added to the weapons of SAC. This bomber, designed to carry either nuclear or conventional bombs, has a speed of more than 1,300 miles an hour. It is a long-range, high-altitude airplane, powered by four jet engines. It carries a crew of three men.

The North American XB-70 Valkyrie was introduced in 1964. Planned as a bomber, it was redesignated a research plane. The Air Force revealed two secretly designed planes in 1964—the Lockheed YF-12A and the SR-71 (strategic reconnaissance), capable of flying more than 2,000 miles per hour (over

Mach 3) and at altitudes over 70,000 feet. Also introduced in 1964 was the General Dynamics F-111A (formerly TFX), a tactical fighter designed to fly at both subsonic speeds and up to about 1,650 miles per hour by means of adjustments in wing position.

A new strategic bomber, a variation of the F-111A fighter, was authorized for development in 1965. The plane, designated the FB-111, will eventually replace the B-58's and the early model B-52's. The FB-111 will carry a two-man crew and fly at altitudes of more than 60,000 feet.

The Air Force's Strategic Missiles

The Northrop Snark, the first United States intercontinental cruise missile, was activated by the Air Force in 1957. Its production was later discontinued. The Douglas Thor intermediate-range ballistic missile (IRBM), designed to carry a nuclear warhead over 1,500 miles, became operational in 1958. Obsolete by 1963, it remained in use as a satellite launcher. The first United States intercontinental ballistic missile (ICBM), the Convair Atlas, became operational in 1959, and the Martin Titan I in 1962. Both liquid-fuel, pad-launched missiles became obsolete in 1965.

Other important Air Force ICBM's are the Boeing Minuteman I, which became operational in 1962, and the Titan II, which became operational in 1963. Both missiles have ranges beyond 6,300 miles. In 1966 the Minuteman II, with a range of over 7,000 miles, was deployed to replace the earlier model; Minuteman III was under development. The Minutemen use solid fuel; the Titan II, liquid fuel. These missiles are launched from deep underground silos, "hardened" to withstand enemy attack.

One of the mobile missiles used by the Air Force is the North American Hound Dog air-to-surface guided missile (AGM). It is designed to be launched from B-52 bombers about 600 miles from the target.

AIRCRAFT MISSION DESIGNATIONS OF THE UNITED STATES AIR FORCE

Aircraft of the United States Air Force are classified by letters and numbers which show the type, the model, and the production series. For example, an F-100D is a fighter, the 100th design model, and the fourth, or D, series of that model. Series letters indicate changes in the engine, structure, or other parts of the basic model.

These type designations are used singly or, if the aircraft serves more than one function, in combinations such as KC—Tanker Transport

A—Attack	**O**—Observation
B—Bomber	**Q**—Target and drone
C—Cargo and transport	**T**—Trainer
F—Fighter	**U**—Utility
H—Helicopter	**V**—Convertiplane
K—Tanker	**X**—Special Research

These letters are used with other mission designations and never alone

D—Director for drones and missiles	**M**—Carrier for missiles or parasites
E—Equipped with special electronic gear	**R**—Reconnaissance
	V—Administrative (staff) transport
H—Search and rescue	
L—Adapted for cold-weather operation	**W**—Weather reconnaissance

These prefixes are also used

X—Experimental	**Z**—Planning
Y—Prototype	

The Role of Tactical Air Power

The Tactical Air Command (TAC) is concerned with gaining air superiority over given areas and supporting ground troops in combat. Two other prime responsibilities of TAC are to disrupt enemy transportation, communication, and supply networks and to strike against enemy emplacements and troops.

MAJOR COMMANDS OF THE UNITED STATES AIR FORCE

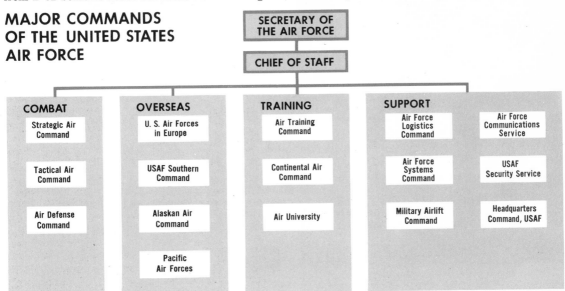

SECRETARY OF THE AIR FORCE

CHIEF OF STAFF

COMBAT
- Strategic Air Command
- Tactical Air Command
- Air Defense Command

OVERSEAS
- U. S. Air Forces in Europe
- USAF Southern Command
- Alaskan Air Command
- Pacific Air Forces

TRAINING
- Air Training Command
- Continental Air Command
- Air University

SUPPORT
- Air Force Logistics Command
- Air Force Communications Service
- Air Force Systems Command
- USAF Security Service
- Military Airlift Command
- Headquarters Command, USAF

FIGHTER PILOT

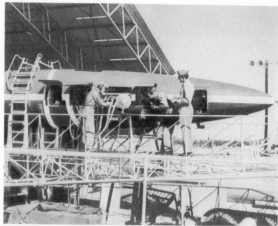

GUIDED-MISSILE MECHANICS

ARMAMENT CREWMEN

JET-ENGINE MECHANICS

TAC's headquarters are at Langley Air Force Base (AFB), near Norfolk, Va. TAC is made up of three numbered air forces—the Ninth, at Shaw AFB, S.C.; the Twelfth, at Waco, Tex.; and the Nineteenth, at Seymour Johnson AFB, N.C. Units of the Ninth and Twelfth air forces are stationed at some 13 air bases throughout the country.

The Nineteenth Air Force is responsible for TAC's Composite Air Strike Force, which is capable of quickly flying tactical and support aircraft to trouble spots anywhere in the world. TAC also contributes elements to the United States Strike Command, a new unified command for which the Strategic Army Corps provides picked combat units.

The Weapons of TAC

TAC planes and missiles include the North American F-100 Supersabre tactical fighter; McDonnell F-101 Voodoo all-weather fighter-interceptor; Douglas RB-66 Destroyer reconnaissance light bomber; Lockheed F-104 Starfighter fighter-interceptor; Republic F-105 Thunderchief all-weather fighter-bomber; and the Martin Mace 1,200-mile-range tactical missile. Supporting aircraft include the Fairchild C-123

Provider, the Lockheed C-130 Hercules, and the Lockheed C-141 Starlifter cargo and troop transports.

The F-104 and the F-105 attain speeds of more than 1,400 miles an hour. They can carry nuclear or conventional bombs and can be armed with the 100-shot-per-second Vulcan automatic cannon. Most of TAC's planes are F-100's, which have speeds of more than 800 miles an hour, and F-101's, which can exceed 1,200 miles an hour. The McDonnell F-4C Phantom is one of TAC's newest and fastest fighters. It is capable of speeds up to 1,600 miles an hour.

The Air Defense Mission

The Air Defense Command (ADC), with headquarters at Ent AFB, Colorado Springs, Colo., guards the nation against airborne attack. It is the USAF component of the North American Air Defense Command (NORAD)/Continental Air Defense Command (CONAD) structure, which includes elements of all the United States armed services and the Royal Canadian Air Force Air Defence Command. NORAD/CONAD's headquarters are at Ent AFB.

The Combat Operations Center (COC), from which air defense forces are directed, is in a hardened site

CONTROL TOWER OPERATORS

RADAR TECHNICIANS

AIRCRAFT LOADMASTER

AEROSPACE RESEARCHER

MEN AND WOMEN OF THE AIR FORCE
The Air Force performs many jobs besides flying aircraft. Airmen and airwomen receive training in more than 40 career fields.

within Cheyenne Mountain, about nine miles northwest of Ent AFB. The ADC has four numbered air forces. The First is at Stewart AFB, N. Y.; the Fourth, at Hamilton AFB, Calif.; the Tenth, at Richards-Gebaur AFB, Mo.; and the Fourteenth, at Gunter AFB, Ala.

Air defense today is based on early warning against attack. It includes the Distant Early Warning (DEW) Line and Ballistic Missile Early Warning System (BMEWS) in the Far North. After airborne radar planes and radar picket ships identify an attacker, the Semi-Automatic Ground Environment (SAGE) electronic system does the "thinking" (*see* Radar).

Air Defense Weapons

Planes of this defense network include the 800-mph Convair F-102 Delta Dagger and the 1,500-mph Convair F-106 Delta Dart, along with the F-101 and the F-104. ADC's prime surface-to-air missile is the Boeing Bomarc. The "A" model of Bomarc, which had a 200-mile range, became obsolete in 1964. The Bomarc "B," operational since 1961, has twice the range of the "A" version. Air Force fighter aircraft can fire a number of air-to-air rockets and

missiles. These include the Hughes Falcon, Philco Sidewinder, Douglas Genie, and Raytheon Sparrow.

Other Major USAF Commands

There are 13 other major USAF commands. The four overseas commands are:

United States Air Forces in Europe (USAFE), with headquarters at Lindsey Air Station, Wiesbaden, West Germany. It provides military support for America's allies. USAFE is charged with tactical and air defense operations and is equipped with the types of planes suited to these missions.

Pacific Air Forces (PAF), Hickam AFB, Oahu, Hawaii. Geographically it is the largest of the Air Force commands. PAF's role in the Pacific and in Southeast Asia is similar to that of USAFE.

Alaskan Air Command (AAC), Elmendorf AFB, Alaska. Strategically located, it is important as part of the electronic warning air defense system.

USAF Southern Command (USAFSC), Albrook AFB, Panama Canal Zone. It is charged with helping Latin

PLANES OF
WORLD WAR I

ALLIES

UNITED STATES

GREAT BRITAIN

CURTISS JN-4A JENNY

SOPWITH PUP

DE HAVILLAND DH-4

HANDLEY PAGE HP-400

American nations develop air forces of their own. The six support commands are:

Air Force Communications Service (AFCS), Scott AFB, Ill. It provides communications, flight facilities, and air-traffic-control service.

Air Force Logistics Command (AFLC), Wright-Patterson AFB, Ohio. AFLC procures, distributes, maintains, and stores supplies for the Air Force.

Air Force Systems Command (AFSC), Andrews AFB, Md. AFSC is responsible for the acquisition and development of new weapon systems.

Headquarters Command, USAF, Bolling AFB, Washington, D. C. It provides administrative services.

Military Airlift Command (MAC), Scott AFB, Ill. It provides aerial transportation for all the armed services of the United States.

USAF Security Service, San Antonio, Tex. It is responsible for service security matters.

The three training commands are:

Air Training Command (ATC), Randolph AFB, Tex. ATC supervises all Air Force training, both for technical and for flight personnel.

Air University (AU), Maxwell AFB, Ala. AU provides advanced education for Air Force officers.

Continental Air Command (CONAC), Robins AFB, Ga. CONAC is responsible for administering the Air

Force Reserve and the Air National Guard programs.

The Air Force also has four separate operating agencies. These are the Air Force Accounting and Finance Center, the Aeronautical Chart and Information Center, the Office of Aerospace Research, and the United States Air Force Academy (*see* Air Force Academy, United States).

Size and Composition of the Air Force

The Air Force is made up of more than 800,000 men and women in uniform. In addition, about 300,000 civilians work for the Air Force in noncombat jobs.

The total number of aircraft of all types is about 20,000. The planes include heavy and medium bombers, fighter-bombers, and fighter-interceptors. Special-purpose types include reconnaissance, transport, trainer, communications, tanker, search and rescue, observation, helicopter, weather, and research.

The combat aircraft are organized into more than 100 operational units known as *wings*. The number of planes in a wing varies from 75 for fighters to 30 for heavy bombers. A wing is usually divided into four *groups*. Each group is further divided into *squadrons*, which are themselves made up of *flights* of aircraft. A flight of fighters is usually composed of four planes.

There are at least two wings in each *air division*.

NIEUPORT 28

SPAD XIII

The air divisions make up the numbered *air forces*, such as the Ninth Air Force of the Tactical command.

Air Force Installations and Man Power

The Air Force has 266 major installations in this country and abroad. These include air bases, missile-launching sites, radar outposts, and supply centers.

The uniformed personnel in the Air Force are either officers or enlisted men and women. (For table of rank and pay, *see* Army, United States. *See also* Uniforms.) A person entering the Air Force as an enlisted man, or "airman," receives basic training and then usually specializes in one of more than 40 basic fields of work. Women in the Air Force (WAF) perform a variety of noncombatant tasks.

All pilots are officers. Officers also occupy administrative posts, navigate aircraft, and hold important technical jobs. They are chosen in a number of ways: through graduation from the Air Force Academy, from the Air Force Reserve Officers' Training Corps (AFROTC) programs at colleges, through flight training programs, from the enlisted ranks, or under special officer-procurement programs.

The Air National Guard (ANG) and the Air Force Reserve (AFRes) supplement the Regular Air Force in times of emergency. The Civil Air Patrol (CAP) is a civilian auxiliary of the Air Force (*see* Civil Air Patrol).

Establishment of an Air Arm

The Air Force has been a separate branch of the United States armed services only since 1947. Before that time it was part of the Army. The first air arm was established in 1907 as the Aeronautical Division of the Army Signal Corps. Two years later the first military airplane, a Wright "Flyer," was purchased. The First Aero Squadron was organized in 1914. It served with the Mexican Border Expedition in 1916, the first United States military air unit to see action. (*See also* Airplane History.)

The Air Service in World War I

In 1914 the Aeronautical Division became the Aviation Section of the Signal Corps. When the United States entered World War I in 1917, it had 103 planes, none of them fit for combat (*see* World War I). In April 1918 the first American air units flew in combat. A month later Army aviation was separated from the Signal Corps. Two air departments were created—the Division of Military Aeronautics and the Bureau of Aircraft Production.

Individual combat in dogfights characterized aerial warfare in World War I. The first "bombs" were grenades dropped from open cockpits. Gradually aircraft and tactics improved.

FOKKER D-VII

GOTHA G-IV

PLANES OF
WORLD WAR II

ALLIES

UNITED STATES

GREAT BRITAIN

NORTH AMERICAN P-51 MUSTANG

SUPERMARINE SPITFIRE XIV

BOEING B-17 FLYING FORTRESS

AVRO LANCASTER

The war produced 71 American "aces," men who shot down five or more enemy planes. The leading ace was Capt. Eddie Rickenbacker of the 94th Pursuit "Hat-in-the-Ring" Squadron, with 26 victories.

End of World War I

When the war ended in 1918 the United States Air Service had 767 pilots and 740 aircraft. Air personnel totaled 195,000 officers and men, about 10 per cent of the Allied air strength.

In 150 bombing attacks the United States pilots dropped 138 tons of explosives and penetrated only 160 miles behind the German lines. American losses were 237 fliers killed and 289 planes.

Most of the aircraft flown in combat by Americans were purchased from the Allies. The Nieuport and the Spad were both built by the French. Another was the British-designed De Havilland DH-4 reconnaissance plane, of which 3,000 were produced in the United States. A few thousand Curtiss JN-4 Jenny trainers were also built in the United States. During the war the United States produced about 14,000 aircraft.

Aviation Developments After World War I

After the war military aviation continued to develop. The first transcontinental flight in a 24-hour period was made by Lieut. William D. Coney in a De Havilland DH-4-B, between San Diego, Calif., and Jacksonville, Fla., in 1921. Two years later Lieuts. Oakley G. Kelly and John A. Macready in a Fokker

T-2 made the first nonstop, coast-to-coast flight from New York to California, in just under 27 hours.

In 1924 Army fliers in Douglas World Cruiser biplanes made history's first round-the-world flight, covering more than 26,000 miles in 363 hours of flying time. The trip took 175 days. In 1929 the *Question Mark*, piloted by Maj. Carl Spaatz (later USAF's first chief of staff) and Capt. Ira C. Eaker, with a crew of three, set a world endurance mark of 150 hours, 40 minutes, using aerial refueling.

Crusade for an Independent Air Force

Earlier, in 1921, Brig. Gen. William Mitchell, an ardent air-power exponent, in a demonstration of strategic bombardment, had sunk the former German battleship *Ostfriesland*. In 1923 Mitchell's bombers sank two obsolete United States battleships. Mitchell's outspoken crusade for an independent air force and criticisms of the high command resulted in his court-martial in 1925 (*see* Mitchell). The following year Congress established the Army Air Corps.

The 1930's were years of development for the Air Corps. A long-range training program was established. Such bases as Randolph and Kelly fields in Texas and Scott and Chanute in Illinois were founded for training pilots. All-metal planes appeared, as did the monoplane and the first of the big bombers—the Boeing B-9 and Martin B-10. In 1935 the Boeing B-17 was flight tested. It became the Flying Fortress, bombardment mainstay of World War II.

RUSSIA

YAK-9

ILYUSHIN IL-3 SHTURMOVIK

The Challenge of World War II

In 1940 when Hitler's forces—spearheaded by the *Luftwaffe* (German Air Force)—overran Europe, President Franklin D. Roosevelt called for production of 50,000 planes a year (*see* World War II). American plants topped this goal, and in 1944 alone they turned out more than 96,000 planes.

In June 1941 the Army Air Forces was established, with Maj. Gen. Henry H. "Hap" Arnold as its first chief. He was made commanding general of the AAF in 1942. General Arnold was to lead the AAF throughout the war, which the United States entered on Dec. 7, 1941, after the Japanese attack on Pearl Harbor.

At the time of the attack the AAF had about 315,000 officers and men. It had 12,000 aircraft, although only 600 were suitable for combat. In the next four years this force was to become the world's most formidable air organization, with almost 2,500,000 men and 80,000 aircraft.

The War in Europe

Military planners directed that Germany should be defeated first, while the Allies maintained a holding action against Japan. On July 4, 1942, the first

AXIS POWERS

GERMANY

JAPAN

JUNKER JU-87 STUKA

MITSUBISHI TYPE "0" (ZERO)

MESSERSCHMITT ME-109

MITSUBISHI MODEL 52 (ZEKE)

BOMBER—Boeing B-52G Stratofortress

TANKER—Boeing KC-135 Stratotanker

TRANSPORT—Lockheed C-130 Hercules

Eighth Air Force squadron flew into action in Europe. Daylight precision bombing proved costly in men and planes. Nevertheless plans were laid at the Casablanca conference in 1943 for a combined bomber offensive against Germany. This called for a round-the-clock air attack, with the AAF bombing by day and the RAF bombing by night. The plan was suggested to the Allied leaders by Gen. Ira C. Eaker.

One of the biggest raids of the war was made on Schweinfurt and Regensburg in 1943, when 376 B-17's dropped 724 tons of bombs with a loss of 60 bombers. In February 1944 began the "big week," a concentrated attack by all available AAF and RAF bombers on German aircraft production centers. In six days 3,800 sorties were flown and 10,000 tons of bombs were dropped.

The Allies had won air superiority over most of Western Europe by the time of the cross-channel invasion on June 6, 1944. On D-Day the AAF flew more than 8,000 sorties. Strategic bombing reached its climax on March 11, 1945, when the AAF dropped the greatest weight of bombs on a single target in Europe. On this raid 1,079 Eighth Air Force planes released 4,738 tons of explosives on the city of Essen. Tactical bombing of targets immediately behind the enemy lines was carried out with equal success by the Ninth Air Force.

War in the Pacific

The air war in the Pacific centered around the operations of the global Twentieth Air Force, activated in 1944. Its major weapon was the Boeing B-29 Superfortress. It operated from bases in China and later from islands in the central Pacific.

The series of strategic, long-range bombing strikes against the Japanese homeland began in 1944. The following year Maj. Gen. Curtis E. LeMay of the Twentieth Bomber Command ordered his Superforts to attack Japanese industrial centers with fire bombs. Seventeen strikes totaling 6,960 sorties dropped 41,600 tons of incendiaries and razed 102 square miles of Tokyo, Nagoya, Kobe, Osaka, and Yokohama.

The age of atomic warfare was ushered in when a B-29, the *Enola Gay*, dropped a nuclear bomb on Hiroshima in 1945. Three days later another B-29 A-bombed Nagasaki. The next day the Japanese sued for peace.

The AAF flew 1,693,505 combat sorties in the European theater, dropping 1,500,000 tons of bombs. In the Pacific there were 669,235 sorties and 500,000 tons of bombs dropped. The AAF lost 18,418 aircraft

FIGHTERS—North American F-100C Super Sabre (left), General Dynamics F-111A (right)

INTERCEPTOR—Lockheed YF-12A

to Germany and 4,530 to Japan. Enemy aircraft destroyed totaled 29,916 German and 10,343 Japanese.

Aces and Aircraft of World War II

World War II produced about 640 aces, headed by Maj. Richard I. Bong, a fighter pilot in the Pacific, who had 40 victories. Next was Maj. Thomas B. McGuire, with 38 kills. About one per cent of American fighter pilots became aces, but this group accounted for 40 per cent of the enemy aircraft downed.

Combat aircraft flown by the AAF included the Boeing B-29 Superfortress (very heavy bomber); the Boeing B-17 Flying Fortress and Consolidated B-24 Liberator (heavy bombers); the North American B-25 Mitchell and Martin B-26 Marauder (medium bombers); and the Douglas A-20 Havoc (light bomber). Fighters included the Lockheed P-38 Lightning, Curtiss P-40 Warhawk, Republic P-47 Thunderbolt, and North American P-51 Mustang.

Aircraft Production in World War II

In 1943 the labor force in the aircraft industry reached a peak of 1,345,600. In the same year more than 85,000 planes were delivered. Douglas, Consolidated, Boeing, and North American produced more

AIRCRAFT OF THE AIR FORCE TODAY
The aircraft of the United States Air Force consists not only of fighters and bombers but also of many specialized craft.

than half the total airframe weight. Production reached a high in 1944 of nearly 100,000 planes.

The bulk of this great force was scrapped when the war ended. From a wartime high of almost 2,400,000 officers and men, the AAF shrank to a little more than 300,000 men and 25,000 planes by 1947. In the same year the National Security Act made the United States Air Force (USAF) an equal member of the three-part National Military Establishment.

The New Air Force

The United States had a monopoly on atomic weapons. The Air Force with its heavy bombers had the only effective delivery system. However, with advances in weapons and jet propulsion a virtually new Air Force had to be created (see Jet Propulsion). In 1946 the Strategic Air Command, Tactical Air Command, and Air Defense Command—the USAF's three basic combat commands—were formed.

Also in 1946 the Convair B-36 Peacemaker made its first flight. It was then the world's largest land-based bomber and could carry 10,000 pounds of

THE ARTILLERYMEN OF THE AIR
At left are the tail guns of a Boeing B-52G Stratofortress. The gunner rides in the cabin and sights by TV camera above the guns. At right is the navigator-bombardier aboard the aircraft. He performs radar navigation and drops the bombs.

bombs for 5,000 miles. The B-36 remained the mainstay of the long-range, nuclear deterrent force until the jet B-47 and later the jet B-52 came into service.

In its first year of separate existence the USAF received a severe test when the Russians blockaded Berlin in 1948. A decision was made to supply the city by air. Before the airlift ended in 1949, some 2,343,000 tons of food, fuel, clothing, and other supplies (1,784,000 tons in USAF aircraft) were flown into Berlin on 277,000 flights.

Three events during this period characterized the USAF's growing global capability. In the first, Capt. Charles E. Yeager, piloting the Bell X-1 rocket-powered research aircraft, in 1947 became the first man to fly faster than sound. In 1949 the Boeing B-50, *Lucky Lady II*, flew around the world nonstop in 94 hours, proving the feasibility of aerial refueling for long-range missions. In another demonstration of in-flight refueling, two Republic F-84–E Thunderjet fighters flew across the Atlantic in 1950 in just over ten hours, completing the first nonstop, transoceanic flight in a jet. Through the years that followed, USAF pilots and aircraft dominated world aviation record flights.

Jets and the Korean War

Germany had introduced jet-fighter aircraft during the closing days of World War II. American jet development, started during the war, was hastened in the late 1940's. In the Korean conflict, which began in 1950, the planes of the USAF were more than a match for the high-performance Soviet-built MiG-15 jets (*see* Korean War).

The first aerial jet victory was won in Korea by Lieut. Russell Brown in 1950 in a Lockheed F-80 Shooting Star. The North American F-86 Sabre became the USAF's entry in jet-age warfare against the MiG. Flying an F-86, Capt. James Jabara became history's first "jet ace." The Korean conflict pro-

ON TARGET IN NORTH KOREA
With deadly effect a Lockheed F-80 Shooting Star strafes a village housing troops, tanks, and jeeps in the Korean war.

duced 38 more jet aces, headed by Capt. Joseph Mc-
Connell, Jr., with 16 victories.

When the armistice was signed in 1953, the USAF
had shot down 984 Communist planes (including 823
MiGs). The USAF lost 941 planes, only 94 of them
in aerial combat. Most of the USAF planes were
shot down by ground fire. In "MiG Alley" over
North Korea the ratio of MiGs downed to Sabres was
14 to 1.

Among the aircraft used in Korea were the F-80 and
the F-84. Bombing was conducted on a limited scale.
Aging B-29's were used to pinpoint rail and industrial
targets, while Douglas B-26's (World War II A-26's)
attacked troops behind the enemy lines.

Air Force Academy Established

In 1954 Congress authorized the establishment of a
separate military academy to train commissioned
officers for the Air Force. The new school, near Colorado Springs, Colo., was opened in 1958. (*See also*
Air Force Academy, United States.)

After the Korean war the development of higher-
flying, faster planes continued. These included the
Century series of fighters—the ultrahigh-performance
F-100, F-101, F-102, F-104, F-105, and F-106—and
the SAC deterrent bombers that succeeded the B-36.
B-52's showed their capabilities in 1957 when three of
them flew nonstop around the world in 45 hours, 20
minutes, averaging 535 mph.

A program for the production of nuclear-powered
military airplanes was canceled in 1961. Work continues on the development of a nuclear rocket engine.

Air Force Power in Vietnam

The participation of the USAF in the Vietnam conflict began in 1962, when it provided advisers for
the South Vietnamese air force. The USAF also helped train South Vietnamese aircrews.

Early in 1965, USAF combat aircraft were employed for the first time in attacks on Viet Cong and
North Vietnamese targets. Such planes as the North
American F-100 Supersabre and the Douglas A-1H
Skyraider were used. Boeing B-52
Stratofortresses based on Guam made
air raids against the Viet Cong forces
and bombed supply routes in North
Vietnam over which Communist troops
infiltrated South Vietnam. Air Force
planes also made reconnaissance flights,
supported attacking ground forces, and
delivered supplies and personnel. (*See
also* Vietnam Conflict.)

Missiles Versus Aircraft

The guided missile can fly faster, farther, and higher than a manned airplane. It is more difficult to detect and
to ward off a missile than an airplane.
In minutes a missile with a nuclear warhead can travel a great distance to inflict
tremendous destruction.

FIREPOWER OF A MODERN FIGHTER-BOMBER
Lined up in front of this supersonic Republic F-105 Thunderchief is the wide assortment of armament that it can carry.

Although missiles are taking on increasing importance, there is a continuing need for manned aircraft
in every type of air combat. The human pilot, with
his intelligence, and his airplane, with its versatility,
are still able to outperform the missile in a wide
range of situations.

In air defense, where missiles have an irreplaceable
role, fighter-interceptor aircraft also play a part. Air-
borne for long periods, they can meet attacking aircraft or missiles far from the target. In strategic warfare, bombers and missiles complement one another.

The manned bomber is flexible. It can be recalled
or it can switch targets. It can take radar-map pictures of the area it has destroyed and use them to plan

AN EARLY INTERCONTINENTAL GUIDED MISSILE
The Snark, a strategic nuclear missile, could be fired from a mobile launching
platform. By 1961 it was being replaced by smaller, more flexible units.

subsequent missions. Jet bombers can carry far heavier and more varied loads of explosives. The manned plane is also essential in search and rescue, transport, evacuation of wounded, antisubmarine patrol, and other missions where the human factor is important.

The Air Force in Outer Space

Even before the first Russian earth satellite, Sputnik I, went into orbit in 1957, the USAF was reaching toward the inner edge of outer space (see Space Travel). In 1956 the Bell X-2, a rocket-powered research aircraft, was piloted to an altitude of nearly 24 miles above the earth.

A more intensive rocket-plane research program began in 1959 with the North American X-15. In 1962 the X-15 was flown up into the lower regions of outer space. In 1963 a more powerful version, the X-15A-2, was developed by modification of an X-15.

In December 1963 the Air Force undertook a new space project—developing a Manned Orbiting Laboratory (MOL). The MOL, consisting of a pressurized cylinder attached to a modified Gemini capsule, will be used primarily to determine the effectiveness of manned space stations for reconnaissance of the earth. The Gemini will enable astronauts to return

to earth from the orbiting MOL after periods in space of up to one month. Launching by a Titan III rocket is scheduled to take place in 1968.

The Air Force has also used ballistic missiles to boost satellites into space to investigate problems of communication and earth observation (see Aerospace Research and Development; Space Travel).

Military Uses of Outer Space

The potential military uses of outer space are almost limitless. Space vehicles or artificial earth satellites could carry out many of the missions performed by traditional aircraft. They might fly space-age bomber or transport missions.

A Satellite Inspector system is undergoing study and preliminary design by the Air Force. These satellites would inspect other nations' satellites in orbit and possibly destroy or capture them.

Other Air Force satellite programs include Samos and Alarm. Samos, designed for reconnaissance of enemy territory, is already operational. Alarm, an early warning satellite formerly designated Midas, is under development. Alarm is designed to "watch" the earth's atmosphere from its orbit. By means of infrared devices, the satellite will detect the exhaust heat of enemy ballistic missiles that rise above the atmosphere on their way to a target. Alarm flight testing began in 1963. The Discoverer satellite program was used primarily to test designs for future spacecraft and to develop techniques for the recovery of space capsules from orbit.

As operations move farther and farther out into space, the Air Force takes the position that space and air are indivisible. Thus, in the airman's lexicon, air power has become "aerospace" power, and the USAF has become more than merely a global force.

HISTORIC EVENTS OF THE UNITED STATES AIR FORCE

1907—U. S. Army creates Aeronautical Division in Signal Corps.

1909—Army buys plane from Wright brothers.

1914—Congress creates Aviation Section in Signal Corps. First Aero Squadron organized; serves in Mexican expedition, 1916.

1918—First units of Aero Squadron fly in combat during World War I. Army aviation separated from Signal Corps.

1921—Brig. Gen. William Mitchell sinks battleship in air-bombing demonstration.

1923—Lieuts. Oakley G. Kelly and John A. Macready fly first nonstop, transcontinental flight.

1924—Army fliers make first round-the-world flight.

1926—Congress establishes U. S. Army Air Corps.

1940—President Franklin D. Roosevelt calls for 50,000 planes a year.

1941—Congress establishes U.S. Army Air Forces.

1945—Army Air Force B-29 drops first atomic bomb.

1947—U. S. Air Force made a separate department on equal basis with Army and Navy. Capt. Charles E. Yeager in a Bell X-1 is first to fly faster than speed of sound.

1948-49—Berlin airlift breaks Russian blockade.

1950—U. S. Air Force ordered to Korea.

1954—U. S. Air Force Academy established.

1957—First ICBM, Atlas, successfully fired.

1962—X-15 rocket plane penetrates outer space.

1965—U. S. Air Force planes initiate raids against Communist forces in Vietnam.

BIBLIOGRAPHY FOR AIR FORCE

Books for Younger Readers

Air Force and Space Digest (Periodical). Our Air Force (Putnam, 1961).

Colby, C. B. Bomber Parade (Coward-McCann, 1960).

Colby, C. B. Fighter Parade (Coward-McCann, 1960).

Colby, C. B. SAC (Coward-McCann, 1961).

Cooke, D. C. Bomber Planes That Made History (Putnam, 1959).

Cooke, D. C. Fighter Planes That Made History (Putnam, 1959).

Coombs, C. I. Airmen and What They Do (Watts, 1958).

Engeman, J. T. U. S. Air Force Academy (Lothrop, 1962).

Books for Advanced Students and Teachers

Air Force and Space Digest (Periodical). The Wild Blue (Putnam, 1961).

Caidin, Martin. Air Force (Holt, 1957).

Caidin, Martin. Thunderbirds! (Dutton, 1961).

Gurney, Gene. Journey of the Giants (Coward-McCann, 1961).

Landis, L. C. The Air Force (Viking, 1962).

Loomis, R. D. The Story of the U. S. Air Force (Random, 1959).

Talmadge, Marian and Gilmore, Iris. This Is the Air Force Academy (Dodd, 1961).

Wagner, Ray. American Combat Planes (Doubleday, 1960).

Whitehouse, A. G. J. Years of the War Birds (Doubleday, 1960).

The United States AIR FORCE ACADEMY

Snowcapped Pikes Peak provides a magnificent background for the United States Air Force Academy. In the rear is the 17-spired Chapel.

AIR FORCE ACADEMY, UNITED STATES. In the foothills of the Rampart Range of the Rocky Mountains, about ten miles north of Colorado Springs, Colo., lies the Air Force Academy. This school educates young men to become officers in the United States Air Force.

About 800 cadets enter the Academy each year. Their four-year course of study includes academic instruction, military training, and physical education. The academic program embraces the basic and applied sciences, the social sciences, and the humanities. Military training is carried out through specialized instruction at the Academy and through summer field trips to military installations in the United States and overseas. Physical education includes courses in conditioning and sports as well as athletic competition.

Each graduating cadet earns a bachelor of science degree and a commission as a second lieutenant in the regular Air Force. If physically qualified he may volunteer for pilot or navigator training. Other graduates may volunteer for a technical school, where they prepare for nonflying assignments such as missile operation or research and development. A few others are selected for advanced graduate work at civilian colleges and universities.

Entrance Requirements

The cadet candidate must be at least 17 and not yet 22 years of age on July 1 of the year he desires to enter the Academy. He must be a male United States citizen, unless applying as a foreign student from the American republics or the Philippines. He must be of good character and never have been mar-

AN AIR FORCE CADET'S GENERAL DAILY SCHEDULE
(based on the Academy's 24-hour-clock system)

0545—Release from Quarters	1150–1215—Lunch
0615—Assembly	1225—Call to Quarters
0625–0655—Early Chapel	1235–1515—Afternoon Classes
0630—Cleanup Call	1515—Release from Quarters
0650–0715—Breakfast	1530–1735—Scheduled Activities
0715—Call to Quarters	1630—Retreat
0730—Sick Call	1835–1905—Dinner
0740–1120—Morning Classes	2230—Tattoo
1120—Release from Quarters	2245—Taps

ried. He must be at least 5 feet 6 inches but not over 6 feet 8 inches tall and have 20/20 vision.

A prospective cadet cannot simply enroll at the Academy as he would at a civilian college or university. He must first obtain an official nomination from a federally authorized source. Most candidates are nominated by their United States senators or representatives.

After nomination, the candidate must pass the College Entrance Examination Board tests, the Air Force Academy qualifying medical examination, and the physical aptitude examination. Successful candidates enter the Academy during the last week in June. Before he is sworn in as a cadet the candidate must sign an agreement stating that he will complete the Academy course of instruction and serve a four-year tour of active duty in a regular component of one of the armed services.

Life at the Academy

The cadet receives his education and his medical and dental care without charge. He has an allowance for food. In addition, he receives $147.30 a month. Out of this he pays for some of his books and clothing and other personal needs. The cadets live two to a room and share a lavatory. Each has his own bed, desk, chair, dresser, bookcase, and closet.

The Air Force cadets live by a strict code of honor: "We will not lie, cheat, or steal, nor tolerate among us those who do."

The curriculum is longer and more intense than at most civilian schools. The cadet receives formal instruction five and a half days a week, ten and a half months a year. The cadet must earn at least $186\frac{1}{2}$ semester hours to graduate. Cadets who are able to carry additional hours above the prescribed courses may take electives. With enough additional credits in a given subject area a cadet may obtain a major with his degree.

Varsity teams in several intercollegiate sports compete against teams from major colleges and universities and from the other service academies. There is also an intramural athletic program. The Academy colors are silver and blue. The falcon was selected as the cadet mascot by the Academy's first class.

History of the Academy

Since the early 1920's, pioneer American airmen such as Gen. William L. (Billy) Mitchell had advocated

A CADET WORKS A SPACE-AGE PROBLEM
This cadet at the Air Force Academy is working out a problem on the placement of a satellite in orbit. He is using an analogue computer.

the establishment of a separate service academy to train commissioned officers for the Air Force. It was not until 1954, however, that Congress authorized such a project.

Three building sites were selected for final consideration. Those at Alton, Ill., and Lake Geneva, Wis., were rejected in favor of a 17,900-acre tract of ranchland near Colorado Springs. The Academy was temporarily set up at Lowry Air Force Base in Denver, Colo. The first class entered there in 1955. The Academy was moved to new buildings at its permanent site in August 1958. The first class was graduated in June 1959. (*See also* Aerospace Careers, section "Aviation Occupations in the Federal Government"; Air Force, United States.)

THE AIR FORCE CADET WING ON PARADE
Clad in dress blues, cadets march down the ramp and onto the parade ground. This view, looking northwest toward the Rampart Range, shows Fairchild Hall (the academic building) in the center and Vandenberg Hall (the dormitory) at the right.

TURBOJET—Douglas DC-8

The airlines fly aircraft with three main types of engines—turbojet, or pure jet; turboprop, or prop jet, with propellers driven by jet engines; and piston engines which drive the propeller.

TURBOPROP (PROP JET)—Lockheed Electra

AIRLINES—
Carriers of
People and Cargo
Through the Skies

PISTON ENGINE—Douglas DC-7C

AIRLINES. The youngest and fastest-growing form of travel in the world's transportation network are the airlines. Today the airliner is as important as the train, bus, truck, and ship (*see* Aviation). Sleek jets streak through the stratosphere crossing continents and oceans in hours. They are as luxurious as plush ocean liners and as safe as trains.

An *airline* is an organization made up of people, airplanes, equipment, and buildings whose purpose is the transporting of passengers, mail, and freight by air. The scheduled airlines of the United States employ some 166,000 people and have assets of over $3\frac{1}{4}$ billion dollars. About 20 per cent of the employees are flight personnel and 30 per cent are mechanics and related workers. The rest are concerned with communications, reservations, and other operations.

The United States has the world's largest air transportation system. It includes about 55 certified

143

SOME MAJOR AIRLINES OF THE WORLD

 **AEROFLOT (AFL):** Civil Aviation Department of U.S.S.R.; operates Soviet airline. TU-104 jet transport began operation in 1956. *Route miles,* 350,000.

 AIR CANADA (AC): Chief airline in Canada; government owned; flies to U.S., Caribbean, Europe. *Organized,* 1937. *Route miles,* 35,000. *Employees,* 12,000.

 AIR FRANCE (AF): One of world's largest airlines; owned and operated by French government; worldwide service. *Organized,* 1933. *Route miles,* 200,000. *Employees,* 24,700.

 AMERICAN AIRLINES (AA): One of largest U.S. airlines in business volume; serves U.S., Canada, Mexico. *Organized,* 1934. *Route miles,* 15,500. *Employees,* 22,000.

 BRITISH OVERSEAS AIRWAYS CORPORATION (BOAC): A public corporation for British overseas air service. *Organized,* 1939. *Route miles,* 163,000. *Employees,* 21,000.

 **CANADIAN PACIFIC AIRLINES (CPA):** Owned by Canadian Pacific Railway; operates in Canada and overseas. *Organized,* 1942. *Route miles,* 47,000. *Employees,* 2,700.

 **DELTA AIR LINES (DL):** Operates in eastern and southern sections of U.S., Caribbean, S. America. *Organized,* 1929. *Route miles,* 11,000. *Employees,* 9,000.

 EASTERN AIR LINES (EA): Serves eastern part of U.S., Canada, Caribbean, Bermuda, Mexico, S. America. *Organized,* 1938. *Route miles,* 19,000. *Employees,* 18,000.

 JAPAN AIR LINES (JAL): Operates in Japan and to U.S. and eastern Asia; private company founded 1951, government participation, 1953. *Route miles,* 47,000. *Employees,* 4,700.

 **LUFTHANSA GERMAN AIRLINES (LH):** Subsidized by German government; serves Europe, Asia, Africa, Americas. *Organized,* 1926. *Route miles,* 69,000. *Employees,* 12,000.

 NORTHWEST ORIENT AIRLINES (NW): Flew mail Chicago-St. Paul-Minneapolis, 1926; serves coast to coast, Alaska, Hawaii, Canada, Orient. *Route miles,* 19,200. *Employees,* 7,000.

 PAN AMERICAN WORLD AIRWAYS SYSTEM (PAA): A large international airline; famous for its Jet Clippers. *Organized,* 1927. *Route miles,* 71,000. *Employees,* 27,000.

 QANTAS EMPIRE AIRWAYS, LTD. (QEA): Owned by Australian government; flies around the world. *Organized,* 1920. *Route miles,* 67,000. *Employees,* 6,600.

 **ROYAL DUTCH AIRLINES (KLM):** World's oldest operating airline; worldwide service. *Organized,* 1919. *Route miles,* 168,000. *Employees,* 15,600.

 **SABENA BELGIAN WORLD AIRLINES (SAB):** Flies in Europe (including helicopters), Africa, Middle East, N. America. *Organized,* 1923. *Route miles,* 87,700. *Employees,* 9,000.

 **SCANDINAVIAN AIRLINES SYSTEM (SAS):** Airlines of Norway, Sweden, Denmark; operates worldwide. *Organized,* 1946. *Route miles,* 130,000. *Employees,* 12,000.

 SWISSAIR-SWISS AIR TRANSPORT COMPANY (SR): A private Swiss company; serves Europe, Asia, Africa, Americas. *Organized,* 1931. *Route miles,* 75,000. *Employees,* 7,500.

 **TRANS WORLD AIRLINES (TWA):** One of oldest airlines in U.S.; serves U.S., Europe, Africa, Asia. *Organized,* 1925. *Route miles,* 50,000. *Employees,* 20,000.

 **UNITED AIR LINES (UA):** The largest U. S. airline in traffic; serves coast to coast, Hawaii, Vancouver, B.C. *Organized,* 1931. *Route miles,* 18,000. *Employees,* 28,800.

 **WESTERN AIRLINES (WA):** Serves western U.S., Mexico City, Calgary, Alta. Began as Western Air Express, 1926; reorganized, 1941. *Route miles,* 9,700. *Employees,* 3,000.

carriers, which fly more than 65 per cent of the world's air commerce. They operate over 250,000 route miles and serve almost 1,000 cities in the United States and abroad. The airlines carry nearly 58 million passengers, about 240 million ton-miles of mail, and over 640 million ton-miles of freight a year. A *ton-mile* is the carrying of one ton of cargo for one mile.

Domestic and International Airlines

The two major classifications of airlines are domestic and international. *Domestic airlines* provide service within a country. *International airlines* operate within a nation and between two or more nations.

A *scheduled*, or *certified*, *airline* operates on a definite timetable between places on a route authorized by the Civil Aeronautics Board (CAB), a government agency (*see* Aviation Regulation). A *nonscheduled*, or *supplemental*, *airline* also functions under government regulation, but it does not have to maintain definite departure or arrival times.

Classes of Air Carriers

There are nine classes of air carriers. *Domestic trunk lines* are carriers which have permanent operating rights between major cities within the country. *Domestic local service*, or *feeder*, *lines* provide flights between the smaller traffic centers and feed into the trunk lines of major cities.

Intra-Hawaiian carriers operate between the islands comprising the state of Hawaii. *Alaskan carriers* provide service within Alaska and between Alaska and the other states except Hawaii.

Helicopter lines are certificated carriers that use helicopters between airports, post offices, and suburbs. *International and overseas lines* are flag carriers which operate between the United States and foreign countries. *All-cargo lines* maintain scheduled cargo flights. *Supplemental air carriers* conduct irregular domestic transport operations. *Other carriers* include air-taxi operators and airfreight forwarders.

Passenger Service

Several service classes and rates of fares are available to airline passengers. *First-class service* is the ultimate in luxury, meals, and speed. Two or more stewardesses see to the passengers' comfort.

Coach service and *economy service* are cheaper than first class. The same types of planes are used but they have more seats. These are narrower and there is less leg room. Meals may or may not be served. Economy service is one of the features of airlines flying between the United States and Europe. Many carriers offer first-class and coach or economy service on the same flight. *Charter service* is provided for athletic teams and other groups at a cost-per-mile rate.

Cargo Service

All aircraft used by the airlines have space available for carrying mail, express, and freight. Some airlines fly special all-cargo planes, such as the Douglas DC-6A and the Douglas DC-7 Cargoliner.

GROWTH OF AIRLINES

CERTIFIED AIR CARRIERS	1939	1949	1960
Number of Airlines	23	45	56
Aircraft in Service	347	1,083	1,848
Cruising Speed of Fastest Transport (Miles per Hour)	220	315	615
Number of People Employed	13,300	76,000	166,400
Total Airline Payrolls	$24,000,000	$349,000,000	$1,106,189,000
Cities Served	286	638	963
Number of Passengers Carried	1,864,000	16,723,000	57,700,000
Seats Available (Daily)	5,100	35,900	121,839
Average Fare (Per Passenger-Mile)	5.62¢	6.23¢	6.01¢
United States Mail, Ton-Miles	8,610,000	61,144,000	240,580,000
Ton-Miles of Freight Carried	2,713,000*	112,500,000	643,792,000
		*Freight and express combined	

The United States air transport industry is scarcely four decades old. Yet it is one of the major means of transportation.

Planes of this type have cargo racks, refrigerated compartments, and cargo-handling winches.

Airmail is divided into two classes. *Priority mail* is regular airmail and parcel post. *Nonpriority mail* is first-class postal matter that is now being carried by air on an experimental basis.

Reserved airfreight (*RAF*) is one of the latest airline developments. It differs from regular freight in that a specific flight is confirmed to the customer before the shipment is accepted by the airline.

TRANSPORTATION COMPARED—

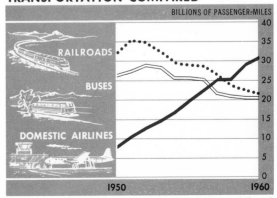

The intercity passenger traffic of the United States airlines is far greater than that of either the railroads or the buses.

TRAVEL by AIRLINER

CHECKING IN AT THE AIRPORT

SERVICING THE JET AIRLINER BEFORE TAKE-OFF

LOADING BAGGAGE

ALL ABOARD!

IN FLIGHT

MEALS IN THE CLOUDS

PERSONAL ATTENTION

RELAXING IN THE LOUNGE

FLIGHT'S END

BEHIND the SCENES at the AIRPORT

PASSENGER SERVICE · FUEL SERVICE CREW · BAGGAGE CO-ORDINATOR · CATERERS · ASSISTANT STATION MANAGER · RADIO MECHANIC · LINE MECHANICS · BAGGAGE LOADERS · UTILITY GROUP · PORTERS · OPERATIONS AGENTS · FLIGHT CREW · TICKET AGENTS

STAFF NEEDED TO GET A JET AIRLINER OFF THE GROUND

RESERVATION CONTROL

COOKS IN THE FLIGHT KITCHEN

The major types of goods carried by the airlines include machines, electrical equipment, cut flowers, printed matter, wearing apparel, aircraft parts and engines, hardware, film and equipment, and animals.

Airline Revenues

The operating revenues of the scheduled airlines of the United States total some $2\frac{1}{4}$ billion dollars annually. About 85 per cent of this comes from carrying passengers and 15 per cent from transporting mail, parcel post, express, and freight.

The revenue received by the airlines averages 5.8 cents per passenger-mile. A *passenger-mile* means the carrying of one passenger a distance of one mile. Such cargo as machines and machine parts, electrical equipment, and printed matter bring major airlines a revenue of 22 cents a ton-mile.

The Post Office Department pays scheduled airlines 30.17 cents per ton-mile, plus a handling charge, for carrying mail. Airlines no longer receive subsidy payments for carrying mail. A *subsidy* is the payment made above that required for the services rendered. Payments in addition to mail revenue are made to local service lines by the CAB. As a local service carrier increases its passenger business, the CAB reduces the amount it gives the airline. Today only 2 per cent of the airlines' revenues are from subsidies, compared with 28 per cent in 1938.

First Airlines Fly Mail

The story of scheduled air transportation in the United States begins with airmail. As early as 1912 the Post Office Department had asked Congress for $50,000 to start a regular airmail service. In 1918 the Post Office opened the first regularly scheduled airmail service, between Washington, D.C., and New York City, with Army fliers. Airmail service between New York and Chicago was begun in 1919 and extended to San Francisco the following year.

Congress aided in the establishment of commercial airlines with the Kelly Air Mail act of 1925. This bill provided for mail-carrying contracts with the airlines. The first carrier to fly under contract, in 1926, between Elko, Nev., and Pasco, Wash., was Varney Speed Lines, one of the predecessor companies of United Air Lines. Early airlines used Ford and Fokker trimotor planes.

In the Air Commerce Act of 1926 the federal government undertook to build airways. Charles Lindbergh's solo Atlantic flight in 1927 made the public airminded. By 1930 there were 43 scheduled airlines. They depended chiefly upon airmail for revenue.

Congress passed the McNary-Watres act of 1930 to encourage the development of passenger traffic. It varied mail payments according to the passenger space provided by the airlines. After mail contracts were canceled briefly in 1934 the Air Mail Act of 1934 reorganized the airlines.

Aircraft developed in this period included the Boeing 247 and Douglas DC-2 and DC-3. Revolving beacons, radio communication, and weather service

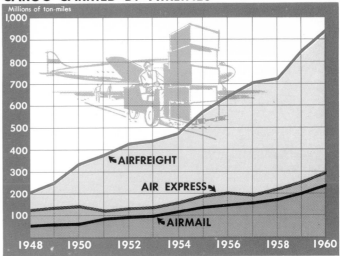

CARGO CARRIED BY AIRLINES

Millions of ton-miles

(Graph showing AIRFREIGHT, AIR EXPRESS, and AIRMAIL from 1948 to 1960, vertical axis 100 to 1,000)

improved airway facilities. In 1936 Pan American World Airways inaugurated transpacific service, San Francisco to Hawaii and Manila, with China Clipper flying boats. In 1939 it began transatlantic service.

In 1938 Congress passed the Civil Aeronautics Act. It created the Civil Aeronautics Authority to

FLYING CARGO

TYING DOWN THE CARGO

UNUSUAL CARGO

CONVEYER BELT SPEEDS LOADING

JACK TRUCK LOADS HEAVY CARGO

149

HOW SPEED OF AIRLINERS HAS INCREASED

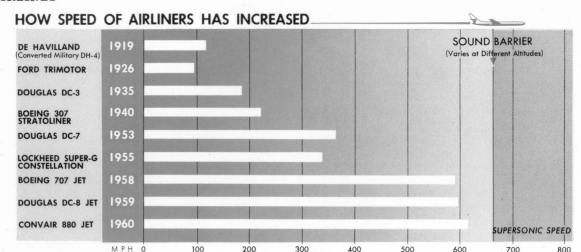

DE HAVILLAND (Converted Military DH-4)	1919	
FORD TRIMOTOR	1926	
DOUGLAS DC-3	1935	
BOEING 307 STRATOLINER	1940	
DOUGLAS DC-7	1953	
LOCKHEED SUPER-G CONSTELLATION	1955	
BOEING 707 JET	1958	
DOUGLAS DC-8 JET	1959	
CONVAIR 880 JET	1960	

SOUND BARRIER
(Varies at Different Altitudes)

SUPERSONIC SPEED

M P H   0   100   200   300   400   500   600   700   800

regulate and promote civil aviation. Airlines were paid subsidies for airmail in the national interest.

Air Transport During and After World War II

During World War II the airlines of the United States provided valuable transport service. They are still important in defense. Hundreds of airliners are in the Civil Reserve Air Fleet. After the war new airliners included the Douglas DC-4, DC-6, and DC-7; Lockheed Constellation; and Boeing Stratoliner. Air travel became about as safe as that of other common carriers (see Airplane Safety).

Air traffic increased rapidly. In the late 1930's the airlines carried 2 per cent of all intercity traffic in the United States. Today they carry as much as all intercity railroads and buses. Congress passed the Federal Aviation Act in 1958. In 1959 all air users, civil and military, came under control of the Federal Aviation Agency.

The airlines achieved even greater passenger and cargo capacity as they switched to jet aircraft (see Airplane Power Plants; Jet Propulsion). British Overseas Airways Corporation began the first turbojet service, London to Johannesburg, South Africa, with Comets in 1952. BOAC and Pan American started regular transatlantic turbojet flights in 1958.

In 1961 Congress approved funds for the development of a supersonic transport (SST). The 2,000-mile-an-hour (Mach 3) plane will be built of titanium and special steels and will be in operation in the early 1970's. In 1962 Britain and France made joint plans to build the *Concorde*, an aluminum SST with a speed of about 1,500 miles an hour (Mach 2.2).

In 1964 the compact Boeing 727 passenger jet, for short-runway airports, entered airline service. In 1965 the rival Douglas DC-9 was introduced. The giant Douglas DC-8 Model 61 jet airliner, with a capacity of 251 passengers, was introduced in 1966.

MILESTONES IN AIRLINE HISTORY

1910—Count Ferdinand von Zeppelin of Germany organizes first commercial airline with airships.

1914—First airline in U.S.—St. Petersburg (Fla.)-Tampa Air Boat Line—begins operation.

1918—U.S. Army flies first scheduled airmail between New York City and Washington, D. C.

1919—New York-Chicago airmail begins. Regular international airmail started, London-Paris.

1920—New York-San Francisco airmail launched.

1925—Air Mail Act (Kelly bill) authorizes mail contracts with private contractors.

1926—Congress passes Air Commerce Act.

1927—American Railway Express and several airlines sign air-express contracts.

1929—Plane-to-ground (2-way) voice radio developed.

1930—A United Air Lines predecessor company uses stewardesses for first time. McNary-Watres act pays operators on space-mile basis.

1931—Air Line Pilots Association organized.

1934—Airmail contracts canceled; Army flies mail briefly. Air Mail Act of 1934 passed.

1936—Air Transport Association of America formed. Pan American World Airways inaugurates transpacific service; transatlantic flights, 1939.

1938—Congress passes Civil Aeronautics Act.

1945—International Air Transport Association formed.

1946—Airlines establish round-the-world service.

1947—International Civil Aviation Organization formed.

1952—British Overseas Airways Corporation begins first jet service, London-South Africa.

1953—Trans World Airlines begins first nonstop transcontinental service, New York-Los Angeles.

1954—Scandinavian Airlines System starts regular transarctic flights, Los Angeles-Europe.

1958—BOAC begins jet flights, New York-London. National Airlines inaugurates regular jet flights in the U.S., New York-Miami. Congress passes Federal Aviation Act.

1959—American Airlines starts first transcontinental jet service, New York-Los Angeles.

AIRPLANE—
The Flying Machine

AIRPLANE. When the Wright brothers mastered the secret of flight, they did not imitate the birds but built a machine for flying. That is exactly what an airplane is, a "flying machine" (*see* Wright Brothers; Airplane History).

An airplane is heavier than air and yet it flies. It does this by propelling itself through the air and by supporting itself on wings so shaped that the air flowing over them gives them lift (*see* Airplane Flight Theory).

Used in a broad sense, the term airplane includes piston-engine and jet-driven aircraft, gliders, helicopters, and winged guided missiles (*see* Glider; Helicopter; Guided Missiles).

LANDPLANE—Champion Challenger

SEAPLANE—Cessna 172   FLYING BOAT—Martin Marlin

TYPES OF AIRPLANES

AMPHIBIAN—Colonial Skimmer IV

GLIDER—Schweizer Sailplane   HELICOPTER—Kaman Huskie

Airplanes are built in many shapes and sizes to do many things. They are designed to take off and land on land or water or both.

FACT FINDER FOR AIRPLANE ARTICLES

The subject of the airplane is a broad one. Readers will find exactly what they want to know about it in the many articles listed here.

AIRPLANES MAY BE CLASSIFIED IN MANY WAYS

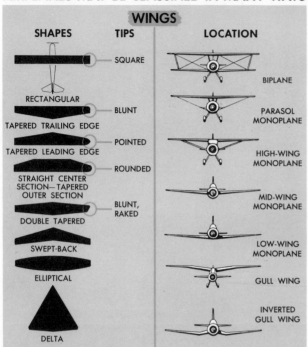

WINGS

SHAPES — TIPS — LOCATION

SHAPES:
RECTANGULAR
TAPERED TRAILING EDGE
TAPERED LEADING EDGE
STRAIGHT CENTER SECTION—TAPERED OUTER SECTION
DOUBLE TAPERED
SWEPT-BACK
ELLIPTICAL
DELTA

TIPS:
SQUARE
BLUNT
POINTED
ROUNDED
BLUNT, RAKED

LOCATION:
BIPLANE
PARASOL MONOPLANE
HIGH-WING MONOPLANE
MID-WING MONOPLANE
LOW-WING MONOPLANE
GULL WING
INVERTED GULL WING

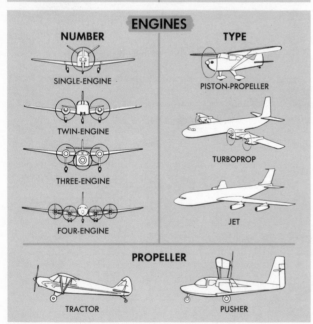

ENGINES

NUMBER — TYPE

NUMBER:
SINGLE-ENGINE
TWIN-ENGINE
THREE-ENGINE
FOUR-ENGINE

TYPE:
PISTON-PROPELLER
TURBOPROP
JET

PROPELLER

TRACTOR — PUSHER

In a more narrow sense, airplane means any power-driven aircraft with a fixed wing. This is the usual meaning of the word. The British use the form *aeroplane*. The word *plane* is short for airplane.

Airplane and Aircraft Distinguished

Airplane and aircraft are widely used to mean the same thing, though *aircraft* is a broader term. It includes both lighter-than-air and heavier-than-air craft.

The lighter-than-air group includes balloons, blimps, and dirigibles, which get lift from gases lighter than air (*see* Balloon). Heavier-than-air craft include airplanes, helicopters, Autogiros, orthopters, and convertiplanes.

The *helicopter* uses power-driven rotating wings for both lift and thrust. The *Autogiro* is another rotary-wing craft, but its blades revolve without power for lift and it uses a conventional propeller for forward motion (*see* Autogiro; Airplane Propeller).

An *orthopter* has wings that flap just as a bird's do. The *convertiplane* can be adjusted to fly as a conventional airplane or as a helicopter or an Autogiro. It is also called a *VTOL* (vertical take-off and landing). A related aircraft is the *STOL* (short take-off and landing).

Parts of the Airplane

An airplane usually consists of an airframe, power plant, instruments, furnishings, and accessories.

The airframe includes the fuselage, wings, tail assembly, landing gear, and engine mount. The *fuselage* is the body of the airplane.

The *wings* are the airfoils that provide lift. Ailerons are hinged portions of the wing that control rolling of the airplane. Flaps are also hinged sections, usually at the rear of a wing. They increase lift or drag, making possible shorter take-offs and slower landings. Spoilers are sections that move up from the top of the wing to increase drag and decrease lift. Slots are narrow, spanwise passages along the leading edge of a wing to improve air flow at high angles of attack.

The *tail assembly*, or *empennage*, consists of the horizontal and vertical stabilizers and their control surfaces. The fixed horizontal stabilizer keeps the plane from pitching. Hinged to it is the elevator. When it is moved up or down it raises or lowers the nose of the plane. The fixed vertical stabilizer, or *fin*, keeps the tail from whipping from side to side. The *rudder* is hinged to it. When the rudder is swung to the left or right it turns the plane.

The *landing gear* is an apparatus for supporting the airplane while on land, water, or snow and when taking off or landing. The *engine mount* is a metal frame for attaching an engine to the airplane. (*See also* Airplane Airframe.)

The power plant consists of an engine, propeller (if any), accessories such as carburetors and fuel pumps, and fuel and oil tanks and lines (*see* Aerospace Fuel). The *engine* is a machine that powers, or propels, the aircraft. (*See also* Airplane Power Plants.)

The instruments are devices for helping the pilot fly the airplane, for navigating, for checking engine performance, and for indicating the operation of equipment, such as deicing systems. (*See also* Airplane Instruments.)

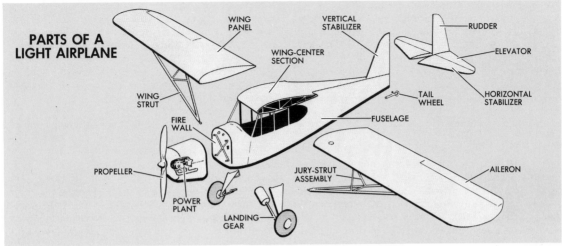

PARTS OF A LIGHT AIRPLANE

Major parts of an airplane are the power plant and airframe, which includes fuselage, wings, tail assembly, and landing gear.

The furnishings include such equipment as seats, safety belts, fire extinguishers, and cupboards.

The accessories are devices that facilitate the use of some piece of equipment. They may be aircraft accessories, such as lighting systems, or engine accessories, such as superchargers.

Many Kinds of Airplanes

Airplanes fall into three broad types, depending upon whether they take off on land, water, or both. A *landplane* has a landing gear for support while at rest or in motion on the ground and during take-off and landing. The landing gear may be wheels, skids, endless tracks, or skis.

A *seaplane* has floats shaped like small airtight boats for landing gear. A *flying boat* has a hull or boatlike fuselage. An *amphibian* can take off and land on either land or water. It has wheels for the ground and a hull or floats for water.

Airplanes may be classified by the number, location, and shape of the wings or by the type, number, and position of the engines. Another designation is by landing gear—fixed or retractable.

Wings as Varied as Those of Birds

The first flying machine was a *biplane*. Almost universal today is the *monoplane*, whose single wing creates less drag. *Triplanes* and other *multiplane* aircraft have been built.

Monoplanes are *high-wing* when the wing is attached high on the fuselage; *low-wing* when it is fastened below the fuselage; and *mid-wing* when it is mounted through the fuselage. A *parasol* monoplane has the wing carried on struts above the fuselage.

The tips of a *dihedral wing* are higher than the wing roots. A *gull wing* slants upward and then straightens out so that it resembles the wing of a gull. An *inverted gull wing* slants downward and then either flattens out or slopes upward. A *flying wing* is an airplane without a tail and with its fuselage incorporated into the wing. Wings are designed in many different shapes, such as rectangular, tapered, and elliptical. A *swept-back*

wing has a backward slant. A *delta wing* looks like an isosceles triangle. Wing tips also vary and may be square, rounded, or pointed.

Power Plants, or Engines

Two types of power plants are the most widely used in aircraft today. They are the reciprocating engine and the jet engine. The *reciprocating*, or *piston-driven*, internal combustion engine is similar to the automobile engine (*see* Internal Combustion Engine).

The most recently developed *jet*, or *reaction*, *engine* may be of two principal types (*see* Jet Propulsion). The *turbojet*, or *pure jet*, does not have a propeller. In the *turboprop*, or *prop jet*, a turbine drives a propeller.

Most combat military aircraft and recently developed airline transports use jet engines. Most of the business-operated planes, trainers, and personally owned aircraft are powered by reciprocating engines.

Another way to classify airplanes is by the number of engines. They may be single-engine, twin-engine, three-engine, and so on. They may also be grouped by location of the propeller. In the more common *tractor* type it is at the front of the engine and pulls the airplane through the air. In the *pusher* type it is at the rear of the engine and pushes the plane.

Civil and Military Aircraft

As airplanes have been required to do more things they have become more specialized in design (*see* Aviation). The bush pilot in Alaska needs an airplane that can take off and land in a small space. The Air Force pilot requires a fighter-interceptor that can climb swiftly. The airline pilot flies an airplane that can carry heavy loads long distances.

This specialization has produced two broad classes, military and civil. *Military aircraft* include bombers, fighters, and other planes of the Air Force, Army, and Navy. *Civil aircraft* are those used in general aviation and those flown by the air carriers.

General aviation aircraft consist of all civil types except air carriers. They range from single-engine, one- and two-place planes flown by sportsmen to large multiengine, multiplace transports used by business corporations.

The *air carriers*, or *airlines*, use many kinds of aircraft, depending upon the service required (*see* Airlines). The planes may be short-, medium-, or long-range aircraft for intercity, transcontinental, or intercontinental flights.

Aircraft of the Air Force

The United States Air Force has many specialized aircraft (*see* Air Force, United States). *Bombers* are classed according to range as heavy, medium, or light. The Boeing B-52 Stratofortress is a heavy bomber that can fly above 60,000 feet at 650 mph and carry a nuclear-bomb load 12,500 miles. The Convair B-58 Hustler is a supersonic medium bomber with a speed of over 1,300 mph. The Douglas RB-66 Destroyer is a reconnaissance light bomber that operates at night and in bad weather in support of ground troops.

Fighters are of two classes, fighter-interceptor and fighter-bomber or tactical fighter. The fast-climbing interceptor meets the enemy as quickly as possible to destroy it. The Convair F-106 Delta Dart is an all-weather jet interceptor that flies at speeds of more than 1,500 mph. The fighter-bomber can both fight and drop bombs. The Republic F-105 Thunderchief can fly over 1,400 mph and deliver nuclear bombs over long ranges.

The *transports* carry passengers, troops, and supplies. The giant Douglas C-133 Cargomaster hauls 50 tons or seats 200 troops. *Tankers* have large fuel tanks and refuel aircraft while in flight. They are equipped with flying booms or with flexible hoses, which have a funnel-shaped drogue at their ends.

Trainers are used to teach aircrews. They are of two types—pilot trainers and observer trainers for instructing navigators, bombardiers, engineers, and radio and gunnery specialists. A pilot trainee graduates from primary to intermediate to basic trainer.

Other types of Air Force aircraft include *reconnaissance, search and rescue, helicopter, observation, utility,* and *research* (or experimental).

Aircraft of the United States Navy have much the same uses as those of the Air Force (*see* Navy, United States). The Navy, however, also has many special types, such as antisubmarine aircraft, carrier planes, and seaplanes. The Army uses airplanes and gliders for observation, hauling cargo, and reconnaissance missions.

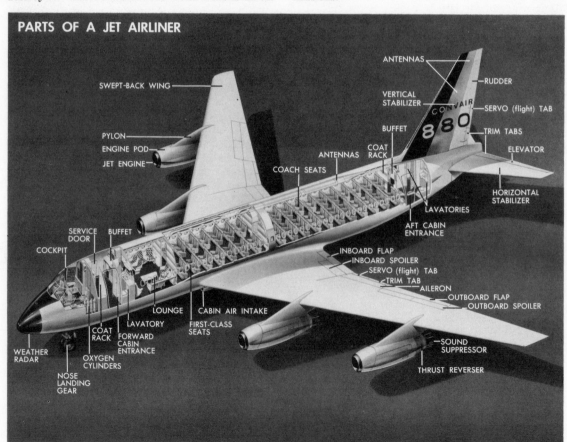

PARTS OF A JET AIRLINER

ANTENNAS — RUDDER — VERTICAL STABILIZER — SERVO (flight) TAB — SWEPT-BACK WING — BUFFET — CONVAIR 880 — TRIM TABS — COAT RACK — ELEVATOR — PYLON — ENGINE POD — JET ENGINE — ANTENNAS — COACH SEATS — HORIZONTAL STABILIZER — LAVATORIES — AFT CABIN ENTRANCE — SERVICE DOOR — BUFFET — INBOARD FLAP — INBOARD SPOILER — SERVO (flight) TAB — TRIM TAB — AILERON — OUTBOARD FLAP — OUTBOARD SPOILER — COCKPIT — LOUNGE — CABIN AIR INTAKE — FIRST-CLASS SEATS — WEATHER RADAR — COAT RACK — FORWARD CABIN ENTRANCE — LAVATORY — NOSE LANDING GEAR — OXYGEN CYLINDERS — SOUND SUPPRESSOR — THRUST REVERSER

This cutaway drawing of a Convair 880 shows the main parts of a jet-powered airliner. This beautiful multijet transport seats 88 first class or 110 tourist class passengers. It cruises at 615 miles per hour at an altitude of 41,000 feet.

AIRLINE TRANSPORTS OF MANY TYPES AND SIZES

TURBOJET—Convair 880

TURBOJET—Boeing 720

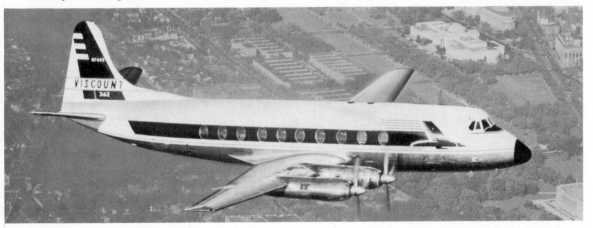

TURBOPROP—British Vickers Viscount 700 Series

TURBOJET—French Sud-Aviation S. E. 210 Caravelle

PISTON-PROPELLER—Douglas DC-7C Seven Seas

BOMBER—Convair B-58 Hustler (Air Force)

ATTACK BOMBER—North American A-5A Vigilante (Navy)

RESEARCH—Ryan X-13
Vertijet (Air Force)

RECONNAISSANCE—Lockheed EC-121K Warning Star (Navy)

TRAINER—Northrop T-38 Talon (Air Force)

BOMBERS, FIGHTERS, AND OTHER SPECIALIZED AIRPLANES

HELICOPTER—Vertol CH-21 Workhorse (Air Force)

ANTISUBMARINE—Grumman S-2A Tracker (Navy)

RECONNAISSANCE-FIGHTER—McDonnell RF-101 Voodoo (Air Force)

UTILITY—Cessna U-3A (Air Force)

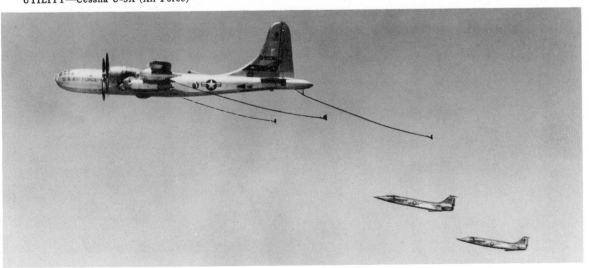

TANKER—Boeing KB-50J Superfortress refueling Lockheed F-104C Starfighters (Air Force)

157

GENERAL AVIATION AIRCRAFT FOR MANY PURPOSES

PIPER COLT 108

BEECHCRAFT MODEL P35 BONANZA

CESSNA 210

CESSNA SKYKNIGHT MODEL 320B

AERO COMMANDER MODEL 1121 JET COMMANDER

AIRPLANE AIRFRAME—
Fuselage, Wing, Tail Assembly, Landing Gear

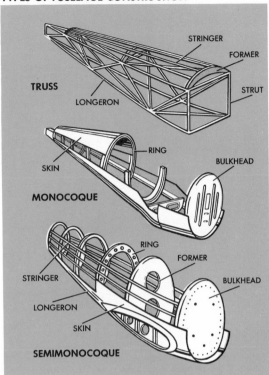

The *truss* fuselage is built up with triangles. The *monocoque* is shaped like a tube; the *semimonocoque* has reinforcements.

AIRPLANE AIRFRAME. An *airframe* is the entire airplane without the power plant and other parts that are regularly replaced (*see* Airplane Power Plants). The major parts of the airframe are the fuselage, wings, tail assembly, engine mounts, and landing gear.

The Fuselage, or Body

The *fuselage* is the body of the airplane. The name comes from the French word *fuselé*, meaning "spindle-shaped." There are two main types of fuselage construction—truss and stressed skin.

The *truss type* is used in light planes. It consists of a framework of steel tubes that are welded, riveted, or bolted together in a series of trusses, or triangles. The tubes running the length of the fuselage are *longerons*. Connecting them are bracing membranes called *struts*. *Formers* and *stringers* are added to give the fuselage a streamlined shape.

Over the framework is a *skin*, or covering, of fabric, sheet aluminum or magnesium, or molded plastic or Fiberglas. Fabric covering is painted with "dope" to shrink and waterproof it.

In the *stressed-skin type* of fuselage the skin bears all or part of the stresses acting on the airplane. The skin is usually sheet aluminum. There are two variations—monocoque and semimonocoque.

In the *monocoque* fuselage the skin is essentially a thin-walled tube that bears all the stresses. Monocoque is a French word meaning "single shell." More common is the *semimonocoque*. Its skin is reinforced by longerons. Rings, frames, and bulkheads shape and strengthen the skin.

The Wings

There are three types of wing structure—cantilever, semicantilever, and externally braced. The *cantilever wing* is made very strong and carries all stresses within itself. It is internally braced and not externally supported by struts or wires to the fuselage or landing gear. The *semicantilever wing* requires some external bracing. It can be made lighter. The *externally braced wing* is supported entirely by struts or wires. It can be made light in weight, but the external

TYPES OF WING CONSTRUCTION

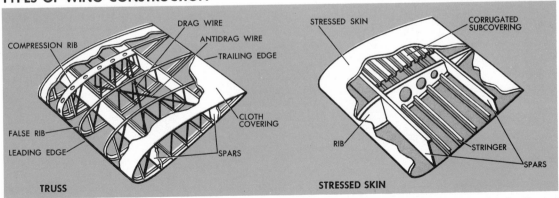

The *truss wing* utilizes the principle of the truss, or triangle. It is a rigid framework of spars, ribs, and braces. In the *stressed-* skin wing the metal covering bears all or part of the bending and twisting stresses arising in the wing.

159

SOME TAIL ASSEMBLY DESIGNS

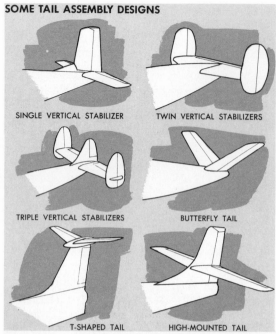

SINGLE VERTICAL STABILIZER

TWIN VERTICAL STABILIZERS

TRIPLE VERTICAL STABILIZERS

BUTTERFLY TAIL

T-SHAPED TAIL

HIGH-MOUNTED TAIL

There are many variations in the arrangement of the tail surfaces of an airplane. Some common types are shown here.

braces increase air drag. It is used for light planes.

Two types of construction are used for wings—*truss* and *stressed skin*. In the first type, truss design and external bracing to the fuselage withstand stresses. In the second type, the wing itself carries all or part of the stresses.

Both truss and stressed-skin wings consist of a frame-

TWO TYPES OF LANDING GEAR

CONVENTIONAL FIXED LANDING GEAR

TRICYCLE RETRACTABLE LANDING GEAR

Both types have three wheels. The Helio Courier (top) has a tail wheel; the Grumman Tiger (bottom), a nose wheel.

work of spars and ribs. Long spars extend the length of the wing and bear most of the load. Fastened to the spars are curved ribs which give the wing its shape. Over the ribs is a covering, or skin. Sometimes corrugated metal sheets or long stringers are placed under the skin for added strength.

The wing parts may be made of wood, but lightweight aluminum is more common. The skin may be doped fabric, plastic-bonded plywood, aluminum or magnesium alloy, stainless steel, or titanium.

The Tail Assembly, or Empennage

At the rear of the fuselage is the *tail assembly*, or *empennage*. The name empennage is derived from the French word *empenner*, meaning "to feather the arrow." Like feathers on an arrow, the empennage stabilizes the aircraft. The tail surfaces, like the wings, are made of spars, ribs, strings, and skin.

Engine Mounts

An *engine mount* is a framework of metal for attaching an engine to an airplane. It is often considered a part of the fuselage. Rubber pads cushion the vibration between the engine and the fuselage. Behind the engine is a fire wall for fire protection. The hollow pod-shaped structure in which an engine is mounted is called the *nacelle*. Detachable sections covering a power plant are *engine cowlings*.

The Landing Gear

The undercarriage on which an airplane rests while taking off or landing is the *landing gear*. It may consist of wheels or skids for land, skis for snow or ice, and floats, or pontoons, for water.

Land planes have conventional, tricycle, or tandem landing gear. A *conventional gear* includes two main wheels and a tail wheel. A *tricycle gear* consists of two main wheels and a nose wheel. A *tandem*, or *bicycle*, *gear* has two main wheels or sets of wheels, one behind the other. Outrigger wheels support the wing tips.

Wheels may be *fixed* or *retractable*. Retractable wheels fold up into the fuselage, wings, or nacelles to reduce air drag. To cushion the impact of landing, the wheels are attached to shock-absorbing devices. Most airplanes use oleo struts which employ oil and air to cushion the blow. Brakes on the wheels are used to stop and steer airplanes. On many aircraft the tail or nose wheel may be steered.

HOW OLEO STRUT WORKS

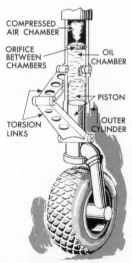

COMPRESSED AIR CHAMBER

ORIFICE BETWEEN CHAMBERS

OIL CHAMBER

PISTON

TORSION LINKS

OUTER CYLINDER

The oleo strut absorbs the shock of landing. Oil and air cushion the impact.

AIRPLANE FLIGHT CONTROLS—
How a Pilot Flies an Airplane

AIRPLANE FLIGHT CONTROLS. To regulate the movement and position, or *attitude*, of his airplane a pilot uses *flight controls.* They consist of a system of levers, pedals, throttles, cables, pulleys, instruments, and other equipment. (*See also* Airplane Instruments.)

Flight controls include a *control stick* between the pilot's knees or a *control wheel*, a pair of *rudder pedals*, and a *throttle.* The pilot pulls the stick backward to raise the aircraft's nose and pushes the stick forward to lower the nose. He moves the stick sideways to bank the plane. He turns the nose right or left with the foot pedals. He controls engine power with the throttle.

Control wheel

Throttle

Ignition switch

Rudder pedals

Primary flight controls on an airplane are the wheel, rudder pedals, and throttle. Some aircraft have a vertical control stick instead of a wheel.

How the Control Stick and Wheel Work

The control stick is connected by cables to the *elevator*, which is hinged to the *horizontal stabilizer* (*see* Airplane). Pushing the stick forward tilts the elevator down. This changes the *angle of attack* of the stabilizer; that is, the angle at which the stabilizer strikes the air flow. It now has more lift so that the tail is raised and the nose is lowered (*see* Airplane Flight Theory). Pulling the stick backward lowers the tail and raises the nose.

The control stick is also connected to cables which run into each wing to the *ailerons*. These are small hinged surfaces on the trailing edge of the wings near the tips. When the control stick is pushed to the right the aileron on the right wing is raised and the aileron on the left wing is lowered. This reduces the air flow over the right aileron and decreases its lift, which lowers the right wing. At the same time the lowered aileron on the left wing increases its lift. This banks the airplane to the right. In a similar manner the aircraft is banked to the left.

Instead of a vertical control stick on the floor, some airplanes have a wheel extending out from the instrument panel. Turning the wheel to the right or left has the same effect as moving the stick in the same direction. Moving the wheel backward or forward raises or lowers the airplane's nose.

The Rudder Controls Direction

The two foot pedals are connected by cables to the *rudder*, which is hinged to the *vertical stabilizer* on the tail. If the left pedal is pushed forward the rudder turns to the left and a sideways force to the right is created on the tail. The airplane's nose then moves to the left.

Some airplanes have a single rudder bar instead of separate pedals. The pilot's feet rest on the bar, which is pivoted in the center.

Secondary Controls

Modern airplanes have secondary high-lift devices and control surfaces. Among these are *flaps*, *slots* and *slats*, and *trim tabs*.

Flaps are hinged control surfaces on the trailing edge of the wing. The pilot lowers them a little in take-off to get lift with a small increase in drag. In landing he lowers them much more for a proportionately greater increase in drag, thus permitting a steeper approach. He controls them with a wheel or crank in the cockpit.

The slot is a narrow air gap on the leading edge of a wing. Air passes through the slot and flows smoothly over the wing to prevent stalls. Slots may be fixed or movable, operating automatically. A movable slot operated by small motors under the pilot's control is called a slat.

161

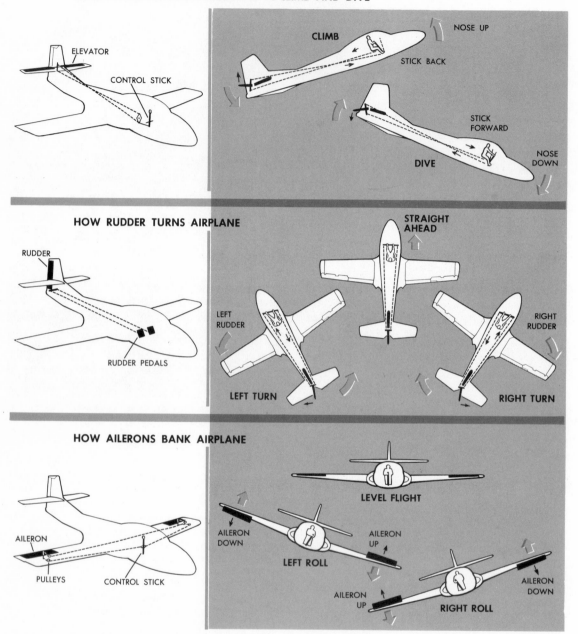

HOW ELEVATORS CAUSE AIRPLANE TO CLIMB AND DIVE

HOW RUDDER TURNS AIRPLANE

HOW AILERONS BANK AIRPLANE

Trim tabs are small control surfaces on the rudder, elevators, and ailerons. They balance the airplane by adjusting for small shifts in weight as fuel is used up or passengers move about. Usually they are operated by small wheels next to the pilot.

Basic Flight Techniques

The flight maneuvers which the pilot masters first are take-off, landing, turns, stalls, climbing, gliding, dives, and sideslips. Spins are usually not taught until the pilot has become proficient in the basic maneuvers, because modern training planes are con-

sidered spinproof. Aerobatics such as loops, rolls, and Immelman turns are learned later.

The Take-Off

Take-off is preceded by a walk-around inspection of the airplane by the pilot. After the engine is started he taxis to the runway. Take-offs are made into the wind rather than downwind or cross wind. The added speed of the air over the wings gives greater lift and permits a shorter take-off run.

The pilot stops the airplane near the end of the runway and opens the throttle wide to check the engine performance. When he sees no aircraft nearby he taxis out on the runway. The throttle is pushed forward until maximum power is obtained.

If the airplane has a conventional landing gear with a tail wheel there is a tendency for the tail to rise. The pilot aids this by pushing the stick forward slightly. When the tail has come up so that the wings are parallel to the runway the pilot centers the stick again. In this attitude the airplane will fly itself off the ground. If the airplane has a tricycle landing gear with a nose wheel, its normal position is suited for quick acceleration.

Once the airplane has lifted off the runway the pilot tries to climb quickly to a safe altitude and to fly out of the airport's traffic pattern. Under normal circumstances the aircraft is leveled off and engine power is reduced from maximum to cruising setting as soon as an altitude of 400 feet is reached. To enter the traffic pattern a level 90-degree left turn is made. If the pilot wants to leave the pattern he then turns away at a 45-degree angle to the right. If he wants to go around the airport and land again he climbs to 600 feet.

The Climb, Glide, and Dive

To *climb* the pilot pulls back on the stick to put the wings at a higher angle of attack for more lift. This raises the nose of the plane. At the same time he opens the throttle.

In a *glide* the pilot reduces or cuts his throttle. Earth's gravity provides the power for descent. As speed is reduced a decrease in lift results. The nose of the airplane is lowered but it is still above the glide path.

To *dive* the pilot pushes the stick forward. This lessens the angle of attack and noses the plane down. Unlike the glide, in the dive the nose is lower than the horizon. The descent, made with or without engine power, is rapid.

Turns

A turn is made by using both the rudder and ailerons at the same time. If the rudder alone is used the airplane will *skid*, or slide sideways, just as an automobile does on an icy street. If the ailerons alone are used the airplane will *sideslip*, or slip sideways and downward. A pilot sometimes purposely sideslips to lose altitude quickly.

Stalls

When an airplane does not have enough lift to keep it air-borne, it *stalls*. A stall may occur when the pilot pulls back on the stick, raising the nose and increasing the angle of attack of the wing to too great a degree for the speed at which the plane is flying. The aircraft continues to lose speed and the controls feel "sloppy." Air burbles over the top of the wing and causes the airplane to shudder. When the stall occurs the nose drops suddenly and the aircraft loses altitude rapidly even though the pilot has the stick pulled back.

The pilot recovers from the stall by pushing the stick forward to lower the nose and build up air speed. When the controls become effective again he pulls the stick back and resumes level flight.

If during the stall the pilot pushes the rudder full right or left the airplane will *spin*. In a spin the airplane dives and spirals at the same time.

Landing

Landings must be made according to government regulations. If the airport is a large one with a traffic control tower, the aircraft should receive a radio or blinker-light signal for clearance to land, except in an emergency. The pilot should fly over a small airport at about 1,500 feet to determine wind direction and which runway is in use. Landings are made into the wind to lower the plane's ground speed.

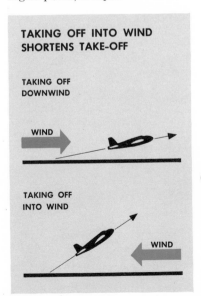

TAKING OFF INTO WIND SHORTENS TAKE-OFF

TAKING OFF DOWNWIND

WIND

TAKING OFF INTO WIND

WIND

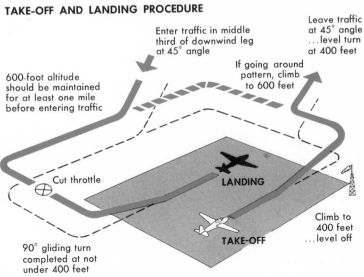

TAKE-OFF AND LANDING PROCEDURE

Leave traffic at 45° angle ...level turn at 400 feet

Enter traffic in middle third of downwind leg at 45° angle

If going around pattern, climb to 600 feet

600-foot altitude should be maintained for at least one mile before entering traffic

Cut throttle

LANDING

Climb to 400 feet ...level off

TAKE-OFF

90° gliding turn completed at not under 400 feet

HOW AN AIRPLANE STALLS AND RECOVERS

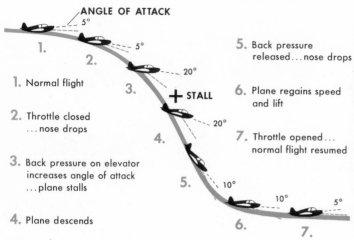

ANGLE OF ATTACK

1. Normal flight

2. Throttle closed ...nose drops

3. Back pressure on elevator increases angle of attack ...plane stalls

4. Plane descends

5. Back pressure released...nose drops

6. Plane regains speed and lift

7. Throttle opened... normal flight resumed

+ STALL

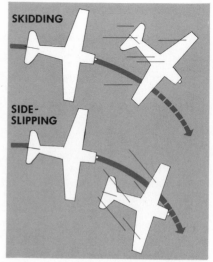

SKIDDING

SIDE-SLIPPING

In preparing to land, the pilot flies at least one mile beyond the airport and descends to 600 feet. He approaches the downwind leg of the traffic pattern at a 45-degree angle. At the end of the runway he makes a 90-degree left turn into the base leg. Then he cuts back his throttle and makes another 90-degree gliding turn to the left into the final approach.

If it looks as though the airplane will touch ground short of the runway the pilot must avoid the danger of trying to stretch his glide. The normal reaction is to pull the nose of the airplane up. This will cut down the air speed and possibly cause a stall. The proper procedure is to nose the airplane down so that it will pick up speed. Even though it will lose altitude it will have sufficient forward speed to remain under control for a safe landing.

Landings are essentially abbreviated stalls made just above the runway so that the airplane's lift is reduced to slightly less than its weight. The plane

then settles gently to the ground. The pilot must accurately control the speed and angle of attack as he skims over the runway. When the wheels are only a few feet above the ground the pilot pulls his stick all the way back. The airplane settles to the runway.

A perfect landing for an airplane with a tail wheel is for all three wheels to touch the ground at once in a *three-point landing*. Usually the two main wheels are touched down first to avoid damaging the tail. The two main wheels should always touch first in landing an aircraft with tricycle landing gear.

If a pilot begins the final stage of landing (called *flare-out*) too high in the air he will stall his airplane. The aircraft then drops down with great force in a *pancake landing*. It will bounce if the pilot begins his flare-out too late or lands too fast.

After all the wheels are on the ground a great deal of forward momentum remains. The pilot must use his brakes to steer and stop the airplane.

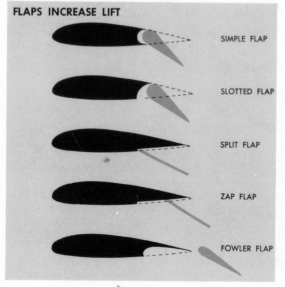

FLAPS INCREASE LIFT

SIMPLE FLAP

SLOTTED FLAP

SPLIT FLAP

ZAP FLAP

FOWLER FLAP

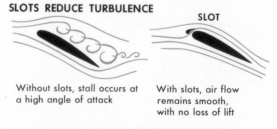

SLOTS REDUCE TURBULENCE

SLOT

Without slots, stall occurs at a high angle of attack

With slots, air flow remains smooth, with no loss of lift

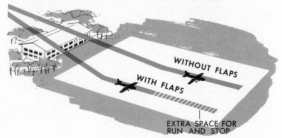

FLAPS PERMIT SMALLER LANDING SPACE

WITHOUT FLAPS

WITH FLAPS

EXTRA SPACE FOR RUN AND STOP

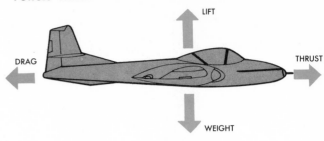

FORCES WHICH ACT UPON AN AIRPLANE IN FLIGHT

LIFT

DRAG

THRUST

WEIGHT

AIRPLANE FLIGHT THEORY—How an Airplane Flies

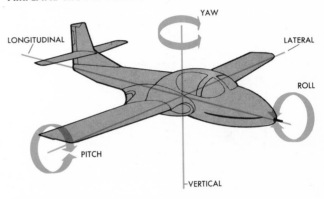

AIRPLANE MOVES ALONG 3 AXES

YAW

LONGITUDINAL

LATERAL

ROLL

PITCH

VERTICAL

AIRPLANE FLIGHT THEORY. How is an airplane able to fly? The answer is explained by the science called *aerodynamics*. This is the study of air in motion and the forces that act on solid surfaces moving through the air. The name aerodynamics is a combination of the Greek terms *aer*, meaning "air," and *dynamis*, meaning "power." It is the reaction of the air on the specially shaped wing, or airfoil, that lifts an airplane off the ground and supports it aloft.

Four Forces of Flight

Lift is one of the four forces that act on an airplane. The others are weight (or gravity), drag, and thrust. *Lift* is an upward force that offsets the airplane's *weight*. *Drag* is air resistance to forward motion. *Thrust* produced by the power plant counteracts drag.

Scientific principles developed by Sir Isaac Newton and Daniel Bernoulli explain what makes lift possible. Newton's third law of motion states that for every action there must be an opposite and equal reaction. Therefore, since a wing is an inclined plane similar to a kite, it deflects the air downward and the air in turn deflects the wing upward. Impact pressure of the air striking the wing's under surface produces about 30 per cent of the lift of a wing.

Bernoulli's law (called the Bernoulli effect) states that an increase in the velocity of air reduces the static pressure. The Venturi tube of a carburetor illustrates this law. It is wide at each end but narrows in the middle. As moving air passes through the throat it speeds up and its static pressure decreases. The low static air pressure in the nozzle leading from the throat draws fuel into the tube from a bowl which is under normal atmospheric pressure.

A wing in cross section is shaped like a side of a Venturi tube. Moving air has farther to go over its curved, or cambered, upper surface than it does over its flatter lower surface. The air moves more rapidly over the top than it does over the bottom and thus

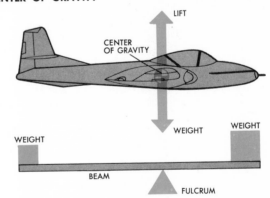

CENTER OF GRAVITY

LIFT

CENTER OF GRAVITY

WEIGHT

WEIGHT

WEIGHT

BEAM

FULCRUM

Airplane is like a beam on a fulcrum.
Lift force must be at or near center
of gravity for plane to be level in flight.

exerts less downward pressure. This pressure differential between the top and the bottom of the wing produces about 70 per cent of its lift.

Factors Affecting Lift

The lift of a wing may be increased by the angle of attack, airfoil shape, outline shape, air speed, wing size, and air density. The *angle of attack* is the angle formed by the airfoil chord and relative wind. The *chord* is the line joining the leading and trailing edges. *Relative wind* is the flow of air in relation to the wing. It is parallel to and opposite the

AIR PRESSURE KEEPS AIRPLANE ALOFT

A simple experiment to
demonstrate lift of a wing

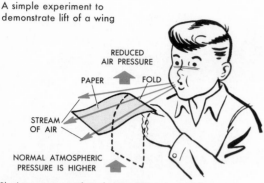

Blowing over upper surface of paper makes it rise, not fall.
Blowing increases speed of air and lowers pressure. Normal higher
atmospheric pressure beneath paper pushes it up. This
illustrates Bernoulli's law.

VENTURI TUBE BASED ON BERNOULLI'S LAW

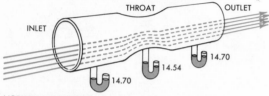

NORMAL ATMOSPHERIC
PRESSURE 14.70 LBS. PER SQUARE INCH

WING WAS DEVELOPED FROM VENTURI TUBE

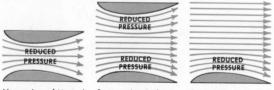

Narrowing of Venturi
tube speeds air flow

Same action in larger
tube as long as there is
any restriction to flow

Same action over half
of Venturi tube which is
like a section of a wing

HOW AIR PRESSURE GIVES LIFT TO A WING

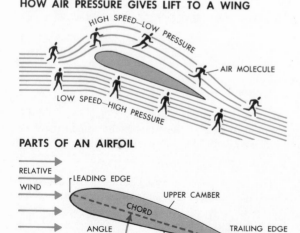

PARTS OF AN AIRFOIL

flight path. The motion may be that of air flowing
past the wing or of the wing moving through the air.

The greater the angle of attack the more the lift.
If a pilot wishes to climb he pulls up the nose of
the plane and thereby increases the angle of attack.
If he points the nose too high, however, the angle
of attack will be too great and the plane will stall.
At too high an angle the air no longer flows smoothly
over the wing but burbles and slows down, decreasing
lift. The angle of attack differs from the *angle of
incidence*, which is formed by the chord of the wing
and the longitudinal axis of the airplane.

Larger wings have more lift, as do wings with
greater camber, or curvature. A long narrow wing
has more lift than a short wide one because less of
a swirl, or vortex, develops at the smaller tip to
produce drag. The ratio between length, or span,
and average chord width is *aspect ratio*. Wings with
high aspect ratio are more efficient.

The faster the airplane flies the greater is the lift.
At higher speeds the air travels faster around the
wing, decreasing the pressure on the top surface
and increasing the impact pressure on the lower
surface. Finally, the density of the air itself affects
lift (*see* Atmosphere). The density varies with altitude, temperature, and humidity.

High-lift devices, such as flaps and slots, reduce
landing speed. A *flap* is a control surface hinged at
the trailing edge of each wing. When lowered it increases the curved surface of the wing for more lift.
It also acts as an air brake by increasing drag. A
slot is a long narrow opening between the leading
edge of a wing and an auxiliary airfoil. It permits
air to flow smoothly over the wing and increases lift.

Forms of Drag

Since drag makes an engine work harder to provide
thrust to overcome it, engineers *streamline* aircraft
(*see* Streamlining). The total drag is the sum of an
airplane's profile, induced, and parasite drag.

Profile drag is caused by the shape of the airfoil
and by skin friction. The clinging of air to the
outer surface of the airplane is called *skin friction*.
Air is fluid and therefore has viscosity, or "sticki-
ness." Aircraft surfaces are made smooth to reduce
skin friction.

The thin layer of air next to the airplane skin is
called the *boundary layer*. Its velocity is slower than
that of the main air stream because of skin friction.
Air flow in the boundary layer may be laminar or
turbulent. In *laminar flow* the air moves in sheets,
or layers, which slide smoothly over each other.
In *turbulent flow* the layers mix and cause drag.

Systems which control the boundary layer reduce
drag. These include porous surfaces, slots, and other
devices for blowing or sucking the air over the wings
(*see* Aerospace Research and Development).

Induced drag is due to lift. It is caused by the
sheet of high-speed air rushing across the wing's
curved upper surface. As this sheet of air leaves the
trailing edge of the wing, it has a slight downward

direction so that it interrupts the smooth flow of lower-speed air under the wing. This causes drag. *Parasite drag* is resistance from parts of the airplane other than the lifting surfaces.

Thrust and Weight

Thrust is the force that drives an airplane forward and opposes drag. A propeller or a jet or rocket engine develops thrust (*see* Airplane Propeller; Airplane Power Plants; Jet Propulsion; Rockets).

Weight is the force of gravity acting on the airplane and its contents. The point where the total weight of the airplane is concentrated is the *center of gravity*. The loading of an airplane must be planned with care so that it will be in balance. The lift force must act on or very near the center of gravity if the airplane is to be level in flight.

Aircraft Stability and Control

Aeronautical engineers design stability and controllability into aircraft. An airplane is *stable* if it flies a straight and level course with no attention to the controls by the pilot. If a gust of wind disturbs a stable plane whose controls are held at neutral it rights itself.

An airplane rotates around three axes—the lateral, vertical, and longitudinal. All three pass through the center of gravity and are perpendicular to each other. The airplane *pitches*, or raises or lowers its nose, along its *lateral axis*, which extends from one wing tip to the other. It *yaws*, or turns right or left, about its *vertical axis*, which runs from the top to the bottom of the fuselage. It *rolls*, or dips its wings up or down, along its *longitudinal axis*, which extends from the nose to the tail.

The tail assembly and the wings provide stability along the axes. The fixed horizontal stabilizer prevents pitching. The fixed vertical stabilizer stops yawing. The wings counteract rolling and sideslipping. *Dihedral*, in which the wings' tips are higher than the roots, contributes to stability. If one wing drops, it has more lift than the raised wing and the plane rights itself. *Sweepback*, or backward slant of the wings, produces stability in almost the same manner. It also corrects yawing by creating more drag farther ahead on the wing than on the aft portion.

An airplane has controllability if it can be flown effectively and easily. The *controls* include the control stick or wheel, rudder pedals, and throttle (*see* Airplane Flight Controls). The *control surfaces* include ailerons, elevators, rudders, flaps, and trim tabs (*see* Airplane).

High-Speed Flight

During World War II fighter planes with piston engines approached the speed of sound (*see* Sound). After the war jet aircraft flew faster than sound. High-speed flight has created problems for engineers.

The basic problem is the compressibility of air. At *subsonic speeds* (less than the speed of sound) the wing creates pressure waves which move in front of

TYPICAL AIRFOIL CROSS SECTIONS

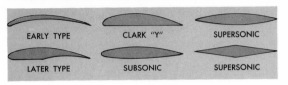

EARLY TYPE CLARK "Y" SUPERSONIC

LATER TYPE SUBSONIC SUPERSONIC

LIFT VARIES WITH ANGLE OF ATTACK

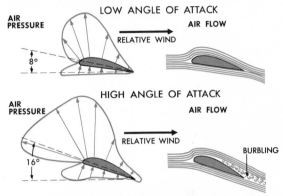

AIR PRESSURE

LOW ANGLE OF ATTACK

AIR FLOW

RELATIVE WIND

8°

AIR PRESSURE

HIGH ANGLE OF ATTACK

AIR FLOW

RELATIVE WIND

BURBLING

16°

Arrows pointing toward wing mean pressure is greater than that of atmosphere. Arrows pointing away from wing mean pressure is less than atmospheric. Lengths of arrows show intensity of pressure.

ANGLES OF ATTACK AND INCIDENCE COMPARED

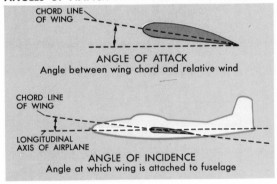

CHORD LINE OF WING

ANGLE OF ATTACK
Angle between wing chord and relative wind

CHORD LINE OF WING

LONGITUDINAL AXIS OF AIRPLANE

ANGLE OF INCIDENCE
Angle at which wing is attached to fuselage

HOW DIHEDRAL RIGHTS AIRPLANE

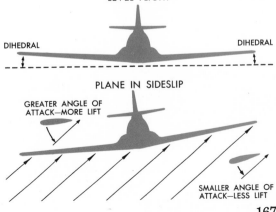

LEVEL FLIGHT

DIHEDRAL DIHEDRAL

PLANE IN SIDESLIP

GREATER ANGLE OF ATTACK—MORE LIFT

SMALLER ANGLE OF ATTACK—LESS LIFT

BREAKING THE SOUND BARRIER

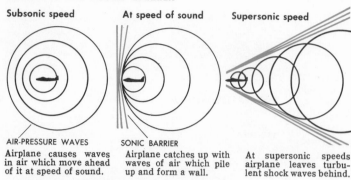

Subsonic speed

At speed of sound

Supersonic speed

AIR-PRESSURE WAVES
Airplane causes waves in air which move ahead of it at speed of sound.

SONIC BARRIER
Airplane catches up with waves of air which pile up and form a wall.

At supersonic speeds airplane leaves turbulent shock waves behind.

CHANGE IN SHAPE MAKES SUCCESS OUT OF FAILURE

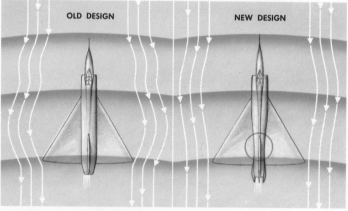

OLD DESIGN

NEW DESIGN

The Convair F-102 (left) failed to fly faster than sound. The redesigned pinched waist F-102A (right) applies the *area rule* and flies at supersonic speed.

BOUNDARY-LAYER CONTROL

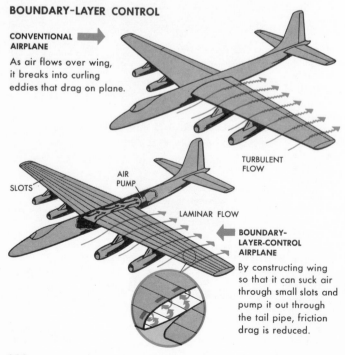

CONVENTIONAL AIRPLANE
As air flows over wing, it breaks into curling eddies that drag on plane.

TURBULENT FLOW

AIR PUMP

SLOTS

LAMINAR FLOW

BOUNDARY-LAYER-CONTROL AIRPLANE
By constructing wing so that it can suck air through small slots and pump it out through the tail pipe, friction drag is reduced.

it at the speed of sound to "warn" air particles in its path of its coming. The alerted particles change their direction and follow the shape of the wing.

At *transonic speeds*, in which different parts of an airplane may be near, at, or beyond the speed of sound, the pressure waves cannot warn air particles ahead that the airplane is coming because it is moving as fast as they are. The air piles up into a *shock wave*. The wings and control surfaces vibrate and buzz, controls become uncertain, and the airplane is buffeted. Swept-back and triangular delta wings and boundary-layer control reduce drag.

A shock wave causes a thunderlike *sonic boom* as it spreads away from the plane. Sometimes persons on the ground can hear the boom. The shock wave may even break windows.

Supersonic speeds are faster than the speed of sound. They are measured by a *Mach number* instead of miles per hour. It is named for Austrian scientist Ernst Mach and expresses the ratio of the speed of an airplane to that of sound. At sea level the speed of sound is 760 mph, but the speed varies with air temperature. At the much colder altitude of 35,000 feet it is only 660 mph. At Mach 1 an airplane is flying at the speed of sound. At Mach 2 it is flying at twice the speed of sound. *Hypersonic speed* is Mach 5 or greater.

After an airplane penetrates the *sonic*, or *sound, barrier*, its flight is smooth because it is moving faster than the pressure waves it produces. They fall behind and cause no shock waves. Airplanes capable of supersonic flight have short, thin wings with knifelike leading edges. Engineers use the *area rule* principle to minimize drag. At the point where the wings are attached they give the fuselage a "wasp-waist," or "coke-bottle," shape.

At extremely high speeds airplanes encounter the *thermal barrier*. The friction of the air heats the airplane's skin to very high temperatures. At Mach 3 the boundary-layer temperature is above 600° F. Only such materials as toughened glass, titanium alloys, and stainless steel retain their strength at such temperatures. The plane may be cooled by internal refrigeration systems; transpiration cooling, which forces a coolant through holes in the skin; and ablation coatings on the plane's surface, which absorb heat by vaporizing.

AIRPLANE HISTORY— How Man Learned to Fly

Within a half century aviation progressed from the 60-mile-an-hour, 80-horsepower pusher-type biplane to the 670-mile-an-hour, 9,000-horsepower F-86 Sabre jet.

AIRPLANE HISTORY. Man's desire to rule the skies has been the driving force behind one of his greatest adventures. In prehistoric times birds and dragonlike flying reptiles sailed through the air. When man appeared on earth, he watched and envied the birds flying in the sky.

Early man also wondered about the smoke climbing from his campfires and about the "falling stars" streaking through the sky. These mysteries of nature—the bird, the smoke, and the meteor—symbolize the three principal types of vehicles that today fly in the aerospace within and above the earth's atmosphere (*see* Aerospace). Heavier-than-air craft and lighter-than-air craft fly in the atmosphere, while spacecraft hurtle through space.

Flights in Myth and Fantasy

Stories of the flight of men, animals, and gods abound in the myths, art, and religions of ancient civilizations. As far back as 3500 B.C. the Babylonians engraved the adventure of Etana, a shepherd who flew on the back of an eagle, on semiprecious stones.

The legendary Chinese prince Ki Kung-shi flew a flying chariot; and the Persian king Kai Ka'us, a flying throne. Khonsu was a winged Egyptian god; and Assur, the chief Assyrian god, had an eagle's wings. In Arabic folklore a magic carpet glided over Baghdad. In a Greek myth Bellerophon rode Pegasus, the flying horse. In Roman mythology Mercury was the winged messenger of the gods. A famous Greek legend of flight is that of Daedalus and his son Icarus. Icarus soared too close to the sun, which melted his wings of feathers and wax. (*See also* Mythology.)

First Man-Made Objects in the Sky

Long before men learned how to fly they sent objects soaring through the air. The arrow dates from

FLIGHT IN FANTASY

ASSUR—chief god of Assyrians, carved about 884 B.C., with wings of eagle

DAEDALUS AND ICARUS— in Greek mythology Icarus disobeys his father and flies too close to the sun, which melts his wings of feathers and wax

MERCURY—winged messenger of Roman gods

DREAMERS OF FLIGHT—DESIGNERS OF MODELS

Leonardo da Vinci, the great Italian genius, designed this bat-like orthopter, with flapping wings, about 1490.

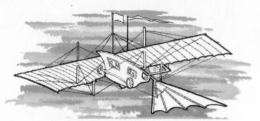

William S. Henson of England patented his "aerial steam carriage" in 1842. It was to provide world-wide airline service.

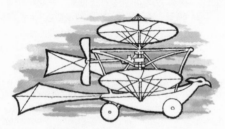

Sir George Cayley designed this "aerial carriage" in England in 1843. It was a combination of an airplane and a helicopter.

John Stringfellow, an English lace machinery manufacturer, flew this model, powered by a tiny steam engine, in 1848.

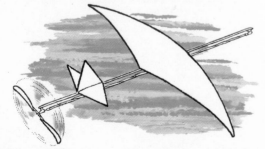

Alphonse Pénaud of France built his *Planaphore*, powered by a rubber band, in 1871. It resembled today's pusher-stick models.

the Stone Age. The ancient Chinese flew kites (*see* Kites). The early inhabitants of Australia invented the boomerang, the blades of which they carved in the shape of an airfoil (*see* Boomerang).

As early as the Middle Ages men of scientific mind prophesied human flight. About 1250 Roger Bacon, an English friar, suggested the *orthopter*, a machine that flaps its wings like a bird (*see* Bacon, Roger). He also conceived the balloon, proposing "a hollow globe filled with ethereal air or liquid fire."

Some 250 years later the great Italian artist and scientist Leonardo da Vinci studied the flight of birds (*see* Vinci). About 1490 he drew sketches for flying machines, also of the orthopter type. Da Vinci made drawings of a propeller and a helicopter and described the principle of the parachute.

Man Flies in the Balloon

An Italian monk, Francesco de Lana, in 1670 proposed a vacuum balloon. Four spheres, from which air had been exhausted, were to support a car equipped with oars and a sail. He overlooked atmospheric pressure, however, which would have crushed the spheres.

Not until a hundred years later was the first balloon flown successfully in public. In 1783 J. Étienne and Joseph M. Montgolfier inflated a big paper balloon with hot air. It rose 6,000 feet (*see* Balloon). That same year the Montgolfier brothers sent up Jean Pilâtre de Rozier in one of their balloons in the first human ascent.

Balloonists sought a way of steering their craft instead of merely floating with the wind. They proposed oars, man-powered propellers, and even harnessed eagles. In 1852 Henri Giffard, a Frenchman, flew a dirigible powered by a steam engine and propeller.

Interest Grows in Heavier-Than-Air Craft

Not satisfied with the limitations of the balloon in controlling flight direction, Sir George Cayley of England turned to the study of heavier-than-air craft. He advanced the basic principle of the airplane and is called the "father of British aeronautics." Beginning in 1810 he built model gliders. In 1843 he proposed the "aerial carriage," which combined the principle of the airplane and the helicopter.

In 1842 William S. Henson, a British inventor, had patented an "aerial steam carriage," the *Ariel*. He and John Stringfellow, a lace machinery manufacturer, organized the Aerial Transit Company, a world-wide airline service, but a model of Henson's airplane failed to fly. Stringfellow continued to experiment and in 1848 flew a steam-powered model.

Alphonse Pénaud of France made models powered by rubber bands. His models of the airplane, orthopter, and helicopter were successful. His *Planaphore* model of 1871 was a single-stick pusher monoplane that looks like the models built today.

Heavier-Than-Air Flight with the Glider

During the second half of the 19th century less attention was given to the idea of flapping the wings

PIONEER GLIDERS

Otto Lilienthal of Germany made more than 2,000 glides until killed in 1896.

An American engineer, Octave Chanute, built this biplane glider in 1898.

In 1905 John J. Montgomery of California launched his glider from a balloon.

of airplanes by means of the arm and leg muscles of the pilot. Instead, gliders were built with wings braced by struts and wires (*see* Glider). They had no engines but relied on gravity and wind for force.

In France Jean Marie le Bris built the *Artificial Albatross*, a birdlike glider, in 1857. Louis Pierre Mouillard, also a Frenchman, in 1881 wrote a book on gliding, which applied bird flight to aviation.

In Germany Otto and Gustav Lilienthal contributed greatly to aeronautics. They made glider flights from an artificial hill. Otto made more than 2,000 glides before he was killed in a flight in 1896. Percy Sinclair Pilcher introduced the Lilienthal glider to Great Britain. He too was killed, while flying his fourth monoplane, the *Hawk*, in 1899.

In Australia Lawrence Hargrave experimented with models, including an orthopter powered by compressed air. In 1893 he invented the box kite, upon which early European airplane designers based their biplanes.

EARLY ATTEMPTS AT POWERED FLIGHT

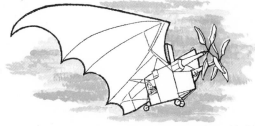

Clement F. Ader of France claimed to have flown his batlike *Avion*, powered by steam engines and twin propellers, in 1897.

In the United States John Joseph Montgomery of California built gliders. His most spectacular demonstration was made in 1905, when his glider was cut loose from a balloon several thousand feet in the air.

Another American, the civil engineer Octave Chanute, influenced the achievement of powered flight by his writings and experiments. From his work with bridges, he developed the truss construction of the biplane. Numerous flights were made with his gliders. Movable control surfaces added to their stability.

Experiments with Powered Flight

At the turn of the century four men came close to actual flight in a power-driven, manned flying machine. They were Ader in France, Phillips and Maxim in England, and Langley in the United States.

Clement F. Ader built batlike monoplanes powered by steam engines. He claimed he flew his *Eole* in 1890 and his *Avion* in 1897. There was some question, however, whether they hopped rather than flew.

Horatio Phillips in 1893 constructed a strange steam-powered multiplane with 50 narrow wings that resembled a Venetian blind. Tethered and without a pilot, it rose a few feet off the ground.

Sir Hiram Maxim, an American-born inventor who lived in England, constructed another curious machine, in 1893. It was a $3\frac{1}{2}$-ton multiplane monster powered by a steam engine. In a test flight on a circular track, it rose, ripped up a guard rail, and then crashed.

Meanwhile in the United States Samuel P. Langley, an American scientist and secretary of the Smithsonian Institution, attempted to solve the problem of

Sir Hiram Maxim built this steam-powered giant in England in 1893. It rose from its railroad track and crashed.

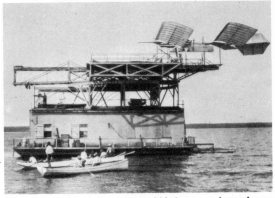

Samuel P. Langley twice catapulted his large aerodrome from a houseboat on the Potomac River in 1903. Both attempts failed.

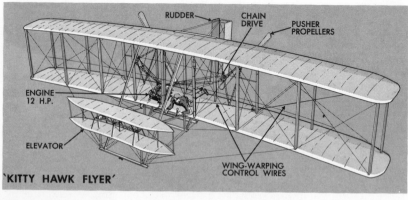

'KITTY HAWK FLYER'

THE FIRST SUCCESSFUL AIRPLANE FLIGHT
This historic photograph shows Orville Wright making the first powered flight by man in a heavier-than-air craft, Dec. 17, 1903, near Kitty Hawk, N.C. His brother, Wilbur, runs alongside.

flight with large powered models after years of scientific research (see Langley). He called his models *aerodromes*, meaning "air runners." In 1896 his *Aerodrome No. 5*, powered by a steam engine, flew for a minute and a half and covered more than a half mile.

In 1898 while at war with Spain the United States government granted Langley $50,000 to build a man-carrying aerodrome for aerial observation. In 1903 a gasoline-engined model flew successfully. Charles M. Manly, Langley's assistant, developed a radial engine that produced 52.4 horsepower. Manly was aboard the aerodrome in two attempted flights in 1903. It

was catapulted from the roof of a houseboat on the Potomac but plunged into the river both times.

Wright Brothers Conquer the Air

Just nine days after Langley's second test, two Americans, Orville and Wilbur Wright, made the world's first successful man-carrying, engine-powered, heavier-than-air flight (see Wright Brothers).

The brothers had read about Lilienthal's gliders and studied the writings of Mouillard, Chanute, Langley, and other pioneers. In their bicycle shop in Dayton, Ohio, they built gliders and a wind tunnel. In their 1902 glider they solved the problem of lateral control with vertical rudders and wing tips that could be warped or twisted up and down. The Wrights added power to their next machine. They built a four-cylinder, 12-horsepower gasoline engine and propellers. The craft weighed 750 pounds, with the pilot. Its wing span was 40 feet, 4 inches.

In the fall of 1903 the Wright brothers shipped their airplane to Kitty Hawk, on the coast of North Carolina. Here they had tested their gliders previously because of the hills and steady winds. On Dec. 17, 1903, Orville made the first flight, which lasted 12 seconds and covered 120 feet.

The Wrights improved their machine so that by 1905 they could fly more than 24 miles in 38 minutes. In

GREAT PIONEER FLIGHTS

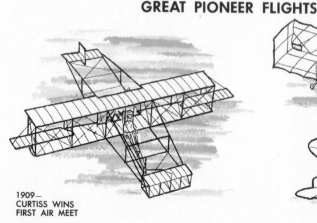

1909—
CURTISS WINS
FIRST AIR MEET

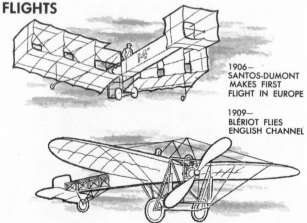

1906—
SANTOS-DUMONT
MAKES FIRST
FLIGHT IN EUROPE

1909—
BLÉRIOT FLIES
ENGLISH CHANNEL

Glenn Curtiss won the first international air meet in his *Golden Flyer* (left), 1909. Alberto Santos-Dumont made the first flight in Europe in his *14 Bis* (upper right), 1906. Louis Blériot flew the English Channel in his *Blériot XI* (lower right), 1909.

1908 Wilbur went to France and flew a Wright machine before the royalty of Europe. That same year Orville demonstrated one of the Wright planes at Fort Myer, Va., before government officials. During one of his flights, Orville took up a passenger, Lieut. Thomas E. Selfridge of the United States Army Signal Corps. Trouble developed and the plane crashed, killing Selfridge. He was the first person to be killed in an airplane crash. In 1909 the trials were successful and the War Department purchased the improved machine. Thus the United States became the first nation to own a military airplane.

Pioneer Daredevils

From 1900 to 1910 many pioneer airmen in many nations flew airplanes. Cash prizes for record flights and air meets stimulated the development of aviation. Fliers were particularly active in France. Alberto Santos-Dumont made the first officially observed airplane flight in Europe in his *14 Bis* in 1906. Henri Farman won a prize in 1908 for flying a kilometer course in a Voisin. In 1909 Louis Blériot flew across the English Channel in his *Blériot XI* and Hubert Latham almost succeeded twice in crossing the channel in an Antoinette monoplane.

Also in 1909 the first international air meet was held, at Reims, France. An American, Glenn H. Curtiss, flew his *Golden Flyer* a record 47.8 miles an hour. In 1910 he won the *New York World* prize of $10,000 for flying from Albany to New York City.

Curtiss had joined the Aerial Experiment Association, organized by Alexander Graham Bell in 1907, and he later became a leading aircraft manufacturer. When he used the aileron for lateral control, the Wright brothers claimed this was based on their wing-warping system and sued him for infringement of their patent. Their claim was sustained by the court.

A remarkable feat was the first transcontinental flight, by Calbraith Perry Rodgers in 1911. He flew a Wright brothers type EX airplane from Long Island, N. Y., to Long Beach, Calif., in 49 days.

The Airplane Becomes a Weapon of War

World War I accelerated the expansion of aviation (*see* World War I). Airplanes were first used for observation and later for aerial duels, bombing, and other purposes. Roland Garros, a French pilot, fired a machine gun through a whirling propeller by attaching steel deflectors on the blades to protect them. Anthony Fokker, a Dutch airplane designer, improved this idea by synchronizing the engine and machine gun.

Aircraft improved in structure and power plants as more military uses were found for them. Famous fighters included the Fokker and Albatros of Germany; the Nieuport and Spad of France; and the Sopwith Camel, Sopwith Snipe, Bristol F2B, and SE-5 of Great Britain. Outstanding bombers were the German Junkers, the British Vickers, and the Italian Capronis.

American fliers flew planes purchased from the Allies. The only United States-built craft used in combat were DH-4's. They were based on the British

NOTABLE LONG-DISTANCE FLIGHTS

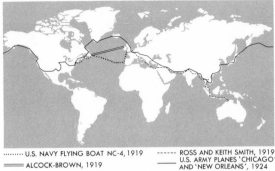

········ U.S. NAVY FLYING BOAT NC-4, 1919   ------ ROSS AND KEITH SMITH, 1919
═══ ALCOCK-BROWN, 1919   U.S. ARMY PLANES 'CHICAGO' AND 'NEW ORLEANS', 1924

This United States Navy flying boat, the NC-4, made the first transatlantic flight, in 1919 from New York to England.

Captain John Alcock and Lieut. A. W. Brown made the first nonstop Atlantic crossing, in 1919 in this Vickers-Vimy.

Captains Ross and Keith Smith and two crewmen made a flight from England to Australia in a Vickers-Vimy in 1919.

United States Army airmen made the first round-the-world flight, in 1924 in two Douglas planes. This one is the *Chicago*.

LINDBERGH'S FLIGHT

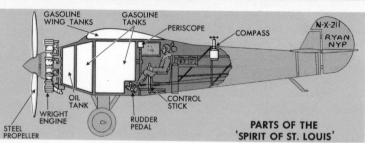

GASOLINE WING TANKS — GASOLINE TANKS — PERISCOPE — COMPASS — N-X-211 RYAN NYP — STEEL PROPELLER — WRIGHT ENGINE — OIL TANK — CONTROL STICK — RUDDER PEDAL

PARTS OF THE 'SPIRIT OF ST. LOUIS'

De Havilland-4 but had American-designed Liberty engines. The United States also produced several thousand Curtiss Jennies for training planes.

During the war continuously scheduled public service airmail began in the United States. In 1918 Army pilots flew regular airmail between Washington, D. C., and New York City by way of Philadelphia.

After the war, pilots found little use for their skills.

OTHER FAMOUS TRANSATLANTIC FLIERS

Clarence D. Chamberlain and his passenger, Charles Levine, flew nonstop from New York to Germany in this Bellanca in 1927.

Commander Richard E. Byrd and a crew of three flew in the Fokker trimotor *America* from New York to France in 1927.

LINDBERGH'S SOLO FLIGHT ACROSS THE ATLANTIC
Charles A. Lindbergh made the first nonstop solo flight across the Atlantic, in 1927. "Lindy" flew his Ryan monoplane, the *Spirit of St. Louis*, from New York City to Paris in 33½ hours.

Many of them bought surplus warplanes and became barnstormers. They offered rides in their craft or did stunt flying at county fairs and carnivals. These courageous and often foolhardy fliers promoted interest in aviation in the United States.

Across the Atlantic and Around the World

Flights over oceans, continents, and poles were made after World War I. In 1919 three huge United States Navy flying boats attempted the first Atlantic crossing. Only one, the NC-4, succeeded. It flew from Rockaway, N. Y., via Newfoundland, the Azores, and Lisbon, Portugal, to Plymouth, England.

A few weeks later Capt. John Alcock and Lieut. Arthur Whitten Brown made the first nonstop Atlantic flight. They flew a Vickers-Vimy from Newfoundland to Ireland. Later in the year Capts. Ross and Keith Smith and two crewmen flew a Vickers-Vimy from England to Australia. The next year the United States Army Air Service flew four DH-4–B's from New York City to Nome, Alaska, and back.

In 1923 Lieuts. John Macready and Oakley Kelly flew nonstop coast-to-coast from New York City to San Diego, Calif., in a Fokker T-2. The following year the first round-the-world flight was made. United States Army airmen took off in four Douglas World Cruisers from Seattle, Wash., but only two completed the trip, in 15 days, 3 hours, and 7 minutes flying time.

In 1926 Lieut. Comdr. Richard E. Byrd of the United States Navy and Floyd Bennett flew over the

North Pole in a Fokker trimotor (*see* Byrd). In 1929 Byrd flew over the South Pole in a Ford trimotor.

The Lone Eagle Defies the Atlantic

The Atlantic Ocean continued to fascinate the airmen. In 1919 Raymond Orteig of France had offered $25,000 for the first nonstop flight between New York City and Paris. Several French and American fliers made unsuccessful and often tragic attempts.

Finally, in 1927, Charles A. Lindbergh succeeded in his Ryan monoplane, the *Spirit of St. Louis* (*see* Lindbergh). His brave solo flight of $33\frac{1}{2}$ hours not only conquered the Atlantic but also made the nation and the world more air-minded.

Two weeks after Lindbergh's feat, Clarence Chamberlain and Charles Levine flew nonstop from New York to Germany in a Bellanca monoplane. A month later Byrd and a crew of three also crossed the Atlantic, in a Fokker trimotor.

With the Atlantic conquered, fliers turned to the Pacific. In 1927 Lieuts. Lester J. Maitland and Albert F. Hegenberger of the United States Army flew from Oakland, Calif., to Honolulu, Hawaii.

The next year Capts. Charles Kingsford Smith and Charles Ulm of Australia and two Americans flew from Oakland, Calif., via Hawaii and the Fiji Islands, to Brisbane, Australia, in the *Southern Cross*. In 1929 Lieut. James Doolittle made the first "blind" flight in history, using instruments to guide him.

General Italo Balbo led a mass flight of Savoia-Marchettis from Rome, Italy, across the South Atlantic to Rio de Janeiro, Brazil, in 1931. Also in that year Wiley Post and Harold Gatty flew around the world in a Lockheed monoplane, the *Winnie Mae*, in 8 days, 15 hours, and 51 minutes. Two years later Post made a solo flight around the world in the same plane.

Women became interested in aviation in increasing numbers. Amelia Earhart flew the Atlantic as the first woman passenger in 1928 in the Fokker *Friendship*. She became the first woman to solo the ocean, in 1932 in a Lockheed Vega. She and her navigator, Fred Noonan, disappeared over the Pacific in 1937.

Commercial aviation also developed in the 1920's and 1930's (*see* Airlines). The Kelly bill of 1925 turned over the airmail routes to private carriers. This encouraged the growth of airlines. More efficient aircraft were produced, including the all-metal Ford trimotor, Douglas DC-3, Sikorsky flying boat, Martin Clipper, and Boeing Stratoliner.

In the 1930's the airplane again became an instrument of destruction. Military craft were used in battles in Manchuria, Ethiopia, Spain, China, and Finland. These conflicts tested the design and tactics of warplanes for their roles in World War II.

Air Power Decisive in World War II

World War II demonstrated the vital importance of air power in modern total war (*see* World War II). Hitler's Junkers JU-87 Stuka dive bombers spearheaded his blitzkrieg of France. When the *Luftwaffe*, Germany's air force, attacked Great Britain, the

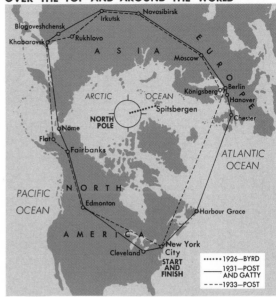

OVER THE TOP AND AROUND THE WORLD

FIRST FLIGHT OVER THE NORTH POLE
Richard E. Byrd and Floyd Bennett flew this Fokker trimotor, the *Josephine Ford*, over the North Pole in 1926.

RECORD-BREAKING ROUND-THE-WORLD FLIGHT
Wiley Post and Harold Gatty flew around the world in the *Winnie Mae* in 1931. Post circled the globe solo in 1933.

Hawker Hurricanes and Supermarine Spitfires of the Royal Air Force fought it to a standstill.

The *Luftwaffe's* planes included the Messerschmitt Me-109, Focke-Wulf FW 190, and Messerschmitt Me-262, all fighters, and the Dornier bombers. Other planes of the RAF were the fighters Hawker Tempest and Westland Whirlwind, the bombers Avro Lancaster, Short Stirling, Halifax, and Bristol Blenheim MK-1, and the fighter-bomber De Havilland Mosquito.

After the Japanese bombers attacked Pearl Harbor, the United States entered the war. Its aircraft production skyrocketed until in 1944 its output was almost 100,000 planes for the year.

Among the American fighters were the North American P-51 Mustang, Lockheed P-38 Lightning, Grum-

1903
'KITTY HAWK FLYER'

1919
NC-4 FLYING BOAT

1924
'CHICAGO'

1926
'JOSEPHINE FORD'

FAMOUS FLIGHTS IN HISTORY

1903 **Dec. 17**—Orville and Wilbur Wright make first successful airplane flight, at Kitty Hawk, N. C.; Orville flies 120 feet in 12 seconds.

1906 **Oct. 23**—Alberto Santos-Dumont makes first officially observed flight in Europe, nearly 200 feet in 6 seconds, in France.

1909 **July 25**—Louis Blériot of France in *Blériot XI* makes first crossing of English Channel by airplane, 25 miles in 37 minutes.

1909 **Aug. 22–29**—Glenn H. Curtiss in *Golden Flyer* wins first James Gordon Bennett international airplane race and other events in first International Flying Meet, Reims, France.

1910 **May 28**—Glenn H. Curtiss flies *Hudson Flyer* in record flight, 135.4 miles, from Albany to New York City, in 2 hours, 32 minutes.

1910 **Nov. 14**—Eugene Ely takes off from deck of U. S. cruiser *Birmingham* at Hampton Roads, Va., in first flight from deck of a ship.

1911 **Sept. 17–Dec. 10**—Calbraith P. Rodgers in Wright EX *Vin Fiz* makes first transcontinental flight, 4,231 miles, from Sheepshead Bay, Long Island, N. Y., to Long Beach, Calif., in 84 days and 70 hops; flying time—82 hours, 14 minutes.

1911 **Sept. 23**—Earle L. Ovington in Blériot monoplane flies first officially sanctioned airmail in U. S., from Hempstead to Mineola, Long Island, N. Y.

1913 **May 13**—Igor Sikorsky, Russian engineer, flies *Grand*, first four-engine airplane.

1914 **Jan. 1**—Anthony Jannus in Benoist flying boat begins world's first scheduled airline service with heavier-than-air craft, from Tampa to St. Petersburg, Fla.

1918 **May 15**—U. S. Army pilots in Curtiss JN4-H Jennies begin first continuous scheduled public-service airmail in U. S., between New York City and Washington, D. C., via Philadelphia.

First Transatlantic Flights

1919 **May 8–31**—Lieut. Comdr. Albert C. Read and crewmen in U. S. Navy flying boat NC-4 make first transatlantic flight, 4,526 miles, from Rockaway, N. Y., to Plymouth, England, via Newfoundland, Azores, Lisbon, Portugal, and other intermediate stops, in 53 hours, 58 minutes.

1919 **June 14–15**—Capt. John Alcock and Lieut. A. W. Brown of Britain in Vickers-Vimy bomber make first nonstop transatlantic flight, 1,960 miles, from Newfoundland to Ireland, in 16 hours, 12 minutes.

1919 **Nov. 12–Dec. 10**—Capts. Ross and Keith Smith and two crewmen in Vickers-Vimy fly from Hounslow, England, to Darwin, Australia, 11,130 miles, in 27 days, 20 hours; flying time—124 hours.

1920 **July 15–Oct. 20**—U. S. Army Air Service pilots in four De Havilland DH-4-B biplanes make New York-Alaska flight and back, 9,329 miles, in 112 flying hours.

1923 **May 2–3**—Lieuts. John A. Macready and Oakley G. Kelly fly Fokker T-2 monoplane in first nonstop transcontinental flight, 2,516 miles, from New York City to San Diego, Calif., in 26 hours, 50 minutes, 3 seconds.

1924 **April 6–Sept. 28**—Two U. S. Army Douglas World Cruisers *Chicago* and *New Orleans* make first round-the-world flight, 26,345 miles, from Seattle, Wash., in 175 days; flying time—363 hours, 7 minutes.

1926 **May 8–9**—Lieut. Comdr. Richard E. Byrd and Floyd Bennett fly Fokker trimotor nonstop from Spitsbergen to North Pole and back, 1,545 miles, in 15½ hours.

1926 **Dec. 21–May 2, 1927**—U. S. Army Air Service pilots starting with five Loening OA-1 amphibians fly Pan American good-will flight, over 22,000 miles, from U. S. to Central and South America and back.

Lindbergh Braves the Atlantic Alone

1927 **May 20–21**—Charles A. Lindbergh flies Ryan monoplane, *Spirit of St. Louis*, in first nonstop solo transatlantic flight, 3,600 miles, from New York City to Paris, in 33½ hours.

1927 **June 4–5**—Clarence D. Chamberlain and Charles Levine in Bellanca monoplane make first nonstop New York-Germany flight, 3,911 miles, in 43 hours, 49 minutes, 33 seconds.

1927 **June 28–29**—Lieuts. Lester J. Maitland and Albert F. Hegenberger of U. S. Army Air Corps fly Fokker C-Z trimotor across Pacific, 2,407 miles, from Oakland, Calif., to Honolulu, Hawaii, in 25 hours, 50 minutes.

1927 **July 14–15**—Emory Bronte and Ernest L. Smith are first civilians to make U. S.-Hawaii flight, 2,340 miles, in 25½ hours.

1928 **April 12–13**—Günther von Huenefeld and Capt. Hermann Koehl of Germany and Comdr. James Fitzmaurice of Ireland fly Junkers monoplane *Bremen* in first nonstop westbound flight over North Atlantic, 2,070 miles, from Ireland to Labrador, in 36½ hours.

---

man F6F Hellcat, and Chance-Vought F4U Corsair (*see* Air Force, United States; Navy, United States). The Boeing B-17 Flying Fortress and the Consolidated B-24 Liberator were used in mass bombings in Europe. The North American B-25 Mitchell attacked Japanese ships. The Martin B-26 Marauder was used in support of ground troops. The Boeing B-29 Superfortresses dropped atomic bombs on Japan.

Famous Japanese fighters were the Mitsubishi Type "0" (Zero) and Mitsubishi Model 52 (Zeke). Russian fighter planes included the Shturmovik and Yak.

Jets Replace Piston-Propeller Power Plants

During World War II the era of jet-propelled airplanes began. In 1939 the Germans flew the world's first successful turbojet airplane, the Heinkel He-178.

Germany and Great Britain were the only nations to have operational jet fighters.

After the war the United States, Britain, and Russia made rapid progress in jet and rocket power (*see* Rockets). In 1947 the rocket plane Bell X-1 became the first aircraft to fly faster than the speed of sound. In the war in Korea American F-86 Sabre jets outflew the Russian MiG–15 jets.

The jet engine also showed its superiority for commercial transports. In 1952 Great Britain began the world's first jet airline service, with De Havilland Comets between London and Johannesburg, South Africa. By 1960 United States airlines had in service the American-built turbojets Boeing 707, Convair 880, and Douglas DC-8 and the turboprop Lockheed Electra. (*See also* Jet Propulsion; Airplane Power Plants.)

| 1927 | 1931 | 1947 | 1959 |
| 'SPIRIT OF ST. LOUIS' | 'WINNIE MAE' | BELL X-1 | NORTH AMERICAN X-15 |

1928 **May 31–June 10**—Capts. Charles Kingsford Smith and Charles T. P. Ulm of Australia and Harry W. Lyon, Jr., and James W. Warner of U. S. in Fokker trimotor *Southern Cross* make U. S.-Australia flight, more than 8,000 miles, in 83 hours, 19 minutes.

1928 **June 17–18**—Amelia Earhart in Fokker trimotor *Friendship* is first woman to fly Atlantic as a passenger.

1929 **Jan. 1–7**—Maj. Carl Spaatz and crew of four in Fokker C-2 trimotor *Question Mark* set refueling endurance record of 150 hours, 40 minutes, 51 seconds, over Los Angeles, Calif.

1929 **Sept. 24**—Lieut. James H. Doolittle makes first demonstration of "blind" flight, at Mitchel Field, N. Y.

1929 **Nov. 28–29**—Comdr. Richard E. Byrd, Bernt Balchen, Harold June, and Capt. Ashley McKinley in Ford trimotor monoplane *Floyd Bennett* make first flight over South Pole, 1,600 miles, from Little America over pole and back, in 18 hours, 59 minutes.

1931 **June 23–July 1**—Wiley Post as pilot and Harold Gatty as navigator fly Lockheed monoplane *Winnie Mae* in round-the-world flight, 15,477 miles, from Long Island, N. Y., in 14 stops, in 8 days, 15 hours, 51 minutes; flying time—107 hours, 2 minutes.

First Nonstop Flight Across the Pacific

1931 **Oct. 4–5**—Clyde Pangborn and Hugh Herndon, Jr., fly Bellanca monoplane *Miss Veedol* in first nonstop transpacific flight, 4,860 miles, from Tokyo, Japan, to Wenatchee, Wash., in 41 hours, 13 minutes.

1932 **May 20–21**—Amelia Earhart in Lockheed Vega monoplane makes first transatlantic solo flight by a woman, 2,026 miles, from Harbour Grace, Newfoundland, to Londonderry, Ireland, in 15 hours, 18 minutes.

1933 **July 1–15**—Gen. Italo Balbo of Italy leads 24 Savoia-Marchetti seaplanes in mass transatlantic flight, 6,100 miles, from Orbetello, Italy, to Chicago, Ill., in 47 hours, 52 minutes.

1933 **July 15–22**—Wiley Post flies Lockheed Vega monoplane *Winnie Mae* in first round-the-world solo flight, 15,596 miles, in 11 stops, in 7 days, 8 hours, 49 minutes; flying time—115 hours, 36 minutes.

1935 **Jan. 11–12**—Amelia Earhart makes first solo flight by a woman, from Hawaii to California.

1935 **Nov. 22–29**—Capt. Edwin C. Musick in Martin China Clipper flies first regular transpacific airmail, between San Francisco and Hawaii and Manila.

1937 **Jan. 19**—Howard Hughes sets transcontinental speed record, 2,453 miles, from Burbank, Calif., to Newark, N. J., in 7 hours, 28 minutes, 25 seconds.

1938 **July 10–14**—Howard Hughes and four crewmen fly Lockheed "14" in round-the-world record flight, 14,971 miles, from Long Island, N. Y., in 3 days, 19 hours, 8 minutes.

The Jet Era Begins

1939 **Aug. 27**—Germans fly Heinkel He-178, world's first turbojet airplane, at Rostock, Germany.

1942 **Oct. 1**—Robert M. Stanley flies first U. S. jet plane, Bell XP-59A Airacomet, at Muroc, Calif.

1946 **Sept. 29–Oct. 1**—Comdr. Thomas D. Davies and crew of three other U. S. Navy fliers in Lockheed P2V Neptune *Truculent Turtle* fly nonstop from Perth, Australia, to Columbus, Ohio, 11,235.6 miles, in 55¼ hours.

1947 **Aug. 7–10**—William P. Odom in Douglas A-26 flies solo around the world, 19,645 miles, in 3 days, 1 hour, 5 minutes, 11 seconds.

1947 **Oct. 17**—Capt. Charles E. Yeager of USAF flies Bell X-1, first plane to fly faster than sound.

1949 **Feb. 26–March 2**—Capt. James Gallagher and crew of 13 fly USAF Boeing B-50 bomber *Lucky Lady II* in first nonstop round-the-world flight, 23,452 miles (4 in-flight refuelings), in 3 days, 22 hours, 1 minute.

1950 **Sept. 22**—Two USAF Republic F-84-E's fly first nonstop jet transatlantic flights (3 in-flight refuelings).

1952 **May 2**—British Overseas Airways Corporation with De Havilland Comets begins first turbojet airline service, between London and Johannesburg, South Africa.

1957 **Jan. 16–18**—Three B-52 Stratofortresses make first nonstop jet round-the-world flight, 24,325 miles (3 in-flight refuelings), in 45 hours, 20 minutes.

1958 **Oct. 26**—Pan American World Airways begins first regular jet service between New York City and Paris, using American-built Boeing 707 jet transports.

1959 **Jan. 25**—American Airlines, using Boeing 707's, begins transcontinental jet service between Los Angeles and New York City; 4 hours, 3 minutes, 53.8 seconds.

1962 **July 17**—North American rocket research plane X-15 penetrates outer space.

1964 **March 19–April 17**—Jerrie Mock makes first round-the-world solo flight by a woman; flies a single-engine Cessna 22,858.8 miles, in 21 stops.

From Buzz Bombs to Earth Satellites

After World War II research was also conducted on many unusual types of aircraft (*see* Aerospace Research and Development). The helicopter was not a new machine, but it was brought to a high degree of efficiency (*see* Helicopter). Other types of aircraft capable of vertical flight were ground-effect and VTOL (vertical take-off and landing) machines, including convertiplanes.

Developments that grew out of World War II research also included missiles and earth satellites (*see* Guided Missiles; Space Travel). These devices marked the transition from craft that flew in the earth's atmosphere to craft that journey in outer space.

During World War II the Germans not only led in jet propulsion but also in rocketry. Among their weapons of vengeance were the jet-propelled V-1, or buzz bomb, and the rocket-propelled V-2.

After the war the United States and Russia also built missiles and experimented with earth satellites using rocket power. The Russians were the first to launch a man-made satellite, in 1957. With satellites in outer space an accomplished fact, scientists turned their efforts to putting humans into space.

Beginning in 1961 both the United States and the Soviet Union sent men into outer space and back. The North American rocket research plane X-15 penetrated the lower reaches of outer space in 1962. Man has thus quickly passed through the Air Age and has now entered the Space Age. (*See also* Space Travel.)

AIRPLANE INSTRUMENTS— Aids to Flight

In the cockpit of the Boeing 707 jet airliner, the captain sits at the left, the copilot at the right, and the flight engineer in the right foreground.

AIRPLANE INSTRUMENTS. The instrument panel of an airliner or a bomber presents a seemingly confusing cluster of dials, switches, and levers. One wonders how a pilot can keep track of these hundreds of instruments. The pilot does not watch all of them at one time, however. In addition, they are conveniently grouped, according to their special use.

Airplane instruments are mechanical, electrical, and electronic devices that tell the pilot many things about his plane and its performance. There are four major classes. *Flight instruments* indicate the plane's speed, altitude, and direction. *Navigation instruments* help the pilot find his way from place to place. *Engine instruments* show how the power plant is functioning. *Equipment instruments* tell how the mechanical and electrical systems are operating.

Early fliers flew "by the seat of their pants." They relied on their senses to tell them the position, or *attitude*, of their plane. Flying by instinct, however, was unreliable because the pilot could easily become confused. He might, for example, confuse the pull of centrifugal force with that of the earth's gravity. Modern airplane instruments prevent such mistakes and thus make flying safer. They also permit "blind," or instrument, flying when the ground or horizon is obscured by fog, rain, clouds, snow, or darkness.

INSTRUMENT PANEL OF A LIGHT PLANE
Even a light plane has an instrument panel with many dials, knobs, and switches. In this Beechcraft Bonanza the instruments for flying the aircraft, navigating, and checking the operation of the engine and equipment are conveniently grouped.

The only flight instruments a light plane actually needs are an altimeter, a turn-and-bank indicator, and an air-speed indicator. A compass and a clock will suffice for navigation. A tachometer, oil-pressure and oil-temperature gauges, and a fuel gauge are the necessary engine instruments. Most planes, however, require many more instruments.

Flight Instruments

The *air-speed indicator* tells the pilot the speed of air flowing past his airplane. If there is no wind, the air speed and the ground speed are the same. A tail wind increases the ground speed. For example, if an airplane has an air speed of 100 mph with a 25 mph tail wind, the ground speed is 125 mph. On the other hand, a head wind decreases the ground speed.

The air-speed indicator operates by air pressure transmitted from the *pitot-static tube*. Actually this is two tubes in one. The *pitot tube* has an open end that protrudes from the wing, nose, or vertical stabilizer. It measures the impact of the air stream. The *static tube* is closed in front, but small holes in its sides supply it with still air. It measures the atmospheric pressure. The air-speed indicator is a hollow diaphragm connected to the pitot tube. Its case is joined to the static tube. The pitot pressure forces the diaphragm to expand or contract with the increase or decrease in speed. The difference between pitot and static pressures is registered by levers and gears leading to a pointer.

The air speed is indicated on the dial in statute miles or nautical miles (knots) per hour. The instrument registers true air speed only in still air at normal atmospheric pressure (*see* Atmosphere). At different altitudes and temperatures the atmospheric pressure varies. The indicated air speed (IAS) must be corrected to true air speed (TAS) by adding 2 per cent to the IAS for every 1,000 feet above sea level.

Jet aircraft have a special air-speed indicator, the *machmeter*. It measures the air speed in relation to the speed of sound and gives the maximum safe speed. High performance aircraft also use the *accelerometer*, or *G-meter*. It shows how great a load is being imposed on the structure in high-speed dives and turns.

The *altimeter* indicates the altitude above sea level or the ground in feet. The *barometric altimeter* is an aneroid barometer (*see* Barometer). It measures variations in air pressure with changes in altitude. A metal diaphragm is housed in a case connected to the static tube. The diaphragm expands and contracts as air pressure in the case changes. Levers and gears connect the diaphragm to a pointer.

The altimeter reads zero at the average sea-level pressure of 29.92 inches. At different geographical locations the barometric pressure varies according to the elevation and weather conditions. The pilot en route radios for the local sea-level barometric reading and adjusts his altimeter to this setting with a knob. When landing he asks the controller for the airport barometric pressure and adjusts his altimeter to show the height above the runway.

The *absolute altimeter*, or *terrain-clearance indicator*, gives the height of the plane above the earth. It measures the time lapse between the transmission of a radio signal to the ground and its return.

The *rate-of-climb*, or *vertical-speed*, *indicator* shows the rate of ascent or descent in thousands of feet per minute. It consists of a metal diaphragm connected to the pitot-static tube. Its case is vented to the static line through a small hole, the "calibrated leak." As the plane changes altitude the pressure change in the case lags behind that in the diaphragm. This pressure difference moves the diaphragm, which is mechanically linked to a pointer.

The *turn-and-bank indicator* is two instruments in one. The *turn indicator* tells the direction and rate of the plane's turn. The dial needle, vertical when the plane is in straight flight, shows turns in degrees per second. A gyroscope operates the needle (*see* Gyroscope).

The *bank indicator* shows slipping or skidding in a turn. A ball is sealed in a curved, liquid-filled

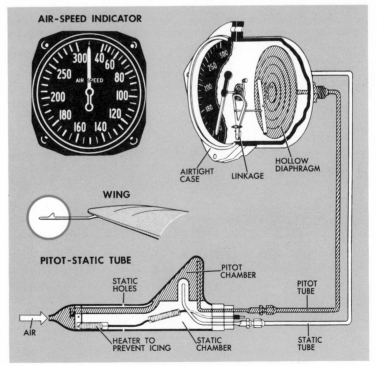

AIR-SPEED INDICATOR OPERATES BY AIR PRESSURE
The air-speed indicator measures the difference between pitot, or impact, and static, or still, air pressures as transmitted from the pitot-static tube.

FLIGHT INSTRUMENTS HELP THE PILOT FLY

ALTIMETER

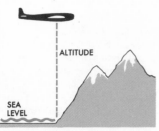

ALTITUDE

SEA LEVEL

The pressure altimeter indicates the altitude of the airplane in feet. It uses an aneroid barometer to measure air pressure.

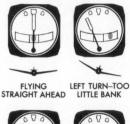

FLYING LEVEL

CLIMBING 1,000 FEET PER MINUTE

DIVING 1,000 FEET PER MINUTE

RATE-OF-CLIMB INDICATOR

Differences in air pressure operate this instrument to indicate the plane's rate of climb or descent in feet per minute.

ATTITUDE GYRO

FLYING LEVEL

BANKING RIGHT

DIVING

CLIMBING

This gyro-operated instrument provides an artificial horizon to show the attitude of the airplane in relation to the earth.

TURN-AND-BANK INDICATOR

FLYING STRAIGHT AHEAD

LEFT TURN—TOO LITTLE BANK

LEFT TURN—TOO MUCH BANK

LEFT TURN— CORRECT BANK

This flight instrument indicates the direction and rate of turn of an airplane and also its skidding or slipping in a turn.

glass tube. If a turn is executed properly, the ball remains in the center. If the plane skids, centrifugal force drives the ball to the high side. If the plane slips, gravity pulls the ball to the low side.

The *gyro horizon*, or *artificial horizon*, helps the pilot keep the wings of the aircraft level and the nose fixed in relation to the horizon. On the dial are a miniature airplane and a horizon bar. In climbs or dives the index airplane appears above or below the bar. When the pilot banks, the index airplane banks. A suction-driven gyroscope operates the instrument. The *attitude gyro* performs the same function as the artificial horizon, but its gyroscope is electrically operated. Instead of an index airplane and horizon

bar it has a horizontal pattern. It can be used even in acrobatic maneuvers when the plane is upside down.

Navigation Instruments

There are many types of navigation aids. The *magnetic compass* shows the heading of the airplane (*see* Compass, Magnetic). Magnetic interference may make the compass inaccurate. A correction card allows for these errors. The compass card swings when the airplane turns or flies in rough weather, making it difficult to read.

The *directional gyro* holds its compass card steady with a gyroscope. It does not seek north but must be set with a knob to agree with the magnetic compass. It must be reset every 15 minutes. The *gyrocompass* needs no resetting. It combines the functions of the magnetic compass and the directional gyro.

Radio and radar are valuable air navigation tools (*see* Radio; Radar). Air-to-ground communications include low to ultrahigh frequency range radio signals. The *radio compass*, or *automatic direction finder*, is a receiving set with a directional antenna that indicates the heading to a transmitter. One of the pilot's most effective course-guidance aids is the *very-high-frequency omnidirectional range* (VOR) *receiver*. *Instrument landing system* (ILS) equipment guides aircraft in landing. (*See also* Air Traffic Control.)

An instrument that relieves strain on long flights is the *automatic pilot*, or *gyropilot*. It keeps the

NAVIGATION INSTRUMENT
The magnetic compass is a directional instrument that indicates to the pilot the heading on which his airplane is flying.

plane on course without the pilot's help. Gyroscopes control the plane's elevators, ailerons, and rudder.

Engine Instruments

A large plane has so many engine instruments that they are mounted on a separate panel under the supervision of a *flight engineer*. These devices indicate when the engine is warmed up, delivering full power in take-offs, or operating at maximum efficiency.

The *tachometer* measures the revolutions per minute (rpm) of the engine shaft. *Thermometers* check the oil, carburetor, and cylinder-head temperatures. One type is a Bourdon tube, a curved, flexible metal device. The liquid inside it expands when it is heated, causing the tube to straighten. The motion drives a pointer. Some thermometers use a thermocouple of two dissimilar metals which generate electricity when heated.

The *oil-pressure gauge* and *fuel-pressure gauge* show the pressures at which lubricants are forced into the bearings and fuel is delivered to the engine. A *manifold-pressure gauge* registers the power the engine is developing by indicating pressure in the intake manifold.

The *engine analyzer* detects ignition and vibration disorders in an engine. The flight engineer scans the screen of a cathode-ray tube for deviations from normal. The *synchroscope* is an indicator on multiengine aircraft that is used to maintain the same rpm on each engine and thereby prevent vibration.

Jet Engine Instruments

Jet aircraft require fewer instruments than those with piston engines (*see* Airplane Power Plants; Jet Propulsion). The *engine-pressure-ratio indicator* (EPR) registers jet thrust by measuring the ratio between the engine compressor inlet pressure and the exhaust pressures.

Tachometers measure compressor speed of rotation in percentage of maximum revolutions per minute. The *exhaust-gas temperature* (EGT) *instrument* monitors overheating of the engine. The *fuel flowmeter* indicates the rate at which fuel is being used by an engine. Each tank has a *fuel gauge*.

Equipment Instruments

The many mechanical, hydraulic, and electrical systems of modern aircraft require instruments to show if they are operating properly. *Loadmeters* measure the generators' output. The *landing-gear-position indicator* tells whether the gear is retracted. Gauges measure air pressure in the cabins and in hydraulic systems for the flaps and brakes. Instruments show the position of the landing flaps, engine cowlings, and other parts not visible from the cockpit. Lights warn of fire and indicate autopilot cutout.

INSTRUMENT PANEL OF THE FLIGHT ENGINEER
The flight, or systems, engineer in the foreground has a separate panel with instruments for monitoring the aircraft's performance in flight.

INSTRUMENTS THAT INDICATE ENGINE PERFORMANCE

TACHOMETER
This electric tachometer shows the rotation speed of a jet rotor.

BOURDON TUBE
Fluid or gas in the hollow tube reacts to measure oil and other pressures.

FUEL FLOWMETER
This instrument indicates the rate of fuel flow to the engine.

OIL-PRESSURE GAUGE
The dial shows the pressure at which oil is being forced into the bearings.

AIRPLANE MODELS— How to Build and Fly Them

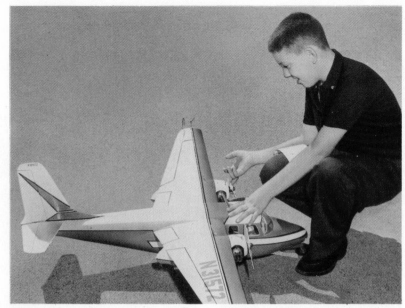

This beautiful model is "checked out" before take-off in a meet sponsored by the United States Navy. The boy's expression reflects his eagerness to see his model fly.

AIRPLANE MODELS. Building and flying model airplanes are fascinating activities. At least 2 million model airplane enthusiasts in the United States participate in this educational hobby. More than 100 manufacturers produce the tools and materials used in making models. The value of this equipment has been estimated at about 30 million dollars a year.

Value of Model Airplanes

Model airplanes are by no means the exclusive interest of hobbyists. Many uses have been found for models by industry and by the armed forces.

The airplane manufacturing industry uses exact scale models of new type airplanes for testing purposes. If any defects are discovered in the model, they can be corrected before the full-scale airplane is put into operation. The wind tunnel test is an ex-

ample. It is performed on all models (*see* Wind Tunnel). In this test the model is subjected to the same stresses and strains that the real airplane will meet.

Models are important also in industries other than airplane manufacturing. For example, the motion-picture industry uses models to depict airplane crashes, aerial dogfights, and similar scenes.

Scale models of all known airplanes are extremely helpful in teaching aircraft identification. Radio-controlled flying models serve as targets in gunnery practice. Other flying models are used to test performance and maneuverability of new aircraft types.

Lindbergh's Flight a Milestone

Model airplane building is not new. Hundreds of years ago inventors made crude models of machines they hoped would enable man to fly. Popular in-

MANY TYPES OF MODEL AIRPLANES

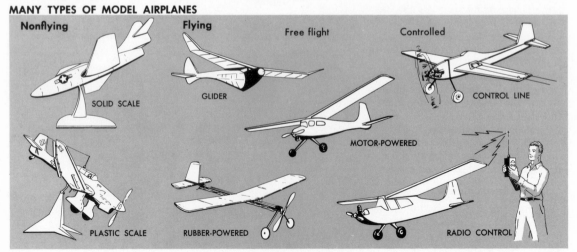

Nonflying · SOLID SCALE · PLASTIC SCALE

Flying · GLIDER · RUBBER-POWERED

Free flight · MOTOR-POWERED

Controlled · CONTROL LINE · RADIO CONTROL

terest in model airplanes did not become widespread, however, until the end of World War I. The present wave of enthusiasm for models probably began in 1927, after Lindbergh's historic transatlantic flight (*see* Lindbergh).

Types of Model Airplanes

There are two general types of model airplanes—nonflying and flying.

Nonflying models are usually built to be exact replicas of actual airplane types. These models may be made of wood such as balsa or pine, or plastic, or any other material. Nonflying models make excellent toys and decorative objects.

Flying models fall into three classes. These are: free flight, control line, and radio control.

Free-flying models cannot be controlled from the ground. They remain in flight until their power source is exhausted. They may be powered either by rubber strands or by some kind of engine. Gliders are free-flying models with no power source (*see* Glider).

Control-line models are regulated in flight by a wire line. One end of this line is fastened to the model. The other end is held by the operator, or "pilot." By holding fast to his end of the line, he is able to keep the model flying in a circular, controlled course. He may "maneuver" the craft by means of special attachments inside it and on his end of the line.

Radio-control models do not have control lines. A model of this type carries a small radio receiver, while the operator holds a small radio transmitter. Radio signals are sent from the transmitter to the receiver. When received these signals regulate the model's controls. By means of these signals the operator can put the airplane through many maneuvers.

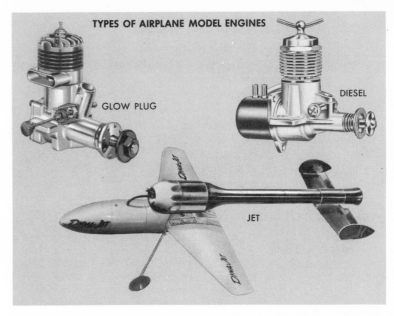

TYPES OF AIRPLANE MODEL ENGINES

GLOW PLUG

DIESEL

JET

Powered Model Airplanes

All flying models, except gliders, carry some form of power source to keep them aloft. This power may be furnished by tightly wound rubber strands. It may also be provided by a miniature engine.

In a *rubber-powered model*, elastic strands are tied at the front end of the airplane to a hook embedded in the propeller hub. The back end is anchored to another hook in the tail portion of the fuselage. When the operator turns the propeller, the rubber strands are wound into a tight spring. Upon release, the unwinding strands spin the propeller.

Model Airplane Engines

The tiny motors used to power model airplanes may be internal combustion or jet engines. They may also be compressed gas engines, deriving their power from the pressure of a gas such as carbon dioxide.

CONTROL-LINE SYSTEMS FOR MODEL AIRPLANES

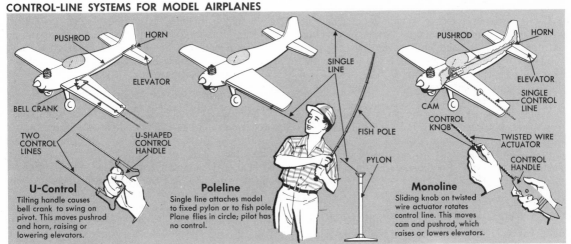

PUSHROD HORN

ELEVATOR

BELL CRANK

TWO CONTROL LINES

U-SHAPED CONTROL HANDLE

U-Control
Tilting handle causes bell crank to swing on pivot. This moves pushrod and horn, raising or lowering elevators.

SINGLE LINE

FISH POLE

PYLON

Poleline
Single line attaches model to fixed pylon or to fish pole. Plane flies in circle; pilot has no control.

PUSHROD HORN

ELEVATOR

SINGLE CONTROL LINE

CAM

CONTROL KNOB

TWISTED WIRE ACTUATOR

CONTROL HANDLE

Monoline
Sliding knob on twisted wire actuator rotates control line. This moves cam and pushrod, which raises or lowers elevators.

HOW TO BUILD A FLYING MODEL

This R.O.G. (rise-off-ground) rubber-powered stick model takes off in a hurry and is a good stunt flyer. It is easy to make—even if you have never built a model before.

Materials

2 balsa strips 36 × 1/8 × 1/8 inches
1 balsa strip 36 × 1/4 × 1/8 inches
1 balsa propeller block 4 × 3/4 × 3/8 inches
14 inches of 1/32-inch music wire
24 inches of 1/8-inch flat rubber

2 corks, 3/4-inch diameter
1 tube model-plane cement
1 tube model-plane dope
1 sheet model-plane tissue
Thread, bead, tin-can metal, rubber band

Directions

1. Cut parts for wing out of balsa with single-edge razor blade. Cement wing parts together, except center rib.
2. After wing dries, cut spars half through on bottom at center and crack slightly. Block up wing tips at proper dihedral angle and cement. Also cement in center rib. When cement is dry, dope top of wing and cover with tissue.
3. Cut out parts for stabilizer and rudder. Cement parts together.
4. Cut motor stick, wide side up. Make propeller hanger and landing gear; bind to motor stick with thread and cement. Make and install wheels. Make tail skid; force end through balsa and bind with thread and cement.

5. Cement stabilizer under motor stick, and rudder on top; line them up square in all directions. Dope top of stabilizer and cover with tissue. Dope both sides of rudder and cover with tissue.
6. Cement small block under center of leading edge of wing to give lift. Hold wing on motor stick with thin rubber band.
7. Carve propeller. Make each blade flat, tapering from 1/8-inch thickness at center to 1/16-inch at tips. Round tips. Bend propeller shaft and cement it to propeller. Install propeller, with bead between it and hanger, then oil.
8. Tie flat rubber in loop; place it between propeller hook and tail skid.

HOW TO FLY THE MODEL

Set wing halfway between prop and rudder. Test-glide plane with gentle shove, nose slightly down. If plane *stalls*, move wing back; if it *dives*, move wing forward. When glide is smooth, wind prop 200 turns.
Hand launching—point nose up a bit; give light shove.
R.O.G.—let plane take off from flat area.

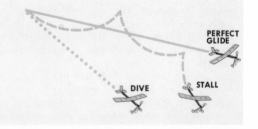

(Courtesy Boy Scouts of America)

Three types of internal combustion engines are widely used. The *ignition type* carries spark plugs, battery, condenser, and coils. The *glow engine* is similar to the ignition type but is equipped with a glow plug instead of spark plugs. The *compression-ignition* engine is really a tiny diesel engine.

A glow plug resembles a spark plug. The insulated electrode of the glow plug, however, connects to a loop of resistance wire instead of ending in a gap.

The jet engine used in models is a *pulse jet*. It consists of a long tube fitted with a system of butterfly valves (*see* Internal Combustion Engine; Jet Propulsion; Diesel Engine).

Building a Model Airplane

The method of building a model airplane depends upon the kind of finished model desired. A simple

model may be made of balsa, tissue paper, and rubber bands. More elaborate models may be made of aluminum or other metals. Such models may also carry accessories such as rubber-tired wheels, plastic windows, and electric wiring.

Materials and Tools for Model Building

The basic material used in the building of most airplane models is balsa, a very light but strong wood. The frameworks for the fuselage, wings, and tail assembly are made of balsa. The frames are then covered with a soft-grained tissue paper. Special cement is used to hold the framework strips together and to glue the paper covering to the frames.

Some models may be covered with *microfilm* instead of tissue paper. A few drops of a liquid plastic material are first placed on the surface of water in

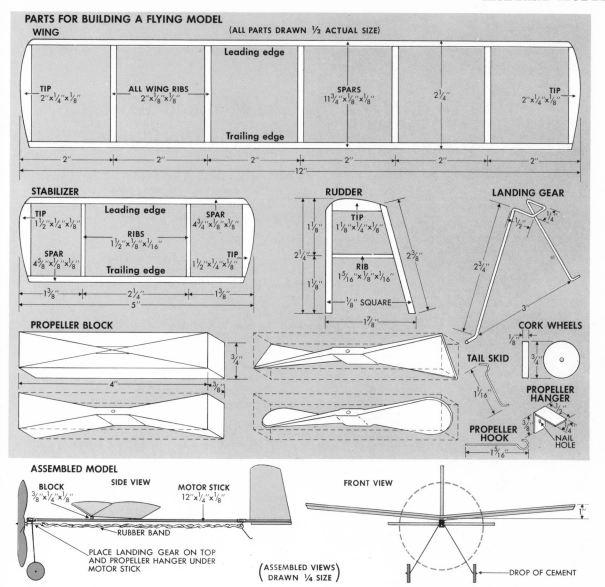

PARTS FOR BUILDING A FLYING MODEL

a pan or tub. These drops spread out over the water, forming a thin sheet, or "film," of microfilm. When the film is partly dry, the modeler slips a wire hoop under it, lifts it from the water, and places it in position on a frame. As the microfilm dries it glues itself to the framework.

Other models are not covered by paper or microfilm but are made entirely of sheets of balsa. Many of the nonflying types are carved from thick pieces of this wood. These models are solid.

The more simple airplane models may be built by using only a few tools. A razor blade, a piece of sandpaper, and perhaps a pair of pliers are all that is needed. Tools such as saws, drills, hammers, screw drivers, metal-cutting shears, soldering irons, clamps, and a vise are required in constructing the more elaborate types of models.

Flying Models in Competition

Model airplane builders fly their craft in numerous local, national, and even international competitions. In the United States such competitive meets are under the jurisdiction of the Academy of Model Aeronautics (AMA).

The AMA is an educational, scientific, nonprofit organization. It was founded in 1934. It is a division of the National Aeronautic Association. The AMA is also the United States representative of the Federation Aeronautique Internationale—the international model airplane organization.

Competitive meets under the guidance of the AMA are sponsored by the United States Navy and Air Force. The American Legion and many industrial organizations also sponsor competitions.

The flight crew for this jet airliner consists of the captain, co-pilot, flight engineer, navigator, and flight attendants.

Airline stewardesses, or hostesses, attend passengers. Airlines operate special training schools for flight personnel.

The Men and Women Who Fly the Planes

AIRPLANE PILOT AND CREW. Many airplanes are operated by one man—a pilot. On airliners, military bombers, transports, and other large and complex aircraft the pilot is assisted by a crew.

Private Pilots

A civilian pilot must have a certificate issued by the Federal Aviation Administration (*see* Aviation Regulation). He may hold a Student, Private, Commercial, or Flight Instructor Certificate. Ratings on the certificate indicate his ability to fly under instrument flight rules or in single- or multiengine aircraft, helicopters, gliders, landplanes, or seaplanes.

A private pilot flies for recreation or business. He must pass a physical examination and both a written and a practical examination in flying. He must also have 20 hours of solo flying. Flight schools or airport operators offer flying instruction.

Airplane Flight Crews

A *flight crew* operates an airliner (*see* Airlines). Smaller planes have a captain and a copilot in the cockpit, or flight deck, and a flight attendant in the cabin. Larger airliners also have a flight engineer, a navigator, and up to six flight attendants.

The *captain*, or *first pilot*, flies the airliner and is responsible for the safety of passengers and cargo. His decision is law at all times. He is like the captain of a ship at sea.

Airlines require the age of a pilot candidate (captain or copilot) to be from 20–23 to 27–30. He must be between 5 feet 7 inches and 6 feet 4 inches tall. Some airlines narrow this to between 5 feet 8 inches and 6 feet. Weight must be normal for height. Most airlines insist on 20/20 vision, uncorrected.

College graduates are preferred, but at least two years of college or the equivalent in experience is required. Pilots must have 400 to 1,000 hours of flying and FAA ratings for flying transports.

Pilots obtain training at private flying schools or while in military service. Airlines give them intensive training before assigning them to flight duty. The average annual salary for captains is $17,700 on domestic flights and $22,300 on international runs.

The *copilot*, or *first officer*, assists the captain. After he serves some time as copilot he may become a captain. Pilots advance according to seniority. A copilot earns about $7,900 annually on domestic flights and $11,000 in international operations.

The *flight engineer* is responsible for mechanical performance of the airliner in flight. Applicants must be from 20–23 to 35 years old. Height and weight requirements are the same as for pilots. Most airlines insist on 20/50 vision, correctable to 20/20. A flight engineer must have a high-school education and an FAA license. One airline requires 600 hours of solo flying; another demands four years of aircraft mechanic experience. Monthly salary ranges from $500 to $1,400 and more for international service.

A *navigator* is carried on some international flights, especially those over water. He determines the aircraft's position at any time (*see* Aviation Navigation).

Flight attendants cater to passenger comfort and needs. Most of them are women *stewardesses* or hostesses, although there are men *stewards*. A *purser* may be in charge of the cabin crew. Before take-off a stewardess helps passengers put away wraps and luggage, takes their names, and instructs them in the use of safety belts and oxygen masks. In flight she serves food and supplies such things as magazines, mints, gum, and pillows.

Age requirements for stewardesses range from 19 to 28. Stewardesses must be single. Preferred height is between 5 feet 2 inches and 5 feet 9 inches; weight, between 100 and 140 pounds. Minimum uncorrected vision must be 20/50 for each eye; but some airlines allow stewardesses to wear contact lenses or plain eyeglasses in flight. Good posture and a pleasing personality and voice are important.

On some airlines stewardesses must have two years of college or be registered nurses. Others require one year of college plus one year of business training. Stewardesses on international airlines must speak foreign languages. Airlines provide special schools for stewardesses. Some courses take six weeks. Flight attendants' salaries range from $250 to $450 a month. They earn more on international routes.

Flight crews fly no more than 85 hours a month on domestic routes and 255 hours in a calendar quarter on international flights. Flight deck personnel must pass a physical examination every six months and demonstrate proficiency in flight to airline and FAA check pilots. The airlines pay expenses of flight crews while away from the base station. They are allowed free or reduced-rate air travel.

Military Aircrews

The size of a military aircrew varies with the type of plane and mission (*see* Air Force, United States; Navy, United States). In a fighter the pilot acts as navigator, gunner, and bombardier. The B-52 bomber has six crewmen, and the B-58 has three. A multiengine plane must have at least a pilot and a copilot. Usually there is a flight engineer. On long flights there may be a navigator and a radio operator.

Military pilots and flight engineers need not obtain FAA licenses but must meet rigid health and proficiency standards. An Air Force cadet receives 12 weeks of preflight training, then 44 weeks of pilot training or 49 weeks of navigation instruction.

REALISTIC TRAINING IN FLIGHT SIMULATOR
The Air Force pilot at right "flies" a Link F-106A interceptor simulator. The two operators set up actual flight problems.

CERTIFIED CIVILIAN PILOTS IN THE UNITED STATES

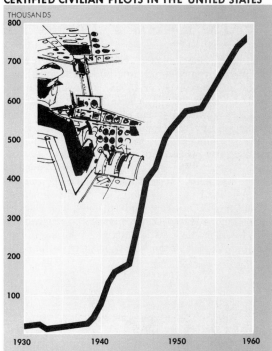

THOUSANDS
800
700
600
500
400
300
200
100

1930   1940   1950   1960

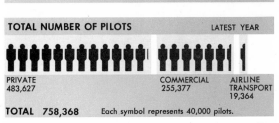

TOTAL NUMBER OF PILOTS		LATEST YEAR
PRIVATE 483,627	COMMERCIAL 255,377	AIRLINE TRANSPORT 19,364

TOTAL 758,368   Each symbol represents 40,000 pilots.

The number of certified civilian pilots has increased steadily. Only about half the total are active pilots, however.

This turbojet with an afterburner (foreground) is the engine for the Lockheed F-104 Starfighter.

AIRPLANE POWER PLANTS—Engines for Flight

AIRPLANE POWER PLANTS. An engine is to an airplane what muscles are to a bird. The muscles of a bird give it the power to flap its wings and fly. Similarly, an engine propels an airplane forward so that its fixed wings develop lift as they move through the air (see Airplane Flight Theory).

Years before the first powered flight, the Wright brothers and others had flown in gliders (see Airplane History). Perhaps the greatest achievement of Orville and Wilbur Wright was the building of an engine for their historic airplane (see Wright Brothers).

The Wright brothers built a 4-cylinder gasoline engine that produced 12 horsepower and weighed 180 pounds. In contrast is the Pratt and Whitney R-4360 Wasp Major, one of the world's most powerful recip-

rocating engines. It has 28 cylinders in four banks, delivers 3,500 horsepower, and has 11,000 parts.

Types of Power Plants

The power plant of an airplane consists of its engine or engines, plus its propeller or propellers (if it has any), accessories, and fuel and oil tanks and lines. Its engine is a machine that converts energy, usually in the form of heat, into work. Accessories include carburetors, fuel and oil pumps, and other elements not actually a part of the engine.

The internal combustion engine powers most aircraft today (see Internal Combustion Engine). The combustion of fuel inside a chamber produces gas pressure that gives the engine power. Two types of internal combustion engines in wide use are the *reciprocating*, or *piston*, *engine* and the *reaction engine*. The automobile has a reciprocating engine, and a skyrocket has a reaction engine. The two general classes of reaction engines are the *jet*, or air-breathing, and the *rocket*, or nonair-breathing, engines.

A number of other types of propulsion systems for aircraft and spacecraft are in the experimental stage (see Aerospace Research and Development; Space Travel). These include nuclear jet and rocket, ionic, photon, solar, and antigravitational propulsion.

Horsepower and Thrust

The power of aircraft engines is rated in different ways. That of reciprocating engines is given in *horsepower*. One horsepower is a unit of power equal to the force necessary to raise 33,000 pounds one foot in one minute.

THE ENGINE THAT POWERED THE FIRST FLIGHT
The Wright brothers could not find a suitable engine to power their airplane, so they built one themselves.

AIRPLANE POWER PLANTS

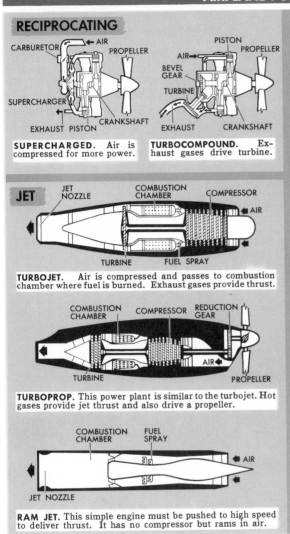

RECIPROCATING

SUPERCHARGED. Air is compressed for more power.

TURBOCOMPOUND. Exhaust gases drive turbine.

JET

TURBOJET. Air is compressed and passes to combustion chamber where fuel is burned. Exhaust gases provide thrust.

TURBOPROP. This power plant is similar to the turbojet. Hot gases provide jet thrust and also drive a propeller.

RAM JET. This simple engine must be pushed to high speed to deliver thrust. It has no compressor but rams in air.

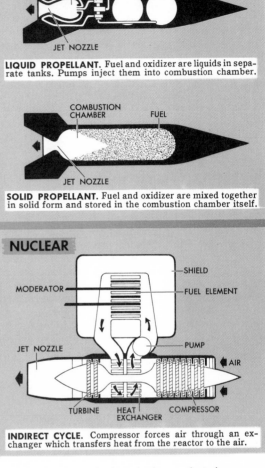

ROCKET

LIQUID PROPELLANT. Fuel and oxidizer are liquids in separate tanks. Pumps inject them into combustion chamber.

SOLID PROPELLANT. Fuel and oxidizer are mixed together in solid form and stored in the combustion chamber itself.

NUCLEAR

INDIRECT CYCLE. Compressor forces air through an exchanger which transfers heat from the reactor to the air.

Turbojet, pulse-jet, ram-jet, and rocket engines are rated by the *pounds* of thrust they produce. One pound of thrust equals one horsepower at 375 miles an hour. The turboprop engine uses almost all the gas turbine's thrust to turn a propeller, and its power is stated as *equivalent-shaft horsepower*.

Reciprocating Engines

The *reciprocating engine* is the type most widely used in aircraft. It gets its name from the back-and-forth movement of a piston in a cylinder (*see* Motors and Engines; Automobile Power Plant). When a fuel-air mixture is ignited, it burns. The expanding gases push the piston downward to rotate a crankshaft and turn a propeller (*see* Airplane Propeller).

Reciprocating engines may be radial, in-line, or opposed, depending upon the arrangement of their cylinders. In the *radial engine* the cylinders are distributed around the crankshaft like spokes on a wheel.

The cylinders may be in a single row, in twin rows, or in multiple rows. The *in-line* engine has one or more rows of cylinders, each behind the other. The rows may be arranged in a "V," "X," or "W" pattern. The *opposed engine* has two rows of cylinders placed across from each other horizontally, one on either side of the crankshaft.

Piston engines may be air-cooled or liquid-cooled. Today most of them are cooled by air blowing over fins on the cylinders. In the automobilelike liquid-cooled system a liquid circulates around the cylinders and through a radiator to carry away heat.

Airplanes that fly in the thin air of high altitudes may be equipped with a *supercharger*. This is a compressor which pumps extra air into the engine for added power. Most superchargers are of the centrifugal type, with an impeller, or bevel gear, which is driven by the crankshaft. In the *turbosupercharger* an exhaust-driven turbine rotates the impeller. The

189

compound, or *turbocompound, engine* also uses exhaust gases for more power by driving a turbine geared to the crankshaft.

Reaction Engines

A reaction engine gets its thrust from gases blasting rearward like a blowtorch. It moves forward, or reacts, in accordance with Sir Isaac Newton's third law of motion. This law states that to every action there is an equal and opposite reaction.

A common example of this principle is the Fourth of July skyrocket. When it is fired, expanding gases escape from it to hurl it high into the sky. It is not the gases rushing out of the skyrocket and pushing against the outside air that drive it ahead. Rather it is the gases inside the skyrocket pressing against the inside front wall that thrust it forward.

Reaction engines are classified according to whether or not they carry their own oxygen for fuel combustion. The *jet engine* obtains oxygen from the atmosphere, but the *rocket engine* does not depend upon atmospheric oxygen and can go into outer space.

Jet Engines

Jet engines are of three types—the gas turbine, pulse jet, and ram jet (*see* Jet Propulsion). The *gas turbine* has a turbine-driven compressor which compresses air for combustion. The *pulse jet* and *ram jet* compress air by other means.

The two main types of gas-turbine engines are the turbojet and turboprop. In the *turbojet* the gases resulting from combustion not only rotate the turbine

to drive the compressor but also create the thrust-producing jet. In the *turboprop,* or prop jet, the turbine drives both the compressor and a propeller. It creates thrust from its jet but produces most of it from its propeller. An *afterburner* added to a turbojet increases its thrust. It is an auxiliary combustion chamber, attached to the tail pipe, in which additional fuel is burned to utilize unused oxygen in the exhaust gases from the turbine.

Another turbojet with increased thrust is the *turbofan engine.* It gets more power by handling more air. It is also called the ducted-fan, aft-fan, or bypass engine. One version has a propellerlike fan enclosed in a duct at the front of the engine. It gulps in air in great quantities and passes some of it around the combustion chamber to add an independent thrust to the exhaust gases in the jet stream. In another type the fan takes in air behind the combustion chamber.

The British bypass engine has a low-pressure compressor in front of a high-pressure compressor. Part of the air flow goes to the high-pressure compressor. The balance bypasses it and mixes with the exhaust.

The pulse jet is an intermittent-firing jet, while the ram jet is a continuous-firing type. Both must be boosted to high speed by some other kind of propulsion to start combustion.

Shutters in the front end of the *pulse jet* open and close to take in air intermittently. This produces power in a series of rapid explosions. It is not as efficient as the turbojet or ram jet. The noisy pulse-jet engine powered the German V-1 buzz bomb during World War II.

The *ram jet* is the simplest jet engine because it has no moving parts. It is an open-end "flying smoke-pipe" which rams air in as it moves forward and burns its fuel continuously to produce forward thrust. It is used for missiles and experimental aircraft.

Rocket Engines

The *rocket engine* powered the German V-2 missile during World War II (*see* Guided Missiles; Rockets). There are two types—liquid propellant and solid propellant. Hybrid-propellant rocket engines under development use a solid fuel and a liquid oxidizer or the reverse. Rocket engines are used in missiles and research planes such as the North American X-15A-2.

Electric Engines

Electric engines will be used to propel spaceships on deep-space missions. These engines produce low thrust for long periods. There are three basic types, each differing in the method used to accelerate the propellant. The *arc-jet,* or *electrothermal, engine* utilizes an electric arc discharge to heat a propellant gas. The gas expands through a nozzle, producing thrust. The *ion,* or *electrostatic, engine* employs cesium ions accelerated by an electrostatic field to create thrust. The *plasma,* or *magnetohydrodynamic* (MHD), *engine* uses an ionized gas accelerated by an electromagnetic field to produce thrust.

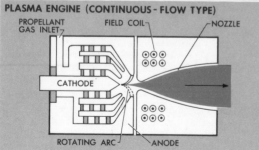

ELECTRIC PROPULSION ENGINES

ION ENGINE (CONTACT TYPE)

IONIZER

ACCELERATING ELECTRODE

DECELERATING ELECTRODE

CESIUM PROPELLANT

NEUTRAL ION BEAM

NEUTRALIZER FILAMENT

PLASMA ENGINE (CONTINUOUS - FLOW TYPE)

PROPELLANT GAS INLET

FIELD COIL

NOZZLE

CATHODE

ROTATING ARC

ANODE

In the ion engine the positive cesium ions are first accelerated, then decelerated to adjust their velocities, and finally neutralized by electrons to prevent the buildup of an electric charge on the spacecraft. The plasma engine uses an ionized propellant gas such as argon or nitrogen.

AIRPLANE PROPELLER.

In today's jet age more and more aircraft have propellerless turbojet engines. Many airplanes, however, are still being powered by piston or turboprop engines that turn propellers (*see* Airplane Power Plants; Jet Propulsion).

A *propeller* is a device so shaped that when it is rotated it produces a force, or thrust, which pulls or pushes an airplane through the air. It is called a *prop* for short. It may have two, three, four or more arms, or blades. They are fastened to hublike spokes in a wheel attached to a crankshaft.

A Propeller Is a Rotating Wing

A propeller blade is actually a small wing. In cross section it is an airfoil (*see* Airplane Flight Theory). When it rotates, its curved front surface creates a low-pressure area in front of it just as the top of a wing does. Its flatter rear surface creates a high-pressure area and pushes air rearward. A forward lift or thrust results that causes the propeller to move forward, pulling the airplane with it.

Most aircraft have *tractor propellers*. They are mounted at the front of the engine ahead of the wing and pull the airplane through the air. A few aircraft have *pusher propellers*. They are at the rear of an engine behind the wing and push the plane. *Counterrotating propellers* have two sets of blades, one behind the other, revolving in opposite directions.

The British call a propeller an *airscrew*, because a propeller bites into the air as a screw bores into wood. It is twisted to provide a small blade angle at its tip, where greater speed is needed, and a large blade angle at its root, where less speed is required.

The angle, or *pitch*, determines the distance the blade moves forward in one revolution. A blade at *high pitch* takes a bigger bite of air than at *low pitch*. A plane with a prop at high pitch is like an automobile in high gear. It moves forward a great distance with each turn of the prop. High pitch is best for cruising; low pitch, for taking off or climbing.

Changing Pitch Is Like Shifting Gears

Many small aircraft use a one-piece *fixed-pitch propeller* whose angle cannot be changed. The blades of the *adjustable-pitch propeller* are clamped in the hub and their angle can be altered on the ground. The pilot can change the blade angle of a *controllable-pitch propeller* while in flight. He operates the controls mechanically, hydraulically, or electrically. A variation is the *constant-speed propeller*. A governor automatically adjusts the pitch to the engine's speed.

If engine failure occurs, a propeller will *windmill*, or continue to rotate, and cause drag. Props on multi-engine planes can be *feathered*, or turned edgewise to the air, to stop rotation. *Reversible-pitch propellers* can be adjusted to change the direction of the thrust. This slows down the plane in flight or when landing.

Light planes usually have laminated wood propellers. Aluminum or magnesium alloy props are machined from forgings. Steel props may be solid or hollow.

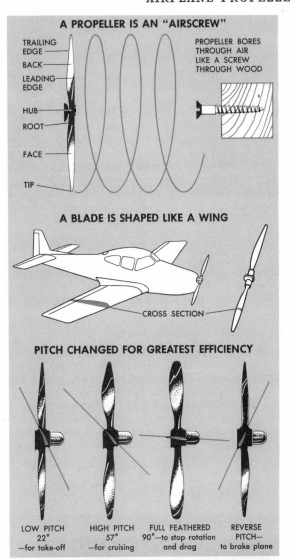

A PROPELLER IS AN "AIRSCREW"

TRAILING EDGE
BACK
LEADING EDGE
HUB
ROOT
FACE
TIP

PROPELLER BORES THROUGH AIR LIKE A SCREW THROUGH WOOD

A BLADE IS SHAPED LIKE A WING

CROSS SECTION

PITCH CHANGED FOR GREATEST EFFICIENCY

LOW PITCH 22° —for take-off

HIGH PITCH 57° —for cruising

FULL FEATHERED 90°—to stop rotation and drag

REVERSE PITCH— to brake plane

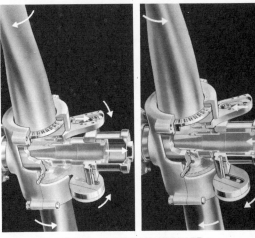

A CONTROLLABLE-PITCH PROPELLER
When the hubcap is moved forward, the blades turn at low pitch (left). For high pitch (right), the cap is pulled back.

AIRPLANE SAFETY. Air transportation today is safer than travel by automobile and compares favorably with that by railroad and bus. Airlines have constantly improved safety for passengers over the years. In 1930 there were 28 passenger fatalities for each 100 million passenger-miles. Today the figure is less than one fatality for the same number of passenger-miles. A far greater number of people die in automobile accidents each year than have been killed in the entire history of peacetime aviation in the United States.

Accidents were numerous in the early days of flying, particularly among "barnstormers." Therefore, Congress in the Air Commerce Act of 1926 established air traffic rules, the licensing of pilots and mechanics, and the licensing and inspection of aircraft.

The rapid growth of airline traffic and the increase in military and civilian flying have crowded the airways and jammed the airports. The coming of the high-speed, high-capacity jet transports has complicated the problem of air safety. Jet aircraft fly so fast that it is difficult for pilots to react in time to avoid accidents.

Aviation Safety Organizations

Many governmental and private organizations are concerned with air safety. The principal federal groups are the Federal Aviation Agency and the Civil Aeronautics Board (see Aviation Regulation). The FAA was created in 1958 to control both military and civilian users of airspace. When the Department of Transportation was established in 1966, it absorbed the FAA and the safety functions of the CAB.

Private aviation safety organizations include the Air Transport Association, composed of airlines; Air Line Pilots Association; Aerospace Industry Association; and Aircraft Owners and Pilots Association.

The National Safety Council, Flight Safety Foundation, Inc., and Guggenheim Aviation Safety Center at Cornell University also promote flight safety.

There are two world-wide air safety organizations, with headquarters in Montreal. These are a United Nations agency, the International Civil Aviation Organization; and the International Air Transport Association. The latter is made up of airlines.

Types of Accidents

Personnel action causes about one half of all air-carrier accidents, with one third of the total attributed to the pilot. Failure of material, such as that in power plants or landing gear, accounts for one fifth of the accidents, with one half of these resulting from power-plant failure. Other causes are the weather and airport terrain (see Aviation Meteorology; Airports).

Some of the hazards of flying are due to fire, icing, high speeds, and poor visibility. The possibility of collision between aircraft, air turbulence, and pilot fatigue are other hazards.

Safety Equipment

Equipment has been developed for the aircraft, crew, and passengers to make civil and military aviation safer. Fireproof fabrics, fire extinguishers, and fire and smoke detectors aid in fire protection.

The airline pilot flashes on the "no smoking" sign during take-offs and landings to guard against ignition of fuel fumes. Safety belts protect passengers during take-offs, landings, rough weather, or crashes.

Anti-icing and deicing aids keep ice from forming on wings, tail assemblies, propellers, windshields, and carburetors. Radio and radar equipment in the aircraft and on the ground assists in air traffic control (see Air Traffic Control; Airplane Instruments).

Parachutes are not carried on most civilian flights but are used by all military personnel (see Parachute). Airliners do not carry parachutes because it is impractical to instruct passengers in their use. Ejection seats on military aircraft hurl pilots from disabled high-speed planes without injury. Military pilots wear special G suits, or antiblackout suits, that exert pressure to prevent the blood from being forced from the head during sharp turns and dives (see Aerospace Medicine).

For protection in ditching at sea, aircraft carry automatically inflating life rafts, life jackets, emergency rations and drinking water, dyes for marking the water, fishing and hunting equipment, maps, and signaling devices such as mirrors and radio sets.

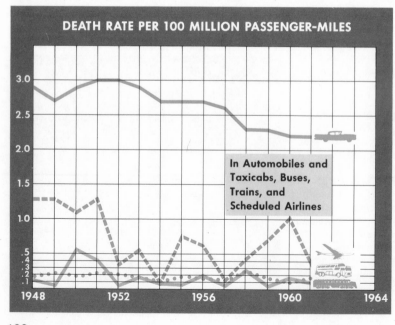

DEATH RATE PER 100 MILLION PASSENGER-MILES

In Automobiles and Taxicabs, Buses, Trains, and Scheduled Airlines

3.0
2.5
2.0
1.5
1.0
.5
.4
.3
.2
.1

1948   1952   1956   1960   1964

Here a huge airfreighter gracefully approaches Runway 13 at La Guardia Airport in New York City. Notice the markings on the runways. The single broken center line indicates a runway. The eight large stripes form a threshold marker.

AIRPORTS—Ports for Ships of the Skies

AIRPORTS. An airplane needs an *airport* just as a ship requires a port, or a train a railroad station. The airplane needs a place for taking off or for landing, either on ground or water. It also needs space for loading, unloading, fueling, repairing, or storing.

Airports vary in size. A large airport is sometimes called an *air terminal*. *Airparks* are small airports. Airports used by the Armed Forces are known as *air bases* or *air stations*.

A *heliport* is an airport for helicopters. Sometimes it is built on the roof of a building. The helicopter alighting pad, or touchdown pad, may not be much larger than a baseball diamond. A *seaplane base* is an airport for water-borne airplanes. It may be located on a river, a lake, or coastal waters.

Visit to an Airport

A visit to a large airport is exciting. Even before it is reached, the roar of airplane engines can be heard. Giant airliners or tiny private planes are taking off and landing. People who drive to the airport may park their automobiles in a large parking lot.

The airport has three types of facilities. One is for passengers, one for airplanes while on the ground, and one for airplanes while in flight. Passenger facilities help to make the change between ground and air transportation rapid. They include roads, taxi stands, bus terminal, airline limousine service, and the terminal building.

Facilities for airplanes on the ground are hangars, service and repair shops, air freight terminal, and fueling system. Some airports have a military area, including hangars for military planes. Other airports have an industrial area with aircraft factories and warehouses. Sometimes there is an aviation school.

Facilities for airplanes while taking off or landing are the airfield, with its runways and taxiways, aprons, control tower, instrument landing system, and lighting system. Some airports also have a heliport for helicopter taxi service to the city or to other airports.

Terminal Building Is the Airplane "Depot"

The most active and interesting building at the airport is the *terminal building*. It is like a big passenger station. In its large *waiting room* are seats for travelers, visitors, and sight-seers. In the *main lobby*, each airline has a ticket counter where passengers make reservations. Behind each counter, agents post information about each departing and arriving flight on a big flight board.

The agents also take baggage and give claim checks for it. They weigh each piece of luggage because the

193

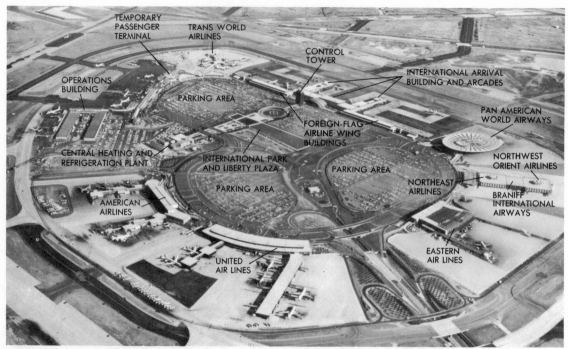

Labels on image: TEMPORARY PASSENGER TERMINAL, TRANS WORLD AIRLINES, CONTROL TOWER, INTERNATIONAL ARRIVAL BUILDING AND ARCADES, OPERATIONS BUILDING, PARKING AREA, PAN AMERICAN WORLD AIRWAYS, FOREIGN-FLAG AIRLINE WING BUILDINGS, CENTRAL HEATING AND REFRIGERATION PLANT, INTERNATIONAL PARK AND LIBERTY PLAZA, PARKING AREA, NORTHWEST ORIENT AIRLINES, NORTHEAST AIRLINES, BRANIFF INTERNATIONAL AIRWAYS, AMERICAN AIRLINES, PARKING AREA, EASTERN AIR LINES, UNITED AIR LINES

THE JOHN F. KENNEDY INTERNATIONAL AIRPORT

This modern airport covers an area of 4,900 acres in the Borough of Queens, New York City. It has the first commercial runway in the world that utilizes flush center-line lighting to guide airplanes in landing and along exits to taxiways.

total load that a plane can carry is fixed by law. Formerly, passengers were weighed, but now an average weight is used. A conveyer belt takes the luggage to the *baggage room*.

In the terminal building passengers may buy insurance at a vending machine and eat at a snack bar or restaurant. There may also be a barbershop, a beauty parlor, a bank, a hotel, and even a theater.

In the terminal building also is the *pilot's ready room*. Here pilots make their flight plans. In the *operations room* flight dispatchers determine the departure schedule, gasoline load, and total weight of each plane. They help to select the routes and altitudes of flights. Meteorologists study and forecast the weather in the *weather bureau office*. Postal clerks sort and bag mail in the *mail room*. In the *flight kitchen* chefs prepare meals for the flights. The manager of the airport and his staff occupy the *airport manager's office*.

Hangars Are Airplane "Garages"

Near the terminal building are the *hangars* where skilled mechanics check and repair the airplanes. Inside the hangars or other buildings are engine and aircraft overhaul shops, stock rooms, radio repair shops, and offices. Other buildings house firefighting trucks, ambulances, maintenance equipment, and heating and power plants. Cargo planes can be loaded and unloaded in the *airfreight terminal*.

The fuel for airplanes is stored in underground tanks. It is pumped into the planes from gasoline service trucks, flush-type service pits, or islands.

FACTS ABOUT THE JOHN F. KENNEDY INTERNATIONAL AIRPORT

Operation: The Port of New York Authority operates the airport under a lease, effective June 1, 1947, with the City of New York.

Location: On Jamaica Bay in the southeastern section of the Borough of Queens, New York City.

Size: 4,900 acres, nine times the size of La Guardia Airport. The longest runway is 14,600 feet. Terminal City occupies 655 acres; International Park, 220 acres. Loading positions for aircraft will total 140.

Construction: Begun in April 1942 when the City of New York contracted for the placing of hydraulic fill over the marshy tidelands on the site of Idlewild Golf Course.

History: In 1943 the airport was named the Maj. Gen. Alexander E. Anderson Airport, in honor of the veteran of both world wars. In 1948 it was renamed the New York International Airport—Anderson Field, but it was popularly known as Idlewild Airport. The first commercial flights began on July 1, 1948. The airport was dedicated on July 31, 1948. On Dec. 24, 1963, it was officially rededicated as the John F. Kennedy International Airport in honor of the assassinated president. The airport's Trifaith Chapel Plaza was scheduled for completion in 1965.

Cost: The City of New York spent about $60,000,000 on construction of the airport. In addition, the Port of New York Authority had invested more than $366,000,000 by 1965.

Control Tower "Traffic Cops"

On top of the terminal building is the *control tower*. Traffic controllers in the tower regulate air traffic at or near the airport (*see* Air Traffic Control). They radio the pilots when to land or take off and what runways to use. At some airports the control tower is in a separate building. It is located so the controllers can see all parts of the airfield. Its walls of tinted glass reduce glare.

The observation deck of the terminal building offers the visitor the best view of the *airfield*. This is the part of the airport from which airplanes land and take off. *Runways* are like long paved streets. On them airplanes gather speed to take off and reduce speed to land. They may be more than two miles long.

Taxiways are like smaller paved streets that enable airplanes to taxi to and from the runway. They connect to *aprons*. These are paved areas in front of the hangars and terminal building where airplanes are parked while they are being loaded, unloaded, or serviced.

AIRPORT FOR SEAPLANES AND FLYING BOATS
At La Guardia Airport in New York City there is a leading seaplane base. It is beside the airfield. Shown here are the round Marine Traffic Building and the hangar.

Marking the Airport for Safety

Airports have markings to make flying safe. The *segmented circle airport marker* helps the pilot to "spot" the airport. It is a large broken circle, 100 feet in diameter, constructed of wooden panels, stone, or concrete. In its center is a wind cone or a tee to indicate wind direction. Other indicators around the circle show the orientation of the landing area and the traffic pattern. Another identification is the *hangar roof marking*. The name of the airport, its latitude and longitude, and an arrow pointing to true north are painted on the roof.

Boundary markers outline the take-off and landing areas of small airports. They are metal or wooden panels or oil drums painted in bright yellow with white or black stripes.

A large number is painted at the start of each runway. It is a compass direction and identifies the runway for the pilot. A *threshold marker* of eight large stripes is also painted at the beginning of the all-weather runway. Other stripes mark the *landing zone*. A broken center line stripe indicates a runway, and a continuous stripe down the center, a taxiway. A runway may also have *side stripes* along its borders. A *holding line marker* on a taxiway warns a pilot not to go

AN AIRPORT ON A ROOF TOP
Heliports for helicopters may be built on the ground or on roofs of buildings. Here, left, is one on the roof of the Port Authority Building in Manhattan. At the right, a helicopter is landing on the touchdown pad.

JET AIRLINERS CLUSTER AT TERMINAL
Hinged, extensible corridors allow passengers to walk directly from the terminal to their planes at La Guardia Airport in New York City. Atop the terminal is a control tower.

beyond the marker until cleared by the controller. Obstructions, such as smokestacks and water tanks, over 150 feet high and within three miles of the airport, are painted in alternate bands of orange and white.

A heliport is marked by a large letter H enclosed in a segmented triangle. The symbol is painted in the center of the touchdown pad.

Lighting Makes Night Flying Possible

Lighting at the airport is essential for flying at night or when daytime visibility is poor. The *rotating beacon* on the roof of the hangar or terminal building locates the airport for the pilot. It flashes two beams —one white, the other green.

Boundary lights show the extent of the landing area. They are white lights mounted on orange-colored cones. *Contact lights* outline the runways. They are white, except for the final 2,000 feet of each instrument runway, where they are yellow. High-intensity *approach lights* help the flier line up on the runway. Green *threshold lights* mark the ends of runways.

Blue *taxiway lights* mark the outlines of the taxiways. Red *obstruction lights* warn of dangerous hazards. *Floodlights* illuminate the aprons. A lighted *wind direction indicator* may be a cone, a tee, or a tetrahedron.

A heliport may have a flashing or a rotating beacon to identify it. It also has boundary lights, floodlights, and a lighted wind direction indicator.

An Airliner Lands

As an airliner approaches the airport, the control tower gives the pilot permission to land and assigns him a runway. To reduce speed, the pilot first lowers the wing flaps. After the wheels touch the ground, he can also re-

BUSY CONCOURSE IN A CHICAGO AIR TERMINAL
Air travelers make reservations, buy tickets, check baggage, and wait for their flights in a lobby at Chicago-O'Hare International Airport.

NERVE CENTER OF THE AIRPORT
Both ground and air traffic are regulated from the control tower at John F. Kennedy International Airport in New York City.

A HUGE GARAGE FOR AIRLINERS
Aircraft are serviced by expert airframe and engine mechanics in vast hangars such as this one at Chicago, Ill.

verse the propeller pitch. In jet planes, engine thrust is "reversed" by closing the *thrust-brake* doors at the rear of the engine.

The plane taxis down a taxiway to the loading apron. A ramp agent then guides the pilot with arm signals. The pilot turns the plane until the passenger door is toward the terminal building and stops the engines. A second ramp attendant rolls a stairway to the airplane, and the passengers descend.

A small army of airport workers services the plane. Cargo handlers open doors in the ship's belly and unload the baggage, mail, and freight. They use a conveyer belt or fork-lift truck. They put the cargo in special trucks drawn by a tractor. After they are finished, they reload the airplane with other cargo.

A ground-service employee connects the ground power unit from a truck to the plane. It supplies electricity while the engines are stopped. Some workers pump fuel from a gasoline truck into the wing tanks. Other men hook an air-conditioning unit from a truck to the plane. This cools it in summer and warms it in winter. Kitchen help unload food containers from a service truck. Maintenance workers check the plane.

Passengers Take to the Air

The airport's loudspeaker announces that the flight is ready to load. A passenger agent checks the tickets of passengers at the loading gate. As the passengers enter the plane the stewardess also looks at their tickets or gate passes. The pilot, copilot, and flight engineer board the plane. They carry with them their dispatch order and flight plan.

The ramp agent closes the door and wheels away the stairway. He salutes the pilot to signal that everything is ready. The propellers begin to spin, one by one. The crew radios the control tower for permission to taxi to the takeoff position. The plane taxis across the apron and down a taxiway. It stops before turning onto the runway. The flight engineer "revs up" the engines to test them. The tower clears the plane for takeoff. The pilot swings it onto the runway. As its engines surge with power, the plane races down the runway and climbs to the altitude mapped out in the flight plan.

How Airports Are Planned

When engineers build airports they first draw up a master plan. Their surveys show what the air traffic will be in the present and the future. They study the types of airplanes that will use the airport. The plan develops the airport by stages and allows for expansion in the future.

The planners determine how the new airport will fit into the system of airports and airways in the

197

TRAFFIC CONTROLLER

METEOROLOGIST

PASSENGER AGENT

FLIGHT DISPATCHER

TELETYPIST

RAMP AGENT

MEN AND WOMEN AT WORK AT THE AIRPORT
It takes many different types of workers to operate an airport. Some help the passengers. Others service the airplanes.

area. They also fit into the National Airport Plan made by the Federal Aviation Agency. The FAA became the governing body regulating civil aviation in 1959.

An airport should be located close to the center of population which it serves. Also the airport should be so planned that residents of surrounding areas are protected as much as possible from airplane noise.

Airplanes must be able to take off and land safely. There must be no obstructions at the airport, in the approach zone, or in the airport vicinity. Clearance over highways and railroads in the approach zone should be adequate.

The airport must be so located that it does not interfere with the traffic of other nearby airports. It must also have good visibility. Swamps, deserts, or factories may cause fog, dust, or smoke.

The direction of prevailing winds is important. Take-offs and landings should be made into the wind. To study wind data engineers construct a *wind rose*. This is a diagram shaped like a wheel. Its spokes indicate the direction and relative strength of the wind. Strong cross winds might overturn lighter aircraft.

The amount and type of traffic serviced by an airport determine its size. The FAA classifies airports into five general categories: *secondary*, for small private airplanes, weighing up to 12,500 pounds, engaged in nonscheduled flying activities; *local*, for airports serving on local-service scheduled air-carrier routes; *trunk*, for airline airplanes serving cities on airline trunk routes; *continental*, for airplanes serv-

ing where long nonstop domestic air-carrier flights originate and terminate; *intercontinental*, for air commerce airplanes making long nonstop flights between countries and transoceanic flights.

Larger and heavier aircraft require longer and stronger runways. The FAA has established standards for the five classes as shown below:

Type of Service	Runway Length (Feet)	Runway Width (Feet)
Secondary	1,600–3,200	75
Local	3,201–4,200	150
Trunk	4,201–7,500	150
Continental	6,001–7,500	150
Intercontinental	7,501–10,500	150

The runway lengths given above are for airports at sea-level sites and on level grades. Runways for airports at higher elevations and where grades are not level must be made longer.

Runway patterns vary. A small airport may have a single runway or it may have two or more runways, either parallel or in the shape of an L, T, or X. Three runways may form a triangular pattern. Larger air terminals may have runways in tangential layouts arranged around the terminal building.

The pavement of runways must be strong enough to support the heaviest planes that will use them. The blast and weight of jet planes may present a special problem. The pavement is built of either rigid or

FIRE FIGHTERS

CARGO HANDLERS

AIRCRAFT MECHANICS

TICKET AGENTS

FLIGHT KITCHEN CHEFS

ENGINE MECHANICS

flexible materials, usually concrete or asphalt. The smaller airports may have turf runways.

Leading Airports of the World

Chicago-O'Hare International Airport is a giant mid-continent terminal for the world's largest jets. Occupying a tract of about 7,000 acres, its facilities have been greatly expanded. Midway Airport, also in Chicago, is used for scheduled airline flights of jet planes designed for airports with short runways.

The nation's chief air traffic hub is in the New York metropolitan area. Four airports operated by the Port of New York Authority serve the area. A 655-acre Terminal City services passengers at the 4,900-acre John F. Kennedy International Airport in New York City. About nine miles to the northwest is La Guardia Airport where, on the average, an airplane arrives or departs every three minutes. In New Jersey are Newark and Teterboro airports, which also serve New York City.

Washington National Airport in the nation's capital is one of the busiest in the country. It is owned and operated by the federal government and regulated by the FAA. Dulles International Airport, west of Washington, and Friendship International Airport, near Baltimore, Md., also serve the capital area.

Famous airports in Europe include London in England; Prestwick in Scotland; Shannon in Ireland; Le Bourget and Orly in Paris; Schipol in the Netherlands; Ciampino in Rome; Tempelhof in West Berlin; and Melsbroek in Brussels. Behind the iron curtain, Vnukovo, in Moscow, and Ruzyne, in Prague, are the busiest airports.

All the large cities of the world have important airports. Gander, in Newfoundland, and Honolulu, in Hawaii, are major transoceanic airports.

FEDERAL AVIATION AGENCY				
FLIGHT PLAN				Form Approved. Budget Bureau No. 04-R072.
1. Type of Flight Plan ☐ IFR ☑ VFR ☐ DVFR	2. Aircraft Identification N 123	3. Aircraft Type APACHE	4. Estimated True Air Speed 140 Knots	5. Departure Time Proposed 1310 z / Actual 1325 z
6. Initial Cruising Altitude 8500	7. Point of Departure WASHINGTON	8. Route of Flight VICTOR 22 FRONT ROYAL VICTOR 144 MORGANTOWN DIRECT COLUMBUS		
9. Destination (Airport & City) PORT COLUMBUS COLUMBUS, OHIO	10. Altitude Changes En Route 6500 MORGANTOWN	11. Estimated Time En Route Hours 2 / Minutes 00	12. Fuel on Board Hours 5 / Minutes 30	
13. Alternate Airport CLEVELAND	14. Remarks None			
15. Pilot's Name JOHN DOE	16. Pilot's Address or Aircraft Home Base WASHINGTON VIRGINIA AIRPORT			17. No. of Persons Aboard 3
18. Color of Aircraft RED AND WHITE	19. Flight Watch Stations (FAA use) MORGANTOWN.			
SEE REVERSE SIDE	CLOSE FLIGHT PLAN UPON ARRIVAL			Form FAA-398 (2-60)

A TYPICAL FLIGHT PLAN
A pilot files a flight plan with an Air Traffic Control Center before taking off. Flight plans help to make air travel safe.

ELEVATED RUNWAY LIGHT

ROTATING BEACON ON CONTROL TOWER   **APPROACH LIGHTS**

LIGHTING THE AIRPORT FOR NIGHT FLIGHTS

Lighting makes flying at night possible. The *runway lights* outline the runway. The *rotating beacon* "spots" the airport for the pilot. The lightninglike flashes of the powerful *approach lights* guide him to the center of the runway.

In the early days of aviation, a cow pasture was often used as a "flying field" and a barn as a hangar. After World War I the Army Air Service encouraged cities to build airports. Between 1932 and 1942 the federal government spent about 393 million dollars to aid airport development. In the Federal Airport Act of 1946 Congress directed the Civil Aeronautics Administration (now the Federal Aviation Administration) to prepare a National Airport Plan. The act authorized expenditures up to 500 million dollars over a period of seven years. In 1955 a new law provided federal aid for four years. The program was extended in 1959 and 1961. In 1964 it was extended for an additional three years.

By 1965 there were over 9,400 civil airports in the United States. In addition, about 55 airports were used jointly by civil and military planes, and about 300 military bases had airport facilities.

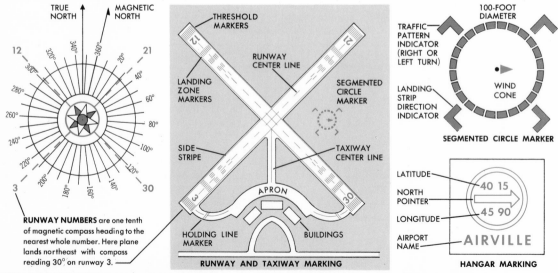

RUNWAY NUMBERS are one tenth of magnetic compass heading to the nearest whole number. Here plane lands northeast with compass reading 30° on runway 3.

RUNWAY AND TAXIWAY MARKING

SEGMENTED CIRCLE MARKER

HANGAR MARKING

AIRPORT MARKING FOR SAFE FLYING

Federal Aviation Administration rules govern airport markings. Runway and taxiway markings help pilots in taking off and landing safely. The segmented circle marker aids in locating and identifying an airport. It also indicates the landing strip direction and traffic pattern. The hangar marker gives the pilot the name and location of the airport.

In the control tower at New York's Kennedy International Airport are the *ground controller,* who directs ground movements; *flight data man,* gets clearances from an air traffic control center; *watch supervisor,* co-ordinates work; *local controller,* signals take-offs and landings.

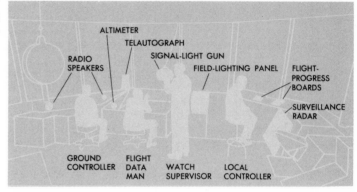

ALTIMETER
TELAUTOGRAPH
RADIO SPEAKERS
SIGNAL-LIGHT GUN
FIELD-LIGHTING PANEL
FLIGHT-PROGRESS BOARDS
SURVEILLANCE RADAR

GROUND CONTROLLER
FLIGHT DATA MAN
WATCH SUPERVISOR
LOCAL CONTROLLER

AIR TRAFFIC CONTROL
of the Skyways

AIR TRAFFIC CONTROL. Airplanes travel "highways," obey traffic signals, and follow traffic laws much as automobiles do. Air traffic control might not seem necessary since the sky extends from horizon to horizon and up to outer space.

In bad weather, however, airplanes that are allowed to fly at any altitude or along any course might collide. Even in good weather, the many planes landing at an airport might cause a traffic jam.

Air traffic control, then, is necessary to make flying safe and to avoid delays. The regulation of airplanes along airways, or air routes between airports, is called *air-route traffic control.* The supervision of aircraft at airports is known as *airport traffic control.* Controlled air space over an airway is a *control area;* at an airport, a *control zone.*

Federal Airways System

The Federal Aviation Administration operates the *Federal Airways System.* It includes more than 220,000 miles of airways in the United States. An airway, ten miles wide, is divided vertically into traffic levels 1,000 feet apart. It extends upward to 25,000 feet. Above this altitude it becomes a *jet route.*

Aircraft follow two types of radio ranges on the airways. The older type is the *low-* or *medium-frequency four-course radio range.* A station sends out four signals shaped like a four-leaf clover. Where they interlock, a radio beam is formed. If the pilot is "on the beam," he hears a hum in his earphones. If he is off course, he will hear a Morse code letter A or N. He follows the beam from station to station.

A pilot learns his position on the beam by flying over radio marker beacons. At the station is a "Z" *marker,* and 20 to 40 miles away is a *fan marker.* Their transmitters cause a light to flash in the cockpit.

A newer type of radio range is the *very-high-frequency omnidirectional radio range,* or VOR. Unlike low or medium frequency, its signal is free of static, even in storms. The VOR station also sends out courses in all directions, instead of only four.

The airman can pinpoint his position by obtaining a bearing on a second VOR station. With *distance measuring equipment,* or DME, he can learn his exact distance from a VOR station. If he also has a *course line computer,* he does not have to follow a route directly over a VOR station. Military aircraft use another distance-measuring device called *tactical*

201

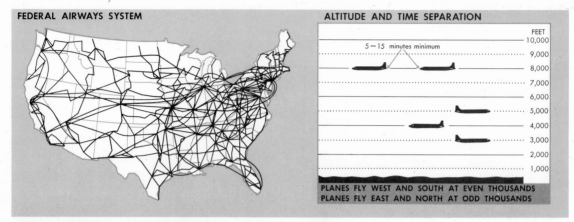

FEDERAL AIRWAYS SYSTEM

ALTITUDE AND TIME SEPARATION

5 – 15 minutes minimum

FEET
10,000
9,000
8,000
7,000
6,000
5,000
4,000
3,000
2,000
1,000

PLANES FLY WEST AND SOUTH AT EVEN THOUSANDS
PLANES FLY EAST AND NORTH AT ODD THOUSANDS

AERIAL HIGHWAYS OF THE FEDERAL AIRWAYS SYSTEM

The map shows airways in the United States, not including Alaska and Hawaii. An airway is a designated route used by commercial, military, and private aircraft. It extends upward to 25,000 feet. Beyond that it is a jet route. Each airplane is surrounded by a block of air space 2,000 feet high, 10 miles wide, and 25 to 50 miles long.

air navigation, or TACAN. When combined with VOR, it is called VORTAC.

Other airway navigation aids are *light beacons, intermediate landing fields* for emergency use, and *en route surveillance radar.* This long-range radar scans the skies for 200 miles in all directions.

Air Traffic Control Centers

The heart of the Federal Airways System is the *air-route traffic control center.* There is an ATC center in each of the 35 control areas in the system. It receives flight plans and reports from pilots. It follows the flight of each plane on a flight-progress board.

The centers communicate with pilots either through direct controller-pilot communications or indirectly through air traffic communications stations, airport traffic control towers, military radio stations, and airline traffic offices.

A pilot follows either of two sets of flight rules. In fair weather he can use *visual flight rules,* or VFR. He watches for landmarks and other planes. In bad weather or in congested air space, he follows *instrument flight rules,* or IFR. He must file a flight plan and radio his position at specified points, or "fixes."

Airport Traffic Control

The FAA also controls traffic at major airports. Airport control towers direct traffic in the *airport traffic zone*—within five miles of the center of the airport. They also regulate traffic in the *airport approach zone*—extending ten miles from the airport.

If too many planes try to land, the controller in the control tower *stacks* them. He orders them to circle a holding point at assigned levels. After he clears the airplane at the lowest level for landing, he steps down the other planes to lower levels.

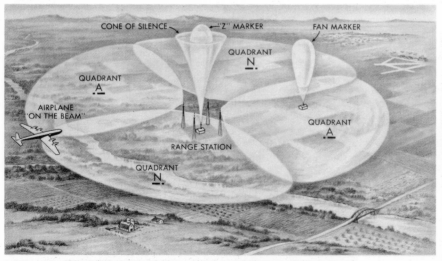

CONE OF SILENCE — "Z" MARKER — FAN MARKER

QUADRANT N.

QUADRANT A.

AIRPLANE "ON THE BEAM"

QUADRANT A.

RANGE STATION

QUADRANT N.

Pilot hears hum when flying "on the beam"

Light flashes when he flys over "Z" or fan markers

LOW- OR MEDIUM-FREQUENCY FOUR-COURSE RADIO RANGE

Each range station sends out four radio signals. Where they interlock a radio beam is formed. A pilot follows the beam from station to station. If he is "on the beam," he hears a hum in his earphones. If he is off course, he hears a code letter A or N. He receives no signal over the station. The "Z" and fan markers are transmitters that tell him where he is along his course.

AIR-ROUTE TRAFFIC CONTROL CENTER

This control center in Washington, D.C., keeps track of aircraft on the airways. Pilots radio their positions which are posted on the flight-progress boards. The controllers also check positions of planes on the horizontal radarscope in the center.

Instrument Landing System and Ground Controlled Approach

A pilot can land even in bad weather with the *instrument landing system*. He follows a "radio runway" down. A runway localizer transmitter sends out a vertical beam to guide him to the center of the runway. A glide slope transmitter sends out a beam sloping upward at the proper glide angle. The pilot watches vertical and horizontal needles on his crosspointer indicator to stay on the beams. An outer marker beacon causes a cockpit light to flash when he is five miles from the runway. A middle marker beacon flashes at 3,500 feet from the end of the runway.

Another system of instrument landing is *ground controlled approach*, or GCA. In the plane is a two-way radio and at the airport are two radar sets (*see* Radar). The *airport surveillance radar*, or ASR, detects all planes within 30 miles of the airport.

As a plane nears a runway the operator sees it on the *precision approach radar*, or PAR. It shows the distance, direction, and elevation of the plane. The operator "talks down" the pilot to a landing. At large airports, aircraft and vehicles on the ground are observed with *airport surface detection radar*.

From Bonfire to Radar

In the early days of flying, airmen flew by watching rivers, railroads, and other landmarks. On the first night flight of airmail in 1921, bonfires marked the route. The first airway lighted by beacons opened in 1924, between Cheyenne, Wyo., and Chicago, Ill.

The Air Commerce Act of 1926 established the Federal Airways System. The next year radio ranges

INSTRUMENTS IN AIRPLANE

Frequency Selector for tuning omnirange station desired

Omnibearing Selector and "To-From" Indicator for selecting magnetic bearing and for indicating whether bearing is to or from station

Course Line Deviation Indicator for indicating whether plane is on course

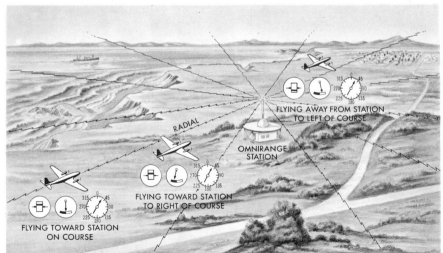

VERY-HIGH-FREQUENCY OMNIDIRECTIONAL RANGE (VOR)

This is a newer type of radio "highway." Its big advantage is that it is free of static. The omnirange station sends out an infinite number of radio signals, or *radials*, like the spokes of a wheel. The pilot uses instruments in his cockpit, shown at the right. He can select any one of the many radio courses. With his receiver he can find his position along his route.

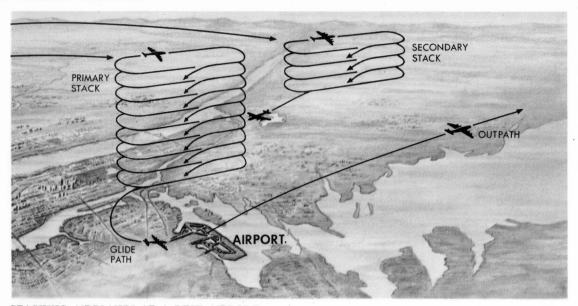

PRIMARY STACK

SECONDARY STACK

OUTPATH

GLIDE PATH

AIRPORT.

STACKING AIRPLANES AT A BUSY AIRPORT

During instrument flying weather too many airplanes may arrive at an airport to land safely. The pilots are instructed to go into a holding pattern. Each plane is assigned a level in a stack. It circles radio marker beacons. If a *primary stack* is filled, the plane is held at a *secondary stack*. When the lowest plane lands, the other planes descend one level.

were installed. By 1930 two-way radio voice communication was possible between aircraft and the ground.

In 1936 a federal bureau, which later became the Civil Aeronautics Administration, took over control of airways. During World War II the CAA also assumed control of airport traffic. In 1946 the Radio Technical Commission for Aeronautics developed a Common System of traffic control for commercial, military, and private flying. Congress approved the

Federal Airway Plan in 1956. It included short- and long-range radar, direct controller-to-pilot communication, and navigation aids such as VORTAC.

Congress established the Airways Modernization Board (AMB) in 1957 to improve air traffic control. In 1959 the CAA and the AMB were incorporated into the Federal Aviation Agency (FAA). In 1966 the FAA, renamed the Federal Aviation Administration, became part of the Department of Transportation.

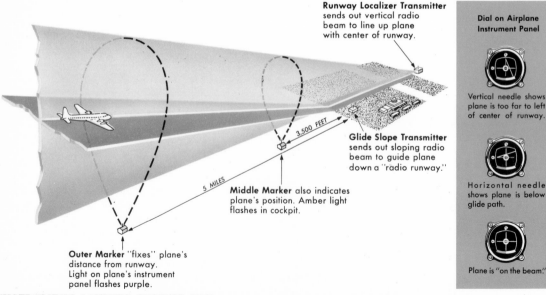

Runway Localizer Transmitter sends out vertical radio beam to line up plane with center of runway.

Dial on Airplane Instrument Panel

Vertical needle shows plane is too far to left of center of runway.

3,500 FEET

Glide Slope Transmitter sends out sloping radio beam to guide plane down a "radio runway."

5 MILES

Middle Marker also indicates plane's position. Amber light flashes in cockpit.

Horizontal needle shows plane is below glide path.

Outer Marker "fixes" plane's distance from runway. Light on plane's instrument panel flashes purple.

Plane is "on the beam."

INSTRUMENT LANDING SYSTEM (ILS)

A pilot can land safely in bad weather on a "radio runway." Two airport transmitters send out a vertical radio beam to line up his plane on the runway and a sloping beam to guide him down. Vertical and horizontal needles on a dial tell him if he is on course. Two other transmitters give him his distance from the runway. Cockpit lights flash when he passes over them.

AISNE (*ān*) **RIVER.** Ever since the time of Julius Caesar, the Aisne River in northeastern France has played an important part in history. The Axona, as the Romans called it, was the scene of Caesar's first battle against the Belgian tribes.

In later centuries too the valley has been a highway for marching armies. It was used in the Napoleonic campaigns, Franco-Prussian War, World War I, and World War II. The Aisne and the Oise offer an easy route between Paris and the Belgian frontier. On this border France has no natural boundaries.

In 1914 the Germans retreated after the first battle of the Marne and made their stand across the Aisne. On the wooded hills north of the river they dug in. The French did the same on the south bank. To keep from being outflanked each side had to extend its trenches. Finally their lines stretched north to the sea and south to the Swiss border.

For three years the Germans held the Chemin des Dames ridge north of the Aisne. A French attack in 1917 resulted in disaster for the army of Nivelle. Later in the year another French army won the ridge.

A great German offensive in 1918 recaptured the heights. They pushed the French back across the Aisne to Chateau-Thierry on the Marne. The second battle of the Marne, however, also went against the Germans. Once more they retreated across the Aisne. Their defeat at Chemin des Dames by Americans and French hastened the end of World War I. (*See also* Marne River.) During World War II the Aisne was one of the fronts along which France made its last stand before surrendering to Germany in 1940.

The Aisne River is narrow, shallow, and only 175 miles long. It rises in the Argonne Forest and turns westward north of Reims. Then it flows through Soissons and enters the Oise near Compiègne. Canals connect the Aisne with the Meuse and the Marne.

AJAX. Among the Greek warriors who besieged Troy, Ajax the Great ranked second only to Achilles in strength and courage. He was the son of Telamon and was half-brother of Teucer. Homer in the 'Iliad' describes him as being gigantic in stature.

At the death of Achilles, Ajax as the bravest of the Greeks claimed Achilles' armor. The prize, however, went to Odysseus (Ulysses) as the wisest. So enraged was Ajax that he went insane and killed himself. His story is told by Sophocles in the tragedy 'Ajax'.

Another Greek hero of the same name was the "Lesser" Ajax, son of Oileus, king of Locris. He was small of stature but brave and skilled in throwing the spear. Only Achilles could run more swiftly. Like the Telamonian Ajax, he was the enemy of Odysseus. Boastful and arrogant, he defied even the gods. As punishment for his rash behavior he was wrecked and drowned on the return voyage from Troy.

AKRON (*ăk′rŭn*), **Ohio.** The rubber capital of the world is Akron. The principal product of its many rubber factories is tires. Several plants, however, make a great variety of other rubber articles. They vary from rubber bands to 142-foot-long logging balloons.

Other manufactures include children's books, plastics, machinery, tools, automobile parts, chemicals, clay and wood products, fishing tackle, and matches.

Akron is located on the Cuyahoga River, 35 miles southeast of Cleveland. Captain Joseph Hart formed the settlement of Middlebury in 1807. That is now East Akron. In 1825 Gen. Simon Perkins laid out a new town on the site of the present city. Because it was among the highest points in Ohio, it was named Akron, from the Greek *akros*, meaning "high."

The town was served by the Ohio and Erie Canal after the section between Akron and Lake Erie opened in 1827. It was also on a north-south railroad that was completed in 1852. Both routes helped Akron become a center of trade. In recent years the Akron area has become an important trucking center.

In 1870 Benjamin F. Goodrich moved his little rubber factory from Melrose, N. Y., to Akron. Here he started the industry which made the city famous. In the 1890's the first "horseless carriages" brought a demand for rubber tires. Akron prospered and grew as the demand for automobile tires increased.

The city is the manufacturing center for lighter-than-air craft in the United States. At its municipal airport is the huge Goodyear Zeppelin airdock. Here the dirigibles *Akron* and *Macon* were built.

Akron is the site of the University of Akron, which is a leader in rubber research. Each year the All-American Soap Box Derby is held here (*see* Soap Box Derby). The city has a mayor-council form of government. Population (1960 census), 290,351.

ONE OF THE WORLD'S LARGEST RUBBER FACTORIES
The B. F. Goodrich Company is one of Akron's many rubber plants. It makes a variety of rubber and plastic goods, including auto tires and industrial hose.

Beautiful gardens abound in and around Mobile, a major seaport and Alabama's second largest city. Here, flanked by azaleas, the Île-aux-Oies River winds through Bellingrath Gardens.

ALABAMA—
Symbol of the New South

ALABAMA. Few states have made as much progress during the 1900's as has Alabama. Before this century the economy of the entire state was based on cotton. Birmingham was little more than a railroad crossing. Today Alabama farms produce a variety of crops and livestock products. Manufacturing is worth more than 2½ billion dollars a year, and Birmingham has become the iron and steel capital of the South.

Most of Alabama's progress can be traced to three factors. The first was the discovery and use of the coal, iron ore, and limestone in the Birmingham area. These resources made possible the development of the city's steel industry. The second was the coming of the boll weevil, which, by destroying cotton crops, forced farmers to turn to other crops and to the raising of hogs and cattle. The third was the development of hydroelectric power.

The name Alabama is from Choctaw Indian words meaning "to clear (or reap) vegetation." The nickname Yellowhammer State originated during the Civil War, when Alabama troops stuck yellowhammer feathers in their caps.

Population (1960): 3,266,740—rank, 19th state. Urban, 54.8%; rural, 45.2%. Persons per square mile, 64.0—rank, 26th state.

Extent: Area, 51,609 square miles, including 549 square miles of water surface (29th state in size).

Elevation: Highest, Cheaha Mountain, 2,407 feet, near Talladega; lowest, sea level; average, 500 feet.

Geographic Center: 12 miles southwest of Clanton.

Temperature (° F.): Extremes—lowest, −24° (Russellville, Jan. 31, 1966); highest, 112° (Centreville, Sept. 5, 1925). Averages at Birmingham—January, 46.5°; July, 81.6°; annual, 64.1°. Averages at Mobile—January, 53.0°; July, 82.6°; annual, 68.2°.

Precipitation (inches): At Birmingham—annual average, 53.05 (including 1.5 snowfall). At Mobile—annual average, 68.13 (including 0.4 snowfall).

Land Use: Crops, 16%; pasture, 9%; forest, 67%; other, 8%.

For statistical information about Agriculture, Communication, Crime, Education, Employment, Finance, Fishing, Forests, Government, Manufacturing, Mining, Population Trends, Selective Service, Trade, Transportation, and Welfare, see ALABAMA FACT SUMMARY.

A Survey of Alabama

The Yellowhammer State lies in the central part of the Deep South. It is bordered on the north by Tennessee and on the west by Mississippi. On the south a panhandle extends along the Gulf of Mexico for 53 miles. The remainder of the southern boundary is shared with Florida. To the east is Georgia, separated in part from Alabama by the Chattahoochee River.

Alabama's greatest length, north to south, is 336 miles. Its greatest width, east to west, is 208 miles.

A State of Five Natural Regions

Almost all the northern part of Alabama lies in four distinct highland regions. Three of these regions form the southern end of the Appalachian Mountains system (*see* Appalachian Highlands). The remainder of the state lies in the coastal plain of the Gulf of Mexico. The boundary between the highlands and the plain is marked by the curving *fall line* of the rivers. The fall line enters the state on the east at Phenix City, passes west to Wetumpka, turns northwest to Tuscaloosa, and then runs north and west to the Tennessee River valley in Colbert County.

The Interior Low Plateaus form a rolling upland in the northwestern corner of the state on both sides of the Tennessee River. This region extends northward into Tennessee, where it is called the Highland Rim. The surface rises 200 to 300 feet above the Gulf Coastal Plain to the southwest.

The Appalachian Plateau, also called the Cumberland Plateau, juts into Alabama from the northeast as far south as Tuscaloosa County. Its highest point is the northern end of Lookout Mountain in De Kalb County, about 2,000 feet above sea level. From here the plateau slopes down to about 1,600 feet in the west and 500 feet in the south.

The Valley and Ridge region lies east of the Appalachian Plateau. It reaches south into Tuscaloosa, Bibb, and Chilton counties. This region is a series of long narrow valleys lying between sharp mountain ridges. The city of Birmingham lies in Jones Valley northwest of Red Mountain. Another important lowland is the valley of the Coosa River.

The Piedmont Plateau is a triangular wedge, 500 to 1,000 feet in elevation, in the east-central part of the state. It is subdivided into the Opelika Plateau to the east and the Ashland Plateau in the west. In the Ashland Plateau is Cheaha Mountain (2,407 feet), the highest point in the state.

The Gulf Coastal Plain is the largest natural region in the state. Its highest part (about 600 feet) is the Central Pine Belt, which borders the Appalachian uplands. From here the surface slopes down to sea level along the coast. Near the center of Alabama a gently rolling prairie, the Black Belt, runs from Sumter County on the west to Russell County on the east. This section, named for its fertile black soil, is 25 to 50 miles wide. South of the Black Belt are the Southern Red Hills, named for their red, sandy clay soil. Pine flats and marshes fringe the coast.

The chief river of northern Alabama is the Tennessee, which bends northward to flow back into Tennessee. The other rivers of the state flow generally south. The Tombigbee and its principal branch, the Black Warrior, drain into the Mobile River, then into Mobile Bay. Also entering the bay is the Alabama, formed by the union of the Coosa and the Tallapoosa near Montgomery. The chief river in the east is the Chattahoochee, along the Georgia border.

Weather and Climate

Most of Alabama has a mild climate, with short, moderate winters and long, warm summers. At Birmingham, in the north-central part of the state, the average annual temperature is about 64° F.; at Mobile, in the southwest, it is about 68° F. De Kalb County, in the north, is the coldest part of the state, with

INDUSTRIAL GIANT OF THE SOUTH

The largest city in Alabama is Birmingham, one of the nation's great producers of iron and steel. This is the city's skyline as seen from Red Mountain. Founded in 1871, Birmingham owes its growth to rich mineral deposits nearby.

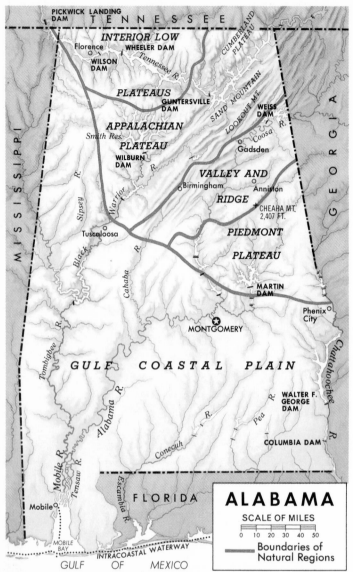

This map shows the five natural regions and the surface features of Alabama. The use that can be made of the land is related to the physical features of each region.

is one of the leading lumber-producing states. The chief commercial trees are pines, followed by oak, gum, and yellow poplar.

The Yellowhammer State has other valuable resources for industry. These include rich deposits of coal, iron ore, and limestone and streams for hydroelectric power. Navigable waterways reach far inland. Mobile Bay provides a huge sheltered harbor. The tourist industry is also important, particularly around the historic cities of the Old South—Mobile and Montgomery.

Alabama's long dependence upon cotton led to the wearing out and eroding of much land. Today farms are being rebuilt by the use of fertilizer, crop rotation, and other conservation methods. Another important conservation program has been the harnessing of water resources. A valuable source of waterpower is at Muscle Shoals, near Florence, where the Tennessee River drops 134 feet in 37 miles. Wilson Dam, completed in 1924, was built at this location to supply power for two nitrate plants. The Tennessee Valley Authority later built Wheeler and Guntersville dams on the river in Alabama. Other large projects in the state include Martin Dam, on the Tallapoosa River, and Wilburn Dam, on the Sipsey Fork.

Most of the natural resources in the state are administered by the Department of Conservation, established in 1939. It has divisions of state parks, forestry, lands, and game and fish.

The People of Alabama

Early inhabitants of the Alabama region were the Mound Builders (see Mound Builders). The first white settlers found the area occupied by four of the Five Civilized Tribes of Indians—Chickasaw, Choctaw, Cherokee, and Creek (the Seminole lived in Florida). The Alabama, or Alibamu, were part of the Creek Confederacy.

The Chickasaw were the most peaceful tribe, the Creek the most warlike. Beginning in 1805 all the tribes but the Creek began ceding their land to the United States. The Creek resisted white settlement until their power was crushed in 1814 by Gen. Andrew Jackson in the battle of Horseshoe Bend on the Tallapoosa River. By 1839 all the major bands of Indians had moved west of the Mississippi River.

Alabama was settled chiefly by people from Georgia, the Carolinas, and other Eastern states. It has attracted few immigrants from abroad. Today less than one percent of its people are foreign born. About one third of the people are Negroes. They are

an average annual temperature about 8 degrees less than that of the Mobile region. The southwest is the wettest part of Alabama. It receives an average of more than 68 inches of precipitation a year. Some areas in the center of the state receive the least precipitation—about 50 inches a year.

The growing season is long throughout the state. It ranges from about 200 days a year in the northwest and northeast to about 300 days along Mobile Bay.

Natural Resources and Conservation

Alabama's rich natural resources for agriculture include a long growing season, plenty of rainfall, and a variety of soils. The land produces much timber, with more than half of the state forested. Alabama

largely concentrated in central Alabama, where some counties have a predominantly Negro population. Alabama is seventh in Negro population, following New York, Texas, Georgia, North Carolina, Louisiana, and Illinois.

Manufacturing and Cities

Before World War II the value of manufacturing in Alabama was less than a quarter of a billion dollars a year. By 1947 it had more than tripled. By the mid-1960's the value of manufacturing had reached nearly 3 billion dollars a year, having increased by almost one billion dollars in the six-year period from 1958 to 1964. Income from manufacturing is more than twice the income from farming, mining, lumbering, and fishing combined.

Today there are in Alabama some 4,500 manufacturing establishments employing approximately 300,000 workers. The growth and diversification of industry in Alabama between 1947 and 1966 has been reflected in a dispersion of workers among more industry groups. In 1947, three traditional industries (textiles, primary metals, and lumbering) accounted for 62 percent of manufacturing employment. In 1963, five industries—primary metals, textiles, apparel, food, and lumbering—accounted for 61 percent of manufacturing employment.

The most important industry is the primary metals industry, centered in the Birmingham district. Here are found all the resources necessary for the manufacture of iron, steel, and related products (see Iron and Steel articles).

Other industries are also important in the Alabama economy. Hydroelectric power plants on the Tennessee River and on streams in the Piedmont Plateau have attracted a concentration of textile mills. The ready availability of fabrics fostered the development of an extensive wearing-apparel industry. Food processing, including meat-packing and the manufacture of soft drinks, is another major industry. The state's forests provide raw materials for the manufacture of paper and paper products.

The state's chief industrial center and largest city is Birmingham, in north-central Alabama. It is a highway and railroad hub and also has a water outlet to the Gulf of Mexico (see Birmingham). Mobile, the second largest city, is a port on Mobile Bay and a ship-repair center (see Mobile). The state capital is Montgomery, the third largest city and the chief trade center of the Black Belt (see Montgomery).

Gadsden, Anniston, and Bessemer are large steel-making cities in the northern half of the state. Tuscaloosa is a lumbering and agricultural center on the Black Warrior River. Huntsville, the largest city in the Tennessee Valley of Alabama, is the home of the United States Army's Redstone Arsenal and of the George C. Marshall Space Flight Center.

LOADING COTTON AT MOBILE
Much of Alabama's cotton is shipped from the government-owned State Docks and Terminals built along the Mobile River.

Agriculture, Mining, and Fishing

Farms occupy about 15 million acres in Alabama. In recent years they have grown fewer in number and larger in size. In the mid-1950's Alabama farms numbered nearly 116,000. By the mid-1960's they numbered some 92,500, with an average acreage of about 165. Only about one fifth were operated by tenants; yet as recently as 1950 more than 41 percent of Alabama farms were tenant operated.

More and more in recent years, Alabama's farmers have turned from growing crops to raising livestock and poultry. In a typical year of the mid-1960's, sales of livestock and livestock products accounted for more than 70 percent of receipts from farm marketings. Most important are poultry, including eggs, and cattle. Swine and dairy products follow. The poultry industry is concentrated in the northern counties. Beef cattle are raised largely in the Black Belt of central Alabama. The leading hog-producing counties are in the southeast.

Automation, which has been the key to increased livestock and poultry production, has also influenced crop production. In general, crops requiring large numbers of workers have given way to crops that can be planted, cultivated, and harvested largely by machine. Cotton, though still an important cash crop, is no longer king in Alabama. In the late 1960's, the acreage devoted to cotton declined to less than that devoted to soybeans.

Corn is another leading crop. The principal corn-producing counties are in the southern part of the state and in the Tennessee Valley of the north. Peanuts are the principal cash crop of many farms in southeastern Alabama. Alabama is usually among the leading states in pecan production.

The state's most valuable mineral is coal. Most of the coal lies in fields in the north-central part of Alabama. The largest is the Warrior field near Birmingham, which covers about 3,000 square miles. To the southeast is the Cahaba; to the east are the Coosa fields. Cement is second in importance after coal. Stone, which is third, is a valuable product of the Piedmont Plateau, especially the marble found in Talladega County around Sylacauga. Red Mountain, adjoining Birmingham, bears a huge seam of hematite (iron ore). It is second in importance in the United States only to the Lake Superior district.

Most of Alabama's fish catch comes from the Gulf of Mexico and from coastal rivers. Among the most valuable catches are shrimp, red snapper, oysters, and mullet. The Tennessee River and its branches yield mussel shells, catfish, and buffalofish.

STATUES SALUTE THE STATE'S ECONOMY

At Enterprise is a statue to the boll weevil, which forced Alabama to grow other crops besides cotton.

Near Birmingham is a statue of Vulcan, representing the iron and steel industry.

Transportation by Land and Water

The first wagon road into Alabama was the Natchez Trace, across the Tennessee River near Muscle Shoals (*see* Roads and Streets). The Federal Road, called the Three Chopped Way from its tree markings, ran from the site of Phenix City to the Alabama River. Branches extended to Natchez, Miss., and to Fort Stoddert.

Alabama's modern road system began in 1911 with the formation of the State Highway Department. There are about 80,000 miles of state and county roads. The major east-west highways are Interstate 10, 20, and 85 and US 72, 78, 80, 82, 84, 90, 98, and 278; north-south, Interstate 59 and 65 and US 11, 31, 43, 45, 231, 331, 411, and 431.

River-barge traffic is heavy on the Tennessee and on the Black Warrior-Tombigbee-Mobile system. Mo-

ON THE TENNESSEE RIVER

Wheeler Dam supplies hydroelectric power for northern Alabama's cotton mills, aluminum plants, and other industries.

bile has a fine harbor. Here are the Alabama State Docks, a multimillion-dollar ocean terminal. A 36-mile channel leads to the Intracoastal Waterway.

One of the first railroads in the South connected Tuscumbia with the Tennessee River at Muscle Shoals in 1832. This two-mile line was extended to Decatur three years later. Today the state is served by some 20 major and secondary railroad lines. Air transportation is also well developed.

Recreation in Alabama

Tourists provide the basis of a multimillion-dollar industry in the Yellowhammer State. Mobile has two of the leading attractions in the nation—the Mardi Gras festival and the Azalea Trail. The Dogwood Trail and the annual state fair attract many visitors to Birmingham. The Deep Sea Fishing Rodeo on Dauphin Island in Mobile Bay is popular.

The Natchez Trace Parkway, Horseshoe Bend National Military Park in Tallapoosa County, and Russell Cave National Monument in Jackson County are administered as national park areas (*see* National Parks, United States). State parks covering many acres preserve scenic, historic, and recreational areas.

Education in Alabama

For many years education in Alabama was limited to tutors and private academies. It was not until 1854 that the legislature was able to provide an effective public school system. The Civil War halted educational activities and forced an extensive program of rebuilding schools and colleges.

In 1907, high schools were established in every county except those which already had normal or agricultural schools. Today each county has at least two

CAPITOL BURNS IN DECEMBER 1849
Two years after Montgomery became Alabama's seat of government, fire consumed the Capitol and many valuable records.

high schools. Consolidation has improved education in many rural schools.

State-supported schools of higher learning include the University of Alabama, at University, near Tuscaloosa, with branch campuses in Birmingham and Huntsville and three resident centers; Auburn University, at Auburn; Jacksonville State University, at Jacksonville; the University of South Alabama, at Mobile; Alabama College, at Montevallo; and Alabama Agricultural and Mechanical College, at Normal. There are also four state colleges, located at Troy, Florence, Montgomery, and Livingston.

Other large schools are Samford University, at Birmingham; Athens College, at Athens; Spring Hill College, at Mobile; and Huntingdon College, at Montgomery. Tuskegee Institute was opened by Booker T. Washington in 1881 (*see* Washington, Booker T.). Alabama-born Helen Keller did much in education for the blind (*see* Keller).

Government and Politics

While Alabama was a territory its capital was at St. Stephens. Huntsville was the first state capital, followed by Cahaba and Tuscaloosa. Montgomery has served as the seat of government since 1847. The state is governed under its sixth constitution, adopted in 1901.

The chief executive officer is the governor, elected every four years. The state legislature consists of a Senate and a House of Representatives. Heading the judiciary is the Supreme Court.

Alabama is a strong Democratic state in both local and national politics. Since 1876 it has voted for the Democratic candidate for president in every election except 1948 and 1964. In 1960 less than half its electoral votes went to the Democratic candidate.

HISTORY OF ALABAMA

Alabama's southern boundary along the 31st parallel of north latitude was fixed while Florida was still a possession of Spain. It was determined by a treaty signed in 1795. The Perdido River boundary with Spanish Florida was established in 1813. By the time Alabama was ready to become a state, its other boundaries had been set by the admission into the Union of neighboring states to the east, north, and west—Georgia (one of the original states), Tennessee (1796), and Mississippi (1817). The following sections tell the development of Alabama into a modern state.

Exploration and Settlement

In 1540 the Spanish adventurer Hernando de Soto became the first white man to explore what is now Alabama (*see* De Soto). A permanent settlement was not made until 1702, when the French built Fort Louis de la Mobile on the Mobile River. The governor was Jean Baptiste le Moyne, sieur de Bienville (*see* Bienville). In 1719 slave ships brought the first Negroes to clear the land for rice and indigo.

France ceded the region to Great Britain in 1763 (*see* French and Indian War). Many British traders and colonists moved in at this time. In 1783 Great Britain surrendered all Alabama except the Mobile area to the United States. In 1813 the Creek destroyed Fort Mims, near the junction of the Alabama and Tombigbee rivers. The following year they were defeated by General Jackson at Horseshoe Bend. In 1817 Alabama was made a territory, and two years later it was admitted to the Union as the 22d state.

The Civil War Period

The first half of the 1800's was a period of extensive cotton planting. Production was encouraged by Abraham Mordecai, who built Alabama's first cotton gin in 1802 at Coosada Bluff near Montgomery. Large plantations with beautiful homes developed in the Black Belt and other rich cotton-growing sections.

211

Wealthy planters who held many slaves dominated the state. One of their chief spokesmen was William L. Yancey, the fiery editor of the *Wetumpka Argus*. Alabama seceded from the Union on Jan. 11, 1861. Montgomery became the first capital of the Confederacy. Here Jefferson Davis was inaugurated as its president. (*See also* Confederate States of America.)

Early in the Civil War Union forces occupied the Tennessee Valley. In August 1864 Adm. David G. Farragut destroyed the Confederate fleet in Mobile Bay. By April 1865 the whole state was occupied by Federal forces. One of the most famous of Alabama's leaders in the war was Adm. Raphael Semmes, commander of the sea raider *Alabama* (*see* 'Alabama' Claims). Other outstanding Confederate leaders from the state were John Morgan, John Pelham, and Joseph Wheeler. (*See also* Civil War, American.)

The carpetbag government which followed the war almost bankrupted the state. The restoration of home rule in 1875 brought a slow but steady economic recovery (*see* Reconstruction Period).

The Modern State

There have been marked industrial changes in Alabama in the 20th century. Many cotton mills have moved there, particularly into the north and east. Steel-manufacturing towns in Alabama send their products all over the world. Hydroelectric power has increased the development of manufacturing and the efficiency of the state's farmlands.

During this time many Alabamians made outstanding contributions to the nation. George Washington Carver pioneered in scientific agriculture (*see* Carver). The Panama Canal could not have been built without the work of William C. Gorgas (*see* Gorgas). Robert J. Van de Graaff invented the high-voltage generator (*see* X Rays).

From 1950 to 1960 the population of Alabama increased by nearly 205,000 persons, a gain of about 7 percent. (*See also* United States, section "The South"; individual entries in Fact-Index on Alabama persons, places, products, and events.)

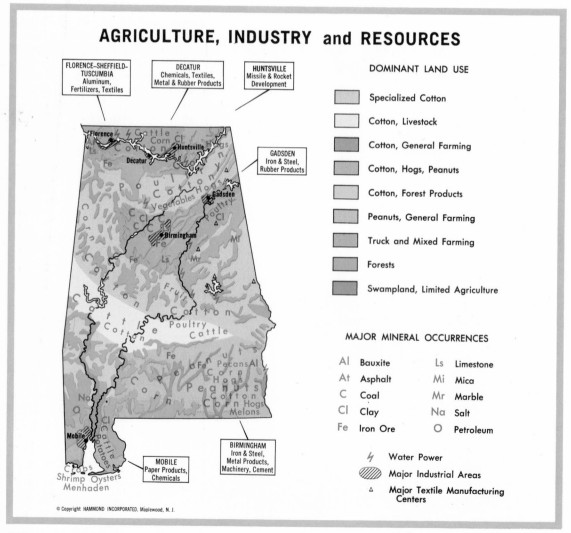

© Copyright HAMMOND INCORPORATED. Maplewood, N. J.

Notable Events in Alabama History

1540—De Soto crosses Alabama; battles Indians at Mauvila, near Choctaw Bluff.

1629—Charles I makes Carolina grant; includes Alabama area.

1682—La Salle explores and claims Mississippi Valley for France.

1699—Pierre le Moyne, sieur d'Iberville, founds colony near Biloxi, Miss. Alabama, as part of Louisiana, is governed from there.

1702—Jean Baptiste le Moyne, sieur de Bienville, builds Fort Louis de la Mobile on Mobile River above Mobile; moves capital from Biloxi to fort.

1711—Fort Louis moved to present site of Mobile; name changed to Fort Condé la Mobile in 1720.

1719—First shipload of slaves arrives at Dauphin Island.

1763—Alabama included in area ceded by France to Great Britain in Treaty of Paris.

1780—Bernardo de Galvez, governor of Spanish Louisiana, captures Mobile from English.

1783—Great Britain cedes Alabama north of 31st parallel to U. S.; Florida, including Mobile, to Spain.

1798—Mississippi Territory created; includes Alabama.

1802—First cotton gin built, in Montgomery County.

1803—U. S. claims Mobile as part of Louisiana Purchase.

1805—Chickasaw, Cherokee, and Choctaw cede part of land claims in Alabama region to U. S.

1813—U. S. Gen. James Wilkinson seizes Mobile from Spaniards. Creek Indians massacre colonists at Fort Mims. Creek defeated by Gen. Andrew Jackson at battle of Horseshoe Bend in 1814; site dedicated as national military park in 1964.

1817—Congress creates Alabama Territory; capital, St. Stephens; governor, William W. Bibb.

1819—Alabama becomes 22d state, December 14; capital, Huntsville; governor, Bibb.

1820—Capital moved to Cahaba. University of Alabama chartered; opened near Tuscaloosa in 1831.

1826—State capital moved to Tuscaloosa.

1832—State's first cotton mill built in Madison County.

1839—Remaining Indians leave state.

1846—Legislature votes to move state capital to Montgomery; holds first session there in 1847.

1851—Present State Capitol completed.

1861—Alabama secedes from Union; Confederate government formed at Montgomery; Jefferson Davis inaugurated Confederate president there.

1862—Federal forces invade Alabama; capture Huntsville, Decatur, and Tuscumbia.

1864—Adm. David Farragut's Union fleet wins battle of Mobile Bay; Mobile captured in 1865.

1868—Alabama readmitted to the Union.

1871—Birmingham founded as railroad junction point.

1880—Blast furnace built at Birmingham.

1881—Booker T. Washington founds Tuskegee Institute.

1901—Present state constitution adopted.

1933—Wilson Dam at Muscle Shoals, completed in 1924, becomes first unit in Tennessee Valley Authority.

1949—Redstone rocket center established at Huntsville.

1962—Alabama's state legislature is first to be reapportioned by federal court order.

1965—Drive for Negro voter registration dramatized by "Freedom March," from Selma to Montgomery. USS *Alabama* enshrined in Mobile state park.

1966—Tennessee Valley Authority awards contract for its first nuclear power plant, at Brown Ferry, near Decatur.

1967—Lurleen Wallace is third U. S. woman to be elected a state governor; dies in 1968.

1802

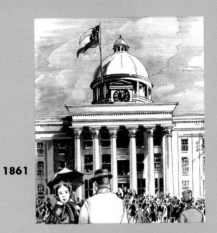

1861

1864

1933

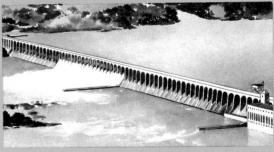

STATE FLOWER:
Camellia

STATE TREE:
Longleaf Pine

STATE BIRD:
Yellowhammer

STATE SEAL: State map shows chief rivers.

Alabama Profile

FLAG: *See* **Flags of the United States.**
MOTTO: Audemus Jura Nostra Defendere (We Dare Defend Our Rights).
SONG: 'Alabama'—words, Julia S. Tutwiler; music, Edna G. Gussen.

For a hundred years, King Cotton ruled in Alabama. Cotton is still a major crop, but the state's diversified agriculture of today, flourishing in a mild climate with adequate rainfall, produces crops ranging from corn to peanuts, from soybeans to watermelons. Cattle, hogs, and chickens are also important farm products of Alabama.

Even more dramatic than its agricultural growth has been Alabama's industrial emergence. The state is situated in the Deep South, commonly considered an agricultural region. Yet its income from manufacturing is twice the combined total obtained from farming, mining, forestry, and fishing. Rich resources of iron ore, coal, and limestone have helped make Alabama a major steel-producing state. Great dams on its rivers provide flood control and hydroelectric power—much of which is consumed by a thriving textile industry. Alabama has the world's largest known deposits of white marble and contains vast areas of pine and hardwood forest. It also has one of the best water-transportation systems in the South. The city of Mobile, linked by Mobile Bay with the Gulf of Mexico, is an important seaport.

Despite all its newly tapped industrial wealth, Alabama is still confronted with problems rooted in the pre-Civil War era. It is working to reclaim hundreds of square miles of land that too many years of one-crop farming left eroded and infertile and to replant vast stretches of cutover forest. The state is also trying to strengthen its educational system and to resolve long-standing problems in human relations. Alabama's Negro citizens are intensifying their efforts to secure the equalities guaranteed by the federal Constitution, and men of goodwill—both whites and Negroes—are working to achieve a climate of mutual understanding and respect.

Alabama picture profile

Floodlit against a night sky, Alabama's State Capitol stands in Montgomery. The Capitol's center section and dome were completed in 1851. It was the first Capitol of the Confederacy and the scene in 1861 of Jefferson Davis' inauguration as president of the Confederate States of America.

Near the center of the University of Alabama's Tuscaloosa campus stands its main library, completed in 1940. The university, which opened in 1831, has branches at Birmingham and Huntsville as well as numerous other facilities.

Many of the rockets and space vehicles for United States space exploration programs are designed and built at the George C. Marshall Space Flight Center at Huntsville. Nearby is the United States Army's Redstone Arsenal.

Alabama picture profile

Images of the grace and elegance of a bygone era are evoked by the many fine plantation homes that Alabama maintains as tourist attractions. Above are exterior and interior views of Gaineswood, an antebellum mansion set in a spacious lawn near Demopolis.

Billets of steel emerge from a continuous casting machine at Birmingham, the largest city in Alabama. Near the city lie rich deposits of iron ore, coal, and limestone. Making iron and steel products is Alabama's major industry. For industrial statistics, *see* ALABAMA FACT SUMMARY.

Connors Steel Division of H. K. Porter Company, Inc.

Now a state park, historic Fort Morgan overlooks the mouth of Mobile Bay. Troops of seven flags have manned the star-shaped fort. It was built in the 1700's and was a key strongpoint in the War of 1812 and the Civil War.

A parade in Mobile is a highlight of the annual Mardi Gras celebration, one of Alabama's colorful festivals. Mobile was the site of the first such carnival parade to be held in the New World.

Helen Keller was born in this tiny cottage at Tuscumbia. Herself both deaf and blind, she devoted a long lifetime of ceaseless effort to helping the handicapped.

This mansion at Montgomery was the first "White House" of the Confederacy. For a short time it was the residence of Confederate President Jefferson Davis and his wife.

A shrine to the state's war dead, the USS *Alabama* is permanently moored at Mobile. The 35,000-ton battleship—veteran of nine major World War II engagements—was saved from the scrapyard by donations.

JOSEPH WHEELER

ALABAMA
PROFILE

some famous people*

HUGO L. BLACK

GEORGE WASHINGTON CARVER

HELEN KELLER

BOOKER T. WASHINGTON

OSCAR W. UNDERWOOD

JABEZ L. M. CURRY

WILLIAM B. BANKHEAD

WILLIAM L. YANCEY

HARPER LEE

*Only a few of Alabama's famous people are shown here. The persons depicted are generally associated with the state, though not all of them were born there. For biographical information, *see* entries in the Fact-Index.

ALABAMA FACT SUMMARY

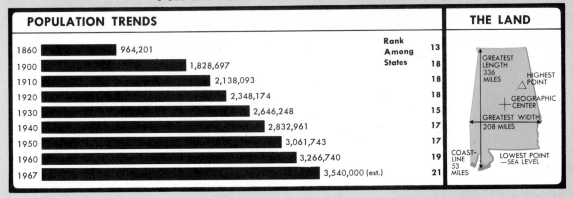

POPULATION TRENDS

Year	Population		Rank Among States
1860	964,201		13
1900	1,828,697		18
1910	2,138,093		18
1920	2,348,174		18
1930	2,646,248		15
1940	2,832,961		17
1950	3,061,743		17
1960	3,266,740		19
1967	3,540,000 (est.)		21

THE LAND

GREATEST LENGTH 336 MILES
HIGHEST POINT
GEOGRAPHIC CENTER
GREATEST WIDTH 208 MILES
COASTLINE 53 MILES
LOWEST POINT —SEA LEVEL

GOVERNMENT

Capital: Montgomery (voted, 1846; first session of state legislature, 1847).

Statehood: Became 22d state in the Union on Dec. 14, 1819.

Constitution: Adopted 1901. Amendment may be passed by three-fifths vote of Legislature; ratified by majority voting on it in a popular election.

Representation in U. S. Congress: Senate—2. House of Representatives—8. Electoral votes—10.

Legislature: Senators—35; term, 4 years. Representatives—106; term, 4 years.
  Convenes 2d Tuesday in January every 4 years after election of Legislature for purpose of organizing. Regular session convenes 1st Tuesday in May in odd years. Session limit—36 legislative days. Special session limit—36 legislative days.

Executive Officers
  Governor—term, 4 years. May not succeed himself.
  Other officials—lieutenant governor, secretary of state, treasurer, and attorney general; all elected; terms, 4 years.

Judiciary: Supreme Court—7 justices; elected at large; term, 6 years. Appellate courts—3 judges; elected; term, 6 years. Circuit courts—31 circuits; 73 judges; elected; term, 6 years. Probate courts—1 in each county; judges elected; term, 6 years.

County: 67 counties. Governed by boards of revenue or boards of commissioners; elected for 4-year terms.

Municipal: Mayor-council plan most common.

Voting Qualifications: Age—21. Residence in state—1 year; in county—6 months; in district—3 months.

Voting Days: General election—1st Tuesday after 1st Monday in November. Primary election—1st Tuesday in May in even years; secondary primary—4th Tuesday thereafter. Preferential presidential primary—1st Tuesday in May.

EDUCATION

Private Elementary and Secondary Day Schools
  Enrollment—elementary, 25,700; secondary, 7,000.
  Classroom teachers—elementary, 990; secondary, 500.

Public Elementary and Secondary Schools*
  Operating school districts—118.
  Instruction rooms available and in use—30,118.
  Compulsory school age—7 to 16.
  Enrollment—elementary, 482,000; secondary, 382,000.
  Average daily attendance—770,704.
  High school graduates—44,000.
  Administrative officials
    Superintendent of education; elected; term, 4 years.
    County superintendents; elected; term, 4 years. In some counties appointed by county boards; terms, 2 to 4 years.
    Superintendents of schools; appointed by city boards of education; terms, serve at pleasure of boards.

Instructional staff—total, 33,350; principals and supervisors, 1,450; elementary teachers, 16,400 (830 men, 15,570 women); secondary teachers, 15,500 (6,075 men, 9,425 women).

Teachers' average annual salaries—elementary, $5,625; secondary, $5,900.

Revenue receipts—$345,000,000.
  Source of receipts (% of total)—federal, 13.6; state, 62.3; local, 24.1.

Nonrevenue receipts†—$15,000,000.

Current expenditures
  For day schools—$319,000,000.
  For other programs—$1,900,000.

State expenditure on education—$390 per pupil.

Head Start programs—participants, 29,554; funds allocated, $5,720,000.

Universities and Colleges‡
  Number of institutions—total (includes junior colleges), 44; public, 24; private, 20; junior colleges, 19. Degree-credit enrollment—88,575.
  Earned degrees conferred—bachelor's and first professional, 7,912; master's except first professional, 1,367; doctor's, 106.

Special Institutions (for the handicapped): Institute for the Deaf and Blind, Talladega; Partlow State School, Tuscaloosa.

Libraries: City and town public libraries—137; county library systems—11; municipal library systems—10; regional library systems—8, serving 24 counties. Alabama Public Library Service aids in developing public libraries. State Department of Education aids in developing school libraries. Noted special library—Air University Libraries, Maxwell Field (near Montgomery).

Outstanding Museums: Birmingham Art Museum; Moundville Historical Museum; Montgomery Museum of Fine Arts, State Department of Archives and History; George Washington Carver Foundation, Tuskegee Institute; Museum of Natural History, University.

CORRECTIONAL AND PENAL INSTITUTIONS

State
  Adult—Kilby Prison and Receiving and Classification Center, Montgomery; Frank Lee Youth Center, Deatsville; Trusty Barracks, Montgomery; Number Four Honor Farm, Montgomery; Atmore Prison; Draper Correctional Center, Elmer; State Cattle Ranch, Greensboro; Julia Tutwiler Prison for Women, Wetumpka. Also 20 road camps throughout the state.
  Juvenile—Alabama Boys' Industrial School, Birmingham; Alabama Industrial School, Mount Meigs; Alabama Training School for Girls, Birmingham.

Federal
  Federal Prison Camp, Montgomery.

All Fact Summary data are based on current government reports.
*Kindergartens are included in the elementary schools; junior high schools, in the secondary schools.
†Money received from loans, sales of bonds, sales of property, and insurance adjustments.
‡Excludes data for service academies

218a

ALABAMA FACT SUMMARY

PRODUCTION—YEARLY VALUE: $3,525,800,000

The chart at left shows the state's major product categories and each category's percentage of the total value.

The charts below list the leading items in each of three important product groups and indicate their dollar values.

Manufacturing* 71%   Agriculture† 19%   Fishing less than 1%

Mining 6%   Forests 3%

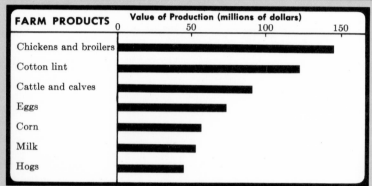

FARM PRODUCTS
Value of Production (millions of dollars)

	0	50	100	150
Chickens and broilers				
Cotton lint				
Cattle and calves				
Eggs				
Corn				
Milk				
Hogs				

AGRICULTURE

Farms and Farm Income
Total farms—93,000.
Land in farms—15,226,000 acres.
Average size of farm—165 acres.
Cash income from crops—$182,254,-000.
Cash income from livestock and products—$464,998,000.
Government payments—$79,617,000.
Realized net income per farm—$2,879.

Principal Crops (amounts produced and acres harvested): Corn—37,840,000 bu., 860,000 acres; cotton lint—200,000 bales, 350,000 acres; hay—780,000 tons, 501,000 acres; peanuts harvested for nuts—234,960,000 lbs., 178,000 acres; soybeans for beans—12,852,000 bu., 476,000 acres.

Livestock on Farms
Cattle (all)—1,877,000.
Chickens—16,850,000.
Hogs and pigs—795,000.
Sheep and lambs—9,000.

FORESTS

Total Acreage: 21,770,000.
Commercial Forest Land (acres)
Total—21,742,000.
Federal—799,000.
State, county, or municipal—202,000.
Private—20,741,000.
Forest Products (value): $106,400,000.
Lumber (board feet cut): 1,078,000,000.
National Forests: 4.

MANUFACTURED PRODUCTS   Value Added by Manufacture*

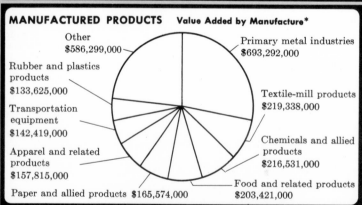

Other $586,299,000
Rubber and plastics products $133,625,000
Transportation equipment $142,419,000
Apparel and related products $157,815,000
Paper and allied products $165,574,000
Primary metal industries $693,292,000
Textile-mill products $219,338,000
Chemicals and allied products $216,531,000
Food and related products $203,421,000

FISHING

Commercial Catch: 35,827,000 lbs.; value—$7,706,000.

TRADE

Wholesale: $3,394,992,000.
Retail: $3,253,433,000.
Service: $362,571,000.

ELECTRIC UTILITIES

Number of Utilities: 5.
Total Capacity: 8,636,306 kw.

MINERALS
Value of Production (millions of dollars)

	0	25	50	75	100	125
Coal						
Cement						
Stone	(exact value not available)					

All Fact Summary data are based on current government reports.
*Value Added by Manufacture—value of manufactured products as they leave the factory, less the cost of materials, supplies, fuel, etc. For complete definition, *see* Fact-Index.
†Cash receipts.

ALABAMA FACT SUMMARY

TRANSPORTATION

Roads and Streets
Total state mileage—76,765; total surfaced—68,483.
Municipal mileage—10,579.
Rural mileage—66,186.
National Interstate Highway System
Total designated mileage—880.
Mileage open to traffic—453.
Mileage under construction or projected—427.

Automobiles, Trucks, and Buses (registrations)*
Total—1,732,000.
Private and commercial—automobiles, 1,400,000; trucks and buses, 308,000.
Publicly owned—24,000.

Motorcycles (registrations): 25,300.

Railroads
Total mileage owned—4,598; Class I—3,918.
First railroad—Tuscumbia to Muscle Shoals, 1832 (now Southern Railway System).

Airports†: Total—119; private 46.

Civil Aircraft: Total—1,877; active—1,326.

COMMUNICATION

Post Offices: 692.

Radio Stations (commercial): AM—125; FM—31. First station—WGH, Montgomery, licensed Feb. 3, 1922.

TV Stations: Commercial—15; educational—6. First station—WAFM-TV, Birmingham, began operation May 29, 1949.

Telephones: Total—1,270,900; residence—935,800.

Newspapers
Daily—22; circulation—710,427.
Weekly—101; circulation—350,407.
Sunday—15; circulation—616,860.
First newspaper—*Mobile Centinel*, Fort Stoddert, 1811.

Periodicals: 71.

WELFARE‡

Old-Age and Survivors Insurance: Beneficiaries—347,683; benefits—$255,235,000.

Disability Insurance: Beneficiaries—54,051; benefits—$42,585,000.

Unemployment Insurance: Beneficiaries (weekly average)—12,190; benefits—$18,796,000.

Workmen's Compensation Benefits: $17,747,000.

Vocational Rehabilitation
Disabled persons rehabilitated—4,818; in process of rehabilitation—8,559.
Total federal and state funds—$12,014,368.

Public Assistance
Old-age—recipients, 113,000; average payment, $60.20.
Dependent children—recipients, 71,300; average payment, $12.70.
Permanently and totally disabled—recipients, 15,200; average payment, $45.35.
Blind—recipients, 1,800; average payment, $70.20.
General assistance—recipients, 94; average payment, $13.80.

Maternity and Child Welfare Services
Federal grants—maternal and child health services, $984,173; crippled children, $1,105,698; child welfare, $1,112,953.
Children receiving services—11,086; rate per 10,000 children—73.

United Fund Campaigns: 47; amount raised—$8,838,927.

All Fact Summary data are based on current government reports.
*Excludes vehicles owned by military services.
†Includes seaplane bases, heliports, and military fields having joint civil-military use.
‡Figures for one-year periods.

EMPLOYMENT

Total Number of Persons Employed: 1,065,897.

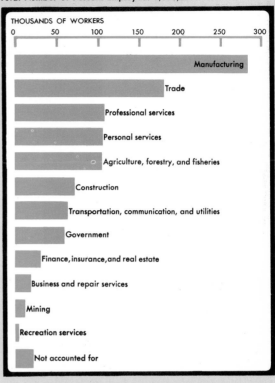

FINANCE‡

Revenue: $953,785,000.

Expenditures: $933,996,000.

Taxation
State tax collections—$483,000,000; per capita—$136.46.
Federal tax collections—$977,000,000; individual income and employment—$758,000,000; per capita—$448.
Local tax collections—$176,000,000; per capita—$50.04.

Personal Income: $7,254,000,000.

Banks: 267; total assets or liabilities—$3,936,000,000.

Savings and Loan Associations: 55, including 8 state associations; assets—$936,000,000, including $129,000,000 of state association assets.

SELECTIVE SERVICE‡

Registrants Subject to Draft: 438,616.

Inductions: 4,929.

Regular Enlistments: 9,627.

Reserves or National Guard Enlistments: 2,217.

CRIME

Rates (per 100,000 population): Murder—10.9; forcible rape—9.7; robbery—32.0; aggravated assault—177.7; burglary—518.4; larceny—329.3; auto theft—130.9.

HOSPITALS AND PHYSICIANS

Hospitals: 144; beds—27,273.

Physicians: 2,675.

ALABAMA FACT SUMMARY

LARGEST CITIES*

Birmingham (340,887): leading iron and steel center of South; industrial city; railroad shops; iron statue of Vulcan (*see* Birmingham, Ala.).

Mobile (202,779): seaport on Mobile Bay; state docks; industrial center; shipyards; 35-mile Azalea Trail; Brookley Air Force Base nearby (*see* Mobile).

Montgomery (134,393): state capital; manufacturing center; Victorian furniture reproductions; cotton and livestock market; first White House of Confederacy (*see* Montgomery, Ala.).

Huntsville (72,365): missile and space research center; textiles, other manufactures; first state capital (1819–20); Redstone Arsenal nearby.

Tuscaloosa (63,370): trade center; University of Alabama; Old Tavern (1827); Gorgas home.

Gadsden (58,088): industrial city; steel and fabricated metal products; Noccalula Falls.

Prichard (47,371): industrial suburb of Mobile.

Anniston (33,657): textiles, cast-iron pipes; Regar Museum of Natural History.

Bessemer (33,054): iron and steel manufacturing.

Florence (31,649): aluminum, fertilizer, and textile manufacturing; livestock; Wilson Dam nearby.

PLACES OF INTEREST

Ave Maria Grotto: at St. Bernard College in St. Bernard; miniature reproduction of the Holy Land.

Bellingrath Gardens: near Mobile along Azalea Trail; azaleas, camellias, and other flowers; moss-hung live oaks.

Bladon Springs State Park: near Bladon Springs; mineral springs; picnicking.

Cathedral Caverns: near Grant; large stalagmite forest; frozen waterfall.

Chattahoochee State Park: near Crosby; fishing; camping.

Cheaha State Park: near Oxford; Cheaha Mountain (2,407 feet), highest point in the state.

Chewacla State Park: near Auburn; rugged valley; cascades; lake.

Chickasaw State Park: near Linden; hiking trail in forest.

Dauphin Island: at entrance to Mobile Bay; French settlement (1669); Fort Gaines.

Demopolis: in Marengo County; Gaineswood, Bluff Hall, and other beautiful plantation mansions.

De Soto State Park: near Mentone; on Lookout Mountain; 120-foot falls.

Fort Morgan State Park: on Mobile Point; historic brick fort.

George C. Marshall Space Orientation Center: at Huntsville; museum of rocketry and space travel.

Gulf State Park: near Foley; beach on Gulf of Mexico; three lakes; swimming and boating.

Horseshoe Bend National Military Park: near Dadeville; Andrew Jackson defeated Creek Indians here on March 27, 1814, during the War of 1812.

Ivy Green: at Tuscumbia; birthplace and home of Helen Keller, noted deaf and blind author-lecturer.

*1960 census.

Joe Wheeler State Park: near Killen on Wheeler Lake; boating and fishing.

Little Mountain State Park: near Guntersville on Lake Guntersville; camping; boating and fishing.

Magnolia Grove: at Greensboro; home of Adm. Richmond P. Hobson, hero of Spanish-American War.

Magnolia Springs: in Baldwin County; fishing resort with only all-water mail route in Alabama.

Mentone: in De Kalb County; resort on top of Lookout Mountain; scenic drives.

Monte Sano State Park: near Huntsville; park on mountain slopes.

Monument to the Boll Weevil: erected by the grateful farmers of Enterprise; damage done by this insect forced them to diversify their crops.

Mound State Monument: near Moundville; prehistoric Indian city of 34 mounds; museum.

Natchez Trace National Parkway: in Alabama, Mississippi, and Tennessee; follows Old Indian Trail between Nashville, Tenn., and Natchez, Miss.

Oak Mountain State Park: near Birmingham; rugged mountains.

Rosemount: near Forkland; elaborate plantation mansion (1830–35); many antiques on display.

Russell Cave National Monument: near Bridgeport; oldest known home of primitive man in southeastern U. S.

Sealy's Hot Salt Mineral Well: near Cottonwood; health resort with curative water.

The Dismals: near Phil Campbell; rock walls rise 100 feet above bottom of ravine; wild flowers.

Tuskegee: in Macon County; old homes; Tuskegee Institute.

TVA dams: Wilson, at Muscle Shoals, Wheeler, near Rogersville, and Guntersville, near Guntersville; fishing, boating, and other recreation on lakes formed by dams (*see* Tennessee Valley Authority).

USS *Alabama:* in Mobile Bay; battleship bought by people of Alabama; established as a state shrine.

Valley Creek State Park: near Plantersville; water sports.

Vestavia Temple and Gardens: near Birmingham; replica of Roman temple.

BOOKS ABOUT ALABAMA

Akens, H. M. and **Brown, V. P.** Alabama Mounds to Missiles (Strode, 1966).

Arnold, Byron. Folksongs of Alabama (Univ. of Ala. Press, 1950).

Bailey, B. F. Picture Book of Alabama (Whitman, 1966).

Baldwin, J. G. The Flush Times of Alabama and Mississippi (Peter Smith, 1959).

Brown, V. P. and **Akens, H. M.** Alabama Heritage (Strode, 1967).

Carmer, C. L. Stars Fell on Alabama (Hill & Wang, 1961) o.p.

Evans, E. K. Araminta (Putnam, 1935) o.p.

Stribling, T. S. The Forge (and sequels) (Doubleday, 1931–34) o.p.

Wellman, M. W. Young Squire Morgan (Washburn, 1956).

Writers' Program. Alabama (Hastings House, 1941) o.p.

ALABAMA

COUNTIES

Autauga	18,739	E 5
Baldwin	49,088	C 9
Barbour	24,700	H 7
Bibb	14,357	D 5
Blount	25,449	E 2
Bullock	13,462	G 6
Butler	24,560	E 7
Calhoun	95,878	G 3
Chambers	37,828	H 5
Cherokee	16,303	G 2
Chilton	25,693	E 5
Choctaw	17,870	B 6
Clarke	25,738	C 7
Clay	12,400	G 4
Cleburne	10,911	G 3
Coffee	30,583	G 8
Colbert	46,506	C 1
Conecuh	17,762	E 8
Coosa	10,726	F 5
Covington	35,631	F 8
Crenshaw	14,909	F 7
Cullman	45,572	E 2
Dale	31,066	G 8
Dallas	56,667	D 6
De Kalb	41,417	G 2
Elmore	30,524	F 5
Escambia	33,511	D 8
Etowah	96,980	F 2
Fayette	16,148	C 3
Franklin	21,988	C 2
Geneva	22,310	G 8
Greene	13,600	C 5
Hale	19,537	C 5
Henry	15,286	H 8
Houston	50,718	H 8
Jackson	36,681	F 1
Jefferson	634,864	E 3
Lamar	14,271	B 3
Lauderdale	61,622	C 1
Lawrence	24,501	D 1
Lee	49,754	H 5
Limestone	36,513	E 1
Lowndes	15,417	E 6
Macon	26,717	G 6
Madison	117,348	E 1
Marengo	27,098	C 6
Marion	21,837	C 2
Marshall	48,018	F 2
Mobile	314,301	B 9
Monroe	22,372	D 7
Montgomery	169,210	F 6
Morgan	60,454	E 2
Perry	17,358	D 5
Pickens	21,882	B 4
Pike	25,987	G 7
Randolph	19,477	H 4
Russell	46,351	H 6
Saint Clair	25,388	F 3
Shelby	32,132	E 4
Sumter	20,041	B 5
Talladega	65,495	F 4
Tallapoosa	35,007	G 5
Tuscaloosa	109,047	C 4
Walker	54,211	D 3
Washington	15,372	B 8
Wilcox	18,739	D 7
Winston	14,858	D 2

CITIES AND TOWNS

Abanda	130	H 4
Abbeville	2,524	H 7
Abernant	200	D 4
Ackerville	25	E 6
Acmar	900	E 3
Adamsville	2,095	D 3
Addison	343	D 2
Adger	600	D 4
Akron	604	C 5
Alabaster	1,623	E 4
Alberta	600	D 6
Albertville	8,250	F 2
Aldrich	950	E 4
Alexander City	13,140	G 5
Alexandria	500	G 3
Aliceville	3,194	B 4
Allen	145	C 7
Allenton	75	E 7
Allgood	147	F 3
Allsboro	150	B 1
Alma	600	C 8
Alpine	156	F 4
Alton	500	E 3
Altoona	744	F 2
Andalusia	10,263	E 8
Anderson	350	D 1
Annemanie	100	D 6
Anniston	33,657	G 3
Ansley	125	F 7
Arab	2,989	E 2
Ararat	65	B 7
Ardmore	439	E 1
Argo	197	E 3
Ariton	687	G 7
Arkadelphia	350	E 3
Arley	400	D 2
Arlington	200	C 6
Ashby	98	E 4
Ashford	1,511	H 8
Ashland	1,610	G 4
Ashville	973	F 3
Athens	9,330	E 1
Atmore	8,173	C 8
Attalla	8,257	F 2
Auburn	16,261	H 5
Autaugaville	440	E 6
Avon	132	H 8
Axis	350	B 9
Babbie	60	F 8
Baileyton	300	E 2
Bakerhill	265	H 7
Banks	201	G 7
Bankston	75	C 3
Barlow Bend	150	C 8
Barnwell		C 10
Barton	250	C 1
Bashi	150	C 7
Batesville	50	H 6
Battles Wharf	500	C 10
Bay Minette	5,197	C 9
Bayou La Batre	2,572	B 10
Bear Creek	243	C 2
Beatrice	506	D 7
Beaverton	162	B 3
Bedford	75	B 3
Belgreen	500	C 2
Belk	150	C 3
Bellamy	750	B 6
Belle Mina	300	E 1
Bellview	75	D 7
Bellwood	273	G 8
Belmont	153	C 5
Beloit	125	D 6
Benton	150	E 6
Bermuda	500	D 8
Berry	645	C 3
Bessemer	33,054	D 4
Beulah	350	H 5
Bexar	94	B 2
Bigbee	30	B 7
Billingsley	179	E 5
Birmingham	340,887	D 3
Birmingham	†521,330	D 3
Black	133	G 8
Blacksher	100	C 8
Bladon Springs	300	B 7
Blalock	15	D 6
Blanton	100	H 5
Bleecker	250	H 5
Blount Springs	100	E 3
Blountsville	672	E 2
Blue Mountain	446	G 3
Blue Springs	94	G 7
Boaz	4,654	F 2
Boligee	134	C 5
Bolinger	200	B 7
Bolling	250	E 7
Bon Air	297	F 4
Bon Secour	500	C 10
Booth	250	E 6
Borden Springs	100	H 3
Boyd	250	B 5
Boylston	1,200	F 6
Bradleyton	75	F 7
Braggs	300	E 6
Branchville	150	F 3
Brantley	1,014	F 7
Bremen	250	E 3
Brent	1,879	D 5
Brewton	6,309	D 8
Brickyard	150	H 6
Bridgeport	2,906	G 1
Brierfield	146	E 4
Brighton	2,884	D 4
Brilliant	749	C 2
Bromley	585	C 9
Brompton	115	F 3
Brooklyn	100	E 8
Brookside	999	E 3
Brooksville	175	F 2
Brookwood	650	D 4
Browns	700	D 6
Brownsboro	100	F 1
Brownville	250	C 4
Brownville	534	*E 4
Brundidge	2,523	G 7
Bryant	150	G 1
Bucks	40	B 8
Buena Vista	200	D 7
Buffalo	75	H 5
Buhl	500	C 4
Burkville	200	E 6
Burl	75	D 7
Burnsville	300	E 6
Burnt Corn	250	D 7
Butler	1,765	B 6
Butler Springs	200	E 7
Cahaba	50	D 6
Calcis	200	E 4
Caledonia	150	D 7
Calera	1,928	E 4
Calhoun	500	F 6
Calvert	500	B 8
Camden	1,121	D 7
Camp Hill	1,270	G 5
Campbell	100	C 7
Canoe	500	D 8
Canton Bend	75	D 6
Capps	100	H 8
Capshaw	650	E 1
Carbon Hill	1,944	D 3
Cardiff	202	E 3
Carlowville	100	D 6
Carlton		C 8
Carrollton	894	B 4
Carrville	1,081	G 5
Carson	200	C 8
Castleberry	669	D 8
Catherine	350	D 6
Cecil	250	F 6
Cedar Bluff	687	G 2
Cedar Cove	100	D 4
Central	175	F 5
Centre	2,392	G 2
Centreville	1,981	D 5
Chance		C 7
Chancellor	200	G 8
Chandler Sprs.	200	F 4
Chapman	617	E 7
Chase	275	E 1
Chastang	200	B 8
Chatom	993	B 8
Chelsea	300	E 4
Cherokee	1,349	C 1
Chestnut	200	D 7
Chickasaw	10,002	B 9
Childersburg	4,884	F 4
China Grove	200	G 7
Choccolocco	300	G 3
Choctaw	600	B 6
Choctaw Bluff	500	C 8
Chrysler		C 8
Chunchula	500	B 9
Citronelle	1,918	B 8
Claiborne	150	D 7
Clairmont Springs	50	G 4
Clanton	5,683	E 5
Claud	500	F 5
Clayton	1,313	G 7
Cleveland	300	E 3
Clinton	200	C 5
Clio	929	G 7
Clopton	140	G 7
Cloverdale	600	C 1
Coaling	150	D 4
Coatopa	100	B 6
Cochrane	73	B 4
Coden	500	B 10
Coffee Springs	205	G 8
Coffeeville	250	B 7
Cohasset	20	E 8
Coker	500	C 4
Collinsville	1,199	G 2
Collirene	100	E 6
Columbia	783	H 8
Columbiana	2,264	E 4
Comer	100	H 6
Consul	30	C 6
Cooks Springs	200	F 3
Cooper	400	E 5
Coosada	250	F 5
Copeland	160	B 7
Cordova	3,184	D 3
Corona	207	C 3
Cottage Grove	200	F 5
Cottondale	500	D 4
Cottonton	100	H 6
Cottonwood	953	H 8
County Line	278	E 3
Courtland	495	D 1
Covin	100	C 3
Cowarts	200	H 8
Coy	950	D 7
Cragford	160	G 4
Crane Hill		D 2
Creek Stand	50	G 6
Creola	500	B 9
Crews	150	B 3
Cromwell	500	B 6
Cropwell	200	F 3
Crosby	25	H 8
Crossville	579	G 2
Cuba	390	B 6
Cullman	10,883	E 2
Cullomburg	300	B 7
Cusseta	250	H 5
Cypress	150	C 5
Dadeville	2,940	G 5
Daleville	693	G 8
Dancy	200	B 4
Danville	100	D 2
Daphne	1,527	C 9
Darlington	150	D 7
Dauphin Island	600	B 10
Daviston	129	G 4
Dawson	75	G 2
Dayton	99	C 6
DeArmanville	375	G 3
Deatsville	275	F 5
Decatur	29,217	D 1
Deer Park	250	B 8
Delmar	72	C 2
Delta	150	G 4
Demopolis	7,377	C 6
Detroit	113	B 2
Devenport	125	F 6
Dickinson	300	C 7
Dixie	50	E 8
Dixons Mills	350	C 6
Dixonville	300	E 8
Dolomite	4,500	D 4
Dora	1,776	D 3
Dothan	31,440	H 8
Double Springs	811	D 2
Douglas	200	F 2
Dozier	335	F 7
Drewry	200	D 8
Duke	200	G 3
Dunavant	100	F 4
Duncanville	300	D 4
Dutton	350	G 1
Dyas	30	C 9
Easonville	200	F 3
East Brewton	2,511	E 8
Eastaboga	600	F 3
Echo	150	G 8
Echola	250	C 4
Eclectic	926	F 5
Edna	500	B 6
Edwardsville	168	H 3
Edwin	150	H 7
Elamville	150	G 7
Elba	4,321	F 8
Elberta	384	C 10
Eldridge	350	C 3
Eliska	75	C 8
Elkmont	169	E 1
Elmore	350	F 5
Elon	300	F 1
Elrod	500	C 4
Emelle	300	B 5
Empire		D 3
Enterprise	11,410	G 8
Eoline	100	D 4
Epes	337	B 5
Equality	100	F 5
Escatawpa	30	B 8
Estillfork	196	F 1
Ethelsville	62	B 4
Eufaula	8,357	H 7
Eunola	124	G 8
Eutaw	2,784	C 5
Eva	180	E 2
Evergreen	3,703	E 8
Excel	313	D 8
Fabius	100	G 1
Fackler	300	G 1
Fairfax	3,107	H 5
Fairfield	15,816	E 3
Fairford	400	B 8
Fairhope	4,858	C 10
Falkville	682	E 2
Farmersville	100	E 6
Faunsdale	124	C 6
Fayette	4,227	C 3
Fayetteville	300	F 4
Fernbank	75	B 3
Finchburg	500	D 7
Fitzpatrick	78	G 6
Five Points	285	H 4
Flat Creek	570	D 3
Flat Rock	500	G 1
Flatwood	250	C 6
Fleta	350	F 6
Flint City	432	D 1
Flomaton	1,454	D 8
Florala	3,011	F 8
Florence	31,649	C 1
Foley	2,889	C 10
Forest Home	500	E 7
Forkland	250	C 5
Forney	100	H 2
Forrester	60	E 6
Fort Davis	300	G 6
Fort Deposit	1,466	E 7
Fort Mitchell	950	H 6
Fort Payne	7,029	G 2
Fosters		C 4
Fostoria	150	E 6
Fountain	150	D 7
Francisco	150	F 1
Frankfort	130	C 1
Franklin	350	D 7
Frankville	500	B 7
Fredonia	50	H 5
Freemanville	100	D 8
Frisco City	1,177	D 8
Fruitdale	800	B 8
Fruithurst	255	G 3
Fulton	688	C 7
Fultondale	2,001	E 3
Furman	300	E 6
Fyffe	230	G 2
Gadsden	58,088	G 2
Gadsden	†68,944	G 2
Gainestown	160	C 8
Gainesville	214	B 5
Gallant	855	F 2
Gallion	300	C 6
Gantt	500	E 8
Gantts Quarry	238	F 4
Garden City	536	E 2
Gardendale	4,712	E 3
Garland	225	E 7
Gasque		C 10
Gastonburg	175	C 6
Gateswood	50	C 9
Gaylesville	144	G 2
Geiger	104	B 5
Geneva	3,840	G 8
Georgiana	2,093	E 7
Geraldine	340	G 2
Gilbertown	270	B 7
Glen Allen	131	C 3
Glencoe	2,592	G 3
Glenwood	416	F 7
Gold Hill	160	G 5
Goodsprings	300	D 3
Goodwater	2,023	F 4
Goodway	40	D 8
Gordo	1,714	C 4
Gordon	222	H 8
Gordonsville	100	E 6
Gorgas	300	D 3
Goshen	260	F 7
Gosport	300	C 7
Grady	150	F 7
Graham	214	H 4
Grand Bay	500	B 10
Grangeburg	35	H 8
Grant	274	F 1
Graysville	2,870	D 3
Green Pond	1,750	D 4
Greenbrier	200	E 1
Greensboro	3,081	C 5
Greenville	6,894	E 7
Greenwood	3,561	G 6
Grimes	175	H 8
Grove Hill	1,834	C 7
Groveoak	250	F 2
Gu-Win	80	C 3
Guin	1,462	C 3
Gulf Shores	356	C 10
Gulfcrest	100	B 8
Guntersville	6,592	F 2
Gurley	706	F 1
Hackleburg	527	C 2
Hacoda	25	F 8
Haleburg	250	H 8
Haleyville	3,740	C 2
Halsell	500	B 6
Hamburg	75	D 5
Hamilton	1,934	C 2
Hammondville	134	G 1
Hamner	100	B 5
Hanceville	1,174	E 2
Hardaway	300	G 6
Harpersville	667	F 4
Hartford	1,956	G 8
Hartselle	5,000	E 2
Harvest	250	E 1
Hatchechubbee	250	H 6
Hatton	550	D 1
Havana	180	C 5
Hayden	187	E 3
Hayneville	950	E 6
Hazel Green	200	E 1
Headland	2,650	H 8
Healing Springs	150	B 7
Heath	125	F 8
Heflin	2,400	G 3
Heiberger	100	D 5
Helena	523	E 4
Henagar	500	G 1
Henderson	50	F 7
Herbert	20	E 8
Hickory Flat	80	H 4
Higdon	350	G 1
Highland Home	85	F 7
Hightower	200	H 3
Hillsboro	218	D 1
Hissop	200	F 5
Hobbs Island	200	F 1
Hobson City	770	G 3
Hodges	194	C 2
Hodgesville	100	H 8
Hokes Bluff	1,619	G 3
Hollins	200	F 4
Holly Pond	193	E 2
Hollytree	239	F 1
Hollywood	246	G 1
Holman	98	C 4
Holt	2,400	D 4
Holy Trinity	350	H 6
Homewood	20,289	E 4
Honoraville	200	F 7
Hope Hull	50	F 6
Hopewell	150	H 3

*No room on map for name. †Population of urban area.

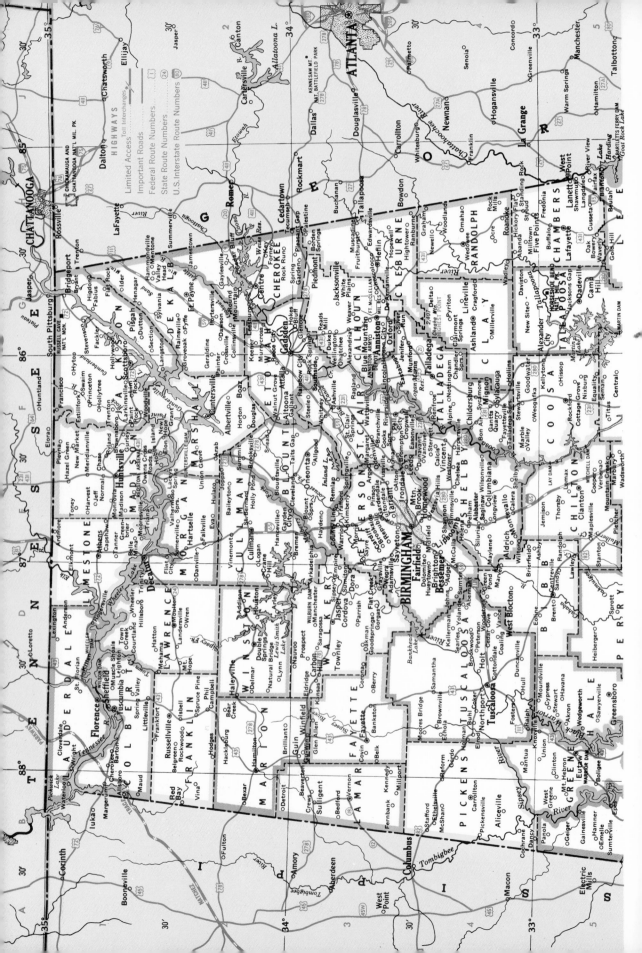

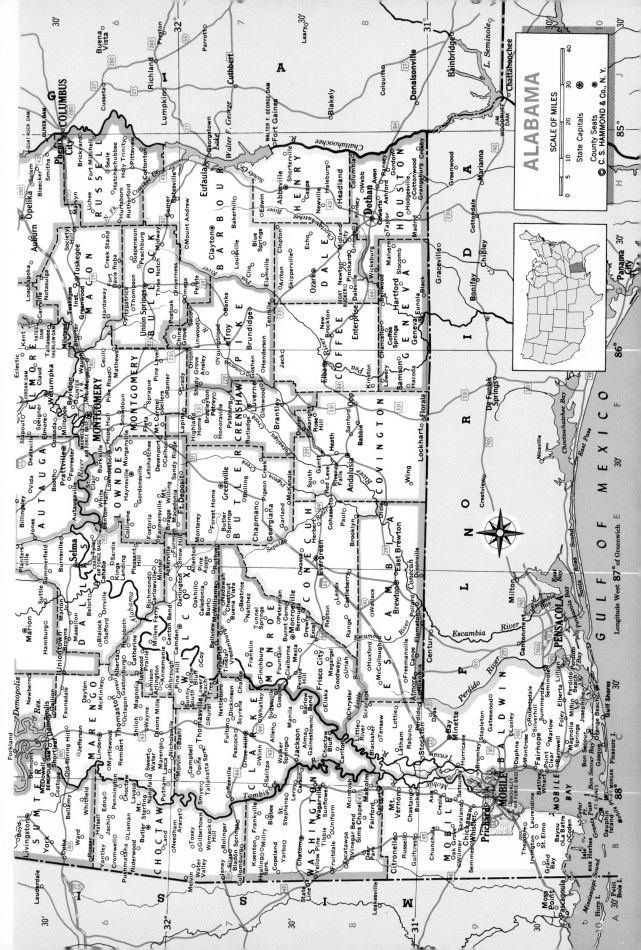

ALABAMA

SCALE OF MILES

0 5 10 20 30 40

⊛ State Capitals
◉ County Seats

C. S. HAMMOND & CO., N. Y.

ALABAMA—*Continued*

Horton	300	F 2
Houston	220	D 2
Hueytown	5,997	D 4
Hulaco	160	E 2
Hull	125	C 4
Huntsville	72,365	E 1
Huntsville	†74,970	E 2
Hurricane	50	C 9
Hurtsboro	1,056	H 6
Huxford	350	D 8
Hybart	200	D 7
Hytop	145	F 1
Ider	300	G 1
Inverness	140	G 6
Irondale	3,501	E 3
Irvington	200	B 9
Isbell	225	C 2
Isney	102	B 7
Jachin	250	B 6
Jack	100	F 7
Jackson	4,959	C 8
Jacksons Gap	600	G 5
Jacksonville	5,678	G 3
Jamestown	90	G 2
Jasper	10,799	D 3
Jeff	100	E 1
Jefferson	600	C 6
Jemison	977	E 5
Jenifer	88	G 3
Johns	338	D 4
Jones	150	E 5
Joppa	178	E 2
Josephine	75	C 10
Kansas	211	C 3
Keener	150	G 2
Kellerman	214	D 4
Kellyton	475	F 5
Kennedy	379	B 3
Kent	500	G 5
Key	175	G 2
Killen	620	D 1
Kimberly	763	E 3
Kimbrough	158	C 6
Kings Landing	200	D 6
Kinsey	283	H 8
Kinston	470	F 8
Knoxville	300	C 4
Koenton	25	B 7
Laceys Spring	350	E 1
Lafayette	2,605	H 5
Lamison	350	C 6
Land	200	B 6
Landersville	100	D 2
Lanett	7,674	H 5
Langdale	2,528	H 5
Langston	250	G 1
Lapine	400	F 7
Larkinsville	400	F 1
Lasca	40	C 6
Latham	300	C 8
Laurendine	200	B 9
Lavaca	350	B 6
Lawley	87	E 5
Leeds	6,162	E 3
Leesburg	350	G 2
Leighton	1,158	D 1
Lenox	100	D 8
Leroy	300	B 8
Letohatchee	325	E 6
Lexington	315	D 1
Lillian	650	D 10
Lim Rock	200	F 1
Lincoln	629	F 3
Linden	2,516	C 6
Lineville	1,612	G 4
Linwood	150	G 7
Lipscomb	2,811	E 4
Lisman	909	B 6
Little River	100	C 8
Littleville	460	C 1
Livingston	1,544	B 5
Loachapoka	500	G 5
Lockhart	799	F 8
Logan	100	E 2
Lomax	100	E 5
Longview	150	E 4
Lottie	150	C 8
Louisville	890	G 7
Lower Peach Tree	725	C 7
Lowery	75	F 8
Lowndesboro	375	E 6
Loxley	831	C 9
Luverne	2,238	F 7
Lynn	531	C 2
Macedonia	150	E 6
Madison	1,435	E 1
Madrid	245	H 8
Magnolia	150	C 6
Magnolia Sprs.	250	C 10
Malcolm	50	B 8
Malvern	213	G 8
Manchester	200	D 3
Manila	150	C 7
Mantua	150	C 4
Maplesville	679	E 5
Marble Valley	70	F 4

Marbury	300	E 5
Marengo	50	C 6
Margaret	715	F 3
Margerum	150	B 1
Marion	3,807	D 5
Marion Jct.	400	D 6
Marlow	100	C 10
Marvyn	200	H 6
Massillon	75	D 6
Mathews	69	F 6
Maud	100	B 1
Maylene	200	E 4
Maytown	297	*D 3
Mc Calla	340	E 4
Mc Cullough	600	D 8
Mc Dowell	275	C 5
Mc Intosh	500	B 8
Mc Kenzie	558	E 7
Mc Kinley	75	C 6
Mc Shan	200	B 4
Mc Williams	250	D 7
Megargel	410	D 8
Mehama	120	D 1
Melvin	300	B 7
Mentone	250	G 1
Meridianville	500	F 1
Mexia	150	D 8
Midfield	3,556	E 4
Midland City	854	H 8
Midway	594	H 6
Miflin	135	C 10
Mignon	2,271	F 4
Millbrook	700	F 6
Millers Ferry	425	D 6
Millerville	150	G 4
Millport	943	B 3
Millry	645	B 7
Milltown	125	H 4
Milstead	200	G 6
Minter	450	D 6
Mobile	202,779	B 9
Mobile	†268,139	B 9
Monroeville	3,632	D 7
Monrovia	500	E 1
Monterey	150	E 7
Montevallo	2,755	E 4
MONTGOMERY	134,393	F 6
Montgomery	†142,893	F 6
Montrose	750	C 9
Moores Bridge	300	C 4
Mooresville	93	E 1
Morganville	300	F 6
Morris	638	E 3
Morvin	100	C 7
Moulton	1,716	D 2
Moundville	922	C 5
Mount Andrew	80	H 7
Mount Carmel	350	F 6
Mount Hebron		B 5
Mount Hope	600	D 2
Mount Meigs	200	F 6
Mount Sterling	350	B 6
Mount Vernon	553	B 8
Mount Willing	172	E 6
Mountain Brook	12,680	E 4
Mountain Creek	100	E 5
Mulga	482	*E 3
Munford	750	F 3
Murrycross	300	G 2
Muscadine	150	H 3
Muscle Shoals	4,084	C 1
Myrtlewood	403	C 6
Nadawah	20	D 7
Nanafalia	400	B 6
Natchez	203	D 7
Natural Bridge	100	C 2
Nauvoo	318	D 3
Needham	108	B 7
Nettleboro	50	C 7
New Brockton	1,093	G 8
New Hope	953	F 1
New Market	500	F 1
New Site	500	G 4
Newbern	316	C 5
Newell	150	H 4
Newton	958	G 8
Newville	546	H 8
Nicholsville	225	C 6
Nixburg	200	F 5
Nokomis	50	D 8
Normal	1,400	E 1
North Johns (Johns)	338	D 4
Northport	5,245	C 4
Notasulga	884	G 5
Nottingham	100	F 4
Oak Bowery	60	H 5
Oak Grove	50	B 9
Oakhill	116	D 7
Oakman	849	D 3
Ocre	50	H 4
Octagon		C 6
Odenville	300	F 3
Ohatchee	437	G 3

Old Spring Hill	100	C 6
Omaha	30	H 4
Omega	400	G 7
Oneonta	4,136	E 3
Opelika	15,678	H 5
Opine	40	C 7
Opp	5,535	F 8
Orange Beach	500	C 10
Orion	50	F 7
Orrville	422	D 6
Owassa	87	E 8
Owens Cross Roads	800	E 1
Oxford	3,603	G 3
Ozark	9,534	G 8
Paint Rock	264	F 1
Painter	250	F 2
Palestine	100	H 3
Panola	400	B 5
Pansey	200	H 8
Parrish	1,608	D 3
Patsburg	70	F 7
Paul	200	E 8
Peachburg	150	G 6
Peacock	36	C 7
Pelham	400	E 4
Pell City	4,165	F 3
Pennington	100	B 6
Perdido	300	C 8
Perdido Beach	128	C 10
Perdue Hill	275	C 8
Perote	84	G 7
Peterman	600	D 7
Peterson	900	D 4
Petrey	165	F 7
Phenix City	27,630	H 6
Phil Campbell	898	C 2
Pickensville	175	B 4
Piedmont	4,794	G 3
Pigeon Creek	110	E 7
Pike Road	150	F 6
Pinckard	578	G 8
Pine Apple	355	E 7
Pine Hill	367	C 7
Pine Level	250	F 6
Pinson	950	E 3
Pisgah	214	G 1
Pittsview	300	H 6
Plantersville	650	E 5
Pleasant Gap	40	H 3
Pleasant Grove	3,097	*E 4
Pleasant Hill	300	E 6
Pletcher	50	E 5
Plevna	100	F 1
Point Clear	750	C 10
Pollard	210	D 8
Portersville	75	G 2
Postoak	35	G 6
Prairie	150	D 6
Prattmont	350	*E 6
Prattville	6,616	E 6
Prichard	47,371	B 9
Princeton	233	F 1
Prospect	80	D 3
Pushmataha	400	B 6
Putnam	289	B 6
Pyriton	100	G 4
Rabun	60	C 8
Ragland	1,166	F 3
Rainbow City	1,625	F 3
Rainsville	398	G 2
Ralph	300	C 4
Ramer	500	F 6
Ranburne	317	H 3
Randolph	200	E 5
Range	140	D 8
Reads Mill	100	G 3
Red Bay	1,954	B 2
Red Level	327	E 8
Reece City	470	F 2
Reform	1,241	C 4
Rehoboth	175	D 6
Rembert	200	C 6
Remlap	102	E 3
Renfroe	400	F 4
Repton	314	D 8
Republic	500	E 3
Richmond	100	D 6
Riderwood	250	B 6
River Falls	401	E 8
River View	1,171	H 5
Riverside	159	F 3
Roanoke	5,288	H 4
Roba	75	G 6
Robertsdale	1,474	C 9
Rock Mills	500	H 4
Rock Run	120	G 2
Rock Spring	350	G 3
Rockford	328	F 5
Rockwood	145	C 2
Rogersville	766	D 1
Rose Hill	60	F 8
Rosser	200	B 6
Round Mtn.	65	G 2
Russell	300	B 8
Russellville	6,628	C 2
Rutherford	100	H 6

Ruthven	100	E 7
Rutledge	276	F 7
Ryland	50	E 1
Saco		G 7
Safford	125	D 6
Saginaw	225	E 4
Saint Bernard	180	E 2
Saint Clair	125	E 6
Saint Clair Sprs.	125	F 3
Saint Elmo	520	B 10
Saint Florian	150	C 1
Saint Stephens	350	B 7
Salem	350	H 5
Salitpa	150	C 7
Samantha	163	C 4
Samson	1,932	F 8
Sandy	50	D 5
Sandy Ridge	325	E 6
Sanford	247	F 8
Saragossa	300	D 3
Saraland	4,595	B 9
Sardis	750	E 6
Satsuma	1,491	B 9
Sawyerville	125	C 5
Sayre	500	E 3
Sayreton	950	E 3
Scottsboro	6,449	F 1
Scranage	100	C 8
Scyrene	100	C 7
Seale	343	H 6
Searight	64	F 8
Searles		D 4
Section	595	G 1
Sellers	400	F 6
Selma	28,385	E 6
Seman	152	F 5
Seminole	250	D 10
Semmes	660	B 9
Shady Grove	125	F 7
Shannon	592	E 4
Shawmut	1,898	H 5
Sheffield	13,491	C 1
Shelby	650	E 4
Shiloh		C 6
Shorter	600	G 6
Shorterville	400	H 7
Shortleaf	125	C 6
Silas	353	B 7
Siluria	736	E 4
Silver Run	125	G 3
Silverhill	417	C 9
Simmsville	100	E 4
Sims Chapel	200	B 8
Sipsey	320	D 3
Skipperville	100	G 7
Slapout	150	F 5
Slocomb	1,368	G 8
Smiths	950	H 5
Smyer	25	B 7
Snead	150	F 2
Snow Hill	50	E 7
Snowdoun	375	F 6
Society Hill	200	G 6
Somerville	166	E 2
South	50	E 8
Southside	436	F 3
Speigner	160	F 5
Sprague	100	F 6
Spring Garden	85	G 3
Spring Valley	300	C 1
Springville	822	E 3
Sprott	100	D 5
Spruce Pine	495	C 2
Stafford	25	B 4
Standing Rock	425	H 4
Stanton	270	E 5
Stapleton	865	C 9
Steele	625	F 3
Sterrett	375	E 4
Stevenson	1,456	G 1
Stewart	200	C 5
Stewartsville	350	F 4
Stockton	950	C 9
Stroud	79	H 4
Suggsville	100	C 7
Sulligent	1,346	B 3
Sumiton	1,287	D 3
Summerdale	533	C 10
Summerfield	300	E 5
Summit	70	F 2
Sumter	300	D 4
Sumterville	100	B 5
Sunflower	100	B 8
Sunny South	200	C 7
Suspension	75	G 6
Suttle	256	D 5
Swaim	136	F 1
Sweet Water	400	C 6
Sycamore	750	F 4
Sylacauga	12,857	F 4
Sylvan Springs	245	*D 3
Sylvania	500	G 1
Taits Gap	300	F 3
Talladega	17,742	F 4
Talladega Sprs.	177	F 4
Tallahatta Sprs.	90	C 7
Tallassee	4,934	G 5

Tallaweka	609	*F 5
Tanner	600	E 1
Tarrant	7,810	E 3
Taylor	150	H 8
Tecumseh	41	H 2
Tennille	100	G 7
Tensaw	55	C 8
Theodore	950	B 9
Thomaston	857	C 6
Thomasville	3,182	C 7
Thompson	150	G 6
Thorsby	968	E 5
Three Notch	125	G 6
Tibbie	200	B 8
Tinela	65	D 7
Titus	100	F 5
Toney	300	E 1
Town Creek	810	D 1
Townley	660	D 3
Toxey	157	B 7
Trafford	529	E 3
Trenton	200	F 1
Triana	150	E 1
Trinity	454	D 1
Troy	10,234	G 7
Trussville	2,510	E 3
Tunnel Springs	150	D 7
Tuscaloosa	63,370	C 4
Tuscaloosa	†76,815	C 4
Tuscumbia	8,994	C 1
Tuskegee	1,750	G 6
Tuskegee Inst.	5,000	G 6
Tyler	250	E 6
Uchee	30	H 6
Uniform	150	B 8
Union	120	C 5
Union Grove	225	E 2
Union Springs	3,704	G 6
Uniontown	1,993	D 6
Uriah	711	D 8
Valhermoso Springs	200	E 2
Valley Head	424	G 1
Vance	125	D 4
Vandiver	500	F 4
Verbena	500	E 5
Vernon	1,492	B 3
Vestavia Hills	4,029	E 4
Vida	30	E 5
Vina	184	B 2
Vincent	1,402	F 4
Vinegar Bend	75	B 8
Vinemont	600	E 2
Vredenburgh	632	D 7
Wadley	605	G 4
Wadsworth	80	E 5
Wagarville		B 8
Walker Sprs.	200	C 7
Wallace	155	D 8
Walnut Grove	237	F 2
Ward	150	B 6
Warrior	2,448	E 3
Water Valley	50	B 7
Waterloo	215	B 1
Wattsville	500	F 3
Waugh	135	F 6
Waverly	250	G 5
Wayne	200	C 6
Weaver	1,401	G 3
Webb	331	H 8
Wedgeworth	300	C 5
Wedowee	917	H 4
Wegra	570	D 3
Wellington	175	G 3
Weogufka	257	F 4
West Blocton	1,156	D 4
West Greene	300	B 5
West Jefferson	272	*D 4
Westover	600	E 4
Wetumpka	3,672	F 5
Whatley	500	C 7
Wheeler	300	D 1
Whistler		B 9
White Hall	100	E 6
White Plains	350	G 3
Whitfield	500	B 6
Whitney	400	F 3
Wicksburg	400	G 8
Wilmer	300	B 9
Wilsonville	683	E 4
Wilton	428	E 4
Winfield	2,907	C 3
Wing	135	E 8
Winn	110	C 7
Womack Hill	306	B 7
Woodland	250	H 4
Woodstock	300	D 4
Woodville	196	F 1
Wren	100	D 2
Wright	125	C 1
Yantley	250	B 6
Yarbo	295	B 7
Yellow Bluff	75	C 7
Yellow Pine	215	B 8
Yolande		D 4
York	2,932	B 6
Youngblood	100	G 7

*No room on map for name. †Population of urban area.

'ALABAMA' CLAIMS. In spite of warnings by the American minister to England, Charles Francis Adams, the British-built steam cruiser *Alabama* was allowed to put to sea on July 29, 1862. Adams said the *Alabama* was intended as a warship for the Confederate government. He was right. For two years the *Alabama* destroyed Northern merchantmen, until it was finally sunk by the cruiser *Kearsarge* on June 19, 1864.

After long discussions the British government agreed to submit to arbitration the claims of the United States for damages arising out of the *Alabama* case. The five arbitrators met at Geneva, Switzerland, in December 1871. They decided that Great Britain had not exercised "due diligence" to prevent the departure of the *Alabama* and awarded the United States $15,500,000 damages. This ended a dispute which threatened to disturb the friendly relations between the two countries. It was also a victory for the principle of the peaceable settlement of international disputes by arbitration (*see* Arbitration).

ALABASTER. Two different mineral substances are called alabaster. The alabaster used by the ancient Greeks and Romans was actually marble, a granular aggregate of crystals of calcium carbonate (*see* Marble). Modern alabaster is a compact form of granular gypsum (*see* Gypsum).

Alabaster is white, pink, or yellow. It often has darker streaks, or bands, of color. The best quality is pure white and translucent. It is so soft that it can be scratched with a fingernail. This softness makes it good for carving.

Alabaster is used for statues, vases, and other ornaments. Florence, Italy, is the center of alabaster production. This mineral is found in England and France. There are small deposits of it in Nova Scotia and New York.

ALAMO. An old mission-fort, the Alamo, in San Antonio, has been called the "cradle of Texas liberty." Its gallant defense and the dreadful massacre of the more than 180 men who fought there inspired the cry, "Remember the Alamo!" Texas soldiers shouted this at the battle of San Jacinto, which brought independence to Texas. (*See also* Texas.)

The Alamo was originally the Mission San Antonio de Valero, founded in 1718 (*see* San Antonio). It ceased to function as a church institution in 1793. At the time of its famous siege the mission chapel was a roofless ruin, but a high rock wall about three feet thick enclosed an area around the chapel large enough to accommodate 1,000 men. Within that enclosure the battle of the Alamo was fought, with a last stand in the chapel.

The Siege of the Alamo

In 1835, during the battle for Texas independence from Mexico, San Antonio had been captured by the Texans. Only 144 soldiers, most of them volunteers, were left to guard the city. They were under the command of Lieut. Col. W. B. Travis. On Feb. 22, 1836, a Mexican force of almost 5,000 troops under Santa Anna arrived at San Antonio. Travis and Col. James Bowie, for whom the bowie knife was named, believed that the Alamo must be held to prevent Santa Anna's march into the interior. On February 23 they and their forces went into the fort, with about 30 refugees, and prepared to withstand attack by the Mexicans.

Santa Anna hoisted a flag of no quarter and demanded unconditional surrender. This was answered by a cannon shot from the fort. The Mexican bombardment began. Meanwhile, on February 22, the frontiersman David Crockett and some of his Tennessee riflemen had arrived to help in the defense. On March 1, 32 more brave volunteers were brought from Gonzales by James Butler Bonham.

The siege lasted 12 days. On the morning of March 6 several thousand Mexicans stormed the fort. As they attacked, a Mexican trumpeter sounded the *deguello*. This is the no-quarter bugle call of Spain. It was a signal to the soldiers to butcher all in the fort. Every Alamo defender died fighting. All the bodies were burned at Santa Anna's order. The only survivors were 16 women and children. About 1,600 Mexicans were killed.

The Alamo is now preserved by Texans as a state park. Located in front of the old fort is a monument to the heroes who died there.

SHRINE OF TEXAS LIBERTY
The Alamo, a famous fort which Texas heroes defended with their lives, is today owned by Texas and maintained by the Daughters of the Republic of Texas.

Mount McKinley, the highest peak in North America, is the crowning glory of Mount McKinley National Park. The park is in the central part of the Alaska Range.

ALASKA—
The 49th State

ALASKA. The Stars and Stripes have flown over Alaska since 1867. In that year Russia sold this vast land to the United States for $7,200,000. In 1912 Alaska was incorporated as a territory. This was the first step toward statehood.

In 1958 the United States Congress approved Alaska's admission to the Union as the 49th state. The news was flashed to the entire territory. The people celebrated with parades and parties. Alaska officially became a state Jan. 3, 1959, when President Dwight D. Eisenhower signed the statehood papers.

Alaska was the first new state to be added since 1912, when New Mexico and Arizona achieved statehood. Its admission required the adding of one more star to the 48 in the United States flag.

Alaska Means "Great Land"

The name Alaska comes from an Aleut word meaning "mainland" or "great land." The state is so large that it increased the area of the United States by a fifth. Texas, long the largest state, had to give up first place to Alaska, more than twice its size.

California lost the distinction of having the highest peak, Mount Whitney. Alaska's Mount McKinley is almost 6,000 feet higher—the tallest mountain in North America (*see* McKinley, Mount).

Population (1960): 226,167—rank, 50th state. Urban, 37.9%; rural, 62.1%. Persons per square mile, 0.40 —rank, 50th state.

Extent: Area, 586,400 square miles, including 15,335 square miles of water surface (1st state in size).

Elevation: Highest, Mount McKinley, 20,320 feet, highest point in North America; lowest, sea level; average, 1,900 feet.

Geographic Center: About 95 miles south of Tanana.

Temperature (° F.): Extremes—lowest, −76° (Tanana, 1886); highest, 100° (Fort Yukon, June 27, 1915). Averages at Barrow—January, −16.2°; July, 39.1°; annual, 9.6°. Averages at Fairbanks—January, −11.1°; July, 59.7°; annual, 25.8°. Averages at Juneau—January, 25.1°; July, 55.3°; annual, 40.1°.

Precipitation (inches): At Barrow—annual average, 4.26 (including 28.9 snowfall). At Fairbanks— annual average, 11.29 (including 63.9 snowfall). At Juneau—annual average, 54.62 (including 102.7 snowfall).

Land Use: Crops and pasture, 1%; forest, 32%; other, 67%.

For statistical information about Agriculture, Communication, Crime, Education, Employment, Finance, Fishing, Forests, Government, Manufacturing, Mining, Population Trends, Selective Service, Trade, Transportation, and Welfare, see ALASKA FACT SUMMARY.

224

The new state also took first place for scenic beauty. Mount McKinley is only one of its many towering snowcapped peaks. Glaciers cover hundreds of square miles. About one third of the entire area is forested. Big-game animals are abundant. Thousands of tourists visit Alaska every summer to hunt or fish or simply to enjoy its spectacular beauty.

In natural resources the immense state also takes high rank. However, it is still a frontier country, waiting to be developed. When the 1960 census was taken, Alaska had fewer people than any of the other states in the Union.

Alaska is of great importance to the defense of the United States. Army, Air Force, and Navy units are stationed there, and billions of dollars have been spent for Alaska defense installations. Radar warning stations situated around Alaska's perimeter are designed to prevent surprise attacks on North America from across the polar regions.

Size and Location

Alaska occupies a huge peninsula, from which hang two long extensions. To the southwest stretch the Alaska Peninsula and the Aleutian Islands chain. To the southeast is a 500-mile-long strip bordering on British Columbia. On its eastern side the Alaskan mainland is adjacent to Canada's Yukon Territory. Alaska's total area is about 586,400 square miles, including 15,335 square miles of lakes and rivers. Its coastline, 6,640 miles in length, is longer than the coastline of all the other states combined—including Hawaii.

Northward, Alaska extends the United States to Point Barrow on the Arctic Ocean. About one third of Alaska is within the Arctic Circle. Westward, the Aleutian Islands chain stretches across the Pacific Ocean into the Eastern Hemisphere. Attu, Alaska's westernmost island, is located at 173° east longitude. This is directly north of New Zealand. The distance from Attu, in the Aleutians, to Ketchikan, in the Panhandle, is greater than the distance from San Francisco, Calif., to New York City.

The tip of Seward Peninsula, on the Alaskan mainland, is a little over 50 miles across the Bering Strait from the Russian mainland. Through the Bering Strait runs the international date line. On one side is Little Diomede Island, a part of the United States. On the other side, less than 3 miles away, is Big Diomede Island, a part of Russia.

Natural Regions and Their Climates

From north to south, the four main natural regions of Alaska are: (1) the Arctic Slope; (2) the Rocky Mountain System; (3) the Interior Plateau, basin of the great Yukon River; and (4) the Pacific Mountain System. The fourth region includes three very different sections: south-central Alaska; the Panhandle; and the Alaska Peninsula and Aleutian Islands chain.

This map shows the four major natural regions and the surface features of Alaska. The use that can be made of the land is related to the physical features of each region.

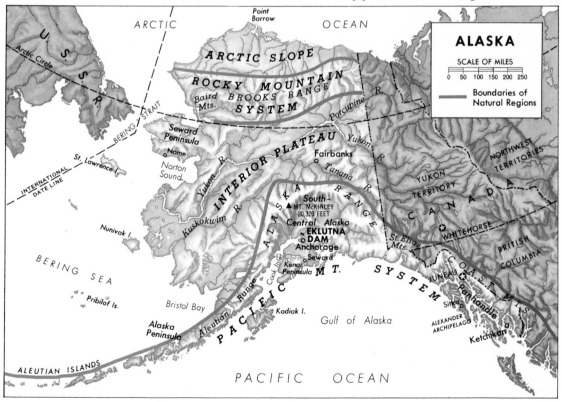

ANCHORAGE BEFORE AND AFTER THE 1964 EARTHQUAKE
In March 1964 a violent earthquake struck southern Alaska. Much of the downtown area of Anchorage, the state's largest city, was demolished. As can be seen from the photograph at the right, the damaged area was subsequently rebuilt.

The Arctic Slope covers about a sixth of Alaska. The climate is the true Arctic type, with light snow and little rain. The soil is tundra (*see* Soil). Continuous sunshine in summer brings up mosses and bright flowers, although the soil thaws only to a depth of one or two feet. At Point Barrow the sun remains above the horizon for 82 consecutive days.

The Rocky Mountain System separates the Arctic Slope from the Interior Plateau. The backbone of the system is the Brooks Range, 600 miles long, a wilderness of ice and snow. Some peaks rise above 8,000 feet. Only the southern foothills are forested. All of the Brooks Range is inside the Arctic Circle.

The Interior Plateau is a vast rolling upland, larger than Texas. Westward across it flows the great Yukon River with its tributaries and the shorter Kuskokwim (*see* Yukon River). On the Bering Sea these rivers have built up huge deltas. There are millions of acres of sub-Arctic forest interspersed with marshes, lakes, and ponds.

The climate in this region is the extreme continental type, with a wide range from summer to winter. Annual precipitation (rain and snow) is 8 to 15 inches. Summers are short, but daylight lasts up to 20 hours, and the temperature has risen as high as 100°F. During the summer the topsoil thaws, but the frozen subsoil causes water to remain on the surface.

The Pacific Mountain System curves around the entire south coast. The climate is the cool wet marine type, tempered by warm ocean currents and warm winds from the Asian mainland. Descriptions of the three sections of this region follow.

Southeastern Alaska—The Panhandle

Geographically, the Panhandle is the coastal section of northern British Columbia. The mainland strip is about 30 miles wide. The Coast Mountains rise sharply almost from the water's edge. Off the coast an outer range of mountains forms the islands of the Alexander Archipelago. The most beautiful approach to Alaska is by boat through the famous Inside Passage between these islands and the shore. The lower mountain slopes are covered with forests. The tops are capped with ice. Glaciers flowing down their sides have deepened the river valleys, forming mountain-walled fjords like those in Norway. Alaskans call these passageways "canals."

The Panhandle is one of the wettest regions in North America. Most of the rain falls from November to March. The heavy rainfall gives rise to great glaciers and to many streams, where Pacific salmon spawn. The largest forest growth of the state is the Tongass National Forest in the Panhandle.

Few peaks in the Coast Mountains are higher than 10,000 feet. To the north, where the coastline turns westward, rise the lofty St. Elias Mountains. Here vast glaciers fill the valleys. Malaspina Glacier, the largest, pours down from Mount St. Elias (18,008 ft.). The beautiful Muir Glacier, in Glacier Bay National Monument, also flows out of the St. Elias Mountains.

South-Central Alaska

South-central Alaska extends from the Panhandle to Cook Inlet. The spectacular Alaska Range, 150 miles wide, sweeps inland in a 400-mile arc, separating the coastal region from the Interior Plateau. The crown of this range is Mount McKinley. Many mountains in this region are more than 15,000 feet high.

Along the coast, west of the St. Elias Mountains, rise the Chugach Mountains. The Chugach National Forest covers their southern slopes. This range blends with the Kenai Mountains, backbone of the Kenai Peninsula, and is continued in the low mountains of Kodiak Island.

The Kenai Peninsula and Kodiak Island, like the Panhandle, have a mild climate and ample rainfall. The mainland climate is colder but drier, and valleys sheltered by mountain walls are suitable for farming.

The Alaska Peninsula and the Aleutians

The Aleutian Range is a continuation of the Alaska Range. It runs the entire length of the Alaska Peninsula (about 500 miles) and is continued by the Aleutian Islands, which are partially submerged peaks of the range. The mountains are of volcanic origin and include some of the world's largest volcanoes.

The climate is windy, wet, and foggy the year round. Scarcely a tree grows in this unfriendly country.

Big Game and Other Wildlife

Alaska offers sportsmen the finest hunting and fishing in the United States. Nowhere else are there so many bears. The most prized trophy of hunters is the Alaska brown bear, found mainly on Kodiak Island. It is the largest of all carnivorous land mammals, weighing up to 1,600 pounds. Other species are the closely related grizzly bear, the black bear, and an occasional polar bear.

Herds of caribou range over the Arctic and central plateau. Among them are sometimes found reindeer, which were introduced into Alaska as domestic animals. Other big-game animals include the moose, the Sitka black-tailed deer, the Dall mountain sheep, and the Alaska mountain goat. Elk and bison have been successfully introduced.

Millions of waterfowl summer on Alaska's rocky islands. Birds of prey include bald and golden eagles, owls, hawks, and falcons. The ptarmigan (white grouse), seen in flocks of several hundred, is Alaska's state bird. Fur seals breed on the Pribilof Islands (see Seal). Sea otter, now carefully protected, are increasing in number.

FIRST STEP IN MODERN PLACER MINING
Before giant dredges scoop up the gold-bearing gravel, this hydraulic hose washes off the overburden of frozen muck. This mine is near Fairbanks.

People and Population

Alaska is so thinly populated that there are about $2\frac{1}{2}$ square miles for each person. Since World War II, however, the population has been growing rapidly. In 1940 it was 72,524; in 1950, 128,643. By 1960 the population had risen to 226,167—an increase of 75.8 percent, or about four times the overall growth rate of the United States.

There are some 40,000 Eskimos, Indians, and Aleuts. Most of them like to be called natives. About 8,000 Alaskans are foreign born. Of the total foreign stock, the largest groups had their origins in Canada, Germany, Norway, Great Britain, Asian nations, and Sweden.

Eskimos are the most numerous of the nonwhite Alaskans. They live along the coast of the Arctic Ocean and Bering Sea and in the great deltas formed by the Yukon and Kuskokwim rivers. They are good fishermen and fur trappers but also gain some support from large herds of reindeer. Hides and meat are sold through cooperative stores that are owned and managed by the Eskimos themselves under government supervision. The Eskimos are friendly and intelligent. They welcome government schools and nurses and take quickly to radios and outboard motors. Many are employed in government construction work and in mining. (See also Eskimos.)

Indians rank second in number among nonwhites. About half of them are Tlingit, living on islands and coasts of the Panhandle. Most of them have their

227

DAIRYING AND FISHING IN ALASKA

This modern dairy farm (left) is in the Tanana River valley, near Fairbanks. The king crabs (right) were taken near Kodiak Island. Fishing is Alaska's biggest industry. Salmon is most important. The crab catch is more than 125 million pounds a year.

own fishing boats. Others work in canneries during the summer and trap and hunt in the fall and winter. Some still carry on the traditions of their people by carving and woodworking. They are famous for their tall, brightly painted totem poles carved with birds, animals, fish, and human figures. They also weave the famous Chilkat blankets, made of cedar bark and mountain-goat wool. (*See also* Indians, American, section "Fishermen of the Northwest.")

The Haida and Tsimshian Indians came to the Panhandle from British Columbia. The Haida are related to the Tlingit. They too carve totems; but they are noted also for their fine slate carvings and delicate articles made of wood, bone, and shell. The Tsimshian were brought to Annette Island by a missionary. Most of them live there in the model village of Metlakatla, which is run partly on a cooperative basis. They own their own fishing boats and operate a salmon cannery.

The Athapaskan Indians live in thinly scattered villages in the interior and in south-central Alaska. Most of them are hunters and trappers.

Aleuts are closely related to the Eskimos but have their own language and customs. They live on the foggy Aleutian and Pribilof islands, the Alaska Peninsula, and Kodiak Island. The early Russian fur traders "civilized" and enslaved the Aleuts and almost wiped them out. Today they number only a few thousand. They still attend services at old Russian-built churches with onion-shaped domes. They are able seamen and fishermen.

Alaska's Four Major Cities

About 38 percent of the Alaskans live in towns and cities. The larger towns are as modern as those in the other states. The chief difference is that they are widely separated and surrounded by sparsely populated areas. Some can be reached only by ship, riverboat, or airplane.

Anchorage is by far the largest city and also the fastest growing. It is situated in south-central

Alaska at the head of Cook Inlet on a bluff overlooking Knik Arm. It was founded in 1914 as a construction camp for the Alaska Railroad. It is now the railroad's headquarters. Highways as well as the railroad link it with ports on the Kenai Peninsula and with the interior. It is also Alaska's chief center for air transportation.

As headquarters for the northern defense, Anchorage has grown rapidly since 1946. Its population in 1960 was 44,237 (with suburbs, more than 80,000), a gain of about 300 percent over 1950. In 1964 much of Anchorage's downtown section was demolished by an earthquake which struck southern Alaska. (*See also* Anchorage.)

Fairbanks is Alaska's second largest city. It is situated on the broad Interior Plateau on the Tanana River, the chief tributary of the Yukon. It began as a mining camp in 1902, and it is still a center for gold-mining operations. Its chief importance, however, is as the transportation hub for the remote hamlets on the plateau and in the Arctic region. It is the terminus of the Alaska Railroad, the Alaska Highway, and the Steese Highway. It is also an important aviation center. Near it are two large United States Air Force bases. At College, four miles away, is the University of Alaska. (*See also* Fairbanks, Alaska.)

Juneau, the capital, is near the northern end of the Panhandle. It is one of many picturesque towns there, hacked out of the mountainsides. Its history goes back to 1880, when gold was discovered nearby. The famous Alaska-Juneau gold mine is now inactive and the chief industries, apart from government, are fishing and lumbering. (*See also* Juneau.)

Ketchikan, at the southern end of the Panhandle, is the first port of call in Alaska for northbound ships. It has the largest pulp mill in the state and is also the chief salmon-canning center.

Alaska Is Rich in Fish and Furs

Salmon is still by far Alaska's leading product, although the catch has been declining because of over-fishing. Sockeye and pink salmon rank first in number, but dog, silver, and king salmon are also taken (*see* Salmon). About 90 percent of the catch is processed in about 80 canneries. The rest is sold fresh, frozen, or cured. Other commercial catches are shellfish (crabs, shrimps, and clams), halibut, and herring.

The most valuable furs come from the Pribilof Islands fur seal herd, which is managed by the federal government. The Alaska statehood bill provided that the state should receive from the federal government 70 percent of the profits from sales of both sealskin and sea otter skin. (*See also* Seal; Otter.)

Mink is the most valuable fur taken by trappers. Also important are beaver, marten, lynx, land otter, and muskrat. Fur farming in Alaska, mostly mink and fox, is also an important industry.

Mining and Mineral Resources

Alaska is known to have large reserves of gold, nickel, tin, lead, zinc, copper, and molybdenum. However, because of transportation difficulties, the development of its mineral resources has been slow. The minerals that reach outside markets are chiefly those of high value and low volume, such as gold, platinum, chrome, mercury, and silver.

The chief minerals produced are petroleum, sand and gravel, coal, gold, and natural gas. Together they make up more than four fifths of Alaska's mineral production. Deposits of subbituminous coal are widespread, but mining has been limited to two areas close to the Alaska Railroad.

Commercial petroleum operations began with the discovery of oil on the Kenai Peninsula in 1957. By the late 1960's there were 7 oil fields and 11 gas fields in south-central Alaska, and production totaled more than 100,000 barrels a day. Other fields were located in and near a Navy petroleum reserve on the Alaskan mainland above the Arctic Circle.

Forests and Forest Products

Alaska's forests are capable of supplying a sustained production of several billion board feet of timber annually. In the interior are extensive stands of white spruce, Alaska birch, cottonwood, black spruce, aspen, and larch. These forests occupy about 32 percent of the land of Alaska. They have been little worked because of transportation difficulties. The usable forests are along the south coast and in the Panhandle, where deep inlets make the timber readily accessible. Here the principal trees are Western hemlock and Sitka spruce, intermixed with some western red cedar and Alaska cedar.

Most of the commercial timber is purchased from Tongass National Forest, which covers more than half of southeastern Alaska, and Chugach National Forest, on the south coast. Logs are manufactured into pulp at a plant at Ketchikan; into plywood at Juneau; and into lumber at a number of sawmills. A second large pulp mill, which supplies great quantities of cellulose to paper and rayon manufacturers in Japan, is in operation about five miles from Sitka.

Farming in Alaska

Alaska imports from the other states about 90 percent of its food. Very little of its vast area is suitable for farming. Good land is usually covered with trees and is difficult and expensive to clear. Farm machinery and fertilizer are also expensive, because they must be imported. The growing season (the time between killing frosts) is short, but plants grow rapidly because of the long summer daylight.

Farmland is being steadily added but totals only about 2 million acres. The best farmlands are in the Matanuska Valley, 50 miles northeast of Anchorage; in the Tanana River valley, near Fairbanks; in the lowlands of the Kenai Peninsula; and in the limited flatland of the Panhandle. The Matanuska district is by far the largest and the most prosperous.

The most profitable crops are perishable products. Garden vegetables, milk, and eggs command a good price in Alaska markets because of their freshness. Long hours of daylight produce potatoes, carrots, and cabbages of enormous size. Potatoes are a standard crop. Almost all kinds of berries can be raised. Dairying is one of the principal farm activities. Oats and legumes take the place of corn for silage and are also used for hay.

Hydroelectric Resources

Alaska's waterpower resources are known to be enormous. They have not yet been fully surveyed, but more than 200 possible sites have been located that could be used for providing electric energy. Most of them are in the Panhandle. Only small projects have so far been developed. The largest, Eklutna, is 34 miles northeast of Anchorage.

Recreation—For Tourists and Alaskans

Thousands of tourists visit Alaska every summer. Most of them come by air, but an increasing number

ON THE "WHITE ALICE" NETWORK
Huge antennas like this relay telephone and telegraph messages. The checkerboard pattern (red and white) is a warning to fliers.

A PUBLIC SCHOOL IN THE INTERIOR
The boy in the front seat is an Athapaskan Indian. This school is located at Nenana, near Fairbanks.

travel by car or bus over the scenic Alaska Highway (*see* Alaska Highway). This highway is linked with Alaska's main tourist attraction, Mount McKinley National Park, in the spectacular Alaska Range. Within the vast park is Muldrow Glacier, more than 50 miles long, fed by snow from Mount McKinley and other peaks. The park is also one of the great wildlife sanctuaries of the nation. Hunting is not allowed here, but fishing and camping are permitted.

Glacier Bay National Monument, 100 miles northwest of Juneau, is famous for its vast ice fields and fjordlike bays. Totem poles are the principal attractions of Sitka National Monument, in the Panhandle. Katmai National Monument, on the Alaska Peninsula, is noted for its volcanoes. (*See also* National Parks, United States.)

Communication and Transportation

Regular telephone communication is now available between Alaska and the other states. Submarine telephone cables from Port Angeles, Wash., to Skagway, at the northern end of the Panhandle, were completed in 1957. An overland system links Skagway to central Alaska. Radiotelephone makes it possible to place calls to many remote towns and villages.

About four families out of five have television. Network programs on tape or film are flown in and shown by Alaska stations.

South-central Alaska is linked with the interior by the Alaska Railroad and by a network of paved roads that connect with the Alaska Highway. The only town in the Panhandle that has access by motor road to the Alaska Highway is Haines, at the northern end of the Panhandle. The Haines Highway runs through Canada.

The backbone of transportation is the airplane. Established routes connect all cities and towns, and many small villages receive mail and freight by airplane only. In addition to scheduled flights, there

are the daring "bush pilots" who own their own planes and will fly anywhere anytime.

State and Local Government

In preparation for statehood, an Alaska convention drafted a constitution, which was ratified by the voters in 1956. It was praised as a model constitution and approved by Congress in the statehood bill.

The voting age is 19. The governor has great power. He appoints the heads of all important departments and the judges. The constitution provides for 24 election districts, based on population. The governor is required to reapportion the districts after each United States census. The people may propose and enact laws by initiative and approve or reject acts of the legislature by referendum. Elected officials are subject to recall by the voters.

Local government is vested in boroughs and cities. A borough is governed by an assembly and a city by a council. The city is represented on the borough assembly by one or more of its council members. The area of a borough is not based solely on population but on common interests, such as its industries.

Conservation of Natural Resources

The United States owned 99 percent of the land in the Territory of Alaska. The statehood act provided for deeding to the state, within 25 years, up to 102,500,000 acres—more than a quarter of Alaska's total area. Alaska may select the lands to take over. The state also gained permission to select from lands within the great national forests up to 400,000 acres. Lands taken over by the state may be sold to individuals or corporations for farms, homesites, or factory sites. Ownership does not include mineral rights. The state reserves the authority to lease such rights. Producing oil wells must pay royalties to the state.

AIR DISTANCES FROM FAIRBANKS
Alaska's strategic location makes it important to the United States both for defensive and offensive operations.

The statehood act also provides that fisheries and wildlife resources should continue to be managed by the federal government until the secretary of the interior decides that Alaska has made adequate provision for the conservation of these resources.

The Alaska constitution provides that all replenishable resources belonging to the state—fish, wildlife, forests, and grasslands—shall be utilized on the "sustained yield" principle.

Public Schools and Universities

Alaska's constitution provides that public schools shall be open to all the children of the state. Schools maintained by the Bureau of Indian Affairs for Indians, Aleuts, and Eskimos are gradually being transferred to the state's public school system.

Alaska has two universities. The University of Alaska, a land-grant college which opened in 1922, is at College, near Fairbanks. It maintains community colleges in Anchorage, Juneau, Kenai, Ketchikan, Palmer, and Sitka. It trains teachers, engineers, and specialists in agriculture, mining, wildlife management, and geophysics. The Geophysical Institute has facilities for studying the Arctic, the sub-Arctic, and all aspects of earth physics. Alaska Methodist University, the state's first private, four-year institution, opened in Anchorage in 1960.

A Bulwark of American Defense

The shortest routes between many of the world's great centers lie across the Arctic region. Many North American defense installations are therefore concentrated in the Far North. Anchorage is the headquarters for the defense of the area. The statehood act provides that in an emergency about 260,500 square miles of state land in northern and western Alaska, including the entire Aleutian Islands chain, will be withdrawn from the state and placed under federal control.

At Anchorage the federal government constructed Elmendorf Air Force Base, one of the world's largest airfields, and Fort Richardson, the Army's headquarters. Near Fairbanks are Eielson Air Force Base and Fort Wainwright, an Army installation. The Arctic Indoctrination Center at Big Delta, near Fairbanks, provides instruction in winter ground operations and tests equipment for Arctic use.

DEW (Distant Early Warning) radar sites have been set up in the Arctic wastes to alert the Air Force against attack. The federal government has also installed the "White Alice" long-distance radiophone and telegraph communications network. To supply fuel for aircraft and motor vehicles in Fairbanks, a 620-mile pipeline was laid to Haines, located in the Panhandle.

HISTORY OF ALASKA

Alaska was once a Russian possession. Russia sold it to the United States in 1867 by a treaty negotiated by Secretary of State William H. Seward during the Administration of President Andrew Johnson. The

STATEHOOD CELEBRATION IN FAIRBANKS
Alaskans celebrated their statehood on June 30, 1958. These youngsters climbed on a fire wagon to join the parade.

following sections trace the growth and development of Alaska from the period of exploration to statehood.

Discovery and Russian Occupation

In 1725 Peter the Great, czar of Russia, ordered Capt. Vitus Bering, a Dane in the service of the Russian navy, to explore the land east of Siberia. On his second trip, in 1741, Bering visited the Alaskan mainland and established Russia's claim to the region. He died on the return voyage, but part of his crew made their way back to Russia (see Bering Sea). Their tales of wealth in furs sent trappers and traders to the new lands.

Russian fur traders set up their first outpost on Kodiak Island in 1784. The natives were cheated, abused, and massacred. Fur-bearing animals of sea and land were wantonly slaughtered. The sea otter was almost exterminated. Some of the abuses were reduced when, in 1799, the czar chartered the Russian-American Company. The director for 19 years was Alexander Baranov, who ruled Russian America like an emperor. In 1804 Baranov moved the capital of the company from Kodiak to a new settlement at Sitka, which the Russians called New Archangel, and made it the most brilliant "court" in America. Alaska's many Russian churches with their onion-shaped domes date from this period.

"Seward's Folly"—The Alaska Purchase

Russia tried to sell its American possession to the United States as early as 1855. United States and British competition had made the Russian-American Company unprofitable, and Russian involvement in the Crimean War left the Alaskan colony vulnerable (see Crimean War). The sale was finally made in 1867 at the insistence of Seward. The price paid was $7,200,000. Charles Sumner supported the measure in the Senate and suggested that the new possession should be named Alaska. The date of the actual transfer of ownership was October 18, Alaska Day.

The American people called Alaska "Seward's folly" and "Seward's icebox." The Army, the Treasury Department, and the Navy in turn took charge. No civil government was provided until in 1884 Alaska became a "district" governed by the laws of the state of Oregon.

The discovery of gold in the Klondike region of Canada in 1896 brought armies of prospectors because the most accessible route was through southeastern Alaska (*see* Klondike; Alaska Boundary Dispute). Before the Klondike strike subsided, a fresh rush began at Nome, on the Seward Peninsula. Again, in 1902, there was a scramble to stake claims in the Fairbanks region. It was a violent, colorful era.

Under Territorial Government

The Organic Act of 1912, signed by President William Howard Taft on August 24, made Alaska an incorporated territory. In 1942, during World War II, Japanese forces occupied and fortified Kiska and Attu islands in the Aleutian chain. In the summer of 1943 United States forces, aided by Canadian troops, recaptured the islands. To ensure Alaska's safety, the United States rushed construction of the Alaska Highway (*see* Alaska Highway). At the same time a huge military construction program was begun. This was continued after the war, bringing about a boom in Alaska's economy and a rapid increase in population.

Steps to Statehood

For more than 40 years the people of Alaska fought for statehood. Finally they had a constitution drafted by a convention of 55 delegates in a meeting held at the University of Alaska, Nov. 8, 1955, to Feb. 6, 1956. In April the voters ratified it, 17,447 to 7,180. At the same time they approved the Tennessee Plan, by which they elected in October two "senators" and one "representative" to plead their cause in the federal Congress.

On June 30, 1958, the United States Senate voted 64 to 20 its approval of the statehood bill passed by the House of Representatives. President Eisenhower signed the statehood proclamation on Jan. 3, 1959 (*see* Statehood), and Alaska became officially the 49th state.

Earthquake!

On March 27, 1964, the most intense earthquake ever recorded on North America struck southern Alaska. More than 100 lives were lost, and damage reached an estimated 500 million dollars. Much of Anchorage's business district was leveled; some of its suburbs, especially Turnagain, suffered heavy damage. Kodiak, Chenega, Seward, Valdez, and surrounding areas were also hard hit. (*See also* United States, section "Alaska"; and individual entries in the Fact-Index on Alaska persons, places, products, and events.)

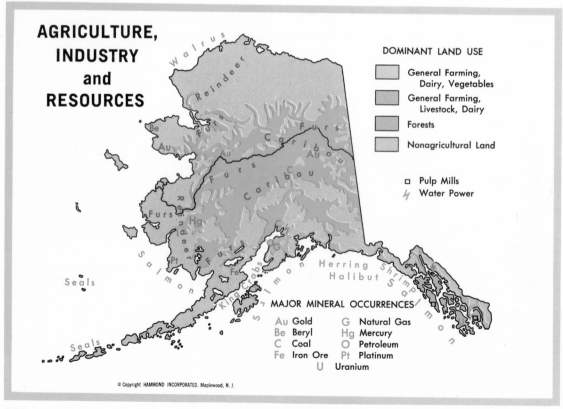

AGRICULTURE, INDUSTRY and RESOURCES

DOMINANT LAND USE

General Farming, Dairy, Vegetables

General Farming, Livestock, Dairy

Forests

Nonagricultural Land

☐ Pulp Mills

⚡ Water Power

MAJOR MINERAL OCCURRENCES

Au	Gold	G	Natural Gas
Be	Beryl	Hg	Mercury
C	Coal	O	Petroleum
Fe	Iron Ore	Pt	Platinum
		U	Uranium

© Copyright HAMMOND INCORPORATED, Maplewood, N.J.

Notable Events in Alaska History

1728—Vitus Bering proves Asia and North America are separate. His lieutenant, Aleksei Chirikov, sights Prince of Wales Island, and Bering, St. Elias Mountains, in 1741.

1774–92—Spanish expeditions explore southeast coast.

1778—British Capt. James Cook surveys Alaskan coast.

1784—Russians make first settlement at Three Saints Bay on Kodiak Island; moved to present site of Kodiak in 1792.

1791—Capt. George Vancouver, British navigator, charts southeast corner of Alaska.

1799—Russian-American Company chartered by Russia for trade; director, Alexander Baranov. Sitka founded; becomes company capital in 1804.

1823—Father Ivan Veniaminov, Russian missionary, begins work among the Aleuts.

1824–25—Limit of Russian colony set at 54° 40' in negotiations with U. S. and Great Britain.

1867—Secretary of State William H. Seward purchases Alaska from Russia for U. S. for $7,200,000.

1878—First commercial Salmon cannery built at Klawock.

1884—District of Alaska created; capital, Sitka; governor, John H. Kinkead.

1891—Rev. Sheldon Jackson, Presbyterian missionary, introduces reindeer into Alaska to aid Eskimos.

1896—Gold discovered in Klondike Basin of Canadian Yukon; at Nome, in 1899; at Fairbanks in 1902.

1900—White Pass and Yukon Route completed, Skagway to Whitehorse, Y. T. Alaska's civil government reformed by U. S. Congress; capital moved to Juneau; government offices transferred in 1906.

1903—Boundary between Panhandle and Canada settled.

1906—Alaska allowed an elected delegate to Congress.

1911—U. S. joins international agreement to regulate seal hunting on Pribilof and other islands.

1912—Territory of Alaska created; capital, Juneau. Katmai volcano erupts.

1916—First statehood bill introduced in Congress.

1917—Mount McKinley National Park established. University of Alaska founded at College; opens in 1922.

1920—Four U. S. Army planes make round trip between New York and Nome.

1923—Naval Petroleum Reserve No. 4 established. Alaska Railroad completed, Seward to Fairbanks.

1924—Lieut. Carl Ben Eielson flies first airmail.

1931—Federal Building, territorial capitol, completed at Juneau; designated State Capitol in 1959.

1935—Families from Middle West resettle in agricultural community in Matanuska Valley.

1942—Japan attacks Dutch Harbor; occupies Attu and Kiska.

1942–43—U. S. constructs Alaska Highway; turns over Canadian section to Canada in 1946.

1943—U. S. recaptures Aleutians from Japan.

1946—Alaskans approve statehood in referendum.

1954—First pulp mill in Alaska completed at Ketchikan.

1955—Eklutna power project operates near Palmer; military fuel pipeline opened, Haines to Fairbanks.

1956—Alaskans adopt state constitution.

1957—Oil discovered on Kenai Peninsula; first oil refinery opens in 1963.

1959—Alaska becomes 49th state, January 3.

1963—Auto ferry system between Prince Rupert, B. C., and Haines and Skagway begins operation.

1964—Alaska devastated by earthquake.

1967—Record floods damage Fairbanks and Nenana. Palmer Seismological Observatory dedicated.

1728

1799

1878

1942–43

STATE FLOWER:
Forget-me-not

STATE TREE:
Sitka Spruce

STATE BIRD:
Willow Ptarmigan

**STATE SEAL: Revised territorial seal
adopted in constitution; shows
natural features and industries.**

Alaska Profile

FLAG: *See* **Flags of the United States.**
MOTTO: None official.
**SONG: 'Alaska's Flag'—words,
Marie Drake; music,
Elinor Dusenbury.**

Alaska is the last United States frontier. The largest of the states in size, this vast, raw, and rugged land is the smallest in population. Twice as big as Texas, it thrusts a chain of volcanic islands more than a thousand miles into the Bering Sea. It juts northward far into the Arctic Circle, and to the south its Panhandle extends about 500 miles between the Pacific Ocean and the Canadian Rockies. Alaska is a land of spectacular contrasts—smoking volcanoes and frozen tundra, hot springs and ice floes, creeping glaciers and virgin forests.

Nearly everything about this 49th state is big. Its Mount McKinley is higher than any other peak in North America. Its Yukon River is one of the longest navigable waterways in the world. Big animals still thrive here—Kodiak, grizzly, and polar bears; moose, caribou, musk-oxen, wolves; otter, walrus, seals.

After its purchase by the United States from Russia in 1867, Alaska remained a remote and lonely fur-trading territory until, late in the 19th century, gold was discovered. The chaotic, primitive life of the gold-rush era is gone. Present-day Alaskans are engaged in a variety of pursuits, including lumbering, commercial fishing and trapping, cattle raising and truck farming, and oil production.

Alaska's Eskimos find it hard to adjust to modern conditions; extinction threatens some wildlife species; and the cost of living is high, since many foods and manufactured goods must be imported. Alaska's unused water resources may provide a solution to the last of these problems. New dams are being planned to generate the power required to attract new industries. In the years ahead, Alaska will have to devise ways of conserving its natural and human resources while utilizing them to meet the needs of an advancing economy.

Columns of Alaskan marble dominate the entrance of Alaska's State Capitol, in Juneau. Completed in 1931 to house federal offices, the building became the Capitol when Alaska attained statehood in 1959. It is the meeting place of the state legislature and houses the governor's offices.

Juneau, the capital since 1900, lies on the Gastineau Channel in southeastern Alaska. It was settled in 1881 by gold miners and named for Joe Juneau, who made Alaska's first major gold discovery here in 1880. Its industrial plants include salmon canneries and lumber mills.

Opened in 1922 as a land-grant college, the University of Alaska achieved its present status in 1935. Its central campus is in College, five miles from Fairbanks. With branches in other cities, the university provides public higher education for the entire state.

The fishing fleet of Kodiak Island brings in an annual catch of halibut, salmon, and shellfish worth millions of dollars. On Kodiak Island are fish canneries, livestock ranches, dairy farms, and Army and Navy bases. The island is also the home of the Kodiak bear.

An offshore oil rig at Cook Inlet, near Anchorage, is evidence of Alaska's developing
petroleum industry. Oil was discovered in
Alaska in 1853 and was produced commercially from 1902 to 1933. Since the 1950's
oil has become one of Alaska's most important products. For industrial statistics,
see ALASKA FACT SUMMARY.

Eskimos in native dress entertain a crowd.
Alaska's 22,000 Eskimos comprise its largest native group. There are also more than
14,000 Indians and over 5,000 Aleuts.

Mendenhall Glacier, north of Juneau, is 17
miles long and 2 to 3 miles wide. A recreation area maintained here by the United
States Forest Service includes trails and
campsites.

236

In the Matanuska Valley, northeast of Anchorage, two thirds of Alaska's farm produce is grown. Other farming areas are the Tanana River valley and the lowlands of the Kenai Peninsula and the Panhandle.

Fairbanks, Alaska's second largest city, is a gold mining, farming, and transportation center. It is the northern terminus of the Alaska Highway and the Alaska Railroad.

Craters, lakes, and the Alaska brown bear are features of Katmai National Monument, one of Alaska's four national park areas. The others are the Glacier Bay and Sitka National monuments and Mount McKinley National Park.

The old Russian Orthodox church at Kenai was built in the early 19th century, when Russian traders dominated Alaska. Russia established Alaska's first white settlement in 1784 on Kodiak Island.

Through the Inside Passage between Prince Rupert, B. C., and Skagway, a modern ferryboat carries motorists and other travelers along the Alaska Marine Highway. Another ferry route lies between the Kenai Peninsula and Kodiak Island.

ALASKA
PROFILE

*some famous people**

E. L. (BOB) BARTLETT
Chase Ltd.

ALEXANDER BARANOV

ERNEST GRUENING

JOHN MUIR

ANTHONY J. DIMOND

SHELDON JACKSON

BERNARD R. HUBBARD

*Only a few of Alaska's famous people
are shown here. The persons depicted
are generally associated with the state,
though not all of them were born there.
For biographical information, *see* entries
in the Fact-Index.

238

ALASKA FACT SUMMARY

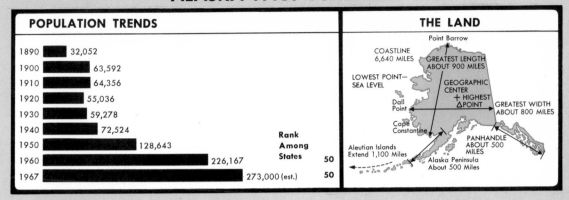

POPULATION TRENDS

Year	Population	Rank Among States
1890	32,052	
1900	63,592	
1910	64,356	
1920	55,036	
1930	59,278	
1940	72,524	
1950	128,643	
1960	226,167	50
1967	273,000 (est.)	50

THE LAND

Point Barrow

COASTLINE 6,640 MILES

GREATEST LENGTH ABOUT 900 MILES

LOWEST POINT— SEA LEVEL

GEOGRAPHIC CENTER + HIGHEST △POINT

GREATEST WIDTH ABOUT 800 MILES

Dall Point

Cape Constantine

Aleutian Islands Extend 1,100 Miles

PANHANDLE ABOUT 500 MILES

Alaska Peninsula About 500 Miles

GOVERNMENT

Capital: Juneau (designated, 1900).

Statehood: Became 49th state in the Union on Jan. 3, 1959.

Constitution: Adopted 1956. Amendment may be passed by two-thirds majority of each house; ratified by majority voting on it in an election.

Representation in U. S. Congress: Senate—2. House of Representatives—1. Electoral votes—3.

Legislature: Senators—20; term, 4 years. Representatives—40; term, 2 years.

Convenes 4th Monday in January annually. Session limit —none. Special session limit—30 calendar days.

Executive Officers

Governor—term, 4 years. May serve two successive terms; then eligible after one term has intervened.

Other officers—secretary of state, elected; term, 4 years. Attorney general, appointed by governor with approval of joint session of Legislature; term, unspecified.

Judiciary: Supreme Court—3 justices; governor appoints; voters approve after 3 years; reelected every 10 years; term, 10 years. Superior Court—9 judges; governor appoints; voters approve after 3 years; reelected every 6 years; term, 6 years.

County: No counties; state divided into boroughs. Assemblies govern organized boroughs.

Municipal: Mayor-council plan usual form. Anchorage has council-manager plan.

Voting Qualifications: Age—19. Residence in state—1 year; in district—30 days. Literacy test—must be able to read and write any article of the U. S. Constitution or furnish proof of 8th grade education.

Voting Days: General election—1st Tuesday after 1st Monday in November. Primary election—1st Tuesday after 2d Monday in August in even years. Preferential presidential primary—none.

EDUCATION

Private Elementary and Secondary Day Schools

Enrollment—elementary, 1,700; secondary, 800.

Classroom teachers—elementary, 80; secondary, 100.

Public Elementary and Secondary Schools*

Operating school districts—27.

Instruction rooms available and in use—2,697.

Compulsory school age—7 to 16.

Enrollment—elementary, 58,600; secondary, 18,400.

Average daily attendance—51,084.

High school graduates—2,750.

Administrative officials

Commissioner of education; appointed by governor from list submitted by Board of Education; approved by both houses; term, 5 years.

Boards of school districts, 3 to 7 members; elected; term, 3 years.

Instructional staff—total, 3,350; principals and supervisors, 151; elementary teachers, 1,886 (428 men, 1,458 women); secondary teachers, 1,184 (638 men, 546 women).

Revenue receipts—$66,500,000.

Source of receipts (% of total)—federal, 29.5; state, 40.3; local, 30.2.

Nonrevenue receipts†—$17,000,000.

State expenditure on education—$877 per pupil.

Head Start programs—participants, 3,303; funds allocated, $1,406,000.

Bureau of Indian Affairs, U. S. Department of Interior—schools operated by this agency for Indians, Aleuts, and Eskimos are being transferred to the public school system.

Universities and Colleges‡

Number of institutions—total (includes junior colleges), 3; public, 1; private, 2; junior colleges, 1.

Degree-credit enrollment—5,836.

Earned degrees conferred—bachelor's and first professional, 212; master's except first professional, 44; doctor's, 3.

Special Institutions: Mission schools teach about 600 Indian, Aleut, and Eskimo children.

Libraries: City and town public libraries—41. Alaska State Library aids in developing public libraries.

Outstanding Museums: Alaska State Museum, Juneau; Sheldon Jackson Museum, Sitka; University of Alaska Museum, College; Aviation Museum, Anchorage.

CORRECTIONAL AND PENAL INSTITUTIONS

State

Adult—Ketchikan State Jail; Adult Conservation Camp, Palmer.

Adult-juvenile—Anchorage State Jail; Fairbanks State Jail; Juneau State Jail; Ketchikan State Detention Home; Nome State Jail.

Juvenile—Youth Conservation Camp and School, Wasilla.

Federal

None.

All Fact Summary data are based on current government reports.
*Kindergartens are included in the elementary schools; junior high schools, in the secondary schools.
†Money received from loans, sales of bonds, sales of property, and insurance adjustments.
‡Excludes data for service academies

238a

ALASKA FACT SUMMARY

PRODUCTION—YEARLY VALUE: $220,400,000

The chart at left shows the state's major product categories and each category's percentage of the total value.

The charts below list the leading items in each of three important product groups and indicate their dollar values.

Manufacturing* 38%   Mining 30%   Fishing 25%   Fur less than 1%
Forests 4%   Agriculture† 2%

FARM PRODUCTS

Value of Production (thousands of dollars)

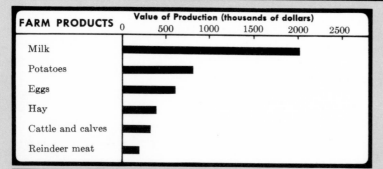

- Milk
- Potatoes
- Eggs
- Hay
- Cattle and calves
- Reindeer meat

MANUFACTURED PRODUCTS

Value Added by Manufacture*

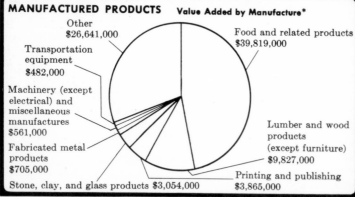

Other $26,641,000

Transportation equipment $482,000

Machinery (except electrical) and miscellaneous manufactures $561,000

Fabricated metal products $705,000

Stone, clay, and glass products $3,054,000

Food and related products $39,819,000

Lumber and wood products (except furniture) $9,827,000

Printing and publishing $3,865,000

MINERALS

Value of Production (millions of dollars)

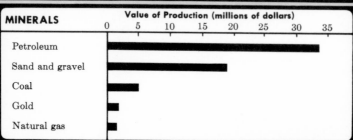

- Petroleum
- Sand and gravel
- Coal
- Gold
- Natural gas

AGRICULTURE

Farms and Farm Income
  Total farms—(estimated less than 500).
  Land in farms—1,959,000 acres.
  Average size of farm—5,129 acres.
  Cash income from crops—$1,228,000.
  Cash income from livestock and products—$3,315,000.
  Government payments—$98,000.
  Realized net income per farm—$2,324.

Principal Crops (amounts produced and acres harvested): Hay—14,000 tons, 9,000 acres; potatoes—138,000 cwt., 1,000 acres; silage—23,000 tons, 4,000 acres; truck crops—600 tons, 105 acres.

Livestock on Farms
  Cattle (all)—8,000.
  Chickens—51,000.
  Hogs and pigs—1,000.
  Sheep and lambs—24,000.

FORESTS

Total Acreage: 118,487,000.
Commercial Forest Land (acres)
  Total—5,761,000.
  Federal—5,585,000.
  State, county, or municipal—146,000.
  Private—30,000.
Forest Products (value): $8,000,000.
Lumber (board feet cut): 92,000,000.
National Forests: 2.

FISHING

Commercial Catch: 581,670,000 lbs.; value—$80,677,000.

TRADE

Wholesale: $180,605,000.
Retail: $284,408,000.
Service: $45,480,000.

ELECTRIC UTILITIES

Number of Utilities: 26.
Total Capacity: 234,081 kw.

All Fact Summary data are based on current government reports.
*Value Added by Manufacture—value of manufactured products as they leave the factory, less the cost of materials, supplies, fuel, etc. For complete definition, *see* Fact-Index.
†Cash receipts.

ALASKA FACT SUMMARY

TRANSPORTATION

Roads and Streets
Total state mileage—6,562; total surfaced—2,663.
Municipal mileage—542.
Rural mileage—6,020.
National Interstate Highway System—None.

Automobiles, Trucks, and Buses (registrations)*
Total—108,000.
Private and commercial—automobiles, 70,000; trucks and buses, 34,000.
Publicly owned—4,000.

Motorcycles (registrations): 4,300.

Railroads
Railroad System—Alaska Railroad, about 540 miles; 470-mile main line, Seward to Fairbanks; opened 1923. White Pass and Yukon Route, Skagway to Whitehorse, Y. T.; 20 miles in Alaska, 91 miles in Canada; completed 1900.

Airports†: Total—551; private—149.

Civil Aircraft: Total—2,900; active—1,821.

COMMUNICATION

Post Offices: 203

Radio Stations (commercial): AM—15; FM—2. First station —KFQD, Anchorage, licensed April 1924.

TV Stations: Commercial—6; educational—0. First station— KENI-TV, Anchorage, began operation Oct. 15, 1953.

Telephones: Total—64,000; residence—35,800.

Newspapers
Daily—6; circulation—65,463.
Weekly—8; circulation—14,650.
Sunday—2; circulation—24,107.
First newspaper (commercial)—*Alaska Times*, Sitka, 1868.

Periodicals: 3.

WELFARE‡

Old-Age and Survivors Insurance: Beneficiaries—8,703; benefits—$7,071,000.

Disability Insurance: Beneficiaries—800; benefits—$733,000.

Unemployment Insurance: Beneficiaries (weekly average)— 2,190; benefits—$6,710,000.

Workmen's Compensation Benefits: $4,138,000.

Vocational Rehabilitation
Disabled persons rehabilitated—127; in process of rehabilitation—304.
Total federal and state funds—$426,658.

Public Assistance
Old-age—recipients, 1,400; average payment, $70.75.
Dependent children—recipients, 5,100; average payment, $34.80.
Permanently and totally disabled—recipients, 350; average payment, $77.20.
Blind—recipients, 96; average payment, $86.90.
General assistance—recipients, 590; average payment, $17.25.

Maternity and Child Welfare Services
Federal grants—maternal and child health services, $167,549; crippled children, $161,672; child welfare, $122,113.
Children receiving services—1,141; rate per 10,000 children—94.

United Fund Campaigns: 2; amount raised—$299,158.

All Fact Summary data are based on current government reports.
*Excludes vehicles owned by military services.
†Includes seaplane bases, heliports, and military fields having joint civil-military use.
‡Figures for one-year periods.

EMPLOYMENT

Total Number of Persons Employed: 58,243.

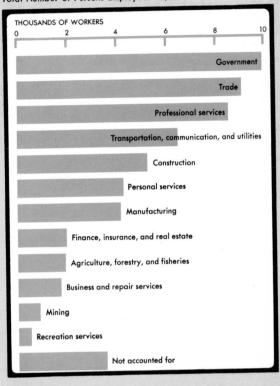

THOUSANDS OF WORKERS

Government

Trade

Professional services

Transportation, communication, and utilities

Construction

Personal services

Manufacturing

Finance, insurance, and real estate

Agriculture, forestry, and fisheries

Business and repair services

Mining

Recreation services

Not accounted for

FINANCE‡

Revenue: $198,561,000.

Expenditures: $203,150,000.

Taxation
State tax collections—$58,000,000; per capita—$213.07.
Federal tax collections—$92,000,000; individual income and employment—$84,000,000; per capita—$673.
Local tax collections—$25,000,000; per capita—$91.91.

Personal Income: $907,000,000.

Banks: 14; total assets or liabilities—$412,000,000.

Savings and Loan Associations: 3; assets—$54,000,000.

SELECTIVE SERVICE‡

Registrants Subject to Draft: 14,783.

Inductions: 228.

Regular Enlistments: 378.

Reserves or National Guard Enlistments: 192.

CRIME

Rates (per 100,000 population): Murder—12.9; forcible rape —19.5; robbery—36.0; aggravated assault—82.0; burglary—593.0; larceny—681.6; auto theft—441.6.

HOSPITALS AND PHYSICIANS

Hospitals: 26; beds—2,006.

Physicians: 165.

ALASKA FACT SUMMARY

LARGEST CITIES AND OTHER PLACES*

Anchorage (44,237): trade and transportation center at head of Cook Inlet; Alaska Railroad headquarters; called Air Crossroads of World; International Airport; Fort Richardson, Elmendorf Air Force Base nearby; Anchorage Fur Rendezvous (*see* Anchorage).

Fairbanks (13,311): on Chena Slough, branch of Tanana River; gold-mining, farming, and transportation center; University of Alaska and Eielson Air Force Base nearby; northern terminus of Alaska Highway and Alaska Railroad (*see* Fairbanks, Alaska).

Spenard† (9,074): community south of Anchorage, on Cook Inlet.

Juneau (6,797): capital of Alaska on Gastineau Channel at foot of Mounts Juneau and Roberts; ice-free sea and fishing port; gold-mining supply center; salmon canneries, lumber mills; Alaska Historical Library and Museum (*see* Juneau).

Ketchikan (6,483): trade center on Revillagigedo Island; port on Inside Passage; called salmon-packing capital of world; saw and pulp mills; Indian totem poles and community house at Ward Lake nearby.

Sitka (3,237): historic town on Baranof Island; Russian blockhouse; Sitka National Cemetery; Pioneers' Home; Sheldon Jackson school; Mount Edgecumbe on nearby Kruzof Island.

Kodiak (2,628): trade center on Kodiak Island; salmon canning; cattle and sheep ranches; dairy farms; Army and Navy bases; home of famed Kodiak bear.

Nome (2,316): port on Seward Peninsula; supply and transportation center; historic gold-rush town; Mark Field; Federal Building; Eskimo crafts.

Graehl Hamilton Acres† (2,162): suburb of Fairbanks.

Seward: (1,891): ice-free port on Resurrection Bay; supply center; gateway to Kenai Peninsula and interior; southern terminus of Alaska Railroad; headquarters for big-game hunters; Silver Salmon Derby.

PLACES OF INTEREST*

Alaska Marine Highway: that part of the Inside Passage between Prince Rupert, B. C., and Skagway; auto traffic via car ferry.

Bell Island Hot Springs: near Ketchikan; resort.

Bethel: fishing and fur-raising village near mouth of Kuskokwim River; placer gold-mining center.

Cordova: On Prince William Sound; old copper mines; Miles and Childs glaciers; Lake Eyak.

Dillingham: fishing metropolis of Bristol Bay; sport fishing and hunting; trapping center.

Douglas: across Gastineau Channel from Juneau; famous Treadwell gold mines; salmon cannery.

Eklutna Dam: 34 miles northeast of Anchorage.

Glacier Bay National Monument: surrounds Glacier Bay and Fairweather Range west of Juneau; Muir and other great tidal glaciers.

*1960 census.
†Unincorporated.

Haines: near end of Lynn Canal; terminus of Haines Highway; gold mining; Chilkoot Barracks.

Homer: in rich farm area; fishing; mining.

Katmai National Monument: on Alaska Peninsula opposite Kodiak Island; Mount Katmai erupted 1912; Valley of Ten Thousand Smokes; home of world's largest brown bear.

Kotzebue: Eskimo fur-farming community.

Malaspina Glacier: west of Yakutat Bay; reaches height of 2,500 feet.

Matanuska Valley: large farming area.

Mendenhall Glacier: north of Juneau; 17 miles long and 2 to 3 miles wide; reached by automobile.

Metlakatla: cooperative Tsimshian Indian village near Ketchikan; salmon cannery; sawmill.

Mount McKinley National Park: between Fairbanks and Anchorage; continent's highest peak, 20,320 feet; large glaciers of the Alaska Range; spectacular wildlife, includes caribou, moose, and grizzly and brown bears.

Nenana: time of ice breakup in Tanana River guessed in annual Nenana Ice Classic.

Palmer: Matanuska Valley civic center; coal mines; moose and bear hunting; sport fishing.

Point Barrow: northernmost point of Alaska; Eskimo village.

Pribilof Islands: fur-seal breeding ground.

Sitka National Monument: adjoins Sitka; site of stockade where Kik-Siti tribe made last stand against Russian settlers; totem poles.

Skagway: port at head of Lynn Canal; terminus of White Pass and Yukon Route.

Taku Valley: 30-mile-long glacier; fishing.

Valdez: ice-free port; Columbia Glacier; Keystone Canyon, Bridal Veil Falls.

BOOKS ABOUT ALASKA

Adams, Ben. Alaska: The Big Land (Hill & Wang, 1959).

Breetveld, Jim. Getting to Know Alaska (Coward-McCann, 1958).

Butler, E. I. and Dale, G. A. Alaska: The Land and the People (Viking, 1957).

Chevigny, Hector. Russian America: The Great Alaskan Venture, 1741–1867 (Viking, 1965).

Gruening, E. H., ed. An Alaskan Reader, 1867–1967 (Meredith, 1967).

Gruening, E. H. The State of Alaska (Random, 1954).

Hoke, Helen, comp. Alaska, Alaska, Alaska (Watts, 1960).

Lindquist, Willis. Alaska, the 49th State (McGraw, 1959).

McNeer, May. The Alaska Gold Rush (Random, 1960).

Smith, F. C. Men at Work in Alaska (Putnam, 1967).

Smith, R. A. The Frontier States (Time, 1968).

Spring, Norma. Alaska: Pioneer State (Nelson, 1966).

Stefansson, E. B. Here is Alaska (Scribner, 1959).

Stull, Edith. The First Book of Alaska (Watts, 1965).

Williamson, Geoffrey. Young Traveller in the Far North (Branford, 1959).

Wood, J. P. Alaska: The Great Land (Meredith, 1967).

ALASKA

240

ALASKA BOUNDARY DISPUTE. Gold was discovered in the Canadian Klondike in 1896. There followed a disagreement between the United States and Canada over the Alaska-Canada boundary.

The Treaty of 1867, by which the United States had bought Alaska from Russia, established the boundary of southeast Alaska (the Panhandle) as 30 miles from the coast. The entrance to the Klondike was through an inlet called Lynn Canal. The Canadians claimed that the boundary ran across inlets from headland to headland. This would have placed Lynn Canal within Canada. The United States held that the line followed all the windings of the coast.

The problem was referred to a joint arbitration commission of six members. Three were American, two were Canadian, and one was British. The commission met in London in 1903. The United States claim was upheld by a vote of four to two.

ALASKA HIGHWAY. The only land route between Alaska and the rest of the mainland United States is the Alaska Highway. Most of it is in Canada. It begins at Dawson Creek, British Columbia, and stretches north 1,221 miles through British Columbia and Yukon Territory. Then it crosses the Alaska border and runs to Big Delta (207 miles). Here it connects with the Richardson Highway (95 miles), which ends at Fairbanks. The total length from Dawson Creek to Fairbanks is 1,523 miles.

United States Army engineers hurriedly constructed the Alaska Highway for defense purposes during World War II. The road was built with the consent and help of Canada. It was originally called the Alcan Highway.

The route was chosen by the United States War Department to connect airfields and to maintain the Canol pipeline system. Construction began in April 1942, and the preliminary road was completed November 20. The initial cost was 115 million dollars.

The Canadian section was transferred to the Canadian government in 1946 and is maintained by the Canadian Army Northwest Highway System. Portions of the highway have been paved, but most of it is gravel, 26 feet wide. (*See also* Roads and Streets.)

A Road for Adventurous Tourists

For tourists, the Alaska Highway offers one of the most spectacular tours in North America. Summer is the ideal time for vacationists. By mid-June maintenance forces have repaired the damage caused by winter freezing and spring thaws. Daytime temperature may reach a high of about 70° F., and there are 16 to 20 hours of daylight.

The highway slashes through almost endless forests of virgin timber; climbs and twists through some of the continent's highest mountains; and skirts great glaciers and clear deep lakes. Fishing is exceptionally good. There are many clearings for parking a car and setting up a camp. For noncampers there are overnight accommodations about every 40 miles.

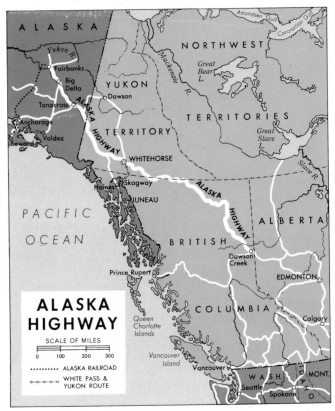

MILEPOST "ZERO"
From Dawson Creek, in British Columbia, the Alaska Highway stretches northwest 1,523 miles to Fairbanks, in the interior of Alaska.

241

STALIN BOULEVARD IN TIRANA, CAPITAL OF ALBANIA
Tirana is a modern city with wide thoroughfares; but very few Albanians own cars. This boulevard was renamed for Stalin; and the traffic policeman stands on the same kind of platform that is used in Moscow.

ALBANIA. The most poverty-stricken country in Europe is the tiny People's Republic of Albania. It is also the most isolated. Its ports on the Adriatic Sea admit few people from Western nations. Its land border is closed against both its neighbors, Yugoslavia and Greece. It can be reached easily only by sea and air. Albania is a Communist country, but since 1961 it has not been allied with Russia or other members of the European Communist bloc.

The Land and the People

Albania has an area of 11,100 square miles, which is about the size of Maryland. From the coast the land rises to wild and rugged uplands, with heights over 8,000 feet in some places. Many streams plunge down from the mountains. There are few roads and bridges and less than a hundred miles of railway. Oxcarts, horses, and donkeys carry people and goods over mountain trails. To cross rivers, the peasants use inflated sheepskins or dugouts.

The people in the north are called Ghegs. Those in the south are Tosks. Their dialects differ but they can understand one another. More than two thirds of the people are Moslems. Most of the remainder are of the Greek Orthodox or Roman Catholic faiths.

In the uplands, mountaineers pasture sheep, cattle, and goats. In the narrow valleys farmers raise corn, wheat, tobacco, grapes, and olives. There are many small villages and only a few large towns. The largest is the capital, Tirana, an inland city. A railway connects Tirana with the chief port, Durazzo.

History of Albania

The Albanians are descended from the ancient Illyrians. Like other peoples of the Balkan Peninsula, they were ruled in turn by Rome and the eastern Byzantine Empire until they fell to the Turks in the Middle Ages (see Balkan Peninsula). The Albanians offered fierce resistance to the Turks under their great national hero Scanderbeg (George Castriota), but soon after his death (1468) the Turks completed their conquest. Albania remained under Turkish rule until it revolted in 1912. For nine years it was a pawn of the European powers. A tribal leader named Ahmed Zogu took over as the premier in 1922 and as the president of a new republic in 1925. In 1928 he proclaimed Albania a kingdom and himself King Zog. Zog fled when Italy conquered Albania in 1939.

Germans and Italians overran Albania in World War II. General Enver Hoxha, a guerrilla leader, became premier of the Communist government formed in 1946. Although he resigned as premier in 1954, Hoxha retained power as head of Albania's Communist party. Albania's bid for United Nations membership, rejected in 1946, was accepted in 1955.

A postwar union with Yugoslavia ended in 1948, when Yugoslavia broke with Russia. After Joseph Stalin's death, Albania—then a Russian satellite—joined Red China in denouncing Russia's "revisionist" policy. Politico-economic ties with Red China were formed after Albania's break with the European Communists. In 1966–67 Albania resumed trade with some European nations, including Yugoslavia. Population (1960 census), 1,626,315; (1967 estimate), 1,938,500.

WATER FROM A MOUNTAIN LAKE
Life is primitive in Albania's mountain villages, but this young water peddler is well equipped for his job.

ALBANY, N.Y. The capital of New York lies on the west bank of the Hudson River. It is 145 miles north of New York City. It is an inland seaport and a center of trade, government, and industry. The Port of Albany, completed in 1932, handles ocean vessels of medium size. The port is connected by river with the New York State Barge Canal.

Advantages of Location

The advantages of Albany's geographical position were known more than 350 years ago. The English explorer Henry Hudson sailed his ship, the *Half Moon*, up the river to the present site of the city. Here he had reached one of the farthest points within the continent to which an ocean vessel could go.

The broad Mohawk Valley begins just above Albany. In the early 1800's it became the route for the Erie Canal (now part of the New York State Barge Canal). Goods were carried on water from New York City, up the Hudson to the Mohawk, and then into the western part of the state. Railroads were built westward through the Mohawk Valley and northward along the level passages of the Hudson.

With its industrial suburb of Rensselaer, across the Hudson, Albany has developed many industries. These include printing; meat-packing; and the manufacture of industrial felts, automotive parts, plastics, chemicals, drugs, and paper, metal, and textile products. The city also has large grain elevators.

Places of Interest

The business district is dominated by the State Capitol. Its construction took more than 30 years—1867–99. Behind the Capitol is the 32-story Alfred E. Smith State Office Building, named for a former governor. South of the Capitol is the South Mall, a complex of state buildings and outdoor facilities under construction. The tower of the nearby City Hall houses the municipal carillon, with its 60 bells.

Among Albany's colleges are the law, medical, and pharmacy schools of Union College and University; the State University of New York at Albany; and College of Saint Rose. Albany Institute of History and Art, the state's oldest museum, was founded in 1791.

Of historical interest are the Schuyler Mansion, home of Philip Schuyler, Revolutionary War general, and the Ten Broeck Mansion, both built in the 18th century. Washington and Lincoln parks and Bleecker Stadium provide public recreation facilities.

One of the Earliest Settlements

In 1614 Dutch fur traders built Fort Nassau on Castle Island near the present site of Albany. In 1624 the first permanent settlers from Holland built Fort Orange, named in honor of the Dutch ruling house. This is now the river-steamer landing.

In 1630 Kiliaen van Rensselaer, with two partners, bought land on both sides of the river, and under the patroon system set up a vast estate. On part of this land Peter Stuyvesant laid out the village of Beverwyck in 1653. In 1664 Fort Orange fell to the English and Beverwyck was renamed Albany for the Duke of York and Albany (later James II). Its city charter was granted in 1686.

In 1754 the Albany Congress met here to establish friendly relations with the Indians and to draw up a plan of union. A plan, largely the work of Benjamin Franklin, was adopted but was rejected by the colonists and the king.

In the Revolutionary War Albany was the objective of Burgoyne's expedition ending in his surrender at Saratoga. In 1797 the city became New York's permanent capital. It has a mayor-council government. (*See also* New York.) Population (1960 census), 129,726.

ALBANY'S CHANGING SKYLINE—THE SOUTH MALL PLATFORM
This sketch of the South Mall of New York's new state-government complex shows (from left) the meeting center, office tower, cultural center, and three of the agency buildings.

ALBATROSS. This great ocean bird follows a ship for days on tireless and apparently motionless wings. It has always held a strange spell over sailors. They believe that it has unnatural power, and rare is the man so bold as to harm one of them. The famous poem by Coleridge, 'The Rime of the Ancient Mariner', is based on this old superstition.

The wandering albatross (*Diomedea exulans*) has the greatest wingspread of any bird. Though only about 9 inches wide, its wings often measure more than 11 feet from tip to tip. Its weight is about 25 pounds. The body feathers of the male are white, the tips of its wings quite black. The female has brownish patches on neck and back. The three front toes of its large feet are webbed.

The albatross lives mostly on the wing. It sits down on the water to eat, floats like a cork, and scoops up small squids, fish, or scraps from ships with its yellow hooked beak. At times it skims the surface of the water, then soars so high it is out of sight. It may stand still in the air, balanced with delicate wing motion against the breeze; yet, when taking advantage of a favorable wind, its speed may exceed a hundred miles an hour.

During the nesting season these birds go to barren antarctic islands where the female lays a single egg in a nest of clay and grass. The parents tend the baby bird until it is able to care for itself.

There are about 17 species of albatrosses and all prefer the tropic seas. The black-footed species (*Diomedea nigripes*) wanders as far north as Alaska and is often seen on the Pacific coast.

THE ALBATROSS "TAXIES" FOR A TAKE-OFF
This photograph shows a black-footed albatross headed into the wind and running on the surface of the ocean, its wings outstretched to catch the air currents. On a calm day it may have to run a hundred yards or more to attain flying speed. Notice how it churns the water with its powerful feet.

ALBERT I, King of the Belgians (born 1875, ruled 1909–1934). The courage displayed by this ruler when Germany invaded his country in 1914 won him the devotion of his people and the admiration of the world. He was well educated in engineering and mechanics and widely traveled. He was a flier in the pioneer days of the airplane and an enthusiastic mountain climber. Artists, writers, and musicians received his help and encouragement.

In 1900 he married Elizabeth, duchess of Bavaria. They had three children, Leopold, Charles, and Marie José. He was interested in social and legal reforms and made a personal investigation of conditions in Belgium's African colony, the Congo State. When he succeeded his uncle Leopold II in 1909, he brought about badly'needed reforms in that colony.

His plans for modernization of the army were long delayed by his parliament. When Germany demanded permission to cross Belgium to attack France (Aug. 2, 1914), his forces were only partly reorganized. Nevertheless Albert refused. As commander in chief he fought beside his soldiers. His many visits to the front-line trenches gave his men courage. His queen was a nurse in army hospitals.

On Feb. 18, 1934, he was found dead at the foot of a cliff he had been scaling alone. His elder son (born 1901) was named king as Leopold III.

Fronting beautiful Lake Louise and with the Canadian Rockies for a backdrop, this luxurious hotel has a magnificent setting.

ALBERTA—
Where Prairies and Mountains Meet

ALBERTA. The rugged Rocky Mountains and the prairies of western Canada meet in the province of Alberta. It is more westerly than the other Prairie Provinces—Manitoba and Saskatchewan. With an area of 255,285 square miles, Alberta is also the largest of the three. It extends about 760 miles northward from the international boundary, which it shares with Montana, to the Northwest Territories. Its width, between Saskatchewan on the east and British Columbia on the west, varies from 180 miles at the 49th parallel to 400 miles at the widest part in the center.

This land of great resources was explored in the late 18th century by Sir Alexander Mackenzie, David Thompson, and other fur traders. Later it became noted for its vast wheat fields, its large cattle ranches, its wealth of oil and gas, and its expanding manufacturing. One of its greatest assets is its spectacular mountain scenery. More than 2 million tourists visit Alberta each year to enjoy its beauty and to engage in mountain climbing, skiing, golfing, camping, trail riding, and fishing.

Alberta is named for Princess Louise Caroline Alberta, a daughter of Queen Victoria. Its nickname is the Princess Province. The husband of the princess was John Campbell, marquis of Lorne (who later became ninth duke of Argyll). He was governor-general of Canada when, in 1882, the name "Alberta" was given to one of four newly organized provincial districts of the Northwest Territories. Alberta and Saskatchewan were created in 1905 out of these districts.

Province of Three Natural Regions

Alberta lies in three natural physiographic regions. These are: the Interior Plains and Lowlands, with their continuation northward in wooded parklands and heavy forests; the Rocky Mountain section of the

Extent.—North and south, 760 miles; east and west, 180 to 400 miles. Area, 255,285 square miles. Population (1966 census), 1,463,203.

Natural Features.—Rocky Mountains on southwestern boundary; North Saskatchewan, South Saskatchewan, Milk, Bow, Oldman, Red Deer, Athabasca, Peace, Hay, and Slave rivers; Lesser Slave Lake, Lake Claire, and Lake Athabasca; highest point, Mount Columbia, 12,294 feet; lowest point, Slave River valley, 573 feet.

Products.—Cattle, hogs, poultry; wheat, barley, tame hay, oats, flaxseed; oil, natural gas; meat, flour, butter, cheese; petroleum and coal products, concrete, structural metal.

Cities.—Edmonton (capital, 376,925); Calgary (330,575); Lethbridge (37,186); Red Deer (26,171); Medicine Hat (25,574); Grande Prairie (11,417).

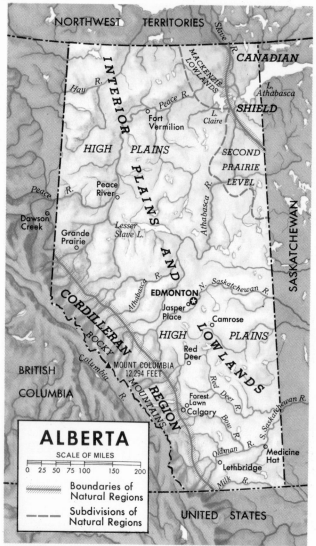

ALBERTA
SCALE OF MILES
0 25 50 75 100   150   200

Boundaries of
Natural Regions
Subdivisions of
Natural Regions

This map shows the three natural regions and the surface features of Alberta. The use that can be made of the land is related to the physical features of each region.

The Southern Plains, lying in the southeast, are gently sloping treeless plains. They rise in elevation steadily from more than 2,000 feet above sea level in the east to about 3,500 feet in the west. The climate is semiarid. Irrigation waters are furnished by the Milk River and by the South Saskatchewan and its tributaries. The area affords good grazing for livestock. In the southwest are rolling grasslands and timber-covered foothills of the Rockies. This too is ideal stock-raising country.

In the Red Deer River valley are the Bad Lands of Alberta. This is a vast expanse of eroded, brilliantly colored land containing fossilized remains of many prehistoric animals. Steveville Dinosaur Provincial Park and the Valley of the Dinosaurs, near Drumheller, draw thousands of visitors yearly.

About 100 miles north of Calgary the country becomes a rolling, wooded parkland. This area, called the Central Parkland, is drained by the North Saskatchewan River. The Central Parkland is the most thickly settled area in the province. Edmonton, the provincial capital, is its center. It is a rich agricultural region, with fertile black soil suited to the raising of a variety of field crops. The farmers also engage in mixed farming, which includes dairying, purebred stock raising, poultry raising, fur farming, and beekeeping. Most of Alberta's great oil wells are in the Central Parkland. East of Edmonton is Elk Island National Park, a big-game reserve.

The Northern Forests occupy the northern half of Alberta. The area consists mostly of forests, lakes, and bogs, called muskegs. It was long frequented only by the lumberman, the trapper, and the hunter. The farmer appeared on the scene when it was found that certain hardy grains (such as Marquis wheat) could be raised in the Peace River country (see Peace River).

The Athabasca River winds across northern Alberta. It originates in Athabasca Glacier in Jasper National Park and flows northeastward into Lake Athabasca. The largest lakes entirely within Alberta are Lesser Slave Lake, Lake Claire, and Lac la Biche.

The High Plains slope downward in the northeast and merge gradually into the Second Prairie Level and the Mackenzie Lowlands. These subdivisions too are a forested wilderness. In this area is Wood Buffalo National Park, home of the largest remaining herd of bison in North America and nesting ground of the rare whooping cranes (see Birds, section "Protecting and Conserving Our Birds").

Canadian Shield. Adjoining the Mackenzie Lowlands and the Second Prairie Level, in the extreme northeastern corner of the province, is the Canadian Shield. It is also called the Laurentian Plateau (see Laurentian Plateau). The Slave River marks its western edge, and the west end of Lake Athabasca lies in

Cordilleran Region in the southwest; and in the extreme northeast, the Canadian Shield. (See also Canada, section "The Natural Regions of Canada.")

Interior Plains and Lowlands. Most of Alberta lies in the *High Plains* subdivision of the Interior Plains and Lowlands. The High Plains extend into the United States, where they are known as the Great Plains. The High Plains are divided into three areas, which vary in elevation, climate, and natural resources. These are the Southern Plains, the Central Parkland, and the Northern Forests. In the northeast, the High Plains slope to a lower elevation. Here they meet two other subdivisions of the Interior Plains and Lowlands—the *Second Prairie Level*, which comes in from northwestern Saskatchewan, and the *Mackenzie Lowlands*, which continue northward into the Northwest Territories.

this region. The lowest point in the province is in the Slave River valley (573 feet above sea level). This is a land of subarctic forest and tundra. Fort Chipewyan, at the junction of the Peace and Slave rivers, and Fort Fitzgerald, to the north, are the only populated centers.

Cordilleran Region. The Rocky Mountain section of the Cordilleran Region straddles the southwestern border between Alberta and British Columbia. The area affords a striking contrast to the low-lying northern wilderness. There are more than 30 peaks over 10,000 feet high. The highest is Mount Columbia (12,294 feet) in Jasper National Park.

Throughout the region there are extensive glaciers, such as the Great Columbia Ice Field, and beautiful waterfalls, such as Athabasca Falls. Among the many mirrorlike lakes are Louise and Moraine in Banff National Park and Maligne in Jasper National Park. In Banff National Park are mineral hot springs. The entire region serves as a forest conservation area and a wildlife sanctuary for the grizzly bear, mountain goat, mule deer, bighorn sheep, and other animals.

From Wilderness Provincial Park in the northwest to Waterton Lakes National Park in the southeast, this portion of the Rockies has won fame for the beauty of its scenery. It is this beauty which has attracted so many tourists and has made the "land of shining mountains" (as the Indians called it) an internationally famous playground (*see* National Parks, Canadian; Rocky Mountains; North America, section "Plants and Animals").

Variable Climate

Alberta has a continental climate, with cold winters and warm summers. In the winter, blizzards are common, with bitterly cold temperatures, high winds, and driving snow. The mean January temperature is 7.7° F. at Edmonton. The lowest on record is −78° at Fort Vermilion. The chinook may blow all winter, bringing almost springlike weather. The chinook is a warm, dry, westerly wind that blows strongly from the mountains (*see* Winds).

Temperatures vary less in the summer. The mean July temperature is 62.9° at Edmonton. The highest recorded was 115° at Gleichen. In the north, temperatures may be almost as high as in the south, owing to the long hours of summer sunlight and the lower altitude. Beaverlodge, in the northwest, has a mean July temperature of 60.2°. Medicine Hat, in the southeast, is only 10 degrees warmer.

Rainfall is usually adequate for crops, except in the southeast. There the chinook prevents much snow from falling in winter and carries off summer moisture, making it necessary to irrigate. The average annual precipitation at Edmonton is 17.63 inches. Edmonton's snowfall amounts to 52.9 inches a year.

The People and Their Origins

The population of Alberta (1966 census) is 1,463,203. The population density is low, with only 5.7 persons to the square mile. The population is 31.2 percent rural and 68.8 percent urban.

About half of Alberta's people are of British origin. Other national groups include Germans, Ukrainians, Scandinavians, French, Dutch, Poles, Russians, and Italians. They poured in from eastern Canada and Europe as well as from the United States in the early part of the 20th century. The most recent influx of immigrants occurred in the wake of the province's oil prosperity.

Alberta has about 25,000 Indians. They live on 87 reserves. They are descended from such tribes as the Assiniboin, Chipewyan, Beaver, Blackfeet, and Slave, who once roamed this region. The Indian Days cele-

STORING ALBERTA'S IRRIGATION WATERS
The St. Mary Dam, 195 feet high and 2,536 feet long, is of earth-fill construction. Erected near Spring Coulee, it is part of the St. Mary-Milk River irrigation project.

bration, held each July in Banff, keeps alive the ancient songs and ceremonial dances of these people.

Agriculture and Irrigation

Ranching and farming have always been the basic industries of Alberta. They account for about two fifths of the value of the province's production. Cattle ranches extend from the Southern Plains to the Peace River district. The ranches in the south are also noted for the raising of sheep and horses, and those in the central and northern parts for the raising of hogs. Cowboys still ride the range and give the ranch country much of the flavor of the old West.

On the smaller farms in the southeastern region, Alberta has more land under irrigation than any other province. The St. Mary-Milk River development is the most important of the major irrigation projects. When completed, it will water some 510,000 acres and bring the total irrigated land to more than one million acres. The project's cost is being divided among the federal and provincial governments and the farmers who use the irrigation waters.

The chief grain raised in Alberta is wheat. In its production the province is outranked only by Saskatchewan. Other important crops are barley, tame hay, oats, and flaxseed. Alberta leads all provinces in the production of sugar beets. A considerable amount of alfalfa is raised. Potatoes, carrots, peas, tomatoes, and other vegetables are also grown.

Immense Mineral Wealth

Alberta is called the Oil Province because it produces more than two thirds of Canada's crude oil. The Turner Valley field, discovered near Calgary in 1913, was long the leading producer. Then in 1947 immense petroleum deposits were found in the Leduc-Woodbend area, near Edmonton. Since then the rich reserves of the Redwater, Bonnie Glen, Pembina, Swan Hills, Sturgeon Lake, and Rainbow Lake fields have also been tapped, and Alberta has experienced one of the greatest booms in Canadian history.

In the "tar sands," an asphaltlike sand bed along the northern course of the Athabasca River, Alberta has one of the greatest known oil reserves. The sands may yield 300 billion barrels of oil. In 1967 the pilot plant near McMurray began the commercial production of oil recovered from these sands.

Gas wells in the Pincher Creek, Viking-Kinsella, and other areas produce about nine tenths of Canada's natural gas. The oldest deposit is the vast pool lying beneath and surrounding Medicine Hat.

Gas and Oil Pipelines

Alberta's oil is carried to the western coast by the Trans-Mountain Oil Pipeline, constructed between Edmonton and Vancouver. Eastern Canada is served by the Interprovincial Oil Pipeline. This pipeline, which extends 1,934 miles from Edmonton to Toronto by way of Superior, Wis., is one of the longest of its kind in the world. Gas pipelines have been constructed from the Peace River district westward to Vancouver and eastward to Montreal.

Also included among Alberta's important mineral products are sand and gravel, coal, cement, clay, sulfur, and salt. At one time the coal mines in the vicinity of Lethbridge and Drumheller yielded half the coal produced in Canada. Today, owing to its emphasis on the development of fuel oil and natural

SUGAR REFINING IN ALBERTA
The trucks in the foreground have brought sugar beets from the irrigated fields to a factory in Taber. Automatic unloaders convey the beets onto the large pile at the left. After processing, the refined sugar is shipped in freight cars.

gas resources, the province accounts for less than a fourth of the national total.

Manufacturing and Cities

Alberta's industrial growth since World War II has been impressive. Based on abundant natural resources, this growth has been aided by ample supplies of low-cost fuels and by excellent road, rail, and other transportation facilities. Highest in value added by manufacture among the province's industries are meat-packing and slaughtering, petroleum refining, industrial chemicals, and pulp and paper.

From the forests of spruce, jack pine, balsam fir, and poplar comes the lumber used by furniture factories, sash and door mills, and pulp and paper mills. Important to Alberta's economy are the province's breweries, distilleries, bakeries, sugar refineries, and vegetable canneries. Other industries include textile factories, feed mills, cement plants, potteries, brick and tile works, and printing establishments. Of growing importance is the petrochemical industry (based on petroleum refining and natural-gas extraction). It manufactures chemicals for making plastics, fertilizers, synthetic rubber, and numerous other products.

The largest city is Edmonton, the oil center of the province and the distributing point for a rich farming district (see Edmonton). Calgary, the second largest city, is not only important industrially, but it is also

LEGISLATIVE BUILDING AT EDMONTON
The Capitol of Alberta was erected on the banks of the North Saskatchewan near the spot where the Hudson's Bay Company's old Fort Edmonton once stood.

a leading financial and transportation center (see Calgary). Lethbridge and Medicine Hat are marketing and industrial centers. Red Deer is noted for dairy and petroleum products.

Educational Opportunities

The elementary and secondary educational system of Alberta is administered by local school authorities, under the general supervision of the Department of Education. It is supported by local taxation and provincial grants. Rural town and village schools

THE UNIVERSITY OF ALBERTA
This aerial view shows the many modern buildings and the campus of the University of Alberta in Edmonton. The university was founded in 1906 by an act of the first session of the provincial legislature.

are almost completely centralized, operating within 32 school divisions and 26 counties. The cities of the province and a few other communities operate as independent school districts. Each district, division, and county has its own school board.

The principal institution of higher learning is the University of Alberta, in Edmonton, with a second campus in Calgary. Provincially supported, it has its own board of governors. The Banff School of Fine Arts is a part of the university. Affiliates of the university are St. Joseph's and St. Stephen's colleges, on the Edmonton campus. The Northern Alberta Institute of Technology is at Edmonton; the Southern Alberta Institute of Technology, at Calgary.

Provincial Government

The government of Alberta, which is centered in Edmonton, is much the same as that of the other Canadian provinces. The Crown is represented by a lieutenant governor, appointed by the governor-general of Canada for a five-year term. The single-chamber Legislative Assembly of 65 members is elected for a maximum period of five years. From it are chosen a premier and an Executive Council (or Cabinet) of Ministers, each of whom has charge of one or more government departments.

Judicial power is vested in the Supreme Court, Court of Appeals, and District Courts. Since 1873 the maintenance of law and order in Alberta has been entrusted to the Royal Canadian Mounted Police.

HISTORY OF THE PRINCESS PROVINCE

For 200 years the history of Alberta was the history of the fur trade in western Canada (*see* Fur Trade, History of). It was a part of vast Rupert's Land, granted to the Hudson's Bay Company in 1670 by Charles II of England (*see* Canadian History; Hudson's Bay Company). Alberta was unoccupied, however, until the rival North West Company built forts in the late 18th century. Sir Alexander Mackenzie of the North West Company established Fort Chipewyan on Lake Athabasca in 1789. Three years later he explored the Peace River district. He was followed by David Thompson, another fur trader, who explored the Rocky Mountain region. The North West and Hudson's Bay companies built forts near present-day Edmonton in 1794–5.

In 1869 the Dominion of Canada bought Rupert's Land from the Hudson's Bay Company for £300,000 (about 1½ million dollars) and organized it as the Northwest Territories. Ranching and farming attracted the pioneer settlers, whose numbers were greatly increased after the Canadian Pacific Railway reached Calgary in 1883. The previous year four provincial districts—Alberta, Saskatchewan, Athabaska, and Assiniboia—had been set up south of the 60th parallel. When, in 1905, the stream of settlers had reached flood proportions, the districts were reorganized as the provinces of Alberta and Saskatchewan.

Social Policies

Ever since the Liberals came to power in 1905, political parties in Alberta have been primarily concerned with the province's agricultural interests and with its social services. The party known as the United Farmers of Alberta gained control of the government in 1921. It owed its popularity to the success of wheat pools and cooperative grain marketing.

During the depression of the 1930's, it was supplanted by the Social Credit party, led by William Aberhart. Aberhart was premier from 1935 until his death in 1943. He advocated radical changes in the control of money and banking, but his more extreme measures were overruled by the Supreme Court of Canada. Under his successor, Ernest C. Manning, the Social Credit party has been victorious in every provincial general election since 1944.

The history of Alberta since World War II has revolved around its oil prosperity. Because the provincial government owns about 90 percent of the mineral rights, it has received vast sums in royalties, rentals, and lease sales. It has almost wiped out the public debt. It has also used much of its income to encourage cultural activities and to improve schools, hospitals, highways, and homes for the aged. (For Reference-Outline and Bibliography, *see* Canada; Canadian History.)

A CHUCK-WAGON RACE AT CALGARY'S FAMOUS RODEO
Known as the world's greatest wild West show, the week-long Calgary Stampede, held each July since 1912, attracts contestants and visitors from all parts of North America.

ALBUMINS.

ALBUMINS. The chemical compounds called *albumins* form an important class of proteins (*see* Proteins). Nearly all animal tissues, and most plants, contain albumins. *Serum albumin*, for example, represents about half the volume of plasma proteins in human blood (*see* Serum, subhead "Serum Proteins").

The albumins were once thought to be a single substance rather than a group of similar but not identical compounds. This single substance was believed to exist in a nearly pure state in egg whites. Its name, "albumen," was derived from the Latin *albus*, meaning "white." Today *albumen* is the name of only one albumin, that of egg white.

Properties of Albumins

Albumins are soluble in water. When an albumin is hydrolyzed, or chemically decomposed by the addition of water, it yields a number of amino acids. Albumins also coagulate when they are heated. Thus an egg's albumen coagulates when the egg is fried.

The exact chemical composition of the albumins is not yet known. All, however, are known to contain carbon, hydrogen, nitrogen, oxygen, and sulfur and to have high molecular weights. That of albumen, for example, varies between 34,000 and 44,000; of horse serum albumin, between 70,000 and 73,000.

Until recently albumins were classified as *simple proteins* (proteins containing only amino acids). It has been shown, however, that albumins contain small amounts of carbohydrates and phosphoric acid in addition to amino acids.

Kinds and Uses of Albumins

Each of the several different kinds of albumins is named for its source. Thus *serum albumin* is prepared from animal blood serum and *ovalbumin* from egg whites. *Wheyalbumin* is made by coagulating casein, the principal protein of milk.

Serum albumin is used to treat certain diseases such as *hypoproteinemia* (in which the protein content of the blood is lowered). It is also administered to prevent or treat conditions of shock (*see* Serum, subhead "The Medical Use of Serum Albumin"). Industrially, serum albumin is used in making photographic paper, in textile printing, and in sugar refining. Ovalbumin is an ingredient in foodstuffs and a clarifying agent in sugar refining. Wheyalbumin is used in the manufacture of adhesives, varnishes, and plastics.

How the Body Uses Albumins

Nutritionally the albumins are almost perfect proteins (*see* Food and Nutrition, subhead "Protein for Building Tissues"). They contain liberal amounts of the 11 amino acids essential for proper growth in children and the 6 amino acids needed to develop and maintain good health in adults. Serum albumin must be present in the blood stream in certain concentrations in order to maintain blood viscosity and osmotic pressure, which regulates the distribution of water in the body.

ALBUQUERQUE (ăl'bŭ-kûr-kē), **N. M.** One of the fastest-growing cities in the Southwest is Albuquerque, New Mexico's largest city. It is situated on the banks of the Rio Grande, about 60 miles southwest of Santa Fe. The Sandia and Manzano mountains are to the east.

Since the city was founded in 1706 by Francisco Cuervo y Valdés, four flags—those of Spain, Mexico, the United States, and the Confederacy—have flown over the Plaza of its Old Town. In early days it was known as San Felipe de Alburquerque. It was named for King Philip V of Spain and the duke of Alburquerque, who was then viceroy of New Spain. Later the name was shortened and changed to Albuquerque.

Albuquerque came under Mexican rule when Mexico gained its independence from Spain in 1821. It became United States property in 1848, at the end

ALBUQUERQUE'S CHURCH OF SAN FELIPE DE NERÍ
The oldest building in Albuquerque is the Church of San Felipe de Nerí. Except for a remodeled façade, it stands exactly as it was built in 1706.

of the Mexican War, when Mexico ceded the province of New Mexico to the United States. During the Civil War Albuquerque was alternately held by Union and Confederate forces. It acquired its New Town in 1881 when the newly completed Atchison and Topeka Railroad (now The Atchison, Topeka and Santa Fe Railway) passed about two miles east of the Plaza and a huddle of shacks was built around the depot. In 1890 Albuquerque was incorporated as a city.

Today, as a division point on the main line of the railway, Albuquerque is the leading commercial and distributing center of New Mexico. The sheep ranches in the surrounding region have made it an important wool-shipping center, and its packing plants process meat from livestock. Canneries utilize the fruits and vegetables raised on the irrigated lands of the Rio Grande Valley.

The varied manufactures of Albuquerque's industries include electronic equipment, machine tools, cement, gypsum wallboard, lumber products, furniture, clothing, trailers, and teaching machines. Large railroad shops are located in the city. Several oil refineries have been erected to accommodate the San Juan Basin oil field in northwestern New Mexico and the city's pipeline connections with Texas oil fields.

A warm, dry climate has made the city a popular health and vacation resort. Indian jewelry and pottery for the tourist trade are made in nearby pueblos.

An Educational and Research Center

Albuquerque has been a noted educational center ever since it was selected as the seat of the University of New Mexico in 1889. The University of Albuquerque, a Roman Catholic institution, is the former College of St. Joseph on the Rio Grande.

During World War II Albuquerque was selected as the site of Defense Department installations and Air Force training centers. Later the Sandia, Kirtland, and Manzano bases were converted into atomic and rocket research centers. They are today playing a vital role in the Space Age. The city has a council-manager form of government, with five commissioners. (*See also* New Mexico.) Population (1960 census), 201,189.

ALCHEMY. During the Middle Ages certain learned men practiced a kind of primitive science that was called alchemy. The objective of alchemy was to discover a substance called the "philosophers' stone." This elusive material was thought to transform common metals such as lead into silver or gold. Another objective of the alchemists' researches was the "elixir of life"—a potion that would cure all diseases and prolong life indefinitely. (*See also* Chemistry, History of.)

Alchemy was based on ideas passed along by older cultures, including the Chinese, Egyptian, East Indian, Greek, Syrian, and Islamic. These ancient peoples had learned how to extract metals from ores. They also knew how to make alloys, soap, glass, leather, alum, dyes, and fermented liquors.

Many alchemists were impostors and fakers who pretended to be able to produce gold. Others, however, were honest men. They performed practical experiments in their quest for the philosophers' stone. They never found it, but they made some contributions to chemistry and developed laboratory techniques. By heating the compound iron sulfate, for example, they produced "oil of vitriol," which is known today as sulfuric acid. They made hydrochloric and nitric acid and compounds such as potash and sodium carbonate. They also identified the elements arsenic, antimony, and bismuth.

Theories of Matter

One of the ancient ideas held by the alchemists was that matter was composed of four "elements"—earth, air, fire, and water—which came from one common source. Matter was thought to have a soul, which could be transferred from one element to another by means of the philosophers' stone.

Some alchemists believed that gold was formed when fire and water combined, under "planetary influences." If the resulting product was only slightly impure, it became silver. If it was markedly impure, it became a base metal such as lead. If, however, fire and water could be brought together in states of "superfine quality," the philosophers' stone would at last have been found.

'THE ALCHEMIST'
This famous painting by the 17th-century Flemish artist David Teniers the Younger shows some of the laboratory equipment that was used by the alchemists.

ALCOHOL. An important chemical substance widely used both in science and in technology is an organic compound known as alcohol (*see* Organic Chemistry). Its name comes from the ancient Arabic word *al-kuhl,* meaning "a powder for painting the eyelids." The term was later applied to all compounds that contain alcoholic spirits. These include beverages such as wine, beer, and whisky. In modern chemistry alcohol usually refers to one type of compound—*ethyl alcohol.* It is also known as *ethanol* or *grain alcohol.*

Man discovered alcohol in early times. He found that certain grains, fruits, and sugars produced an intoxicating liquid when they fermented (*see* Fermentation). Today the manufacture of alcoholic beverages is a major industry. The distillation and sale of beverages containing ethyl alcohol have a direct effect on a nation's economy. The United States derives about 5 billion dollars each year from taxes levied on the manufacture and sale of drinking alcohol. Most other countries impose similar taxes.

Government regulations maintain rigid control over the quality and purity of drinking alcohol. If such beverages do not meet prescribed standards, they cannot be legally sold. In the United States drinking alcohol is sold by "proof," or "degree proof." A 100-degree-proof spirit, for example, contains 50 per cent absolute alcohol at 60° F.

PRODUCTION OF ALCOHOL

KIND	MANUFACTURE	USES
Methyl (wood alcohol, methanol)	By destructive distillation of wood. Also by synthesis from hydrogen and carbon monoxide under high pressure.	Solvent for fats, oils, resins, nitrocellulose. Manufacture of dyes, formaldehyde, antifreeze solutions, special fuels, plastics.
Ethyl (grain alcohol, ethanol)	By fermentation of sugar, starch, or waste sulfite liquor. Synthesis from ethylene or acetylene. Direct hydration of ethylene.	Solvent for products such as lacquers, paints, varnishes, glues, pharmaceuticals, explosives. Also as "building block" in making high-molecular-weight chemicals.
Isopropyl (isopropanol)	By hydration of propylene from cracked gases. Also as by-product of certain fermentation processes.	Solvent for oils, gums, alkaloids, resins. Making acetone, soap, antiseptic solutions.
Normal propyl	As a coproduct of air oxidation of propane and butane mixtures.	Solvent for lacquers, resins, coatings, films, waxes. Also as brake fluid, in manufacture of propionic acid, plasticizers.
Butyl (n-butanol)	By fermentation of starch or sugar. Also by synthesis, using ethyl alcohol or acetylene.	Solvent for nitrocellulose, ethyl cellulose, lacquer, urea-formaldehyde, urea-melamine plastics. Diluent of hydraulic fluids, extractant of drugs.
Isobutyl	By synthesis from carbon monoxide and hydrogen at high pressure, then distillation from products formed.	Solvent for castor-oil-base brake fluids. Substitute for n-butyl alcohol in making urea resins.
Secondary butyl	By hydration of 1-butane, formed in petroleum cracking.	In making other chemicals such as methyl ethyl ketone. Solvent in nitrocellulose lacquers. Production of brake fluids, special greases.
Tertiary butyl	By hydration of isobutylene, derived from petroleum cracking.	In perfume making. As wetting agent in detergents. Solvent for drugs and cleaning compounds.
Amyl (pentyl)	By fractional distillation of fusel oil, a coproduct of ethyl alcohol manufacture by fermentation.	Solvent for many natural and synthetic resins. Diluting brake fluids, printing inks, lacquers. In medicinal products.
Ethylene glycol	By oxidation of ethylene to glycol. Also by hydrogenation of methyl glycolate made from formaldehyde and methanol.	Deicing fluid, antifreeze, brake fluid. In production of explosives. Solvent for stains, oils, resins, enamels, inks, dyes.
Diethylene glycol	As coproduct in manufacture of ethylene glycol.	Solvent for dyes, resins. Antileak agent. In gas drying. Softening agent in adhesive printing inks.
Triethylene glycol	Coproduct in manufacture of ethylene glycol.	Air disinfectant and dehumidifier. Production of resins, plasticizers.
Glycerol (glycerin; 1-, 2-, 3- propanetriol)	From treatment of fats in soapmaking. Synthetically, from propylene. By fermentation.	In alkyd resins, explosives, cellophane. Tobacco humectant.
Pentaerythritol	By condensation of acetaldehyde and formaldehyde.	In synthetic resins. As tetranitrate in explosives. Also as drug for treatment of heart disease.
Sorbitol	By reduction of sugar, usually corn sugar, with hydrogen.	In foods, pharmaceuticals, in chemical manufacture. Conditioning agent in paper, textiles, glue, cosmetics. Source of alcohol in resin manufacture.
Cyclohexanol	By catalytic hydrogenation of phenol. By catalytic air oxidation of cyclohexane.	Intermediate in making chemicals used in nylon manufacture. Stabilizer and homogenizer of soaps, synthetic detergents. Solvent.
Phenyl ethyl	By synthesis from benzene and ethylene oxide.	Principally in perfumes.

Alcohol has certain physiological effects on the human body. It acts specifically on the central nervous system. When taken in excess, it may become habit-forming. This leads to a condition called alcoholism. Organs such as the brain, liver, and kidneys may be damaged by excessive indulgence in alcohol. Mental impairment may also result. Several private organizations are dedicated to influencing legislation that would outlaw the manufacture and sale of alcoholic beverages (see Prohibition; Temperance; Woman's Christian Temperance Union).

Industrial Alcohol

The main value of alcohol is not as an intoxicating drink. It is important in the making of thousands of products. Many of its uses are listed in the table on the preceding page.

Methyl alcohol, or wood alcohol, was originally made by the destructive distillation of wood. Now it is produced synthetically by passing compressed hydrogen and carbon monoxide over catalysts, then condensing the reaction product. Some methyl alcohol is still made by distillation of wood. It is used chiefly in the manufacture of denatured alcohol.

Denatured alcohol is ethyl alcohol to which other substances have been added to make it unfit to drink. Because it is not sold as a beverage, denatured alcohol is not subject to heavy taxation. It is made under government regulations. Wood alcohol and benzene are the two most common denaturing additives. In certain cases, however, substances such as pyridine, diethyl phthalate, and nicotine may be added.

Chemistry of Alcohols

Chemically, alcohol is defined as the hydroxyl derivative of a hydrocarbon (see Acids and Alkalies; Hydrocarbons). The chemist represents one hydroxyl molecule by the symbol OH. The hydroxyl group is also called a *hydroxide*, or "a combination of hydrogen and oxygen." When a hydrogen atom contained in a hydrocarbon molecule is replaced by a hydroxyl group, a molecule of alcohol is produced. One molecule of *ethane*, a hydrocarbon, is written as CH_3CH_3. If one "H" in the second "CH_3" is replaced by an OH, the ethane molecule becomes a molecule of ethyl alcohol, CH_3CH_2OH.

Alcohols may be classified according to the OH groups in each molecule. Ethyl alcohol, with one OH group, is a *monohydric* alcohol. *Ethylene glycol* (CH_2OHCH_2OH) has two OH groups and is a *dihydric* alcohol. A *trihydric* alcohol such as *glycerol*, or glycerin ($CH_2OHCHOHCH_2OH$), has three hydroxyl groups. *Hexahydric* alcohols have four OH groups, and *polyhydric* alcohols have many.

The manufacture of alcohol for industry is based on the principle of replacing hydrogen atoms with hydroxyl groups. Until 1930 this process was carried out by simple fermentation of grains such as corn, wheat, rice, and barley. Other alcohol was obtained from the fermentation of starches and sugars—principally of blackstrap molasses. Some industrial alcohol is still produced by fermentation.

Most of the industrial alcohol produced in the United States, however, is made synthetically. It is usually synthesized from ethylene gas that comes from natural-gas deposits or from petroleum cracking processes (see Gas, Natural; Petroleum).

ALCOTT, Louisa May (1832–1888). Everyone who has read 'Little Women' knows the Alcott family well. The tempestuous and lovable Jo was Louisa herself. Her sisters May, Elizabeth, and Anna were Amy, Beth, and Meg. Louisa drew on her own girlhood experiences for most of the incidents. She wrote the book for young girls, and it was immediately successful. The story still has a wide appeal because of its warm account of New England family life.

Louisa May Alcott was born in Germantown, Pa., on Nov. 29, 1832, and grew up in Boston and Concord, Mass. Her father, Amos Bronson Alcott, was a teacher and a transcendental philosopher, a close friend of Ralph Waldo Emerson. Alcott's "conversational" method of teaching was far in advance of his time and won him few pupils. It was, however, very successful with Louisa. She began to write poems and stories. When she was 15, she was writing and producing amateur theatricals. By 1860 her verses and stories were appearing in *The Atlantic Monthly*.

Civil War Nurse; Financial Success

In 1862, during the Civil War, Louisa Alcott served as a nurse in the Union hospital at Georgetown, now part of Washington, D.C. A fever contracted there forced her to return home after six months and left her in poor health for the rest of her life. Her letters home telling of her hospital experiences were published in 1863 under the title 'Hospital Sketches' and brought her $2,000. With this money she made her first trip to Europe, in 1865.

On her return she began 'Little Women'. This book, published in 1868, made her famous and enabled her to pay off all the family debts. Enough money was left for Louisa and her sister May to take a long tour of Europe. In Rome she wrote 'Little Men'.

Louisa Alcott took an active part in the temperance and the woman's suffrage movements. She never married. She died on March 6, 1888, two days after her father. Orchard House, in Concord, where she wrote 'Little Women', was made a memorial in 1911.

Louisa Alcott's best-known works are 'Little Women' (1868); 'An Old-Fashioned Girl' (1869); 'Little Men' (1871); 'Eight Cousins' (1874); 'Under the Lilacs' (1878); and 'Jo's Boys' (1886).

ALDEN, John (1599?–1687). Among the Pilgrims who arrived in America on the *Mayflower* in 1620 was John Alden. He was a cooper (barrelmaker) hired at Southampton before the ship sailed. He was successful enough in business in Plymouth to become one of the eight bondsmen who assumed responsibility for the colonial debt. Later he moved to Duxbury and took over a farm near his friend Miles Standish.

Henry Wadsworth Longfellow made the name of John Alden famous in his poem 'The Courtship of Miles Standish'. The poem tells how Alden courted Priscilla Mullins (or Molines) for his friend Miles Standish until Priscilla asked, "Why don't you speak for yourself, John?" There is little historical foundation for this story. John did marry Priscilla, however, and they had 11 children.

For many years Alden was assistant to the governor of Plymouth Colony. He died in Duxbury and was buried near Standish. The John Alden house, near the site of the original home, has been occupied by Alden's descendants since colonial days. It is owned by the Alden Kindred Society. (*See* 'Mayflower'.)

ALDER. Along stream banks from Saskatchewan and Nebraska eastward, the speckled alder is a beautiful and familiar tree. It is often a large shrub, but it may grow to a height of 60 feet. The leaves are oval, coarse, and irregularly notched. They are dark green above with a whitish down underneath. In late summer male and female catkins form on the same twig. The mature fruit resembles small fir cones. The wood is soft, light, and of little value.

On the Pacific coast the red alder grows to a height of 80 to 130 feet. The wood is commercially important. It is used for inexpensive furniture, veneers, and wooden novelties. It is one of the first trees to appear on burned and logged areas. The European alder, introduced as a park and lawn tree, has become naturalized.

Alders belong to the birch family, *Betulaceae*. The scientific name of the speckled alder is *Alnus incana*; red alder, *A. rubra*; European alder, *A. glutinosa*.

THE SPECKLED ALDER
The male catkins fall off after their pollen is scattered. The shorter female catkins develop into seed-bearing cones.

ALEWIFE. Each spring tremendous numbers of alewives, or river herring, swim in from the Atlantic Ocean to spawn in the tidal parts of rivers. They then return to the sea. Large numbers are caught at spawning time, from the St. Lawrence River to the North Carolina sounds. The largest fisheries are in Chesapeake Bay. The average annual catch in the United States is about 50 million pounds. Only a small portion are marketed fresh. The rest are canned, salted, or cured in salt and vinegar.

Alewives are small fish of the herring family. They average 8 to 10 inches in length and weigh about a half pound. There are two species: the "true" alewife, or branch herring (*Pomolobus pseudoharengus*), and the blueback (*Pomolobus aestivalis*).

ALEXANDER, Emperors (Czars) of Russia. Three Romanov rulers of Russia were named Alexander.

ALEXANDER I (born 1777, ruled 1801–1825) came to the throne after the murder of his father, Paul I, the "mad czar." At the beginning of his reign he carried out many important reforms.

In 1805 Alexander joined with England, Austria, and Prussia in

ALEXANDER II

the European coalition against Napoleon I. After the Russian defeat at Friedland, in 1807, he deserted his allies, and in the Treaty of Tilsit he and Napoleon agreed to divide the world between them (*see* Napoleon I). Rivalry soon developed, and Napoleon invaded Russia in 1812. After the disastrous winter retreat of the French forces, Alexander himself carried the war to French soil. At the Congress of Vienna (1814–15) he was a leading figure (*see* Vienna).

In 1815 Alexander tried to create a world order based on Christian principles. It was called the Holy Alliance. The name was later applied to the Grand Alliance, which virtually ruled Europe (*see* Europe, History of). Before he died Alexander undid many of the reforms of the first part of his reign.

ALEXANDER II (born 1818, ruled 1855–1881) was the son of Nicholas I. He was called the "czar liberator" because in 1861 he freed the serfs (*see* Russian History). He also relaxed the censorship of the press and extended education. Nevertheless attempts were made on his life. In 1880 part of the Winter Palace was blown up. The next year Alexander was killed by a bomb while driving in his carriage.

ALEXANDER III (born 1845, ruled 1881–1894) came to the throne after the assassination of his father, Alexander II. Unlike his father, he was a firm believer in autocracy and practically suppressed revolutionary agitation. He was succeeded by his son, Nicholas II, the last of the Russian czars.

ALEXANDER THE GREAT (356–323 B.C.).
More than any other world conqueror, Alexander III of Macedon deserves to be called "the Great." Although he died before he was 33 years old, he conquered almost all the then known world and gave a new direction to history.

Alexander was born in 356 B.C. at Pella, the capital of Macedon, a kingdom north of Hellas (Greece). Under his father, Philip II, Macedonia had become strong and united, the first real nation in European history. Greece was reaching the end of its Golden Age. Art, literature, and philosophy were still flourishing, but the small city-states had refused to unite and were exhausted by wars. Philip admired Greek culture. The Greeks despised the Macedonians as barbarians. (*See also* Macedonia; Greece.)

Alexander's Early Years

Alexander was extraordinarily handsome and had the physique of an athlete. He excelled in hunting and loved riding his horse Bucephalus. When Alexander was 13 years old, the great Greek philosopher Aristotle came to Macedonia to tutor him. From Aristotle Alexander learned to love Homer's 'Iliad'. He also learned something of ethics and politics and the new sciences of botany, zoology, geography, and medicine. (*See also* Aristotle.) His chief interest, however, was military strategy. He learned this from his father, who had reformed the Greek phalanx into a powerful fighting machine (*see* Warfare).

Philip was bent on the conquest of Persia. First, however, he had to subdue Greece. The decisive battle of Chaeronea (338 B.C.) brought all the Greek city-states except Sparta under Philip's leadership. Young Alexander commanded the Macedonian left wing at Chaeronea and annihilated the famous "sacred band" of the Thebans.

Two years later (336 B.C.) Philip was murdered. Alexander's mother, Olympias, probably plotted his death. Alexander then came to the throne. In the same year he marched south to Corinth, where the Greek city-states (except Sparta) swore allegiance to him. Thebes, however, later revolted, and Alexander destroyed the city. He allowed the other city-states to keep their democratic governments.

Alexander's Campaign in Asia Minor

With Greece secure Alexander prepared to carry out his father's bold plan and invade Persia. Two centuries earlier the mighty Persian Empire had pushed westward to include the Greek cities of Asia Minor—one third of the entire Greek world (*see* Persian History; Persian Wars).

In the spring of 334 B.C., Alexander crossed the Hellespont (now Dardanelles), the narrow strait between Europe and Asia Minor. He had with him a Greek and Macedonian force of about 30,000 foot soldiers and 5,000 cavalry. The infantry wore armor like the Greek hoplites (*see* Armor) but carried a Macedonian weapon, the long pike. Alexander himself led the "companions," the elite of the cavalry. With the army went geographers, botanists, and other men of science who collected information and specimens for Aristotle. A historian kept records of the march, and surveyors made maps that served as the basis for the geography of Asia for centuries.

In Asia Minor Alexander visited ancient Troy to pay homage to Achilles and other heroes of the 'Iliad'. At the Granicus River, in May, he defeated a large body of Persian cavalry, four times the size of his own. Then he marched southward along the coast, freeing the Greek cities from Persian rule and making them his allies. In the winter he turned inland, to subdue the hill tribes.

Alexander's efficient intelligence service reported that Darius III of Persia was gathering a huge force. The two armies met at Issus in October 333 B.C. Alexander himself charged with his cavalry against Darius. Darius fled, leaving behind his mother, wife, and two daughters. Alexander treated the captives with kindness and respect.

Alexander Destroys Tyre and Visits Egypt

Alexander then marched south along the coast of Phoenicia to cut off the large Persian navy from all its harbors. Tyre, on an island, held out for seven months until Alexander built a causeway to it and battered down its stone walls.

Late in 332 B.C. the conqueror reached Egypt. The Egyptians welcomed him as a deliverer from

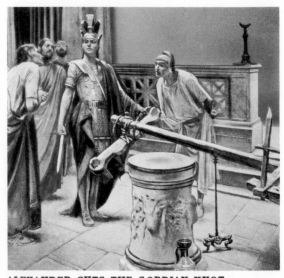

ALEXANDER CUTS THE GORDIAN KNOT
At Gordium, in Asia Minor, Alexander was shown this curious knot. An oracle had declared that the man who untied it would rule Asia. Alexander dramatically cut it with his sword.

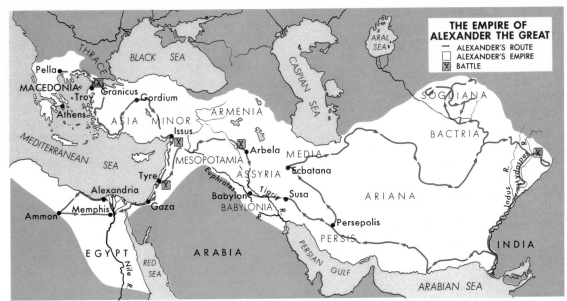

THE EMPIRE OF
ALEXANDER THE GREAT
— ALEXANDER'S ROUTE
☐ ALEXANDER'S EMPIRE
☒ BATTLE

Alexander the Great's conquests freed the West from the menace of Persian rule and spread Greek civilization and culture into Asia and Egypt. His vast empire stretched east into India.

Persian misrule and accepted him as their pharaoh (king). In Memphis he made sacrifices to Egyptian gods. Near the delta of the Nile River he founded a new city, to be named Alexandria after him (*see* Alexandria). At Ammon, in the Libyan desert, he visited the oracle of Zeus, and the priests saluted him as the son of the great Greek god. Deification of living men was not uncommon in the ancient world.

Battle of Gaugamela and Death of Darius

Leaving Egypt in the spring of 331 B.C., Alexander went in search of Darius. He met him on a wide plain near the village of Gaugamela, or Camel's House, some miles from the town of Arbela.

Darius had gathered together all his military strength—chariots with scythes on the wheels, elephants, and a great number of cavalry and foot soldiers. Alexander again led his cavalry straight toward Darius, while his phalanx attacked with long pikes. Darius fled once more, and Alexander won a great and decisive victory (July 331 B.C.) After the battle he was proclaimed king of Asia.

Babylon welcomed the conqueror, and Alexander made sacrifices there to the Babylonians' god Marduk. The Persian capital, Susa, also opened its gates. In this city and at Persepolis an immense hoard of royal treasure fell into Alexander's hands. In March (330 B.C.) Alexander set out from Persepolis to pursue Darius once more. He found him dying, murdered by one of his own attendants.

Searches for the Limits of the Earth

His men now wanted to return home. Alexander, however, was determined to press on to the eastern limit of the world, which he believed was not far beyond the Indus River. He spent the next three years campaigning in the wild country to the east. There he married a chieftain's daughter, Roxane.

In the early summer of 327 B.C. Alexander reached India. At the Hydaspes River (now Jhelum) he defeated the army of King Porus whose soldiers were mounted on elephants. Then he pushed farther east.

Alexander's men had now marched 11,000 miles. Soon they refused to go farther, and Alexander reluctantly turned back. He had already ordered a fleet built on the Hydaspes, and he sailed down the Indus to its mouth. Then he led his army overland, across the desert. Many died of hunger and thirst.

The Death of Alexander

Alexander reached Susa in the spring of 324 B.C. There he rested with his army. The next spring he went to Babylon. Long marches and many wounds had so lowered his vitality that he was unable to recover from a fever. He died at Babylon on June 13, 323 B.C. His body, encased in gold leaf, was later placed in a magnificent tomb at Alexandria, Egypt.

Confusion followed Alexander's death as his generals fought over the succession. Finally three kingdoms emerged. Ptolemy, one of Alexander's generals, ruled Egypt. Seleucus made Antioch the capital of his Asiatic kingdom. Antigonus became supreme in Macedonia. Alexander IV, who was born after his father's death, was put to death with his mother, Roxane, in 310 B.C.

Effects of Alexander's Conquests

The three centuries following the death of Alexander are called the Hellenistic Age because Greek culture—Hellenism—became widespread.

Alexander thought of mankind as citizens of one great community, "the inhabited world." He bound his empire together by founding cities along great trade routes and by giving the entire realm a uniform coinage. Macedonians and Greeks colonized the new cities and made Greek the international language for both government and commerce. Trade flourished.

Alexandria, in Egypt, replaced Athens as the cultural capital (*see* Alexandria). From Alexandria Greek culture flowed later to Rome. When Christianity appeared, there was a world with a common civilization in which the new religion could spread.

ALEXANDRIA, Egypt. Egypt's chief seaport is Alexandria, located on the Mediterranean Sea. It is also the country's most popular summer resort. A railway joins Alexandria with Cairo, the national capital, 110 miles to the southeast. A canal connects the city with the Nile.

Alexandria lies just west of the muddy Nile delta, on a narrow strip of land between the sea and Lake Maryut. A T-shaped peninsula divides the east and west harbors. The east harbor is shallow and is used only for fishing. Beautiful beaches and gardens line the shore. Behind them is an attractive residential section, formerly Alexandria's European quarter.

The deep west harbor accommodates seagoing vessels. Around it are factories and warehouses and the homes of the working people. The principal industries are cotton ginning and cottonseed-oil extraction. The chief export is cotton.

Origin of the City

Alexandria takes its name from Alexander the Great, who founded the city in 332 B.C. (*see* Alexander the Great). He had brought Egypt into his empire because he wanted a port to replace Tyre, in Phoenicia, which he had destroyed. Up to this time Egypt had no good harbor. The Nile served as a highway through the interior, but its outlets in the delta were choked with silt. West of the delta the shore was sandy and sheltered by a long rocky island, Pharos. Here Alexander traced on the ground the plan for a new city. Building began immediately, and a narrow stone causeway was constructed to connect Pharos with the mainland. Deposits of silt gradually widened this causeway, and it is now a peninsula a half mile wide.

When Alexander died, in 323 B.C., one of his generals, Ptolemy, became pharaoh (king) of Egypt. He and the Greek pharaohs who followed him—called Ptolemies—made Alexandria their capital. About 300 B.C. a great stone lighthouse, 400 feet high, was erected on Pharos to guide mariners into the harbor (*see* Seven Wonders of the World).

A hundred years after its founding, Alexandria was the largest and richest city in the world, with a population of about a million. To its port came products from Mediterranean lands, Arabia, and India. From it were shipped grain, papyrus, perfumes, linen, and blown glass.

A Center of Greek Culture

The royal Greek section of the city contained parks and gardens, the magnificent palace of the Ptolemies, luxurious villas, temples, theaters, and gymnasiums. Even the ordinary houses were impressive, being several stories high. The tomb of Alexander was in the center of the city. The greatest glory of the city, however, was its library and its university, called the Museum (home of the Muses). The earlier Ptolemies searched the world for valuable manuscripts and collected about 500,000 papyrus rolls for the library.

From all over the Greek world, philosophers and scientists came to Alexandria to study and teach. Here Euclid wrote his geometry and Eratosthenes studied the heavens from an observatory and calculated the circumference of the earth. So great were their achievements that for about 2,000 years few improvements were made in their work.

Throughout the Hellenistic Age Alexandria remained the cultural capital of the Greek world. It also became a center of Hebrew culture.

From Roman to Modern Times

Egypt was formally joined to Rome in 30 B.C. after the suicide of Cleopatra, the next to last of the Ptolemaic line. Under Roman rule the city became even more magnificent. In the 3d century it acquired new importance as a seat of Christian learning.

After A.D. 640, when Egypt fell to the Arabs, Alexandria declined rapidly. In the 19th century a new canal to the Nile revived its trade and made irrigation possible in the vicinity. All that remains today to recall the city's past are catacombs and Pompey's Pillar, a tall granite shaft. The Museum has a large collection of antiquities. (*See also* Egypt.) Population (1960 census), 1,516,234.

CROWDS WATCH A PARADE IN ALEXANDRIA
Corniche Drive, lined with handsome apartment houses and hotels, faces the shore of the eastern harbor on the Mediterranean.

ALFALFA. One of the most useful and widely grown hay crops is alfalfa. It is a nourishing and well-liked animal food used as pasturage, cut and dried for hay, or cut for filling silos. Because it is high in protein, it is a particularly valuable feed for milk- or meat-producing animals. Alfalfa will yield abundantly for many years. Unlike many other crops, it improves the soil. Because of these valuable qualities, the United States usually grows more tons of alfalfa each year than of any other hay crop.

The plant adapts itself to different climates and soils, and so it is raised in many parts of the world. In the United States it is grown below sea level in southern California and in high altitudes in Colorado; in the dry regions of the West and in the Gulf states of heavy rainfall; in the tropical climate of the South and in the Northwest.

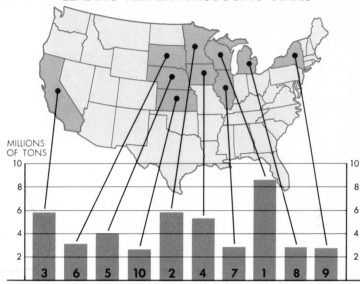

LEADING ALFALFA-PRODUCING STATES

MILLIONS OF TONS

CALIF. S.D. NEB. KAN. MINN. IOWA ILL. WIS. MICH. N.Y.
3   6   5   10   2   4   7   1   8   9

Numbers on bars show rank among states.   *(Little alfalfa is grown in Alaska and Hawaii.)*

Alfalfa flourishes where other crops fail because of its long roots. These are usually about 6 feet long. They may, however, extend to lengths of 30 or more feet. The roots draw moisture and nourishment from deep within the subsoil. Alfalfa is often rotated with other crops that draw heavily upon surface soil.

A Valuable Legume

Alfalfa is one of the valuable legumes that enrich the soil. It belongs to the same family as clover, beans, and peas (*see* Clover), and the scientific name is *Medicago sativa*. Tiny bacteria that grow on alfalfa roots gather nitrogen from the air and transform it into nitrates on the roots (*see* Bacteria; Nitrogen). When alfalfa is harvested, the nitrates remain in the soil. Often the whole plant is plowed under to improve soil worn out by other crops.

Of the many varieties of alfalfa, *common* and *Grimm* are most generally grown. Alfalfa is a heavy user of lime, and so acid soils must be limed before they are seeded. Seed may be sown broadcast or drilled. Dodder, grasses, and other weeds are the most harmful enemies of the young plants. It is well, therefore, to plant alfalfa after a clean cultivated crop such as corn, potatoes, or cotton. The most serious disease of alfalfa is bacterial wilt, and grasshoppers are the plant's worst insect pest.

Uses of Alfalfa

Most alfalfa is cut for hay. It is usually cut soon after the plants have begun to bloom. It yields from two to seven crops a year depending upon the variety, climate, and soil. Alfalfa produces more than two tons of hay per acre, compared with less than two for clover and timothy and one for most other hays. Some alfalfa is ground into meal. In this form it is less wasteful and can be shipped more conveniently.

About 28 million acres of alfalfa are harvested for hay each year in the United States. This is about 40 per cent of the total hay acreage. In 1960 nearly 70 million tons of alfalfa hay were produced.

Growing alfalfa for seed is also important and is most dependable in dry climates, as in the West. Cross-pollination results in much more seed than self-pollination, but it is complicated. Bees are the main carriers of pollen from plant to plant. The stamen, loaded with pollen, is folded down within the blossom. When a bee visits a flower, its weight releases, or "trips," the stamen, which deposits pollen on the bee.

When alfalfa hay is made, parts of the leaves may be destroyed—by drying, handling, or being rained on. Special care thus must be taken in harvesting.

Although alfalfa is one of the newer crops in the United States, it is one of the oldest forage crops known to man. It may have originated in southwest Asia, China, or Siberia. In central Asia it was called *al-façfaçah*, which means "the best feed." It was introduced into Greece about the time of the Persian Wars. The Romans carried it from Greece to Italy and then to Spain and France. It got its European name of *lucerne*, a corruption of the Catalan *userdas*, from Spain and not from the Swiss canton of Lucerne.

Food Value

The chief food value of alfalfa is contained in the leaves. Alfalfa-leaf meal contains more than 20 per cent protein. This is about one and a half times more protein than is found in corn or wheat. Alfalfa protein supplies essential amino acids such as arginine, lysine, threonine, and tryptophan. Vitamins such as choline, folic acid, pantothenic acid, E, K, and C are also present.

ALFONSO XIII, King of Spain. Thirteen rulers of Spain have borne the name Alfonso. Alfonso XIII (1886–1941), the last of the line, was the most important. He was born a few months after his father, Alfonso XII, died. In the first 16 years of the king's life his mother ruled for him.

It was a time of violent internal disorders and of the Spanish-American War of 1898, by which Spain lost practically the last of its colonial possessions. Alfonso took personal charge of the government in 1902. Charming and politically adroit, he held the crumbling monarchy together with the aid of a dictatorship until April 1931. Elections at that time showed the overwhelmingly republican sentiment of his people. The "last of the Bourbons" then quit his throne and went into exile (*see* Bourbon).

The name Alfonso (or Alphonso) has also been a favorite one in Portugal, where six monarchs have been so called. The last was King Alfonso VI, who reigned from 1656 to 1667.

ALFRED THE GREAT (born 848? ruled 871–899). The course of English history would have been very different had it not been for King Alfred. He won renown both as a statesman and as a warrior and is justly called "the Great."

The England of Alfred's time was a country of four small kingdoms. The strongest was Wessex, in the south. Alfred was the youngest son of Ethelwulf, king of Wessex. Each of Alfred's three older brothers, in turn, ruled the kingdom. Alfred was by temperament a scholar, and his health was never robust. Nevertheless in his early youth he fought with his brother Ethelred against the dreaded Danish invaders. He was 23 when Ethelred died, but he had already won the confidence of the army and was at once acclaimed king (871). By this time the Danes, or Vikings, had penetrated to all parts of the island, plundering the rich monasteries and burning villages. Three of the Saxon kingdoms—Northumbria, Mercia, and East Anglia —had one after another fallen to them.

The Soldier

Under Alfred's leadership, the Saxons again took courage. The worst crisis came in the winter of 877,

when the Danish king, Guthrum, invaded Wessex with his whole army. In 878 Alfred was defeated at Chippenham, where he was keeping Christmas, and was forced to go into hiding. According to an old story, he went to a herdsman's hut for shelter. The housewife, not knowing who he was, asked him to watch her cakes while she went out. When she returned, she found them burned and scolded her royal guest.

A few months later he forced Guthrum to surrender at Chippenham. The Danes agreed to make the Thames River and the old Roman road called Watling Street the boundary between Alfred's kingdom and the Danish lands to the north. The treaty, however, did not mean permanent peace. The Danes harried London and the coast towns repeatedly. Not until about 896 did they admit defeat and cease to struggle for a foothold in southern England.

The Scholar and Builder

Alfred was much more than the defender of his country. He took a keen interest in law and order and was much concerned in improving the cultural standards of his people. He encouraged industries of all kinds and rebuilt London, which had been partly destroyed by the Danes. He collected and revised the old laws of the kingdom. He invited learned men from other countries to instruct the people because even the clergy of Wessex had largely ceased to know Latin, the international language of the church. He established a school like the Palace School of Charlemagne.

The "books most necessary for all men to know" were translated from Latin into English so that the people might read them. Alfred himself took a part in preparing the translations. The 'Anglo-Saxon Chronicle' was probably begun under his direction. The translations and the 'Chronicle' have survived.

Alfred died at the age of 51. He was in no sense king of England, for he ruled less than half the island. After his death, however, his capable son, Edward the Elder, and his grandsons extended their rule over all England. (*See also* English History.)

ALGAE (ăl′gē). The first and simplest plants were the water plants called algae. As they floated about in the water, the living drops of jellylike material called protoplasm soaked food through the thin walls of the cells. One cell budded from another and broke away to start a new family or clung to the parent cells to form a beadlike string or a knot. Sometimes they budded all around the sides and formed mats and flat networks of cells.

Some of these nets and mats floated on rocks, in quiet places where the motion of the water was not strong enough to float them off again. As the rocks sheltered them, the plants were not so easily torn apart. The cells that lay on the rocks could not gather much food. Thus they learned to cling, while the floating cells gathered food and budded and spread into feathery, leaflike fronds. The plants lived in a colony and divided the labor just as people do in a village. It was the business of some plants or

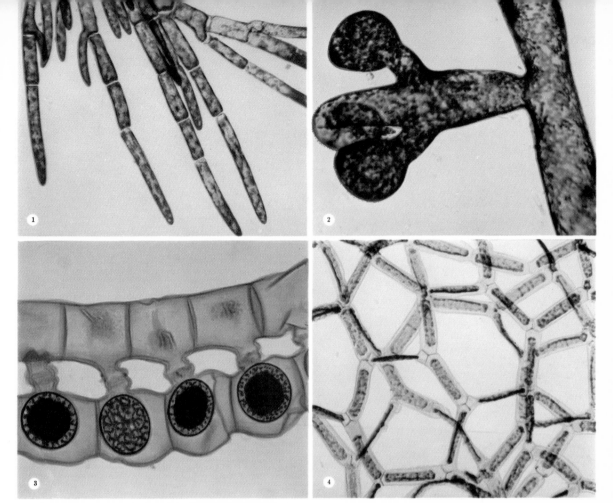

PATTERNS AMONG MICROSCOPIC ALGAE

The waters of the earth contain various kinds of algae. The characteristic designs of most types can be observed only through a microscope. The algae shown here are (1) Cladophora, (2) Vaucheria, (3) Spirogyra, and (4) Hydrodictyon.

cells to cling to the rocks. Others waved in the water and gathered food. It was not necessary any longer, and there was not room, for each cell to bud, though it could have done so. Certain cells began to collect budding material in little raised dots on the fronds. When these dots ripened they were washed off. These bud dots were spores. They were not seeds but merely the hints of seeds. The cells that clung to the rocks were hints of roots, and the cells that spread out and floated were hints of leaves. All together they formed seaweeds. Seaweeds belong to the plant family called algae.

All algae contain a green coloring matter called *chlorophyll*, which acts as a catalyst in the production of food in the plant cells. By the process called osmosis, raw materials such as carbon, hydrogen, nitrogen, and magnesium are obtained from the air and water. The energy of sunlight is used to manufacture carbohydrates for the plant from these inorganic materials by the process of *photosynthesis*.

Most algae live in water. They are found in oceans, rivers, lakes, ponds, marshes, and warm springs. The most common alga is the green scum that forms on ponds and swamps. This scum, which

is known by the scientific name *Spirogyra*, is composed of a mass of filaments, each having a chain of cells which can be studied under a microscope.

Algae are of special interest because they represent the most primitive forms of the plant kingdom, from which all other groups of plants have probably been derived. Some are only a single cell and are microscopic in size, while others, such as the giant kelps of the ocean, are very huge and complex.

Algae are classified for scientific purposes according to three main characteristics: (1) color, or pigmentation; (2) the nature of the food reserves stored in their cells—for example, starch; and (3) the nature of the motile cells—especially the number, arrangement, and length of the flagella, or whiplike appendages, used for movement by the cells.

The blue-green algae and the green algae dwell mainly in fresh water. The brown algae contain, in addition to chlorophyll, a yellowish to brown pigment which gives their bodies various shades from olive to yellow and brown. The red algae have a red pigment in addition to chlorophyll; they are among the most attractive plants on the seashore. (*See also* Plants, Kinds of; Seaweed.)

261

FUNDAMENTAL CONCEPTS IN ALGEBRA

ALGEBRA. An important branch of mathematics, algebra today is studied not only in high school and college but, increasingly, in the lower grades as well. Taught with insight and understanding of the new mathematics programs, it can be an enjoyable subject. Algebra is as useful as all the other branches of mathematics—to which it is closely related. For some careers, such as those in engineering and science, a knowledge of algebra is indispensable. (*See also* Arithmetic; Geometry; Calculus; Mathematics; Numeration Systems and Numbers.)

Parents are aware of the growing emphasis upon mathematics in present-day school programs. They may not realize, however, that they have many opportunities at home to help their children take the natural step from solving arithmetic problems to solving algebra problems.

For example, suppose a father is asked his age by his eight-year-old son. Instead of answering the boy directly, the father can attempt an experiment by replying that he is 30 years older than the boy. This is a problem that the son is interested in solving. He can quickly perform the addition and find that his father is 38 years old:

$$8 + 30 = 38$$

Suppose the boy then asks the age of his mother. The father might at this point present a more challenging problem. For example, the father may answer that if the boy added six years to his mother's age, the result would be equal to the father's age. The father has thus found an excellent opportunity to help his son understand how an *algebraic equation* may be made up and solved.

The father writes the mother's age on a slip of paper and turns the slip over so the boy cannot see the numeral. He then lays the slip, blank side up, on a tablet. Next to the slip he writes the symbols that will help solve the problem:

$$\blacksquare + 6 = 38$$

The son takes only a moment to guess that his mother is 32 years old. When the father turns the slip of paper over, they see this answer is correct:

$$\boxed{32} + 6 = 38$$

This will have been the boy's first lesson in algebra because he essentially solved the equation

$$x + 6 = 38 \text{ [say "x plus 6 is equal to 38"]}$$

The father did not say anything about a mysterious letter "x" that can stand for any number. Nor did he tell the boy about any rule such as "changing the sign of the six and writing it on the other side of the equation." Instead, the boy's first lesson in algebra evolved in a natural way from a problem in arithmetic.

When the boy studies algebra in school, he will learn more about the relationship between algebra and arithmetic. Some of the fundamental concepts of algebra that are taught in school are explained here. Their applications in solving various types of mathematical problems are discussed in the section "Applying the Fundamental Concepts of Algebra."

OPEN SENTENCES

The open sentence is a commonly used teaching device. It is also often used in giving students examinations. In a test consisting of a list of sentences to be completed, the first three sentences might be, for example:

1. ⬜⬜⬜ is the capital of Pennsylvania.
2. _____ is the capital of California.
3. ⬭⬭⬭ is the capital of Illinois.

The student is expected to fill in the blanks with the correct answers to convert these sentences into **true statements.**

A student taking the test converted the first sentence into a *true statement* as follows:

1. *Harrisburg* is the capital of Pennsylvania.

He converted the second sentence into a *false statement:*

2. *Hollywood* is the capital of California.

He didn't know the name of the city which is the capital of Illinois, so he went on to the other sentences, leaving the third sentence open:

3. ⬭⬭⬭ is the capital of Illinois.

By not filling in the blank in the third sentence, the student did not convert it into a true statement or into a false statement. Sentences which are neither true nor false are called *open sentences.*

The problem of converting open sentences into true

statements is quite common in mathematics. Here are some examples of open sentences that you may easily convert into true statements by filling in each of the blanks or frames with an appropriate numeral:

1. $6 + 32 = \square$ 3. $5 - 3 = \bigcirc$

2. $\_ + 2 = 5$ 4. $5 \times \diamondsuit = 10$

These open sentences may be converted into true statements by writing '38' in the frame in the first sentence, '3' in the blank in the second sentence, '2' in the frame in the third sentence, and '2' in the frame in the fourth sentence:

T 1. $6 + 32 = \boxed{38}$ 3. $5 - 3 = \textcircled{2}$ T

T 2. $\underline{3} + 2 = 5$ 4. $5 \times \boxed{2} = 10$ T

If, however, you write '10' in the frame in the first sentence, you will convert it into a false statement:

$6 + 32 = \boxed{10}$ F

VARIABLES

Consider the following short composition written by a student:

> Every year many people visit it. It is a famous city. Abraham Lincoln lived in it. It is the capital of Illinois.

Since none of these sentences asserts a definite statement that can be judged to be true or false, each one is an open sentence. The teacher might ask the student to convert each of the sentences into a true statement by replacing the pronoun 'it' with a proper noun—the name of the correct city.

If in each sentence the student had replaced the pronoun 'it' with the proper noun 'Washington', the first three sentences in his composition would have been converted into true statements, but the fourth sentence would have become a false statement. However, if he had used the proper noun 'Springfield', all four of the sentences would have been converted into true statements:

> Every year many people visit Springfield. Springfield is a famous city. Abraham Lincoln lived in Springfield. Springfield is the capital of Illinois.

In mathematics, as in ordinary language, open sentences may be written without using blanks or frames. For example, the open sentence

$$\square + 3 = 5$$

may also be written

$$x + 3 = 5$$

Just as the open sentence

It is the capital of Illinois.

may be converted into a true statement or a false statement by replacing the mark 'It' with a name, the open sentence

$$x + 3 = 5$$

may be converted into a true statement or a false statement by replacing the mark 'x' with a name. The mark 'It' serves as a *placeholder* for a name of a city; the mark 'x' serves as a placeholder for a name of a number.

We may of course use other marks to serve as placeholders. Letters such as 'a', 'b', 'c', or 'x' which are serving as placeholders are called *variables*.

The sentence

$$m + 3 = 8$$

may be converted into a true statement by replacing the variable 'm' with the numeral '5':

$$\textcircled{5} + 3 = 8 \quad T$$

It may be converted into a false statement by replacing the variable 'm' with the numeral '2':

$$\textcircled{2} + 3 = 8 \quad F$$

Here are some other examples of open sentences which you may easily convert into true statements or false statements:

1. $y - 5 = 4$ 3. $k \div 3 = 4$

2. $3 \times a = 12$ 4. $\frac{m}{4} = 3$

These sentences may be converted into true statements by replacing 'y' with '$\textcircled{9}$', 'a' with '$\textcircled{4}$', 'k' with '$\textcircled{12}$', and 'm' with '$\textcircled{12}$'.

In mathematics the multiplication sign '$\times$' is often replaced by a dot '$\cdot$'. Sometimes, as between a numeral and a variable, or between two variables, it is omitted altogether. Thus, for example, the sentence '$3 \times a = 12$' may be written as

$$3 \cdot a = 12 \text{ or } 3a = 12$$

The sentence '$k \div 3 = 4$' may be read as

The result of dividing k by 3 is 4.

The sentence '$k \div 3 = 4$' may also be written

$$\frac{k}{3} = 4$$

NUMBERS, NUMERALS, AND EQUATIONS

The number of eggs in this carton

has many names. For example,

$\frac{1}{2}$ dozen, 6, $3 + 3$, $\frac{18}{3}$, and $3 \cdot 2$

are all different *names* for the number of eggs in the carton.

A name for a *number* is called a *numeral* or a *numerical expression*. The open sentence

$$x - 4 = 2$$

may be converted into a true statement by replacing

'x' with any numeral which names the number of eggs in the carton pictured above. For example,

$$6 - 4 = 2,$$

$$(3 + 3) - 4 = 2, \text{ and}$$

$$(3 \cdot 2) - 4 = 2$$

are true statements. We say that

> the number *6* **satisfies** the open sentence 'x − 4 = 2'.

We may also say that

> the number *3 + 3* satisfies the open sentence 'x − 4 = 2'.

Since

$$5 - 4 \neq 2 \text{ [say ''5 minus 4 is not equal to 2''],}$$

we say that

> the number *5* does not satisfy the open sentence 'x − 4 = 2'.

Although the variable 'x' may be replaced by many numerals to convert the open sentence 'x − 4 = 2' into a true statement, all such numerals are names for the same number because there is one and only one *number* which satisfies this open sentence. It is true that the number 6 satisfies this open sentence, and that the number 3 + 3 also satisfies this open sentence, but '6' and '3 + 3' are just different names for the same number.

The sentence

$$6 - 4 = 2 \quad T$$

is called an *equation*. This equation tells us that 6 − 4 is the same number as 2. It is a true statement because the numerals '6 − 4' and '2' name the same number. The equation

$$5 - 4 = 2 \quad F$$

is a false statement because '5 − 4' and '2' are not names for the same number.

The equation

$$(3 + 3) - 4 = (3 \cdot 2) - 4$$

is a true statement because '(3 + 3) − 4' and '(3 · 2) − 4' are names for the same number. The parentheses in the numeral '(3 + 3) − 4' tell you that you may find another name for the number (3 + 3) − 4 by first adding 3 and 3 and then subtracting 4 from their sum:

$$\left. \begin{array}{c} (3 + 3) - 4 = 6 - 4 \\ 6 - 4 = 2 \end{array} \right\} \text{ so, } (3 + 3) - 4 = 2$$

The parentheses in the numeral '(3 · 2) − 4' tell you that you may find another name for the number (3 · 2) − 4 by first multiplying 3 by 2 and then subtracting 4 from their product:

$$\left. \begin{array}{c} (3 \cdot 2) - 4 = 6 - 4 \\ 6 - 4 = 2 \end{array} \right\} \text{ so, } (3 \cdot 2) - 4 = 2$$

The open sentence

$$x - 4 = 2$$

264

is also called an equation. The set of all numbers which satisfy this equation is called the *solution set* of the equation. The solution set of this equation consists of just the number 6, because 6 is the only number which satisfies this equation.

A shorthand notation for the set of all numbers which satisfy the equation 'x − 4 = 2' is

$$\{x : x - 4 = 2\}$$

We may read this as "the set of all numbers x such that x − 4 = 2."

The sentence

$$\{x : x - 4 = 2\} = \{6\}$$

says that the set of all numbers which satisfy the equation 'x − 4 = 2' consists of just the number 6.

Notice, for example, that the sentences

$$\boxed{3} \cdot 0 = 0 \text{ and } \boxed{7} \cdot 0 = 0$$

are true statements. In fact, if any number is multiplied by 0, the result is 0. Thus the open sentence

$$\boxed{} \cdot 0 = 0$$

is satisfied by every number. In other words, the solution set of 'x · 0 = 0' consists of every number:

$$\{x : x \cdot 0 = 0\} \text{ consists of all numbers.}$$

GENERALIZATIONS

Since the sentence

$$\boxed{Springfield} \text{ is the capital of Illinois.}$$

is a true statement, we may say that

> there is a city which is the capital of Illinois.

Similarly, since the equation

$$\boxed{8} - 5 = 3$$

is a true statement, we may say that

> there is a number with such a property that when 5 is subtracted from it the result is 3.

More briefly, we say that

> there exists a number x such that x − 5 = 3.

This last sentence tells us about a property of numbers, and it is called a *generalization*. Since it tells us that there exists among the numbers one which has a certain property, the sentence is called an *existential generalization*.

Existential generalizations are often written in an abbreviated form by using a turned-around 'E'. The sentence

$$\exists_x \, x - 4 = 2$$

is a shorthand notation which tells you that there exists a number with such a property that when 4 is subtracted from it the result is 2. The sentence '∃x x − 4 = 2' may be read as follows:

> There exists x such that x minus 4 is equal to 2.

Sentences such as

$$\boxed{5} - 4 = 2 \quad \mathcal{F}$$

$$\text{or} \quad \boxed{8} - 4 = 2 \quad \mathcal{F}$$

are called *instances* of the above generalization. These instances are, of course, false statements. The instance

$$\boxed{6} - 4 = 2 \quad \mathcal{T}$$

is, of course, a true statement. The existential generalization

$$\exists_x \, x - 4 = 2$$

is a true statement because it has *at least one true instance*. That is, the existential generalization is true because there exists at least one number with such a property that when 4 is subtracted from it the result is 2.

Recall that the sentences

$$\boxed{3} \cdot 0 = 0 \quad \text{and} \quad \boxed{\tfrac{1}{2}} \cdot 0 = 0$$

are true statements. In fact,

each number has such a property that when it is multiplied by 0 the result is 0.

More briefly, we may say that

for each number x, x · 0 = 0.

This last sentence tells us about a property of numbers, and it too is called a generalization. Since it tells us that each number has a certain property, the sentence is called a *universal generalization*.

Universal generalizations are often written in an abbreviated form by using an upside-down 'A'.

The sentence

$$\forall_x \, x \cdot 0 = 0$$

is a shorthand notation which tells you that each number has such a property that when it is multiplied by 0 the result is 0. The sentence '$\forall_x \, x \cdot 0 = 0$' may be read as follows:

For each x, the product of x by 0 is 0.

Sentences such as

$$\boxed{5} \cdot 0 = 0 \quad \mathcal{T}$$

$$\text{or} \quad \boxed{6} \cdot 0 = 0 \quad \mathcal{T}$$

are instances of the above generalization. This universal generalization is a true statement because *all of its instances are true statements*.

Notice that there is no number which satisfies the open sentence x · 0 = 5. That is, the existential generalization

$$\exists_x \, x \cdot 0 = 5 \quad \mathcal{F}$$

is a false statement. This is equivalent to saying that each number satisfies the open sentence

$$\boxed{} \cdot 0 \neq 5$$

Therefore, the universal generalization

$$\forall_x \, x \cdot 0 \neq 5 \quad \mathcal{T}$$

is a true statement.

Notice, for example, that '$2 \cdot \boxed{4} = 6$' is a false statement. Thus it is not the case that each number satisfies the open sentence '$2x = 6$'. That is, the universal generalization

$$\forall_x \, 2 \cdot x = 6 \quad \mathcal{F}$$

is a false statement. This is equivalent to saying that there is a number which satisfies the open sentence

$$2 \cdot \boxed{} \neq 6$$

Therefore the existential generalization

$$\exists_x \, 2 \cdot x \neq 6 \quad \mathcal{T}$$

is a true statement.

The symbol '$\exists$' is called the *existential quantifier*. The symbol '$\forall$' is called the *universal quantifier*.

Here are some other examples of generalizations. Some are true and some are false:

1. $\exists_x \, x + 3 = 8$ 3. $\exists_x \, x \cdot 0 = 0$
2. $\forall_x \, x + 3 = 8$ 4. $\exists_x \, x + 3 = 3$

The first generalization is true because '$\boxed{5} + 3 = 8$' is a true instance of it. The second generalization is false because not all of its instances are true statements. For example, '$\boxed{6} + 3 = 8$' is a false statement. The third generalization is true because, for example, '$\boxed{1} \cdot 0 = 0$' is a true statement. The fourth is true because '$\boxed{0} + 3 = 3$' is a true statement.

PATTERNS AND PRINCIPLES

Let us consider the following question:

Does there exist a number with such a property that the result of adding it to 3 is the same as the result of subtracting it from 15?

This amounts to asking if there is a number which satisfies the open sentence

$$3 + \boxed{} = 15 - \boxed{}$$

The number 2 does not satisfy this open sentence because the sentence

$$3 + \boxed{2} = 15 - \boxed{2} \quad \mathcal{F}$$

is a false statement. The number 6 does satisfy the above open sentence because

$$3 + \boxed{6} = 15 - \boxed{6} \quad \mathcal{T}$$

is a true statement.

Notice that although the equation

$$3 + \boxed{5} = 15 - \boxed{7}$$

is a true statement, it does not follow the *pattern* suggested by the open sentence

$$3 + \boxed{} = 15 - \boxed{}$$

A sentence follows the pattern of this open sentence if and only if the *same* numeral is written in both square frames.

For each frame we may substitute an 'x'. Consider the open sentence

$$3 + x = 15 - x$$

This open sentence may be converted into a true statement by replacing each occurrence of the variable 'x' with the numeral '6'. It may be converted into a false statement by replacing each occurrence of the variable 'x' with the numeral '2'.

Thus we see it is true that

$$\exists_x \; 3 + x = 15 - x \qquad T$$

and it is false that

$$\forall_x \; 3 + x = 15 - x \qquad F$$

Let us now consider a very important fundamental property of numbers. Notice that, for each pair of numbers, the result of adding the second number to the first is the same as that for adding the first number to the second. For example:

$$\boxed{2} + \bullet\!3 = \bullet\!3 + \boxed{2} \qquad \begin{cases} 2 + 3 = 5 \\ 3 + 2 = 5 \end{cases}$$

$$\boxed{5} + \bullet\!15 = \bullet\!15 + \boxed{5} \qquad \begin{cases} 5 + 15 = 20 \\ 15 + 5 = 20 \end{cases}$$

Because of this property, each pair of numbers satisfies the open sentence

$$\square + \bullet = \bullet + \square$$

We agree that we shall be following the pattern suggested by this open sentence if a first numeral is written in each square frame and a second numeral is written in each circular frame.

Using variables instead of frames, we may say that each pair of numbers satisfies the open sentence

$$x + y = y + x$$

We agree that each occurrence of the variable 'x' is to be replaced by a first numeral and that each occurrence of the variable 'y' is to be replaced by a second numeral.

The property of numbers to which we have been referring may be stated as follows:

$$\forall_x \; \forall_y \; x + y = y + x$$

This universal generalization is called *the commutative principle for addition*. It tells you that

for each x and each y, x + y = y + x.

This is a true generalization because all of its instances are true statements.

The universal generalization

$$\forall_{x \neq 0} \; x \cdot \frac{1}{x} = 1$$

tells you that each *nonzero* number satisfies the open sentence $\square \cdot \dfrac{1}{\square} = 1$. This generalization is also a true statement because all of its instances are true statements. For example, the following instances are true statements:

$$\boxed{2} \cdot \frac{1}{\boxed{2}} = 1 \qquad\qquad \boxed{4} \cdot \frac{1}{\boxed{4}} = 1$$

The first of these sentences tells you, for example, that two halves of a pie is one pie. The second sentence tells you, for example, that four quarters of a pie is one pie. The number $\frac{1}{2}$ is called 'the *reciprocal* of 2';

the number $\frac{1}{4}$ is the reciprocal of 4.

Another basic property of numbers is suggested by the multiplication tables. For example, consider the following:

$$
\begin{aligned}
1 \cdot 2 &= 2 \\
2 \cdot 2 &= 4 \\
3 \cdot 2 &= 6 \\
4 \cdot 2 &= 8 \\
5 \cdot 2 &= 10 \\
6 \cdot 2 &= 12 \\
7 \cdot 2 &= 14
\end{aligned}
$$

$$3 + 4 = 7 \qquad\qquad 6 + 8 = 14$$

We see that the following sentence is a true statement:

$$\left(\diamond\!3 + \blacktriangle\!4 \right) \cdot \boxed{2} = \left(\diamond\!3 \cdot \boxed{2} \right) + \left(\blacktriangle\!4 \cdot \boxed{2} \right)$$

The open sentence

$$\left(\diamond + \blacktriangle \right) \cdot \square = \left(\diamond \cdot \square \right) + \left(\blacktriangle \cdot \square \right)$$

is converted into a true statement if a first numeral is written in each diamond-shaped frame, a second numeral is written in each triangular frame, and a third numeral is written in each square frame.

The universal generalization

$$\forall_x \forall_y \forall_z \; (x + y) \cdot z = (x \cdot z) + (y \cdot z)$$

tells you that

for each x, each y, and each z, the result of multiplying the sum of x and y by z is the same as the result obtained by multiplying x by z and y by z and then adding the products.

This universal generalization is called the *distributive principle* [technically: the distributive principle for multiplication over addition]. It is a true generalization because all of its instances are true. Thus, for example, the complicated numerical expression

$$(27 \cdot 18) + (73 \cdot 18)$$

may be simplified quite easily by noticing that, by the distributive principle,

$$\left(\diamond\!27 \cdot \boxed{18} \right) + \left(\blacktriangle\!73 \cdot \boxed{18} \right) = \left(\diamond\!27 + \blacktriangle\!73 \right) \cdot \boxed{18}$$

$$= 100 \cdot \boxed{18}$$

$$= 1800$$

So, $(27 \cdot 18) + (73 \cdot 18) = 1800$

REAL NUMBERS

Numbers-of-arithmetic are numbers which are used as measures of *magnitude*. For example, we use numbers-of-arithmetic when we speak of a 10-mile trip, a 15-pound package, or a 7-day vacation.

Real numbers are numbers which are used as measures of *directed change*—they measure *direction* as well as *magnitude*. For example, if you gain 10 pounds, the change in your weight is measured by the real number

$^+10$ [say "positive ten"].

If you go on a diet and lose 10 pounds, the change in your weight is measured by the real number

$^-10$ [say "negative ten"].

The set of real numbers consists of all the positive numbers, all the negative numbers, and 0. The real number 0 corresponds to the number-of-arithmetic 0. Corresponding to each nonzero number-of-arithmetic there are exactly two real numbers: one positive number and one negative number. For example, $^+10$ and $^-10$ are the two real numbers corresponding to the number-of-arithmetic 10. The number-of-arithmetic 10 is called the *arithmetic value* of $^+10$ and of $^-10$.

The sum of a pair of real numbers is the real number which is the measure of the *resultant* of the corresponding pair of directed changes. For example, if you gain 10 pounds [a change in weight measured by the real number $^+10$] and then lose 6 pounds [a change in weight measured by $^-6$], the resultant change in weight is a gain of 4 pounds [measured by $^+4$]. For short,

$$^+10 + {}^-6 = {}^+4$$

If you gain 6 pounds [$^+6$] and then lose 10 pounds [$^-10$], your net change in weight is a loss of 4 pounds:

$$^+6 + {}^-10 = {}^-4$$

If you gain 10 pounds and then lose 10 pounds, your net change in weight is 0:

$$^+10 + {}^-10 = 0$$

We say that

the **opposite** of $^+10$ is $^-10$

and that

the **opposite** of $^-10$ is $^+10$.

A short name for the opposite of $^+10$ is $- {}^+10$,

and a short name for the opposite of $^-10$ is

$$- {}^-10.$$

Since $\quad - {}^+10 = {}^-10,$

the sum of $^+10$ and its opposite is 0:

$$^+10 + - {}^+10 = {}^+10 + {}^-10$$

$$^+10 + {}^-10 = 0$$

So, $\quad \boxed{^+10} + - \boxed{^+10} = 0$

Similarly, $\quad \boxed{^-10} + - \boxed{^-10} = 0$

In fact, for each real number the sum of that real number and its opposite is 0. Moreover, if the sum of a pair of real numbers is 0, then each is the opposite of the other. For example,

$$^+10 + {}^-10 = 0,$$

and $^+10$ and $^-10$ are each the opposite of the other.

Notice that

$$0 + 0 = 0,$$

so the opposite of 0 is 0.

The opposite of a given real number is called the *additive inverse* of the real number. For example, the additive inverse of $^+10$ is $^-10$, and the additive inverse of 0 is 0. Each real number has an additive inverse.

Basic Principles for Addition

We shall list certain principles concerning addition of real numbers. These are called *basic principles*. We start our list with three principles mentioned above:

(A0) $\begin{cases} \text{(a) The sum of a pair of real numbers} \\ \quad \text{is a real number.} \\ \text{(b) 0 is a real number.} \\ \text{(c) The opposite of a real number is} \\ \quad \text{a real number.} \end{cases}$

Notice that a gain of 10 pounds followed by a loss of 6 pounds,

$$^+10 + {}^-6,$$

results in the same change in weight as a loss of 6 pounds followed by a gain of 10 pounds,

$$^-6 + {}^+10$$

Thus,

$$\boxed{^+10} + \bigcirc{^-6} = \bigcirc{^-6} + \boxed{^+10}$$

This suggests that addition of real numbers is a commutative operation, and we accept this as another of our basic principles for addition of real numbers:

(A1) $\qquad \forall_x \forall_y \ x + y = y + x$

A gain of 10 pounds followed by no further gain or loss of weight results in a gain of 10 pounds:

$$\boxed{^+10} + 0 = \boxed{^+10}$$

This suggests our next basic principle:

(A2) $\qquad \forall_x \ x + 0 = x$

We mentioned in the last section that the sum of a real number and its opposite is 0. We accept this as another basic principle:

(A3) $\qquad \forall_x \ x + - x = 0$

Finally we complete our list of basic principles with the *associative principle* for addition of real numbers. Before stating this principle, let us consider an example.

Suppose that you go on a two-week vacation. If you gain 2 pounds the first week and lose 3 pounds the second week [a resultant change in weight measured by the real number $^+2 + {}^-3$] and then come home and gain 4 pounds [$^+4$], your resultant change in weight is measured by the real number

$$(^+2 + {}^-3) + {}^+4$$

If, instead, you gained 2 pounds [$^+2$] the week before going on vacation and then lost 3 pounds the first week and gained 4 pounds the second week [$^-3 + {}^+4$] of vacation, your resultant change in weight is measured by the real number

$$^+2 + (^-3 + {}^+4)$$

Since $(^+2 + {}^-3) + {}^+4 = {}^-1 + {}^+4 = {}^+3$

and $^+2 + (^-3 + {}^+4) = {}^+2 + {}^+1 = {}^+3,$

it follows that

$$\left(\boxed{^+2} + \blacktriangle{^-3}\right) + \bullet{^+4} = \boxed{^+2} + \left(\blacktriangle{^-3} + \bullet{^+4}\right)$$

This suggests that the open sentence

$$\left(\square + \blacktriangle\right) + \bullet = \square + \left(\blacktriangle + \bullet\right)$$

is converted into a true statement if a first numeral is written in each square frame, a second numeral is written in each diamond-shaped frame, and a third numeral is written in each circular frame.

The universal generalization

(A4) $\quad \forall_x \forall_y \forall_z \, (x + y) + z = x + (y + z)$

is called the *associative principle* for addition of real numbers. This basic principle tells you that

> for each x, each y, and each z, the result of adding (x + y) and z is the same as the result of adding x and (y + z).

A short way of saying that addition of real numbers satisfies the basic principles (A0) through (A4) is to say that the set of real numbers is a *commutative group under addition*.

Basic Principles for Multiplication

Consideration of real numbers as measures of directed change suggests basic principles for multiplication of real numbers.

Let us first consider some examples. If you gain 3 pounds [a change in weight measured by $^+3$] each week, then 2 weeks from now [a change in time measured by $^+2$] you will be 6 pounds heavier [$^+6$]. We say that the product of $^+3$ and $^+2$ is $^+6$. For short,

$$^+3 \cdot {}^+2 = {}^+6$$

If you gained 3 pounds [$^+3$] each week, then 2 weeks ago [$^-2$] you were 6 pounds lighter [$^-6$]:

$$^+3 \cdot {}^-2 = {}^-6$$

If you lost 3 pounds [$^-3$] each week, then 2 weeks ago [$^-2$] you were 6 pounds heavier [$^+6$]:

$$^-3 \cdot {}^-2 = {}^+6$$

If a given real number is multiplied by the real number $^+1$, the product is the given real number. For example:

$$\boxed{^+2} \cdot {}^+1 = \boxed{^+2} \qquad \boxed{^-2} \cdot {}^+1 = \boxed{^-2}$$

We stated earlier that each real number has an additive inverse. It is also the case that each real number [except 0] has a *multiplicative inverse*. It is called the *reciprocal* of the real number. The result of multiplying a real number by its reciprocal is $^+1$; if the product of a pair of real numbers is $^+1$, then each is the reciprocal of the other. So, for example, the

reciprocal of $^+3$ is named by the fraction

because $\quad \boxed{^+3} \cdot \dfrac{^+1}{\boxed{^+3}} = {}^+1 \qquad \dfrac{^+1}{^+3}$

Each nonzero real number satisfies the open sentence

$$\square \cdot \dfrac{^+1}{\square} = {}^+1$$

Notice also that multiplication of real numbers satisfies the commutative principle. That is, the open sentence

$$\square \cdot \blacktriangle = \blacktriangle \cdot \square$$

is converted into a true statement if a first numeral is written in each square frame and a second numeral is written in each triangular frame. For example:

$$\boxed{^+2} \cdot \blacktriangle{^-3} = {}^-6$$

$$\blacktriangle{^-3} \cdot \boxed{^+2} = {}^-6$$

So, $\quad \boxed{^+2} \cdot \blacktriangle{^-3} = \blacktriangle{^-3} \cdot \boxed{^+2}$

Multiplication of real numbers also satisfies the associative principle. For example:

$$\left(\boxed{^+2} \cdot \blacktriangle{^-3}\right) \cdot \bullet{^+4} = {}^-6 \cdot {}^+4 = {}^-24$$

$$\boxed{^+2} \cdot \left(\blacktriangle{^-3} \cdot \bullet{^+4}\right) = {}^+2 \cdot {}^-12 = {}^-24$$

So, $\quad \left(\boxed{^+2} \cdot \blacktriangle{^-3}\right) \cdot \bullet{^+4} = \boxed{^+2} \cdot \left(\blacktriangle{^-3} \cdot \bullet{^+4}\right)$

These investigations of properties of real numbers suggest a list of basic principles for multiplication of real numbers which are similar to the basic principles for addition of real numbers. Corresponding to the basic principle (A0), we accept the basic principle:

(M0)
- (a) The product of a pair of real numbers is a real number.
- (b) $^+1$ is a real number, and $^+1 \neq 0$.
- (c) The reciprocal of a nonzero real number is a real number.

Corresponding to the basic principles (A1) through (A4), we accept the basic principles:

(M1) $\quad \forall_x \forall_y \, x \cdot y = y \cdot x$

(M2) $\quad \forall_x \, x \cdot {}^+1 = x$

(M3) $\quad \forall_{x \neq 0} \, x \cdot \dfrac{^+1}{x} = {}^+1$

(M4) $\quad \forall_x \forall_y \forall_z \, (x \cdot y) \cdot z = x \cdot (y \cdot z)$

The basic principle (M3) tells you that the product of each nonzero real number ($\forall_{x \neq 0}$) and its reciprocal is $^+1$.

Finally we complete our list of basic principles for addition and multiplication of real numbers by adding the distributive principle to the list:

(D1) $\quad \forall_x \forall_y \forall_z \, (x + y) \cdot z = (x \cdot z) + (y \cdot z)$

A short way of saying that addition and multiplication of real numbers satisfies the basic principles (A0) through (A4), (M0) through (M4), and (D1) is to say that the set of real numbers is a *field*.

In the next section we shall give some examples of how we may use these principles to deduce other properties of addition and multiplication of real numbers.

Using the Basic Principles

Let us use the basic principles to obtain some other principles of addition and multiplication of real numbers. We agree that the basic principles are true statements, and we show that other sentences are true statements by proving that they are logical consequences of the basic principles.

We begin with a very simple example. Notice that the sentence

$$\boxed{^{+}3} + 0 = \boxed{^{+}3}$$

is a true statement because it is an instance of the universal generalization (A2). The sentence

$$0 + \boxed{^{+}3} = \boxed{^{+}3}$$

is not an instance of (A2) because it does not follow the pattern suggested by 'x + 0 = x'. But it is a true statement. Do we need to do any computing to discover that it is true?

No! We can show that the sentence

$$0 + \boxed{^{+}3} = \boxed{^{+}3}$$

is true by showing that it is a consequence of (A1) and (A2). Here is how we might do this. The following sentence is an instance of (A1):

$$0 + \boxed{^{+}3} = \boxed{^{+}3} + 0$$

and this is an instance of (A2):

$$\boxed{^{+}3} + 0 = \boxed{^{+}3}$$

From these two sentences it follows that

$$0 + \boxed{^{+}3} \qquad = \boxed{^{+}3}$$

This suggests a pattern which we may follow in order to show that any instance of the universal generalization

$$(*) \quad \forall_x \, 0 + x = x$$

is a consequence of the basic principles (A1) and (A2). In view of this we say that the universal generalization itself is a consequence of (A1) and (A2).

The generalization (*) differs in an important respect from the generalizations listed in the basic principles. We accept the basic principles on the basis of computation with some examples. We accept (*) because it follows *logically* [that is, by reasoning alone] from the accepted basic principles. We *postulate* the basic principles, but we can *prove* (*).

Notice that the sentence

$$\boxed{^{+}3} \cdot {^{+}1} = \boxed{^{+}3}$$

is a true statement because it is an instance of the universal generalization (M2). The sentence

$${^{+}1} \cdot \boxed{^{+}3} = \boxed{^{+}3}$$

is not an instance of (M2). Can you show that it is a true statement by proving that it is a consequence of (M1) and (M2)? [Try it!]

Notice that none of the basic principles which we have listed says that the product of 0 and each real number is 0. We do not need a basic principle which says this because we can *prove* the universal generalization

$$\forall_x \, 0 \cdot x = 0$$

by showing that it is a consequence of our basic principles. As an example of the argument that may be used, here is a proof of the sentence

$$0 \cdot \boxed{^{+}3} = 0$$

First we notice that the following sentence is an instance of (A2):

$$\boxed{0} + 0 = \boxed{0}$$

So, $\qquad 0 \cdot {^{+}3} = (0 + 0) \cdot {^{+}3}$

By (D1), $\qquad (0 + 0) \cdot {^{+}3} = (0 \cdot {^{+}3}) + (0 \cdot {^{+}3})$

So, $\qquad 0 \cdot {^{+}3} = \underbrace{(0 \cdot {^{+}3}) + (0 \cdot {^{+}3})}$

It follows that

(I) $(0 \cdot {^{+}3}) + - (0 \cdot {^{+}3}) = [(0 \cdot {^{+}3}) + (0 \cdot {^{+}3})] + - (0 \cdot {^{+}3})$

Now by (A3),

(II) $(0 \cdot {^{+}3}) + - (0 \cdot {^{+}3}) = 0$

But, by (A4), (A3), and (A2),

$[(0 \cdot {^{+}3}) + (0 \cdot {^{+}3})] + - (0 \cdot {^{+}3}) = (0 \cdot {^{+}3}) + [(0 \cdot {^{+}3}) + - (0 \cdot {^{+}3})]$
$= (0 \cdot {^{+}3}) + 0$
$= 0 \cdot {^{+}3},$

and so it follows that

(III) $[(0 \cdot {^{+}3}) + (0 \cdot {^{+}3})] + - (0 \cdot {^{+}3}) = 0 \cdot {^{+}3}$

From sentences (I), (II), and (III), it follows that

$$0 \cdot {^{+}3} = 0$$

Thus we have shown that '$0 \cdot {^{+}3} = 0$' is a consequence of (A2), (D1), (A3), and (A4).

We may follow the pattern of argument to show that *any* instance of the universal generalization

$$\forall_x \, 0 \cdot x = 0$$

is a consequence of our basic principles. In view of this we say that the universal generalization itself is a consequence of our basic principles.

Recall now that our basic principle (M0)(b) tells us that

$$^{+}1 \neq 0$$

We therefore know that for each real number, the product of 0 and that real number is not $^{+}1$. That is,

$$\forall_x \, 0 \cdot x \neq {^{+}1}$$

This explains why 0 has no multiplicative inverse: the

269

result of multiplying a real number by its multiplicative inverse is $^+1$, but the result of multiplying 0 by any real number is not $^+1$.

Many other generalizations concerning addition and multiplication of real numbers may be shown to be consequences of our basic principles.

Subtraction of real numbers may be defined in terms of addition of real numbers. For example:

$$\boxed{^+10} - \triangle_{^+3} = \boxed{^+10} + - \triangle_{^+3}$$

$$\boxed{^+10} - \triangle_{^-3} = {}^+10 + - \triangle_{^-3}$$

Subtraction of real numbers may be defined by the universal generalization

$$\forall_x \forall_y \; x - y = x + -y.$$

We may show, for example, that the universal generalization

$$\forall_x \forall_y \; (x - y) + y = x$$

is a consequence of our basic principles and the definition of subtraction.

The reader should try to show that a particular instance of this universal generalization is a true statement. For example, try to show that the sentence

$$(^+3 - {}^-4) + {}^-4 = {}^+3$$

is a consequence of the definition of subtraction, (A4), (A1), (A3), and (A2). Here is how you might start:

By the definition of subtraction,

$$(^+3 - {}^-4) + {}^-4 = (^+3 + - {}^-4) + {}^-4$$

By (A4),

$$(^+3 + - {}^-4) + {}^-4 = {}^+3 + (- {}^-4 + {}^-4)\ldots.$$

[You complete the argument, using (A1), (A3), and (A2).]

In an analogous manner we may define division of a real number by a nonzero real number in terms of multiplication and reciprocating. For example:

$$\boxed{^+10} \div \triangle_{^+3} = \boxed{^+10} \cdot \frac{^+1}{\triangle_{^+3}}$$

Division of a real number by a nonzero real number may be defined by the universal generalization

$$\forall_x \forall_{y \neq 0} \; x \div y = x \cdot \frac{^+1}{y}$$

We may show, for example, that the universal generalization

$$\forall_x \forall_{y \neq 0} \; (x \div y) \cdot y = x$$

is a consequence of our basic principles and the definition of division.

The reader should try to show, for example, that the sentence

$$(^+3 \div {}^-4) \cdot {}^-4 = {}^+3$$

is a consequence of the definition of division, (M4), (M1), (M3), and (M2). [Start in a manner analogous to the manner in which you started to derive the sentence '$(^+3 - {}^-4) + {}^-4 = {}^+3$'.]

(For a more complete study of the algebra of real numbers, *see* the section "Applying the Fundamental Concepts of Algebra" later in this article. *See also* Numeration Systems and Numbers.)

THE BEGINNINGS OF ALGEBRA

More than 3,500 years ago an Egyptian named Ahmes collected together a set of mathematical problems and their solutions. Included were problems such as finding the number which satisfies the equation

$$x(\tfrac{2}{3} + \tfrac{1}{2} + \tfrac{1}{7} + 1) = 37$$

About 2,500 years ago the Greek mathematician Pythagoras started a religious-mathematical brotherhood. Its members were called Pythagoreans. Intensely interested in geometry, they classified numbers according to geometrical properties. For example, they studied properties of the triangular numbers

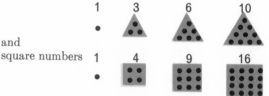

and square numbers

The famous Greek geometer Euclid discovered important properties of numbers through a study of geometry. For example, the truth of the sentence

$$2 \cdot (3 + 4) = (2 \cdot 3) + (2 \cdot 4)$$

is verified geometrically by noting that the area of the following rectangle:

$$\text{area} = 2 \cdot (3 + 4)$$
$$= 2 \cdot 7$$
$$= 14$$

is the same as the sum of the areas of the following rectangles:

$$\text{area} = 2 \cdot 3 \qquad \text{area} = 2 \cdot 4$$
$$= 6 \qquad\qquad = 8 \qquad [6 + 8 = 14]$$

Diophantus, another famous early Greek mathematician, has been called the "father of algebra." He treated algebra from a purely numerical point of view. He made a special study of certain types of equations which are today called Diophantine equations.

Our modern word "algebra" comes from the Arabic *al-jabr*, which appeared in the title of an algebra text written about A.D. 825 by the Arab astronomer and mathematician al-Khwarizmi. The words "algorism" and "algorithm" are derived from his name.

MODERN ALGEBRA

Our algebra of real numbers developed through the centuries from considerations of problems in arithmetic. The study of the algebra of real numbers and the recent recognition of the fundamental importance of the *basic principles* have led to the development of what is now called *modern algebra* or *abstract algebra*.

One of the earliest pioneers in this direction was the

French genius Évariste Galois (1811–32). Although he lived a tragic life and died in a foolish duel at the age of 20, his work led to the development of the modern *theory of groups and fields*.

The concepts of modern algebra have been found to be extremely useful in other branches of mathematics, as well as in the physical and social sciences. A chemist may use modern algebra in a study of the structure of crystals; a physicist may use modern algebra in designing an electronic computer; a mathematician may use modern algebra in a study of logic.

In the algebra of real numbers we study the properties of addition and multiplication of real numbers which follow as a consequence of certain basic principles. In modern algebra we may work with any set of objects. [We need not work just with real numbers.] We consider certain operations on these objects. [These operations need not be addition and multiplication.] We agree that certain basic principles are satisfied by these operations. [These basic principles need not be the same as our basic principles for addition and multiplication of real numbers.] Then we derive various properties which follow as consequences of the assumed basic principles.

BOOLEAN ALGEBRA

An important branch of mathematics is called *Boolean algebra* for the English mathematician and logician George Boole (1815–64). It combines algebraic methods and logic. Let us consider a simple example.

Suppose that two sources of electric power are connected to a motor which we shall label 'Motor ⊕ ':

We suppose that Motor ⊕ is operating if at least one of the power sources is in operation but is not operating if neither power source is operating. We now ask a series of three questions, each of which can be answered 'Yes' or 'No', and such that the answers to the first two questions determine the answer to the third question. We list the different possible combinations of answers to the first two questions, and the corresponding answers to the third question:

Is source A in operation?	Is source B in operation?	Is Motor ⊕ in operation?
No	No	No
No	Yes	Yes
Yes	No	Yes
Yes	Yes	Yes

Given the answers to the first two questions, we can determine the answer to the third question. The above list suggests that we may define an operation which we shall denote by the symbol '⊕':

No	⊕	No	= No
No	⊕	Yes	= Yes
Yes	⊕	No	= Yes
Yes	⊕	Yes	= Yes

Suppose now that Motor ⊕ is replaced by a new motor, which we shall label 'Motor ⊗':

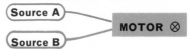

We suppose that Motor ⊗ is not operating unless both sources of electricity are in operation. We may ask the same series of three questions, and again the answers to the first two questions determine the answer to the third question:

Is source A in operation?	Is source B in operation?	Is Motor ⊗ in operation?
No	No	No
No	Yes	No
Yes	No	No
Yes	Yes	Yes

This list suggests another operation, which we shall denote by the symbol '⊗':

No	⊗	No	= No
No	⊗	Yes	= No
Yes	⊗	No	= No
Yes	⊗	Yes	= Yes

The operations ⊕ and ⊗ suggest a type of miniature arithmetic in which we work with the objects

No and **Yes**

instead of real numbers. These operations satisfy certain basic principles which qualify the arithmetic to be called a Boolean algebra.

For example, just as in the algebra of real numbers, ⊕ and ⊗ satisfy the commutative principles

(A1) $\square \oplus \bullet = \bullet \oplus \square$

(M1) $\square \otimes \bullet = \bullet \otimes \square$

Thus, for example, the sentences

$$\text{No} \oplus \text{Yes} = \text{Yes} \oplus \text{No} \quad \begin{cases} \text{No} \oplus \text{Yes} = \text{Yes} \\ \text{Yes} \oplus \text{No} = \text{Yes} \end{cases}$$

and $\text{No} \otimes \text{Yes} = \text{Yes} \otimes \text{No}$ $\begin{cases} \text{No} \otimes \text{Yes} = \text{No} \\ \text{Yes} \otimes \text{No} = \text{No} \end{cases}$

are, by our rules, true statements.

These are only a few of the basic principles of a Boolean algebra. The basic principles of a Boolean algebra are very much like those of the algebra of real numbers. A knowledge of Boolean algebra is very useful in fields requiring the application of mathematics and logic. Electronic-computer programming and the construction of electronic circuits are examples of such fields.

At this point, the student has developed an understanding of the fundamental algebraic concepts and of algebra's relationship to other branches of mathematics. The following section will deepen this understanding by explaining how the fundamental concepts of the algebra of real numbers may be applied in solving various kinds of mathematical problems.

271

Applying the Fundamental Concepts of Algebra

AN UNDERSTANDING of the fundamental concepts of algebra and of how those fundamental concepts may be applied is necessary in many professional and most technical careers. For engineers and scientists it is an essential requirement.

The fundamental concepts of algebra are described in the preceding section of this article. How these concepts may be applied to aid in the solution of various types of mathematical problems is explained here.

USING REAL NUMBERS

An example of the use of real numbers is in the measurement of temperatures. If it is a very cold day, it may not be enough to tell someone that the temperature is **5** degrees; you may have to indicate whether it is **5** degrees "above zero" or **5** degrees "below zero." You may use the real numbers $^+5$ [say "*positive* **5** "] or $^-5$ [say "*negative* **5** "] to indicate the temperature. The degree temperatures "above zero" are measured by positive real numbers, and the degree temperatures "below zero" are measured by negative real numbers.

It may be helpful to picture the set of real numbers as the set of points on a line:

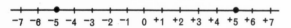

A diagram such as this is often called a *picture of the number line*. The point labeled '0' is called the *origin* (*see* Numeration Systems and Numbers).

The *number-of-arithmetic* **5** is the arithmetic value of the real numbers $^+5$ and $^-5$. The numbers-of-arithmetic are used as measures of *magnitude;* the real numbers are used as measures of *magnitude and direction.*

As another example of how real numbers are used, consider the measurement of distances above and below sea level. The elevation of Mount McKinley is 20,320 feet *above* sea level, measured by the real number $^+20,320$. Death Valley has an elevation of 282 feet *below* sea level, measured by the real number $^-282$. The elevation at sea level is 0; distances above sea level are measured by positive real numbers, and distances below sea level are measured by negative real numbers.

OPERATIONS ON REAL NUMBERS

In the preceding section of this article, it was mentioned that the *sum* of a pair of real numbers is the real number which is the measure of the *resultant* of the corresponding pair of directed changes. To gain further insight into addition of real numbers it may be convenient to refer to a picture of the number line.

For example:

$^+3 + \, ^+2 = \, ^+5$

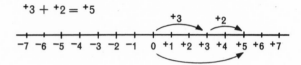

$^-3 + \, ^-2 = \, ^-5$

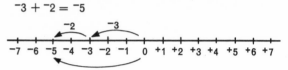

Notice that we may apply our knowledge of addition of numbers-of-arithmetic when we wish to add a pair of positive numbers [or a pair of negative numbers]; for the arithmetic value of the sum of a pair of positive numbers [or of a pair of negative numbers] is the sum of their arithmetic values:

$$3 + 2 = 5$$

If we wish to find the sum of a positive number and a negative number, for example:

$^+3 + \, ^-2 = \, ^+1$

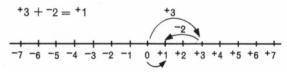

or the sum of a negative number and a positive number, for example:

$^-3 + \, ^+2 = \, ^-1$

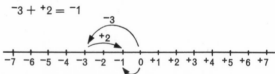

we may apply our knowledge of subtraction of numbers-of-arithmetic:

$$3 - 2 = 1$$

In the preceding section of this article, subtraction of real numbers was defined in terms of addition and oppositing. For example:

$$^+3 - \, ^+2$$

is simply a shorthand notation for

$$^+3 + - \, ^+2$$

Since

$$- \, ^+2 = \, ^-2$$

it follows that

$$^+3 - \, ^+2 = \, ^+3 + - \, ^+2 = \, ^+3 + \, ^-2 = \, ^+1$$

Thus, the result of subtracting $^+2$ from $^+3$ is $^+1$.

Similarly, the result of subtracting $^+3$ from $^+2$ is $^-1$:

$$^+2 - {}^+3 = {}^+2 + - {}^+3 = {}^+2 + {}^-3 = {}^-1$$

Multiplication of real numbers is similarly related to multiplication of numbers-of-arithmetic:

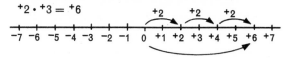

$^+2 \cdot {}^+3 = {}^+6$

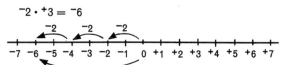

$^+2 \cdot {}^-3 = {}^-6$

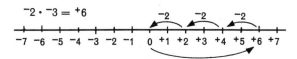

$^-2 \cdot {}^+3 = {}^-6$

$^-2 \cdot {}^-3 = {}^+6$

Notice that the arithmetic value of the product of a pair of real numbers is the product of their arithmetic values:

$$2 \cdot 3 = 6$$

Notice also that the product of a positive number by a positive number [or of a negative number by a negative number] is a positive number. The product of a positive number by a negative number [or of a negative number by a positive number] is a negative number.

In the preceding section of this article, division of a real number by a nonzero number was defined in terms of multiplication and reciprocation. For example:

$$^+6 \div {}^+3$$

is simply a shorthand notation for

$$^+6 \cdot \tfrac{^+1}{^+3}$$

Let us see what it means to divide $^+6$ by $^+3$. We wish to find the real number which satisfies the open sentence

$$^+6 \cdot \tfrac{^+1}{^+3} = \square$$

A real number satisfies this open sentence if and only if it satisfies the following open sentence:

$$\overline{\left(^+6 \cdot \tfrac{^+1}{^+3}\right) \cdot {}^+3} = \square \cdot {}^+3$$

But,

$$\overline{\left(^+6 \cdot \tfrac{^+1}{^+3}\right) \cdot {}^+3} = {}^+6 \cdot \left(\tfrac{^+1}{^+3} \cdot {}^+3\right)$$

$$= {}^+6 \cdot \left(^+3 \cdot \tfrac{^+1}{^+3}\right)$$

$$= {}^+6 \cdot {}^+1$$

$$= \underline{{}^+6}$$

So a real number satisfies the open sentence

$$^+6 \cdot \tfrac{^+1}{^+3} = \square$$

if and only if it satisfies the open sentence

$$\underline{^+6} = \square \cdot {}^+3$$

We notice that $^+2$ is the real number which satisfies the last open sentence

$$\underline{^+6} = \boxed{^+2} \cdot {}^+3$$

So it follows that

$$^+6 \cdot \tfrac{^+1}{^+3} = \boxed{^+2}$$

or, equivalently, that

$$^+6 \div {}^+3 = \boxed{^+2}$$

Here are some other examples to illustrate division of real numbers:

$^+15 \div {}^+5 = \boxed{^+3}$ because $^+15 = \boxed{^+3} \cdot {}^+5$

$^+16 \div {}^-2 = \boxed{^-8}$ because $^+16 = \boxed{^-8} \cdot {}^-2$

$^-12 \div {}^+2 = \boxed{^-6}$ because $^-12 = \boxed{^-6} \cdot {}^+2$

$^-9 \div {}^-3 = \boxed{^+3}$ because $^-9 = \boxed{^+3} \cdot {}^-3$

Notice the similarity between division of real numbers and division of numbers-of-arithmetic. For example:

$15 \div 5 = \boxed{3}$ because $15 = \boxed{3} \cdot 5$

$16 \div 2 = \boxed{8}$ because $16 = \boxed{8} \cdot 2$

Notice also that the result of dividing a positive number by a positive number [or of dividing a negative number by a negative number] is a positive number. The result of dividing a positive number by a negative number [or of dividing a negative number by a positive number] is a negative number.

FORMULAS, FUNCTIONS, AND GRAPHS

A fruit dealer sells apples priced at 12 cents each. He may find it convenient to make a list of the cost of various quantities of apples:

Number of apples	Cost
0	\$ 0
1	.12
2	.24
3	.36

He may, of course, extend this list as far as necessary.

Notice that to find the cost of any quantity of apples he may use the *formula*

$$C = .12 \cdot N$$

If he substitutes a numeral for 'N', he can find the corresponding cost by using this formula. For example, to find the cost of 17 apples he substitutes '17' for 'N':

$$C = .12 \cdot 17$$

ALGEBRA

If he multiplies .12 by 17, he finds that the cost of 17 apples is $2.04.

We assume that the dealer is not interested in knowing the cost of fractional parts of an apple. Thus the *values* of 'N' are simply the whole numbers

$$0, 1, 2, 3, \ldots$$

and the values of 'C' are simply the multiples of .12.

It is also useful to consider the set of *ordered pairs*:

$$\{(0, 0), (1, .12), (2, .24), \ldots \}$$

The first member of an ordered pair is called the *first component*, and the second member of an ordered pair is called the *second component*. For example, the first component of the ordered pair (3, .36) is 3, and its second component is .36. Notice that in the set of ordered pairs which we are considering, no two ordered pairs have the same first component. [For example, the two ordered pairs (1, .12) and (2, .24) have different first components.]

A set of ordered pairs which satisfies the condition that no two ordered pairs in the set have the same first component is called a *function*. Thus, the set of ordered pairs given above is a function.

The set of ordered pairs given above may be described as the set of all ordered pairs (n, c), where the first component is a whole number, such that

$$c = n \cdot .12$$

The *domain* of a function is the set of first components of the set of ordered pairs of which the function consists. The *range* of a function is the set of second components. In the example considered above, the domain of the function is the set of whole numbers, and the range of the function is the set of multiples of .12.

Instead of listing the costs of various quantities of apples, the dealer may make a *graph:*

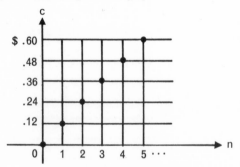

The dot which is above '1' and to the right of '.12' illustrates the point which corresponds to the ordered pair (1, .12). The dot which is above '2' and to the right of '.24' illustrates the point corresponding to the ordered pair (2, .24). By referring to the graph, the dealer can see at a glance that the cost of 4 apples is 48 cents.

The domain of the function whose graph is pictured above consists of only the whole numbers. For this reason, the graph of this function consists of only a sequence of points.

272b

Linear Functions

Consider the set of all ordered pairs of real numbers (x, y) which satisfy the condition that the sum of the first and second components is $^+5$:

$$x + y = {}^+5$$

Some ordered pairs which belong to this function are:

$$({}^+5, 0), \left({}^+3\tfrac{1}{2}, {}^+1\tfrac{1}{2}\right), ({}^+6, {}^-1)$$

This set of ordered pairs may also be described as the set of all ordered pairs of real numbers (x, y) such that

$$y = {}^-1 \cdot x + {}^+5$$

This set of ordered pairs of real numbers is a function whose domain and range is the set of all real numbers. The graph of this function is a line:

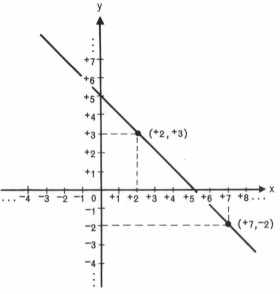

The points on the graph which correspond to the ordered pairs ($^+2$, $^+3$) and ($^+7$, $^-2$) are marked on the graph. You may find it worthwhile to locate the points on the graph which correspond to the following ordered pairs:

$$(0, {}^+5), ({}^+1.5, {}^+3.5), ({}^-1, {}^+6)$$

Since the graph of the function is a line, the function is called a *linear function*, and the equation

$$y = {}^-1 \cdot x + {}^+5$$

is called a *linear equation*.

Since the graph of a linear function is a straight line, many geometric problems which involve lines and line segments may be solved by algebraic methods. The properties of linear functions are studied in analytic geometry and calculus (*see* Geometry; Calculus).

Another example of a linear function is the set of all ordered pairs of real numbers (x, y) such that

$$y = x + {}^+1$$

Some ordered pairs which belong to this function are:

$$(0, {}^+1), ({}^-1, 0), ({}^+2.5, {}^+3.5), ({}^-2.5, {}^-1.5)$$

The graph of this function is a line:

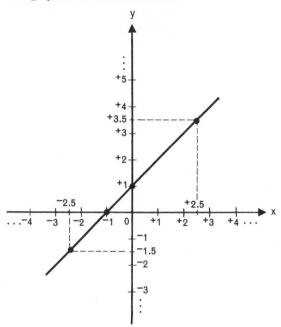

Here are other examples of linear equations:

$$y = x + {}^-6 \quad y = {}^+5x + {}^-2 \quad y = {}^-4x + {}^+1$$

In fact, if 'a' and 'b' are real numbers, and 'a' $\neq$ 0,

$$y = ax + b$$

is a linear equation. The corresponding function is a linear function, and its graph is a straight line.

Quadratic Functions

The formula for computing the area of a *rectangle* is

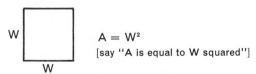

$$A = L \cdot W$$

This formula tells you that the area of a rectangle may be found by multiplying its length by its width. For example, the area of a rectangle 5 inches long and 2 inches wide may be found by substituting '5' for 'L' and '2' for 'W' in the formula and then multiplying:

$$A = 5 \cdot 2 = 10$$

Hence the area of the given rectangle is 10 square inches.

If the rectangle is such that the length is the same as the width, the rectangle is called a *square*, and the formula for its area is

$$A = W^2$$

[say "A is equal to W squared"]

The numeral '2' is called an *exponent*. The expression 'W²' is a shorthand notation for

$$W \cdot W$$

The set of all ordered pairs of real numbers (x, y) such that

$$y = x^2$$

is a function. Some ordered pairs which belong to this function are:

$$(0, 0), ({}^+1, {}^+1), ({}^-1, {}^+1), ({}^+2, {}^+4), ({}^-2, {}^+4)$$

The graph of this function is not a line; the function is not a linear function. It is an example of a *quadratic function*. Its graph is a *parabola:*

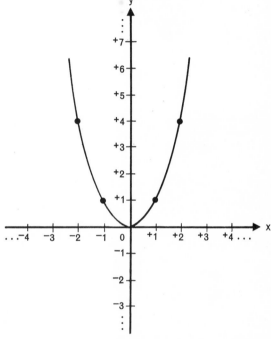

Another example of a quadratic function is the set of all ordered pairs of real numbers (x, y) such that

$$y = {}^+2x^2 + {}^+5x + {}^-1$$

If 'a', 'b', and 'c' are real numbers, and 'a' $\neq$ 0, then the set of all ordered pairs (x, y) such that

$$y = ax^2 + bx + c$$

is called a quadratic function. The properties of quadratic functions are studied in analytic geometry and calculus.

Functions of Higher Degree

Consider the function consisting of all ordered pairs of real numbers (x, y) such that

$$y = x^3 \text{ [say "y is equal to x cubed"]}$$

The expression 'x³' is a shorthand notation for

$$x \cdot x \cdot x$$

Some ordered pairs which belong to this function are:

$$(0, 0), ({}^+1, {}^+1), ({}^-1, {}^-1), ({}^+2, {}^+8), ({}^-2, {}^-8)$$

272c

This function is an example of a *third degree* function:

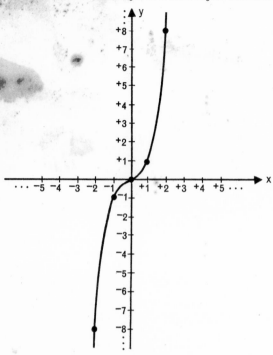

The function consisting of the set of all ordered pairs of real numbers (x, y) such that

$$y = x^4 \text{ [say "y is equal to x to the fourth"]}$$

is an example of a *fourth degree* function. The expression 'x⁴' is, of course, a shorthand notation for

$$x \cdot x \cdot x \cdot x$$

Some ordered pairs which belong to this function are:

$$(0, 0), (^+1, ^+1), (^-1, ^+1), (^+2, ^+16), (^-2, ^+16)$$

You might find it interesting to draw a graph of this function.

Properties of Exponents

In the preceding section of this article, the basic principles for addition and multiplication of real numbers were listed. From these basic principles, other principles were derived. We now note some properties of exponents which follow easily from the basic principles.

Notice, for example, that

$$2^2 \cdot 2^3 = (2 \cdot 2) \cdot (2 \cdot 2 \cdot 2)$$
$$= 4 \cdot 8$$
$$= 32$$

and that $2^5 = 2 \cdot 2 \cdot 2 \cdot 2 \cdot 2 = 32$

In fact, it is easy to prove the following principle:

$$\forall_x \ x^2 \cdot x^3 = x^5$$

This principle tells you that for each real number 'x', the product of 'x²' by 'x³' is 'x⁵'. [Notice that $2+3=5$.]

Note also, for example, that

$$\frac{2^5}{2^2} = \frac{2 \cdot 2 \cdot 2 \cdot 2 \cdot 2}{2 \cdot 2} = \frac{32}{4} = 8 = 2 \cdot 2 \cdot 2 = 2^3$$

and that $\frac{2^2}{2^5} = \frac{2 \cdot 2}{2 \cdot 2 \cdot 2 \cdot 2 \cdot 2} = \frac{4}{32} = \frac{1}{8} = \frac{1}{2 \cdot 2 \cdot 2} = \frac{1}{2^3}$

These examples suggest the following principles which are easily proved to be consequences of the basic principles:

$$\forall_{x \neq 0} \ \frac{x^5}{x^2} = x^3 \qquad \forall_{x \neq 0} \ \frac{x^2}{x^5} = \frac{1}{x^3}$$

[Notice that $5-2=3$.]

The principles suggest methods you may use to solve problems like the following without using pencil and paper:

(a) $3^3 \cdot 3^5 = ?$ [Solution: $3^3 \cdot 3^5 = 3^8$]

(b) $\frac{2^6}{2^2} = ?$ [Solution: $\frac{2^6}{2^2} = 2^4$]

(c) $\frac{2^2}{2^6} = ?$ [Solution: $\frac{2^2}{2^6} = \frac{1}{2^4}$]

You may, of course, check the answers by computing. For example, in the last problem we have:

$$\frac{2^2}{2^6} = \frac{2 \cdot 2}{2 \cdot 2 \cdot 2 \cdot 2 \cdot 2 \cdot 2} = \frac{4}{64} = \frac{1}{16} = \frac{1}{2 \cdot 2 \cdot 2 \cdot 2} = \frac{1}{2^4}$$

Products and Factoring

You already know that, for each real number 'a',

$$2 \cdot a + 3 \cdot a = 5 \cdot a$$

This follows from the distributive principle (*see* section on fundamental concepts)

$$2 \cdot a + 3 \cdot a = (2 + 3) \cdot a$$

and the fact that $2+3=5$.

Consider now the *indicated product:*

$$(a + 2) \cdot (a + 3)$$

From the basic principles it follows that:

$$(a + 2) \cdot (a + 3) = (a + 2) \cdot a + (a + 2) \cdot 3$$
$$= (a^2 + 2 \cdot a) + (a \cdot 3 + 2 \cdot 3)$$
$$= (a^2 + 2 \cdot a) + (3 \cdot a + 6)$$
$$= a^2 + (2 \cdot a + 3 \cdot a) + 6$$
$$= a^2 + 5 \cdot a + 6$$

Thus,

$$(a + 2) \cdot (a + 3) = a^2 + 5 \cdot a + 6$$

We say that the expression $a^2 + 5 \cdot a + 6$ is the *expanded* form of the indicated product

$$(a + 2) \cdot (a + 3)$$

When we transform an expression into an indicated product, we say that the expression has been *factored*. We see that the expression

$$a^2 + 5 \cdot a + 6$$

may be factored, and that its *factors* are

$$(a + 2) \text{ and } (a + 3)$$

Notice that for each pair of real numbers 'a' and 'b':

$$(a + b) \cdot (a + b) = (a + b) \cdot a + (a + b) \cdot b$$
$$= (a^2 + b \cdot a) + (a \cdot b + b^2)$$
$$= a^2 + (a \cdot b + a \cdot b) + b^2$$
$$= a^2 + 2 \cdot a \cdot b + b^2$$

Thus,

$$(a + b) \cdot (a + b) = a^2 + 2 \cdot a \cdot b + b^2$$

and we see that for each pair of real numbers 'a' and 'b', the expression

$$a^2 + 2 \cdot a \cdot b + b^2$$

may be factored.

For each pair of real numbers 'a' and 'b', the expression

$$a^2 - b^2$$

may also be factored. This is demonstrated as follows:

$$(a - b) \cdot (a + b) = (a - b) \cdot a + (a - b) \cdot b$$
$$= (a^2 - b \cdot a) + (a \cdot b - b^2)$$
$$= (a^2 + - a \cdot b) + (a \cdot b - b^2)$$
$$= a^2 + (- a \cdot b + a \cdot b) - b^2$$
$$= a^2 + 0 - b^2$$
$$= a^2 - b^2$$

Thus,

$$(a - b) \cdot (a + b) = a^2 - b^2$$

A knowledge of factoring may be helpful when we wish to simplify a given expression. The following two examples illustrate this:

Example 1: $\dfrac{5 \cdot a + 5 \cdot b}{5} = ?$

Solution: $\dfrac{5 \cdot a + 5 \cdot b}{5} = \dfrac{5 \cdot (a + b)}{5}$

$$= 5 \cdot (a + b) \cdot \frac{1}{5}$$
$$= (a + b) \cdot (5 \cdot \frac{1}{5})$$
$$= (a + b) \cdot 1$$
$$= a + b$$

Example 2: $\dfrac{a^2 - 4}{a - 2} = ?$ [$a \neq 2$]

Solution: $\dfrac{a^2 - 4}{a - 2} = \dfrac{a^2 - 2^2}{a - 2} = \dfrac{(a - 2) \cdot (a + 2)}{a - 2} = a + 2$

A knowledge of factoring may also provide a shortcut in computing. The following example illustrates this:

Example 3: $19 \cdot 21 = ?$

Solution: $19 \cdot 21 = (20 - 1) \cdot (20 + 1)$
$$= 20^2 - 1^2$$
$$= 400 - 1$$
$$= 399$$

The ability to factor is also important in finding the solutions of quadratic equations. This will be shown under the subhead "Quadratic Equations."

It will be instructive for you to try to factor the following expressions by transforming each expression into an indicated product:

 (a) $3 \cdot 3 + 3 \cdot 4$
 (b) $a^2 - a \cdot b$
 (c) $a^2 - 2 \cdot a \cdot b + b^2$

Answers: (a) $3 \cdot 3 + 3 \cdot 4 = 3 \cdot (3 + 4)$
 (b) $a^2 - a \cdot b = a \cdot (a - b)$
 (c) $a^2 - 2 \cdot a \cdot b + b^2 = (a - b) \cdot (a - b)$

Quadratic Equations

Consider the equation

$$x^2 - {}^+25 = 0$$

This equation is an example of a *quadratic equation*. The real numbers $^+5$ and $^-5$ both *satisfy* the above open sentence:

$$\boxed{^+5}{}^2 - {}^+25 = 0$$

$$\boxed{^-5}{}^2 - {}^+25 = 0$$

The solution set of the given equation consists of simply the real numbers $^+5$ and $^-5$. We say that $^+5$ and $^-5$ are the two *roots* of the given quadratic equation.

When we are trying to find the roots of a quadratic equation, we often make use of an important principle of real numbers. This principle, which is derived from the basic principles listed in the preceding section, states that the product of a pair of real numbers is 0 if and only if one of the numbers is 0. That is,

$$\forall_x \forall_y \; xy = 0$$

if and only if

$$x = 0 \text{ or } y = 0$$

Let us see how we may use this principle to find the roots of the quadratic equation

$$x^2 - {}^+16 = 0$$

We first notice that the expression

$$x^2 - {}^+16$$

may be factored:

$$x^2 - {}^+16 = x^2 - {}^+4^2 = (x - {}^+4) \cdot (x + {}^+4)$$

Thus, we may transform the given equation

$$x^2 - {}^+16 = 0$$

into the *equivalent* equation

$$(x - {}^+4) \cdot (x + {}^+4) = 0$$

A real number satisfies the last equation if and only if it satisfies the given equation.

We know that

$$(x - {}^+4) \cdot (x + {}^+4) = 0$$

if and only if

$$x - {}^+4 = 0 \text{ or } x + {}^+4 = 0$$

Thus, a real number satisfies the equation

$$(x - {}^+4) \cdot (x + {}^+4) = 0$$

if and only if the real number satisfies one of the following equations:

$$x - {}^+4 = 0 \text{ or } x + {}^+4 = 0$$

The solution set of the equation

$$x - {}^+4 = 0$$

consists of simply the number $^+4$, since

$$\boxed{^+4} - {}^+4 = 0$$

The solution set of the equation

$$x + {}^+4 = 0$$

consists of simply the number $^-4$, since

$$\boxed{^-4} + {}^+4 = 0$$

Thus, the solution set of the equation

$$(x - {}^+4) \cdot (x + {}^+4) = 0$$

consists of the numbers $^+4$ and $^-4$. Hence the roots of the given quadratic equation

$$x^2 - {}^+16 = 0$$

are the numbers $^+4$ and $^-4$. We may check this result:

Check: $\boxed{^+4}^2 - {}^+16 = 0$ and $\boxed{^-4}^2 - {}^+16 = 0$

Here is another example which shows how factoring aids us in finding the roots of a quadratic equation:

Example: Find the roots of the equation

$$x^2 - {}^+3x = 0$$

Solution: The expression $x^2 - {}^+3x$ may be factored

$$x^2 - {}^+3x = (x - {}^+3) \cdot x$$

Hence the given equation may be transformed into the equivalent equation

$$(x - {}^+3) \cdot x = 0$$

A real number satisfies this equation if and only if it satisfies one of the following equations:

$$x - {}^+3 = 0 \text{ or } x = 0$$

The only real number which satisfies the equation

$$x - {}^+3 = 0$$

is $^+3$, and the only real number which satisfies the equation

$$x = 0$$

is 0. Thus, the roots of the given equation are $^+3$ and 0.

Check: $\boxed{^+3}^2 - {}^+3 \cdot \boxed{^+3} = 0$ and

$\boxed{0}^2 - {}^+3 \cdot \boxed{0} = 0$

SOLVING PROBLEMS

The following are some typical problems which, in a natural way, lead us to algebraic equations. In each problem, the solution to the problem is found by finding the solution set of an equation. When we find the solution set of an equation, we say that we have *solved* the equation.

Example 1: A number has such a property that when 6 is subtracted from twice the number, the result is 16. What is the number?

Solution: The required number must satisfy the open sentence

$$2 \cdot \square - 6 = 16$$

or, equivalently, the required number must satisfy each of the following open sentences:

$$(2 \cdot \square - 6) + 6 = 16 + 6$$
$$2 \cdot \square = 22$$
$$\tfrac{1}{2} \cdot (2 \cdot \square) = \tfrac{1}{2} \cdot 22$$
$$\square = 11$$

Since the only number which satisfies the last equation is 11, 11 is the required number. We may check our result:

Check: $2 \cdot \boxed{11} - 6 = 22 - 6 = 16$

Example 2: A number has such a property that when 10 is subtracted from twice the number, the result is the same as when 6 is added to the number. What is the number?

Solution: A number has the required property if and only if it satisfies the open sentence

$$2 \cdot x - 10 = x + 6$$

or, equivalently, a number has the required property if and only if it satisfies each of the following open sentences:

$$(2 \cdot x - 10) + 10 = (x + 6) + 10$$
$$2x = x + 16$$
$$-x + 2x = -x + (x + 16)$$
$$(-x + x) + x = (-x + x) + 16$$
$$x = 16$$

The only number which satisfies the last open sentence is 16. Therefore, 16 is the required number.

Check: $2 \cdot \boxed{16} - 10 = \boxed{16} + 6$

Example 3: Suppose that Tom has $6.00 more than Bill and that together they have a total of $12.00. How much money does Tom have? How much money does Bill have?

Solution: Suppose that Tom has 't' dollars and that Bill has 'b' dollars. Since Tom has $6.00 more than Bill, then

$$(1) \quad t = 6 + b$$

Since Tom and Bill have together a total of $12.00, then

$$(2) \quad t + b = 12$$

Equation (1) tells us that

t is the same as 6 + b

We may therefore replace 't' by '6+b' in equation (2):

$$(6 + b) + b = 12$$

Thus,
$$6 + 2b = 12$$
$$2b = 6$$
$$b = 3$$

Therefore Bill has $3.00. It follows that

$$t = 6 + b = 6 + 3 = 9$$

and so Tom has $9.00.

Check:

$(1) \quad \boxed{9} = 6 + \triangle{3}$

$(2) \quad \boxed{9} + \triangle{3} = 12$

These examples show how a knowledge of algebra may be applied to solve a variety of mathematical problems. An understanding of the fundamental concepts of algebra and practice in using them to solve problems will enable anyone to discover how useful and enjoyable algebra may be.

This modern industrial city is Algiers, the capital of Algeria. Once a refuge for the Barbary pirates, the city is now a major port on the Mediterranean Sea.

ALGERIA—Land of Fertile Fields and Desert Wastes

ALGERIA. Situated on the north coast of Africa, Algeria was part of the French colonial empire in that area for more than a century. In 1962— after a long, bitter struggle— Algeria attained independence. The nation covers an area of 919,353 square miles—more than four times the area of France. Its boundaries touch the territories of seven nations. To the west and southwest are Morocco, Spanish Sahara, Mauritania, and Mali. To the east and southeast are Tunisia, Libya, and Niger.

The Land and the People

Along the Mediterranean coast in the north is a fertile, 50-mile-wide, 600-mile-long strip. Behind this plain are the Atlas Mountains. South of the mountains are the vast wastes of the Sahara, composing about two thirds of the country.

Along the coastal strip, or Tell, are great vineyards which produce grapes for wine. Orchards of olives, citrus fruits, and figs and fields of grain, tobacco, and cotton are also found here. Once owned by European settlers, the farms are now run mostly as communes, governed by workers' "management committees."

The Atlas Mountains lie south of the coastal strip in two parallel ranges. Wedged between these ranges is a plateau containing a long chain of lakes. Here industrious Berbers raise wheat and barley on small farms. Wild esparto grass (alfa) is collected on the plateau and used in the manufacture of paper. Palms supply fiber for upholstery padding and rope. Cork oaks grow in the large forests on the northern slopes. On the dry southeastern slopes, Arab nomads wander with herds of camels and sheep.

The Sahara region is important for the production of oil and natural gas. Pipelines link the oil and gas fields to cities on the Mediterranean coast.

Few people live in the Sahara. Nomads tend sheep, goats, and camels along the desert's fringe, where rain sometimes falls (*see* Nomads). Some crops are raised on irrigated land near oases (*see* Sahara).

The population of Algeria is 10,453,000 (1964 estimate). Most of the people are Arab and Berber farmers, herders, and city workers. They are of the Moslem faith. French and other Europeans had been migrating to Algeria since the last century. Most of these *colons* left the country after it won independence, however.

Minerals, Cities, and Transportation

Along with the valuable deposits of oil and gas found in the Sahara, Algeria has rich resources of iron ore. Phosphates and manganese are also mined.

Algeria's major cities are Mediterranean ports. Algiers, the capital, and Oran are the largest. Constantine is a leading inland city.

The country's chief exports include wine, crude oil, fruits and vegetables, iron ore, hides and skins, and phosphates. Local industries produce cement and other materials for construction purposes. Chemicals and textiles are also produced.

Modern highways connect the chief centers of commerce. A railway with spurs reaching into the Sahara

273

crosses Algeria from Morocco to Tunisia. There is an international airfield at Algiers.

History and Government

In ancient times the native Berbers of Algeria were conquered by successive waves of invaders—Phoenicians, Carthaginians, Romans, and Vandals. Later, Arabs and Turks spread the Moslem religion throughout the land. By the 16th century the Algerians had become dreaded pirates. They plundered shipping in the Mediterranean Sea until 1815, when they were defeated by an American fleet under Stephen Decatur (see Decatur).

In 1827 the French consul was struck in the face with a flyswatter by the native Algerian ruler. France avenged this insult by seizing Algiers in 1830 and driving the Turks out. The country was not wholly conquered by France until 1848. In 1919 some literate Moslems were given French citizenship. In 1947 citizenship was extended to all Algerians. Nonetheless, a Moslem revolt against French rule began in 1954. In the more than seven years of fighting that followed, many civilians on both sides lost their lives in terrorist violence.

When Charles de Gaulle came to power in France, in 1958, he sponsored Algerian independence. He was bitterly opposed by the colons. A truce was signed in March 1962. After a referendum in which Algerians overwhelmingly approved independence, Algeria was proclaimed a republic on July 3, 1962. A struggle for power ensued. Ahmed Ben Bella triumphed, becoming premier in September. One year later, after a new constitution was adopted, he became president. (See also France, History of.)

Northwestern Africa is ribbed by the parallel ranges of the Atlas Mountains. Fertile fields and groves cover their seaward slopes. Between the ranges lie the salt lakes known as "chotts." To the south spreads the vast Sahara.

ALGERIA FACT SUMMARY

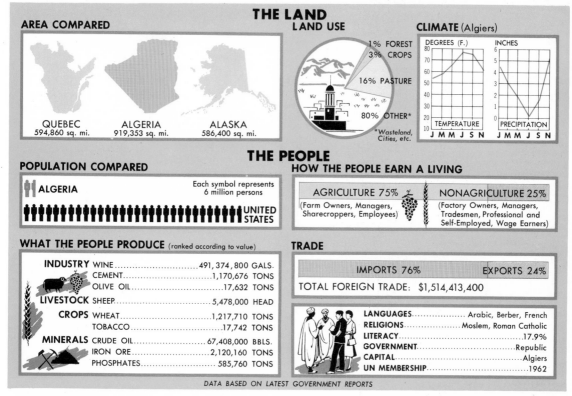

THE LAND

AREA COMPARED

QUEBEC
594,860 sq. mi.

ALGERIA
919,353 sq. mi.

ALASKA
586,400 sq. mi.

LAND USE

1% FOREST
3% CROPS
16% PASTURE
80% OTHER*

*Wasteland, Cities, etc.

CLIMATE (Algiers)

DEGREES (F.)   INCHES

TEMPERATURE   PRECIPITATION

J M M J S N   J M M J S N

THE PEOPLE

POPULATION COMPARED

ALGERIA

Each symbol represents 6 million persons

UNITED STATES

HOW THE PEOPLE EARN A LIVING

AGRICULTURE 75%
(Farm Owners, Managers, Sharecroppers, Employees)

NONAGRICULTURE 25%
(Factory Owners, Managers, Tradesmen, Professional and Self-Employed, Wage Earners)

WHAT THE PEOPLE PRODUCE (ranked according to value)

INDUSTRY WINE............................491,374,800 GALS.
CEMENT....................................1,170,676 TONS
OLIVE OIL......................................17,632 TONS
LIVESTOCK SHEEP....................................5,478,000 HEAD
CROPS WHEAT....................................1,217,710 TONS
TOBACCO....................................17,742 TONS
MINERALS CRUDE OIL......................67,408,000 BBLS.
IRON ORE............................2,120,160 TONS
PHOSPHATES........................585,760 TONS

TRADE

IMPORTS 76%   EXPORTS 24%
TOTAL FOREIGN TRADE: $1,514,413,400

LANGUAGES.................... Arabic, Berber, French
RELIGIONS.................... Moslem, Roman Catholic
LITERACY..17.9%
GOVERNMENT..............................Republic
CAPITAL..Algiers
UN MEMBERSHIP................................1962

DATA BASED ON LATEST GOVERNMENT REPORTS

The constitution provides for a one-party state, with socialism as its goal. The ruling party, the National Liberation Front, nominates the president and the candidates for the National Assembly.

In the mid-1960's Algeria's shattered economy was bolstered by extensive aid from France. Ben Bella nationalized farms and other property of the colons and began a gradual take-over of many industries. Between 1962–64 Ben Bella put down revolts against his leadership. In June 1965, however, he was overthrown in a surprise coup led by Col. Houari Boumedienne, chief of the armed forces.

ALHAMBRA. On the flat top of a hill above the roofs of Granada stands the Alhambra. This fortress-palace testifies to the power of the old Moorish civilization of southern Spain. Towered walls of red brick encircling the hill explain the name Alhambra, which is Arabic for "the red house."

From the Gate of Judgment can be seen vaulted ceilings, arches, pillars, arabesques, and carvings. Vaulted passages lead to the Court of the Lions, with its marble and alabaster fountain. They lead also to the Hall of the Abencerrages, where the princes of that name, sitting at a banquet, were massacred by Boabdil, the last Moorish king of Granada.

The Alhambra of today is only a marred remnant of what it was in the 13th and 14th centuries. Ferdinand and Isabella drove Boabdil from this last stronghold in 1492 (see Moors).

ALIEN AND SEDITION LAWS. The administration of President John Adams drew sharp criticism from newspaper editors and public speakers. To check these attacks Congress passed four measures in 1798. These were called the Alien and Sedition Laws.

These measures were: (1) a naturalization act, making a residence of 14 years necessary before foreigners could become citizens; (2) an alien act, giving the president power to deport any aliens judged "dangerous to the peace and safety of the United States"; (3) an alien enemies act, still in force, by which subjects of an enemy nation might be deported or imprisoned in wartime; (4) a sedition act, providing heavy penalties for conspiracy against the government or for interfering with government operations. This also included printing anything scandalous against the government.

A strong reaction against the Alien and Sedition Laws reinforced American faith in the Bill of Rights (see Bill of Rights). Not until World War I did Congress again restrict these rights. In 1917 and 1918 laws were passed imposing heavy penalties for interfering with the conduct of the war or for making disloyal statements.

During World War II Congress compelled aliens to register and be fingerprinted by the government. It was also made unlawful for any person to advocate the forcible overthrow of the government or to spread ideas which might injure the loyalty, morale, or discipline of the United States military forces.

ALKALI METALS.

A family of chemical elements identified as *alkali metals* occupies the first column of the periodic table (see Periodic Table). These elements are named alkali metals because they form powerful alkalies when they combine with other elements (see Acids and Alkalies). The alkali metals are lithium, sodium, potassium, rubidium, and cesium and an extremely rare element called francium, about which little is known.

Properties of Alkali Metals

Alkali metals bear little resemblance to more familiar metals such as iron or tin. All alkali metals are silver-white, malleable, and soft enough to be cut with a knife. They react quickly, sometimes violently, with other chemical substances, particularly with oxygen and water. Because they react readily, alkali metals are never found pure in nature. In the laboratory pure alkali metals must be kept submerged in oil or kerosene to prevent them from forming compounds with other elements.

Each atom of every alkali metal has only one electron in its outer shell (see Atom; Chemistry). Such an atom tends to give up its single outer electron to atoms of other elements. This causes the alkali metal atom to combine chemically with the atom to which it surrenders its outer electron. Thus a molecule of a compound is formed.

Uses of Alkali Metals

Sodium and potassium have many important compounds and uses. They are therefore discussed in separate articles (see Sodium; Potassium).

Metallic lithium is used in the heat treatment of steel and to purify various metals. Alloyed with lead it forms a heat-resistant bearing metal. Lithium compounds are used to eliminate gas pockets in castings of copper and copper alloys. They are also used as catalysts in certain organic chemical reactions. Lithium salts are added to glass, porcelain enamels, and ceramic glazes to help these materials resist heat. Tritium, the triple-weight hydrogen isotope important in atomic physics, is made from lithium (see Atomic Energy; Hydrogen).

Rubidium and cesium are relatively obscure members of the family. All the alkali metals are sensitive to light, and cesium alloys and compounds are used in photoelectric cells (see Photoelectric Devices). Cesium compounds are also used as *getters* to remove traces of gas from vacuum tubes (see Vacuum). Rubidium has few practical uses.

Francium

Francium was long a scientific mystery. Its place (atomic number 87) in the periodic table of the elements remained blank, though chemists searched diligently. Finally in 1939 francium was discovered in the laboratory as a radioactive decay product of the element actinium (see Radioactivity).

The half-life of francium is only about 20 minutes. Therefore it exists only briefly, if at all, in nature. Its atomic weight has not been determined.

ALKALINE EARTH METALS.

The members of the family of alkaline earth metals are beryllium, magnesium, calcium, strontium, barium, and the radioactive element radium. This family occupies the second column of the periodic table (see Periodic Table). The designation "earth" for these metals is very old. In the Middle Ages alchemists referred to many nonsoluble substances as earths (see Alchemy).

Properties of Alkaline Earth Metals

All alkaline earth metals are grayish white. They are malleable but vary in hardness. Beryllium, for example, is hard enough to cut glass; barium is as soft as lead. They are not found freely in nature because they react readily with oxygen and other elements. Unlike the alkali metals, many alkaline earth metals are insoluble in water. Each alkaline earth atom has two electrons in its outer shell.

In general, calcium, strontium, and barium resemble each other closely. Beryllium and magnesium do not. For this reason these two elements are often considered a group apart from the other alkaline earth metals. Radium is classified chemically as an alkaline earth metal but is placed in a special order because of its unique properties (see Radium).

Uses of Alkaline Earth Metals

Magnesium and calcium are by far the most important members of the family. They are treated in separate articles (see Magnesium; Calcium).

Beryllium alloys are highly resistant to wear and fatigue. They are used in springs and in engine parts. Beryllium salts are important in the manufacture of fluorescent lamps and in ceramics. Pure beryllium is used as a window for X-ray tubes because it is more transparent than most substances. Strontium nitrate provides the "red fire" for fireworks, signal lights, and star shells.

Barium oxide coating on the filaments of vacuum tubes used in the electronics industry increases their electrical activity. This reduces the power required for long-distance telephone service (see Electrons and Electronics). Barium sulfate is used to make a pigment, *permanent white*. Mixed with zinc sulfide it forms lithopone, a substitute for white lead. It is also used to give body and weight to some types of paper.

THE ALKALI METALS			
Lithium	Li	Rubidium	Rb
Sodium	Na	Cesium	Cs
Potassium	K	Francium	Fr

THE ALKALINE EARTH METALS			
Beryllium	Be	Strontium	Sr
Magnesium	Mg	Barium	Ba
Calcium	Ca	Radium	Ra

ALLEN, Ethan (1737?–1789). One of the first heroes of the American Revolution was Ethan Allen. He was especially famed for leading a small force against the British at Fort Ticonderoga and winning a bloodless surrender on May 10, 1775.

Ethan Allen was born in Litchfield, Conn., on Jan. 10, 1737 or 1738. In 1757, during the French and Indian War, he served at Fort William Henry, on the New York frontier. In 1762 he married Mary Bronson. They had five children.

Soon after he was married, Allen moved to the "New Hampshire Grants" (now Vermont) and bought farm lands. Both New York and New Hampshire claimed this area under their colonial grants. Allen was a leader among the New Hampshire claimants, and in 1770 he was made the head of an irregular force called the "Green Mountain Boys." Their attacks upon the "Yorkers" led the New York governor to offer a reward of £100 (about $485) for Allen's capture.

When the American Revolution started, Allen and members of the Connecticut assembly raised a small force. He led this band and his Green Mountain Boys against Fort Ticonderoga. They arrived at dawn, and the astonished British commander surrendered. In the autumn Allen joined an expedition against Canada but was captured while attacking Montreal. In 1778 an exchange of prisoners between the British and Americans brought Allen's release. Washington then named him a brevet colonel.

During this time the Hampshire Grant settlers had organized a provisional government and asked Congress for statehood (*see* Vermont). This government made Allen a major general. It also sent him with a mission that failed to win statehood from Congress.

Allen then plotted with the British to make Vermont a separate British province. For his part in this affair, Allen was accused of treason, but later the charge was dropped. During the rest of the Revolution, Allen contented himself with harassing the "Yorkers." In 1783 Allen's wife died, and about a year later he married Frances Buchanan, a widow. They had three children. Allen died on Feb. 12, 1789.

ALLENTOWN, Pa. Nearby deposits of anthracite, iron, and rock suitable for cement making changed Allentown from a country town to a manufacturing city during the 19th century. Today Allentown and its neighbor, the steelmaking city of Bethlehem, form one of the large industrial centers in Pennsylvania.

The site was laid out in 1762 by Judge William Allen, then chief justice of Pennsylvania. He named the place Northampton (or Northamptontown). Its location on the Lehigh River, at the junctions of Jordan Creek and Lehigh Creek, made it a good meeting place for the settlers nearby.

During the Revolutionary War the town made arms for the American forces. In 1777 the Liberty Bell was brought here from Philadelphia and hidden under the floor of Zion Reformed Church to safeguard it from the British. Today the Liberty Bell Shrine marks the hiding place. Completion of the Lehigh Canal in 1829 stimulated the growth of the community, which was renamed Allentown, after the founder, in 1838. It was chartered a city in 1867. Industrial progress was accelerated by the establishment of a cement plant and an iron-rolling mill before the Civil War and of a barbed-wire plant in 1886. Today the chief manufactures are trucks and buses, electronic devices, electrical appliances, cement, woven and knitted textiles, apparel, and machinery.

Educational centers in the city include Muhlenberg, Cedar Crest, and Eastern Pilgrim colleges, and a commonwealth campus of Pennsylvania State University. Trout Hall, erected as a fishing lodge in 1770 by a son of Judge Allen, is now headquarters of the county historical society. An art museum houses masterpieces of the Kress collection. A county fair, held in August, attracts thousands of visitors.

Many descendants of Germans who settled here before the Revolutionary War live in Allentown, and many customs and language oddities of the area's Pennsylvania Dutch have been preserved. Allentown, the seat of Lehigh County, has a commission form of government. Population (1960 census), 108,347.

ALLERGY. Some people suffer attacks of hay fever when pollen is in the air. Others develop skin rashes if they touch certain substances. Still others experience cramps after eating particular foods.

These are only a few examples of conditions known as allergies. An *allergy* is the unusual or abnormal reaction that a person may have to some specific substance which is harmless to most other people.

Most people feel no ill effects from breathing air containing pollen. If a certain type of person breathes the same air, however, unusual reactions occur in his body. He sneezes. His eyes fill with tears. His eyelids become reddened and irritated. His nasal passages become congested. Such a person is the victim of a common allergic disease called hay fever.

Allergy Resembles Immunity

An allergy to a certain substance develops in much the same way as does an immunity to a disease (*see* Diseases, Infectious; Vaccines). In both cases—allergy and immunity—the blood contains specific antibodies against invading substances which are known as antigens. An *antigen* is any substance that upon entering the blood stream incites the production of antibodies against itself.

Antigens which cause allergies are called *allergens*. The most common include pollens, foods, dust, animal dander (bits of flaky skin or fur), cosmetics, soaps, bleaches, dyes, and drugs. Heat, cold, sunlight, and emotions may also act like allergens.

The Allergy Victim

About one person in ten has some kind of allergic condition. This would indicate the disease develops in only certain types of people. Heredity may be an important factor. Most sufferers come from families in which the parents or other close relatives had allergies (*see* Heredity).

Specific allergies are not inherited, however. A hay fever victim, for example, does not inherit that disease. He becomes sensitive to pollen (usually ragweed pollen) by exposure to it.

How an Allergy Develops

Since different allergies develop in a similar way, the process can be described in general terms.

COMMON ALLERGIC CONDITIONS

Urticaria—commonly called "hives." Smooth, slightly raised patches erupt on the skin. Their centers are much whiter than the skin surrounding them. Urticaria is accompanied by severe itching.

Angioneurotic Edema—or "giant hives." Skin, mucous membranes, and sometimes the viscera are filled with fluid (edema) and swell. There is redness and urticaria.

Contact Dermatitis—an acute inflammation of the skin caused by contact with substances of animal, vegetable, or chemical origin.

Hay Fever—an acute inflammation of the mucous membranes of the nose, eyelids, and upper respiratory tract. It usually is caused by pollens and occurs only at certain times of the year.

Vasomotor Rhinitis—resembles hay fever but occurs throughout the year. It is not caused by pollens but by airborne dusts from animals, birds, cereals, fabrics, and grains.

Asthma—difficult breathing produced by smooth-muscle contractions in the respiratory tract, particularly in the bronchial tree. It is caused by the reaction of respiratory mucous membranes to an antigen. Asthma is not exclusively an allergy. Infections and heart conditions may also be causes.

Gastrointestinal Allergies—probably caused by the action of food on mucous membranes of the digestive tract.

Physical Allergies—can be brought on by cold, heat, drafts, and solar radiations.

First, a person must be particularly susceptible to some specific substance, or allergen. When he is initially exposed to this allergen, his body develops antibodies against it. In a person who is susceptible to hay fever, for example, antibodies against ragweed pollen are produced the first time he is exposed to that allergen.

The next time he is exposed to that allergen, the antibodies now present in his blood react against it. This reaction is accompanied by the violent liberation of a chemical substance, *histamine*, from the tissues. This is perhaps the most significant factor in producing his allergy.

The Role of Histamine

Histamine is present in all animal and vegetable tissues. It is harmless while it remains enclosed inside a cell. When it is released, however, it triggers a series of violent reactions. The blood vessels dilate, or become wider. The velocity of the blood flowing through these expanded vessels decreases. This leads to a seepage of fluid through the blood vessel walls into the surrounding tissues. The result is *edema*—an abnormal accumulation of fluid. (*See also* Diseases, Noninfectious, section on diseases of the blood.)

Swelling accompanies edema. If this happens in the nasal membranes, the nose becomes swollen, as in hay fever. Tissues are irritated and swollen when they become inflamed (*see* Diseases, Infectious). Redness of the eyelids in hay fever is an example.

Histamine also causes smooth-muscle tissues to contract. If the contraction, or spasm, occurs in the bronchial smooth muscle, asthma results. Similarly, a smooth-muscle spasm may occur elsewhere in the body and cause such symptoms as pain and cramps.

Treatment of Allergies

Every person suffering from an allergy should have medical care. Almost all allergic diseases can be temporarily relieved by the use of medication. Physicians frequently prescribe *antihistaminic drugs* for this purpose (*see* Drugs). If the offending allergen is known, the simplest way to prevent a reaction is to avoid the substance. Thus a person susceptible to hay fever is advised to go during the hay-fever season to a section of the country where ragweed does not grow.

A person may be desensitized to, or become tolerant of, the allergen causing his discomfort. A small amount of an extract made from the allergen is injected under the skin. The dose is gradually increased until a tolerance to the allergen is built up.

A person who is known to be allergic to a certain kind of food is advised not to eat it. This is not difficult to do if the allergen is found in chocolate, strawberries, or other foods that are not essential to good nutrition. If the allergen is a vital food such as milk, the physician may attempt to desensitize the person against his allergy.

ALLIGATOR. The alligator is one of the ugliest and most terrifying of all animals. It is a reptile that lives in coastal swamps and waters. There are only two species of true alligator. One lives in China's Yangtze Kiang. The other inhabits the Southern United States from North Carolina to Florida and west to the lower Rio Grande. Close relatives of the alligator are the several species of cayman of South and Central America.

The alligator is related also to the crocodile, but it has a broader head and blunter snout. Alligators prefer fresh water; crocodiles are usually found in salt water. The alligator's lower teeth fit inside the edge of the upper jaw and cannot be seen when the lipless mouth is closed. The crocodile's teeth are always visible.

Alligators reach a maximum length of about 16 feet, but 6 to 8 feet is the average. The back is covered with a rough armor of rows of bony shields. The underside, tail, and legs have leathery scales.

The long, powerful tail enables the animal to swim with speed and skill. Despite its short legs and awkward body, the alligator can run with surprising speed. Practically all its food is animal—fishes, birds, other reptiles, and muskrats. It will attack man if it is cornered, and it can kill with a lash of the powerful tail. Alligators have been hunted extensively, however, and have become extremely shy.

The animal's teeth are designed only for seizing prey. Creatures too large to be swallowed whole are torn to pieces with twisting motions of the whole body or are drowned and permitted to decay for several days. Alligators live in underwater dens in swamps and in the banks of streams. Well-marked trails, or "crawls," lead to the dens.

In spring the thundering bellow of the male may be heard a mile away. It is probably a challenge to other males. As the male roars, musk is emitted from glands under the chin.

The female lays from 30 to 60 eggs in a nest which she covers with leaves and mud. Heat from the decomposing leaves incubates the eggs for about two months.

A newly hatched alligator is about eight inches long. Its hide is striped with yellow, but the yellow fades as the animal matures. Alligators grow about a foot a year until they reach adult size.

Commercial Value

The hide is made into a valuable leather. For years the animals were hunted, for sport and for their hides, until the species was threatened with extinction. Florida maintains a state alligator refuge and since 1950 has limited hunting. Also in the state are alligator farms where the reptiles are raised commercially. The Chinese alligator is too small and too rare to be commercially important. No specimen over five feet eight inches has been recorded.

Spanish explorers, mistaking the nature of the reptile they first saw along the Florida coast, called it *el lagarto* (the lizard). The scientific name of the American alligator is *Alligator mississipiensis;* of the Chinese alligator, *A. sinensis.* (*See also* Crocodile.)

A BABY ALLIGATOR ENTERS THE WORLD

A baby alligator takes its first look at the world. Eight inches long when hatched, it will grow about a foot a year until it reaches the average adult length of six to eight feet.

A FULL-GROWN ARMORED MONSTER

The alligator can gulp down small animals whole. Its broad tongue, attached to the lower jaw, can be raised to keep water out of the throat when the jaws are open.

ALLOYS—
Metallic Mixtures
with Special Properties

ALLOYS. Mixtures of various elements called *alloys* are used in millions of ways every day. Airplanes, trains, automobiles, building metals, tools, cooking pots, and thousands of other machines and objects are made of alloys. We usually speak of metal articles as though they were made of such pure elements as iron, aluminum, copper, tin, or lead, but almost all of them are combinations of two or more metals or of metallic and nonmetallic elements.

Metals in their pure states do not have a great many uses. A cooking pot of pure aluminum would be weak and soft and would wear away quickly, whereas one made of aluminum alloyed with copper or silicon can be used daily year after year. A pure-iron knife blade will dull almost the instant it is first used because pure iron is relatively soft; but one made of iron alloyed with carbon and other elements will cut well and will retain its sharp edge for some time.

About three fourths of the elements are classed as metals. Few are in common use; and many are so rare, so difficult to extract from their ores, or so unstable that they cannot be made into useful objects. To obtain desirable qualities, men combine the more available metals and nonmetals. Several thousand such alloys are made of the elements listed below.

The Steel Alloys

Iron is the major constituent of the most frequently used alloys. These are called *ferrous alloys*, from the Latin *ferrum*, meaning "iron." A large number are *steels* (see Iron and Steel, Properties of). Basically, steels are alloys of carbon and iron; these alloys are

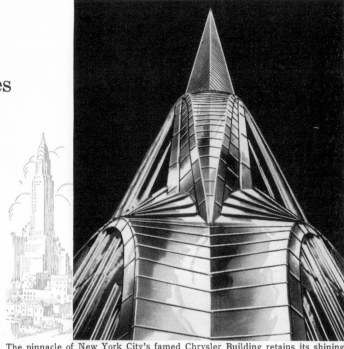

The pinnacle of New York City's famed Chrysler Building retains its shining brightness, though it has been subjected to years of snow, wind, rain, and sunshine, because it is surfaced with a steel alloy containing chromium.

called *plain carbon steels*. Plain carbon steels are given characteristics to meet special needs by alloying them with other elements. Among the elements added are manganese, nickel, chromium, and silicon. Steels containing manganese are shaped more easily in rolling mills; consequently most steels contain manganese. Nickel steels are rust resistant. Chromium steels are hard and strong. Silicon steels have superior magnetic properties and are used in electric generators and many other electrical devices.

The so-called *stainless steels* are highly resistant to rust and acid corrosions. Generally, stainless steels are alloys of iron with 10 to 20 per cent chromium and 5 to 10 per cent nickel. Table knives, light fixtures, kitchen cabinets, decorative trimming for automobiles, and many other articles are made of them. Stainless steels are used in machinery and vats for processing and storing chemicals that would "eat away" ordinary steels.

Special-purpose steels are of many kinds. They include *automotive spring* steels, *high-speed tool* steels, and several kinds of steels used in the manufacture and distribution of electric power.

Automotive spring steels absorb road shocks well because alloying elements give the steels a continuing elastic property. The principal alloys of spring steels are silicon and manganese, or chromium.

High-speed tools (the name comes from their use as cutting tools on high-speed machinery) retain a cutting edge even when red-hot. They can be made hard enough to cut almost any material, including other very hard steels. High-speed tool steels are

THE ELEMENTS MOST USED IN ALLOYS			
Aluminum*	Chromium*	Manganese*	Silver*
Antimony*	Cobalt*	Mercury*	Sulfur*†
Beryllium	Copper*	Molybdenum*	Thorium
Bismuth*	Gold*	Nickel*	Tin*
Boron†	Iridium	Palladium	Titanium*
Cadmium*	Iron*	Phosphorus*†	Tungsten*
Carbon*†	Lead*	Platinum*	Vanadium*
Cerium	Magnesium*	Silicon*†	Zinc*

There are other alloying elements besides those listed here. Almost all alloys now used, however, are made up of two or more of the elements in this list. *Element is discussed in a separate article. †Nonmetal.

SOME SPECIAL-PURPOSE STEEL ALLOYS

Type of Steel	Typical Uses*
Carbon Steels	
Plain carbon†	Sheets for auto bodies, tinplate for cans, structural shapes (for example, I-beams), bars, plates, saw blades, pipe, railroad-car axles
Free cutting‡	Screws, nuts, bolts, heavily machined parts
Alloy Steels§	
Chromium	Auto and truck springs
Silicon, manganese	Auto and truck springs
Chromium, nickel	High-strength structural shapes; stainless steel
Nickel	Gears
Manganese	Wear-resistant parts (for example, rail intersections, excavating equipment)
Tungsten, chromium, vanadium	High-speed tools
Titanium	Stoves, refrigerators, and other enameled products
Silicon	Electric motors, generators

*Only some examples are given. †Plain carbon steels ordinarily contain one per cent or less of carbon and limited amounts of manganese, silicon, phosphorus, and sulfur. ‡Higher sulfur content. §These contain small amounts of other elements not listed above.

made of iron, tungsten, chromium, and vanadium. Tungsten is the most important element in tool steels because it melts at the unusually high temperature of 6,098° F. It is also used to make other than steel cutting tools. *Tungsten carbide* (a compound of tungsten and carbon) is one of the hardest substances known, but it is brittle. To keep tungsten carbide from chipping and breaking while cutting, particles are embedded in cobalt.

Nonferrous Alloys

Alloys that do not have an iron constituent are called *nonferrous alloys*. Of these the copper alloys are the largest group. Most of the copper alloys are *brasses* and *bronzes* (*see* Brass; Bronze). Brass is copper alloyed chiefly with zinc. It is easily shaped and has a pleasing appearance. Bronze is copper alloyed chiefly with tin. Many different alloys classed as bronzes are made by substituting other elements for part of or all the tin. Bronze possesses strength, toughness, and elasticity.

Various amounts of copper, alloyed with other metals, are used in coins. Copper also is alloyed with nickel and small amounts of other elements to make exceptionally corrosion-resistant *Monel metal*.

Certain alloys are both structurally strong and light in weight. These are alloys of aluminum or magnesium with various other metals. They are used in airplanes, railroad cars, kitchen ware and equipment, and automobile parts. Use of the lightweight alloys

results in a saving of power because there is less "dead weight" to be moved.

Low-Melting-Point Alloys

A *low melting point* is an important property of some alloys. Bearings, printing types, solders, and electric fuses, as well as safety plugs are made of low-melting-point alloys.

One of the most important of the low-melting-point alloys is *Babbitt metal* (an alloy of tin, antimony, and copper). In general, less friction develops between dissimilar metals than between metals which resemble one another. Because Babbitt metal melts at a low temperature, it can be poured into a mold fitted around a steel shaft without harm to the shaft. The Babbitt metal becomes a bearing in which the shaft rotates with little wear to either shaft or bearing.

When antimony forms part of an alloy, it causes the metal to expand as it cools. This special quality is the reason for its use in Babbitt metal and in type metals. Its expansion, as it hardens into a bearing, ensures a smooth, close fit around a shaft. In type metal its expansion causes the metal to fill out the tiny molds to the finest hairline. The printing on this page is sharp and clear because the type metal contained about 16 per cent antimony.

The common kinds of solder are alloys of lead and tin, the tin ranging from one third to two thirds. Alloyed, these metals melt at a lower temperature than either will by itself. Brazing solder, or *spelter*, used for forming stronger joints than ordinary solder, usually is made of equal parts of copper and zinc. Silver is added to spelter for jewelry work.

Bismuth, lead, tin, and cadmium combine in a very low-melting-point alloy called Wood's metal. It makes a good fuse for an electric line. When heated by an excess of current that might damage electrical apparatus or set fire to a building, the fuse melts, leaving a gap in the line the current cannot jump. Safety plugs made of such alloys are used in boilers, water heaters, and sprinkler and fire-alarm systems.

Electric Wire Alloys

Electric wire must offer little resistance to the passage of electric current. A highly resistant wire

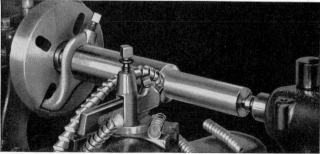

DURABLE ALLOY CUTTING EDGE
High-speed tool steels retain sharp edges even when heated red-hot by friction. One of the important metals in high-speed tools is tungsten. Tungsten is hard and brittle; it can be melted only at extremely high temperatures. Alloyed with steel it retains hardness and gains strength.

ALLOYS THAT FIT SPECIAL NEEDS

Type metal (1) expands as it hardens because it contains antimony. Brass drawer handles (2) are decorative. The stove (3) is constructed of an alloy to which enamel can be firmly baked; the top and oven heating elements (4) are Nichrome, which resists the passage of electric current but does not burn out; the pot is stainless steel.

tungsten and thorium is used in the filaments of light bulbs. Radio, television, X-ray, and other vacuum tubes must have filaments that release large quantities of electrons over long periods of time. The cores of such filaments are made of an alloy of nickel, cobalt, iron, titanium, and manganese called *konel*. A coating of either barium or strontium emits electrons (*see* Electrons and Electronics; Radio). The composition, name, qualities, and typical uses of some much-used nonferrous alloys are shown in the table on this page.

would waste much current and cause the wire to heat. Silver sets up the least resistance to electric current. But it is too expensive to use. So copper, only slightly higher in resistance, is used. Copper wire is almost pure metal (99.92 per cent). It is strengthened and hardened by drawing it into wire while cold.

Yet alloys highly resistant to electric current are needed to produce electric light and heat. Heating units for toasters and electric stoves are made of nickel-chromium alloys. These are not only highly resistant to electricity but can withstand great heat without burning out. A highly resistant alloy of

Some Other Alloys

Gold, silver, and platinum are alloyed to make them more durable. Silver coins would wear rapidly if they were not hardened with 10 per cent copper. Sterling contains 7.5 per cent copper. Laboratory apparatus that must resist heat and chemical action is usually made of an alloy of platinum and iridium.

Small amounts of some elements are added to alloys because they work chemically to rid the alloys of undesired constituents. They do not necessarily become a valuable constituent. Elements commonly used thus are aluminum, titanium, calcium, zirconium, and lithium (*see* Chemistry). An alloy of rare-earth metals called *misch metal* is one of the materials so used. Small quantities of misch metal will remove sulfur, gases, and oxides. Misch metal also is alloyed with 35 per cent iron to make flints for cigarette lighters, miners' lamps, and gas lighters. Added to carbon in carbon-arc lamps, misch metal gives the intense, brilliant light required in photography and the projection of motion pictures.

SOME NONFERROUS ALLOYS

General Composition*	Name of Alloy	Special Qualities	Typical Uses†
Aluminum and copper	Lynite	Hard, strong	Machinery housings, cooking utensils
Bismuth, lead, tin, and cadmium	Wood's metal	Very low melting point	Safety plugs in water heaters
Cerium and iron	Ignition pin alloy	Emits hot spark with friction	Lighter flints
Cobalt, tungsten, and chromium	Stellite	Extreme hardness	Cutting tools
Copper and zinc	Brass	Easily shaped, good appearance	Hardware
Copper and beryllium	Beryllium copper	Very hard, high strength	Nonsparking tools, rifle parts, small castings
Gold and palladium	White gold	Color, durability	Jewelry
Lead, antimony, tin, and copper	Type metal	Low melting point, expansion on cooling	Printing type
Lead and tin	Plumber's solder	Low melting point	Sealing metal joints
Magnesium, aluminum, and zinc	Dowmetal	Lightweight, high strength	Airplane parts, complex die castings
Nickel, copper, and iron	Monel metal	Corrosion resistance	Steam valves, turbine blades
Nickel and chromium	Nichrome	Electrical resistance, nonoxidizing	Heating elements in stoves, irons, toasters
Tin, antimony, and copper	Babbitt metal	Low melting point, low friction	Bearings
Tungsten and thorium	Tungsten filament	High melting point, electrical resistance	Light-bulb filaments

*The largest constituent is listed first. †These alloys have many additional uses.

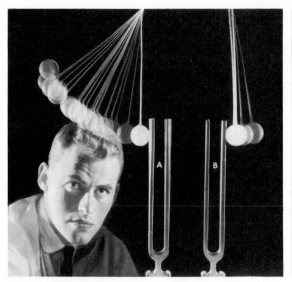

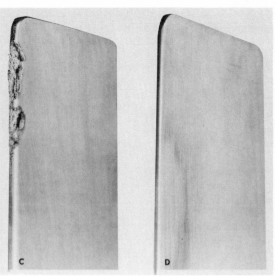

ALLOYS DESIGNED FOR SPECIAL JOBS
Minimum vibration of metals is a desirable quality in many industrial products. The tuning fork (B), made of a special alloy containing seven metals, vibrates much less than a steel tuning fork (A). Notice how they both affect a Ping-pong ball.

The edge of the aluminum propeller blade (C) is severely pitted and corroded after a test exposure to a stream of high-speed water. The same blade, covered with a special nickel coating (D), remains undamaged after identical treatment.

Platinite is a very useful industrial alloy containing nickel and iron. When heated, this alloy expands at exactly the same rate as glass. Platinite is used to connect the socket contact and the filament through the glass of a light bulb.

Crystalline Structure of Alloys

Many facts about the crystalline structure of alloys have been revealed by microscopic and spectroscopic studies. They show that crystals are made from tiny grains which have a boundary material between grains. (*See also* X Rays; Spectrum and Spectroscope.)

Some grains are hard and some are soft because of the different elements mixed in the alloy. The hard grains support the load and resist wear. The soft grains, being more pliable, permit the hard grains to move. Thus if an attempt were made to bend a piece of metal that had only hard grains, it would break. But if hard and soft grains are intermixed, the piece of metal can be bent because the soft grains deform when the hard grains press against them.

In general, fine-grained metals are tougher than large-grained metals. The materials making up the boundaries between grains may be either stronger or weaker than the grains. In large-grained alloys the boundaries may be continuous. Such a structure is weak because fewer grains interlock. A large-grained alloy is generally brittle and will fracture readily along its boundary lines. The sizes and shapes of the crystalline structure determine the physical properties of an alloy—its hardness and strength.

Heat Treatment of Alloys

Heating and cooling can change the sizes and shapes of the grains of metal. An alloy is heated to a certain temperature and then cooled in different ways and at different rates to get various degrees of hardness and strength. The heating temperatures are all below the melting point of the alloy.

When high-carbon steel is heated to a temperature above 1,400° F. and then cooled suddenly, it becomes hard and brittle. This happens because the crystalline structure does not have time to change gradually as it would during a longer cooling period. It is usually desirable to soften an alloy below this extreme hardness by the process of annealing. This consists of reheating the alloy and then cooling it slowly. Annealing often follows forging or rolling operations.

ALMOND (ä′mŏnd). The almond is a nut-bearing tree of the rose family. It is related to the plum and the peach and reaches a height of from 20 to 30 feet.

Early in the spring delicate white or pink flowers bloom on the almond tree. The flowers are followed by leaves which are oval, pointed, and notched at the edges. The fruit has a soft outer coat enclosing the shell, within which is the seed, or kernel. (For picture of an almond, *see* Nuts.)

A tree with white blossoms produces bitter almonds. A tree with pink blossoms bears sweet almonds. Bitter almonds are used in the manufacture of flavoring extracts and prussic acid. Sweet almonds are classified as paper-shell, soft-shell, standard-shell, and hard-shell. They may be cooked and salted for eating. Sweet almonds are also processed into paste and butter for use as baking ingredients and into oil for use in medicines and cosmetics.

Almonds are grown extensively in western Asia, in the Mediterranean countries, and in California. They were probably first grown in the Mediterranean region and were considered valuable in Biblical times. The scientific name is *Amygdalus communis*.

ALPACA. A full-grown alpaca stands about 3½ feet high. It looks like a large goat with a camel's head. Thick, woolly hair, from 6 to 24 inches long, grows on the body and legs. From it is woven one of the world's finest fabrics. The color may be white, brown, black, or mixed on the same animal.

The alpaca is found only in the Andes, usually at heights ranging from 13,000 to 15,000 feet. The chief food of this animal is a grass called ichu. An alpaca can go without food or water for long periods because its three-chambered stomach serves as a reservoir. Cleft feet with hooked spurs help it to climb steep crags. No region other than the high Andes suits the living habits of the alpaca. Attempts to raise it elsewhere have failed.

The alpaca, the llama, the guanaco, and the vicuña belong to the same family. The vicuña, which lives wild in Peru, yields the lightest, warmest, and strongest wool known. It is estimated that alpacas number less than 2 million.

Alpaca Wool and Fabrics

Ever since the days of the ancient Incas, the people of Peru and Bolivia have used alpaca wool for clothing and the skin for rugs. Most of the alpaca wool for commerce is still grown in these countries. The people keep small herds which graze over the bleak plateaus by day and follow leaders into rude stone corrals at night.

An alpaca is sheared every year or two. To overcome the animal's resistance, it is necessary for the herders to throw the alpaca to the ground and tie its feet together before shearing. Most of the wool is

A FINE CROP OF ALPACA WOOL
The long fleece of these alpacas shows that the animals are almost ready for shearing. An adult alpaca yields from four to ten pounds of valuable wool every second year.

shipped to Arequipa, Peru. It is sorted according to color, length, and quality, and then marketed.

Genuine alpaca fabrics are soft, strong, light, and durable. Many fabrics called alpaca are actually made from mohair, cotton, or rayon, while others are a mixture of cotton and alpaca. The scientific name of the alpaca is *Lama glama pacos*.

ALPHABET—The Foundation of Written Language

The writings on this sphinx, found on the Sinai Peninsula, date from about 1500 B.C. The lower, in Sinaitic, a Semitic tongue, reads "Beloved of Ba'alat." Above are Egyptian hieroglyphics, "Beloved of Hathor." The Egyptian goddess Hathor corresponded to the Sinaitic Ba'alat. The known Egyptian writing gave scholars the key to Sinaitic.

ALPHABET. To write the letters c, a, and t for "cat" seems as natural as pronouncing the word. Each letter stands for one sound in the spoken word. To write the word, the sign for each sound is simply set down in the proper order.

This kind of writing is called *alphabetic*, from the names *alpha* and *beta* —the first two letters in the Greek alphabet. Because the method is so simple, it is hard to imagine anybody writing in any other way. Actually alphabetic writing came late in human history, though its prehistory dates to very ancient times.

Origin of the English Alphabet

Most people would designate as "English" the writing which is used to express the English language. It might also be termed "Latin," for even in its modern form English writing differs little from the Latin writing of more than 2,000 years ago.

The history of Latin writing can be traced backward in a series of steps.

The Latin alphabet is a development from the Greek alphabet. The Greek alphabet, in turn, is an adaptation of a writing which was developed among the Semites of Syria about 1500 B.C. Outwardly, this first Semitic writing seems to be an original and individual creation. Its principles, however, are certainly based on the Egyptian word-syllabic writing, which, together with the Sumerian, Hittite, Chinese, and other writings, belongs to the great family of ancient Oriental systems of writing. The history of the oldest of these writings, Sumerian, can be followed from about 3100 B.C. (*See also* Writing.)

Egyptian Word-Syllabic Writing

Two kinds of signs are found in the Egyptian writing. These are word-signs and syllabic signs. The word-signs are signs which stand for words of the language, as in the English signs + for "plus," $ for "dollar," and ¢ for "cent."

The definition of syllabic signs is more difficult. The word Toledo, for example, has three syllables. In English writing the division in syllables is disregarded and only the single sounds are expressed. The ancients, however, did not know how to write single sounds, and they expressed only syllables. The ancient syllabic signs consisted of one or more consonants. Thus Toledo could be written with three signs, *To-le-do*, or with two signs, *Tole-do* or *To-ledo*. These syllables end in vowels. However, syllables ending in a consonant were written the same way. The name Lester, for example, might be written *Le-s(e)-te-r(e)*, *Les(e)-te-r(e)*, or the like. It would be taken for granted that certain vowels, here put in parentheses, would not be pronounced.

The Semitic Writings

Sometime between 1500 and 1000 B.C. the Semites of Syria and Palestine created their own systems of writing patterned after the Egyptian. They refused, however, to be burdened with the hundreds of different signs contained in the Egyptian system. They discarded all the Egyptian word-signs and all the syllabic signs with more than one consonant. The Semites retained a simple syllabary of about 30 signs, each consisting of one consonant plus any vowel.

In the Semitic writing the same sign stood for the syllables *pa*, *pi*, and *pu*. In other systems these syllables would be represented by three different signs. In Mycenaean and Japanese writings the distinctions in vowels were regularly indicated but not the distinctions in some related consonants. In these syllabaries three different signs would be used to indicate the vowel distinctions in *pa*, *pi*, and *pu*, but the same sign would stand for *pa*, *ba*, and *pha*.

Although the syllabic type of writing was an idea that the Semites borrowed from the Egyptians, they did not borrow the forms of the individual signs from the Egyptians. They created their own. Several early Semitic systems were used within limited areas and for a very short time only. They all died out without leaving any direct descendants.

Phoenician Syllabic Writing

About 1000 B.C. a new syllabic writing originated which was destined to have world-shaking influence upon the subsequent evolution of writing. This writing was created by the Phoenicians at Byblos, the city famous for export of the writing material known as papyrus. From this Phoenician city's name were derived the Greek word *biblia* (books) and

	BYB-LOS	LATE GREEK	LATIN	
'	Κ	A A (A)	A A	A
B	ϟ	Β Β (Β)	Β B	B
G	٦	Γ ((Γ)	(C	C
D	◁	Δ Δ D (Δ)	D D	D
H	⅄	Ε Ε Ε (Ε)	·· E	E
W	Υ	F F F ···	·· F	F
Z	I	I I ··· (Z)		··
··	··		·· G	G
Ḥ	Ħ	Β Η (Η)	·· H	H
Ṭ	⊕	⊗ Θ (Θ)	···	···
J	?	Ϛ ς Ι (Ι)	·· I	I
··	··			J
K	ψ	Κ Κ (Κ)	·· K	K
L	Ϲ	Γ V Λ (Λ)	ϲ L	L
M	ξ	Μ Μ (Μ)	·· M	M
N	ς	Ν N (Ν)	·· N	N
S	∓	∓ ··· (Ξ)		··
C	O	O O (O)	·· O	O
P	?	Γ Γ ··· (Π)	Γ P P	P
Ṣ	ħ	···	···	··
Q	φ	φ Q ···	Q Q	Q
R	ϟ	P R (P)	R R	R
Š	w	Ϛ ς Σ (Σ)	ς S	S
T	+X	T ··· (T)	·· T	T
··	··	U Υ (Υ)	·· V	U
··	··	··· (Φ)		V
··	··			W
··	··	+ ··· (X)	·· X	X
··	··	··· (Ψ)	·· Y	Y
··	··	··· (Ω)	·· Z	Z

DEVELOPMENT OF THE ALPHABET
The writings of the Phoenicians in Byblos had great influence on the development of the alphabet. The sounds of the letters in the Semitic language (left) did not correspond to those in the Greek language.

THE OLDEST GREEK WRITING

This inscription, on a vase from Athens, dates from about the beginning of the 8th century B.C. It reads: "Whoever of the dancers makes merry most gracefully, let him receive this"— that is, the vase as a trophy.

the English word Bible. The Phoenician writing consisted of only 22 signs, because the Phoenician language had fewer consonants than the earlier Semitic languages.

After 1000 B.C. the Phoenician writing spread in all directions. The Phoenicians carried it with them on their seafaring activities along the Mediterranean coast. A form of the Phoenician system was used in Palestine by the old Hebrews and their neighbors. Another branch developed among the South Arabs, who lived in an area which corresponds roughly to modern Yemen. From the South Arabs this writing spread to Ethiopia, where it is still in use today.

One of the most important branches of the Phoenician writing is Aramaic. A form of this writing was adopted by the Hebrews. It replaced their older system, which was derived directly from the Phoenician. This new Hebrew writing is still used among the Jews of today. It is called "the square writing," after the square shape of its characters. The North Arabs took over a form of the Aramaic system and, in the course of the centuries after the rise of Islam, spread it to the far corners of the world.

The Greeks Borrow Phoenician Writing

The most important writing derived from the Phoenician is Greek, the forerunner of all the Western alphabets. All indications favor the 9th century B.C. as the time when the Greeks borrowed Phoenician writing, but this is still in some doubt. The Greeks took over from the Phoenicians the forms and names of signs, the order of the signs in the alphabet, and the direction of the writing. They made many changes, however.

The older Greek writing resembles the Phoenician very closely. Anyone who has had practice with the Phoenician writing would have no difficulties in reading correctly the individual signs of the Greek system. The later Greek forms changed considerably. They resemble more the forms of Latin, and consequently English, writing.

The names of the Greek signs were taken over, with very slight changes only, from the Phoenician. For example, the Greek names *alpha, beta, gamma,* and *delta* correspond to the Phoenician *'aleph, beth, gimel,* and *daleth*.

The orders of the signs in the Phoenician and Greek systems were originally identical. The Phoenician signs *waw, sade,* and *qoph* were used by the Greeks under the names *digamma, san,* and *koppa* in the earlier periods but were later dropped. The three signs are still used for the numbers 6, 900, and 90 in the scheme of writing numbers by means of the letters of the alphabet.

Changes in the Greek System

While the direction of signs and lines in the Phoenician writing was from right to left—as it is in modern Hebrew and Arabic—the direction in the Greek writing varied greatly in the older periods. It could run from right to left; from left to right; or from right to left and from left to right in the same inscription, changing direction alternately from line to line. Only gradually did the method of writing from left to right prevail in the Greek system. This method passed on to the Latins and then to the Western world.

The most radical changes in the Greek system were in regard to the values of the signs. Three signs, as has been noted, were dropped; two changed their original values, namely the Phoenician *ṭ* and *s*, which became *th* and *x*; and five new signs, called *upsilon, phi, chi, psi,* and *ōmega,* were added at the end of the Greek alphabet.

Signs for Vowels

The changes which were to become revolutionary in the history of writing involved the creation of signs for vowels. Phoenician, like other West Semitic writings, consisted of syllabic signs beginning with a consonant and ending in any vowel. In this system the name *Dawid* (in English, David) could have been written by means of three signs, *da-wi-d(i)*. Because the vowels in these signs were not indicated, this writing could stand also for *di-wi-di, du-wi-di, da-wa-du,* and so on. In most cases people who were familiar with the common words and names of their language had no difficulties in reading such a writing. *Y cn fnd prf fr ths sttmnt n ths sntnc.* In cases where two readings were possible, however, for example, in *Dawid* or *Dawud,* new ways had to be found in order to insure the correct reading. They were found in the use of some weak consonants, such as *y* and *w.* In the writing of *da-wi-yi-d(i)* for *Dawid* the sign *yi* did not stand for an independent syllable; its sole function was to make sure that the preceding syllabic sign, *wi,* would be read as *wi* and not as *wa, we, wo,* or *wu.*

While the Phoenicians only occasionally employed such full spellings, the Greeks used them systematically after each syllabic sign. They used for this purpose six signs with weak consonants which they inherited from the Phoenicians. Since most of these sounds were used only in the Phoenician, the Greeks had no use for them as consonants. They turned them into the vowels *a, e, u, ē, i,* and *o.*

Once the six signs developed their values as vowels in Greek, the natural step was to reduce the remaining syllabic signs to consonants. If, in the writing of *da-'a-wi-yi-d(i)*, the second sign, *'a*, is taken as a vowel *a* to help in the correct reading of the first sign as *da* (not *de*, *di*, *do*, or *du*) and if the sign *yi* is taken as *i* to indicate *wi*, then the value of the signs *da* and *wi* must be reduced from syllables *da* and *wi* to consonants *d* and *w*. Once this was done the Greeks developed for the first time a full alphabet, composed of both vowels and consonants.

The Spread of the Greek Alphabet

From the Greeks the alphabet passed on to the Etruscans of Italy; to the Copts of Egypt (where it replaced their old Egyptian hieroglyphic writing); and to the Slavonic peoples of Eastern Europe. The Latin writing of the Romans was derived from the Etruscan.

Like the earlier Greek, the Latin writing consisted of 24 signs; but the similarity in number was coincidental, for Latin underwent a different set of changes and replacements. The Greek *digamma* sign of *w* became *f* in Latin, and the Greek *eta* became *h*. The Greek sign *gamma* for *g* was used in older Latin for both *c* and *g*. Later the *g* sign was differentiated from *c* by the addition of a small horizontal bar (recognizable in the English capital letter *G*).

The Greek letters *th*, *z*, and *x* were dropped altogether in the early Latin writing. The later additions to the Latin writing were placed at the end of the alphabet. The *v* sign developed from the same sign as *f*, which stood for both the sounds *u* and *v* (pronounced as *w* in English). Later the sign *v* developed two forms, *v* for the sound *v* and *u* for the sound *u*. The signs for *x*, *y*, and *z* were added by the Latins when they became aware of the need to spell the many words and names which they borrowed from the Greek during the imperial Roman period. With the addition of the letters *j* (developed from *i*) and *w* (developed from *v* or *u*) in the Middle Ages, the number of letters of the Latin alphabet increased to 26. This became the basic alphabet of the English language and the languages of Western Europe and of Western civilization. The sounds of different languages are further differentiated by combining letters, as in the English *sh* or the German *sch*, or by diacritic marks, as in the Czech *š*. The sound of all these letters is the same.

The Alphabet Returns to the Semites

The alphabet passed in the course of time from the Greeks back to the Semites, thus repaying the debt of the original borrowing of the Phoenician writing by the Greeks. In the Semitic writings, however, the vowels were generally indicated by means of diacritic marks in the form of small strokes, dots, and circles, placed either above or below or at the side of consonant signs. Thus *ta* would be written as *ṯ* in Hebrew and as *ï* in Arabic.

The development of a full Greek alphabet expressing single sounds of language by means of consonant and vowel signs was the last important step in the history of writing. (*See also* Alphabet in the Fact-Index at the end of this volume. The history of each letter is given at the beginning of the Fact-Index of the respective volume.)

Capitals and Small Letters

In English handwriting and print two kinds of letters are used: capitals (called "majuscules") and small letters (called "minuscules"). This is a relatively modern innovation. The Romans, Greeks, and Oriental peoples never distinguished capitals from small letters, as is done in English writing. All these earlier peoples employed two forms—a carefully drawn form of writing with squarish and separate signs on official documents and monuments and a less carefully drawn form of cursive (running) writing with roundish and often joined signs on less official documents, such as letters.

During the Middle Ages a form of capital letters called "uncials" was developed. Uncials (from a Latin word meaning "inch-high") were squarish in shape, with rounded strokes. They were used in Western Europe in handwritten books, side by side with small-letter cursive writing, used in daily life. After the Renaissance and the introduction of printing in Europe, two types of letters were distinguished: the majuscules, which were formed in imitation of the ancient Latin characters, and the minuscules, which continued in the tradition of the medieval cursive writing. Another distinction in printing form developed at the time was between the upright characters of the roman type and the slanting characters of the italic type. (*See also* Books.)

ALPS. Among the most important high mountains in the world are the Alps of Europe. (The word *alp* is German for "high mountain meadow.") The Alps divide the central part of Europe into northern and southern portions. This division has done much throughout history to shape nations, languages, and ways of life.

The peaks and higher crests rise more than 10,000 feet above sea level and catch abundant snow and rain from moisture-laden westerly winds. Above the "snow line," at 8,000 feet (or 9,500 in some places), snow never melts. Hence it accumulates, turns to ice, and flows down the valleys as "frozen rivers," or glaciers. At lower levels the ice melts, and the water feeds four great rivers of Europe—the Rhone, the Rhine, the Danube, and the Po. The unfailing water supply and sharp fall of the rivers furnish abundant hydroelectric power. (For maps showing the Alps, *see* Danube River; Switzerland.)

The Alps occupy an area about equal to that of Illinois and Indiana together. Switzerland lies in the central portion. Outlying ranges extend in sweep-

BEAUTIFUL JUNGFRAU MOUNTAIN IN THE BERNESE ALPS

The white purity of this peak inspired the Swiss to name it Jungfrau (meaning "maiden"). From the famous resort town of Interlaken, in the foreground, a many-tunneled rail line runs to the saddle of the mountain, called the Jungfraujoch.

ing curves into southeastern France, West Germany, Austria, and northern Italy. The Austrian and Italian portions are commonly called the Tyrol. On the Italian side the Alps descend steeply into the valley of the Po. On the other sides the slope is less abrupt. The highest peak is Mont Blanc (15,781 feet), in southeastern France.

Winding roads lead up the valleys to passes between the peaks and crests. The lowest pass is the Brenner, (summit, 4,511 feet above sea level). It connects the Inn River valley in Bavaria and western Austria with the eastern part of the Po Valley. Men have used this pass since prehistoric times. Through it northern barbarians descended to complete the ruin of the western Roman Empire. The western passes (St. Gotthard, Simplon, Mont Cenis, and so forth) are higher and often snow choked. But conquerors from Hannibal to Napoleon have led armies over them. Today railroads travel in tunnels beneath these passes.

The Alps attract tourists from all over the world. Thousands of people go each year to Luzern (Lucerne), Interlaken, Chamonix below Mont Blanc, and dozens of other beautiful places. Winter sports attract thousands more to St. Moritz and Davos Platz. Many adventurers climb the Matterhorn and other famous peaks. Gemlike lakes nestle in the valleys. Lakes Geneva, Luzern, Como, Garda, and Maggiore are particularly famous. Excellent roads are provided for motor travel. High on the slopes of the Great and Little St. Bernard Passes stand the Hospices of St.

Bernard. Through many centuries monks from the hospices and their St. Bernard dogs rescued travelers caught by storm in the passes.

The most common rocks in the Alps are sedimentary (*see* Geology). Geologists say that the rock was laid down in an ancient sea called Tethys. Then an earth convulsion turned the Tethys rocks into mountains. It acted just as though Italy had moved north and had folded up the sea bottom rocks against ancient mountains in central France, Bavaria, and Czechoslovakia. Some folds, such as the Jura Mountains, were pushed on top of the older rocks. The folding also cracked the crust and let molten rock well up, forming "massifs" such as Mont Blanc. Outcroppings of magnesian limestone called dolomite give the name Dolomites to mountains in the Italian Tyrol. (*See also* Switzerland; Tyrol.)

ALSACE-LORRAINE (ăl′săs-lŏ-rān′). The fortunes of France's two old northeast provinces—Alsace and Lorraine—have filled many pages of history. They lie along the boundary of France and West Germany at a crossroads of trans-European travel. This position helped bring them wealth from commerce, but it also placed them in the path of war and invasion. Their nationality has shifted repeatedly as the great powers fought for possession of their fertile fields and rich resources. Today they compose one of France's most important industrial areas.

Although the two are often spoken of as a single

territory, they are quite distinct regions. Alsace starts as a gentle plain west of the Rhine. It rises to a western boundary in the Vosges. Lorraine lies to the west on a stream-carved plateau that merges with the Paris Basin. Its chief streams are the Moselle and the Meuse. (*See also* France, section on geographic regions.)

Trade and Industry

In Alsace the terraces rising from the Rhine bear meadows and fields and vineyards that yield Rhine wines. Higher slopes are clothed in forests and dotted with picturesque old castles and monasteries. Beside the Vosges streams are textile mills, founded when their power came from water wheels. The old cities near the Rhine and its parallel tributary, the Ill, had their start as medieval trading centers. They grew

NANCY, HISTORIC CAPITAL OF LORRAINE
This view is from the Place Stanislas toward the Arch of Triumph and the Government palace, built in the 18th century.

with the building of canals, railways, highways, and industries in recent centuries.

The chief cities of Alsace are Strasbourg, its historic capital, population 225,964 (1962 census), and Mulhouse, population 107,946. Picturesque Strasbourg has been the seat of the Council of Europe since 1949. The city is famous for its 13th-century Gothic cathedral (*see* Strasbourg). Industries of Alsace are diversified. The leading products are foods, chemicals, textiles, machine tools and equipment, and other engineering products. Potash salts are mined and processed, and some petroleum is produced.

The noted iron and steel and chemical industries of Lorraine are based on its iron mines—the largest in Europe—coal reserves, and rock-salt deposits. A vast industrial district reaches south from the Luxemburg and German borders. Here are many mining and manufacturing towns. Nancy, the historic capital of Lorraine, population 127,729 (1962 census), and Metz, 101,496, are the largest cities (*see* Metz).

Political History of the Provinces

Lorraine took its name from that of Charlemagne's grandson Lothair I. He was given the territory of Lotharingia when Charlemagne's empire was divided at the partition of Verdun in 843. In feudal times the rulers of the duchy of Lorraine were chiefly French nobles. In 1766 Lorraine was joined to France, but it retained special privileges and legislation until the French Revolution.

Alsace was a part of Germany for several centuries but was given to France in 1648 by the Treaty of Westphalia. In 1681 the French seized and retained Strasbourg, the chief city of the region.

Germany's victory in the Franco-Prussian War brought it all of Alsace and a large part of Lorraine. The area saw some of the bloodiest fighting of World War I. France regained the "lost provinces" through the Allied victory in that war. (*See also* Franco-

Prussian War; World War I; Meuse-Argonne, Battle of; Verdun.)

In World War II the Germans outflanked the fortifications of the Maginot Line in 1940 and occupied Alsace-Lorraine. In 1945 American armies swept across the provinces, driving the Germans out.

After the war the French reconstructed and re-equipped the damaged and obsolete plants in the area and built modern iron and steel mills. Manufacturing and mining production outstripped prewar records.

ALUM. The chemical compound alum has wide use in industry and medicine. An *alum* is a double salt made up of two metals and one acid group. It forms colorless eight-sided crystals. *Common alum* occurs when potassium sulfate is dissolved in aluminum sulfate. The two salts combine and crystallize as potassium aluminum sulfate. The formula is $K_2SO_4 \cdot Al_2(SO_4)_3 \cdot 24H_2O$. The crystals contain about 45 percent water. When these crystals are heated until the water evaporates, the powdery mass remaining is known as *burnt alum*. Other alums may contain sodium, ammonium, or chrome in place of potassium.

Alum's Use in Medicine and Industry

Alum's value in medicine is due to its having the property of an *astringent*, which binds, or contracts, the tissues. It is applied to check bleeding and retard perspiration and in treating wounds and canker sores.

In the dyeing industry alum is used as a mordant. Combined with certain dyes it serves to fix the colors to the fibers. Alum is used in making baking powder, paper sizing, and leather tanning compounds. Aluminum sulfate is added to water to settle out bacteria, industrial wastes, and other impurities.

Alum is sometimes found in a natural state. This accounts for its use since very early times in the tanning of leather and for medicinal purposes.

ALUMINUM—The Most Abundant Metal in the Earth's Crust

This long bank of electrolytic cells uses vast amounts of electric power to convert alumina into aluminum.

ALUMINUM. Strong, lightweight, and rustproof, aluminum is a versatile metal. Except for magnesium and beryllium, it is the lightest structural metal. It is therefore widely used in buildings, aircraft, trains, boats, and automobiles. Aluminum cables carry high-voltage electricity. Tubes, cans, and foil wrappings of aluminum protect perishables.

More than 25 per cent of the aluminum consumed in the United States is used for construction. Siding, roofing, insulation, window frames, and builder's hardware are among the construction materials often made of the metal. The transportation industries account for more than 20 per cent of all the aluminum used. Other large consumers are the electrical appliance industry, the electric power and communications industries, and the container industry.

Aluminum is a good conductor of electricity. It reflects heat and is widely used for radiant insulation. It can be cast, rolled, forged, stamped, drawn, machined, or extruded. It combines with other elements to form alloys, which greatly increases its usefulness (see Alloys).

More aluminum is produced in the world than any other nonferrous metal. Total production capacity is nearly 6 million tons annually. Enormous amounts of electric power are required to make aluminum. About 20 per cent of the output cost is for electrical energy. The United States produces about 40 per cent of the world's aluminum. Canada and the Soviet Union each produce about 15 per cent.

Aluminum's Raw Material —Bauxite

Aluminum is the most plentiful metal in the earth's crust. As a silicate or oxide compound it is found in every clay bank and in most of the common rocks. At present, however, it is not economical to extract the metal from clay. Nearly all aluminum for American use comes from one rich ore, called *bauxite* (pronounced *bôks'ĭt* or *bō'zĭt*, from Les Baux, France, where plentiful sources were first found).

Bauxite is mainly aluminum hydroxide, $Al(OH)_3$, usually combined with impurities of iron, silicon, and titanium

oxides. The ore itself may be as soft as clay or as hard as rock and may appear in any of several colors. Bauxite deposits are usually near the earth's surface, where open-pit mining methods are used. For deeper deposits, miners dig shafts and tunnels to reach the ore (see Mines and Mining).

The principal bauxite-producing countries are Jamaica, the Soviet Union, Surinam, Guyana, France, the United States, Guinea, and Hungary. Almost all the bauxite mined in the United States comes from Arkansas. Imported ore is chiefly from South America and the West Indies. Canada imports most of its bauxite from Guyana and Guinea.

Bauxite is a mineral of strategic military importance. Nations compete for control of large deposits outside their borders, for aluminum products are needed in nearly every phase of modern warfare.

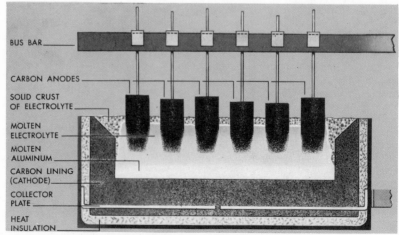

BUS BAR

CARBON ANODES

SOLID CRUST OF ELECTROLYTE

MOLTEN ELECTROLYTE

MOLTEN ALUMINUM

CARBON LINING (CATHODE)

COLLECTOR PLATE

HEAT INSULATION

HOW AN ELECTROLYTIC CELL WORKS

A strong electric current goes from the bus bar down through the anodes to the cathode, splitting the alumina in the electrolyte into oxygen and aluminum.

ALUMINUM CUTS WEIGHT
The structural rigidity and the light weight of aluminum are used to good advantage in the construction industry.

At mills near the mines the bauxite is crushed and sometimes dried out before shipment to treatment plants. The first step in treatment is to remove impurities from the ore. This refining process turns bauxite into aluminum oxide, or *alumina*. Four to six pounds of bauxite yields two pounds of alumina, making one pound of pig aluminum.

One important process for making alumina was developed by Karl Josef Bayer, an Austrian chemist. In the Bayer method, powdered bauxite is mixed with hot caustic soda (sodium hydroxide). In large pressure tanks, called *digesters*, the bauxite turns into a solution of sodium aluminate. The impurities remain in solid form and are filtered out as "red mud."

The hot solution is then pumped into tall precipitating tanks. As it cools, crystals of aluminum hydroxide appear. Kilns heat the crystals white hot and drive off the chemically combined water. This turns the aluminum hydroxide into alumina.

Alumina is reduced to pure aluminum by *electrolysis* (*see* Electrochemistry). In the electrolytic cell used in making aluminum, the aluminum oxide is dissolved in a *bath*, or *electrolyte*. Then a strong electric current is passed through the solution. The action reduces the alumina (takes out the oxygen) and deposits nearly pure aluminum on the bottom of the bath. When enough has accumulated, the aluminum is tapped, or siphoned off, and cast into pigs.

The electrolytic cell is a rectangular steel shell lined with carbon. The carbon lining serves as the cathode. Carbon anodes hanging in the bath from overhead bus bars lead in the current. Oxygen given up by the alumina and carbon from the anodes form carbon dioxide gas, which bubbles out of the bath. Ten kilowatt-hours of electricity and about 12 ounces of carbon anode are required to produce one pound of aluminum.

The bath itself is a melted mineral called *cryolite*, or "ice stone." It is not consumed in the refining process and may be used over and over again. Large deposits of natural cryolite are found only in Greenland. Synthetic cryolite is also used.

A recent production method involves making aluminum directly from bauxite ore, eliminating the alumina refining process. This is expected to reduce the cost of production, though the electric power requirement will remain about the same.

Pig aluminum contains some impurities as it comes from the bath. These are removed by remelting it before the aluminum is made into useful objects. "Commercially pure" aluminum is actually more than 99 per cent pure. During the remelting process, aluminum can be alloyed with other metals. The remelted metal is cast into ingots of various sizes and shapes.

Early Work with Aluminum

Ever since Biblical times, men have been using alum, one of the aluminum compounds found in nature (*see* Alum). Its chemical identity was not discovered until 1746. Then Andreas Marggraf, a German chemist, proved that alum has as its base an unknown metal which is now called aluminum. For decades men tried to isolate aluminum. The Danish scientist Hans Christian Oersted succeeded in 1825, but he could not repeat his experiment. Friedrich Wöhler, of Germany, continued the search for a method to create pure aluminum. In 1845 he isolated a small quantity of the metal by decomposing anhydrous aluminum chloride with potassium.

PROPERTIES OF ALUMINUM	
Symbol............Al	Density at 32°F...2.699
Atomic Number.....13	
Atomic Weight..26.9815	Boiling Point..3,272°F.
Group in Periodic	Melting Point
Table........IIIA	..........1,219.46°F.

A few years later Henri Sainte-Claire Deville substituted the cheaper sodium for potassium and exhibited an aluminum ingot at the Paris Exposition in 1855. Emperor Napoleon III realized that the new metal could lighten his army's equipment and permit more mobility. He commissioned Sainte-Claire Deville to find a way to make large amounts of aluminum cheaply. The French chemist was not able to produce more than a few tons yearly, but it was enough to acquaint scientists and manufacturers with aluminum and its possibilities.

In the United States a young Oberlin College student had been trying to discover a commercially profitable method of aluminum production. Eight months after graduation, in February 1886, Charles Martin Hall worked out his electrolytic method of reducing alumina. He used a solution of alumina, with cryolite as the electrolyte (*see* Hall).

METROPOLIS OF THE TEXAS PANHANDLE
The curving roadways feed into downtown Amarillo's one-way street system. In the rear are the tracks of the Burlington and Rock Island railroads.

Unknown to Hall, Paul Louis Toussaint Héroult, a Frenchman his own age, discovered the same method in the same year. In 1886 Hall applied for American patents (which he secured in 1889) on his electrolytic method of making aluminum; and Héroult applied for French patents.

AMARILLO, TEX. Once the scene of wild buffalo hunts and thundering cattle drives, Amarillo now is the metropolis of the Texas Panhandle. Tall buildings rise beside its busy streets. There are several landscaped parks. The surrounding treeless prairie is a checkerboard of broad pastures and waving fields of wheat and grain sorghum.

Amarillo is a major airline, highway, and railroad junction. With a population that almost doubled between 1950 and 1960 it is one of the fastest-growing cities in the United States.

A marketing center for cattle, grain, petroleum, and natural gas, Amarillo is also an industrial hub. Meat-packing, flour milling, oil refining, and zinc smelting are important. Among the city's many manufactures are leather goods, farm equipment, and chemical and sheet-metal products. Much of the helium produced in the United States is extracted from natural-gas deposits by government plants at Exell, to the north, and at Soncy, nearby to the west.

Amarillo has a popular Little Theater and its own symphony orchestra. Each September the city is host to the Tri-State Fair. There is also an annual rodeo and livestock show. A United States Air Force base lies on the eastern city limits.

The city operates a municipal junior college. To the south, in Canyon, is West Texas State College, which has an evening extension center in Amarillo. On the main campus is the Panhandle Plains Historical Society Museum. Nearby, along a headstream of the Red River, is the 1,100-foot-deep trench of Palo Duro Canyon State Park.

History of the City

The Spanish conquistador Francisco Vázquez de Coronado, in his fruitless search for the Seven Cities of Cibola, visited the area in 1541 (*see* Coronado). A monument to the missionary Juan de Padilla, who accompanied Coronado, now stands in the city.

Amarillo began as a collection of buffalo-hide huts near a railway construction camp in 1887. Then called Ragtown, it was a supply center and shipping point for the cattle ranchers and buffalo hunters. Renamed Amarillo (Spanish for yellow), it soon grew into a cowboy town crowded with hotels, cafes, saloons, and gambling houses. It had no local government, and it was run by Texas Rangers stationed there to curb cattle rustling. Industry developed after the discovery of natural-gas and oil fields in 1918.

Amarillo is the seat of Potter County, but its 55 square miles also sprawl southward into Randall County. It was incorporated in 1892. Amarillo has a home-rule charter adopted in 1913 and a city manager-council form of government. (*See also* Texas.) Population (1960 census), 137,969.

AMAZON RIVER. This great river of tropical South America is a gigantic water reservoir. It drains an area of 2½ million square miles—about one third of the continent. It is the "biggest" river on the globe in volume of discharge. Its flow is greater than that of the Mississippi, the Nile, and the Yangtze combined. It pushes fresh water more than 100 miles into the Atlantic Ocean. Its load of silt and debris totals 160 million tons or more a year.

The Amazon is about 3,900 miles long. The uppermost portion, called the Marañon, rises in the Andes of Peru within 75 miles of the Pacific Ocean. It sweeps across Brazil, gathering the waters from about 1,100 tributaries. Its mouths empty into the Atlantic in a huge estuary that straddles the equator. With its branches the Amazon is navigable by steamboats for 15,000 to 20,000 miles. Ocean vessels can steam 1,000 miles to Manaus, Brazil, at low-water season and 2,300 miles to Iquitos, Peru, at high.

The main stream is 60 miles wide at its mouth. Even 2,000 miles from the sea it still is almost two miles wide. The depth of the main channel is at least 175 feet for 750 miles.

The Atlantic tides are felt for about 400 miles up the river. Incoming tides make the tidal bore, which the natives call *pororoca*. It throws up a wall of salt water from 10 to 15 feet high on top of the river water. The bore may travel 100 miles. Except for the Andean headwaters region, most of the Amazon Basin lies less than 800 feet above sea level. In its last 2,000 miles the river falls only about 35 feet.

The vast Amazon Basin is hot and rainy. Its tremendous rainfall and the melted snows of the Andes account for the river's enormous flow. Plants grow swiftly in the moist heat. Most of the basin is covered with a dense tropical rain forest, though higher lands away from the stream bear prairie grass. No part of the earth has a greater variety of plant and animal life and no stream holds more types of fish.

The entire region has but a few hundred thousand people. Only a few hundred square miles are under cultivation. Visitors have been repelled by the humid heat, jungle plant growth, swarms of insects, and malaria and other diseases.

How the Amazon Indians Live

The only inhabitants in a great part of the basin are scattered tribes of Indians. They live in this hot, wet land much as their ancestors did before America was discovered. They supply themselves with food by hunting, fishing, gathering wild nuts and fruits, and planting gardens. The women plant yams, corn, and cassava for a season or two. Then the fertility is washed from the soil by the heavy rain, so they must move and make another clearing.

They build a new house by erecting a frame of poles, weaving branches for walls, and thatching the steep roof with palm leaves. They have little to move—a few pottery vessels, baskets, and fiber hammocks. Their clothing is a strip of fiber cloth. (*See also* South America, section "The Amazon Basin.")

THE AMAZON AS A COMMERCIAL LIFELINE
These boats are drawn up at a marketplace in Manaus, Brazil. Their owners trade jungle produce for goods from the cities.

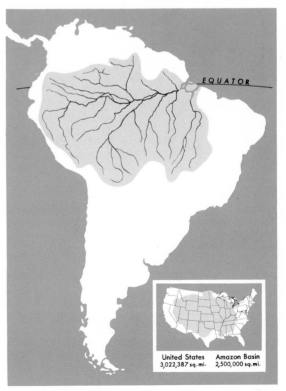

United States
3,022,387 sq. mi.   Amazon Basin
2,500,000 sq. mi.

THE GREAT AMAZON RIVER BASIN
The immense drainage basin of the Amazon is almost as large as the continental United States without Alaska, as the smaller map shows. The region covers northern Brazil and parts of Peru, Bolivia, Ecuador, Colombia, and Venezuela.

Travel is mainly by water in this land of streams and swamps. The Indians hollow out logs by burning and scraping to make long, sturdy dugout canoes. Steamers carry traders, travelers, and goods to the few cities and the trading posts beside the river. Roads and railroads are rare. The longest railway is the 200-mile Madeira-Mamoré line around the rapids of these streams. A highway from Tingo María in Peru crosses the Andes to the Pacific.

The products of the basin come mainly from the forest—wild rubber; Brazil nuts; oil nuts and seeds; gums; resins; mahogany, ebony, and other rare woods; plants and barks yielding quinine, cocaine, curare, and rotenone. Petroleum was discovered on Nova Olinda Island in 1956. Crude oil from this field and from eastern Peru is refined at Manaus, Brazil. Other minerals have not been exploited.

The Brazilian government is trying to attract settlers to develop the basin. Its public health services are eradicating mosquitoes, improving sanitation, and providing health centers and visiting nurses. Agricultural experts are testing various tropical crops on experimental farms. Brazil has inventoried the forest resources of the huge basin with technical aid from the United Nations. (*See also* Brazil, subhead "Geographic Regions—the Amazon Basin.")

AMAZONS. In Greek mythology the Amazons were a nation of female warriors ruled by a queen. No man was permitted to dwell in their country, located on the south coast of the Black Sea. The boy babies were sent to their fathers, the Gargareans, of a neighboring land. The girls were trained in agriculture, hunting, and the art of war.

The Amazons were fearsome warriors. Usually they fought on horseback. Their weapons were the bow, spear, ax, and a shield. According to the myths, they invaded Greece, Syria, the Arabian peninsula, Egypt, Libya, and the islands of the Aegean. Legends tell of the adventures of Hercules and Theseus in the land of the Amazons. Achilles is said to have slain their queen in a fierce battle under the walls of Troy. Many Greek works of art portray the Amazons.

In various parts of the globe anthropologists have found peoples among whom the rights of the mother exceed those of the father and where women have an importance which elsewhere belongs to men. Such a society is called a *matriarchate*. It is thought that the Amazon myths arose from travelers' tales of such societies. Legends of women warriors are told in India, the Arabian peninsula, England, and Ireland.

History records many instances of women warriors. In modern times the king of Dahomey, in western Africa, had an army of women. A female "battalion of death" fought in the Russian Revolution of 1917. Women soldiers served with Soviet troops in World War II, and the South Korean army had women fighters in 1950. The Amazon River gained its name from the fact that an early explorer there was attacked by a savage tribe among whom the women fought alongside the men.

AMBER. Millions of years ago in the Oligocene epoch of the earth's history, clear resin seeped from pine trees growing in the Baltic Sea basin. As centuries passed, lumps of this resin were covered by layers of soil. The Ice Age glaciers poured over it. The resin was hardened by time and pressure into a fossil called amber. It is a brittle, yellow-to-brown, translucent substance. It is hard enough to be carved but not as hard as marble or glass.

When the resin was fresh, soft, and sticky, sometimes leaves, flowers, or live insects were trapped in it. They may be seen in the amber today.

The ancient Phoenicians, Greeks, and Romans valued amber highly. They believed it would cure certain diseases. Amber takes a charge of static electricity when it is rubbed, so the Greeks called it *elektron*. The word "electricity" comes from the term.

The amber-producing pines grew chiefly on the site of the Baltic and North seas. The land was later submerged. Today when violent storms disturb the seas, pieces of amber may be washed up on the shores. Most amber, however, is obtained by mining. Lumps weighing up to 15 and 18 pounds have been discovered. Small amounts are found in Great Britain, Sicily, Siberia, Greenland, and the United States, but the chief source is the Baltic region.

Other fossil resins include *burmite, copalite*, and *retinite*. Pressed amber, or *ambroid*, is made by heating and compressing amber fragments. Amber has been used for jewelry and ornaments since prehistoric times. Its use for such items as mouthpieces of pipes has declined since plastics have been manufactured (*see* Plastics).

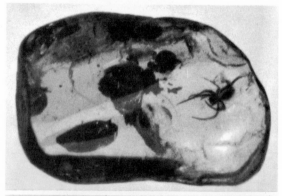

A SPIDER AND A MOTH IN AMBER
The spider in the top lump was trapped in the resin before it fossilized. A moth is in the bottom piece. Where insects have become extinct, the fossils make them available for study.

Columbus is honored as the discoverer of America. His voyages were sponsored by the Spanish crown and were widely publicized. This is an early artist's conception of his first landing.

AMERICA—How the New World Was Discovered

AMERICA. Suppose a space explorer were to return to earth and announce a landing on a new planet. He reports that it is huge, beautiful, and rich. Its atmosphere and climate are suitable to man and his familiar plants and animals. Such a discovery would scarcely promise more to people of today than the discovery of America offered Europeans of 1492.

The New World contained all the natural wealth for which 15th-century people longed—and far more. Here were great deposits of the gold which they sought so eagerly. Here also were vast reserves of other minerals. Mile upon mile of plains, valleys, and mountains held fertile farm lands and pastures.

The New World was scantily settled by its people, the American Indians. Large areas where the Indians lived by hunting, fishing, or gathering had no permanent settlements. The tribes that lived by farming had, however, domesticated many valuable plants. Corn, potatoes, pumpkins and squash, peanuts, and other new crops from America were to play a big role in nourishing mankind. (For picture map in color of crops raised by the American Indians, see Indians, American.)

Size and Extent of the American Continents

America or the Americas is the name given the two continents of the Western Hemisphere, with their adjacent islands. They lie between the Atlantic Ocean on the east and the Pacific on the west. North America and South America together contain some 16,250,000 square miles. This area is about 4.3 times as large as Europe. The two continents are about two thirds as large as Europe and Asia together.

The New World is scarcely comparable with the Old in population. The estimated total population of the Americas is about 429,000,000, compared with the 604,000,000 of Europe alone.

North and South America together have the greatest north-south extent of any land mass on earth. With Greenland, usually considered as part of North America, the two Americas extend from 83° 39′ North latitude to 55° 59′ South—or nearly 140 degrees. This is more than 9,500 miles. North America's greatest width is some 3,000 miles; South America's, about 3,200 miles. (See also the articles North America and South America and their Reference-Outlines.)

LEIF ERICSON SIGHTS THE NORTH AMERICAN COAST

Storms drove Leif's Viking ship to Vinland almost 500 years before Columbus discovered America. Norse settlements there were abandoned and forgotten for centuries. This painting by Christian Krohg hangs in the National Gallery in Oslo, Norway.

tomac. (For map of river drainage in the United States, *see* United States.)

South America's greatest streams drain the basins that make up its central plains. They flow into the Atlantic. They are the Amazon, the Orinoco, and the Paraná-Paraguay.

Broad Range of Climate

America affords every type of climate on earth and almost every class of vegetation. Temperature, rainfall, growing season, and wet and dry seasons are affected by the physical features of the continents as well as by the wide range of latitude.

North America is broadest in the high and middle latitudes. Three quarters of its area lies in the middle latitudes so favorable to human activity and to the growth of many of the most useful crops. Three quarters of South America lies in the tropics. Its greatest width is near the equator. Heat and humidity have delayed development here. South America's middle latitude lands are in the narrower south. (*See also* Climate; Rainfall; Grasslands.)

Varied Natural Resources

America's great natural wealth is widely distributed. The resources of one region contribute to the development of another through trade. Bolivia's tin, Chile's copper, Argentina's wool, Brazil's manganese, Venezuela's iron, and Canada's nickel are used by industries in the United States. Canada's wood pulp and paper, grain, and fish are traded for the coffee, bananas, cacao, sugar, and cotton of the tropical and semitropical sections. Manufactured wares from the United States include machinery for the industrial development of all America.

When the Northmen Sailed to America

The first European to land in America was Leif Ericson, a Viking seaman from Greenland (*see* Ericson). The ancient sagas give different accounts of this voyage made in the year 1000. Leif landed on a forested shore which he called Vinland. He did not realize he had found a new continent, and Europe heard nothing of his discovery. In 1963 archaeologists uncovered the remains of a Viking settlement on the northern tip of Newfoundland. According to radiocarbon dating it was occupied about A.D. 1000. This was the first proof that white men had lived in North America before Columbus.

Most medieval Europeans were ignorant of other places in the world. Maps of the time showed only

America's Shape and Structure

The two continents are similar in physical structure. Each forms a rough triangle, with the base in the north. They are joined by the Isthmus of Panama —part of Central America, a division of North America. South America lies southeast of North America. Between them in the Caribbean Sea stretch the West Indies islands, geographically part of North America. (For map, *see* World.)

Near the west coast of both continents rise the Cordilleras. This is a great system of young fold mountains which in places encircles plateaus and basins. It is made up of a number of parallel ranges. They are fringed by a narrow Pacific coastal plain. Both North and South America contain broad interior plains. From them the land rises again to lower, older highlands in the east.

Rivers of America

These vast continents are drained by some of the world's greatest rivers. The rivers of North America fall mainly into two groups—those which drain the western mountain system and flow into the Pacific and those which drain the Interior Plains and send their waters directly or indirectly into the Atlantic. Those flowing into the Pacific include the Yukon, Fraser, Columbia, and Colorado. The waters of the Great Lakes reach the Atlantic through the St. Lawrence. The Mississippi River flows southward to the Gulf of Mexico, carrying the waters of its huge tributaries—the Missouri, Arkansas, Red, Ohio, and Tennessee. East coast rivers are shorter, but they are important for the gaps they have cut through the Appalachian Highlands and for the fine harbors at the drowned mouths of the Hudson, Delaware, and Po-

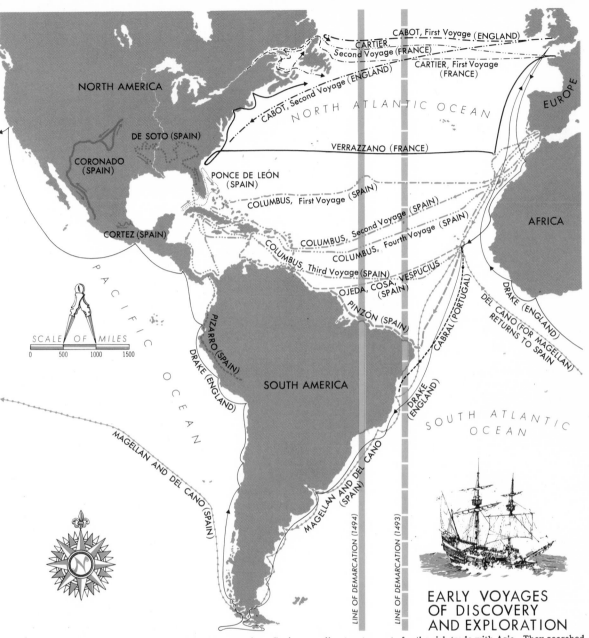

NORTH AMERICA

CABOT, First Voyage (ENGLAND)

CARTIER, Second Voyage (FRANCE)

CARTIER, First Voyage (FRANCE)

CABOT, Second Voyage (ENGLAND)

NORTH ATLANTIC OCEAN

EUROPE

DE SOTO (SPAIN)

VERRAZZANO (FRANCE)

CORONADO (SPAIN)

PONCE DE LEÓN (SPAIN)

COLUMBUS, First Voyage (SPAIN)

CORTEZ (SPAIN)

COLUMBUS, Second Voyage (SPAIN)

COLUMBUS, Fourth Voyage (SPAIN)

COLUMBUS, Third Voyage (SPAIN)

OJEDA, COSA, VESPUCIUS (SPAIN)

PINZÓN (SPAIN)

AFRICA

DRAKE (ENGLAND)

DEL CANO (FOR MAGELLAN) RETURNS TO SPAIN

PACIFIC OCEAN

SCALE OF MILES

0   500   1000   1500

PIZARRO (SPAIN)

DRAKE (ENGLAND)

SOUTH AMERICA

CABRAL (PORTUGAL)

DRAKE (ENGLAND)

SOUTH ATLANTIC OCEAN

MAGELLAN AND DEL CANO (SPAIN)

MAGELLAN AND DEL CANO (SPAIN)

LINE OF DEMARCATION (1494)

LINE OF DEMARCATION (1493)

EARLY VOYAGES OF DISCOVERY AND EXPLORATION

Europe's great powers of the 15th and 16th centuries—Spain, Portugal, England, and France—rivaled one another in sending expeditions of discovery across the Atlantic. They sought a direct water route for the rich trade with Asia. They searched for gold and for land to build overseas empires. The general outlines of America emerged and colonization advanced.

a broad strip of land and water reaching from Greenland south to the Mediterranean coasts of Europe and Africa and far eastward to China's Pacific shore.

Events and developments in the next 500 years had served to make Europeans curious about the world by the time Columbus rediscovered America in 1492. Christian knights from Europe had been fighting in wars, called Crusades, in western Asia (*see* Crusades). The crusaders had brought wonderful products home from Asia. There were cloves, pepper, and other spices to make food taste good and keep it from spoil-

ing. There were sheer, colorful silken cloths, rich carpets, and sparkling jewelry. Europeans wanted these luxuries so much that Venice and Genoa, in Italy, grew rich trading in them. People were excited by the story of Marco Polo, which told of a trip to China and the greater wonders there (*see* Polo, Marco).

Discoveries in the science of the stars—astronomy—now helped seamen navigate their ships better. Some men believed that the earth was round. Part of the new knowledge came from the long-forgotten writings of great thinkers of ancient Greece and Rome. This rebirth of interest in ancient learning was called the Renaissance (*see* Renaissance).

The magnetic compass had reached Europe in the 1100's. Within a hundred years or so sea captains learned to rely on it. Men began to make better maps. Little by little it became safer for sailors to venture into unknown seas.

Trade Routes Enlarge the World

At first the wealth of the East trickled into Western Europe mainly by overland routes. Goods changed hands many times before they reached the consumer, and at each exchange the cost increased. Shipping costs were also high. Goods were transported by camel or horse caravans, each animal carrying only a comparatively small load. After 1453 the Moslem Turks controlled Constantinople, which was the crossroads of important trade routes. They permitted cargoes from the East to pass through the city only on their own terms.

Western European merchants thought that if they could find sea routes to the Orient they could import goods directly to their own cities. Soon they were prepared to outfit ships for sea captains sailing in search of new routes. Each contributed only a portion of the expense, so that no one would be completely ruined if the venture failed. They also secured the king's approval of their enterprises and his promise to defend their claims to lands discovered along the way. The king of Spain always demanded a fifth of the gold and silver found by his explorers.

The Italian port cities were satisfied with their monopoly of the old routes. The Scandinavian countries were far removed. Germany was split into many small states. Thus the work of discovery fell to Portugal, Spain, England, and France.

Portuguese Exploration Around Africa

Under the sponsorship of Prince Henry the Navigator, Portugal took the lead in the 1400's (*see* Henry the Navigator). Portuguese sea captains made ever-

lengthening voyages along the western coast of Africa. Bartholomew Diaz first saw the cliffs of the Cape of Good Hope at Africa's southern tip in 1488 (*see* Diaz, Bartholomew). In 1497–98 Vasco da Gama rounded the Cape and reached India by sea. He brought back a cargo of spices that netted a huge profit (*see* Gama). Portugal occupied key cities on the sea lanes between China and the Red Sea. Its wealth became the envy of Western Europe.

Others before Vasco da Gama had planned new sea routes to the Orient, and some had guessed that such a route might be found by sailing west. Few men could agree on how *far* west Asia lay from Europe by sea, and no one dreamed that the American continents stood in the way.

Columbus Sails West

One of the most optimistic advocates of the western route was Christopher Columbus (*see* Columbus, Christopher). For years he begged the courts of Portugal, England, France, and Spain for a grant of ships and men to prove that Asia lay only a few thousand miles west of Europe. Finally in 1492 Queen Isabella of Castile provided the money, and Columbus sailed with three ships. Pressing onward over the growing objections of his captains and crews, he finally sighted one of the Bahamas and shortly thereafter discovered Cuba and Hispaniola.

On three later voyages he found the mainlands of Central and South America. Until his death, in 1506, Columbus never swerved from his belief that the lands he discovered were actually part of Asia.

Spain and Portugal Divide the New World

When Columbus first returned to Spain, the Portuguese claimed that he had merely visited a part of their dominion of Guinea in Africa. Spain and Portugal accordingly asked Pope Alexander VI to settle the dispute. He complied by drawing a north-south Line of Demarcation in 1493. If Spain discovered lands west of this line, the Spanish king was to have them if they were not already owned by a Christian ruler. In 1494 the line was drawn through a point 370 leagues west of the Cape Verde Islands.

In 1500 a Portuguese mariner, Pedro Alvarez Cabral, sailing along Africa en route to India, was carried by a storm to Brazil. He claimed the land for Portugal since it lay east of the line. When the Portuguese king heard of Cabral's discovery, he sent out an expedition which sailed hundreds of miles along the South American coast.

New Land Named for Vespucius

An Italian merchant, Americus Vespucius, asserted he was a member of exploring parties to the New World and wrote a letter telling of what he had seen. Martin Waldseemüller, a German

SIR FRANCIS DRAKE'S GLOBE-CIRCLING 'GOLDEN HIND'
Only this ship from Drake's fleet passed through the stormy Strait of Magellan. With it he captured Spanish treasure ships off Peru and sailed around the world to England. He was knighted by his queen, Elizabeth I.

NICOLET FINDS AND EXPLORES LAKE MICHIGAN

Jean Nicolet was one of the explorers Samuel de Champlain sent into the Great Lakes region of New France. This painting shows Nicolet at Green Bay in 1634. He was the first white man to set foot in what is now Wisconsin.

scholar, included the letter in a popular geography and suggested that the new land be called America. The name caught on and brought Vespucius an honor he did not deserve (*see* Vespucius).

By 1510 men realized that the new land was not part of the Orient, but they still thought that China and India were just beyond. In 1513 Vasco Nuñez de Balboa, the Spanish adventurer, crossed the Isthmus of Darien and became the first European to see the Pacific Ocean from American shores (*see* Balboa).

By this time Spain claimed that the Line of Demarcation extended around the globe, but no one knew where it fell in the Eastern Hemisphere. A Portuguese captain, Ferdinand Magellan, believed there might be a water passage through the New World that would lead to the Orient. He convinced the king of Spain that the richest lands in the Far East lay in the region reserved for Spain by the papal line. The king commissioned Magellan to find a western route.

Magellan's Ship Circles the Globe

In 1519 Magellan sailed from Spain to Brazil. Then he proceeded south along the coast to the tip of the continent and passed through the strait that now bears his name. He sailed into the ocean which he named the Pacific. Magellan was killed in the Philippine Islands, but one of his ships went on to India and finally in 1522 to Spain by way of the Indian Ocean and the Cape of Good Hope (*see* Magellan).

The voyage established Magellan as the foremost navigator in history. For the first time the globe was circled and the vast expanse of the Pacific was revealed. No longer could America be regarded as an outlying part of Asia.

Spain and Portugal each claimed that the rich Spice Islands of the East lay within its allotted territory. Spain's westward route was so much longer than Portugal's eastern route that Spain could not profit from the trade. In 1529 Spain surrendered to Portugal its claims in Asia and received the Philippine Islands in return. Magellan's voyage thus failed to break Portugal's supremacy in the Orient.

The Spanish Penetrate America

The Spanish took the lead in exploring and colonizing the New World. The earliest settlements were in the West Indies. Hispaniola had the first towns. Santo Domingo, established in 1496, became the first capital of New Spain. Other settlements rose in Cuba, Puerto Rico, and Jamaica. From island harbors sailed expeditions to explore the coasts and penetrate the continents. They found gold, silver, and precious stones and enslaved the Indians. Ambitious men became governors of conquered lands. Missionaries brought a new religion to the Indians.

One adventurer, Juan Ponce de León, sailed from Puerto Rico in 1513. He landed on a new shore that he called Florida. He was interested in exploration and slave trading. He also wanted to find a fabled fountain whose waters made men perpetually young. He returned to Florida in 1521 to build a settlement, but he was slain by Indians (*see* Ponce de León).

Riches for Spain from Mexico and Peru

The Spanish dream of finding great riches in America was realized when Hernando Cortez conquered the empire of the Aztecs in Mexico in 1519–21 (*see* Cortez). A few years later Francisco Pizarro with a small force vanquished the Inca empire and seized the treasure of Peru in South America (*see* Pizarro). Gold and silver from these lands poured into the Spanish king's treasury, rousing the envy of other rulers. The treasure ships attracted bloodthirsty pirates and privateers (*see* Pirates and Piracy).

Spanish and Portuguese in North America

Other Spanish conquerors (called in Spanish *conquistadores*) turned north to the lands now forming the southern part of the United States. In 1539 Hernando de Soto came from Spain by way of Cuba to the east coast of Florida. From there he trekked overland to the Mississippi. He wandered into what is now Arkansas and Oklahoma and later floated down the Arkansas River to its mouth. In 1542 he died and was buried in the Mississippi (*see* De Soto).

Indian traditions and stories of Spanish wanderers told that somewhere north of Mexico the golden towers of the Seven Cities of Cibola gleamed in the sun. Francisco de Coronado, governor of a province in western Mexico, set out in 1540 to find them. He

299

crossed the deserts and plains between what is now western New Mexico and central Kansas, but he found only poor Indian towns (pueblos). Coronado returned to Mexico without gold and jewels. Although Coronado had traveled well into the heart of North America, the Spaniards did not care to explore further the disappointing lands he had seen (*see* Coronado; Southwest, American).

Earlier, in 1524–25, a Portuguese sea captain, Estevan Gómez, serving the king of Spain, explored the coast of North America from Maine to New Jersey. His descriptions led the Spaniards to consider this region far less valuable than the lands they had in the south. Thus they ignored the greater part of the east coast of North America.

The Portuguese made one important discovery in this northern region. In 1501 Gaspar Corte-Real reached Newfoundland. His voyages were not followed up, for Portugal soon needed all its resources to develop its East India empire and its colony in Brazil.

The English Seamen

England's first port for mariners sailing west was the city of Bristol. Bristol merchants hoped that if a new route to the Orient lay directly west across the Atlantic, their city would become the principal trade center. In 1497 they sent John Cabot, a Genoese sea captain, in search of this new passage. Cabot touched land between Newfoundland and Nova Scotia and returned believing that he had visited the outlying parts of Asia. His voyage gave England its later claim to North America (*see* Cabot).

After realizing that Cabot had not reached Asia, England tried to open a route to the Orient around northern Europe—the "Northeast Passage." In 1576 Sir Humphrey Gilbert wrote his 'Discourse of a Northwest Passage', in which he reasoned that a water route led around North America to Asia. A few years later Gilbert sailed to establish a base in Newfoundland but died on the way home. Two other captains, Martin Frobisher and John Davis, each made three voyages between 1575 and 1589 to the network of

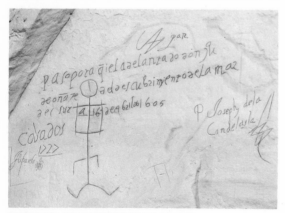

HISTORY ON 'INSCRIPTION ROCK'
El Morro mesa, now a national monument in New Mexico, was for 170 years a camping place for Spanish explorers. Here is the record of an encampment by Juan de Oñate in 1605.

straits and inlets north of the St. Lawrence River, but neither could find a way to the Pacific.

Search for Northwest Passage

To give England a foothold in the Far East, Queen Elizabeth I chartered the East India Company in 1600. In 1602 the company sent George Weymouth to find a passage through the continent to the Pacific, but he did not sail beyond Labrador. Another expedition the same year, under Bartholomew Gosnold, explored the New England coast. When the Virginia Colony was founded in 1607, John Smith and other settlers hoped to find a waterway across the country that would lead them to the Pacific.

England had another motive for entering the competition: to weaken Spain as a European power. In the 1500's England had established a national Protestant church. Spain wished to restore the pope's authority over England. The Spanish military might was largely supported by the gold and silver from Mexico and Peru. Another source of revenue was the high duty levied on the Spanish traders, who held a monopoly on importing Negro slaves into Spanish colonies. John Hawkins, an English sea rover, began smuggling Negroes from Africa into the Spanish West Indies. He made three such voyages and reaped huge profits. On his third voyage he was attacked by a Spanish fleet and lost all but two ships (*see* Hawkins).

The Adventures of Drake

Hawkins escaped the Spaniards, taking with him his daring partner and cousin, Francis Drake (*see* Drake). Drake realized that England could gain more by seizing Spanish treasure in the West Indies than by smuggling slaves. He sailed to the Caribbean on a raiding expedition, but the Spaniards were well guarded and he won little spoil. Then he planned a bolder move. Knowing that the Spanish ships and ports on the Pacific were unprotected, he sailed from England, passed through the Strait of Magellan, and fell upon the Spaniards off Chile and Peru. He took so much plunder that he used silver for ballast. He sailed north, seeking an eastward passage through North America. Failing in this, he sailed across the Pacific and followed the route of Magellan's party back to Europe.

The English raids on the Spaniards in America helped plunge the two nations into open war. In 1588 the great Spanish Armada preparing to invade England was completely crushed (*see* Armada, Spanish). Spain's sea power swiftly declined and with it Spain's strength to keep England from the opportunities of the New World.

The riches of Spanish America prompted many Englishmen to search for gold in their own holdings in North America. In 1576 Martin Frobisher found samples of a "black earth" that he thought was a gold ore. He was wrong, but for a time England thought it was on the track of great wealth. Walter Raleigh sent out parties between 1584 and 1587 to explore and colonize the area named Virginia, but his ventures failed (*see* Raleigh, Sir Walter).

The French in Canada

While the conquistadors were busy in Central America, Spain and France were at war at home. Francis I, king of France, wanted a share of the Oriental trade to finance his armies. He commissioned a Florentine navigator, Giovanni da Verrazzano, to find a passage to Asia. In 1524 Verrazzano touched the American coast at North Carolina and then sailed north to Newfoundland. His report to the king contained the first description of the northeastern coast of North America and gave France its claim to American lands.

The next explorer from France was Jacques Cartier. He made three voyages between 1534 and 1541 in quest of the Asia route. He ascended the St. Lawrence as far as the site of Montreal (*see* Cartier). After Cartier's voyages, a series of religious wars at home stopped France from sending out other parties. France made attempts, however, to establish two colonies as refuges for the Huguenots (French Protestants). One colony, in Brazil (1555–58), was destroyed by the Portuguese. The other, in Florida (1562–65), was wiped out by the Spaniards. Starting about 1540 French fishermen annually fished off the Newfoundland coast and in the Gulf of St. Lawrence.

THE CONQUISTADORS IN AMERICA
A host of Spanish conquerors (*conquistadores*) came to win fortunes in the American wilderness. With them came soldiers to enslave and priests to convert the Indians. Courageous and cruel, the Spanish left their imprint on America.

Under the vigorous rule of Henry IV (1589–1610) France was again united and at peace. Once more French explorers began to seek a strait to the Pacific.

Samuel de Champlain sailed to Quebec in 1608 and set up the first permanent French colony in North America. Then he probed westward, always hoping the St. Lawrence led to the western sea (*see* Champlain).

Exploring the Great Lakes and the Mississippi

A memorable voyage by Jean Nicolet in 1634 carried the French flag across Lake Michigan to the Fox River in Wisconsin. Here the Indians told of a mighty river nearby that flowed into a great body of water. The French thought this water might be the western sea they were seeking. In 1673 Louis Joliet, a fur trader, and Father Jacques Marquette, a Jesuit missionary, followed the Fox and Wisconsin rivers to the Mississippi and descended it (*see* Marquette).

René Robert Cavelier, sieur de La Salle, France's great empire builder, was inspired by stories of the river valley. In 1682 he reached the mouth of the Mississippi and claimed the valley for France. He named it Louisiana, after King Louis XIV. He returned to the Gulf of Mexico to settle a colony but was slain by his men (*see* La Salle).

The Dutch Come Last

The Netherlands was the last to begin exploration in the New World. For years the Dutch struggled to win their independence from Spain. During this struggle, Spain in 1580 annexed Portugal and gained control of the Oriental trade. The Dutch realized that Spain might be weakened by striking at its trade. They formed the Dutch East India Company and dispatched Henry Hudson, an English sea captain, to find a short cut to the Orient. Hudson entered the Hudson River in 1609 and ascended it to the site of Albany (*see* Hudson). About 14 years later the Dutch established their first colony, on Manhattan Island. The story of the colonization of North America is told in the articles American Colonies; American Colonies, Life in; Southwest, American.

Thirteen Colonies That Became a Great Nation

AMERICAN COLONIES. Thirteen colonies were established in the wilderness along North America's Atlantic coast in the 1600's and early 1700's. Weak and struggling settlements at first, they grew and developed to become the 13 original states of the United States.

Eleven of the colonies were founded by the English —Virginia, the first permanent colony (1607); Massachusetts (1620); New Hampshire (1623); Maryland (1634); Connecticut (1635); Rhode Island (1636); North Carolina (1653); New Jersey (1664); South Carolina (1670); Pennsylvania (1682); and Georgia (1733). New York (1624) was settled by the Dutch as New Netherland. Swedes established the first settlement in Delaware (1638). These territories were later taken over by the English. All the American colonies thus became English in speech and custom. (For history of the colonies, *see* articles on the 13 states.)

Founders of the Nation

Americans honor the men and women of the colonies as the founders of their nation. These people courageously crossed a wide, stormy ocean to build homes in a raw, unknown land. They developed the land into farms and villages and cities. They set up schools and churches, courts and legislatures.

Forced to rely upon themselves, they grew resolute and independent. The colonists and their children became a new people—the Americans. In 1776 they

From the *Arbella*, June 30, 1630, Governor Winthrop and his Puritan colonists view the unknown shore that will be their home. They came to Massachusetts seeking religious freedom.

declared the colonies independent of England. They won freedom in the Revolutionary War and established a new nation. The democratic constitution their leaders created is the basis of the United States government. (*See also* Revolution, American; United States Constitution; United States History.)

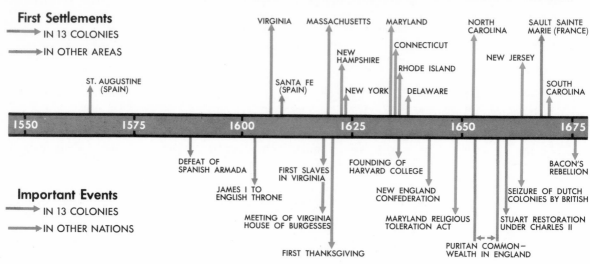

THE AMERICAN COLONIAL ERA

First Settlements

→ IN 13 COLONIES

➡ IN OTHER AREAS

ST. AUGUSTINE (SPAIN)

VIRGINIA   MASSACHUSETTS   MARYLAND   NORTH CAROLINA   SAULT SAINTE MARIE (FRANCE)

CONNECTICUT

NEW HAMPSHIRE   NEW JERSEY

SANTA FE (SPAIN)   RHODE ISLAND

NEW YORK   DELAWARE   SOUTH CAROLINA

1550   1575   1600   1625   1650   1675

DEFEAT OF SPANISH ARMADA   FIRST SLAVES IN VIRGINIA   FOUNDING OF HARVARD COLLEGE   BACON'S REBELLION

JAMES I TO ENGLISH THRONE   NEW ENGLAND CONFEDERATION   SEIZURE OF DUTCH COLONIES BY BRITISH

Important Events

→ IN 13 COLONIES

➡ IN OTHER NATIONS

MEETING OF VIRGINIA HOUSE OF BURGESSES   MARYLAND RELIGIOUS TOLERATION ACT   STUART RESTORATION UNDER CHARLES II

PURITAN COMMON-WEALTH IN ENGLAND

FIRST THANKSGIVING

Rivalry for Empire in the New World

Few people of the early 1600's would have foretold that the English colonies would grow into a great nation. Spaniards and Frenchmen were settling in North America too. England appeared to be the underdog in the struggle for empire.

Spain had taken the lead in exploration and discovery in the New World (see America). Its expeditions had conquered rich Indian kingdoms in Mexico and Peru and had discovered gold and silver. Spaniards had settled the first town in what is now the United States—St. Augustine, Fla.—in 1565. Later they spread from Mexico into the high, dry regions of present New Mexico, Arizona, California, and Texas. The Spanish expeditions included soldiers to conquer the Indians and priests to convert them to Christianity and teach them manual skills. Their colonies usually took the form of missions, military posts (presidios), and huge ranchos. The land of New Spain belonged to the Spanish king and he made its laws.

Relatively few Spaniards who came to America intended to make it their home. After more than 200 years, there were only several thousands living north of the Rio Grande. Spanish influence, however, remained strong in the Southwest. Spanish missions and presidios here developed into famous American cities (see Southwest, American; Santa Fe; San Antonio; San Diego).

French Power in Interior America

The French were attracted to the rich fishing grounds off Newfoundland and the fur-trading country along the St. Lawrence River and inland around the Great Lakes. Traders, missionaries, and explorers followed the rivers west and south. La Salle traced the Mississippi all the way to its mouth and claimed its vast basin for France (see La Salle).

In all their huge territory there were but two provinces—Louisiana in the south and New France in the interior and along the St. Lawrence. Migration to the wilderness attracted relatively few Frenchmen. Settlers were widely scattered, since agriculture was neglected for the greater profits in the fur trade. The provinces were rigidly ruled from the French throne. During the 1600's a strong chain of forts was established along the waterways from Quebec to New Orleans. They formed a menacing arc around the English colonies along the coast. The forts and missions founded by France developed into important cities of the United States (see New Orleans; Mobile; Detroit).

England Bids for Empire Through Colonies

The English had not been as active in exploration as had the Spanish and French. Their claim to North America was based on John Cabot's voyage of 1497 (see Cabot). In the latter 1500's they determined to develop the land they claimed and to hold it by setting up colonies. Progress was slow. The first colony sent out by Sir Walter Raleigh failed (see Raleigh, Sir Walter). Others survived only after losing hundreds of settlers to hunger and disease. Finally, however, a string of colonies stretched along the Atlantic coast from French Canada on the north to Spanish Florida on the south.

This part of North America had its advantages and its disadvantages. The English were disappointed because the land did not yield the gold and silver that had brought great wealth to Spain. In the long run, however, the abundant fertile soil and good growing weather proved more valuable than gold. If the colonists had found precious metals, they might have exploited the minerals and returned to England. To earn a living from the soil they had to work patiently year after year and make permanent homes. About nine tenths of the colonists became farmers.

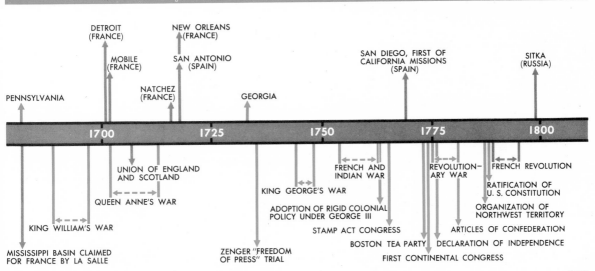

303

Learning to Use the Land's Resources

The seaboard afforded good harbors for fishing and for trading with Europe and other parts of America. Many streams were available for water transportation and for turning mill wheels. The land was thickly wooded for the most part. Although it was difficult to clear for fields and pastures, the forest afforded building material, fuel, and timber for shipbuilding and for export.

Inland the Appalachian Highlands long served as a barrier to westward expansion. On their limited strip in the East, the English were not spread thin like the French and Spanish in their wide territories. The colonies formed a solid block of settlement to oppose the scattered French forts beyond the mountains. By 1750 the English settlers outnumbered the French 14 to 1.

As time went by the people of the different colonies and regions learned to use the resources of their areas. Different economies and ways of life developed in the South, the Middle Colonies, and New England (see American Colonies, Life in).

Who Came to the Colonies and Why

Who were the people that dared to leave their old homes and settle in this strange, wild land? Why did they come? They were farmers and ministers and laborers, rich men and poor men, families with children, and men alone. Most of them were simple folk of small means who were eager to work and to think for themselves. A few were daring men seeking wealth and adventure.

Many came to worship God in their own way. They were not permitted to do so in England and in other parts of Europe (see Church, Christian).

WHERE VIRGINIA COLONISTS PRAYED
This ivy-covered church tower, rising amid the graves of the forefathers, is the only standing ruin at Jamestown. The memorial church behind it was built on the 1639 foundation.

Among those who came for religious freedom were the Pilgrims and Puritans of New England, the Catholics for whom Lord Baltimore made a refuge in Maryland, and the Quakers and other sects who followed William Penn to Pennsylvania. (See also Baltimore, Lords; 'Mayflower'; Penn; Plymouth, Mass.; Puritans.)

There were other freedoms for which the colonists hoped. In Europe, long ruled by kings, the idea of political freedom was stirring men's minds. In new communities across the sea they believed they might have more to say about how they were governed.

Poverty and Injustice Lead to Migration

Although religious and political freedom led many to America, poverty and trouble led more. During the 17th century it was sometimes thought that England had more people than it could feed. Many farmers had found it more profitable to raise sheep than to grow crops. They had enclosed their lands and driven the farm hands from the cottages. The unemployed crowded the roads seeking homes and work.

Even those who had work were discontented. The English class system kept a man confined to his occupation. He had no chance to advance or improve his fortune. If he fell into debt he might be sent to the overcrowded prisons. As time went by, England sent prisoners overseas by the thousands. Ship captains made a profit by selling them as indentured servants. They were bound by a contract to work for a certain time in payment for their passage. The last of the 13 colonies, Georgia, was founded by Gen. James Oglethorpe to provide a home for poor debtors (see Oglethorpe).

England supplied most of the colonists in the 1600's. Later, increasing numbers poured in from neighboring lands—Germans, Scotch-Irish, Scottish highlanders, Swiss, French Protestants, and others. Religious persecution, war, taxation, poverty, and ambition were factors in leading them to migrate. Negro slaves from Africa also helped to people the New World and do its work. They were brought to Virginia as early as 1619.

How the Colonies Were Set Up

From the beginning there were people willing to come to America, and the English government was eager to establish colonies. The matter of paying for them presented a problem. A great deal of money was needed to equip settlers, transport them to a colony, and maintain them until they became self-supporting. The government encouraged rich merchants and other private investors to furnish capital.

The investors demanded a charter from the king giving them privileges in return. The king made them lords of a tract of land and allowed them to govern their settlement. They secured a favored position in its trade.

Companies and Proprietors Get Charters

Sometimes the promoters organized a stock company, and it received the charter. Shareholders elected the governor of the company and his council, passed laws for the settlement and provided it with officers, and made grants of land. As the colony developed, the profits from the labor of the settlers were to pay dividends to the shareholders. The London Company used this method for establishing the first permanent settlement, Jamestown. It was also used by the Dutch in New Netherland. The Puritans organized the Massachusetts Bay Company in 1629. Their motive was not profit but religious freedom.

In other cases the king gave a whole colony to one person or a group not organized into a company. These men were called proprietors. Cecil Calvert, the second Lord Baltimore, became the proprietor of Maryland in 1632. Eight important men became the proprietors of the Carolinas in 1663. When New Netherland was taken from the Dutch in 1664, Charles II turned it over to his brother James, duke of York. Lord John Berkeley and Sir George Carteret received New Jersey. In 1681 Charles II gave the land between New York and Maryland to Penn.

Rhode Island and Connecticut were founded by settlers from Massachusetts acting without authority from the king. They established independent towns, agreeing to live under a government of their own making. Then those towns were combined into colonies. Rhode Island received a charter in 1644, and Connecticut got its royal charter in 1662.

How Self-Government Developed

Various forms of self-government soon began to appear in the colonies. The Virginia House of Burgesses was founded in 1619. Some charters required the company or proprietor to get the assent of the settlers to laws and taxes. Assemblies were thus set up. Most colonial legislatures had two branches— an elected assembly and a governor's council. Massachusetts' Puritans created a theocracy—a partnership of church and state. Self-rule flourished in early America partly because the colonies were too poor to be valued highly and partly because England was busy with its Civil War and other troubles.

In a period of 50 years following 1679, England changed all the colonies except Pennsylvania, Maryland, Rhode Island, and Connecticut into royal provinces. The king appointed the governor and council and told them what to do. Both were supposed to guard England's interests and to enforce acts of the British Parliament regarding the colonies. Particularly offensive to the colonists were acts restricting their trade with nations other than England and "punitive" taxes levied after George III ascended the throne in 1760. Opposition to these laws helped unite the colonists in rebellion against England.

Unity Grows Slowly

Unity among the colonies was long retarded by poor communications. It was well into the 1700's before roads, inns, and stagecoach lines were developed and news could spread by means of newspapers and a routed postal system. (*See also* American Colonies,

REGIONS OF THE THIRTEEN COLONIES

This map shows the three regions of colonial America. Within each, land, climate, resources, and ways of life were similar. Western boundaries are omitted since most were in dispute.

Life in, section "The Colonies Grow Together.")

Wars and the need of a common defense also drew the colonies together. There were frequent danger from Indian raids and intermittent warfare between the French and English. Every time a general conflict broke out in Europe it spread to America. Wars with the French included King William's War (1689–97), Queen Anne's War (1702–13), and King George's War (1744–48). The final conflict was the French and Indian War (1754–63). English victory sounded the doom of French dominion in North America and gave Britain control of Canada and all the French-held land east of the Mississippi, except New Orleans. The colonists came to know and respect one another fighting side by side in these conflicts. Wilderness warfare prepared fighters and leaders for the Revolution. (*See* articles on these wars.)

Critical Years and a New Nation

By 1776 there were some $2\frac{1}{2}$ million people in the colonies. The growing unity among them had been intensified by resentment against laws that hampered their struggling economy. Leaders rose to preach freedom and the rights of man. Delegates to the Second Continental Congress adopted the Declaration of Independence. The colonies were thrown into a war that cautious men thought hopeless. Thirteen years later, however, the war had been won, a constitution adopted, and George Washington had become first president of the United States. (*See also* Revolution, American; United States History.)

Peoples and Ways of Life in Colonial America

Colonists in the three regions differed in views and dress. The Puritan couple (left) wore drab garments relieved by white. The Quakers (center) had richer attire in quiet colors. Southern Cavaliers (right) delighted in colorful, elaborate clothes.

AMERICAN COLONIES, LIFE IN THE. The people who settled the American Colonies came to a new life as well as a new land. Their old way of life in Europe had developed slowly over hundreds of years. A craftsman made a tool just as his father had taught him. A farmer knew which standard crop would grow best on a field and when to expect rain or frost. A merchant was familiar with the market for his wares. Everyone knew which family belonged in a castle and which in a cottage, for people seldom moved from the social class in which they were born.

A different way of life was necessary in the wilderness. At first the settlers suffered from their ignorance of the new surroundings. Malaria from Jamestown's swamps and the severe cold of New England brought sickness and death. Food was scarce until crops could be raised. Nine tenths of Jamestown's settlers died in the "starving time" of 1609.

The colonists invented ways to cope with their problems and adapted old methods. The English learned from their Indian neighbors and from other settlers. The Indians taught them how to raise new crops. They showed them which fish and wild plants to eat and how to track game. The Swedes of Delaware introduced the first practical wilderness house—the log cabin.

Gradually the people in each region of colonial America learned to use their natural resources in making a living and developed a way of life suited to their environment. The three regions within which land, climate, and conditions were similar were the Southern Colonies—Virginia, Maryland, North Carolina, South Carolina, and Georgia; the Middle Colonies—New York, New Jersey, Pennsylvania, and Delaware; and the New England Colonies—Massachusetts, New Hampshire, Connecticut, and Rhode Island. (See also United States, sections "New England," "Middle Atlantic Region," and "The South.")

The Southern Colonies

WHEN the London Company founded Jamestown it had hopes that gold and silver would be discovered in Virginia. An early illustration of life in Jamestown shows 20 gentlemen setting out with pickaxes and shovels to dig for minerals. There was great disappointment in the colony and in London when no precious metals were found.

The Company had the colonists make experiments in growing a variety of crops—grapevines, flax, oranges, tobacco, and mulberry trees to feed silkworms. Tobacco succeeded. It brought the wealth denied the gold seekers. For a long time Virginia, eastern Maryland, and northeastern North Carolina were known as tobacco colonies. John Rolfe, the planter who married the Indian princess Pocahontas, showed the way to this wealth (see Pocahontas).

The Story of Tobacco

The settlers had found the Indians smoking tobacco in their pipes. The smoke tasted bitter to the Englishmen when they tried it. Rolfe watched the Indians grow the plants and dry the leaves in the sun. He decided that the bitter taste was due to their lack of skill. He planted tobacco and tried out many methods for curing the leaves. Not until 1616 did he succeed in producing tobacco which he was willing to ship to London.

Tobacco was just then becoming very popular in England. It came chiefly from the Spanish West Indies. One can imagine how anxiously Rolfe waited during the months before he could hear of the result of his venture. When the report came, it was good.

His tobacco was declared to be as "strong, sweet, and pleasant as any under the sun." It brought a high price in the London market.

Tobacco Growing Brings Prosperity

Life in the Jamestown colony had been very hard (see Jamestown; Virginia; Smith). Many of the settlers wanted to return to England. The success of Rolfe's tobacco changed this. Other planters followed his methods with good results. Everyone turned to raising tobacco, and the colony was saved. The plant was even grown on the streets of the little town. Within a few years there were laws requiring planters not to use all their land for tobacco but to save a certain amount for food crops. The settlers had gone a long way from their "starving time." As early as 1627 half a million pounds of the yellow leaves were being sent to England.

The rich soil, warm climate, and abundant rain made the Southern Colonies a fine place for plantations producing rich crops for export. The geography of the area too helped decide how and where the colonists should live.

Virginia's Waterways

A French traveler who came to Virginia in 1686 described the region as he saw it. "Nature gave this country," he wrote, "a feature at once beautiful and useful. The sea from time to time extends into the land by little arms one hundred or one hundred and fifty feet wide."

The colonists went up each waterway in their boats until they came to its end or to the hills. Then they laid out their farms, or plantations, along the streams. They needed a great deal of space for the tobacco fields, so even in the early days the plantations were rather far apart. This was different from other parts of America, especially New England, where the people set up villages.

The first colonists did not have to begin by building roads. "These waters," said the traveler, "serve all the inhabitants as a common highway, as do also the four great rivers. No plantation house is more than one hundred or one hundred and fifty feet from the water." He observed with interest that people made their visits from one house to another in boats and carried all their supplies and the products of their farms in the same way.

The Pioneer Virginia Planter

Suppose a man from the little settlement of Jamestown obtained a piece of land in about the year 1650. How was he to go about starting his plantation? He was living in the colony's pioneering time. All through that century the wilderness lands were opening up.

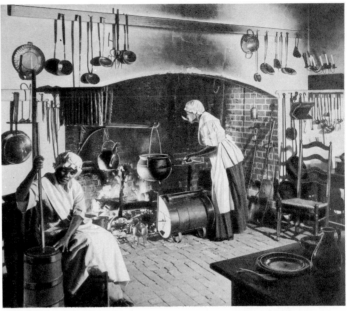

COOKING MEALS OVER AN OPEN FIRE
Planters built outside kitchens like this one in colonial Williamsburg. One cook is sampling the soup from a kettle while another is churning. Notice the copper and iron utensils and the Dutch oven where roasts turned on a spit.

AROUND THE FIRE IN A PLANTATION GREAT ROOM
This picture re-enacts a colonial family gathering. It was photographed at Kenmore, home of the family of George Washington's sister, Betty Lewis, in Fredericksburg, Va. It has been restored and furnished with antiques.

DINNER AT GEORGE WYTHE'S HOUSE IN WILLIAMSBURG

The planters enjoyed gay company and fine food at their dinner parties. Here the butler offers fowl and potatoes which he has carried in a covered dish from the outside kitchen. Candles and a centerpiece filled with fruit decorate the table.

his passage and agree to give him his food, a place to live, and clothes. The agreement was called an "indenture," and the man became an "indentured servant," or "bond servant." When such a man's term of service was over, he was wholly free. He might even be given 50 acres of land by the colony. If not, he could get land for himself and start his own plantation. It was no disgrace for any man to have been an indentured servant.

The Planter's House

For his home the planter usually wanted to copy the house in which he had lived in England. He learned that a Virginia house should be somewhat different because of the mild climate. He built two chimneys, one at each end of the house, with space between for a big open room which would be cool in the summer months. He had high ceilings too to let the air pass freely.

The house of the pioneer planter was 30 or 40 feet long and 15 or 20 feet wide. Its broad, front door was on the long side, opening into the great room. There were usually two other rooms on the first floor and one or two upstairs under the steep roof.

It was not like the 18th century in which George Washington and Benjamin Franklin and other founders of the nation lived.

This pioneer planter first had to clear the land where he wanted to build his house and plant his tobacco. The trees had to be cut down and burned or taken away. From those trees could be cut the logs and boards for his house. These tasks were hard, and planting and tending tobacco plants were hard too. The planter needed one or two strong helpers even though his farm was to be a small one.

Indentured Servants on the Plantation

The planter could get help from England. Many men living there wanted to come to the New World, but they had no money. They could not pay for the ocean voyage, or for land, or for a new home; but they wanted so much to come that they would sell themselves as servants. They would agree to work for three, five, or sometimes seven years to pay off the cost of getting to Virginia and making a start. The planter could have one of these men if he would pay

Because of the mild climate, the kitchen did not have to be in the house. It was in a small building nearby. Other workrooms too were outside the main house. This seemed strange to the early colonists.

A few of the 17th-century houses were of brick, made in the colony or brought from England as ballast in ships. Most were built of wood. The inner walls were covered with a plaster made of mud or clay and coated with whitewash. Some materials were hard to get. Nails were so scarce that pegs of wood were often used in their place. A man moving inland would sometimes burn his old house simply to get its nails for the new one. In 1645 a law was passed forbidding this. The colony agreed to allow him as many nails as there were in his old house if he would leave it standing. Two officers were appointed to look his house over and decide how many nails he should have.

The Plantation Wharf

The planter built his house and planted his fields. Then he did the next thing that was needed most. He built his own private wharf on the stream near his house. This waterway was his street or road, and he had to have a place for loading boats.

He did not have to build a road even to this wharf. If there was already a trail or path to the water, he began by using that. Then as soon as his first crops were ready, he packed them in big barrels and rolled them to the wharf. The heavy wooden barrels filled with tobacco widened and smoothed the path. When hundreds of barrels had been hauled along it, there would be what was called a "rolling road."

Indian Neighbors

It took courage for a pioneer planter to go into the wild country to live. His house was a long way from that of his nearest neighbor. Probably there were not more than two or three plantations on the entire creek or stream beside which he planned to build. Tobacco growing required large plantations. A man had to have the fields he was using and space for many more. After three or four years the tobacco wore out the soil, and he had to plant in a new place.

He knew too that he would have Indian neighbors in the wilderness. When the white men first came to Virginia the Indians were very friendly. They taught the Englishmen to plant corn and showed them how to get food by hunting and fishing. The Indians, however, soon found that the Englishmen wanted their land. Sometimes the colonists made agreements and paid for the land. At other times they simply took it. Naturally the Indians were angry at being pushed off the land which had always been theirs.

The first time the Indians attacked Jamestown was within a few years of its founding. Before the middle of the century there were other attacks. The Indians fought with great cruelty, and the white men fought cruelly too. The Indians lost many men and were driven back farther into the wilderness. Between the wars there were long periods of peace. Then the colonists traded with the Indians for corn and game and learned their customs (see Indians, American, section "Woodland Indians of the Eastern Wilderness").

Social Life and Clothing

Although the tobacco plantations were far apart, the Southern colonists were usually social people.

FAMILY AND GUESTS GATHER FOR A DANCING LESSON

The ballroom in the palace of the royal governor of colonial Virginia is the setting for this party. Scores of candles in crystal chandeliers and on convenient stands are needed to supply light. Notice the harpsichord with its two keyboards.

They gathered together as often as they could. They came to Jamestown for services in the Anglican church and for meetings of the legislature, called the House of Burgesses. At the church service small and large boats were tied up at the wharves, and horses were fastened to the fences. The planters had brought their families many miles on the water or along narrow trails through the woods for the service.

They came in their best clothes brought by ship from England. On his farm a planter wore work clothes made of coarse materials spun on the plantation. When he went visiting he dressed as any gentleman of the time would dress in London. His coat and breeches (short trousers fastened at the knee) were of dark red or green velvet or broadcloth. He wore a linen shirt and embroidered vest and had white ruffles at his neck and wrists. He had long silk stockings and shoes with silver buckles. His lady donned a heavy silk or satin overdress, slashed or draped in front to show a gay petticoat.

Small boys wore long coats until they were seven years old. After that they dressed like their fathers,

309

with breeches and long stockings. Little girls looked like grown-up women in their long, full skirts beneath which red shoes with silver buckles showed. Like their mothers they wore lace collars and caps.

There was much visiting between plantations even in the early years. A traveler about the middle of the century tells how any stranger was welcomed and entertained without charge. He adds a report on how planters, even though living far apart, helped one another. If the word got around that a man was ill, his neighbors arranged it so that one of them would be there every day to do his work.

Plantations Became Larger

As time went on, plantation life changed. The soil yielded such fine crops of tobacco that the rich planter acquired more and more land. Many planters owned thousands of acres. It took a small army of workers to cultivate these huge farms. The planter got them by buying Negro slaves. Since the early days of the colony a few slave ships had brought Negroes from Africa. Toward the end of the 17th century many Negroes were being brought in, and in the next 50 years most of the hard labor in the fields was done by slaves. The Negroes were used to working in a warm climate. They were able to work better than white men through the long, hot hours in the tobacco fields and the rice plantations of the Carolina low country.

With more workers available the planter could cultivate more fields. He also had to look after his many workers and their families. A plantation became like a small village. It carried on an independent life and supplied the needs of its people.

Around the Great House

All the plantation life centered around the owner and the great house which he had built for his family as his wealth increased. The mansion was large and comfortable looking, with balconies and porches for outdoor living. It usually stood on a little hill or on high ground which sloped down to the river or stream. From its windows there was a wide view of fields and orchards and of the river with its slow-moving boats.

A wide path with borders of flowering shrubs led from the wharf or road to the front door. On both sides of this path were spacious green lawns and gardens. Often there were summerhouses half hidden in the trees. Inside the house was

a large central hall out of which opened big rooms with high ceilings. The rooms were richly furnished with articles brought from England.

Back of the house there was usually a yard with a large kitchen garden. Nearby were one or more separate kitchens with their big brick fireplaces where all the cooking was done. Other small buildings were a laundry, a separate dairy for the care of milk and cream and the making of butter and cheese, and a smokehouse for curing hams and bacon. Beyond these houses were the stables for the farm horses and the fine horses which later came to be the planter's special pride. There were barns and pens for the oxen, cows, and pigs and storehouses for tobacco and other crops. These buildings went with the main house. A big plantation, however, had many more.

Community Life

There were cottages for the overseers and the indentured workers. At a little distance from the great house stood a group of cabins for the slaves. These were likely to be poorly built and unpainted.

Such a community had many needs, which were met by the people who lived in these houses. Indentured servants did most of the skilled work, and slaves were trained for certain tasks. There was a blacksmith who with his helpers kept the horses shod and the plows, harnesses, tools, and wagons in repair. Near his forge there was a carpenter's shop where skilled workers were busy all the time. Coopers made barrels for shipping tobacco overseas. Fences had to be kept in good repair so that cattle and pigs could not

WILLIAMSBURG'S COURTHOUSE BUILT IN 1770

Here a Virginia lady is passing the court-house in her imported carriage. The wealth of the colonists and their pride in local self-government are reflected in this fine structure. It is one of the Williamsburg buildings restored to show Americans how their forefathers lived.

SHIPPING TOBACCO AT A TIDEWATER WHARF
Here the ship for England lies at a planter's wharf. Slaves head the tobacco casks while planters and merchants discuss the sale. This old engraving was made by Joshua Fry and Peter Jefferson for the North American Atlas printed for William Faden, London, 1777. By this time most planters were shipping from merchants' warehouses instead of their private wharves.

get out and deer and other wild creatures could not get in. Buildings were put up as they were needed.

Food and Clothing for Family and Slaves

It was the duty of the planter to keep his slaves and other workers clothed. Flax and hemp were grown in the fields, and women worked at spinning and weaving in a special weaving house. A tanner made leather from animal skins; and a shoemaker spent all his time turning out shoes for the host of men, women, and children of the plantation.

Food for community needs was produced on the plantation. Slaves tended the corn and wheat crops and cared for the farm animals which supplied the meat and dairy products. They raised garden vegetables for table use. Every plantation had large orchards which added to its beauty when the trees were in blossom and provided fruit for the plantation folk. Gathering and preserving the fruit kept the women busy for many weeks. Indian corn was the chief food of the slaves and other workers. It was ground or crushed and made into hominy by boiling. No worker need go hungry on the plantation of a good master.

With the Mistress of the House

While the planter rode on horseback over the broad acres of his farm, his wife was busy with the care of her household. At times it must have seemed to her that the large number of servants were more care to her than help, but they were all needed.

She taught the girls and women to sew and spin and weave. She made sure that there were candles to light every room in the house, as well as special ones for the dining table and for parties. Every day a servant replaced the candles used the night before.

She gave out the supplies of food and planned the meals. Meat or game, along with vegetables, fruits, and pastries, was served three times a day. It was for her to see that there was always an abundance for the entertainment of unexpected guests. No one could tell in the morning how many might appear before the day was over. The big houses had room for 10 or 20 visitors, who might stay for several weeks.

One of the special interests of the mistress was the garden. Seeds and plants ordered from England were set out in the rich soil and grew well. No favorite English flower was missing from the garden beds and borders. There were roses, hollyhocks, and peonies, as well as tulips and columbine, pansies,

A MINOR OFFENDER IN A PILLORY
The cruel and humiliating punishments in colonial times contrast sharply with the otherwise high standards of personal dignity. Passers-by scoffed and threw things at prisoners.

311

lilies, and many others. Neighbors and friends exchanged plants. A Southern lady did not think any visit complete without admiring her friend's garden.

Educating the Children

Much of the children's education was carried on at home. Plantations were too far apart for setting up schools easily. Sometimes several families arranged for what was called an "old-field school" to which the younger boys rode on their ponies or were taken by boat. Young George Washington went to such a school for a short time. But its term was short, and the teaching was poor. Usually the mother or an educated indentured servant taught the young boys, or a teacher was brought from England to live with the family. When the sons of the house were older, they were likely to go away to school. Fathers liked to send them to college in England for two or three years.

Girls' formal education from books was not thought as important as it was for boys. However, every girl was expected to learn the household arts. She was supposed to be ready to manage her own home when she married.

Plantation children had their share of fun outside school hours. For the boys there was riding, hunting, and fishing. They found it interesting to watch the many fascinating activities of the plantation. Small girls enjoyed their dolls and played "keeping house." A visitor wrote of watching a child tying a string to a chair and pretending to spin, and sweeping the floor with a splintered stick. They had pets of all kinds—deer, squirrels, lambs, and calves, as well as cats and dogs. In the evening the children might join their elders at a fish fry or barbecue.

Music and Dancing

The planters of Virginia and Maryland were fond of music. In the wealthier homes there were violins and guitars which were played by the gentlemen of the house. There were also harpsichords and spinets, which look like small pianos (see Piano). Young ladies were expected to learn to play these instruments. The boys liked the drum, fife, or horn. Always on every plantation the sound of banjos came up from the cabins of the Negroes. Above the twanging of their strings there rose and fell the refrain of songs brought from Africa. As time went on, there were Christian hymns too, telling of the sorrows of these workers in a strange land. A new kind of American music, the Negro spiritual, was being born. (See Folklore, subhead "Negro Folklore.")

Dancing was a favorite pastime of young and old in the great house. It was part of the education of every boy and girl to take lessons in this art. A dancing master came to the plantation occasionally and stayed for a week. In the evening when the candles were lighted in the large central chandelier, all the family and their guests took part in the dancing. There were minuets and other stately English dances and the popular Virginia reel. Often Negro musicians came up to the house to play for the dancing.

When the Ships Came in

Everyone on the plantation looked forward to the great day when a ship would arrive from England. The planter had sent tobacco and other products of the plantation to London with an order for the goods he needed. England was still "home" to the older colonists. Clothes, furniture, a new coach, farming tools, books—all came from London. The Virginian did his buying there as if he lived only a few miles away instead of across an ocean.

It was a gala day when the ship came in with a big order. There might be a new chest, one of those useful pieces of furniture which served in these colonial days as closets. There might be a big bed for the master and his wife. This bed was a four-poster. Its tall posts and frame (tester) supported curtains that could be closed at night.

Handsome Furniture

Today pieces of furniture which are called "colonial," "early American," or "18th century" may be patterned after the beds, tables, chests, chairs, and mirrors brought in these ships from England. In the colony's first 60 or 70 years the furniture was plain. The dining table was made by laying boards on wooden supports, or trestles. Only the master had a big chair. Others sat at the table on stools and benches. As the houses grew finer, more furniture was needed for the rooms, and so a ship might bring one or more of the beautiful tables and graceful chairs of 18th-century style. There might be

HOSPITABLE BRANDON-ON-THE-JAMES
Plantation mansions grew with the wealth of their owners. Brandon's land was first granted in 1616. The east wing was built early in the 18th century and the porticoed central structure later. The low connecting buildings were called "hyphens."

A RICE PLANTATION
A. Formal Garden
B. Carpenter Shop
C. Loomhouse
D. Great House
E. Kitchen
F. Washhouse
G. Smokehouse
H. Blacksmith Shop
I. Stables
J. Slave Quarters
K. Kitchen Garden
L. Winnowing House
M. Rice Barn
N. Wharf

THE RICE PLANTER'S MANSION, FIELDS, AND WATER SUPPLY

Here one can see why it took a rich man to set up a rice plantation in the Carolina lowlands. He had to dam a stream to make a reservoir and dig canals for the water to flood the fields.

Gates kept the salt water from the tidal river from seeping onto his land. His mansion and buildings were costly. He chose a fine site and beautified it with lovely gardens and trees.

a big mirror to add to the many which hung on the walls. There would be fine china and pewter, silver, and table linens too. (The Interior Decoration article describes furniture of colonial times and pictures show rooms in fine colonial houses.)

The children never knew what had been ordered for them. When the boxes and barrels were being opened, they could hardly wait to find out. Their mother and the other ladies were almost as excited. There would be clothes for every member of the family, all in the latest London fashion. Little Nelly Custis, adopted daughter of George Washington, once had 12 pairs of shoes on a single ship that came to the wharf at Mount Vernon. There were cloth shoes and leather shoes and two pairs of slippers for parties.

There were toys also. A planter often put in an order for some of the latest English or French toys. One year many of the ships brought the new music boxes.

How Rice Came to South Carolina

Some time between 1686 and 1690 a ship landing at the port of Charleston (then Charles Town), S. C., started that colony on a new and important industry. It had sailed from the distant island of Madagascar and was blown off its course in a storm. The captain gave a bag of seed rice to one of the colonists. The proprietors and planters were always interested in new

plants which might thrive in America. The rice grew very well. The planters knew that England bought large quantities of rice from the tropics. They thought this might be a valuable crop; and so it proved to be. Within ten or twelve years South Carolina's rice had started the region on its way to a prosperity which matched that of the tobacco colonies.

The colony had much low land bordering broad rivers. These marshy places, covered at times by water, were exactly right for the rice plants. To flood them at the proper times and to tend and harvest the crops required many laborers. The answer to that need was to bring in slaves from the West Indies, where many South Carolina planters had formerly lived.

Wealthy Planters and Merchants in Charleston

Only a rich man could build the irrigation works to flood the fields and buy the slaves. The planters and their families became a class apart. They built fine houses on their lands and in Charleston to which they came to escape the malaria of the swampy plantations. A visitor to that city just before the Revolution found there "a show of riches and luxury far greater than are to be found in northern towns." It was the colony's capital, and social life was especially gay when the assembly met. Charleston had theaters and concert halls before most towns in America.

The city was the first important southern port. It had its wealthy merchants as well as its rich planters. They made their wealth shipping rice and other produce of the fertile colony. They traded with London and with the prosperous sugar-growing colonies in the West Indies. During the 18th century planters elsewhere in the South gradually stopped dealing directly with London merchants. Then ports developed in the other colonies. The most important were Savannah in Georgia, Wilmington in North Carolina, Norfolk in Virginia, and Baltimore in Maryland.

Eliza Lucas Raises Indigo

A 16-year-old girl introduced another plantation crop to South Carolina. Eliza Lucas was left by her father, a British army officer, in charge of their big plantation. She acted as schoolmistress for her young brothers and sisters and the Negro children. Her real interest, however, was in the plantation. Her father had trained her to look after its business.

In the year 1740 he sent her some indigo plants from the West Indies. The blue dye made by boiling and working over indigo leaves was in demand in England at this time. Eliza put the plants in her garden and tried various experiments with the leaves. When she got good results she shared her experience with her neighbors. She gave all the seed from her first crop to them. They began to raise the plants.

No industry grew more quickly. Planters were already raising rice on their marshlands. However, they owned high lands too. These proved to be excellent for the new plant. Thousands of acres which had not been planted before were turned into indigo fields. Until the time of the American Revolution, indigo was one of the chief products of South Carolina and other parts of the South.

As the Southern Colonies Grew and Spread

Life on the great plantations was amazingly comfortable, even elegant, for so new a land, but it was not the only way of life in the Southern Colonies. All southern farms were not big plantations and most of the people were not rich planters. Not all the region was suited to plantation agriculture. Fertile land and ready transportation were needed for profitable tobacco growing. For more than a century all the great tobacco plantations lay in the coastal lowlands of Maryland, Virginia, and northern North Carolina, with their tidewater transportation. Rice could be grown profitably only in the "low country" of South Carolina and parts of North Carolina and Georgia.

All Southern Colonies had many smaller farms where the people raised corn, wheat, barley, flax, and other crops, as well as stock, for their own use. They planted tobacco fields for a cash crop. In the pine forests of eastern Virginia and the Carolinas lived poor whites and Negroes who worked at making tar and pitch, gathering turpentine, and cutting timber. Georgia was founded later than the other colonies, and farms of 500 to 1,000 acres were the rule there.

CRAFTSMEN IN COLONIAL TOWNS

After southern towns began growing in the 18th century, they offered work for a few mechanics and artisans, such as this cabinetmaker shown working on a graceful table.

A good part of the barber's work consisted of making wigs and keeping them cleaned, curled, and powdered. Often he served as "surgeon" too, bleeding a patient or pulling a tooth.

The colony was intended as a refuge for English debtors, and for a time its laws forbade the sale of slaves, on which plantation riches depended (see Georgia).

It was not easy to get land in the tidewater region, and a freed bond servant considered himself lucky to acquire 100 to 200 acres and a modest house. Some owned no land and worked as overseers or at other plantation tasks. As towns grew, skilled men found work as mechanics and artisans. The towns too had professional men and well-to-do merchants, at one end of the scale, and "poor white trash," at the other.

Life in the "Back Country"

Able and vigorous newcomers and small farmers were not limited to the opportunities in the tidewater area. There was land to be had up the river valleys where the hilly Piedmont (foothills) rose in the west. Here was fertile soil, not sapped of its richness by tobacco like the lowland farms. Here, however, the settlers were face to face with the wilderness again. A man had to build his cabin, clear his land, plant and harvest his fields and orchards, with only the help of his wife and children. He had to make home furnishings and farm tools. In the Piedmont he lived on the "shallow water" above the first falls of the rivers, and it was even harder to bring in goods than it was to transport his tobacco crop to tidewater ports.

RAISING A FRONTIER CABIN
Loneliness and danger were the lot of the "backwoods" family. The father hewed the logs and built the house. The mother was nurse and doctor when the children sickened. They accepted the hardships to get land of their own.

Life was full of danger and hard work, and luxuries were rare. For meals the family was lucky to get corn bread, bacon and greens, "hog and hominy," cider, wild berries, and game. They had to spin and weave every spare moment to supply linsey-woolsey for clothing. Men and boys turned to long-wearing buckskin. Living far from friends or neighbors, they welcomed the passing stranger to share their crowded cabin. (*See also* Pioneer Life.)

Despite the hardships settlement spread rapidly, and before the Revolution the Piedmont had become a region of substantial farms. It had its rich plantations too, for some of the tidewater planters had sent in overseers and slaves to establish homes in the Piedmont when their tidewater lands wore out. Settlers had also spread through gaps in the Blue Ridge Mountains to the Great Valley (*see* Appala-chian Highlands). There they met a stream of immigrants who had entered through Pennsylvania and Maryland. Many took up land in the valley. Others pushed on to the Carolina or Georgia Piedmont.

Varied Settlers in the "Melting Pot"

Among the inland settlers were Scotch-Irish and Highland Scots, Germans, and Swiss. French Huguenots had also come directly to Charleston. The American melting pot was already beginning to "boil."

The sturdy society of pioneer farmers in the Piedmont was a valuable addition to the South. More democratic, less closely tied with England, and less dependent on slavery than the big planters, their representatives brought a new spirit to the House of Burgesses in Virginia.

The Middle Colonies

EARLY MAPS of the Middle Colonies rarely show the names of the separate colonies: New York, New Jersey, Pennsylvania, and Delaware. Colony names and boundaries were still changing. European nations were disputing ownership of this region. Its first settlers were not English like the original colonists in the South and New England. The Dutch claimed the land on both sides of the Hudson River because they had sent out its first explorer, Henry Hudson. They set up fur-trading posts and forts, then settlements, and called their colony New Netherland (*see* New York; New Jersey).

Swedish and Finnish settlers founded the first town in Delaware where Wilmington now stands (*see* Delaware; Wilmington). Their method of building log cabins was a great gift to America. These houses were the easiest and most practical kind in a forested land, and pioneers built them as they pushed into the wilderness.

By the year 1700 the names of two port cities, New York and Philadelphia, stood out plainly on all maps. These were the ports through which people came from many parts of the Old World and from which the produce of the Middle Colonies was shipped. They were the trading centers for the people of the area.

If there had been picture maps like those made today, they would have shown how close the farms came to the towns. Almost next door to the houses and the masts of the ships at the wharves, there would be green spots marking cultivated lands with big barns in their midst. The green of the farms would reach far back into the country, especially along the banks of the broad rivers. Farming and trading were the chief occupations in these regions.

Most of the people who came to settle in the Middle Colonies knew more about agriculture than about any other way of making a living. Whether they came from the Netherlands, Sweden, France, Germany, or the British Isles, they belonged to the land. They and their fathers and grandfathers and great-grandfathers had practiced the art of cultivating fields and raising crops and animals. Few of them were rich or of high rank, but they were skilled workers.

People on the Land

The soil of the Middle Colonies pleased these people greatly. At the seacoast and reaching back along the rivers it was rich and level. When the trees were cleared away, they found that it was free from stones. These colonists began at once to plant many kinds of crops. Before long they were not only raising their own food but also having crops they could sell. In one region or another they were raising large crops of corn, wheat, beans, and peas. They also had many farm animals. They made butter, cheese, and lard which they sold in England and Europe and in the West Indies. People abroad used to call this whole region the "bread colonies."

There were also animals in the forests and along the banks of the streams whose furs were valuable. New Amsterdam, which became New York, started as a Dutch fur-trading post.

So in all this middle region between the South and New England the land and the waters provided riches for those who would work for them. There were also good harbors along the seacoast. Harbors were important, for these colonists were trading as well as farming people. They came from countries which sent out many ships. Their leading men welcomed every chance to carry on the exchange of goods with other lands. A class of merchants sprang up to do business in the chief ports. The merchant was to be as important a person here as the planter was in the South.

The Dutch in New York

A stranger visiting New Amsterdam in the 17th century might have thought himself still in Holland. The colonists from the Netherlands who settled here had built houses like those at home. Here were steep roofs reaching out beyond the house and many houses set with their ends to the street instead of their long sides. Windmills turned slowly in the wind. It was all as Dutch as the full skirts of the women and the broad-brimmed hats of the men.

On a pole beside the trading office floated the flag of the Dutch West India Company. This company had established the settlement and ruled it all the years it was under Dutch control.

Families Join the Traders on Manhattan

Only men came to the colony at first, intending to do their trading in furs and then leave for home. Then in 1624 two families from a group of colonists coming to New Netherland chose to stay on Manhattan Island, where Fort Amsterdam was being built (see New York, N. Y.).

In 1626 Peter Minuit arrived to be director general for the Company. He saw that if there was to be a colony, the people must be made more comfortable. He had ships sent over with horses, cows, sheep, and pigs. He also gave the settlers seeds so that they could plant flowers and vegetables. Two years later the first minister of the official Dutch Reformed Church came. When the people were counted for the first report of the colony, there were 270 men, women, and children.

New Amsterdam was under Dutch rule for about 40 years. Then it was taken over by the English and

DUTCH TRADE AND TREATIES WITH THE INDIANS

A Dutch trading ship lies in the Hudson River off New Amsterdam (left). The traders offer the Indians arms and trinkets in exchange for their furs. A Dutch official (right) shows an Indian chief where to place his mark on a treaty. The setting in this painting by John Ward Dunsmore is the home of Jonas Bronck, the Dane, for whom Bronx borough was named.

DUTCH HOUSES ALONG THE EAST RIVER IN OLD NEW YORK

This painting by Edward L. Henry in the collection of the Title Guarantee and Trust Company shows Pearl Street in busy downtown Manhattan as it looked in the 17th century. The big house was the residence of Captain Kidd, the pirate. It has the stepped gables and stoop found on Dutch homes. The house at its left boasts two settles, or benches, outside the divided Dutch door.

named New York, but town life continued much the same until well into the 18th century. A traveler wrote in 1760 that more than half the people and almost all the merchants were Dutch.

Waterways and Walls in Old New York

New Amsterdam also seemed like a Dutch town because water surrounded it on three sides and canals cut through it. Waterways were the chief and most convenient highways. Yet in the area near the fort there were curving and crooked streets. Soon after 1650 the Company made these streets official and gave them names.

A little later a wall, or palisade, was built which was to give its name to one of New York's most famous streets. The palisade was made of stakes driven deep into the ground with rails across the top. Beside it was a deep ditch, and earth was piled against the stakes. Fortunately the palisade was never needed for defense in war, and it was allowed to fall to pieces in the next century. The line of the old wall is the line of the modern Wall Street.

A boy walked along the streets each morning, blowing his horn. At its call cattle came out from the yards and fell into line behind him. They followed him to a big pasture beyond the edge of town.

Animals and Waste in the Streets

Other animals, sheep, goats, geese, and especially pigs, wandered along the streets. Town officials tried in every way to have them kept behind fences; but they broke through. Streets were laid out with a narrow ditch for water in the middle. Steppingstones were placed at the crossings for people to use when rain flooded the ditches. But house owners threw waste into the ditches. Again and again they were ordered not to block the ditches and to keep their animals at home. Finally the order was given that each householder was to clean the part of the street in front of his house once a week. As late as 1750, Friday was street-cleaning day for the people of New York City.

At night four watchmen, wearing blue coats with yellow on collar and cuffs, marched up and down the streets. They carried staffs, lanterns, and large rattles. No Dutch town was complete without its rattle watch. They patrolled the streets from nine in the evening until daylight, calling the hours at the street corners. They sounded their rattles loudly in case of fire or if they came upon thieves or other persons who had no business abroad at night.

There was no street lighting until 1700. Then it was arranged that a lantern was to be hung outside every seventh house. The six nearest neighbors helped pay for the candles, which burned all night.

The Houses from the Outside

From the street the Dutch houses made a pleasing appearance. Travelers visiting New Amsterdam or early New York spoke of their charm.

The houses stood close together, for they usually turned their narrow ends to the street. They were built high from the ground and had a little platform with steps leading up to it in front of the main door. This platform was called a "stoop" from its Dutch name *stoep*. From it came the idea of the American front porch. During the long summer evenings families sat outside, talking back and forth with neighbors on their front stoops. The streets looked and sounded friendly to visitors as they walked along.

A TOWN CRIER IN NEW AMSTERDAM
Dutch folk hurried out to hear the news when the town crier and drummer appeared. Notice the wide hats and knickerbockers of the men and the woman's full skirt, cap, and apron.

Another thing which strangers noticed was the style of the front door in the houses. It was in two sections, so that the upper half could be left open in warm weather. The lower half was kept closed, partly to keep wandering animals out of the house. Like the stoop this Dutch door became part of an American way of building.

Colored bricks gave the houses a cheerful look. The houses were tall, two or three stories high. The ends, and in later years the whole of the houses, were built of brick; and the bricks were of different colors. These colors were not simply in rows running right and left. They were put together in patterns. A house of yellow brick might have designs with brown, blue, and red bricks fitted in. Roofs were usually of tiles made of clay. They too were colored, usually red. Sometimes there were pots of flowers at the windows. When the tulips in the garden were in bloom and the peach trees blossomed, the streets looked gay.

Inside the Houses

The streets might sometimes need cleaning, but inside the houses everything was scrubbed and shining. The floors were polished, then sprinkled with white sand which was swept into patterns by the broom. The great fireplace which was the center of family life was shining too. It was decorated with blue and white tiles with pictures on them. A child could sit by the fireplace and study the stories—probably from the Bible—told in a series of pictures. Hung beside

and around the fireplace were the pots, pans, kettles, and other cooking utensils, all polished brightly.

Furniture in the houses of the well-to-do citizens was solid and comfortable. There were big beds, strong carved chairs, and cupboards with open shelves for showing the treasures of fine china and shining silver and pewter. One kind of bed was built into the wall with doors that closed during the day. There was always the *kas*, or chest, a huge piece of furniture in which great piles of household linens, quilts, towels, and other supplies were stored. This chest was decorated, often in color, as were other pieces of furniture.

The Dutch burgher and his wife took great pride in their possessions. The housewife took pride also in keeping the house and all that was in it spotless. She kept busy with brushes and brooms every day.

The Clothes the Dutch Wore

This was a period of gay dress. The colonists tried to keep up as well as they could with the fashions of Amsterdam and Paris. Some ordered their clothes abroad. Others had them made in the colony, but in the foreign styles. Materials for their costumes were broadcloth, velvet, and satin, with fine white linen for ruffled collars and fur and lace for trimming.

Men's breeches were short and rather loose, gathered in at, or just below, the knee. This style has continued to be known by the name "knickerbocker." They were trimmed up and down the sides with rows of silver or cloth buttons. The long stockings were of wool, and the leather shoes were tied with big bows. The costume was completed by a fancy waistcoat, or vest, a white collar, either flat or ruffled, and a felt hat with a broad brim and a sweeping feather.

A SKATING PARTY IN 18TH-CENTURY NEW YORK
The Dutch made skating popular on Manhattan, and the later English settlers enjoyed it too. John Ward Dunsmore chose the date of Jan. 13, 1753, for his painting. It grew so cold that day that daring people crossed the frozen East River to Long Island on the ice.

That was the way the merchant or wealthy land-owner dressed for going out in public; and his lady was not behind him in elegance. She wore a very full skirt, usually in bright colors and sometimes striped. Under it were many petticoats. A rather tight bodice had big sleeves and stiffly starched white ruffles at the neck. Indoors or out the ladies wore the close-fitting Dutch cap made of linen or lace.

Women of the middle class dressed more simply. They too had many petticoats under a full skirt. A white kerchief at the neck, a cap, and a bright-colored apron made the women look very attractive as they went to church or market. Children, both boys and girls, wore clothes like those of their parents, with yellow, brown, or red stockings.

Training in School and Church

Religion and education were important in Dutch life. The two went together. In the colony the schoolmaster was an official of the church. It was part of his work to train the children for the worship of the church. He also gave them regular lessons.

Fathers in New Amsterdam wanted their children to learn how to write well and to use numbers. Arithmetic was important, for the boys would grow up to carry on different kinds of trade. A father paid the schoolmaster a small sum every three months according to the age of the child. The "poor and needy" were taught free. The school had three grades. In the first the child was taught his A B C's and how to spell, with first lessons in reading out of an alphabet book. In the next grade reading, writing, and numbers were taught, and in the third grade, arithmetic.

Girls went to school with the boys and had the same lessons, but they sat apart from the boys and recited by themselves. Most of them dropped out of school early. Their learning came from their mothers in the home. The Dutch women were splendid housewives. They taught their girls how to spin and weave, knit, sew, and embroider, and how to prepare meals. Music was also part of a girl's training.

Few families had clocks in those days. The children were called to school each day by a bell, horn, or drum. Classes were held in the master's house, if there was no other place. He sat at a chair behind a desk. The children sat through the long days on benches without backs. There were tables for their writing lessons. A boy raised his cap to the master when he entered the room in the morning and took it off again when he recited. For the rest of the time he kept it on his head.

There were few books, and the teaching was not very good. But the people did not let the Company in Holland forget that there must be schoolmasters. They complained again and again when they were not satisfied. After the colony fell under English rule, the Dutch citizens tried to keep their Dutch schools where the Dutch language was spoken.

Religion was important to the Dutch colonists. The people went to church, summoned by an officer who not only rang a bell but also knocked on their doors with his stick. Every household had its Bible, which was kept in the best room. In the wealthy homes this Bible was a very large, heavy book, beautifully printed and bound. The head of the house read from the Bible before or after breakfast each day.

Family and Social Life

Meals were the times when the family gathered, with the father at the head of the table. There was little talk, but everyone enjoyed the food and ate heartily. They were healthy meals, with meat or fish as one dish, and plenty of vegetables and fruits drawn from the garden and orchard or bought at the market. Vegetables were often made into a stew. Cabbage was chopped and served raw in what is still called "cole-slaw" from the Dutch words *kool sla*, meaning "cabbage salad." Tea was the favorite drink. But the housewife gave special attention to her cakes, pies, and sweets. She baked them in a brick oven after a fire of logs had heated it. Every holiday had its feast with its own customary dishes.

The people of New Amsterdam worked hard but they enjoyed themselves.

A RECEPTION IN NEW YORK'S JUMEL MANSION
The elegance of dress and manners in New York City's 18th-century society is shown in this Dunsmore painting from the Title Guaran-tee and Trust collection. George Washington used the mansion as his headquarters in the fall of 1776. It is a famous city landmark today.

319

TEDIOUS TASKS IN MAKING LINEN AND WOOLEN THREAD

The man (left) is working a flax brake. It mashes the rotted woody stalk of the flax plant, so it can be removed from the fiber within. The woman (right) is spinning on a big wool wheel.

As the wheel turns she steps backward three steps, holding the yarn as it twists, then suddenly glides forward and lets it wind onto a spindle. In a day's work she may "step" 20 miles.

They liked to go on picnics, carrying their food to some spot reached by water or on foot. They celebrated holidays. On New Year's Day they made calls and received them. Housewives served on that day a little cake called *koekje*, from which comes the word "cooky." If a person did not stay to eat the cake offered him, he was expected to carry it away in his pocket. May Day was a popular holiday, with its dancing around a Maypole. The Dutch also enjoyed attending the lectures, concerts, and theater and puppet performances offered in the growing city.

Games and Sports

A favorite game was bowling on the grass with wooden balls. A small park in New York City is still called Bowling Green. Chief of all the sports were those that belonged to winter. The Dutch had always been accustomed to canals and streams which froze over in cold weather. They delighted to use sleighs and sleds in winter and to skate on the canals and streams. One traveler speaks of seeing men and women "flying upon their skates from place to place" with market baskets on their heads. Another visitor tells of a trip when 40 or 50 sleighs were met, all being driven very fast. Postmen sometimes carried the mail on skates in winter.

So the Dutch colony had a pleasant social life, without too many hard laws or rules. When it became an English colony, it continued to be friendly and hospitable. Many travelers went through it,

and some who came to trade at its port stayed and made homes. There were always people from many countries on the streets of New York City.

A New City—Philadelphia

While New York was changing from a Dutch to an English town, a new city was growing up which was to be a busy seaport. Philadelphia was founded by William Penn in 1682 to be the capital city for his big province of Pennsylvania. Other colonial towns grew from small settlements. Penn planned from the

A 17TH-CENTURY ROOM FROM LONG ISLAND

This room is plainer than the later one opposite. Open beams support the ceiling. Chairs have slat backs or simple turnings. A Bible box is on the chest at right. These rooms are in the Henry Francis du Pont Winterthur Museum.

DIFFICULTIES IN MAKING AND USING COLONIAL LIGHTS

The girl is pouring tallow from the kettle into candle molds, with strings in them for wicks. Molding was an improvement over the more tedious method of dipping candles. Whale oil was burned in "Betty lamps," or "Phoebe lamps." They were hanging cups with a spout from which the wick dangled. The expression on the man's face shows they gave a poor light for reading.

first for a city at this spot, with its good harbor and its broad river, the Delaware (*see* Penn).

In 1690 the American Colonies had five towns which were on their way to becoming cities. All were seaports. Two were in New England—Boston in Massachusetts and Newport in Rhode Island. One was in the South, Charleston. New York and Philadelphia were in the Middle Colonies. In that year New York had about 3,900 people, while Philadelphia had 4,000. New York was then 65 years old, while Philadelphia was only eight years old. During its first years, 600 houses were built there. In 1697 it was said to have a population of 7,000. No other city grew so fast. (*See also* Philadelphia; Pennsylvania.)

Quaker Beginnings

William Penn had many dreams for his city and colony. He was a Quaker with a deep sympathy for all needy and oppressed people. His colony was to be a place of refuge where they could build homes and start new lives. Europe had many who needed such a place. Countless thousands there were suffering from religious persecution, harsh rule, bitter poverty, and the cruelties of war.

Penn did careful planning before any building was begun. He laid out broad streets which crossed one another in a pattern of squares. Between them he left spaces for parks and public buildings. It was to be, he said: "a green and open country town." Philadelphia was to become one of the finest cities in America. Its early builders developed an architecture of their own. They built houses of brick, on simple, straight lines, without ornament. Little stone steps led to the front door, and each house had a small square of grass in front and a little garden.

Education and Welfare

As the city grew and prospered, Georgian architecture came into fashion here as elsewhere. Many stately mansions and handsome churches and public buildings rose along the streets of Penn's town.

AN 18TH-CENTURY ROOM FROM NEW JERSEY

These fine chairs, table, and highboy are of Queen Anne style made by skilled Philadelphia cabinetmakers. Colored tiles and delft vases came from Holland. This room and the one opposite have "Turkey" carpets from Asia Minor.

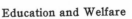

A HISTORIC SCHOOL AND HOUSE STANDING IN GERMANTOWN

Concord School, built by public subscription in 1775, was named for the battle of Concord. The wall at its left surrounds a grave-yard for Revolutionary War soldiers. The house of Billmeyer, the printer, was erected in 1727. It is a typical colonial farm-house of the area. In front of it Washington and his officers held the council that resulted in the battle of Germantown.

Philadelphia became a leader in education and welfare too. It had the first medical school and hospital in the colonies, the first circulating library, and the first organization for fighting fire.

Travelers coming from New York in the early 18th century were interested in the differences between the two towns and their people. The Dutch were fond of gay colors. Philadelphia began as a Quaker colony. Even its rich merchants dressed in quiet grays and browns. Its houses were patterned after English homes; but its people were never all of one kind. Many came from the British Isles, but the colony also attracted people from other countries. Among those who came in large numbers were Germans from the Palatinate area, who came to be known as Pennsylvania Dutch; and Scotch-Irish, Welsh, Swiss, and French Huguenots.

European Settlers Bring Valuable Skills

Besides being good farmers, many of these settlers had been trained abroad in making goods the colonists needed. A list of new arrivals in 1709 included masons, carpenters, shoemakers, tailors, butchers, millers, tanners, stocking weavers, locksmiths, cloth and linen weavers, coopers, saddlers, glass blowers, hatters, lime-burners, engravers, brickmakers, silversmiths, blacksmiths, and potters.

Some of them lingered to work in the industries of the thriving city. Others set up shop or found employment in the growing villages elsewhere in the colony. Still others took up a tool kit and set out as journeymen, offering their services to farm folk. Because of its expert workmen Pennsylvania got an early start in glass, pottery, iron, and fine furniture manufacturing. It contributed the "Kentucky rifle" to the winning of the Revolution and the Conestoga wagon to the settling of the West.

Farm Produce Moves to Philadelphia

Many farmers went up the river valleys. Theirs was a hard pioneer life, such as people in all new regions live. They did not leave the city wholly behind, for with their industry and farming skill they were able to raise produce to sell in the city. From their fertile acres they brought a stream of wheat, corn, salt, meat, flax, hemp, flour, peas, furs, cattle, and lumber and other wood products.

Ships waited at the wharves to be filled with supplies for the West Indies, England, and the other

A FIRE ENGINE BUILT IN 1720

This fire engine was imported from England for the King George III fire company, founded in 1761. The firemen pulled it by hand. The Insurance Company of North America owns the relic.

A RIVER-FRONT VIEW OF THRIVING PHILADELPHIA ABOUT 1753

Only the center panels of an 'East Prospect of Philadelphia' made under the direction of the province surveyor are shown here; but it is easy to see that the city had grown in its 70 years. The building with the tower, left of center, is the State House, later famed as Independence Hall. This old print came from the archives of the Historical Society of Pennsylvania.

colonies. Philadelphia's port was the outlet for the produce of Pennsylvania and New Jersey.

Philadelphia's Big Market

The city also depended on the farms for food. Almost as soon as the town began, the officials set apart two days a week as market days. At first the market was held in a long, wooden shed with separate stalls. As the city grew, a one-story brick store with open stalls was built. In time it extended for nearly a mile. Market days were Wednesday and Saturday. Early in the morning the market was opened with the ringing of a bell. Here were sold meat, fish from river and ocean, fowl, butter, eggs, cheese, peaches, apples, and other fruits. All the products of the land were spread out in these stalls in their season.

Other things besides food were sold on these market days. On their lonely farms the men and women practiced many home industries. They had to do their own carpentry and shoemaking, their candlemaking and soapmaking, and their own weaving and dyeing of homespun cloth. At first they did these things only for themselves. Then they brought samples of their work to the city and sold them there.

City and Country People Meet

These market days were a marvel to the travelers who watched them. Here were well-to-do Quakers in their plain, dark-colored clothes. Next to them might stand several hunters, dressed in buckskins, with furs for sale. Germans and Swedes from their little settlements were there in their peasant costumes, speaking their own languages. Next to them might be city young ladies in their fashionable clothes, perhaps with Negro maids at their sides to carry home the market baskets. Farm women were visiting, and city neighbors were chatting with their friends.

These early market days were a symbol of the new America which was being born. Farming and trade were bringing people together.

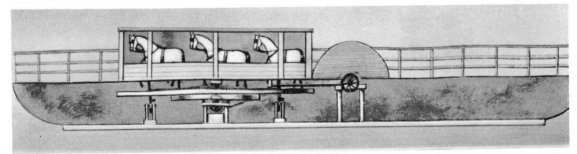

A THREE-HORSEPOWER FERRY ACROSS THE DELAWARE

This ingenious boat, called a "wherry," was put into service between Philadelphia and Kaighn's Point (now part of Camden, N. J.) by Arthur Donaldson in 1765. The horses walked on a flat treadmill wheel which revolved, turning the upright wheel behind them. It rotated the paddle wheel that pushed the ferry through the water. The ferry was able to carry several vehicles.

The New England Colonies

FROM the day of the landing of the Pilgrims in 1620, New England developed a way of life which was wholly its own. Its people came from the British Isles and made it truly a *new* England. But they gradually changed the English pattern in the years they lived along the rocky shores of the Atlantic and in the valleys and the hills of New England.

They found no easy way of life. Most of them were farming people, but the soil and climate did not provide the chance for quick cash crops in tobacco and rice. However, there were other kinds of wealth for those who would work for it. Forests of tall trees grew almost to the edge of the ocean. The colonists had never seen such magnificent trees with such tall, straight trunks. England had become a merchant nation with a need for ships to go to the far parts of the world. These trees would make fine masts for English vessels. New Englanders cut the trees and sent them to England. Later they began to build ships for themselves and for sale abroad. Another source of wealth was the sea. The colonists turned to fishing and built up a profitable industry.

Stern Wills and a Stony Land

Above all else the founders of New England wanted freedom to worship as they chose. They came to America with the purpose of setting up godly communities centered around the church of their faith. They wanted to create a pattern of free government. Only by ruling themselves could they be sure of a government that would support their faith.

Because of their deep faith, strong desires, and stern wills, they were the right people for such a land. They were not frightened by difficulties but moved forward to overcome them. The articles 'May-

flower' and Plymouth, Mass., tell of the hardships and struggles of the Pilgrims and describe their contributions to the American heritage.

The Great Puritan Migration

The Pilgrims were a small company of people—weak and almost alone in the wilderness. After the Massachusetts Bay Company obtained a charter from King Charles I in 1629, however, a flood of English Puritans poured into the colony. In the next dozen years some 14,000 came to Massachusetts alone.

The Puritans were Protestants with religious beliefs regarded as advanced for their time. They belonged to the Anglican church, the state church of England, but were trying to "purify" it of ritual and doctrine retained from the Roman Catholic church (*see* Puritans). They wanted each congregation to govern itself instead of by bishops and archbishops. They had succeeded in some parishes of eastern England, where the ministers preached their beliefs. Then King Charles and Archbishop William Laud demanded that all churches follow the Anglican doctrine. Ministers with Puritan views were dismissed, imprisoned, and even hanged. Puritan government officials lost their posts. The leaders determined to go to the New World and found a church reflecting their beliefs, with a government to uphold its teachings.

When John Winthrop, first governor of the Massachusetts Bay Colony, brought 1,000 settlers to the colony in 1630, he carried the charter with him so he could set up a government free of English control (*see* Winthrop; Massachusetts). It had a governor, a deputy governor, 18 assistants, and a general court made up of "freemen." Only church members could serve in the court or elect its members.

EARLY HOUSES OF THE PILGRIMS AND THE PURITANS

Villages have been set up in Plymouth and Salem to show how the first settlers lived. The Pilgrim house (left) is made from clapboards and has a thatched roof. The Puritan house (right) is a dugout. To build it the Salem Puritans dug into a bank, then set up a wall of vertical logs with a door and window. The window panes were of greased paper because glass was scarce.

The Winthrop group founded Boston. Here they had one of the best harbors on the Atlantic coast. It became the entry port for a large share of the swarm of settlers and developed into one of the chief trading centers in the colonies (*see* Boston).

As the great migration swelled, other towns sprang up around Massachusetts Bay, along the coast, and inland beside the rivers. When a company of settlers arrived after their dangerous and disagreeable voyage in small, pitching ships, they would study the maps of the colony and select a location. Then they petitioned the general court for a grant of land for their town. When they were given perhaps ten square miles of meadow and forest, these land-hungry Englishmen could hardly believe their good fortune.

Organizing a Puritan Town

Settling in towns rather than on separate farms was part of the Puritan plan. In a village the people were near the church they loved and under the eye of the pastor and the elders. The tight-knit group had its own local government, with a town meeting which only the men of the congregation could attend. At these meetings they decided upon the affairs of the town and elected such officers as fence viewers, field drivers, hog reeves, tax assessors, and selectmen. (The Township article tells how the town meeting and the township unit of government have been retained in much of New England.)

Settlers in a new town first parceled out the land in the village proper, giving a home lot to every family. These lots were narrow and long. The Puritan built his house on the front and left plenty of room at the back for a garden nearly as big as an English farm and for an orchard in which he planted apples and other English fruit. Land in the village was set aside for the meetinghouse and for the minister and there was "common land" for pasturing the stock.

Advantages of Village Life

After the lots had been cleared, fenced, and planted, the woods beyond were divided into fields for the settlers. After the backbreaking labor of felling the trees, they could plant Indian corn, as well as the wheat, rye, and oats they had brought across the sea. The aim was to have every field near enough to the village so the farmers could live near the church and walk or drive their oxcarts back and forth to the fields each day. Only later when lands farther away were given out did the people begin living on separate farms and drifting away from the influence of the church.

Living in villages was a good plan in the wilderness, because it afforded protection against the

HOUSES GROW AS FAMILIES INCREASE

This drawing from the National Life Insurance Company collection shows the busy main room of a 17th-century house. A boy brings in firewood. The women churn and spin flax, and the man is cobbling a shoe.

The middle section of the Fairbanks Family house in Dedham, Mass., was built in 1636. Because the roof sloped over a shed like a lid, such houses were called "salt boxes." Wings were added in 1648 and 1654.

Indians. Nobody could forget that beyond the settlement lay the forest in which the Indians roamed. Defense was a first duty of the town fathers. The history of New England towns is filled with tragic stories of attacks on farms and settlements.

The village settlement was the usual plan in all New England Colonies. People from Massachusetts helped to settle them. Some folk left the older towns to find better farm lands. Others broke away because of religious disputes. Thomas Hooker, a Cambridge minister, preached that all the people should be allowed to choose the general court, in disagreement with the powerful Boston clergy. He and his congregation moved to Connecticut, founding Hartford (see Connecticut; Hartford).

Roger Williams was banished because he questioned the right of the government to act in religious matters. He fled to Rhode Island and founded Providence in 1636. Anne Hutchinson, banished for her beliefs, helped to settle Newport (see Williams; Hutchinson; Rhode Island; Providence).

The Reverend John Wheelwright, another exile for conscience' sake, led the settlers who founded Exeter in New Hampshire. Settlements had already been made in New Hampshire and in Maine. Massachusetts extended its control over these two areas. New Hampshire broke away and became an English province in 1741; but Maine remained part of the colony until it became a state (see New Hampshire; Maine).

A SCHOOL IN COLONIAL NEW ENGLAND

Children huddle around the open fire in this colonial school. The 'New England Primer', first printed about 1688, was the text from which the little ones learned to read such improving rhymes as: "The idle fool is whipt at school."

Living in a New England Village

The early house was a plain building, a story and a half high, shaped like a long box. It had two rooms—the main room, which was also the kitchen, and a family bedroom. The ceilings were low, and the windows small and high. Above was the attic under the thatched roof. To it the boys of the family climbed by a ladder or steep stairs. Later, two-story houses were built.

In the center of the long wall was the great fireplace. Around it the family gathered for warmth in winter and for all their activities. Here all the cooking was done. The wide open mouth held great logs cut by the men and boys. The long iron arm of the crane supported large iron kettles, while hooks ("pothooks," as they were called) held smaller pots over the flames or red-hot coals. On one side of the fireplace was a brick oven built for baking. In the corners of the chimney the children sat on three-legged stools, while their parents sat on a high-backed bench, or settle. Its back protected them from the cold air which blew in around the windows or came in from the opening of the doors.

Beside the fireplace hung covered pans with long handles. These were warming pans, made of brass or copper. They were filled at night with live coals and passed back and forth in the beds to warm the cold sheets. The fire was seldom allowed to go out. If it did, someone had to go to a neighbor's house and borrow coals to start it again. To kindle a fire by rubbing a flint stone on steel was a difficult process.

A Family Day

The day began with very early rising. The father and the boys went out to milk the cows and feed the hogs, while the mother and the girls cooked a cereal dish, called porridge, made of Indian corn. This was the grain which had saved the lives of the Pilgrims in their first years. The Indians taught them how to plant and cultivate it, and it was the main article of food for many years.

When the father came in from the barnyard all members of the household seated themselves at the long, narrow table. The father read from the Bible; all joined in prayers; and then he led in a word of thanks for the meal. The porridge was served in bowls of wood or pewter, known as porringers.

Hard Work and Plain, Hearty Meals

Then the father and sons went to work in the fields while the mother and daughters did the household chores. At noon a horn was blown to call the workers from the fields. A plain but abundant meal was now served—a boiled dish of Indian corn and beans, probably with a slice of deer meat added for flavor. The Indian name for this dish of corn and beans was "succotash," a name which is used to this day. The housewife brought out from the brick oven the pumpkin or other pies which she had prepared, as well as brown bread and puddings. Meat for stews was from deer or elk or pigeons; and on many days wild turkey was served.

Again the family went about their tasks, usually for four or five hours, until the animals were driven home from the pasture. Supper was a simple meal; once more there was reading from the Bible; and the family went to bed early.

THE CHURCH DOMINATES THE NEW ENGLAND VILLAGE GREEN

Many New England towns are built around a green that began as a Puritan common. Storrowton, pictured here, is a model village created from old buildings found in the region. Captain John Potter, a Revolutionary War officer, built the big house at the right alone, making nails and hardware by hand. Storrowton is part of the Eastern States Exposition at West Springfield.

The life was hard but healthy. That was according to Puritan beliefs. Children had school to break the routine, and all went to church on the Sabbath.

Establishing Public Schools

A church and a school were as much a part of the Puritan idea of a town as were the houses to live in. There is a story of a famous minister who came to Massachusetts in 1631. He used to get up in the colonial assembly and pray for schools. "Lord, for schools everywhere among us," he would pray, "that every member of this assembly may go home and procure a good school in the town where he lives!"

Puritans opened schools in the first settlements so their children would not grow up without education. As new towns were started, laws required that there be a grammar school or at least a teacher of reading and writing in each one (see Education).

How the Teachers Were Paid

Making a law did not make things happen at once. But schools did begin in the settlements. The first school might be only a dame school, set up in a house and taught by a woman who gathered the neighborhood children together. Sometimes she was paid only what the parents could give. It might be fourpence a week for each child for 12 or 20 weeks. Then the town might add a little for the support of the school. The masters of the town schools were glad to have the boys learn to spell and read a few words and do numbers before they entered their classes.

The public schools were open to the children of the town; but those who could afford to pay were expected to do so. Sometimes this payment was made by bringing a load of wood for the school fires. The master "boarded around" in different houses. He stayed a few weeks in each one, and so got part of his small salary in food and lodging.

Churches and Sabbath Observance

There was a strong community life. This centered largely about the church. At first the people held their services of worship in such small square build-

OLD SHIP MEETINGHOUSE AT HINGHAM

The oldest in Massachusetts, this square church was put together by ship's carpenters in 1681. They built a lookout station around the cupola, like the widow's walk on a shipowner's house.

A CHILD'S SAMPLER

Every colonial girl made a sampler like this to show her skill at needlework. She stitched letters, figures, designs, and a pious verse on it. Hannah Harforth, aged 13, made this one.

ings as they could afford. They were called to them by a drum or by a bell rung by the town crier. As time went on the buildings became more satisfying. The best builders gave their skill, and the lovely New England churches with their graceful spires rose in many parts of the colonies.

Sunday—the Sabbath—was observed very strictly by the Puritans. No work was done from Saturday evening till Sunday night. Such food as was eaten was prepared beforehand. Everyone gathered at the church for two long services. This was part of the strict Puritan rule which prevailed in all ways of life in the first 75 or 100 years in New England.

Community Doings

The colonists had a friendly way of working together and helping one another. They knew how to make a success of living together in a community. They set apart a piece of land in the center of every village as public land. Here anyone could pasture his cows. The green common still remains as a pleasant park in the center of New England towns. They also had their public lands on the edge of the town in which all shared. When there was need of more pasture land for cattle or sheep, the men were expected to come together and cut down the trees. Connecticut made a law that every male citizen was to work one day a year clearing away brush to make pasture land.

Some pieces of work were too hard for a man and his sons to do alone. A large group of neighbors came together for a barn-raising or a house-raising. The side of a building would be built on the ground and then lifted into place. While the men worked, the women prepared food to be eaten out of doors. A "raising-day" was a welcome social event to which everyone came gladly.

There was a name for social gatherings for work or for amusement. They were called "bees." Farmers had husking bees when young and old came together to help in pulling the outer husks off ears of corn piled high on his barn floor. These were gay parties with much fun. Women had quilting bees and knitting bees. Modern spelling bees had their beginnings in colonial times.

The Puritans did not approve of religious holidays such as Christmas. They had their own special Thanksgiving Day (*see* Thanksgiving). They also had Training Day, when the men who met for military training gathered for public drill and parade. It was a festive day, with marching and beating of drums.

Tools and Methods from Old England

New England settlers were prepared by their lives in England for the kind of life they were to live. Most of them came from the eastern part of England.

BEDS AND A CRADLE IN A NEW ENGLAND HOUSEHOLD

In the bedroom at the left are a four-poster bed and a trundle bed that was pulled out at night for a child. The cradle at the right had a hood to keep out drafts.

HOUSEHOLD WARES MADE IN NEW ENGLAND AND IN'THE MIDDLE COLONIES

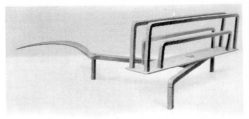

A blacksmith may have made the iron toast rack above, but it took a skilled and artistic silversmith to create the beautiful bowl in the center. It was made between 1680 and 1710. The sturdy pewter jug, or pitcher, at the right, was cast in a mold.

This pewter lamp and porringer are simple. The soft metal does not lend itself to intricate detail. Pennsylvania-Dutch pottery bore quaint designs. The silver coffeepot is a mid-18th-century piece. Articles are in the Metropolitan Museum of Art.

There they had been farmers, fishermen, shipbuilders, and cloth weavers. They raised many of the same crops in spite of colder weather and rocky land.

Though they were skilled farmers, they had only the poorest kind of tools, but these were the same as those they had used in England. Hand tools—hoes and forks for turning up the soil—were mostly of wood. The only plow was huge and clumsy. It took two men to handle it and four or six oxen to pull it through the ground. The farmer was fortunate who had one with an iron tip. Yet by their own labor and strength these farmers somehow plowed and culti-

MILES STANDISH'S CHEST
A chest was an important item in an early colonial home. Miles Standish probably brought this one from England, though his friend, John Alden, was a carpenter, so he might have made it.

vated their fields and raised the crops needed for their families. They had cattle, and in the meadowlands by the rivers they soon began to carry on the dairy industry for which New England was to be noted.

Clothing the Family

Much labor and skill went into the business of clothing the family. Here also they used arts which they used in England. The colonists grew flax plants in their fields and went through the many processes to prepare the fibers to be spun into linen thread. The women had to be skilled in spinning both linen and wool. Every colonial kitchen had its big spinning wheel before which the woman spinner stood or walked, holding and turning the fibers with quick motions as the wheel turned. In a corner of the room stood the great loom for weaving. The father often was the one to do the heavy work of running the loom. The children might tend the dye pot.

The dress of the early colonist was simple and plain, according to the Puritan rule. He wore a short close-fitting garment that came to his waist and was of dark color. His breeches were full, and he wore bright-colored stockings. Women wore gowns of gray or brown cloth, with white linen kerchiefs and cuffs. In a group of people, however, there were always touches of color from those same dye pots. The dress might be purple instead of gray or brown. The children's caps and stockings might be colored.

Home Industries

Winter was the time for many of the home industries. In the long evenings while the women were spin-

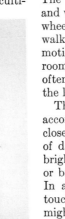

329

ning and knitting, the men and boys whittled. With their knives they shaped new wooden tools and household articles such as bowls and spoons. They also built the simple pieces of furniture needed in the home. It was not until the 18th century that some men, called cabinetmakers, gave all their time to the making of fine furniture.

Fishing and Shipbuilding

New England farms could not support all those who wanted to come to the colonies. The seacoast, however, made New England a land of opportunity. No man or boy had to say to himself: "I have no chance except as I make it on my own piece of land." He had only to go a few miles to get the smell of salt water. A little farther on there might be salt codfish drying on the beach; or he would hear the sound of hammers as a ship was being built.

Fishing as a colonial industry goes back to the days of the Pilgrims. Indeed, the idea goes back farther, to Capt. John Smith. He had been disappointed not to find gold mines in Virginia. Then as he explored the North American coast, he learned of the great fishing grounds that lay between Cape Cod and Newfoundland. These, he declared, would be worth as much as any gold mine.

Those who came out to New England were ready and eager to take up the dangerous occupation of deep-sea fishing. They lacked small fishing ships, however, and could not afford to buy them from England. The forests were close at hand, with trees ready for cutting; and there were skilled men among the colonists who knew how to build ships. Governor John Winthrop launched the first ship, the *Blessing of the Bay*, in 1631. From that time on, shipyards were built all along the coast and up the river valleys.

Large numbers of men went to the fishing grounds and brought in huge catches. Other men dried the fish and prepared them for sale. Two new industries had come into being: commercial fishing and the building of ships for use in fishing and later for foreign trade.

Whaling and Foreign Trade

Many New Englanders turned to the even more dangerous and difficult business of whaling. Gloucester, Salem, Marblehead, and Boston were the chief centers for the fishing industry. Whaling ships used

NEW ENGLANDERS WORK AT FISHING AND MILLING

This quaint drawing from Moll's 'Map of North America', printed in 1715, shows "Ye Manner of Fishing for, Curing, and Drying Cod." The fish were cleaned and salted in the shed. They were then spread out on the platform to dry.

Gristmills were important to grind the grain for daily use and to make flour for export. Henry Ford had this 17th-century mill put in working order when he restored the Wayside Inn in nearby Sudbury, Mass. Its great wheel is turned by a small stream.

the ports of New Bedford and the island of Nantucket. New England was reaching out. These captains went far beyond the usual fishing grounds.

Ships built in New England soon won a proud name. People from across the Atlantic wanted to buy them. New England merchants used them to carry logs, lumber, fish, and furs to British ports; fish, lumber, and other produce to southern Europe and the West Indies; and a variety of products to the other colonies. In distant ports the ship's master found cargoes wanted in the colonies—the sugar and molasses of the West Indies; fruits, wines, and cloth from France; and slaves from Africa. The wharves of Boston were crowded with ships unloading their varied cargo. This profitable

WEALTH FROM LUMBERING AND SHIPBUILDING

One of New England's first exports was timber. The Royal Navy got the tallest, straightest pines to make masts for men-of-war. Woodsmen marked them with an arrow. Ox teams snaked them to a stream and they floated down to the port.

This drawing from the National Life Insurance Company collection shows the building of war vessels on Lake Champlain in 1776. The same methods were used in the busy shipyards of the northern ports. Notice the crude two-man pit saw used to cut boards.

trade was the basis of many New England fortunes.

Other industries followed. As the call for lumber increased, New Englanders pushed farther into the wilderness and built sawmills on the swift-moving streams. They no longer needed to do all their work by slow hand labor. Water power could turn their mill wheels. Iron was needed for the ships and for farm tools. When iron ore was discovered, furnaces and mills for working it were set up. (*See also* Iron and Steel, History of.)

A New Prosperity

With the rise of commerce and industry, skilled workers were needed. A stream of men of many trades came in at the ports. They helped to build better houses and finer public buildings. Famous architects planned beautiful churches. The new prosperity was in the towns as well as in the few cities. Two-story houses replaced the early dwellings.

Merchants took the lead, as planters had done in the South. They built their houses on the same English pattern as those of the other colonial centers. A fine New England house was likely to have four rooms on each floor with the added beauty of a handsome doorway. Inside there was a graceful carved stairway, and the woodwork in the downstairs rooms was also carved. Many of these houses were painted white. The furniture matched the beauty of the rooms in pattern and style. While the Virginia planter had brought his furniture across the ocean, much of the 18th-century furniture was made by American craftsmen in New England and the Middle Colonies. The towns also had their silversmiths, clockmakers, and makers of fine glass.

The merchants and their families lived well and dressed in the latest London or Paris fashions. "Ladies and gentlemen appear as gay as courtiers in England," declared a traveler. In portraits of the leading statesmen and merchants, men's wigs and elaborate coats are seen. The men wore two-cornered or three-cornered hats.

Changes from Puritan Ways

This elegance belonged only to the "upper classes." Workers dressed in leather breeches and coats of homespun. The Puritans had passed laws forbidding the workers to copy the clothes worn by the wealthy; but their regulations were not always obeyed. With growing prosperity New England relaxed many of the stern Puritan rules. The influx of merchants and workers of many nationalities and religious beliefs had changed the make-up of New England society. In the early days the Puritans had attempted to keep out strangers and had deprived them of citizenship. Now the church was no longer in control of the government. Religious qualifications for voting had all but disappeared, though Puritan influence remained strong.

New England was building up a strong society of leaders and plain citizens. They were to serve well in the coming days of revolution and independence.

The Colonies Grow Together

FROM the South to the Middle Colonies and on to New England each colony was growing during the 1700's. That was important, but something still more significant was happening. They were growing together. Transportation, travel, communication, and trade, as well as common interests, were bringing the colonies and their people into touch with one another.

Travel in the Early Colonies

No one could believe travel in the colonies could be so difficult unless he tried it. It was not only that the roads were bad. Travelers used every word they knew to describe them—"frightful," "wretched," "savage," and more. Rivers and streams presented other problems. For George Washington to get from his home in Mount Vernon to a meeting at Philadelphia he had to ford many rivers and make frequent use of ferries. The journey might take a week or more.

A ferry might be a rowboat or a flatboat big enough for a horse or even a wheeled vehicle. When the ferryman decided the crossing was dangerous, travelers might have to wait until a flood subsided. Frequently they got mired in the mud and had to stay until the road dried or help arrived.

Transportation Improves in the 18th Century

In the early colonial days people lived practically without wheels. Later farmers began to use crude carts and wagons. Wealthy people brought coaches across the ocean. These vehicles, however, were exceptional even in prosperous places such as Philadelphia, Boston, and Williamsburg. It was not till the early 18th century that travel on wheels became common, and then the bad roads made it uncomfortable

CARRYING THE MAIL ON HORSEBACK
The postman in this painting by Stanley M. Arthurs blows a horn as he enters a village. Anyone who expects mail hurries to the tavern or store for it. He must pay the postal fee.

and slow. People who took long journeys usually rode horseback. (*See also* Transportation, section "Early Travel in North America"; Roads and Streets.)

The latter half of the century, however, saw highways of one sort or another connecting the colonies and the main towns within them. Regular lines of stagecoaches plied between Boston and New York City and New York City and Philadelphia. Sea travel had improved too, as vessels became larger. A regular packet sailed between New York City and Charleston.

The Inn, or Tavern

Because travel was slow and possible only during daylight hours, people built inns, or taverns, where men and horses could be kept overnight. Some were poor, small, and so crowded that several men might share a bed or even the floor. The inns became centers for news and small public gatherings. Some have been restored and now cater to tourists.

The cities had their fine taverns where notable travelers could be entertained. Some of them became famous as places of meeting during the struggle for independence. Especially noted was Raleigh Tavern in the city of Williamsburg, which had become Virginia's capital in 1699 (see Williamsburg). In 1774 the royal governor of Virginia brought the session of the colony's House of Burgesses to an end because it had passed a vote of sympathy with the rebellious colonists of Massachusetts. The gentlemen promptly

A HISTORIC INN OF COLONIAL VIRGINIA
Raleigh Tavern in Williamsburg has been restored and looks as it did in 1774. Since many people of the day could not read, signs bore pictures as well as words. On this one Sir Walter Raleigh's portrait is painted.

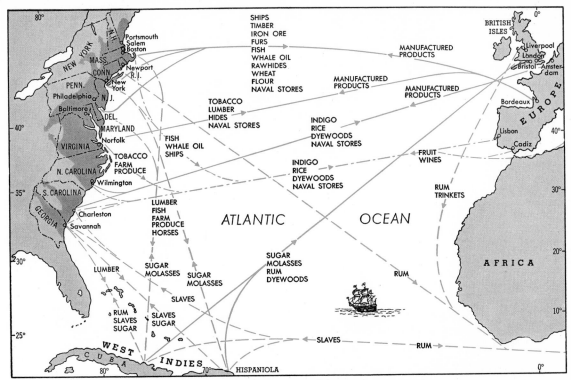

HOW THE TRIANGULAR TRADE BROUGHT PROSPERITY

Trade among northern ports, the West Indies, and Africa enabled the New England and the Middle Colonies to sell their produce and pay for English goods. Crops of the Southern Colonies could be traded direct to England. Here the colonies are drawn to a scale twice that used for Europe and Africa. The shading denotes the westward advance in 1763.

adjourned to Raleigh Tavern where they voted to recommend to the colonies that they call a congress to plan for united action.

Letters and Newspapers Link the Colonies

Communications had improved too. A postal system had been developed to carry mail between the colonies. In 1753 the system came under Benjamin Franklin's guidance, and he greatly improved it. Postriders on horseback carried letters from Maine to Florida, and boats bore them along the waterways (see Postal Service, United States).

The first successful newspaper had been published in Boston in 1704. Before the Revolution each city had its press. Publishers also brought out books and pamphlets. A fiery political pamphlet might circulate throughout the colonies.

Dangers Shared Serve as a Bond

People of the different colonies found new reasons to communicate with one another as their interests drew them together. As English colonists, they felt a common danger from the hostile Indians and from the ring of foreign settlements that surrounded them. The Spanish held Florida, and troops there threatened the rich southern rice and indigo colonies. The French had established fur-trading posts in Canada, around the Great Lakes, and down the Mississippi. They had made allies of many Indian tribes with whom they traded. The Indians and the French traders each had an interest in keeping the country a wilderness hunting ground. The Indians feared the English. Their settlers from the coastal colonies took the land and cleared it for farms and townsites.

The French and English had fought three wars for possession of North America. When the French and Indian War broke out in 1754 both sides knew it was a war to the finish for control of the Ohio Valley, the Mississippi with its port of New Orleans, and other western lands. This region was the frontier to which the Atlantic colonies hoped to expand. Their people were deeply concerned over this struggle. To them it was not simply a fight between England and France —part of a European rivalry. It was their own struggle, and they played a big part in winning it (see French and Indian War).

A Westward Movement from Each Colony

Each colony had its western movement. Pioneer settlers from the Southern Colonies and from Pennsylvania had met in the Great Valley of the Appalachians. In New York the prosperous town of Albany had developed from a Dutch trading post, and from it settlers had pushed along the fertile Mohawk Valley (see Albany). From the New England Colonies hardy pioneers had started seeking better lands to the West. Trail blazers like Daniel Boone and land speculators told wonderful stories of faraway places (see Boone).

333

NEWSPAPERS AND ADVERTISED WARES

Colored flint Stiegel glassware, made in Pennsylvania, was popular in the colonies. It is now a collector's item.

Franklin's fireplace saved fuel and radiated heat in all directions. Advertising helped make it a "best seller."

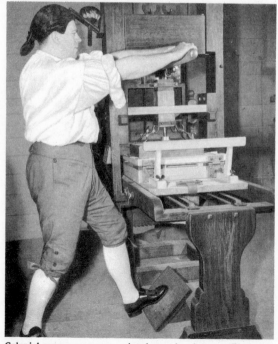

Colonial newspapers were printed on a hand press. They contained news articles, political discussions, poems, and essays.

The threat of war on the frontier was a common threat to all the colonies.

Politics and Trade

All the colonies had political problems. Over the years the king of England had revoked the charter of one colony after another and made all but four royal provinces. He appointed the governor and the council of the province and told them what to do. Each province had its assembly, with representatives elected by the voters. The powers of the assemblies, however, were threatened by the royal governor. Each colony had its fight to maintain and extend self-government, and the lawmakers consulted one another about it.

Growing trade broke down barriers as merchants from different areas competed or co-operated in ventures. Trade was so important a source of wealth that when Parliament passed laws restricting foreign commerce the colonists drew together in their resentment.

They had always bought most of their manufactured goods from England. Their problem was to find the means to pay for the imports. The Southern Colonies were in a favored position, since they could market the bulk of their great crops in England.

New England and the Middle Colonies had little they could sell England. The furs, whale oil, whale bone, and ship timber England wanted did not pay for more than a fifth of their imports. Their merchants entered into widespread trade to get bills of exchange to pay the English. They sent fish and other produce to southern Europe. They exchanged grain, lumber, and fish with French and English planters in the West Indies for sugar and molasses. They traded rum made from the molasses to the Indians for furs and sold it to African slave traders.

English Laws Hamper Trade

The British Parliament's Molasses Act of 1733 forbade the shipment of molasses to the colonies except from English possessions. It was a threat to the profitable triangular trade among the northern ports, the West Indies, and Africa. When smuggling became widespread, Parliament passed more stringent trade acts. Certain "enumerated articles" had to be shipped only to England. Imports from Europe had to go through English ports. There the goods were taxed so their price exceeded that of English goods.

Wealth gained from trade and land speculation financed manufacturing concerns in the colonies. The center of ironmaking shifted from New England to Pennsylvania. High-grade ore was found in many places, and the forests supplied wood for charcoal.

Many plants began processing the wealth of raw materials. These concerns turned out articles so bulky or perishable that they did not compete with similar European goods. Others made new products for which the colonies had once depended upon England. As colonial factories began cutting into the profits of English merchants and industrialists Parliament passed new laws. These forbade the making of certain products and the exporting of others.

Interests of City Folk

People living alike in the different colonies were coming to resemble one another in viewpoints and attitudes. City people in the various colonies had more in common with one another than with the farmers of their own region.

Clubs had become a fad. As their members gathered for fun and sociability, they talked over the affairs of the day. Together with the increase in newspapers and books, this contributed to the development of public opinion. Educated people in all colonies had similar backgrounds, ideas, and enthusiasms. When Benjamin Franklin formed the American Philosophical Society in 1743, members from half a dozen colonies joined it.

Frontier Problems

Frontier folk had nearly the same problems everywhere. In the backwoods they met settlers from other colonies and from Europe and found much in them to like and admire. Their constant danger, their hard lives, their struggle to win representation in the assemblies and protection against the Indians divided them from people in the coastal towns and united them with each other.

They too had their quarrel with the government of King George III. When England gained control of the frontier through the French and Indian War, it issued the Proclamation of 1763. This forbade settlers to buy lands beyond a line through the headwaters of rivers flowing into the Atlantic. Although this act was designed to pacify the Indians, it roused a fighting spirit on the frontier.

They Were Americans

Colonial self-confidence increased with experience. When colonial soldiers fought shoulder to shoulder with British troops in the French and Indian War and in other military ventures, they found that as men they were as good—or maybe better. An "American type" was developing. A man might still call himself a Virginian or a Rhode Islander, but he was beginning to think of himself as an American. Pride in their achievements, self-confidence, and a spirit of independence were characteristics of the American colonists. Here are two quotations about them from travelers of the time. Dr. Alexander Hamilton said:

VIRGINIA'S HOUSE OF BURGESSES IN WILLIAMSBURG

First of the elected assemblies was Virginia's House of Burgesses, which met in this hall. The royal governor and his council made up the upper house. The burgesses were mainly tidewater planters. Frontier farmers demanded representation too.

"I found but little difference in the manners and character of the people in the different provinces I passed thro. . . . As to politeness and humanity they are much alike, except in the great towns, where the inhabitants are more civilized, especially in Boston."

Peter Kalm, a Swedish botanist who traveled through the colonies in 1748–51, wrote: "Everyone who acknowledges God to be the Creator, preserver, and ruler of all things, and teaches or undertakes nothing against the state or against the common peace, is at liberty to settle, stay and carry on his trade here. And he is so well secured by the laws and enjoys such liberties that a citizen here may be said to live in his house like a king. It would be difficult to find anyone who could wish for and obtain greater freedom."

Slowly increasing common interests were drawing the colonists together in the 18th century. Yet they might have remained separate for decades but for the growing hostility against oppressive British laws and policies. They united to meet the threat to the freedom they had come to believe was their right.

The articles Declaration of Independence and Revolution, American describe the events, issues, and movements that led to the war for the independence of the colonies and the creation of a new nation. (For Reference-Outlines and Bibliography, *see* United States History; American Heritage Outline.)

THE

AMERICAN

HERITAGE

. . . AN OUTLINE

Proud of their American heritage, these United States Marines plant the Stars and Stripes. This memorable scene took place atop Mount Suribachi during the height of the battle of Iwo Jima in the second World War.

THE VERY FOUNDATIONS of American democracy and freedom have been threatened in recent times by world forces bent on destroying them. These threats have aroused in the American people a new interest in the principles that underlie their national life. They want to understand clearly the things to which they, as a people, are dedicated—the principles for which they fought in two world wars and on which their hopes of world peace are founded.

The manner in which Americans will meet tomorrow's problems will be determined by the kind of nation they have built. The fabric of their past is the pattern also of their future.

This is what we mean by the "American way." It is the character the nation acquired as it grew. To chart that character, as it is represented in these volumes, is the purpose of this outline.

I. THE PEOPLE

CAME FROM EUROPE

LOOKING

FOR FREEDOM

THEY *found wilderness and Indians—and it was a question which was the more savage. But they did not turn back, these bold colonists. Let the Old World perish! They had a New World to conquer!*

A. They left England and crossed an ocean A-302, A-324, J-361a, E-238

　1. Some sought freedom of worship P-395, A-304, A-324, A-344, M-129, P-539, picture A-302

　2. Others wanted freedom of economic opportunity A-304, G-83, V-335, N-248
　3. Still others looked for adventure in the mysterious New World A-300, A-304, R-91

B. Among their number were many brave men

　1. John Smith was a natural leader S-219
　2. Roger Williams risked death for his convictions W-166
　3. William Penn pioneered in democracy P-162

II. A NATION FOUNDED BY REVOLUTION

THE *Americans were strange. In a world of tyranny they dared to say—every individual is born with the rights of life, liberty, and the pursuit of happiness! To win these rights, the Americans fought a war. Thirteen colonies versus the British Empire—that was the lineup. Almost everyone said it was crazy, but they did it. They built a nation and became heir to a continent.*

3. Then, to safeguard the individual liberties of each citizen, they appended a Bill of Rights B-157, U-144, 151-2, H-140, C-353b-5
4. They had created a republic founded on democracy U-173-4, R-174, D-84

5. The Stars and Stripes became its symbol F-185, 188a, 190, color picture F-191
6. 'The Star-Spangled Banner', written in the struggle of 1812, was later adopted as its anthem N-50-1

III. DEMOCRACY GREW AS THE FRONTIER MOVED WESTWARD

Raw, *reckless, with the vigor of a growing giant, America advanced from colonies to nation and from nation to empire. As the frontier pushed to the Pacific, the Americans marveled at their continent— at its incredible wealth, its vast proportions, its sprawling loveliness. It was a heroic setting for their experiment in freedom.*

A. The Americans drove to the Pacific

1. They followed paths broken by early explorers and missionaries A-301: Champlain C-205-6; Marquette and Joliet M-113, J-438a; I-41; La Salle and Tonti L-128, L-367, I-41; Hennepin H-133, M-389; Nicolet W-197, M-275, picture A-299
2. They took the land U-29
   a. By the irresistible advance of the people U-175-8, F-66-71, N-362
   b. By dispossessing the Indians I-145-6, P-340-1, F-67
   c. By fantastic bargains, such as the Louisiana Purchase L-379, map U-177
   d. Even by war, as with Mexico M-237-8, P-438, C-43, T-38-9, S-75
3. Free land attracted a steady stream of settlers U-177, L-107-8, P-334, 337, 340, S-323, 326
4. Discovery of gold brought a swarm C-41, S-2, P-337, F-71, C-458, N-147-8, S-326

B. Pioneer days produced rough-and-ready heroes

1. Daniel Boone led his band across the mountains into Kentucky B-266, K-31
2. Lewis and Clark traversed the continent L-202-3, C-381, L-202, M-415, F-65, map U-176
3. Kit Carson, John C. Frémont, Buffalo Bill, Zebulon Pike, and Jim Bridger explored the West E-356, F-66, 69-71, C-142, F-434, B-362, B-328
4. Fur traders penetrated the northern wilderness F-497-8, F-66-7, S-326, N-344

C. Democracy flowered on the frontier

1. The pioneers were self-reliant and independent, yet cooperative U-177, 178, P-332, 335-335a

2. They were prodigal of nature's resources C-535
3. They dispensed justice with rude honesty P-335a
4. And they became a power in the nation U-177-8

D. New agricultural states brought a fresh western breeze

1. The state constitutions followed the liberal pattern of the federal Constitution S-428, S-429a-b
2. The backwoods produced leaders of a new variety U-177-8
   a. Davy Crockett couldn't read, but he talked himself into Congress C-608
   b. Andrew Jackson represented the "common man" in the White House J-348
   c. After Jackson came other presidents from the South and West H-42, P-436, T-37

E. Democracy moved from theory to practice

1. The system of checks and balances was perfected
   a. It consisted of the executive (P-492), the legislative (C-515), and the judicial (C-593)
   b. Marshall established the authority of the Supreme Court M-119, U-146
2. The two-party system developed P-432
   —Opposing ideas of Hamilton and Jefferson laid the foundation H-15, J-403
3. The Alien and Sedition Laws were rejected as attempts to abridge liberties A-275, U-173

F. The republic adopted a foreign policy of isolation

1. George Washington — avoid permanent foreign alliances with the Old World W-26
2. Monroe—keep the Old World out of America M-457

G. Democracy's culture—it seemed barbaric to aristocratic foreigners, but the people liked it

1. Because it offered education for every citizen E-78, 91, N-362, L-108, picture P-336
   —Horace Mann, missionary for knowledge M-91, E-91
2. Its press was free N-231-2, N-249

3. Its religious spirit was unrestricted C-337, P-332
4. Its social life was homely and informal P-335a

5. And its literature sprang from the life of the people A-345-9

IV. THE NATION
TESTED BY
INTERNAL STRIFE

Yes, *the young republic grew. But was it outgrowing the bonds that held it together? Were the very energy of its growth and the force of its freedom destined to split it asunder? The test was at hand—"whether that nation or any nation so conceived and so dedicated can long endure."*

A. Grave issues divided the people C-372-4

1. There was the question of States' Rights S-429d
   a. Webster said, "Liberty and Union, now and forever, one and inseparable!" W-91
   b. Calhoun said that a state had the right to nullify a federal law C-30
2. There was the tariff question, with the industrial North opposed to the agricultural South T-24, 25, C-372
3. There was the question of slavery U-179
   —and the Abolitionist movement led by Garrison (G-34) and Sumner (S-512)
4. All efforts at peaceful compromise failed C-374-5, M-412, C-501-2
   —despite the genius of Henry Clay C-382

B. War broke out between the states C-375

1. They fought it out on the battlefield: at Fort Sumter (F-349), at Bull Run (B-372), at Shiloh (S-163), at Antietam (A-449), at Fredericksburg (F-430), at Chancellorsville (C-206), at Vicksburg (V-311), at Gettysburg (G-119), at Chattanooga (C-221), in the Wilderness Campaign and at Petersburg (C-378), and at Atlanta (A-669)
2. Both sides produced great leaders
   a. In the North Lincoln towered granitelike L-279; and with him stood Sherman (S-163), and Sheridan (S-162), and the unconquerable Grant (G-171-2)
   b. In the South shone the nobility and genius of Robert E. Lee L-180b; and with him Jefferson Davis (D-38), Stephens (S-443), and Stonewall Jackson (J-356)

C. In the end, the nation stood the test and there were abiding results for democracy R-113

1. The slaves were emancipated E-190
2. Constitutional amendments reinforced the liberties of every citizen U-145-6, B-157
3. Never again did the threat of secession seriously arise S-429d

V. A UNITED NATION
WAXED RICH
AND POWERFUL

"Government *of the people, by the people, and for the people shall not perish from the earth." Abraham Lincoln said that was the issue. And*

when the passions of war had subsided, everyone agreed. It did not, it shall not perish. So the wounds healed and the nation grew wondrously. It flung skyscrapers into the heavens; its ships encompassed the earth. And it became a refuge for the oppressed, a proper land for the brave and the bold.

A. With war's end came tremendous developments U-182-4
1. Many new large enterprises were launched H-136-7
2. The magnet of high wages drew waves of immigrants from Europe I-57-8

B. American inventive genius was born and grew up with the nation I-247
1. There had been men like Fulton of the steamboat (F-479), Whitney of the cotton gin (W-158), Howe of the sewing machine (H-263), McCormick of the reaper (M-5), and Morse of the telegraph (M-491)
2. And now came Bell of the telephone (B-130) and Edison, the electrical wizard (E-69)

C. Railroads and communication lines webbed the land R-74, 82-3, T-244, T-54-6, T-64, picture T-65

D. The United States became the greatest industrial nation in the world I-176-88
1. It had abundant raw materials and a vast domestic market U-103-11, T-230-1

2. Great fortunes were built up by oil kings such as Rockefeller (R-230), steel kings such as Carnegie (C-138)
3. And presently came the automobile industry A-775-7, F-144, S-490b
   a. Led by Henry Ford, it worked out mass-production methods F-339, A-775, 777
   b. With it came an amazing program of highway building R-212, T-195
4. The Wright brothers invented the airplane and America took to the air W-305, A-172-3
5. Electric power transformed the life of the people E-153-4
6. De Forest and Armstrong perfected the radio and vast broadcasting networks brought the people closer together R-57, 55-6, D-62

E. Out of this new industrial revolution came the modern American pattern U-186-7
1. Great cities throbbed with industries and people C-363-6
2. "Big Business" grew and consolidated I-177-86
3. The American labor movement followed a typically independent course L-86
4. The American farmer learned how to produce more at lower costs A-101, 106-7, F-63-4
5. Mass consumption of mass-produced products created the "American Standard of Living" L-184, A-38, T-228, picture I-176
6. Americans pioneered in automation A-746-53

VI. OLD IDEALS
FOUND NEW
EXPRESSION

I𝚃 *was time to take stock. The Americans, abating their breathless expansion, began to look at one another. They found that in the swift race many had been left behind. They found injustice—poverty in the midst of plenty. So they crusaded for reform. They found their culture backward. So they rushed to "conquer culture," as they had the West. But their achievements were great, and greatest of all was this—they had made democracy work!*

A. The Americans sought to perfect their democracy
1. They broadened popular participation in government V-386-8
   —They provided for direct primaries (P-496), initiative, referendum, and recall (I-189), direct election of senators (C-515), and suffrage for women (W-214)
2. They regulated industry in the interest of public welfare U-182-4
   —They launched the antitrust movement (M-449-50, T-282); they set up the Interstate Commerce Commission (I-246) and the Federal Trade Commission (F-83)
3. And they tried to improve the living conditions of the underprivileged
   —They provided for employers' liability (E-201) and other kinds of social insurance (S-236)

B. The nation was coming of age
1. Its frontiers were disappearing M-312, F-71
2. It began to restrict immigration I-57-8
3. It became a world power U-183-4, M-19-22

VII. NEW PROBLEMS IN THE NEW WORLD

THIS *American—this Uncle Sam, lean and tall, awkward, abundant in his love, stern in his sense of justice—this American—born in revolution, cradled in a continent, maturing in a world of violent change . . . how will he fare? Let us follow his progress as the days stride forward. Let us look into his record as set forth in the Reference-Outline for United States History—pages U-200-1.*

AMERICAN LEGION. The American Legion was formed in 1919 by veterans of World War I who wanted an organization to keep alive their comradeship and to honor the memory of their dead. In 1942, it opened its ranks to veterans of World War II. Later veterans who served during the Korean War and the Vietnam conflict became eligible for membership.

Ever since its founding, the Legion has been a powerful force in American life. It has helped many veterans to obtain work, hospital care, and compensation. It has promoted laws helpful to veterans and brought about the reorganization of government agencies engaged in their behalf. A campaign during 1925–26 produced a 5-million-dollar endowment fund to support rehabilitation and child-welfare work.

In education for good citizenship, the work of the Legion includes school awards, citizenship schools for the foreign born, flag education, and occupational guidance for boys. The Legion, together with the National Education Association, started the observance of American Education Week. The National Americanism Commission strives to educate school children as well as adults to be "100 per cent" Americans. It also fights subversive activities.

Youth activities include sponsoring the Boy Scouts, the Reserve Officers' Training Corps, Citizens' Mili-

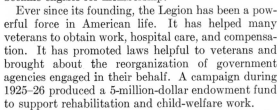

tary Training Camps, 4-H Clubs, Junior Rifle Clubs, drum and bugle corps and bands, and National Boys' and Girls' Week. The Legion's Junior Baseball League, founded as a national activity in 1926, provides recreation for hundreds of thousands of boys throughout the country and trains them in sportsmanship. The Boys States are citizenship organizations to teach boys democratic procedure. (*See also* Juvenile Organizations.)

Women who were in the armed forces during World War I, World War II, the Korean War, or the Vietnam conflict are eligible for Legion membership. Wives, sisters, mothers, and daughters of legionnaires have banded together in the American Legion Auxiliary. The Auxiliary sponsors Girls States and a Girls Nation to give high school girls training in citizenship. (*See also* Girls State in Fact-Index.)

Until 1959 another Legion subsidiary was a secret organization known as the Society of the Forty and Eight. It aided child-welfare programs and membership campaigns. The Legion, however, disagreed with the society's membership policies and forbade the group to use either the Legion's name or its emblem in connection with its activities.

The Sons of the American Legion is a group composed of sons of legionnaires. Its purpose is to cooperate with the parent organization. It is represented in each state.

Headquarters of the Legion are in Indianapolis, Ind. The Legion's official publications are the *American Legion* and the *National Legionnaire*.

In Melville's 'Moby-Dick', one of the great books in American literature, Ahab scans the sea for the white whale. This picture is by Rockwell Kent (copyright by R. R. Donnelley & Sons Co.).

AMERICAN LITERATURE Reflects American Life

AMERICAN LITERATURE. Wherever there are people there will be a literature. A literature is the record of human experience, and people have always been impelled to write down their impressions of life. They do so in diaries and letters, in pamphlets and books, and in essays, poems, plays, and stories. In this respect American literature is like any other. There are, however, many characteristics of American writing that make it different from all others. This has not always been true.

American literature began with the first English colonies at Plymouth and Boston. The colonists came to the New World to find religious freedom and prosperity. They came, however, in no spirit of revolution. They came as Englishmen, bringing with them the literary wealth of English legends, ballads, and poems and the richness of the English language. They were loyal to the Crown. These settlers did not even call themselves Americans.

How the English colonists slowly came to think and act as "Americans" is a familiar and proud story. How their literature slowly grew to be "American" writing is less well known. The growth of American literature, however, follows closely the history of the nation from its beginning to the present time.

American authors have written countless essays and songs, poems and plays, novels and short stories. There is space here to discuss only the most important and the best. Even a short summary, however, shows something of the splendid accomplishment of American literature since it emerged from its crude colonial beginnings more than 300 years ago.

Colonial Times in America

THE MAN SOMETIMES called the first American writer was Capt. John Smith (1580–1631). He was a soldier-adventurer who came to Virginia in 1607 and wrote pamphlets describing the new land. His first, 'A True Relation of Virginia' (1608), aimed at attracting settlers and winning financial support for the colony.

His 'General History of Virginia' (1624) elaborates on his experiences. In it he tells how his life was saved by Pocahontas. Smith was an able leader and an interesting reporter. His books are valued because he was the first person to write about the English settlements. (*See also* Smith.)

Colonial life in Virginia was best described by William Byrd (1674–1744), owner of Westover, an estate of almost 180,000 acres on the James River. The beautiful house is a showplace today. Educated in England, Byrd returned home to lead the life of a country gentleman. He worked hard managing his affairs. His most notable public act was to survey the boundary between Virginia and Carolina, fighting his way through the great Dismal Swamp. He described this adventure of 1728–29 in 'History of the Dividing Line', published in 1841. He told, often amusingly, of settlement life in the backcountry. Byrd's 'Secret Diary', discovered in 1940, gives intimate glimpses of colonial times and helps bring to life this refined and witty colonial gentleman.

Plantation life in Virginia was civilized, even elegant. The people were not intellectual, however, and they produced little writing. The inhabitants, descended from the Royalist, or "Cavalier," group in England, were faithful members of the Church of England. They accepted religion as a matter of course and felt no need to write about it. In addition, the system of plantation life produced a number of isolated communities, as did the feudalism of the Middle Ages. This kept people from gathering in cities.

People in the Southern Colonies therefore had little need to write, and social conditions did not encourage them to do so. The South's great contributions, both to statecraft and to literature, came later. The significant writing of colonial times was done in New England, where American literature may properly be said to have begun.

Colonial life began in New England with the landing of the Pilgrims at Cape Cod in 1620. Before going ashore they signed the Mayflower Compact, an agreement to live together in harmony under law (*see* 'Mayflower'). It is found in 'History of Plimoth Plantation'. This moving account of the early struggles of the colonists was written by William Brad-

COTTON MATHER
Cotton Mather, the leading Boston clergyman in the early 1700's, was one of the most influential Puritans.

ford (1590–1657), who was governor for 30 years. A similar journal was kept by Governor John Winthrop (1588–1649) of the Massachusetts Bay Colony, founded ten years after Plymouth (*see* Winthrop). Present-day knowledge of Thanksgiving, the Pilgrims' dealings with Indians, and other experiences of the first settlers comes from these two narratives of the colonization.

The Influence of Puritanism

For more than 100 years after the Pilgrim landing in 1620, life and writing in New England were dominated by the religious attitude known as Puritanism. To un-

THE DEVIL IN NEW ENGLAND
In colonial times in America many women were believed to be witches in league with the devil. Cotton Mather wrote exten-

sively of them. These old woodcuts are from his 'On Witchcraft', published by the Peter Pauper Press.

343

THE HARSHNESS OF PURITAN LIFE
Nathaniel Hawthorne's 'Scarlet Letter', from which this illustration is taken, well portrays the stern ideas of the Puritans.

derstand colonial life and literature one must understand Puritanism, one of the major influences in American life.

The early settlers in New England were Protestants. England had become a Protestant country when Henry VIII broke away from the Roman Catholic church. Some Englishmen, however, felt that the break was not complete. They wanted to "purify" the church of Catholic features; they were therefore known as Puritans. Another group, the Separatists, wanted to separate, or break away entirely, from the Church of England. These were the Pilgrims. Both groups came to the New World in order to worship God in their own way. They felt they had a divine mission to fulfill. It was the will of God, they believed, that they establish a religious society in the wilderness. This belief must have helped them endure the hard life they faced as colonists.

In the Puritan view, God was supreme. The Puritans held that He revealed His will through the Bible, which they believed literally. Clergymen interpreted the Bible in sermons, but each man and woman was obliged to study it for himself too. The people had to be educated in order to read the Bible, to discuss it, and to write about it. Harvard College was founded in 1636 partly to meet this demand for an educated populace. Other colleges and public schools followed. Indeed, the intellectual quality of New England life, which later influenced other parts of the country, is traceable to the Puritans' need for a trained and literate population.

Religious Quality of Puritan Writing

New Englanders have always been industrious writers. Most of what they wrote in colonial times was prompted by their religious feeling. Many sermons were published and widely read. Cotton Mather (1663–1728), the leading clergyman in Boston in the early 1700's, wrote more than 400 separate works. The most ambitious was his 'Magnalia Christi Americana' (Christ's Great Achievements in America), published in 1702.

Clergymen encouraged some people to keep personal diaries or journals. The most readable of these today is the diary of Samuel Sewall (1652–1730). The 'Diary of Samuel Sewall 1674–1729' (published 1878–82) is lively and often amusing, as when the author wrote of his courtship of Madame Winthrop: "Asked her to acquit me of rudeness if I drew off her glove. Enquiring the reason, I told her 'twas great odds between handling a dead goat and a living lady."

Sewall was a courageous man. A judge during the witchcraft trials in 1692, he concurred in the decision to hang 19 persons condemned as witches. After the hysteria had died down, however, he alone among the judges stood up in meeting and publicly asked "to take the blame and shame" for his part in the executions. He was also an early foe of slavery. His 'Selling of Joseph' (1700) was perhaps the earliest antislavery pamphlet in America.

The Puritans wrote little imaginative literature. The theater was not welcomed by them any more than it was by the Puritans who closed the London theaters in 1642. Fiction writing (stories and novels) was in its infancy in England, and it probably did not occur to men and women in the New World to write stories. The only imaginative Puritan literature was poetry; and that, like everything else in Puritan life, was prompted by religion.

The first book in English to be published in the New World was the 'Bay Psalm Book' (1640). The new translations of the Biblical psalms were plain; the meter and rhyme were regular, as in Psalm xxiii, which begins as follows:

The Lord to me a shepherd is, want therefore shall not I.
He in the folds of tender-grass doth cause me down to lie.

This familiar rhythm was used by Michael Wigglesworth (1631–1705) in 'The Day of Doom' (1662), a 224-stanza account in verse of the Last Judgment. Based on the Puritan religious belief in Calvinism, the poem presents in dramatic terms the divine judgment of those condemned to eternal torment in hell and also of those who, by God's grace, are elected to gain eternal salvation in the world to come. Many Puritans, both young and old, committed 'The Day of Doom' to memory.

More interesting, because it is better poetry, are the religious verses of Edward Taylor (1642–1729). These were first published in 1939. Taylor was a devout clergyman, but his poems are not harsh and gloomy. Instead, they express his feeling of joy and delight in the Christian life. For instance, in one poem he pictured the church members as passengers in a coach, Christ's coach, singing as they rattle along to salvation in the next world:

> For in Christ's coach they sweetly sing,
> As they to Glory ride therein.

Taylor's verse is full of such vivid and exciting metaphors. His is the most interesting American poetry of colonial times.

Jonathan Edwards—The Last Puritan

Puritanism could not maintain its authority forever. As the seaboard settlements grew and people became prosperous, as more political power was given to the people, and as a more scientific attitude challenged the old religious way of thinking, men and women in New England came to be more worldly and to take their religion for granted. It was to combat this worldliness that Jonathan Edwards (1703–58),

the last and the greatest Puritan, taught and preached and wrote. Puritanism was fated to die out, but not before Edwards made heroic efforts to keep it alive.

Edwards believed that the people were too matter-of-fact about religion. To be religious, one must feel deeply, he thought. He therefore joined with others in preaching emotional sermons. These produced a wave of religious revivals. After the enthusiasm had passed, however, Edwards was dismissed from his congregation and became a missionary to the Indians. He was a brilliant theologian and philosopher, and most of his writings are difficult to read. His 'Personal Narrative', however, which tells the story of his youthful religious experiences, is an honest and moving revelation. It was written about 1740.

The nation owes a great debt to Puritanism. It is true that in several ways Puritan life was harsh and unlovely, as one learns from reading 'The Scarlet Letter', Nathaniel Hawthorne's great novel. Nevertheless one must admire the Puritans for their zeal, their courage, and their strong moral nature. They recognized that man is often guilty of evil actions. Their hardheaded view of human nature has much truth in it. The 20th century has seen enough cruelty and depravity for one to believe that the Puritan view of human beings was valid in some respects.

The Shaping of a New Nation

AMERICAN WRITING in colonial days, as has been seen, dealt largely with religion. In the last 30 years of the 18th century, however, men turned their attention from religion to the subject of government. These were the years when the colonies broke away from England and declared themselves a new and independent nation. It was a great decision for Americans to make. Feeling ran high, and people expressed their opinions in a body of writing which, if not literature in the narrow sense, is certainly literature in the sense of its being great writing.

Since World War II moves for national independence have been numerous throughout the world. Historically, however, the first people to throw off a colonial yoke were those of the American Colonies. The literary record of their struggle thus is a fascinating and inspiring story to people everywhere.

Franklin—Spokesman for a Nation

The birth of the United States was witnessed by Benjamin Franklin (1706–90) in his last years. His career began in colonial days. At 17 he ran away from his home in Boston and went to Philadelphia. How he took up printing, made enough money to retire at 42, and educated himself is the subject of his 'Autobiography', first published in book form in English in 1793. This is the first and most celebrated story of the American self-made man. Many of his rules for self-improvement ("Early to bed, early to rise," and so forth) appeared in his 'Poor Richard's Almanack', first published in 1732.

Franklin was simple in manners and tastes. When

THOMAS PAINE
The fiery pamphlets of Thomas Paine inspired the American people to declare their independence from Great Britain.

he represented the colonies in the European courts, he insisted on wearing the simple homespun of colonial dress. He used the plain speech of the provincial people. He displayed the practical turn of mind of a people who had shrewdly conquered a wilderness. (*See also* Franklin, Benjamin.)

Franklin embodied the American idea. That idea was defined by Michel Guillaume St. Jean de Crèvecoeur (1735–1813), a Frenchman who lived in America for many years before the Revolution. In his 'Letters from an American Farmer' (1782) he described the colonists as happy compared with the suffering people of Europe. In one letter he asked, "What then is the American, this new man?" This is a challenging question even today, nearly 200 years later. Crèvecoeur's answer then was:

"*He* is an American, who, leaving behind him all his ancient prejudices and manners, receives new ones from the new mode of life he has embraced, the new government he obeys, and the new rank he holds. He becomes an American by being received in the broad lap of our great *Alma Mater* (nourishing mother). Here individuals of all nations are melted into a new race of men, whose labours and posterity will one day cause great changes in the world . . . The American is 'a new man, who acts upon new principles; he must therefore entertain new ideas and form new opinions . . . This is an American."

The immigrant prospered in America, and he became fiercely loyal to the system that made possible his prosperity. That system, which included a large measure of personal freedom, was threatened by the British. Americans tried to preserve it by peaceful means. When this became impossible, they chose to become a separate nation.

Thomas Paine Arouses the Patriots

The power of words to affect the course of history is clearly seen in the writings of Thomas Paine (1737–1809). The shooting had started at Lexington and Concord in April 1775, but for months there was no move to break away from England. Then, in January 1776, appeared Paine's pamphlet 'Common Sense'. In brilliant language, logical and passionate, yet so simple that all could understand, Paine argued in favor

NOAH WEBSTER—MOLDER OF THE "AMERICAN" LANGUAGE

Perhaps no man has so greatly influenced the "American" language as Webster.

Because of him Americans spell many words differently from the English.

of declaring independence from Britain. The effect was electric.

By June the Continental Congress resolved to break away; and on July 4, 1776, the Declaration of Independence appeared. Paine continued his pamphleteering during the war in 'The Crisis', a series of 16 papers. The first one begins, "These are the times that try men's souls." George Washington said that without Paine's bold encouragement the American cause might have been lost. (*See also* Paine.)

The famous Declaration of Independence was largely the work of Thomas Jefferson (1743–1826). In justifying the American Revolution to the world he stated the political axioms on which the revolution was based, among them the proposition that "all men are created equal." This phrase is at the very heart of democracy. (*See also* Jefferson.)

After the war Americans, having rejected their rulers, were faced with the job of governing themselves. They attempted "to form a more perfect Union." The result was the Constitution. Although the United States has flourished under the system of government outlined in the Constitution, not all Americans favored adopting the new plan when it was proposed. In the great debate over adopting it, Alexander Hamilton (1755?–1804) and others wrote 85 essays, known as 'The Federalist' (1787–88), in support of the Constitution. These are models of clear and forceful writing.

Poets during these years wrote patriotic verses on political themes. Some of the poems of John Trumbull (1750–1831) and Joel Barlow (1754–1812) are interesting, but in style they were imitative of English poetry. Novels too resembled those written of England. Susanna (Haswell) Rowson (1762–1824) wrote 'Charlotte Temple' (1791), a sentimental tale of a betrayed heroine. 'Wieland' (1798), by Charles Brockden Brown (1771–1810), is patterned after an English novel. This imitativeness is not surprising: writers were in the habit of writing like Englishmen.

More and more, however, authors wanted to write as Americans. They had won political independence; they now wanted literary independence. The poet Philip Freneau (1752–1832) pleaded for a native literature. So did Noah Webster (1758–1843). "Customs, habits, and language," he wrote, "should be national." He did his part by compiling 'The American Spelling Book' (1783) and his 'American Dictionary of the English Language' (1828). "Center," instead of "centre," and "honor," instead of "honour," are typical of Webster's "Americanized" spelling. (*See also* Webster, Noah.)

Literature of the Early Republic

IT WAS ONE thing for writers to want to create a native American literature; it was quite another thing to know how to do it. For 50 years after the founding of the nation, authors patterned their work after the writings of Englishmen. William Cullen Bryant was known as the American Wordsworth; Washington Irving's essays resemble those of Addison and Steele; James Fenimore Cooper wrote novels like those of Scott. Although the form and style of these Americans were English, the content—character and especially setting—was American. Every American region was described by at least one prominent writer.

Frontier life in western Pennsylvania is pictured in 'Modern Chivalry' (1792–1815), written by a friend of James Madison and Philip Freneau, Hugh Henry Brackenridge (1748–1816). This episodic narrative, modeled on Miguel de Cervantes' 'Don Quixote', shows how people in the backcountry behaved politically under the new Constitution. Henry Adams called 'Modern Chivalry' a "more thoroughly American book than any written before 1833." American it is, in character, setting, and theme.

The beauties of New England's hills and forests were sung by William Cullen Bryant (1794–1878). 'Thanatopsis' (1817) and 'A Forest Hymn' (1825) show a reverence for nature. The English critic Matthew Arnold thought 'To a Waterfowl' (1818) the best short poem in the English language. (*See also* Bryant.)

New York City and its environs were the province of Washington Irving (1783–1859). 'Salmagundi' (1807–8), which he coauthored, describes the city's fashionable life. 'A History of New York . . . by Diedrich Knickerbocker' (1809), an imaginary Dutch historian, is an amusing account of its history under Dutch rule.

Irving's masterpieces were his sketches 'The Legend of Sleepy Hollow' and 'Rip Van Winkle', both published in 1820. These tales—the first of Icha-

EXCITING ACTION IN 'THE DEERSLAYER'
This is one of the thrilling episodes in 'The Deerslayer', by Cooper. The picture (originally in color) is by N. C. Wyeth (copyright by Charles Scribner's Sons).

ICHABOD CRANE FLEES IN TERROR

Here the Headless Horseman (in reality the reckless horseman Brom Bones) chases luckless Ichabod Crane in 'The Legend of Sleepy Hollow', by Washington Irving. This picture by F. O. C. Darley was drawn for an early edition of the story.

RIP VAN WINKLE RETURNS

Another of Irving's well-known characters, Rip Van Winkle, left his shrewish wife to seek peace in the Catskills. He returned after his 20-year nap to find his world entirely altered. His wife was dead, and even his faithful dog did not recognize him.

bod Crane, a superstitious schoolmaster, the second of Rip, who sought refuge in the Catskills from his shrewish wife and slept for 20 years—are among the best-loved American stories. Irving's literary skill was appreciated in England too. There he was recognized as the first important American writer. (*See also* Irving.)

James Fenimore Cooper

James Fenimore Cooper (1789–1851) wrote more than 30 novels and many other works. He was an enormously popular writer, in Europe as well as at home. Of interest to readers today are his opinions on democracy. Reared on an estate near Cooperstown, N. Y., the writer had a patrician upbringing. When he criticized democracy, as in 'The American Democrat' (1838), he criticized the crudity he saw in the United States of Andrew Jackson. Yet he defended the American democratic system against attacks by European aristocrats.

In his day Cooper was best known as the author of the 'Leatherstocking Tales', five novels of frontier life. These stories of stirring adventure, such as 'The Last of the Mohicans' (1826) and 'The Deerslayer' (1841), feature Cooper's hero Natty Bumppo, the skillful, courageous, and valorous woodsman. This character embodied American traits and so to Europeans seemed to represent the New World. (*See also* Cooper.)

The South too was portrayed in fiction in these years. 'Swallow Barn' (1832), by John Pendleton Kennedy (1795–1870), pictures life on a Virginia plantation. Later portrayals of life in the Old Dominion, in fiction and in motion pictures, often follow the idealized picture of Virginia given in 'Swallow Barn'. In South Carolina many adventure novels of frontier life, such as 'The Yemassee' (1835), came from the pen of William Gilmore Simms (1806–70), sometimes called the Cooper of the South.

Thus by 1835 American writers had made a notable start toward creating a new and independent national literature. In Scotland in 1820 Sydney Smith, a famous critic who wrote for the *Edinburgh Review*, had asked: "In the four quarters of the globe, who reads an American book?" Sensitive Americans, conscious of their cultural inferiority, winced at this slighting remark. More and more, however, they had reason to be proud of their writers. In the next 20 years American literature would come to the full flowering which had been hoped for since the Revolution.

The Flowering of American Literature

THE MIDDLE of the 19th century saw the beginning of a truly independent American literature. This period, especially the years 1850–55, has been called the American Renaissance.

More masterpieces were written at this time than in any other equal span of years in American history. New England was the center of intellectual activity in these years, and Ralph Waldo Emerson (1803–82) was the most prominent writer.

Emerson and Thoreau

Emerson began his career as a clergyman. He came to feel, however, that he could better do his work outside the church. Thus he became an independent essayist and lecturer, a lay preacher to Americans. He preached one message—that the individual human being, because he is God's creature, has a spark of divinity in him which gives him great power. "Trust thyself," Emerson said in his essay 'Self-Reliance' (1841). He believed it made no difference what one's work is or where one lives. Emerson himself lived in the village of Concord. There, as oracle and as prophet, he wrote the stirring prose that inspired an entire nation. (*See also* Emerson.)

One person who took Emerson's teaching to heart and lived by it was his Concord neighbor Henry David Thoreau (1817–62). Thoreau lived a life of independence. He was a student of wildlife and the great outdoors. He was also a student of literature, who himself wrote fresh, vigorous prose. His masterpiece is 'Walden, or Life in the Woods' (1854), an account of his two-year sojourn at Walden Pond. "I went to the woods," he wrote, "because I wished to live deliberately"—that is, to decide what is important in life and then to pursue it.

The simplicity of Thoreau's life makes a strong appeal to modern readers. They are impressed too by his essay 'Civil Disobedience' (1849), which converted Emersonian self-reliance into a workable formula for opposing the power of government. He advocated passive resistance, including, if necessary, going to jail, as he himself did. Mahatma Gandhi, who was jailed so many times in his fight to free India from British rule, was strongly influenced by the ideas contained in this essay of Thoreau's. (*See also* Thoreau.)

Popular New England Poets

More conventional and less challenging than the Concord writers were the popular poets of New England. Oliver Wendell Holmes (1809–94) won early renown with 'Old Ironsides' (1830), which told the story of the *Constitution* in such stirring words that people rallied and saved it from destruction. His 'Last Leaf' (1833) and 'Chambered Nautilus' (1858) were also favorites. Holmes took time from his medical practice to write 'The Autocrat of the Breakfast-Table' (1858), which first appeared in the newly founded *Atlantic Monthly*. The autocrat is a thin

HOW JOHN ALDEN COURTED FOR HIS FRIEND
In Longfellow's well-known poem 'The Courtship of Miles Standish', John Alden intends to speak for Miles Standish but actually wins Priscilla for himself. This painting is by W. L. Taylor.

disguise for Holmes himself. Holmes was a witty conversationalist; and through his mouthpiece, the autocrat, he gave lively expression to a variety of opinions (*see* Holmes, Oliver Wendell).

The poems of James Russell Lowell (1819–91) were admired in his day. This wellborn Bostonian was versatile. He was editor of the *Atlantic Monthly*, a professor at Harvard, United States minister to Spain and then to England, a literary critic, and a poet.

Lowell's 'Vision of Sir Launfal' (1848) has long been popular. Fresher and more native is his 'Biglow Papers' (1848–67), rhymed verse in Yankee dialect used for humor and satire. Hosea Biglow, the pretended author, is blessed with common sense and a strong New England conscience. By capturing the thought and speech of the American rustic, Lowell showed one way in which American literature could be truly national. (*See also* Lowell, James Russell.)

The favorite American poet in the 19th century was Henry Wadsworth Longfellow (1807–82). He was a storyteller in verse. 'The Courtship of Miles Standish' (1858), 'Evangeline' (1847), and 'The Song of Hiawatha' (1855) use native incident and character. Longfellow was trying to give the United States legends like those of Europe. His lyrics too were admired. 'A Psalm of Life' (1839) was memorized by generations of school children. (*See also* Longfellow.)

Nearly as popular as Longfellow was John Greenleaf Whittier (1807–92), author of such well-known ballads as 'Barbara Frietchie' (1863). Whittier was a Quaker and thus a foe of slavery, which he attacked in both verse and prose. After the Civil War he wrote 'Snow-Bound' (1866). This homely poem, based on the poet's childhood experiences, pictures farm life in an earlier day. It must have reminded many readers of their own rural childhoods. (*See also* Whittier.)

Poe and Hawthorne

The major writer in the South during these years was Edgar Allan Poe (1809–49). Instead of American characters, themes, and settings, Poe wrote of timeless places and people. He did brilliant work in three areas: poetry, short fiction, and criticism. Poems such as 'The Raven' (1845), 'The Bells' (1849), and 'Ulalume' (1847) are vague in thought but hauntingly beautiful in sound.

Poe's short stories are of two kinds: (1) tales of detection, such as 'Murders in the Rue Morgue' (1843) and 'The Purloined Letter' (1845) (Poe's Dupin being the forerunner of Sherlock Holmes and other later fictional detectives); and (2) psychological tales of terror, such as 'The Fall of the House of Usher' (1839) and 'The Masque of the Red Death' (1842). Both types of stories observe the principles he outlined in his critical writing—that a story should be short, that it should aim at a definite effect, and that all its parts should contribute to the effect, thus making for unity. Modern short-story

THOREAU AT WALDEN
In a quiet meadow near Walden Pond, Thoreau found time to analyze life's essentials. The result of his thoughts was the famous 'Walden'. This picture is by Rudolph Ruzicka (copyright by R. R. Donnelley & Sons Co.).

RALPH WALDO EMERSON
The New England essayist Ralph Waldo Emerson preached that man has a spark of divinity in him which gives him power.

OLIVER WENDELL HOLMES
This popular poet won early fame with 'Old Ironsides', a poem which saved the ship *Constitution* from destruction.

writers owe much to Poe's critical ideas. (*See also* Poe.)

Although Poe disliked most New England writing because it was too obviously moral in intention, he greatly admired the stories of Nathaniel Hawthorne (1804–64). The son of a sea captain from Salem, Mass., Hawthorne grew up in that old port city rich in legends of the past. He steeped himself in the history of Puritan times and laid many of his stories in that period. The earlier settings made his tales shadowy and, because the Puritans were conscious of sin, gave the author a chance to explore the sinful human heart in his fiction. He did so in the stories 'Young Goodman Brown' (1835) and 'The Minister's Black Veil' (1837), as well as in his full-length masterpiece, 'The Scarlet Letter' (1850). His fiction, seemingly simple, is rich and subtle. It is also often profound in its treatment of life's darker side, the side which the Puritans had freely acknowledged but which Hawthorne's contemporaries often chose to ignore. (*See also* Hawthorne.)

Herman Melville

Modern readers are warm in their praise of Hawthorne. They have come to admire also the work of his neighbor and spiritual ally, Herman Melville (1819–91). All but forgotten by the public in his later years, Melville in modern times is regarded as one of the great writers in American literature. He was the first to treat the South Seas in fiction;

'Typee' (1846) and 'Omoo' (1847) give fascinating pictures of this exotic region.

These books and the three that soon followed them prepared Melville to write 'Moby-Dick' (1851), considered by some as the greatest contribution of American letters to world literature. This work is many books in one: an epic, a tragedy, a novel, a treatise on the whaling industry, and a spiritual autobiography. At the story's center is Captain Ahab, who obsessively searches the seven seas to kill the white whale which bit off his leg. Melville's later works, short pieces such as 'Benito Cereno' (1856) and 'Billy Budd' (written shortly before his death), are artfully done and full of meaning. Few writers wrestled more heroically with the basic problems of existence than did Herman Melville. (*See also* Melville.)

Whitman—Poet of the People

The other major writer at mid-century, Walt Whitman (1819–92), was unique. His 'Leaves of Grass' (1855) was new in form and in content. Whitman wrote about his country in a way never done before. At first the little book of strange verse seemed a failure. Emerson, however, recognized its greatness; and now most people agree that it was the first book of truly American poetry.

Here, at last, was the fresh, distinguished bard destined to create an art wholly American. Through

351

Whitman's poetry the new nation is caught in its largeness, its variety, and its great energy. 'One's-Self I Sing' and his major poem, 'Song of Myself', are brilliant and complex utterances of the human spirit freed in the New World.

Walt Whitman's poems are a love letter to his country. To accomplish his purpose of singing the praise of the untrammeled American spirit, Whitman forsook the confining poetic forms of his day. His poems are melodic chants, suited to the ear.

Readers of American literature around the world have turned to Whitman as the spokesman for the new democratic society. No poet has celebrated that society with more enthusiasm or more poetic genius than Walt Whitman. His verses are charged with the energetic American spirit. They are a striking contrast to the neat meters and rhymes of conventional poetry previously written. Since Whitman's death, his writing has influenced many other American poets. (*See also* Whitman, Walt.)

A CLEVER DETECTIVE STORY BY POE

Edgar Allan Poe's famous story 'The Purloined Letter' turns on the fact that a completely obvious hiding place will be overlooked. This picture is by W. A. Dwiggins (copyright by R. R. Donnelley & Sons Co.).

Transition to the Modern Age

THE CIVIL WAR sharply interrupted American literary activity. Although seven of the ten major authors of the American Renaissance continued to write after the war years, most of these had done their best work by 1860. Literary leadership passed to a new generation of writers. Their work is interesting in itself. It is interesting also because it prepared the way for the excellent writing which followed in the 20th century.

The Civil War was a harsh experience. In addition to enduring the pain and sorrow of war, Americans were shocked by the threat to the nation itself. They realized that democracy was not an inevitable system of government; it could fail, though it had survived the test of civil war. It was subject to further strains, however, from corruption in Washington, D. C.; from growing industrialism, which moved people from farms to cities and led to bitter quarrels between workers and employers; and from immigration and westward expansion.

These problems and disappointments were perplexing. No longer could men look to the future with complete optimism. In place of the exuberant chants to democracy he had written in 1855, Whitman, in 'Democratic Vistas' (1871), was urging Americans to look critically at their society and work hard to keep it healthy. In short, postwar conditions prompted the people to view their world directly and honestly.

Writing in the War Years

The most memorable writing of the war years came from the pen of Abraham Lincoln (1809–65). The prairie president had earlier shown his mastery of the art of cogent and compelling argument. In his wartime utterances he rose to new heights. The Gettysburg Address and his second inaugural address are prose of haunting beauty.

The Confederacy is represented in verse by Henry Timrod (1828–67) and Paul Hamilton Hayne (1830–86). Had not the war shaken their health and devastated their region, they might have achieved more. Timrod's 'Ode' (1873) on the graves of the Confederate dead in a Charleston cemetery is an excellent poem.

Sidney Lanier (1842–81) is the most interesting Southern poet of the period. He is best known for his musical verse, such as 'The Song of the Chattahoochee' (1883), and for poems of vague mysticism, such as 'The Marshes of Glynn' (1878). (*See also* Lanier.)

Whitman wrote some of his best verse after the war. 'Drum-Taps' (1865) contains brilliant and moving war vignettes; and the excellent long poem 'Passage to India' (1871) voices his hope for world unity and his belief in the oneness of creation.

The outstanding poet of these years, however, wrote works as different from Whitman's as they could possibly be. The lyrics of Emily Dickinson (1830–86) are short, compressed, rhymed, and metrical; whereas Whitman's lines, in free verse, are loose, unrhymed and somewhat diffuse. There is another difference as well: whereas Whitman had his poetic fingers on the nation's pulse, Emily Dickinson lived in a world not much larger than the garden of her father's house in Amherst, Mass. The world of her imagination, however, was as vast as the universe. In tight, rhyming hymn meters she wrote of the nature she knew intimately, of love, and of the ultimate questions of death and immortality.

The works of Emily Dickinson were hardly known during her lifetime beyond a small circle of friends, for they were not published until after her death. Modern readers have come to value her as one of the truly great American poets. (*See also* Dickinson.)

Regional Prose After the Civil War

The postwar years seemed better suited to prose than to verse. The regional story or novel became popular. Bret Harte (1836–1902) acquainted the country with the Western miner in such stories as 'The Luck of Roaring Camp' (1868) (*see* Harte). Joel Chandler Harris (1848–1908), through his character Uncle Remus, depicted plantation life in the Deep South (*see* Harris). George Washington Cable (1844–1925) wrote of Creoles and the bayou country near New Orleans. Indiana was the province of Edward Eggleston (1837–1902), whose 'Hoosier Schoolmaster' (1871) became a favorite.

Harriet Beecher Stowe (1811–96) is best known for her novel about slavery, 'Uncle Tom's Cabin' (1852); but her 'Oldtown Folks' (1869) is a fine portrayal of life in New England (*see* Stowe). New England is also pictured in the stories of Sarah Orne Jewett (1849–1909) and Mary E. Wilkins Freeman (1852–1930).

Every section of the country was represented in these local-color stories. The customs, manners, and especially the speech ways of the locality were carefully portrayed. Such elements made the stories realistic. However, because the authors usually depicted their regions as they were in their own youth, they often flavored their stories with sentiment. The mixture of realism and sentiment was appealing, and local-color stories filled the pages of the leading magazines until the end of the century.

Three Major Novelists

The three major novelists in this period stand in an interesting relationship to one another. At one extreme is Mark Twain (1835–1910), self-educated, a product and a depicter of the frontier. At the other extreme is Henry James (1843–1916), wealthy, educated by tutors, a resident in Europe, a man of cosmopolitan tastes. His novels portray Americans traveling or living in Europe and so confronting an old, rigid, and traditional society. Twain and James were not personally acquainted, but each was a good friend of William Dean Howells (1837–1920), who in several ways embodied both the provincial and the cosmopolitan interests of his two friends.

Mark Twain's works are of several kinds. 'The Innocents Abroad' (1869) and 'Roughing It' (1872) are books of travel which combine personal anecdotes, description, and humorous comment in a delightful mixture. Twain's interest in the past is seen in 'The Prince and the Pauper' (1882); in the

WALT WHITMAN AND 'LEAVES OF GRASS'
The poet sprawls on a high point above the shore of Long Island Sound and contemplates the grass that gave him the title for his most famous work. This picture is by Lewis C. Daniel (copyright by Doubleday, Doran & Co., Inc.).

MARK TWAIN'S 'HUCKLEBERRY FINN'
No boy in fiction is more beloved than Huck Finn. His adventures on the Mississippi River have been relived by generations of readers. This picture is by E. W. Kemble (drawn in 1884 for the first edition).

Americans in the process of experiencing Europe, thereby contrasting two cultures, the old and the new. In this contrast the manners of Americans sometimes suffer by comparison with those of Old World aristocrats. Morally, however, James's Americans compare favorably with Europeans. The author saw good in both groups and was less interested in taking sides than in exploring, in an elaborate and elegant style, the many differences between them. 'The American' (1877), 'The Portrait of a Lady' (1881), and 'The Ambassadors' (1903) all develop the international theme. James's fiction is not always easy to read, but it is as rich and subtle as any in American literature.

William Dean Howells was a champion of realism. Novels, he believed, should present life as it is, not as it might be. Accordingly his books study types of persons prominent in American life of the time: women in the professions, in 'Dr. Breen's Practice' (1881); the self-made man, in 'The Rise of Silas Lapham' (1885); factory workers and summer resort people, in 'Annie Kilburn' (1889). His books also discuss serious social questions honestly: divorce, in 'A Modern Instance' (1882); and social justice, in 'A Hazard of New Fortunes' (1889). Taken together, Howells' novels give a full, clear picture of American life in the last years of the 19th century. (*See also* Howells.)

The Birth of Naturalism

The novels of Howells and James presented life truthfully as the authors saw it. In the opinion of a later generation, however, their fiction omitted great areas of life: Howells was too polite, too proper; and James was too exclusively concerned with the leisure classes. Several novelists at the turn of the century therefore undertook to portray those sides of life, often ugly, which they felt had not been fully recognized in literature.

Stephen Crane (1871–1900) depicted life in New York City slums in 'Maggie: A Girl of the Streets' (1893); and in the excellent 'The Red Badge of Courage' (1895) he wrote of how the Civil War, in all its horror, impinged on the consciousness of a youthful recruit. Frank Norris (1870–1902) showed the ugly violence in economic life in 'The Octopus' (1901), which depicts the struggle between railroads and wheat ranchers in California, and in 'The Pit' (1903), a story of speculation on the Chicago wheat exchange. The vigorous, often ruthless, activities of men in the business world were also the province of Theodore Dreiser (1871–1945). His 'Sister Carrie' (1900), 'The Financier' (1912), and 'The Titan' (1914) show men and women caught up in the cruel, raw forces of commercial life. In his best work, 'An

hilarious 'A Connecticut Yankee in King Arthur's Court' (1889); and in 'Personal Recollections of Joan of Arc' (1896), which Twain thought his best work.

Favorites with most readers are his Mississippi River books: 'The Adventures of Tom Sawyer' (1876), a delightful treatment of a boy's life in a small town; 'Life on the Mississippi' (1883), which re-creates vividly the colorful days of steamboating on the great river; and 'The Adventures of Huckleberry Finn' (1884), Twain's masterpiece.

The adventures of Huck, the boy, and Jim, the runaway slave, as they float downstream on a raft, appeal to all readers. It is Huck who tells the story throughout, and his language, so limited yet so expressive, is a literary achievement of the first order (*see* Writing, Creative). One of the great novels of the world, Mark Twain's story set a new style in fiction by showing the literary possibilities in common, everyday American speech. (*See also* Twain.)

Henry James studied the American character in his stories and novels but by a method quite different from Twain's. James's usual way was to depict

American Tragedy' (1925), youthful Clyde Griffiths is victimized by these forces.

All these novels were written in the mode of literary naturalism, which invited writers to examine human beings objectively, as a scientist studies nature. In portraying ugliness and cruelty, the authors refrained from preaching about them; rather they left readers to draw their own conclusions about the life so presented. Naturalistic fiction shocked many readers; but in revealing hitherto neglected areas of life, it greatly broadened the scope of fiction.

The 19th century closed with the Gay Nineties. In the opinion of many, however, the times were more somber than gay. Political corruption, violent conflicts between capital and labor, loss of religious certitude, concern over the developments of science —these causes, among others, gave to literature a darker cast than it had had in earlier times. The writer who best caught this mood was Henry Adams (1838–1918), historian and descendant of two presidents of the United States. In 'The Education of Henry Adams' (1918) he depicts himself as a misfit and, he would have readers believe, a failure. A failure he certainly was not, but the book shows why he thought he was. Unlike his forbears, Adams felt powerless to affect the course of history. Men were at the mercy of great social and economic forces, which worked for the disintegration of society. This view seemed sound to many. For them the 'Education' summed up an era. (*See also* Adams, Henry.)

Modern American Literature

AMERICAN LITERATURE of the 20th century is different from earlier literature in significant ways. It is possible to list several of its characteristics which are implied in the term *modern:*

1. The scope of modern literature is broad. For example, writers are able to treat ugliness and violence freely.

2. The meanings of modern literature are deeper and more complex than in earlier writing because life itself has become more complex. Present-day writers have learned much about economics, sociology, anthropology, and especially psychology; and their works often embody ideas drawn from these new areas of thought.

3. Modern writing is technically sophisticated. To write about the life of today, authors have discovered new ways to express their ideas. These ways are fresh and stimulating, but they sometimes make severe demands on readers.

4. If technique is complicated, the language of modern writing is simpler than that of earlier times. In place of the old formal language, thought proper for literature, contemporary writers have substituted language much closer to that of everyday speech.

5. Modern literature exhibits more variety than that of earlier periods. Because life today is varied, so is the writing that reflects it varied—in subject, in region portrayed, in philosophical outlook, in scope (broad and sociological or concentrated and psychological), and in form and technique.

In a short space, only some of the outstanding writers and their works can be noted. The following discussion groups the chief modern writers by literary field—poetry, drama, and fiction.

SINCLAIR LEWIS' MAIN STREET
This 1920 scene shows Main Street in Sauk Centre, Minn., from which Sinclair Lewis took the name for his novel 'Main Street'. A satirical novelist, Lewis wrote of small-town life during the years following World War I.

Poetry in the Middle West

In the years following the Civil War, poetry, except for the work of Whitman and Emily Dickinson and two or three minor poets, was at low ebb. The age was one of prose. Early in this century, however, poetry once again came into its own.

In 1912 Harriet Monroe (1860–1936) founded the little magazine *Poetry: a Magazine of Verse*, in Chicago. She sought to encourage struggling poets everywhere and to train readers in the art of reading verse. The first issue of *Poetry* quoted Whitman for its motto: "To have great poets there must be great audiences too." The founding of *Poetry* was a timely act, for, as Harriet Monroe soon found out, there were a number of unknown poets who needed just such an outlet for their work. *Poetry* published the first or early work of nearly every distinguished modern American poet. (*See also* Monroe, Harriet.)

Poetry magazine discovered excellent new writers in its own backyard, the Middle West, never until then known for its poets. One such discovery was Edgar

Lee Masters (1869–1950), known primarily for 'Spoon River Anthology' (1915). It is a series of poems in free verse (that is, unrhymed and not in strict meters). Each poem is a report on his own life by a character now buried in the village graveyard. As each person reveals himself he helps build up the picture of an entire Illinois village. More than 200 people are there: "The weak of will, the strong of arm, the clown, the boozer, the fighter." Not all the poems are good, but some are excellent, and the total effect of the book is strong.

Vachel Lindsay (1879–1931) was another *Poetry* discovery. 'The Congo and Other Poems' (1914) secured him fame, especially the title poem, with its jazz rhythms and its strong refrain:

Then I saw the Congo, creeping through the black,
Cutting through the Jungle with a golden track.

Almost as popular are 'General William Booth Enters into Heaven' (1913) and the more stately poem 'Abraham Lincoln Walks at Midnight' (1914).

The third striking discovery by *Poetry* was Carl Sandburg (1878–1967). Like Masters and Lindsay, Sandburg made poetry out of the materials of the Midwest. He first won a prize with 'Chicago' (1914), still his best-known poem, which begins:

Hog-butcher for the World,
Tool-maker, Stacker of Wheat,
Player with Railroads and the
Nation's Freight-handler;
Stormy, husky, brawling,
City of the Big Shoulders.

The importance of Whitman's influence on modern American poetry is unmistakably shown in Sandburg's lines. Sandburg also used the sprawling unmetered and unrhymed line, and he too was the spokesman for all the American people. Like the martyred Lincoln, whom he portrayed in a great biography, Sandburg affirmed a faith in the democratic process and in the people for whom it operates. "The people will live on," the poet asserted confidently in 'The People, Yes' (1936), his book of democratic chants. (*See also* Sandburg.)

Poets of Modern New England

About the time that *Poetry* was first published in the Middle West, two Eastern poets attracted favorable attention. The first, Edwin Arlington Robinson (1869–1935), had for years been writing poems ignored by all but a few. After 1912, with the newly awakened interest in poetry, Americans began to read his verse. Today he is ac-

THOMAS WOLFE'S 'LOOK HOMEWARD, ANGEL'
'Look Homeward, Angel', the first of Wolfe's long, passionate novels, is in many ways his best. This scene was taken from the stage version of the book.

TWO FAMOUS AMERICAN POETS
Robert Frost (left), a New Englander, and Carl Sandburg, a Midwesterner, wrote poetry which was universally loved.

INFLUENTIAL INNOVATOR IN POETRY
T. S. Eliot, shown here receiving an honorary degree in Great Britain, his adopted country, influenced many modern poets.

knowledged to be one of the most important American poets of the 20th century.

Robinson wrote about defeated people, those who found the complexities of life baffling and wearing. Everything he wrote, however, had a dry humor and wit as well as a profound sense of pity for men's suffering. Although most of his best poetry concerned New England, Robinson wrote several long poems about King Arthur's knights. 'Tristram' (1927) was a best seller. (*See also* Robinson.)

The second New England poet to win both popularity and fame was Robert Frost (1874–1963). His poems, such as 'Mending Wall' (1914) and 'Birches' (1916), deal lovingly with the country Frost knew as a New Hampshire farmer. As Emily Dickinson described her own poetry, he wrote "New Englandly," particularly in his early poems. His writing treats of simple, enduring experiences, with a delightful humor and tenderness. Simple his poems are, but at the same time they are deep and provocative. Some poets appeal to masses of readers; others appeal chiefly to persons of sophisticated taste. Frost is admired by both groups. (*See also* Frost, Robert.)

T. S. Eliot and New Techniques

The Middle West and New England both appear in the poetry of T. S. Eliot (1888–1965). Born and educated in the United States, Eliot later became a British subject. Nonetheless the sights and memories of his earlier years make up the substance of his best poetry, with a few exceptions.

Although Eliot has published few poems, they have had a tremendous influence on modern poetic technique. 'The Love Song of J. Alfred Prufrock' (1915) was the first poem of Eliot's to be widely read. 'Prufrock' describes the thoughts of a timid, well-educated man on his way to an elegant party. He fears what the people there will say about his clothes, his figure, his thinning hair—"in short, I am afraid." Prufrock stands for the fearful people of the world, who, though outwardly prosperous, are inwardly defeated.

Eliot's second important poem was 'The Waste Land' (1922). Here modern life is portrayed as a land of desert and rocks, lacking water upon which life depends. The rich, heroic stories of the past are referred to repeatedly, as a contrast to the sterile, empty present. The poem is an immediate reflection of the disillusionment which many artists felt after World War I, when life seemed meaningless and trivial. 'The Waste Land' at first puzzled critics with its technique of placing splintered fragments of thought against one another in striking combinations.

Eliot's later poetry, as complicated in technique as 'The Waste Land', is more affirmative than disillusioned. 'Four Quartets' (1943) is a reasoned discussion of the foundations of the Christian faith. The influence of Eliot's ideas and his technique has been very great. Other modern poets have followed his lead. (*See also* Eliot, Thomas Stearns.)

E. E. Cummings (1894-1962) satirized modern pettiness and emptiness, as Eliot had done, but Cum-

357

WILLA CATHER'S 'MY ÁNTONIA'
The novelist Willa Cather won fame with regional stories, such as 'My Ántonia'. This picture is by W. T. Benda (copyright by Houghton-Mifflin).

book-length epic of the Civil War. Elinor Wylie (1885–1928) and Sara Teasdale (1884–1933) wrote poetry of delicate perception.

Mention should be made also of popular light verse. Although not "great," such verse, when skillfully written, is enjoyed by many. Ogden Nash (born 1902) was noted for his playful satires, deliberately rendered in bad versification which includes outrageous rhymes. The verse of Phyllis McGinley (born 1905), which often appeared in *The New Yorker* magazine, is more conventional in form. In her verse she captured the details of modern living and implicitly commented on life satirically or with affection. Feeling is subdued, however, because of the detachment afforded by her clever versifications.

mings also wrote lyrics of tenderness and beauty. His technique is arresting, because his verse usually omits punctuation marks and capitalization (he signed his name "e e cummings").

Another exciting modern poet is Hart Crane (1899–1932), whose early death cut short a promising career. His poem 'To Brooklyn Bridge', a portion of the longer work 'The Bridge' (1930), is reminiscent of Whitman's 'Crossing Brooklyn Ferry'. As in the Whitman poem, the scene of New York Harbor is used symbolically to say things about man and human relations.

The poetry of Wallace Stevens (1879–1955) is also distinguished modern verse. An insurance executive in Hartford, Conn., Stevens in a sense was a poetic amateur, yet his verse is brilliant. Like all true poets, he was in love with the medium of language. In his verse every word counts, for it is made to carry subtle shades of meaning and to affect the reader through its sound as well. 'Peter Quince at the Clavier' (1923) is one of his best-known poems. Marianne Moore (born 1887) also used poetic symbols extensively in her work.

The old traditional appeals of poetry were not forgotten with increased use of new techniques. Edna St. Vincent Millay (1892–1950) used the sonnet form to express age-old concepts of romantic love. Archibald MacLeish (born 1892) wrote stirringly of the Spanish conquest of Mexico in 'Conquistador' (1932), and Stephen Vincent Benét (1898–1943) re-created the American past in 'John Brown's Body' (1928), a

Modern American Drama

Thus far no mention has been made of the drama. The reason is that although the theater was active during the 19th century, the American plays produced were mostly sensational melodrama and hence of small literary importance. The case is different with drama of the 20th century, however. As the country has matured culturally, audiences have encouraged serious playwrights to write plays which, if not so great as those of Sophocles and Shakespeare, are interesting and important as literature.

The first step in creating a serious drama was to abandon the improbable situations of melodrama and to adopt the realistic approach of the Norwegian dramatist Henrik Ibsen. 'Street Scene' (1929), by Elmer Rice (1892–1967), and 'Dead End' (1935), by Sidney Kingsley (born 1906), show life as it is lived, using realistic scenery and authentic dialogue.

Realism on the stage was an improvement over melodrama, but too frequently it was unable to get beneath the surfaces of life. For this reason dramatists experimented with new techniques. 'Beggar on Horseback' (1924), by George S. Kaufman (1889–1961) and Marc Connelly (born 1890), and 'The Adding Machine' (1923), by Rice, use the technique of expressionism, in which realism is clearly abandoned in favor of fantasy and other representational devices in an effort to show meanings beneath appearances.

'Our Town' (1938), by Thornton Wilder (born 1897), was also experimental. No scenery is used, and actors are planted in the audience. With such unconventional methods the playwright presented a sympathetic picture of life in a small American town.

Another technical experiment in the modern theater was drama in verse. Sophocles and Shakespeare used verse in their plays, and some modern dramatists have sought to follow their example in an effort to achieve emotional intensity. Several of the plays of Maxwell Anderson (1888–1959), such as 'Winterset' (1935), are written in blank verse (see Anderson, Maxwell). The same is true of T. S. Eliot's 'Murder in the Cathedral' (1935), a dramatization of the martyrdom of Thomas Becket, archbishop of Canterbury. These experiments in verse drama were interesting but have had no lasting influence on dramatic construction in the modern theater.

Eugene O'Neill—Leading American Playwright

It is generally agreed that the leading American dramatist is Eugene O'Neill (1888–1953). He tried bold experiments in dramatic technique. In such plays as 'The Emperor Jones' (1920) and 'The Hairy Ape' (1922) all the attention is concentrated on the central character, the other characters being unimportant. In 'The Great God Brown' (1926) the actors use masks to distinguish between the real thoughts and the assumed thoughts of the characters. In 'Strange Interlude' (1928) the characters reveal their true opinions by uttering two kinds of remarks: one to the other characters, the other to the audience, as a dramatic aside.

O'Neill's most ambitious work was 'Mourning Becomes Electra' (1931), a trilogy that presents in American terms Sophocles' drama of Agamemnon's return from the Trojan War. It is a somber work, as are most of O'Neill's plays. He was versatile enough, however, to achieve many different kinds of dramatic success. 'Ah, Wilderness!' (1933), a study of adolescence, is an amusing and refreshing folk comedy of New England life. In quantity, variety, profundity, and technical boldness, O'Neill is clearly the leading figure in modern American drama. (See also O'Neill.)

Williams and Miller

The most important playwrights since O'Neill were Tennessee Williams (born 1914) and Arthur Miller (born 1915). Williams portrayed a decadent Southland with tarnished or frustrated belles in 'A Streetcar Named Desire' (1947) and 'Cat on a Hot Tin Roof' (1955). 'The Glass Menagerie' (1944) also portrays faded grandeur, but more tenderly.

'Death of a Salesman' (1949), written by Miller, reveals the aloneness of an ordinary, undistinguished man. Undeniably poignant, the play approaches true tragedy. 'The Crucible' (1953), based on the witchcraft persecutions in colonial New England, reminds modern audiences that fear of the unknown, mass hysteria, and perversions of justice infect life in the 20th century as they did in the 17th.

'GONE WITH THE WIND'
Margaret Mitchell's massive book is a good example of the historical novel which has become popular in recent years. The book, dealing with the Civil War, became an all-time best seller. This scene is from the movie made from the novel.

'MOURNING BECOMES ELECTRA', BY EUGENE O'NEILL
This masterpiece by O'Neill, who is generally agreed to be the leading American dramatist, presents in American terms a three-part drama by Sophocles.

tion formed the background for 'Drums Along the Mohawk' (1936), by Walter Edmonds (born 1903), and for 'Northwest Passage' (1937), by Kenneth Roberts (1885–1957).

The American frontier West has been a favorite subject for historical romancers. Standing considerably above most Westerns is 'The Big Sky' (1947), by A. B. Guthrie (born 1901). His narrative skill did justice to the great epic theme of the West.

Regional Novelists

A number of modern novelists have sought to picture the region of the country that they knew best. As a rule these "regionalists" are more authentic than their predecessors, the post-Civil War local-color writers. Willa Cather (1875–1947) is best remembered for depicting Nebraska of frontier days. 'O Pioneers!' (1913) and 'My Ántonia' (1918) are heartwarming stories of settlement on the prairie. (*See also* Cather.)

The Norwegian-born novelist O. E. Rölvaag (1876–1931) wrote a moving story of Norwegian settlers, 'Giants in the Earth' (translated 1927), which can be claimed for American literature. The Midwest in more recent times is the subject of 'The Folks' (1934) and 'Iowa Interiors' (1926), by Ruth Suckow (1892–1960).

The list of Southern regionalists is long, for the American South has produced an impressive number of fine writers in recent years—Eudora Welty (born 1909), Carson McCullers (1917–1967), Jesse Stuart (born 1907), and, most notable, William Faulkner (1897–1962).

The works of Robert Penn Warren (born 1905) are laid in his native Southland. The best is perhaps his study of a political demagogue in Louisiana, 'All the King's Men' (1946). One of the outstanding novelists of recent years, Warren was also a skillful poet and critic.

The metropolitan sections of the East have formed the settings of several distinguished novelists. Edith Wharton (1862–1937), a disciple of Henry James, wrote of the well-to-do classes of New York City, as in 'The House of Mirth' (1905). Equally gifted was Ellen Glasgow (1874–1945), who studied changing attitudes and social behavior in and near Richmond, Va., in 'Barren Ground' (1925) and 'Vein of Iron' (1935). New England aristocrats, genteel and rather stuffy, were the special concern of John P. Marquand (1893–1960). The best of his kindly satires is per-

Modern American Fiction

Poetry has enjoyed a rebirth, and drama has come of age artistically. It is prose fiction, however, that is the major form of literary expression in the 20th century.

Writers of important modern fiction are numerous, the level of their achievement is high, and the variety of their work is remarkable. Grouping of some of the more significant writers reveals their variety.

Historical Novelists

The historical novel has appealed to Americans eager to discover their cultural roots. Although the form has been popular since the days of James Fenimore Cooper, the massive best seller 'Anthony Adverse' (1933), by Hervey Allen (1889–1949), gave a new vogue to the historical novel. 'Gone with the Wind' (1936), by Margaret Mitchell (1900–49)—about the Civil War and also a big book—was an all-time best seller. The times of the American Revolu-

haps 'The Late George Apley' (1937), the story of a vigorous Boston aristocrat who succumbs to the pressures of social convention, until his life is stunted and meaningless.

Although Pearl S. Buck (born 1892) did not deal with American themes, she ranks high among modern American writers. She portrayed Chinese peasants sympathetically in 'The Good Earth' (1931) and other novels. (*See also* Buck.)

Depicters of Their Eras

Just as some novelists are associated with the regions of which they write, others are associated with the times of which they seem to be the spokesmen. F. Scott Fitzgerald (1896–1940) caught the mood of the Roaring Twenties in 'This Side of Paradise' (1920) and 'The Great Gatsby' (1925). A volume of his stories was appropriately titled 'Tales of the Jazz Age' (1922). (*See also* Fitzgerald.)

Small-town life in the postwar years is the theme of 'Main Street' (1920), by Sinclair Lewis (1885–1951). His 'Babbitt' (1922) satirizes the dull, unimaginative life of a middle-class businessman. (*See also* Lewis, Sinclair.)

In the following decade, the years of the big depression, novelists concerned themselves with problems of a people caught in hard times. 'The Grapes of Wrath' (1939), by John Steinbeck (born 1902), tells of the Joads, a family of Oklahoma farmers who are driven from their drought-stricken land and make a heroic trek West in an old jalopy. It is a memorable and moving tale. John Dos Passos (born 1896) is also associated with the depression years. His anger toward the system that permitted wholesale misery fired several novels openly critical of abuses of the economic system. His major work is the trilogy 'U.S.A.' (1937), which chronicles the lives of several persons over a 30-year period. It is not a flattering picture of American life; but the portrait is vivid, made so by the unique way in which the story is told. (*See also* Steinbeck; Dos Passos.)

The novels of Thomas Wolfe (1900–38) have moved many readers. A physical giant of colossal appetites, Wolfe wrote novels proportionately huge. They tell of a young man finding his place in the world and so are full of the passion, ecstasy, anger, and frustration of youth. The first to be written, 'Look Homeward, Angel' (1929), is in many ways the best; but almost equally powerful is the last, 'You Can't Go Home Again' (1940). (*See also* Wolfe, Thomas.)

Hemingway and Faulkner

The two greatest American novelists of recent times are Ernest Hemingway (1899–1961) and William

TENNESSEE WILLIAMS' 'GLASS MENAGERIE'
This powerful play portrays, as do many dramas by Tennessee Williams, faded grandeur. It is, however, tenderer than his later works.

Faulkner. Both are representative of the modern world, yet in several important ways they are quite different. Hemingway's novels are about man alone, uprooted and facing the Great Enemy (which takes several forms) as bravely as he can. Faulkner, on the other hand, presented a society, a variety of persons of differing colors and classes, in his native Mississippi. His work is a saga of the South, and the same characters reappear in his successive novels.

Both writers were concerned with moral values. For Hemingway courage was the paramount virtue. Man cannot win in the struggles in which he engages, but the important thing is how he behaves. If he meets his defeat without flinching, then he achieves "grace under pressure," which is a triumph of sorts, that gives meaning and dignity to his struggle. Faulkner's moral values were social rather than personal. The South was cursed with slavery, which bred countless problems before, but especially since, the Civil War. The good people, white and black, do what they can to solve the problems; but they are

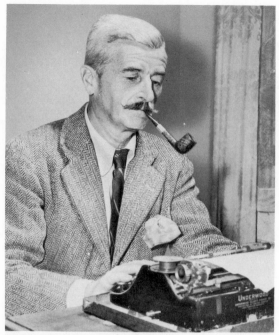

NOVELIST WILLIAM FAULKNER
The novels of William Faulkner constitute a saga of the American South. His characters reappear in successive books.

often helpless before the conniving, unscrupulous ones.

Finally, the writing styles of the two men are markedly different. Faulkner's prose is ornate and complex; his sentences are long and complicated; and many nouns and adjectives are used. Hemingway's style is quite the opposite. His sentences are short and pointed; adjectives are used sparingly. The effect is one of great power and compression.

The level of performance of these two writers is high. The outstanding works by Hemingway include 'The Sun Also Rises' (1926); 'A Farewell to Arms' (1929); 'For Whom the Bell Tolls' (1940); and the minor masterpiece 'The Old Man and the Sea' (1952). Among Faulkner's best-known books are 'The Sound and the Fury' (1929), 'Light in August' (1932), 'Absalom, Absalom!' (1936), and 'The Town' (1957). (*See also* Faulkner; Hemingway.)

The Modern Short Story

Although the novel seems to be the dominant form of prose fiction in modern times, at least equally impressive is the short story. It is a form to which American literature has some claim. The features of the short story were first defined by Poe, and many Americans practiced in the form to fill the newly founded magazines after the Civil War. Most of the important 20th-

century authors have written at least a few excellent stories. In former years authors spoke of trying to write the "great American novel," envisioning, apparently, a gigantic work of fiction which somehow would capture the entire American experience. Such an intention has come to seem more and more like a fond dream, as the country has grown and as modern life has become more varied. In place of the broad canvas, many writers prefer the vignette; they feel that fiction can best explore and reveal life if it does so in small, manageable units.

In addition to the novelists discussed above, these are outstanding short-story writers: Ring Lardner (1885–1933), Sherwood Anderson (1876–1941), Katherine Anne Porter (born 1894), Irwin Shaw (born 1913), James Thurber (1894–1961), Eudora Welty (born 1909), John Cheever (born 1912), and J. D. Salinger (born 1919). Many other authors have distinguished themselves in this art form.

The story of American literature is far from finished. One thing is clear: after years of tentative and shaky beginnings, American literature has matured to the point where it is probably the most widely read literature in the world today. Some 140 years after Sydney Smith's scornful query, "Who reads an American book?", one feels it more appropriate to ask, "Who does not read an American book?" Today people everywhere are curious about American civilization and culture; and they have been able to satisfy that curiosity by reading in the rich and varied body of writing known as American literature.

NOVELIST-ADVENTURER ERNEST HEMINGWAY
A Nobel prize winner, as was Faulkner, Ernest Hemingway wrote of man alone facing life bravely without flinching at danger.

Representative American Writers

COLONIAL TIMES IN AMERICA

BETWEEN the founding of Jamestown (1607) and the signing of the Declaration of Independence (1776), scattered English settlements grew into a group of colonies ready to declare themselves a nation. The colonists changed from thinking and acting as Englishmen to full awareness of themselves as Americans.

During this time almost all writing was devoted to spiritual concerns and to practical matters of politics and promotion of settlements. In New England, fiction was considered sinful and little poetry was written. A few interesting personal journals and diaries survive.

Bradford, William (1590–1657), historian—'History of Plimoth Plantation'.

Byrd, William (1674–1744), historian and diarist—'History of the Dividing Line'; 'Secret Diary'.

Edwards, Jonathan (1703–58), theologian—'Personal Narrative'; 'The Freedom of the Will'.

Mather, Cotton (1663–1728), theologian—'Wonders of the Invisible World'; 'Magnalia Christi Americana'.

Sewall, Samuel (1652–1730), diarist—'Diary of Samuel Sewall 1674–1729'; 'The Selling of Joseph'.

Taylor, Edward (1642–1729), poet—'God's Determinations'; 'Sacramental Meditations'.

Ward, Nathaniel (1578?–1652), essayist—'The Simple Cobler of Aggawam'.

Wigglesworth, Michael (1631–1705), poet—'The Day of Doom'.

THE SHAPING OF A NEW NATION

THE GREAT questions in the last years of the 18th century were political ones. Should the colonists declare independence from England? Once they had done so, how, they asked, should they govern themselves? The literature of political discussion and debate in these years is of high quality. Immediately following independence, writers also made efforts to develop a native literature. This is the period of beginning for poetry, fiction, and drama in the United States.

Barlow, Joel (1754–1812), poet—'The Vision of Columbus' ('The Columbiad'); 'The Hasty Pudding'.

Brown, Charles Brockden (1771–1810), novelist—'Wieland'; 'Edgar Huntly'; 'Jane Talbot'.

Crèvecoeur, Michel Guillaume St. Jean de (1735–1813), essayist—'Letters from an American Farmer'.

Franklin, Benjamin (1706–90), prose writer—'Autobiography'; 'Poor Richard's Almanack'.

Freneau, Philip (1752–1832), poet—'The Indian Burying-Ground'; 'The British Prison Ship'.

Hamilton, Alexander (1755?–1804), essayist—'The Federalist' (coauthor).

Hopkinson, Francis (1737–91), poet—'The Battle of the Kegs'.

Jefferson, Thomas (1743–1826), historian—'Notes on the State of Virginia'.

Paine, Thomas (1737–1809), political philosopher—'Common Sense'; 'The Crisis'; 'The Rights of Man'.

Payne, John Howard (1791–1852), playwright—'Clari, or the Maid of Milan' (with song 'Home, Sweet Home').

Rowson, Susanna (Haswell) (1762–1824), novelist—'Charlotte Temple'; 'Rebecca'.

Trumbull, John (1750–1831), poetic satirist—'M'Fingal'; 'Progress of Dullness'.

Webster, Noah (1758–1843), lexicographer—'Spelling Book'; 'American Dictionary of the English Language'.

Weems, Mason Locke (1759–1825), biographer—'The Life and Memorable Actions of George Washington'.

LITERATURE OF THE EARLY REPUBLIC

IN THE EARLY years of the 19th century several full-fledged American writers developed. The most notable among them were Bryant, Cooper, and Irving. These writers were recognized even in England. In different ways each of them tried to make his works American.

Bird, Robert M. (1806–54), novelist and playwright—'Nick of the Woods'; 'The Gladiator'.

Brackenridge, Hugh Henry (1748–1816), novelist—'Modern Chivalry'.

Bryant, William Cullen (1794–1878), poet—'Thanatopsis'; 'To a Waterfowl'; 'A Forest Hymn'.

Cooper, James Fenimore (1789–1851), novelist—'The Pilot'; 'The Last of the Mohicans'; 'The Spy'; 'The Deerslayer'; 'The Pathfinder'; 'The Pioneers'.

Irving, Washington (1783–1859), essayist and short-story writer—'A History of New York, by Diedrich Knickerbocker'; 'The Alhambra'; 'The Sketch Book'.

Kennedy, John Pendleton (1795–1870), novelist—'Swallow Barn'; 'Horse-Shoe Robinson'.

Simms, William Gilmore (1806–70), novelist and poet—'The Yemassee'; 'Atalantis'.

Thompson, Daniel Pierce (1795–1868), novelist—'The Green Mountain Boys'; 'The Rangers'.

THE FLOWERING OF AMERICAN LITERATURE

FROM 1836 to the Civil War was a period of rapid growth in the United States. The nation was self-sufficient in agriculture, and the Eastern cities buzzed with commerce. War with Mexico brought California into the Union just when gold was discovered there. This event and the opening of Oregon sent thousands of pioneers westward. However, slavery in the South and in new Western territories became a fighting issue.

In the East the period was a golden age. Essays by Emerson and Thoreau vied with tales by Poe. Novels were popular, and Longfellow's poems were best sellers. Historians such as Parkman and Prescott added knowledge of the American past.

Bancroft, George (1800–91), historian—'History of the United States'.

Dana, Richard Henry, Jr. (1815–82), autobiographer—'Two Years Before the Mast'.

Emerson, Ralph Waldo (1803–82), poet and essayist—'Self-Reliance'; 'Compensation'; 'Nature'; 'Poems'.

Fuller, Margaret (1810–50), sociological writer and critic—'Woman in the Nineteenth Century'; 'Papers on Literature and Art'.

Hawthorne, Nathaniel (1804–64), novelist and short-story writer—'The Scarlet Letter'; 'The House of the Seven Gables'; 'Tanglewood Tales'.

Holmes, Oliver Wendell (1809–94), poet, essayist, novelist—'Old Ironsides'; 'The Chambered Nautilus'; 'The Autocrat of the Breakfast-Table'.

Longfellow, Henry Wadsworth (1807–82), poet—'The Song of Hiawatha'; 'Paul Revere's Ride'; 'Evangeline'; 'The Courtship of Miles Standish'.

Longstreet, Augustus Baldwin (1790–1870), novelist—'Georgia Scenes'.

Lowell, James Russell (1819–91), poet, critic, essayist—'The Vision of Sir Launfal'; 'Biglow Papers'; 'Among My Books'; 'My Study Windows'.

Melville, Herman (1819–91), novelist—'Moby-Dick'; 'Typee'; 'Omoo'; 'White-Jacket'; 'Billy Budd'.

Motley, John Lothrop (1814–77), historian—'The Rise of the Dutch Republic'.

Parkman, Francis (1823–93), historian—'The Oregon Trail'; 'A Half-Century of Conflict'.

Poe, Edgar Allan (1809–49), poet, critic, short-story writer—'The Raven'; 'The Poetic Principle'; 'Tales of the Grotesque and Arabesque'; 'The Bells'.

Prescott, William Hickling (1796–1859), historian—'Conquest of Mexico'; 'Conquest of Peru'.

Thoreau, Henry David (1817–62), essayist—'Walden; or, Life in the Woods'; 'Excursions'; 'Cape Cod'.

Whitman, Walt (1819–92), poet—'Leaves of Grass'; 'November Boughs'; 'Drum-Taps'; 'Democratic Vistas'.

Whittier, John Greenleaf (1807–92), poet—'Snow-Bound'; 'The Barefoot Boy'; 'Barbara Frietchie'.

TRANSITION TO THE MODERN AGE

THE CIVIL WAR scarred the United States for four bloody years. The North was quick to recover; the South less so. As the nation revived, however, the pulse of expansion and growth quickened. Cities boomed; industries expanded; and rail lines stretched from coast to coast. The conquest of the wilderness was nearly complete. Great fortunes were made, by a few individuals, and many social and economic injus-tices arose from the ruthless competition of getting ahead.

Writers reacted in various ways. Some wrote of the lawless West, others of the culture of the East. Many found subjects for fiction and poetry among their sur-roundings; these were the first *regional*, or *local-color*, writers. A few protested against what they considered the evils of the age.

Adams, Henry (1838–1918), historian—'The Education of Henry Adams'; 'Mont-Saint-Michel and Chartres'.

Alcott, Louisa May (1832–88), novelist and short-story writer—'Little Women'; 'Little Men'; 'Moods'.

Bierce, Ambrose (1842–1914?), short-story writer—'In the Midst of Life'; 'Can Such Things Be?'.

Cable, George Washington (1844–1925), novelist and short-story writer—'The Grandissimes'; 'Old Creole Days'.

Crane, Stephen (1871–1900), novelist—'The Red Badge of Courage'; 'The Little Regiment'; 'Maggie: A Girl of the Streets'.

De Forest, John William (1826–1906), novelist—'Miss Ravenel's Conversion from Secession to Loyalty'.

Dickinson, Emily (1830–86), poet—'Poems'; 'Letters'.

Dreiser, Theodore (1871–1945), novelist—'Sister Carrie'; 'An American Tragedy'; 'The Genius'.

Eggleston, Edward (1837–1902), novelist and historian—'The Hoosier Schoolboy'; 'The Hoosier School-master'; 'The Circuit Rider'.

Frederic, Harold (1856–98), novelist—'The Damnation of Theron Ware'; 'The Copperhead'.

Freeman, Mary E. Wilkins (1852–1930), novelist and short-story writer—'A New England Nun'; 'Madelon'.

Garland, Hamlin (1860–1940), novelist and short-story writer—'Main-Travelled Roads'; 'A Son of the Middle Border'; 'Prairie Folks'.

Hale, Edward Everett (1822–1909), novelist—'The Man Without a Country'.

Harris, Joel Chandler (1848–1908), short-story writer—'Uncle Remus' stories; 'On the Plantation'.

Harte, (Francis) Bret(t) (1836–1902), short-story writer—'The Luck of Roaring Camp'; 'The Outcasts of Poker Flat'; 'The Twins of Table Mountain'.

Hayne, Paul Hamilton (1830–86), poet—'Legends and Lyrics'; 'The Broken Battalions'.

Hearn, Lafcadio (1850–1904), essayist—'In Ghostly Japan'; 'Creole Sketches'; 'Chita'.

Howe, E(dgar) W(atson) (1853–1937), novelist, journal-ist—'The Story of a Country Town'; 'Plain People'.

Howells, William Dean (1837–1920), novelist—'A Modern Instance'; 'The Rise of Silas Lapham'.

James, Henry (1843–1916), novelist—'Daisy Miller'; 'The American'; 'The Portrait of a Lady'.

James, William (1842–1910), psychologist and philosopher—'Principles of Psychology'; 'Pragmatism'; 'Varieties of Religious Experience'.

Jewett, Sarah Orne (1849–1909), novelist and short-story writer—'Betty Leicester'; 'Tales of New England'.

Kilmer, (Alfred) Joyce (1886–1918), poet—'Trees and Other Poems'; 'Rouge Bouquet'.

Lanier, Sidney (1842–81), poet—'The Marshes of Glynn'; 'The Song of the Chattahoochee'.

London, Jack (1876–1916), novelist—'The Call of the Wild'; 'The Sea Wolf'; 'Martin Eden'.

Miller, Joaquin (Cincinnatus Hiner Miller) (1841?–1913), poet—'Songs of the Sierras'.

Moody, William Vaughn (1869–1910), playwright and poet—'Gloucester Moors'; 'Ode in Time of Hesitation'.

Norris, Frank (1870–1902), novelist—'The Octopus'; 'The Pit'; 'McTeague'.

O. Henry (William Sydney Porter) (1862–1910), short-story writer—'The Four Million'.

Page, Thomas Nelson (1853–1922), novelist and short-story writer—'In Ole Virginia'.

Riley, James Whitcomb (1849–1916), poet—'Rhymes of Childhood'; 'The Old Swimmin' Hole'.

Stowe, Harriet Beecher (1811–96), novelist—'Uncle Tom's Cabin'; 'Oldtown Folks'.

Timrod, Henry (1828–67), poet—'Ode'; 'A Cry to Arms'.

Twain, Mark (Samuel Langhorne Clemens) (1835–1910), novelist and humorist—'The Adventures of Tom Sawyer'; 'The Adventures of Huckleberry Finn'; 'Life on the Mississippi'.

Wister, Owen (1860–1938), novelist—'The Virginian'.

MODERN AMERICAN LITERATURE

THE 20th century began quietly, but soon new forces brought profound changes. Although science and technology enriched material life, two World Wars and the prospect of a third raised grave concern about the future. The federal government intervened increasingly in the activities of the people. The nation also learned that it was involved in the problems of peoples around the globe.

Literature reflected various reactions to the new circumstances. Some writers were deeply pessimistic; others viewed the same realities with hope for the future. One literary school surveyed the American past in an attempt to find meaning for the present. The writing that seemed most likely to survive emphasized enduring human values and the unquenchable vitality of man's spirit.

Allen, Hervey (1889–1949), novelist and biographer—'Anthony Adverse'; 'Action at Aquila'.

Anderson, Maxwell (1888–1959), playwright—'Elizabeth the Queen'; 'Mary of Scotland'; 'Valley Forge'; 'Winterset'; 'Key Largo'; 'Joan of Lorraine'.

Anderson, Sherwood (1876–1941), novelist and short-story writer—'Poor White'; 'Dark Laughter'; 'Winesburg, Ohio'; 'The Triumph of the Egg'.

Barry, Philip (1896–1949), playwright—'Holiday'; 'The Philadelphia Story'; 'White Wings'.

Benét, Stephen Vincent (1898–1943), poet, novelist, short-story writer—'Five Men and Pompey'; 'John Brown's Body'; 'The Devil and Daniel Webster'.

Bradford, Roark (1896–1948), novelist—'Ol' Man Adam an' His Chillun'; 'John Henry'.

Bromfield, Louis (1896–1956), novelist—'Early Autumn'.

Brooks, Van Wyck (1886–1963), critic—'America's Coming-of-Age'; 'The Flowering of New England'.

Buck, Pearl S(ydenstricker) (born 1892), novelist—'The Good Earth'; 'The Mother'; 'The Patriot'.

Carmer, Carl (born 1893), short-story writer and folklorist—'Stars Fell on Alabama'.

Cather, Willa (1875–1947), novelist and short-story writer—'O Pioneers!'; 'My Ántonia'; 'A Lost Lady'; 'Death Comes for the Archbishop'.

Cheever, John (born 1912), novelist and short-story writer—'The Wapshot Chronicle'.

Coffin, Robert P(eter) Tristram (1892–1955), poet, novelist, essayist—'Strange Holiness'; 'John Dawn'; 'An Attic Room'.

Connelly, Marc(us) (born 1890), playwright—'The Green Pastures'; 'Beggar on Horseback' (coauthor).

Crane, (Harold) Hart (1899–1932), poet—'White Buildings'; 'The Bridge'.

Cullen, Countee (1903–46), poet—'Color'; 'Copper Sun'.

Cummings, E(dward) E(stlin) (1894–1962), poet and novelist—'No Thanks'; 'The Enormous Room'.

Dos Passos, John (born 1896), novelist—'Manhattan Transfer'; 'U.S.A.' (trilogy).

Dunne, Finley Peter (1867–1936), humorist—'Mr. Dooley in Peace and in War'; 'Mr. Dooley's Philosophy'.

Durant, Will(iam James) (born 1885), philosopher and historian—'The Story of Philosophy'; 'The Story of Civilization'.

Edmonds, Walter D(umaux) (born 1903), novelist—'Drums Along the Mohawk'.

Eliot, T(homas) S(tearns) (1888–1965), poet, critic, playwright—'Prufrock and Other Observations'; 'The Waste Land'; 'Four Quartets'; 'The Sacred Wood'; 'Murder in the Cathedral'.

Farrell, James T(homas) (born 1904), novelist—'Studs Lonigan' (trilogy).

Faulkner, William (1897–1962), novelist—'The Sound and the Fury'; 'Light in August'; 'Sanctuary'; 'Absalom, Absalom!'; 'The Town'.

Ferber, Edna (1887–1968), short-story writer and novelist—'So Big'; 'The Girls'; 'Show Boat'; 'Cimarron'; 'Giant'; 'Ice Palace'.

Field, Rachel (1894–1942), novelist—'All This, and Heaven Too'; 'Time Out of Mind'.

Fisher, Dorothy Canfield (1879–1958), novelist—'The Bent Twig'; 'The Brimming Cup'.

Fitzgerald, F(rancis) Scott (1896–1940), novelist and short-story writer—'The Great Gatsby'; 'This Side of Paradise'; 'The Last Tycoon'; 'Tales of the Jazz Age'.

Freeman, Douglas Southall (1886–1953), biographer—'R. E. Lee'; 'George Washington'.

Frost, Robert (1874–1963), poet—'A Boy's Will'; 'North of Boston'; 'In the Clearing'.

Gale, Zona (1874–1938), novelist and short-story writer—'Miss Lulu Bett'; 'Friendship Village'.

Glasgow, Ellen (1874–1945), novelist—'Barren Ground'; 'The Romantic Comedians'; 'Vein of Iron'.

Green, Paul Eliot (born 1894), playwright—'In Abraham's Bosom'.

Guthrie, A(lfred) B(ertram) (born 1901), novelist—'The Big Sky'; 'The Way West'.

Hart, Moss (1904–61), playwright—'You Can't Take It with You' (coauthor); 'Act One' (autobiography).

H. D. (Hilda Doolittle) (1886–1961), poet—'Sea Garden'; 'Red Roses for Bronze'.

Hellman, Lillian (born 1905), playwright—'The Little Foxes'; 'Watch on the Rhine'.

Hemingway, Ernest (1899–1961), novelist and short-story writer—'A Farewell to Arms'; 'For Whom the Bell Tolls'; 'The Old Man and the Sea'.

Howard, Sidney (Coe) (1891–1939), playwright—'They Knew What They Wanted'; 'The Silver Cord'.

Hughes, (James) Langston (1902–67), poet—'The Negro Mother'; 'A New Song'.

Hughes, Rupert (1872–1956), biographer and novelist—'George Washington'; 'No One Man'.

Jeffers, Robinson (1887–1962), poet—'Roan Stallion'; 'Give Your Heart to the Hawks'.

Kaufman, George S(imon) (1889–1961), playwright—'Beggar on Horseback' (coauthor); 'You Can't Take It with You' (coauthor).

Kingsley, Sidney (born 1906), playwright—'Dead End'.

Lardner, Ring(gold Wilmer) (1885–1933), humorist and short-story writer—'You Know Me, Al'.

Lewis, Sinclair (1885–1951), novelist—'Main Street'; 'Babbitt'; 'Arrowsmith'; 'Dodsworth'.

Lindsay, (Nicholas) Vachel (1879–1931), poet—'The Congo'; 'General William Booth Enters into Heaven'.

Lowell, Amy (1874–1925), poet and critic—'Sword Blades and Poppy Seeds'; 'John Keats'.

McCullers, Carson (1917–1967), novelist—'The Heart Is a Lonely Hunter'; 'Member of the Wedding'.

McGinley, Phyllis (born 1905), poet—'Times Three'.

MacLeish, Archibald (born 1892), poet and playwright—'Conquistador'; 'Land of the Free'; 'J. B.'.

Markham, Edwin (1852–1940), poet—'The Man with the Hoe, and Other Poems'.

Marquand, John P(hillips) (1893–1960), novelist—'The Late George Apley'; 'Wickford Point'.

Masters, Edgar Lee (1869–1950), poet and novelist—'Spoon River Anthology'; 'Domesday Book'.

Mencken, H(enry) L(ouis) (1880–1956), essayist and critic—'Prejudices'; 'The American Language'.

Millay, Edna St. Vincent (1892–1950), poet—'Renascence'; 'Second April'; 'Conversation at Midnight'.

Miller, Arthur (born 1915), playwright—'All My Sons'; 'Death of a Salesman'; 'The Crucible'.

Mitchell, Margaret (1900–49), novelist—'Gone with the Wind'.

Moore, Marianne (born 1887), poet—'Poems'; 'Collected Poems'; 'What Are Years'.

Morley, Christopher (1890–1957), essayist, poet, novelist—'Romany Stain'; 'Kitty Foyle'.

Nash, Ogden (born 1902), writer of satirical verse—'The Primrose Path'; 'I'm a Stranger Here Myself'.

Neihardt, John G(neisenau) (born 1881), poet—'The Song of Hugh Glass'.

O'Neill, Eugene (Gladstone) (1888–1953), playwright—'The Iceman Cometh'; 'Mourning Becomes Electra'.

Parker, Dorothy (1893–1967), short-story writer and poet—'Not So Deep as a Well'; 'Laments for the Living'; 'Here Lies: the Collected Stories'.

Porter, Katherine Anne (born 1894), short-story writer and novelist—'Flowering Judas'; 'Ship of Fools'.

Ransom, John Crowe (born 1888), poet—'Chills and Fever'.

Rice, Elmer (1892–1967), playwright—'The Adding Machine'; 'Street Scene'; 'Dream Girl'.

Roberts, Kenneth (Lewis) (1885–1957), novelist and essayist—'Northwest Passage'; 'Oliver Wiswell'.

Robinson, Edwin Arlington (1869–1935), poet—'The Man Who Died Twice'; 'Tristram'; 'Merlin'.

Rölvaag, O(le) E(dvart) (1876–1931), novelist—'Giants in the Earth'.

Salinger, J(erome) D(avid) (born 1919), short-story writer and novelist—'Nine Stories'; 'The Catcher in the Rye'; 'Franny and Zooey'.

Sandburg, Carl (1879–1967), poet and biographer—'The People, Yes'; 'Abraham Lincoln: The Prairie Years'; 'Abraham Lincoln: The War Years'.

Saroyan, William (born 1908), short-story writer, novelist, playwright—'The Time of Your Life'; 'My Name Is Aram'; 'The Human Comedy'.

Shapiro, Karl (Jay) (born 1913), poet—'V-Letter'.

Shaw, Irwin (born 1913), playwright, short-story writer, novelist—'Bury the Dead'; 'The Young Lions'.

Sheean, (James) Vincent (born 1899), journalist and novelist—'Personal History'; 'A Day of Battle'.

Sherwood, Robert E(mmet) (1896–1955), playwright—'Abe Lincoln in Illinois'; 'The Petrified Forest'.

Sinclair, Upton (born 1878), novelist—'The Jungle'.

Steinbeck, John (born 1902), novelist and short-story writer—'Of Mice and Men'; 'The Grapes of Wrath'.

Stevens, Wallace (1879–1955), poet—'Harmonium'; 'Transport to Summer'.

Stribling, T(homas) S(igismund) (1881–1965), novelist—'The Forge'; 'The Store'; 'Unfinished Cathedral'.

Stuart, Jesse (Hilton) (born 1907), novelist and poet—'Taps for Private Tussie'; 'Beyond Dark Hills'.

Suckow, Ruth (1892–1960), novelist and short-story writer—'Iowa Interiors'; 'The Folks'.

Tarkington, (Newton) Booth (1869–1946), novelist and short-story writer—'Penrod'; 'Monsieur Beaucaire'.

Teasdale, Sara (1884–1933), poet—'Rivers to the Sea'.

Thurber, James (Grover) (1894–1961), humorist and essayist—'My Life and Hard Times'.

Van Doren, Carl (1885–1950), critic and biographer—'American Literature'; 'Benjamin Franklin'.

Warren, Robert Penn (born 1905), poet and novelist—'All the King's Men'; 'Night Rider'.

Welty, Eudora (born 1909), short-story writer and novelist—'A Curtain of Green'; 'The Ponder Heart'.

Wharton, Edith (1862–1937), novelist and short-story writer—'Ethan Frome'; 'The House of Mirth'.

Wilder, Thornton (Niven) (born 1897), playwright and novelist—'The Bridge of San Luis Rey'; 'Our Town'.

Williams, Tennessee (Thomas Lanier Williams) (born 1914), playwright—'The Glass Menagerie'; 'A Streetcar Named Desire'.

Williams, William Carlos (1883–1963), poet and novelist—'The White Mule'; 'Paterson'.

Wolfe, Thomas (Clayton) (1900–38), novelist—'Look Homeward, Angel'; 'You Can't Go Home Again'.

Wright, Richard (1908–60), novelist and short-story writer—'Native Son'; 'Black Boy'.

Wylie, Elinor (1885–1928), poet and novelist—'Nets to Catch the Wind'; 'The Orphan Angel'.

BIBLIOGRAPHY FOR AMERICAN LITERATURE
HISTORY AND CRITICISM

Abel, Darrel. American Literature (Barron's, 1963).

Bogan, Louise. Achievement in American Poetry, 1900–1950 (Regnery, 1951).

Brooks, Van Wyck. Makers and Finders: a History of the Writer in America, 1800–1915, 5v. (Dutton, 1936–52).

Brooks, Van Wyck. Writer in America (Avon, 1964).

Brooks, Van Wyck and Bettmann, O. L. Our Literary Heritage (Dutton, 1956).

Cambridge History of American Literature, 3v. in 1 (Macmillan, 1954).

Cantwell, Robert. Famous American Men of Letters (Dodd, 1956).

Gassner, John, ed. Best American Plays (Crown, published annually).

Hart, J. D. Oxford Companion to American Literature (Oxford, 1965).

Larrabee, Eric, ed. American Panorama (N.Y. Univ. Press, 1957).

Parrington, V. L. Main Currents in American Thought (Harcourt, 1939).

Perry, Bliss. American Spirit in Literature (Chronicles of America Series) (Yale Univ. Press, 1918).

Scherman, D. E. and Redlich, Rosemarie. America: the Land and Its Writers (Dodd, 1956).

Spiller, R. E. and others. Literary History of the United States (Macmillan, 1964).

Wagenknecht, E. C. Cavalcade of the American Novel (Holt, 1952).

West, R. B. Short Story in America, 1900–1950 (Regnery, 1956).

ANTHOLOGIES

Benét, W. R., comp. Poems for Youth (Dutton, 1925).

Benét, W. R. and Pearson, N. H., eds. Oxford Anthology of American Literature, 2v. (Oxford, 1938).

Fadiman, Clifton, ed. American Treasury (Harper, 1955).

Foerster, Norman, ed. American Poetry and Prose (Houghton, 1960).

Foley, Martha, ed. Best American Short Stories (Houghton, published annually).

Johnson, J. W., ed. American Negro Poetry (Harcourt, 1931).

Matthiessen, F. O., ed. Oxford Book of American Verse (Oxford, 1950).

Quinn, A. H. Representative American Plays (Appleton, 1953).

Untermeyer, Louis, ed. Anthology of the New England Poets (Random, 1948).

Untermeyer, Louis, ed. The Britannica Library of Great American Writing, 2v. (Encyclopaedia Britannica, 1960).

Untermeyer, Louis, ed. Modern American Poetry (Harcourt, 1962).

Williams, Oscar, ed. A Little Treasury of American Poetry (Scribner, 1955).

Woods, R. L., ed. Family Reader of American Masterpieces (Crowell, 1959).

AMIENS (*ăm-yăn'*), **France.** The ancient cathedral city of Amiens lies on the Somme River in northern France. The river valley is a natural route both for trade and for invading armies. Hence its largest city is an important center of commerce and has been the scene of a number of decisive battles. Since the Middle Ages it has also been a center of the textile-weaving industry. But it is noted above all for its magnificent Cathedral of Notre Dame. Amiens is the capital of the department of Somme.

THE GOTHIC CATHEDRAL OF AMIENS
The western façade of the Cathedral of Notre Dame of Amiens is a marvel of medieval decoration.

Celebrated as one of the most splendid monuments of Gothic architecture, the cathedral dates from the 13th century. Begun in 1220 by the architect Robert de Luzarches it was enlarged from time to time, and completed about 1288. The interior is unusually spacious and beautiful. At its highest point the ceiling of the nave is nearly 140 feet above the floor. The choir stalls are adorned with more than 3,500 wood figures, carved in the 16th century.

Invasions and bombardments of the city have several times threatened the cathedral with destruction. In the Franco-Prussian War (1870) Amiens fell to Germany, and early in World War I it was stormed and held briefly by German troops. Because of its importance as a railway center and its commanding position on the Somme River, it became a British army base in that war (*see* Somme River). In 1918 it withstood another German attack. The cathedral, damaged by bombs and artillery shells, was repaired after the war. During the German conquest of France in 1940, Amiens was heavily bombed before it fell, but the cathedral remained practically intact.

The city was captured by Caesar and became a stronghold of the Roman Empire. One of the most momentous events associated with its name is the signing of the Treaty of Amiens between Napoleon and Great Britain. This occurred in the city hall on March 27, 1802. The treaty gave the British the only breathing spell they had during the wars following the French Revolution. It was the rupture of this treaty, in 1803, which enabled the United States to purchase from Napoleon the Louisiana Territory, a possession too remote to be defended by the French.

Amiens today is a commercial and industrial center. Its manufactures include silk, woolen, and cotton cloths, velvet, and carpets. Amiens is 80 miles north of Paris. Population (1962 census), 101,677.

AMMONIA. Few people realize that they may never have seen ammonia. The household cleaner called "ammonia" is actually a water solution of the true ammonia. This is an invisible gas under ordinary conditions, a compound of one nitrogen atom and three hydrogen atoms (NH_3).

The manufacture of ammonia is a big and important part of the chemical industry. Today most ammonia is produced by the direct union of nitrogen and hydrogen through the Haber-Bosch process or similar processes (*see* Nitrogen). Great quantities are used in the manufacture of fertilizers. Ammonia is also used in refrigeration (*see* Refrigeration) and in the manufacture of nitric acid.

Ammonia is released as proteins decompose, and long ago it was produced by distilling the horns and hoofs of animals. The old name *spirits of hartshorn* (for ammonia water) refers to that process.

In combination with acids ammonia yields several *ammonium salts*. Ammonium chloride is the *sal ammoniac* used in the manufacture of dry-cell batteries (*see* Battery) and also as a deoxidizer in soldering. Ammonium nitrate is used in making explosives, ammonium carbonate (*sal volatile*) for smelling salts, and ammonium bicarbonate for certain kinds of baking powder. Fertilizers also contain ammonium compounds. In all these compounds, the gas unites with a fourth atom of hydrogen to form the especially close combination called a *radical*. The ammonium radical behaves as an alkali metal (*see* Alkali Metals).

At normal pressure, ammonia gas liquefies at $-28°$ F. ($-33.3°$ C.) and freezes at $-107.9°$ F. ($-77.7°$ C.). It is easily liquefied by compression and is shipped in steel tanks as *anhydrous* (water-free) *ammonia*.

AMMUNITION. Since the invention of the hand cannon in the 1300's there has been a steady improvement in guns and in the types of ammunition fired. Today ammunition ranges from the small but deadly cartridge of a boy's hunting rifle to the huge shells fired by naval guns. It also includes the powerful atomic artillery shell of the United States Army.

All modern ammunition has three basic parts—projectile, propellant, and primer. The *projectile* is the bullet, slug, shot, or warhead that is actually fired at the target. The *propellant* is the main charge of powder that throws, or propels, the projectile out of the gun barrel. The *primer* contains the high-explosive material that ignites the powder.

A firearm such as a rifle or a pistol is loaded with a *cartridge*. This is a brass case containing the projectile (bullet), powder charge, and primer. Shotgun ammunition is also a self-contained unit called a *shotshell*. It differs from a cartridge in that it has a heavy paper

MODERN AMMUNITION IN ACTUAL SIZE
Three common types of sporting ammunition are: 30-06 (.30 caliber, 1906 model) rifle cartridge (left); 12-gauge shotgun shell (center); and .22-caliber rifle cartridge (right).

case enclosing powder and projectile (shot pellets and wadding or a rifled slug). The paper case is joined to a metal base which holds the primer. (For a definition of the bore sizes, or calibers, of cartridges and the gauges of shotgun shells, *see* Firearms.)

Large military weapons fire several different types of ammunition. One type is self-contained. In another type, the projectile can be removed to alter the kind or amount of propellant, or the projectile and the metal case which contains powder and primer may be two separate units. Ammunition for the largest guns is assembled at the gun site in three separate units. The projectile, bags of powder, and primer are then inserted into the breech in that order.

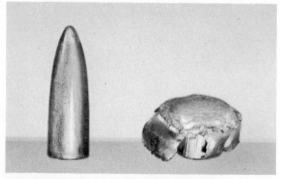

THE "STOPPING POWER" OF A BULLET
Shown here is a .220-caliber Swift soft-point bullet before and after striking a target of gelatin. The bullet travels at an initial rate of 4,110 feet per second and mushrooms on impact.

The firing action in most ammunition begins with a sharp blow from a firing pin on the primer. The impact sets off the high-explosive priming material. This sends a jet of flame into the main powder charge. The burning powder produces expanding gases which propel the projectile out of the barrel at high speed.

Bullets for Hunting and for War

The first projectiles were stones and balls of iron or bronze. Later lead came into use because it was heavier and could more easily be molded into balls. Beginning about 1840 the shape of bullets gradually changed from a spherical to a rounded-cone design. This shape helped overcome air resistance and provided far greater accuracy and range.

Modern military bullets fired by rifles and machine guns are sharply pointed with a lead or hardened steel core completely enveloped by a copper and zinc (gilding metal) jacket. This jacket prevents the bullet from mushrooming, or expanding, when it strikes. Such bullets are of three main types: *ball*, or regular; *armor piercing* (AP), which has a hardened steel core; and *tracer*, which is treated with a compound that burns for about 700 yards in flight.

Hunters want a bullet to mushroom, for this provides "stopping power." Soft-point bullets are jacketed except for the tip, which mushrooms during penetration. Hollow-point bullets have an open cavity in the tip. They mushroom and break into fragments after penetration. Bullets with controlled expansion, such as the silvertip, mushroom only after hair, hide, and outer tissues have been penetrated. These bullets have a thin layer of metal at the tip and a harder, thicker metal jacket over the remainder of the core. Lead bullets without jackets are used chiefly in .22-caliber rifles and in some types of pistol ammunition.

From Black to Smokeless Powder

The first propellant used in ammunition was black powder made from a mixture of saltpeter, sulfur, and charcoal. Its major fault was that its rate of burning could not be controlled and much effective energy was lost; that is, a bullet would be forced out of the barrel before all the powder had turned into gas. Other drawbacks were the loud noise and heavy smoke cloud that accompanied firing.

Despite these disadvantages black powder remained in use until the late 1800's. Then the development of nitrocellulose (cotton treated with nitric acid) provided the basis for the first smokeless powder. It was made by coating the powder grains with various chemical agents and by varying the length and diameter of the grains. In this way the rate of burning could be controlled and the maximum force of the explosion utilized. This increase in the power of propellants permitted a reduction in the size of cartridges. It also led to use of hard metal jackets on bullets so that the powerful powder would not cause them to jump the rifling or to melt in the barrel.

Another improvement in propellants came in 1932 with the development of "ball" powder—round rather than cylinder-shaped grains of nitrocellulose. The added energy derived from this powder permitted the manufacture of still smaller cartridges such as the .308-caliber Winchester.

The "Quick-Tempered" Primers

In the early days of ammunition the propellant was ignited from a small quantity of gunpowder spread near the touchhole at the breech of the gun. This priming powder was itself ignited by lighted sticks or by sparks from a piece of pyrite or flint.

A long step forward came in 1807 when a Scottish clergyman, Alexander Forsyth, discovered that certain compounds, called fulminates, could be ignited with a sharp blow. By the mid-1800's fulminate of mercury primers in the form of percussion caps were used. Today primers are made of such compounds as lead azide or lead styphnate plus oxidizing materials.

Development of Self-contained Ammunition

For hundreds of years loading ammunition into guns was a slow, crude process. First a certain amount of powder was poured down the barrel. The bullet was then rammed down on top of the powder charge. Finally, the gun had to be primed.

It was not until about 1865 that the first true self-contained cartridge was produced in the United

BULLETS USED DURING THE ERA OF BLACK POWDER

Shown here (left to right) are a lead ball; .58-caliber Springfield; Volcanic bullet and cutaway view of Volcanic bullet showing space for propellant; .44 caliber; 44-40 Winchester (.44 caliber, 40 grains of powder); 45-70 Ballard; and 40-70 Ballard. After the rounded-cone shape came into use bullets changed little until the introduction of smokeless powder.

States. The priming material was placed in the outer rim of a metal case which enclosed both powder and bullet. The cartridge was fired by a blow of the firing pin on the rim. Today the .22-caliber rimfire cartridges still use this principle.

Center-fire cartridges were designed later. The priming material was placed in a small cup inserted in a pocket in the center of the metallic case. Center-fire cartridges gained wide use after 1873.

The history of shotgun ammunition parallels that of other firearms. Shotshells with heads of brass and cases of paper have been used since about 1900. The use of smokeless powder permitted a reduction in the size of shotshells. In the days of black powder a shotgun as large as 2 gauge was used. The largest gauge manufactured now is 10, and the trend is toward still smaller sizes.

AMOEBA (a-mē'ba). A tiny bit of shapeless jelly with a dark spot inside it—this is what an amoeba looks like when seen through a microscope. The amoeba is the lowest form of animal life. Various kinds dwell in fresh and salt water, in soil, and in the digestive tract of man and other animals.

The amoeba consists of a single cell of *protoplasm*, the substance of which all living things are made (*see* Protoplasm). The surface of the cell is a membrane. Water passes in and out of the membrane, but the fats, salts, proteins, and carbohydrates of the protoplasm cannot escape through it. If the amoeba is cut apart, the pieces instantly form new membranes.

The protoplasm consists of two parts—the *cytoplasm* and the *nucleus*. The cytoplasm is a simple jellylike material with a clear outer layer and a granular inner part in which the nucleus lies embedded. The amoeba cannot live without the nucleus. It is necessary to reproduction and to the digestion of food. The nucleus makes a new amoeba by simply pinching in two in the middle (called *fission*). The two halves then pull apart, each half forming a new amoeba (*see* Cell). In this way amoeboid life is continued and increases indefinitely.

One of the most interesting things about the amoeba is the way it moves its shapeless body. The fluid cytoplasm pushes forward and forms a projecting lobe called a *pseudopod*, meaning "false foot." As new pseudopods form the old ones flow back into the general mass of cytoplasm. Thus the creature slowly progresses by an irregular, flowing movement from one side to the other. The name amoeba comes from a Greek word that means "change," referring to this constant change of shape by throwing out pseudopods.

The amoeba has no mouth, but may take in food at any point on its surface. It feeds by flowing over and surrounding a smaller one-celled plant or animal. Food particles are enclosed in a drop of water called a *food vacuole*. There may be several food vacuoles in the body at the same time. When the food is digested, the temporary "stomach" disappears. Indigestible portions are eliminated in the simplest way possible. They are pushed to the outer surface and the creature moves away, leaving the refuse behind.

Another body located in the cytoplasm is the *contractile vacuole*. Its purpose is to regulate the water

CHIEF EVENTS IN AN AMOEBA'S LIFE

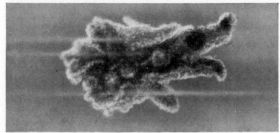

The film of water between two pieces of glass on a microscope stage is an ocean for *Amoeba proteus*. Here it is magnified about 1,000 times. The lobes at the right are pseudopods.

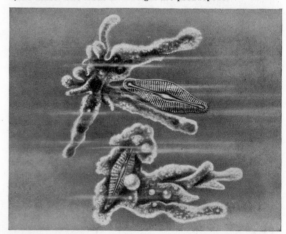

Meeting a small boat-shaped plant called a diatom, the amoeba simply reaches out and surrounds it. The food is enclosed in a drop of water in which digestion takes place.

Here are shown the steps by which an amoeba becomes two amoebas. The nucleus divides in half, and the cytoplasm pinches together in the middle until the two pieces separate. Each new amoeba has a nucleus and half of the parent cytoplasm.

content of the amoeba. It pumps water out through a tiny pore to keep pace with any excess water in the cytoplasm. (For a drawing of the amoeba, showing the nucleus and vacuoles, *see* Life.)

Like all animals, the amoeba "breathes." It absorbs oxygen from the water and discharges carbon dioxide through the cell membrane. It has reactions to stimuli (*tropism*). If it is touched or shaken, it rolls into a round ball (*thigmotropism*). It moves away from a strong light (*negative phototropism*) or from water that is too hot or too cold.

A few species of amoebas live in the digestive tract of man. Most of them are harmless. One species, however, *Endamoeba histolytica*, causes a serious disease, amebic dysentery. Carried by sewage, polluted water, unclean hands, and unwashed fruits and vegetables, it lives in the large intestine and eats cells and tissues. Amoebas belong to the phylum *Protozoa* (*see* Protozoa).

AMPÈRE, André Marie (1775–1836). While awaiting execution during the French Revolution, Jean Jacques Ampère wrote that his greatest expense had been for books and scientific instruments for his son, André Marie, whom he had tutored. The investment proved worthwhile. André Marie Ampère became known as the father of the theory of electromagnetism.

André Marie Ampère was born Jan. 22, 1775, in the village of Polémieux, near Lyons, France. His father was a justice of the peace. André Marie was recognized as a prodigy in his early years. In 1793, the year his father was guillotined, he devised an international language intended to unite mankind and promote peace. Compassion for all humanity was one of Ampère's lifelong traits.

Marriage; Honors

From about the age of 21, Ampère gave private lessons at Lyons in chemistry, mathematics, and language. In 1799 he married his childhood sweetheart, Julie Carron, and the following year their son, Jean Jacques Antoine, was born. In 1801 Ampère accepted a professorship of physics and chemistry at Bourg. His sick wife and infant son remained in Lyons, where Julie Ampère died of tuberculosis three years later. This was a tragedy from which Ampère never wholly recovered; but he dedicated himself with greater zeal to his experiments. A second marriage, in 1807, was a failure, lasting only two years. There was one child, a daughter. In 1809 Ampère was appointed professor of mathematics at the École Polytechnique in Paris. Five years later he was honored by membership in the Institut National.

Develops Electromagnetic Theory

In 1820 Ampère heard of the work of the Danish physicist Hans Christian Oersted, who had observed that an electric current deflects a magnetic needle. The news of this phenomenon stimulated Ampère, and he quickly formulated a theoretical explanation of electromagnetism and related phenomena. His paper on the subject was presented to the Académie des Sciences one week after he first heard of Oersted's work. Ampère applied mathematical formulas to the reactions between magnets and electric currents (Ampère's Law). (*See also* Electricity.) His theories formed the basis for the modern science of electrodynamics.

Ampère also invented the astatic needle, which led to the development of the galvanometer (*see* Galvanometer). In 1824 Ampère became a professor of physics at the Collège de France in Paris. His son, who became a famous lecturer and literary historian, also taught there.

Ampère later wrote a remarkable work on the philosophy of science in an attempt to classify all human knowledge. He also wrote on differential and integral calculus; the theory of probability; optics; animal physiology; and other scientific subjects. The intimate details of his life were carefully recorded in his journals and in his personal letters. André Marie Ampère died in Marseilles, France, on June 10, 1836. The ampere, or unit of flow of an electric current, was named for him.

AMSTERDAM, Netherlands. The *hoofdstad* (head city) of the Netherlands is Amsterdam. It is one of Europe's most picturesque capitals. It is also a leading commercial, financial, industrial, and cultural center. The city is situated in the province of

North Holland on the Amstel River and on the IJ River, an arm of the IJsselmeer (formerly called the Zuider Zee). Since the restoration of the House of Orange in 1815, Dutch rulers have been crowned in the 17th-century Nieuwe Kerk (New Church). Most governmental activities, however, are conducted at The Hague, the seat of government (*see* Hague, The).

Industries and Places of Interest

Amsterdam is in the shape of a crescent, with the Dam Square as its center. It has some 40 canals, bordered by elms and crossed by nearly 400 bridges. These canals so divide the city that it consists of about 100 islands. (For airview of Amsterdam, *see* Netherlands.) Because the sand and loam on which the city is built cannot support large structures, Amsterdam's tall, narrow, gabled houses are perched on wooden piles driven down to the clay subsoil. Many of the more elaborate buildings date back to the 17th century, Amsterdam's "Golden Age" of commerce.

A WATER HIGHWAY OF AMSTERDAM
A typical street scene in Amsterdam shows one of the many canals that link the city with the North Sea and the Rhine River.

During this Golden Age the city's merchant princes traded not only with all parts of Europe but with the recently acquired Dutch East Indies and Dutch West Indies. In later years Rotterdam outstripped Amsterdam as a port, but Amsterdam has kept the lead in finance and industry and is noted for its commodity, marine, and stock exchanges. Its thriving industries include iron mills, shipyards, glass factories, chemical plants, food-processing factories, breweries, textile mills, printing plants, and diamond-cutting works.

Amsterdam is the cultural center of the Netherlands. It is the seat of the University of Amsterdam (1632) and the Free (Protestant) University (1880). Its Concertgebouw Orchestra is world-famous. The city has about 40 museums. Its Rijksmuseum, the national art gallery, houses the works of Rembrandt, Vermeer, Hals, and other Dutch masters. The Municipal Museum is noted for its Van Gogh collection.

The city's name (originally Amsteldam) refers to a dam which the lord of Amstel built in 1240 to protect his castle and a nearby fishing village from being flooded by the Zuider Zee. The oldest building is the 14th-century Oude Kerk (Old Church). The old

PLACES OF INTEREST IN CENTRAL AMSTERDAM

1. Anne Frank House
2. West Church
3. Central Station
4. Nieuwe Kerk (New Church)
5. St. Nicolas Church
6. Royal Dam Palace
7. Dam Square
8. National Monument
9. Stock Exchange
10. Oude Kerk (Old Church)
11. Schreierstoren (Weeping Tower)
12. Weighing House (Amsterdam Historical Museum)
13. Beguines' Courtyard
14. City Hall
15. Montelbaan Tower
16. University of Amsterdam
17. Munt Tower
18. Rembrandt House (museum)
19. Municipal Theater
20. Leidseplein
21. Rembrandtsplein
22. Zoological Gardens
23. Rijksmuseum (national art gallery)
24. Stedelijk Museum (Municipal Museum)
25. Olympic Stadium
26. Scheepvaart (Maritime Museum)
27. Concertgebouw (Concert Hall)
28. New RAI Building (Exhibition Hall)
29. Museum of the Royal Tropical Institute

MONTELBAAN TOWER
According to tradition, this is one of the towers from which Dutch seamen's wives waved good-bye to their husbands centuries ago.

Weighing House (formerly St. Anthony's Gate) with its historical museum recalls the days when Amsterdam belonged to the Hanseatic League (*see* Hanseatic League). Another historic structure is the 17th-century Royal Dam Palace. Originally a town hall, it was the residence of Napoleon's brother Louis when he ruled the Kingdom of Holland (1806–10). (*See also* Netherlands.) Population (1960 census), 849,335.

AMUNDSEN (*äm′ŭn-sĕn*), **Roald** (1872–1928). One of the most important men in the history of polar exploration was Roald Amundsen. He was the first man to reach the South Pole, the first to sail around the world via the Northwest and Northeast passages, and the first to fly over the North Pole in a dirigible.

Roald Amundsen was born in Borge, Norway, on July 16, 1872. His father, a shipowner, died when the boy was 14. In school young Amundsen read stories about Sir John Franklin and other polar explorers and set his heart on becoming one himself. Exercising to toughen his body, he also trained himself to endure bitter cold by sleeping with his windows open during the harsh Norwegian winters.

Young Amundsen's mother, however, wanted him to become a physician. To please her, he studied medicine for two years at the University of Christiania (now Oslo). When his mother died, Amundsen dropped his studies at the university and went to sea.

At the age of 25 Amundsen became the first mate of the ship *Belgica* on a Belgian expedition to the Antarctic. After he returned to Norway, he prepared for his first independent venture.

Arctic and Antarctic Exploration

In 1903 Amundsen set sail in the ship *Gjöa*, hoping to locate the north magnetic pole. For 19 months he remained at King Wilhelm Land, in the northeastern part of Greenland, making observations. His studies indicated that the magnetic pole has no stationary position but is in continual movement.

While on this expedition, he also traversed, in 1905, what explorers had been seeking for more than 300 years—the Northwest Passage from the Atlantic to the Pacific. He sailed through bays, straits, and sounds to the north of Canada. Thus Amundsen justified the search for a shorter route to the Orient which had challenged and frustrated countless navigators—from Martin Frobisher to John Davis to Henry Hudson.

Amundsen had planned next to drift across the North Pole in Fridtjof Nansen's ship *Fram*. When he learned that the American explorer Robert E. Peary had reached the North Pole in April 1909, he decided to seek the South Pole instead. He arrived there Dec. 14, 1911—just 35 days before the arrival of Robert F. Scott (*see* Scott, Robert Falcon).

In the summer of 1918 Amundsen once again set sail for the Arctic, in the newly built ship *Maud*. He planned to drift across the North Pole from Asia to North America, but he failed in this purpose because the ship was unable to penetrate the polar ice pack. Two years later, however, when Amundsen reached Alaska, he had sailed also through the Northeast Passage, by way of Siberian coastal waters connecting the Atlantic with the Pacific.

Dirigible Flight over the North Pole

After he had sent the *Maud* back to the Arctic to continue observations, Amundsen turned to the project of flying over the North Pole. His efforts were crowned with success on May 11–13, 1926. In the dirigible *Norge*, piloted by Col. Umberto Nobile, an Italian, he flew over the pole on a 2,700-mile flight between Spitsbergen and Teller, Alaska. He was accompanied by Lincoln Ellsworth, an American explorer.

Two years later came Amundsen's last adventure. In June 1928 he left Norway to fly to the aid of Nobile, whose dirigible had crashed on a second Arctic flight. Amundsen's plane vanished, though Nobile was later rescued. Months afterward the discovery of floating wreckage told the tragic story of how Amundsen met his death. (*See also* Polar Exploration.)

371b

AMUR (*ä-mŭr'*) **RIVER.** The most important waterway in the far-eastern part of Russia is the Amur River. It is formed by the union of the Argun and Shilka rivers. For 1,100 miles the river provides a natural boundary between Russia to the north and the People's Republic of China to the south. It then flows some 650 miles northeastward across Russia to the Tatar Strait, an arm of the Pacific Ocean. To the north the Amur's principal tributaries are the Zeya, the Bureya, and the Amgun rivers; to the south its main tributaries are the Sungari and the Ussuri (which constitutes another portion of the border between Russia and China). Including its headstreams, the length of the Amur River is 2,700 miles.

River of the Black Dragon

Known to the Chinese as the "River of the Black Dragon," the Amur reaches its high point in midsummer during the monsoon rains. From May to November, when the river is free of ice, the Amur is navigable for its entire length.

Russia first became interested in the Amur River region about 1640, when explorers penetrated westward to the Sea of Okhotsk. Chinese troops, however, resisted Russian efforts to settle the region, and the Treaty of Nerchinsk, signed in 1689, gave the territory to China. In 1849 Capt. Gennadi Nevelskoy of the Russian navy explored the Amur's mouth and realized that the river could be of great commercial value. The Treaty of Aigun, signed in 1858, gave the left bank of the Amur to Russia. Today the Amur River provides an important waterway for several Russian industrial centers, including Khabarovsk, Blagoveshchensk, and Komsomol'sk.

ANAHEIM, Calif. One of the fastest-growing cities of the Los Angeles metropolitan area is Anaheim. The largest city in prosperous Orange County, it is situated some 20 miles southeast of Los Angeles.

Much of the economy of Anaheim is based on the processing of citrus fruits and walnuts raised in the surrounding area. The city is also noted for its dairy products and for the canning of vegetables.

Manufacturing and the tourist industry are other important sources of income. Anaheim's factories produce spray chemicals, feeds, paints, wire, hosiery, batteries, electric motors, and industrial alcohol. Disneyland is an internationally famous amusement park that attracts several million visitors to the city annually (*see* Disney).

History and Government

Anaheim is known as the "mother colony" of southern California. It was founded in 1857 by German settlers from San Francisco as an experiment in communal living. The city was named after the nearby Santa Ana River, which provides water for irrigation. The German word *heim* (home) was added as a suffix.

Originally, the main crop in the Anaheim area was grapes, which were raised for making wine. However, the vines were destroyed by a blight in the 1880's, and attempts to restore the vineyards proved unsuccessful. Later, walnuts and citrus fruits, principally Valencia oranges, were introduced.

Since the late 1920's Anaheim has had a rapid industrial development. In 1966 it became the home of the California Angels baseball team (formerly the Los Angeles Angels) of the American League. The city has a council-manager form of government. (*See also* California.) Population (1960 census), 104,184.

THE AMUR RIVER—A VITAL ARTERY FOR SIBERIA'S INDUSTRY
The runoff of monsoon rains over the permafrost soil gives the Amur River great volume in late summer. From May to November ships ply its entire length, providing valuable transportation for industrial centers along the river's banks.

ANATOMY—
The Structure
of the
Human Body

An understanding of the human body is important to everyone. These students are using special models to compare the structures of a human and an animal skeleton.

ANATOMY. It is common practice to divide the human body into eight systems. The principal parts of each of these systems and their relationships are shown in the drawings in this article.

The Skeleton

The skeleton consists of the bones, joints, and cartilages, which make up the framework of the body. There are between 200 and 212 bones in the body, depending upon how many small accessory bones there are around certain joints. Bones are of two principal types—the long and the flat. The long bones are those in the arms, legs, hands, and feet. The flat bones are the breastbone and ribs, the face bones, and the cranial, or skull, bones. Some of these are curved, and some are more massive than flat. Small bones in the wrist and ankle have various shapes, neither round nor flat.

Joints are formed where two bones come together. In the skull these are simple irregular lines where the bones join without moving. Joints that have movement are of three principal kinds. In the shoulders and hips there are joints in which a ball fits into a socket, giving a wide range of circular motion. In the elbows, knees, jaw, fingers, and toes, there are hinged joints. They permit back-and-forth motion, largely limited to one plane. In the ankles, wrists, and between the bones in the spine, sliding motion is limited.

Joints are made of the adjacent surfaces of bones which are covered with cartilage, or gristle. Large strips of cartilage connect the ribs to the breastbone. The joints are further secured in place by heavy sheets of fibrous connecting tissue known as joint capsules or ligaments. In each joint is a small amount of slippery lubricating fluid.

The spine gives strength with flexibility to the back through small bones called vertebrae. There are 7 of these in the neck (cervical), 12 in the chest (thoracic), and 5 in the back (lumbar). The hipbones are attached to a united mass of 5 more (sacrum). The spine ends with 4 small bones fused together (coccyx). The long and the flat bones have cavities filled with marrow. The marrow makes the red and certain kinds of white blood cells. (*See also* Skeleton; Bone.)

The Muscles

Muscles in the body are of three kinds. These are voluntary, or striped; involuntary, or smooth; and heart muscles, which are striped and branched.

The voluntary muscles move parts of the body and help hold the head and body upright. Each of these muscles is attached by a fibrous cord (ligament) to a bone. The voluntary muscles are composed of fibers which can contract. Thus they pull on the bones and move the limb or other body part.

Most smooth muscles act automatically under control of the nervous system. They are found in the lungs, the intestines, and the bladder.

Heart muscle fibers are branched and striped. The heart has a bundle of fibers which combines the qualities of muscles and nerves. This originates and regulates the automatic heartbeat. (*See also* Muscles.)

Circulation and Respiration

All parts of the body depend upon the circulation of blood and a fluid called lymph for nourishment, oxygen supply, and the removal of waste products. Circulation is maintained by the heart, the blood-vessel system, and the lymph circulation. The lungs

373

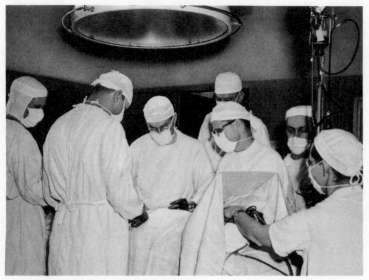

ANATOMY EXPERTS AT WORK
Doctors, particularly surgeons, must have a thorough knowledge of anatomy. The patient's life depends upon the skill of these men.

may be regarded as part of the circulatory system also. (*See also* Blood; Lungs; Respiration.)

The heart is a muscular pump. Its beat circulates the blood through the body. Its two parts are nearly identical. The heart's system of valves permits the blood to flow in at the top and flow out through the principal arteries only. The left side of the heart receives blood from the lungs, where it has taken up oxygen. The blood is then pumped through the arteries to all parts of the body. The arteries branch into smaller and smaller tubes and finally end in a network of microscopic thin-walled capillaries. (*See also* Heart and Circulation.)

The lymph is a fluid closely allied to blood. It is circulated toward the heart by the pressure of blood in the capillaries and other body activity.

Portal circulation consists of the capillaries in the digestive system. These unite into veins and finally form a large vein which carries the blood to the liver.

The lungs fill the entire chest that is not taken up by the heart and the great blood vessels. They are a spongy structure consisting of fibrous tubes leading to air sacs. These small tubes merge into larger ones that unite to form the windpipe. At the upper end of the windpipe is the larynx, or voice box, which opens into the throat. The larynx admits air from the nose or the mouth. It is protected from inhaling food particles by a valvelike structure, the epiglottis.

The diaphragm is a sheet of muscular tissue dividing the chest from the abdomen. When one breathes in, the chest is raised by the ribs and the diaphragm is drawn downward, thus increasing the chest cavity. (*See also* Diaphragm.)

The spleen is an accessory organ to the circulatory system. It is located on the left side of the abdomen, under the liver. The spleen destroys red blood cells when they are no longer useful.

The Digestive System

The digestive system is a modified tube (*see* Digestion). Food enters the body and is digested; useful food is absorbed, and waste is expelled.

In the mouth are the tongue, the teeth, and the glands which produce saliva. Food is chewed and mixed with saliva in the mouth. Sugar digestion begins. When it is swallowed through the long, elastic esophagus, the food enters the stomach. There it is mixed with acid and two principal digestive ferments. One of these curdles milk. The other begins the digestion of protein.

The stomach mixes the food before passing it into the small intestine. There bile from the liver and digestive ferments from the pancreas are added. The liver is the body's largest internal organ. (*See also* Stomach; Liver.)

The small intestine is about 21 feet long and is packed into the abdominal cavity in coils. Its inner lining provides more digestive juices and the means of absorbing food substances into the blood. The muscular coat moves the liquified contents onward by stages. Finally they reach the large intestine. Here they encounter a valvelike barrier which relaxes from time to time to allow liquid to enter the large intestine. Attached to the large intestine near its junction with the small intestine is the appendix.

The large intestine is a six-foot-long muscular structure. Its main function is to reduce its almost liquid contents to a semisolid form by the absorption of moisture. It then expels waste materials.

The Urinary System

The body automatically maintains its water balance through a complicated system centering about the kidneys. These two organs are each about the size of a human fist and shaped like a bean.

The kidneys are complicated filters. In addition to regulating the amount of water in the body, they control the concentration of many substances in the blood. The final secretion of the kidneys is urine. It trickles through long tubes which pass from each kidney to the bladder. The bladder is an elastic and muscular vessel that holds the urine until it can be voided. (*See also* Kidneys.)

The Glandular System

The actions of the body are controlled in part by a system of interrelated organs known as endocrine glands, or glands of internal secretion. Their products, known as hormones, are absorbed directly into the blood. (*See also* Gland; Hormones.)

The chief gland is the pituitary, located under the brain. The gland is in two parts. Its hormones

Continued on page 384

KEY TO ANATOMICAL DRAWINGS*

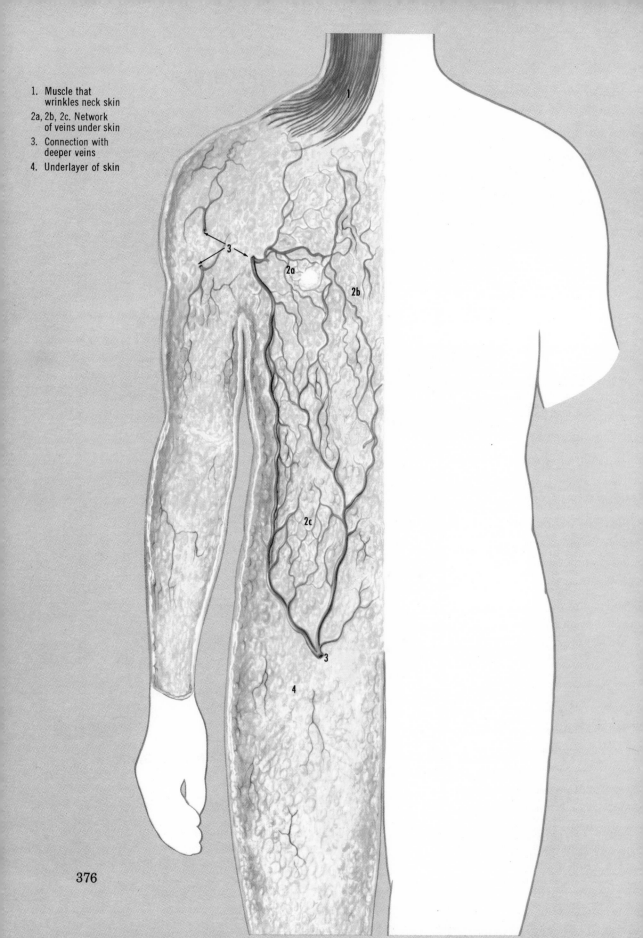

1. Muscle that
   wrinkles neck skin
2a, 2b, 2c. Network
   of veins under skin
3. Connection with
   deeper veins
4. Underlayer of skin

1

3

3

2a

2b

2c

3

4

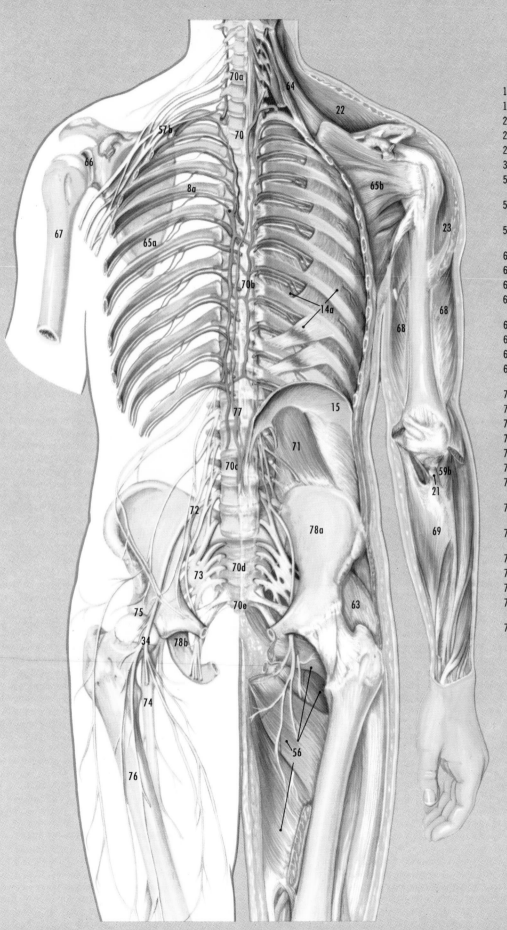

8a. Rib
14a. Rib muscle
15. Diaphragm
21. Biceps muscle
22. Trapezius muscle
23. Deltoid muscle
34. Leg nerve
56. Muscles that pull
    thighs together
57b. Nerves of neck
    and shoulder
59b. Muscle that
    rotates forearm
63. Hip muscle
64. Deep neck muscles
65a. Shoulder blade
65b. Shoulder blade
    muscles
66. Shoulder joint
67. Upper arm bone
68. Triceps muscle
69. Deep muscles of
    forearm
70. Backbone
70a. Neck vertebrae
70b. Rib vertebrae
70c. Lumbar vertebrae
70d. Sacrum
70e. Coccyx
71. Main lower back
    muscle
72. Lumbar nerve
    network
73. Sacral nerve
    network
74. Sciatic nerve
75. Hip joint
76. Long thighbone
77. Principal lymph
    vessel
78a, 78b. Hipbones

383

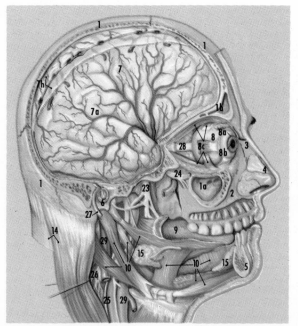

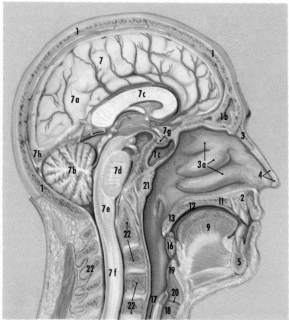

KEY TO HEAD DRAWINGS

1. Skull bones	7. Brain	8c. Muscles that move	19. Epiglottis
1a. Maxillary sinus	7a. Cerebrum	eyeball	20. Vocal cords of larynx
1b. Frontal sinus	7b. Cerebellum	9. Tongue	21. Adenoid
1c. Sphenoid sinus	7c. Corpus callosum	10. Throat muscles	22. Neck bones
2. Upper jawbone (maxilla)	7d. Pons	11. Hard palate	(cervical vertebrae)
3. Nose bone	7e. Medulla oblongata	12. Soft palate	23. Mandibular nerve
3a. Turbinates	7f. Spinal cord	13. Soft palate muscles	24. Maxillary nerve
covered by mucosa	7g. Pituitary gland	14. Muscles that move head	25. Vagus nerve
4. Nose cartilages	7h. Covering membranes	15. Salivary glands	26. Cervical nerves
5. Lower jawbone	8. Eyeball	16. Tonsil	27. Facial nerve
(mandible)	8a. Iris	17. Esophagus	28. Optic nerve
6. Ear canal	8b. Pupil	18. Trachea	29. Arteries and veins

govern growth and development (in conjunction with the thyroid and the sex glands); water balance (in conjunction with the kidneys); and the action of involuntary muscles.

At the base of the neck is the thyroid gland. This controls the speed of body chemistry, known as metabolism. The thyroid is closely related to the pituitary and the sex glands. The sex glands make hormones and reproductive cells.

Near the thyroid and sometimes buried in it are the parathyroid glands. These are concerned with the use of calcium in the body and with muscular action.

Perched like a cap on each kidney is a gland known as the adrenal. It produces cortisone and epinephrine, popularly called adrenalin.

The pancreas is located in the upper abdomen. It secretes a hormone known as insulin. This controls the body's ability to use sugars and starches.

The Nervous System

The brain is in the head protected by the skull. It is the control center for the nervous system, which regulates body movement. The lower portions of the brain are concerned mainly with automatic functions.

Here are the nervous centers that control balance and breathing and, in conjunction with the glands and internal secretions, regulate body functions.

In the higher brain are the centers for vision, touch, hearing, taste, and smell and the functions of memory and thought. Here too are the centers which control the speech and the voluntary muscular actions. Nerve fibers run to all portions of the body through a channel in the spinal column. These fibers make up the spinal cord, which is a two-way nerve pathway with many intermediate nerve connections to body parts such as arms and legs. (*See also* Brain and Spinal Cord; Nerves.)

The Skin

The skin protects the structures underneath. Through its network of blood vessels, it helps control body temperature with the aid of sweat glands. These glands pour sweat onto the surface, where it cools by evaporation. Coloring matter guards the skin against too much sunlight. The skin contains the nerve endings, which give sensations such as heat, itching, and pain. Oil glands waterproof the skin. It absorbs almost nothing, thus protecting the body from harmful contacts. (*See also* Skin.)

DIGESTIVE SYSTEMS COMPARED

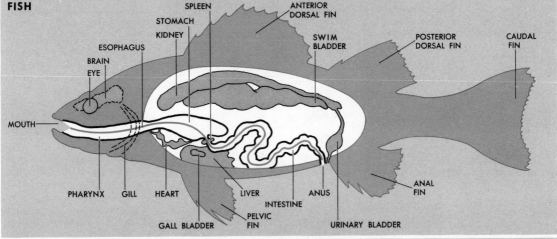

EARTHWORM

BRAIN
HEARTS
CROP
INTESTINE
MOUTH
PHARYNX
ESOPHAGUS
GIZZARD
EXCRETORY TUBULES
EXCRETORY PORES
ANUS

FISH

SPLEEN
STOMACH
KIDNEY
ESOPHAGUS
BRAIN
EYE
ANTERIOR DORSAL FIN
SWIM BLADDER
POSTERIOR DORSAL FIN
CAUDAL FIN
MOUTH
PHARYNX
GILL
HEART
LIVER
INTESTINE
ANUS
ANAL FIN
GALL BLADDER
PELVIC FIN
URINARY BLADDER

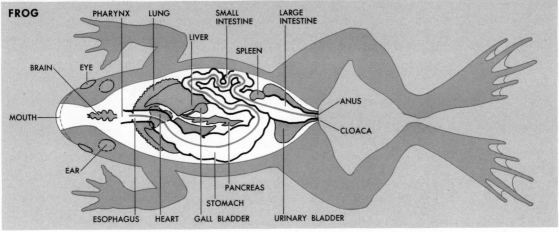

FROG

PHARYNX
LUNG
SMALL INTESTINE
LARGE INTESTINE
LIVER
SPLEEN
BRAIN
EYE
ANUS
MOUTH
CLOACA
EAR
PANCREAS
STOMACH
ESOPHAGUS
HEART
GALL BLADDER
URINARY BLADDER

ANATOMY, COMPARATIVE. The job any machine can do depends upon its parts and their arrangement. A saw is able to cut wood because it has teeth. A sewing machine can pierce cloth because it has a needle. Every kind of animal and every kind of plant also has its own peculiar structure. How and where it can live depends upon its structure.

In comparative anatomy the structures of various animals are studied and compared. The drawings on this page show the digestive systems of the earthworm, the fish, and the frog. The colored lines trace the animals' digestive tracts. As can be seen, the systems are alike in many ways. Each animal has a mouth, a pharynx, an esophagus, an intestine, and an anus. There are also differences. For example, the frog and the fish have livers whereas the earthworm has a gizzard. The differences enable each animal to digest the food found where it lives.

The drawings show other organs that equip each animal for its way of life. The fish, which lives in water, has gills through which it breathes. It has no lungs. The frog, which lives on land as well as in water, is equipped with lungs for air breathing. The earthworm has neither lungs nor gills. It breathes through its skin. (*See also* Animals, Kinds of; Earthworm; Fish; Frog; Frog, Anatomy of.)

385

Strategically located Anchorage has become an important transportation center in Alaska.

After a devastating earthquake in 1964, the city began to rebuild quickly.

ANCHORAGE, Alaska. In the early evening of Good Friday, March 27, 1964, a mighty earthquake struck southern Alaska. A major portion of downtown Anchorage was demolished. Hundreds of homes, apartment buildings, and places of business were ruined, and many lives were lost. There was also widespread damage in some nearby residential areas, especially Turnagain, and in surrounding cities and towns. In a surprisingly short time, however, Anchorage had dug out from under the rubble and had begun the giant task of reconstruction.

This fast-growing city is nearly as far west as Honolulu and is farther north than Helsinki, Finland. Only 375 miles south of the Arctic Circle and some 1,450 air-line miles northwest of Seattle, Anchorage has a surprisingly pleasant climate, with comparatively moderate winters and mild summers. Unlike most Alaska cities, it has wide, regular streets. The city was carefully planned and laid out.

The Z. J. Loussac Public Library and the Anchorage Municipal Auditorium are in the heart of the city. The downtown district also contains restaurants, hotels, theaters, the Federal Building, the City Hall, and the Post Office. Modern office buildings stand side by side with log cabins which were built in Anchorage's early days.

Within walking distance of the downtown area are the industrial district and the Alaska Railroad yards. North of the railroad yards is Government Hill, a residential area affording a fine view of Mount Mc-Kinley, 140 miles away. The city-operated airport and some residential areas are in the eastern part of the city. To the south are a golf course and another residential area. Nearby is Anchorage International Airport.

Industry and Transportation

The economy of the Anchorage area depends largely upon government and military activities. The construction of Elmendorf Air Force Base and Fort Richardson during World War II made Anchorage a defense center and started the rapid growth of the city.

In addition, Anchorage is a major railroad transportation center. Its strategic location and favorable year-round flying weather have also made the city a key spot in world aviation. Trucking is important too, with direct roads leading to other major Alaska cities and to the Alaska Highway. The port of Anchorage, which was inaugurated in 1961, opened south-central Alaska to ocean trade.

Anchorage has a large concentration of seaplane activity. In winter the planes are equipped with skis for landing on snow. Many bush pilots take passengers from Anchorage to remote areas.

Anchorage has an excellent education system with modern elementary- and high-school buildings. There are also a community college and a small university.

In the Anchorage area are more than 90 churches. The city has television and radio stations and two daily newspapers. There are the Anchorage Community Chorus, Little Theater, Symphony Orchestra, and figure-skating and ski clubs. An important annual event is the Alaska Music Festival, featuring guest artists, which is held in the summer.

The major entertainment event of the year is the Anchorage Fur Rendezvous, held in February. The winter carnival celebration is climaxed by a fur auction. Other entertainment features of the carnival are the All-Alaska Dog Sled Races, a seal-hunt pageant, and skiing exhibitions.

History and Government

Anchorage was founded in 1914 as a railroad construction port for the Alaska Railroad. In 1915 the first sales of town lots were held. In 1920 the United States government relinquished control of Anchorage affairs and an election was held. The city was incorporated on Aug. 15, 1938.

The government is administered by an elected mayor and council and a city manager. (*See also* Alaska.) Population (1960 census), 44,237.

ANCIENT HISTORY—Rise and Fall of Civilizations

ANCIENT HISTORY. The period which is called ancient history began with the invention of writing about 3100 B.C. This period lasted more than 35 centuries—a comparatively short time in the known history of mankind. The long ages before there were written records are known as *prehistoric* ("before history").

Evidences of prehistoric man unearthed from deposits in eastern Africa have been dated at 1,750,000 years (*see* Man; Prehistoric Life). Early man advanced from barbarism into what is called the Old Stone (Paleolithic) Age. He lived in a cave and developed crude tools of stone (*see* Stone Age). The New Stone (Neolithic) Age came next. Men began to live together in tribes and developed a primitive form of agriculture (*see* Family). When the use of metals was discovered man stood on the threshold of true civilization (*see* Civilization).

The historical period began when by writing it was possible to keep records of happenings. Civilization

had begun in the river valleys of Mesopotamia and Egypt. It spread westward through the Mediterranean region and reached its height in the classical cultures of Greece and Rome. The record of events in this part of the earth is often called the history of ancient *western civilization* to distinguish it from the history of ancient eastern Asia. The ancient period ended in the 5th century after the birth of Christ when the Roman Empire of the West fell to the barbarian invaders from northern Europe (*see* Europe, History of). The Dark Ages which followed lasted for almost 400 years.

The outline which follows will enable the reader to trace the development of the ancient nations and their cultures as detailed in articles throughout the encyclopedia. Further material will be found in the outline for World History. For the phase of history which follows the period outlined here, *see* the Reference-Outline for the Middle Ages.

REFERENCE-OUTLINE FOR STUDY OF ANCIENT HISTORY

HOW HISTORY BEGAN IN MESOPOTAMIA AND EGYPT

I. River valleys produced the first civilizations and city life M-226, E-117-18: Tigris and Euphrates T-177, E-304; Nile N-290. See also the Reference-Outline for World History

II. Need for record keeping brought the invention of writing about 3100 B.C. C-367, 368, S-57e, W-306-7, H-159, C-489, picture S-57d: alphabet A-285, W-308a. See also the alphabet story at the beginning of the Fact-Index in each volume; and the Reference-Outline for Communication

A. Cuneiform writing (Sumeria, Babylonia, Assyria) C-629, W-306a, B-7-8, pictures B-7, W-307, P-214

B. Hieroglyphics (Egypt) W-306a, 306b, E-125: Rosetta stone E-125-6, picture E-125

C. Early calendars C-28, Y-336

EARLY MESOPOTAMIA

I. The rise of civilization on the Tigris and Euphrates rivers M-226-7, C-369, T-177, E-304, map P-212

A. Sumerians B-6: capital at Kish K-61; calendar C-28; cuneiform writing C-629; geometry P-544;

schools for reading, writing, and arithmetic B-8; conquered by Sargon of Akkad B-9

B. Babylonians B-9-10: capital at Babylon B-5; agriculture B-6; architecture A-489, picture A-490; astronomy A-659; government and religion G-163, D-82 (Hammurabi's laws B-9-10, P-506); sculpture S-82-3; slavery S-212; sundial and water clock W-59; water supply W-70b; writing B-5, C-629, A-485, pictures W-307, P-214

II. Rise and fall of an ancient city—Babylon B-5, B-9

ANCIENT EGYPT TO DECLINE OF THE NEW KINGDOM

I. Rise of civilization on the Nile E-117, C-368, chart H-161: dynasties—union of Upper and Lower Egypt E-118, list E-119

A. Old Kingdom (2700–2200 B.C.) E-119: construction of Djoser's tomb begins Pyramid Age, picture P-543; the pyramids of Gizeh and the Great Sphinx P-542-3, S-378-9, pictures E-117, P-542; King Khafre, picture E-118; a scribe, picture E-125

B. Middle Kingdom (2050–1800 B.C.) E-119: pharaohs begin construction of Temple to Amun at Karnak, in Thebes E-119, T-157, picture A-490; Hyksos invade and conquer Lower Egypt E-119

C. New Kingdom (1570–1090 B.C.) E-119-20: Hatshepsut's temple at Deir el-Bahri, picture E-124; Amenhotep III builds temple at Luxor and Colossi of Memnon M-219, pictures E-120, 123;

AEGEAN REGION AND GREECE

PALESTINE AND SYRIA

ASSYRIA, CHALDEA, AND PERSIA

THE ANCIENT GREEKS

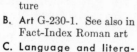
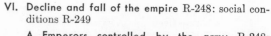
Note: For the next phase of the history of Western civilization, see the Reference-Outline for the Middle Ages.

BIBLIOGRAPHY FOR ANCIENT HISTORY

Books for Younger Readers

Barker, D. R. The Story of Ancient Athens (St. Martin's, 1960).

Bowra, C. M. Classical Greece (Time, 1965).

Corney, L. C. The Story of Rome (St. Martin's, 1965).

Duggan, A. L. The Romans (World Pub., 1964).

Erdoes, Richard. A Picture History of Ancient Rome (Macmillan, 1967).

Horizon (Periodical). Pharaohs of Egypt (American Heritage, 1965).

Renault, Mary. The Lion in the Gateway (Harper, 1964).

Robinson, C. A., Jr. The First Book of Ancient Egypt (Watts, 1961).

Robinson, C. A., Jr. The First Book of Ancient Rome (Watts, 1964).

Sporry, J. T. The Story of Egypt (Nelson, 1964).

Winer, B. K. Life in the Ancient World (Random, 1961).

Books for Advanced Students and Teachers

Baumann, Hans. The World of the Pharaohs (Pantheon, 1960).

Chubb, T. C. The Byzantines (World, 1959).

Coolidge, O. E. Men of Athens (Houghton, 1962).

Cottrell, Leonard. Land of the Two Rivers (World Pub., 1962).

Cowell, F. R. Everyday Life in Ancient Rome (Putnam, 1961).

Durant, W. J. Story of Civilization, vols. 1-3. (Simon & Schuster, 1935–44).

Falls, C. B. The First 3000 Years (Viking, 1960).

Finley, M. I. The Ancient Greeks (Viking, 1963).

Gibbon, Edward. The Decline and Fall of the Roman Empire (Putnam, 1962).

Lloyd-Jones, Hugh, ed. The Greeks (World Pub., 1963).

Mertz, Barbara. Red Land, Black Land: the World of the Ancient Egyptians (Coward-McCann, 1966).

Sellman, R. R. Ancient Egypt (Roy, 1962).

Swain, J. W. The Ancient World, 2v. (Harper, 1950).

Taylor, D. B. Ancient Greece (Roy, 1958).

Taylor, D. B. Ancient Rome (Roy, 1961).

ANDERSEN, Hans Christian (1805–1875).

Like many young sons in fairy tales, Hans Christian Andersen came of poor and humble parents. His father was a cobbler and his mother washed the clothes of her neighbors. While a boy, Hans Christian was considered a fool. People said he was fit for nothing except to dream. He was tall for his age and thin, homely, and awkward, easy prey for the pranks and jokes of his companions. At last, however, he came to success and honor, like the traditional fool in folklore. Kings and queens, scholars, poets, and artists of many countries honored Andersen and delighted to share his company.

'The Ugly Duckling' and Other Tales

Hans Christian Andersen is one of the immortals of world literature. The fairy tales he wrote are like no others written before or since. People everywhere remember them for the wise things they say about life, for the wit and fun in them, and for their compassion. The stories are unforgettable too for the fantastic and incredible adventures they describe.

'The Steadfast Tin Soldier', 'The Snow Queen', 'The Swineherd', 'The Nightingale'—these are stories that have been translated into almost every language. All over the world people know what it means to be an ugly duckling. Andersen's story of the swan who came from among the ducks is a story in which each person recognizes something of himself. No one can equal him for his power to give life to common things—to matches, balls, and darning needles and to pots and pans. He describes conversation among kitchen utensils as if he had heard it himself: " 'My fate was a different sort', said the Iron Pot, '. . . ever since I came into the world, there has been a great deal of scouring and cooking done in me. I look after the practical part and am first here in the house . . . our only newsmonger is the Market Basket'."

Birth and Boyhood

On the island of Fünen (Fyn), off the coast of Denmark, stands a bleak, wind-swept, fishing village called Odense. Here, in a one-room house, on April 2, 1805, Hans Christian Andersen was born, and here he spent the early years of his childhood. He described the room in his 'Story of My Life':

"The one and only little room, almost filled by the cobbler's bench and the bedstead and the folding bench in which I slept, this was my childhood home, but the walls were covered with pictures, there were pretty cups, glasses, and knickknacks on the chest of drawers, and over the cobbler's bench by the window was a shelf with books and songs."

The books and songs were to bring great pleasure to the boy. His father, though poorly educated, could read. He shared with his son the tales from the 'Arabian Nights' and plays by Danish writers. Hans Christian learned to recite many of these plays before he could read or write.

On Sundays and holidays there were walks to the beech woods and trips with his devoted grandmother—his father's mother—through the gardens of the asylum where she worked. From his grandmother he heard old folk tales of Denmark and legends of goblins and ghosts. His mother's own garden was one wooden box in which grew chives and parsley. It was on the top of the house in the gutter that divided the roof of their house from the roof of the adjoining house. This was the garden that was to bloom, in 'The Snow Queen', into the "wall of flowers" where Gerda and Kay sat "among the roses" and played happily. All that Andersen saw as a child he remembered with intense emotion. His wonder stories abound in descriptions of woods, forests, flowers, birds, snow, the sea, and gardens under the sea.

Hans Christian was sent first to a Dame School. This was a school usually taught by a woman in her own home. Later he attended a school for poor children. He preferred to stay at home, however, playing with the toys his father made for him or making costumes for his puppets. In his puppet theater he acted out plays he knew and also invented stories of his own. He was delicate, and his parents indulged him in his desire to be let alone to dream and play.

When Hans Christian was 11, his father died. The boy was left more alone than ever because his mother and grandmother were hard at work. He went to school only at intervals and spent most of his time imagining stories rather than reading lessons. He could memorize very easily and learned some of his lessons by listening to a neighborhood boy who was in the habit of studying aloud. He memorized and recited plays to anyone who would listen. He haunted the theater in Odense and startled his mother by imitating everything he saw or heard—ballet dancers, acrobats, or pantomimists. He felt himself quite capable of becoming all of these.

To put an end to this, his mother apprenticed him first to a weaver, then to a tobacconist, and finally to a tailor. Hans knew these occupations were not for him. The only things that held his interest were the theater, books, and stories.

He Leaves Home to Seek His Fortune

When he was 14, Hans Christian decided to go to Copenhagen, the capital of Denmark, and seek

ANDERSEN'S HOBBY
To amuse children Andersen used to cut silhouettes out of paper. This is his picture of a ballet dancer.

MOUNTAIN CHIEF AND ELFIN MAID
In 'The Elfin Mount' the chief sets out to select wives for his sons. Instead he chooses his own young bride. The picture is by Rex Whistler, from 'Fairy Tales and Legends' by Hans Christian Andersen (Oxford).

his fortune. "It is quite simple," he said to his mother. "One suffers greatly for a while and then one becomes famous." His mother consulted a gypsy fortuneteller. The gypsy said that one day the whole town of Odense would be illuminated in her son's honor. With this assurance and with seven dollars in the pocket of his only suit, which had been cut from one of his father's, Hans Christian bade farewell to his old grandmother and mother and took the stage-coach to Copenhagen.

A printer in Odense, who had published handbills for the theater, had given Hans Christian a letter of introduction to a dancer. The boy presented himself to her and sang and danced in his stocking feet before her astonished guests. They laughed uproariously at his absurd manner and brash behavior.

Years of Poverty and Despair

There followed three bitter years of poverty. Hans Christian earned a little money singing in a boys' choir until his voice changed. He tried to act and to join the ballet, but his awkwardness made these careers impossible. He attempted to work with his hands, but this too he could not do. Not once did it occur to him, however, to return home and admit defeat. Sometimes he went down to the wharves and looked long at the ships that were going to Odense.

At last, when he was 17, Andersen came to the attention of Chancellor Jonas Collin, a director of the Royal Theater. Collin had read a play written by Andersen and he saw that the youth had talent, though he lacked education. He procured from the king money for Andersen's education and sent him to a school at Slagelse, near Copenhagen. Here the young man suffered the humiliation of being in classes with students younger than he was. His teacher, a

bitter man, treated him harshly and took particular delight in taunting him about his ambition to become a writer. Andersen had an unusually sensitive nature and suffered intensely. Nevertheless, he studied hard, encouraged by the kindness of Collin.

Finally Collin, convinced that the teacher was actually persecuting Andersen, took the youth from the school and placed him under a private tutor in Copenhagen. In 1828, when he was 23, Andersen passed his entrance examinations to the university in Copenhagen.

Success at Last

Andersen's writings began to be published in Danish in 1829. In 1833 the king gave him a grant of money for travel, and he spent 16 months wandering through Germany, France, Switzerland, and his beloved Italy. His first works were poems, plays, novels, and impressions of his travels. He was slow to discover that he especially excelled in explaining the essential character of children.

In 1835 Andersen published 'Fairy Tales for Children'—four short stories he wrote for a little girl, Ida Thiele, daughter of the secretary of the Academy of Art. The stories were 'Little Ida's Flowers', 'The Tinderbox' (which he had heard from his grandmother), 'Little Claus and Big Claus', and 'The Princess and the Pea'. He seems to have sent them into the world with little appreciation of their worth and returned to the writing of novels and poems. However, people who read the stories—adults as well as children—wanted more.

Andersen published in all 156 fairy tales. He wrote the stories just as he would have told them. "The real ones come of themselves," he said. "They knock at my forehead and say, 'Here I am'." Although he had no children of his own, he was at his best as an interpreter of child nature. In some respects he remained a child himself and looked at life with a youngster's eyes.

It was his fairy tales that brought Andersen the affection of the world as well as the friendship of great men and women. The famous writer Charles Dickens was his friend, and Andersen paid him a long visit in England. Jenny Lind, the great Swedish singer, was also his devoted friend, and they shared a Christmas tree together one year in Berlin.

The prophecy of the gypsy woman came true. Forty-eight years after Andersen left Odense, the town was illuminated in his honor. There was a great fete for him, with everyone in the city to do him honor and messages from the great of the world.

Hans Christian Andersen lived to be 70 years of age. He died on Aug. 4, 1875. He never married, but he had many friends who felt the greatest affection for him, and they sustained him through a lifetime. When he came to write the account of his life, he began with the words, "My life is a lovely story, happy and full of incident."

ANDERSON, Maxwell

(1888–1959). The American playwright Maxwell Anderson was a strong believer in the dignity of man and the importance of democracy. Many of his plays express his ideas of liberty and justice. He was also an expert writer of blank verse, and he popularized the use of poetry in modern drama.

Maxwell Anderson was born on Dec. 15, 1888, in Atlantic, Pa. His father was the Rev. William Lincoln Anderson, a Baptist minister. His mother was Premely Stevenson Anderson. Because the Andersons, with their four children, moved frequently, Maxwell attended many different schools.

Education and Early Work

The writer received an A.B. degree at the University of North Dakota in 1911. While attending the university he played football and first became interested in the theater. He earned an M.A. degree at Stanford University while he taught English in a San Francisco high school. Three years later he turned from teaching to newspaper work, first in Grand Forks, N. D., then in San Francisco.

In 1918 he went to New York City. While working on the *New York World*, Anderson met Laurence Stallings, a book reviewer, who helped him get his first play, 'The White Desert', produced. With Stallings, Anderson wrote his first really successful drama, 'What Price Glory?'. It was produced in 1924.

Anderson later resigned from the *World* and devoted himself exclusively to writing plays. For more than 30 years he turned out a play nearly every season, with varied but generally great success.

Prizewinning Playwright

The shy, serious author chose to write in solitude on his farm, shunning the busy life of New York and refusing to attend the opening nights of his plays. He wrote very quickly, composing in longhand in a large ledger.

Anderson won the Pulitzer prize in 1933 for his drama 'Both Your Houses', a study of corrupt politics. He received the New York Drama Critics' Circle Award in 1935 for 'Winterset', a social protest play, and again in 1936 for 'High Tor', a comic fantasy combining blank verse with prose.

Other plays by Anderson include 'Elizabeth the Queen' (1930); 'Mary of Scotland' (1933); 'Knickerbocker Holiday' (1938); 'Key Largo' (1939); 'Joan of Lorraine' (1946); and, with composer Kurt Weill, 'Lost in the Stars' (1949).

Anderson died on Feb. 28, 1959, in Stamford, Conn. He was married three times; his first two wives died before he did. He had three sons and one daughter.

ANDERSON, Sherwood

(1876–1941). In his short stories and novels, the American writer Sherwood Anderson protested against the frustrations of ordinary people and against what he believed to be the narrow-minded conventions of his time. He was a master of colloquial speech. His concern with "little" people probably came from his experiences early in life.

Sherwood Anderson was born in Camden, Ohio, on Sept. 13, 1876, the third child of a family of five boys and two girls. His father, Irwin, was an irresponsible man who could not hold a job long, but he was a colorful talker and storyteller. His mother was Emma Smith Anderson.

Boyhood and War Service

Most of Anderson's boyhood was spent in the small town of Clyde, Ohio, where he attended school irregularly. When he was only 14 his mother died and Anderson ended his formal education altogether.

The young man drifted from one job to another, finally welcoming the chance to serve in the Spanish-American War. When the war was over he returned to Ohio and eventually became manager of a paint factory in Elyria. It was at this time that Anderson began to write. He became more and more absorbed in writing. Finally one day he walked out of the factory, apparently on a sudden impulse, never to return.

Writing Career Begins

Sherwood joined his brother Karl, a magazine illustrator, in Chicago and took a job with an advertising agency. He became acquainted with the "Chicago group" of writers, which included Theodore Dreiser, Carl Sandburg, Ben Hecht, and Floyd Dell. Dreiser and Dell helped get Anderson's first novel, 'Windy McPherson's Son', published in 1916. It was a story of factory life, based on his own experiences.

His next books were 'Marching Men' (1917), a novel about mines, and 'Mid-American Chants' (1918), a book of poetry. Anderson was best as a short-story writer, and his most successful book was 'Winesburg, Ohio', published in 1919. The book is made up of short stories about small-town people. Although a fictional place, Winesburg is modeled after Clyde, the town where Anderson spent his boyhood years.

After going abroad in 1921, Anderson returned to live in New Orleans and, later, New York. He finally settled in Marion, Va., where he edited two newspapers and continued to write. His autobiographical books are 'A Story Teller's Story' (1924); 'Tar: a Midwest Childhood' (1926); and 'Sherwood Anderson's Memoirs' (1942). He died in Colón, Panama, on March 8, 1941. Anderson was married four times.

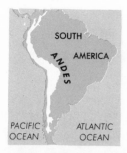

ANDES. Ages ago geologic forces pushed the bed of the Pacific Ocean against land masses in both North and South America. The rocks lying between the rising Pacific bed and the old lands were squeezed and forced up into a towering mountain system—the *Cordilleras* (kôr-dĭl-yêr'az). The word comes from a Spanish term meaning "little ropes." The South American Cordilleras are called the *Andes*, from an Indian word of uncertain origin.

The giant Andean system stretches along the entire western side of South America, a distance of about 4,500 miles. In elevation it is exceeded only by the Himalayas in central Asia. Many of its peaks are higher than Mount McKinley, the highest mountain in North America. The tallest peak is Mount Aconcagua, 22,834 feet (*see* Aconcagua).

The width of the Andean chain is about 200 miles or less, except in Bolivia, where it broadens to about 400 miles. Bolivia shares with Peru the lofty central plateau, called the altiplano (high plain), between the eastern and western ranges. This is one of the highest inhabited regions in the world.

Throughout much of their length the Andes rise close to the Pacific coast and descend abruptly to low plains on the east. As the main watershed of the continent, the system is the source of short streams flowing to the Pacific and also of most of the head-streams of rivers flowing east and north. It is a formidable barrier to transportation. The only railroad crossings are those connecting Chile with Argentina and Bolivia.

The Andes are rich in nonferrous metals but have no coal. Many deposits are inaccessible. The chief minerals obtained are gold and silver, copper, tin, antimony, lead, zinc, bismuth, and vanadium.

Volcanoes and Earthquakes

When the Andes were formed, sedimentary rocks were crushed into long ridges, called *sierras*. In some

IRRIGATED FIELDS IN THE ANDES
In Peru and Bolivia agriculture is concentrated on the altiplano (high plain). Fields extend to the foot of the mountains.

places huge cracks allowed molten granite and other igneous rock to well up from the depths. Wherever this rock reached the surface, it built up volcanic cones. Most of the highest peaks in the Andes, including Aconcagua, are volcanoes. Some are active; hundreds are dormant or extinct. The mountains are still settling. Severe earthquakes occur, and volcanoes occasionally erupt, with terrific destruction.

How the Andes Affect Climate

The Andes affect the climate by influencing precipitation. In northern Colombia three ranges spread out to catch and hold the moisture of the northeast trade winds, making this a region of heavy rainfall. On the Pacific side, from the Isthmus of Panama to the equator, the Colombian Andes catch the southwesterly winds, and rains fall almost daily.

From the Gulf of Guayaquil through northern Chile the west coast is extremely dry. This stretch lies in

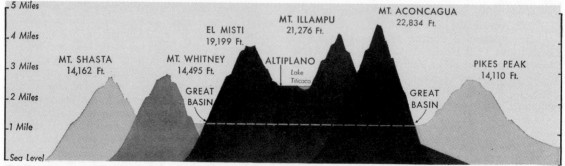

HOW THE ANDES COMPARE WITH THE ROCKY MOUNTAINS AND THE SIERRA NEVADA
This comparison profile shows two important differences between the Andes (*black shading*) and the Cordilleras of the Western United States. Notice how Mount Aconcagua, the highest peak in the Andes, towers over Mount Whitney, the highest peak in the Sierra Nevada. Compare also the heights of the central plateaus. The altiplano and Lake Titicaca lie at a height of more than two miles—about double the average height of the Great Basin in the United States.

A HIGH VALLEY IN THE ANDES
Peruvian Indians graze llamas in steep mountain valleys. Llamas supply meat and wool and also serve as beasts of burden.

the trade wind belt. Winds tend to come from the east and southeast, and they drop their moisture on the eastern slopes. In summer, however, they have moisture enough to give rain on the western slopes also.

In northern Chile cool trade winds from the Pacific become warmed as they reach the hot coast and hold their moisture as fog. The great desert of Chile is one of the driest places in the world.

In the latitude of Valparaiso the coast has a Mediterranean climate, with drying trade winds in summer and moisture-laden westerly winds in winter. Farther south the winds come from the west the year around and the Chilean slopes of the Andes catch their moisture as drenching rain or heavy snow. The eastern slopes in Argentina are relatively dry. (*See also* South America; and articles on the countries named.)

ANDORRA. The little country of Andorra is an oddity in the modern world. This principality, high in the Pyrenees between the Spanish province of Lérida and the French department of Ariège, is a strange survivor of medieval Europe which retains many feudal practices. The inhabitants pay no taxes. Instead they pay a tribute every two years to France and to the Spanish bishop of Urgel. Members of Andorra's small army receive no pay or uniforms. All soldiers are officers, and the army has not fought for hundreds of years. Only the head of a household may vote.

The country, only 175 square miles in size, is a cluster of narrow valleys and gorges surrounded by the high peaks of the Pyrenees. Puig de la Coma Pedrosa (9,665 feet) is the highest. The climate is severe, with cold winters and cool summers. Drought is a serious problem. The passes are snowbound most of the year.

The best soil is on artificially terraced slopes. The chief crop is tobacco, much of which is smuggled into France and Spain. Sheep raising is the main occupation in Andorra.

The People of Andorra

The Andorrans are mostly of Spanish origin. They are Roman Catholic and speak Catalan.

The population is scattered in six villages. The only person with legal rights in each family is the head of the house. When he retires, at the age of 60, another person, usually his oldest son, is chosen to replace him.

History and Government

In 1278 the principality of Andorra was placed under the joint suzerainty of the French count of Foix and the Spanish bishop of Urgel. The rights of the House of Foix passed to that of Béarn and later to the French crown. Today these rights are exercised by the president of France.

The government of Andorra is administered by a General Council. Its 24 members are elected for four years. The executive consists of a First Syndic and a Second Syndic chosen by the council. Actually, the real government power rests with the French president and Spanish bishop. Both "princes" have set up a Permanent Delegation for Andorran Affairs. Population (1965 estimate), 11,000.

A PASTORAL SCENE IN ANDORRA
During the summer, sheep graze on the slopes of the Pyrenees. Sheep raising is the major occupation in Andorra.

ANDRÉ (*än′drä*), **John** (1751–1780). During the American Revolution young John André, a British army officer, was hanged by the Americans as a spy. His fate aroused sympathy in America as well as in England. Although the sentence was justified, blame for the tragedy belongs to Gen. Benedict Arnold. André was merely carrying out orders to negotiate with the American traitor. (*See also* Arnold, Benedict.)

John André was born in London in 1751. His father, who had come to England from Genoa, was a prosperous merchant. An unhappy love affair caused the youth, at 20, to join the British army in America. He was strikingly handsome, charming, and witty and had considerable literary and artistic ability. He was also an able soldier and won rapid promotion.

The West Point Plot

In 1780 Major André was in New York, serving as aide to Sir Henry Clinton, commander in chief of the British land forces. General Arnold had been given command of West Point and was plotting with Clinton to surrender the important fortress to the British. Clinton arranged for André to meet secretly with Arnold to work out details of the plot.

On September 20 André ascended the Hudson in the British sloop of war *Vulture*. On the night of September 21–22 he met with Arnold in a house near Stony Point. Before he could return to the *Vulture*, the ship was forced downstream by an American battery. André put on civilian clothes and started for New York on horseback.

On September 23, near Tarrytown, three American militiamen captured him and found incriminating papers in his boots. Arnold had time to flee in the *Vulture* to the British army.

André was taken to Gen. George Washington's headquarters at Tappan, N. Y. A military court, which included the Revolutionary War hero Lafayette, convicted him on Sept. 29, 1780. On October 2 he was hanged. A tablet in his memory was placed in Westminster Abbey, and his remains were taken there in 1821.

ANEMONE (*ǫ-nĕm′ō-nē*). The anemones are delicate wild flowers that grow in northern woods and on prairies. According to myth, these are the plants that sprang from the ground where Aphrodite's tears fell when she mourned for Adonis (*see* Adonis). Their name comes from the Greek word *anemos*, which means "wind." Some kinds of anemones are also known as windflowers because they sway on their slender stems in the breeze.

The anemones have no petals, but their sepals resemble petals. Stamens and pistils are numerous. About two thirds of the way up the stem is a whorl of leaves, usually three in number. Each leaf is compound and deeply cleft. The upper stem, topped by a single blossom, springs from this whorl.

Four Types of Anemones

Prairie anemone (*Anemone canadensis*) grows on moist prairies and stream banks from Labrador to Pennsylvania and west to Kansas and Colorado. It blossoms from May to August. It is from one to two feet high. The flower has five white sepals. Wood anemone (*A. quinquefolia*) grows in forests in April and May. It is from four to nine inches high. The white or pink-tinged blossom has from four to seven sepals. (For picture in color, *see* Flowers, Wild.)

Tall anemone (*A. virginiana*) is also called thimbleweed because the seed head of this flower resembles a thimble. It blossoms in woods and meadows from June to August. The stout, hairy stem is from two to three feet tall.

The pasqueflower (*A. ludoviciana*) is native to dry western prairies from Illinois and Wisconsin to British Columbia and southward into Texas. The name means "Easter flower," referring to its early blossoming at Easter time. The plant has a thick underground stem and an upright stem from 6 to 16 inches high, covered with silky hairs. The single purple or white flower has from five to seven sepals. It is the state flower of South Dakota. (For picture in color, *see* Plants.)

A GARDEN VARIETY OF ANEMONE
The Anemone Coronaria is also called the poppy-flowered anemone. The flowers grow in a variety of colors.

ANESTHETICS—Drugs That Kill Pain

ANESTHETICS. Certain drugs have the power to cause complete or partial loss of feeling (*see* Drugs). These drugs are *anesthetics*. The loss of feeling they produce is known as *anesthesia*.

The name "anesthetic" for these types of drugs was proposed by Oliver Wendell Holmes (*see* Holmes, Oliver Wendell). It comes from Greek terms meaning "without sensation."

The introduction of anesthetics into medical practice helped eliminate pain. Modern anesthetics can safely produce several hours of anesthesia in patients undergoing surgery. This permits the surgeon to perform long, delicate operations. (*See also* Medicine, History of; Surgery.)

Kinds of Anesthetics

There are two broad types of anesthetics—general and local. *General anesthetics* produce unconsciousness in the patient. *Local anesthetics* cause a loss of feeling in some restricted ("local") area of the body.

A general anesthetic produces unconsciousness by depressing the activities of the central nervous system (*see* Brain; Nerves). The most commonly used methods of administering general anesthetics are *inhalation*, in which the patient breathes a gas or vapor into his lungs, and *intravenous injection*, in which the drug is injected into a vein.

How General Anesthetics Act

The exact manner in which general anesthetics produce their effects is not yet clearly understood. It is known, however, that a general anesthetic is first absorbed by the blood. The circulating blood transports the drug to the nervous system.

In the nervous system a general anesthetic so alters the normal activities of nerve cells that the body's communications network temporarily ceases to function. Sensory impulses are not carried to the central nervous system. Thus a person under general anesthesia cannot feel sensations, such as pain. At the same time his central nervous system cannot issue the command impulses which move the parts of his body. The anesthetized person remains in this state until the drug's effect is eliminated by his body.

Substances Used As General Anesthetics

Listed here are some of the more important drugs used as general anesthetics:

Ether (Diethyl Ether). A colorless, volatile (easily vaporized) liquid. It is highly flammable and explosive; therefore it is never used near an open flame or in a place where sparks may be produced.

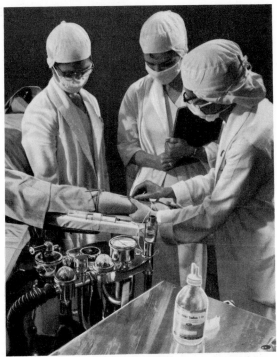

Here a soluble, quick-acting anesthetic is being injected directly into a vein in the patient's arm.

Ether is breathed in and absorbed into the blood from the lungs. It depresses the central nervous system, producing sleep, loss of feeling, and loss of reflexes. Ether is a powerful anesthetic, yet it has a good margin of safety when properly administered.

Cyclopropane (Trimethylene). A colorless, sweet-smelling, inflammable, explosive gas. It is inhaled in combination with oxygen. Cyclopropane is a very potent anesthetic gas but is considered less irritating to respiratory membranes than ether.

Nitrous Oxide (Laughing Gas). A colorless, sweet-smelling, nonflammable, nonexplosive gas. It is a relatively weak anesthetic. To obtain surgical anesthesia, it is most commonly used in combination with such drugs as narcotics and muscle relaxants.

Ethylene. A slightly stronger gas than nitrous oxide. It is highly flammable, explosive, and nonirritating. Ethylene has an unpleasant odor.

Chloroform. A clear, nonflammable fluid. It is more potent than ether but has a narrow margin of safety.

Vinethene (Divinyl Ether). A liquid that has an onionlike (but nonirritating) odor. Because it produces rapid anesthesia, Vinethene is recommended for operations of short duration.

Trilene (Trichloroethylene). A liquid that produces a light analgesic (pain-killing) effect in operations of short duration. It is preferably administered in combination with nitrous oxide and oxygen.

Fluothane. A new synthetic anesthetic. It is nonflammable, nonexplosive, and more potent than ether or chloroform. A calibrated apparatus is used to deliver measured amounts of the drug into the body.

Barbiturates. The molecules of certain barbiturate drugs contain sulfur. These sulfur-containing barbiturates are called *thiobarbiturates*. They appear as yellow powders and are soluble in water. They may be dissolved in saline or glucose solutions and then injected intravenously to produce general anesthesia. Thiobarbiturates are most commonly used in combination with inhaled anesthetics, such as nitrous oxide or ethylene, or with narcotic drugs. One example of a thiobarbiturate is *thiopental sodium* (Pentothal Sodium), also known as a "truth serum."

Local Anesthetics

When certain drugs are injected into the tissues, they prevent impulses from traveling through nerves which come in contact with the drug solution near the point of injection. Sensations of pain and touch are not transmitted while these nerves are bathed in the anesthetic. This effect, known as local anesthesia, makes possible the performance of some operations without placing the patient under general anesthesia.

The injection of a local anesthetic into the tissues is known as an *infiltration*. The drug may also be injected around the main nerves leading to the area to be operated upon. The nerves supplying this area are then rendered incapable of transmitting sensory impulses. This is called a *block anesthesia*, because the impulses traveling in those nerves are blocked by the anesthetic drug.

The most commonly used local anesthetics are Novocain (procaine), Pontocaine, Metycaine, Nupercaine, and Xylocaine. All are synthetic drugs.

Cocaine, a drug derived from coca leaves, was once a widely used local anesthetic. Today its use is confined to topical application to mucous membranes. It is not injected because it is too irritating. The synthetic local anesthetics listed above are far superior to cocaine.

The effect of local anesthesia may also be obtained by applying cold (ice packs, ethyl chloride spray) to the tissues, by cutting off the circulation to the area, or by applying pressure to the nerve trunks.

Spinal Anesthesia

Local anesthetics may be injected into the space surrounding the spinal cord (*see* Brain and Spinal Cord). Such administration produces complete insensitivity to pain as well as muscular relaxation in the part of the body below the site of injection.

Spinal anesthesia can only be used below the level of the cord that gives rise to spinal nerves which help control breathing and heart action. These nerves are located in the upper chest region.

Anesthesiology

Numerous anesthetics have been developed since 1842, when Dr. Crawford W. Long first used ether to anesthetize a patient (*see* Long). New information is constantly being obtained about these drugs and about the techniques of using them. This knowledge has become so extensive that a new medical

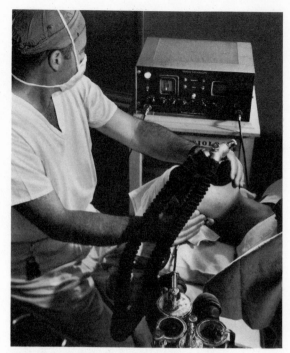

ADMINISTERING AN ANESTHETIC GAS
The anesthesiologist monitors the action of the patient's heart on a Cardio-tachoscope while administering gas to him.

specialty dealing with all phases of anesthesia has been founded. The specialty is called *anesthesiology*.

A practitioner of anesthesiology is an *anesthesiologist*. He is a graduate physician who has undertaken additional training and education in this particular field. Like the specialists recognized in other areas of medicine, the anesthesiologist must take the examinations given by a board of qualified experts in his field. After passing these examinations, he is *certified* by the board. (*See also* Medicine, subhead "Certification of Specialists.")

The anesthesiologist is an important member of any surgical team engaged in performing a major operation. He usually prepares the patient for such an operation by prescribing certain drugs. For example, he may administer a sedative to calm the patient's anxiety about the coming operation, a hypnotic to assure him a good sleep before surgery, or an analgesic to dull any pain he might have.

The anesthesiologist selects the drug best suited for the patient and for the type of operation to be performed. He also determines the best method of administering the anesthetic. During the operation he watches over the patient's condition. For example, he frequently checks the patient's heart action, blood pressure, and respiration. He reports his findings to the surgeon at regular intervals.

Sometimes the anesthetic is administered by an *anesthetist*, who may be either a physician or a nurse. An anesthetist is trained to give certain types of anesthetics but does not have the highly specialized training of the anesthesiologist.

ANGELICO, Fra (1387-1455). One of the greatest Renaissance religious painters was the Dominican monk best known by the nickname Fra Angelico. He is also known as Guidolino di Pietro and Giovanni da Fiesole.

Fra Angelico was born in 1387 at Vicchio, Tuscany, Italy. With his brother Benedetto, he entered the Dominican cloister at Fiesole in 1407. There he learned and practiced the art of manuscript illumination.

In 1436 the Fiesole monks were transferred to Florence, where Cosimo de' Medici had commissioned the restoration of the cloister of San Marco. Fra Angelico and his pupils did much of the fresco decoration.

Fra Angelico was invited to Rome in 1445 by Pope Eugenius IV. The artist painted frescoes in two chapels for Eugenius IV and for Pope Nicholas V. He also began frescoes in a chapel at Orvieto but left before the work was completed to go back to Rome. In 1449 he returned to Fiesole and became prior. He died in Rome in 1455 and is buried there.

A pious man, Fra Angelico painted many religious subjects. He was one of the first to paint Christ as a simple baby. In his 'Madonna of the Linen Weavers', the central figure is surrounded by angelic musicians. Some people believe that it is from these and other angels in his work that the painter got the nickname Angelico. Others believe his nickname refers to his excellent character.

ANGOLA. Since it was discovered in the 15th century, Angola has been associated with Portugal. The African territory has grown increasingly restless under Portuguese domination, however, and has been the scene of violence and revolt.

Angola has a 1,000-mile Atlantic Ocean coastline, and it is bounded by the Republic of the Congo, Zambia, and South-West Africa. The country, 481,352 square miles in area, consists of a great dissected tableland rising abruptly from a coastal lowland and then sloping gently eastward. This central plateau is one of Africa's major watersheds.

Agriculture and Chief Cities

On tropical lowland plantations sugarcane, cacao, and cotton are grown. On the central plateau coffee, sisal, and beeswax are produced for export. Beans, rice, and corn are also grown, and the people gather wild rubber and palm products for export. Some cattle are raised in the plateau areas where they are not threatened by tsetse flies. Angola possesses valuable diamond deposits. Iron ore, crude oil, copper, and manganese are also produced.

The important cities are Luanda, the capital (population, 1960 census, 224,540), Benguela, Moçâmedes, Lobito, Sá da Bandeira, and Malange. Most of the Europeans living in Angola are Portuguese. The native population is mostly of Bantu stock. There are several tribes of Bushmen in the southeast.

Railways link coastal towns with the interior, and the principal cities are connected by regular air service. Heavy traffic passes through ports on the Atlantic. There are elementary and secondary schools as well as professional and technical institutions in the larger towns. Angola constitutes an archdiocese of the Roman Catholic church.

History and Government

The north coast of Angola was discovered in 1482 by the Portuguese navigator Diogo Cam (or Cão). The first settlers arrived in 1491. Luanda, founded in 1575, was occupied by the Dutch from 1641 to 1648. From the 17th to the 19th century the colony prospered by slave trade with Brazil.

Angola is an overseas province of Portugal. It is administered by a governor-general, who is assisted by a council. A revolt in 1961 against Portuguese rule was ruthlessly quelled. The rebels then adopted guerrilla warfare tactics. In 1965 Portugal began a three-year plan for the economic and educational development of Angola. Population (1965 estimate), 5,119,000.

COFFEE HARVEST IN ANGOLA
Coffee, grown on plantations on the central plateau, is one of Angola's major exports. The workers harvesting the crop are of Bantu stock.

ANIMALS—
The Diversity of
Life in the
Animal Kingdom

A mother polar bear holds her sleepy cub and seems to gaze tenderly into its face. She will teach it to swim and will feed and care for it for more than a year.

ANIMALS. What is an animal? Everyone will agree that horses, dogs, cats, bears, and monkeys are examples. People usually think of an animal as a warm-blooded creature with a backbone, four legs, and a coat of hair or fur. This is but one kind of animal, called a mammal. There are many other kinds. Insects and birds, worms and fishes, corals, sponges, frogs, and snails are only a few.

All living things are divided into two main "kingdoms"—the animal kingdom and the plant kingdom. What is the difference between a horse, for example, and the grass? A horse moves about in the pasture eating the grass. It trots toward you when you offer it a lump of sugar and shows pleasure when you stroke its head. The grass, however, is rooted to one place. It does not respond to you or to the horse in any way. (*See also* Life; Plants.)

Animals Move About and Sense Surroundings

Here then are two differences: Animals *move* freely from place to place, and they *sense* their surroundings; that is, they can taste, smell, hear, see, touch, and think. Certain lowly animals, such as the corals and barnacles, spend most of their lives fastened to one spot, but they are able to swim freely when they are young. Even these "rooted" animals have parts that move in order to capture food. Plants, however, cannot shift about by their own will. They react to heat, light, chemicals, and touch, but the responses are automatic, quite different from those of animals.

All living things, plants and animals alike, are made up of cells of protoplasm. They may consist of a single cell, such as the amoeba, or billions of cells, such as a tree or a horse. The cell wall of a plant is composed of a woody material called cellulose. Wood, cotton, linen, and paper are forms of this substance. *No true animal contains cellulose.* Animal cells are bounded by a membrane composed chiefly of fat and protein. (*See also* Cell; Cellulose.)

Both plants and animals require food. Green plants make their own food. With the aid of the green substance called chlorophyll, they use the energy in sunlight to change carbon dioxide and water into carbohydrates and other food materials. *No true animal contains chlorophyll.* Animals must eat the food manufactured by plants. A horse cannot stand in the sun and wait for his body to make fat and proteins. It must move about the pasture in search of green grass. Even meat eaters—for example, lions—live on animals, such as zebras, which in turn subsist on plants.

The chief differences between plants and animals are these:

1. Animals move about freely at some period of their lives.
2. Animals sense and respond to their surroundings.
3. Animals live on ready-made foods.
4. No true animal contains woody material.

400

BABY RED FOXES

Foxes, bright and alert, are among the most intelligent of wild animals. They are famous for their cleverness in outwitting dogs, hunters, and other enemies.

The Variety of Animal Life

More than a million different kinds of animals inhabit the earth. The exact number is not known, for new kinds are continually being discovered. They live in the seas, from the surface down to the black depths where no ray of light penetrates. On mountaintops and in deserts, in mud and in hot pools some form of animal life may be found.

Animals are infinitely varied in form, size, and habits. The smallest animals are bits of protoplasm that can be seen only with a microscope. The largest are the blue whales. They may be 100 feet long and weigh 300,000 pounds. (*See also* Animals, Kinds of.)

The Shapes of Animals

The most familiar animals, such as dogs, birds, frogs, and fish, all have a backbone and a central nervous system. They are called *vertebrates*, meaning animals with backbones (*see* Vertebrates). They have a head. Sense organs are located in the head. These animals usually move head foremost. They have limbs, wings, or fins by which they move about.

Vertebrates have what the scientists call *bilateral* (meaning "two-sided") *symmetry*. If they were divided down the middle, they would have an eye, an ear, an arm or wing, and a leg or fin on each side. One side matches the other, but in reverse; that is, vertebrates have a right and a left side.

It seems obvious that if an animal is to move and capture food it must have a backbone, a head, and limbs. There are many kinds of animals, however, that lack these advantages. These are the *invertebrates*—the animals *without* backbones.

One-celled animals called *protozoans* live in fresh and salt water (*see* Protozoa). They are shapeless creatures, with no top or bottom, no head or rear, no right or left sides. Such animals cannot swim toward their food. They move along by squeezing out a fingerlike projection from the body. This is called a *pseudopod*, meaning "false foot." The pseudopod fastens to something solid, and the rest of the body flows into it. The amoeba also moves in this manner. One-celled animals are very small. A single blob of liquid enclosed in a thin membrane cannot reach large size or a very definite shape.

Many-celled animals without backbones include the sponges, hydras, corals, jellyfishes, and sea anemones. They are shaped somewhat like a wheel. They are said to have *radial symmetry*. If they were divided down the middle, the two sides would be identical.

All these animals live in water. Some drift with the currents, unable to swim in any definite direction. Others become attached to a solid object by the "down" end and float with the mouth end upright. Tentacles arranged in a circle around the mouth sweep in food particles and ward off enemies.

Animals with Outside Skeletons and Feet

Mollusks have soft bodies that are not divided into specialized sections (*see* Mollusks). Many mollusks are enclosed in hard, hinged shells. These are the lowliest form of animals with feet. The feet appear in strange places, however. Snails are "stomach-footed" mollusks. They have a single large, fleshy foot on the stomach side. The octopus and the squid are "head-footed." The head is surrounded by a circle of eight or ten tentacles which act as arms and feet. Oysters, clams, mussels, and scallops are "ax-footed." They have a single ax-shaped foot with which they burrow into sand.

Most mollusks do not move around efficiently. Oysters fasten themselves to something solid and settle down for life, letting food drift to them. Scallops move in zigzag leaps by clapping their shells together.

SOME WILD ANIMALS
OF NORTH AMERICA

OPOSSUM. This is America's only marsupial. It sleeps in a hidden place by day, coming out at night to hunt for food.

RACCOON. Alert and bright-faced, the raccoon is one of the most intelligent of wild creatures. It is a night prowler.

SKUNK. A beautiful, playful animal, the skunk uses its famous scent gland only when it is frightened or injured.

BADGER. The badger has a long, flat body, with grayish fur on the sides that almost conceals its sharp-clawed feet.

WEASEL. This weasel, pictured in Walt Disney's 'White Wilderness', is trying to open the egg of a ring-billed gull.

BROWN BEAR. A mother bear and her cub look for handouts in Yellowstone National Park.

SNOWSHOE RABBIT. Also called varying hare, this little animal's coat changes from brown to white in the wintertime.

THIRTEEN-LINED GROUND SQUIRREL. This relative of the chipmunk and squirrel lives on the prairies of North America.

RED NEWT, or **EFT.** This is one of the salamanders in the three-year period when it lives on land, in the woods.

HOG-NOSED SNAKE. This harmless snake frightens intruders by flattening its head, inflating its body with air, and hissing.

403

WILD ANIMALS OF AFRICA AND ASIA

CHEETAH. The cheetah, found in Africa and India, is a gentle member of the cat family. It is trained to help hunters.

ELEPHANT. The Asiatic elephant has smaller ears than its African relative and can be trained to serve man.

OSTRICH. The ostrich lives on the plains and deserts of Africa. It cannot fly, but it can outrun a horse. This is a female.

ELAND. The largest of the many kinds of African antelopes, the eland lives in the central and southern part of the continent.

404

SOME WILD ANIMALS
AROUND THE WORLD

KOALA. Australia's attractive little "teddy bear" is a rare marsupial. The country no longer permits its export to zoos.

GIBBON. The gibbon is an ape of Southeast Asia. The baby clings to its mother's fur as she swings through the jungle trees.

TIMBER WOLF. Timber wolves live in sub-Arctic regions. This wolf appeared in the Walt Disney picture 'White Wilderness'.

GUANACO. In remote regions of the Andes of South America lives the guanaco. It is a relative of the camel.

ANIMAL SPEED RECORDS

TWO-TOED SLOTH, ½ mph   AFRICAN ELEPHANT (charging 120 yards), 24.5 mph   WHITE-TAILED DEER, 30 mph   GIRAFFE, 32 mph
DESERT TORTOISE, ½ mph   ROAD RUNNER, 15 mph   EMU (10 miles), 31 mph   WART HOG, 30 mph   RHINOCEROS, 35 mph

The Joint-Legged Animals

Joint-legged animals have a far better body plan than that of any of the animals mentioned so far. Their bodies are divided into segments which have specialized functions. They have many jointed legs. Most of them are covered with a jointed skeleton made of a horny material. This outside skeleton is lighter than the shells of the mollusks. The legs and muscles and many other organs are attached to it. The joint-legged animals, or arthropods, include insects, lobsters, crabs, centipedes, millepedes, and spiders. Many of them have wings. They can run, jump, swim, creep, or fly. They live on land, in fresh water, and in salt water.

The grasshopper and flea are champion jumpers. The flea can make a standing high jump of 100 times its own height and a broad jump of 200 times its own length. The flea is a better jumper than the kangaroo, which can leap only five times its length. The horsefly is one of the fastest insect fliers. It can soar through the air at the rate of $31\frac{1}{2}$ miles an hour. The botfly can reach a speed of 25 miles an hour.

How Backboned Animals Move About

The animals with backbones move through the water, the air, and over the ground with the greatest speed and skill. Birds, with their feathered wings, are the greatest of all fliers. Fish are the champion swimmers. Other backboned animals, however, also can fly and swim. The bat flies on wings of membrane. The flying squirrel glides on a broad membrane between its legs. The flying fish soars over the surface of the water with its great back fin.

Turtles swim with paddlelike front legs. Some water birds can swim under water with their wings. Old squaws and shearwaters are examples. The mudskipper is a fish that walks on mud by pulling itself along on its front fins. It can also hop on its tail and fins.

Frogs and kangaroos and the various cats are superior jumpers. There are also some good jumpers among fish. Salmon leap up waterfalls when they travel from the sea to their home streams to lay their eggs. Tarpon, swordfish, and sailfish make great leaps out of the water when they are pursuing their prey

MONGOLIAN WILD ASS, 40 mph   OSTRICH (½ mile), 50 mph   GOBI GAZELLE, 60 mph   PRONGHORN ANTELOPE, 60 mph
GREYHOUND (¼ mile), 36 mph   RED FOX, 45 mph   JACK RABBIT, 45 mph   CHEETAH (100 yards), 70 mph

or trying to escape an enemy. Snakes are the most well-known "creepers" (*see* Snake, subhead "How a Snake Gets About").

Various Ways of Breathing

All animals must take in oxygen in order to change food into a form that the body can use. One-celled animals that live in water absorb oxygen directly through their membranes. The sponge is a very simple many-celled animal. The surface of a sponge is covered with millions of tiny pores. Water, bearing dissolved oxygen and minute food particles, flows through the pores and out of the opening at the top of the sponge.

Fish and tadpoles breathe by means of gills (*see* Fish, subhead "How Fish Breathe"). Insects and caterpillars take air into the body through breathing pores called spiracles (*see* Insects, subhead "The Internal Organs").

Mammals, birds, and reptiles obtain oxygen from the air. They take it into the lungs. The oxygen goes through membranes in the lungs into blood particles called corpuscles. The blood stream then carries the oxygen to every part of the body (*see* Blood; Lungs; Respiration). Frogs and other amphibians have lungs, but they also have thin, moist skins which absorb oxygen directly (*see* Frog, Anatomy of).

How Animals Reproduce

All animals reproduce their own kind. One-celled creatures such as the slipper animalcule, or paramecium (shown on a later page), pinch together in the middle and divide in two. The process is called *cell division* or *fission*.

A kind of sea squirt reproduces by budding. Lumps appear along a branchlike organ and develop into young sea squirts. Sea squirts, sponges, corals, and other creatures that bud often remain together and form large colonies. The picture of a sea squirt on a later page shows the beginning of a colony. The hydra also reproduces by budding, but in time the young bud separates and goes off to live alone.

Reproducing by Eggs

Many animals reproduce by means of eggs which develop into new animals. Fish, snails, clams, crabs

407

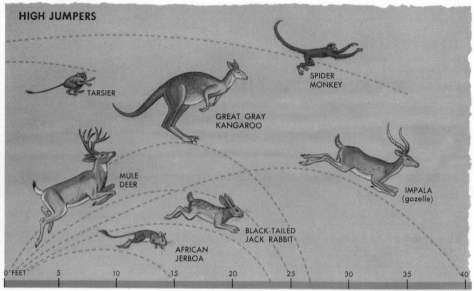

HIGH JUMPERS

DOLPHIN (straight up)

FEET
—15

SALMON

—10

—5

ADÉLIE PENGUIN (straight up)

TARSIER

GREAT GRAY KANGAROO

SPIDER MONKEY

MULE DEER

IMPALA (gazelle)

BLACK-TAILED JACK RABBIT

AFRICAN JERBOA

0 FEET   5   10   15   20   25   30   35   40

and lobsters, insects, frogs, snakes, and birds are some of the egg-laying animals.

Water-dwelling species generally lay their eggs and pay no more attention to them. The same is true of turtles and most spiders and insects. Ants, bees, and wasps have worker "nurses" that care for the eggs and young. Mother lobsters carry their eggs about, and some fish guard both their eggs and their young. Most birds and certain snakes protect their eggs. Other snakes and some lizards produce eggs with shells, but they keep the eggs in their bodies until they hatch. When the young animals come out of the eggs, they are ready to take care of themselves.

Most mammals begin as tiny eggs which have no shells and develop inside the mother's body (see Mammals; Egg). In time the baby animals are born. The mother cares for them and feeds them with her milk.

Homes of Animals

Many animals build temporary or permanent homes for themselves and their young. Birds occupy their nests only while they are incubating eggs and feeding the helpless nestlings (see Birds). A few fish make temporary nests for their young (see Fish).

No animal dwelling has excited more wonder and interest than the lodge built by the beaver. Almost as remarkable is the dome-shaped winter home of the muskrat. Underground burrows with sleeping rooms, food-storage rooms, connecting tunnels, and emergency exits are constructed by ground hogs, prairie dogs, European rabbits, gophers, kangaroo rats, and field mice. Chimpanzees and gorillas build temporary nests and sleeping platforms of sticks in trees. As wonderful as the lodges of mammals are the living

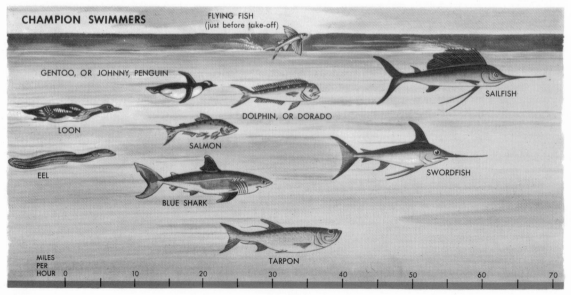

CHAMPION SWIMMERS

FLYING FISH (just before take-off)

GENTOO, OR JOHNNY, PENGUIN

SAILFISH

LOON

DOLPHIN, OR DORADO

SALMON

EEL

SWORDFISH

BLUE SHARK

TARPON

MILES PER HOUR   0   10   20   30   40   50   60   70

TERMS FOR CERTAIN ANIMALS AND THEIR GROUPS

ANIMAL	MALE	FEMALE	YOUNG	GROUP
Bear	Boar	Sow	Cub	Sloth*
Beaver	....	....	Pup, Kitten	Colony
Bee	Drone	Queen, Worker	....	Hive; Swarm (in flight)
Bison	Bull	Cow	Calf	Herd
Cat	Tomcat	....	Kitten	Litter; Clowder*
Cattle	Bull	Cow	Calf	Drove; Herd
Chicken	Rooster	Hen	Chick	Flock; Brood (of chicks)
Crow	....	....	....	Murder*
Deer	Buck; Stag	Doe	Fawn	Herd
Dog	Dog	Bitch	Pup	Litter; Pack (wild); Kennel
Donkey	Jackass	Jennet	Colt	Drove; Herd
Duck	Drake	Duck	Duckling	Flock
Eagle	....	....	Fledgling	Aerie
Elephant	Bull	Cow	Calf	Herd
Fish	....	....	....	School; Shoal
Fox	Reynard	Vixen	Kit; Cub; Pup	Skulk
Goat	Buck	Doe	Kid	Herd; Trip
Goose	Gander	Goose	Gosling	Flock; Gaggle; Skein (in flight)
Grouse; Partridge; Quail	Cock	Hen	Chick	Covey
Hog	Boar	Sow	Shoat; Farrow	Drove; Herd; Litter (young)
Horse	Stallion; Stud	Mare; Dam	Foal; Colt (male); Filly (female)	Stable; Herd; String or Field (of race horses)
Jay (bird)	....	....	....	Band
Kangaroo	Buck; Boomer	Doe; Flyer	Joey	Troop; Herd
Lion	Lion	Lioness	Cub	Pride
Locust	....	....	....	Host
Ox	Steer	Cow	Stot	Drove; Herd
Pheasant	Cock	Hen	Chick	Nye
Rabbit	Buck	Doe	Kitten	Colony; Warren
Seal	Bull	Cow	Pup	Herd; Rookery; Harem
Sheep	Buck; Ram	Ewe; Dam	Lamb	Flock; Hurtle*
Swallow; Dove	....	....	....	Flight
Swan	Cob	Pen	Cygnet	
Trout	....	....	....	Hover*
Turtle	....	....	....	Bale*
Walrus	Bull	Cow	Cub	Herd
Whale	Bull	Cow	Calf	Gam; Herd
Wolf; Coyote	....	....	....	Pack
Zebra	Stallion	Mare	Colt	Herd

*Obsolete but still used in literature.

quarters made by the different kinds of ants. Certain tropical bats cut palm fronds in such a way that they droop to form a leafy shelter from the hot sun and torrential rains.

Defenses Against Enemies

All animals have some means of defending themselves against enemies. Cats can usually outrun a dog and climb the nearest tree. If they are cornered, they scratch and bite. Dogs, wolves, foxes, and coyotes have swift legs and sharp fangs.

Porcupines and hedgehogs roll into a ball and raise their sharp quills. The quills come off at a touch, their barbed tips sticking into the nose of an unwary dog or some other enemy. Skunks spray a foul-smelling fluid from a gland when they are frightened.

Deer, moose, and antelope fight with their antlers. An elephant's trunk is a powerful weapon. It can be used to pick up another animal and smash it to the ground.

Squids shoot out a cloud of inky material and escape in a smoke screen. Torpedo fish and several other kinds of fish have built-in electric storage cells by which they can deliver a paralyzing shock. Some snakes and lizards protect themselves with their poison.

Many animals hide by means of *protective coloration*. A baby deer is almost invisible in the forest because its spotted coat looks like patches of sunlight in the brown leaves. Many fishes, birds, insects, lizards, and snakes use nature's camouflage to avoid observation. (*See also* Protective Coloration.)

HOW SOME ANIMALS CAPTURE FOOD

FOOD PARTICLES

CILIA

FLAGELLUM

PSEUDOPODS

FOOD PARTICLE

VORTICELLA

FOOD PARTICLES

COLLAR FLAGELLATE

FOOD VACUOLES

HELIOZOAN

TENTACLES

HYDRA

HEAD OF BUTTERFLY

SIPHONING TUBE

BARN SWALLOW

KANGAROO RAT

S.N.SWAIN

How Some Animals Capture Food

One-celled animals, such as the vorticella, collar flagellate, and heliozoan, live in fresh or salt water. The pictures of them above are very greatly magnified, for they can be seen only under a microscope. They feed on even tinier organisms in the water. The vorticella is attached by its stalk to some solid object. At the upper end is a mouth surrounded by tiny hairs called *cilia*. The hairs sweep food particles into the mouth by setting up a whirlpool action in the water. The food is enclosed in a bubble called a *food vacuole*, where it is digested.

The collar flagellate has a delicate, transparent collar. From the center of it grows a whiplike organ, the *flagellum*. The beating of the whip draws a current of water toward the cell. Food particles in the current pass through the wall of the cell into the food vacuoles.

The heliozoan, also called "sun animal," moves about and captures food by means of pseudopods. In this case the pseudopods are stiff spines that radiate from the center of the cell. The spines wrap around the food and enclose it in a vacuole.

The hydra in the picture is capturing the larva of a kind of shellfish. It has a mouth surrounded with long tentacles. The tentacles sting and paralyze the prey and then shove it inside the mouth.

Butterflies and moths have tubelike mouth parts. With these they suck nectar from flowers. Grasshoppers and beetles have chewing, grasping, and tearing mouth parts. (For picture of insect mouth parts, *see* Insects.)

The barn swallow catches insects in flight. Some birds hammer into the bark of trees for grubs, comb the leaves with their bills for small insects, swoop down on rodents and on other birds. (For picture of the feeding habits of birds, *see* Birds.)

HOW OTHER ANIMALS CAPTURE FOOD

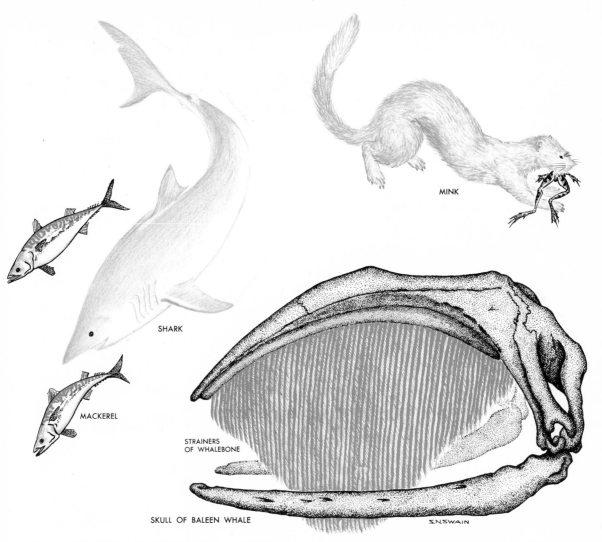

MINK

SHARK

MACKEREL

STRAINERS
OF WHALEBONE

SKULL OF BALEEN WHALE

I.N.SWAIN

The kangaroo rat is an attractive, harmless little animal that lives in the deserts of the Southwestern United States. It lives on dry thistle and cactus leaves, seeds, and small juicy tubers that grow abundantly in the desert an inch or two below the surface. It collects seeds in its cheek pouches and stores them in underground chambers. Gophers and chipmunks also collect food in their cheek pouches and store it in underground pantries for future use.

How Other Animals Capture Food

The shark is a fierce meat eater. It lives on smaller fish such as mackerel. Some fish subsist on plant and animal life known as plankton (*see* Fish, subhead "The Endless Food Chain"). The baleen whale is an enormous animal, from 20 to 100 feet long. It feeds upon shrimplike creatures only an inch or two in length. When it finds a school of shrimp, it opens its mouth and gulps in several barrelfuls of water. Horny strainers that hang from the roof of its mouth catch the shrimp and drain out the water.

The mink lives on frogs, fish, and lizards. It is swift moving, with dagger-sharp teeth and claws. Many other mammals are meat eaters (*carnivorous*). They all have special kinds of teeth for tearing their food into chunks and chewing it (*see* Teeth). Most of them have claws for catching and holding their prey. Among the meat eaters are cats, dogs, raccoons, weasels, bears, hyenas, and civet cats.

Plant- and Insect-Eating Mammals

A large group of animals are plant eaters (*herbivorous*). Many of them are victims of the meat eaters. The plant eaters include the horse family, cattle, sheep, goats, rabbits, rodents, elephants, deer and antelope, and monkeys and apes. A few mammals live on insects—moles, shrews, and hedgehogs, most bats, armadillos, aardvarks, and anteaters.

411

How Animals Sense Their Surroundings

The ability of animals to sense and respond to their surroundings is one way in which they differ from plants. Animals have sense organs to perceive light, sound, touch, taste, smell, and other sensations (*see* Sensation and Perception).

Eyes are very important to most mammals. Animals that hunt and feed by night have very large eyes. The flying squirrel is an example. Cats' eyes have pupils that can open wide in the dark and narrow down to slits in the sunlight. Insects have compound eyes, made up of tiny units which break up the image into many small pictures. They also have two or three simple eyes which probably detect motion. (For pictures of some interesting animal eyes, *see* Eye.) The eyesight of some fish is especially keen (*see* Fish, subhead "Senses of Fish").

Ears are perhaps as important as eyes. The fennec is a foxlike animal that lives in the Sahara and hunts by night. Its large ears help it detect its prey in the darkness of a hot, dry climate where food is very scarce. The cat is also a night prowler, and it too has large, erect ears. The "ears" of the field cricket and katydid are located on their forelegs. The ear is a thin membrane that vibrates in response to sound waves.

Many animals have sense organs unlike those of the mammals. The antennae of the moths, butterflies, and other insects seem to correspond to the organs of taste, touch, smell, and hearing. (For pictures of different kinds of antennae, *see* Insects.)

The barbels of the catfish and the whiskers of the flying squirrel and the cat are organs of touch. They are very useful for animals that explore in the dark. The lateral line of the fish is a rod of nerve cells the length of the body. It probably helps it feel movements in the surrounding water.

The delicate forked tongue of the snake "tastes" the air. With it the snake can locate food and other snakes. The rattlesnake has sensory pits on the head. It can detect a nearby warm-blooded animal through these pits. Even the simplest one-celled animals respond to touch. If the amoeba is touched, it curls up into a ball. It moves away from strong light or from water that is too hot or too cold.

In the warm, muddy rivers of western Africa there are fish that send out small electric impulses and surround themselves with an electric field. Whenever another fish or other object approaches, the fish is made aware of it by the changes in the charged field. Thus a built-in electrical system takes the place of eyesight in the dark waters and keeps the fish informed of its surroundings. Bats have built-in radar enabling them to "see" with their wings.

Migration and Hibernation

When winter comes in northern regions, animals must find some way to keep warm. Many birds and some mammals move south and seek a mild climate. They are said to *migrate*. Other kinds of mammals (bears, chipmunks, and woodchucks, for example) store up fat in their bodies in the fall by eating all they can stuff into themselves. Then they curl up in a cave

HOW ANIMALS SENSE THEIR SURROUNDINGS

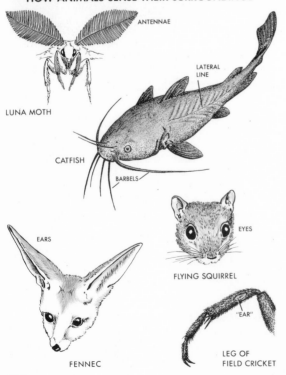

ANTENNAE

LUNA MOTH

LATERAL LINE

CATFISH

BARBELS

EARS

EYES

FLYING SQUIRREL

FENNEC

"EAR"

LEG OF FIELD CRICKET

TWO WAYS OF REPRODUCING

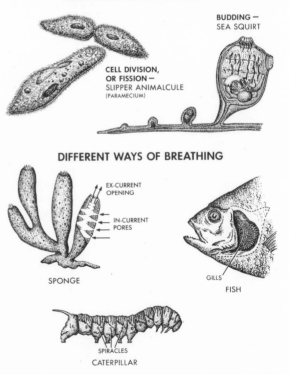

BUDDING — SEA SQUIRT

CELL DIVISION, OR FISSION — SLIPPER ANIMALCULE (PARAMECIUM)

DIFFERENT WAYS OF BREATHING

EX-CURRENT OPENING

IN-CURRENT PORES

SPONGE

GILLS

FISH

SPIRACLES

CATERPILLAR

MANY ANIMALS CARE FOR THEIR YOUNG

BOBWHITE TURNING EGGS

MOTHER DOG NURSING PUPS

or some other protected place and sleep during the cold period. They are said to *hibernate*.

Most insects die in the wintertime. They leave well-protected eggs, which hatch in the spring. Ants, however, hibernate. Water-dwelling animals, such as fishes and frogs, may hibernate in mud, or they may move to deeper water and remain inactive. (*See also* Hibernation; Migration of Animals.)

Living Together in Colonies

Some animals live with others of their own kind. Ants, honeybees and bumblebees, and wasps are called *social insects* because they live together in highly organized societies. It is fascinating to observe the lives of these insects. (*See also* Nature Study, section "Ways of Watching Ants and Bees".)

Some birds live in large colonies. They help incubate one another's eggs and care for the young. Penguins, anis, and eider ducks are examples. Weaver finches work together to build huge community "apartment houses."

South American monkeys travel through the jungles in family groups. They scatter while they are searching for food but stay within sight or hearing of one another. Toward evening they rejoin and spend the night together. Baboons live in large bands. They co-operate in food getting and post sentries to watch for danger when the group stops.

Intelligence in Animals

Most animal activities that appear to indicate intelligence are simply instinctive. The most intelligent animals are the apes and monkeys. Chimpanzees can be taught to do many things that a child can do (*see* Circus; Learning; Zoo). Dogs and elephants serve man in many ways. Horses, seals, porpoises, and even lions and tigers are taught to perform in circuses and aquariums. Talking birds, such as the parrots, para-

SOME ANIMALS LIVE TOGETHER IN COLONIES OF THEIR OWN KIND

ANTS

PRAIRIE DOGS

MONKEYS

PENGUINS

HOW LONG DO ANIMALS LIVE?

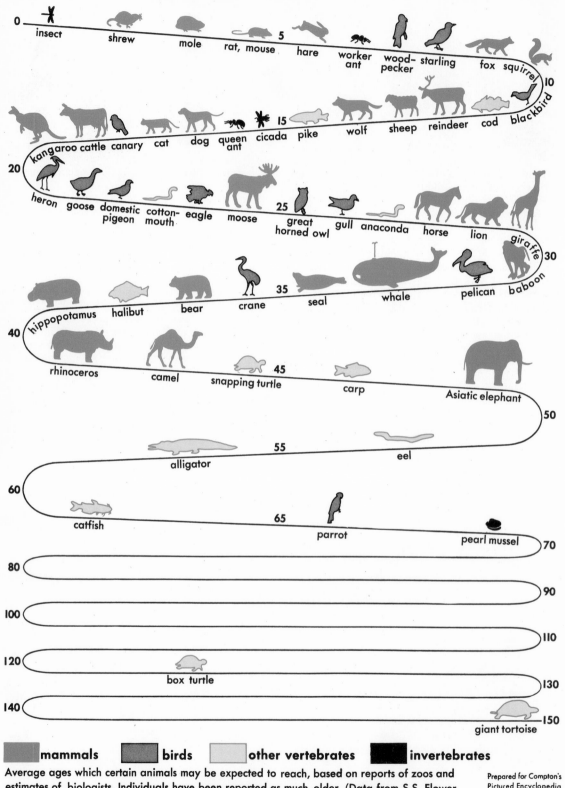

Average ages which certain animals may be expected to reach, based on reports of zoos and estimates of biologists. Individuals have been reported as much older. (Data from S.S. Flower, 'The Duration of Life in Animals', in *Proceedings of the London Zoological Society*.)

THE GREAT VARIETY OF ANIMAL LIFE

The Portuguese man-of-war, a kind of jellyfish (left), carries a sail, or crest, that projects above the sea. Ocean breezes blow it about like a tiny rudderless boat. The spiny oak-slug caterpillar (center) terrifies possible enemies with its strange spines. The baby wanderoo monkey (right) is tucked into the pocket of a nurse in the zoo. It sucks its thumb and clings to the nurse's hand.

keets, and mynas learn to imitate sounds, but they do not *think* what they are talking about.

Animals as Friends and Enemies of Man

Without the help of animals man would never have become civilized. (For the story of the important part played by domestic animals, *see* Animals, Domestic.) In pollinating flowers bees make possible fine orchard fruits, alfalfa, clover, and many vegetables. The lowly earthworm by churning up the soil improves the growth of plants.

Birds eat insect pests, weed seeds, and rodents (*see* Birds, subhead "What Birds Do for Man"). Certain bats eat so many mosquitoes and other insects that some communities erect huge shelters for them to encourage their help. Hyenas and vultures keep country regions clean by devouring dead animals.

Countless animal products are used by man: pearls (from the oyster), shellac and lacquer (from the lac insect), glue, and fertilizers are only a few. Important drugs are produced from the blood and glands of animals. Smallpox vaccine, for example, is cultivated in calves. Serums and antivenins for snake bite are made from the blood of horses. Experiments performed on such animals as rats, mice, and guinea pigs have been responsible for great advances in medical knowledge and the conquest of disease.

Animal enemies include the organisms in the human body that cause serious diseases (*see* Parasites). Fleas, lice, rats, and malarial mosquitoes are also disease carriers. Insect pests cause billions of dollars' worth of damage every year. (*See also* Insects; Animals, Distribution of; Animals, Domestic; Animals, Extinct; Animals, Kinds of; Animals, Legendary; Animal Tracks; Life; Nature Study. For Reference-Outline, *see* Zoology.)

BIBLIOGRAPHY FOR ANIMALS

Books for Younger Readers

Bailey, J. S. Our Wild Animals (Nelson, 1965).
Baker, Mary and Bridges, William. Wild Animals of the World (Doubleday, 1957).
Barker, Will. Winter-Sleeping Wildlife (Harper, 1958).
Berrill, Jacquelyn. Wonders of Animal Migration (Dodd, 1964).
Blough, G. O. After the Sun Goes Down (Whittlesey, 1956).
Brown, Vinson. How to Understand Animal Talk (Little, 1958).
Burton, Maurice. In Their Element (Abelard, 1960).
Cosgrove, M. L. The Strange World of Animal Senses (Dodd, 1961).
Green, I. E. Animal Masquerade (Coward-McCann, 1955).
Mason, G. F. Animal Habits (Morrow, 1959).
Peattie, D. C. The Rainbow Book of Nature (World, 1957).
Pettit, T. S. The Book of Small Mammals (Garden City, 1958).
Selsam, M. E. The Language of Animals (Morrow, 1962).
Weyl, P. K. Men, Ants and Elephants (Viking, 1959).
Zim, H. S. Mammals (Golden, 1955).
Zim, H. S. What's Inside of Animals? (Morrow, 1953).

Books for Advanced Students and Teachers

Breland, O. P. Animal Facts and Fallacies (Harper, 1948).
Breland, O. P. Animal Life and Lore (Harper, 1963).
Cahalane, V. H. Mammals of North America (Macmillan, 1953).
Devoe, Alan. This Fascinating Animal World (McGraw, 1951).
Ditmars, R. L. Reptiles of North America (Doubleday, 1936).
Drimmer, Frederick, ed. Animal Kingdom, 3v. (Greystone, 1954).
National Geographic Society. Wild Animals of North America (National Geographic, 1960).
Palmer, R. S. The Mammal Guide (Doubleday, 1954).
Sanderson, I. T. How to Know the American Mammals (Little, 1951).
Sanderson, I. T. Living Mammals of the World (Garden City, 1955).
Scheele, W. E. First Mammals (World, 1955).
See also bibliographies for Birds; Hobbies, section "Nature Hobbies"; Insects; Nature Study; and Zoology.

This is a marsh scene, showing some of the animals that live in such a *habitat*. In the cattails are red-winged blackbirds, black terns, coots, rails, and phalaropes, and along the shallow edges, the mounds of muskrats.

Distribution of Animals

ANIMALS, DISTRIBUTION OF. On a walk through the countryside, one may notice that different kinds of animals live in different kinds of surroundings. Along the lake shore, gulls wheel overhead looking for fish. In the seaweed on the edge of the waves, sandpipers search for insects.

Back from the shore line may be a swampy pond edged with cattails. Red-winged blackbirds and marsh wrens nest in them. A muskrat has a home of mud and weeds in the shallow water. A meadow stretches from the marsh to a distant woodland. Meadow larks nest on the ground. Grasshoppers and crickets leap from under one's feet, and a frightened meadow mouse scurries away. A herd of cattle graze nearby. In the quiet woods the plants and wildlife are quite different from those of shore line, marsh, and meadow. Owls nest in the evergreens. At nightfall one may catch a glimpse of a fox, a raccoon, or an opossum.

Distribution by Habitats

The various plant and animal communities are called *habitats*. There are many kinds of habitats—seashore, fresh-water ponds, treeless tundra of the Far North, grasslands, deserts, tropical rain forests, temperate forests. The science of the association between plants and animals is called ecology (*see* Ecology). Ecology, then, is one way to explain animal distribution.

Distribution by Regions

There is another kind of distribution of animals. Scientists have found that the land area of the earth can be divided into six *faunal* (meaning "animal") regions. These, with some of the mammals characteristic of each region, are shown on the next three pages. (The drawings are adapted from 'Life: An Introduction to Biology' © 1957 by Harcourt, Brace and Company.)

The regions are Nearctic (meaning "New World northern"); Palaearctic ("Old World northern"); Neotropical ("New World tropical"); Ethiopian; Oriental; and Australian. The division line between the Oriental and the Australian regions passes through the narrow straits between the islands of Bali and Lombok and between Borneo and the Celebes. It is called Wallace's line, after the naturalist Alfred Russel Wallace (*see* East Indies).

Within each of these regions the plants and animals are different from those of any other region. The explanation is to be found in the geological history of the earth. Over the ages old land connections between the continents were cut off by the sea. Mountain barriers rose. Climates changed. The animals that live in a certain region developed, over a period of tens of thousands of years, into various *kinds* of animals. Each region developed its own distinctive species *if* there was no contact with the animals of other regions because of high mountains, seas, or deserts.

Thus the animals of southern Asia are of different kinds than those of Asia north of the Himalayas. These lofty mountains prevented animals from moving from one side of them to the other. On the other hand, the animals of northern Europe, Asia, and North America are similar. There were no barriers in the past, and animals could move freely across the top of the world. Only in comparatively recent times has the land connection between eastern Siberia and Alaska been cut off by the Bering Strait.

Australia for countless ages has been an island continent. At the time when it became separated from the Asiatic mainland, a primitive kind of mammal called a marsupial lived in the region. The kangaroo is a marsupial. Australia's marsupials developed while those in the rest of the world almost disappeared. The only marsupial in North America is the opossum. The higher mammals in Australia were brought there by settlers.

DISTRIBUTION OF LAND ANIMALS

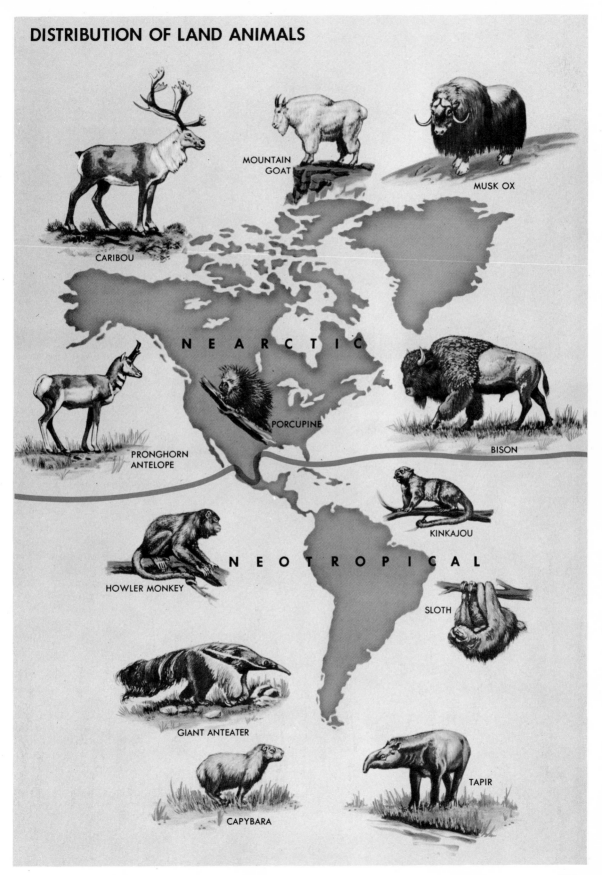

CARIBOU

MOUNTAIN GOAT

MUSK OX

NEARCTIC

PRONGHORN ANTELOPE

PORCUPINE

BISON

KINKAJOU

HOWLER MONKEY

NEOTROPICAL

SLOTH

GIANT ANTEATER

CAPYBARA

TAPIR

DISTRIBUTION OF LAND ANIMALS

REINDEER

BISON

HEDGEHOG

PALAEARCTIC

POLECAT

AARDVARK

BINTURONG

ETHIOPIAN

AFRICAN ELEPHANT

GORILLA

ZEBRA

GIRAFFE

GNU

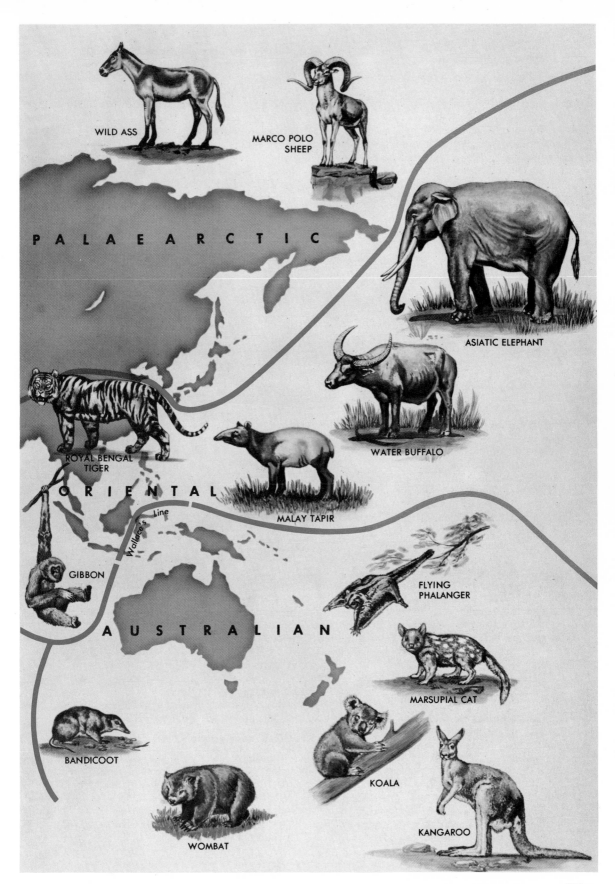

WILD ASS

MARCO POLO
SHEEP

PALAEARCTIC

ASIATIC ELEPHANT

WATER BUFFALO

ROYAL BENGAL
TIGER

ORIENTAL

MALAY TAPIR

Wallace's Line

GIBBON

FLYING
PHALANGER

AUSTRALIAN

MARSUPIAL CAT

BANDICOOT

KOALA

KANGAROO

WOMBAT

419

Distribution of Sea Animals

Marine life is divided into three groups. *Planktonic* animals are those that float on the surface of the sea, drifting with the currents. They are microscopic forms of sea life, including eggs and larvae, which together with plants constitute the plankton.

Nektonic creatures are free-swimming, like fish, and able to roam the seas in search of food. *Benthonic* animals are those which live on the bottom of the sea. Some are fixed, such as sponges and corals; some burrow, such as certain worms and shellfish; and others creep about, such as starfish and mollusks. (*See also* Fish; Ocean; Oceanography.)

Ocean currents control the distribution of the planktonic animals. Water temperature is an important factor in determining where the nektonic creatures are found. Many fish are able to live only within a narrow range of temperature variation. Warm-water fish that have been carried into cold water by storms or other unusual disturbances have been known to die by the millions. In general, therefore, the distribution of marine life depends upon ecological factors.

How Man Put Animals to Work for Him

ANIMALS, DOMESTIC. Man's success on earth has been due in part to the animals that he has been able to put to work for him. They carry him and his burdens. They pull his machinery and cultivate his fields. They feed and clothe him. As pets they amuse him and console him in his loneliness.

Domesticated animals are those that have been bred in captivity for many generations. One speaks of *taming* a single animal. Only a *group* of animals can be domesticated. In the course of time, by selective breeding, they have greatly changed from their wild ancestors. There is a vast difference between the scrawny little red jungle fowl of southern Asia and its descendant, the heavy-breasted, egg-laying "machine" produced on the modern chicken farm.

Not all domestic animals are tame at all times. An angry bull, a mother goose, or a mother sow with young pigs can be vicious. Some creatures confined in zoos breed in captivity. The lion is an example. These animals are not domesticated, however, for they remain wild and dangerous.

Dogs, the First Domesticated Animals

There seems to be little doubt that the dog was the first animal domesticated by man. Its bones are common in campsites of the late New Stone Age, dating back more than 10,000 years. At least five different kinds of dogs similar to the household pets of today have been identified from these remains. The beginnings of their domestication must, therefore, date many thousands of years earlier than that.

Possible wild ancestors of the domesticated dog are found on every continent. They include wolves and coyotes in North America, Europe, and Asia;

Cattle have been called the most useful of domesticated animals. As beasts of burden and providers of milk, meat, and leather, they are unequaled. This little girl is feeding a Hereford calf.

jackals in Africa; and dingoes in Australia. One theory suggests that the wild dog "adopted" Old Stone Age hunters of 100,000 years ago by trailing on the edges of their camps for scraps of food. The hunters probably discovered that a litter of pups, raised in camp, became attached to their human companions and yet retained their hunting instincts. They joined in the hunt and shared in the feast. In some such way the hunting dog became man's first helper. (*See also* Dogs; for picture in color of Stone Age men hunting with dogs, *see* Man.)

When Domestication First Came About

Beginning about 8000 B.C. and continuing over a period of about 5,000 years, all the other animals important to man today were domesticated. Remains of cattle, sheep, and pigs have been found in Mesopotamia in ruins dating some time before 3000 B.C. About the same time, in the Indus River valley, in India, people were raising buffaloes, sheep, fowls, elephants, and two kinds of cattle. Fayum, Egypt,

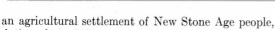

PET (Pony)

LABOR (Water Buffalo)

an agricultural settlement of New Stone Age people, dating about 3000 B.C., kept cattle, pigs, and sheep or goats.

As suddenly as it began, man's control over wild animals came to an end. Not one creature has been added in the past 4,000 years, unless laboratory animals such as mice, rats, guinea pigs, and monkeys can be considered domesticated.

Of the many thousands of species in the world, only a very few have been domesticated. The early peoples of central and southwestern Asia were the most successful in domesticating animals. They gave modern man cattle, sheep, pigs, goats, camels, horses, and asses, or donkeys. Indochina was the original home of the water buffalo, zebu, ox, chicken, and elephant. The yak, domesticated in Tibet, has never left its high mountain home. Northern Europe contributed

only the reindeer. Africa, with the greatest variety of animals in the world, domesticated only the cat, the ass, and the guinea fowl. South America has domesticated three animals—the llama, the alpaca, and the guinea pig. Only the turkey came from North and Central America.

Why Animals Were Domesticated

It is interesting to observe that cattle, sheep, pigs, goats, and horses—the most important and widespread of the domestic animals—are all hoofed grass eaters and can be kept in herds. All of them were first mastered by the early peoples of southwestern Asia. It has been suggested that the grassy plains of that region began slowly drying up some 10,000 years ago. Men and animals were forced to share smaller and smaller oases of fertile land. Men grad-

HUNTING (Cheetah)

CLOTHING (Alpaca)

TURKEY (Meat)   **CHICKENS** (Eggs, Meat)   **GOAT** (Milk, Cheese)

ually learned how to control the animals. Some bred in captivity, and the domestic strains developed.

Another theory on how domestication came about points to the widespread human practice of making pets of captured young and crippled animals. Certain kinds of creatures became attached to their human masters. They followed the camps, and slowly herds were built up. Several factors, rather than any one simple cause, must have led to the association of men and animals.

Cattle, the Most Important Animals

Cattle are the most useful of all domestic animals. It has been said that when people first drank cow's milk and put the ox before the plow, modern civilization began. Cattle have wild relatives in many parts of the world. They must have been domesticated in Asia first, however, for their bones are found in earlier settlements there than anywhere else. Short-horned cattle are supposed to have been introduced into Europe from central Asia when the long-horned urus was still running wild. The urus (now extinct) and the Celtic ox were domesticated later than the Asiatic kinds of cattle.

Sheep have been so changed by breeding that their wild ancestors are hard to identify. The domestic sheep of Egypt in 3000 B.C. had coats of coarse hair, as all wild sheep do. The dense wool is developed by selective breeding.

Pigs were derived from the wild boar, which is still widely distributed in Europe, Asia, and Africa. In Egypt their flesh was not eaten. They were kept as scavengers. They loosened the soil by their rooting and so prepared it for planting. They were also used to trample down the seeds after sowing and to thresh the grain at harvesttime.

Chickens first appear in archaeological records in the cities of the Indus Valley about 3000 B.C. The donkey of Mediterranean lands is thought to be a descendant of the wild ass of western Asia.

Domestication of the Horse

The horse was the last important animal to be domesticated. The only wild horse still living in the 20th century is Przhevalski's horse. Very small numbers survive in western Mongolia. The tarpan, a wild horse of Europe and northern Asia, became extinct about a century ago. These two were probably the ancestors of the modern breeds. The "wild horses" of western North America are domesticated creatures that have returned to the wild.

A Semitic people who conquered the Mesopotamian region about 2300 B.C. were mounted on horses. This fact may explain their success in war. The first sight of a man riding a horse must have struck terror in the hearts of a simple people. The myth of the centaur, half horse and half man, probably had its origin in just such an experience. The 15 horses brought to Mexico by Cortez sent the Aztecs in terrified flight.

In North America before the arrival of the Europeans, the only domesticated animal was the dog. The Indians remained in a primitive state of culture until the white people brought horses to America. The horse effected great changes in the ways of living of the Plains tribes (*see* Indians, American). The far more highly civilized Incas of pre-Columbian Peru domesticated the llama and the alpaca.

Other Attempts to Tame Animals

Men have tried to domesticate many animals, but, as has been noted, they succeeded with very few. Dozens of kinds have been kept as pets and raised in menageries and zoos. Attempts have been made with the bison, related to cattle; with the zebra, related to the horse; and with the peccary, a cousin of the pig. The Egyptians kept herds of antelopes and gazelles in pastures. Why a few animals yielded to domestication while the majority refused to be mastered by man remains a mystery.

ANIMALS, EXTINCT. Many kinds of animals that once inhabited the earth have entirely disappeared. Man knows about the most ancient ones from their fossil remains (*see* Fossils). The bones of some extinct prehistoric creatures have been found with the remains of the hunters who killed them. Other animals that died out long ago can be seen in the artistic and realistic paintings made by Stone Age cave dwellers of France and Spain (*see* Man). Some species now extinct were still alive in historic times. A few vanished in the 20th century, and some are disappearing today as their numbers steadily grow smaller.

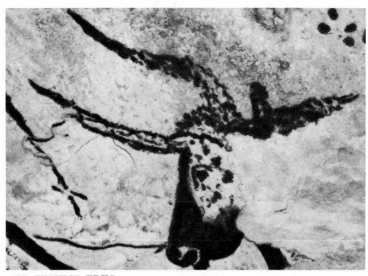

THE EXTINCT URUS

This painting of a urus, an extinct ox, is in the Lascaux Cave of southern France. It was made by a New Stone Age artist some 20,000 years ago. (From 'The Lascaux Cave Paintings', by Fernand Windels, © Viking Press, 1949.)

Why Animals Become Extinct

Animals can survive only as long as they remain adapted to their environment. Changes in the climate and in the geology of any one part of the earth usually occur very slowly. Some animals can adapt their eating and other living habits to meet these changes. Others apparently cannot. This is one explanation for the disappearance of the dinosaurs and other giant reptiles of prehistoric times (see Dinosaur; Prehistoric Life; Reptiles).

A modern example is the ivory-billed woodpecker. It can live only in large cypress forests. With the disappearance of such forests, the birds too are disappearing (*see* Woodpecker). Other extremely rare animals are becoming extinct because they are victims of *too great specialization*. The little koala bear of Australia, for example, refuses to eat anything but eucalyptus leaves. The everglade kite, a beautiful hawk of Florida fresh-water lakes, lives only on snails. Inability to change the specialized diet and other habits in response to a changed environment is, then, one important reason why animals become extinct.

Some prehistoric animals *evolved* into the animals of today. The extinct *Eohippus*, the "dawn horse" of 55 million years ago, was one of the ancestors of the horse. Archaeopteryx was an ancestor of the birds. The urus (*Bos primigenius*), also called giant ox, or aurochs, is one of the ancestors of domestic cattle. (*See also* Birds, subhead "The First True Bird"; Cattle; Horse.)

Overhunting Wipes Out Entire Species

Man exterminates animals directly by overhunting. Prehistoric hunters may have wiped out the mammoth and mastodon, the cave bear, the Irish elk, the saber-toothed tiger, and the other great animals of remote times. Probably changes in climate due to the melting of the Ice Age glaciers also contributed to their disappearance. (*See also* Mammoth and Mastodon; Saber-Toothed Tiger.)

In Europe, only a century before Christ, lions, tigers, leopards, wild cats, and great herds of wild cattle abounded in the region then known as Dacia, north of the Danube River. None of these animals now exist in Europe.

With modern weapons the destruction is rapid and complete. Hunters within recent times wiped out the dodo and solitaire, the great auk, the Carolina parakeet, the passenger pigeon, and the moa (see Auks; Birds, section "Protecting and Conserving Our Birds"; Dodo; Parakeets; Pigeons).

Other Ways in Which Man Affects Animals

Wild animals cannot live in competition with domestic animals. On the range lands of the Western United States, the rancher wages constant warfare with the coyote, wolf, puma, and other predators on livestock. In Africa the cattle herders are driving the antelope, gazelle, zebra, elephant, and other unique animals out of their old grazing grounds in order to give the available grasslands to the animals upon which their livelihood depends.

Introducing an animal into a country where it is not native and has no natural predators can be disastrous to the resident species. Mongooses in the West Indies and dogs and hogs on the island of Mauritius are examples of introduced species which helped wipe out native animals (*see* Mongoose). The myna, introduced into Hawaii from Asia, drove out most of the more desirable native birds.

Modern man also makes rapid and violent changes in environment. By chopping down forests, plowing prairie lands, draining marshes, and polluting waterways, he destroys the dwelling places of the animals in those habitats. Only wise conservation measures can save many of the earth's fine animals which are now threatened with extinction (see Conservation).

The Basic Forms of Animal Life and How They Differ

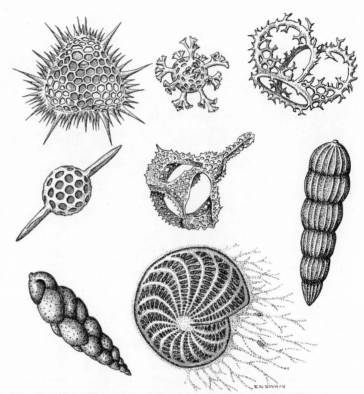

These beautiful objects are the skeletons of one-celled animals called *protozoans*. Two kinds are pictured here. The radiolarians (first five) build up their skeletons from silica extracted from sea water. The skeletons of the foraminifers (last three) are composed of calcium carbonate.

ANIMALS, KINDS OF. More than a million different kinds of animals inhabit the earth. No one knows exactly how many kinds there are, for some 10,000 new ones are found every year.

The Beginnings of Animal Life

The first animals in the history of the earth must have been one-celled bits of protoplasm floating in shallow seas and ponds. Here they remained for millions of years. They developed from one cell to many cells, becoming more and more complex. In time some of the more hardy animals moved into fresh water. Others began to live on land. In these surroundings they changed still more, until today there is a bewildering variety of forms. (*See also* Evolution; Fossils; Life.)

The creatures that developed a backbone and internal skeleton are called *vertebrates*. They include all the familiar animals—the mammals; reptiles; birds; fish; and frogs, toads, and salamanders. Animals without backbones are called *invertebrates*. They include insects, sponges, corals, jellyfish, clams, lobsters, and starfish. (*See also* Vertebrates.)

The vertebrates make up only about 5 per cent of the million or more species of animals. Invertebrates comprise the remaining 95 per cent. There are some 3,500 species of mammals in the world. Insects alone number more than 800,000 species.

How Animals Are Classified

To study the many forms of animal life in a systematic way, scientists have divided the animal kingdom into groups. These groups are based upon the structure of the animal's body. The largest division is the *phylum* (plural, *phyla*). The word means "race" or "tribe." The phyla are groups of animals with fundamentally different body plans.

Each phylum is divided into *classes;* the classes into *orders;* and the orders into *families.* Families are subdivided into *genera* (plural of *genus*), and each genus is divided into *species.* The word "kind" of animal means the species. All members of the same species are closely related. They are capable of interbreeding and producing fertile offspring. Animals of different species cannot interbreed. Every

animal has a Latin term which is the name of its genus and species. (*See also* Biology.)

How Classification Shows Relationships

Classification shows relationships between animals in a decreasing order, from closely related species within a genus to remotely related members of the same phylum. House cats (*Felis domesticus*) and jaguars (*Felis onca*) belong to the same genus and family (*Felidae*) but to different species. Dogs and cats do not appear to be related at all. Both, however, are backboned, meat-eating mammals. Hence they belong to the same phylum, *Chordata* (vertebrates), class *Mammalia* (mammals), and order, *Carnivora* (flesh eaters), but to different families (dog, *Canidae;* cat, *Felidae*).

Whales and sharks, on the other hand, appear to be kinds of fish. Both are strong, streamlined swimmers in the sea. The scientist who has studied these animals knows that the whale is a *mammal*. It has lungs and warm blood, gives birth to living young in the same way a cat does, and nurses the offspring with the mother's milk. Whales therefore belong to the same class (*Mammalia*) as the cat. The shark, on the other hand, is a primitive kind of fish with a skeleton of cartilage instead of bone. It belongs to a different class than the whale and is related to it only in having a backbone (phylum *Chordata*).

Classification also suggests which kinds of animals

may have descended from other types. All many-celled animals, for example, are supposed to be descendants of one-celled animals. This does not mean descent from one *living* kind of animal to another. All living animals are believed to have descended from common ancestors which were less specialized than they. These relationships may be shown on a treelike diagram called a *phylogenetic tree*. The word comes from two Greek words meaning "race history." (For a diagram, *see* Zoology.) The chief phyla are described below, starting with the simplest animals and progressing to the most complex.

Animals Without Backbones—Invertebrates

The simplest animals consist of a single cell—a bit of protoplasm containing one nucleus. One-celled animals differ endlessly in detail, but the one-celled nature is fundamental. The phylum of these creatures is called *Protozoa*. The term comes from Greek words meaning "first animal." Protozoans live in salt and fresh water, in moist earth, and as parasites in other animals. (*See also* Amoeba; Animals; Life; Protozoa. For pictures in color of glass models of radiolarians, *see* Glass.)

All other animals have many cells and belong to the group called *Metazoa* ("higher animal"). The simplest many-celled animals make up the phylum *Porifera* ("pore bearers"). The most familiar kinds are the sponges. They are called pore bearers because they are covered with millions of tiny holes. Water flows through the holes, filtering out the organisms that comprise their food. Sponges have no mouth or digestive cavity and no nervous system. All the cells are essentially alike. (*See also* Sponge.)

Pouchlike Animals

The next structural pattern is a hollow pouch. The phylum is *Coelenterata*, from the Greek words *koilos* ("hollow") and *enteron* ("intestine"). Among the coelenterates are the corals, hydras, jellyfish, and sea anemones. The body is composed of two tissue layers. *Tissues* are groups of similar cells bound together to perform a common function. The inner layer (*endoderm*) lines the central digestive cavity. The outer layer (*ectoderm*) protects the animal.

The coelenterates have a mouthlike opening which takes in food and ejects waste material. Food-getting and protective structures such as tentacles and stinging cells surround the mouth. There is a primitive nervous system. (*See also* Coral; Hydra; Jellyfish; Sea Anemone.)

Bilateral Animals with Heads

All the animals described above are headless creatures, shaped like a wheel, a globe, or a blob of jelly. They are said to have radial or spherical symmetry. They drift about in ocean currents, unable to swim efficiently in any particular direction. Some of them in their adult stages—the corals, for example—fasten themselves to fixed objects and do not move at all.

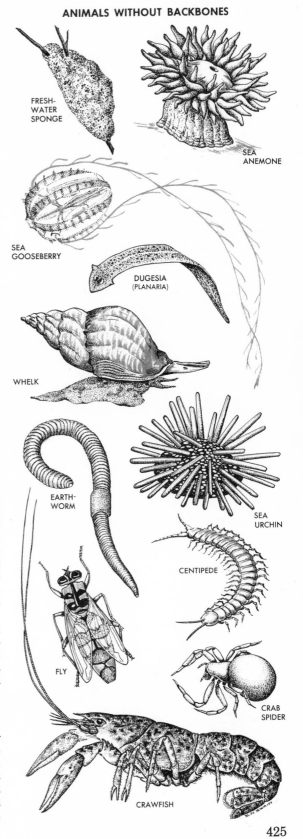

ANIMALS WITHOUT BACKBONES

FRESH-WATER SPONGE

SEA ANEMONE

SEA GOOSEBERRY

DUGESIA (PLANARIA)

WHELK

EARTH-WORM

SEA URCHIN

CENTIPEDE

FLY

CRAB SPIDER

CRAWFISH

ANIMALS WITH BACKBONES

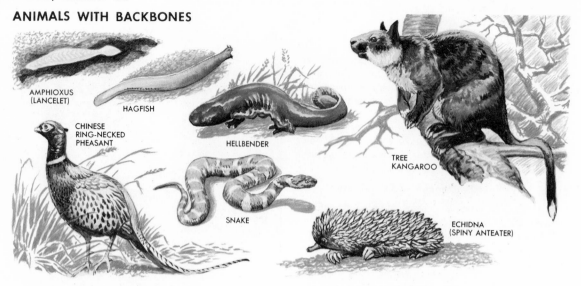

AMPHIOXUS (LANCELET)

HAGFISH

CHINESE RING-NECKED PHEASANT

HELLBENDER

TREE KANGAROO

SNAKE

ECHIDNA (SPINY ANTEATER)

A flatworm called dugesia, or planaria, is interesting because it shows two very important improvements in body structure. It belongs to the phylum *Platyhelminthes* ("flat worms"). It is the most primitive animal with a definite head bearing eyes and sense organs. The mouth is on the underside of the triangular head. The body is differentiated into a front end and a rear end, a top and a bottom. It is said to have *bilateral symmetry*. Each half of the body is a mirror image of the other half. All the higher animals, including man, are built on this pattern of body structure.

Dugesia is also the first animal to have three cell layers. Between the ectoderm and endoderm, which first appeared in the jellyfish and their relatives, is a middle layer (*mesoderm*). Two-layered animals are small and fragile. The third layer gives solidity to the body and permits the animal to grow to large size. Muscles and other complex organs develop from this layer.

Segmented Worms

Segmented worms have a far more efficient body plan. Dugesia takes in food and ejects waste material through the same opening in the head. Segmented worms have a digestive tube with two open-

ings—an anus through which wastes are expelled and a mouth. The phylum *Annelida* ("ringed" or "segmented") has a digestive system built on the same plan as the vertebrates. Earthworms are familiar annelids. (*See also* Anatomy, Comparative; Earthworm; Worm.)

The Soft-Bodied Animals

The phylum *Mollusca* ("soft-bodied") includes the clam, oyster, chiton, snail, octopus, and squid. Mollusks have soft, fleshy bodies not divided into segments. The main part of the body is enclosed in a fold of tissue called the mantle. They have bilateral symmetry. Many of them are covered by a shell. Here is still another type of body pattern—a protective and stiffening structure outside the body. Such a structure is called an *exoskeleton*. (*See also* Clams and Mussels; Mollusks; Nautilus; Octopus; Oyster; Scallop; Snails and Slugs; Squid.)

The Largest Group of Animals

The phylum *Arthropoda* ("jointed feet") has the largest number of species. In fact, about 90 per cent of the million or more species living on the earth today are arthropods. The insects total more than 800,000 species. Other arthropods include the cen-

SEA-DWELLING MAMMALS OF TWO DIFFERENT ORDERS

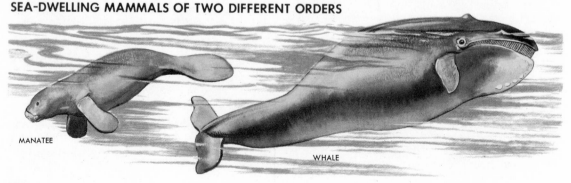

MANATEE

WHALE

MAMMALS OF EIGHT DIFFERENT ORDERS

BAT

FLYING LEMUR

MOUSE

MOLE

HYRAX (CONY)

HAIRY ANTEATER

AARDVARK

PANGOLIN (SCALY ANTEATER)

tipedes and millepedes; the arachnids (spiders, scorpions, ticks, mites), and the crustaceans (barnacles, crabs, crawfish, lobsters, shrimp, water fleas).

Obviously, the arthropod body plan has been highly successful. The members of this great phylum live on land, in fresh water, and in salt water. They can walk, fly, burrow, and swim. This is the only invertebrate group with jointed appendages (legs, feet, and antennae).

Arthropods, like mollusks, wear a supporting framework, or exoskeleton, on the outside of the body. It is much more highly developed, however, than the heavy, clumsy shell of the clams and snails. It is made of a substance called chitin. Rigid, waterproof plates of chitin are joined by thin, flexible

membranes of chitin so that the animal can move freely and quickly. The muscles are attached to the inner surface of the armor. Many important structures are connected to the outer surface. For example, the wings, legs, jaws, and antennae of the insects are all made of chitin and are attached to the outer skeleton. The body is divided into sections, or segments. (*See also* Barnacle; Centipedes and Millepedes; Crab; Crawfish; Insects; Lobster; Scorpion; Shrimp; Spiders and Mites.)

Spiny-Skinned Animals

One strange phylum seems to have the characteristics of several others. The *Echinodermata* ("spiny-skinned") group includes starfishes, sea urchins, sea

MAMMALS OF FIVE DIFFERENT ORDERS

DONKEY

BOBCAT (LYNX)

HARE

PECCARY

ASIATIC ELEPHANT

427

cucumbers, and sea lilies. The young, called larvae, have bilateral symmetry, but the adults have radial symmetry, like the coelenterates. The mouth is in the center of a disk on the undersurface. A number of arms radiate from the disk.

These are the most primitive creatures with an *endoskeleton*, or skeleton embedded in the flesh. It consists of a meshwork of plates made of calcium. They are joined by connective tissue and muscles. Spines project from these plates. (*See also* Sea Cucumber; Starfish and Sea Urchins.)

Animals with Backbones—Vertebrates

At the top of the animal kingdom is the phylum *Chordata* ("spinal cord"). The great subdivisions, or classes, of the vertebrates are the fish, amphibians (the frog, salamander, and toad), reptiles, birds, and mammals. Members of this phylum possess the following structures at some period of their life, either as adults or as embryos:

1. A notochord. This is an internal supporting rod extending the length of the body. It is found in the embryos of all chordates, including man. Only the most primitive forms, such as the amphioxus, or lancelet, the lamprey, and the hagfish, retain it as adults. Remnants of it are present in sharks.

In the higher chordates (amphibians, reptiles, birds, and mammals) the notochord is replaced during development of the embryo by a bony column of vertebrae, which give the column flexibility.

2. A nerve tube. This lies in the mid-line of the body on the backside (dorsal side) of the notochord. In the annelid worms and the arthropods the main nerve is solid and lies on the underside (ventral side). In most chordates the forward end of the nerve tube is enlarged to form a brain; the remainder is the spinal cord.

3. Pharyngeal gill slits or pouches. The lower chordates, such as the fish, breathe through openings in the side of the neck in the region of the pharynx. The embryos of the higher chordates have these slits, but they disappear in the adult.

4. A skeleton. The framework is internal and composed of bone and cartilage or, in the lower chordates, of cartilage alone. (*See also* Skeleton.)

Primitive Chordates

The most primitive backboned animal is the amphioxus. This chordate is a laterally compressed, semitransparent sea dweller from 2 to 3 inches long. Scientists believe that it may be one of the ancestors of the vertebrates. It has a notochord and a tubular nerve cord along the back. It has no well-developed brain, however, and only traces of eyes and ears. Pigment spots along the body are sensitive to light. The pharyngeal gill slits strain food from the water. The tunicates, or sea squirts, and acorn worms are other primitive chordates.

Lampreys and hagfishes are the most primitive of the true vertebrates. They have a notochord. The skeleton is composed of cartilage. They lack jaws and paired limbs. (*See also* Lamprey.)

The Mammals

Mammals differ from other vertebrates in having bodies covered with hair at some period of their lives. They are warm-blooded. The females have milk glands to feed their young. The most primitive mammals are the egg-laying duckbill, the echidna, or spiny anteater, and the marsupials (*see* Duckbill; Mammals). The remaining mammals carry their unborn young in a placenta and give birth to fully developed offspring. These *placental mammals* are divided into 16 orders. The pictures on this and the two preceding pages show one animal for each of 15 orders and three for the Primates, as follows:

Edentata ("toothless")—hairy anteater
Pholidota ("scaled")—pangolin, or scaly anteater
Tubulidentata ("tube-toothed")—aardvark
Carnivora ("flesh eater")—bobcat, or lynx
Cetacea ("whale")—whale
Perissodactyla ("odd-toed")—donkey
Artiodactyla ("even-toed")—peccary
Hyracoidea ("shrew mouse")—hyrax, or cony
Proboscidea (*pro*, meaning "before," and *boskein*, meaning "eat")—elephant
Sirenia ("siren")—manatee
Rodentia ("gnawers")—mouse
Lagomorpha ("hare")—hare
Insectivora ("insect eater")—mole
Dermoptera ("skin wing")—flying lemur
Chiroptera ("hand wing")—bat
Primates ("chief" or "highest")—ring-tailed lemur, marmoset, chimpanzee

(*See also* Animals; Birds; Fish; Frog; Mammals; Reptiles; Salamander; Skeleton; Toad; Vertebrates. For Reference-Outline, *see* Zoology.)

PRIMATES—THE HIGHEST ANIMALS

RING-TAILED LEMUR

CHIMPANZEE

MARMOSET

CHINESE DRAGON

ANIMALS of Legend and Hearsay

ANIMALS, LEGENDARY. People have always been interested in animals. Very early in the history of civilization men hunted and domesticated the animals of their own surroundings. They were interested too in the marvelous and unknown. They listened eagerly to the travelers in far places who told of strange beasts they had seen and even stranger ones they had only heard about.

Early writers, lacking scientific knowledge, confused fact with hearsay. Several books of travel and natural history dating from pre-Christian times and the Middle Ages were widely read, and their reports of fantastic animals were firmly believed. The Roman writer Pliny the Elder (A.D. 23–79) published a 37-volume 'Natural History', which was a massive compilation of 2,000 earlier works.

Fifteen hundred years later Sebastian Münster (1489–1552) wrote the popular 'Cosmographia Universalis', which had pictures and descriptions of dragons and basilisks. Even the great Swiss naturalist Konrad von Gesner (1516–65), in 'Historia Animalium', described the unicorn and winged dragons.

The most famous travel book of the Middle Ages was 'Narrative of Travels', written in the mid-14th century by a "Sir John Mandeville." It is now believed to have been compiled by Jean de Bourgogne from earlier works. His descriptions of monsters probably were derived from Pliny's 'Natural History'.

Dragons, Centaurs, and Griffins

Winged *dragons* with flame and smoke pouring from their nostrils enter into the legends of many countries (*see* Dragon). The *centaurs* of Greek mythology were part human and part horse (*see* Centaurs). They may have originated in stories about the wild horsemen of prehistoric Asia. Never having seen men ride upon the backs of animals, people were filled with awe and terror of these mounted invaders.

The *griffin* had the head and wings of an eagle, the body of a lion, and the tail of a serpent or a lion. In legends of the Far East, India, and ancient Scythia, griffins were the guardians of mines and treasures. In Greek mythology they guarded treasures of gold and drew the chariot of the sun.

Basilisk, Mermaids, Sea Serpents

The *basilisk*, or *cockatrice*, was a serpent so horrible that it killed with a glance. Pliny the Elder described it simply as a snake with a small golden crown. By the Middle Ages it had become a snake with the head of a cock or sometimes a human head. It was born of a spherical egg, laid during the days of Sirius, the Dog Star, by a seven-year-old cock. The egg was then hatched by a toad. The sight of a basilisk was so dreadful that if the creature saw its own reflection in a mirror it died of fright. The only way then to kill it was to hold a mirror before it and avoid looking at it directly. The original of the basilisk could have been a horned adder or the hooded cobra of India.

Mermaids lived in the sea. They had the body of a woman to the waist and the body and tail of a fish from the waist down. Irish legend says that mermaids were pagan women banished from earth by St. Patrick.

429

VEGETABLE LAMB

CENTAUR

BASILISK

GRIFFIN

MERMAID

UNICORN

SEA SERPENT

Sea serpents are still reported in the newspapers. Gesner's 'Historia Animalium' has a picture of a sea snake about 300 feet long wrapping its coils around a sailing vessel. The *kraken* of Scandinavian myth and the modern Loch Ness monster of Scotland have many similarities.

The Vegetable Lamb

A mixture of fact and fable is the *vegetable lamb*. A picture of it appears in the book by "Sir John Mandeville." Various explanations have been advanced to explain the origin of this myth. It is easy for uneducated people to give a literal meaning to figurative language. For example, a figure of speech like "the fleece that grows on trees" is a colorful description of the cotton plant. It could be misinterpreted as referring to a *lamb* that grows on trees.

Another explanation points to a fern that grows in some Asiatic countries. It has an odd root system that could be imagined to look like four legs and a head. It is covered with fine furlike fibers and has a reddish sap like thin blood.

The Unicorn

One of the most charming and beautiful of legendary animals is the *unicorn*. It is a white horse, with the legs of an antelope, and a spirally grooved horn projecting forward from the center of its forehead. The horn is white at the base, black in the middle, and red at the tip.

The earliest reference to the unicorn is found in the writings of Ctesias. He was a Greek historian, at one time physician to the Persian king Artaxerxes II. Ctesias returned from Persia about the year 398 B.C. and wrote a book on the marvels of the Far East. He told of a certain wild ass in India with a white body and a horn on the forehead. The dust filed from this horn, he said, was a protection against deadly drugs. His description was probably a mixture of reports of the Indian rhinoceros, an antelope of some sort, and the tales of travelers.

In early versions of the Old Testament, the Hebrew word *rĕ'ēm*, now translated as "wild ox," was translated "monokeros," meaning "one horn." This became "unicorn" in English. By the Middle Ages this white animal had become a symbol of love and purity. It could be subdued only by a gentle maiden. The story of 'The Lady with the Unicorn' was a theme in the finest of medieval tapestries. In church art the unicorn is associated with the lamb and the dove. It also appears in heraldry.

The connection between the unicorn and the rhinoceros may be traced through the reputation of the powdered horn as a potent drug. Drinking beakers of rhinoceros horn, common in medieval times, were decorated with the three colors described by Ctesias. As late as the 18th century, rhinoceros horn was used to detect poison in the food of royalty. In Arabian and other Eastern countries, rhinoceros horn is still believed to have medicinal powers. (*See also* Pegasus; Sphinx.)

430

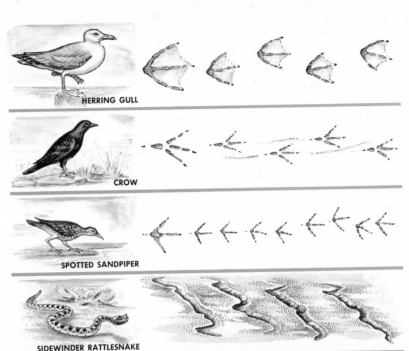

HERRING GULL

CROW

SPOTTED SANDPIPER

SIDEWINDER RATTLESNAKE

GRASSHOPPER

ANIMAL TRACKS—
Tales in Snow, Sand, and Mud

ANIMAL TRACKS. Indians, fur trappers, hunters, and other observant outdoorsmen notice the tracks of animals. They know just what creatures have passed by from the impressions they left behind in snow, sand, soft earth, or mud. A nature walk is more interesting if one can learn to be a good "tracker." Some of the commonest tracks are shown on these pages. They include tracks of mammals, insects, snakes, and ground-walking birds.

The size of the prints of all four feet gives one a clue to the size of the animal. The distance between front and hind feet should be noted, the number of toes, and the toenails. The tracks of the front and back feet may occur in pairs or they may alternate. All these details help to determine the identification.

Sometimes tracks tell a dramatic story of flight and pursuit, of capture or escape. (For a picture of tracks left by a rabbit who was attacked by a large bird and made his escape, *see* Nature Study.)

Where to Look for Tracks

The muddy bank of a stream may have a great variety of tracks, for all animals must come down to the water to drink. In winter the animals who do not hibernate are very active. Finding a food supply is more difficult at this time, and they roam far and wide in search of it, especially at night. Early in the morning after a fresh snowfall is the ideal time to look for winter tracks.

On the wet edges of lake shores lapped by the waves and along the marshy shore of a pond one finds the tracks of gulls, sandpipers, and herons. There are also footprints of crabs, turtles, insects, raccoons, and muskrats. A few feet from the sides of a sandy desert road one may see the tracks of the black-tailed jack rabbit, the kangaroo rat, or the kit fox. Sand dunes carry the impressions of snakes and insects, as well as tracks of bird and mammal travelers. A trip to the national parks and wilderness areas is made more interesting if one can identify the tracks of the big mammals. These include deer, antelope, and elk, bobcat and mountain lion, coyote, and grizzly and black bears.

How to Make Plaster Casts

Making a collection of animal tracks in plaster casts is an interesting hobby. The equipment consists simply of plaster of Paris, a tin can, strips of cardboard two inches wide and two to three feet long, and paper clips.

First make a hoop of the cardboard, fastening the ends together with the paper clips. The hoop should be a little larger than the print. Place the hoop over the track. Put some water in a bowl and add plaster slowly until all the water is absorbed and the plaster stands up in a peak. A quick stir and it is ready to pour into the hoop around the track. Be sure that every indentation is completely filled and

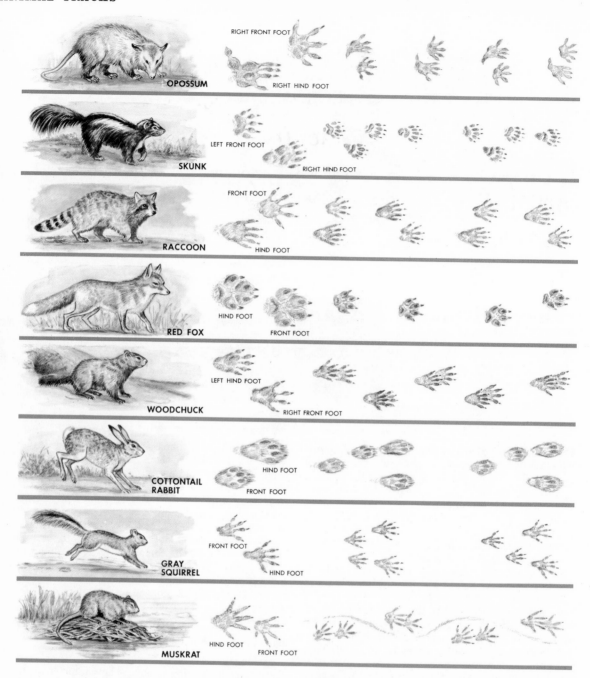

that the plaster overflows the margins of the track.

In ten or fifteen minutes the mold should be hard enough to pick up. Wrap it in a newspaper to carry it home. This mold will be in *relief*. The next step is to make a cast that duplicates the original print. Brush off all loose dirt or sand and smear the print side with oil or vaseline. Again place a hoop around the cast, print side up, and pour plaster of Paris into it. When the plaster has set, the two casts can be separated. The cast now looks just like the original print. To make it still more realistic, paint it with white shellac. While the shellac is still damp, dust it with fine sifted sand or dirt.

Making a cast in snow is difficult because the plaster of Paris may melt the bottom of the track. Some naturalists dust in a fine layer of dry plaster as a lining in the track before they pour in ice-cold wet plaster. Another trick is to spray cold water over the track with an atomizer and let it form a thin coating of ice before making the impression. (For books on the identification of animal tracks, *see* the Bibliography for Animals.)

®The Easy Reference Fact-Index

Guide to all volumes
for subjects from

A to **Annamese**

*To find a single fact
or all the facts
easily and quickly*

USE THIS FACT-INDEX

INDEX

Aa *Aa* Aa

THE LETTER A probably started as a picture sign of an oxhead, such as is found in the Egyptian hieroglyphic writing (1) and in a very early Semitic writing which was used about 1500 B.C. on the Sinai Peninsula (2).

Beginning about 1000 B.C. in the city of Byblos and in other Phoenician and Canaanite centers, the sign was given a linear form (3), from which all later forms are derived. In the Semitic languages this sign was called *aleph,* meaning "ox." It had the sound of the glottal stop, produced in the glottis, a vocal area on either side of the larynx. This sound is not found in the English language.

The next change occurred when the Greeks borrowed the alphabet from the Phoenicians. Because the Greeks had no use for the *aleph* sound, they made the *aleph* sign stand for the vowel "a." They also changed the name to *alpha,* which is found in the English word *alpha-* bet. They used several different forms of the sign, including the ancestor of the English capital A (4). The Romans took this form of the letter over into Latin. From the Latin the capital letter has come unchanged into English.

The English small "a" first took shape in Greek handwriting in a form (5) quite similar to the present English capital letter. In about the 4th century A.D. this was given a circular shape with a projection (6). This shape was the parent of both the English handwritten character (7) and the printed small "a" (8).

NOTE.—For the story of how alphabetic writing began and developed, *see* the articles Alphabet; Writing.

A, letter. *See* story on preceding page

A-1, a shipping term used to denote that a vessel is in good condition; applied also to other things of the highest class: C-602–3

A. & P. Company. *See in Index* Great Atlantic & Pacific Tea Company

A.A. *See in Index* Alcoholics Anonymous

AAA. *See in Index* Agricultural Adjustment Agency; American Automobile Association

Aachen (ä'ĸĕn), or **Aix-la-Chapelle** (āks-lä-shä-pĕl'), West Germany, city near Belgian border; pop. 174,-300: A-1–2, *maps* G-115, W-252, *picture* A-1
Charlemagne's capital C-210, A-1
treaties: (1668) A-1; (1748) M-107, A-1; (1818) A-1
World War II W-289

Aalborg (ôl'bôrḡ) ("Eel-town"), Denmark, chief port of n. Jutland, 20 mi. inland from the Kattegat on Lim Fjord; pop. 85,800; exports fish, grain; important commercially from medieval times; plundered by Wallenstein and by Swedes in 17th century: *map* D-91

Aalto, (Hugo) Alvar (Henrik) (born 1898), Finnish architect, born Kuortane, near Vaasa; identified with moderns; functional, trimly designed, and finely proportioned buildings; research professor in architecture (1940, 1945) at Massachusetts Institute of Technology.

Aardvark (ärd'värk) ("earth pig"), a mammal A-2, *pictures* A-2, A-418, A-427

Aard'wolf ("earth wolf"), a hyena-like carnivorous mammal A-2

Aare (är), or **Aar,** largest river (180 mi.) entirely within Switzerland; from Bernese Alps, flows n.w.; passes through Bern, thence n.e. into the Rhine: S-539, *map* S-537
Bern on B-143, *picture* S-544

Aarhus (ôr'hŭs), Denmark, seaport and 2d largest city; pop. 120,069; large trade in grain, cattle; shipyards, iron foundries; seat of bishop since 10th century; fine 13th-century cathedral: *map* D-91

Aaron (ĕr'ŏn), first high priest of Israelites, brother of Moses; with Moses led Israelite exodus from Egypt; made idol, golden calf, while Moses was on Mt. Sinai: M-495. *See also in Index* Golden calf

Aaron's rod, various tall flowering plants (goldenrod, mullein, etc.) named from budding and flowering of Aaron's rod (Num. xvii); in architecture, ornamental rod with leaves or entwined serpent.

AAU. *See in Index* Amateur Athletic Union

Aba (ä'bạ), or **abayah** (ạ-bä'yä), a sleeveless outer garment, usually of camel's or goat's hair, frequently of striped pattern, worn by Arabs: N-295, *picture* C-398

Abaca (ăb-ạ-kä'), or **Manila hemp** H-133, F-105, R-291, P-258, *pictures* H-133, R-292, P-259, *table* F-105

Abacus (ăb'ạ-kŭs), a calculating device A-2–3, *pictures* A-3, D-133

Abacus, in architecture A-491, *pictures* A-491

Abadan', Iran, city on island of same name in the Shatt-el-Arab; pop. 302,189: A-3, *maps* A-636, I-280, *picture* A-621
location, *locator map* A-3

Abaft, *diagram* B-230. *See also in Index* Nautical terms, *table*

Abalone (ăb-ạ-lō'nē), or **ear shell,** a shellfish A-3
black abalone shell, *color picture* S-151

Ab'ana, or **Amanah** (now **Barada**), and **Pharphar** (now **Awaj**), two famous "rivers of Damascus" mentioned in Bible (II Kings v, 12).

Abarbanel, Isaac. *See in Index* Abrabanel

Abbai River. *See in Index* Blue Nile River

Abbas (ăb-bäs') **I, the Great** (1557–1628), ruler of Persia P-214

Abbas II, full name Abbas Hilmi Pasha (1874–1944), 3d khedive of Egypt, born Cairo; ruled under British supervision 1892–1914; deposed for plotting with Turks.

Abbasids (ạ-băs'ĭdz), second great dynasty of Mohammedan caliphs; ruled at Baghdad 750–1258; based claim on descent from Abbas, uncle of Mohammed; most famous sovereign Harun al-Raschid.

Abbaye-aux-Hommes, or **St. Étienne,** church in Caen, France A-496, *picture* A-495

Abbe (ăb'ē), **Cleveland** (1838–1916), meteorologist and astronomer, born New York City; as director of Cincinnati Observatory, in 1869 established daily telegraphic weather reports for Middle West; he and Joseph Henry first practical weather forecasters in U. S.; served U. S. weather office 1871–1916.

Abbe (ăb'ē), **Ernst** (1840–1905), German physicist, born Eisenach; associated with Zeiss optical firm at Jena, Germany, after 1866, owner after 1888; made important improvements in optical glass.

'Abbé Constantin, L'' (läb-bā kôn-stän-tăn'), romance by Halévy in which an old priest unconsciously acts as matchmaker for a young officer and an American heiress.

Ab'bess, head of a convent M-448

Abbeville (ăb-vēl'), France, town on Somme, 12 mi. above English Channel; pop. 21,744; cloth manufacturing; point at which German thrust to channel cut off Allies from Belgium in 1940: *map* F-404
prehistoric relics M-79

Abbeville, La., town 65 mi. s.w. of Baton Rouge; pop. 10,414; oil wells; milling of rice, sugar; dairy products: *map* L-376

Abbevillians (ăb-vĭl'ē-ạns), a prehistoric people, *color picture* M-77

Ab'bey, Edwin Austin (1852–1911), artist, born Philadelphia, Pa.; lived many years in England; gained first success as a pen-and-ink illustrator; later became famous both as historical and mural painter.

Abbey, a monastic house M-445, *pictures* M-444, F-411

Abbey Theatre, on Abbey Street, Dublin, Ireland; center for Irish literary revival; many Irish plays first produced there 1904–51; received subsidies from Annie E. F. Horniman and Irish government; Abbey Theatre Company toured Europe and U. S.: I-292, Y-339
new building, *picture* I-285

Abbot, head of a monastery M-446

Abbot, Anthony. *See in Index* Oursler, (Charles) Fulton

Abbot, Charles Greeley (born 1872), astrophysicist, born Wilton, N. H.; director, Astrophysical Observatory 1907–44, secretary 1928–44, Smithsonian Institution; studies in solar radiation, weather cycles, effect of sunspots on climate.

Abbot, George (1562–1633), English prelate, born Guilford, Surrey; archbishop of Canterbury 1611–33; staunch Puritan; rose through favor of James I and used position for persecution of Roman Catholics; lost power through his accidental killing of gamekeeper and through accession of Charles I.

Abbot, Willis John (1863–1934), newspaper editor and author, born New Haven, Conn.; editor *Christian Science Monitor* 1922–27 ('Blue Jackets of '76'; 'Battle Fields and Camp Fires').

'Abbot, The', historical novel by Sir Walter Scott (1820); hero, Roland Graeme, becomes involved in fortunes of Mary, queen of Scots, imprisoned at Lochleven; the abbot, Father Ambrose, plays a minor part
critical estimate S-74

Ab'botsford, baronial home of Sir Walter Scott on Tweed River, 3 mi. from Melrose Abbey, Scotland, where most of his novels were written: S-73, *picture* S-74

Abbott, Douglas Charles (born 1899), Canadian jurist, born Lennoxville, Que.; member House of Commons 1940–54; minister of finance 1946–54; judge of the Supreme Court of Canada 1954–.

Abbott, George (born 1889), producer, director, and playwright; born Forestville, N. Y. (coauthor and director 'Three Men on a Horse'; 'Where's Charley?'; 'A Tree Grows in Brooklyn'; 'Pajama Game'; 'Fiorello', awarded 1960 Pulitzer prize; autobiography, 'Mister Abbott').

Abbott, Grace (1878–1939), social worker, born Grand Island, Neb.; resident Hull-House, Chicago, 1908–15; chief of U. S. Children's Bureau 1921–34; made professor of public welfare administration at University of Chicago 1934 ('The Immigrant and the Community'; 'Immigrant in Massachusetts').

Abbott, Jacob (1803–79), writer of juvenile books, educator, and Congregational preacher; born Hallowell, Me.: L-307

Abbott, Sir John Joseph Caldwell (1821–93), Canadian jurist and statesman: A-4, *picture* A-4

Abbott, John Stevens Cabot (1805–77), historian, brother of Jacob Abbott; born Brunswick, Me.; popular histories ('History of Napoleon Bonaparte'; 'The French Revolution').

Abbott, Lyman (1835–1922), Congregational preacher and author, born Roxbury, Mass.; Beecher's successor at Plymouth Church, Brooklyn, N.Y.; editor of the *Outlook;* son of Jacob Abbott.

ABDICATIONS OF IMPORTANCE

(For biographical information, *see in Index* names below)

Name	Title	Country	Date	Cause
Diocletian (245–313)	Emperor	Roman Empire	305	Wearied of rule
Romulus Augustulus (born 461?)	Emperor	Roman Empire	476	Revolt of German mercenary troops
Richard II (1367–1400)	King	England	1399	Insurrection
Charles V (1500–1558)	Emperor	Holy Roman Empire	1556	Wearied of rule
Mary Stuart (1542–87)	Queen	Scotland	1567	Insurrection
Christina (1626–89)	Queen	Sweden	1654	Distaste for rule
James II (1633–1701)	King	England	1688	Insurrection
Napoleon I (1769–1821)	Emperor	France	1814, 1815	Defeat by foreign powers
Pedro II (1825–91)	Emperor	Brazil	1889	Revolution
Manuel II (1889–1932)	King	Portugal	1910	Revolution
Pu-yi (Hsuan T'ung) (1906–67)	Emperor	China	1912	Revolution
Nicholas II (1868–1918)	Czar	Russia	1917	Revolution
Ferdinand I (1861–1948)	Czar	Bulgaria	1918	Defeat in World War I
William II (1859–1941)	Emperor	Germany	1918	Revolution
Charles I (1887–1922)	Emperor	Austria-Hungary	1918	Revolution
Mohammed VI (1861–1926)	Sultan	Turkey	1922	Revolution
Edward VIII (born 1894)	King	Great Britain	1936	Clash over marriage
Carol II (1893–1953)	King	Rumania	1940	Ousted by dictator
Victor Emmanuel III (1869–1947)	King	Italy	1946	Gave crown to son Humbert
Michael I (born 1921)	King	Rumania	1947	Communists dominated government
Wilhelmina (1880-1962)	Queen	Netherlands	1948	Gave crown to daughter Juliana
Leopold III (born 1901)	King	Belgium	1951	Gave crown to son Baudouin
Farouk I (1920-65)	King	Egypt	1952	Forced to abdicate
Charlotte (born 1896)	Grand Duchess	Luxemburg	1964	Gave crown to son Jean

Abbreviations A-4. *See also table* on following pages

ABC (American Broadcasting Company) R-56

"A B C Powers," the three chief South American powers: Argentina, Brazil, and Chile

Mexico and United States M-256

Abd-el-Kader (*ăb-dŭl-kä'dĭr*) (1807?–83), Arab chief, born near Mascara, Algeria; struggled for 15 years against French conquest of Algeria; surrendered 1847: F-206

Abd el Krim, Mohammed ben (1880?–1963), Riffian chief; imprisoned by French on Réunion Island 20 years; escaped from French 1947; given sanctuary in Alexandria, Egypt; operetta 'The Desert Song' based on his exploits.

Abdication, renunciation of an office, usually by a ruler. *See table* on this page

Abdomen (*ăb'dŏ-mĕn* or *ăb-dŏ'mĕn*) human body, *color pictures* A-379–82: muscles, *color pictures* A-377–8; nerves, *diagram* N-131
insects I-197, *diagrams* I-197

'Abduction from the Seraglio, The', comic opera by Mozart O-463, *picture* O-464a

Abdul-Aziz (*ăb-dŭl-ạ-zēz'*) (1830–76), sultan of Turkey; came to throne in 1861; misgovernment caused many uprisings; deposed 1876.

'Abdu'l-Baha (*ăb-dŭl-bạ-hä'*) (1844–1921), Persian religious leader; imprisoned by Turks 1868–1908; inherited leadership of Baha'i movement from father 1892; knighted 1920: B-20

Abdul-Hamid (*ăb-dŭl-hä-mēd'*) **II** (1842–1918), sultan of Turkey; came to throne in 1876; deposed 1909: T-305

Abdullah ibn-Hussein (*ăb-dŭ-lä'ĭb-ĕn-hụ-sän'*) (1882–1951), king of Jordan 1946–51, born Mecca, Arabia; 2d son of Hussein ibn-Ali; assassinated July 1951: J-439

Abdul-Medjid (*ăb-dụl-mĕ-gēd'*) (1823–61), sultan of Turkey; to throne in 1839; kind but weak would-be reformer; France and England fought Crimean War in his behalf.

Abeam. *See in Index* Nautical terms, *table*

Abel (*ā'bĕl*), a shepherd, second son of Adam and Eve; killed by his elder brother Cain, a tiller of the soil, because Abel's offering was more acceptable to God (Gen. iv): A-15

Abel, Sir Frederick Augustus (1827–1902), English chemist, born London; improved manufacture of guncotton and other explosives; with James Dewar invented cordite; consulting chemist to British War Dept. 1854–88.

Abel, John Jacob (1857–1938), pharmacologist, born Cleveland, Ohio; professor pharmacology, Johns Hopkins University after 1893; noted for isolation of epinephrine and of insulin in crystal form.

Abel (*ä'bĕl*), **Niels Henrik** (1802–29), Norwegian mathematician, born on island near Stavanger; known for work in elliptic functions.

Abelard (*ăb'ĕ-lärd*), **Peter** (1079–1142), French scholar and philosopher A-4, P-264

Abele. *See in Index* White poplar

'Abe Lincoln in Illinois', tragedy by Robert E. Sherwood, *picture* D-175

Abelmosk, species of hibiscus H-153

Abelson, Philip Hauge (born 1913), physicist, born Tacoma, Wash.; director of Geophysical Laboratory, Carnegie Institution of Washington, after 1953; with E. McMillan, discovered element neptunium 1940: P-394

Abencerrages (*ȧ-bĕn'sĕ-rä-gēs*), Moorish family of Granada, eminent in 15th century
princes massacred A-275

Abercrombie (*ăb'ĕr-krŏm-bĭ*), **Lascelles** (1881–1938), English poet and critic, born Ashton-on-Mersey, Cheshire; professor University of Leeds 1922–29, Bedford College, London, 1929–35; Goldsmiths' reader at Oxford University after 1935 ('Interludes and Poems'; 'Deborah'; 'Sale of Saint Thomas').

Abercromby, or **Abercrombie, James** (1706–81), British general, born Scotland; repulsed by French under Montcalm at Ticonderoga, N. Y. (1758).

Abercromby, Sir Ralph (1734–1801), British general, born Scotland; commander in chief in the West Indies (1795–97), in Ireland (1797–98), and in Netherlands (1799); commanded expedition to Mediterranean and defeated French in battle of Alexandria (1801) but was fatally wounded.

Aberdare (*ăb-ēr-dâr'*), Wales, urban district in s.e.; pop. 39,155; coal mining; refractories (firebrick), electric cable, television and radio sets, record players: *map* G-199h

Aberdeen', Scotland, city on e. coast; pop. 185,390: A-5, *maps* G-199g, S-67
Balmoral Castle, *picture* A-5
location A-5, *locator map* A-5

Aberdeen, S. D., city in n.e.; pop. 23,-073; railroad center and wholesale distribution point; food processing, machinery; Northern State College; home of Fischer quintuplets: *maps* S-335, 323, U-40
climate, *list* S-321

Aberdeen, Wash., port city on Grays Harbor, adjacent to Hoquiam and about 45 mi. w. of Olympia; pop. 18,741; lumber products; fishing; vegetable, fruit, and fish canneries: *maps* W-52, U-40

Aberdeen, University of, Scotland A-5

Aberdeen and Temair, John Campbell Gordon, first marquis of (1847–1934), British statesman, born Edinburgh, Scotland; appointed lord-lieutenant of Ireland by Gladstone 1886, and again held that office 1905–15; governor-general of Canada 1893–98; distinguished himself by friendship with all parties.

Aberdeen Angus, also called **Angus**, a breed of cattle C-167–8, *pictures* C-165, F-367
Brahman-Angus crossbreeding C-168

Aberdeen Proving Ground, U. S. reservation for testing ordnance; near Aberdeen, Md.: A-583, *map* M-139

Aberdeen'shire, county of n.e. Scotland; 1971 sq. mi.; pop. 321,783; stock raising, agriculture, granite quarrying, fishing
Balmoral Castle, *picture* A-5

Aberhart, William (1878–1943), Canadian political leader, born Seaforth, Ont.; an organizer of Social Credit party in Alberta; premier of Alberta 1935–43: A-250

Ab'ernethy, George (1807–77), pioneer colonist and merchant in Oregon, born New York, N. Y.; sailed 1839 with *Lausanne* party as financial manager of Oregon Methodist mission; elected provisional governor of Oregon district 1845, 1847.

Aberration A-5–6
in lenses P-284
chromatic and spherical A-6, L-195, T-66–7, *diagrams* L-195, A-5: chromatic studied by Newton S-371
of light A-5–6, *diagrams* A-660

Aberystwyth (*ăb-ēr-ist'wĭth*), Wales, municipal borough, resort on Cardigan Bay; pop. 10,427; seat of one of colleges of University of

ABBREVIATIONS AND SYMBOLS IN COMMON USE

(See also Chemical elements, *table* C-236; New-math symbols, *list* M-163b; Punctuation P-534; Roman numerals N-379c; Weights and measures, *tables* W-95-7; Zodiac, *picture* Z-356. *See also in Index* Knighthood, *table,* for abbreviations of chief orders.)

Abbreviations

A

a.—acre; ampere; anode.
A—angstrom unit.
AAA, A.A.A.—American Automobile Association.
AAU—Amateur Athletic Union.
A.B.—*Artium Baccalaureus,* Bachelor of Arts.
ABA—American Bar Association.
ABC—American Broadcasting Company.
AC, A.C., or a.c.—alternating current.
accel.—*accelerando,* with increasing rapidity (music).
acct—account.
A.D.—*anno Domini,* in the year of our Lord.
ADC—aide-de-camp.
ad lib.—*ad libitum,* at pleasure.
Adm.—Admiral.
AEC—Atomic Energy Commission.
A.E.F.—American Expeditionary Forces.
AFAM—Ancient Free and Accepted Masons.
A.F.L.-C.I.O.—American Federation of Labor-Congress of Industrial Organizations.
AID—Agency for International Development.
A.L.—American League.
Ala.—Alabama.
Alta.—Alberta.
A.M.—*ante meridiem,* before noon; *Artium Magister,* Master of Arts.
AMA—American Medical Association.
amu—atomic mass unit.
anon.—anonymous.
AP—Associated Press.
Apr.—April.
apt.—apartment.
aq—*aqua,* water.
ARA—Associate of the Royal Academy.
Ariz.—Arizona.
Ark.—Arkansas.
ASCAP—American Society of Composers, Authors and Publishers.
assn—association.
asst—assistant.
Aug.—August.
AV—Authorized Version (of the Bible).
av—average; avoirdupois.
Ave.—Avenue.
awol—absent without leave (military).
awu—relative atomic weight unit.

B

B.A.—*Baccalaureus Artium,* Bachelor of Arts.
Bart., Bt.—Baronet.
BBC—British Broadcasting Corporation.
bbl.—barrel.
B.C.—before Christ; British Columbia.
B.C.E.—Bachelor of Civil Engineering.

B.C.L.—Bachelor of Civil Law.
B.D.—*Baccalaureus Divinitatis,* Bachelor of Divinity.
B.D.S.—Bachelor of Dental Surgery.
bev—billion electron-volts.
bk—bank; book.
B.L.—*Baccalaureus Legum,* Bachelor of Laws.
bldg—building.
B.Lit.—*Baccalaureus Literarum,* Bachelor of Literature.
blvd.—boulevard.
B.M.—*Baccalaureus Medicinae,* Bachelor of Medicine.
B.M.E.—Bachelor of Mining Engineering.
BMEWS—Ballistic Missile Early Warning System.
B.Mus.—*Baccalaureus Musicae,* Bachelor of Music.
B.Phil.—*Baccalaureus Philosophiae,* Bachelor of Philosophy.
BPOE—Benevolent and Protective Order of Elks.
Br—British.
Brig. Gen.—Brigadier General
bros—brothers.
B.S., B.Sc.—*Baccalaureus Scientiae,* Bachelor of Science.
B.T.U.—British thermal unit.
bu.—bushel; bushels.

C

c—carat; cent; circa; copyright.
C.—centigrade.
cal—calendar; calorie.
Calif.—California.
Can.—Canada.
CARE—Co-operative for American Remittances to Everywhere.
C.B.—*Chirurgiae Baccalaureus,* Bachelor of Surgery; Companion of the Bath.
CBS—Columbia Broadcasting System.
cc—cubic centimeters.
CC—carbon copy.
CCC—Commodity Credit Corporation.
C.C.F.—Co-operative Commonwealth Federation.
CENTO—Central Treaty Organization.
cf.—*confer,* compare.
ch, or chap—chapter.
Chron.—Chronicles.
CIA—Central Intelligence Agency.
cm.—centimeter.
c/o—care of.
Co., co.—company; county.
CO, C.O.—Commanding Officer.
COD—cash on delivery; collect on delivery.
Col.—Colonel; Colossians.
Colo.—Colorado.
Comdr.—Commander.
Commo—Commodore.
Conn.—Connecticut.
Cor.—Corinthians.
CORE—Congress of Racial Equality.
Corp.—Corporal; Corporation.
cp—compare.
C.P.A.—Certified Public Accountant.
cr—cathode ray; credit.
cresc.—*crescendo,* gradual increase of tone (music).
CST—central standard time.
cts.—cents.
cu.—cubic.
cwt—hundredweight.
C.Z.—Canal Zone.

D

d.—*denarius,* a penny.
D—Democrat.

Dan.—Daniel.
DAR—Daughters of the American Revolution.
D.C.—*da capo,* from the beginning (music); District of Columbia.
DC, D.C., d.c.—direct current.
D.C.L.—Doctor of Canon Law; Doctor of Civil Law.
D.D.—*Divinitatis Doctor,* Doctor of Divinity.
D.D.S.—Doctor of Dental Surgery.
Del.—Delaware.
D.Eng.—Doctor of Engineering.
dept.—department.
Deut.—Deuteronomy.
DEW—Distant Early Warning.
D.F.—Distrito Federal (Federal District).
dim.—*diminuendo,* gradual decrease of tone (music).
dist—district.
D.Lit.—Doctor of Literature.
dm.—decimeter.
D.M.D.—Doctor of Dental Medicine.
D.Mus.—*Doctor Musicae,* Doctor of Music.
DNA—deoxyribonucleic acid.
do.—*ditto,* the same.
doz.—dozen.
Dr.—Doctor.
D.S., D.Sc.—Doctor of Science.
D.S.C.—Distinguished Service Cross.
D.S.M.—Distinguished Service Medal.
D.S.O.—Distinguished Service Order.
DST—Daylight-saving time.
D.V.M.—Doctor of Veterinary Medicine.
dwt.—deadweight ton; pennyweight.

E

e., E, or E.—east.
Eccles.—Ecclesiastes.
ed—edition; editor; education.
EDC—European Defense Community.
EE—electrical engineer.
EEC—European Economic Community.
EFTA—European Free Trade Association.
e.g.—*exempli gratia,* for example.
E.M.F.—electromotive force.
Ens.—Ensign.
Eph.—Ephesians.
esp—especially.
Esq.—Esquire.
est—established.
et al.—*et alibi,* and elsewhere; *et alii,* and others.
etc.—*et cetera,* and so on.
et seq.—*et sequens,* and the following; *et sequentes, et sequentia,* and those that follow.
Euratom—European Atomic Energy Community.
Exod.—Exodus.
Ezek.—Ezekiel.

F

f—*forte,* loud.
f.—franc (French money); following (page).
F.—Fahrenheit.
FA—field artillery.
FAA—Federal Aviation Agency.
FAM—Free and Accepted Masons.
FBA—Fellow of the British Academy.
FBI—Federal Bureau of Investigation.
FCC—Federal Communications Commission.
Feb.—February.

fed—federal; federation.
ff—folios; following (pages).
ff—*fortissimo,* very loud (music).
FHA—Federal Housing Administration.
fl.—flourished.
Fla.—Florida.
FM—frequency modulation.
FOB—free on board.
FOE—Fraternal Order of Eagles.
FRB—Federal Reserve Board.
FRCP—Fellow of Royal College of Physicians.
FRCS—Fellow of Royal College of Surgeons.
FRGS—Fellow of Royal Geographical Society.
Fri.—Friday.
FRS—Fellow of the Royal Society.
ft.—feet; foot; fort.

G

g.—gram; gravity.
Ga.—Georgia.
Gal.—Galatians.
gal.—gallon; gallons.
GAR—Grand Army of the Republic.
GATT—General Agreement on Tariffs and Trade.
gcd—greatest common divisor.
GCT—Greenwich civil time.
Gen.—General; Genesis.
GMT—Greenwich mean time.
GNP—gross national product.
G.O.P.—Grand Old Party (Republican party, U. S.).
Gov.—Governor.
govt—government.

H

Hab.—Habakkuk.
Hag.—Haggai.
hdkf—handkerchief.
hdqrs—headquarters.
Heb.—Hebrews (Book of).
hgt—height.
H.I.H.—His (or Her) Imperial Highness.
H.I.M.—His (or Her) Imperial Majesty.
H.M.S.—His (or Her) Majesty's Ship (or Service).
Hon.—Honorable.
hon.—honorary.
Hos.—Hosea.
hp—horsepower.
hr.—hour.
HR—House of Representatives.
hwy—highway.

I

I.—Island, Isle.
ib., ibid.—*ibidem,* in the same place.
ICBM—intercontinental ballistic missile.
I.C.C.—Interstate Commerce Commission.
id.—*idem,* the same.
ID—identification.
i.e.—*id est,* that is.
IHS—symbol meaning Jesus, formed by a contraction of Greek letters.
Ill.—Illinois.
illus.—illustrated.
in.—inch; inches.
inc.—incorporated; inclusive.
incog—incognito.
Ind.—Indiana.
I.N.R.I.—*Iesus Nazarenus, Rex Iudaeorum,* Jesus of Nazareth, King of the Jews.
intl—international.
IOOF—Independent Order of Odd Fellows.
IOU, I.O.U.—I owe you.
IQ—intelligence quotient.
IRS—Internal Revenue Service.

(Continued on the next page)

ü = French *u,* German *ü*; g� in: ǵem, ḡo; thin, then; ǹ = French nasal (Jeaǹ); zh = French *j* (*z* in azure); ᴋ = German guttural *ch*

Isa.—Isaiah.
I.S.O.—Imperial Service Order.
ITO—International Trade Organization.
IWW, I.W.W.—I n d u s t r i a l Workers of the World.

J

Jan.—January.
Jas.—James.
J.C.D.—*Juris Civilis Doctor*, Doctor of Civil Law.
J.D.—*Jurum Doctor*, Doctor of Laws.
jg—junior grade.
Josh.—Joshua.
JP—justice of the peace.
Jr.—Junior.
J.U.D.—*Juris Utriusque Doctor*, Doctor of both Civil and Canon Law.
Judg.—Judges.

K

K—Kelvin (scale).
Kan., Kans.—Kansas.
kg.—kilogram.
kl.—kiloliter.
km.—kilometer (km²—square kilometer).
KP—kitchen police.
kw.—kilowatt.
kw-hr—kilowatt-hour.
Ky.—Kentucky.

L

l.—liter.
La.—Louisiana.
L.A.—Los Angeles.
Lab.—Labrador.
Lam.—Lamentations.
lat—latitude.
lb.—*libra*, pound.
lc—lower case (type).
LCD—lowest common denominator.
LCM—least common multiple.
Lev.—Leviticus.
L.I.—Long Island.
Lieut., Lt.—Lieutenant.
Lit.B.—*Literarum Baccalaureus*, Bachelor of Literature.
Lit.D.—*Literarum Doctor*, Doctor of Literature.
LL.B.—*Legum Baccalaureus*, Bachelor of Laws.
LL.D.—*Legum Doctor*, Doctor of Laws.
LL.M.—*Legum Magister*, Master of Laws.
loc. cit.—*loco citato*, in the place cited.
log—logarithm.
long—longitude.
ltd—limited.

M

μ (Greek letter)—micron.
m.—*meridies*, noon.
M.—Monsieur.
m., m—meter.
mμ—millimicron.
M.A.—*Magister Artium*, Master of Arts.
Ma.E.—Master of Engineering.
Maj.—Major.
Mal.—Malachi.
Man.—Manitoba.
Mar.—March.
Mass.—Massachusetts.
Matt.—Matthew.
M.B.—*Medicinae Baccalaureus*, Bachelor of Medicine.
MBS—Mutual Broadcasting System.
M.C.—*Magister Chirurgiae*, Master of Surgery; Master of Ceremonies; Member of Congress.

M.C.E.—Master of Civil Engineering.
M.D.—*Medicinae Doctor*, Doctor of Medicine.
Md.—Maryland.
M.D.S.—Master of Dental Surgery.
mdse—merchandise.
Me.—Maine.
M.E.—Mining (or Mechanical) Engineer; Methodist Episcopal.
Messrs.—*Messieurs*, Gentlemen, Sirs.
mev—million electron volts.
mf—*mezzo forte*, moderately loud (music).
mfg—manufacturing.
mg.—milligram.
Mgr., or Msgr.—Monsignor.
mi.—mile.
Mic.—Micah.
Mich.—Michigan.
Minn.—Minnesota.
misc—miscellaneous.
Miss.—Mississippi.
Mlle.—Mademoiselle.
MM.—Messieurs.
mm.—millimeter (mm², square millimeter; mm³, cubic millimeter).
Mme.—Madame.
Mo.—Missouri.
mo.—month.
Mon.—Monday.
Mont.—Montana.
MP, M.P.—Member of Parliament; military police.
mph—miles per hour.
MRAS—Member of the Royal Academy of Science; Member of the Royal Asiatic Society.
MRCP—Member of the Royal College of Physicians.
MRCS—Member of the Royal College of Surgeons.
MRGS—Member of the Royal Geographical Society.
MRI—Member of the Royal Institution.
M.S., M.Sc.—Master of Science.
MS—manuscript (plural, MSS).
Mt.—Mount, Mountain.
Mus.B.—*Musicae Baccalaureus*, Bachelor of Music.
Mus.D.—*Musicae Doctor*, Doctor of Music.

N

n., N, or N.—north.
NAACP—National Association for the Advancement of Colored People.
Nah.—Nahum.
NASA—National Aeronautics and Space Administration.
NATO—North Atlantic Treaty Organization.
N.B.—New Brunswick.
N.B., n.b.—*nota bene*, note well.
NBC—National Broadcasting Company.
N.C.—North Carolina.
NCAA—National Collegiate Athletic Association.
NCO—noncommissioned officer.
n.d., ND—no date (of publication).
N.D., N. Dak.—North Dakota.
N.E.—New England.
Neb., Nebr.—Nebraska.
Neh.—Nehemiah.
nem. con.—*nemine contradicente*, "no one contradicting," unanimously.
Nev.—Nevada.
Newf., Nfld.—Newfoundland.
NG—national guard; no good.
N.H.—New Hampshire.
N.J.—New Jersey.
N.L.—National League.
N.M., N.Mex.—New Mexico.

No.—*numero*, number.
non seq.—*non sequitur*, it does not follow.
Nov.—November.
NP—notary public.
N.S.—Nova Scotia.
N.S.W.—New South Wales.
NT., N.T.—New Testament.
Num.—Numbers.
N.W.T.—Northwest Territories.
N.Y.—New York.

O

OAS—Organization of American States.
ob.—*obiit*, died.
Obad.—Obadiah.
OCS—officer candidate school.
Oct.—October.
OK, okay—all right (slang).
Okla.—Oklahoma.
Ont.—Ontario.
o.p.—out of print.
op. cit.—*opere citato*, in the work cited.
Ore.—Oregon.
OT—Old Testament.
oz.—ounce.

P

p—page; *piano*, soft (music).
Pa., Penn., or Penna.—Pennsylvania.
par—paragraph.
PAU—Pan American Union.
PC—Privy Council; Privy Councilor.
pd—paid.
Pd.M.—Master of Pedagogy.
P.E.I.—Prince Edward Island.
pf, pfd—preferred.
p.f.—*piu forte*, a little louder (music).
pfc—private first class.
Phar.D.—Doctor of Pharmacy.
Ph.B.—*Philosophiae Baccalaureus*, Bachelor of Philosophy.
Ph.D.—*Philosophiae Doctor*, Doctor of Philosophy.
Ph.G.—Graduate in Pharmacy.
Phil.—Philippians.
Phila.—Philadelphia.
P.I.—Philippine Islands.
pk.—peck.
pkg—package.
pkwy—parkway.
P.M.—*post meridiem*, after noon.
PO—Post Office.
pp—pages; *pianissimo*, very soft (music).
P.P., p.p.—parcel post.
P.P.C.—*pour prendre congé*, to take leave.
ppd—postpaid; prepaid.
P.R.—Puerto Rico.
Prof.—Professor.
Prov.—Proverbs.
PS—*post scriptum*, postscript; public school.
Psa.—Psalms.
pt.—point; port; part; pint.
PTA—Parent-Teacher Association.
Pvt.—Private.

Q

Q.E.D.—*quod erat demonstrandum*, which was to be shown.
Q.E.F.—*quod erat faciendum*, which was to be done.
QMG, Q.M.G.—Quartermaster General.
qt.—quart.
qu, ques—question.
Que.—Quebec.
q.v.—*quod vide*, which see.

R

R—Republican.
R.—*regina*, queen; *rex*, king.

RA—royal academy.
R.A.F.—Royal Air Force.
R.A.M.—Royal Academy of Music.
R.A.M.C.—Royal Army Medical Corps.
RCAF—Royal Canadian Air Force.
R.C.M.P.—Royal Canadian Mounted Police.
RCN—Royal Canadian Navy.
re—reference; regarding.
Rep—Representative.
Rev.—Revelation; Reverend.
R.F.C.—Royal Flying Corps.
R.F.D.—Rural Free Delivery.
R.I.—Rhode Island.
R.I.P.—*Requiescat in pace*, May he rest in peace.
rit., ritard.—*ritardando*, gradually slower (music).
riten.—*ritenuto*, retarding (music).
R.M.S.—Royal Mail Steamship.
RN—registered nurse; Royal Navy.
ROTC—Reserve Officers Training Corps.
rpm—revolutions per minute.
RR—railroad; rural route.
R.S.F.S.R.—Russian Soviet Federated Socialist Republic.
R.S.V.P.—*Répondez, s'il vous plaît*, Answer, if you please.
ry—railway.

S

s.—*solidus*, a shilling (English money).
s., S, or S.—south.
SAC—Strategic Air Command.
Sam.—Samuel.
SAR—Sons of the American Revolution.
Sask.—Saskatchewan.
Sat.—Saturday.
S.B.—Bachelor of Science.
sc.—*scilicet*, that is to say.
S.C.—South Carolina.
Sc.B.—*Scientiae Baccalaureus*, Bachelor of Science.
Sc.D.—*Scientiae Doctor*, Doctor of Science.
S.D., S. Dak.—South Dakota.
SEATO—Southeast Asia Treaty Organization.
SEC—Securities and Exchange Commission.
sec, secy—secretary.
Sen.—Senator.
Sept.—September.
seq.—*sequentia*, the following.
s.g.—specific gravity.
sgd—signed.
Sgt., Sergt.—Sergeant.
SHAPE—Supreme Headquarters, Allied Powers, Europe.
SJ—Society of Jesus (Jesuits).
SOP—standard operating procedure.
SPCA—Society for the Prevention of Cruelty to Animals.
SPCC—Society for the Prevention of Cruelty to Children.
sp. gr.—specific gravity.
S.P.Q.R.—*Senatus Populusque Romanus*, the Roman Senate and People.
sq.—square.
Sr.—Senior.
SRO—standing room only.
SRS—*Societatis Regiae Socius*, Fellow of the Royal Society.
SS—steamship.
SSR, S.S.R.—Soviet Socialist Republic.
St.—Saint; Strait; Street.
S.T.B.—*Sacrae Theologiae Baccalaureus*, Bachelor of Sacred Theology.

(Continued on the next page)

Wales and of National Library of Wales: *map* G-199h

Abidjan (*ăb-ĭ-gän'*), Ivory Coast, capital and port, on lagoon connected with Atlantic Ocean; pop. 212,000: I-346, *map* A-94, *picture* I-346

Abies (*ā'bĭ-ēz*), the fir genus F-121

Abigail (*ăb'ĭ-gāl*), wife of Nabal; ministered to the fleeing David, who married her on Nabal's death (I Sam. xxv, 14–42); name used to mean a waiting maid.

Abilene (*ăb'ĭ-lēn*), Kan., city on Smoky Hill River about 85 mi. n. of Wichita; pop. 6746; shipping point for farm produce; Old Abilene Town, restored village: *map* K-17
Eisenhower memorials E-127, 137, K-7, *color pictures* K-12
former cattle town C-171, 175: cattle trail, *map* F-71; Hickok, Wild Bill H-153

Abilene, Tex., city about 140 mi. s.w. of Fort Worth; pop. 90,368; trade and shipping center for farming and ranching region; petroleum products, packed meats, cottonseed products, clothing, candy; Hardin-Simmons University, Abilene Christian College, McMurry College; military installations nearby: *maps* T-128, U-40

Abilene Christian College, at Abilene, Tex.; Church of Christ; founded 1906; liberal arts; graduate study.

Abimelech (*ă-bĭm'ĭ-lĕk*), a judge of Israel, son of Gideon; made himself king of Shechem by killing all except one of his 70 brothers; in an uprising a woman struck his head with a millstone and he had himself slain by his armor bearer rather than die by the hand of a woman (Judges viii, ix).

Abington, Pa., urban township n. of Philadelphia; pop. 55,831.

Abiogenesis. *See in Index* Spontaneous generation

Abiti'bi, Lake, on Ontario-Quebec boundary, Canada; 2 lakes joined by narrows; total area 356 sq. mi.: *map* O-456a

Abitibi River, Ontario, Canada, flows 340 mi. n. from Lake Abitibi to Moose River: O-456b, *map* C-99

Ablation. *See in Index* Aerospace, *table of terms*

Abnaki (*ăb-nä'kĭ*), Indian tribe in Maine M-53, N-171, *map* I-134, *table* I-136

Abnormal psychology P-522

Åbo, Finland. *See in Index* Turku

Aboli'tionist movement, to end Negro slavery in United States C-373
Garrison leads G-34, 35, *pictures* G-35, J-352
Liberty and Free Soil parties P-433
Sumner S-512
Tubman, Harriet T-284
Whittier W-158, 159
women's rights movement W-214

"Abominable snowman" M-443, *picture* M-443

Aborigines (*ăb-ō-rĭġ'ĭ-nēz*), name given by Romans to a people of central Italy, traditionally said to have descended from their mountain home upon Latium, where they settled down as Latini. Term now applied to original, or earliest known, inhabitants of any country or area; primitive as against invading or colonizing people. *See also in Index* Pygmy
Australia A-716–17, *picture* A-717: boomerang B-265, *picture* B-265; skull type, *picture* R-27
Japan (Ainu) J-366, *picture* J-366

'Abou Ben Adhem' (*ä'bo̱ bĕn ä'dĕm*), title and hero of Leigh Hunt's poem. In a vision Abou Ben Adhem sees an angel writing "the names of those who love the Lord"; asks to be counted as one who loves his fellowmen, and learns that the love of man is the love of God.

Aboukir (*ä-bo̱-kēr'*) **Bay**, or **Abukir Bay**, on n. coast of Egypt, w. of Rosetta mouth of Nile; here Nelson destroyed French fleet (1798): N-127, N-11

About (*à-bo̱'*), **Edmond François** (1828–85), French author; wrote prodigious number of novels, plays, essays, newspaper articles, pamphlets; friend of Second Empire, but became republican after its fall; published paper *XIXe Siècle*.

Abrabanel (*ä-brä-bä-nĕl'*), or **Abarbanel, Isaac** (1437–1508), Jewish scholar and statesman, born Lisbon, Portugal; treasurer of Alfonso V of Portugal; banished after king's death, became minister of state in Spain under Ferdinand and Isabella until expulsion of Jews in 1492; later in Naples, Corfu, and Venice; noted Bible commentator.

Ab'racadab'ra, a magic word, formerly used as a charm.

A'braham, founder of Hebrew nation A-6, J-426
Moslem beliefs M-195
sacrifice of Isaac, *picture* A-6

Abraham, Plains of. *See in Index* Plains of Abraham

Abraham Lincoln Birthplace National Historic Site, in Kentucky N-29, *pictures* K-31, L-280

Abrahamson, James A. (born 1933), aerospace research pilot (astronaut candidate); U.S. Air Force officer chosen for Air Force Manned Orbiting Laboratory program 1967.

Abramovitz, Max (born 1908), architect, born Chicago, Ill.; partner of Wallace K. Harrison 1940–; designed Corning Glass Center and Philharmonic Hall, Lincoln Center Corning Glass Center, *picture* U-112

ü=French *u*, German *ü*; *ġem*, *ġo*; *thin*, *then*; *ṅ*=French nasal (Jeaṅ); *zh*=French *j* (*z* in azure); *ᴋ*=German guttural *ch*

Abrams, Creighton Williams (born 1914), U.S. Army officer, born Springfield, Mass.; Army vice chief of staff 1964–67; deputy commander U.S. forces in Vietnam 1967–68, commander 1968–.

Abrantes (ä-brän'tĕsh), Portugal, town on river Tagus, 75 mi. n.e. of Lisbon; founded about 300 B.C.; strongly fortified; trade in olive oil, wine, grain, and fruit; captured by French (1807) under General Junot, who received title duke of Abrantes.

Abrasives, substances used for grinding or polishing, for sharpening tools, etc. I-182a. *See also in Index*
Aloxite; Carborundum; Sandpaper
corundum E-197
diamond D-102, M-338
diatomite D-104, M-332, F-357
electric furnace for making, *picture* N-240
emery E-197
glass grinding and polishing G-138, L-164, L-195
grinding machines T-206, *pictures* T-206: emery wheel E-197; grindstone O-416
pumice L-164
quartz Q-7
sandblast S-38, P-399

Abruzzi (ä-brụt'tsē), **Luigi, duke of** (1873–1933), Italian royal prince, explorer, and scientist; born Madrid, Spain; first to ascend Mt. St. Elias, Alaska (1897); commanded expedition which attempted to reach North Pole (1899–1900); commanded Italian fleet World War I.

Abruzzi and Molise (mō-lē'zā), region in central Italy; 5881 sq. mi.; pop. 1,564,318; includes highest point of Apennines, Gran Sasso d'Italia ("great rock of Italy"), culminating in Mt. Corno (9560 ft.): I-328, *map* I-338

Ab'salom, handsome, unscrupulous son of David; rebelled against his father; caught by his long hair in tree when riding, and slain by Joab; deeply mourned by David (II Sam. xiv–xviii)
tomb, *map* J-411

'Absalom and Achit'ophel', political satire in verse by Dryden, in which duke of Monmouth figures as Absalom and the earl of Shaftesbury as Achitophel.

Absaroka Range, n.w. Wyoming R-234a, *maps* W-315, 326, U-80, Y-340

Ab'scess, a collection of pus in a body tissue
dental D-92

Absent-mindedness H-290

Ab'solute, Sir Anthony, in Sheridan's comedy 'The Rivals', blustering kind-hearted old gentleman: *picture* D-171

Absolute altim'eter, or **terrain-clearance indicator,** airplane instrument A-179

Absolute pitch, the ability to identify or sing any given musical tone; may be inborn or acquired.

Absolute zero H-111
scale shows, *pictures* H-111

Absorption
air-conditioning system A-125
energy A-680, R-34–5, E-207, S-373–4, *diagrams* R-35, E-209
food D-118
light C-447–52: analyzing the sun S-371–2; experiments with color C-448–51, *color pictures* C-449, 451
refrigeration R-136
spectrum S-371

Abstract art P-68
finger painting and, *color pictures* F-115–16

mobiles and stabiles C-27, *pictures* C-27, S-93

Abstraction, in writing W-309

Abt (äpt), **Franz** (1819–85), German composer, born Eilenburg, Saxony; songs noted for melodic simplicity ('When the Swallows Homeward Fly'; 'Good Night, My Child'; 'Sleep Well, Sweet Angel').

Abu (ä'bụ), Arabic word meaning "father," the first element in many personal and place names, as Abu Bakr, "father of the virgin."

Abu, Mount, in Rajputana, India; 5653 ft.
temples I-70

Abu Abdullah. *See in Index* Boabdil

Abu Bakr (băk'ẽr), also **Abu Bekr** (bĕk'ẽr) (573–634), first Mohammedan caliph, born Mecca, Arabia: M-421

Abukir Bay, Egypt. *See in Index* Aboukir Bay

'Abundance', drawing by Botticelli D-181, *picture* D-181

Abury, England. *See in Index* Avebury

Abu Simbel, Egypt, two temples of Rameses II hewn in rock near 2d cataract of Nile: A-663, *map* E-109, *pictures* S-79, A-662

Abu'tilon, genus of plants of the mallow family, mostly tropical or semitropical; some species with red, pink, yellow, or white pendant blossoms, called flowering maples, are grown in pots, like geraniums

Abutment, in architecture B-324, *diagrams* M-205, A-477

Abydus (a-bī'dŭs), or **Abydos,** Asia Minor, ancient city at narrowest point of Hellespont, where Xerxes built bridge of boats: *map* G-221
home of Leander H-146

Abydus, or **Abydos,** Egypt, ancient city on Nile, once second only to Thebes; held sacred as burial place of Osiris: *map* E-109

Ab'yla, in ancient geography, one of the Pillars of Hercules; on African coast opposite modern Gibraltar; now called Apes' Hill
legendary origin H-143

Abyssal fauna. *See in Index* Deep-sea fish

Abyssal hill, of the ocean floor O-398d, *map* O-395c

Abyssal plain O-395a, O-398, *map* O-395c–d

Abyssinia (ăb-ĭ-sĭn'ĭ-a), another name for Ethiopia A-7. *See also in Index* Ethiopia

Abyssinian cat C-155, *color picture* C-155. *See also in Index* Cat, *table*

A.C. *See in Index* Electric current, *subhead* alternating

Acacia (a-kā'sha), genus of shrubs and trees A-7, *picture* A-7
leaf A-7
mulga, dwarf acacia A-713, *picture* A-711

Academic freedom, liberty of teacher or research worker to discuss and investigate problems of his field without arbitrary interference from school or public officials.

Académie Goncourt, French literary society established 1896 by will of Edmond de Goncourt for encouragement of independent art among young writers; in operation after 1903; ten members; annual prize for best imaginative prose work.

Acad'emy A-7–8
ancient Athens A-7, P-385
British A-7–8
French A-7, R-204
Russian R-332h
various meanings of word A-7

Academy award, in motion pictures M-527, *picture* M-527. *See also in Index* Oscar

Academy of Model Aeronautics A-185

Academy of Motion Picture Arts and Sciences M-527
award M-527, *picture* M-527

Academy of St. Luke R-254

Academy of Sciences, Russian R-332h

Academy of Television Arts and Sciences, Hollywood, Calif., established 1946 for the advancement of television; first president, Edgar Bergen. *See also in Index* Emmy

Academy of the New Church, at Bryn Athyn, Pa.; General Church of the New Jerusalem; founded 1876; liberal arts, theology.

Acadia (a-kā'dĭ-a), former French colony in North America A-8, N-374, N-164, M-55, *picture* A-8
location A-8, *locator map* A-8

Acadia National Park, in Maine N-29, *map* N-30, *picture* N-29, *color picture* M-59

Acadia University, at Wolfville, N. S., Canada; founded 1838 by Baptist church; nonsectarian; arts and sciences, commerce, education, engineering, home economics, music, theology.

Acajutla (ä-kä-hụt'lä), El Salvador, seaport on Pacific; pop. 3662; shipping port for El Salvador's chief coffee section.

Acala cotton C-592

Acanthus (a-kăn'thŭs), a plant A-9, *picture* A-9
Corinthian capital decoration A-9, *pictures* A-9, A-491

Acanthus family, or **Acanthaceae** (ăk-ăn-thā'sē-ē), a family of plants, native chiefly to the tropics; includes red justicia, ruellia, and bear's-breech.

A cappella. *See in Index* Music, *table* of terms and forms

Acapulco (ä-kä-pụl'kō), Mexico, seaport on Pacific, 180 mi. s.w. of Mexico City; pop. 49,149; pleasure resort; sugarcane, fruit, hides; deep-sea fishing: M-240, *maps* M-241, 260e, *picture* M-252
historic trade with Manila M-87

Acari'na, order of arthropod animals; includes the mites and ticks: S-388

Acarnania (ăk-är-nā'nĭ-a), district of ancient Greece on w. coast, n. of Gulf of Patras; inhabitants, hunters and herdsmen, lingered behind rest of Greece in culture; now forms, with Aetolia, a prefecture of modern Greece (2137 sq. mi.); pop. 237,407: *map* G-221

Accad. *See in Index* Akkad

Accault, Michel. *See in Index* Aco, Michel

Accelerando. *See in Index* Music, *table* of terms and forms

Accelera'tion
mechanics M-209–10, G-195, *diagram* G-196
physics G-195, *diagram* G-196: gravitational acceleration measured by pendulum P-160; space travel A-58–9, S-348f, 342–4, *pictures* A-58–9

Accelerometer, or **G-meter,** instrument A-179, T-58–9

Accent, in music M-554. *See also in Index* Music, *table* of terms and forms

Accent, in pronunciation, stress or emphasis placed on certain syllables in pronouncing a word. If a word has more than one accent, the most important is called the primary, the less important, the secondary; many foreign languages have definite rules of accent; English has no definite rules, but usually stresses the first syllable in short words.

Acceptance, or trade acceptance C-603

Acciaccatura. *See in Index* Music, *table* of terms and forms

Accident
causes S-7–8, 3, *chart* S-4, *pictures* S-9
cost S-3
decreased by education S-4
employers' liability E-201
first aid. *See in Index* First aid
insurance I-216
lightning L-275
police role P-426, 428, *color picture* P-425
prevention. *See in Index* Safety; Safety devices and measures
traffic. *See in Index* Automobile driving, *subhead* traffic accident

Accidental, in music M-564

Accipiter, a genus of hawks H-74
silhouette, *picture* H-74

Accipitridae, a family of birds, including the kites, hawks, and ospreys.

Accolade (ăk-ō-lād') K-66

Accordion (à-kôr'dĭ-ŏn) M-568
making, *picture* I-329
reed used R-121

Accounting A-9. *See also in Index* Bookkeeping
automatic typewriters used T-321
bibliography A-9
financial report, *table* B-59a
vocation A-9, V-367: tax accountant V-368, *picture* V-368

Accounting Office, General, United States U-166

Accra (à-krä' or ăk'rà), Ghana, capital and railroad terminus; pop. 337,828, including suburbs: G-122, *map* A-94, *pictures* G-121–2

Accredited colleges C-433–4

Accretion, of land
international law I-238

Accrington, England, manufacturing town in Lancashire. 34 mi. n.e. of Liverpool; pop. 39,018: *map* B-341

Ace, term for an aviator who has brought down five or more enemy planes; originated in World War I.

Acer (ā'sēr), trees, maple genus M-92

Aceraceae. *See in Index* Maple family

Acerola. *See in Index* Barbados cherry

Acesines River, in Kashmir and the Punjab. *See in Index* Chenab

Acetal'dehyde, a colorless volatile liquid (CH₃CHO) important in synthesis of organic compounds: A-9

Acetan'ilid, a drug derived from aniline; used in headache and fever remedies; obtained from coal tar.

Acetate (ăs'ē-tāt), a salt of acetic acid
cellulose acetate C-184–5, *picture* C-185, *table* C-184: rayon R-98–9
fabric, *picture* F-102, *table* F-9
fiber F-102, *picture* F-101: use of generic name F-103
lead, in secret ink I-191
photographic film P-291

Ace'tic acid, an organic acid; gives vinegar its characteristic taste V-326, O-503. *See also in Index* Acetate
acetylene a source A-9
photographic stop-bath solution uses P-292
white lead manufacture P-73

Acetobacter (ăs-ē-tō-băk'tēr), a genus of bacteria B-17

Ace'tone, an organic compound, (CH₃)₂CO, used as a solvent

bacteria produce B-17
dissolves acetylene A-10
formula O-502

Acetylene (à-sĕt'ĭ-lēn), an unsaturated hydrocarbon used as illuminating gas A-9–10, *picture* A-10
buoys A-9
cutting with oxyacetylene flame, *picture* S-9
formula O-502, V-255
illuminating gas G-39
neoprene P-228
synthetic rubber R-308
welding A-9, *picture* A-10

Acetylsalicylic acid. *See in Index* Aspirin

Acevedo Díaz, Eduardo (1851–1924), Uruguayan novelist L-153

Achaea (à-kē'à), Latinized name of ancient Greek **Achaia,** district on n. coast of Peloponnesus, *map* G-221
Achaeans conquer Hittites H-180
people in time of Homer G-220

Achaean League, a confederation of the cities of Achaea, crushed by Rome 146 B.C.

Achates (à-kā'tēz), in Vergil's 'Aeneid', Trojan hero noted for loyalty to Aeneas; hence phrase *fidus Achates,* "faithful Achates," for a faithful friend.

Achene, or akene (à-kēn'), fruit F-257

Achernar (ā'kēr-när), a star S-414, *chart* S-417. *See also in Index* Star, *table*

Acheron (ăk'ēr-ŏn), in Greek mythology, river of underworld; also the underworld in general.

Acheson (ăch'ĕ-s'n), **Dean (Gooderham)** (born 1893), lawyer and statesman, born Middletown, Conn.; undersecretary of treasury 1933; assistant secretary of state 1941–45, undersecretary of state 1945–47, secretary of state 1949–53; Presidential Medal of Freedom 1964; author of 'A Democrat Looks at His Party', 'Sketches from Life of Men I Have Known', 'Morning and Noon'.

Acheson, Edward Goodrich (1856–1931), inventor, born Washington, Pa.; had little schooling and went to work when young; was assistant to Thomas Edison 1880–81; invented method of making artificial graphite
carborundum S-195b

Achievement, in heraldry H-141–2

Achievement tests P-523, I-223

Achillea (ăk-ĭ-lē'à), a genus of perennial plants with white or yellow flower heads in open clusters; includes yarrow and sneezewort.

Achilles (à-kĭl'ēz), Greek hero of Trojan War A-10–11, T-266, *picture* A-11
Amazons and A-294
slays Hector H-122–3

Achilles' heel A-10

Achilles tendon T-80
origin of name A-11

Achinese (ăch-ĭ-nēz'), people of Achin, or Atcheen, a former kingdom at n. end of Sumatra; shorter and darker than other Sumatrans.

Achmet I, also **Ahmed I** (1589–1617), sultan of Turkey 1603–17
mosque, *picture* T-298

Achroite, a colorless variety of tourmaline.

Ach'romatic colors C-446

Achromatic lens L-195
use in telescope T-67

Achromatic telescope T-67

Achronite J-424

Acid, in chemistry A-11–12, C-239. *See also in Index* chief acids listed below
acetic, in vinegar V-326, O-503
amino B-160d, P-514, O-503–4, F-309, N-293
antidotes F-148, 149, P-410
barbituric N-15
carbolic (phenol) C-131
chromic C-335
citric: lemon L-188; lime L-278
concentrations and equilibriums C-241–2
fatty, in soapmaking S-229, 231
formula O-502
hydrochloric (muriatic) H-287
hydrocyanic (prussic) C-632–3: deadly poison P-411
hydrofluoric G-140
lava L-164
litmus test L-313
nitric N-292
noble metals resist G-150, P-384
normal and molar solutions S-256
oxalic, antidote L-278
picric E-361
poisonous properties P-410, 411
salicylic: formula O-501
sulfuric S-510: in explosives D-210
tartaric T-26–7
testing and measuring acidity A-12, Q-4, 6

Acidophilus (ăs-ĭ-dŏf'ĭ-lŭs) **milk** D-4

Ackley, Edith Flack (born 1887), author, designer of dolls, puppets, and marionettes; born Greenport, N.Y. Her books are useful, the directions clear. They may be used by adults, also by boys and girls ('Dolls to Make for Fun and Profit'; 'Paper Dolls'; 'Holiday Cards for You to Make'; 'Marionettes, Easy to Make, Fun to Use').

Ackley, (Hugh) Gardner (born 1915), economist, born Indianapolis, Ind.; joined faculty University of Michigan 1946, became professor 1952; served government in various posts; on presidential Council of Economic Advisers 1962–68, chairman 1964–68; ambassador to Italy 1968–.

Aclin'ic line, or **magnetic equator,** an imaginary irregular and varying line around the earth, near geographical equator, marking perfect balance between attraction of north and south magnetic poles; at any point on this line the compass needle does not dip.

Ac'ne, a skin disease characterized by pimples, or papules; caused by inflammation of the sebaceous glands: D-130

Aco, or **Accault** (à-kō'), **Michel** (flourished 1680–1702), French explorer, born Poitiers; leader of party captured by Sioux near St. Anthony Falls, but freed by Du Lhut; married daughter of chief of Kaskaskia tribe: I-267

Acoma (ä'kō-mä), a pueblo 55 mi. s.w. of Albuquerque, N.M.; Acoma people belong to the Keresan language group of Pueblo Indians: N-207, 208
woman, *picture* S-339

Aconcagua (äk-ŭn-kä'ḡwà), highest peak of Andes (22,834 ft.); also name of river and province in Chile: A-12, *diagrams* A-394, S-295, *maps* A-516, S-299, *picture* A-12
height, comparative. *See in Index* Mountain, *table*

Aconite. *See in Index* Monkshood

Acon'itin, poisonous white crystalline alkaloid from aconite P-411

Acorn, nut of oak tree O-387, *picture* O-388

ü=French *u*, German *ü*; *ġ*em, *ḡ*o; *th*in, *th*en; *n̂*=French nasal (Jean̂); *zh*=French *j* (*z* in azure); *ᴋ*=German guttural *ch*

Acorn barnacle, or **rock barnacle** B-66

Acorn woodpecker, or **California woodpecker,** a bird (*Balanosphyra formicivora*) of the Pacific coast oak and pine forests; black-backed with white rump, white wing patch, black, white, and red head pattern: B-182d

Acorn worm, a wormlike marine animal of the genus *Balanoglossus*; possesses features of both invertebrates and vertebrates
animal groups, *chart* Z-366

Acosta, Joaquin (1799?–1852), Colombian author, explorer, and general; born Guaduas, central Colombia; famous for books on Colombia.

Acoustic nerve E-5, *diagram* E-4

Acoustics P-305–6, S-61e, *picture* S-61e, *Reference-Outline* P-309

Acoustic torpedo T-214

Acoustimeter. *See in Index* Decibel

Acquittal. *See in Index* Law, *table* of terms

Acre (äk′rĕ), Brazil, state situated in w. and bordered by nations Peru and Bolivia; 58,915 sq. mi.; pop. 160,208; cap. Rio Branco: B-307

Acre (ä′kēr or ä′kēr), also **Akka,** Israel, port 10 mi. from Haifa across Bay of Acre; pop. 28,100: *map* I-318
Crusades C-616
Napoleon's defeat N-11

Acre, unit of land measure, *table* W-95
origin of name W-94
surveying S-520

Acre-foot, unit of measure for irrigation water; quantity that would cover one acre of land one foot deep (43,560 cubic feet, equal to 325,851 U. S. gallons).

Acres (ā′kērz), **Bob,** in Richard Brinsley Sheridan's 'The Rivals', a swaggering coward.

Acrididae (ăk-rĭ-dĭ′dē), an insect family consisting of the locusts, or short-horned grasshoppers.

Acrilan, a man-made fiber P-228, *table* F-9

Acrisius (ă-krĭs′ĭ-ŭs), in Greek mythology, king of Argos, grandfather of Perseus: P-210

Acroclinium, an annual plant (*Helipterum roseum*); flowers daisylike, red or white; dried and used as everlastings; native to Australia.

Acrocorin′thus, citadel of Corinth G-221

Acromegaly (ăk-rō-mĕg′a-lĭ), a disease H-225

Acropolis (a-krŏp′ō-lĭs), citadel of an ancient Greek city G-221, A-14
Thebes T-157

Acropolis, in Athens A-12–14, A-664, *pictures* A-13, A-665–6, G-222. *See also in Index* Parthenon
Acropolis Museum A-14
law tablets displayed B-247

Acrostic (a-krŏs′tĭk), a verse form in which the initial, and sometimes final, letters of the lines form words; was popular with monks of Middle Ages, and with poets of Middle High German period and of Italian Renaissance. The term acrostic is also applied to some of the Hebrew psalms in which in the original the verses begin with the letters of the alphabet in order.

Acrylic, *picture* P-382
fiber F-103
uses, *table* P-384

ACTH (adrenocorticotropic hormone) H-225, *list* M-192

Actia Nicopolis, Greece. *See in Index* Nicopolis

Acting, methods in theater T-151

Actinide (ăk′tĭ-nĭd) **series,** of chemicals, *table* P-207

Actinism (ăk′tĭn-ĭz′m), the property of radiant energy, particularly light, to produce chemical change, or the change produced light L-269
photography P-291, 282–3, *diagram* P-291
photosynthesis. *See in Index* Photosynthesis

Actin′ium (Ac), a radioactive chemical element, also a series of radioactive elements: R-64, *tables* P-207, C-236

Actinomycete (ăk-tĭ-nō-mĭ-sēt′), moldlike organism related to bacteria B-16

Actinomyco′sis, an infectious disease of cattle and swine; lumpy tumors form in the mouth and jaws; caused by a fungus; sometimes transmitted to man.

Actium (ăk′shĭ-ŭm), promontory of n.w. Acarnania, in Greece
battle (31 B.C.) C-385, A-451, A-706

Act of bankruptcy B-63

Act of Chapultepec (1945) S-292, L-146

Act of Havana (1940) L-146

Act of Settlement, in English history. *See in Index* Settlement, Act of

Act of Supremacy (1534 and 1559) C-337

Act of Uniformity (1559) C-337

Act of Uniformity (1662) E-239

Act of Union
Canada (1840) C-112, *map* C-112a
Ireland and Great Britain (1801) E-243, I-287: O'Connell works for repeal O-401
Scotland and England (1707) S-71, A-433, E-240
South Africa (1909, effective 1910) S-267

Ac′ton, John Emerich Edward Dalberg Acton, first **Baron** (1834–1902), English historian and editor, born Naples, Italy; led liberal Catholic movement in England; opposed declaration of papal infallibility.

Actor, performer in a play T-151, 154, *table* T-151
Chinese C-295e
director and T-149–50

Acts of the Apostles, 5th book of New Testament giving history of the Church from the ascension of Christ to the imprisonment of St. Paul in Rome; book attributed to St. Luke.

Acts of Trade, British R-166

Actuary, in insurance I-212

Acushnet (a-kŭsh′nĕt) **River,** Mass., short river on which New Bedford is situated; flows south into Buzzards Bay.

Acute angle, in mathematics, *diagram* G-69

Ada (ā′da), Okla., city 75 mi. s.e. of Oklahoma City; pop. 14,347; cement and glass; oil fields; East Central State College: *maps* O-447, U-41

Adagio (a-dä′ġō), in music, term meaning slowly; in dancing, a slow duet dance in which the woman, supported by her partner, performs difficult feats. *See also in Index* Music, *table* of terms and forms

Adair, James (1709?–83?), American pioneer and trader, said to have been born in Ireland; lived among Cherokee and Chickasaw Indians; 'History of American Indians' expounds his theory of Jewish origin of Indians.

Adam, Robert (1728–92) and **James** (1730–94), British architects and furniture designers; most celebrated of four brothers
interior decoration, influence on I-226, *picture* I-230
Stowe School, *picture* E-227

Adam and Eve, story in the Bible A-14–15, *picture* A-14
Michelangelo's 'Creation of Adam', *picture* M-264
Rodin's sculpture, *pictures* R-237

Adamawa (ăd-a-mä′wa), former native kingdom of w.-central Africa, divided between Nigeria and Cameroon; largely mountainous, with thick forests; 50,000 sq. mi.

'Adam Bede', novel by George Eliot (1859), named from hero, a simple, righteous country carpenter; Hetty Sorrel, his first love, betrays his affections, and he finally marries Dinah Morris, an evangelist.

Adam de la Halle (a-dän′ dē là àl′) (1240?–88?), French dramatist, songwriter, and troubadour; born Arras, France.

Adamic (ăd′a-mĭk), **Louis** (1899–1951), American writer, born Slovenia, Austria-Hungary (now Yugoslavia); to U. S. 1913, became citizen 1918; 'The Native's Return' is story of his visit to Yugoslavia; 'My America' and 'From Many Lands' about the immigrant in America; 'My Native Land', war and politics in Yugoslavia.

Adaminaby Dam, in Australia, over Eucumbene River, *picture* A-729

Adams, Abigail Smith (1744–1818), wife of President John Adams W-140, 144, 152, A-16–17, *pictures* W-144, A-18
portrait, *picture* A-24

Adams, Alvin (1804–77), a pioneer expressman, born Andover, Vt.: E-362

Adams, Brooks (1848–1927), historian and lawyer, born Quincy, Mass. ('America's Economic Supremacy'): A-25
genealogy, *chart* A-25

Adams, Charles Francis (1807–86), American minister to Great Britain during Civil War A-15, A-24, 25, *picture* A-15
genealogy, *chart* A-25

Adams, Charles Francis (1835–1915), lawyer, historian, and railroad expert; born Boston, Mass.: A-24
genealogy, *chart* A-25

Adams, Charles Francis (1866–1954), secretary of Navy under President Hoover, born Quincy, Mass.; lawyer and officer in many business corporations; yachtsman of note.

Adams, Franklin Pierce (1881–1960), pen name F.P.A., humorist, born Chicago, Ill.; conductor of 'Conning Tower' column in *New York World, Herald Tribune,* and *Post;* writer of light, satiric verse ('Tobogganing on Parnassus'; 'In Other Words'; 'The Melancholy Lute').

Adams, Henry (1838–1918), American historian A-15, A-355, *pictures* A-15, B-163
'Education of Henry Adams, The' A-355, A-744, A-15
genealogy, *chart* A-25
quoted A-347
Saint-Gaudens memorial to wife, *picture* S-18

ü=French *u*, German *ü*; *g̑*em, *g̑*o; *th*in, *then*; *ṅ*=French nasal (Jea*ṅ*); *zh*=French *j* (*z* in azure); *ᴋ*=German guttural *ch*

ADDRESSING OFFICIALS

Air Force, U.S. Same as Army officers. *See* Army, U.S., below

Ambassadors

American ambassador. "The Honorable——, American Ambassador." Begin letter: "Sir" or "My dear Mr. Ambassador."

Foreign ambassadors in Washington, D. C. "His Excellency —— (name and title if known), Ambassador of ——" or "The —— Ambassador" (British, French, etc.). Begin letter: "Sir" or "Excellency."

Archbishop. "His Excellency, the Archbishop of ——" or "The Most Reverend ——, Archbishop of ———." Begin letter: "Your Excellency" or "Most Reverend Archbishop."

Army, U.S. Officers and enlisted men should be addressed by their titles, as "General ——," "Colonel ——," "Corporal ——" (titles may be abbreviated). Business salutation for all ranks and grades is "Dear Sir." In informal letters, the titles may be used in the salutations, as "My dear General," "My dear Lieutenant," "My dear Corporal." For all ranks and grades below Second Lieutenant, the title "Mr." may be used in the salutation.

Associate Justice of the Supreme Court. "Mr. Justice ——, The Supreme Court." Begin letter: "Sir" or "My dear Mr. Justice."

Attorney General. "The Honorable ——, Attorney General" or "The Attorney General." Begin letter: "Sir."

Bishop. "The Most (or Right) Reverend ——, Bishop of ——" (Protestant Episcopal and Roman Catholic); "The Reverend Bishop ——" (Methodist). Begin letter: "Most (or Right) Reverend Sir," "Your Excellency," or "Dear Bishop ——."

Cabinet officer (man or woman). "The Honorable, The Secretary of ——" or "The Honorable ——, The Secretary of ——." Begin letter: "Sir," "Dear Sir," or "My dear Mr. Secretary (or Madam Secretary)." *See also* Attorney General in this *table*.

Cardinal. "His Eminence Cardinal ——." Begin letter: "Your Eminence."

Chief Justice of the Supreme Court. "The Chief Justice of the United States" or "The Chief Justice." Begin letter: "Sir" or "My dear Mr. Chief Justice."

Clergyman, Protestant. "The Reverend ——," or if entitled to a degree, "The Reverend Dr. ——." Begin letter: "Dear Sir," "My dear Sir," or "Reverend Sir."

Governor. "The Honorable Governor of ——" or "The Honorable ——, Governor of ——," also "His Excellency, the Governor of ——." Begin letter: "Sir," "Dear Sir," or "My dear Governor."

House of Representatives, Member of "The Honorable ——, House of Representatives." Begin letter: "Sir," "Dear Sir," or "Dear Madam."

King. "His Majesty the King." Begin letter: "Sir" or "Your Majesty."

Marine Corps, U.S. Same as Army officers. See Army, U.S., in this *table.*

Mayor. "The Honorable ——, Mayor of ——" or "The Mayor of the City of ——." Begin letter: "Sir," "My dear Mayor ——," or "My dear Mr. Mayor."

Member of Parliament. "The Honorable ——, M.P." Begin letter: "Sir" or "Dear Sir."

Monsignor. "The Right Reverend Monsignor ——" or "The Very Reverend Monsignor ——." Begin letter: "Right Reverend Monsignor" or "Dear Monsignor ——."

Navy, U.S. Officers and enlisted men should be addressed by their titles, as "Admiral ——," "Commander ——," "Ensign ——" (titles may be abbreviated). For petty officers the title is written after the name, as "——, Gunner's Mate 1." Business salutation for all ranks, rates, and grades is "Dear Sir." For officers of high rank the titles may be used in the salutation, as "My dear Admiral," "My dear Captain." For all ranks, rates, and grades below Commander, the title "Mr." should be used in the salutation.

Pope. "His Holiness, Pope ——" or "His Holiness the Pope." Begin letter: "Your Holiness" or "Most Holy Father."

President. "The President, The White House, Washington, D.C." Begin letter: "The President," "Mr. President," or "My dear Mr. President."

Priest, Roman Catholic. "The Reverend Father ——." Begin letter: "Dear Reverend Father" or "Dear Father ——."

Queen. "Her Majesty the Queen." Begin letter: "Your Majesty."

Rabbi. "Rabbi ——." Begin letter: "Sir" or "My dear Rabbi (or Doctor, if Rabbi is entitled to a degree)."

Senator. "The Honorable ——, The United States Senate." Begin letter: "Sir," "Dear Sir," or "Dear Madam."

Speaker of the House of Representatives. "The Honorable ——, The Speaker of the House of Representatives" or "The Speaker of the House of Representatives." Begin letter: "Sir" or "My dear Mr. Speaker."

Vice-President. "The Vice-President" or "The Honorable, The Vice-President of the United States." Begin letter: "Sir," "Mr. Vice-President," or "My dear Mr. Vice-President."

---

ease of the suprarenal glands.

Addition, in mathematics A-27–30, A-530, 531, *pictures* A-27–30
algebra A-262, 263, 266, 267–8, 269, 272, 272b–c, *d–e*
base-two, or binary, system N-379a
calculating machines C-19–20
decimals D-47
fractions F-375, 376
magic square M-164b–c, *diagrams* M-164b–c, A-529
new-math methods M-164–164c, *diagrams* M-164–164a, *list* M-163b

Additive system of numeration N-379

Addra gazelle, an antelope, *picture* A-443

Address, forms of. Custom has established forms to be used in addressing persons of high rank or official position. For a list of those in common use, *see table* on this page

Addressograph, machine for printing addresses and other matter; embossed metal printing plates are used; these return automatically to original order after printing.

Ade (*ād*), **George** (1866–1944), American humorist and playwright A-31, *pictures* A-31, L-98, I-98
time line, *chart* A-31

Adelaide (*ăd′l-ād*), South Australia, capital and trade center; 7 mi. from sea on Torrens River; pop. 587,957, with suburbs: A-31–2, A-716, *map* A-733, *picture* A-31
location A-31, *locator map* A-31

Adelboden (*ä′dĕl-bō-dĕn*), a picturesque valley and village in Switzerland, about 25 mi. from Lake of Thun; mineral springs
Girl Scout Chalet G-131

Adélie (*à-dā-lē′*) **Coast,** a portion of the Antarctic Continent, discovered by Dumont d'Urville, a Frenchman, in 1840; French claim recognized 1924: *map* A-439

Adélie penguin P-162, *picture* P-161, *color picture* A-408
courtship, *picture* B-177

'Adelphi' (*ă-dĕl′fī*) ('The Brothers'), Latin comedy by Terence based partly on one in Greek by Menander; treats question of whether it is better to bring up children indulgently or sternly; influenced number of later playwrights

Adelphi University, at Garden City, N. Y.; private control; founded 1896; liberal arts; graduate studies; branch, Adelphi Suffolk College.

Aden (*ä′d′n* or *ā′d′n*), South Yemen, seaport city in s.w., on Gulf of Aden; pop. 150,000; formerly in Aden Colony and Protectorate now included in South Yemen: A-32, *maps* A-470, A-637. *See also in Index* South Yemen, People's Republic of
location A-32, *locator map* A-32

Aden, Gulf of, an indentation of the Arabian Sea; joins Red Sea at Bab el Mandeb: A-32, *maps* A-470, A-637

Adenauer, Konrad (1876–1967), German political leader A-32, G-112, *pictures* A-32, G-103
addresses the Bundestag, *picture* G-111
Erhard and E-283
Kennedy and, *picture* K-24f
time line, *chart* A-32

Adenoids, a pharyngeal tonsil, *color picture* A-384, *diagrams* N-371

Adenosine (*q-dĕn′ō-sēn*), in biochemistry B-160b, P-273

Ader, Clement F. (fl. 1889–97), French aircraft designer and experimenter;

Addison, Joseph (1672–1719), English poet and essayist A-26, E-260, *picture* A-26
Swift and S-531

Addison, Thomas (1793–1860), English physician, born near Newcastle, England; taught at Guy's Hospital, London; discovered Addison's dis-

---

Key: cāpe, ăt, fär, fȧst, whạt, fạll; mē, yĕt, fērn, thêre; īce, bĭt; rōw, wón, fôr, nŏt, dọ; cūre, bŭt, rw̧de, fw̧ll, bûrn; out;

flew his airplanes secretly on grounds of Château d'Armainvillier, near Paris: A-171

Avion, picture A-171

Adhesion (ăd-hē'zhŏn) M-166
surface tension L-300

Adhesives
dextrin D-99, *diagram* C-577
glue G-145, *pictures* G-145
gums G-263
mucilage, *diagram* C-577
plastics P-380: in plywood P-397

Adige (ä'dē-gā) River, n. Italy, rises in Tyrolese Alps and empties into Gulf of Venice, *maps* I-338, 325

Adirondack (ăd-i-rŏn'dăk) **Forest Preserve**, in New York N-49, *picture* N-49

Adirondack Mountains, in n.e. New York A-33, N-237, *maps* N-239, 261, U-36, 50, *pictures* A-33, N-238, F-345, *color picture* N-255
geologic history G-67
location, *locator map* A-33

Adja, tribe in Dahomey D-1b

Adja'cent colors C-447

Ad'jective A-33, *table* G-166
confusion with adverb A-37
phrase or clause S-111

Adjustable-pitch propeller, airplane instrument A-191

Adjusted Compensation Act (1924), as amended, an act providing for the payment of a bonus to veterans of World War I by issuance of adjusted service certificates in the form of a 20-year paid-up endowment insurance policy; by cash payment to those veterans whose adjusted service credit did not exceed $50, and to the dependents of those veterans who died without filing application.

Adjustment, social M-173, 175, S-61h, *pictures* M-173, 175

Adjutant General's Corps, U. S. Army A-576
insignia, *picture* U-10

Adjutant stork, or marabou, a large East Indian bird S-456

Adlai E. Stevenson Institute of International Affairs, *picture* D-94a

Adler (äd'lēr), **Alfred** (1870–1937), Austrian psychologist, born Vienna; associated with Freud, but dropped psychoanalysis and founded Society for Individual Psychology; established first child-guidance clinics in Europe; explained maladjustment as due to "inferiority complex" ('Understanding Human Nature')
individual psychology P-519

Adler (äd'lēr), **Cyrus** (1863–1940), educator and scholar, born Van Buren, Ark.; president Dropsie College for Hebrew and Cognate Learning, Philadelphia, after 1908; president Jewish Theological Seminary of America, New York City, after 1924.

Adler, Elmer (1884–1962), printer, born Rochester, N. Y.; successful under name Pynson Printers; leader in group which drew inspiration from Rogers and Updike and raised artistic standards; editor *Colophon*, graphic arts quarterly, 1928–40; graphic arts consultant Princeton University 1940–52.

Adler, Felix (1851–1933), American ethical leader, born in Alzey, near Worms, Germany; founded, in New York, Society for Ethical Culture 1876; professor of social and political ethics, Columbia University, 1902–33.

Adler, Felix (died 1962), American clown C-410d, *color picture* C-410d

Adler, Larry (born 1914), harmonica virtuoso, born Baltimore, Md.; largely self-taught; concerts in U. S., England, Africa, Australia; recitals with Paul Draper, dancer.

Adler, Mortimer Jerome (born 1902), educator and author, born New York City; won wide recognition as philosopher; taught philosophy of law at University of Chicago 1930–52; associate editor 'Great Books of the Western World' 1945–; was editor 'The Syntopicon of the 102 Great Ideas'; director Institute for Philosophical Research, Chicago, 1952– ('Dialectic'; 'St. Thomas and the Gentiles'; 'How to Read a Book'; 'How to Think About War and Peace'; 'The Conditions of Philosophy'; 'The Difference of Man and the Difference It Makes').

Adler Planetarium and Astronomical Museum, Chicago, Ill., in Grant Park, *map* C-261. See also in Index Museums, *table*
interior, *picture* A-656

Ad libitum. See in Index Music, *table* of terms and forms

Adlumia (ăd-lū'mi-ą), a biennial vine (*Adlumia fungosa*); flowers white or purplish, in branching clusters; leaves pinnate; also called Allegheny vine, mountain fringe, or climbing fumitory.

Admetus (ăd-mē'tŭs), in Greek mythology, king of Pherae in Thessaly; saved from death by his wife, Alcestis, who offered her life for his.

Administrator, in law. See in Index Law, *table* of terms

'Ad'mirable Crichton, The', play by Sir James Barrie. See in Index Crichton

Ad'miral, in U. S. Navy, *tables* A-584, N-96
chief of naval operations N-94, *table* A-584
first appointments F-64, P-451, *picture* F-64
fleet admiral. See in Index Fleet admiral
insignia, *pictures* U-8

'Admiral Graf Spee', German armored cruiser W-267

Ad'miralty, department of British government which administered naval affairs; became part of combined Ministry of Defence 1964.

Admiralty Island, Alaska, south of Juneau, about 90 mi. long; part of Alexander Archipelago.

Admiralty Islands, group of small islands in Bismarck Archipelago; 800 sq. mi.; pop. 14,420; coconuts, pearls: N-168, *map* P-4

Admiralty law, legal system governing criminal and civil cases arising on the high seas; originally administered in England by lord high admiral; in U. S. administered by federal judiciary.

Adobe (ą-dō'bē), sun-dried brick, or a clay for bricks B-318, C-383, *picture* M-245
houses S-159, *pictures* M-245, S-35, S-338, A-536
oven, *picture* S-338
village. See in Index Pueblo

Adolescence (ăd-ō-lĕs'ĕns), transition period from childhood to adult life A-34–6, *pictures* A-34–6
baby-sitting, *picture* A-36
bands, *pictures* B-54, A-36
bibliography A-36, P-525
change of voice V-377
dancing D-17, *pictures* D-17
diet, *charts* F-313–14: calories F-309, *chart* F-310; milk M-317–18, *chart* M-316
emotion A-34–5, *pictures* E-198–9

juvenile courts J-444
maturity M-173–6, *pictures* M-174
play and P-388
psychology of P-522, A-34–6, *pictures* A-34–6
training for C-275–80
youth organizations. See in Index Youth organizations

'Adona'is', elegy by Shelley on death of Keats S-154

Adonijah (ăd-ō-nī'ģą), son of King David, deprived of his succession to the throne by the supporters of his younger half brother, Solomon, and later murdered by Solomon's orders (I Kings i–ii).

Adonis (ą-dō'nis), in Greek mythology A-37, *picture* A-37

Adonis, a genus of annual and perennial plants of the crowfoot family with finely dissected leaves; garden species are *Adonis vernalis* with large yellow solitary blossoms, and *Adonis aestivalis*, or pheasant's-eye, with scarlet flowers; native to temperate regions of Asia and Europe.

'Adoration of the Kings', fresco by Giotto, *picture* C-325

'Adoration of the Shepherds', medieval mystery play, *picture* M-298

'Adoration of the Shepherds', painting by Giorgione, *picture* G-126

Adoula, Cyrille (born 1921), Congolese public official, born Léopoldville; premier of Democratic Republic of the Congo 1961–64: C-511

Adrenal (ăd-rē'năl) **glands**, or **suprarenal glands** H-226, 225, *color picture* A-381, *diagram* H-225

Adrenaline, hormone H-226

Adrenocorticotropic hormone (ACTH) H-225, *list* M-192

Adrian, or **Hadrian**, popes. For list, see in Index Pope, *table*

A'drian I, pope 772–795, invited Charlemagne in 773 to invade Italy.

Adrian IV (Nicholas Breakspear) (1100?–1159), only English pope; elected 1154; quarreled with Emperor Frederick Barbarossa, initiating long contest between papacy and house of Hohenstaufen.

Adrian VI (1459–1523), pope 1522–23; born Utrecht, Netherlands; became pope through influence of his ex-pupil Emperor Charles V
house in Utrecht U-236

Adrian, Edgar Douglas (born 1889), English physiologist, born London; shared 1932 Nobel prize in medicine and physiology with Sir Charles Scott Sherrington for their discoveries on function of neuron; at Cambridge University since 1937, professor of physiology 1937–51, Master of Trinity College 1951–65.

Adrian, Mich., city on Raisin River 30 mi. n.w. of Toledo, Ohio; pop. 20,347; aluminum products, automobile parts and chrome plating, cable controls and linkage, laboratory and hospital furniture, concrete and metal products; Siena Heights College and Adrian College: *map* M-285

Adrian College, at Adrian, Mich.; Methodist related; founded 1845 at Leoni, Mich., moved to Adrian 1859; liberal arts.

Adrianople (ā-drĭ-ăn-ō'pl), Turkish **Edirne** (ĕ-dĭr'nĕ), Turkey, historic city on Maritsa River, 135 mi. n.w. of Istanbul; pop. 39,410; grapes, wine, silk, cotton; leather products; named Adrianople for Roman Emperor Hadrian; battle of Adrianople (378), in which Visigoths defeated Roman Emperor Valens, marked

beginning of Rome's decline; city fell to Turks 1361 and for nearly a century was their capital; awarded to Greece 1920; regained by Turkey 1923: *maps* T-299, B-25, E-335
siege (1912–13). *See in Index* Siege, *table*

Adrianople, Peace of (1829) G-215

Adriatic (*ā-drĭ-ăt'ĭk*) **Sea,** an arm of the Mediterranean, e. of Italy A-37, *maps* E-334, I-338, 325. *See also in Index* Ocean, *table*
location, *locator map* A-37
Trieste harbor T-260

Adsorption C-436
charcoal used to adsorb gases C-208
glue C-437

Adua, Ethiopia. *See in Index* Adwa

Adul'lam, Cave of, the cave in which David hid when he fled from King Saul (I Sam. xxii, 1–2; II Sam. xxiii, 13–17; I Chron. xi, 15–19).

Adult education E-91, P-449, U-113
Argentina A-522
audio-visual materials A-699
citizenship training C-353a, N-53
co-operatives C-565
Denmark D-90, *picture* D-90
Italy I-331
Kenya, *picture* K-45
Latin America L-139
Mexico M-247–8, *picture* M-250
Turkey T-302
YMCA Y-345
YWCA Y-346: Ethiopia, *picture* Y-346

Adulteration, food. *See in Index* Food adulteration

Adultery M-117

Aduwa, Ethiopia. *See in Index* Adwa

Ad valorem (*ăd vạ-lō'rĕm*) duty T-22

Advanced Research Projects Agency A-62

Advent (from Latin *adventus,* meaning "coming"), in Christian churches, a period including the four Sundays before Christmas; spent in prayer and fasting, in preparation for the feast of the Nativity; beginning of the ecclesiastical year in the Roman Catholic church.

Ad'ventists, various religious denominations believing in second coming of Christ; movement in U. S. originated with William Miller. Adventist bodies include Advent Christian church, Seventh-day Adventist Denomination, Church of God (Adventist), Church of God (Oregon, Ill.), Life and Advent Union, and Primitive Advent Christian church. For membership, *see in Index* Religion, *table; see also in Index* Miller, William; Seventh-day Adventists

'Adventure', Captain Kidd's ship K-48b

Ad'verb A-37, *table* G-166
confusion with adjective A-37
conjunctive C-518
phrase or clause S-111

Advertising A-38–42, *pictures* A-38–42
agencies A-41–2
billboard A-39–40, *pictures* A-41, C-483
chain store C-204
circular, *picture* F-69
circus, *color pictures* C-347: Barnum C-348c, B-67
copy writing A-41–2, *picture* A-38
economic effects A-38–9
fraud prevention A-40–1, F-83
free instructional materials A-699
ink I-191
Lusitania warning, *picture* S-177e
magazine M-33–4, A-39, 40, 41
mail A-40
methods, or techniques A-39–40, U-109–10, *pictures* A-39, 41–2
national A-41
newspaper N-230, A-39, 40, 41, 42
poster, *picture* F-66
propaganda. *See in Index* Propaganda

publicity. *See in Index* Publicity
radio R-48, 55, A-39, 40, 41, 42
television T-70, 79, R-48: censorship A-40
vocational opportunities A-42, V-365: commercial artist V-365, *picture* V-365

Adwa, also **Aduwa,** Italian **Adua** (*ä'dụ-ä*), Ethiopia, town in n.; pop. 6000; Italians defeated (1896); captured by Italians (1936); freed from Italy in World War II: *maps* E-294, A-94

Adz, a tool
Indians, American, *picture* I-131

Æ. *See in Index* Russell, George W.

Aeacus (*ē'ạ-kŭs*), in Greek mythology, son of Zeus; king of the Myrmidons; renowned for his piety and justice, and after his death became a judge of the underworld.

AEC. *See in Index* Atomic Energy Commission, United Nations; Atomic Energy Commission, U. S.

Aëdes aegypti (*ā-ē'dēz ē-ġĭp'tĭ*), new name for Stegomyia mosquito M-497, 500, P-93, *picture* M-498

A.E.F. *See in Index* American Expeditionary Forces

Aegean (*ē-ġē'ạn*) **civilization,** flourished (3000–1200 B.C.) in Crete and neighboring islands and mainland A-43–4, *map* A-43, *pictures* A-43–4
costumes, *picture* D-189
Crete C-604–5, *picture* C-604
history, *chart* H-161
Homer's poems H-211, A-485–6
influence on Greece G-220
octopus vase, *picture* D-94b
painting, *picture* D-93e
remains at Troy T-266: jewel, *picture* A-479

Aegean Islands, Italian, a former name for the Dodecanese. *See in Index* Dodecanese

Aegean Sea, arm of Mediterranean between Greece and Asia Minor A-43, *maps* A-43, G-213, E-334. *See also in Index* Ocean, *table*
origin of name T-159

Aegeus (*ē'ġūs* or *ē'ġē-ŭs*), mythical king of Athens T-159

Aegina, or **Egina** (*ē-ġī'nạ*), island of Greece, in Saronic Gulf 15 mi. s.w. of Athens; 40 sq. mi.; important ancient state; conquered by Athens 458 B.C.; antiquities include beautiful temple.

Aegina, Gulf of. *See in Index* Saronic Gulf

Aegis (*ē'ġĭs*), in Greek mythology A-45, Z-355, *picture* A-45
Athena A-45, *picture* A-45
Zeus A-45, *picture* A-45

Aegisthus (*ē-ġĭs'thŭs*), in Greek mythology, son of Thyestes and adopted son of Atreus, whom he slew; aided Clytemnestra in slaying of Agamemnon, his cousin.

Aegospotami (*ē-ġŏs-pŏt'ạ-mī*), meaning "goat rivers," ancient name of a maze of rivulets on peninsula of Gallipoli, emptying into Hellespont battle of G-225

Aelfric (*ăl'frĭk*) (955?–1020?), English abbot and writer; called the "grammarian"; abbot of Cernel, later of Eynsham; author of theological works: E-273

Aemilian (*ē-mĭl'ĭ-ạn*) **Way,** road in ancient Italy 185 mi. long, Rimini to Milan; built 187 B.C.

Aeneas (*ē-nē'ạs*), fabled ancestor of Romulus and Remus, hero of Vergil's epic 'Aeneid': A-45, A-455
'Dido and Aeneas', opera O-464

Aeneas Sylvius (Pius II) (1405–64), pope P-347

'Aene'id', epic poem by Vergil V-283,

L-155, M-579, S-473
Aeneas A-45

Aeolian (*ē-ō'lĭ-ạn*) **harp,** or **Eolian harp** A-45

Aeolian Islands. *See in Index* Lipari Islands

Aeolians, one of four great divisions of the ancient Greek race G-220

Aeolian soil S-249

Aeol'ic, dialect in ancient Greece G-236

Aeolina, early name of harmonica H-34

Ae'olus, in Greek mythology, ruler of the winds A-45
aids Odysseus C-343
Michel sculpture inspired by, *picture* A-45

Aepinus (*ē-pē'nụs*), **Franz Maria Ulrich-Theodor** (1724– 1802), German physicist, born Rostock; improved microscope; discovered electric properties of tourmaline; research in electricity and magnetism; surname originally Hoch.

Aepyornis (*ē-pĭ-ôr'nĭs*), bird M-23

Aequians (*ē'kwĭ-ạnz*), Italic tribe, opposing Romans C-343, R-244

Aeration, of water supply W-70a

Aerial. *See in Index* Antenna

Aerial perspective P-220

Aerial photography. *See in Index* Photography, *subhead* aerial

Aerial tramway, *picture* C-130b

Aerobee, a rocket G-255, V-259

Aerocar, airplane-automobile, *picture* A-791

Aerodrome (*ā'ĕr-ō-drōm*), an early type of flying machine (this spelling also used for airdrome, an airport): A-172, *pictures* A-171, L-113

Aerodynamics S-61d, *picture* S-61d
airplane flight A-165–8, *diagrams* A-165–8. *See also in Index* table on following pages
origin of word A-165

Aeroembolism, or **decompression sickness** A-58

Aeroflot A-144, R-334c
airplanes, *picture* R-330b
insignia, *color picture* A-144

Aerogram P-460b

Aerolite (*ā'ĕr-ō-līt*) ("air-stone"), meteorite M-232

Aeronautical Chart and Information Center, U. S. Air Force
lunar charts N-91

Aeronautical engineering E-212, 215, A-167, *picture* E-216
area rule A-168

Aeronautics, the science or art of designing, manufacturing, and operating aircraft. *See also in Index* Aerospace; Airplane; Airship; Autogiro; Aviation; Aviation, military and naval; Balloon; Glider; Helicopter; Sailplane
bibliography S-65

Aeronautics, National Advisory Committee for, created 1915 for study of problems of flight and to direct and conduct research and experiment; its duties absorbed by National Aeronautics and Space Administration.

Aeronautics and Space Administration, National. *See in Index* National Aeronautics and Space Administration

Aeronautics Board, Civil, U.S. *See in Index* Civil Aeronautics Board

Aeroplane. *See in Index* Airplane

Aerosol (*ā'ĕr-ō-sŏl*), a liquid or solid finely dispersed in air A-46, *diagrams* A-46, *pictures* A-46
"bomb" M-499–500
detecting ozone in smog, *pictures* A-46
how aerosol dispenser works A-46, *diagrams* A-46

AEROSPACE AND AVIATION TERMS

Ablation. The melting of nose cone materials of vehicles reentering the earth's atmosphere at hypersonic speeds (Mach 5 or greater).

Aerodynamics. The science that studies the motion of air and other gases and the forces that act on bodies moving through them.

Aeronautics. The science or art of designing, manufacturing, and operating both lighter-than-air and heavier-than-air craft.

Aerospace. The earth's atmosphere and the space above it, in which fly aircraft, missiles, and spacecraft.

Afterburner. An auxiliary combustion chamber at rear of a jet engine into which additional fuel is injected and burned, utilizing unburned oxygen in the exhaust gases to increase thrust.

Aileron. A movable control surface, usually on trailing edge of wing, used to control rolling of airplane.

Airfoil. A surface designed to obtain a reaction from air, such as a wing for lift, fin for stability, elevator for control, and propeller blade for thrust.

Airspeed. Speed of an aircraft relative to the air in contrast to *ground speed*, or its speed relative to the ground.

Airway. A designated air route equipped with navigational aids.

Angle of attack. The angle formed by the chord of an airfoil and the line of air flow, or relative wind.

Angle of incidence. Angle made by the chord of an airfoil and the longitudinal axis of the aircraft; that is, the angle at which the airfoil is attached to the airplane.

Area rule. A method of aircraft design for minimizing drag. The cross-sectional area of transonic aircraft is distributed to resemble that of an ideal body of minimum drag by lengthening the nose, adding a tail blister, or indenting the fuselage in a *Coke-bottle* shape.

Aspect ratio of airfoil wing. Ratio of span of a wing to its mean chord.

Attitude. The position of an aircraft as determined by the relationship of its three axes to the horizon.

Automatic direction finder (ADF). A radio compass that automatically indicates the direction of the station to which it is tuned.

Automatic pilot, or autopilot. A device that maintains an aircraft in straight and level flight or set course by means of a gyroscope that automatically governs the elevators, rudder, and ailerons.

Aviation. The art or practice of operating heavier-than-air craft.

Axis. A line passing through an airplane about which it may revolve. An airplane has three mutually perpendicular axes, each passing through the center of gravity—*longitudinal* from nose to tail, measuring roll; *lateral*, from wing tip to wing tip, measuring pitch; and *vertical*, from back to belly, measuring yaw.

Bail out. To make a parachute jump.

Bank. To incline an airplane laterally.

Beacon. A device that guides aircraft with light, radio, or radar beams.

Beam. A stream of radio or radar impulses or light rays used for aircraft guidance. An aircraft following a radio beam is *on the beam*.

Blackout. Temporary loss of vision, sometimes followed by unconsciousness, in making a fast turn or pulling out of a dive when centrifugal force decreases blood pressure in the head, resulting in insufficient oxygen. A *redout* results at the top of a dive when blood rushes to the head.

Blind flying. Flight with the use of instruments when the pilot cannot see out because of darkness or weather or of a hood.

Boundary layer. A thin layer of air next to an airfoil, distinct from the main air flow, with flow characteristics resulting from friction. Its flow may be *laminar* (smooth) or *turbulent* (eddying).

Braking ellipses. A series of orbital approaches to the atmosphere of the earth or other planet to slow a spacecraft before landing.

Ceiling. 1. Maximum altitude an aircraft can attain. 2. Upper limit of flying visibility because of clouds.

Chord. The dimension between the leading and trailing edges of an airfoil section.

Clearance. Authorization for a flight to depart from an airfield or to fly a specified route.

Collective pitch stick. The control in a helicopter for changing the pitch of all the main rotor blades simultaneously to regulate lift.

Condensation trail, or vapor trail. A visible trail of water droplets or ice crystals formed in the wake of high-altitude aircraft by disturbing supercooled air and by ejecting water vapor of the exhaust into cold air.

Control stick, or stick. A lever which controls movements of a plane by operating elevators and ailerons. Some aircraft have a *wheel* on a *control column* instead of a stick.

Convertiplane. An aircraft designed to fly vertically (like a helicopter) and horizontally (like a fixed-wing plane).

Crabbing. To point an aircraft partly into the wind to offset drift.

Crosswind landing gear. A landing gear with wheels that turn from side to side enabling the airplane to land in a crabbed attitude.

Cruising speed. Speed at which a plane flies best under given conditions.

Cyclic pitch stick. Helicopter control for changing angle of each rotor blade during the cycle of rotation to regulate horizontal flight.

Dead reckoning. Calculation of position using earlier known position, elapsed time, speed, heading, and wind.

Deicer. Device for removing ice from wings, propeller, or control surfaces.

Dihedral. Upward (positive) or downward (negative) inclination of a wing or stabilizer from the horizontal.

Drag. Resistance to the passage of an airplane through the air.

Ejection seat. A seat designed to be catapulted with its occupant from high-speed aircraft in an emergency.

Elevator. A control surface hinged to a horizontal stabilizer for rotating an aircraft about its lateral axis.

Empennage, or tail assembly. Horizontal and vertical stabilizers and control surfaces at rear of an aircraft.

Feather. 1. To turn a propeller blade edgewise into the airflow to minimize resistance. 2. To change blade angle or a rotor blade or rotating wing.

Flap. A movable control surface at rear of wing for increasing lift or drag in takeoff or landing.

Flight plan. A detailed statement about a proposed flight submitted to Air Traffic Control prior to takeoff, including point of departure and destination, flight route, altitude, airspeed, and amount of fuel.

Free fall. The drop of a parachutist before opening his parachute.

Fuselage. The main body of an airplane.

G-force. A force exerted by gravity or by reaction to acceleration or deceleration when direction is changed. Measured in g's, or multiples of the force of gravity.

Glide path. The line of flight of an aircraft in controlled descent.

Ground controlled approach (GCA). An instrument landing system, used during poor visibility, in which a ground operator observes a plane's position and direction on a radarscope and directs the pilot by radio.

Ground loop. A violent turn made while moving on the ground.

Gull wing. A wing which slants upward from its roots and then flattens out or angles upward. An *inverted gull wing* slants downward and then straightens out or slants upward.

Heat barrier. *See in this table* Thermal barrier.

Helicopter. An aircraft, capable of both vertical and horizontal flight, which derives both lift and thrust from rotating wings power-driven about a vertical axis.

High-wing monoplane. An airplane whose wing is mounted at, near, or above the top of the fuselage. A *parasol monoplane* has its wing mounted above the fuselage on struts.

Hypoxia. Oxygen deficiency in the blood in high-altitude flight, impairing physical faculties.

Icing. Atmospheric moisture freezing on the surfaces of an aircraft.

(Continued on the next page)

ü = French *u*, German *ü*; *ġ* em, *ḡ* o; *th* in, *th* en; *ṅ* = French nasal (Jea*ṅ*); *zh* = French *j* (*z* in azure); *ᴋ* = German guttural *ch*

AEROSPACE AND AVIATION TERMS—*Concluded*

Instrument flight rules (IFR). Traffic and procedure rules governing flight under instrument conditions.

Instrument flying. Navigating and controlling an aircraft solely by the use of instruments.

Instrument Landing System (ILS). Radio system for guiding aircraft in landing during poor visibility. Directional radio transmitters indicate direction of runway and angle of glide path, and radio marker beacons establish position along approach path.

Jet. *See in this table* Turbofan; Turbojet.

Jet stream. 1. Narrow band of high-speed wind in upper troposphere or in stratosphere moving west to east. 2. Stream of combustion products expelled from a reaction engine.

Lift. Aerodynamic force which acts on an airfoil perpendicular to the relative wind and is usually exerted upward, opposing force of gravity.

Loop. Maneuver in which an airplane makes a circular path in the vertical plane, with its lateral axis horizontal.

Low-wing monoplane. An airplane whose wing is mounted at or near the bottom of the fuselage.

Mach number. A number expressing the ratio of the speed of a moving body or of air to the speed of sound, with Mach 1.0 equal to the speed of sound.

Mid-wing monoplane. An airplane whose wing is mounted halfway between the top and bottom of the fuselage.

Mush. To settle or to gain little or no altitude while flying with the airplane's nose held high.

Nacelle. A streamlined housing for engines, personnel, or equipment.

Nose cone. The shield that fits over, or is, the nose of an aerospace vehicle; constructed to resist the high temperatures generated by friction with air particles.

Omnidirectional radio range, or omnirange. A radio station that gives bearings in all directions from a transmitter.

Pilotage. Navigation by visual reference to check points and by comparing landmarks with symbols on a chart.

Pilot chute. A small parachute which pulls out main parachute from pack.

Pitch. 1. The up-and-down, or vertical, movement of an aircraft about its lateral axis. 2. Blade angle of a propeller or rotor blade.

Pitot-static tube. A device, consisting of a pitot tube and a static tube, that measures impact and static pressures. The pressure difference registers airspeed in an air-speed indicator. The static pressure may operate an altimeter or similar instruments.

Pressurize. To maintain normal pressure in a cabin at high altitudes.

Radius of action, or radius. The distance an airplane can fly and return to its starting point.

Range. Maximum distance an aircraft can fly from takeoff until its fuel supply is exhausted.

Reaction engine. An engine, such as a jet or rocket type, which derives thrust by its reaction to a substance ejected rearward.

Reciprocating engine. An engine which develops thrust by back-and-forth motion of pistons in cylinders to rotate a crankshaft.

Reduction gear. A gear assembly used to run a propeller or a rotor at a slower rate than the engine.

Relative wind. Flow of air with reference to an object passing through it.

Rendezvous. The meeting in flight of two or more aerospace vehicles at a planned time and place; also, the point in aerospace where the meeting occurs.

Rev, or rev up. To revolve or to increase the revolutions per minute of an engine.

Reversible-pitch propeller. A propeller whose blade angle can be changed to give reverse thrust for braking the airplane in landing.

Rocket. An engine which derives thrust from expulsion of hot gases and carries an oxidizer, making it independent of atmosphere for combustion.

Roger. 1. A code word meaning "message received and understood." 2. An expression of agreement meaning "O. K." or "all right."

Roll. Rotation of an airplane about its longitudinal axis.

Run, or run up. To increase engine speed while the aircraft is standing still to check or to warm up the engine.

Sideslip. 1. To slide sideways and downward along the lateral axis with wings sharply banked. 2. In a turn, a sidewise movement toward the inside of a turn. A *skid* is a slide sideways away from the center of the turn.

Solo. Flying alone.

Sonic. Pertaining to speed of sound.

Sonic barrier, or sound barrier. Large increase in drag when approaching the speed of sound.

Space platform. A large habitable satellite for scientific and military uses.

Span. The dimension of an airfoil from tip to tip or from root to tip.

Spar. The principal spanwise member in a wing or other airfoil.

Spin. A maneuver, controlled or uncontrolled, in which an airplane dives and spirals at the same time.

Stability. Ability of an aircraft to return to level flight.

Stabilizer. An airfoil which keeps an aircraft steady in flight; includes *horizontal stabilizer* and *vertical stabilizer*, or *fin*.

Stall. A condition which occurs when an airplane flies at insufficient airspeed and with the nose too high, creating an excessive angle of attack on the wings and resulting in a loss of lift.

Strut. A rigid member that bears compression loads, such as between longerons in a fuselage or in a landing gear.

Subsonic. Less than speed of sound.

Supercharger. A pump or compressor for forcing air into a reciprocating engine for high-altitude flights.

Supersonic. Greater than speed of sound.

Sweepback. The backward slant of a wing or other airfoil.

Tab. A small airfoil hinged to a control surface and used to move the larger surface or to trim or balance the plane. May be a *balancing tab, servo tab* or *trim tab.*

Taxi. To move an airplane over ground or water under its own power.

Thermal barrier, or heat barrier. Zone of speed at which friction heat generated by passage of an object through air endangers its operation.

Three-point landing. A landing in which the tail skid or tail wheel of an airplane and its two main wheels touch ground at the same instant.

Torque. A force which produces twisting, such as rolling of an airplane in reaction to the rotating propeller or turning of a helicopter fuselage because of the revolving rotor.

Transonic. The transitional speed between subsonic and supersonic.

Turbofan. A jet engine of the bypass, or ducted-fan, type in which part of the air taken in at the front by a compressor or fan bypasses the combustion chamber to give extra thrust; one type has a fan at the rear.

Turbojet. A jet engine with a turbine-driven compressor that takes in and compresses air for combustion of fuel, producing hot exhaust gases that rotate the turbine and create a jet steam for thrust.

Turboprop, or prop jet. A jet engine whose exhaust gases drive a turbine-connected propeller and also produce thrust.

Visual flight rules (VFR). Rules for minimum altitudes and limits of visibility to govern contact flight by visual reference to the ground.

Warm-up. Running an engine to heat it to operating temperature.

Wind sock. A cloth cone pivoted on a pole to show wind direction.

Wind tee. A pivoted T-shaped device that indicates wind direction.

Wing loading. Gross weight of loaded airplane divided by the wing area.

Yaw. Movement about vertical axis.

Zoom. A brief, steep climb.

Key: cāpe, ăt, fär, fȧst, whạt, fạll; mē, yĕt, fẽrn, thêre; īce, bĭt; rōw, wȯn, fôr, nŏt, dǫ; cūre, bŭt, rụde, fụll, bûrn; *out;*

ü=French u, German ü; g̣em, g̣o; thin, then; ṅ=French nasal (Jeaṅ); zh=French j (z in azure); ᴋ=German guttural ch

shelter. *See in Index* Shelter, *subhead* Africa

slavery S-214, A-81: Congo C-511; Ethiopia E-293; Gambia G-9; Ghana G-122; Mozambique M-538; Nigeria N-287

Sudan S-501

trade routes: India via Cape of Good Hope G-7–8, *picture* G-8

transportation and communication A-82, 84, *Reference-Outline* A-98

water R-120, *map* C-5. *See also in Index* Suez Canal

vegetation A-79, *maps* A-80, G-193, *Reference-Outline* A-97

veld. *See subhead* savanna

waterfalls, *table* W-73c: Victoria V-315, W-73a–b, *color picture* W-73c, *maps* A-95, S-264

watermelons as water source W-74

African buffalo, or **Cape buffalo** B-361–2

African civet cat C-366

African cobra C-422

African daisy. *See in Index* Dimorphotheca

African elephant E-174–80, *pictures* E-174, 177, A-418, *color picture* A-72

speed E-176, 178, *color picture* A-406

African mahogany. *See in Index* Khaya

African Methodist Episcopal church, a religious organization established in Philadelphia, Pa., in 1816 for Negroes, its doctrines in accord with those of the Methodist church, of which it had been a part.

African millet M-325, *picture* M-325

African sleeping sickness, contagious disease T-283

cause, *picture* D-128e

African violet. *See in Index* Saintpaulia

African Violet Society, Inc. F-269

Afrikaans, South African language S-264, *map* A-89

Afrikaner, in South Africa S-265, *color picture* A-71

Afro-Malagasy Common Organization, flag F-214, *color picture* F-213

Aft, or **after,** *diagram* B-230. *See also in Index* Nautical terms, *table*

Afterburner, of automobile engine A-782

Afterburner, or **tail-pipe burner,** of turbojet engine J-417, A-190, *diagram* J-416a, *picture* A-188

Afterimage C-452

'Afternoon of a Faun, The', tone poem by Debussy D-44

ballet B-31

Aft-fan engine. *See in Index* Turbofan engine

Aftonian, interglacial period I-5

Agade. *See in Index* Akkad

Agadir (ä-gä-dĭr'), Morocco, seaport on Atlantic; pop. 16,722: E-32, *maps* A-94, A-274

Aga Khan I (ä'gä kän) (Hasan Ali Shah) (1800–1881), born in Persia of ancient and royal family; for political reasons fled to India; as Mohammedan leader, he greatly helped to reconcile Moslems to British.

Aga Khan III (Aga Sultan Sir Mohammed Shah) (1877–1957), born Karachi, Pakistan; grandson of Aga Khan I; Mohammedan leader of vast influence which he exerted to raise Indian standards and to encourage cooperation with British ('India in Transition').

Aga Khan IV (Shah Karim el-Huseini) (born 1936), born Geneva, Switzerland; grandson of Aga Khan III, whom he succeeded as Mohammedan leader Oct. 1957; attended Harvard University.

Agamemnon (ăg-ạ-mĕm'nŏn), in Greek mythology, king of Mycenae, leader of Greeks in the Trojan War, brother of Menelaus; upon his return from victory over Troy, Agamemnon was murdered by his wife, Clytemnestra: T-266

'Agamemnon', ship used in laying early cable C-8

Agana (ä-gä'nyä), capital of Guam; pop. 1642; College of Guam: G-245, *map* P-4

Aganippe (ăg-ạ-nĭp'ē), in Greek mythology, fountain at the foot of Mount Helicon sacred to Apollo and the Muses; those who drank from it were inspired to write beautiful poetry.

Agar-agar (ä'gär-ä'gär), vegetable gelatin, obtained from seaweeds; used as a culture medium, and as a laxative; also, in China, to render silk and paper transparent: P-378, *picture* D-128c

Agar'icus campestris, edible mushroom M-552, *color picture* M-553

Agassiz (ăg'ạ-sē), **Alexander** (1835–1910), American zoologist, mine operator, ichthyologist, and oceanographer; born Switzerland; son of Jean Louis R. Agassiz: A-100

Agassiz, Jean Louis Rodolphe (1807–73), American naturalist and geologist A-99–100, I-4, *picture* A-99

Hall of Fame, *table* H-11

time line, *chart* A-99

Agassiz, Lake, prehistoric glacial lake in North America M-88

Red River valley R-120

Agate, James Evershed (1877–1947), English author and critic, born Manchester, England; dramatic critic for *Manchester Guardian* ('At Half-past Eight'; 'First Nights').

Agate, a semiprecious stone found in the British Isles, both Americas, and India J-422

quartz in Q-7

Agate, a size of type T-316

Agateware E-202

Ag'atha, Saint, Sicilian noblewoman; martyred about A.D. 251; patroness of Malta; feast day February 5.

Agathea. *See in Index* Felicia

Agave (ạ-gā'vē), a genus of American plants A-100, *picture* A-100, *color picture* F-277f. *See also in Index* Maguey

leaf A-100, *picture* A-100

sisal S-206, *pictures* R-292

Age. *See also in Index* Life, *subhead* length of; Man, *subhead* antiquity; Old age

Chinese method of reckoning C-291e

Age, or **era,** as "Age of Bronze." *See in Index* Bronze Age, etc.

Agee (ā'gē), **James** (1909–55), writer, born Knoxville, Tenn. (poems: 'Permit Me Voyage'; novels: 'The Morning Watch', 'A Death in the Family' awarded 1958 Pulitzer prize; 'Letters to Father Flye'): *picture* T-94

Agena, an upper-stage rocket used in space exploration by NASA and the military services; also the target vehicle for rendezvous and docking maneuvers: S-345h, 346a-b, c-d, 348, *diagrams* S-345a, *picture* S-346b

Agency for International Development (AID), United States A-112, U-156, P-19, L-125b

Agency shop, in industry L-84

Agenor (ạ-ġē'nôr), in Greek mythology, king of Phoenicia, father of Cadmus and Europa.

Ageratum (ăg-ēr-ā'tŭm or ạ-ġĕr'ạ-tŭm), a species of annual garden flower of the composite family with blue or white flower heads; leaves heart-shaped; dwarf and tall varieties.

Agglutina'tion, of blood B-224

Agglu'tinative languages L-114

Aggradation, of land surface E-15

Aggregate, crushed stone or gravel in concrete C-503, *picture* C-504

Aghrim, or **Aughrim** (ġκ'rĭm), **battle of** (1691), decisive victory of forces of William III over those of James II at village of Aghrim, Galway County, w. Ireland.

Agincourt (ăg'ĭn-kôrt), French **Azincourt** (ạ-zăṅ-kūr'), France, village in n.; pop. 106; decisive battle of Hundred Years' War (1415): A-100, H-272, H-136, *picture* H-137

Aglaia (ạ-glā'yạ), in Greek mythology, one of the three Graces. *See also in Index* Graces

Agnes (ăg'nĕs), **Saint,** Roman martyr (A.D. 304); patron saint of young girls; symbol, a lamb; festival, Roman Catholic church January 28, Anglican January 21.

Agnes Scott College, at Decatur, Ga.; for women; founded 1889 by Presbyterians; nonsectarian; arts and sciences; observatory has 30-inch telescope, largest in southeast.

Agnew, Spiro T. (born 1918), lawyer and public official, born Baltimore, Md.; governor of Maryland after 1967; Republican vice-presidential nominee 1968.

Agnon, Shmuel Yosef (born 1888), Israeli writer, born Buczacz, Galicia (present Buchach, Russia); lived in Palestine (present Israel) 1907–13, 1924–; wrote of Jewish ghetto traditions ('The Bridal Canopy'; 'A Guest for the Night'); shared 1966 Nobel prize in literature with Nelly Sachs.

Agnosticism (ăg-nŏs'tĭ-sĭz'm), the theory that the nature or existence of ultimate realities, especially God and the human soul, can neither be proved nor disproved. The word was first used by Thomas Huxley.

Agora (ăg'ō-rạ), marketplace of ancient Greek cities, particularly of Athens A-667, G-224

Agouti, or **aguti** (ạ-ġọ'tĭ), a rodent of South America and the West Indies (*Dasyprocta aguti*); about size of rabbit; coarse hair; brownish above and yellowish underneath.

Agra (ä'grä), former province, now part of Uttar Pradesh state, India.

Agra, India, ancient city, 110 mi. s.e. of Delhi; pop. 462,020: I-76, *maps* I-66, A-637

Taj Mahal T-10–11, *picture* T-11

Agram, Yugoslavia. *See in Index* Zagreb

Agramonte, Aristides (1869–1931), Cuban bacteriologist, born Puerto Príncipe (present Camagüey); as U. S. Army surgeon, member of yellow fever commission in Cuba: M-499

Agrarian Reform Law (1960), Venezuela L-143

farmer receives title, *picture* L-148

Agricola (ạ-grĭk'ō-lạ), **Georgius** (Georg Bauer) (1490–1555), German scientist, born Saxony; called "father of mineralogy"; author of *'De re metallica'*, first scientific textbook on mining and metallurgy: S-57g, W-149

isolates zinc Z-355

Agricola, Gnaeus Julius (A.D. 37–93), Roman general and governor of Britain (A.D. 78–85); father-in-law of Tacitus, who wrote his life

discovers Scottish Highlands, *table* E-358

Key: cāpe, ăt, fär, fạst, whạt, fạll; mē, yĕt, fērn, thêre; īce, bĭt; rōw, wón, fôr, nŏt, dọ; cūre, bŭt, rụde, fụll, bûrn; out;

ü=French *u*, German ü; ġem, ḡo; thin, then; ṅ=French nasal (Jeaṅ); zh=French *j* (*z* in azure); ᴋ=German guttural *ch*

Alcott, Louisa May (1832–88), American author A-254, A-364, R-110d, 111a, *picture* A-254
home in Concord, Mass. C-502h

Alcuin (*ălk'wĭn*) (735–804), English scholar and churchman, in Charlemagne's court E-253, C-210

Alda, Frances (Frances Davis) (1883–1952), operatic soprano, born Christchurch, New Zealand, of English parents; studied in Paris; sang leading roles with Metropolitan Opera Co., New York City, for many years (Gilda in 'Rigoletto'; Marguerite in 'Faust').

Aldabra (*ăl-dä'brä*), group of coral islands in Indian Ocean, part of British Indian Ocean Territory 265 mi. n. of Madagascar; home of giant tortoise: *map* A-95

Aldanov (*ŭl-dà'nôf*), Mark, pseudonym of Mark Aleksandrovich Landau (1888–1957), Russian novelist, born Kiev; to France 1919, to U. S. 1941: R-360a

Aldebaran (*ăl-dĕb'ạ-rän*), a reddish star, the brightest in the constellation Taurus (Bull): S-414, 417, *charts* S-415, 421, 423. *See also in Index* Star, *table*

Aldehyde, a compound intermediate between a simple alcohol and an organic acid O-502
formula O-502

Alden, John (1599?–1687), *Mayflower* Pilgrim, assistant to governor of Plymouth Colony: A-255, M-182, *picture* A-349
courts and marries Priscilla Mullens A-255, M-182, A-349

Alder, Kurt (1902–58), German chemist, born near present Katowice, Poland; with O. Diels won 1950 Nobel prize in chemistry for work on diene synthesis, method of making organic chemicals synthetically.

Alder (*ăl'dēr*), a genus of shrubs or trees A-255, *picture* A-255
swamp plants W-75

Alder fly, species of large net-veined insect peculiar to America; larvae (dobsons) used as bait for stillfishing; eggs laid on leaves or branches overhanging water, in which young live until maturity
eggs, *picture* E-107

Alderman, Edwin Anderson (1861–1931), educator, lecturer, and writer; born Wilmington, N. C.; president University of North Carolina, Tulane University, University of Virginia ('The Growing South'; 'Some Tests of an Educated Man').

Alderman (from Anglo-Saxon *ealdor*, "elder"), in England and in the United States member of a city legislature: M-547

Alderney (*ăl'dēr-nĭ*), one of Channel Islands; pop. 1321; 3 sq. mi.: C-207, *map* G-199h

Aldershot (*ăl'dēr-shŏt*), England, a town 34 mi. s.w. of London; pop. 31,225; in military training area: *map* G-199h

Alderson-Broaddus College, at Philippi, W. Va.; Baptist; formed 1932 by merger of Alderson Junior College and Broaddus College; liberal arts, education.

Aldine Press. *See in Index* Aldus Manutius

Aldington, Hilda Doolittle ("H. D."). *See in Index* Doolittle, Hilda

Ald'ington, Richard (1892–1962), English writer, born Hampshire, England; lived much in U. S.; one of leaders of "imagist" school; married Hilda Doolittle ("H. D."), later divorced (poems: 'Images of

Desire'; novel: 'The Romance of Casanova'; biography: 'The Duke', life of Wellington, and 'D. H. Lawrence').

Aldis, Dorothy Keeley (Mrs. Graham Aldis) (1897–1966), writer, born Chicago, Ill. (verses for children: 'Everything and Anything', 'Before Things Happen', 'Hello Day'; novels: 'Poor Susan' and 'Dark Summer').

Aldrich (*ạl'drĭch*), Bess Streeter (1881–1954), novelist, born Cedar Falls, Iowa; early work issued under name of Margaret Dean Stevens; wrote chiefly of pioneer life in small prairie towns ('Mother Mason'; 'The Rim of the Prairie'; 'A Lantern in Her Hand'; 'A White Bird Flying'; 'Song of Years').

Aldrich, Nelson W (ilmarth) (1841–1915), U. S. senator from R. I. (1881–1911), born Foster, R. I.; father of Winthrop W. Aldrich; authority on tariff and finance (Payne-Aldrich Tariff, Aldrich-Vreeland Currency Law)
Stalwart Republican leader T-8

Aldrich, Thomas Bailey (1836–1907), poet and novelist, born Portsmouth, N. H.; editor *The Atlantic Monthly* 1881–90; known for story based on his own boyhood ('Story of a Bad Boy'), short stories ('Marjorie Daw'), and graceful verse: R-111a

Aldrich, Winthrop W (illiams) (born 1885), banker and diplomat, born Providence, R. I.; son of Nelson W. Aldrich and brother-in-law of John D. Rockefeller, Jr.; admitted to New York bar 1912; president of Chase National Bank of the City of New York 1930–34, chairman of the board 1934–53; U. S. ambassador to Great Britain 1953–57.

Aldrin, Edwin E., Jr. (born 1930), astronaut, born Glen Ridge, N. J.; U. S. Air Force officer chosen for NASA program 1963: S-346d

Aldus Manutius (*ạl'dŭs mạ-nū'shĭ-ŭs*) (1450–1515), Venetian printer; founder of the Aldine Press: T-317, P-534
italic type, *picture* B-251

Alecto (*ạ-lĕk'tō*), in Greek mythology, one of the Furies F-480

Aleichem, Shalom. *See in Index* Rabinowitz, Shalom

Alemán (*ä-lā-män'*), Mateo (1547?–1614?), Spanish novelist, born Seville; official in Spanish treasury for many years; later emigrated to Mexico: S-366

Alemán, Miguel (born 1902), Mexican lawyer and statesman, born Sayula, Veracruz; governor of state of Veracruz 1936–40, minister of government in Camacho's cabinet 1940–45; president of Mexico 1946–52: M-256

Alemanni (*ăl-ĕ-măn'ī*) ("all-men"), confederacy of German tribes; conquered 496 by Clovis. French call Germans "Allemands" and Germany "Allemagne." Descendants today in Switzerland, Alsace, and Swabia: G-102

Alembert (*à-län-bêr'*), Jean le Rond d' (1717–83), French mathematician and philosopher, born Paris; made important contributions to the theories of mechanics
contributor to 'Encyclopédie' R-124
Laplace and L-125c

Alembic. *See in Index* Retort

Alemtejo (*ä-lĕń-tā'zhö*), province of s.e. Portugal, known for cork P-455

Alençon (*ä-län-sôń'*), France, city 107

mi. s.w. of Paris; pop. 24,299; textiles: *map* F-404
lace L-95, 96, *picture* L-95

Alep'po, French Alep, Arabic Haleb, Syria, city of n.w.; pop. 425,029; trade center; textiles, wool, hides, wheat, vegetable oils, sugar, soap, copper products: S-550, *maps* A-636, I-280, T-299

Alessandria (*ä-lĕs-sän'drē-ä*), Italy, city in Piedmont, 47 mi. n. of Genoa; pop. 92,760; railroad center: *map* I-338

Alessandri (*ä-lä-sän'drē*) Palma, Arturo (1868–1950), Chilean lawyer and liberal statesman; president of Chile 1920–24, 1930–38.

Aletris. *See in Index* Star grass

Aletschhorn (*ä'lĕch-hôrn*), a peak (13,773 ft.) in the Swiss Alps; the Aletsch glacier, 16 mi. long, is the greatest in the Alps.

Aleut (*ạ-lūt'*), Indian tribe that lives in Aleutian Islands E-288, A-228, I-152, *map* I-134, *table* I-136

Aleutian (*ạ-lū'shạn*) Islands, Alaska, chain of islands extending 1100 mi. s.w. from Alaska Peninsula to Attu Island; pop. 6011. Geologically, the Aleutian chain includes Commander (Komandorskiye) Islands, belonging to Russia, and extends to Kamchatka Peninsula, a total of 1500 mi.: A-225, 227, *maps* A-225, U-94, A-513, A-636, *inset* A-239, U-39
World War II W-272, 294

Aleutian Range, mountains of s.-central Alaska A-227, *map* U-94

Alewife, or gaspereau, a fish of the herring family A-255

Alexander, popes. *See in Index* Pope, *table*

Alexander I, Saint, pope from 105 to 115; frequently identified with Alexander, a martyr, and represented with chest pierced with nails; festival May 3.

Alexander VI (1431–1503), pope B-269
division of New World A-298, *map* A-297
excommunicates Savonarola S-52d

Alexander I (1777–1825), emperor of Russia A-255, R-353
Peace of Tilsit N-12

Alexander II (1818–81), emperor of Russia A-255, R-353, *picture* A-255
emancipates the serfs R-339

Alexander III (1845–94), emperor of Russia A-255, R-353

Alexander (1893–1920), king of Greece G-217

Alexander I, Obrenovitch (1876–1903), king of Serbia, born Belgrade; succeeded 1889; assassinated by Karageorgevitch supporters: S-113

Alexander I (1888–1934), king of Yugoslavia, of Karageorge line; born Cetinje, Montenegro: Y-351

Alexander, of Battenberg (1857–93), first prince of Bulgaria; elected by Bulgarians to newly created throne in 1879; abdicated in 1886; nephew of Czar Alexander II.

Alexander, Chief (died about 1662), Indian of Wampanoag tribe in Massachusetts; son of Massasoit, brother of "King" Philip; put in Plymouth prison by Governor Winslow, where, according to Indian belief, he was killed by poisoning.

Alexander, Grover Cleveland. *See in Index* Baseball Hall of Fame (elected 1938), *table*

ü=French *u*, German *ü*; *ġ*em, *ġ*o; *th*in, *th*en; *ṅ*=French nasal (Jeaṅ); *zh*=French *j* (*z* in azure); *к*=German guttural *ch*

Alexander, Harold Rupert Leofric George, first **Earl Alexander of Tunis** (born 1891), British field marshal, born Tyrone, Northern Ireland; served in France 1914–18; led British at Dunkirk and in Burma in World War II; made British commander in chief in Middle East 1942, deputy Allied commander in chief in North Africa 1943, Allied commander in chief in Italy Dec. 1943, in Mediterranean theater Nov. 1944; governor-general of Canada 1946–52; minister of defense in British cabinet 1952–54: W-273, 277

Alexander, John White (1856–1915), portrait, figure, and mural painter; born Allegheny (now part of Pittsburgh), Pa. (Murals in Harrisburg Capitol; 'The Evolution of the Book', in Congressional Library; 'The Pot of Basil', in Museum of Fine Arts, Boston).

Alexander Archipelago, group of more than 1100 islands along coast of s.e. Alaska: A-226, *maps* A-225, U-39, 94, *inset* A-239

Alexander City, Ala., city in e., 45 mi. n.e. of Montgomery; pop. 13,140; dairying, lumber, textiles, foundries, mobile homes: *map* A-220

Alexander Nevsky (1220–63), Russian hero and saint; devoted life to Russia and Orthodox Church; distinguished himself in constant warfare with Germans, Swedes, and Lithuanians, receiving surname of Nevsky from victory over Swedes on river Neva; order St. Alexander Nevsky founded in his honor.

Alexander Severus (să-vĕr'ŭs) (208?–235), Roman emperor, born Phoenicia; succeeded his cousin Heliogabalus in 222; able, public-spirited, but too indulgent; murdered in insurrection.

Alexanderson, Ernst Frederik Werner (born 1878), American electrical engineer and inventor, born Uppsala, Sweden; to U. S. 1901; with General Electric Company, Schenectady, N. Y., 1902–47; pioneer in railroad electrification, television, and electric ship propulsion; inventions include high frequency alternator and multiple tuned antenna.

Alexander the Great (356–323 B.C.), king of Macedon, son of Philip of Macedon A-256–8, *pictures* A-256
Alexandria named for A-258
Aristotle instructs A-528
conquers Egypt E-120, A-256–7
exploration A-256, E-355
Persian campaigns A-256, 257, P-212
route of army, *maps* A-257, M-7

Alexan'dra (1844–1925), queen of Edward VII of England, daughter of Christian IX of Denmark; born Copenhagen, Denmark.

Alexandra Feodorovna (1872–1918), empress of Russia, wife of Nicholas II; born Princess Alix of Hesse, granddaughter of Queen Victoria: N-284, *picture* N-284

Alexandretta, sanjak of, Turkey, former name of Hatay. *See in Index* Hatay

Alexandri, or Alecsandri, Vasile (1821–90), Rumanian poet, born Bacau, Moldavia; known for his collection of songs and ballads.

Alexandria, Egypt, chief seaport; pop. 1,516, 234; center of ancient Hellenic culture: A-258, C-15, *maps* E-109, A-94, M-7, *picture* A-258
banner, medieval, *color picture* M-294
bookselling and publishing B-263

caravan stop in ancient times, *picture* S-381
library A-258, L-211–12, *picture* L-212
location A-258, *locator map* A-258
medical center, ancient M-215
Pharos (lighthouse) S-116, *picture* S-116

Alexandria, La., city on Red River, near center of state; pop. 40,279; in timber, agricultural, oil, and salt region; railroad center; lumber and cotton products, chemicals: L-367, *maps* L-376, 364, U-41
climate, *list* L-362

Alexandria, Minn., city 120 mi. n.w. of Minneapolis; pop. 6713; summer resort in lake area; farm trade: *map* M-363

Alexandria, Va., historic city on Potomac River 6 mi. s. of Washington, D.C.; pop. 91,023; railroad shops; electronic equipment, metal products, chemicals, dairy products, *maps* V-349, 331, U-41
Christ Church, *picture* V-334

Alexandria Conference (1785) U-139–40

Alexandrian library A-258, L-211–12, *picture* L-212

Alexandrine manuscript, of Bible B-149

Alexan'drite, a variety of chrysoberyl discovered in Russia J-422
birthstone, *color picture* J-422

Alexandroúpolis, formerly **Dede Agach,** Greece, seaport on Aegean Sea, near Turkey, 10 mi. n.w. of estuary of Maritsa River; pop. 18,712; exports grain; belonged to Turkey till 1913–14, to Bulgaria till 1919: *map* G-213

Alex'is (1629–76), czar of Russia 1645–76; 2d in Romanov line; father of Peter the Great; death attributed to poisonous mushrooms.

Alexis (1690–1718), Russian czarevitch, son of Peter the Great by his first wife: P-226

Alexis, Willibald, pen name of Georg Wilhelm Heinrich Häring (1798–1871), German historical novelist, born Breslau ('Der falsche Waldemar'; 'Roland von Berlin').

Alexius (ă-lĕk'sĭ-ŭs) **I, Comnenus** (1048–1118), Byzantine emperor, born Constantinople; succeeded 1081; brilliant soldier, efficient administrator; inspired First Crusade: C-615

Alfal'fa, or lucerne A-259, *chart* A-259
honey H-214, B-108
meal A-259
nitrogen gatherer N-292, A-259
pests I-209, *picture* I-209
producing regions A-259, *chart* A-259
root A-259, *picture* R-291

Alfa plant. *See in Index* Esparto grass

Al Fayyūm, Egypt. *See in Index* El Faiyûm

Alfieri (äl-fyĕ'rē), **Count Vittorio** (1749–1803), Italian tragic dramatist, born Asti, Piedmont, Italy; adhered to classic rules; loved the heroic; tried to revive national spirit in Italy; his eventful life recounted in autobiography: I-322

Alfilaria, an annual tufted grass (*Erodium cicutarium*); flowers rose-purple; leaves oblong; found wild and cultivated from Rocky Mountains to Pacific; also called pin clover or filaree.

Alföld (ŏl'fŭld), large fertile plain of central Hungary H-274

Alfon'so I, king of Castile. *See in Index* Alfonso VI (1030–1109)

Alfonso I (1109?–85), founder of Portuguese kingdom; proclaimed king after victory of Ouriques (1139) over Moors.

Alfonso VI (1643–83), king of Portugal A-260

Alfonso VI (1030–1109), Spanish king of Leon (1065–1109) and of Castile as Alfonso I (1072–1109); became most powerful Christian ruler in Spain; took Toledo from Moors (1085), but was defeated by them in 1086 and 1108; built alcazar at Segovia; court at Toledo became meeting place of Christian and Moslem culture; reign noted for exploits of the Cid.

Alfonso XII (1857–85), king of Spain, born Madrid; succeeded mother (Isabella II) to throne after collapse of first Spanish republic (1874); defeated the Carlists; suppressed Cuban rebellions; reduced national debt; father of Alfonso XIII: S-360

Alfonso XIII (1886–1941), king of Spain A-260, S-360–1, *picture* A-260
son and grandson S-284

Al'ford, Henry (1810–71), English preacher, Biblical scholar, and poet; born London; dean of Canterbury 1857–71; greatest work his edition of 'New Testament for English Readers' (4 vols.); also wrote 'The School of the Heart and Other Poems'; 'A Plea for the Queen's English'; and hymns.

'Alfred', flagship of the first commander of the American Navy (Esek Hopkins)
first display of American flags J-438b

Alfred the Great, king of Wessex (848?–99) A-260, E-231, *picture* A-260
literary work A-260, E-253–4, 273
son, Edward the Elder E-100

Alfred University, at Alfred, N.Y.; private control; chartered 1857; liberal arts, nursing; graduate school; college of ceramics branch of State University of New York.

Algae (ăl'jē), a low type of plants, including seaweed A-260–1, P-370, *picture* P-370, *color pictures* A-261
classification A-261, L-259, *picture* L-258, *Reference-Outline* B-279a–b
diatoms D-104, O-398b, *pictures* L-256, M-291
lichens contain L-250, *pictures* L-250
pond scum A-261, *color pictures* N-54b, i
seaweed S-104, *pictures* S-104
sloth covered with S-218

Algardi (äl-gär'dē), **Alessandro** (1602–54), Italian sculptor and architect of the baroque period, born Bologna, Italy; court sculptor under Pope Innocent X (statue of Pope Leo XI and of Innocent X; 'Beheading of St. Paul'; altarpiece of St. Leo and Attila in St. Peter's church).

Algaroba (ăl-gȧ-rō'bȧ), another name for the carob tree.

Algarve (äl-gär'vä), province of s. Portugal P-455

Algebra (ăl'jē-brȧ), a branch of mathematics A-262–72f
new-math methods M-164d–e
powers and roots P-484–5, *table* P-484

Algeciras (ăl-jē-sē'rȧs), Spain, seaport 6 mi. across bay from Gibraltar; pop. 51,096
conference (1906) R-286

Alger (ăl'jēr), **Horatio, Jr.,** (1832–99), author of boys' books, born Revere, Mass.; Harvard University graduate; Unitarian minister;

ü=French *u*, German *ü*; *ġ*em, *ġ*o; *th*in, *th*en; *ṅ*=French nasal (Jea*ṅ*); *zh*=French *j* (*z* in azure); *ĸ*=German guttural *ch*

$\ddot{u}$=French *u*, German $\ddot{u}$; $\dot{g}$em, $\dot{g}$o; t*h*in, *th*en; $\dot{n}$=French nasal(Jea*ṅ*); *zh*=French *j* (*z* in azure); *к*=German guttural *ch*

ALPHABETS

	GERMAN		HEBREW		GREEK		RUSSIAN		ARABIC		
A	𝔄 𝔞	(art)	א ALEPH[2]		Α α ALPHA		А	(art)	١[5]	ALIF[2]	
B	𝔅 𝔟	(bat)	ב BETH	(bat)	Β β BETA		Б	(bat)	ب بـ ـبـ ـب	BE	(bat)
			ב (VETH)[3]	(vat)			В	(vat)	ت تـ ـتـ ـت	TE	(tea)
C	ℭ 𝔠	(can, its)	ג GIMEL	(go)	Γ γ GAMMA		Г	(go)	ث ثـ ـثـ ـث	SE	(thin)
D	𝔇 𝔡	(day)	ד DALETH	(day)	Δ δ DELTA		Д	(day)	ج جـ ـجـ ـج[9] JIM		(go, jour)
E	𝔈 𝔢	(egg, ate)	ה HEH	(ha)	Ε ε EPSILON		Е	(yell)	ح حـ ـحـ ـح[9] HE		(ah!)
F	𝔉 𝔣	(fat)	ה (FEH)[3]	(fat)					خ خـ ـخـ ـخ[9] KHE		(hoch)
			ו VAV	(vat)			Ж	(azure)	د ـد	DAL	(day)
G	𝔊 𝔤	(gay)	ז ZAYIN	(zeal)	Ζ ζ ZETA		З	(zeal)	ذ ـذ	ẒAL	(djug)
H	ℌ 𝔥	(ha)[1]	ח CHETH[4]	(hoch)	Η η ETA		И (I,V)[6]	(eel)	ر ـر	RE	(rod)
			ט TETH	(tea)	Θ θ THETA				ز ـز	ZE	(zeal)
I	ℑ 𝔦	(it)	י YOD	(yet)	Ι ι IOTA		Й	(oil)	س سـ ـسـ ـس SIN[2]		
J	ℑ 𝔧	(yet)							ش شـ ـشـ ـش SHIN		(shop)
K	𝔎 𝔨	(kit)	ךכ CAPH[5]	(can)	Κ κ KAPPA		К	(kit)	ص صـ ـصـ ـص SAD[4]		
			ךכ CHAPH[3, 5]	(hoch)					ض ضـ ـضـ ـض[9] DAD[4]		
L	𝔏 𝔩	(let)	ל LAMEDH	(let)	Λ λ LAMBDA		Л	(let)	ط	TA[4]	
M	𝔐 𝔪	(man)	םמ MEM[5]	(man)	Μ μ MU		М	(man)	ظ	ZA[4]	
N	𝔑 𝔫	(no)	ןנ NUN[5]	(no)	Ν ν NU		Н	(no)	ع عـ ـعـ ـع AIN[2]		
			ס SAMEKH	(see)	Ξ ξ XI				غ غـ ـغـ ـغ	GHAIN	(gem)
O	𝔒 𝔬	(more)	ע AYIN[2]		Ο ο OMICRON		О	(other)	ف فـ ـفـ ـف[9] FE		(fat)
P	𝔓 𝔭	(pay)	ףפ PEH[5]	(pay)	Π π PI		П	(pay)	ق قـ ـقـ ـق[9] QAF		(qaow)
			ץצ TSADI[4]						ك كـ ـكـ ـك[5] KEF		(kit)
Q	𝔔 𝔮	(kvass)	ק KOPH	(kit)					ل لـ ـلـ ـل[9] LAM		(let)
R	𝔕 𝔯	(her)	ר RESH	(rod)	Ρ ρ RHO		Р	(her)	م مـ ـمـ ـم	MIM	(man)
S	𝔖 𝔰 𝔰[5]	(see, is)	ש SIN	(see)	Σ σ ς[5] SIGMA		С	(say)	ن نـ ـنـ ـن	NUN	(no)
			ש (SHIN)[3]	(shop)					ه	HE	(ha)
T	𝔗 𝔱	(tea)	ת TAV	(tea)	Τ τ TAU		Т	(tea)	و	WAW	(way)
			ת (THAV)[4]	(the)					ي ـى	YE	(yet)
U	𝔘 𝔲	(boo)			Υ υ UPSILON		У	(boo)			
V	𝔙 𝔳	(fat)			Φ φ PHI		Ф (Θ)	(fat)			
W	𝔚 𝔴	(vat)	**VOWEL POINTS**								
X	𝔛 𝔵	(hicks)	ָ (awe)		Χ χ CHI		Х	(hoch)			
Y	𝔜 𝔶	(yet)	ֳ (of)		Ψ ψ PSI		Ц	(its)			
Z	𝔷 𝔷	(its, adze)	ֲ (am)		Ω ω OMEGA		Ч	(church)			
			ֵ (ere)				Ш	(shop)			
			ֶ (egg)				Щ	(Christian)			
	Pronounced with		ִ (it)				Ъ[7]				
	Rounded Lips		ֹ (no)				Ы[8]	(nymph)			
	𝔄̈ ä	(ayee)	ֹ (boo)				Ь[8]				
	𝔒̈ ö	(oeh)	ֻ (full)				Э	(egg)			
	𝔘̈ ü	(uee)					Ю	(unit)			
							Я	(yard)			

PRONUNCIATIONS are shown by italicized letters in English words, as *g* in (*go*).

[1] Pronounced at start of word, otherwise silent.

[2] Harsh vowel or silent—used in Hebrew to take vowel points.

[3] A variant of another character with a dot omitted or shifted; not counted in the alphabet.

[4] Sound not used in English.

[5] Second form final—used at ends of words.

[6] First form preferred to others.

[7] Used like ' to indicate division of words.

[8] Indicates that preceding consonant is soft.

[9] First form initial, second within words, third final.

SPECIAL LETTERS IN CERTAIN ALPHABETS

SCANDINAVIAN		POLISH				PORTUGUESE	
Æ, Ä	(care)	C, CZ	(its, itch)	Ó	(boo)	Ã	(aany)
Å	(law)	DŹ, DŻ	(edge)	Ś	(shop)	Ç	(cent)
Ø, Ö	(German 𝔒̈)	Ł	(wood)	Ź	(jour)	Õ	(ony)

Key: cāpe, ăt, fär, fȧst, whạt, fạll; mē, yĕt, fẽrn, thêre; ĭce, bĭt; rōw, wón, fôr, nŏt, dọ; cūre, bŭt, rụde, fụll, bûrn: out:

Alphege (ăl'fĕġ), or Aelfheah (ălf'hê-ąк), Saint (954–1012), archbishop of Canterbury; had been an anchorite monk at Bath; murdered by the Danes; festival April 19.

Alpheus, a river-god in mythology. See in Index Arethusa

Alpheus (ăl-fē'ŭs), modern Ruphia, river of Peloponnesus, Greece; drains part of Arcadia; enters Mediterranean Sea near Pyrgos; 100 miles long
in mythology H-143

Alphonso. See in Index Alfonso

Alphonsus Crater, on moon M-485, 486, S-347, map M-480

Alpine fir, evergreen tree (Abies lasiocarpa) of pine family, native to high altitudes from Alaska to New Mexico. Grows to 90 ft.; leaves flat, bluish green, to 1½ in. long, with white bands. Cones to 4 in. long, purple. Sometimes called Rocky Mountain fir. Wood similar to, and marketed as, "white fir." Cork-bark fir, a related species, sometimes considered a variety.

Alpine hare R-22, 23

Alpine phlox P-266

Alpine subrace, of the Caucasoid race R-27, chart R-26

Alpine system of mountains E-306

Alps, greatest mountain system of Europe A-287–8, maps I-325, S-537, E-334, picture A-288
altitude. influence on vegetation and population, pictograph E-49
Austria A-738, pictures A-738, E-311
Brenner Pass T-322, A-288, map D-32
climbing the Alps A-288
France F-388
geologic history A-288, E-312, G-68
Gross Glockner A-738, diagram E-329
Hannibal crosses H-21
Italy I-323, 326, A-287–8, picture I-324
Jungfrau, picture A-288
lakes in S-541
location, locator map A-287
Matterhorn S-541, diagram E-329, map S-537, picture S-540
Mont Blanc F-388, diagram E-329
Monte Rosa S-541
origin of word A-287
St. Bernard dog, color picture D-145, table D-152
Semmering Pass A-738
Switzerland S-539, 541–2, A-287–8, pictures S-536, 538–40, A-288, E-307, W-239
tunnels T-291, 292, 293, picture T-292. See also in Index Tunnel, table
Tyrol T-322
winter sports W-186–7

Alsace-Lorraine (ăl'săs-lŏ-rān'), region in n.e. France; taken by Germany in 1871, restored to France 1919 after World War I, taken by Germany 1940, by Allies 1944: A-288–9, map F-405, picture A-289
history A-289: Charles the Bold invades C-217; Franco-Prussian War F-420
Metz M-236

Alsatia (ăl-sā'shǐ-ą), Latin name for Alsace; also, popular name for Whitefriars, London, once a refuge for criminals; described in Scott's 'Fortunes of Nigel'.

Alsike (ăl'sǐk) clover C-410

Alster River, in West Germany, flows into Elbe at Hamburg H-13, picture H-13

Altadena, Calif., community n.e. of Los Angeles; in fruit-raising area; pop. 40,568: map, inset C-53

Altai Mountains. See in Index Altay Mountains

Altair', star S-414, charts S-419–20, 422. See also in Index Star, table

Altamaha (ąl-tą-mą-hą') River, in Georgia, formed by confluence of Oconee and Okmulgee rivers; flows s.e. 155 mi. into Altamaha Sound; navigable all the way for boats drawing 5 ft. of water: maps G-79, 93, U-59

Altamira (äl-tä-mē'rä), Cave of, in n. Spain; here in 1879 Old Stone Age relics and colored drawings of animals were discovered: D-180

Altamont, Ore., community on Lost River s.e. of Klamath Falls; pop. 10,811; livestock, grain, lumbering: map O-492–3

Altar, in church architecture, picture M-115
altar screen, picture M-231
Brazzaville cathedral, picture C-512
Escorial, near Madrid, picture M-31
Holy Trinity Church, Stratford-on-Avon, picture S-132
Salisbury Cathedral, England, picture A-603
Temple Emanu-El, New York, N.Y., picture J-427

Altar of the Innocents, Bethlehem B-144

Altay Mountains, or Altai (ăl'tī) Mountains, between People's Republic of China and Mongolian People's Republic and between Kazakh S.S.R. and Siberia; highest point Kuiten (15,266 ft.); silver, lead, zinc: maps R-322, 344–5, A-636, C-291, C-312

Altdorf (ält'dôrf), correctly Altorf, Switzerland, capital of canton of Uri, on Lake Lucerne; pop. 7477
scene of story of William Tell T-79

Altenburg (äl'tĕn-buřк), East Germany, city 24 mi. s. of Leipzig; pop. 46,905; lignite and clay mined; textiles, machinery; old castle celebrated as scene of abduction (1455) of Saxon princes Albert and Ernest: map G-115

Alte Pinakothek, museum at Munich, West Germany. See also in Index Museums, table
Dürer's 'Four Apostles' P-38–9, color picture P-39

Alter, David (1807–81), physicist and physician, born Freeport, Pa.; noted for pioneer work in spectral analysis: S-58

Alternate angles, in geometry G-69, diagram G-69

Alternating current. See in Index Electric current, subhead alternating

Alternation of generations, type of reproduction in which one generation reproduces sexually and the next asexually: S-396, pictures S-396
ferns F-87–8, pictures S-396
jellyfish J-408, picture J-407
liverwort L-315
moss M-500–1, pictures M-501, S-396

Alternator, an electric generator furnishing alternating current E-148, 149, A-781

Altgeld (ąlt'ġĕld), John Peter (1847–1902), governor of Illinois 1893–97; born Nieder-Selters, Nassau, Germany; pardoned Haymarket anarchists; furthered prison reform; friend of the "underdog": I-42, picture I-48

Althaea, shrubby. See in Index Rose of Sharon

Al'thing, the legislative body of Iceland; founded 930, has functioned almost continuously for more than 1000 years: I-13, 14, N-360
entry to Thingvellir, picture D-84

Altim'eter, airplane instrument A-179, picture A-180

Altiplano, plateau in South America A-394, B-236, 237, 238, diagrams

A-394, S-295, pictures A-394, B-236, S-269
Indians, picture S-281c

Al'titude, angular elevation of a heavenly body above horizon; arc of circle between body and horizon.

Altitude, distance or elevation above the ground or sea level
airplane. See in Index Airplane, subhead altitude
balloon records B-41–2
barometer measures B-67–9, diagrams B-68
boiling point varies W-68–68a, diagram W-68
climate, vegetation, and population affected by C-394, E-48, pictograph E-49
cloud types C-409
greatest heights, diagram A-673
maps show M-97, 99, D-126, maps M-99, D-126

Altitude, of geometric figure M-186

Altmühl (ält'mül) River, tributary of Danube, in central Bavaria; connection with Main River by canal makes it link in Danube-Rhine communication.

Alto. See in Index Contralto

Alto Adige (äl'tō äd'ĭ-ġä), n. Italy, district in Tyrol; forms Bolzano, n. province in Trentino-Alto Adige region. See also in Index Bolzano, province

Altocumulus cloud C-409, picture C-408

Alto horn, a musical instrument H-227, picture M-569

Al'ton, Ill., manufacturing and railroad center, 20 mi. n. of St. Louis, Mo., on Mississippi River; pop. 43,047; glass, oil, munitions, chemicals; Elijah Lovejoy, abolitionist, was killed here in 1837: maps U-41, inset I-51

Al'tona, West Germany, industrial and commercial seaport on Elbe River; part of Hamburg: map G-114

Altoo'na, Pa., city in s-central part of state, about 85 mi. e. of Pittsburgh, near famous Horseshoe Curve; pop. 69,407; railroad shops; machinery and electrical products, clothing and shoes, bearings, garment patterns, food products: maps P-184, U-41

Alto-relievo, in sculpture. See in Index High relief

Altorf, Switzerland. See in Index Altdorf

Altostratus cloud C-409

Al'truist (from Latin alter, "other"), one devoted to interests of others
philosophy P-263

Altsheler, Joseph Alexander (1862–1919), journalist and author of tales for boys, born Three Springs, Ky.; wrote books on Indians, frontiersmen, Civil War.

Altus, Okla., city in s.w. part of state; pop. 21,225; wheat, cotton, maize; chemicals; Altus Air Force Base: map O-446

Altyn Tagh (äl'tĭn tä'), People's Republic of China, n. branch of Kunlun Mts.; extends along s. edge of Taklamakan Desert: maps C-291, C-312, A-636

Al'um A-289
baking powder, content B-20
chrome alum C-335
fireproofing, use in F-144

Alumina, aluminum oxide, most abundant of earths, and common constituent of silicate minerals forming basis of many rocks, clays, and soils
abrasive T-206
bauxite yields A-291
clay contains C-383
corundum M-335, E-197
rubies and sapphires J-424, M-335: synthetic J-421, picture J-423

ü=French u, German ü; ġem, ġo; thin, then; ṅ=French nasal (Jeaṅ); zh=French j (z in azure); к=German guttural ch

reduction to aluminum A-291, *diagram* A-290, *picture* A-290
refractory brick B-320
'Aluminaut', a research submarine S-496
Aluminum (*a-lū'mĭ-nŭm*), or **aluminium** (*ăl-ŭ-mĭn'ĭ-ŭm*) (Al), a very light metallic element A-290-2, *diagram* A-290, *pictures* A-290-1, *tables* A-291, P-207
alloy cleanser A-282
alloys A-281: bronze B-345, C-569; German silver C-569
brickmaking B-318
building industry B-366, A-290, *picture* A-291
cementmaking C-187
chemical test for, *table* Q-4
compounds
chloride S-256
fluoride M-335
oxide. *See in Index* Alumina
phosphate (turquoise) J-424
silicates M-336, 337, B-136b, P-73; feldspar F-83, *picture* F-83; mica M-263b
sulfate, in alum A-289
earth's crust, percentage in, *diagram* C-237
electrochemical activity E-167
extrusion plant, *picture* F-12
foil A-290
forging operation, *picture* T-207
glass manufacture G-137
Hall discovers cheap metallurgical process H-11, A-292
ingots, *pictures* C-79, Q-9b
ion, *table* C-238
manufacture A-291, *diagram* A-290, *picture* A-290: Canada A-290, Q-11, *picture* C-79; United States A-290, *picture* U-89
ore A-551, A-290: world distribution, *map* O-497
periodic table, *diagram* C-235, *table* P-207
photolithographic plate P-277
properties, *tables* M-229, A-291
radioactivity induced R-64
uses A-290: airplane A-290, A-150, A-159, 160, A-57, 61, A-191; fireworks F-145; office building, *picture* A-507; telescope mirrors T-68
wire W-190, A-290
Aluminum brass B-301
Aluminum bronze B-345, C-569
Alum Rock, Calif., community 4 mi. e. of San Jose; pop. 18,942: *map, inset* C-52
Alumroot (*Heuchera americana*), a perennial garden plant of the family *Saxifragaceae* with round heart-shaped leaves springing chiefly from the rootstock and long racemes of greenish flowers.
Al'unite, or **alum stone**, a mineral M-336
Alva (*äl'vä*), or **Alba, Fernando Alvarez de Toledo, duke of** (1508-83), Spanish general, in war with Netherlands: N-138
William the Silent opposes W-165
Alva B. Adams Tunnel, in Colorado T-292, C-455, C-469, *maps* C-470, C-466. *See also in Index* Tunnel, *table*
Alvarado (*äl-vä-rä'thŏ*), **Pedro de** (1485-1541), Spanish cavalier, companion of Cortez in conquest of Mexico
conquers Mayas G-248b
conquers, names El Salvador S-33
Alvarez (*äl'vä-rĕz*), **Luis Walter** (born 1911), physicist, born San Francisco, Calif.; physics professor University of California 1945-; in radar research for U.S. in World War II, he guided development of ground-controlled approach (GCA)

system for landing aircraft; did atomic bomb research 1943-45; in 1947, drafted a system, called triple-coincidence navigation (Tricon), for controlling air traffic; awarded National Medal of Science 1964.
Alvarez Quintero (*äl'vä-rāth kēn'tä-rŏ*), family name of two Spanish brothers, **Serafín** (1871-1938) and **Joaquín** (1873-1944), who together wrote comedies of manners and short musical dramas ('The Women Have Their Way'; 'A Sunny Morning'; 'One Hundred Years Old'; 'The Lady from Alfaqueque'): S-365b, A-365b
Alve'oli, small cavities
lungs L-395, *diagram* L-395: diseases D-129e
udder of cow M-317
Alverno College, at Milwaukee, Wis.; Roman Catholic; for women; founded 1887; liberal arts, business education, education, home economics, medical technology, music therapy, nursing.
'Alvin', a research submarine S-496, *color picture* O-396
Alvsborg Bridge, Göteborg, Sweden. *See in Index* Bridge (suspension), *table*
Alyssum, sweet, a genus of low spreading plants (*Alyssum*) of the mustard family, with small fragrant yellow, rose, or white flowers; used for garden borders: G-21, 22
A.M., abbreviation of Latin *ante meridiem*, "before noon" T-178
Amadeo (*ä-mä-dê'ŏ*), also **Omodeo, Giovanni Antonio** (1447?-1522), eminent sculptor and architect of the Renaissance, born Pavia, Italy; works include Colleoni Chapel in Bergamo; façade of the Certosa (monastery) of Pavia, and Gothic spire of Milan Cathedral.
Amadeus. *See in Index* Felix V
Amadeus I (*ăm-a-dē'ŭs*) (Amadeo, duke of Aosta) (1845-90), king of Spain, born Turin, Italy; son of Victor Emmanuel II of Italy; accepted crown from Spanish revolutionists 1870; abdicated in 1873.
Amadeus, Lake, in central Australia, s.w. part of Northern Territory, *map* A-732
Amager (*ä'mä-gēr*), island, Denmark; 25 sq. mi.; pop. 178,184: C-566
'Amahl and the Night Visitors', Christmas opera by Menotti, *picture* A-609
book R-111
Amalekites (*ăm'a-lĕk-īts*), an ancient tribe of Edomites, hereditary foes of the Israelites; crushed by Saul and David.
Amal'fi, Italy, port 22 mi. s.e. of Naples; pop. 7163; 13th-century cathedral and old Capuchin monastery; medieval rival of Genoa and Pisa: *map* I-339, *picture* I-330
Amal'gam, an alloy containing mercury G-150c, 150, M-226, M-228
Amalgamated Clothing Workers of America, labor union formed 1915; headquarters in New York City; organizations in United States and Canada: L-90
Amalgamation, in metallurgy G-150c, M-228
Amami Islands, of Japan. *See in Index* Ryukyu Islands
Amanah, river in Syria. *See in Index* Abana
Amana (*a-măn'a*) **Society**, a corporation since 1932, formerly a religious community incorporated in Iowa in 1859; outgrowth of organization

founded in Germany by Johann F. Rock and Eberhard Gruber 1714; community, n.w. of Iowa City, is made up of seven villages: I-261
old cooper's shop, *color picture* I-270
Amanita (*ăm-a-nī'ta*), a genus of poisonous fungi
deadly amanita M-552: danger signals, *picture* M-551
fly amanita M-552, *color picture* M-553
Amanul'lah (1892-1960), king of Afghanistan; succeeded his father as amir 1919; took title of king 1926; tried to modernize Afghanistan; forced to abdicate 1929: A-69
Amapá', Brazil, territory, created 1943 from 53,013 sq. mi. taken from n.e. of state of Pará; pop. 68,889; cap. Macapá: B-307
Amapa'la, Honduras, chief Pacific port, on Tigre Island in Gulf of Fonseca; pop. about 3000; exports lumber, coffee, livestock: H-213
Amaranth (*ăm'a-rănth*), or **love-lies-bleeding**, a hardy annual garden herb with spikes of red flowers; introduced from India.
Amaranth family, or **Amaranthaceae** (*ăm-a-răn-thā'sē-ē*), a family of plants including many garden plants, as cockscomb, gomphrena, prince's-feather, Joseph's-coat, and tassel flower.
Amargosa (*ä-mär-ḡō'sä*) **River**, in Nevada and California, flows into Death Valley and becomes a series of dry channels: *map* C-53
Amaril'lo, Tex., city in Panhandle 65 mi. from w. border; pop. 137,969: A-292, *maps* T-128, 111, U-40, *picture* A-292
climate, *list* T-109
helium plant, *picture* T-114
location, *locator map* A-292
Amar'na, El, also **Tell el-Amarna**, Egypt, site of city built by Akhenaton (Amenhotep IV) during his rule but soon deserted: E-120, L-197, *map* E-109
Amarna letters, also **Tell el-Amarna letters** L-197
Amaryl'lis, a genus of bulbous-rooted plants of the amaryllis family; a well-known species is the belladonna lily (*Amaryllis belladonna*), introduced from s. Africa, with long narrow leaves and clusters of large fragrant rose-red funnel-shaped flowers.
Amaryllis family, or **Amaryllidaceae** (*ăm-a-rĭl-ĭ-dā'sē-ē*), a family of plants, native chiefly to tropical and subtropical regions, including the amaryllis, century plant, spider lily, snowdrop, star grass, narcissus.
Amaterasu (*ä-mä-tē-rä'sụ*), Japanese sun-goddess J-367
Amateur athletics A-668, T-225-7, *pictures* A-667, T-225-6, *table* T-227. *See also in Index* Olympic Games
Amateur Athletic Union of the United States (AAU), founded 1888; conducts competitions among its more than 40 amateur athletic associations; purposes: to improve and promote amateur sports, to establish rules for eligibility and competition; founder of American Olympic Association in 1921.
Amateur radio operator, or **ham** R-43, 55, *pictures* R-52, A-699
Amati (*ä-mä'tē*), celebrated Italian family of violinmakers at Cremona; **Andrea** (1530?-1611?), first to gain international reputation; his sons **Antonio** (1550-1638) and **Girolamo**, or **Geronimo** (1551-1635), continued the tradition; Girolamo's son, **Nicolo** (1596-1684), was most famous member: V-327, S-484

ü = French *u*, German *ü*; *ġ*em, *ḡ*o; *th*in, *th*en; *ṅ* = French nasal (Jea*ṅ*); *zh* = French *j* (*z* in azure); *ᴋ* = German guttural *ch*

American Theatre Wing, Inc., New York, N. Y., founded 1941 by a committee representing all branches of entertainment industry to help in war effort; later amended to render service, on part of theater, to community as a whole and to entertainment profession; presents Antoinette Perry Memorial Award (Tony). *See also in Index* Tony

'American Tragedy, An', novel (1925) by Theodore Dreiser about a New York murder A-354–5

American Tree Farm System F-344, L-386–7, *picture* F-346

American Turners, gymnastic association G-267b

American University, at Washington, D. C.; Methodist; chartered 1893; opened 1914 by President Wilson; arts and sciences, business administration, government and public administration, international service, law; graduate school: *map, inset* W-32

American University of Beirut, at Beirut, Lebanon L-180a, B-121, *picture* L-180a

American Veterans Committee, organization of men and women of U.S. armed forces in World War II; aim, to work for "a more democratic and prosperous America and a more stable world"; headquarters, New York, N. Y.; local chapters: P-140

American Veterans of World War II (Amvets), founded 1944, open to veterans of World War II also to veterans of Korean conflict; devoted to defense of the U.S. Constitution, development of a sound democratic American program, and the welfare of veterans; headquarters, Washington, D. C.: P-140

American Volunteer Group (A. V. G.). *See in Index* Flying Tigers

American War Mothers, organization for American women whose sons were in service in World War I; founded 1918.

American Water Ski Association A-462

American water spaniel, *table* D-150

American Woman Suffrage Association W-214

American Youth Hostels, Inc. *See in Index* Hostels

America's Cup B-232–3, *table* B-233

'America the Beautiful', patriotic song of the United States N-51

Americium (Am), chemical element, *tables* P-207, C-236

Americo, Pedro (Pedro Americo de Figueiredo e Mello) (1843–1905), Brazilian painter, born Parahyba; versatile artist, but noted especially for battle scenes ('The Battle of Avahy'; 'Joan of Arc').

Amer'icus, Ga., city 33 mi. n. of Albany; pop. 13,472; center for farming region; shirt factory, lumber mills, cottonseed- and peanut-oil mills, mobile homes; Andersonville, Confederate prison, 11 mi. n.e.; Georgia Southwestern College: *map* G-93

solar battery C-625, 621–2, *picture* C-621

Amerigo Vespucci. *See in Index* Vespucius, Americus

Amerongen (*ä'mĕr-ŏng-ĕn*), Netherlands, village 21 mi. s.e. of Utrecht; pop. 2981

William II, retreat of W-162

Ames (*āmz*), **Fisher** (1758–1808), orator and congressman, born Dedham, Mass.; made speech for Jay's Treaty in Congress (1796); a prominent Federalist.

Ames, Winthrop (1871–1937), theatrical producer, born North Easton,

Mass.; experimented with repertory theater and successfully produced plays in his Little Theater and in the Booth Theater in New York, N. Y.; pioneered in production of plays for children.

Ames, Iowa, city about 30 mi. n. of Des Moines; pop. 27,003; canned goods, collegiate supplies; Iowa State University of Science and Technology: *map* I-274

Atomic Energy Laboratory, *list* A-692

Amesbury, Mass., town on Merrimack River 36 mi. n.e. of Boston; pop. of township 10,787; hats, shoes, boats, foundry products, plastics; once the home of the poet Whittier: *map* M-161

Ames Research Center A-62, S-44

Amethyst, semiprecious stone J-423 birthstone, *color picture* J-422

Amfor'tas, in Arthurian legends, chief of Knights of Holy Grail; loses possession of sacred spear and is wounded by it; healed by Parsifal after years of suffering.

Amhar'ic, the official language of Ethiopia E-490

Am'herst, Jeffrey Amherst, Baron (1717–97), British soldier, born Kent, England; succeeded Abercromby as commander in conquest of Canada from French; led successful expeditions against Louisbourg, Ticonderoga, Crown Point, Montreal; governor-general of British North America 1759–63; commander in chief British army 1772–82, 1783–95

military road across Vermont V-289

Amherst, Mass., about 19 mi. n. of Springfield; pop. of township 13,718; named for Baron Amherst; Amherst College; birthplace of Emily Dickinson and Helen Hunt Jackson: *map* M-160

Massachusetts, University of, *color picture* M-155

Amherst, N. S., Canada, manufacturing town near New Brunswick boundary, about 90 mi. n.w. of Halifax; pop. 10,551; agriculture; salt, coal, lumber; enamelware, aircraft, leather products, structural steel: *maps* C-99, N-373a

Amherst College, at Amherst, Mass.; private control; for men; opened 1821; chartered 1825; liberal arts; graduate studies; excellent scientific museums

Noah Webster a founder W-92

Amicis (*ä-mē'chēs*), **Edmondo de** (1846–1908), Italian novelist and writer of books of travel, born Oneglia (now part of Imperia), Italy; 'Cuore' (The Heart of a Boy), which he wrote for children, has passed through 300 editions in Italian and been translated into 20 foreign languages.

Am'ide, in organic chemistry, a compound in which an organic acid radical takes the place of one or more of the hydrogen atoms in ammonia (NH_3); for example, acetamide (CH_3CONH_2) consisting of acetic acid radical (CH_3CO) plus NH_2 formula O-502, F-103

Amidships, *diagram* B-230. *See also in Index* Nautical terms, *table*

Amiel (*ȧ-myĕl'*), **Henri Frédéric** (1821–81), Swiss author, born Geneva; known for one book ('Journal', revelation of an introspective, Hamletlike soul).

Amiens (*ȧm-yăṅ'*), France, important manufacturing city; pop. 101,677:

A-367–8, *maps* F-381, 404, E-334, *picture* A-367

cathedral A-367, A-497, *pictures* A-367, A-496, D-94

location A-367, *locator map* A-367

World War I, *map* W-252

Amiens, treaty of (1802) A-367, N-11

Amine', in organic chemistry, a compound in which a hydrocarbon radical takes the place of one or more of the hydrogen atoms in ammonia (NH_3); for example, methylamine (CH_3NH_2) consisting of the methyl radical (CH_3) plus NH_2

formula O-502

vitamins V-354

Amino acids, several organic acids, derived from metabolism of protein in body, all containing amine radical NH_2: B-160d, P-514, O-503–4, F-309, M-190, N-293

formulas B-160d

genetic code G-43e–f, *diagram* G-43f

glycine O-503

measuring B-17

Amir, or **ameer** (*ạ-mēr'*), also **emir** (*ĕ-mēr'*), title used in Mohammedan countries, corresponding roughly to British title of lord; used to denote ruling power or distinct office; also as title of honor for descendants of Mohammed through his daughter Fatima.

Amish, a branch of the Mennonite church, named from Jacob Ammon, or Amen, who founded it in Switzerland and s. Germany 1698, insisting on strict interpretation of Mennonite principles; many members migrated to Pennsylvania in 1730–40, later to Ohio, Indiana, and other states: *picture* P-170

Amitosis, in biology, direct cell division, in which the nucleus and the rest of the cell are squeezed into two parts by constriction. *See also in Index* Mitosis

Amman', Biblical **Rab'bath Am'mon,** ancient **Philadelphia,** modern capital of Jordan; pop. 246,475; textiles, tobacco products, tiles, cement, flour; extensive ruins: J-439, *maps* A-470, A-636, I-318

libraries L-241

Ammann, O(thmar) H(ermann) (1879–1965), American bridge designer, born Schaffhausen, Switzerland; to U.S. 1904, became citizen 1924; chief engineer (1930–37), director of engineering (1937–39) of Port of New York Authority; B-327

Ammersee (*äm'ēr-zā*), a lake of s. Bavaria, 10 mi. long, 4 mi. wide, traversed by the Ammer River.

Am'meter, a galvanometer showing current strength directly in amperes G-6, E-147, *diagrams* G-6, E-147, *picture* G-6

Ammobium (*ă-mō'bǐ-ŭm*), a biennial plant; tubular florets form small flower heads of yellow, surrounded by silvery-white sheath; used as everlasting; native to Australia; name from Greek for "living in sand."

Ammo'nia A-368

air contains, *diagram* A-672

antidotes F-148

copper separation C-568

electronic structure, *diagram* M-170

fertilizer A-368, F-89; applying, *picture* A-106

gas manufacture yields G-38

manufacture C-241: calcium cyanamide process C-18–19; catalytic methods N-293; electric arc process N-293

nitric-acid production N-292

refrigerating systems R-136, 137

stimulant for poisoning cases P-411

ü=French *u*, German *ü*; *ǵ*em, *ǵ*o; *th*in, *th*en; *ṅ*=French nasal (Jea*ṅ*); *zh*=French *j* (*z* in azure); *κ*=German guttural *ch*

Ammonite (ăm'ŏn-īt), an extinct type of mollusk having a flat spiral shell like nautilus; a common fossil.

Ammonites, Semitic tribe living e. of the Jordan; hostile to Israelites; subdued by Judas Maccabaeus.

Ammonium (NH₄), a chemical radical A-368
alums A-289
carbonate A-368: fireproofing, use in F-144
chemical test for nitrogen, *table* Q-4
chloride, or sal ammoniac A-368: electric dry cell B-93, A-368, *diagram* B-93; soda production S-247
ion, *table* C-238
nitrate A-368: in explosives D-210
sulfate: as fertilizer N-293; fireproofing, use in F-144

Ammunition A-368-70, *pictures* A-368-9
bullets L-167
explosives E-361
gunpowder G-263-4, *picture* G-263
machine gun M-9-12, *diagrams* M-11-12, *table* M-9
shell. *See in Index* Shell (artillery projectile)
small arms F-129-30

Amnesia B-299

Amnesty, a pardon
criminals P-505b
pirates P-342a

Amnesty Act (1872), United States R-116

Amnesty proclamation (1863), Lincoln's offer of pardon to all citizens of the seceded states (except certain prominent leaders) who would lay down their arms and take an oath to support the Constitution.

Am'nion E-194
human fetus, *diagram* M-542a

Amoeba (ạ-mē'bạ), the simplest form of animal life A-370-1, L-254-5, C-181, *pictures* A-370, L-254, C-180b
breathing A-371, R-159
classed among *Protozoa* P-515
reproduction A-370, *pictures* A-370
vacuole A-370-1, C-180b, *picture* L-254

Amoebic dysentery, or **amebic dysentery** A-371

Amor (ā'môr), Cupid C-629-30, A-455

'Amore dei Tre Re, L' (lä-mō'rä dā'ē trā rā) (The Love of the Three Kings), opera by Montemezzi
Garden as Fiora, *picture* O-462

Amorites (ăm'ō-rīts), an ancient people living in mountainous Palestine and Syria
land where they lived, *map* B-6

Amor'phous substances M-170
sulfur S-510

Amortization, in economics, the liquidation or reduction of debt through a fixed scale of payments; usually a sinking fund; also the process of writing off each year the premium above par or discount below par, so that the payment at maturity will not show either a loss or a profit.

Amory (ā'mō-rĭ), **Cleveland** (born 1917), social historian, born Nahant, Mass. ('The Proper Bostonians'; 'The Last Resorts'; 'Who Killed Society?'; editor in chief 'Celebrity Register').

Amos, Hebrew prophet (8th century B.C.) P-508, 509, J-426, *picture* P-509

Amosite, a variety of asbestos A-613

'Amos 'n' Andy'. *See in Index* Correll, Charles; Gosden, Freeman

Amoy (ä-moi'), People's Republic of China, port on Amoy Island, Fukien Province; pop. 308,000; sugar, tobacco, fruit, wine; food processing; became treaty port 1842: *maps* C-313, A-636-7

Ampelopsis (ăm-pĕ-lŏp'sĭs), a plant genus of climbing shrubs, using twining tendrils and not disks for support. The Boston ivy, Engelmann's creeper, and Virginia creeper sometimes classed here, but botanically belong to genus *Parthenocissus*.

Ampère (än-pĕr'), **André Marie** (1775-1836), French mathematician and physicist A-371, *picture* A-371
unit of electricity named for him E-144

Ampere (ăm-pēr') **and amperage**, in electricity E-144-6, 152

Ampere meter. *See in Index* Ammeter

Amphetamines, drugs N-15

Amphibia (ăm-fĭb'ĭ-ạ), a class of vertebrate animals including frogs, toads, and salamanders, *Reference-Outline* Z-368. *See also in Index* Frog; Toad; Salamander
animal groups, *chart* Z-366
bibliography Z-369, S-64g
breathing, or respiration R-159
eggs E-193
evolution F-162, R-152-3
first appearance G-67, P-487, *pictures* G-60, P-487-8
fish distinguished from F-153
gill slits in young V-304
heart R-152

Amphibian plane, an airplane able to take off and alight on water or land A-153, *picture* A-151

Amphibious warfare N-99, 106, 97, 94, 101
landing craft N-99, 94, *pictures* N-97, 100, 106, M-110, W-10

Amphibole (ăm'fĭ-bōl), a silicate mineral M-336

Amphibrach (ăm'fĭ-brăk), poetic foot P-405

Amphictyon'ic league, or **Amphic'tyony** ("dwellers around," "neighbors"), confederation of ancient Greek communities centering about some convenient shrine, where they held periodical festivals and discussed political questions; most celebrated of these was the Delphic Amphictyony at the shrine of Apollo.

Amphimacer (ăm-fĭm'ạ-sēr), poetic foot P-405

Amphineu'ra, class of mollusks M-424

Amphion (ăm-fī'ŏn), in Greek mythology, a son of Zeus; by playing a magic lyre which he had received from Hermes, Amphion charmed stones so that they built themselves into walls of the city Thebes.

Amphioxus, or **lancelet**, a fish-shaped sea animal; several species known; classed in the phylum *Chordata*, subphylum *Leptocardia*: A-428, V-304, *picture* A-426
animal groups, *chart* Z-366

Amphisbaena (ăm-fĭs-bē'nạ), a legless lizard L-318

Amphithe'ater, building in which the spectators' seats surround the place used by the performers. *See also in Index* Stadium
Arles, France, *picture* F-410
Colosseum at Rome A-492, R-257, *map* R-250, *pictures* A-492, R-254, E-318
Epidaurus, Greece, *picture* T-152
Hollywood Bowl, *list* L-354, *map* L-352, *pictures* C-40, F-90
Melbourne music bowl, *map* M-217a, *picture* M-217b
Red Rocks Park, *color picture* C-461
Verona, Italy, *picture* I-343b

Amphitrite (ăm-fĭ-trī'tĭ), in Greek mythology, sea queen, wife of Poseidon; daughter of Nereus and mother of Triton.

Am'phora, earthenware jar used by ancient Greeks and Romans, especially to keep oil, honey, or wine.

Amphoteric substance, one having both acid and basic properties C-235

Amplification, in electric circuits
cables C-6, *diagram* C-6
electron tube E-170
phonograph P-268f-9, *diagrams* P-269-70
photoelectric devices P-274
radio R-60-1, E-170, *diagrams* R-46-7, 57

Amplitude, in physics, measure of strength of a wave, similar to height from trough to crest of a water wave
radio waves R-46, 47
sound waves S-260

Amplitude modulation
radio R-46-7, 49-50, *diagram* R-50

Amr ibn-al-As (ăm-rụb-nil-äs'), or **Amru** (ăm-rụ') (594?-664), Arab general and statesman who subjugated Egypt C-15

Amritsar (ŭm-rit'sēr), India, city in Punjab state; pop. 376,295; center of Sikh faith; silks, shawls, carpets: *maps* I-66, A-636

Amru. *See in Index* Amr ibn-al-As

Am'sterdam, Netherlands, capital, on Amstel River; pop. 849,335: A-371-371b, *maps* A-371a, N-133, E-334, *pictures* A-371a-b, N-137
canals A-371, *pictures* A-371a-b. *See also in Index* Canals, *table*
climate, *graphs* N-141
diamond-cutting industry D-102
location A-371, *locator map* A-371
Montelbaan Tower, *map* A-371a, *picture* A-371b
name, origin of A-371a
places of interest, *map* A-371a
Rijksmuseum (State Museum) A-371a, *map* A-371a. *See also in Index* Museums, *table*
tea auction T-43

Amsterdam, N. Y., city on Mohawk River and New York State Barge Canal, 30 mi. n.w. of Albany; pop. 28,772; rugs and carpets, clothing, plastics, boats, fiber glass, electronics: *map* N-261

Amu-Dar'ya (ä'mụ där'yạ), ancient **Oxus**, river of w. Asia, rising on Pamir Plateau and flowing about 1500 mi. n.w. to Aral Sea: *maps* R-322, A-636, P-212

Am'ulet, a small object worn as a charm against evil M-38, 40, I-31

Amun, god of ancient Egypt E-123
temple at Karnak T-157, E-119: "Avenue of Sphinxes" S-379; columns, *picture* A-490

Amundsen (ăm'ụn-sĕn), **Roald** (1872-1928), Norwegian navigator and explorer A-371b, *picture* A-371b
discovers South Pole P-421: route, *map* A-439; tent, *picture* P-419
Gjöa in San Francisco S-41a
Northwest Passage A-371b, P-420, *map* P-417

Amundsen Sea, in South Pacific Ocean off Marie Byrd Land, Antarctica; discovered 1928-29 by Nils Larsen, a Norwegian, and named for Roald Amundsen: *maps* A-439, W-242

Amurath, name of several Turkish sultans. *See in Index* Murad

Amur (ä-mụr') **River**, great navigable river of n.e. Asia A-372, *maps* R-322, A-636, M-82, C-291, C-313, *picture* A-372
Komsomol'sk on, *picture* S-188
length, comparative. *See in Index* River, *table*
location A-372, *locator map* A-372

Amusement parks P-126, *color picture* G-88

Amusements. *See also in Index* Ballet; Carnival; Circus; Dance; Drama; Fairs and expositions; Folk dance; Games; Motion pictures; Pageant; Play; Puppets and marionettes;

Radio; Sports; Television; Theater; Toys; Winter sports
Barnum's museum B-67
cards, history C-135–6
charades C-208
hobbies H-181–95, *pictures* H-181–95
leisure-time activities L-185–7
magic M-41–4, *pictures* M-37, 41–4
Northmen, *picture* N-359
riddles R-205
Russia R-331
Tivoli Gardens, Denmark C-566
vacation activities V-237–48, *pictures* V-237–47, *Reference-Outline* V-240–8

Amvets. *See in Index* American Veterans of World War II

Amyl acetate, clear liquid ester ($CH_3CO_2C_5H_{11}$) with fruitlike odor; popularly called banana oil or pear oil; prepared from amyl alcohol and sodium acetate.

Amylase (ăm′ĭ-lās), an enzyme E-281, H-87

Amylop′sin, a starch-digesting enzyme secreted by pancreas, *table* E-281

Amyot (à-myō′), **Jacques** (1513–93), French writer and bishop of Auxerre, born Melun, France; his translation of Plutarch's 'Lives' into French served as basis for Sir Thomas North's English translation.

Anabap′tists, a religious sect P-539

'Anab′asis', Xenophon's account of the expedition sent by Cyrus the Younger against Artaxerxes: X-329

Anableps. *See in Index* Four-eyed fish

Anab′olism, in physiology P-312, 313, B-160a

Anacardiaceae. *See in Index* Cashew family

Anacon′da, a snake B-226, S-226a
length of life, average, *pictograph* A-414

Anaconda, Mont., city about 25 mi. n.w. of Butte; pop. 12,054: M-460, *maps* M-470, U-40

Anacos′tia, part of Washington, D.C.; naval air station; experimental and new model planes tested: *map, inset* M-138

Anacostia River, tributary of the Potomac W-35, *maps, insets* W-32, M-138

Anacreon (à-năk′rē-ŏn) (6th century B.C.), Greek lyric poet; famous for songs of love and wine.

Anadolu. *See in Index* Anatolia

Anadyomene (ăn-à-dī-ŏm′ē-nē), another name for Aphrodite.

Anadyr′, Gulf of, arm of Bering Sea; in n.e. Siberia: *maps* U-39, R-322, A-636

Anadyr′ River, in n.e. Siberia, 450 mi. long; empties into Gulf of Anadyr′, Bering Sea: *map* A-636

Anaemia. *See in Index* Anemia

Anaero′bic bacteria B-15

Anaesthetics. *See in Index* Anesthetics

Anagallis (ăn-à-găl′ĭs), genus of plants of primrose family, including the pimpernel.

Anagram, a word or sentence formed out of another by reading the letters backward or by transposing them; thus, "violence run forth" is an anagram of "French Revolution." The best anagrams relate in meaning to the words or phrases from which they are formed.

Anagrams, a game in which players form words from letters molded or printed on flat wooden blocks, dice, or small cards.

Anaheim, Calif., city 20 mi. s.e. of Los Angeles; pop. 104,184: A-372, *map, inset* C-53
Disneyland D-131, *picture* D-131, *color picture* C-47
location, *locator map* A-372

Anakim (ăn′à-kĭm), children of Anak, giant race dwelling in mountains of Palestine before Israelitish conquest (Deut. i, 28); Hebron their chief city; "son of Anak," figurative term for a giant.

An′alects of Confucius C-509

Analemma, on terrestrial globe T-180, *diagram* T-180

Analog calculator C-19
meters M-234–6, *diagrams* M-234–5
slide rule S-217, *picture* S-217
weighing machines W-94

Analog computer. *See in Index* Computer, *subhead* analog

Anal′ogous colors C-447
interior decoration plan I-230

Analogy, a similarity in relations I-222

Anal′ysis, separation into its parts or elements
chemical: qualitative and quantitative analysis Q-3–6, *pictures* Q-3, 5–6, *table* Q-4
grammatical G-167
light, spectroscopy S-371–4, *diagrams* S-372–3

Analytical chemistry C-241

Analytical psychology P-519

Analytic geometry, a form of mathematics in which geometric positions and relations are defined and studied by algebraic methods: G-73, C-22

Ananias (ăn-à-nī′ăs), a Christian who, with wife Sapphira, was struck dead for lying (Acts v, 1–10).

Anansi, West Indian folk hero S-476–7

An′apest, poetic foot P-405

An′archism, theory that all government is unnecessary; modern anarchist movement founded by Pierre Joseph Proudhon, violent anarchism (nihilism), by Mikhail Bakunin: T-297
bar to U.S. immigration I-58

Anasazi (from a Navajo word meaning "old peoples" or "ancient ones"), an Indian civilization, including the Basket Makers and the Pueblos, which has flourished from about A.D. 100 to the present time, in n.e. Arizona, n.w. New Mexico, s.e. Utah, and s.w. Colorado: I-143. *See also in Index* Basket Makers; Cliff Dwellers; Pueblo Indians
relics, *picture* I-141

Anastigmat′ic lens P-284, *picture* P-284

Anathema, a punishment administered by the church C-336

Anatidae (à-năt′ĭ-dē), family of birds including swans, geese, ducks.

Anatolia (ăn-à-tōl′yà), Turkish **Anadolu** (ä-nä-dō-lọ′), modern name for Asia Minor A-639, *picture* A-639. *See also in Index* Asia Minor; Turkey

Anat′omy A-373–84, *pictures* A-373–4, *color pictures* A-376–84. *See also in Index* Morphology; Physiology; and names of organs and regions of the body
frog F-452–62, *color pictures* F-455–62, *diagrams* F-452, A-385, *table* F-453
history M-215b: Vesalius S-57f, *pictures* S-57f, M-215b
human A-373–84, *pictures* A-373–4, *color pictures* A-376–84
bone B-242–3, *diagram* B-242
brain B-295–9, *diagrams* B-295–9
diaphragm D-103
digestive system D-114–18, *color pictures* A-379–82, *diagrams* D-115–17
ear E-4–5, *diagram* E-4, *pictures* E-4–5
eye E-366–70, *diagrams* E-366–7
foot F-328, 330

hair H-5, *color picture* M-293, *diagram* H-5
hand H-17–18, *diagram* H-18
heart H-105–8, *color pictures* H-105–8
intestines A-374
kidneys K-48b–9, *diagrams* K-49
liver L-313–14
lungs L-395, *diagram* L-395
muscles M-548–50, *pictures* M-549–50
nerves N-128–31, *diagrams* N-129–31, *table* N-130
nose N-371, *diagrams* N-371
skeleton S-208–10, A-373, *diagrams* S-208, 210, *picture* A-373, *color pictures* A-377–9, 381–3
skin S-210d–11, *diagram* S-211
stomach S-454–5, *diagram* S-454
teeth T-52–4, *charts* T-53, *diagram* T-53, *pictures* T-52–3
tendon T-80, *picture* T-80
tongue T-197, *diagrams* T-197
voice organs V-377, *diagrams* V-377
kinds S-61e
microscopic (histology) Z-365
plant B-278

Anatomy, comparative A-385, *diagrams* A-385
bills of birds, *pictures* B-171
Cuvier's work C-632
eyes of animals, *picture* E-368
feet of animals F-328, *pictures* F-329
feet of birds, *pictures* B-170
frog and man F-452–3
"hands" of animals, *diagram* H-18
skeletons of animals, *diagram* S-209
teeth T-52, *pictures* T-52
tongues of animals T-197

'Anatomy of Melancholy, The', one of most famous books in English literature; written by Robert Burton; much admired by Dr. Johnson and Charles Lamb: E-258

Anaxagoras (ăn-ăks-ăg′ō-răs), Greek philosopher of 5th century B.C., teacher of Pericles; introduced philosophy into Athens; helped prepare way for atomic theory.

Anaximander (à-năk-sĭ-măn′dēr) (611?–547? B.C.), Greek philosopher and astronomer; conceived of the universe as endless, unaging mass.

Anaximenes (ăn-ăk-sĭm′ē-nēz), Greek philosopher of 6th century B.C., born Miletus, Asia Minor; pupil of Anaximander; held that air is primary substance and that all things are formed from it by compression or by rarefaction.

Ancestor worship
Japan (Shintoism) J-367

Anchises (ăn-kī′sēz), in Roman mythology, Trojan hero, father of Aeneas: A-455, A-45

Anchor. *See also in Index* Nautical terms, *table*
flukes F-278

Anchorage, Alaska, seaport in s. at head of Cook Inlet; pop. 44,237: A-386, A-228, 231, *maps* A-239, 225, U-39, 94, N-308, A-794, *pictures* A-226, A-386
climatic region, *map* U-119: temperature and precipitation, *graph* U-119
earthquake A-232, A-386, *pictures* A-226
fur-collection center, *picture* F-489
location A-386, *locator map* A-386

Anchorage, of harbor H-25

Anchor bend, a knot K-71, *picture* K-70

Anchor ice I-3

Anchor nail, *picture* N-2

'Anchors Aweigh', U. S. Navy song N-51

Anchovy (ăn′chō-vē), small herring-like fish, abundant in Mediterranean; related species in America sold under same name; 1966 U.S. catch 62,284,000 lbs.

Anchusa (ăng-kū'sạ), a genus of annual and perennial plants of the borage family; flowers blue or purple; leaves hairy; also called alkanet; dropmore is one species; roots of some used medicinally.

Ancient history A-387-90, W-245-7, *chart* H-161-3, *pictures* A-387-90, *Reference-Outline* A-387-90. *See also in Index* Archaeology; Civilization; *also* names of countries
bibliography A-390
scope of H-160

Ancient Mariner. *See in Index* 'Rime of the Ancient Mariner, The'

Ancient Order of Foresters. *See in Index* Foresters, Orders of

Ancient Order of Hibernians. *See in Index* Hibernians, Ancient Order of

Ancient Order of United Workmen, a fraternal, beneficiary society providing life insurance for members; founded at Meadville, Pa., 1868.

Ancona (än-kō'nä), Italy, seaport on n.e. coast; pop. 100,485; triumphal arch in honor of Trajan, A.D. 115; sugar refining, shipbuilding, silk, paper: *maps* I-338, 325, E-334

Ancona, a breed of poultry P-482

Ancre (än'kr̆), a small French river flowing s.w. into Somme 8 mi. e. of Amiens; plateau between Ancre and Somme, scene of various "battles of the Somme" in World War I.

Ancus Martius (än'kŭs mär'shĭ-ŭs), legendary king of Rome, reigned 638?-614? B.C.: R-241

Andalu'sia, Ala., city in s., 73 mi. s.w. of Montgomery; pop. 10,263; timber, naval stores, textiles: *map* A-221

Andalusia, beautiful fertile district (formerly province) in southern Spain; fruit, olives, grain: S-358
people S-352
Seville chief city S-118

Andalusian, breed of poultry P-482, *picture* P-481

Andalusite (än-dạ-lū'sĭt), a transparent or opaque aluminum silicate; a gem; various colors; variety chiastolite bears design of a cross; found in Spain, Ceylon, Brazil.

Andaman and Nicobar Islands, federally administered territory of India, in Bay of Bengal, composed of Andaman Islands, on the north, and Nicobar Islands, on the south; total area 3215 sq. mi.; pop. 63,548; cap. Port Blair, on South Andaman Island; from 1858, Port Blair was headquarters for India's convict settlement (abolished 1945): *maps* I-162, A-637, I-81
skull type, *picture* R-27

Andaman Sea, e. of Bay of Bengal between Andaman and Nicobar islands and Malay Peninsula: *maps* I-162, A-637. *See also in Index* Ocean, *table*

Andante (än-dän'tā or ăn-dän'tĕ), in music, rather slow but flowing; used also as name for the slow movement of a symphony, sonata, or other composition. *See also in Index* Music, *table* of terms and forms

Andantino. *See in Index* Music, *table* of terms and forms

Andean condor C-505, 506, *picture* S-273

Anders, William A. (born 1933), astronaut candidate, born Hong Kong; U. S. Air Force officer selected for NASA program 1963.

Andersen, Hans Christian (1805-75), Danish author A-391-2, *picture* A-391
children's literature, place in L-310, S-461

fairy tales A-391, 392, L-310, S-471, R-110b: illustration for, *pictures* A-392, S-462, 470
Grimm brothers and G-242
paper cutout by Andersen, *picture* A-391

Anderson, Alexander (1775-1870), first wood engraver in the United States, born New York, N. Y.; works show skillful craftsmanship.

Anderson, Carl D(avid) (born 1905), physicist, born New York, N. Y.; professor at California Institute of Technology; shared 1936 Nobel prize in physics with Victor Hess: A-696

Anderson, Clarence William (born 1891), illustrator and author, born Wahoo, Neb.; attended Chicago Art Institute; interest in horses reflected in all his work. For children ('Billy and Blaze' and 'Salute'), for older boys and girls ('Big Red', 'Thoroughbreds', 'Horses Are Folks', 'Twenty Gallant Horses').

Anderson, Clinton P(resba) (born 1895), political leader, born Centerville, S. D.; U.S. congressman from New Mexico 1941-45; U.S. secretary of agriculture 1945-48; U.S. senator 1949-; prominent Democrat: *color picture* N-218

Anderson, Elizabeth Garrett (1836-1917), one of earliest English women physicians, born London; women's rights pioneer; first English woman mayor.

Anderson, Eugenie (Helen Eugenie Moore Anderson) (born 1909), diplomat, born Adair, Iowa; first woman ambassador from U.S. (to Denmark, 1949-53; to Bulgaria 1962-64); Democrat: *picture* M-360

Anderson, George Whelan, Jr. (born 1906), U. S. Navy officer, born Brooklyn, N.Y.; commissioned ensign 1927; commands include Sixth Fleet 1959-61; became full admiral 1961; chief of naval operations 1961-63; ambassador to Portugal 1963-66.

Anderson, Dame Judith (born 1898), actress, born Adelaide, South Australia; appeared on U. S. stage from 1918 ('Strange Interlude'; 'Mourning Becomes Electra'; 'Macbeth'; 'Medea'); also in motion pictures ('Rebecca'; 'Kings Row'; 'The Edge of Darkness') and on television; won Emmy for 'Macbeth' 1954 and 1960.

Anderson, Leroy (born 1908), composer and conductor, born Cambridge, Mass.; musical director Harvard University Band 1932-35; guest conductor Boston Symphony Orchestra Pops concerts (popular compositions: 'The Syncopated Clock', 'Fiddle-Faddle', 'Sleigh Ride', and 'Blue Tango').

Anderson, Marian (Mrs. Orpheus H. Fisher) (born 1902), contralto, born Philadelphia, Pa.; studied in Germany 1932 and gave concerts in European capitals until Arturo Toscanini heard her at 1935 Salzburg Festival; New York debut the same year, Metropolitan Opera Company debut 1955; delegate to United Nations 1958; awarded Spingarn medal for music 1939 and Presidential Medal of Freedom 1963; announced retirement 1965: R-111d, *picture* A-606, *color picture* P-180

Anderson, Mary (Mrs. Antonio de Navarro) (1859-1940), Shakespearean actress (Rosalind, Juliet, Perdita); born Sacramento, Calif.; retired at age of 30 and lived in England.

Anderson, Maxwell (1888-1959), American playwright A-393, A-359, 365, D-176, *picture* A-393

Anderson, Patrick (born 1915), Canadian poet, born England C-114

Anderson, Rasmus Björn (1846-1936), author and editor, born Albion, Wis.; professor Scandinavian languages and literature University of Wisconsin 1875-83 ('Viking Tales of the North').

Anderson, Robert (1805-71), major general, born near Louisville, Ky.; served in Second Seminole, Mexican, and Civil wars
defends Fort Sumter F-350

Anderson, Robert Bernerd (born 1910), lawyer and public official, born Burleson, Tex.; professor of law University of Texas 1932-34; Texas state tax commissioner 1934-36; general counsel for W. T. Waggoner estate (ranching and oil) 1937-41, general manager 1941-52; secretary of the navy 1953-54; undersecretary of defense 1954-55; secretary of the treasury 1957-61.

Anderson, Sherwood (1876-1941), American short-story writer and novelist: A-393, A-365, *picture* A-393, *color picture* O-426

Anderson, Ind., city about 34 mi. n.e. of Indianapolis, in fertile agricultural area; pop. 49,061; automobile electrical equipment and other parts, steel and wire products, tile; Anderson College; Mounds State Park nearby: *maps* I-100, 92, U-41

Anderson, S. C., city in n.w. part of state, 28 mi. s.w. of Greenville; pop. 41,316; in farm area; cotton and rayon textile products, sewing machines, glass fibers: *maps* S-318, U-41

Anderson College, at Anderson, Ind.; affiliated with Church of God; opened 1917; chartered 1925; arts and sciences, theology.

Anderson Ranch Dam, in Idaho, on South Fork of Boise River D-13, *picture* I-30
reservoir, *map* I-17

Andersonville, Ga., village 52 mi. s.w. of Macon; pop. 263; site of Civil War Confederate prison in which over 12,000 died; burial ground now a national cemetery: *map* G-93

Andersson, Johan Gunnar (1874-1960), Swedish geologist, born near Orebro, Sweden: M-80

Andes (ăn'dēz), mountains in w. South America; highest peak 22,834 ft.: A-394-5, *diagram* A-394, *map* S-298-9, *pictures* A-394-5
Aconcagua A-12, *picture* A-12
animals: alpaca A-284, *pictures* A-284; condor C-505, 506; llama L-321, *pictures* L-321, A-395; tapir T-21
Argentina A-515, 519, *pictures* A-519-20: Aconcagua A-12, *picture* A-12
Bolivia B-236-7, *pictures* L-125c, S-287
Chile C-281, 282, *pictures* C-284, S-281b, 284
'Christ of the Andes, The', statue, *picture* A-474
climate, effect on A-394-5, S-271, A-516
Colombia C-439
Ecuador E-64, 65, *picture* S-274
geologic history G-68, S-269
I.G.Y. studies I-236d
location, *locator map* A-394
minerals and mining A-394, / S-279, *pictures* S-287
North American mountains compared, *diagram* A-394
Peru P-221, 222, *pictures* P-221, S-269, 287, A-394-5, W-239

---

transportation, *pictures* S-289: railroads A-394, C-286
Venezuela V-273

Andhra Pradesh, state in s.e. India; area 110,250 sq. mi.; pop. 35,983,-447; cap. Hyderabad; formed 1956 from parts of former Madras and Hyderabad states: *map* I-81

Andirons (*ănd'ī-ĕrns*), a pair of metal supports for wood in a fireplace
colonial America, *pictures* A-321, I-228, S-160

Andizhan', Russia, city in e. Uzbek S.S.R.; pop. 130,083; railroad center; cotton ginning: *maps* A-636, R-345

Andor'ra, principality in valley of Pyrenees between France and Spain; 175 sq. mi.; pop. 11,000 (1965 est.); cap. Andorra: A-395, *Fact Summary* E-327, *maps* S-350, E-334, *picture* A-395
flag F-202, *color picture* F-203
government A-395: elections A-395
location A-395, *locator map* A-395

Andover, Mass., about 22 mi. n. of Boston; pop. of township 15,878; rubber products, woolens, plastics, electronics; Phillips Academy, Abbot Academy; incorporated 1646: *map* M-161
Ryder's 'Toilers of the Sea', in gallery at Phillips Academy P-54, *color picture* P-55

Andrada e Silva (*ăn-drä'tha ē sĭl'vą*), **José Bonifácio de** (1763–1838), Brazilian statesman, geologist, and author; born Santos; one of chief leaders in movement which resulted in establishment of a limited monarchy and independence of Brazil; minister of interior under Pedro I; banished to France by Pedro I 1823, returned to Brazil 1829; became tutor to Pedro II.

Andrade (*än-drä'dē*), **Olegario Víctor** (1841–82), Argentine poet, born Gualeguaychú, near Paraná, Argentina: L-149a, *picture* L-149b

Andrássy (*ŏn'drä-shĭ*), **Gyula (Julius), Count** (1823–90), Hungarian statesman, born Kassa (now Kosice, Czechoslovakia); supported Kossuth in 1848–49 rebellion against Austria; in 1861, with Deák, brought about compromise leading to formation of Austro-Hungarian Empire in 1867; first premier of Hungary under Dual Monarchy; foreign minister of Austria-Hungary 1871–79; negotiated alliance with Germany in 1879. *See also in Index* Deák, Ferencz; Kossuth, Louis

Andrássy, Julius, Count (1860–1929), Hungarian statesman, son of preceding; figure in Austrian politics during World War I; as minister of foreign affairs tried to make separate peace with U. S.

André (*ăn'drā*), **Brother** (1845–1937), Canadian Roman Catholic, born St. Grégoire d'Iberville, Que.; was baptized Alfred Bissette; school porter for 40 years; lay brother of Congregation of the Holy Cross; erected shrine to St. Joseph in Montreal.

André (*än'drā*), **John** (1751–80), British spy, executed in Revolutionary War: A-396, *picture* A-396

'Andrea Chenier', opera by Umberto Giordano
Tebaldi as Maddalena, *picture* O-466

Andrea del Sarto. *See in Index* Sarto

Andreanof Islands, in Aleutian group, *maps, inset* A-239, U-39

Andrée (*än-drā'*), **Salomon August** (1854–97), Swedish scientist and aeronaut, born Grenna, near Jönköping, Sweden: P-420
wreck of balloon, *picture* P-422

Andreev, or **Andreyev** (*ŭn-dryā'yĕf*), **Leonid** (1871–1919), brilliant Russian writer, mystic, and fatalist; born Orel, central Russia: D-174
chief works R-361

Andrew, Saint, one of the Twelve Apostles; patron of Scotland and Russia; festival Nov. 30: A-457

Andrew, Prince (Andrew Albert Christian Edward) (born 1960), son of Queen Elizabeth II of England: E-188

Andrew, John Albion (1818–67), "war governor" (1860–66) of Mass.; born Windham, Me.; raised first regiment of free Negroes in North.

Andrew Johnson National Monument, in Tennessee N-29, *map* N-30, *picture* J-433

Andrews, Charles McLean (1863–1943), historian and educator, born Wethersfield, Conn.; professor American history Yale University 1910–33 ('Fathers of New England'; 'Colonial Folkways'; 'Colonial Period of American History').

Andrews, Elisha Benjamin (1844–1917), educator, born Hinsdale, N. H.; with Union army in Civil War; became president of Brown University 1889, superintendent of Chicago schools 1898, chancellor of University of Nebraska 1900 ('History of the United States').

Andrews, Frank Maxwell (1884–1943), U.S. Army officer, born Nashville, Tenn.; graduated West Point 1906; commander G.H.Q. Air Force 1935–39; named commander U.S. Air Force at Panama Nov. 1940, of Caribbean Defense Command Jan. 1942, of U.S. forces in Middle East Nov. 1942, and of U.S. forces in European theater Feb. 1943; killed in airplane crash in Iceland 1943.

Andrews, Julie, real name Julia Elizabeth Wells (born 1935), English actress, born near London; on Broadway in 'The Boy Friend', 'My Fair Lady', and 'Camelot'; movies: 'Mary Poppins' (1964 Oscar), 'The Sound of Music'
'My Fair Lady', *pictures* O-468, D-173

Andrews, Mary Raymond Shipman (1865?–1936), author, born Mobile, Ala.; won fame with 'The Perfect Tribute', story of Lincoln (1906).

Andrews, Roy Chapman (1884–1960), explorer and naturalist, born Beloit, Wis.; director American Museum of Natural History, New York, N. Y., 1935–41; explored Alaska, East Indies, Korea, China, Mongolia, central Asia; discovered huge fossil fields in The Gobi; found first dinosaur eggs ever discovered, about 10,000,000 years old, and skeleton of largest land mammal (natural history): 'This Amazing Planet', 'Nature's Ways'; autobiography: 'An Explorer Comes Home'; for younger readers: 'Quest in the Desert', 'All About Dinosaurs', 'All About Whales', 'Quest of the Snow Leopard', 'In the Days of the Dinosaurs'): *picture* W-131
Gobi E-357, M-432: dinosaur eggs, *picture* F-356

Andrews, Tex., city 40 mi. n.w. of Midland; pop. 11,135; cattle, cotton, sorghum; oil: *map* T-128

Andrews University, at Berrien Springs, Mich.; Seventh-day Adventist; founded 1960; Emmanuel Missionary College, undergraduate school, founded 1874; liberal arts; graduate school; theological seminary.

Andreyev, Leonid. *See in Index* Andreev

Andric, Ivo (born 1892), Yugoslav diplomat and writer, born near Sarajevo, Bosnia, now Yugoslavia; won 1961 Nobel prize in literature ('The Bridge on the Drina'; 'Devil's Yard'; 'The Woman from Sarajevo').

'Androcles (*ăn'drō-klēz*) **and the Lion',** story L-296

Andromache (*ăn-drŏm'ą-kĭ*), in Greek mythology, wife of Hector H-122, 123

Andromeda (*ăn-drŏm'ē-dą*), in Greek mythology, daughter of King Cepheus and Queen Cassiopeia of Ethiopia; offered to sea monster to appease Poseidon and sea nymphs, who had been angered by Cassiopeia's boasting of her own beauty
Perseus saves P-210

Andromeda, a constellation, *charts* S-415, 420–1, 423
galaxy, *picture* M-233: distance from earth, *table* A-643

Androni'cus, Livius (3d century B.C.), Roman poet (Greek by birth) L-154

An'dros, Sir Edmund (1637–1714), English colonial governor of New York (1674–81), New England (1686–89), and Virginia (1692–98); born London; tyrannical and unpopular: R-185
Connecticut charter hidden from, *picture* C-525
flag F-188a, *color picture* F-189

Ándros, Greece, fertile mountainous island in Aegean Sea, 50 mi. s. of Athens; one of Cyclades: *map* G-213

Androscoggin (*ăn-drŏs-kŏg'ĭn*), river in New Hampshire and Maine; flows 180 mi. to Merrymeeting Bay; abrupt descent gives immense waterpower: *maps* M-53, 65, N-170, 182, U-44

Andros Island, largest island in Bahama archipelago, 125 mi. s.e. of Miami Beach, Fla.; area, 1600 sq. mi.; pop. 7136; pine, mahogany, hardwood; fish, sponges; pineapples; oil wells: *maps* B-19, W-104

Ane'mia, or **anaemia,** term (meaning "bloodless") for various forms of a blood disease D-129d–e, B-224, H-85
folic acid prevents V-355
normal and anemic blood, *diagram* B-222
sickle-cell H-145, B-160d
vitamin B₁₂ V-356

Anemom'eter, for measuring velocity of wind, *picture* W-89

Anemone (*ą-nĕm'ō-nē*), or **windflower** A-396, *picture* A-396
Greek myth A-37, A-396
origin of name A-396
wood A-396, *color picture* F-274

Anemone, sea. *See in Index* Sea anemone

Anemotropism (*ăn-ē-mŏt'rō-pĭz'm*), in biology I-206

An'eroid barometer B-69, *diagram* B-69, *picture* B-69

Anesthesia (*ăn-ĕs-thē'zhĭ-ą*), a temporary or permanent loss of sensation A-397
general and local A-397–8

produced: by damaged nerve N-131; by hypnosis H-290
spinal A-398
Anesthesiol'ogist, specialist in anesthesiology A-398, *pictures* A-398, S-519a
Anesthesiology, science of anesthesia and anesthetics A-398
Anesthet'ics A-397–8, *pictures* A-397–8
cocaine N-15, A-398
discovery L-345
first uses L-345, M-215c, *pictures* M-215d, G-85, T-314
general and local A-397–8
opiates O-470
Anes'thetist, one who administers certain types of anesthetics A-398, *picture* A-397
Aneto, Pico de (*pē'kō thä ä-nä'tō*), French **Pic de Néthou** (*pēk' dē nä-tọ'*), highest mountain of Pyrenees (11,168 ft.), in Spain, about 50 mi. w. of Andorra: *diagram* E-329
Aneurysm (*ăn'ū-riz'm*), local enlargement in artery D-129d
Angara (*ŭn-gŭ-rả'*) **River**, in Siberia; outlet of Lake Baikal (Baykal); flows 1150 mi. to Yenisey River; also called Upper Tunguska in lower course: *maps* A-636, R-345
Angary (*ăng'gạ-ri*), a right, under international law, of a belligerent to seize, use, or destroy property of neutrals if necessary; exercised in taking over use of neutral ships during World Wars I and II.
Angel, John (1881–1960), American sculptor, born Newton Abbot, Devon, England; to U. S. 1925, became citizen 1936; known for religious figures and war memorials: S-85
statues for Cathedral of St. John the Divine, *picture* S-84
Angel, in theology, a supernatural being, serving as messenger or minister of God
Bosch's 'Vision of Tondalys', *color picture* P-33
Cimabue's 'Madonna of the Angels', *color picture* P-29
El Greco's 'Assumption of the Virgin', *color picture* P-40
fallen angels, 'Satan and Beelzebub', *picture* E-453
Giotto's 'Descent from the Cross', *color picture* P-29
Memling's 'Madonna and Child with Angels', *color picture* P-32
St. Michael, *picture* J-429
Angel Falls, in Guiana Highlands, Venezuela; drops from Auyantepui plateau; highest known falls (3212 ft.): W-73, *map* V-274, *picture* V-273, *table* W-73c
Angelfish, popular name of several freshwater and saltwater fishes.
Angel food cake B-314
Angel'ica, a genus of stout perennial herbs of the parsley family with pinnately compound leaves and small white or greenish flowers; name often incorrectly applied to other plants; *archangelica*, a closely related genus, is used for flavoring and in medicine.
Angelico, Fra, title given to Giovanni da Fiesole (*gō-vän'nē dä fyē'zō-lä*) (1387–1455), Italian religious painter A-399, *picture* A-399
'Madonna and Child', *picture* M-29
Angel Island, largest island in San Francisco Bay; under Spanish occupation a rendezvous of pirates; seat of U.S. immigration and quarantine stations; Fort McDowell military reservation, established 1865 as Camp Reynolds, abandoned by Army 1946: *map* S-41b, *inset* C-52
An'gell, George Thorndike (1823–1909), philanthropist, born South-

bridge, Mass.; advocated laws for prevention of cruelty to animals; criminologist; worked against adulteration of foods.
Angell, James Burrill (1829–1916), educator, born Scituate, R. I.; president University of Michigan 1871–1909; minister to China 1880–81, to Turkey 1897–98.
Angell, James Rowland (1869–1949), educator, born Burlington, Vt., son of James Burrill Angell; professor of psychology and dean of faculty, University of Chicago 1911–20; president of Yale University 1921–37: P-520
Angell, Sir Norman (Ralph Norman Angell Lane) (1874–1967), English writer and lecturer, born Holbeach, England; at various times resident of U. S.; in early career Paris correspondent for U. S. newspapers; general manager *Paris Daily Mail*; lecturer U. S. universities; awarded Nobel peace prize 1933 ('The Great Illusion'; 'The Fruits of Victory'; 'Let the People Know'; 'After All', autobiography).
Angelo, Valenti (born 1897), American artist and children's author, born Massarosa, Tuscany, Italy; to U. S. 1905, became citizen 1923; wrote and illustrated 'Nino', 'Golden Gate', 'Paradise Valley', 'Hill of Little Miracles', 'Marble Fountain', 'Acorn Tree', and 'Honey Boat': R-111, 111a
'Bells of Bleecker Street, The' R-110c–d, *picture* R-110c
Angel of the Battlefield, Clara Barton B-72, *picture* B-72
Angelo State College, at San Angelo, Tex.; founded 1928, senior college 1965; liberal arts.
Angel shark, or monk fish S-145
Angel's trumpet, a common name for 2 species of datura, or thorn apple; one is a shrub, and the other a tree native to South America.
Angelus (*ăn'gĕ-lŭs*), in Roman and Greek Catholic church, a devotion recited morning, noon, and evening at the sound of a bell, the Angelus bell; named from opening word of Latin form, *Angelus Domini nuntiavit Mariae* ('The Angel of the Lord declared unto Mary').
Angel wings (*Barnea costata*), mollusk shell, *color picture* S-149
Anger
child development C-270, *picture* C-277
physical effect of E-200
Angers (*äṅ-zhā'*), **Sir Auguste Réal** (1838–1919), Canadian lawyer and statesman, born Quebec, Que.; held various political offices; as lieutenant governor of Quebec caused sensation in 1891 by dismissing Honoré Mercier, premier of province.
Angers, Félicité. *See in Index* Conan, Laure
Angers, France, historic city on Maine River 165 mi. s.w. of Paris; pop. 109,614; varied manufactures; slate quarrying nearby: *maps* F-404, E-334
Angiospermae (*ăn'ji-ō-spĕr'mē*) (**angiosperms**), a class of plants P-371, T-258, 259, *pictures* P-371, S-106, *Reference-Outline* B-279b
Angkor (*ăng'kôr*), a group of Khmer ruins in Cambodia; includes Angkor Wat and Angkor Thom: C-56a, *map* I-162, *picture* C-56
Angle
geometry G-68–74, *diagrams* G-68–72
light (incidence, refraction, and reflection) L-263, 265, *diagrams* L-265; mirrors M-371
trigonometry T-261–3, *diagrams* T-261–3

Angle of aberration, in astronomy A-6
Angle of attack, of airplane wing A-165–6, *diagrams* A-167. *See also in Index* Aerospace, *table* of terms
Angle of incidence, of airplane wing A-166, *diagram* A-167. *See also in Index* Aerospace, *table* of terms
Angler fish, marine fish; family *Lophiidae:* F-154
deep-sea F-154, 161, *picture* F-161
Angles (*ăng'g'lz*), Teutonic tribe which invaded Britain E-230, E-318. *See also in Index* Anglo-Saxon
Anglesey (*ăng'g'l-sē*), Wales, island in Irish Sea connected with mainland by two bridges; pop. 39,155; with nearby Holy Island constitutes the county of Anglesey; area 276 sq. mi.; pop. 51,705; cattle, sheep, grain; megalithic remains: W-3, *map* G-199h
Llanfair, *picture* N-3
Angleworm. *See in Index* Earthworm
Anglia, East, early kingdom in Britain. *See in Index* East Anglia
Anglican church. *See in Index* England, Church of
Anglicans, members of Church of England and of other churches in communion with it. *See also in Index* England, Church of
Ang'lin, Margaret (1876–1958), American actress, born Ottawa, Ont., Canada; noted for her character portrayals in modern plays as well as in Greek and Shakespearean drama.
Anglo-Egyptian Sudan. *See in Index* Sudan, Republic of the
Anglo-Japanese Alliance (1902). *See in Index* Treaties, *table*
Anglo-Saxon, term applied to Teutonic tribes that conquered Britain in 5th and 6th centuries and by the time of Alfred the Great had become one people; also used of the English race today, wherever found, as in Europe, America. *See also in Index* Angles; Jutes; Saxons
'Anglo-Saxon Chronicle' A-260, E-253, quoted W-163
Anglo-Saxon language and literature, also called **Old English** E-252, 253–4
'Anglo-Saxon Chronicle' A-260, E-453; quoted W-163
'Beowulf' E-254, B-137, S-472, L-116, M-580
Caedmon C-13
only manuscript in America, *picture* B-262
Anglo-Saxon law L-165
jury system J-442–3, *pictures* J-441
Anglund, Joan Walsh (born 1926), author and illustrator, born Hinsdale, Ill.; wrote and illustrated children's books ('A Friend Is Someone Who Likes You'; 'The Brave Cowboy'; 'Love Is a Special Way of Feeling'; 'In a Pumpkin Shell'; 'Cowboy's Secret Life;' 'A Year Is Round').
Angoff (*ăn'gŏf*), **Charles** (born 1902), American author, born Minsk, Russia; to U. S. 1908, became citizen 1923; noted for novels of Jewish life ('The Sun at Noon').
Ango'la, or **Portuguese West Africa**, an overseas province of Portugal on s.w. coast of Africa; area 481,352 sq. mi.; pop. 5,119,000; cap. Luanda: A-399, *Fact Summary* A-85, *map* A-95, *picture* A-399
location A-399, *locator map* A-399
Portugal retains A-82
Angora, Turkey. *See in Index* Ankara
Angora cat C-154
Angora goat G-147, *picture* G-146
Angora rabbit R-22

Key: cāpe, ăt, fär, fȧst, whạt, fạll; mē, yĕt, fẽrn, thêre; īce, bĭt; rōw, wŏn, fôr, nŏt, dọ; cūre, bŭt, ryde, fụll, bûrn; out;

Ankle, or tarsus F-328, 330, S-210

Ankoli cattle, *color picture* A-72

Ankor Thom. *See in Index* Angkor

Ankor Wat. *See in Index* Angkor

Ankylostoma (*ăng-kĭ-lŏs'tō-mạ*), a genus of nematode worms which includes hookworm.

Ann, Cape, promontory of n.e. Mass.; site of Gloucester and Rockport; granite quarries: *map* M-161

Anna, a nickel-copper coin used in India, equals sixteenth part of a rupee, historical value about 2 cents.

Annaba, also **Bône** (*bōn*), formerly **Bona** (*bô'nä*), Algeria, seaport and industrial city about 80 mi. n.e. of Constantine; pop. of greater city 164,844; just south of Bône lie the ruins of Hippo, see of St. Augustine: *maps* A-274, A-94

'Anna Karenina' (*kä-rĕn'yĭ-nạ*), novel by Leo Tolstoi, also name of its heroine; psychological study with background of 19th-century social life in Russia; character of Levin partly autobiographical: R-112i

'Annals', of Tacitus T-3

Annam, or **Anam** (*ä-năm'*), former French protectorate in Indochina; principal city Hue; divided at 17th parallel in 1954, one portion included in North Vietnam, the other in South Vietnam: I-163

Anna Maria College for Women, at Paxton, Mass.; Roman Catholic; founded 1946; liberal arts.

Annamese (*ăn-ạ-mēz'*), or **Vietnamese,** a Mongoloid people of Indochina I-161, 163, V-318

ü＝French *u*, German *ü*; *ġ*em, *ḡ*o; *th*in, *then*; *ṅ*＝French nasal (Jea*ṅ*); *zh*＝French *j* (*z* in azure); *ᴋ*＝German guttural *ch*